Inside Game/Outside Game

A CENTURY FOUNDATION BOOK

INSIDE GAME OUTSIDE GAME

Winning Strategies for Saving Urban America

DAVID RUSK

BROOKINGS INSTITUTION PRESS
Washington, D.C.

ABOUT BROOKINGS

The Brookings Institution is a private nonprofit organization devoted to research, education, and publication on important issues of domestic and foreign policy. Its principal purpose is to bring knowledge to bear on current and emerging policy problems. The Institution was founded on December 8, 1927, to merge the activities of the Institute for Government Research, founded in 1916, the Institute of Economics, founded in 1922, and the Robert Brookings Graduate School of Economics and Government, founded in 1924.

The Institution maintains a position of neutrality on issues of public policy. Interpretations or conclusions in Brookings publications should be understood to be solely those of the authors.

Copyright © 1999
THE CENTURY FOUNDATION

Library of Congress Cataloging-in-Publication Data

Rusk, David
    Inside game/outside game: winning strategies for saving urban America
/ by David Rusk.
    p. cm.
Includes bibliographical references and index.

ISBN 0-8157-7650-0 (cloth : alk. paper)
    1. Urban policy—United States. 2. Metropolitan areas—United
States. 3. Metropolitan government—United States. 4. Land
use—United States—Planning. 5. Urban poor—Housing—United
States. 6. Revenue sharing—United States. I. Title.
    HT123.R843 1998
    307.76'0973—ddc21   98-25430
                                                                    CIP

9 8 7 6 5 4 3 2 1

The paper used in this publication meets minimum requirements of the American National Standard for Information Sciences—Permanence of Paper for Printed Library Materials: ANSI Z39.48-1984.

Typeset in Minion

Composition by Cynthia Stock
Silver Spring, Maryland

Printed by R. R. Donnelley and Sons
Harrisonburg, Virginia

To
Dean and Virginia Rusk
Carlos and Delcia Bence
Irving and Adele Moskovitz

Foreword

FOR A TIME in the 1960s to 1970s, urban problems occupied center stage in American public policy debates, remaining an important part of politics well into the succeeding decade. Republican President Nixon, for example, felt the need for a prominent urban strategist—Daniel Patrick Moynihan, a Democrat at that—on his personal staff. Gradually, however, the plight of the cities, like many other pressing matters, was pushed aside, first by the central drama of the Vietnam War and subsequently by the Watergate scandal and, still later, the oil crisis.

Urban problems finally lost what little remained of their glamour during the 1980s. Today, in fact, the Clinton White House boasts no similar special competence in this area at all. The dominant topic of political conversation since the early 1980s has been the question of how to get government out of the way of the quest for personal wealth. Unfortunately, this change in subject was not the result of resolving urban issues. In fact, throughout this period the segregation by race and income in most of the older and some of the not so old core cities and bordering suburbs has been increasing. Persistent division by race and income underlies the recent subtle, but unmistakable, reemergence of the exploitation of racial tensions to influence political outcomes.

More recently, these trends have taken a new form. Perhaps as a logical consequence of modern economic dislocations and increasingly expensive and abrasive politics, the basic functions of government, more and more, have taken on a two-tier character. What sort of government you get depends not only on where you live but on what you can afford. There is a new sharpening of the disparity between the services, often privatized, available to the well-off and those provided by government for average-income and poor citizens. The consequences of this development are magnified by the steepening of inequality in income and wealth over the past twenty-five years. In the present climate, the bold and expensive urban initiatives that might directly address these developments are, in effect, political nonstarters.

On the other hand, not all of the changes in America have been negative, either for city dwellers in general or for the ethnic and racial minorities who comprise the bulk of the urban poor in particular. African Americans, especially, have made great strides. The Census Bureau reports, for example, that the share of black households earning more than $35,000 a year (inflation-adjusted) increased from 24.9 percent in 1970 to 32 percent in 1995. And the surge in Hispanic populations is changing the calculus of politics in some of the nation's largest states. An optimist might say that the apparently intractable nature of urban problems is a passing phase—that the economic, social, and political conditions necessary for a rekindling of the spirit of constructive change in our cities are already discernable.

In the pages that follow, David Rusk, former mayor of Albuquerque and currently a nationally recognized consultant to numerous American cities, is at once realistic about the current situation in many cities and re-markably positive about the potential for future improvement. The key to his optimism is his belief that a cluster of specific and practical public policy changes could reverse recent trends and spark an urban renaissance. The core of his prescriptions involves three strategies: regional land use planning, regional fair-share affordable housing, and regional revenue sharing. Most important is mandatory mixed-income housing policy for all new residential construction. He makes a compelling case for each, explaining the dramatic changes that implementation could bring.

Rusk is no Pollyanna, and his ideas will not appeal to everyone. Even a critic, however, would be hard put to argue that he fails to come to grips with the scale of the problem and the constraints on potential solutions. If Rusk is right when he says that no typical cocktail of government programs will make enough of a difference, then his approach may serve as the foundation for a set of priorities for those who, over the next generation, will engage in the immense task of revitalizing the urban cores of metropolitan areas.

Finally, Rusk knows that any discussion of public policy in urban areas would be incomplete without an interpretation of the complex interaction of racial attitudes and politics. His personal view in this area is, again, that of an optimist: one who stresses the significance of the progress made on these matters, even while acknowledging that we have miles to go.

Rusk's book continues a long history of concern with urban problems at The Century Foundation, ranging from the work of a group of task forces in the 1970s and 1980s (*CDCs: New Hope for the Inner City, A Nice Place to Live, New York World City, Living Cities*) to August Heckscher's *Open Spaces: The Life of American Cities* to the more recent *Breaking Away: The Future of Cities*, edited by Julia Vitullo-Martin.

On behalf of the Trustees of The Century Foundation, I thank David Rusk for this, his latest contribution to our thinking about one of the great unfinished issues of the twentieth century.

Richard C. Leone, President
The Century Foundation
November 1998

Acknowledgments

FOR THE INFORMATION and insights in this book, I am indebted to the hundreds of individuals and organizations that, as clients and colleagues, have invited me into their communities over the past six years.

This book was written with the encouragement and generous support of The Century Foundation. Greg Anrig first proposed this project, which subsequently received the enthusiastic support of Richard Leone and the foundation's board of trustees. Sarah Ritchie ably shepherded the project along, and Beverly Goldberg guided me through the process of securing a publisher.

With its long history of publishing influential works, I am fortunate that the Brookings Institution Press accepted this project. This has given me the opportunity to work with Nancy Davidson, who has shown both patience and persistence in dealing with a manuscript that has always been a work in progress. She was ably assisted by Venka Macintyre, whose stylistic judgment greatly improved the clarity of my writing; Carlotta Ribar, who proofread the pages; and Julia Petrakis, who prepared the index.

I have benefited from the comments of many colleagues who have reviewed my work at various stages. These have included Carl Abbott, Thomas Bier, Michael Burton, Jack L. Dustin, Linda Gum, Mossik Hacobian, John Klofas, Myron Orfield, Charles Palms, john powell, Henry Richmond, Paul Scully, Joyce Segal, Ralph Sell, Ethan Seltzer, Bernard Tetreault, Richard Tustian, Donald Vermillion, and Marc Weiss. My brother, Richard Rusk, a gifted writer, also read several chapters and provided valued suggestions. I am, of course, solely responsible for all judgments and statements of fact.

In addition to all the hosts of my field work, I am indebted to the re-search staff of the Census Bureau library, in particular Douglas Carroll, Paul Neuhaus, Justin Murray, and William Turner, for their assistance.

I also thank my children, Gregory, Patrick, and Monica, their spouses, Becky Brown and Mark Maghini, and my grandchildren, Daniel and Dylan, for their forbearance, since book writing is always a family undertaking.

Finally, my most valued collaborator has been Delcia, my wife and part-ner. We have visited many communities together, sharing impressions and ideas. She has entered tens of thusands of data items in spreadsheets and has relieved me of all of the administrative detail of our small but busy enter-prise. She is always my most insightful reviewer and loving critic.

Contents

TABLES

FIGURES

1

Journeying through Urban America

"WHERE YOU STAND depends on where you sit." The old adage certainly applies to my perspective on urban America. For the twenty years before researching and writing my first book, *Cities without Suburbs,* I sat in Albuquerque, New Mexico, four of those years in the mayor's chair (1977–81). Having lived previously in the San Francisco Bay area, outside New York City, and in Washington, D.C., I found Albuquerque a very different setting indeed.

Despite several decades of dramatic regional growth, even today Albuquerque remains an almost metropolitan city. Between 1940 and 1990, the population of Bernalillo County, Albuquerque's home county, grew almost sevenfold, from 69,391 to 480,577. Through aggressive annexation of land and subsequent development, Albuquerque expanded its boundaries as well: from just 3 square miles in 1940 to 132 square miles by 1990, while its population ballooned from 35,449 to 384,736.[1] The city captured 86 percent of the region's population growth and almost 90 percent of the new tax base.

Such expansion had big advantages. Tapping most of the region's tax base, the city government was able to keep tax rates relatively low and apply

---

1. By 1996 Albuquerque's municipal area had expanded further to 150 square miles, and its population was 419,681, making it the country's thirty-sixth largest city.

1

them uniformly. (Businesses paid the same property tax rates, for instance, as homeowners.) The city's biggest source of revenue was its share of the state-collected gross receipts tax applied to the sale of all goods and services; the overall tax rate was 5.75 percent (of which the city government received 1.75 percent). Used primarily for construction bonds, the city's property tax was about 11–12 mills (about one-third of 1 percent of market value). Periodically, the city government might go through a local budget crunch, but, compared with the fiscal crises many other cities faced, Albuquerque's problems were minor. Having near-metropolitan jurisdiction, the city government could balance its needs and revenues at moderate tax rates.

Being an almost metropolitan city brought nonfiscal benefits as well. Albuquerque society was much more open than in other communities I had lived in. There were still economic disparities. "Anglos" averaged higher incomes and lower poverty rates than Hispanics, blacks, or Indians.[2] Albuquerque had its richer neighborhoods and its poorer neighborhoods. But, overall, Anglos, Hispanics, blacks, the wealthy, middle class, and poor mixed together much more than in many other places.[3]

Though New Mexico remained one of the nation's poorer states, steady economic growth was certainly one cause of this greater melding. Another factor was undoubtedly the community's relative newness. Founded in 1706, Albuquerque grew primarily after World War II, a period in which racially restrictive housing covenants were declared unconstitutional and civil rights legislation began reshaping the behavior of people and institutions (even if hearts and minds were slower to change).

Albuquerque's greater social wholeness was also helped by the relative unity of its major public institutions. The city served 80 percent of the region's population, for there were only two other small municipalities in the area.[4]

2. In Southwestern parlance, all non-Hispanic whites are "Anglos," whether their names are Jones, Schmidt, Puccini, Pulaski, or Goldstein.

3. Later research confirmed my impressions. Among the country's 117 largest metropolitan areas in 1990, Albuquerque had the third most integrated neighborhoods and third most integrated public schools for the region's small African American population (2.7 percent). For its much larger Hispanic population (37 percent) it ranked somewhat lower on the scale—twenty-fourth for neighborhoods (out of seventy-eight metro areas) and fifty-third for schools (out of 107 metro areas). Black and Hispanic median family incomes were both 63 percent of Anglo median family income, both percentages above national averages. In terms of segregation of the poor, Albuquerque ranked twenty-ninth of the eighty-six largest metro areas.

4. These were the village of Los Ranchos de Albuquerque (5,075 residents) in the North Valley and the tiny mountain village of Tijeras (340 residents). Two self-governing Indian pueblos, Isleta and Sandia, were such different worlds that, as mayor, I saw them as merely blank spaces on the Bernalillo County map.

County government looked after the 18 percent of the region's residents who lived in unincorporated areas. More remarkable, the region had a single, unified public school system, the Albuquerque Public Schools, which even jumped county boundaries to serve urbanizing portions of an adjacent county.

From time to time some citizens might complain about the city government's or the school district's "bigness," but, supported by broad tax bases, both the city and the school district generally served all neighborhoods and schools well.[5] The city and county adopted a common comprehensive land use plan. City zoning encouraged relatively small subdivisions with varied housing types. By design, public housing complexes were small and scattered into many areas of the city. Although the public schools never had a court-ordered busing plan, the school board tweaked boundaries periodically to reduce social and economic disparities.

During my two decades in New Mexico, Albuquerque was certainly not exempt from the ills of American society. But racial and ethnic disparities were less prevalent and more muted than in other metro areas. Albuquerque was simply a more relaxed, more open, more integrated community, and the better for that.

The Theory of Relative Elasticity

In 1991 my wife, Delcia, and I returned to Washington, D.C., where we had lived before moving to Albuquerque. Upon turning my attention to urban trends across the nation, I was immediately struck by the contrast between Albuquerque and many other cities, Washington included. Albuquerque stood out for its sound economic, social, and fiscal health. Were there others like it?

With a personal computer and spreadsheet, I began to build a database from census reports: first for the 50 largest metro areas, then for the 100 largest, finally for all 320 metro areas in the country. I published articles

---

5. With almost 80,000 students, Albuquerque Public Schools was the nation's twenty-fourth largest school district in 1990. Indeed, Albuquerque Public Schools tapped the broadest possible tax base: the entire state of New Mexico. The state government funds 94 percent of the annual operating budgets of the eighty-eight local school districts through a statewide school equalization funding formula. The other 6 percent are federal funds. Like city governments, New Mexico school districts turn to property tax only for capital projects (construction and major renovation of school buildings).

about my findings in the *New York Times* and the *New Democrat* magazine of the centrist Democratic Leadership Council. These led to an invitation to spend the summer of 1992 as a guest scholar on urban affairs at the Woodrow Wilson International Center for Scholars in Washington, D.C. The center's press made a commitment to publish my research.

By summer's end I had written the first draft of a book. I had categorized all metro areas by the population trends in their central cities: "longtime losers," "past-their-peakers," "old suburban boomers," "new suburban boomers," and "cities without suburbs" (a phrase I had coined for the *New Democrat* article). Cities without suburbs, like Albuquerque, had expanded rapidly. Their regions contained many suburban-type subdivisions, but most were found within the city limits. Cities without suburbs dominated their metropolitan regions.

But this typology was unsatisfactory. It merely indicated where all central cities fell on a demographic scale by the 1990s. The classifications did not suggest why the cities had come to be where they were.

During my research I had tracked the geographic and population expansion of all metro areas from 1950 to 1990. I had measured each city's territorial expansion. The almost universal drop in city population densities decade by decade had intrigued me. Late one October night, having finished a major revision of my draft, I was pondering the matter. Suddenly, the thought struck me. "Initial density times rate of boundary expansion equals *elasticity*."[6] My inspiration hardly matched Einstein's "$E = mc^2$" in cosmic significance, but I was excited enough about my own Theory of Relative Elasticity to spend the next thirty-six hours without sleep, pushing around data on spreadsheets.

What emerged was a new way to describe something that had been happening to America's 522 central cities for the past four decades.[7] Postwar development had been horizontal, not vertical. America's urban areas were growing outward (becoming less densely populated), not upward (becoming more densely populated). Cities that had expanded their boundaries through annexation, as had Albuquerque and Charlotte, or through city-county consolidation, as in the case of Nashville-Davidson County and Indianapolis-Marion County, were *elastic* cities.[8] Elastic cities defended them-

6. Subsequent analysis showed that it was more accurate to place three times greater weight on a city's rate of boundary expansion than on its initial population density. This revision was incorporated into the second edition of *Cities without Suburbs*.

7. For more detailed discussion of urban elasticity, see Rusk (1995).

8. A few cities, Los Angeles being one, had begun the postwar period having already annexed

selves against suburban sprawl by capturing a substantial share of new development.

By contrast, many other cities entered the postwar era already densely populated and unable to expand their boundaries at all. New York, Detroit, Cleveland, Baltimore, and Washington would fall into this category.[9] These inelastic cities could not defend themselves against suburban sprawl. They not only did not capture their share of new growth; they *contributed* to suburban expansion. Inelastic cities steadily lost middle-class households, retail stores, offices, and factories to their new suburbs. Despite the revival of many downtown business districts in the 1980s and 1990s, more and more city neighborhoods became warehouses for the region's poor, particularly blacks and Hispanics. With shrinking tax bases and burgeoning service needs, many inelastic city governments slid into fiscal crisis.

Elasticity's consequences for cities were clear. What fascinated me was that the social and economic profile of entire metro areas could be characterized to a large extent by the relative elasticity of their central cities. Schools and neighborhoods in "inelastic" metro areas, for example, were more racially segregated than they were in "elastic" metro areas. Inelastic metro areas were more economically segregated as well, as shown in table 1-1 (the higher the segregation index rating, the greater the degree of segregation of poor households from the rest of the nonpoor).

Over several decades, elastic regions also had higher rates of job creation and income growth than inelastic regions.[10] Income disparities between city and suburban residents were less pronounced. Particularly after adjusting for relative costs of living, many elastic regions had higher real incomes.

Would many of the same explanations I offered for Albuquerque's greater social and economic mobility apply to whole categories of cities and metro areas, classified by elasticity? Is there a regional bias in the data? Yes. Most elastic regions are found in the South and West. Does more vigorous eco-

---

vast areas that were still largely undeveloped. With relatively low initial density, they had room internally to accommodate more growth and were also classified as elastic cities.

9. In the 1950 census 28 central cities had population densities of more than 10,000 persons per square mile. New York City topped the list with 25,046 residents per square mile (Manhattan's population density was 69,017 per square mile). Some 100 central cities would be unable to expand their existing municipal boundaries at all (that is, they were *zero-elastic* cities).

10. A heated academic debate surrounds the issue of the economic interdependence of cities and suburbs. As a practical matter, I have found that when a chamber of commerce must produce an alibi for the sad state of the central city, the whole region is in trouble.

Table 1-1. *Segregation of Poor Households in 117 Major U.S. Metro Areas, by Census Tract, 1990*

Elasticity category	Number of metro areas	Segregation index[a]
Zero	23	47
Low	22	43
Medium	24	40
High	23	39
Hyper	25	34

a. This table employs a common "dissimilarity index" that measures the relative evenness or unevenness of the distribution of a target population across census tracts, schools, and the like. A score of 100 would indicate total segregation (that is, all poor households, and only poor households, live in certain neighborhoods and all nonpoor live everywhere else).

nomic growth facilitate social mobility? Certainly. Social change comes easier in good economic times, and the Sun Belt has outperformed the Rust Belt in recent decades. Have the crises faced by America's old-line manufacturers affected local economic growth differentially? Of course. In the early 1970s, if a region's economy was heavily dependent on "smokestack" industries, it was headed for hard times, regardless of the central city's elasticity. Are elastic regions generally younger, growing up in an era of civil rights laws? Yes.

Metropolitan regions are complex systems influenced by many factors, and I have never meant to suggest that elasticity explains all metropolitan trends. However, a city's past elasticity—its ability to defend its market share of sprawling new development—is an excellent barometer of its current social, economic, and fiscal health.

Big Boxes versus Little Boxes

The way local governance is organized regionally is an important factor shaping regional social, economic, and fiscal patterns. The more fragmented local governance, the more fragmented regional society by race, ethnic group, and income class. I have seen these patterns over and over again, not only in census data but also in visiting scores of metropolitan areas themselves. In regions with "big-box" governments, different racial, ethnic, and income groups tend to mix together more readily than in regions with multiple "little-box" governments.

School integration is a straightforward example of this phenomenon. In 1990 about one-quarter of all school-age children in both metro Charlotte and metro Cleveland were African American. With its countywide school systems, including the unified Charlotte-Mecklenburg County district, metro Charlotte had only nine school districts. For almost a quarter-century Carolina school districts have operated under federal court-ordered desegregation plans. Metro Charlotte's school segregation index measured a low 33, and a 22 within the Charlotte-Mecklenburg unified system.[11]

By contrast, metro Cleveland had fifty-six separate school systems, including thirty-two in Cuyahoga County. Federal desegregation orders covered only the Cleveland Public Schools.[12] By 1990 the city school system enrolled less than 30 percent of the region's public school students and was two-thirds black, whereas most suburban systems were overwhelmingly white. Metro Cleveland's school segregation index measured a high 79, the nation's seventh worst.[13]

In a less obvious way, the same kinds of factors help produce more racially and economically mixed societies in regions with large, constantly expanding central cities. Public housing is often more scattered across a broader range of neighborhoods within elastic cities than within the combination of inelastic cities and their independent suburbs. City neighborhoods tend to feature a greater mixture of owner-occupied and rental housing than suburban neighborhoods. Many black families may be readier to move into largely white neighborhoods within the city itself than into almost totally

11. The segregation index used here, as in table 1-1, is a "dissimilarity index" that, in this case, measures the relative unevenness of the distribution of black students among the region's public high schools. A score of 100 would equal total apartheid; a score of 0, in metro Charlotte or metro Cleveland's case, would mean that one-quarter of the population in every public high school in the metropolitan area is African American. A 22 means that only 22 percent of the African American high school students in the Charlotte-Mecklenburg system would have to shift schools in the "right" proportions for every high school's enrollment to mirror the districtwide minority enrollment.

12. Under the U.S. Supreme Court's 1974 decision in *Milliken* v. *Bradley*, suburban school districts do not have to participate in desegregation plans with central-city systems.

13. Moreover, the Charlotte region's more integrated public schools retained a higher proportion of school-age children (93 percent) than did the Cleveland region's public schools (81 percent). Undoubtedly, the greater availability of Catholic education in the urban North contributed to the lower share of school-age children in the Cleveland region's public school systems. However, relatively few white parents appeared to be fleeing the Charlotte area's more integrated systems. Some 91 percent of white school-age children attended metro Charlotte's public schools (84 percent within Charlotte-Mecklenburg) compared with only 76 percent in metro Cleveland's fifty-six school districts. (Only 56 percent of Cleveland's white school-age children attended the Cleveland public schools.)

white-dominated suburbs. If necessary, they can still find black champions down at city hall.

What happens *inside* large, expanding, elastic cities, however, is probably less important than what does *not* happen *outside* in many suburbs surrounding inelastic cities. Again, metro Cleveland has 89 municipalities and 42 townships, including 60 local governments in Cuyahoga County alone. There is always another level of local government below county government. Suburban cities, villages, and townships cover every square foot of the four-county region, and all 131 exercise their own independent planning and zoning powers. A few communities, such as Shaker Heights and Cleveland Heights, have welcomed racial integration in recent decades. The unspoken mission of most little city councils, little township boards, and little school boards, however, is "to keep our city/our town/our schools just the way they are for people just like *us*" (whoever "us" happens to be). This tacit agenda is often enforced through fierce resistance to multifamily housing (not to speak of the public firestorm that greets any proposed suburban public housing project). Suburbs invented and perfected the practice of "exclusionary zoning."

By contrast, Charlotte's seven-county region, with almost two-thirds of metro Cleveland's total population, counts only fifty local governments, and dominant Mecklenburg County encompasses only the city of Charlotte and six suburban municipalities. By 1990 more than half of Mecklenburg County's 527 square miles was still unincorporated and under the county government's authority. Even now, a countywide joint planning commission and single planning staff serve all eight jurisdictions. Any new development will ultimately be incorporated into one of the seven existing municipalities. Charlotte and its six suburban neighbors have executed formal agreements specifying zones of future annexation for each. The Charlotte area is not beset by the intense turf protection that afflicts the Cleveland area.

Elasticity: An Elusive Tool

As mentioned earlier, most elastic cities are found in the South and West and most inelastic cities in the Northeast and Middle West. In writing my first book, I realized that elasticity analysis might therefore create the false impression that it is just a way of describing contrasts between the Sun and Rust belts. My initial analysis was based on trends in all 320 metro areas. To communicate the central themes more effectively, however, I paired specific communities that many readers could relate to. To minimize the Sun Belt–Rust Belt dichotomy, in *Cities without Suburbs* I intentionally contrasted elastic and inelastic cities and their metro areas within the same section of the country or even within the same state. Rather than comparing high-elastic Charlotte with zero-elastic Cleveland, for example, I looked at Cleveland alongside high-elastic Columbus, Ohio's capital city. Matching regions by population size and racial composition, I paired high-elastic Indianapolis with low-elastic Milwaukee; hyperelastic Nashville with low-elastic Louisville; hyperelastic Raleigh with low-elastic Richmond, two southern state capitals; and high-elastic Madison with zero-elastic Harrisburg, two northern state capitals. In every instance, the anticipated demographic, economic, and social contrasts appeared as expected.

The primary policy recommendation of *Cities without Suburbs* was that cities should try to maintain or reacquire elasticity: they should secure or defend workable annexation laws, promote city-county consolidations, and support unifying school districts. They should create, in effect, quasi-metropolitan, more unified, big-box governance structures that could help diminish the racial and economic segregation that has created an underclass in many of America's major urban areas.

At the same time, I already understood how difficult it is to change formal government structures. In the past half-century, voters around the country have turned down five times as many proposed city-county consolidations as they have approved. If anything, *Cities without Suburbs* was meant to be just a wake-up call. To say to much of the Northeast and Middle West, whose experiences dominate the perceptions of federal urban policymakers: "Hey, we do things differently in the other half of the country and it works better." And to say to the South and West: "Watch out. Hold on to the good policies you've got. Don't follow the rest of the country down the failed path of growth-constrained cities."

"Where you stand depends on where you sit." Since *Cities without Suburbs* first appeared in April 1993, I have hardly sat down anywhere. I have made over 300 trips to more than ninety metro areas as a speaker and consultant on urban affairs. I have completed a dozen statewide studies and analyzed fifty-eight metro areas in depth.

Two-thirds of my work has been in the Northeast and the Middle West, where local governance is much more highly fragmented than in the South and West. In some northern regions, the policy prescriptions set out in *Cities without Suburbs* regarding a city's elasticity are still relevant. In most of the northern tier of states, they are not. Local government boundaries are cast in concrete from Maine through Pennsylvania. In the Middle West, annexation is still a possibility for some cities (Columbus and Springfield, Ohio, for example). Sometimes formal governmental consolidation can occur in extraordinary circumstances. In 1969, then-mayor Richard Lugar maneuvered the consolidation of Indianapolis and Marion County through Indiana's Republican-controlled political system. In Michigan, the Kellogg Corporation hammered local voters into merging Battle Creek City and suburban Battle Creek Township in 1982. Both mergers stimulated an almost Sun Belt–like dynamism in the expanded Indianapolis and Battle Creek. Where annexation or consolidation is still feasible, my advice is "Do it."

Acting as One

But from the outset I have had to answer this question: if a highly fragmented region cannot, in effect, *become one* governmentally, can the many individual governments be brought to *act as one?* What are the most critical issues on which they must collaborate? What are the qualities of highly elastic cities that might be duplicated without formally changing local government structure? In other words, what policies might serve as substitutes for elasticity?[14]

The central issue facing most cities is the concentration of poverty, particularly the existence of high-poverty ghettos and barrios. In highly fragmented regions, high concentrations of poverty also produce wide fiscal disparities among different jurisdictions. In more unified regions, consolidated city-county governments or constantly expanding central cities serve as quasi-regional revenue-sharing mechanisms. Elastic city governments convert taxes from wealthier neighborhoods into services for poorer neighborhoods. Fiscally, highly fragmented regions could "act as one" if they adopted regional revenue or tax base sharing.

Second, moving people is far more important than moving money. In America's metropolitan areas three out of four poor whites live in middle-class, often suburban neighborhoods; most poor whites are part (albeit a marginal part) of mainstream society. By contrast, one out of two poor Hispanics and three out of four poor blacks live in poor inner-city neighborhoods. All cities have their poorer neighborhoods, but elastic cities tend to show less severe concentrations of minority poor; a somewhat higher percentage of poor minority households are mainstreamed in middle-class

14. John Blair of Wright State University has referred to such policies as "elasticity mimics."

neighborhoods. To "act as one," regional housing policies could require a fair share of low- and moderate-income housing in all suburban jurisdictions in order to help disperse high concentrations of poor households from central cities.

A third critical issue has emerged in my own thinking since I first wrote *Cities without Suburbs:* the need to control suburban sprawl. My policy perspective in *Cities without Suburbs* was "Sprawl happens; capture it." A central theme of this book is "It is better to control sprawl than just capture it."

I am indebted to many people for educating me about sprawl's consequences, but above all to Henry Richmond, a long-time leader of Oregon's growth management movement. Sprawl has most often been criticized for ravaging the natural landscape, but its impact on the human landscape has been even more deplorable. In the prewar era, city neighborhoods typically developed piecemeal at different periods of time.[15] Older cities featured different styles and types of housing and were much more diverse communities economically. By contrast, postwar suburban subdivisions were almost always built all at once, tended to offer only one type of housing in limited styles, and targeted a relatively narrow income range.

Most metropolitan areas are now slowly becoming less segregated by race but steadily more segregated by income. Elastic cities may sprawl across the landscape, but they tend to have higher densities than the uncoordinated developments mushrooming in the multiple little cities and townships around inelastic cities. Most elastic cities have substantial power to control regional development more tightly (though they rarely use such power fully). Limiting sprawl through regional land use planning would also help metropolitan areas "act as one."

Playing the Outside Game

This book's primary concern is the plight of central cities in the Northeast and Middle West. Most cannot annex and most cannot consolidate. How can they be helped? My answer is a three-pronged agenda:

—To help control sprawl, require regional land use planning.

—To help dissolve concentrations of poverty, ensure that all suburbs have their fair share of low- and moderate-income housing.

—To help reduce fiscal disparities, implement regional revenue sharing.

15. I am old enough that "prewar" and "postwar" refer to World War II.

These are the key policies that form the "outside game." Part 2 of this book details the best practices I have seen for each of these regional strategies.

Chapter 8 discusses the history and impact of Oregon's statewide land use law in the Portland area. After two decades of implementing an antisprawl "urban growth boundary," the Portland area is clearly marching to a different drummer than most of urban America—and reaping enormous benefits from a booming economy and high quality of urban life.

Chapter 9 examines the nation's best and oldest mixed-income housing laws in Montgomery County, Maryland. For twenty-five years a county ordinance has mandated that all new subdivisions and apartment developments—many in the county's wealthiest neighborhoods—provide for a minimum of 15 percent low- and moderate-income housing.

Chapter 10 explores the Dayton area's ED/GE plan, the nation's most significant voluntary, multijurisdictional revenue-sharing program. It is both a remarkable success story and a reminder of the limits of voluntary cooperation among fiercely independent local governments. The state-mandated tax base–sharing program in the Minneapolis-St. Paul area, for example, has more than 100 times the fiscal impact of the Dayton area's voluntary system.

Chapter 11 points out who realistically must put such regional programs into effect—state legislatures—and how to build majority legislative coalitions. Minnesota shows how: ally central cities and older, now declining suburbs.

Part 3 examines other tools and organizing strategies for regionalism. Chapter 12 details the struggles in Washington, D.C., to end the federal public housing program's impact as the greatest instrument of economic segregation in American life. Chapter 13 provides case studies of key members of regional reform movements—coalitions of inner-city and suburban churches, business organizations, universities, grass-roots citizens' groups—and ends with assessments of the role of philanthropic foundations and city mayors.

Finally, chapter 14 sums up my thoughts on what it will take to break out of the grip of our growing divisions and become the America we say we want to be.

Grading the Inside Game

But first, in part 1, we need to explore further how many of our cities got into their present sad state and the attempts to counter urban neighborhood decline over the past three decades. For three decades the federal government has targeted poor areas with a succession of antipoverty initiatives—community action programs, model cities programs, community development block grants, urban development action grants, empowerment community and enterprise zone funds and tax credits—all variations on what I call the "inside game." Chapters 2 and 3 analyze the impact of thirty-four widely lauded "community development corporations." These are private, nonprofit, community-based organizations engaged in housing development, commercial redevelopment, and local social service programs. Chapter 4 highlights the twin factors—sprawl and race—shaping metropolitan development patterns. Chapter 5 elaborates on "the Sprawl Machine," chapter 6 on "the Poverty Machine," and chapter 7 on "the Deficit Machine."

In part 1, based on hard, cold facts on income and population, I conclude that playing only the "inside game" is a losing strategy for even the most exemplary players. For both poverty-impacted cities and poverty-impacted neighborhoods, even the strongest inside game must be matched by a strong "outside game"—the regional strategies outlined in part 2.

In a sense this book traces a personal journey. In 1963, fresh out of the University of California at Berkeley, I began my professional career as a civil rights and antipoverty organizer with the Washington Urban League. With the advent of the federal war on poverty, our local Urban League took responsibility for spurring community action in one of Washington's poorest black ghettos. Neighborhood residents themselves were the primary organizers, but in the 1960s I spent many nights and weekends in meetings of block clubs, neighborhood improvement clubs, a self-help organization for ex-convicts, and other community action groups.

Moving on to New Mexico, in the early 1970s I was active in Albuquerque's Model Cities program as director of the city-county comprehensive manpower program. Later, in 1974, I was a citizen member of the Citizens Advisory Group shaping Albuquerque's initial allocation of community development block grant (CDBG) funds.[16] As mayor of Albuquerque, I oversaw CDBG expenditures and secured the first "pocket of poverty" grant from the Carter administration's urban development action grant (UDAG) program in 1979.

Since returning to Washington in 1991, I have revisited the scene of my 1960s antipoverty work. Part of the old neighborhood has literally disap-

16. The community development block grant program was the Nixon administration's largely cosmetic repackaging of the model cities program.

peared in the wake of "progress." A bare parking lot, hugging a wide trench for an aborted interstate freeway, has replaced my old office building. The tenements of DeFrees Street have vanished under the new Astroturf athletic field of Gonzaga High School. Row houses on lower New Jersey Avenue were bulldozed to make way for two new hotels and several office buildings. Parts of upper New Jersey Avenue and adjacent streets have a gap-toothed look: rubble-strewn, weed-covered empty lots and boarded-up, sometimes partly burned, abandoned buildings alternate with aging, but still-occupied row houses. Elsewhere there are newer, modest, garden-style apartments and townhouses, clearly an improvement over past conditions.

Thirty-three years ago the Urban League helped local residents set up a tent city on several vacant acres of land on New York Avenue and North Capitol Street. The tent city, proclaimed "the nation's first Demonstration City," stood in protest of bureaucratic foot-dragging on a long-promised public housing project.[17] Today that project, a combination high-rise for senior citizens and family townhouses, is undergoing total renovation after more than two decades of hard use. Some of the residents displaced by new hotels, office buildings, and the high school ball field still live there. It is hard to see, however, that life is significantly better in a neighborhood that so many, including many residents themselves, tried to improve over three decades.

A word of explanation for the very personal tone of this book. *Cities without Suburbs* and *Baltimore Unbound,* my second book, were both written for what several years ago were fashionably called "policy wonks." Those earlier books featured tables and tables of statistics. Of the 140-plus pages of *Cities without Suburbs,* only 5 or 6 contained personal references.

There will be plenty of data in this book as well. Over the past six years many listeners at the hundreds of speeches I have given have said that, though I am a good enough speaker, it is the data I present that make such a compelling case. I am not going to abandon my most persuasive sales technique.

But successful political reform movements are not about data. They are about real people in real situations: inspired legislators, courageous city and county officials, determined citizen activists. I hope that the success stories told here will inspire some readers to step forward in their own communities. There is nothing so special about a Portland, a Montgomery County (Maryland or Ohio), or a Minnesota that their successes cannot be repeated elsewhere.

17. Within a week, the Johnson White House had renamed the just authorized demonstration cities program the model cities program.

I also appear personally at many points in these pages. I am not trying to insert myself Forrest Gump–like into the middle of significant events. In fact, I had nothing to do with creating the policies and programs I most admire.

Over the past six years, however, I have been at least periodically on the scene in many communities in which regional reform movements are gathering momentum. Often I have been the "national expert" brought in to help local sponsors attract added attention to their reform agenda. Any major success requires local leaders to do all the heavy lifting, and they, not I, will deserve most of the credit.

It has long been a saying in my family that "there is a tremendous difference between the world of opinion and the world of decision." As a former federal official, city department head, state legislator, and mayor, I have been part of the world of decision. As an author, speaker, and consultant, I am now clearly part of the world of opinion. Many of the judgments I make and policies I recommend are easy for me to discuss but very difficult for elected officials to embrace.

I recognize that. Everything recommended in these pages, however, has been adopted by some group of city or county officials or state legislators. They have stepped up to make the tough decisions. Their states and communities are much better places for their vision, tenacity, and courage.

PART ONE

The Inside Game

PART 1 OPENS with a visit to the Bedford Stuyvesant Restoration Corporation. Founded in 1967 primarily by New York Senator Bobby Kennedy, "Restoration" is the grandfather of all nonprofit community development corporations (CDCs), which now number more than 2,000 nationwide. In the early 1990s CDCs became popular organizations to support in business, foundation, and government circles. Any pretense of devoting serious federal money to fighting inner-city poverty had vanished during the Reagan-Bush years. Nor would the Great Society be revived with the return of a Democrat to the White House in 1993.[1] In his 1996 State of the Union speech, President Bill Clinton would proclaim that "the era of Big Government is over."

CDCs, embodying all the characteristics emphasized in the political buzzwords of the day, seemed the logical choice to fill the vacuum. They are "private sector" entities (though most rely heavily on government grants). Technically nonprofit organizations, CDCs seem to operate "like a business," at least more than government agencies do. CDCs deal primarily in "hard services" rather than "soft services." Almost all are bricks-and-mortar operations. CDCs build or renovate low- and moderate-income housing. They struggle to revive neighborhood shopping centers. Though some CDCs run extensive recreation and social service programs as well, one can visit a new CDC-built housing development, shop at a CDC-

---

1. In actuality, the high-water mark of federal urban aid occurred during the Nixon years, especially with the creation of general revenue sharing.

revived supermarket, or (more rarely) walk through a new, CDC-recruited factory, warehouse, or telemarketing center in an inner-city neighborhood.

"Self-help," "citizen participation," "empowerment" are constantly invoked. Each new generation of aspiring inner-city activists, I have observed, assumes that the decay and decline around them reflect, in part, the fact that *they* have not been involved. Empower the new generation, and we will lead the neighborhood to the Promised Land. Generation after generation, "empowerment" is always a surefire rallying cry.

To the world beyond ghettos and barrios, part of the CDC movement's bedrock appeal is no doubt its commitment to solving inner-city poverty *in place*. To improve the lives of inner-city residents, most CDC advocates believe, new opportunities for low-income residents have to be created in inner-city neighborhoods, although more progressive CDCs may seek to attract some middle-income households from the outside, dabbling in the import market. CDCs rarely design programs for the export market, that is, to help neighborhood residents move out.

As chapters 2 and 3 show, these tactics are producing discouraging results: even the nation's best CDCs, despite some block-by-block victories, are losing the war against poverty itself. In effect, CDCs are expected to help a crowd of poor people run up a down escalator, an escalator that is engineered to come down faster and faster than most poor people can run up.

In these pages I do not mean to criticize CDCs themselves. Those that I have visited or worked with have had many able and extraordinarily committed staff and volunteers (both residents of the target neighborhoods themselves as well as recruits from the larger business, professional, and governmental community). In fact, given the adverse conditions they face, most CDCs are engaged in a truly heroic struggle.

My exasperation stems from the way in which the CDC paradigm allows powerful institutions to shirk once again their responsibility to confront racial and economic segregation. It is easier to pair corporate money and volunteers with inner-city schools than to allow inner-city students to attend the schools that corporate executives' own children attend. It is easier to give foundation grants for affordable housing projects in inner-city neighborhoods than to demand a "fair share" of low- and moderate-income housing in neighborhoods where many foundation executives dwell. It is easier for a governor, senator, or president to thump the drum of inner-city revitalization: "Let's solve (and keep) the problems *in there*" rather than admit that part of the solution must be found *out here,* where the bulk of the voters now live. Easier? Not easier at all, if the goal is to achieve substantial progress. It is "easier" only in that this path is more socially and politically comfortable.

A small case in point: in 1992 Senator Bill Bradley (D-N.J.) made headlines with a remarkable speech (at least, for the 1990s) on the U.S. Senate floor. It was reprinted many times and widely distributed as a pamphlet titled "Race and the American City."[2] "Slavery was our original sin, just as race remains our unresolved dilemma," the senator said. "The future of American cities is inextricably bound to the issue of race and ethnicity." He then gave a blunt, unflinching, eloquent analysis of American cities, decrying the fact that they "are poorer, sicker, less educated, and more violent than at any time in my lifetime." Bradley predicted that "the future of urban America will take one of three paths: abandonment, encirclement, or conversion."

—*Abandonment* means that "like the small town whose industry leaves, the city will wither and disappear. . . . The self-destruction has reached a point of no return and [cities] will crumble from within."

—*Encirclement* means "that people in cities will live in enclaves. The racial and ethnic walls will go higher. The class lines will be manned by ever increasing security forces and communal life will disappear."

—*Conversion* means "winning over all segments of urban life to a new politics of change, empowerment, and common effort. It is as different from the politics of dependency as it is from the politics of greed."

"When politicians don't talk about the reality that everyone knows exists, they cannot lead us out of our current crisis," the senator warned. "Institutions are no better than the people that run them."

Senator Bradley talked the talk, but his legislative proposals several months later hardly laid a hand on the "current crisis." His multipoint program, as I recall, was a watery gruel of more federal assistance for neighborhood-level, miniproject activities. Once again, a national leader was treating symptoms rather than systemic causes.

Among all states, New Jersey has the ninth most racially segregated metro areas and the seventh most racially segregated schools, but there were no proposals to combat what the senator targeted as "racism . . . alive and well." Among all states, New Jersey's central cities have the second largest gap between city and suburban incomes, the third lowest average

2. Quotations are taken from the reprint by the Massachusetts Mutual Life Insurance Company distributed by Senator Bradley's office.

incomes, and the fifth worst poverty burden, but there was no effort to amend federal tax policies that continue to favor suburban homeowners over city apartment dwellers. During the 1980s new development in New Jersey consumed land at almost twice the rate of population growth, yet there were no proposals to curb the massive federal subsidies for sprawl-inducing highways and sewage lines.

Knowing how the Congress actually works, my guess is that Senator Bradley's proposals were a hastily approved pastiche of ideas that caught the attention of some junior aide or of the senator himself during tours of New Jersey's distressed cities. But all in all, in a state where voters are 70 percent white and 85 percent suburban, the senator's package was a politically comfortable set of proposals. As part 1 shows, sprawl and race—the two factors underlying the senator's description of America's cities as "poorer, sicker, less educated, and more violent" than at any time in his life—have become deeply institutionalized.

2

Bedford Stuyvesant: Beginnings

"AREN'T THE offices of Bedford Stuyvesant Restoration Corporation located near here?"

The desk sergeant at New York City's Seventy-Ninth Precinct looked up at me.

"The 1300 block of Fulton Street," he replied. "We'll have a squad car take you there."

"No thanks. I can walk. It must be only four or five blocks away." A little startled by his suggestion, I did not want to be any trouble to my impromptu hosts. As a middle-aged white man in a business suit with a briefcase in one of Brooklyn's toughest black ghettos, I would probably have accepted his offer if it had been eleven o'clock at night. The time, however, was eleven on a beautiful, sunny May morning.

Located catty-corner to Von King Park, the one-story, 1960s-style precinct house was not at all like the gritty, cacophonous New York police stations portrayed on TV cop shows such as *Hill Street Blues* or *NYPD Blue*. In fact, it looked like a typical police substation in Albuquerque. The tree-shaded streets were lined with elegant old brownstones and bland, mid-rise apartment buildings. In the morning sunlight the scene looked benign enough.

"Wait for a squad car," the sergeant firmly insisted. "You don't know the neighborhood."

I waited for the squad car.

I had come to Bedford Stuyvesant on the spur of the moment. That afternoon I was to address the 1995 national conference of the Council on Foundations, meeting nine miles away in Manhattan's New York Hilton. The topic of the three-day conference was foundation support for private anti-poverty programs in the nation's inner cities. The conference organizers had scheduled field trips to the South Bronx and Brownsville. These were the sites of the latest showcase programs by widely praised community development corporations such as Banana Kelly Neighborhood Improvement Association and the East Brooklyn Congregations.

The neighborhood tours were sure to be spiritually uplifting and professionally reassuring for the many foundation participants. They would be shown examples of renovated, not-for-profit, low-income housing projects and trim high-rises for senior citizens. They would visit colorful, lively day care centers and job training programs with encouraging initial placement results. A highlight of the tour would be Charlotte Street, a suburban-style neighborhood of new, single-family townhouses with neat, postage-stamp front yards where, just a few years before, the ruins of abandoned tenements smoldered in the midst of Fort Apache, The Bronx.

Having been a civil rights and antipoverty worker in the 1960s, however, I had more institutional memory than many of the younger foundation officials I would be addressing. There are *always* exemplary new programs to see. But do this year's success stories translate into long-term progress for many inner-city neighborhoods?

So, without any advance planning, after getting off the shuttle from Washington, D.C., I opened the Brooklyn volume of the New York City phone book and located what looked like a police station serving the Bedford Stuyvesant area. After verifying that fact with a brief phone call, I took the long cab ride from La Guardia to the Seventy-Ninth Precinct.

From Bedford Corners to Bed-Stuy

While waiting to talk with the precinct's community relations officer (who was off at a neighborhood meeting), I brushed up on Bedford Stuyvesant's history from a four-page mimeographed brochure the desk sergeant handed me. The community began as Bedford Corners, a Dutch farming community in the 1600s. By the mid-nineteenth century Bedford Corners had become a suburban locale of large houses and great lawns for white middle- and upper-income families. The opening of the Brooklyn Bridge in 1883 and the coming of elevated railroads shortly thereafter intensified development. Dozens of blocks of impressive brownstone, graystone, and gray brick homes in the Romanesque Revival style were built in Bedford and neighboring Stuyvesant.

The new republic's first census in 1790 had recorded a population of 204 for Bedford Corners, one-third of whom were identified as black slaves. With the free black communities of nearby Weeksville and Carrsville, these formed the core of the area's black population. In the 1920s this core began expanding rapidly as tens of thousands of black migrants moved into the area. Many came from deteriorating Manhattan neighborhoods (soon to be connected to Brooklyn by the A-train, immortalized by Duke Ellington). Legions more arrived from Deep South cotton states during the Great Migration.

The racial turnover was swift and often bitter. In fact, the handout noted, "the *Brooklyn Eagle* first coined the term Bedford Stuyvesant in its reports of whites and Blacks stockpiling arms to be used against each other." The handout continued:

> Not unlike Harlem, considered the center of Black activity for decades, Bedford Stuyvesant was a Mecca with flaws. Limited employment gains made during the labor shortage of World War I were erased by the Depression. Single-family homes were subdivided into single-room dwellings to accommodate the influx of newcomers. High interest mortgage rates encouraged neglect by absentee landlords. Real estate associations promoted racially exclusionary zoning. Police protection dwindled as did sanitation service when the white population fled. Prohibitive prices and ethnic and class discrimination, coupled with a deterioration of city services, gave rise to Bedford Stuyvesant's reputation as a large American ghetto.

By the 1950s, most white residents had fled to new subdivisions in Queens and Long Island. With almost 400,000 black residents, "Bed-Stuy" had become the nation's second largest black community, surpassed only by Chicago's South Side.

Having finished the pamphlet, I learned what I could from the police station's walls. There were graphs showing the crimes reported over the previous three months.[1] Not knowing the precinct's current population, I could not calculate a rough crime rate. Coming from the mayhem of Washington,

---

1. For January–March 1995, Precinct Seventy-Nine recorded 11 murders, 454 robberies, 325 burglaries, 132 grand larcenies, 26 rapes, 220 felony assaults, 139 grand larceny auto, and 322 other felonies. I later calculated, in roughest terms, that Bed-Stuy's murder rate was about half of Washington, D.C.'s rate.

D.C., where I now lived, the eleven homicides recorded for the three months struck me as relatively low. (With just under 600,000 residents, the nation's capital would record 469 murders that year.) A map of the precinct charted where crimes had occurred by "community policing district," the 1990s revival of the 1890s police beat. On the walls were the name, rank, and photograph of each officer assigned to the precinct. The command reflected the New York Police Department's citywide demographics (overwhelmingly white and male) rather than Bedford Stuyvesant's demographics (86 percent black, 55 percent female).

The community relations officer returned from the neighborhood meeting. His responses to my unscheduled interview were polite, professional, and unmemorable. It was after the interview that I had asked about the location of the Bedford Stuyvesant Restoration Corporation.

Once in the squad car, I suggested that I was in no hurry and would be happy to see some of the neighborhood as we cruised. We drove back and forth along one-way streets, weaving steadily closer to Fulton Street. It was a quiet morning, no calls on the radio, nothing happening on the sidewalks. I asked about crime levels in the precinct. "Better than some, worse than others" was the noncommittal reply. If the officers could wish for one thing for the neighborhood, what would it be? "Get rid of the drugs. Without drugs, 90 percent of the problems would go away," the older officer responded.

Restoration: Vanguard of Hopes and Dreams

Restoration Plaza could not be missed. A converted, abandoned milk bottling factory, now doubled in size, it was easily the largest building complex for blocks. It surrounded a courtyard where various neighborhood retail businesses were located: a Baskin-Robbins, a Lerner Shops, Chemical Bank, Citibank, Consolidated Edison, Brooklyn Union Gas. I walked through the lobby, past the Billie Holiday Theater, and was directed to the sixth-floor offices of "Mr. Palms."

White, mustached, late-sixties, Charley Palms was the organization's vice president. Hired in October 1967, he was almost an original staff member and was specially recognized in Restoration's twenty-fifth anniversary booklet.[2] Our chat about Restoration's history and accomplishments reaffirmed the reasons why I had made the pilgrimage to Bedford Stuyvesant.

---

2. Facts and quotations about Restoration's history and achievements are taken from *Bedford Stuyvesant Restoration Corporation 1967–92: 25 Years of Making a Difference* and other agency handouts.

Bedford Stuyvesant Restoration Corporation is the progenitor of about 2,000 community development corporations serving many of the nation's poorest urban ghettos and barrios. Restoration was the first, intended as the model for all that were to come. Its pedigree could not have been more high-powered. The organization was conceived in 1966 in the wake of Senator Robert F. Kennedy's highly publicized walk through Bed-Stuy. New York's junior senator was naturally eager to help one of the poorest districts in his state. He was also rankled by Lyndon Johnson's putting the LBJ brand on what Bobby Kennedy viewed as a piece of his assassinated brother's legacy. During Bobby Kennedy's years as John F. Kennedy's attorney general, many antipoverty program concepts, including "community action," had been incubated in the President's Committee on Juvenile Delinquency, housed in the Department of Justice. Renamed and expanded manyfold, the war on poverty was now the keystone of President Johnson's Great Society.

Responding to neighborhood appeals, Kennedy decided to initiate a new poverty-fighting vehicle, a community-based, private, not-for-profit "community development corporation." "The program for the development of Bedford Stuyvesant will combine the best of community action with the best of the private enterprise system," Kennedy told a neighborhood gathering in December 1966. "Neither by itself is enough, but in their combination lies our hope for the future."

As political godfathers for the new organization, Kennedy recruited New York's charismatic mayor, John Lindsay, and New York's senior U.S. senator, Jacob Javits. Business muscle could not have been stronger: IBM chairman Thomas B. Watson Jr., Citibank chairman Walter Wriston, CBS chairman William Paley, former secretary of the treasury Douglas Dillon, and a half dozen other blue-chip corporate and foundation leaders.

Kennedy and Javits joined forces to amend the federal Economic Opportunity Act to launch a "special impact program." The Kennedy-Javits amendment mandated federal funding for the infant community development corporation. Kennedy announced a seven-point action plan that, he hoped, would serve as a national model for inner-city revival. The plan called for the formation of two key organizations:

—Bedford Stuyvesant Renewal and Rehabilitation Corporation (forerunner of the Bedford Stuyvesant Restoration Corporation). Directed by a board of distinguished community representatives, the group would spearhead the neighborhood's economic, social, and physical development by sponsoring housing construction and rehabilitation, cultural and recreational facilities, job training programs, industrial and small business development, and programs to improve public schools.

—Its big business partner, the Bedford Stuyvesant Development and Services Corporation (D & S), would "involve and draw on the talents, energies, and knowledge of some of the foremost members of the American business community."

Other steps included recruiting a professional staff, enlisting the support of city and state governments, securing major federal grants from the Department of Housing and Urban Development and the Labor Department as the core financial support, and acquiring additional private foundation funding. New York's Pratt Institute and internationally renowned architect I. M. Pei would develop a series of plans for the area's physical redesign.

On the eve of the program's inauguration, Kennedy summed up the task ahead and the stakes involved:

> This is a unique effort—the only one of its kind and scope in the country. We have to show that it can be done. . . . We are striking out in new directions, on new courses, sometimes without a map or compass to guide us. We are going to try, as few have tried before, not just to have programs like others have, but to create new kinds of systems for education and health and employment and housing. We here are going to see, in fact, whether the city and its people, with the cooperation of governments and private business and foundations, can meet the challenges of urban life in the last third of the Twentieth Century.
>
> And it is Bedford Stuyvesant that is the vanguard—Bedford Stuyvesant that can take the lead. If we here can meet and master our problems; if this community can become an avenue of opportunity and a place of pleasure and excitement for its people, then others will take heart, and men all over the United States will remember your contribution with the deepest of gratitude. . . . But if this community fails, then others will falter, and a noble dream of equality and dignity in our cities will be sorely tried.[3]

Touring Bed-Stuy: A Different Burger King

Now, that last third of the twentieth century was almost over. Had Bedford Stuyvesant succeeded or failed? To pursue the answer, my wife, Delcia, and I returned several months later for a follow-up visit. Arriving early for our

---

3. *Bedford Stuyvesant Restoration Corporation 1967–92.*

appointment, we decided to have a cup of coffee at the Burger King across the street from Restoration's offices. A Burger King was a good sign. Taken for granted by millions of suburbanites, a new Burger King, Pizza Hut, or McDonald's franchise is tangible evidence of economic progress in scores of dusty southwestern crossroad towns, and in big-city ghettos as well. (A McDonald's was just down Fulton Street.)

This was almost a standard Burger King: same menu, same prices, scrubbed, cheery, and well lit. It was more interesting than most Burger Kings. In a glassed-in eating area toward the back, what may have been "the oldest, established, permanent, floating *chess* game in New York" was in progress. Shouting good-natured taunts and slapping their timers with a flourish, two black men were playing the kind of speed chess depicted in the film *Searching for Bobby Fischer*. Vanquishing a younger opponent, the champion—wiry, gap-toothed, of indeterminate middle age—and his new challenger greeted each other with well-honed trash talk worthy of two NBA point guards. Neither of the players was visibly a customer of Burger King, but the staff seemed to welcome the chess tournament as a local variation from the standard Burger King formula.

In two other ways, however, this was not a typical suburban Burger King. Heading for the rest rooms, we found the rest room doors could be opened only by special tokens (free but dispensed judiciously by the counter personnel). In addition, customers and staff had to slide tokens, cups of coffee, hamburgers and fries, or handfuls of bills and change through narrow openings cut through the inch-thick, ceiling-high, bulletproof Plexiglas shields that spanned the entire counter area.

Leaving the Burger King, over the next several hours we took a windshield tour of the neighborhood. Our host again was Charley Palms, joined by Lester Matthews, a courtly black man who had been a lifelong neighborhood leader and now was, like Charley, a Restoration staff member.

Pathmark Supermarket

Driving out of Restoration's underground garage, both men pointed out the Pathmark supermarket taking up one whole end of Restoration Plaza. Except for the large Pathmark sign, the supermarket was easy to miss. The blank, fortress-like brick walls gave no hint of the nature or volume of the business inside.

The Pathmark was one of Restoration's proudest victories. Opened in 1979, the 30,000-square-foot store was the first new supermarket to be built in Bedford Stuyvesant in nearly thirty years. At a cost of $2.5 million, the project was a joint venture; two-thirds was owned by Restoration and one-third by Supermarkets General of New Jersey, owner of the Pathmark chain.

Chalking up annual sales of over $25 million, Restoration Supermarkets Corporation is listed annually among the top fifty black-owned companies in the United States each year by *Black Enterprise* magazine. Of more importance, an evaluation study found that Pathmark shoppers pay more than 30 percent less than they would at the few, small-volume corner grocery stores scattered throughout the neighborhood.

Housing Renovation

Better housing was always one of Restoration's priorities. To demonstrate quick, tangible community impact, its first program in 1967 was a crash effort to renovate the faces of 394 brownstones covering 11 blocks of Bedford Stuyvesant; in the process, Restoration trained seventy-two unemployed neighborhood residents to do the work. Over a period of almost three decades the pilot effort expanded, giving facelifts to the exteriors of 4,200 homes covering 150 blocks. During the same period Restoration built or renovated 2,225 housing units. Some new projects fit right into the neighborhood's historic fabric. Fulton North blended forty apartment units onto second and third floors over street-level retail shops in the classic New York tradition. Other housing developments sought to transform the area. The 267 units in Restore Village were spread among four new, four- to eight-story brick buildings grouped around an interior park and playground in an I. M. Pei–designed "superblock."

To promote homeownership, in April 1968 Restoration persuaded a consortium of eighty New York banks, insurance companies, and savings and loan associations, led by Citibank, to commit approximately $65 million in Federal Housing Administration (FHA) insured loans to a new home mortgage pool for Bedford Stuyvesant residents.[4] About 1,500 homeowners received mortgages or major renovation loans from the pool, which became a for-profit, wholly owned subsidiary called Restoration Funding Corporation. (By 1994 Restoration Funding was no longer active.) In 1986–88 alone, Restoration took over, renovated, and resold more than $3 million of predominantly one- to six-unit brownstone or brick townhouses. Some hous-

---

4. This was nine years before the federal Community Reinvestment Act of 1977 made such lending practices mandatory for all federally regulated mortgage lenders.

ing improvements were less visible from the street. From 1980 onward, under a state contract, Restoration "weatherized" more than 5,800 apartments for low-income and elderly residents.

To our practiced eyes, which had seen poor neighborhoods in almost fifty metro areas, the physical proof of Restoration's housing programs was evident during our windshield tour. There were still a few tough-looking blocks of deteriorated tenements, and most streets did not have the spruced-up look of wealthier neighborhoods. But nowhere did we see the unmistakable signs of wholesale urban abandonment found in Detroit or Saint Louis: weedy lots strewn with bricks, concrete blocks, broken glass, crumpled beer cans, rusting auto hulks, evicted sofas and rotting mattresses interspersed among the tottering, broken-sash structures still standing.

Brownstones

What left a lasting impression of Bedford Stuyvesant were the magnificent Victorian brownstone and graystone townhouses that still lined so many blocks. It was these very brownstones, filled with hard-working black owners, "committed to raising their families and building their neighborhood," that had initially captured Bobby Kennedy's attention.

With a veteran real estate agent's curiosity, Delcia asked about estimated sales prices. A four-story brownstone in good condition? Probably $80,000 to $90,000, Lester estimated. An equal architectural gem but in visible need of major renovation? Perhaps $40,000 to $50,000. (In Manhattan's East Sixties, now-scarce brownstone mansions sold for up to one hundred times as much.)

Frankly, we were amazed. Just a scant ten minutes by the A-train from lower Manhattan and almost abutting downtown Brooklyn, where new office towers housed Wall Street's back office operations, were undoubtedly the best housing values in metropolitan New York. "Location, location, location" is the real estate industry's mantra. The brownstones of Bed-Stuy actually have perfect "location," but, like so much in American life, the realtor's adage is just code. "Location, location, location" really means "neighborhood, neighborhood, neighborhood." The difference between the $5,000,000 brownstone of the East Sixties and the $50,000 brownstone of Bedford Stuyvesant was not the physical geography of their location but the human geography of their surroundings. It was a sad truth we had seen affirmed in scores of cities.

"With this supply of wonderful houses," Delcia said to Charley and Lester, "Bedford Stuyvesant always has the potential to make a strong comeback."

"We know," Lester replied. "In fact, Rod [Roderick Mitchell, Restoration's current president] has ended our low-income housing programs. He feels we have too much low-income housing already and would like to emphasize new affordable housing for working people."

"I think he's right on the mark," I responded.

IBM Plant

Our tour was approaching another Restoration icon, a modern, two-story factory occupying an entire city block on the corner of Nostrand and DeKalb.

"Is this where the IBM plant was located?"

"Still is," Charley replied.

"I thought IBM recently closed it down?"

"They did," Charley explained, "but the plant was sold to IBM's former employees. It still operates as a supplier to IBM and others under contract."

"Is it doing OK?"

"As far as I know."

I hoped so. The IBM plant had been Restoration's biggest economic development coup. In 1968 Restoration and D & S, its big business-dominated twin, persuaded IBM to take a long-term lease on an old, eight-story brick warehouse at the corner of Gates and Nostrand and convert it into a computer component factory. (It was not a hard sell since IBM's chairman and chief executive officer, Thomas B. Watson Jr., was a founding director of D & S.)

Initially employing 120 local residents, the facility soon grew to 400 employees. Needing a new facility, in 1975 IBM built a new $10.2 million factory just several blocks up Nostrand Avenue on a site previously reserved for a new school. Bedford Stuyvesant, local representatives stated, ranked among IBM's top ten plants in efficiency and productivity, a claim shrouded in some doubt when the operation failed to survive IBM's cost-cutting corporate downsizing in 1993. However, sold to its employees and renamed Advanced Technological Solutions, a year later the plant was the biggest minority employee–owned manufacturing company in the United States.

As the former IBM plant faded in our rearview mirror, I wanted to draw out Lester more.

The Crack Cocaine Plague

"What are some of the changes you've seen over these years?"

"For one thing, as we're driving around today, we haven't seen anybody 'nodding,'" he replied, describing a familiar phenomenon of heroin addiction. "When Restoration started, even early in the morning, you'd see all sorts of men and women nodding out on the streets. We pretty well got rid of that."

"When did crack hit the neighborhood?" (Almost any knowledgeable inner-city activist, as Lester Matthews certainly was, can name the year, often the month, when crack cocaine moved into the neighborhood.)

Lester flinched, almost as if he had been jabbed in the solar plexus. "Let's see," he said finally. "That must have been the early summer of 1986. I remember that I'd be driving around, and I suddenly began noticing all these young men congregated on different street corners . . . same corners every day. I thought maybe something good was happening, until I found out what was going on."

"I have the impression that real progress was being made until crack hit."

Lester nodded in agreement. "That's true, that's true," he said wistfully, almost to himself.

Islands of Progress

As our tour was coming to a close, we set out to locate two census tracts where the poverty level had dropped significantly in the past two decades. In tract 277 the poverty rate had fallen from 36 percent to 27 percent; in adjacent tract 279, from 42 percent to 26 percent. Something dramatic had to have happened.

As indeed it had. We found several blocks lined with dozens of new, brick-faced, two-story townhouses, all obviously the work of the same builder. They lacked the style and craftsmanship of the brownstones of a century before, but the new townhouses undoubtedly had the modern kitchens, bathrooms, and family rooms that many middle-class households demand today.

Saying good-bye to our hosts back at Restoration's offices, Delcia and I walked back down Fulton Street toward the subway station at the intersection with Nostrand Avenue. Fulton was alive as crowds of people brushed by sidewalk vendors. We almost had to step out into the street to pass the busiest corners. The sidewalk vendors actually upgraded the appearance of Fulton Street. Obscured by the vendors' overhanging umbrellas and awnings, more and more storefronts were shuttered and padlocked as we moved farther away from Restoration Plaza.

Our windshield tour had given us only a surface impression of Restoration's work in Bedford Stuyvesant. We had not visited the Family Health Center, serving 55,000 outpatients annually. We had not been among the 40,000 people who attend performances at the Billie Holiday Theater every year. We were not among the 20,000 residents whom Restoration had placed in temporary and permanent jobs over the quarter-century. In many ways it was hard not to be impressed with Restoration's achievements.

But was the Bedford Stuyvesant community better off than it had been before Bobby Kennedy's walk in 1966? For that answer we turned to cold, hard census statistics.

Tale of the Tracts: Vanishing Populations

Boxing fans look to the "Tale of the Tape" to handicap a boxing match. Social analysts and economists must look to the Tale of the Tracts to judge how well the battle against neighborhood decline is going. Beginning with the 1970 census, the U.S. Bureau of the Census has published detailed income data, census tract by census tract, for each of the country's metro areas. This allows independent researchers to study neighborhood trends readily, without the assistance of big mainframe computer centers found only at universities, government agencies, and major think tanks. Taking the list of eighty-five census tracts Charley Palms supplied, I was able to construct my own profile of Bedford Stuyvesant from 1970 to 1990, a period covering the bulk of Restoration's twenty-eight years of activity.

During that period Bedford Stuyvesant lost 100,000 residents. The figure dropped from 375,761 residents recorded in 1970 to only 275,457 in 1990, which amounted to a 27 percent decline. Of course, having a smaller population is not automatically a negative development, particularly in communities suffering from overcrowded housing. With a general trend toward smaller household size, even among poor households, most neighborhoods must increase the total number of households just to maintain a constant population level. However, Bedford Stuyvesant lost households as well. Their number dropped from 114,887 households in 1970 to 94,879 in 1990 (a 17 percent decrease). Because the figures reflected occupied housing units, the number of households was not as subject to the Census Bureau's notorious undercounting of poor urban residents. In effect, the neighborhood was slowly depopulating.

Bedford Stuyvesant was also becoming blacker and browner. The proportion of African American residents rose from 81 percent in 1970 to 82 percent in 1990. By 1990, most of the non-black residents were Hispanic (14 percent). In fact, a majority of residents were Hispanic in almost 10 percent of Bedford Stuyvesant's census tracts, forming a barrio within a ghetto.

The area's "Anglo" population (that is, non-Hispanic whites, to use the southwestern term) had shrunk to 9,020. Most were clustered in blocks along Washington Avenue and Eastern Parkway, the western and southern edges of Bedford Stuyvesant. Since several census tracts span Bedford Stuyvesant's traditional boundaries, a block-level analysis would probably show that many of these Anglo households actually lived just outside Bedford Stuyvesant itself.

Rising Poverty

What about reducing poverty, Restoration's reason for being? In 1970 an estimated 21,352 families in the area were under the poverty threshold. Twenty years later that figure was unchanged: 21,233 families. With a smaller population base, the poverty rate among families had increased from 23.7 percent to 34.4 percent. If all persons in poverty are measured (including unrelated individuals who were not family members), the total number of poor persons had declined from 103,402 in 1970 to 93,557 in 1990. Again, measured against a smaller population base, the poverty rate for individuals had increased from 27.5 percent to 34.0 percent.

What would be the effect of the "census undercount" on these figures? Census enumerators do not miss many doctors, lawyers, business executives, factory workers, secretaries, and civil servants. They miss street people. To the extent that a more accurate count could be made in Bedford Stuyvesant, it would probably reveal even higher poverty rates.

The overall figures also masked changes at the tract level. Tracts with 20 percent to 40 percent of the residents below the poverty level are typically designated "poverty neighborhoods." In "high-poverty neighborhoods," the poverty level ranges from 40 to 60 percent. Those with more than 60 percent poverty are "hyperpoverty neighborhoods."

Of eighty-five census tracts in 1970, Bedford Stuyvesant recorded sixty-four poverty neighborhoods and seven high-poverty neighborhoods. In only fourteen census tracts was the poverty level below 20 percent. The lowest poverty rate (13.7 percent) was found in a tract spanning Washington Avenue, Bed-Stuy's western boundary.

By 1990, however, the number of high-poverty neighborhoods (40 to 60 percent poor) had increased from seven to thirty-seven, because many neighborhoods had become much poorer. Meanwhile, the number of relatively more affluent neighborhoods had shrunk from fourteen to only three, leaving the remaining forty-five tracts with poverty neighborhood status.

Overall, poverty rates increased significantly in sixty-four tracts, were stable in seventeen tracts, and decreased significantly in only four tracts (including tracts 277 and 279 just discussed). In only tract 197 (again on the area's western boundary) had economic conditions improved to the point where that neighborhood escaped poverty classification.[5]

In short, during two decades in which the poverty level in the Greater New York region dropped from 14 percent to 12 percent, poverty in Bedford Stuyvesant increased from 27.5 percent to 34.0 percent, and only one out of seventy-one poverty neighborhoods rose out of poverty status.

Shrinking Markets

Looking at another set of statistics, I found a partial explanation for the juxtaposition of a successful Pathmark supermarket and the many shuttered storefronts along Fulton Street. Bedford Stuyvesant's total neighborhood buying power was $811 million in 1970. By 1990 neighborhood buying power had risen to a nominal $2.4 billion. Yet, adjusted for twenty years of inflation, neighborhood buying power had actually decreased 12 percent.

In effect, Bedford Stuyvesant offered a big enough market for a Pathmark, a Baskin-Robbins, a Burger King, or a McDonald's, all of which have established products and formulas for selling them successfully. But marginal mom-and-pop stores faced the reality of fewer customers with fewer dollars to spend. After two decades of effort, as measured by poverty levels and neighborhood buying power, Bedford Stuyvesant was poorer than when Restoration began. Had Restoration failed?

Developing Minority Leadership

Restoration has had many individual success stories. One of the high-profile success stories was that of Franklin Thomas, Restoration's first president. He joined Restoration with impeccable credentials. Born in Bedford

---

5. I was puzzled, however, about why poverty levels never rose above 60 percent in Bedford Stuyvesant. During our tour we had seen many large public housing complexes. Across urban America, a large public housing complex is almost invariably the core of a high-poverty or hyperpoverty neighborhood. Several months later I found out that New York City's housing policies differ from the federal standard. Whereas federal policies give priority to the poorest of the poor, New York City allocates about one-third of every project to the elderly (of whatever income level), one-third to working-class households, and only a third of the units to welfare recipients and other desperately poor households. Although all residents of city housing complexes have no more than modest incomes, the city's policy promotes some degree of social and economic diversity.

Stuyvesant, Thomas was a basketball star at Columbia University, where he also received a law degree. Deputy police commissioner of the city of New York at age thirty-one, he authored the civilian review board plan. An original board member, he became Restoration's president when political infighting within the new organization led to its reorganization in May 1967. Assembling a top-level staff, he helped write the application that resulted in a $7 million first-year grant from the U.S. Department of Labor, with the required local match coming from the Ford Foundation. After a decade leading Restoration, he left to head the Ford Foundation itself, becoming the first African American chief executive of a major national foundation.

Many other Bedford Stuyvesant residents were also propelled into broader community leadership roles after serving on Restoration's board, committees, and task forces. Staff jobs were key rungs on the ladder to professional careers for many young African American college graduates. Scores of other community residents found their first clerical or paraprofessional jobs with Restoration.

These comments are not offered (nor should they be read) from a cynical point of view. One of the success stories of community-based, antipoverty programs has been leadership development. Antipoverty jobs have opened doors to opportunity for a whole generation of African American and Hispanic mayors, city council members, state legislators, members of Congress, public administrators, corporate executives, and other professionals.

Grading Restoration's Twenty-Five Years

In evaluating Restoration's success or failure, one must also consider the fate of Bed-Stuy's 100,000 "missing" residents. Some of the population decline was just the effect of an aging community. However, over the two decades tens of thousands of residents also left Bedford Stuyvesant. Many would have been helped by Restoration's job training and placement programs. Others would have used steady wages at the IBM plant or other local businesses created by Restoration to move out.

"Where have most people moved to?" I had asked Lester. He had thought for a minute. "Queens. Long Island."

In short, today's black emigrants from Bedford-Stuyvesant move out in the same general direction as white Bedford Stuyvesant residents a generation before. (Often black emigrants move into the same set of suburban communities that are now rapidly resegregating. Long Island's suburbs are as racially segregated as New York City itself.)

What would have happened without Restoration's efforts? Would Bed-Stuy be even poorer, more disorganized, more crime-ridden? Common sense suggests the answer would be "probably." Since it began, Restoration's slogan has been "making a difference." I believe that Restoration has made a difference for the good, including beyond its neighborhood boundaries.

Several months after our second visit, Charley Palms made the latter point in a letter to me. "The back offices of Chase Manhattan, Morgan Stanley, Goldman Sachs, Bear Stearns, Charles Schwab, and other businesses have moved in from lower Manhattan and currently occupy the newly developed One Pierrepoint Plaza and MetroTech in downtown Brooklyn," Charley wrote. "They employ more than 12,000 people. It is projected that by the year 2000, MetroTech Center, combined with other new developments in downtown Brooklyn, will have more than 30,000 new jobs."

"Many of us believe," Charley concluded, "that if Restoration had not maintained stability in central Brooklyn, the redevelopment of downtown Brooklyn would never have happened—a view corroborated in a conversation I had with a Vice President at Chase Manhattan two years ago."[6]

Charley makes a fair point. I will concede that, to some degree, Restoration's efforts contributed to the revival of downtown Brooklyn. Nevertheless, the hard fact remains: the Bedford Stuyvesant community is poorer today than when Restoration began. And, with a rising concentration of poverty, falling relative incomes, and slowly declining real buying power, Bedford Stuyvesant's capacity to be, in Bobby Kennedy's words, an "avenue of opportunity" (much less to be a "place of pleasure and excitement") grows less and less with each passing decade.

If Bedford Stuyvesant Restoration Corporation, the vanguard, is failing as a neighborhood antipoverty program, are other community development corporations that followed faltering as well? Or was Restoration's failure really an exception to a general pattern of success?

6. Letter to the author, March 27, 1996.

3

Walnut Hills, Jamaica Plain, and Other Neighborhoods

THE OHIO RIVER lay at my feet. From my vantage point on top of Cincinnati's Walnut Hills, I could see a handful of sailboats and powerboats dotting the river, blue and shimmering under a crisp October sky. An occasional barge or river freighter bulled its way along. Two large boat marinas hugged the opposite shore of Kentucky's Kenton County. All in all, it was a beautiful view. Our ancestors knew where to build cities.

"Cincinnati discouraged building any private marinas on the north side of the river," commented Ed Burdell, who, with his partner Bill Woods, was my guide. "All the marina development—and much of the high-end housing associated with boat owners—is now happening over on the Kentucky side."

"We do have one boat tied up on the north side," Bill said, pointing to a large, enclosed barge down on the river off to our left. "That's the only floating high school classroom in the country . . . specializes in teaching nautical sciences. The Cincinnati Public Schools are very proud of it."

To my right, Cincinnati's downtown, one of the country's more vigorous and interesting central business districts, was screened from direct view by the bulge of Mount Adams. At the foot of Walnut Hills a narrow ribbon of concrete—the Columbia Parkway—wound its way. Set far back from the riverbank, a few grim, rusting industrial hulks and warehouses still marked the area. Otherwise, the Ohio River's floodplain had been largely left as natural areas or grassy playing fields. Abandoned riverfront and lakefront industrial districts, now available for recycling into high-end condominiums and townhouses, are one of the great, underexploited assets of many of America's aging industrial cities. Successful urbanites will pay big money for a glimpse of moving water.

That idea was obviously not original with me. To my left, on East Walnut Hills, three large condominiums—the Edgecliff, the Ingleside, River Terrace—shot into the air. Condo owners probably paid quite a premium to have a balcony looking out over the Ohio rather than backward into the city. In the Walnut Hills neighborhood itself, once fine Victorian mansions had shed more recent lives as partitioned rooming houses and were made whole again, sparkling under new paint and trim applied by their young urban professional owners. What was happening in Walnut Hills? In a word, regentrification.

Walnut Hills: Regentrification and Decline

I had come to Cincinnati to address a seminar of business and civic leaders. My side trip to Walnut Hills was prompted by intense curiosity. Out of thirty-four of the country's best community development corporations, the Walnut Hills Redevelopment Foundation target area was one of only four in which average household income had risen as a percentage of average household income in the whole metropolitan area. And Walnut Hills's progress was a minuscule advance, at best. In 1980 the income of the average Walnut Hills household was 43 percent of the metro Cincinnati average; by 1990 the ratio had nudged upward to 44 percent.

I was standing in the middle of the sole reason for the Walnut Hills neighborhood's economic resurgence. Census tract 19 is the only tract of the five in the Walnut Hills Redevelopment Foundation's target area that has riverfront views. The other four are away from the river, stretching back into one of Cincinnati's poorest black ghettoes.

Parts of the area had long been African American, Ed and Bill explained. The big houses were built beginning in 1895, when Walnut Hills was opened up as a streetcar suburb for Cincinnati's wealthier families. Behind us, across what was once Lincoln Avenue, shotgun homes had been built for the mansion owners' black servants.[1]

In the decades after World War II, the wealthy families moved away to new suburban havens, and the mansions went into a long decline. The 1980 census had outlined tract 19's dismal numbers. Totaling 838 households (three-quarters black, one-quarter white), tract 19 was a high-poverty neighborhood. Some 43 percent of families and individuals were poor. In fact, tract 19 had the highest poverty rate of the five tracts. Its average household income, at $9,251, was only 44 percent of the Greater Cincinnati average.

By contrast, the 1990 census reflected a rapid regentrification. The number of total households had increased to 929 (a growth rate approaching 10 percent). Single-person households—young lawyers, architects, stockbrokers, and other professionals—accounted for almost all of the increase. There was a net increase of only fifteen family households in tract 19 during the decade.

Also, the net increase was entirely white. During the decade, tract 19's black population dropped from 1,400 in 1980 to 1,035 in 1990, but its white population climbed from 468 to 750. (Although the net increase was white, some black middle-class professionals had undoubtedly moved into tract 19 as well.) Its poverty rates had been halved, to 21 percent of family households and 25 percent of all residents. Most impressively, tract 19's average annual household income had risen from 44 percent to 74 percent of the Greater Cincinnati average.

Without the stimulus of river view location, however, the other four census tracts of the Walnut Hills Redevelopment Foundation's target area had not only shown no signs of regentrification, but they had followed the familiar pattern of deepening poverty and racial segregation. The four "inland" tracts combined dropped from 3,673 households in 1980 to 3,300 in 1990 (a 10 percent decrease). Already hypersegregated by 1980, the four tracts saw the percentage of black residents inch upward, from 94 percent to 95 percent. Both the absolute numbers of poor families and poor persons and rates of poverty increased. The family poverty rate jumped from 33 percent to 40 percent, and poverty among all individuals climbed from less than 39

1. After 1968 Lincoln Avenue was renamed Martin Luther King Jr. Drive. It was another bittersweet example of how, as a gesture to black communities, the name of the great champion of an integrated society had been so often attached to streets, schools, and parks in the heart of many of America's most segregated black neighborhoods.

percent to almost 46 percent. Nominal buying power among residents of the four inland tracts increased from $32.6 million in 1980 to $44.5 million in 1990, but, adjusted for inflation, real buying power declined by 20 percent.

However, back in tract 19, with its middle-class resurgence, nominal buying power grew from $7.8 million in 1980 to $26.3 million in 1990. Adjusted for inflation, the real buying power of tract 19 residents almost doubled (registering a 97 percent growth rate) in just ten years. Tract 19's surging prosperity more than offset the steady decline of its four neighboring tracts, producing the small increase in overall buying power (1 percent) that had drawn me to visit the area. Except for the regentrification of tract 19, the Walnut Hills Redevelopment Foundation's target zone would have been yet another example of unrelieved economic decline.

Boston's Urban Edge Housing Corporation

A second CDC-served neighborhood in my national survey that had experienced relative improvement in average household income was in the Boston area.[2] Since 1974 the Urban Edge Housing Corporation has served parts of Boston's Roxbury and Jamaica Plain neighborhoods. Overall, the buying power of these areas increased 17 percent between 1970 and 1990, and average household income rose from 73 percent of the Boston area average in 1980 to 76 percent in 1990. However, like Walnut Hills, these two communities did not experience uniform improvement during these two very different decades.

The Target Area

Urban Edge's primary service area covers a cluster of three census tracts in Roxbury and two in Jamaica Plain that I will call the "target area." In the 1970 census the target area had almost 20,000 residents: more than 40 percent were African American and about one-quarter Hispanic. It was one of the poorest sections of Boston; 22 percent of all families and 25 percent of all individuals fell below the poverty line (this was three times the Boston region's poverty rates). Average household income was only 61 percent of the regional average.

2. The other CDCs whose target areas gained ground economically were San Francisco's Mission Housing Corporation and Phoenix's Chicanos por La Causa.

The 1970s brought further economic decline. The target area's overall population dropped by 10 percent, while poverty rates escalated to 33 percent for families and individuals, and average household income declined to 57 percent of the regional average.

During the 1980s, however, the "Massachusetts Miracle" took hold. The Boston region boomed with new high-tech firms springing up all along Route 128. Relatively few target-area residents may have gone to work for Wang or Digital Electronics Corporation, but the benefits of the economic boom clearly trickled down to the neighborhood. The target area's population became stabilized; only 24 household units were lost (compared with more than 200 during the previous decade). Poverty rates inched back downward for families (28 percent) and individuals (30 percent), though average household incomes slipped further, to 55 percent of the regional average.

Meanwhile, the target area had become more racially isolated. The 1990 census showed that the African American population had increased to 50 percent, and most of the remaining population was Hispanic (41 percent), largely first- and second-generation Puerto Rican immigrants.

Jamaica Plain

Beyond Urban Edge's target area, the rest of the Jamaica Plain neighborhoods (which I will call "Jamaica Plain") presented an entirely different face. Jamaica Plain was neither predominantly minority nor poor. In 1970 these four census tracts were almost 90 percent non-Hispanic whites. African Americans constituted just 2 percent of the residents, and Hispanics totaled about 10 percent. Individual poverty rates in the four census tracts ranged from 8 percent to 14 percent, with the overall level at 12 percent. Average household income was a relatively healthy 84 percent of the Boston area average.

For Jamaica Plain, the 1970s were stressful as well. The community shrank by about 350 households. The number of poor residents rose by one-fifth, and, with middle-class households leaving, the individual poverty rate in Jamaica Plain as a whole pushed up to 17 percent. Average household income dipped to 71 percent of the regional average.

The economic boom of the 1980s again made Jamaica Plain a hot residential area. Almost 500 households were added back to the community, some of them minority households. As a result, Jamaica Plain became one of Boston's more racially diverse neighborhoods. Its black population rose to 12 percent and its Hispanic population to 23 percent. The poverty rate dropped back to 12 percent, and household income rebounded to 78 percent of the regional average. Most remarkably, Jamaica Plain's overall buying power increased 56 percent during the 1980s (compared with a 24 percent decline during the previous decade). Combined with a lesser resurgence in the target area's buying power, the overall neighborhood buying power in Urban Edge's service area increased 17 percent during the two decades. It was this statistic that had drawn my attention to Roxbury-Jamaica Plain originally.

Which would be the pattern of the 1990s—the decline of the 1970s or the resurgence of the 1980s? With the bloom off the Massachusetts Miracle, was Urban Edge's target area sinking deeper into ghetto poverty in the 1990s? Was Jamaica Plain continuing to prosper as a racially diverse but stable community, or was it losing ground again? What had been the contribution of Urban Edge Housing Corporation? Its housing programs accounted for only about 5 percent of all housing units but a larger percentage of the new housing created. Had Urban Edge made a crucial difference?

Touring Roxbury and Jamaica Plain

To try to answer these questions, I visited Urban Edge in June 1996 to meet with Mossik Hacobian, its veteran executive director, and to take a tour of the neighborhood. Urban Edge's headquarters filled four apartments converted to offices in a forty-unit, low-income apartment complex located on what is euphemistically called Egleston Square. The "square" was simply the intersection of two major streets—Columbus Avenue and Washington Street—without any park, plaza, or other monumental space, which, anywhere but Boston, would be required to justify the designation *square*. As I climbed out of my cab in front of the Urban Edge offices, I saw a half dozen men wearing bright blue shirts with "Urban Edge Property Management" stitched over the chest. They were busy sweeping around the housing complex and around Cleaves Court, another Urban Edge–managed property across the street.

Using a slide presentation, Mossik outlined the history of Urban Edge. It had begun as a fair housing brokerage business. Urban Edge's original offices had been located on Centre Street deep in Jamaica Plain. "But we realized that the 'urban edge'—the boundary between the haves and the have-nots—was moving east toward Roxbury," Mossik explained. "Columbus Avenue was the boundary between black Roxbury and the Latino section of Jamaica Plain. There might as well have been a Berlin Wall running right down the middle of Columbus Avenue. Urban Edge consciously placed our new offices on the African American side of the avenue to break through that boundary."

Over the years Urban Edge had grown into a major operation. With an annual budget of $3.8 million and a staff of sixty, Urban Edge is now one of the five largest employers in the target area. It has developed 670 units of affordable housing, which it continues to manage through an affiliated property management company. In September 1995 it was awarded a contract by the Boston Housing Authority to manage Walnut Park tower, a 168-unit high-rise apartment for senior citizens located a block from Urban Edge's headquarters. In the last half-dozen years, Urban Edge has expanded its role beyond housing development and management to provide a wide range of social services for its tenants, including youth programs and antigang activities.

A focal point of Urban Edge's recent activity has been the development of Egleston Center, a small, 7,000-square-foot neighborhood shopping center on the corner of Columbus Avenue and Washington Street. It features a McDonald's and a branch of Fleet Bank. Three blocks away the bank had earlier opened a temporary facility in a trailer in order to build up its clientele. The new Fleet Bank is the first bank branch ever on Egleston Square. "Fleet Bank isn't coming as an act of charity," Mossik commented. "It saw a market opportunity."

"Market opportunity" certainly characterizes Urban Edge's latest plans. "We feel that we have largely succeeded in the Egleston Square area," Mossik continued. "We're shifting our focus northward a half-mile up Columbus Avenue to the Jackson Square area. Egleston Square is one important meeting ground between Boston's Roxbury and Jamaica Plain neighborhoods. Jackson Square is another important geographic connector between these two communities. With 10,000 people living near Jackson Square, 8,000 rail commuters passing through the MTA station, and 70,000 cars driving through the intersection, Jackson Square also represents a tremendous commercial opportunity."

"I'd like to see it very much," I said. "I also very much want to visit census tract 812 in Roxbury. During the 1970s and 1980s that tract experienced an enormous drop in the number of poor families. I'm curious to find out what happened. It's almost as if a major public housing project shut down."

Mossik and his colleague, Fiona O'Connor, my tour guide, checked a map. "Bromley-Heath . . . the largest public housing project in Massachusetts . . . it's located right there," they confirmed. "In the mid-1980s the Boston Housing Authority began a major renovation of Bromley-Heath. Whole buildings have been vacated for long periods of time. The Census Bureau must have counted the project midway through that process."

Jamaica Plain: Where the Mixes Match

For the next two hours we crisscrossed much of Roxbury and Jamaica Plain. Several highlights of the tour stood out.

—Saint John Street in the heart of Jamaica Plain. It was an excellent example of an urban neighborhood of an earlier age: a dense collection of varied buildings with wood-frame, single-family homes and duplexes mixed in with small apartment buildings. Mature broad-leafed trees hung over the narrow, one-way street, reduced to barely one lane by the parked cars on either side, which further shielded the sidewalks from the flow of traffic. Ivy, honeysuckle, and other flowering plants climbed the sides of many of the buildings. Within Jamaica Plain, Saint John Street was not atypical, and it was easy to understand why the neighborhood had undergone such a strong revival. "Everybody lives on this street," Fiona said, "from Ph.D.'s to car mechanics, of every racial and ethnic background. Over the last fifteen or so years Jamaica Plain has become very proud and very protective of its diversity. The slogan of our Jamaica Plain Business Association is 'Jamaica Plain— Where the Mixes Match.'"

—The subtle transitions along Centre Street. Centre Street began among vacant lots and low-slung auto shops near Jackson Square in Roxbury, moved through a zone of bodegas and tiendas catering to the Hispanic population, and metamorphosed into a trendy, upscale collection of boutiques, coffee shops, and restaurants in the heart of regentrified Jamaica Plain. Outside a newly opened sushi bar, we saw a film production crew setting up on the corner of Hyde Square. "What are you filming?" I yelled out as we slowed. "A commercial for the Boston Tourism Bureau," a crew member replied. Jamaica Plain had arrived.

—Stoney Brook Co-operative, a new cluster of gray-and-white, affordable townhouses developed by Urban Edge near a long, linear park created by relocation of the Metropolitan Transit Authority's Orange Line. The townhouses were very attractive, and, though new, matched the style of the neighborhood. What I most remember was how the tenants were selected. "There were over 500 qualified applicants for just fifty units," Fiona explained, "but because this would be a co-op project, and our goal was to create a real community, Urban Edge added a special screening criterion. Specifically, we were looking for a demonstrated history of community involvement, the ability to join together for common goals. Past membership in a PTA, being a church leader, an active member of a political ward organization. As a result Stoney Brook is filled with real community activists. Later this year the co-op's board will take over all ownership and management responsibilities from Urban Edge. More important, all these live wires have had a tremendous impact on the surrounding neighborhood. They've energized a whole range of community organizations."

—The Bromley-Heath public housing complex, a jumble of massive, four- and six-story, brown concrete boxes covering about a dozen square blocks. Major renovations were still under way, as construction crews could be seen working around several vacant buildings. Undoubtedly, when Bromley-Heath was first built in the 1950s, it was considered the last word in safe, sanitary, decent housing for low-income families. By comparison with almost every neighborhood surrounding it, however, Bromley-Heath looked sterile and massively institutional.

Bromley-Heath was the first tenant-managed public housing project, constantly touted as a national model. Shortly after my visit I wrote "perhaps tenant management has made a difference, but I doubt that the social environment faced by hundreds of children growing up in Bromley-Heath is better than in scores of massive public housing projects around the country." Sadly, in October 1998, after thirty-eight residents were arrested as drug traffickers, amid charges of widespread mismanagement, the Boston Housing Authority took back control of Bromley-Heath.

Guaranteeing Permanent Diversity?

Back at Urban Edge's offices, I congratulated Mossik for his organization's visible success. We chatted about the delicate balancing act the CDC faced on the "urban edge," that boundary between the haves and the have-nots. One of Mossik's comments, in particular, struck me. "Fifteen years ago we realized that if we could create strong, stable, multifamily developments for low-income families, that would change everything. The neighborhoods would no longer be in the hands of speculators."

What was Mossik really saying? I wondered. Community development corporations are typically characterized as antipoverty programs. Would Jamaica Plain, if not Roxbury itself, have regentrified even more uniformly without Urban Edge's involvement? Were market forces in Jamaica Plain so

hout Urban Edge, the neighborhood would have become
ie, with poor Hispanics and African Americans being
ut into some other forgotten corner of the Boston area? In
, Urban Edge had performed a different—but invaluable—role:
guaranteeing that there would always be a place in the Jamaica Plain community for low- and moderate-income households. Urban Edge's housing programs had been a mechanism for creating the very diversity of income classes (with the resultant racial and ethnic diversity) that Jamaica Plain's middle-class activists might exalt, but that market mechanisms are incapable of keeping in place.

"You know," I concluded, "Urban Edge's greatest contribution may turn out to be showing how a stable, truly diverse community can really be established and maintained for the long run. That would be a great lesson for America."

The CDC Movement

Since the birth of the Bedford Stuyvesant Restoration Corporation in 1967, the number of community development corporations has grown dramatically. In the wake of the Kennedy and Javits initiative, perhaps one hundred CDCs had been organized by 1970 under the provisions of the amended federal Economic Opportunity Act. By the early 1990s the National Council for Community Economic Development, the CDCs' national trade association, estimated that as many as 2,000 CDCs had been organized in urban and rural areas around the country. The greatest concentrations are found in inner-city neighborhoods in the Northeast and industrial Middle West.

The most extensive study of community development corporations was completed in 1992 by the Community Development Research Center, an arm of the New School for Social Research in New York City. Through a combination of data collection and field visits, the Community Development Research Center reviewed a sample of 130 established CDCs in twenty-nine cities.

Averaging twelve years in existence, the sampled CDCs were "larger, more complex, and more accomplished" than the average CDC. Just over one-quarter (27 percent) were founded before 1973. As the Research Center noted, "These groups were born of the activist spirit of the '60s—product of the War on Poverty and the Civil Rights Movement, and reactions to the negative effects of the federal urban renewal program." About twice as many groups (53 percent) were founded between 1973 and 1980, while the final one-fifth were established during the Reagan years (1981–88), "a period in which federal funding for CDCs and their programs fell dramatically. Reliance on state and local government, the establishment of public/private partnerships to support local development, and regional and national nonprofit organizations helped these CDCs meet 'the bottom line.' "

Most CDCs are small. In the sample of 130, the typical CDC has an annual operating budget of $700,000 and employs a full-time paid staff of seven: five professionals and two clerical support staff. ("Even these figures overstate CDCs' financial strength," the study noted, "since sampled CDCs have budgets about four times larger than the typical CDC nationally.")

Housing Programs

Low-income housing development is the principal activity of most CDCs. Eighty-seven percent of the sample CDCs are engaged in housing, with most of these (86 percent) assuming the role of developer or co-developer. Most CDCs are involved in both rehabilitating existing housing (87 percent) and building new units (67 percent). In recent years the typical CDC's output has been twenty-one new or rehabilitated housing units a year. (That level of production actually compares favorably with that of private homebuilders. Three-quarters of for-profit developers build fewer than twenty-five units a year.) Over the course of its twelve-year existence, the typical CDC has built or rehabilitated 150 units, of which it still actively manages about 75 low-income rental properties. Other common housing activities include counseling first-time homebuyers, sponsoring paint-up and clean-up campaigns, and operating home-repair and weatherization programs.

Commercial Development

Two-thirds of the CDCs sampled develop commercial real estate as well, most taking on the same roles as catalyst, developer, and manager that they carry out in housing development. CDCs are more likely to develop retail, office, and mixed-use properties than industrial sites. With their housing emphasis, CDCs are naturally drawn to renovating or building local shopping districts that serve neighborhood residents. The typical CDC studied has produced 33,000 square feet of retail and office space, about the size of a small department store in a community shopping center. CDCs active in commercial development commonly organize promotional campaigns for neighborhood shopping districts, work to upgrade streetscapes and security, and administer loan funds to commercial tenants for property improvements.

Slightly more than half of the CDCs sampled (57 percent) also are engaged in developing business enterprises. Most offer technical assistance and counseling to local firms. Many also provide management training and administer Small Business Administration loans. However, only one out of five CDCs currently owns or operates a business. Forty percent of CDCs that have ever been venture capital investors and more than 25 percent that have ever been active business owners have withdrawn as business owners because of the considerable financial risks and staff time and energy consumed. Though a few firms owned by older CDCs have become major businesses, two-thirds of CDC-owned businesses report annual gross sales of less than $1 million, and most management training programs have trained fewer than one hundred people. In short, as housing developers, as commercial developers, as business promoters, the typical CDC is a small business serving small businesses.

Grading Exemplary CDCs

A substantial body of literature has grown up around the community development movement, analyzing and promoting it. Most studies focus on process and projects. Only a few have assessed the impact of CDC activity on economic conditions in their target neighborhoods. It was that information gap that I set out to help fill.

For guidance I turned to two outstanding national support organizations at the core of the community development movement, mentioned earlier in the chapter: the National Council for Community Economic Development and the Community Development Research Council. I asked each organization to recommend a list of the nation's outstanding urban CDCs. My only stipulation was that each CDC had to have been established before 1980, so that I could track social and economic changes over at least a decade in its target neighborhood, through the 1980 and 1990 censuses.

From their recommendations emerged a list of thirty-four "exemplary" CDCs. The organizations ranged from Newark's New Community Corporation (1,200 employees; $200 million annual budget) to Omaha Economic Development Corporation (4 employees; $170,000 annual budget).

Through the national groups' own reports or direct contacts with the CDCs, Delcia and I verified when each began operations and the identification of the census tracts that most closely define their target neighborhoods.

Then we began to crunch the numbers, dividing the CDCs into two groups. Those founded by 1970 were evaluated over the twenty-year span between the 1970 and 1990 censuses; those founded between 1971 and 1979 were evaluated over a ten-year span between the 1980 and 1990 censuses.

Between 1980 and 1990, poverty rates in the twenty-three newer CDC target areas increased from 23 percent to 26 percent for families and from 25 percent to 29 percent for individuals (see figure 3-1). By contrast, rates for the metropolitan areas in which the CDCs were located remained stable over the same period, hovering around 8 percent for families and 10 percent for individuals.

Over the twenty-year period from 1970 to 1990, the family poverty rate in neighborhoods served by older CDCs increased from 19 percent to 28 percent, and the rate for individuals jumped from 23 percent to 30 percent. Over the same period the metrowide family and individual poverty rates were stable at 7 and 9 percent, respectively.

A second measure of neighborhood economic trends is the ratio of average household income in CDC target areas to average household income metrowide. For the ten-year group, average household income in target areas declined from 64 percent to 58 percent of average household income metrowide; for the twenty-year group, the figure dropped from 61 percent to 53 percent (see figure 3-2).

Neighborhood buying power also showed significant trends. For the ten-year group, CDC neighborhood buying power was flat (showing no growth), while metrowide buying power increased 22 percent. For the twenty-year group, CDC neighborhood buying power plummeted 18 percent, while metro-area buying power averaged a 64 percent increase.

Chapter 2 posed the question: is the steady economic decline experienced by Bedford Stuyvesant "an exception to a general pattern of success" among CDCs in general? The sad answer is "not at all." Bedford Stuyvesant's record was about the average experience over the two decades; in fact, Bed-Stuy's decline in neighborhood buying power (12 percent) was considerably less than the decline in neighborhoods served by older CDCs as a group (22 percent). In short, in cities across the country, the thirty-four target areas served by the most successful CDCs as a group still became poorer, fell farther behind regional income levels, and lost real buying power.

A brief summary, of course, blurs substantial variations among the different communities. From a detailed analysis of the thirty-four CDCs, it is evident that a handful of target areas have experienced some economic improvement. (See appendix tables A-1, A-2, and A-3.)

Figure 3-1. *Family and Individual Poverty Rates in Thirty-Four Communities Served by Exemplary CDCs, 1970–90*

Percent

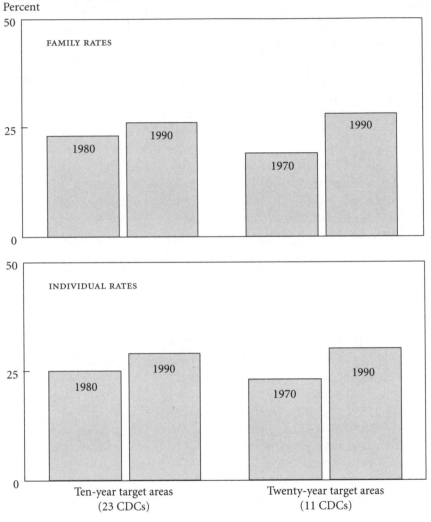

—Family poverty rates, individual poverty rates, or both, stabilized or declined slightly in only seven target areas (Boston's Urban Edge Housing Corporation, the area of the South Bronx served by MBD Community Housing Corporation, San Francisco's Mission Housing Development Corporation and Chinese Community Housing Corporation target areas, Washington, D.C.'s Marshall Heights CDC, Newark's New Community Cor-

Figure 3-2. *Income Levels in Thirty-Four Communities Served by Exemplary CDCs, 1970–90*[a]

Percent

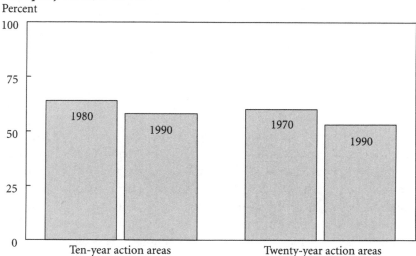

Ten-year action areas
(23 CDCs)

Twenty-year action areas
(11 CDCs)

a. Ratio of average household income in CDC to average household income in metro area.

poration, and La Casa de Don Pedro). As the earlier discussion of the experiences of Walnut Hills and Urban Edge shows, an improvement in a target area's overall statistics can almost always be attributed to the impact of some highly localized development. Family poverty rates in the Marshall Heights neighborhood, for example, declined slightly because two large public housing projects were all but abandoned.

—Average household incomes rose slightly as a percentage of regional average household income in only four target areas (Urban Edge, Mission Housing, Walnut Hills, and Phoenix's Chicanos por La Causa). All other target areas lost ground in comparison with the rest of their metropolitan areas.

—Virtually every target neighborhood registered a decline in overall population and, more significantly, in total households. Only target areas served by East Boston and Urban Edge, Cleveland's Miles Ahead, San Francisco's Chinese Community Housing Corporation, and the South Bronx's MBD and Banana Kelly added households.

—Higher poverty rates and declining numbers of households translate into declining neighborhood buying power. In twenty-three of thirty-four target areas, real neighborhood buying power dropped. Efforts to stimulate local retail businesses typically faced a neighborhood market with fewer—and poorer—potential customers. Real neighborhood buying power plummeted by one-third to one-half in areas served by Chicago's Bickerdike Redevelopment Corporation and Bethel Housing, Inc., the Community Development Corporation of Kansas City, Newark's New Community Corporation, New York's West Harlem Community Organization, and Phoenix's Chicanos por La Causa.

By contrast, regional buying power increased in all seventeen metro areas covered, ranging from almost negligible 2 percent growth in Lima, Ohio, and 4 percent in metro Cleveland, to 54 and 85 percent in Greater Los Angeles and the San Francisco-Oakland Bay Area, respectively, to 199 percent in metro Phoenix. Almost invariably, growth in real neighborhood buying power was associated with in-migration of new households, whether new households were primarily yuppies (as in East Boston, Urban Edge, and Walnut Hills), Hispanics (as in Los Angeles's Vermont-Slausson and the South Bronx), or Asians (as in San Francisco's target neighborhoods).

—Fifteen of the thirty-four target neighborhoods had predominantly African American populations (40 percent or more). Ten of the fifteen lost between 6 and 45 percent of their households and had rising poverty rates. Of the five target areas with stable or slightly rising numbers of households, New York City's Jamaica area, for example, is a quasi-suburban community that would not qualify as a high-poverty area; the poverty rate rose from only 12 percent in 1970 to 14 percent in 1990, and average household income has been stable at 85–90 percent of the regional average. A tremendous influx of Hispanics and Asians, replacing white out-migration, has also brought great economic and social vitality to the Jamaica area. Cleveland's Miles Ahead neighborhood is a long-established, stable, middle-class black community in which poverty rates have also been relatively low (13–16 percent).

South Bronx Miracle: A Pyrrhic Victory

The South Bronx deserves special attention. It is the poster child of the community development movement, and deservedly so. Neighborhood-based groups such as Banana Kelly and MBD Community Housing Corporation hung on through neighborhood conditions rivaling the devastation experienced by European cities during World War II and fought for reinvestment to rebuild their communities. With substantial assistance facilitated by the Local Initiatives Support Corporation (LISC), which helped mobilize a massive injection of private mortgage financing, and a revival of services from the city of New York, areas of the South Bronx have been reborn as livable communities for moderate- and middle-income households.[3] Fifteen years ago, smoldering, abandoned tenements and rubble-filled vacant lots dominated the cityscape. As they whizzed past on their way to midtown's Grand Central Station, suburban rail commuters shuddered at the hellish scenes until they, too, became so inured to the destruction that they stopped even glancing up from their morning *New York Times* or *Daily News.*

Today, Fort Apache, The Bronx, has disappeared beneath the trim front yards and modest, new single-family row houses of Charlotte Street, an almost suburban-style subdivision recreated in the heart of the city. It is a remarkable achievement. The statistics in appendix table A-1 covering Banana Kelly and MBD's impact pick up the story at rock bottom (around 1980). Table 3-1 provides a slightly longer view of what has happened in the South Bronx. Between 1970 and 1980 (shortly after both CDCs began their activities) the MBD neighborhoods had lost 71 percent of their households. Banana Kelly's target area was almost abandoned.

The impact of the two CDCs' housing programs is reflected in part in the household growth in the MBD area and Banana Kelly during the 1980s. Since many of the organizations' new housing construction and rehabilitation projects did not open until the 1990s, the census for the year 2000 will undoubtedly record further revival. It is, as I stated earlier, an impressive record for the coalition of neighborhood-based organizations, major mortgage finance institutions, and city government.

Yet what is the long-term prognosis? Even if one acknowledges the South Bronx's mini-renaissance, these two target areas had higher poverty rates in 1990 than in 1970, lower household incomes in relation to regional averages, and far fewer resident households. Overall, real neighborhood buying power had dropped by two-thirds.

---

3. Founded in 1979 by the Ford Foundation (shortly after Franklin Thomas left Bedford Stuyvesant Restoration Corporation to head up the foundation), LISC is the nation's largest provider of financing and technical support for CDCs that are "transforming distressed neighborhoods into healthy communities." Since its creation, LISC has raised more than $3.1 billion from 1,900 individuals and corporate and foundation donors. LISC's loans, grants, and equity investments, leveraging another $3.8 billion in mortgage loans, helped 1,500 CDCs build or rehab over 80,000 homes and create 10.3 million feet of commercial and industrial space.

Table 3-1. *Population and Economic Trends in the South Bronx, 1970–90*
Percent unless otherwise noted

Trend	Target area	
	MBD Community Housing Corporation	Banana Kelly Community Association
Family poverty rate		
1970	37	34
1980	45	49
1990	43	51
Individual poverty rate		
1970	41	38
1980	47	46
1990	45	53
Local income/regional average		
1970	49	51
1980	43	46
1990	41	37
Total number of households		
1970	20,330	24,783
1980	5,850	9,897
1990	6,279	11,689
Change in total households		
1970–80	−71	−60
1980–90	7	18
1970–90	−69	−53
Change in neighborhood buying power		
1970–80	−78	−69
1980–90	37	28
1970–90	−69	−60

In effect, what happened in the South Bronx was urban renewal by abandonment and arson. The neighborhood organizations have seized victory from the ashes, but it is a Pyrrhic victory for the city. Many more such victories and the city of New York, like the "victorious" Greek King Pyrrhus, will be completely undone.

Do CDCs Make a Difference?

Would target neighborhoods have declined faster without the efforts of the thirty-four CDCs? Did the CDCs "make a difference"? In my review of the census data, I did not try to answer these questions. "What if?" is a question that history can never answer, and complex social issues do not readily lend themselves to controlled laboratory experiments.

One study has compared four CDC-served neighborhoods and four similar ("control") neighborhoods not served by CDCs in Philadelphia and Pittsburgh between 1970 and 1980 (or between 1970 and 1990 in terms of noneconomic data).[4] All eight neighborhoods lost between 20 percent and 51 percent of their population over the 1970–90 period; population loss was reflected in a drop in housing units, which ranged from 4 percent to 37 percent. During the 1980s real median incomes declined between 16 percent and 46 percent in all eight neighborhoods. In six of the eight, poverty rates increased during the decade. In Pittsburgh's Lincoln-Lemington and Hazelwood areas (both *non*-CDC neighborhoods), poverty rates edged downward from 26.7 percent to 24.0 percent and 25.6 percent to 21.3 percent, respectively, even though unemployment increased from 5 to 27 percentage points in all eight neighborhoods, including these latter two.

Between 1970 and 1990 married-couple families as a percentage of all households declined precipitously from 44–77 percent in 1970 to 13–56 percent in 1990. Conversely, the percentage of female-headed households ballooned everywhere, from 19–51 percent in 1970 to 32–72 percent two decades later. By 1990 the North Central neighborhood of Philadelphia (called "the grimmest ghetto in all of America" by one expert) had almost five times as many female-headed households (72 percent) as married-couple households (13 percent).

In head-to-head matchups there was little to choose between the CDC target areas and the control neighborhoods. The four sets of neighborhoods performed about equally in terms of population loss, loss of housing units, increased housing vacancies, and increased unemployment rates. Control neighborhoods actually fared slightly better than CDC neighborhoods, with a smaller increase in poverty rates, smaller losses of married-couple families and smaller increases in female-headed households, and less decline in median income.

---

4. All statistics and quotations regarding the Philadelphia-Pittsburgh study are drawn from McDevitt (1992).

The only statistic in which CDC neighborhoods outperformed control neighborhoods was in achieving modest increases in owner-occupied housing. At the low percentage changes observed, the increases may well reflect some direct impact of CDC homeownership programs. However, in the north central Philadelphia neighborhood served by National Temple Non-Profit Development Corporation, after homeownership increased marginally from 13.1 percent to 19.7 percent during the 1980s, it dropped again to 14.7 percent by 1990. Improving percentages of homeowners in ghetto communities may be as much a reflection of wholesale abandonment of rental housing by landlords as an increase in actual homeowners.

"What would the National Temple neighborhood be like without the CDC?" the study asked. "In a neighborhood as desolate as National Temple [the CDC area] or North Central [the control area], CDCs may not make the physical impact in new businesses and housing that is possible in other [less impoverished] neighborhoods. However, neighborhood-based agencies [such as the National Temple CDC] which also provide social services can make a great deal of difference in the 'quality of life' for local residents, reducing a desperate life to one at least able to meet some basic needs."

Commenting on a Pittsburgh-area matchup, the study observed that "Homewood has seriously deteriorated over the last 20 years. The impact of the Homewood-Brushton Revitalization and Development Corporation has yet to be demonstrated in the neighborhood demographics. . . . Yet, looking into the future, the CDC is creating a perception of progress and the perception may carry the neighborhood into the future. Lincoln-Lemington [the control neighborhood] lacks such an effort, and its business district is boarded up. Without such intervention, what will the impression of Lincoln-Lemington be in the future?"

Summing up the overall study, the report concluded: "These are neighborhoods where life is becoming more difficult for the residents and those who can flee are doing so. Clearly community development corporations have not been able to stem the massive market and demographic forces at work. . . . Perhaps the fairest way to assess CDC contributions is to look at specific programs over time with reference to what the CDC has done and what the need is in the neighborhood."

Clearly, in trying to assess the neighborhood-wide impact of CDCs, there is a problem of scale. Against the "massive market and demographic forces" are arrayed CDCs that I have characterized as small businesses. How valid is it to evaluate the effectiveness of relatively small neighborhood organizations against the much larger panorama of the neighborhoods they target with their housing, commercial development, and social service programs?

Newark's New Community Corporation

Inadequate scale, however, hardly describes Newark's New Community Corporation. Commonly regarded as the nation's most successful CDC, New Community Corporation dominates life in Newark's Central Ward. It was founded in 1968 in the wake of Newark's bloody, destructive riot the previous summer. Led since its inception by Monsignor William J. Linder, the CDC still works closely with Saint Rose of Lima parish. New Community has built or renovated 2,706 units of rental housing, about half for senior citizens. Almost 60 percent of all units are covered by federal rent subsidies. Three-quarters of all housing in the Central Ward is owned and managed by New Community.

With its staff of more than 1,200 persons, New Community provides extensive social programs for its tenants and other Newark residents. Seven Babyland Nurseries provide day care for 700 children. A new Pathmark supermarket and shopping center attract 50,000 shoppers a week. New Community operates a nursing home, an elementary school, medical offices, a job placement center, a restaurant, a wellness center, and a newspaper. As journalist Nicholas Lemann has remarked, "In the neighborhood where New Community operates, there is almost no private-sector economic activity. New Community, an imaginative and energetic harvester of grants, loans, subsidies and tax abatements from government, foundations and business, owns outright almost everything there."[5]

The Tale of the Tracts traces an intriguing picture of the Central Ward's recent history. Already in steady decline, by the 1970 census New Community's target area still had almost 23,000 residents (88 percent black). Exactly one-third of all residents (33.3 percent) fell below the poverty line, and average household income was only 44 percent of the average income for the whole Newark region.

By the 1990 census the area's population had been halved to less than 11,000. The number of total households had dropped from 6,199 to 3,613. In part, New Community's housing programs had come to dominate the

5. Nicholas Lemann, "The Myth of Community Development," *New York Times Magazine*, January 9, 1994, p. 27.

Central Ward because the community had shrunk to meet the CDC almost halfway. Almost everyone who had the power of choice had chosen to move, except for those housed in New Community's housing developments.

Almost everyone, but not all. In 1988 New Jersey's largest private homebuilder began developing market-rate townhouses in census tract 64, the first such housing built in the Central Ward in two decades. By 1994, more than 600 units were occupied, and the Society Hill project will have 1,100 townhouses when completely redeveloped. Located near Newark's central business district and New Jersey's University College of Medicine and Dentistry, the townhouses have found a strong market among largely black, professional households.

In 1970, census tract 64 was the Central Ward's poorest area. Almost 45 percent of its 824 households were poor; the average household income was only 34 percent of the metropolitan average. Over the next two decades tract 64's previous population virtually vanished. By the 1990 census the 824 households had dropped to 297, but most were newcomers, residents of the new Society Hill townhouses. The number of poor families had dropped from 216 to 16; the number of poor residents, from 1,313 to 88. The 1990 poverty rate was 14.2 percent (only 11.4 percent among families). Average household income had shot up to 68 percent of the regional average, and 135 percent of the citywide average itself. In short, Society Hill was being transformed into one of Newark's more prestigious neighborhoods.

Throughout the rest of the New Community target area, however, poverty levels had remained high (32 percent), and average household incomes continued to slide to 37 percent of the regional average. Despite the 64 percent reduction in total households, because of the much greater affluence of newcomers to Society Hill, tract 64's real buying power declined only 15 percent. By contrast, the rest of the New Community neighborhood lost 39 percent of its buying power.

Society Hill "is a vote of confidence in New Community's ability to stabilize the area," Lemann decided. "The neighborhood feels organized and safe," in part, a result of the 120 unarmed security officers who patrol New Community's housing developments. And perhaps the Society Hill townhouses, occupied by middle-class residents very different from New Community's core constituency, are the greatest testimonial to New Community's impact. It may not be necessary to destroy a neighborhood in order to save it, the basic vision of federal urban renewal programs of the 1950s and 1960s. But New Community, like Walnut Hills and Jamaica Plain, demonstrates the hard reality of inner-city poverty. Poor, minority neighborhoods escape poverty only when new, middle-class households move in. Regentrification has been the only escape route for poverty neighborhoods.

Up the Down Escalator

To an audience of foundation executives on the afternoon of my first visit to Bedford Stuyvesant, I reached for a metaphor to describe the tragic dilemma of community-based, antipoverty programs in a place such as Bedford Stuyvesant. "It is like helping a crowd of people run up a down escalator. No matter how fast they run, the escalator comes back down at them faster and faster. Some individuals can run so hard—some programs will function so well—that they succeed in getting to the top of the down escalator. But then they jump off. *They move.* All the others are carried back down to the bottom, and the climb out of poverty becomes steeper and steeper for those that try later."

"Most foundations support programs to help people run up the down escalator," I told the audience. "The real challenge is to rewire the direction of the escalator so that it is moving with, not against, ghetto residents. That escalator has to carry ghetto residents upward, and generally outward as well. The true 'empowerment zone' is the whole regional economy and the whole regional society."

Old Data or Current Trends?

That speech to the Council on Foundations was in May 1995. My visits to Bed-Stuy, Walnut Hills, Urban Edge, and others occurred in 1995 and 1996. The data I have presented end with the 1990 census. (Income and poverty data actually are reported for 1989.) In late 1997 *Time* magazine's lead article, "City Boosters," proclaimed that "a new breed of activist mayors is making City Hall a hothouse for innovation." Among the mayors cited were Cleveland's Michael White, Philadelphia's Ed Rendell, Chicago's Richard Daley, and Milwaukee's John Norquist. The first three cities were all placed among my cities "past the point of no return" in *Cities without Suburbs* (Milwaukee just barely missed the list). For such cities—and the thirty-four CDCs just analyzed—am I guilty of relying on old 1990 census data that no longer reflect the realities of the late 1990s?

As I continue to present my trend analyses in different communities, I face the constant challenge of updating census data. The census itself releases periodic raw population updates for states, counties, and the largest cities. Income data at the city and neighborhood level are either nonexistent (Census Bureau) or highly unreliable (some commercial consulting services).[6]

For political jurisdictions, I have found two useful and reliable sources of annual data: annual property valuation records and reports on home sales from local boards of realtors. For the 1990s the general picture these records show is that the sustained economic boom has helped cities, but the gaps between cities (and some older suburbs) and their surrounding, more prosperous suburbs continue to grow.

In 1990, for example, Baltimore accounted for 31 percent of its metro area's population but only 20 percent of the gross assessed valuation of all commercial, industrial, and residential property. By 1995 Baltimore had lost another 50,000 residents and dropped to 28 percent of the region's population and only 15 percent of the property tax base. The spectacular revival of Baltimore's Inner Harbor–Downtown area, fueled by substantial public (and therefore tax-exempt) investments like Camden Yards, Ravens Stadium, the National Aquarium, a mammoth convention center expansion, and the University of Maryland's Medical School, was not sufficient to offset the lost value hemorrhaging out of commercial, industrial, and residential property elsewhere in the city. Similarly, while between 1990 and 1995 Detroit slipped from having 24 percent to 22 percent of its region's population, the city's share of the region's state-equalized valuation of all property declined further, from 7.4 percent to 6.1 percent.

The regional housing market did testify to Detroit Mayor Dennis Archer's hard, courageous efforts to revive Detroit: in 1996 home sale prices in the city increased faster than the rate of inflation for the first time in twenty-five years. Indeed, the city's rate of increase was the best in the region that year. Detroit's recent performance, however, has been the exception. As housing markets revived around the country in the 1990s, the improvement in city home prices typically lagged suburban housing markets.

To update neighborhood-level economic trends between decennial census reports, however, one can turn to local school records. Throughout the nation, every public elementary and secondary school and most parochial and private schools receive federal aid to provide children from low-income

6. The Internal Revenue Service does release fascinating, annual county-by-county summaries of median household incomes based on tax returns.

households with free or reduced-price school lunches. Although the income eligibility standards are higher than the poverty level, school lunch figures, particularly for elementary schools, serve as a rough indicator of neighborhood income trends.[7]

Studies that I have done in a dozen regions (Baltimore, Buffalo, Dayton, and others) show that the percentages of low-income children have increased in central-city school systems even as regional unemployment rates have plummeted. This suggests that, in the midst of regional prosperity, many low-income neighborhoods targeted by CDCs are continuing to decline.

Median home sale prices in Chicago's West Garfield Park, the target area of Bethel Housing, Inc., doubled from 1990 to 1995—an eye-catching success story. Yet during the same period the percentage of children receiving free or reduced-price lunches in the neighborhood's five elementary schools climbed from 95 percent in 1990–91 to 99 percent in 1996–97.

Matching local public schools with CDC target areas is tricky. Boundaries generally do not coincide, and enrollment patterns can be affected by citywide busing programs. In many northern cities, in particular, parochial schools provide a low-cost alternative for many inner-city families. In some communities charter schools are also beginning to offer alternatives to the local public schools.

Undoubtedly, many housing programs are having a positive impact. Over fifteen years (1982–97) the New York City Housing Partnership Homeownership Program had built or begun construction on over 13,500 housing units in the city's five boroughs.[8] (I passed one of its construction sites during my tour of Bedford-Stuyvesant.) New owners are primarily working-class families, often new immigrants grasping the first rung on the ladder of homeownership.

However, I have encountered only one instance where a housing revitalization program has probably helped reduce the percentage of low-income children in local public schools: Battle Creek, Michigan's Neighborhoods, Inc. In all others that I have tracked, regentrification has not begun to improve the school environment of the neighborhood's remaining low-income children.

---

7. High school students are well known for avoiding even applying for free lunch support, no matter how stressed financially.

8. Orlebeke (1997, p. 212).

A definitive evaluation must await the Tale of the Tracts, Census 2000-style. Until then, the evidence of my experience is that, even in the midst of what is now a seven-year economic expansion, prosperity has not reached into the heart of many of America's poorest ghettos and barrios. The down escalator just goes faster and faster. The good guys are not winning with just an inside game.

4

Pilot Small's Airport and the RKO Keith's Balcony: Sprawl and Race

WHAT IS THIS "down escalator"? How does it work? Any American—black *or* white—who has grown up in or around an American city can answer these questions by just thinking about his or her own personal experiences. My own answers begin with "Pilot Small's airport." For a half dozen years immediately after the end of World War II, my family lived in Alexandria, Virginia, in a new, sprawling, garden apartment development called Parkfairfax. Constructed in 1944–45, Parkfairfax was created to house the postwar crush of young government and military families, busily launching the baby boom.

As a child, I would leaf through a popular series of children's books: *Farmer Small, Sailor Small, Fireman Small,* and so on. My favorite was *Pilot Small.* On those Sundays when my father could rip himself away from General George C. Marshall's State Department, he would often bundle the family into our GI-style 1946 Ford and drive out to "Pilot Small's airport." It was somewhere off in the country, what seemed like half an hour's drive away. We would watch Piper Cubs, Cessnas, and (a real thrill) an occasional biplane land and take off from the little "general aviation" airport (as I learned to designate such a facility three decades later as mayor of Albuquerque).

When I was a little older, my parents would let me take the bus to downtown Washington by myself, where I would go to RKO Keith's or the Warner

Theater to see *Task Force,* or *Thunderbolt,* or *The Sands of Iwo Jima.* I scarcely noticed that, on the trip into Washington, colored people always had to ride in the back of the bus. As I watched my war movies, I occasionally cast a jealous glance back up into that mysterious balcony where colored people had to sit: a great place to watch a movie, I thought, but where white kids like me rarely ventured.

One-quarter of the 1.2 million residents of metropolitan Washington were "non-white," in the terminology of the 1950 census, but (except for Margaret, our once-a-week cleaning lady) I rarely came in contact with any colored people. None lived in Parkfairfax. There were none at my legally segregated Charles Barrett Elementary School. There were few colored customers in neighborhood stores we frequented, and no colored employees behind the counters. Whether in Virginia or in the District of Columbia, I was rarely in a colored neighborhood, except when my father and I would go to Griffith Stadium to watch the Washington Senators play. (Griffith Stadium was located on Georgia Avenue near the intersection with Florida Avenue, a neighborhood that, over the previous four decades, had become the heart of "the other Washington.")

During the 1960s, after a dozen years away in New York and California, I lived again in the Washington area, this time in the District of Columbia itself. For five years I was a civil rights staffer with the Washington Urban League, working with antipoverty programs in Negro neighborhoods, before moving on to a job with the Labor Department's Manpower Administration.

Now, in the 1990s, I again live in the Washington area after twenty years in Albuquerque, New Mexico. I have revisited the sites of many childhood memories, seen now with a keener professional eye.

I automatically assumed that Pilot Small's airport had vanished, but vague childhood memories left me with no idea where it had been located. A check with local planning departments turned up a small pamphlet, "Ghost Airports of Fairfax County." Pilot Small's Airport must have been the Washington and Virginia Airport, located just three to four miles from Parkfairfax near Bailey's Crossroads and built in 1947. At its peak, 135 Piper Cubs, Cessnas, and PT-19s were tied down at the little airport with its two graveled runways.

Pilot Small's airport had, indeed, vanished. In 1970 the property was sold to a developer, who built Skyline Center, a hundred-acre complex of stores, offices, apartments, and townhouses. Some 38,000 people now live on the site of my Pilot Small's airport and in the surrounding Bailey's Crossroads area (equal to one-third of Fairfax County's entire population in 1950).

In fact, Skyline Center is practically the geographic center of a vast metropolitan region embracing 4.5 million people spread across the federal district, five Maryland counties, a dozen Virginia counties, and three counties in West Virginia. Metropolitan Washington today stretches roughly 80 miles north-south from Frederick, Maryland, to Fredericksburg, Virginia, and 110 miles east-west from Saint Mary's City, Maryland, to Martinsburg, West Virginia.

RKO Keith's, the Warner Theater, and every other movie palace in downtown Washington have also disappeared. (In fact, not a single movie theater is still open in any predominantly black area of the nation's capital.) Griffith Stadium also has long since crumbled under the wrecker's ball, making way for Howard University Hospital. The Washington Senators are gone, too, not once but twice. In 1961 the Griffith clan moved the original fifty-eight-year franchise north to Minneapolis–Saint Paul to become the Minnesota Twins. (The Griffiths were rumored to be looking for a whiter community in which to do business.) Then, in 1971, the David Rusk family and the born-again Washington Senators, an expansion franchise, both went west, the Rusks to New Mexico, the Senators to Dallas-Fort Worth to become the Texas Rangers.

Parkfairfax, though, remains a vale of memories. Completely built out at its inception and always well maintained, Parkfairfax looks exactly the same today, over 200 eight-unit, two-story, red brick or white brick buildings, just as I remember them. There are a few small changes. The bus stops have "Metro" signs rather than "WM&VA" signs. The trees and bushes have forty-five years' more growth on them. In 1978–79 Parkfairfax converted to condominiums; all 1,684 remodeled units are now owner-occupied. Whether occupants are renters or homeowners, of course, would not be visible to the eye, but another change is. A modest level of diversity has come to Parkfairfax. Parkfairfax is no longer all white, but 3.7 percent African American, 3.3 percent Hispanic, and 2.7 percent Asian.

African Americans are hardly invisible in today's Washington area. There are black anchormen and anchorwomen on all the local newscasts. Three of the nine members of the Alexandria City Council are black, as were two members of the seven-member Alexandria school board.[1] The federal government has three black cabinet secretaries, forty members of the Black

---

1. In 1997, after Virginia switched from appointed to elected school boards, the Alexandria school board suddenly found itself without a single black member for a district in which 40 percent of the pupils were African American.

Congressional Caucus, and 79,000 black employees at all levels in the national capital area.

Clearly, blacks and whites have traveled some distance toward Martin Luther King's dream. However, the hard truths of the Bedford Stuyvesants, Roxburys, and Central Wards, or, in the Washington area, the Anacostia or the Shaw neighborhoods, testify that our nation still has a long path to travel.

My emblematic Pilot Small's airport and the RKO Keith's balcony—sprawl and race—are the twin forces that have dominated urban America since World War II. Urban sprawl and racial segregation feed upon and reinforce each other. The greater the sprawl, the more far-flung the dispersion of middle-class households. The greater the dispersion of middle-class households, the greater the abandonment of older neighborhoods in central cities and older suburbs. The greater the abandonment of older neighborhoods, the greater the concentration of poor minorities in those areas. The greater the concentration of poor minorities, the greater the increase in crime and violence, drug and alcohol addiction, family disintegration, unemployment and welfare dependency, school failure, and neighborhood deterioration. The greater the social meltdown of the "inner city" (which now connotes a set of social conditions more than location), the greater the incentives for those remaining residents who can choose where to live—middle-class households—to join the suburban diaspora.

And so, the cycle of peripheral growth and core abandonment accelerates in many metropolitan areas across the country. Under the impact of regional development patterns, Pilot Small's airport vanished, but, ephemerally integrated, RKO Keith's vanished as well.

Sprawl, Metropolitan Style

It is hard to exaggerate the sprawling geographical expansion of urban America and its impact on both land and people. In 1950 (when I was still looking wide-eyed at Pilot Small's airport), the national census identified 168 metropolitan areas. These I will call "old metro areas." Some 84 million people, or 56 percent of the nation's population, lived in these old metro areas. Typically, they contained one large "central city" and its surrounding county. Of the 168 such areas, 115 covered only one county. Larger, more complex metro areas usually included several counties. In all, the 168 old metro areas contained 304 counties, covering almost 208,000 square miles.

At the middle of the twentieth century, the central cities of these areas dominated the urban landscape and housed much of its population, to an extent largely forgotten now, on the threshold of the twenty-first century. The 193 old central cities contained almost 60 percent of their regional populations; their suburbs were home to only 40 percent.[2] Under the city's dominance, a sense of unity spread over the surrounding region. Most area children attended the city school system. Most area residents used city parks and libraries. Most area workers rode city buses, streetcars, and subways to blue- and white-collar jobs within the city, or, occasionally, to nearby factories just outside the city limits. Most of the region's voters cast their ballots for the same set of local offices. Although there were often fierce rivalries among ethnic and racial groups, common city-based public institutions were unifying forces (except in the legally segregated South, with its sets of parallel institutions).

By 1990 the demographic proportions were reversed. The original 168 old metro areas had sprawled to embrace 345,000 square miles in 536 counties. Some 159 million people, or 66 percent of the nation's population, lived in these old metro areas. However, their central cities had shrunk in relative importance, now housing only one-third of their metropolitan populations; two-thirds now lived in their suburbs.

As the population of the central cities declined, local governance became increasingly balkanized. Just four decades earlier, 60 percent of the nation's metropolitan residents had been governed by 193 city councils and commissions and by 193 mayors or city managers. By 1990, almost 70 percent of the population of the same 168 regions fell under the governance of approximately 9,600 suburban cities, towns, villages, townships, and counties.

Urban growth, of course, has not been limited to long-established urban centers. Another 152 urban areas have grown to a scale to achieve metropolitan status, containing another 34 million persons in 1990. Some of the "young" metro areas are far-flung outliers of great metropolitan centers such as New York, Chicago, or Los Angeles. But most young metro areas have developed as independent urban centers in their own right. Many are located in southern and western states, a result of the long-term population shift to the Sunbelt. Many are also blessed with favorable annexation laws, such that their central cities have been able to capture much of their regional growth within their expanded borders. By 1990 these cities contained 21 million people, or 62 percent of their metropolitan populations, and covered 240,000 square miles in 211 counties.

2. Some metro areas, like Albany-Schenectady-Troy, New York, had several central cities.

Thus, after four decades of urban sprawl, metropolitan America (including old and new metro areas) had grown from an area of 208,000 square miles housing 84 million people to an area of 585,000 square miles housing 193 million people. Almost three-quarters of all Americans live in the nation's 320 metro areas. The total population in these areas has increased 128 percent, but the land area accommodating that population has increased by 181 percent. The density of population of these metropolitan areas has fallen from 407 persons per square mile in 1950 to 330 persons per square mile in 1990. By this measure, the postwar development of America's urban areas has been consuming land about 50 percent faster than the growth in population.

Exploding Urbanized Areas

Calibrating the phenomenon of urban sprawl according to the county-by-county expansion of metropolitan areas, however, understates the voracious consumption of land in the postwar period. On the basis of commuting patterns to major job markets, the Census Bureau defines metro areas as groups of entire counties. Yet, on first being added to a metro area, only a small portion of a county may be urbanized. County-based tabulation of the growth of metro areas may add either too much land or too little.

As an example of understated urban growth, from 1950 through 1990 the census defined the Albuquerque metro area as 1,163-square-mile Bernalillo County. By this measure, in the above discussion, the Albuquerque metro area does not register as having grown at all in land area: in 1950 the metro area was Bernalillo County; in 1990 it was the same, geographically unaltered, Bernalillo County.[3]

In reality, from 1960 to 1990 what the census also defined as Albuquerque's "urbanized population" grew from 241,216 to 487,120, and the amount of "urbanized land" from 78 square miles to 226 square miles. While its urbanized population doubled, Albuquerque's urbanized land area almost tripled.

What picture emerges from calculating the growth of America's "urbanized areas" (as contrasted with the growth of county-defined metropolitan areas)? The 1950 census also reported that 69 million people resided in 157 urbanized areas covering almost 13,000 square miles. By 1990 the population of these same 157 areas had grown to more than 130 million people occupying almost 46,000 square miles. While the urbanized population grew

3. In 1992, having assessed the results of the 1990 census, the federal government added two more counties to the Albuquerque metro area.

88 percent, urbanized land expanded 255 percent (which amounts to three times the rate of population growth). By 1990 the average resident of these 157 communities was consuming 90 percent more land area than just forty years before.

I have analyzed data on urban sprawl for all 396 urbanized areas designated in the 1990 census; continuous data are available for only 157 for the four decades discussed above. However, as a speaker and consultant, I have worked in depth in fifty-eight metro areas. On my initial visit I have always taken an auto tour of the region, trying to see examples of new and old neighborhoods, ranging from the best to the worst. (I pay less attention to new commercial areas. After the first dozen tours, I realized that all suburban strip commercial centers and shopping malls look alike.)

Appendix table A-4 presents sprawl data for these fifty-eight regions. Overall, from 1950 to 1990 urbanized land expanded 305 percent while urbanized population grew only 80 percent—an almost 4-to-1 ratio. During the 1980s new suburban growth occurred at an average of about 1,500–2,000 persons per square mile. The density of new development in the 1980s was about one-fourth of the density of population of central cities in 1950 in these fifty-eight metro areas.[4]

No Room at the Inn

This pattern of sprawling growth embodies a vision of metropolitan development dominated by universal ownership of a single-family home in a small, self-governing community distant from the workplace; universal car ownership; and a workplace in a low-rise, parklike setting with immediately adjacent parking.[5]

It is a vision that, in many respects, has been substantially achieved. Since mid-century, home ownership has risen from 40 percent to 65 percent, one of the world's highest rates of homeownership. While the nation's population has increased by only 75 percent since 1950, motor vehicles have increased by 300 percent—and vehicle miles traveled by over 200 percent.[6]

4. Appendix table A-4 shows that several urbanized areas experienced new growth at *negative* densities (for example, Buffalo, Detroit, Peoria, and Pittsburgh). Clearly, that is impossible. What the data reflect is that these suburban areas are experiencing overall population loss as older suburbs are now beginning to lose population just as their central cities have for decades. Without doing tract-by-tract analysis, it is not possible to factor out suburban population losses to calculate actual density of new development.

5. See Downs (1994).

6. Bureau of the Census (1975; 1997, table 1010).

By 1990, the average American household owned 1.77 cars, trucks, minivans, or recreational vehicles that were driven over 15,000 miles annually. Over 91 percent of all workers (nine out of ten driving alone) logged one-third of those total annual miles commuting to their jobs, 55 percent of which were now located in suburbs outside central cities.[7]

Critics of this vision object to its wastefulness, citing the high costs of the infrastructure needed to serve low-density development; the loss of precious farmland, greenbelt, and recreational areas; the increased air and groundwater pollution; the growing dependence on oil (particularly foreign oil); and other environmentally based concerns. In the 1990s these issues have fueled the "sustainable communities" movement.

To return to the metaphorical down escalator, this vision of metropolitan development makes no room for low-income households. Although postwar housing construction moved from a retail to wholesale scale, factory-produced, prefabricated homes never succeeded (despite some initial enthusiasm by both private investors and the federal government). Instead, factory-type assembly-line techniques moved outdoors to the building site. Postwar builders such as William Levitt learned to develop giant subdivisions, moving specialized work crews from site to site.

In the early postwar years, homebuilders targeted the moderate-income market, seeking to meet the pent-up demand for new homes by returning veterans and blue-collar workers. In more recent decades, however, homebuilders have increasingly concentrated on a more upscale market, aimed at higher-income households (in fact, the higher the better). Though several builders may be involved in developing a typical subdivision, offering a number of housing styles, all build for a relatively narrow band of the income scale. New subdivisions designed for a wide range of household incomes are uncommon. New subdivisions are rare indeed that purposefully mix middle-income households and low-income households (even if the latter are supported by generous government subsidies).

If not in new suburbs, then, where are low-income families to be housed? According to Oliver Byrum, former planning director for Minneapolis,

> After enough observation and thought, the obvious finally becomes obvious. Low-income people and poverty conditions are concentrated in inner city areas because that is where we want them to be. It is, in fact, our national belief, translated into metropolitan housing policy, that this is where

7. Bureau of the Census (1997, table 1015).

they are supposed to be. Additionally, they are to have as little presence as possible elsewhere in the metropolitan area.

It is only a slight overstatement to suggest that an unspoken agreement has been struck between the city and suburbs. Suburban communities don't want poor people, and in some ways the central cities need the needy. The poor don't fit the image of the suburban good life with its neighborhoods, schools, parks, shopping centers and jobs. The cities need them to occupy housing and neighborhoods that the more affluent market has rejected, as statistics to make the case for special funding consideration from higher levels of government, as voters, as clients for the public and nonprofit social service and housing bureaucracy and system. Cities need their housing assistance as a source of financing, and as occupants for redevelopment areas.

Summing up, Byrum continues,

> Cheap shelter is to be mostly created by the devaluation of inner city neighborhoods.... Revitalization [of inner-city neighborhoods] is in direct conflict with our national housing policy of devitalization as a means of providing low-income shelter.[8]

Concentrated Poverty: A Racial Phenomenon

Not *all* low-income households are concentrated in poverty-stricken inner-city neighborhoods, however. The country's 320 metropolitan areas in 1990 contained 10.8 million poor whites, 6.9 million poor blacks, and 4.8 million poor Hispanics, almost as many poor whites as poor blacks and Hispanics combined. In a typical metro area, however, three out of four poor whites lived in middle-class, mostly suburban neighborhoods. By contrast, three out of four poor blacks and one out of two poor Hispanics lived in inner-city "poverty neighborhoods" where at least 20 percent of the residents were poor.

Using the 1990 census, I calculated the relative concentration of poor persons by racial and ethnic group for fifty-eight metro areas where I have spoken and consulted. At that time, only 26 percent of poor whites lived in poverty neighborhoods, whereas 54 percent of poor Hispanics and 75 percent of poor blacks did so (see appendix table A-5).

The concentration by race and ethnicity was even more dramatic in high-poverty neighborhoods, where 40 percent or more of the residents were

8. See Byrum (1992, pp. 12–13).

poor: only 5 percent of all poor whites lived in high-poverty neighborhoods, in contrast to 18 percent of poor Hispanics and 32 percent of poor blacks. In effect, only one of out every twenty poor whites lived in a high-poverty neighborhood, the grim circumstance faced by one out of every three poor blacks.

Living in poverty is tough enough for any household, regardless of race. For the great majority of poor whites, however, poverty is an individual household condition. Most poor whites are not surrounded by other poor people. For most poor blacks, and, to a lesser degree, for poor Hispanics, poverty is a communal crisis, as well as an individual hardship.

Segregated housing markets have created this disproportionate concentration of poor blacks and poor Hispanics. There has certainly been progress in breaching the walls of residential apartheid. Progress can be measured first in changes in social attitudes. A poll taken in 1942 found that only 36 percent of whites felt that it would make no difference to them "if a Negro with the same income and education as theirs moved into their block."[9] By 1972 that percentage had risen to 85 percent.[10]

Slow Racial Desegregation

Slow progress can also be measured in actual results. The dissimilarity index first mentioned in chapter 1 can be used to determine how evenly or unevenly a minority group is distributed, for instance, across neighborhoods or classrooms. A score of 0 indicates an absolutely mathematically even distribution, or complete integration; a score of 100 indicates an absolutely uneven distribution, or complete segregation.

For example, if the population of a metro area is 25 percent black, then a dissimilarity index of 0 would mean that blacks make up 25 percent of the population (neither more nor less) in every neighborhood in the metro area. A dissimilarity index of 100 would mean that all blacks, and only blacks, live in certain neighborhoods, and all whites, and only whites, live everywhere else. A dissimilarity index of 65 would mean that 65 percent of all blacks would have to move to other neighborhoods (in the mathematically appropriate proportions) for all neighborhoods to be 25 percent black.

Table 4-1 traces the movement toward greater residential integration in thirty-two of the country's largest metropolitan areas between 1970 and 1990.

9. Thernstrom and Thernstrom (1997, p. 141).
10. Thernstrom and Thernstrom (1997, p. 221).

Table 4-1. *Black Residential Segregation in Thirty-Two Major Metro Areas, 1970–90*

Dissimilarity index (100 = total segregation)

Metro area	1970	1980	1990	1970–90
Northern				
Boston	81	78	68	−13
Buffalo	87	79	82	−5
Chicago	92	88	86	−6
Cincinnati	77	72	76	−1
Cleveland	91	88	85	−6
Columbus	82	71	67	−15
Detroit	88	87	88	0
Gary-Hammond-East Chicago	91	91	90	−1
Indianapolis	82	76	74	−8
Kansas City	87	79	73	−14
Los Angeles-Long Beach	91	81	73	−18
Milwaukee	91	84	83	−8
New York	81	82	82	1
Newark	81	82	82	1
Philadelphia	80	79	77	−3
Pittsburgh	75	73	71	−4
St. Louis	85	81	77	−8
San Francisco-Oakland	80	72	66	−14
Average	85	80	78	−7
Southern				
Atlanta	82	79	68	−14
Baltimore	82	75	71	−11
Charlotte	67	61	53	−14
Dallas-Ft. Worth	87	77	63	−24
Greensboro-Winston-Salem	65	56	61	−4
Houston	78	70	67	−11
Memphis	76	72	69	−7
Miami	85	78	70	−15
New Orleans	73	68	69	−4
Norfolk-Virginia Beach-Newport News	76	63	50	−26
Oklahoma City	90	71	60	−30
San Antonio	77	63	54	−23
Tampa-St. Petersburg	80	73	69	−11
Washington	81	70	66	−15
Average	79	71	64	−15

Sources: Douglas S. Massey and Nancy A. Denton. *American Apartheid: Segregation and the Making of the Underclass* (Harvard University Press, 1993), p. 64; Roderick J. Harrison and Daniel H. Weinberg, "Racial and Ethnic Segregation in 1990," U.S. Bureau of the Census, April 1992; and author's calculations based on census data.

At the outset, segregation levels were very high in both northern metro areas and southern metro areas. Over the next two decades, southern communities progressed at almost twice the rate of northern areas. The largest improvement was recorded in San Antonio, Dallas-Fort Worth, Norfolk-Virginia Beach-Newport News, and Oklahoma City. In other metro areas, such as Detroit, New York, and Newark, progress was nonexistent. By 1990, however, of the thirty-two metro areas listed, only Norfolk-Virginia Beach, Charlotte, and San Antonio had moved from being highly segregated into a status of more "moderate" segregation. Despite some progress, all other twenty-nine metro housing markets were still highly segregated.

Atlanta: Desegregation . . . and Resegregation

How would this statistical index translate into a more practical description of racial residential patterns? In the Atlanta metro area, for example, the African American percentage has held constant at about 27 percent for several decades. Metro Atlanta's dissimilarity index dropped from 82 in 1970 to 68 in 1990, a substantial improvement over twenty years. During these two decades, much of Atlanta's large black middle class moved out of the city into the suburbs, primarily into southern Fulton, DeKalb, and Clayton counties. For the most part, however, new black suburbanites were not moving into new subdivisions but into hand-me-down, older suburban neighborhoods. These older neighborhoods were either rapidly being vacated by former white residents or, at least, were no longer considered choice neighborhoods for middle-class whites moving into the Atlanta area.

In the metro area's ten core counties, the 1980 census showed only twenty-four census tracts with reasonably proportionate racial balance. (As a rule of thumb, I would define racial balance as being within ten percentage points of the regional racial percentages, that is, 17–37 percent black and 63–83 percent white in the Atlanta region). By the 1990 census, the proportion of black residents had increased substantially in twenty-one of the twenty-four tracts. In the space of ten years, eight tracts had gone from racial balance to 60–87 percent black. Steady resegregation accompanied black suburbanization almost everywhere in the Atlanta area.

Atlanta's dissimilarity index score of 68 still left most blacks and most whites living in substantially segregated communities in 1990, but the most extreme apartheid was reduced over the two decades. In 1970, 59 percent of the area's blacks lived in forty-one census tracts that were 90 percent or more black; one-quarter of all blacks lived in eighteen tracts that were totally seg-regated (that is, 99 percent black). On the other side of the color line, in 1970 more than 81 percent of all whites lived in 143 tracts that were 90 percent or more white, and 49 percent—almost half of all whites—lived in totally segregated tracts (that is, 99 percent white).

By 1990, however, only 6 percent of all whites and 10 percent of all blacks lived in totally segregated tracts. The hard edges of total apartheid had been rounded off. However, almost two-thirds of whites still lived in 90 percent or more white tracts, and more than one-third of all blacks still lived in 90 percent or more black tracts.

The Atlanta area offers a test of the proposition that rising economic prosperity will reduce the concentration of poverty. It would be hard to con-ceive of a more vibrant regional economy than that experienced by the At-lanta area in recent decades. From 1970 to 1990 real per capita income in metro Atlanta grew 49 percent, and during the 1980s alone the growth rate was 29 percent, both figures far above the national metro averages for the same periods.

In the wake of the region's strong economic growth, particularly during the 1980s, overall poverty levels dropped from 11.8 percent to 9.6 percent. Among white residents, the poverty rate fell steadily, from 7.0 percent in 1970 to 4.9 percent in 1990. The poverty rate among black residents was 28.6 percent in 1970, or four times the white poverty level. Over the twenty years, black poverty also dropped, to 22.4 percent regionwide, but was still more than four times the white poverty level.

During that same period, however, the number of poverty neighbor-hoods grew dramatically, from fifty-six to ninety-one. Most poverty neigh-borhoods were (and are) located in the city of Atlanta. Atlanta had fifty of the region's fifty-six poverty neighborhoods in 1970 and seventy-two of ninety-one in 1990. As these trends show, however, concentrations of pov-erty formed in older suburban areas as well. Six suburban poverty neigh-borhoods in 1970 grew to nineteen, with the greatest number being in the inner suburbs: DeKalb County and the Tri-Cities area of southern Fulton County.

Equally ominous is the greater intensity of poverty within many of the neighborhoods. In 1970 Atlanta had only fourteen high-poverty neighbor-hoods (40 to 60 percent poor) and five hyperpoverty neighborhoods (more than 60 percent poor). By 1990 the number of high-poverty neighborhoods had increased to twenty-one, and the number of hyperpoverty neighbor-hoods almost tripled to fourteen.

These were not neighborhoods of concentrated white poverty, but of concentrated black poverty. Of the ninety-one poverty neighborhoods in the region, only thirteen (half in the suburbs) had whites in the majority. There were probably only eight in which poverty among white residents themselves exceeded 20 percent; higher poverty levels among black residents probably pushed the other five tracts over the 20 percent threshold. There were *no* high- or hyperpoverty census tracts in which the majority of residents were white.

Although the region's black upper middle class had grown and become suburbanized, many still lived in poverty neighborhoods. Almost one out of five black households with incomes above the regional household median lived in poverty neighborhoods (down from one out of three in 1970). In the Atlanta region an upper-middle-class black household was twice as likely to live in a poverty neighborhood as a poor white household because of continued racial segregation in housing markets.

Despite the region's two decades of unparalleled prosperity, the city of Atlanta itself ended the period more burdened by concentrated poverty than it began, and some inner suburbs were becoming poverty-stricken as well.

Higher Economic Segregation

The trends in poverty neighborhoods for the fifty-eight metro areas I have studied firsthand are analyzed in appendix table A-6. There is a striking contrast between regional poverty trends and neighborhood poverty trends. Between 1970 and 1990 the overall poverty rate for the fifty-eight metro areas increased slightly from 10.7 percent to 11.7 percent. The increase for the group as a whole was due entirely to increasing poverty levels in the industrial heartland, which accounted for all of the twenty-six metro areas (except Oklahoma City) whose poverty levels increased by more than one percentage point. By contrast, over the two decades poverty levels dropped by more than one percentage point in sixteen metro areas, all located along the northeastern seaboard or in the Sun Belt.

However, the number of poverty neighborhoods increased in almost every metro area from 1970 to 1990. In the fifty-eight regions the number of poverty tracts almost doubled; within those totals, the number of high-poverty tracts (that is, with greater than 40 percent poverty rates) almost tripled.

Only in Norfolk-Virginia Beach-Newport News, which experienced the greatest reduction in its regional poverty rate, and Mobile, Alabama, did the total number of poverty neighborhoods decrease. All of the Mobile area's net decrease was accounted for by new development in Baldwin County (located across the bay from Mobile itself). In 1970 fourteen census tracts in then largely rural Baldwin County still had many poor farm families. As the Mobile area prospered, many whites sought out new homes in Baldwin County rather than in Mobile County. Over a period of two decades suburbanization dropped Baldwin County's poverty rate from 22.6 percent to 14.3 percent, and the number of poverty tracts in the county shrank from fourteen to four. Across Mobile Bay, on the other hand, the number of poverty neighborhoods in the cities of Mobile and majority-black Pritchard grew from forty to forty-seven, and all but six of the poverty neighborhoods had African American majorities.

Several other metro areas held their own. In Tallahassee, whose economic progress was spurred by the growth of the state government and Florida State University, the number of poverty tracts was stable, as was the case in Gainesville, home of the University of Florida. In metro Charlotte the number of poverty neighborhoods barely increased. In metro Richmond the number of poverty neighborhoods increased modestly. All were regions with solid economic growth and sustained progress toward greater racial integration.

But economic growth alone is not sufficient to stem the growth of poverty neighborhoods. The Grand Rapids area has had one of the country's most prosperous economies. The poverty rate has been stable (around 8 percent). Between 1973 and 1988, the Grand Rapids area experienced a 55 percent increase in jobs, a rate of increase equal to that in metro Charlotte. Most remarkably, the area had a 22 percent *increase* in manufacturing employment, although undoubtedly education and skill requirements rose for jobs in the manufacturing sector. But Grand Rapids is also a very racially segregated society (a dissimilarity index of 72). Any adverse economic adjustments affecting black workers were magnified within highly segregated black neighborhoods. Despite the region's prosperity, the number of poverty neighborhoods grew from twelve to twenty-two, and almost half of these had minority populations even though the entire region had less than a 10 percent minority population.[11]

In a study of the dynamics of high-poverty districts in 318 metro areas, Paul Jargowsky, a social scientist at the University of Texas at Dallas, found

---

11. Immigration of low-skilled Hispanics into the city of Holland in neighboring Ottawa County also helped increase the region's poverty neighborhoods.

that ghetto poverty increased significantly between 1980 and 1990.[12] The number of all blacks living in ghetto areas increased from 4.3 million in 1980 to 5.9 million in 1990. The percentage of the total black population (of all income levels) living in ghetto areas increased from 20 percent to almost 24 percent. This, however, means that more than three-quarters of the black population does not live in urban ghettos (as defined by Jargowsky). Booming postindustrial economies around Boston, New York, Philadelphia, Baltimore, Washington, and Atlanta, for example, allowed many middle-class blacks to leave what Jargowsky terms ghettos for new suburban homes (even though racial resegregation often followed).

Most ominous for many central cities, the geographic scope of urban ghettos expanded dramatically during the 1980s even as, with the flight of the black middle class to the suburbs, the population density of ghettos declined. The number of census tracts Jargowsky classifies as ghettos grew from 3,256 to 5,003—a 54 percent increase—while population density declined 11 percent in ghetto areas.

In a follow-up study, Jargowsky devised an ingenious "neighborhood sorting index" to measure the degree of economic segregation within different racial and ethnic groups. Jargowsky noted:

> Metropolitan areas usually show incredible diversity, with widely varying levels of and changes over time on most socio-demographic indicators. In contrast, the trend toward greater levels of economic segregation was remarkably widespread. In the 1980s, 108 out of the 111 metropolitan areas for which I calculate a change in Neighborhood Sorting Index had an increase in [economic segregation] among blacks. For whites, [economic segregation] increased in 253 out of 318 metropolitan areas; for Hispanics, [economic segregation] increased in 39 out of 49 metro areas.
>
> This trend is characteristic of virtually every region as well as metropolitan areas of different sizes. For whites, the increases [in economic segregation] were modest but consistent over time. For blacks and Hispanics, the increases were modest in the 1970s but much larger on average in the 1980s. The rapid increases in economic segregation, especially among blacks, have contributed to ghetto poverty. Against the backdrop of modest decreases in racial segregation in the 1980s, these trends suggest that class may come to rival race as the organizing principle of the metropolis.[13]

12. Jargowsky (1994). In this study Jargowsky defined a ghetto as a majority-black neighborhood with a poverty rate of 20 percent or more.
13. Jargowsky (1996).

Table 4-2. *Percentage of Racial Groups Living in High-Poverty Neighborhoods, 239 Metro Areas, 1970–90*

Percent

Racial group	1970	1980	1990
All income levels			
White	0.8	0.8	1.4
Black	14.4	15.2	17.7
Hispanic	9.6	8.6	10.5
Poor			
White	2.9	3.3	6.3
Black	26.1	28.2	33.5
Hispanic	23.6	19.2	22.1

Source: Paul A. Jargowsky, *Poverty and Place: Ghettos, Barrios, and the American City* (New York: Russell Sage, 1997), pp. 38, 41.

In 1997 Jargowsky published his most comprehensive analysis of neighborhood poverty.[14] This work focuses on what I have termed "high-poverty neighborhoods," those in which 40 percent or more of the population is poor. Such neighborhoods are clearly in extreme economic and social crisis. In my work I have emphasized the lower poverty threshold (that is, more than 20 percent) because most neighborhoods just past that poverty level (particularly minority neighborhoods) steadily deteriorate into high-poverty status within one or two decades.

In Jargowsky's terminology, high-poverty neighborhoods in which two-thirds of the residents are black are called "ghettos," those with two-thirds Hispanic residents are "barrios," and those with two-thirds white residents are "white slums." High-poverty areas with no dominant racial group are "mixed slums." Jargowsky used these definitions to categorize 2,866 high-poverty census tracts in the country's 318 metro areas. Of the total, 1,329 (or 46 percent) were black ghettos; 334 (or 12 percent) were Hispanic barrios; 387 (or 14 percent) were white slums; and the rest (816, or 28 percent) were mixed slums.

Table 4-2 again shows the disproportionate experience of concentrated poverty among the nation's different racial groups. The percentage of whites of *all* income levels living in high-poverty neighborhoods grew slightly from

14. Jargowsky (1997).

1970 to 1990, but by 1990 barely one white out of one hundred lived in a high-poverty neighborhood. By contrast, for all income levels more than one out of ten Hispanics and one out of six blacks lived in high-poverty neighborhoods. When the situation of *poor* persons is examined in each racial group, their isolation increased across all groups. Barely one out of twenty poor whites was living in a high-poverty neighborhood in 1990, compared with one out of five poor Hispanics and one out of three poor blacks.[15]

Thus poor whites rarely live in "deadly neighborhoods" (that is, high-poverty census tracts), and poor whites infrequently reside in "transitional" or "depressed" neighborhoods (that is, poverty census tracts) where neighborhood conditions and opportunities are usually steadily getting worse.

Jargowsky's findings bring us back full circle to the intersection of race and urban sprawl. Patterns of sprawling metropolitan development divide Americans more and more by income class. Every suburban enclave of privilege is balanced by an inner-city enclave of social misery.

That poor blacks have become more isolated than ever in poor inner-city neighborhoods is, in part, an ironic result of the success of the civil rights movement. The black middle class has expanded dramatically over the past generation. Between 1970 and 1990 the percentage of African Americans in executive, managerial, and professional occupations increased, the result of higher educational levels, general economic prosperity, lowered discriminatory barriers, and affirmative action. As Jargowsky's neighborhood sorting index along racial lines confirms, many black middle-class households have moved from old inner-city neighborhoods to new suburban opportunities.

I do not begrudge their decisions. Every family head must make the best decisions for the family's future, and black families have no greater responsibility to put up with rising crime, declining schools, and deteriorating neighborhoods than anyone else. But black suburbanization has contributed significantly to the greater isolation of poor African Americans.

The dynamics of poverty neighborhoods can perhaps be better understood through an analogy from nuclear physics. Every person, every family can be said to live with a certain level of stress that yields (metaphorically) a low level of radiation. Generally, that radiation is benign and easily contained within a stable community. However, many things can happen to

---

15. The proportions of poor of different racial groups living in high-poverty tracts in Jargowsky's study of 318 metro areas matches almost exactly the proportions in my sample of fifty-eight metro areas visited (see appendix table A-3).

increase the level of radioactivity within a family: sudden unemployment, a divorce, a severe illness, and the like. Nothing generates more stress, however, than sustained poverty.

As poverty increases, the interaction between stressed families also increases, particularly as stable, middle-class families move away. Once these "control rods" are removed and the concentration of poverty reaches a critical level, a chain reaction begins in the community: crime and delinquency rise, alcoholism and drug addiction increase, schools fall into decline, neighborhoods deteriorate, unemployment and welfare dependency increase, and social meltdown begins.

Poor blacks almost invariably live in neighborhoods that have reached these critical levels. Poor whites almost never do. There is a world of difference.

5

The Sprawl Machine

A FABLE

The Chairman looked up from the well-thumbed, back issue of *Time* magazine as his chief of staff led the procession into the conference room. This is "The American Century," *Time*'s publisher, Henry Luce, had confidently proclaimed a year before Pearl Harbor. America's massive mobilization had indeed keyed the Allied victory over the Axis powers, and, though the Americans would not know it for four anxious decades, America's economic strength and, above all, its message of freedom would ultimately smother the Soviet Union, the third of the century's great totalitarian powers. The Chairman knew that the next fifty years were already a lost cause. The task he had set his chief of staff and the strategic planning group was to determine how to so weaken America that the twenty-first century would be his century once again.

The Chairman nodded almost imperceptibly, and several chairs squeaked as the dozen committee members nervously took their assigned places. The thirteenth, the chief of staff, remained standing by the briefing board at the opposite end of the room.

"America is the most formidable instrument ever created by the Other Side," the chief of staff began. "We have concluded that America can never be defeated by an external threat. America can only be vanquished from within. We must destroy Americans' confidence in themselves."

The Chairman's eyes bored into his chief of staff, expectantly.

"The Strategic Planning Group recommends that we concentrate on eroding American civilization at its most visible points. We propose to destroy America's cities—New York, Chicago, Los Angeles, Philadelphia, Detroit—all their great urban centers. Destroy the core, and within fifty years a majority of Americans will be convinced that America is 'headed in the wrong direction,' that 'government cannot do anything right,' and that 'you cannot trust the government.' Whatever else America achieves—eradicating polio, reaching the moon, inventing the computer, winning the cold war itself—the very visible failure of its cities will erode American self-confidence."

The Chairman frowned as he remembered Sherman burning Atlanta in '64 . . . the Great Chicago Fire of '71 . . . the San Francisco earthquake of '06 . . . the Big One in Los Angeles in . . . (when will that be?). Whatever we've thrown at them, he reflected, only challenges the Americans to redoubled effort.

Another might have trembled at the slightest hint of the Chairman's displeasure, but the chief of staff had stood at the Chairman's right hand for eons and he ignored the Chairman's frown. "We propose to persuade many Americans to abandon their cities voluntarily. We have a plan to encourage them to do just that," the chief of staff continued. "Belial argued that we should exploit that common American view that cities are inherently bad places— Sodom and Gomorrah, stress Jefferson's yeoman tradition, all that— but, having actually spent time among them, Aaron urged that we play to Americans' innate optimism. Aaron," he said, calling one of the committee members up to the front.

Still wearing his hair pulled back in the old style, wearing a frayed brown frock coat, knee breeches, and white stockings, Aaron took his place at the briefing board. "We will subtly recast the American Dream. The American Dream has always been based on a naive belief in opportunity: work hard, play by the rules, and you can build a better life for your children. For millions, the start was a farm on the frontier. For millions more just coming off the boat, a factory job in the cities. And schools, always schools, whether the one-room, little red school house or PS 141."

Aaron could sense the Chairman's impatience, so he hurried on. "We shall give the American Dream a new, more material form: a house outside the city in the 'suburbs,' as we'll call them, a little private yard, a car, 'television' to isolate people in their own homes. No need to weaken America by trying to create another breakaway republic in the Mississippi Valley again. We will create a new vision of the Good Life that will lure millions of Americans into willingly dividing their nation up all by themselves."

Aaron was warming to his argument. "Everything will be organized to sell this new American Dream. Advertising, newspapers, magazines, radio, movies, this 'television' I mentioned, politicians' promises, laws, easy loans, everything. We'll make it just easy enough for certain people to achieve this new American Dream. The politicians will be convinced that every step, every policy is for the public good."

He uncovered a flip-chart headed "Operation Suburban Sprawl." A series of dates and events ran down the page. "These new suburbs will be massively subsidized, but in ways that ultimately jeopardize city life. Cheap mortgage financing for new houses, but no help for apartment renters. Tax deductions for homeowners' mortgage interest, for property taxes, for home sale profits (but only if the seller buys another, even bigger house). Billions of tax dollars to build new highways leading out of the cities into the suburbs, but a relative pittance for city subway and bus systems. We'll make it easy for business to plow over 'greenfields' for new suburban office buildings and factories. We'll make it tough to recycle 'brownfields,' old abandoned factory sites in the cities. Families, jobs, stores will be drawn out of the cities into the new suburbs. The cities will slowly be abandoned by all except the poorest. The cities will be converted into giant almshouses."

The chief of staff stepped back. "The brilliance of this plan is that just as we are succeeding in making the cities a Hell on Earth, these suburbs will become the new Purgatory. Suburban highways will become choked with traffic as driving more and more miles becomes the only way to shop or get to work. The air will fill with exhaust fumes, and runoff from new development will foul streams and lakes. Farmlands and forests will disappear under the bulldozer's blade. And we'll promote a soul-deadening sameness—residential streets that all look the same, strip shopping centers, shopping malls—two-thirds of all businesses will be the same stores from coast to coast. Variety and uniqueness will disappear."

"Why would Americans willingly let all this happen?" One of the committee members had dared to interrupt. It was more objection than question. Old Anarch had always been a skeptic.

"Americans will readily divide themselves to be conquered," the chief of staff responded. "Part of their national myth is the little community of stalwart citizens that govern themselves 'democratically,' the New England town meeting and all that. We have already laid the groundwork for fragmenting these new suburbs into many, many little governments. Each will follow its own perceived self-interest. 'One man's sprawl is another man's tax base.' It will be more effective than another Tower of Babel in dividing these Americans. And they will defend each little town and each little school district fiercely under the banner of 'local home rule.' They will forget that, to achieve great purposes, Americans have always banded together. We failed to keep those lovely Articles of Confederation in effect. We lost the War between the States. But this strategy will divide Americans more than ever. Many will truly believe Jefferson's nostrum about 'that government governs best which governs least.' They will be incapable of uniting to solve their common problems."

("Jefferson didn't even believe that himself," Aaron muttered. "He illegally bought Louisiana.")

"It all will be," the chief of staff concluded, with a deferential bow to the Chairman, "truly diabolical."

"I'm still unconvinced," Anarch interjected. "It just doesn't seem enough. It's too bloodless . . . too lacking in emotional impact. The Americans have many, many fine city neighborhoods . . . good city school systems . . . excellent streetcar systems . . . some with subway systems as well. The cities are all linked by the world's greatest network of railroads. How can we rely on the appeal of this new American Dream to pull millions of Americans away from all they already have? Is there not some factor that can drive them away as well?"

"Race." The Chairman's first word echoed throughout the room. "We have always confounded the Americans over race." With great deliberation, he ordered, "Play the race card."

Finally, the chief of staff broke the silence. "We have many acolytes to recruit. There is, for example, a promising young homebuilder on Long Island outside New York City: Levitt... William Levitt, I believe. Great attitude. Levitt recently said, 'America can solve its housing problem or America can solve its race problem. America cannot solve both problems.' Have we your permission to proceed with Operation Suburban Sprawl?"

"Execute."

National Suburban Policy

This is, of course, just a fable. There never was a cabal (satanic or otherwise) that plotted the postwar downfall of so many American cities. But such a conspiracy would have been redundant. It would have been hard to devise consciously a more coherent set of national policies to undermine our cities than those that the federal government adopted piecemeal. Collectively, federal laws have added up to a "national *sub*urban policy" that has reshaped urban America during the postwar decades. (We can safely focus our survey on federal government policies, knowing that human nature has created enough devilry at state and local levels without any master plan.)

Low-Cost Home Mortgages

The earliest installment of our national suburban policy was probably the National Housing Act of 1934, which created the Federal Housing Administration in an effort to stabilize and then to expand homeownership. The successor to the Home Ownership Loan Corporation, the FHA insured low-interest mortgage loans made by banks and savings and loan associations to middle-income households. In and of itself, such a program inherently favored newer suburbs, with their predominantly single-family homes, over older cities, with their much higher proportions of rental housing.

During its early decades, however, the FHA also promulgated rating standards that systematically discriminated against poorer urban neighborhoods, particularly those with substantial minority populations. The FHA would insure mortgages, its regulations stated, only in "racially homogeneous" neighborhoods. It even issued officials maps "redlining" certain city areas (generally minority neighborhoods), placing them off-limits for mortgage loans, whereas no such strictures applied to the emerging suburbs.[1]

The Servicemen's Readjustment Act of 1944, or the "GI Bill of Rights," was undoubtedly one of the most beneficial pieces of social legislation ever enacted in this country. Almost 8 million GIs returning from World War II, and 12 million more servicemen and -women from the cold war years were able to attend colleges, universities, and trade schools to build the skills that have been the basis of much of America's postwar prosperity. Low-cost mortgage loans from the Veterans Administration (VA) financed homeownership for 14 million veterans. Like FHA-insured mortgages, however, VA-guaranteed mortgages had the effect of accelerating the growth of new suburbs and reducing the demand for housing in older city neighborhoods.

The FHA and VA made the members of the white working class and middle class an offer they could not refuse. In 1934 the FHA began by requiring a 20 percent down payment and single-digit interest loans; by the early 1950s, the FHA required only 5 percent down. The VA went one better, requiring no down payment. As one committed city dweller described the postwar market,

> We could find nothing that could meet our needs in any [city] neighborhood we cared to live in at a [rent] we could afford. Instead, what we did find, poring over the real estate pages of the paper, was ad after ad urging us to buy a house in the suburbs. We weren't interested in living in the suburbs, and had not planned on buying a home, but the terms made us rub our eyes in disbelief. It was impossible to resist at least going out to look. Imagine, a six-room house with a yard of its own which could be 'carried'—amortization, taxes, insurance—for a monthly payment lower than the rent on our one-room apartment.[2]

1. In the 1930s, the FHA was struggling "for all the community support [it] could muster. [It] was not going to pioneer in the thicket of race relations. [The FHA was] going to follow sound business principles in order to protect the solvency of its programs. The FHA wanted its housing to be in harmonious and stable neighborhoods. The insurance manuals suggested the use of zoning ordinances and physical barriers to protect racial stability, and racially restrictive covenants were a precondition of mortgage insurance. The FHA Insurance Manual used in the thirties and forties 'read like a chapter of the Nuremberg Laws.'" Welfeld (1988).

2. Louis Schlivek, *Man in Metropolis*, quoted in Welfeld (1988).

By the early 1950s, the FHA and VA were insuring half the mortgages in America and accounted for one-third of all new housing starts. By 1996 the FHA and VA were insuring just 20 percent of the home mortgage market, but the amount of outstanding mortgage loans covered was still massive: the FHA's mortgage portfolio was $423 billion, while mortgages guaranteed by the VA topped $212 billion.

The Secondary Mortgage Market

Established by federal statute in 1938, the Federal National Mortgage Association (FNMA) did not come into its own until after World War II, when it created the secondary mortgage market. Most of the nation's largest banks, thrifts, insurance companies, and pension funds—the primary sources of mortgage money—were located in the slow-growing East. Much of the new housing demand was developing in the fast-growing South and West, where local financial institutions could not scrape together enough money to meet mortgage needs. The FNMA bridged regional imbalances between the supply and demand for mortgage money.

By 1968, the FNMA became "Fannie Mae," a quasi-private corporation, stockholder-owned and federally regulated. It was joined by "Freddie Mac" (the Federal Home Loan Mortgage Corporation, owned, in effect, by the nation's private savings and loan associations) and "Ginnie Mae," a government agency created to guarantee mortgages backing various federal housing subsidy programs. By the 1970s all three financial cousins had perfected the marketing of "mortgage-backed securities." They would package tens of thousands of FHA, VA, and conventional mortgages as collateral for bonds sold on Wall Street, raising billions of dollars more that Fannie Mae, Freddie Mac, and Ginnie Mae would loan back to frontline mortgage lenders.

The avalanche of mortgage money from the secondary mortgage market gave further impetus to suburban development. Until congressional action in the early 1990s, these government-sponsored enterprises (GSEs) were not required to direct a minimum share of funds raised for mortgages to city-based homebuyers.

The financial impact of the federally chartered mortgage pools was even greater than the FHA and VA backing of private lenders. In 1995 the total value of Fannie Mae's mortgage portfolio was $767 billion, Freddie Mac's $559 billion, Ginnie Mae's $472 billion, and that of other federal programs (primarily the Farmers Home Administration) $44 billion. That amounted to more than $1.8 trillion in the federally organized mortgage pools, the great bulk of it invested in suburban, single-family homes.

By contrast, in 1995 direct federal subsidies for low-income households totaled less than $26 billion, of which one-third was for 1.4 million units in public housing projects and two-thirds paid various forms of rent subsidies for low-income households in private apartments. Attributing an amortized value to the public housing inventory would raise the federal government's annual support of low-income rental housing to about $60 billion.

To sum up FHA, VA, and GSE intervention in the home mortgage market, the federal government provides about forty times more support for suburban-oriented, middle-income homeownership than it does for largely city-based, lower-income rental housing.

Pro-Homeowner Tax Policies

From the dawn of the federal income tax (1913), according to the Internal Revenue Service, taxpayers have been able to deduct home mortgage interest against their tax liability. The intent once again was to encourage homeownership. No such tax offsets were provided for apartment renters. For fiscal year 1999 the annual value of the mortgage interest deduction was estimated to be $54.4 billion in tax breaks for 40 million homeowners (only about one-quarter of whom itemize their deductions).[3] Treating this "tax expenditure" just as if it were a budget appropriation has turned the mortgage interest deduction into the federal government's sixth largest expenditure after social security payments, national defense, medicare, interest paid on the national debt, and medicaid assistance.

Stimulating higher homeownership through mortgage interest deductibility may even be unnecessary. Canada and Australia have achieved America's high level of homeownership without such tax subsidies. However, the home mortgage interest deduction is widely viewed as politically untouchable. Even several "flat tax" proposals discussed during the 1996 Republican presidential primary season incorporated continued deductibility of home mortgage interest.

The Internal Revenue Act Amendments of 1951 created the rollover

3. Bureau of the Census (1997, tables 521, 1204).

requirement for home sales. Ostensibly motivated by the capital gains tax problems faced by defense workers shifting from regions with high housing costs to those with low costs, Congress exempted homesellers from any capital gains tax liability if they bought a home of equal or greater price. The effect was to encourage homebuyers to step up constantly in price, and often step out of central cities and older suburbs as well.[4]

Urban Renewal

Title 1 of the Housing Act of 1949 created the federal urban renewal program. At first glance, this would seem to have been a pro-cities measure. Between 1953 and 1986, the federal government provided $13.5 billion for slum clearance and urban redevelopment. Cities used urban renewal money to redesign central business districts, build multilevel parking garages (above and below ground), and convert city streets into pedestrian malls for specialty stores to attract suburban shoppers again. Luxury hotels and apartments were built to attract rich visitors and residents alike. Efforts were made to upgrade the neighborhood environs of major medical centers, museums, concert halls, and theaters that served city residents and suburbanites.

Unfortunately, the era of urban renewal coincided with the era of international-style architecture: giant glass and steel, single-purpose boxes, sometimes perched on stilts, surrounded by concrete and marble plazas, filled with planters but no people. The varied, chaotic, busy street life that historically defined vital cities was designed out of countless urban renewal areas. Sometimes the traditional grid patterns of city streets disappeared as urban renewal areas aped suburban office campuses. In the many cities I have visited, I have found few urban renewal areas of the 1950s and 1960s to be interesting. Many of the most vital downtown areas of the 1990s are those that had the good sense or good luck to escape the federal bulldozer of the 1960s.

More ominous for the future of cities, however, was the bitter truth of the axiom that urban renewal meant "Negro removal." Needless to say, physical housing conditions in many of the black ghettos that were bulldozed were bad. In the long run, however, the replacement homes of many displaced residents were worse: massive, new high-rise public housing complexes often located in isolated sections of the city. Such massive projects as Robert Taylor Homes and Cabrini-Green in Chicago or Baltimore's Lexing-

4. See chapter 13 for a fuller discussion of the impact of federal capital gains tax treatment on housing markets.

ton Terrace and Lafayette Courts became black holes of high crime and poverty that expelled, rather than attracted, middle-class households within gravitational range. In many communities, the federal urban renewal program created both dull, lifeless downtown areas that failed to pull suburbanites back into the city and high-poverty, high-crime public housing complexes that pushed other households into the suburbs even faster.

Federal Transportation Policy

The National Interstate and Defense Highway System Act of 1956, espoused by President Dwight D. Eisenhower during the cold war, was ostensibly justified as a national defense measure. The national network of interstate highways would supposedly allow more effective mobilization of the nation's military resources. Ike remembered the difficulty encountered in moving military units and supplies across the country during the Great War.[5] Broad highways radiating outward also would allow quicker evacuation of America's cities under the threat of nuclear attack. Of course, new highways were two-way streets. Ribbons of concrete allowed new suburbanites to flee the residential areas of cities permanently while still commuting daily back to their city-based jobs.

In launching the most massive peacetime expenditure program ever, President Eisenhower permanently reshaped metropolitan America. From 1956 to the mid-1990s, when the 54,714-mile interstate highway system was nearing completion, the federal government spent a total of $652 billion (in 1996 dollars) on highway aid. Despite the program's original emphasis on long-distance interstate roads, over half of the funds had gone into building 22,134 miles of new highways *within* metropolitan areas. This fostered a vast decentralization of the country's urban centers. By contrast, under the Urban Mass Transit Act of 1964, federal aid to public bus and subway systems, which tend to promote greater centralization, totaled only $85 billion (in 1996 dollars). Federal transportation policy, in effect, channeled almost seven times more money into suburban sprawl than into helping maintain more compact urban centers.

"9.9 cents a gallon" is the price on an old gasoline pump, part of a Depression-era gas station preserved in the Museum of Albuquerque, "2.3 cents

---

5. After World War I, on General Pershing's orders, Major Eisenhower led a convoy of seventy-nine military vehicles over the partly paved Lincoln Highways from Washington, D.C., to San Francisco. The trip took fifty-six days.

federal and state taxes included." Sixty years later, in 1996, the average gallon of gas cost 128.8 cents, including a federal tax of 18.4 cents and state tax of 19.3 cents.

Faced with a short-term spike in nominal gas prices in 1996, Republican presidential candidate Bob Dole was quick to call for a repeal of the 4.3 cents per gallon that had been added as part of President Clinton's deficit reduction package three years earlier. Just weeks before, the national media had heralded the fact that, in inflation-adjusted terms, the cost of a gallon of gasoline had reached an all-time low.

Indeed, by a wide margin, Americans enjoy the cheapest gasoline in the world. Filling up the tank costs about one-third as much as it does in European countries, where gasoline sells at the equivalent of about $3–$4 a gallon. In Europe the untaxed cost of gasoline is about $1 a gallon, the same level as in the United States. The difference is almost entirely in the level of taxes paid. U.S. national policy is to promote cheap gasoline, maximize the use of private automobiles, and, in the process, subsidize the massive decentralization of urban activity across the suburban landscape. European countries keep gasoline relatively expensive, subsidize public transportation extensively, and generally encourage a more compact urban lifestyle.

Does cheap gasoline mean that Americans spend less on transportation than Europeans? Not at all. It is estimated that the average, auto-dependent American household spends almost 20 percent of its annual income on transportation compared with half that level for the average European family. In theory, we may value the high degree of mobility many American households have. In practice, most of those same households have no alternative to driving an average of 1,000 miles a month per vehicle in order to reach their job sites, basic shopping areas, and essential services.

Sewage Plant Expansion

In the Clean Water Act of 1972, the federal government moved, with salutary intent, to clean up the country's polluted lakes and streams. Since 1956 the federal government has provided $130 billion (in 1996 dollars) in grants to state and local governments for new sewage treatment plants and major sewer lines. Much of the money (perhaps one-third) has been spent not to remedy old problems but to provide new capacity to support new suburban growth. The federal grants have covered 75 percent of the costs of wastewater treatment plants, thus creating heavy subsidies for new development.

Redlining Black Americans

Who benefited from new suburban opportunities created? As Melvin Oliver and Thomas Shapiro have written, "Home ownership represents not only an integral part of the American Dream but also the largest component of most Americans' wealth portfolio. . . . The value of the average housing unit tripled from 1970 to 1980, far outstripping inflation. Thus households that owned homes before the late 1970s had an opportunity to accumulate wealth in the form of home equity, while those that did not missed an excellent opportunity."[6]

Though the gap had closed slowly over the decades, in 1988 homeownership among blacks (42 percent) seriously lagged homeownership among whites (64 percent). Part of the gap could be ascribed to lower incomes among blacks in comparison with whites; in the 1990 census black median family income was only 58 percent of white median family income. But it is clear that the past exclusion of blacks from new suburban housing still limited access (though it was much improved) to good mortgages, and the price exacted by segregated housing patterns has shrunk the black community's wealth. Blacks make up approximately 11 percent of the nation's population and earn about 7 percent of the nation's income, but own only 3 percent of the nation's accumulated wealth.

The home equity and wealth gap remains wide even though blacks with comparable education have almost closed the income gap with whites. Table 5-1 charts the median household incomes of white and black households headed by individuals with comparable educations. In 1988 black college graduates earned 80 percent of the income of white college graduates. Black householders with postgraduate degrees earned 77 percent of the income of white householders with postgraduate degrees. True income equality was attained only at the bottom of the social heap. Whites and blacks with no more than an elementary school education had virtually identical earnings.

By contrast, the gap in home equity is staggering (table 5-1). Even black college graduates and professionals have less than one-third the value of home equity that their white counterparts do. In fact, white high school dropouts typically have greater home equity than black professionals.

As mentioned earlier, segregated housing patterns add to this disparity in home equity–based wealth. Income and home values calculated for fifty-

6. Oliver and Shapiro (1995, p. 198).

Table 5-1. *Median Household Income and Home Equity of Blacks and Whites with Comparable Educational Attainment, 1988*

Thousands of dollars unless otherwise noted

Educational attainment	White median	Black median	Percentage of black-to-white
	Median household income		
Elementary	7,001	6,942	99
Some high school	11,554	8,724	76
High school degree	17,328	11,534	67
Some college	27,594	21,076	76
College degree	35,068	28,080	80
Postgraduate	40,569	31,340	77
	Median home equity		
Elementary	23,044	2,500	11
Some high school	22,310	430	2
High school degree	29,424	1,199	4
Some college	33,489	5,714	17
College degree	49,365	15,170	31
Postgraduate	56,373	17,796	31

Source: Adapted from Melvin L. Oliver and Thomas M. Shapiro, *Black Wealth/White Wealth: A New Perspective on Racial Inequality* (London: Routledge, 1995), table A5.2.

eight metro areas for 1990 are particularly revealing. In the Baltimore metro area, for instance, the average black homeowner had an income of $39,000 and a home worth $69,000. By contrast, the average white homeowner in metro Baltimore had an income of $55,000 and a home worth $133,000. In effect, for every dollar of income, the black homeowner received $1.68 in home value, whereas the white homeowner received $2.40. Within metro Baltimore's still segregated housing market (its segregation index was 71 in 1990), the average black homeowner got only 70 percent of the home value per dollar of income that the average white homeowner received. (See appendix table A-7.)

I have driven through many Baltimore-area neighborhoods, including many well-maintained, black middle-class neighborhoods. I know that the lesser value of black-owned homes rarely reflects the widely held white prejudice that "blacks don't keep up their neighborhoods." I also have no doubt that a black neurosurgeon joining the faculty of Johns Hopkins Medical

School could buy a home of any value he or she could afford anywhere in the Baltimore area.

What the racial home equity gap does reflect is that most black homeowners live in majority-black neighborhoods where whites will no longer buy homes. When the 74 percent of the Baltimore area's potential homebuyers that are white take themselves off the market for houses in black neighborhoods, the potential demand and competition for those homes are automatically reduced. With the demand for homes in predominantly black neighborhoods solely dependent on the buying power of the black community, increases in home value are automatically dampened.

Because metro Baltimore still has segregated housing markets, its black homeowners pay, in effect, a 30 percent "segregation tax." Black homeowners in fifty-eight metro areas typically paid a segregation tax of 17 percent in 1990. In only a handful of metro areas (including Albuquerque) did black homeowners receive about the same housing value for each dollar of income as did white homeowners. With a low segregation index (39), Metro Albuquerque is also one of the nation's most integrated communities.

In fact, relative segregation of housing markets has a statistically significant impact on the variation in segregation tax among different regions. Simple regression analysis shows that for every point increase in the segregation scale, the segregation tax increases by five-tenths of a percent. Thus it is not surprising to find that black homeowners pay little or no segregation tax in the least segregated housing markets (like Albuquerque) and the highest segregation tax in the most segregated housing markets (for example, 43 percent in metro Detroit).

Playing the "race card" has thus robbed black Americans of many of the benefits of the redefined, postwar American dream. "America can solve its housing problem or America can solve its race problem. America cannot solve both problems." While the civil rights movement struggled to unite Americans, the sprawl machine inexorably worked to divide them.

An Insider's Testimony

Perhaps the best way to sum up the full impact of the sprawl machine is to cite expert testimony from within the real estate development industry itself. Christopher B. Leinberger is the managing partner of Robert Charles Lesser & Company, the largest independent real estate advisory firm in the country. Leinberger's firm specializes in helping real estate investors identify the hottest places to invest in metropolitan areas across the nation. Leinberger is also a thoughtful analyst of his industry who has written perceptively about the very trends he has helped to promote.

Over the past thirty-five years, Leinberger writes, what has become the fundamental unit of metropolitan areas is the "metro core," the area in which the vast majority of export and region-serving jobs are located.[7] First-generation metro cores are, of course, the original downtown hubs and immediately adjacent areas. Shortly after World War II, most upper-middle and high-end households abandoned the gracious, traditional neighborhoods around these downtown cores for new suburban communities. Retailing followed into new regional shopping malls, and almost all new jobs were being created in office complexes and new industrial parks outside the original core areas.

The second generation of metro cores emerged during the 1960s, typically providing new office space and industrial locations two to six miles from downtown. Examples would be the Stemmons Freeway area in Dallas, mid-Wilshire in Los Angeles, and the area around the Northeast Expressway in Atlanta. Typically, the prosperity of these office-oriented, second-generation metro cores has been brief, and most are now failing. They have fallen victim to the decline of the neighborhoods around them, in the wake of the poverty expanding outward from inner-city ghettos and barrios, or, merely as a result of their own inadequacies: as sterile strips of boxy, 9-to-5 office buildings with few surrounding mixed uses and amenities, they have been unable to compete with newer, third-generation metro cores.

Edge Cities

The spectacular growth of third-generation metro cores, dubbed "edge cities," has attracted much attention.[8] All metro areas in the country, regardless of population size, have a third-generation metro center, Leinberger claims, and they all share a unifying characteristic: they are located adjacent to the vast concentration of upper-middle and high-end housing districts. "All such metro cores in the country have this characteristic," Leinberger explains, "because the bosses live in the high-end housing districts and want to minimize their commutes and the commutes of the firm's senior management."[9]

7. Leinberger (1996).
8. Garreau (1991).
9. All quotations from Leinberger are from Leinberger (1996, pp. 203–22).

"Upper-middle and high-end housing tends to heavily concentrate in most metropolitan areas," Leinberger continues. "By understanding the limited access highway system, [and then] by placing a point in the downtown and drawing a roughly 90 degree arc that encompasses the high-end housing concentration, [one can] define the 'favored quarter.' This is where upwards of 80 percent of all commercial real estate activity and job growth took place over the past generation."

Third-generation metro cores, such as Tyson's Corner on the I-95 beltway outside Washington, the Perimeter Center outside Atlanta, and the O'Hare Airport area in Chicago, experienced explosive growth in the 1970s and 1980s. Despite only two decades of existence, by the end of the 1980s many had more occupied office space than the old downtowns.

Following the real estate slump of the late 1980s and early 1990s, many third-generation metro cores have resumed their growth, but generally at rates only slightly higher than those of their metro areas as a whole. Some even grew less rapidly than their metro rates for the first time. Leinberger identifies three reasons for the slowdown: traffic saturation, growing neighborhood opposition to further growth, and the "character" of many such edge cities. All began with a suburban character: relatively low densities with upward of 70 percent of their land area dedicated to moving and parking cars. Third-generation metro cores that are becoming denser, more urban environments with a greater emphasis on pedestrian-scale activities are still growing vigorously. Those that have retained their excessively suburban character are sliding toward stagnation as fourth-generation metro centers are now evolving in many regions.

Fourth-generation office-oriented metro cores, such as Fair Lakes on I-66 west of Washington and Plano on the Dallas Tollway, lie four to twelve miles farther out from the third-generation metro cores, always moving away from the center city. They are characterized by very low-density, heavily landscaped office campuses.

The Future of Metro Cores

What does the future hold for the different generations of core areas? Leinberger sees only three possibilities for the original downtown cores: stability, moderate decline, or severe decline. Downtowns consistently capture their share of employment in only three sectors: professional services, finance, and government. Relative stability can probably be found in a few downtown areas: Washington, Seattle, Portland, San Francisco, midtown

Manhattan, and Boston, all of which have strong employment bases in those three sectors, combined with substantial high-end housing and retail sectors serving large influxes of tourists, as well as the residents of nearby, still affluent city neighborhoods.

In the not-too-distant future, the majority of downtowns will experience a moderate decline. Some may see their retail sector flourish to a degree, buoyed by successful convention centers, sports stadiums and arenas, and tourist attractions. Yet these activities will do little to regenerate the downtown employment base. Leinberger places Denver, Baltimore, and San Diego solidly in this category. Others, such as Atlanta, Philadelphia, and Los Angeles, "could slip into the severe decline category if remedial action is not taken, because all product categories (office, industrial, housing, and retail) are in relative decline."

Severely declining downtowns—those of Detroit and Saint Louis are prime examples—have retained virtually no upper-end housing or any retail base, nor do they have any prospect of developing either. The impact of convention business or sports facilities is very limited because visitors flee the downtown immediately after the event. Office occupancy is stagnant or even declining. "In essence, there is 'no there there,'" Leinberger concludes.

Most second-generation metro centers also suffer from having "no there there." Most were created solely for the office market and have little retail or nearby high-end housing. Among second-generation metro cores, an extraordinary public investment, such as the Washington area's Metro system (which Leinberger characterizes as "the longest subway system in the world and the safest in the country") can spur office, retail, and housing development at major subway stops, as has happened around Court House and Ballston in Arlington County, Virginia, and Chevy Chase and Bethesda in Montgomery County, Maryland.

Some third-generation metro cores are "densifying" by becoming mass transit hubs, developing high-density apartments and condominiums, upgrading and expanding retail stores, and generally creating a more urban feel. The key to the success of such urbanizing metro cores as Atlanta's Buckhead area and Perimeter Center, Denver's Cherry Creek, and Country Club Plaza in Kansas City is, in Leinberger's view, that they offer "one of the few, if not the only, safe urban environments in the metropolitan area."

As noted above, however, Leinberger expects suburban-character, third-generation metro cores to decline slowly. Part of the reason is racial.

Research has shown that the white population has an aversion to shopping or living in a community where there is more than a 20 or 25 percent minority population. Whenever a community or shopping center goes over the line, it becomes virtually 100 percent minority very rapidly. This kind of change generally affects a metro core in the demographics of the shopping centers and malls and then the rental apartment housing stock. Both can change very quickly. . . . In an overbuilt local rental apartment market, for example, owners can offer minority occupants low rents in a better neighborhood than they live in. Where this has occurred, the new minority residents have tended to have children who attend the local elementary schools initially. White flight from the school district occurs, generally in a rolling fashion as the minority children get older and enter junior and senior high school. The impact on the surrounding single-family housing, which almost exclusively will have a majority white population, and the office market is delayed. There has not been enough experience around third generation metro cores to document this impact or how fast it occurs. Conventional wisdom, however, suggests that there will be a decline in values, white flight from the neighborhoods, and a movement of office users to alternative metro cores when their leases, which generally average five years in length, expire.

Continuing the general theme, Leinberger believes "the underlying reason for the growth of fourth-generation metro cores is undoubtedly fear. In spite of the fact that violent crime has remained stable over the past 20 years . . . , the perception persists that crime has become significantly worse. Much of this perception is based on rapidly growing gang activity, which is wrongly assumed to be a predominant factor in every minority community regardless of its socioeconomic base. The majority white population moving to the residential districts serving fourth generation metro cores sees the move as a way to ensure safety."

Pondering the social and environmental implications of these trends for the future of our metropolitan areas, Leinberger foresees some grim changes:

—The poor and working poor in central cities and inner suburbs will become increasingly isolated from new employment growth in far-distant fourth- and fifth-generation metro cores.

—Inner suburbs will go into a rapid decline without new jobs or the cultural and civic institutions that still claim regional support successfully for downtown areas.

—Declining tax bases in the central city and inner suburbs will exacerbate existing social problems, and state governments will step in to take over more and more functions of the local governments and school systems.

—Urbanized land will increase at rates eight to twelve times faster than underlying population and employment growth.

—Air and water pollution and traffic congestion will all grow worse because of the nearly exclusive reliance on automobile transportation. ("If the economics of oil-based automobile transportation ever radically change," Leinberger cautions, "we will have painted ourselves into a corner with few good options.")

Though "this is both the best of times and the worst of times for our metropolitan areas," Leinberger concludes, "as a nation, we continue to ignore the negative consequences of how we are building [our metropolitan areas] where 75 percent of all Americans live." Like some atomic scientists in World War II's Manhattan Project, Chris Leinberger is clearly troubled by the kind of world he is helping to create.

6

The Poverty Machine

AMERICA KNOWS HOW to fight a successful war on poverty. In the early 1960s, when Michael Harrington was writing his classic study, *The Other America: Poverty in the United States,* which seized the attention of Jack and Bobby Kennedy, almost 39 million persons, 22 percent of all Americans, would have been classified as poor.[1]

Fighting the Elderly's War on Poverty

Of that total, 5.5 million persons were aged sixty-five and older. More than 35 percent of all elderly persons lived in poverty. Just one generation later, in 1995, the poverty rate among the elderly was down to 10.5 percent. In fact, the poverty rate among America's senior citizens was less than the poverty rate for everyone else (14.1 percent).[2] On the threshold of the New Frontier and the Great Society, more than one out of three elderly persons lived in poverty. Three decades later, barely one out of ten senior citizens was poor. By any definition, that was surely one victory in the war on poverty.

---

1. Harrington (1962).
2. Bureau of the Census (1970, table 502). The federal government did not officially define a poverty level until 1964, so all calculations for earlier periods are retrospective.

Expanding Social Security

The war on poverty among the elderly was fought primarily by federal government programs and policies. The first milestone was the enactment of the New Deal's Social Security Act of 1935. Nevertheless, by 1960, after social security's first twenty-five years, the average retired couple's monthly check still was barely $113, or about 28 percent of median household income that year.[3]

Beginning in the 1960s, successive Congresses and administrations boosted social security benefits dramatically. One key step occurred in 1965, when Representative Wilbur Mills, all-powerful chairman of the House Ways and Means Committee, shepherded through a 25 percent increase in retirement benefits unmatched by any increase in payroll taxes. Another occurred in 1972, when benefit levels were automatically indexed to the increase in the consumer price index (to be effective in 1975). Indexing social security benefits yielded a steady increase in the real buying power of retirement checks if, as Congress determined in 1997, the consumer price index, as constructed by federal bureaucrats, systematically overstated the real increase in the cost of living.

By 1995 the average married couple's monthly retirement benefit from social security was $1,221, or some 43 percent of median household income that year.[4] Since 1960 the typical social security check had risen 110 percent (adjusted for inflation). During the thirty-four years since 1960 the federal government had more than doubled the real value of direct cash support of elderly citizens.

Protecting Pensions

Another significant federal policy was the Employee Retirement Income Security Act (ERISA) of 1974. ERISA extended federal regulatory oversight to private pension plans, which, by 1992, covered 41 percent of all private sector workers. ERISA helped assure workers that company and union pension plans would not be abused or mismanaged but could be counted on as building blocks for their retirement years. By 1993 private pension plans were paying out $156.3 billion in annual benefits to retirees, which represented a 9,200 percent increase in total payments since 1960, when just

---

3. Bureau of the Census (1997, table 739).
4. Bureau of the Census (1997, tables 588, 717).

$1.7 billion was paid out to private pensioners.[5] Adjusting for a fourfold increase in inflation, the average retiree's private pension in 1993 was worth more than five times its monthly value in 1960.

With government employment approaching 18 percent of the total labor force, public employee retirement plans also played a significant role in the lives of elderly Americans. The average federal annuitant's monthly benefit grew from $107 in 1960 to $1,698 in 1996, or about 200 percent in real value. Total payments to retired state and local government retirees increased from $12 billion in 1980 to $53.4 billion in 1994, which amounted to another 150 percent increase in *total* real value in just fourteen years.[6]

Despite periodic recessions, recent decades have been characterized by steady economic growth, allowing many households to build their own retirement nest eggs. Once again, federal tax policy played an important role. Internal revenue code amendments promoted tax-deferred savings plans such as Keogh plans and individual retirement accounts ($152.4 billion in assets in 1995), and 401(k) employee savings plans ($44 billion paid out in benefits in 1993).[7]

Increasing Home Equity

The rising value of the family home also helped build retirement incomes. Until the 1997 tax reform (see chapter 13), any gain from selling one's home was subject to federal capital gains taxes. However, tax law did permit a one-time exclusion of $125,000 in capital gains for home sellers after age fifty-five. This allowed many older homeowners to convert some home equity into retirement income.

Creating Medicare

Public subsidies for the elderly were not restricted to money income. Medicare's passage in 1965 put another major building block in place. By 1994 medicare reimbursements were worth more than $4,800 a year for each elderly enrollee.[8] The program's comprehensive health coverage vastly improved the health care of seniors and alleviated the threat of major medical bills depleting their savings. Also, by relieving employers of providing high-

5. Bureau of the Census (1997, tables 592, 593).
6. Bureau of the Census (1997, tables 590, 591).
7. Bureau of the Census (1997, table 594).
8. Bureau of the Census (1997, table 161).

cost health insurance for older employees, medicare allowed many older workers to continue working in full- or part-time jobs, effectively extending their earning power.

Other Federal Subsidies for the Elderly

There have been many more in-kind subsidies for the elderly. By 1993 HUD had financed the construction of 507,500 units of public housing for the elderly. Some 1.7 million seniors either lived in federal public housing projects or received rental assistance through federal rent vouchers. Hundreds of thousands of additional housing units for elderly tenants have been built by nonprofit organizations, aided by federal subsidies. In 1992, 1.2 million lower-income senior citizens were assisted by the federal food stamp program.[9] Under the Older Americans Act, the federal government makes grants to states for a wide range of social services, counseling, and recreation programs for senior citizens; the act's appropriations topped $865 million in fiscal year 1998.

Through almost four decades of successive presidents, senators, and congressmen, U.S. society has sanctioned spending the money necessary to ensure that, if retirement would not exactly bring guaranteed golden years for all Americans, raw want would be minimized and a comfortable retirement provided for most. By 1996 at least 38 cents of every federal dollar was spent on direct cash assistance, medical services, and programs for the elderly.

With the huge baby boom generation beginning to reach retirement around the year 2010, this massive commitment of society's resources cannot be sustained without significant reforms. Will Congress and the president muster the political courage to take the necessary actions? (The earlier changes are enacted, the more modest they need be.) The 1997 balanced budget agreement was not reassuring. At the last moment, President Clinton and the Republican congressional leadership backed down on Senate-enacted measures to postpone modestly the age of retirement eligibility and boost monthly medicare premiums for wealthier retirees. I am confident, however, that, crablike, Washington politicians will soon edge their way into adopting modest but essential changes rather than face the draconian cuts that continued procrastination would ultimately require. America's future retirees will not be thrust back into pre-1960s conditions. The war on poverty among the elderly, I believe, has been won permanently.

9. Bureau of the Census (1996, tables 1203, 579).

Reducing Poverty among Urban Whites

I would also argue that our nation has fought a successful war on poverty among urban white Americans. As noted in chapter 3, in urban America the 1990 census counted 10.8 million poor whites, about as many as poor blacks (6.9 million) and poor Hispanics (4.8 million) combined. But the white population of the country's 320 metropolitan areas was 140 million in all. Only about one out of every thirteen white residents of our metro areas (7.7 percent) was poor in 1990. By contrast, the poverty rate among Hispanics was 24.5 percent and among blacks 27.5 percent, or three to four times as great as poverty among whites.

Furthermore, as both my analyses and field observations and Paul Jargowsky's extensive census studies showed (cited in chapter 4), there were relatively few poor white neighborhoods. At the higher poverty level (more than 40 percent poverty rate), Jargowsky found that only 14 percent of all high-poverty neighborhoods were "white slums" (where whites constituted at least two-thirds of the residents).

I have not calculated a comparable percentage for poverty neighborhoods (more than 20 percent poverty rate) in all fifty-eight metro areas I have visited. Undoubtedly, the proportion of poverty neighborhoods in which whites constituted at least two-thirds of all residents would be somewhat higher than 14 percent.

An extreme example would be metro Pittsburgh, where poor whites outnumbered poor blacks by three to one. With the collapse of the steel industry in the 1970s and 1980s, poverty soared in both Pittsburgh itself and in the "Mon Valley" steel towns. The number of poverty tracts jumped from 82 to 144 during the two troubled decades. Categorizing poverty neighborhoods by predominant racial group (at least two-thirds of residents were of one group or another), by 1990 there were 85 white poverty tracts (twice the number in 1970), 35 black poverty tracts, and 24 mixed-race poverty tracts.

At the other extreme would be metro Memphis, where the racial proportions of poverty were reversed: poor blacks outnumbered poor whites by three and a half to one. In 1990 there were 7 white poverty tracts (the same number as 1970), 63 black poverty tracts, and 17 mixed-race poverty tracts. Thus, between my two extreme examples, white poverty neighborhoods as a percentage of all such neighborhoods ranged from 59 percent (metro Pittsburgh) to 8 percent (metro Memphis).

In regions like Pittsburgh, the growth in poor white neighborhoods reflected both the impact of major factory layoffs on traditional white, blue-collar neighborhoods and the constant tendency toward greater income segregation promoted by ever-outward suburbanization. Compared with the expansion of poor black and poor Hispanic neighborhoods, however, the growth of poor white neighborhoods in central cities and older suburbs was still relatively small.

The result is that, although poverty affects millions of white households at any given moment, it is rarely a *community* crisis for white residents of any metropolitan area. Among the seventy-five largest metropolitan areas in the 1990 census (excluding Honolulu, Hawaii), the region with the highest poverty rate among white families (9.9 percent) was Knoxville, Tennessee. The one with the lowest black family poverty rate was the Washington area, with 10.1 percent.[10] For all areas, the highest poverty rate for white families was still lower than the lowest poverty rate for black families.

Moreover, nowhere was the poverty rate for white residents even half the rate for black residents. In only two large metro areas (El Paso and Tucson) was the white (that is, Anglo) poverty rate even 40 percent of the black rate. In both those communities, Hispanics occupied the bottom rung of the economic ladder.

As discussed in chapter 4, poor whites are also rarely concentrated in poor neighborhoods. In the fifty-eight metro areas in which I have consulted, in 1990 barely one out of four poor whites lived in poverty neighborhoods, and only one out of twenty poor whites lived in high-poverty neighborhoods. For the most part, poor whites living in poor neighborhoods found either blacks or Hispanics in the majority. By contrast, one out of two poor Hispanics and three out of four poor blacks lived in poverty neighborhoods (30 percent of the latter in high-poverty neighborhoods).

To repeat, three out of four poor whites live in working-class or middle-class neighborhoods, whereas one out of two poor Hispanics and three out of four poor blacks live in poverty neighborhoods.

I repeat these facts because this disproportion is what fuels the dynamics of poverty in urban America. To be poor and white is, in general, still to be part (albeit often a marginal part) of the mainstream of white, middle-

---

10. The poverty rates of metro Knoxville and metro Washington are not that easy to compare. Because Washington's cost of living is 37 percent higher than the national metro average, its poverty rate is significantly understated; the poverty rate in metro Knoxville, where the cost of living is 13 percent below the national average, is somewhat overstated. In addition, located on the fringe of Appalachia, the Knoxville region has many genuinely poor people, but its statistics are somewhat ballooned by the disproportionate presence of university students at Vanderbilt and the University of Tennessee (though this latter factor would not affect the *family* poverty rate significantly).

class society with its values, expectations, and above all, access to educational and employment opportunities. To be poor and Hispanic or poor and black is, in general, to be isolated from mainstream society.

The success of the war on poverty among poor urban whites can be traced, not to some government agency's master plan, but to a core of assumptions flowing from the fact that American society is still heavily organized along lines of race and ethnicity:

—One assumption is that the majority of poor white households will live in local communities with sufficient fiscal health to provide adequate public services. Indeed, the majority of poor whites live in suburbs or in "elastic" southern and western central cities. Despite the strains felt by many older, inner suburbs, most suburban jurisdictions are in better fiscal shape than poverty-stricken central cities.

—Two, even in the face of the wrenching economic transformations that lie at the heart of much poverty in America, the majority of poor whites will live in sectors of their metro areas where most new job creation is occurring. Nationwide, 55 percent of poor whites live in suburbs outside central cities, where in the last two decades 80 percent of all new jobs have been created. By contrast, 67 percent of poor Hispanics and 77 percent of poor blacks live in central cities where low-skilled employment, in particular, has been vanishing.

—Three, the majority of poor white children will have access to better educational opportunities. Local public schools typically mirror local housing patterns. Because most poor white children do not live in poor neighborhoods, most poor white children do not attend neighborhood schools heavily attended by other poor children. Attending predominantly middle-class schools has a positive effect on educational outcomes.

The Importance of Family Structure

The issue of opportunity for children is certainly an important one. By 1995, 14 million children constituted almost 40 percent of all poor persons in the United States: 35 percent of the white poor, 46 percent of the Hispanic poor, and 47 percent of the black poor.[11] Appendix tables A-8 and A-9 show how family structure affects the incidence of poverty among children. At the same time, they highlight the most hopeful set of statistics

11. Bureau of the Census (1997, tables 736, 737).

I have yet encountered regarding urban America: of all white married couples with children, 96 percent are *not* poor; of all black married couples with children, 89 percent are *not* poor, and of all Hispanic married couples with children, 87 percent are *not* poor.

Among the fifty-eight metro areas in which I have analyzed this phenomenon, the variation in *non*poverty rates of white married couples is small, from a low of 93 percent to a high of 99 percent (appendix table A-8). The variation in nonpoverty rates for Hispanic and black married couples is somewhat greater. However, across all racial and ethnic lines the basic observation holds: the odds are nine out of ten that children in two-parent, often two-wage-earner, families will *not* be poor.

The dismal side of the argument, illustrating the "feminization" of poverty, is also summarized in appendix table A-9: of all white single mothers with children, 33 percent are poor; of all black single mothers with children, 56 percent are poor; of all Hispanic single mothers with children, 56 percent are poor. The two-parent, two-wage-earner family is the most effective anti-poverty program for children. That is not a statement of social values. That is a demographic and economic fact. It is true that many single mothers, often through great effort, are able to keep themselves and their children above the raw poverty level. Two-thirds of all white single mothers and almost half of all Hispanic and black single mothers are not poor. Nevertheless, the surest path to poverty is to be the child of a single mother.

The dramatic differences between poverty rates for married couples and for single mothers highlights a growing social concern for white and Hispanic society, one that has already become a clear and present disaster for black society. Appendix table A-10 shows the number of married-couple families for every 100 single-mother families in 1990. In the fifty-eight metro areas there were 501 white married couples with children for every 100 white single mothers with children, a ratio of 5 to 1. The ratio dropped within the Hispanic community: 310 married couples with children per 100 single female family heads, or 3 to 1. But within the black community there were only 80 married couples with children for every 100 single mothers, a ratio of less than 1 to 1.[12]

In the fifty-eight metro areas that I analyzed, the white ratio ranged from more than 6 to 1 in prosperous, highly educated labor markets such as

12. By 1995 these ratios had shrunk even further. In just five years, the national ratio of white married couples with children to white single mothers with children had dropped to 455 to 100; for Hispanics, to 285 to 100; and for blacks, to 77 to 100.

Atlanta, Minneapolis-Saint Paul, Washington, and south central Pennsylvania to around 4 to 1 in less prosperous, more blue-collar labor markets such as Battle Creek, Kalamazoo, Akron, Dayton-Springfield, and Youngstown-Warren. (The Ohio industrial communities all had substantial numbers of long-term immigrants from Appalachia, initially recruited for lower-skilled factory jobs that had substantially disappeared by 1990.)

Among blacks, the same economic factors are at work. High-education, high-tech job markets with substantial black middle classes (Atlanta, Fort Worth, Washington) still have slightly more married couples raising children than single mothers. Hard-hit factory towns such as Buffalo, Erie, and Muskegon have very low ratios of black married-couple families to single-mother families. However, the patterns are uneven (note Minneapolis–Saint Paul's low ratio). The variations in black family structure, however, range from social disaster to social catastrophe.

Even more dramatic is the imbalance between married-couple families and single-mother families in the poorest neighborhoods. Appendix table A-11 presents the ratio of married-couple families to single mothers in the poorest tracts (those with poverty rates higher than 40 percent) and in the rest of the metro areas excluding these poorest tracts. As a group, the poorest neighborhoods averaged only 43 married couples raising children for every 100 single mothers with their children. Throughout all the other neighborhoods of these metro areas, subtracting the high-poverty areas, the average was 347 married-couple families for every 100 single-mother households.

There was an 8-to-1 swing between the typical family structure of the poorest neighborhoods and that of all other neighborhoods. As a result, a child growing up in one of these poorest neighborhoods has little exposure to what constitutes the successful formula in adulthood for child-rearing: married-couple families. Regionwide, 90 percent of two-parent families will not be poor; even in these poorest neighborhoods, typically three-quarters of two-parent families are not poor. But in high-poverty neighborhoods a society of single mothers and their children will be the norm, and in these poorest neighborhoods three-quarters of all single mothers are poor.

The connection between these ratios regarding family structure and a population group's poverty rates can be illustrated through a mathematical exercise. Suppose that, across the fifty-eight sample metro areas, the black population had the same family structure ratio as the white population while maintaining the same relative poverty rates associated with their own group's family structure. In other words, in this hypothetical exercise 11 percent of black married-couple families would still be poor (the converse of 89 per-

Table 6-1. *Impact of Family Structure on Poverty Rates*

Community and family structure	Married couples		Single-mother families		Combined poverty rate, all families with children
	Number	Poverty rate	Number	Poverty rate	
Black community					
Black family structure	80	11	100	56	36
Hispanic family structure	310	11	100	56	22
White family structure	501	11	100	56	18
Hispanic community					
Hispanic family structure	310	12	100	56	23
Black family structure	80	12	100	56	36
White family structure	501	12	100	56	19
White community					
White family structure	501	4	100	33	9
Hispanic family structure	310	4	100	33	11
Black family structure	80	4	100	33	20

cent of black married-couple families *not* being poor), and 56 percent of all black single-mother families would still be poor. I will only vary the ratio of family structures. Instead of 80 married-couple families for every 100 single-mother families (the actual black community ratio), in this exercise I calculate poverty rates for the black community on the basis of 501 married-couple families for every 100 single-mother families (the actual white community ratio).

Table 6-1 summarizes the results. With the current black family structure, the poverty rate for black families with children is 36 percent. With the shift to a white family structure (that is, 501 rather than 80 married-couple families for every 100 single-mother families), the black family poverty rate would be halved to 18 percent. (With a Hispanic family structure, the black family poverty rate would decline to 22 percent.)

Similarly, the Hispanic family poverty rate (23 percent) drops slightly to 19 percent with a white family structure but shoots up to 36 percent under a black family structure. In like fashion, the poverty rate for white families with children is 9 percent. Applying the Hispanic family structure ratio,

Table 6-2. *Ratio of Married-Couple Families to Single-Mother Families Nationwide, 1960–95*

Census year	Ratio married/100 single-mother			Ratio white married/black married
	White	Black	Hispanic	
1960	1,539	413	n.a.	3.7
1970	1,125	197	390	5.7
1980	592	95	375	6.2
1985	500	78	252	6.4
1990	494	75	248	6.6
1995	422	63	225	6.7

n.a. Not available.

the white family poverty rate increases slightly to 11 percent, but it would more than double, rising to 20 percent, if the black population's family structure ratio were applied to the white population.

If such hypothetical calculations are set aside, empirical evidence shows a significant and persistent difference in family structure between blacks and whites. The earliest census information on family structure by racial group dates from 1960. Table 6-2 summarizes the changes over the intervening thirty-five years.

In 1965 U.S. Senator Daniel Patrick Moynihan, then a young assistant secretary of labor, wrote a confidential report to President Lyndon Johnson entitled "The Negro Family: The Case for National Action." In it Moynihan stated:

> At the heart of the deterioration of the fabric of Negro society is the deterioration of the Negro family. It is the fundamental source of the weakness of the Negro community. . . . In essence, the Negro community has been forced into a matriarchal structure which, because it is so out of line with the rest of American society, seriously retards the progress of the group as a whole.[13]

Moynihan's document was leaked to the press (probably by liberal critics of his thesis) and caused an immense controversy at the time. Yet black family structure was much less tilted toward single-mother families when Moynihan

13. Moynihan (1965).

was writing than it would be three decades later. In the 1960 census, for every 100 black single mothers there were still 413 black married couples with children rather than just 63 black married couples for every 100 black single mothers, as in 1995. In 1960 white married couples with children also dominated the white family structure much more than a generation later. In 1960 there were 1,539 white married couples with children for every 100 white single mothers, compared with a ratio of only 422:100 by 1995.[14]

Throughout earlier decades, the ratio of white married couples to single mothers was about 3.5 times that among blacks, a very substantial, but relatively stable, differential. For purposes of argument, I will assume that this roughly 3.5 to 1 differential sums up the consequences of the historical experience of African Americans in U.S. society: 250 years of slavery, 100 years of Jim Crow segregation in the South and de facto segregation in the North, the transition from rural poverty to the lowest rungs of the urban economic ladder, substantial education gaps between whites and blacks, and active discrimination in housing and job markets. I will not try to separate out the impact of all these factors on family structure. I will just assume that this is the starting point.[15]

From the 1960 census onward, however, the historic differential between white and black family structures deteriorated sharply, from 3.7 in 1960 to 6.7 in 1995. How could this be? During these very same decades America dismantled Jim Crow laws, eased racial discrimination in the job market, and, to a lesser degree, reduced de facto segregation in housing markets and public education.

Most notably, long-standing educational gaps were narrowed significantly. Table 6-3 shows the long-term achievements of African Americans in striving for educational parity with white Americans. In fact, in September 1996 the Census Bureau announced that a historic milestone had been passed. For the first time, among persons aged twenty-five to thirty-five, blacks and whites had attained the same high school completion rate. While

14. Hacker (1992, p. 231).
15. Note, too, that the ratio of married-couple families to single-mother families has been changing outside the United States as well, most notably in northern and western Europe. Certain demographic and economic factors are contributing to this trend across many societies. Among them are the increasing age at marriage, higher divorce rates, increasing social acceptance of having children outside marriage, women's greater participation in the paid labor force and hence greater economic independence, and, in many societies, a substantial decline in the wages of millions of male blue-collar workers. In the United States these factors are operating across all racial and ethnic lines.

Table 6-3. *Educational Attainment, Persons Aged 25–35 Nationwide, 1940–90*

Census year	Completed high school		Ratio black/ white	Completed four years college		Ratio black/ white
	Black	White		Black	White	
1940	12.3	41.2	3.35	1.6	6.4	4.00
1950	23.6	56.3	2.39	2.8	8.2	2.93
1960	38.6	63.7	1.65	4.8	11.8	2.45
1970	58.4	77.8	1.33	7.3	17.3	2.36
1980	82.2	89.8	1.10	11.5	25.3	2.20
1989	82.2	89.3	1.09	12.7	24.4	1.92

Source: Andrew Hacker, *Two Nations: Black and White, Separate, Hostile, Unequal* (Scribner's, 1992), p. 234.

the percentage of black college graduates in that age group still lags behind the percentage of white college graduates, the gap continues to close.

Disparities still exist in the quality of education provided by many central-city school systems (from which the majority of blacks graduate) compared with many largely suburban school systems (from which most white students graduate). The disparities are probably less significant among the college-educated. It is reasonable to conclude that parity in educational attainment (as measured by years of education completed) does not yet translate into parity in the skills with which each group has been equipped by their years in school. Black Americans' substantial achievements in closing the educational attainment gap are not yet matched by equivalent gains in the job market. By 1995 the median wage for black males was only 73 percent of the median wage for white males (though the gap had narrowed from 43 percent in 1940, but less markedly from the 1970s level of 64 percent).[16]

Too Few Jobs versus Too Much Welfare

Taking the long view, several measures suggest that by the 1990s many black Americans were less isolated from mainstream society and less overtly constrained in their opportunities for advancement than in decades past. What accounted for the startling deterioration in family structure associated with higher poverty rates? Two basic schools of thought have emerged on that

16. Robert J. Samuelson, "The Jobs Are There," *Washington Post*, September 11, 1996.

question, which in the 1970s and 1980s stirred up a good amount of academic debate. By the 1990s the battle lines had been drawn in Congress and statehouses across the country, one camp crying "Too few jobs," the other "Too much welfare." In fact, both groups are complaining about the same phenomenon: the rise in urban poverty as a direct result of low-skilled city residents, particularly African Americans, working less regularly than they did. The question is why? One side argues that joblessness is involuntary, imposed on the poor by sweeping economic changes; the other that it is voluntary, the product of a rational economic choice by many poor persons themselves.

For the proponents of "too few jobs," high inner-city joblessness is the result of the sharp decline in city-based blue-collar jobs. Many of these jobs vanished under the impact of technological change or global competition. In many cities they were partially replaced by new white-collar jobs. These required higher education and skill levels than disadvantaged city residents had. The skills mismatch arose. Other blue-collar jobs were relocated from central cities to their own suburbs. Low-skilled African Americans faced greater barriers than low-skilled whites in either moving or commuting to the city's suburbs. The spatial mismatch was born.

The proponents of "too much welfare" say that extensive federal welfare programs have made not working more attractive than working. Conservative scholar Charles Murray popularized this point in his influential book, *Losing Ground.* Marshaling an extensive array of statistics, Murray argued that the ready availability of welfare payments, medicaid, food stamps, and subsidized housing allowed poor families to improve their economic position by not working and instead relying on the public dole. Short-term economic improvement, however, was simply the precursor of long-term social disaster, as two-parent families dissolved, births out of wedlock increased, and succeeding generations of inner-city residents became locked in a cycle of poverty. "We tried to provide for the poor and produced more poor instead. We tried to remove the barriers to escape from poverty and inadvertently built a trap," Murray wrote.[17]

Counterattacking Murray with his own array of statistics was William Julius Wilson, the former president of the American Sociological Association, who now heads Harvard University's black studies program:

Murray's thesis in *Losing Ground* does not begin to come to grips with the complex problem of the rising number of female-headed families and out-

17. Murray (1984, p. 9).

of-wedlock births because he overemphasizes the role of liberal welfare policies and plays down what is perhaps the most important factor in the rise of black female-headed families—the extraordinary rise in black male joblessness. . . . The decline in the incidence of intact marriages among blacks is associated with the declining economic status of black men. . . . Black women nationally, especially young black women, are facing a shrinking pool of "marriageable" (i.e., employed) black men. . . . The sharp rise of black female-headed families is directly related to increasing black male joblessness.[18]

University of North Carolina economist John Kasarda and Kwok-fai Ting, a statistician at the Chinese University of Hong Kong, have attempted to adjudicate the scholarly battle by statistically assessing the relative contribution of both factors—economic structural change and welfare dependency—to joblessness.[19] They examined trends in joblessness, poverty, and welfare for the non-Hispanic white and non-Hispanic black residents of sixty-seven large cities between 1980 and 1990. To test the skills versus spatial mismatch hypothesis, Kasarda and Ting measured the relative importance of low-skilled industries located within each city itself in 1980, the size of the city's low-skilled work force, and the degree of economic restructuring that occurred during the next decade (such as the loss of low-skilled jobs and their partial replacement by high-skilled jobs in the city itself). Residential segregation within the city, measured by a dissimilarity index, was also incorporated into the model. The impact of welfare participation was measured by its "feedback" effect on joblessness.

Low-skilled industry jobs averaged almost 42 percent of all city-based jobs in 1980; over the next decade the cities lost 15 percent of their low-skilled industry jobs. By 1990 a large skills mismatch had developed for black city residents compared with white city residents. Almost 58 percent of all jobs located in the cities were filled by workers with more than a high school education. Some 56 percent of adult white city residents had more than twelve years of education (a negligible skills shortfall) compared with only 37 percent of adult black city residents (a 21-point gap between skills available and skills required).

The researchers attempted to measure spatial mismatch by the average travel time of city residents to city-based jobs (an "imperfect measure of

18. Wilson (1987, pp. 104–05). Wilson has elaborated on his themes more recently in Wilson (1996).

19. Kasarda and Ting (1996). In addition to the information quoted, my discussion of the two schools of thought was substantially modeled on this article.

spatial mismatch," they commented). One-way commuting times of white residents to city-based jobs averaged about twenty minutes. For black city residents average commuting times were a slightly longer twenty-three minutes. This was, in part, a reflection of the loss of jobs within segregated black neighborhoods as well as the greater isolation from newer job locations within the cities.[20]

In 1990, joblessness, poverty, and rates of welfare participation were substantially higher for blacks than whites in the sixty-seven cities. About 33 percent of white women and 15 percent of white men were jobless compared with almost 40 percent and 27 percent of black women and black men, respectively. Only 14 percent of white women and 10 percent of white men fell below the poverty line compared with 37 percent of black women and 24 percent of black men. Welfare participation of black women was more than three times the welfare participation of white women. Given restrictive eligibility rules, welfare participation rates were substantially lower for both white men and black men than for women.

The question, of course, is the extent to which all of these factors contributed to joblessness. From their detailed multiple regression analyses, Kasarda and Ting concluded that "economic restructuring and the welfare disincentive paradigms are not necessarily conflicting explanations of urban joblessness and poverty. They may, in fact, operate side by side to reinforce joblessness and poverty." Furthermore,

> Resident education levels, urban industrial structure, and racial segregation all play roles in influencing skill and spatial mismatches for both African Americans and . . . whites. Urban industrial structure and racial segregation, however, have a greater impact on skill and spatial mismatches for African-Americans than for whites. In turn, these mismatches, as well as welfare program participation, contribute to urban joblessness.
>
> Skill and spatial mismatches, in general, have greater effects on joblessness among white residents than among African Americans, despite a quite strong association between spatial mismatch and joblessness for African-American women. Conversely, welfare program participation contributes more to joblessness among African-American city residents than among white residents, with the complete welfare-joblessness-poverty cycle strongest among female African Americans.[21]

20. The average dissimilarity index of black residential segregation was 66 for the fifty-eight cities.

21. Kasarda and Ting (1996, p. 409).

Kasarda and Ting also found that joblessness had its greatest impact on poverty rates among African American women and the least impact among white women. Family structure, they added, was largely to blame for this difference, "since it has been well documented that a lower percentage of African American women have working spouses." Combined with welfare programs, these fewer job opportunities and lower wages in all likelihood discourage poor African Americans from seeking employment alternatives. The solution to all these problems, Kasarda and Ting concluded, lies not only in policies designed to reduce inner-city unemployment and poverty but also in a concerted effort to mitigate spatial and skill mismatches and to reform welfare. Above all, structural barriers to job access, such as housing segregation, and the traps welfare can create for the poor need to be eliminated.

The weight Kasarda and Ting give spatial mismatch as a cause of joblessness would no doubt increase considerably if the dynamics of whole metropolitan areas were taken into account. The impact of changes in the city-based job supply on city residents alone is far from the central phenomenon. Two-thirds of all whites (including 55 percent of poor whites) now live in suburbs outside central cities where, in recent decades, more than 80 percent of new job creation has occurred (including most low-skilled job creation). Almost 70 percent of all blacks (including 77 percent of poor blacks) live in central cities, from which, as Kasarda and Ting noted in their sample of sixty-seven major cities, about 15 percent of low-skilled industry jobs vanished in just one decade.

Paul Jargowsky's metropolitan work sheds somewhat more light on the subject. Using a sophisticated statistical model to measure the factors that contribute to the growth and number of high-poverty neighborhoods, Jargowsky was first startled by the "alarming" growth rate of *all* high-poverty neighborhoods since 1970, whatever their racial composition: over this period, the number of persons living in ghettos, barrios, and slums has grown by 92 percent and their poor population by 98 percent. For the 8 million people now living in these neighborhoods, "reduced economic opportunities and social isolation add insult to the injury of being poor. Within some of these communities, the deprivation does irreparable harm." In Jargowsky's view,

> the primary factors behind the increasing concentration of poverty are metropolitan economic growth and the general processes that create and sustain segregation by race and class. Metropolitan-level variables for economic opportunity and segregation [both economic and racial] can ex-

plain about four-fifths of the variation among metropolitan areas [of the number of high-poverty neighborhoods] and about the same proportion of the changes in neighborhood poverty over time. Although such factors as spatial location, neighborhood culture, and social policy may play a role, they are secondary to income generation and neighborhood sorting, which together explain most of the observed variations in ghetto poverty.[22]

The fundamental need on the policy side, Jargowsky adds, is to increase productivity and reduce inequality. "Policies that affect the spatial organization of metropolitan areas and reduce racial and economic segregation will also affect the formation of ghettos and barrios. In contrast, policies that aim to alter the culture, values, and behavior of ghetto residents are unlikely to make much difference without larger changes in the metropolitan economy and in rates of segregation."[23]

For Jargowsky, two principal factors—the level and changes in average metropolitan household incomes and the neighborhood sorting process—explain four-fifths of the variations observed in what he terms "neighborhood poverty," or the percentages of residents of all income levels in each metro area of different racial and ethnic groups that live in high-poverty neighborhoods. Assuming that the same factors apply comparably to the "concentration of poverty" (the percentages of poor whites, blacks, and Hispanics who live in high-poverty neighborhoods), I would suggest that a third factor explains most of the remaining one-fifth variation in the concentration of poverty among different metro areas: federal public housing policy.

The Impact of Public Housing Projects

There is no sadder example of the unintended consequences of a well-motivated social policy than the federal public housing program, especially in its efforts to address highly concentrated poverty. Take the case of Cleveland, which in 1990 had sixty-three high-poverty census tracts. Tracking the location of housing projects operated by the misleadingly named Cuyahoga Metropolitan Housing Authority (whose effective jurisdiction is limited to the city of Cleveland), I found a high-density housing project in or right next to every high-poverty census tract. The situation was no different in

22. Jargowsky (1997, pp. 185–86).
23. Jargowsky (1997, p. 186).

the city of Baltimore's thirty-four high-poverty census tracts. After touring more than sixty metropolitan areas, I have concluded that nothing in private housing markets compares with the intense concentration of poor minorities in federal public housing units. By the 1990s federal public housing had become the biggest poverty trap in American society.

It was not always that way. When the New Deal Congress approved the Wagner-Steagall Act, public housing was intended to be transitional housing for low-income working families. The federal government financed only the construction of low-rise, small-scale, generally attractive projects. The projects were maintained and managed by local housing authorities whose operating budgets had to be self-sustaining from the rents collected. As a result, local authorities worked hard to maintain a diversity of tenants, at least where income was concerned. Racial diversity would have been impossible since most projects were rigidly segregated in the North as well as in the South.

In many communities I have visited, some middle-aged black leaders (businessmen, agency administrators, city council members, and mayors among them) have said that "I was raised in Lafayette Terrace (Baltimore)," or "As a child I lived ten years in Techwood Homes (Atlanta)." "Is that project today the same place you grew up in?" I'll ask. "Oh, no," is the instant answer. "In my day the housing project was a real community: lots of families with the fathers going off to work every day. Today the projects are very different. Nothing but women on welfare and their children."

The shift started in Washington, D.C., in Julia Vitullo-Martin's view (many others would agree). She blames the regulations that the Department of Housing and Urban Development (HUD) imposes on public housing and the complexities added to them by Congress: "A program can start out fairly simple and straightforward and quickly become a mess."[24]

The unraveling of public housing began in the 1950s. To accommodate hundreds of thousands of low-income black migrants pouring into the nation's cities from the rural South (and to house tens of thousands of others displaced by federal urban renewal programs and urban freeway construction), many of the nation's larger public housing authorities began to build huge high-rise projects. Such projects were thought to be cheaper (they were not), modern, and beautiful, "stunning though that idea may seem today," Vitullo-Martin wrote.

---

24. Vitullo-Martin (1996, p. 105). This sixteen-page article is the best short history and critique of the country's public housing program I have found, and my briefer history is patterned on it.

In the 1920s Germany's Bauhaus architects had put forward a new vision for workers' housing: clean, high, pure, well-constructed buildings that rejected the false trappings of the bourgeoisie—curtains, clutter, space, individual entrances. Intent on avoiding the picturesque, the Bauhaus Modernists advocated severe horizontality in composition and perfect simplicity in design. This worked well enough when the finest materials were exquisitely crafted into housing for the wealthy, but worked deplorably when shoddy materials were carelessly employed in huge repetitive buildings.[25]

Over the decades the inherent ills of the Modernists' antihuman vision were compounded by the evolution of HUD's minimum design standards. During the 1930s and 1940s public housing projects were often better built and more attractive than privately owned, low-rent apartments and row housing in many communities. Faced with private landlords' criticisms and the ever-present federal desire to slash costs, HUD subsequently outlawed such "amenities" (HUD's term) as basements, doors on closets, ceiling fans, and individual entrances. A few communities gained HUD exemptions to upgrade their new projects by supplementing HUD funds with local support, but by the 1970s most public housing, as the saying went, "looked like public housing."

The final blow to humane, positive public housing came neither from design nor density but from congressional meddling with tenant selection standards. In 1967, Congress approved a series of reforms introduced by Edward Brooke of Massachusetts, the Senate's only black member at the time. To assist public housing tenants who were paying high proportions of their incomes in rent, the Brooke amendments mandated that no tenant should pay more than 25 percent of his or her income in rent. With incredible speed, this well-intentioned reform had terrible results, converting "a low-rent but self-sustaining program into a low-income—and eventually deeply subsidized—program."[26]

The impact of the Brooke amendments was twofold. Faced with immediate rent increases, working families found that much better housing was available for the right price in the private market. Tens of thousands of stable, working-class households quickly deserted public housing projects. With their best tenants gone, local authorities found rental income plummeting; 25 percent of welfare recipients could not cover basic maintenance and

25. Vitullo-Martin (1996, p. 107).
26. Vitullo-Martin (1996, p. 109).

management costs with their monthly stipends. For their first three decades, local housing authorities had been basically self-sufficient. In fiscal year 1969, the first year of the Brooke amendments, operating subsidies for local authorities were $14 million. By fiscal 1999, HUD's annual operating subsidies had ballooned to $2.8 billion, with federal subsidies now covering the greater share of local authorities' annual operating budgets.[27]

Directives from Washington continued to compound local authorities' problems. In 1981, seeking to focus an admittedly scarce supply of subsidized housing on the neediest, Congress required that 95 percent of residents be in the "very low income" bracket, that is, with incomes below 50 percent of the area median income. Simultaneously, Congress raised the standard rent level to 30 percent of adjusted gross income. In 1987 Congress further mandated that local authorities give preference to applicants who were already receiving other welfare assistance and had been displaced by other federal programs (such as highway construction), or who were living in substandard housing, or who were paying more than 50 percent of their income to private landlords.

The federal preference list was further expanded in 1992 to include young disabled persons. Incredibly, the new federal mandate defined "former" drug abusers and alcoholics as being among the disabled. This last congressional intrusion almost shredded the one public housing program universally recognized as successful: public housing for the elderly. Placing supposedly recovering young drug addicts (and traffickers) into apartment buildings formerly reserved exclusively for the elderly created terrifying conditions for many elderly tenants. One local housing authority official explained: "We messed it up. It was fixed and we broke it. Or Congress broke it and we let them."[28]

Private Rent Subsidies

By the mid-1970s, it was clear that the nationwide network of public housing projects had broken down. During the early years of the Nixon administration several successful experiments had been carried out providing rent vouchers for households eligible for public housing. The experiments became a full-fledged program with the passage of section 8 of the Housing and Community Development Act of 1974.

27. Data provided by HUD's Public and Assisted Housing Division.
28. Vitullo-Martin (1996, p. 109).

Section 8 subsidies took two forms: unit-based and tenant-based. Under the unit-based approach, local authorities would contract with private landlords for a specified number of units; in fact, whole private apartment complexes were often financed under section 8. Ultimately, though privately built and managed, many such "section 8 ghettos" became little different from housing authority–operated projects.

More beneficial was the more flexible use of tenant-based section 8 certificates and vouchers. A section 8 certificate allowed an eligible family to obtain private rental housing. Under a three-way rental agreement, the housing authority would pay the landlord the difference between the tenant's monthly payment (30 percent of the tenant's income) and the negotiated rent. Rent levels could not exceed HUD-established fair market rents (FMRs), which varied by size of unit and local market. Under the section 8 vouchers, tenants could opt for more expensive housing by using more than 30 percent of their income to supplement HUD's FMR ceiling.

Over the next two decades the section 8 program grew rapidly. It began by providing rental assistance to 330,000 poor households in 1976. By 1998, section 8 was aiding some 2.8 million poor households, twice the 1.4 million poor households living in public housing projects.[29] But here again the politics of race distorted the program. Administration of the section 8 program was assigned to the same local public housing authorities. The legal powers of most authorities (particularly big-city agencies) were limited to the boundaries of the government that established them. Few authorities spanned city and suburbs. Certificates and vouchers could be used only within each authority's jurisdiction. Within cities the use of section 8 certificates and vouchers often became concentrated in working-class neighborhoods already destabilized by nearby public housing projects. At the same time, section 8 was a boon for many suburban jurisdictions that had resisted building public housing projects (except for the elderly). Allocation of section 8 assistance expanded rapidly and was used in more dispersed patterns.

In 1987, in one of its rare constructive actions, Congress amended section 8 to make certificates and vouchers "portable" across jurisdictional lines. However, few local authorities aggressively promoted areawide use of this assistance since it was difficult to administer when tenants carried vouchers from one jurisdiction into another while still reporting back to the first.

By the 1990s the federal public housing assistance program was still maintaining historic, racially segregated patterns, now de facto rather than

29. Bureau of the Census (1994, table 577).

de jure. Of the 1.4 million tenants in projects, 48 percent were black and 18 percent were Hispanic in 1997. The great majority of family projects were located in central cities. Suburban housing assistance relied heavily on section 8 certificates and vouchers. Overall, in 1997, about 45 percent of all section 8 beneficiaries were white, 39 percent were black, and 15 percent were Hispanic. For poor blacks, housing assistance typically meant living in a public housing project or "section 8 ghetto" in a high-poverty city neighborhood. For poor whites, housing assistance meant receiving a rent subsidy for a privately owned apartment or house in the lower-poverty suburbs.

High-Poverty "Neighborhood Effects"

Like the nation's public housing programs, the neighborhood sorting process Jargowsky analyzes is not color blind but color coded. Is the net result just the grouping together into high-poverty ghettos and barrios of poor blacks and Hispanics who would otherwise face the same problems if they were scattered in communities with less poverty? Or do high-poverty ghettos and barrios themselves generate and perpetuate poverty?

This question has spawned a lively debate over the issue of "neighborhood effects." I believe that the preponderance of the evidence—and my own experience and observations—supports the view that poor neighborhoods are poverty machines that generate poverty itself. The much greater concentration of poor blacks and Hispanics than poor whites in poverty and high-poverty neighborhoods contributes substantially to minority poverty rates, which are three and four times the poverty rate among whites nationally.

Another old adage is that "you can take the boy out of the farm, but you can't take the farm out of the boy." Can you take the ghetto out of the boy by taking the boy out of the ghetto?

Several years ago the Urban Institute and I studied the test results of pupils from public housing households in the Albuquerque Public Schools.[30] We chose Albuquerque for two reasons. First, as its former mayor, I had excellent contacts with both the local housing authority and the public school system. This facilitated data gathering. Second, Albuquerque has an unusu-

---

30. Rusk and Mosley (1994). Our study was supported by a grant from the Carnegie Corporation of New York, the nation's leading philanthropic foundation in the field of early childhood education.

ally high number of public housing children living in middle-class neighborhoods and attending middle-class neighborhood schools. With 80 percent of the metro area's population, Albuquerque is a near-metropolitan city. Its small housing projects and rental subsidies are widely scattered across the city. Thus Albuquerque operates a quasi-regional public housing policy.

On the other side of the equation, Albuquerque Public Schools, with the nation's twenty-fifth largest enrollment, is one of only five metrowide school systems. There is a high degree of uniformity in the distribution of school resources. Albuquerque also has a predictable pattern of test score results. Outcomes mirror inputs, as measured by the socioeconomic status of the children's families, since all other inputs (per pupil expenditures, facilities, teacher qualifications, and so on) are substantially equal. Among Albuquerque's seventy-eight elementary schools, the percentage of pupils who qualified for free and reduced-price school lunches accounted for almost 80 percent of the variation in school-by-school test scores. The high correlation between socioeconomic status and test scores has been confirmed by many educational studies since the massive report prepared by sociologist James Coleman for the U.S. Office of Education in 1966.[31]

We examined the third- and fifth-grade test scores of 1,108 children from public housing over a ten-year period. The results? Having statistically controlled carefully for sex, race and ethnicity, and household characteristics, we found that for every percentage point decrease in poverty among a public housing child's classmates, that child's test scores improved 0.22 of a percentile. In other words, attending a middle-class neighborhood school with 20 percent poor children rather than a high-poverty neighborhood school with 80 percent poor children meant a 13 percentile point improvement in an average public housing child's test scores.

When we switched the focus from the school's socioeconomic mix to the school's average test performance, the results were even more dramatic. For every percentile increase in the school's average test scores, the public housing child's scores improved 0.53 percentile point. Attending a school whose students ranked on average in the 80th percentile in the national tests as opposed to a school whose students were in the 20th percentile meant a 32 percentile improvement in the average public housing child's test scores.

Good teaching makes a difference. However, champions of typical school-centered reforms should not get too excited about these last results.

31. Coleman and others (1966).

In Albuquerque (and elsewhere almost invariably) the high-performance schools all drew most of their pupils from households with high socioeconomic status. In a school with 80 percent of the children from poor households, I doubt that any combination of educational reforms and enhanced resources would produce a 13 percentile improvement in test scores (much less a 32 percentile improvement).

How much of the improvement can be attributed to what happened in that middle-class, high-achieving classroom where the public housing children spent six hours a day, 180 hours a year? How much can be attributed to what happened in the middle-class neighborhood or in the children's own households, where the children spend all the rest of their time? Our Albuquerque study could not determine. Neighborhood effects could be modest. At the very least, those children were probably exposed to standard English much more in the middle-class neighborhood than in a poorer neighborhood. Black English or Chicano English (and certainly Spanish itself) are legitimate vehicles of communication, but standard English is the language in which the child is tested and must communicate in the adult world of work.

In 1996 Hillary Rodham Clinton published *It Takes a Village*, proposing a wide range of reforms for improving the lives of the country's children.[32] At the Republican National Convention, presidential candidate Bob Dole thundered in rebuttal that Republicans believe that it takes not a village but a *family* to raise a child. In my view, it takes a family, a neighborhood, and a school to raise a child successfully. Where families are weak, neighborhoods and schools must be correspondingly stronger to compensate.

Implicitly, American society functions in a way that fulfills that formula for many poor white children. For most poor black and Hispanic children, however, the formula works in reverse. Those with the weakest families are consigned overwhelmingly to the weakest neighborhoods and the weakest schools. High-poverty ghettos, barrios, and slums are substantially the outcomes of the middle-class dispersion and disinvestment promoted by the sprawl machine. Such high-poverty neighborhoods themselves—and the neighborhood schools that struggle to serve them—become the poverty machine for the next generation.

32. Clinton (1996).

7

The Deficit
Machine

IT WAS HARD to decide which looked more fearsome, the Speaker of the House or the life-sized skull of *Tyrannosaurus rex* displayed in the Speaker's conference room in the Capitol building. It was June 1995, and Newt Gingrich was at the height of his power and notoriety. Most of his Contract with America had just been successfully rammed through the U.S. House of Representatives in the previous 100 days.

A dozen presidents of major chambers of commerce from around the country and I had remained standing until the Speaker motioned us to sit down around his conference table. They had come to Washington for a seminar on the federal budget that the association of American Chambers of Commerce Executives had asked me to organize. I had prevailed on Senator Pete Domenici, Senate Budget Committee chairman, to meet with the group.[1] The Atlanta chamber president had arranged the audience with Speaker Gingrich.

---

1. Domenici had been chairman of the Albuquerque City Commission from 1967 to 1970, just before I arrived in Albuquerque. He often talked about his experiences as "mayor" of Albuquerque, although Albuquerque did not shift from a commission-manager to mayor-council form of government until 1974. In reality, with his energy and ability Domenici exercised mayoral-type leadership even without the formal executive powers of a mayor.

126

Gingrich began with his standard ten-minute talk, sprinkled with quotations ranging from Alexis de Tocqueville to futurist Alvin Toffler. Then he invited questions.

"What are the prospects for real collaboration between cities and suburbs on some of the tough issues like schools and housing?" asked Jim Dunn, president of the Richmond Chamber of Commerce. Jim had been pushing regionalism in Virginia, ultimately with substantial success (see chapter 13).

"Never happen," the Speaker snapped. "Why should Cobb County or Gwinnett County, for example, get involved with Atlanta?[2] What's in it for them? The city's got too many problems. The solution for Atlanta's problems is for city government to get its own house in order. Eliminate union featherbedding. Cut the bureaucracy. Slash high tax rates that are driving families and jobs out of Atlanta. Become a lean, well-run, low-cost government like its suburbs. Then Atlanta can compete on even terms." The Speaker's imperial dictum stifled any follow-up response from the chamber executives (though several others, I knew, were actively pushing regional strategies in their communities).

"If your analysis is correct, Mr. Speaker," I interjected, "how do you explain this fact? Most major cities that annex new development have high credit ratings and low tax rates. Older cities cut off from annexing new development have lousy credit ratings and high tax rates. Let me illustrate the point with this chart."

I distributed copies of a multicolored, three-dimensional chart (see figure 7-1) that looked vaguely like the island of Manhattan. The "island" was traversed by five "avenues." Buildings of successively greater heights were arrayed along the length of each avenue. The relative heights of the buildings, I explained, represented different cities' credit ratings. The tallest buildings (AAA credit ratings) towered over "downtown." The buildings scaled back progressively in size (AA1, AA, A1, and A) until one came to the low-rise fiscal slums "uptown" (BAA1, BAA, BA1, BA, and B).

On First Avenue were represented all the "zero-inelastic cities" that since 1950 (or for decades earlier) had been unable to annex new suburbs at all. First Avenue had only one AAA tower downtown

2. Gingrich's 6th congressional district embraces part of suburban Cobb, Fulton, Gwinnett, and Cherokee Counties, known locally as the "golden crescent."

Figure 7-1. *Elasticity and Municipal Bond Ratings for America's Largest Cities*

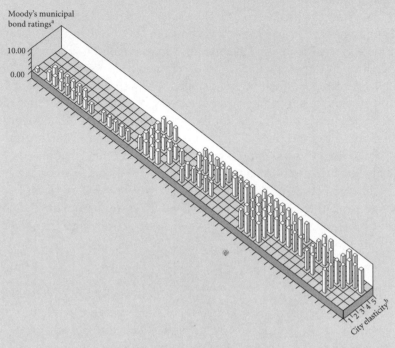

Moody's municipal bond ratings[a]

a. Bond ratings (or "building heights") range from B (1.0) to AAA (10.0).
b. 1 = zero; 2 = low; 3 = medium; 4 = high; 5 = hyper.

(Minneapolis) and only four slightly shorter AA towers (Cincinnati, Hartford, Syracuse, and San Francisco).[3] Most First Avenue buildings were squat tenements clumped uptown in the fiscal slums.

Average building heights (that is, credit quality) improved steadily along Second Avenue (low-elastic cities) and Third Avenue (medium-elastic cities, including Atlanta, which quadrupled in size

3. Both Minneapolis and Saint Paul (an AA1 rating) are traditionally major net beneficiaries from the Twin Cities fiscal disparities plan, the nation's only significant regional tax base–sharing program (see chapters 10 and 11). The assurance that Minneapolis and Saint Paul will benefit proportionally from any new commercial and industrial development in the region encourages the credit rating agencies to maintain high credit ratings for the two central cities.

during the 1950s). The great bulk of downtown high-rise towers, however, were clustered along Fourth and Fifth avenues (high- and hyperelastic cities, such as Indianapolis, Nashville, Charlotte, Houston, Raleigh, and Austin).

"I call your attention to the fact," I continued, "that there isn't a single low-rise building—that is, a low-credit city—located along Third, Fourth, and Fifth avenues. Credit ratings have little to do with having strong unions or weak unions, Republican- or Democratic-controlled city halls, commission-manager or mayor-council governments. Credit ratings substantially reflect a city's ability to defend—even expand—its market share of the regional tax base through its ability to annex new suburban growth."

The Speaker was rendered speechless.

Of course, it was all a Walter Mittyesque daydream. In reality, it was not my meeting. I was just the consultant, not a principal, at the conference table. Had I been a mayor again and part of a delegation of mayors, it would have been a different story. As it was, I just bit my tongue and let the moment pass.

The Conservative Party Line

The Speaker's approach to urban problems, however, was straight conservative party line: a city's fiscal distress was basically its own fault, thanks to profligate, undisciplined spending; the dead weight of municipal bureaucrats; and the iron grip of city employee unions. Of course, middle-class families and businesses had deserted many cities. Quite simply, they were driven out by high taxes and poor services.

Speaker Gingrich's remarks echoed the findings of a policy analysis recently issued by the Cato Institute, a right-wing, libertarian think tank located in Washington.[4] (Renowned as a voracious reader, Gingrich had probably read the report.) The analysis was apparently triggered by (or at least framed as a response to) the U.S. Conference of Mayors' call for a new $35 billion "Marshall Plan for the cities" in the wake of the 1992 Los Angeles

4. Moore and Stensel (1993).

riot. The report examined economic and population growth and fiscal policies for seventy-seven of America's largest cities.

"Unquestionably, there are regional factors at play in determining the relative rates of growth of cities," the report's introduction acknowledged. "Most of the declining cities in our survey are the once-mighty industrial centers in the Northeast and the Midwest—the Rustbelt. Most of the growth cities are in the Sunbelt, on the West Coast, and in the Southeast. . . . Still, the fact that for long periods of time some cities have flourished as others have been deteriorating suggests that the self-imposed policies of cities play an important role in determining their economic fates. We believe an important factor is that their spending and taxing policies are very different. Growth cities have pro-growth fiscal policies; declining cities have anti-growth fiscal policies."[5]

The study divided the seventy-seven cities into five groups based on population and economic growth during the 1970s and 1980s. The first category was highest-growth, with ten cities (for example, San Jose, Lexington, Jacksonville, Raleigh, Charlotte), then came high-growth with eleven (notably, Las Vegas, Nashville, Phoenix, Austin, Albuquerque, and San Diego), average-growth with ten (for example, Boston, Los Angeles, Houston, Dallas, San Francisco, Indianapolis), low-growth with twenty-six (such as Denver, Kansas City, Minneapolis, Seattle, Portland, New York, Atlanta, Baltimore, Philadelphia, Saint Louis, Chicago), and lowest-growth with five (Milwaukee, Buffalo, Cleveland, Rochester, Detroit).

The authors of the Cato Institute study asserted that cities "do have some direct control over their own economic fortunes. Cities in decline are victims of bad public policies that are at least *partially* self-generated" [emphasis added]. They did acknowledge that "in some case they are also victims of high state taxes." Upon comparing the fiscal policies of low-growth and high-growth cities, they concluded that low-growth cities spend, on average, $1.71 for every $1.00 of expenditures in high-growth cities; have tax burdens about 50 percent higher; impose tax burdens on families often about $1,000 higher; have much higher government payroll costs; on average, have more than twice the number of municipal employees per 10,000 residents; are much more likely to impose a local income tax; tend to rely heavily on income and property taxes for revenues, whereas high-growth cities rely heavily on sales taxes; routinely spend $1,400 more per student on education; and are characterized by a substantially higher burden in combined state and local taxes

5. Moore and Stensel (1993, p. 11).

for their residents. Consequently, through their high spending and taxes, low-growth cities promote their own decline.[6]

To restore economic vitality and capital investment to declining cities, the Cato Institute report continued, it would be necessary to bring down the costs of municipal services, and lighten the tax burdens that pay for them. This could be done, it was felt, "without sacrificing vital services." Without such measures, no amount of federal aid would be able to "reverse the decline of urban America."[7]

I agree with that very last statement, suitably amended: without basic changes in *metropolitan systems,* "no amount of federal aid can reverse the decline of urban America."

"City Problems"

The Cato Institute's perspective is widely shared. In my travels to more than ninety metro areas, I have often heard suburban officials and suburban residents upbraid the region's core city government for being wasteful, inefficient, incompetent, costly, too bureaucratic, and corrupt. High taxes or poor services are another complaint. But by far the strongest objection that suburbanites raise concerns what they call "city problems." Just what are city problems? Most often they refer to high crime and, more tellingly, poor schools. When challenged about the city's "poor schools," critics rarely provide specific facts about the competence of teachers, principals, or administrators, or pupil-teacher ratios, or the availability of textbooks and teaching aids, or the quality of school buildings. Sometimes "poor schools" does not even refer to comparative levels of expenditures per pupil. As the Cato Institute study itself observed, some city school systems have higher per pupil expenditure levels than many suburban school systems. What most suburban critics implicitly mean by the city's "poor schools," I find, is that the city system has many schools *with a lot of poor children in them.*

The real issue, then, is the social structure of the city within its metropolitan context rather than the city's specific fiscal policies. This again brings up the idea of the city's elasticity, its ability to absorb new development within its city limits. In the postwar era of low-density development, a city could only do this if it had vast amounts of undeveloped land within existing city

---

6. Moore and Stensel (1993, pp. 26–28).
7. Moore and Stensel (1993, pp. 37–38, 39–40).

limits (as Los Angeles did around 1950) or if it could expand through annexation (which is what three-quarters of the country's central cities did).

However, dismissing the importance of annexation, the Cato Institute remarked, "Annexation is as much a consequence of a city's economic success as it is an explanation of that success. In many cases localities have merged with central cities because it has been in their economic interests to do so. By the same token, more and more localities are now attempting to secede from declining central cities because their economic policies, such as tax rates and service costs, have grown too burdensome."[8]

The passage just quoted is a vintage example of looking at public policy through thick ideological glasses. In the mid-nineteenth century some smaller municipalities did voluntarily merge with larger municipalities for improved city services. (The mergers of Roxbury and Charleston with the city of Boston in 1857 and 1864, respectively, come to mind.) By the mid-twentieth century, however, residents of existing communities almost never voluntarily merged with larger cities unless they were beset by severe groundwater pollution problems from a proliferation of septic tanks that could only be solved by annexation into a city's water and sewer system.

Even the handful of successful city-county consolidations (a form of superannexation) occurred because a preponderance of central-city voters swung countywide elections over the opposition of many voters in unincorporated areas.[9] Other consolidations were a defensive measure against city annexation. In 1963, for example, largely rural Queen Anne's County merged with the tiny city of Virginia Beach (2,000 residents) to immunize the county against further encroachment by the city of Norfolk.[10]

Most annexations occur in one of two circumstances. First, an owner of a large tract of land may want to develop the land and needs municipal utilities and other services; annexation is the city's price for extending services. (Albuquerque, Columbus, Ohio, and Midland, Michigan, are good examples of such service-motivated annexation requests by major developers. Typically, such cities control regional water and sewer systems.) Second,

8. Moore and Stensel (1993, p. 12).

9. In the case of Nashville-Davidson County and Jacksonville-Duval County, voters of all existing smaller municipalities elected to remain independent of the larger, unified governments. The merger of Indianapolis-Marion County was the direct handiwork of the Indiana legislature, accomplished without any local referendum. In this case also, existing municipalities were exempted from "Unigov."

10. The resulting city of Virginia Beach, with 432,545 residents by 1997, is not only Virginia's largest "city" but regularly ranks at the top of the list as America's healthiest central city. Virginia Beach, of course, is a municipalized suburban county.

Table 7-1. *Elasticity Scores of Seventy-Seven Central Cities, by Growth*

Cato Institute growth rating	Number of cities	Elasticity score	Capture-contribute percentage[a]
Highest	10	32	47
High	11	29	53
Average	25	22	33
Low	26	13	−22
Lowest	5	7	−40

a. The degree to which the central city either captured a percentage of the metro area's net population growth or contributed to suburban growth by a net population loss over the period from 1950 to 1990.

some state laws give nearby cities unilateral power to annex unincorporated residential, commercial, and industrial developments without landowner approval. (Texas, Tennessee, and, in particular, North Carolina law virtually mandate such annexations.) When cities have the power to annex, they use it.

To explore annexation's possible influence on city growth and fiscal health, I assigned elasticity scores to each of the seventy-seven central cities studied by the Cato Institute, according to the methodology I developed in *Cities without Suburbs* (see table 7-1). The scores range from a minimum of 4 for the cities that were the most densely developed in 1950 and subsequently could not expand their boundaries at all (such as New York, Newark, and Detroit) to a maximum in the high 30s for those that were least densely developed in 1950 and subsequently expanded their city limits the most (notably, Phoenix, San Jose, and Tucson).

The Cato Institute's categorization by population and economic growth corresponds almost exactly to my categorization of cities by relative elasticity, or geographic expansion. The average elasticity of the Cato Institute's ten highest-growth cities is 32, which falls within the range of my hyperelastic cities (31–40). The eleven high-growth cities (average elasticity 29) fall within my high-elasticity category (25–30). The twenty-five average-growth cities (average elasticity 22) correspond to my medium-elasticity category (18–24). The twenty-six low-growth cities (average elasticity 13) correspond to my low-elasticity cities (9–17), while the five lowest-growth cities (average elasticity 7) fit firmly into the zero-elasticity category (4–8).

Table 7-1 also shows my calculation of the average "capture-contribute percentage" for the Cato Institute's city growth categories. On the average,

Table 7-2. *Elasticity Scores of Seventy-Seven Cities, by Fiscal Health*

Cato Institute fiscal rating (taxes/spending)	Number of cities	Elasticity score	Capture-contribute percentage[a]
Very low	19	30	47
Low	20	26	36
Average	15	20	5
High	21	17	3
Very high	11	10	−18

a. See table 7-1.

cities in the top three growth categories captured shares of their regions' new growth. The low- and lowest-growth cities, however, suffered substantial population losses and were net contributors to their suburbs' growth.

A city that captures a positive share of its region's growth is adding to its tax base. It is also maintaining a more socially and economically balanced population that proportionally has a less acute demand for many services. A city that is losing population and steadily contributing to the growth of its suburbs is not only losing potential tax base, but its residual population is also concentrated in low-income households that have high service needs.

Table 7-2 considers the Cato Institute's rankings of municipal fiscal health. These rankings are based on six factors: per capita city expenditures, city expenditures as a share of personal income, growth in per capita expenditures, combined state and city per capita tax burden, city tax revenues as a share of personal income, and city employees per 10,000 residents. The nineteen cities categorized as having very low taxes and spending levels per capita are, on average, hyperelastic cities that have captured 47 percent of their region's growth. In other words, low-tax/low-cost cities have maintained broad tax bases and strong middle-class populations. They have incorporated half of their suburbs into the city.

At the other end of the spectrum are eleven cities with very high taxes and expenditures per capita. They are typically zero-elastic cities that were unable to expand territorially. They have suffered a steady drain of middle-class households and tax base into their suburbs.

Each of these groupings varies greatly, of course. Social scientists typically use regression analysis to assess the interrelationship between different factors. The Cato study reports that "the correlation between fiscal variables and economic performance variables ranged between 0.3 and 0.5." (A correlation of 1.0 would mean that a city's economic performance can be completely explained by municipal tax and expenditures levels. A correlation of 0.0 would mean there is no relationship.)

I ranked the study's seventy-seven cities by economic growth and fiscal outcomes and analyzed the relationship with each city's elasticity. The correlation between elasticity and fiscal outcomes was 0.38; between elasticity and the city's growth rate, a more substantial 0.56. In short, a city's annexation policy is a somewhat better explanation for its economic growth and fiscal health than its tax levels and city service costs.

In reality, an apples-to-apples study would undoubtedly yield an even greater explanatory margin for elasticity over fiscal policy. All my elasticity calculations cover a city's territorial and population trends for four decades (1950–90). All but one of the Cato Institute's data series start in 1965 or 1970. The positive elasticity ratings of a number of major cities are based on annexations undertaken in the 1950s (for example, in Milwaukee, Atlanta, and Norfolk). Adjusting my analysis for more comparable time periods, I believe, would yield an even better "fit" between elasticity and the Cato study's assessment of economic and fiscal health.

America's Ailing Cities

A much more thorough study of the relationship of a city's demographic profile, economic base, and fiscal health was undertaken by Helen F. Ladd and John Yinger.[11] They analyzed both the hypothetical (or "standardized") and actual revenue-raising capabilities and service costs of eighty-six of the nation's largest cities for 1972, 1982, and 1988. On the revenue side, Ladd and Yinger concentrated on property taxes, earnings taxes (payroll or income), and sales taxes. To determine a city's "standardized" revenue-raising capability, they assumed that every city has the legal power to levy all three types of taxes. They also assumed that the standardized city received 50 percent of its revenue from property taxes and 25 percent each from earnings and sales taxes. The key variables then were the relative well-being of city residents (measured by per capita income) and the ability of the city to "export" its revenue-raising needs through taxes on noncity residents.

11. Ladd and Yinger (1991).

Revenue-Raising Capacity

For a sample of seventy-eight cities with comparable revenues, Ladd and Yinger hypothesized that, on average, for every dollar of city property taxes, nonresidents would pay 34 cents and city residents 66 cents. (The authors termed this an "export ratio" of 0.52.) Nonresidents paid property taxes as customers of city-based retail stores, employees in city-based offices, and consumers of city-based manufacturing goods. Nonresidents would pay a proportionate share of property taxes paid by stores, offices, and factories. The authors also calculated that of each dollar of sales taxes paid, nonresidents would pay 17 cents and residents would pay 83 cents (export ratio = 0.21). This ratio reflected the fact that households did the bulk of their shopping (at grocery stores, pharmacies, gasoline stations, dry cleaners, and the like) close to where they lived. Finally, of every dollar paid in earnings taxes (in large part hypothetical, I would remind the reader), nonresidents paid 56 cents and residents paid 44 cents, on the assumption that the typical city would still be the surrounding region's primary job center (export ratio = 1.27).

In general, the wealthier the city's residents, the greater the revenue-raising capability of city government. On the other hand, the more the city serves as an employment and retail center for its region (and manufacturing center for the nation), the greater its capability to export revenue raising onto nonresidents. Table 7-3 illustrates how these concepts applied to particular cities in 1982. Denver, Boston, and Oakland all had resident income levels higher than the average city. The residents of Atlanta, Baltimore, Detroit, and San Antonio had less than average income levels. This would mean that, on the basis of residents' income, inherently the first three cities would have higher revenue-raising capabilities than the latter three.

With regard to the second factor (the revenue export ratio), both Boston and Atlanta had notably high potential ability to raise revenues from nonresidents. Within their metropolitan areas, both are relatively small cities with large job bases. In 1980, zero-elastic Boston held only 15 percent of the regional population, and medium-elastic Atlanta 20 percent. By contrast, high-elastic San Antonio both had a high proportion (76 percent) of its region's population and the smallest manufacturing base (less than 8 percent of all workers).

From the point of view of their potential revenue-raising capabilities, Denver, Atlanta, Boston, and Oakland all had higher than average potential, and Detroit, Baltimore, and San Antonio all substantially lower than average revenue potential. These calculations were based on a standardized (or

Table 7-3. *Indexes of Standardized and Actual Revenue-Raising Capabilities of Seven Representative Cities, 1982*

City	Per capita income	Estimated export ratios	Revenue-raising capability Standardized	Revenue-raising capability Actual[a]
Atlanta	92	178	119	116
Baltimore	83	86	78	57
Boston	91	178	118	100
Denver	121	110	125	134
Detroit	83	92	80	44
Oakland	108	123	115	93
San Antonio	81	48	65	79

Source: Helen F. Ladd and John Yinger, *America's Ailing Cities: Fiscal Health and the Design of Urban Policy* (Johns Hopkins University Press, 1991), p. 57.

a. Actual taxing authority under state law.

hypothetical) package of taxes that all cities would share. As already noted, all cities were assumed to levy a property tax (50 percent of local revenues), earnings tax (25 percent), and sales tax (25 percent).

That, of course, is not the reality. Table 7-4 summarizes the cities' actual taxing powers. Only six cities out of the eighty-six analyzed levied all three taxes as the standardized model hypothesized.[12] Twenty-nine cities were restricted to the property tax alone, which accounted for 82 percent of all their tax revenues. (These were primarily in New England, New York, New Jersey, and North Carolina.) A dozen cities combined property and earnings taxes in some proportions. Thirty-nine cities depended on the combination of property and sales taxes.

For the eighty-six cities as a group, property taxes represented 53 percent of total tax revenues, other taxes (utility franchise taxes, business licenses, and the like) 20 percent, sales taxes 17 percent, and income, earnings, or payroll taxes only 10 percent. Note, too, that only eighteen of the group had some form of income, earnings, or payroll taxes, which are the principal revenue source for state and federal governments. Twelve major cities had the power to tax incomes earned in the city in full by residents and commuters alike. These were Louisville, Newark, San Francisco, Birmingham, Kansas City (Missouri), Philadelphia, Saint Louis, and five Ohio cities

12. These were Kansas City (Missouri), New York, Saint Louis, San Francisco, Birmingham, and Washington.

Table 7-4. *Revenue Mix of Eighty-Six Cities, by Category of Tax Use, 1982*

Category of tax use	Number of cities	Percentage of total tax revenues			
		Property	Earnings	Sales	Other
Property only	29	82	0	0	18
Property and earnings	3	66	18	0	16
Earnings and property	9	23	71	0	6
Property and sales	21	52	0	23	25
Sales and property	18	29	0	48	23
All three	6	28	29	18	25
Average	86	53	10	17	20

Source: Ladd and Yinger, *America's Ailing Cities*, p. 127.

(Akron, Cincinnati, Cleveland, Columbus, and Dayton).[13] Toledo, Detroit, and New York partly tax commuters, while Pittsburgh, Baltimore, and Washington tax residents' incomes but not commuters'.[14]

When real-world limitations were used to calculate cities' standardized revenue-raising potential, their taxing capacities were generally lower. Boston, Oakland, Baltimore, and, in particular, Detroit all suffered significant reductions in underlying revenue-raising capability, while Denver and San Antonio improved their positions. What do these calculations mean? They mean, for example, that, with identical tax policies (as represented in the third column of table 7-3), the city of Denver had more than 50 percent greater inherent revenue-raising capacity than the city of Detroit. In terms of the two cities' actual taxing authority under different Colorado and Michigan laws (column 4), the city of Denver was endowed with *three times* the actual inherent revenue-raising capacity of the city of Detroit. Contrary to conclusions reached in the Cato Institute study, these projections were entirely or almost entirely independent of each city government's taxing policies.

Of course, a city's actual revenues are not determined solely by its ability to collect local taxes and service fees. State and federal aid make important contributions and, on balance, partly offset disparities in local revenue-

13. Earnings taxes (including self-employment earnings and profits from unincorporated businesses as well as salaries and wages) are the primary revenue source for all Ohio municipalities.

14. In 1973, on granting the federal District of Columbia extensive home rule powers, the Congress explicitly prohibited the District government from enacting a commuter tax, basically, the only revenue limitation imposed on the District City Council that otherwise received all of the taxing authority of cities, counties, and states combined.

raising capabilities. (Ladd and Yinger undertake a thorough analysis of the differential impact of state and federal aid as well.) However, the basic picture of the revenue side of the equation has been set.

Standardized Expenditures

On the expenditure side, Ladd and Yinger calculated standardized expenditure needs by first assuming that service responsibilities are the same for all city governments. The goal was to describe external constraints on a city government's ability to provide public services. They divided public services into three basic groups: police services, fire services, and general services (including airports, public health, highways, housing and urban renewal, corrections, libraries, parking, parks and recreation, sanitation, water and sewer utilities, and, in some cities, education and hospitals). They then analyzed the impact that different environmental factors (that is, factors beyond the city government's control) had on service costs per city resident in the eighty-six cities.

Police Protection

Many factors affect the cost of police services, such as private sector wage rates (with which police departments must compete for personnel) and the percentage of commuters in the work force (who also must receive police services). However, the one factor with the greatest impact on the cost of police services per city resident was the city's poverty rate. For every 1 percent increase in the poverty rate, the cost of police services per resident increased 5.5 percent. As measured by variations from the average for the eighty-six cities, a city whose poverty rate was one standard deviation from the mean would pay 36 percent more per resident for police services; a poverty rate one standard deviation less than the mean would mean a 27 percent reduction in the cost of police services per resident. In terms of the poverty factor, then, the city of Norfolk (with a poverty rate of 19 percent) would pay 70 percent more for police protection per resident than its suburban neighbor, Virginia Beach (with a poverty rate of 6 percent).

Fire Protection

Ladd and Yinger also found a significant relationship between a city's poverty rate and the cost of fire services: one standard deviation above the average municipal rate would raise fire protection costs 27 percent, and one standard deviation below would lower fire protection costs by 21 percent. As measured by standard deviations from the means, other significant influences were the percentage of older housing (+13 percent versus −12 percent); the regional consumer price index, which influences firemen's wage levels and equipment costs (+12 percent versus −11 percent); and the proportions of higher fire-risk rental housing and retail property that had to be protected in comparison with lower fire-risk offices, factories, and owner-occupied homes.

Infrastructure

The percentage of older housing also served as a proxy for the age of a city's infrastructure. Thus cities with older infrastructure had higher costs than cities with newer infrastructure (+11 percent versus −10 percent). Interestingly, the cost of general services was also significantly affected by a city's population density. As the authors explained, "Cities with low densities face high transportation and coordination costs, whereas cities with high densities face severe congestion." Given that water, sewer, and street maintenance are included in the category of general services, low-density cities must also have high capital costs per resident. The minimum cost for general services, the authors calculated, is "at a density of about 15,800 people per square mile, well above the 1982 average of 5,468. . . . The cost at a density of 15,800 is about 11 percent below the cost at the average density and about 6 percent below the cost at the maximum density. All else equal, therefore, both New York with its relatively high density [23,550 people per square mile] and cities with very low densities, such as New Orleans (2,870 people per square mile) . . . face relatively high costs for general services."[15]

Table 7-5 illustrates the differences in costs for ten cities and summarizes the variation in the three services across all eighty-six cities. The cost of general services in 1982 was more than twice as high in the city with the toughest setting (163) as in the one with the most favorable setting (70), but most cities were grouped within 10 percent (plus or minus) of the average (for a standard deviation of 30).

The variation across cities was much greater for police services, largely because of dramatic differences in city poverty rates. The cost per resident

15. Ladd and Yinger (1991, p. 85). New Orleans's apparent low density results from having 60 percent of its municipal area in swampland or under Lake Ponchartrain.

Table 7-5. *Indexes of Public Service Costs and Standardized Expenditure Needs, Ten Selected Cities, 1982*

| Cities | Cost index | | | Standardized expenditure need[a] |
	General	Police	Fire	
86 cities				
Average	112	159	133	115
Standard deviation	30	22	111	52
Maximum	163	710	343	214
Minimum	70	35	43	58
Selected cities				
Albuquerque	77	64	83	71
Cleveland	151	300	218	172
Houston	118	130	95	112
Kansas City, Mo.	144	106	99	126
Miami	75	280	194	114
Newark	102	710	344	214
New Orleans	113	461	110	162
Richmond	112	148	188	118
Salt Lake City	163	145	141	149
Tampa	112	141	138	112

Source: Ladd and Yinger, *America's Ailing Cities,* p. 100.
a. As an index of the 1982 index for these cities.

of police services was more than twenty times as high in the city with the harshest conditions (Newark, 710) as in the city with the most favorable conditions (Virginia Beach, 35), and the range among most cities was very wide (plus or minus 55 percent).

The variation in fire costs fell between the cost variation for general services and police service. The highest-cost city (once again, Newark, 344) had to pay almost eight times as much for the same quality fire protection as the lowest-cost city (Virginia Beach, 43). The fire costs of most cities were grouped within 25 percent (plus or minus) of the average for all cities.

In discussing variations among the selected cities, Ladd and Yinger explained:

> Albuquerque has relatively low police costs because its poverty rate [14 percent in 1980] is somewhat below average and its share of metropolitan population [80 percent] is relatively large, and Cleveland has relatively high

police costs primarily because of its high concentration of poverty [29 percent in 1980]. High poverty is also the main cause of high fire costs in Cleveland, high police costs in New Orleans, and high police and fire costs in Newark and Miami. Population density does not affect police and fire costs, but high or low densities boost the cost of general services. Miami has relatively low general service costs despite its high other costs because it has relatively low wages and because its population density, about 12,300, is near the lowest-cost density. Salt Lake City and Richmond have relatively high general service costs because their population densities, below 2,500, are extremely low. Finally, New Orleans has low fire costs despite its high poverty because it has a high value of service and manufacturing property . . . which are relatively inexpensive to protect from fire.[16]

Finally, the three categories were summarized to calculate the standardized expenditure needs.[17] Standardized expenditure needs varied widely across cities (table 7-5). The highest-cost city (Newark, 214) had to spend almost four times as much per resident to provide the same level and quality of services as the lowest-cost city (Virginia Beach, 58). Again, standard deviation indicated that most cities' standardized expenditure needs were grouped within 15 percent (plus or minus) of the average city.

As with standardized revenue-raising capability, the preceding calculations do not reflect actual city expenditures and the quality of services. Service quality will vary significantly among different cities. In addition, the specific package of services that a given city government provides will vary significantly from city to city. Albuquerque operates an airport, bus system, and water and sewer systems as municipal departments, for example. In many communities these services may be operated by independent regional authorities. In like manner, Albuquerque's city government has no responsibility for health care, a function that most consolidated city-county governments must assume. Some city governments, such as New York, Baltimore, and Richmond, are responsible for financing local public schools. In most cities, local school districts are independent governments with separate taxing authority.

16. Ladd and Yinger (1991, p. 92).
17. The 1982 standardized expenditure needs were expressed as an index of the 1972 index for the same eighty-six cities. At an index of 115 in 1982, the average city had to spend 15 percent more (after adjusting for inflation) to achieve the same level and quality of services it had in 1972. In effect, further deterioration in the economic and social environment of the average city during the 1980s had upped the cost of meeting a standardized service level.

Ladd and Yinger explore real world costs versus standardized model costs as well. Their standardized models, however, were the most revealing. Combining a city's standardized revenue-raising capability with its standardized expenditure needs yielded a city's "standardized fiscal health." A city with a standardized fiscal health of 20 percent would have 20 percent more revenue-raising capability than expenditure needs. It could provide its residents with the standard quality and level of services, while cutting taxes 20 percent. Alternatively, it could maintain the same revenue level and improve the quantity and quality of services by 20 percent. On the other hand, a city with a standardized fiscal health of −20 percent would either have to slash the level of services or receive sufficient state and federal aid to cover the revenue gap.

I have spent some time here countering the Cato Institute's arguments with Ladd and Yinger's observations in order to reinforce my central point about municipal finances: the foremost reasons for substantial disparities in taxes and services among cities—and among cities and suburbs—are factors over which local officials have *minimal control*.

A city's revenue-raising capabilities are based primarily on what taxes it can collect from whom. City councils do not control that basic decision. State legislatures do. State legislatures determine what a city's basic revenue-raising authority will be. For the most part, mayors and city councils can set tax rates only within narrow, legislatively prescribed limits.

Equally important for both revenue-raising potential and service needs is the social and economic profile of the city's work force and residents within the metropolitan framework. As I have argued, in the age of sprawl, the ability or inability of a city to be territorially "elastic"—to be able to defend its market share of the region's population and economic growth through annexation—is vital. Here again state legislatures control the rules of the game. In effect, annexation is impossible in one-third of the nation (the Northeast and Middle Atlantic states). It is difficult to carry out in one-third of the nation (generally, in the Midwest and Sun Belt states that require property owner approval for annexations), and relatively easier in the remaining one-third of the nation (mostly Sun Belt states, notably Texas, Tennessee, and North Carolina).

"Geography is fiscal fate," I told an audience of several thousand in a keynote address to the national convention of the Government Finance Officers Association in June 1997. (At the convention I actually did use my three-dimensional "island" graphic of bond ratings with which, in my Walter Mittyesque musings, I had confounded Speaker Gingrich.) A city's territo-

Table 7-6. *Standardized Fiscal Health Scores for Sixty Major Cities, by Elasticity*

Elasticity category	Number of cities	Capture-contribute percentage	Fiscal health
Hyper	10	49	6
High	8	28	−5
Medium	11	11	7
Low	11	−2	−14
Zero	20	−38	−26

Source: Author's calculations based on Ladd and Yinger, *America's Ailing Cities,* pp. 121–22.

rial elasticity roughly conforms to Ladd and Yinger's calculations of standardized fiscal health (table 7-6). Limiting the comparison to sixty central cities, I found that the twenty-nine reasonably elastic cities (medium- to hyperelastic) captured both positive shares of their regional growth (11–49 percent) and had generally positive standardized fiscal health scores. Eleven low-elastic cities, however, contributed modestly (−2 percent) to suburban growth and averaged negative standardized fiscal health scores (−14 percent). The linkage becomes acute for zero-elastic cities. They not only lost a substantial amount of their population to their suburbs (−38 percent) but had to face constant underlying fiscal crises (−26 percent fiscal health score).

Inelasticity and Incompetence

Are the Cato Institute and the hundreds of suburban officials and residents whom I have heard condemn their core city governments totally wrong? Of course not. There are demonstrable instances of waste, featherbedding, sclerotic bureaucracy, even outright corruption. Nevertheless, beyond the specific history of many inelastic cities, the sprawl machine and the poverty machine combine to create a deficit machine. Until the interlocking cycles of sprawling peripheral growth and the core disinvestment and abandonment are reversed, inelastic cities will be unable to make themselves healthy solely through what they do.

Ed Rendell became mayor of Philadelphia in 1992 at the City of Brotherly Love's lowest moment. It was bankrupt. Its credit rating had dropped so low that it could no longer market its municipal bonds. With courage, determination, and hard work, Mayor Rendell brought Philadelphia back from the brink of total collapse. Within six months, Rendell's reforms had succeeded in raising the city's bond rating from B (meaning "imminent danger of nonpayment") to BA (the "speculative investment" or "junk bond" grade).

We were chatting at a conference in Philadelphia about city-suburb relations. Mayor Rendell told me, "Back in the darkest days, our suburban neighbors told me, 'Cut back on the city unions' power. Slash city payrolls to get rid of the deadwood. Get rid of the bureaucracy. Balance the budget. Get your bond rating back. Get your house in order and then we suburbs will be happy to help out.'

"Well," Rendell continued, "I did all that. I backed the unions down. I chopped the deadwood out of the bureaucracy. I balanced the budget. I got our bond rating raised. I got Philadelphia's house back in order—and it didn't make a darned bit of difference. Our suburbs are no more ready to help now than they were before."

In this generation many central cities are sinking under the burden of too many poor people and too little tax base. In the next generation, that will be the fate of many older suburbs. To fix the deficit machine, we absolutely must change the rules regarding metropolitan housing and development patterns and add regional revenue sharing to ease the transition.

PART TWO

The Outside Game

SPRAWLING DEVELOPMENT patterns, growing concentrations of minority poor, and widening fiscal disparities define America's urban crisis. Part 2 shows how a handful of communities have adopted policies to combat these destructive forces. They have used regional land use planning to help control sprawl; regional fair-share low- and moderate-income housing to help dissolve concentrations of poverty; and regional revenue sharing to help reduce fiscal disparities.

Rather than survey the range of various state and local initiatives in growth management, affordable housing, and revenue sharing, I have focused on the best practices available. For those who follow urban affairs, my choices are not surprising: Oregon and Portland for strong regional growth management (chapter 8); Montgomery County, Maryland, for long-tested mixed-income housing policies (chapter 9); and the Twin Cities area for regional revenue sharing, though in this case, I have chosen to focus on Minnesota's recent experience in political coalition building as its most important lesson for the country (chapter 11).

In its place I have described the voluntary program devised in the Montgomery County–Dayton, Ohio, region (chapter 10). Dayton's economic development and government equity (ED/GE) plan is ten parts economic development to one part revenue sharing. Within the context of Ohio's highly fragmented system of local governance, the countywide collaborative effort is a remarkable achievement, but the minimal impact of its revenue-sharing component illustrates the limitations of voluntary intergovernmental compacts.

With suitable adaptations from state to state, these new rules for local governments would substantially reverse sprawl and the growing concentrations of poverty, and ease fiscal disparities. These three rules would, in effect, bring the built-in benefits of elasticity to inelastic cities and their older, built-out suburbs.

Actually, these rules are essential for elastic cities as well. Many elastic cities have the legal tools to control sprawling development better. Yet few actually do. The recent actions by the city of San Jose and three other California cities to adopt urban growth boundaries—and enforce their goals through supportive utility policies limiting new extensions—stand out as positive examples.

A number of communities have mandatory affordable housing requirements for all new development, but (to my knowledge) only Montgomery County, Maryland, and neighboring Fairfax County, Virginia, require that a modest percentage of the affordable housing created must be sold to the county housing authority, a crucial step in fighting the concentration of poverty. Any region would benefit from adopting Montgomery County's housing policies.

Elastic cities serve as internal revenue-sharing mechanisms, but as they mature, other communities (both incorporated and unincorporated) spring up on their outskirts. Multijurisdictional growth management and housing compacts, buttressed by revenue-sharing arrangements, are becoming more and more necessary around the Albuquerques, the Charlottes, the Columbuses, the Indianapolises. The old formula—defending your market share of regional growth through annexation or consolidation—becomes less and less effective.

Despite tripling their municipal territory from 1960 to 1990, even the fifty most expansion-minded central cities lost market share: from 65 percent (1960) to 51 percent (1990) of their urbanized populations and from 60 percent (1960) to 43 percent of their metropolitan populations.

Only two regions that I have visited successfully do it all. The first is Toronto, Canada. For four decades the Toronto region was served by Metro Toronto, a regional government. Formed in 1954 when the city of Toronto was one-half of the region's population and about three-quarters of its tax base, Metro Toronto successfully guided the metropolitan area's growth. Today Toronto is generally proclaimed North America's most livable city. (That certainly was our reaction when Delcia and I visited Toronto in November 1996.)

Metro Toronto was responsible for overall transportation and land use planning; all major infrastructure systems (water, sewer, highways, transit, regional parks); financing local public schools; and a regionwide police department. The city of Toronto and five suburban municipalities provided fire protection, maintained local streets, picked up the trash, and provided other purely local services.

Within its 240-square-mile jurisdiction, Metro Toronto carried out all the measures I would later recommend: regional land use planning, regional revenue sharing, and regional "social housing." Where subsidized housing would be located, for example, has never been a matter for local governments to decide. Social housing has always been controlled by Metro Toronto or even by the provincial government of Ontario. As a result, social housing is widely dispersed and concentration of Toronto's poorest residents is averted.

Metro Toronto's Achilles' heel is that, once established by the Ontario parliament, Metro's jurisdiction was never allowed to expand beyond its original 240-mile territory. For two decades that was sufficient, but in recent decades growth has leaped past Metro Toronto's reach. The Greater Toronto Area (GTA) now has a population of 4.5 million people scattered over 2,700 square miles.

In 1996 the Conservative party took control of Ontario for the first time in decades. Taking a page out of the Republican party's manual in America, the Tories campaigned on a platform of "less government." Fulfilling their pledge, in early 1997 the provincial government "amalgam-ated" the city of Toronto, its five suburban municipalities, and Metro Toronto itself into one unitary government. In the process, the Tories claimed, they had simplified local government and eliminated almost half of all local elected offices.

This was a better outcome than one alternative: abolishing Metro Toronto itself and leaving Toronto and its five immediate suburban neighbors without any overall mechanism. But the newly elected parlia-mentary majority rejected Metro Toronto's own preference: extend Metro's powers to the full 2,700-square-mile Greater Toronto Area. (The Tories' political stronghold is Toronto's outer suburbs.)

Instead, what was long viewed by American eyes as the model of regional collaboration (Canadian-style) has been converted into some-thing much more familiar, a central city surrounded by hostile suburban counties (called, in Toronto's case, "regional municipalities").

The new amalgamated city of Toronto is a much healthier central city than its American counterparts. Toronto, of course, is the business and financial capital of Canada, New York, and Chicago rolled into one. Long characterized as "Toronto the Good," Toronto has been transformed from the straitlaced head of British Canada into the heart of a world city. It is populous (2.5 million residents) and amazingly cosmopolitan.[1] With approximately 10,500 residents per square mile, the new Toronto is also much more densely populated than all but a dozen U.S. cities.[2] Yet with carefully interconnected subway lines, bus routes, and a viable streetcar system, Torontonians move around readily and quickly. All the ills of city life that many Americans tolerate are refuted by Toronto.

Yet Canada no more escapes the influence of American styles in its metropolitan development patterns than it does in business or popular culture. New suburban communities springing up in the Greater Toronto Area (outside the influence of Metro Toronto) are indistinguishable from American suburbs. Whether Toronto will still be North America's most livable city in another half century is an unanswered question. There is now no counterpart to Metro Toronto to deal with the new regional challenges across a region ten times the size of that successfully managed by Metro Toronto.

The other community that has done it all is Montgomery County, Maryland. Someone might object that Montgomery County is only one-fifth of the national capital region. It is a fair objection. Silver Spring or Bethesda would never have supplanted Washington itself as Montgomery County's central city; county government does not have to contend with true inner-city problems in all their intensity. Yet Silver Spring, in particular, could have evolved into an extremely distressed area if county policies had allowed that to happen. Instead, it is simply a somewhat frayed and aging community that the county is trying hard to reinvigorate.

With 826,766 residents in 1997, Montgomery County, standing alone, would be the nation's sixty-ninth largest metro area. It offers, in the words of a former county planner, "a big enough canvas to work on." A large enough portrait of a complex urban community has been drawn on that canvas to be judged critically.

Montgomery County has its problems. The Montgomery County Public Schools are constantly struggling to meet the needs of many

---

1. In 1991, only 65 percent of Metro Torontonians reported English as their mother tongue.
2. All except New York City (23,698 per square mile) and San Francisco (15,502) have been steadily depopulating since mid-century.

minority students whose numbers are steadily approaching half the county's school population. Tragic murders occur. Yet with a poverty rate one-quarter that of neighboring District of Columbia, Montgomery County has one-twentieth the murder rate. These points serve as reminders that the world is not perfect. Yet the perfect should not be made the enemy of the good. Montgomery County is an exceptional community in which many people of different racial and ethnic backgrounds and different economic status live side by side. Any region that adopts the model policies detailed in part 2—and as practiced in Toronto and Montgomery County—will be much closer to being all that America can be.

8

Portland, Oregon: Taming Urban Sprawl

"IN THE GOOD OLD DAYS, where did Portlanders love to go to get a break from city life?" Our guides as Delcia and I toured Oregon's metropolis in February 1996 were Carl Abbott and Ethan Seltzer, two Portland State University professors.

"Sauvie Island," my hosts agreed, "a very special place . . . forty square miles of prime farmland on an island where the Columbia and Willamette rivers come together . . . just ten miles from Downtown Portland. Strawberries, pumpkins, other vegetables, dairy farms. On weekends families would come out from the city to buy fresh produce and show their children real cows and horses. Businessmen could even go duck hunting at dawn, then make it into the office by 9 A.M."

"Sauvie Island was right in the path of urban development?" (The Portland area's population had more than tripled in fifty years.)

"Yes, flat land, great views, linked by highway to Portland. Some potential flood and drainage problems, but nothing that enough money couldn't fix," Carl replied. "The turning point came in 1976 when a developer first proposed subdividing the 3,000–4,000-acre Douglas Farm."

Carl paused. "Let's go see what Sauvie Island looks like today."

Leaving Portland's skyscrapers behind us, we drove north on U.S. 30, following the Willamette River. Overshadowed by towering cargo cranes, low-slung factories and warehouses lay on either side of the highway. In a steady procession, oceangoing freighters and container ships lined the wharves of the Port of Portland on our right. Three-quarters of American wheat exported to Japan, China, and other Pacific Rim destinations passes through Portland.

Several hundred yards to the west, a steep, wooded ridge, Forest Park, rose up. A mile-wide ribbon, Forest Park stretches from almost the edge of downtown nine miles northward. A guidebook claims that, with its more than 5,000 acres, Forest Park is the largest municipal park in the world.

"What's in Forest Park?"

"Bike trails, jogging trails, even some old growth forest. It's very popular with city residents. Much of it was assembled by the city in the 1930s through tax foreclosures," Ethan explained.

Just as the Willamette veered northeastward to join the Columbia, a sign announced "Sauvie Island," pointing toward a concrete bridge arching high over the Multnomah Ship Channel. At the highest point of the bridge we had a brief, panoramic view of what had become of Sauvie Island.

It was still farmland stretching as far as we could see!

"How is this possible?"

"Senate Bill 100, Oregon's Statewide Land-Use Planning Act, passed in 1973. Aroused neighbors blocked subdividing Douglas Farm, and by 1979 Sauvie Island was placed outside Portland's urban growth boundary. It should always be farmland." Carl's faint grin betrayed a touch of pride. "Or nature preserve. Most of the northern end of the island is a wildlife refuge."

"There's the Pumpkin Patch." Ethan pointed out several reddish, white-trimmed farm buildings. "Tens of thousands of Portlanders come out here every fall to get their Halloween pumpkins. It's a real urban-rural ritual."

Our car cruised virtually alone along the two-lane road that hooked around three sides of the island. Gazing across fields and orchards, we could see downtown Portland's tallest buildings to the south and Mount Hood etched sharply against the eastern horizon. To the northeast was the truncated remnant of Mount Saint Helens, its upper 1,500 feet having been pulverized and ejected into the atmosphere by the cataclysmic eruption fifteen years earlier. Even more startling for us visitors was the sight of giant ships sailing along the Columbia River, their superstructures towering above the riverbank levee that hid their hulls.

We turned westward to cut across the island's neck. Several lookout points and parking areas punctuated the southern edge of the state nature sanctuary. Farther along, discreet wooden signs pointed up roads leading to two private duck-hunting clubs. "You should see this road before dawn during duck season. Real traffic jams out here with cars lined up, hunters waiting to get their turn in the duck blinds," Ethan commented.

"What would prevent Sauvie Island from being turned into five to ten-acre 'farms' with big mansions for 'gentlemen farmers,' which happens in so many places?"

"Oregon's laws preserving agricultural land around urban areas are really tough," Carl explained. "On this island no single property can be less than sixty-seven acres except for a few smaller parcels that were 'grandfathered.' Land has to be actively farmed, producing at least $80,000 in annual revenue. A farmer who wants to build another house must show that the new house is essential to farming the land. No hobby farms allowed. You know, keep a few horses but commute to your law office in Portland."

As the sun set, we turned southward back toward the city. Houseboats lined sections of the Multnomah Ship Channel, dividing Sauvie Island from the mainland. "That's one way to have a 'detached' house in the suburbs without spending weekends cutting the grass!"

"A houseboat's really a lot of work, constant maintenance," Ethan cautioned. "But, you just tie up, pay your docking fee to the wharf owner, no property taxes. Some people really like it. Portland provides for lots of different lifestyles."

Saving the Farm

Over breakfast the next morning I sought more information on Oregon's land use planning law from two nationally recognized experts, Henry Richmond and Bob Stacey. For many years they led 1000 Friends of Oregon, the state's leading watchdog group over land use planning and growth management. I had been praising the environmental organization's success.

"Do you know who really passed Senate Bill 100 back in 1973?" Henry said. "A small group of conservative Republican farmer-legislators. The one who got it started was Hector MacPherson, a dairy farmer who was a member of the Linn County Planning Commission for many years. County planning commissions might try to preserve farmland, but state laws were so weak back then that the commissions were really powerless whenever developers waved enough money around in front of hard-pressed farmers. The Willamette Valley has some of the most productive agricultural land in the world. Agriculture's 20 percent of the state's economy. But Hector saw that the farming economy—and a whole way of life—was being paved over by urban sprawl year after year."

"The story is told," Bob interjected, "that one day Hector was driving past a neighbor's farm. A big Caterpillar was shoving the soil around. 'What ya plannin' to grow here?" Hector called out. "Houses," the Cat operator answered.

"That finally tore it for Hector," Henry continued. "He was fed up and got himself elected to the state Senate. He was determined to change state law to make exclusive farm use zoning stick."

"So, Oregon's landmark growth management law wasn't really the handi-work of liberal Democrat tree-huggers from Portland?"

Henry smiled at my gentle dig. "Oh, some of us were there at the state capitol, plugging away, but at every critical legislative juncture there was a conservative Republican farmer-legislator in the middle of the reform battle. Hector MacPherson, of course, Jim Smart and Randy Smith from Polk County, Stafford Hansell from Umatilla County. Salt-of-the-earth types with real dirt under their fingernails. At legislative hearings they spoke with the moral authority of Old Testament prophets. They're the ones who really put Oregon's land use law on the books."

"And, of course, we had Tom McCall as governor then," Bob added. "An-other Republican, from an old Oregonian family. McCall had a deep feeling for what makes Oregon so special. He once said that he loved Oregon more than life itself.

"The growth management act set statewide land use goals, but the key was how strongly the goals would be interpreted and enforced. Governor McCall appointed L. B. Day, a top Teamsters Union leader, as first chairman of the state Land Conservation and Development Commission." Bob chuck-led. "L. B. was a tough son-of-a-gun. He proclaimed that urban sprawl was 'a stinking cancer on the lush, green breast of the Willamette Valley.'

"L. B. drove the commission members through seventy-eight public hearings. They came out with tough interim rules. Until the state commis-sion approved new local comprehensive plans, L. B. ruled, the statewide goals applied to all local rezoning actions. His commission had to approve all lo-cal, nonconforming proposals. That stopped a lot of quick land grabs by developers."

"I have the impression that growth management is now primarily an urban issue," I said. (That week Representative Ron Wyden, a liberal Demo-crat from Portland, had narrowly beaten State Senator Gordon Smith, a con-servative Republican from eastern Oregon, for Bob Packwood's vacated U.S. Senate seat. Wyden's narrow victory margin was widely credited to over-whelming support by Portland area environmentalists.)[1]

1. In November 1996 Smith was elected to fill the other U.S. Senate seat vacated upon Mark Hatfield's retirement.

"No. In the last legislative session, the Farm Bureau was one of 1000 Friends' best allies in fighting the law's repeal. But with the strong, antigovernment ideology of many Republican legislators these days, statewide growth management has lost its clear, bipartisan flavor," Bob explained. "If the legislature repealed the law, 1000 Friends would probably push for a popular referendum. Oregon voters have twice solidly rejected repealing our growth management law. But we haven't had a popular vote since 1982. A referendum might be a tough fight, but I'm confident that most Oregonians want strong, statewide land use planning."

State Ends, Local Means

Strong, statewide land use planning is precisely what Senate Bill 100 provides. The legislature set fourteen statewide goals that must be met by all local governments. These cover a wide range of concerns. All local governments must encourage urban development, but only within urban growth boundaries. They must curb urban sprawl. Local plans must identify and preserve historically or archaeologically significant sites and buildings. They must set aside open space, conserve fish and wildlife habitats, protect air and water quality, and develop parks. Saving productive forests and farmlands, the bill's original objective, is a high priority.

Oregon's land use planning law extends beyond concern over the natural environment to address the human environment. All local plans must encourage the availability of affordable housing for all income groups. Local plans must promote a variety of residential densities and housing types and encourage the preservation of existing housing stock. Continued economic growth, especially for unemployed and disadvantaged persons, is another key goal. Local plans must also favor efficient, energy-saving light rail and bus systems for more densely populated areas. All must be accomplished through a process of continuous citizen participation. Senate Bill 100 gives the state's Land Conservation and Development Commission the power to review and approve (or reject) all local plans, depending on whether they conform with statewide goals.

In the rest of Oregon, county government has the key coordinating role. In metropolitan Portland, however, officials who manage the growth process are directly accountable to all area residents through Metro, the nation's only elected regional government. Metro is a state-chartered regional government that covers Multnomah, Clackamas, and Washington Counties, the city of Portland, and twenty-three other municipalities. The region's voters elect directly the seven-member Metro council and Metro's executive officer.

"The constant debate about growth issues around here is really remarkable." Our dinner companion that night was Mike Burton, Metro's current executive officer. Tall, mustachioed, good-looking, fiftyish, Burton is a former state senator with a career politician's easy presence. He was elected to his first four-year term as head of Metro in November 1994. I seconded his observation. "As just one example of what you say, I picked up this morning's *Daily Oregonian,* and what was the 'Question of the Day' in the reader poll but 'Should Portland's urban growth boundary be extended or not?' Call such and such an '800' number to vote 'yes', another to vote 'no'."

"Metro is truly unique. We're the only elected level of government in the country whose mission is really to focus on the future," Burton responded. "Oh, we have some service functions. We run the Washington Park Zoo and the Oregon Convention Center. But you could strip away all these other functions. What's really important is our responsibility for regional land use planning.

"And that's made even stronger by Metro's home rule charter, adopted by the citizens of the region in 1992," Burton continued. "Our charter gives Metro an unparalleled grant of responsibility for growth management. In section 9 our citizens direct the courts to interpret Metro's land use planning powers liberally. That's an unparalleled set of instructions for the courts."

A liberal interpretation of local government powers, I thought, is standard language in most home rule charters. Burton's larger point, though, was right on the mark: Portland Metro is indeed a unique regional government with growth management powers that are unparalleled in the United States.

Electing to Go Metro

Metro had a long gestation. For seventy years the Portland area has been experimenting with regional governance. As early as 1925 a state study commission raised the alarm that rapid, unplanned, automobile-based suburbanization was outrunning Portland's ability to annex new areas. The commission called for Portland and Multnomah County's consolidation, a proposal the Oregon legislature studiously ignored.

The postwar boom revived the concern over sprawl. During the 1950s Multnomah, Clackamas, and Washington Counties all adopted their first zoning codes. By 1961 the number of special districts for fire, water, zoning, sewers, parks, and street lighting had exploded to 218 (from just 28 in 1941). Political wars raged over Portland's aggressive annexation efforts. Suburban subdivisions struggled to incorporate as a defense against "big city" annexation.

To bring some order out of chaotic local governance, the League of Women Voters, business leaders, and other good government groups persuaded the state legislature to establish the Portland Metropolitan Study Commission (1963–71). Unlike its predecessor four decades earlier, this commission made recommendations that ultimately transformed regional governance. The study commission first helped organize a voluntary Columbia Region Association of Governments (CRAG) in 1967. Then the study commission got the legislature to set up two other regional bodies: the Local Government Boundary Commission (1969), which would adjudicate annexation disputes, and the Metropolitan Service District (1970).

From the outset CRAG was embroiled in frustration and controversy. Its original membership was composed of officials representing four counties and fourteen cities. Over the years its governing board mushroomed to delegates from five counties and thirty-one member cities. All had coequal status. Though CRAG had a good professional staff, it had neither the authority nor the ability to forge a consensus around difficult regional policy issues.

As Carl Abbott, my Portland State host, explained, "CRAG board members were often torn between what was good for the region and what would protect their own constituents from unwanted costs, programs, or development." In short, CRAG had all the virtues and defects that characterize most of some 600 voluntary councils of government scattered across the nation today. CRAG was a useful setting for local officials to convene and exchange views. Its staff produced insightful studies and thoughtful recommendations. However, CRAG acted only on the easy issues, meaning that member jurisdictions thought they had nothing to lose.

The Metropolitan Services District (MSD), on the other hand, proved to be a more promising regional initiative. The MSD was created by the Oregon legislature as a "metropolitan municipality of greater Portland," covering Multnomah, Clackamas, and Washington Counties. The MSD did not supplant county government or any of the 24 municipalities. It was only an empty governmental "box" to be filled by whatever duties the legislature or the voters approved for it.

The MSD began life uncertainly and modestly. In May 1970 the region's voters swept aside the mayor of Portland's implacable opposition and activated the MSD by a 54 to 46 margin. It was initially governed by a seven-member board of local elected officials from Portland, the three counties, and three other cities. A second voter referendum turned down the MSD's request for a general property tax levy. The MSD's first project—planning a regional solid waste disposal system—was financed by a small tax on used auto tires. In 1976, this time with Portland's agreement and voter approval of an earmarked tax levy, the MSD added a second regional function, operating the Washington Park Zoo.

In 1977 the legislature injected more direct democracy into the MSD. The state lawmakers shelved having it governed by elected officials from member counties and cities in favor of having the region's voters elect a twelve-member board and an executive officer. The legislature also gave the MSD broader taxing authority (but only with local voter approval).

As Carl Abbott remembered the change, "The legislature saw direct elections as the best, and perhaps only, way to secure an effective areawide government. Like CRAG, the mayors and county officials who served on MSD's board still looked out for their own jurisdictions first."

"Why an elected executive officer rather than hiring a professional administrator?"

"A hired chief administrator wouldn't have a political base. A city manager-type simply couldn't survive in a role as increasingly controversial as MSD chief executive," Carl responded. "The MSD needed an elected head honcho."

In May 1978 the region's voters approved the revised MSD by a 55 to 45 margin. In the bargain, the voters abolished CRAG. The newly democratized MSD took over CRAG's regional planning role, including overseeing Oregon's Statewide Land-Use Planning Act for the three-county Portland area. In 1979 the state Land Conservation and Development Commission endorsed the Portland area urban growth boundary drawn up by the MSD. The boundary line was based on CRAG staff work begun five years earlier.

There were still more setbacks (two other tax referendums were defeated). Nevertheless, under Rena Cusma, its first elected executive officer, the MSD slowly matured. Attendance at the Washington Park Zoo boomed. Buttressed by an advisory council of local officials, the MSD took over planning for federal transportation funds. In 1986 the region's voters approved a $65 million bond issue for the Oregon Convention Center, which the MSD would plan, build, and run.

In 1987 the legislature gave the executive officer veto power over council actions. The council itself began to act less like a board of directors and more like a legislative body. Finally, in 1990 the Oregon constitution was amended to allow the MSD to have its own home rule charter. Drawn up by a citizens' charter commission, the document was approved by area voters in November 1992.

The structural changes provided in MSD's home rule charter—now officially called "Metro"—were minimal; the council was reduced from twelve members to seven. Metro's state-conferred growth management powers, however, received a resounding endorsement from local voters. In the new charter the voters affirmed that regional planning would be Metro's "primary function."

The charter charges Metro with developing a fifty-year "future vision" and a "regional framework plan." Metro has the power to resolve conflicts between regional and local plans and, by ordinance, require compliance with the regional framework plan.

Growth Boundaries and Good Sidewalks

Metro is merely the framework for regional planning, however. The substance flows from Oregon's Statewide Land-Use Planning Act. Of all the goals, the most innovative is state goal 14, which requires that each municipality establish an urban growth boundary in a perimeter around each urbanized area. There must be sufficient capacity within an urban growth boundary for twenty years of anticipated growth. Indeed, within an urban growth boundary, local land use plans, zoning regulations, and the building permit process must expedite private development.

But outside an urban growth boundary, the land is reserved for exclusive farm use, exclusive forest industry use, or for parks and natural areas. The county government must prevent both suburban development and rural sprawl. No water lines, no sewer lines, no wider county roads, no permissive zoning. Oregon draws a sharp line between what is urban and what is rural.

"When it was first designated in 1979, Portland's urban growth boundary was really just an imaginary line on a map.[2] Now, almost twenty years later, you can actually see it," our tour guide, Ethan Seltzer, commented, as we had continued our drive around the Portland area. "If we were flying over the area, in many sections you could actually see the growth boundary now from the air. Subdivisions extend up to a point, then they stop, and

2. The Portland area's initial urban growth boundary added about 20 percent more vacant land to the region's already urbanized area.

farmland takes over. Actually, we're driving along part of the growth boundary now—Sunnyside Road—in northern Clackamas County."

We continued looking around. To our right—inside the urban growth boundary—were relatively new subdivisions. Denser townhouse developments alternated with more traditional, single-family, split-level homes grouped around their cul-de-sacs. But to our left—outside the urban growth boundary—were working farms.

We turned into Sunnyside itself, a new subdivision being built in the "neotraditional" style. Though there were some attached townhouses, most were stand-alone, single-family homes. However, Sunnyside felt more like a neighborhood constructed a century before. Unlike the brick or stucco ranch houses and split-levels of classic postwar suburbs, Sunnyside's houses were two and three stories, wood frame construction, with pitched roofs, garrets, and dormer windows. Many had front porches where parents could sit and watch their children play in front or greet neighbors as they passed by. Sideyards were small, and houses situated close together lined the streets.

There was something notably absent from this neotraditional neighborhood: the blank expanse of the two-car garage doors, the dominant aesthetic feature of postwar suburban houses. With rare exceptions, garages were not visible in Sunnyside. They had been tucked into separate structures at the back of the deep lots, reached by sideyard driveways or, more often, off midblock alleyways.

Sunnyside was a good effort, but perhaps (I noted to myself) with a design shortcoming: its sidewalks. In more conventional suburban fashion, Sunnyside's sidewalks were narrow and flush to roll curbs. In effect, they were unusable by pedestrians, a seemingly small but crucial design issue that will significantly reduce casual contact among neighbors.

I had come to appreciate the importance of good sidewalks years earlier when we lived in a genuine "traditional" neighborhood in Washington. Our sidewalks in Barnaby Woods were set back from the curb about five feet. The setback was sufficient to provide a flat ribbon of concrete unbroken by drive pads and to allow stately old elm trees to line both sides of the street, creating a cool green canopy along its entire length. Parallel-parked cars provided further separation from automobile traffic.

The sidewalks in Barnaby Woods were little highways of neighborhood activity. Having been taught *never* to step into the street, toddlers to teenagers played up and down the sidewalks. Young mothers rolled baby carriages along. Elderly residents walked their dogs. Working men and women walked to and from bus stops morning and evening. All we lacked was neighborhood shopping within easy walking distance; the nearest neighborhood grocery store was a half mile away. (Sunnyside residents, I could see, would also be auto-dependent for all shopping.)

The poet Robert Frost once wrote (perhaps ironically) that "good fences make good neighbors." He had it wrong. Good sidewalks make good neighbors. With good sidewalks, neighbors are thrown together in casual encounters all the time.

Typical postwar suburban subdivisions isolate residents from one another. Where they even exist, sidewalks usually serve only to prop up curbs (as, unfortunately, Sunnyside's new sidewalks do). Wide, empty streets encourage fast traffic. Typical subdivision residents live in self-contained cocoons—either driving their cars in and out of two-car garages or disappearing into family rooms and fenced backyards.

In pursuit of the American Dream suburban-style, many Americans have bought into the notion that a big house on a big lot is a satisfactory substitute for being part of a real neighborhood. Public space disappears. Private space reigns. Residents only become "neighbors" when they take some specific action to get together—such as a car pool or an occasional backyard barbecue.

Picture This!

My sense of what constitutes a well-designed neighborhood is clearly shared by a majority of Portland area residents. Several days after my auto tour, I met with Portland City Commissioner Earl Blumenauer (now a member of Congress, having won Ron Wyden's vacated seat). He gave me a copy of *Picture This!* It was the final report of a "visual preference survey" commissioned by Metro, Tri-Met (the three-county transit authority), the city of Portland, and a dozen other local governments.

During several weeks in 1995 more than 3,000 Portland area adults and 1,500 youth participated voluntarily in thirty-five sessions conducted by Nellesen and Associates, an architectural and planning firm based in Seattle and Princeton. They were shown more than 200 pictures of commercial areas, neighborhood streets, and houses and were asked to grade their visual preferences on a scale of −10 to +10.

The results? Despite the fact that two-thirds of participants were Portland suburbanites, typical suburban shopping centers (even high-design efforts) uniformly were graded negatively. No amount of cosmetic design could hide the reality of acres of parking lots and the visual monotony of shopping center storefronts. By contrast, with their parallel parking, street trees, and variegated building styles, older city commercial streets graded positively.

The same was true for neighborhoods. Typical suburban subdivisions with low-slung homes widely spaced, one to five to an acre along curving streets or around cul-de-sacs, were graded negatively; even some very tony-looking, upper-income subdivisions were rejected. By contrast, tree-arced city streets (with good sidewalks), lined more densely with two- and three-story frame houses, brick townhouses, or even modest one-story bungalows (with screen porches) graded very positively. The highest-rated residential neighborhood was a street scene from Toronto with thirty to forty dwelling units per acre.

Picture This!, as Nellesen and Associates themselves emphasized, was merely an expression of visual preferences. How much do visual preferences actually govern consumer preferences in the Portland area? ("A lot of suburban areas around here look like everywhere else despite our growth management policies," Metro's Mike Burton had told me.) What the suburban dream has been selling successfully for decades is not just two-car garages, backyard barbecues, all-electric kitchens, and modern bathrooms. It has also been selling social uniformity and escape from "city problems."

Segregation and Revival

The Portland region has not been exempt from racial and economic segregation, I reminded a Portland City Club audience to whom I spoke the day after my auto tour. Portland's African American population is relatively small; it amounts to some 3 percent of the region's population (the same proportion as the Albuquerque area). However, as of the 1990 census, the degree of racial segregation was surprisingly high. On the dissimilarity index scale of 0–100 (with 100 representing total segregation), the Portland region measured 66. (Albuquerque's index was 39.) By this statistical measure, the Portland area was as racially segregated as the Dallas-Fort Worth, Columbus (Ohio), or Washington metro areas.

One-quarter of the Portland region's 41,000 African Americans lived in just six majority-black census tracts across the Willamette River from downtown in the city's Albina area. The poverty rate in those six tracts was 30 percent in 1970; by 1990, the poverty rate had risen to 38 percent.

In fact, race aside, the number of poverty neighborhoods with more than

20 percent poor residents had grown from twenty-three in 1970 to thirty-eight in 1990, including several now-poverty neighborhoods in suburban Gresham, Beaverton, and Forest Grove. Of the twenty-three poverty neighborhoods in 1970, over the next two decades the poverty rate had increased in eleven, was stable in five, and had declined in eight neighborhoods.

"Your growth management policies are admirable, but you need to adopt more rigorous requirements for mixed-income housing development," I advised the City Club audience. "Some communities require that 15 or 20 percent of all new construction be affordable housing.[3] Over the past two decades such a mixed-income housing policy for the Portland region would have resulted in another 10,000 moderate-income homes and apartments for working-class households and another 5,000 units acquired by a regional low-income housing assistance program. This would have been sufficient to close down Columbia Villa and other public housing projects or to convert them to mixed-income housing."

Nevertheless, measured statistically through the 1990 census, the concentration of poverty in the Portland area was more moderate and the isolation of poor households was less extreme than in most other metropolitan areas. By the same dissimilarity index, but this time measuring the segregation of poor households (regardless of race), in 1990 the Portland area measured 27, the lowest of all metropolitan areas with more than 1 million residents.[4]

Poverty neighborhoods in the Portland area *felt* different as well. As we drove through Albina and other poor neighborhoods in February 1996, they did not look like poverty neighborhoods we would see in other cities. There were too many signs of revival: renovated homes, new townhouses, and refurbished stores. In fact, our visit to Portland in February 1996 may have been one of the few occasions when my analysis was truly the victim of old data. Six years had passed since the 1990 census had identified Albina as Portland's poorest neighborhood. By early 1996 the Portland economy was booming. The region's urban growth boundary had been in place for seventeen years. Both were dramatically transforming inner-city Albina.

Seven months after our visit, the *Sunday Oregonian* provided conclusive documentation of Albina's resurgence.[5] From 1990 to 1995 the total

3. See chapter 9 on Montgomery County, Maryland.

4. The fact that three out of four poor persons were white but were not highly segregated contributed to the Portland region's low economic segregation index.

5. Jim Barnett and Steve Suo, "Albina: Up or Out?" *Sunday Oregonian*, September 8, 1996. Information and comments about Albina are drawn liberally from this article.

value of all commercial, industrial, and residential property in Albina rose from $1.4 billion to $2.6 billion. In just five years Albina's homes, stores, and factories had almost doubled in value.

Targeted public investment had made its contribution. The newspaper estimated that since 1986 government agencies had committed at least $145 million to programs designed to move low-income residents into jobs, homes, or business ownership in Albina. A red-hot real estate market, however, had pumped eight times as much value into Albina's homes and stores. Since 1990 at least 844 properties, the reporters found, had "flipped," meaning they were bought and resold within twelve months.

In 1990 city inspectors counted 700 derelict buildings in Albina. At that time some buildings' values had sunk so low that it would have cost more to bring them up to code than leave them vacant. Other buildings were seized by the county for unpaid taxes. The real estate boom hastened the rehabilitation of hundreds of dilapidated properties. Where once banks would not lend, today they welcome customers, the article reported. By September 1996 the number of derelict buildings had dropped to 100. The demand for investment property in Albina is so great that the city sells lists of derelict buildings for $10 apiece.

How was such a revival triggered in Albina? "Government and volunteer social programs can take credit for planting the seeds of renewal," the article observed. "The urban growth boundary can take credit for herding people inward. Community patrols can take credit for standing toe-to-toe with crime. . . . But the gains blossoming in Albina these days have much more basic roots: *profit*. In five years, a booming real estate market has done for Albina what fifty years of government and social programs alone could not."

In the 1990s Albina's revival is not unique in the Portland region. New investment is flowing into older blue-collar suburbs such as Gresham, Milwaukie, and Oregon City. The *Oregonian,* I think, understated the urban growth boundary's impact. By controlling peripheral growth the urban growth boundary has turned market demand inward. Albina, Gresham, Milwaukie, and Oregon City are reviving because of Metro's growth management policies. The "inside game" succeeds because the "outside game" succeeds.

Progress brings new problems, of course. "As home values rise, Albina's poorest residents are finding it harder to rent, much less buy," the *Oregonian*'s story noted. "The inner-city's revival is walking hand-in-hand with gentrification. Most home loans are made to whites, encouraging a shift in

Table 8-1. *Change in Segregation Indexes in Metro Portland High Schools, 1989–98*

Racial or ethnic group	Percentage of students		Segregation index	
	1989–90	1997–98	1989–90	1997–98
All minorities	13.6	17.7	39.0	30.5
Black	4.7	4.1	65.7	62.5
Hispanic	2.5	6.1	30.0	27.0
Asian	5.4	6.4	39.1	36.4
Native American	1.0	1.0	43.7	32.2

the racial character of Portland's largest African-American community. As Albina residents celebrate their long-awaited shot at economic redemption, some wonder: As we save our neighborhood, will we lose our neighbors?"

It is certainly a fair question, but it can be overdramatized. Despite a 33 percent poverty rate among Albina's black residents in 1990, more than half were already homeowners. They have benefited from what few black homeowners experience nationally, a sustained increase in the value of their home. In the five-year period, home values at least doubled in each of Albina's thirteen neighborhoods.

The newspaper also found that credit is flowing more readily to black homeowners. More than 260 African Americans applied for home loans in 1994, an increase of 50 percent over 1992.[6] During the 1990s, however, housing prices have increased four times as fast as the average incomes of Albina residents. According to the *Oregonian*'s calculations, in 1990 nine out of ten Albina properties were affordable for its residents. By 1995 only six out of ten were still affordable. Low-income renters—black and white—faced a growing squeeze.

School enrollments offer some measure of trends in racial segregation between census reports (table 8-1). In *Cities without Suburbs* I had calculated segregation indexes for all public high schools in the nation's 320 metro areas for 1989–90. The school segregation index for black students in Portland (66) matched the region's housing segregation index (also 66). (With-

6. Applications from whites rose 53 percent, to 2,645, in the same period, and were approved at a slightly higher rate. As a result, more than 80 percent of the increased lending activity from 1992—both in dollars and number of loans—involved white buyers.

out a court-ordered school desegregation plan for the Portland area, school enrollment patterns would be expected to mirror housing patterns.) Seven years later, the level of school segregation had dropped for all racial groups, including for black students, who saw it fall from 66 to 62. The change reflects changing housing patterns, of course. The diminished isolation of black students, for example, was due both to white regentrification of areas of black concentration (such as Albina) and to the steady movement of blacks into other neighborhoods throughout the Portland region.

Growth Boundaries and Housing Affordability

Until the 1990s, the affordability of housing had not been a pressing regional issue. From the original legislative debates in the early 1970s onward, critics argued that urban growth boundaries would artificially inflate land costs, thus reducing housing affordability and inhibiting economic development. During the urban growth boundary's first decade, Portland's urbanized population grew 14 percent while urbanized land grew only 11 percent. (Portland was one of the few urban areas in which population grew faster than land use.) New suburban areas had about 4,500 residents per square mile, about three times the typical density of new suburbs in the 1980s.

Until the mid-1980s, the Oregon economy languished as forest products, the state's leading industry, weathered a fifteen-year slump. With modest amounts of land available within the urban growth boundary and slow economic growth, area housing costs went down relative to national inflation for much of the period.

To evaluate the impact of the urban growth boundary and Metro's Housing Rule, the 1000 Friends of Oregon and the Home Builders Association of Metropolitan Portland jointly studied trends in the Portland housing market for 1985–89.[7] They found that the public policies had achieved their goals:

—Multifamily housing construction increased to 54 percent of all new housing in the region during 1985–89. Before the Housing Rule, multifamily housing (apartments, row houses, duplexes, four-plexes, and so on) rep-

---

7. Metro's Housing Rule requires that each of the region's three counties and twenty-four municipalities adopt comprehensive plans that allow for a construction mix that includes at least 50 percent apartments and townhouses. In addition, the Housing Rule sets minimum target housing densities of ten units per buildable acre in the city of Portland and six to eight units per buildable acre for most suburban areas. The Housing Rule was based on the premise that restricting development to smaller lots would result in more affordable housing.

resented only 30 percent of the region's planned, twenty-year supply of new housing.

—Lot sizes (and prices) on new single-family housing had been lowered. About two-thirds of the new homes were being built on lots smaller than 9,000 square feet, whereas the average lot measured 13,000 square feet for new housing already approved under local zoning plans in effect before the Housing Rule's enactment. Homes on large lots (larger than 9,000 square feet), on average, cost twice as much as homes on small lots (smaller than 7,000 square feet).

—Both policies helped manage regional growth while promoting affordable housing. During the five-year period, if the same amount of development had occurred under densities prevailing before the Housing Rule took effect, it would have consumed an additional 1,500 acres, an area in excess of two square miles. Because of the savings in land use realized, another 14,000 housing units could be built within the urban growth boundary. In communities throughout the region, the density of new development increased by 13–32 percent over levels before the Housing Rule, the most significant gains being in single-family development.

In terms of overall affordability, the study found that 77 percent of the region's households could afford to rent the median-priced two-bedroom apartment while 67 percent could afford mortgage payments on the median-priced two-bedroom home, and 43 percent could afford the median-priced three-bedroom home. "Without state-mandated housing policies," the study concluded, "[local] zoning would exclude low and moderate income housing from some communities, and the Portland area would likely be suffering from the same 'affordability crisis' other fast-growing areas are now experiencing."[8]

By the time of our visit in February 1996—a half-dozen years after both the 1990 census and the Housing Rule study—the Portland area was clearly drifting toward a crisis over affordable housing that extended well beyond the Albina neighborhood. The trigger was rapid economic growth. The long, forest industry–based recession was a memory. High-tech industry was "bustin' out all over." Some $13 billion worth of new high-tech plants for corporate heavyweights such as Intel, Fujitsu Microelectronics, and LSI Logic was under construction.[9] Unemployment had dropped to less than 4 per-

8. 1000 Friends of Oregon and Home Builders Association of Metropolitan Portland (1991).
9. In fact, in 1995, for the first time in Oregon's history, forest products were supplanted as the state's leading industry by Portland's high-tech companies.

cent. The "local" labor force was tapped out, and new jobs were being filled by newcomers moving from around the country.

With the sudden, heavy demand for new homes created by the new-comers (especially former Californians with substantial home equities to reinvest), housing prices had been shooting up. The *Washington Post* reported that "the median price of a single-family home had risen from $64,000 in 1989 to $139,900 in 1996. During that same period Portland has gone from being ranked by the National Homebuilders Association as one of the most affordable U.S. cities for housing to being the fifth least affordable city."[10]

Amid the rising concern over housing costs, Portland Metro and several other local groups sponsored an affordable housing conference in September 1997. Attention focused mainly on Maryland's Montgomery County, whose long experience with affordable housing policies I had championed in my visit to Portland (as I have everywhere). For almost a quarter-century, Montgomery County laws have mandated that at least 15 percent of major new construction be sold or rented at prices within the reach of low- and modest-income households (see chapter 9). Veterans of Montgomery County's path-breaking housing policies (including Bernard Tetreault, long-time head of its Housing Opportunities Commission; Eric Larson, zoning administrator of the moderately priced dwelling unit policy; and Gus Baumann, former chairman of the planning commission) made effective presentations. In the aftermath, Portland Metro began seriously considering whether to require mixed-income housing in all major new development in the Portland region.[11]

10. William Claiborne, "Cracks in Portland's 'Great Wall,'" *Washington Post,* September 29, 1997, p. A1. Aside from the fact that the survey figures report home sales for metro areas rather than just cities (as the *Post* article stated), the National Homebuilders Association's national "housing affordability index" must be approached with caution. Calculated each quarter, the index is highly volatile, matching median income estimates (soft data) with median prices of single-family homes sold (harder data). During the 1990s, other western boomtowns—Salt Lake City, Denver, Albuquerque, for example—also emerged as "least affordable housing" regions like Portland. The factors were the same: rapid influxes of job-seeking workers (holding wage rates down) put sudden pressure on housing markets that could not expand as rapidly. The impetus for Portland and Albuquerque's booms was the same: multibillion-dollar new Intel plants. As boomtown conditions recede, such housing markets adjust back to their more regular equilibrium.

11. Metro's authority to adopt such measures is well tested. In November 1996, for example, Metro enacted ten ordinances to help implement its regional framework plan, among them an ordinance banning any further retail stores in excess of 60,000 square feet on industrially zoned land. In other words, no more Sam's Club or Costco warehouses or Home Depots. Metro's goals were many: conserve industrial sites for future Intels, reduce vehicle miles traveled ("big box category killers" rely on fifteen- to twenty-mile commuter sheds), and strengthen smaller retailers (particularly in pedestrian- and transit-friendly commercial areas). Though the measures were hotly

After the conference, Portland Metro wrestled with what additional measures to take to generate construction of more affordable housing. The Metro Council adopted a series of financial incentives and eased certain regulatory requirements that were barriers to lower-cost housing. However, the Metro Council backed away from adopting a Montgomery County–type "inclusionary" zoning ordinance mandating a minimum level of affordable housing in all new developments. Responding to pleas from homebuilders and some local governments, it announced a one-year delay to allow local groups to develop their own voluntary affordable housing initiatives. If voluntary local plans did not show promise of major results, the council warned, it would resume consideration of an areawide mandatory zoning ordinance.

I believe that Portland Metro will have to adopt just such a decisive measure. From the evidence of public school records, even as racial and ethnic segregation is diminishing, economic segregation (at least among the school-age population) appears to have risen during the prosperous 1990s. From 1989–90 to 1997–98 the percentage of low-income elementary school children in a four-county region receiving free or reduced-price school lunches increased substantially, from 24 percent to 33 percent. I have calculated dissimilarity indexes regarding the distribution of these low-income pupils throughout the region's 266 public elementary schools. In the eight-year period the economic segregation index among elementary school children increased slightly from 37 to 40, suggesting that residential segregation of low-income families (at least, those with school-age children) is increasing as well.

How could the percentage of low-income schoolchildren be increasing in the midst of the Portland area's thriving economy? The reality is that boomtowns have downsides as well as upsides. Many of the newcomers migrating into the region are filling low-wage retail and service-sector jobs that leave their families still eligible for free or reduced-price lunches.[12] The irony of continued want in the midst of record low unemployment was highlighted in a cover article entitled "The Revenge of the 'Baristas'" that analyzed the expansion of low-wage jobs in the boomtown economy.[13] ("Baristas" is a slang term coined by Hispanic immigrants for jobs as bartenders, waitresses, and busboys in Portland's yuppie bars and restaurants.)

---

debated, the Metro Council approved the measures, and the area's cities and counties must conform to the new rules.

12. The nationwide eligibility cut-off levels were 135 percent and 185 percent of the poverty level ($16,036 for a family of four in 1996) for free and reduced-price lunches, respectively.

13. Metroscape (1996).

Of course, with such a substantial increase in low-income schoolchildren, the modest rise in the segregation index might have been higher in another metro area that did not have Portland's activist growth management and affordable housing policies. Conventional housing industry practices nationwide promote greater economic segregation. Without changing the local ground rules, the Portland area is likely to follow the national trend.

Revisiting the Urban Growth Boundary

Portland's boom spurred Metro to make yet another assessment of the existing urban growth boundary. By the early 1990s Metro had begun an extensive program to update its long-range regional plans. It forecast that the four-county area (including Clark County, Washington) would grow by an additional 1.1 million people during the next fifty years, for a total of 2.5 million people. Furthermore, the region's population would have a much older average age by the year 2040, a lower average household size, and a more diverse racial and ethnic makeup. By 1996, however, just five years later, the region had already added almost 40 percent of the population growth expected for the next fifty years. Most of the inventory of vacant land within the original urban growth boundary had been used up.

Even though the best plans can be overcome by events and must be modified further to accommodate new realities, it is instructive to examine the Portland area's planning process. An early step was Metro's development of four alternative "concepts for growth" in June 1994. The base case anticipated no change in current development patterns and densities. Under the base case, the current urban growth boundary would have to be expanded by about 120,000 acres (a 50 percent increase) to accommodate new population. The three alternative concepts assumed new local, state, and federal land use and transportation policies. Concept A would expand the boundary modestly while promoting higher-density development. Concept B would seek to absorb all population growth within the current boundary at much higher densities and with the most intensive public transit system. Concept C projected that much of the region's growth would be directed toward relatively compact "satellite cities" outside, separated from the urban growth boundary by extensive greenbelts; the remaining growth would be absorbed within the current boundary.

Metro held 182 public meetings with local government officials and citizens. To supplement these presentations, Metro produced a video and made it available through area Blockbuster Video stores and libraries. It mailed a tabloid and questionnaire, featuring multicolored maps of the alternative concepts, to all 550,000 households in the Portland area. More than 17,000 questionnaires were mailed back, 10,000 with additional written comments beyond the choices checked off on the questionnaire.

The Metro staff consolidated all sources of information and reaction into a "recommended concept." Among the major provisions, the staff recommended that the urban growth boundary be expanded by 14,500 acres during the fifty-year period. The average lot size for new single-family homes regionwide would be 6,650 square feet, or 6.5 units per net acre. The ratio of single-family to multifamily homes would be 62 percent to 38 percent (compared with the current 70:30 ratio). One-third of the buildable acres would allow mixed uses and two-thirds would remain in single-use categories such as residential or industrial. About 19,300 acres of currently developed urban land would be redeveloped for more intensive uses, while open space would be conserved in 14 percent of the boundary area.

In effect, Metro's recommended concept was a melding of concept B and concept C, with the satellite cities renamed "neighbor cities." It envisioned twenty-five town centers throughout the metropolitan region, each with its own downtown offering shops and services within walking or biking distance from nearby housing. Most of the nine "regional centers" projected would be built along the light rail lines linking major suburban municipalities to downtown Portland. The recommended concept was adopted by the Metro Council in December 1994.

However, pressures kept building within the urban growth boundary. In early 1997 the Metro council amended the "urban growth reserve" area from 14,500 acres to nearly 19,000 acres, including 2,500 acres of current farmland (the latter over Executive Officer Mike Burton's strong objections). By late 1997, the council was poised to extend the urban growth boundary formally into some portion of the reserved lands. Burton recommended an expansion of 3,000–4,000 acres. Don Morissette, a conservative Republican who is the only builder-developer on the council, proposed a boundary expansion of 8,000–10,000 acres. Adopting a middle ground was Metro council's presiding officer, Jon Kvistad, who stated: "I think we're looking at a 6,000-acre expansion this time. I know that it's not very politically correct to expand the urban growth boundary, but we have to do it."[14] In compari-

14. Beyond the vocal opposition of many environmentally concerned groups and citizens, all twenty-four area mayors, including the mayors of municipalities abutting the current boundary that would likely annex any new development within the expanded territory, testified against boundary expansion.

son with the rate of uncontrolled sprawl in other communities, Kvistad observed, "our 6,000 acres is not very much. It is just a pittance."[15]

Finally, in November 1997 the Metro Council voted 5–2 to add less than 4,000 acres (about 6 square miles) to Portland's existing 342-square-mile urban growth boundary. (The two dissenting voters, Morissette and Kvistad, felt the expansion was too little.) As Metro Councilor Ed Washington, whose District 6 includes Albina, explained his vote for the small boundary expansion, "We are having redevelopment in my district for the first time in forty years; we don't want to lose it."

Individual Goals, Community Means

Beyond the statistics, beyond official planning documents, beyond consultant studies, the best evidence of the success of Portland's growth management policies is the quality of life in so much of the region. It is found in Forest Park and Sauvie Island and in other parkland and natural areas to be acquired through the $138 million bond issue for open space acquisition approved by the voters of the three-county area in November 1995. It is found in strong, healthy city neighborhoods such as Hawthorne, Northwest Twenty-Third, and Irvington. Even the poorest neighborhoods, such as the majority-black Albina area or Brentwood-Davlington, do not exude the odor of despair, decay, and abandonment so typical of poverty neighborhoods in other cities that are being sucked dry by uncontrolled urban sprawl. Indeed, with its growth management policies, the Portland area is clearly experiencing an economic resurgence in many of its "traditional" neighborhoods within the city and some older suburbs.

Downtown Portland is also being rejuvenated. Of the many vibrant, interesting downtowns I have visited and admired—such as downtown Baltimore, Pittsburgh, or Cincinnati—Portland certainly relies more on public transportation than the others. Tri-Met's east-west light rail line and extensive bus routes converge on Portland's downtown transit mall; some 45 per-

15. As indeed it is. To place the issue in some perspective, anticipating a 50 percent growth in population by 2040, the Portland region plans to urbanize an additional 8 percent of its land. By contrast, the Detroit region projects only 6 percent population growth by 2020 but will consume 40 percent more land. Farmland conservation? The 2,500 acres of farmland the Portland region will take forty-five years to convert would be paved over in the state of Michigan in just ten days (on the basis of estimates of the South East Michigan Council of Governments and the Michigan Society of Planning Officials).

cent of all workers and shoppers in downtown Portland enter by public transportation, bicycle, or on foot. By contrast, more than 80 percent of users of downtown Baltimore, Pittsburgh, or Cincinnati arrive one per car. And, with another $445 million bond issue just approved, Portland's light rail system will be extended south from downtown into Clackamas County (with hopes for a future northward extension across the Columbia River to Vancouver, Washington).

Yet, beyond transportation distinctions, each of these other downtown areas feels fragile and threatened, even threatening, at night. These downtowns are surrounded by poverty neighborhoods. By contrast, Portland's downtown is surrounded by strong, mixed-income neighborhoods. There is a depth and solidity to downtown Portland that compels confidence in its future.

There is much to praise about Portland, and in my talk to the City Club, I had more praise for Portland's achievements than for any other of the seventy communities I had visited. Beyond even the value of its growth management policies, I concluded, the Portland community exemplifies an ideology that can breathe hope into our nation's despairing cities.

"Living now in Washington, D.C.," I told the audience, "I am bombarded daily by the ideology of the so-called 'Conservative Revolution.' But it seems to me that this revolution is based on two false propositions.

"The first is that as a society we Americans are overtaxed . . . that if we just get government off our backs, we will all prosper. Well, as a matter of fact, an annual study done by the Organization for Economic Cooperation and Development [OECD] shows that all national, state, and local taxes add up to slightly more than 29 percent of our gross domestic product. That is the second lowest tax level of any of the twenty-three member countries. We are slightly more taxed than Australians and slightly less taxed than the Japanese (who don't have big military forces to support). Our level of taxation is far below, for example, that of the Norwegians, the Swedes, or the Dutch, whose tax levels approach half their gross domestic product.

"Yet another report of the OECD," I continued, "shows that the United States has the widest income disparities of any economically developed society and that income inequality in our society is growing rapidly. I think that these two trends—a low tax level and growing economic inequality—are related. This trendy ideological notion that we are overtaxed has one clear sponsor and one clear beneficiary—the already rich. Public taxation is the vehicle through which we can afford collectively what most of us, unlike the rich, cannot afford individually.

"As a region, Portlanders have been willing to tax themselves for things that are important to you—for example, $134 million for parklands and wildlife preservation, $445 million to expand your light rail system. In a nation where many communities are consuming the seed corn of their future through blind adherence to antitax apostles, Portland's example is important.

"The second false proposition is that government cannot do anything right," I continued. "It is particularly ironic to hear that philosophy expressed by elderly persons. Thirty years ago the largest group of poor Americans consisted of the elderly. Through tremendous improvements in social security, medicare, federal private pension regulation, poverty among the elderly has been almost abolished. Almost 38 cents of every federal dollar is spent on aid to the elderly. The elderly are better off today as a group than the rest of American society. It's just wrong to claim that government can't do *any-thing* right. Having largely eliminated poverty and want among the elderly is just the first of a long list of things that government has done right.

"But the people of this region are a constant example of citizens who recognize that some individual goals can only be achieved through collective action, and that government is the vehicle for such collective action. Time and again you have reaffirmed that faith: in your three different referenda authorizing Metro's powers, in your constant participation in the regional planning process, in key bond votes to provide the money to achieve important land use and transportation goals.

"You are constantly engaged in the struggle to balance individual rights and individual initiatives with community goals and communal effort. There are no permanent 'right' answers. The task is always to keep pursuing the proper balance. But Portland serves as the school for America. You teach us that our most precious inheritance is precisely government of the people, by the people, and for the people."

Portland has, of course, a better way to convey what I took thirty-five minutes to tell that City Club audience. Three months later Mike Burton, Metro's executive officer, and I were sharing the podium at an Albuquerque Chamber of Commerce retreat. Mike was asked to comment on the Goals for Albuquerque, a community-wide "visioning" process in which a dozen committees involving several hundred volunteers had participated for over a year.

"We produced a wonderful Goals for Albuquerque report but very little has actually happened since," the local questioner complained.

"How long was your goals statement?" Mike asked.

"About 200 pages."

"Well, for starters, that is probably 199 pages too long," Mike responded. "We express our vision for Portland in just two sentences:

Everyone can always see Mount Hood.

Every child can walk to a library.

An almost electric charge surged through me on first hearing Portland's vision statement. As I thought more and more about it, the more layers of complexity the simple words contained. "Everyone can always see Mount Hood." Of course, that did not mean everyone would have a big picture window facing eastward. It meant that everyone could always look through forty miles of urban air and see Mount Hood clearly. Controlling sprawl. More buses and trolleys, fewer autos. Clustering homes, stores, and offices in walkable communities. Less air pollution.

And "Every child can always walk to a library." This is not a statement of the American Library Association's wildest dream, but a vision in which all children (and their parents) would feel safe from bad traffic and bad people on the streets, that many stores, schools, parks, and playgrounds as well as the library would be within walking distance, that all children would *want* to walk to a library. Is it any wonder that the Intels of the world are flocking to Portland?

9

Montgomery County, Maryland: Mixing Up the Neighborhood

MARYLAND'S MONTGOMERY COUNTY, lying outside Washington, is the nation's sixth richest county—and as I drove along River Road on a warm, sunny Saturday afternoon in mid-June, it looked every bit that wealthy. Leaving behind imposing country houses set back a quarter mile from the road, behind their white, horse farm–style wooden fences, I passed through the upscale, white-and-gray trim stores of Potomac Village, then turned right up Falls Road. To the left, the Falls Road Golf Course was moderately crowded, a public course masquerading as a private country club. To the right, the red brick manorial buildings and spacious grounds of the private Bullis Prep School were deserted that day. Colorful banners advertised soccer and lacrosse clinics that, on summer weekdays, would fill acres and acres of well-manicured playing fields with the sons and daughters of many of the national capital's most successful and powerful people.

I turned left off Falls Road onto Eldwick Way, the golf course still on my left. A half mile's drive up this country lane, a low brick sign in the center of a tastefully landscaped traffic island announced my destination: Fallswick. Turning into the Fallswick neighborhood, I cruised slowly past large homes, pulled into Lost Trail Way, parked in a space marked off around a landscaped berm at the end of a cul-de-sac and, walking down the gently sloping street, set off to interview the neighbors.

As I surveyed the 9500 block of Lost Trail Way, I noticed a paved path running between two houses. Fifty yards down the path was a four- or five-acre lake, surrounded by a discreet, wood-and-wire fence to keep toddlers out. It was certainly an attractive, well-maintained neighborhood amenity. New-mowed lawns carried right down to the water's edge. The lake served as the neighborhood's principal storm drainage facility. Whether it also doubled as a recreational lake, I could not tell.

Talking with the Neighbors

Returning to Lost Trail Way, I began to canvass the homes along the 9500 block. Each was different, yet basically the same. All were large, detached, two-story, brick colonial homes with peaked roofs and relatively narrow sideyards. Color schemes varied: red brick, white brick, cream-colored brick, gray brick; red shutters, black shutters, gray shutters. Attached two-car garages extended either left or right from the houses. Landscaping was similarly varied, yet almost all yards were immaculately groomed. These were expensive homes even for Montgomery County, probably around $500,000–$550,000 each.

One of the verities of the American way of life is that, no matter what hour a political candidate or neighborhood canvasser selects, most people are not home. This Saturday afternoon was no exception. But, working up both sides of the two-block street, I developed a rough profile of the residents of Lost Trail Way, using a "neighborhood satisfaction survey" as a tool to gather information.

A grandmother from Taiwan, living with her divorced son (an employee of Hughes Communications) and two grandchildren . . . a Chinese American physicist at the Applied Physics Lab, his wife, and two young children . . . a white woman, too busy with two young children to talk . . . two different homes where the women of the house, through security intercoms, indicated no interest in being interviewed . . . the military attaché of the Spanish Embassy, his wife and three children . . . the teenage son of a Korean couple who owned a beer and wine delicatessen in the District of Columbia . . . a white couple in their mid-thirties with one child, who just moved into the neighborhood five months earlier . . . an Asian American couple with two children (he worked as a computer consultant, she as a part-time administrator of her local church) . . . another young Asian American man, a bookkeeper, living with his two parents . . . a young white man.

There were seven houses with no one home and few visual clues: a proliferation of basketball backboards in the driveways, Jewish mezuzahs on a couple of front doors, and one house belonging to a University of Michigan graduate (judging by the doorbell, which played a stanza of "The Victors," the Wolverines' fight song).

I reached the 9400 block of Lost Trail Way, where the housing type shifted from detached, single-family houses to large, elegant townhouses. These cost about $350,000–$400,000 each. One- or two-car detached garages, thrusting forward from the townhouses, dominated the streetscape. A peculiar design. Yet walking up to each front door, I realized that the arrangement created more privacy for the front yards and little patios tucked behind the detached garage structures. Again, each property was well landscaped. If anything, the townhouse residents seemed to invest more of themselves into their patio gardens. Probably a greater proportion of "empty nesters" lived here, though all the townhouses were three- and four-bedroom units.

I began my survey again. A white attorney with two teenage children . . . another white family . . . a white management consultant, his wife (manager of the local furniture store), and their grown son (a computer consultant) . . . another Jewish household (judging by the religious symbol on the front door) . . . an Asian American household, busily greeting young guests to a child's party . . . a white vice president of Lockheed Martin, the huge defense contractor, which has its headquarters in Montgomery County . . . two more Jewish households (again with religious symbols displayed; Congregation Har Shalom and the Washington Hebrew Congregation's Julia Bindman Center both lie within a mile of Fallswick) . . . a realtor, originally from a South Asian country, watching his two young girls bicycling around the landscaped island at the end of the cul-de-sac . . . another Asian American household . . . a white couple, a phone call cutting short our conversation before I could find out more about them . . . another white couple . . . a red-haired young woman (more likely the family's daughter) who declined to be interviewed . . . a retired army colonel (white) now serving as a defense industry consultant . . . a white vice president of a local biotech company, his wife (a radiologist in private practice), and their twenty-three-year-old son, a student at the nearby University of Maryland . . . another young white woman . . . the largest townhouse on the block with a substantial sideyard, with a notice to call a certain telephone number "in case of emergency" (a doctor's house? a plumber's?) . . . ten townhouses with nobody home, though one with a "for sale" sign in front was already "under contract."

I reached the end of the 9400 block. The housing style changed once more. Tidy, more compact, two-story brick townhouses, in two rows obliquely angled to each other, formed the head of the cul-de-sac. They were separated from the rows of larger townhouses only by grassed alleys. These were clearly more modest, but still tastefully done units, each with two or three bedrooms. The most visible difference between these townhouses and those of their neighbors was that they lacked private garages. Residents' cars were parked in marked spaces either in front of the units or perpendicular to the landscaped berm in the middle of the cul-de-sac (where I had parked). Though closer to the street than any other homes, the shallow front yards were also neatly landscaped and well cared for. Whatever their market value, I already knew that these homes sold for about $80,000 each.

I continued the canvass: an African American couple, she calling out instructions to him about how to drive their two young children to the local library branch . . . a Taiwanese computer consultant, with wife and eight-year-old daughter . . . another African American woman, little girl tugging at her skirt, declining to be interviewed . . . a white loan manager at a local credit union and his wife (salesperson for the Yellow Pages) . . . a woman from El Salvador with a nine-year-old son (she worked as an assistant in a private laboratory) . . . another black woman in her mid-thirties and her six-year-old son; she was a customer service representative in the Metro system's special paratransit service for the mobility handicapped but hoped to shift to a job with county government . . . a fourth African American household, a woman and her eleven-year-old son; she was an accounts payable supervisor for a local land development company . . . four households with nobody home.

The longest conversation took place with a young white mother with two children of preschool age. Her son and an older playmate (the son of the Salvadoran woman) were playfully brandishing their Super Soakers at the two little girls riding their bicycles around (daughters of the South Asian realtor across the street). Throughout the conversation, the young daughter clung to her mother. Her husband, she told me, worked in computer operations at the headquarters of Fannie Mae, the mortgage market giant, the nation's largest financial institution, which is headquartered in Washington. She herself took occasional assignments organizing auctions of property confiscated by the U.S. Customs Service. They had lived in their townhouse for more than eight years.

"How do you like the neighborhood?" (One of my standard questions.) "Would you say that you are very satisfied, somewhat satisfied, somewhat dissatisfied, or very dissatisfied?"

"Oh, very satisfied," she replied emphatically.

"What do you like best about the neighborhood?"

"Everything . . . it's clean . . . quiet . . . safe . . . a good mix of different people . . . friendly."

"Does your son go to Wayside Elementary?"

"Not yet. He's still at Potomac Village, a private preschool. But I've heard wonderful things about Wayside," she added.

"How would you rate Montgomery County government: very satisfied, somewhat satisfied, somewhat dissatisfied, very dissatisfied?"

"I have no complaints. I don't get involved."

I thanked her, and began to turn away.

"Do you know that all these townhouses are 'MPDUs'?" The question seemed to explode eagerly from her.

I confessed that I did know about the MPDUs, or moderately priced dwelling units. (Indeed, they were the reason for my neighborhood survey.)

"These thirteen townhouses are all MPDUs," she continued, waving her hand at the two rows of smaller townhouses. "Eight years ago my husband had just graduated from college and was working for the government. He wasn't earning half of what we earn now so we qualified for an MPDU. We entered the lottery the county conducted to allocate them. Our number was pulled out, and we bought this townhouse.

"It's been great for us," she continued. "Oh, with two children now, our townhouse is a bit small. Now that we're doing a lot better, we're saving up our money. If we moved up today to the kind of house I'd really like, though, I'd probably have to go back to work full time. I wouldn't trade the opportunity to stay home with my children now for any dream house. So we'll wait for the ten-year grace period to be up and hope to sell this house afterwards for a good enough price that we can buy a bigger home without my having to go back to work full time."

(If MPDU purchasers sell their townhouse within ten years after the first purchase, I had read in the county's program description, the resale price must still fall within control levels. After the ten-year period, when they can sell at market price, the owners have to split any equity increase with the county's revolving Housing Initiative Fund. This young couple was waiting out the ten-year period before putting their townhouse on the market in order to benefit from any price increase.)

"You know that five of these thirteen townhouses are owned by the county?" she asked, indicating, with unerring accuracy, which five belonged to the Montgomery County Housing Opportunities Commission (HOC). Three of the HOC units, I knew, were federally financed "public housing units" whose tenants qualified at the lowest end of the income scale. The other two the county dubbed "McHomes," subsidized by a special county fund; typically, their residents were slightly higher up the income scale.

"How are your neighbors?"

"Fine," she replied. "Oh, there was one that caused some trouble some time back, but they're gone. I'm sure that the county moved them out. The county keeps a pretty careful eye on things."

"How about maintenance on the properties?"

"The county keeps up their property, and we owners keep up ours. Of course, the Homeowners Association takes care of all the common areas and picks up all the trash as well. I think that our fees in these townhouses are actually higher than the fees paid by the owners of bigger houses." It was the first real complaint that she'd had. (As a "homeowner" of five townhouses, the Housing Opportunities Commission pays the requisite assessments to the Fallswick Homeowners Association on behalf of its tenants.)

"The MPDU program is a great program," she concluded. "It's given us a chance." Indeed, the MPDU program had given a real chance to thirteen families in Fallswick, both the eight owner-occupant families like hers and the five renter families of the HOC-owned townhouses.

In all the interviews only two other neighbors mentioned the MPDUs. The retired colonel was "a little apprehensive when I first moved into the neighborhood, but it's turned out OK." (His judgment was not based just on being a neighbor located four doors from the nearest MPDU. He also was an officer of the Homeowners Association.) And the realtor expressed the thought that his own property might appreciate a little more in value if the MPDUs were of the same quality. "They look just fine from over here," he noted from his front yard, "but up close you can see that they're not of the same quality of construction.

"However, the county's housing laws are the best laws we have," he observed. "I haven't lived in a lot of places in this country, but overall Montgomery County is a very good place. Montgomery County stands out."

The Moderately Priced Dwelling Unit Policy

Within Montgomery County, the Fallswick subdivision is not unique. Much the same social diversity is found in many mixed-income housing developments, such as Normandie Crest, Deer Park at Fairland Green, or North Sherwood Forest, scattered throughout Montgomery County. Among Ameri-

can communities, Montgomery County stands out for its integrated neighborhoods, integrated both by racial and ethnic group and, most uncom-
monly, by income class.

The level of economic integration is not the result of any progressive
business ethic among local developers and builders (although several builders active in Montgomery County have become national champions of
mixed-income communities). Montgomery County's neighborhoods have
mixed-income housing because Montgomery County law requires it.

The county government has the nation's most progressive mixed-income housing laws, in particular, the Moderately Priced Dwelling Unit Ordinance, adopted in 1973. By law, all new subdivisions in Montgomery
County must contain a mix of housing for different income groups: 85 percent market rate (at whatever income levels the developer targets) and 15
percent priced for moderate-income households.[1]

Though Montgomery County was the earliest, a number of communities now have mandatory mixed-income housing laws. What sets Montgomery County apart is the extra mile county government travels in its
commitment to mixed-income housing. The county government requires
builders to give first right of purchase for one-third of the MPDUs to the
Montgomery County Housing Opportunities Commission, the county's
public housing authority. For almost a quarter century Montgomery County
has not built public housing projects for low-income families. Its Housing
Opportunities Commission simply buys standard new housing in regular
new subdivisions—up to 5 percent of all that is built by private developers—as an inventory of rental units for its low-income families.[2]

A "Big Box" Government

To understand how this happened one must look at the special role of county
government in Maryland. From colonial days onward, county government
has been Maryland's primary form of local government. State law provides
for the creation of municipalities, but relatively few Marylanders actually

1. The county sets the maximum eligible income at 65 percent of the county's median household income. In other words, moderate-income households fall within the lowest third of the population economically.

2. Fallswick fulfilled the formula exactly. By my count, Fallswick contained fifty-five detached
homes, twenty-six market-rate townhouses, and thirteen MPDUs (five owned by the county housing authority).

live within municipalities. There is, of course, Baltimore City (1997 estimated population: 657,256), which is, however, organized as its own county government as well. There are also the cities of Annapolis (33,234), Frederick (46,227), Hagerstown (34,633), Rockville (46,019), Gaithersburg (45,361), and 149 other smaller municipalities.[3]

However, Baltimore County, which geographically almost surrounds, but is a separate jurisdiction from Baltimore City, has 720,662 residents (1997 estimate) and no municipal governments whatsoever. With budgetary control over the unified, countywide school system, county government is the only local government in Baltimore County. Likewise, in fast-growing Howard County (1997 estimated population: 228,797), county government stands alone. In fact, classifying Baltimore City as a county rather than a municipality (as an "independent city," city government exercises all county powers), only about one-quarter of Maryland's 5.1 million residents live within municipalities.

Montgomery County is a prime example of a "big box" community. Under Maryland law, Montgomery County, like all counties, has a single, unified, countywide school system. With over 128,000 students, the Montgomery County Public School system is one of the nation's twenty largest and clearly one of the best. Under another state law enacted in 1927, county government exercises exclusive planning and zoning control throughout the 495-square-mile county, except for the cities of Rockville and Gaithersburg and five small villages whose existing zoning powers were grandfathered. (These seven municipalities total only about 12 percent of the county's population.) Though there are nominally seventeen municipalities within Montgomery County, county government is the only local government of real consequence.[4] Well-known areas such as Bethesda and Silver Spring are just place names, not incorporated municipalities; county government is their residents' only government.

For decades Montgomery County was primarily a suburb of Washington. By 1950 the county population was still just 164,401 residents; about three-quarters worked in Washington. Median family income was $5,259 (about one-third higher than the District of Columbia's median family in-

---

3. All municipal populations are based on the 1996 census estimates, except Baltimore City.

4. Montgomery County's empowerment by the Maryland legislature has led to perhaps the nation's most comprehensive growth management system. Key elements are the long-range "wedges and corridors" comprehensive plan, the annual growth policy, the Adequate Public Facilities Ordinance (linking subdivision approval to the orderly construction of public facilities), and the transferable development rights program (to help preserve one-third of the county as agricultural land).

come). Though middle-class subdivisions were beginning to spring up, at midcentury many Montgomery County residents still paid nonresident tuition to send their children to the more prestigious (and still racially segregated) public schools in the District of Columbia.

Over the next two decades, however, Montgomery County boomed. Thousands of high-quality professional and technical jobs were created at Bethesda Naval Hospital, the National Institutes of Health, the National Bureau of Standards, and other federal installations. By 1970 the county's population had ballooned to 522,809. More than half now worked at jobs located in Montgomery County itself. Average incomes were high; median family income was $16,710, now almost 75 percent higher than in the District of Columbia. The racial cleavage was also clear. The District's population was 65 percent black; Montgomery County's population was 92 percent white.

The Campaign for Affordable Housing

County government was highly respected, activist, and progressive. In response to a vigorous campaign conducted by the League of Women Voters, Suburban Maryland Fair Housing, and other citizen groups, the county council adopted a model Fair Housing Ordinance. The county acted several years before Martin Luther King's assassination fueled congressional support for passage of the Civil Rights Act of 1968.

By the end of the 1960s, a severe shortage of affordable housing had developed in the county. The economic boom, subdivision restrictions, and a temporary moratorium on new water and sewer connections had caused the price of building lots to accelerate much faster than general inflation. To maintain profitability in the face of curtailed volume, builders were constructing the largest and most profitable houses possible on virtually irreplaceable land. The prices of both new and existing housing escalated rapidly. Price escalation, civil rights advocates feared, could well negate the practical effects of the new Fair Housing Ordinance. An adequate supply of low- and moderate-income housing, the groups recognized, would be essential to achieve meaningful racial integration. They set out to secure county policies to diversify the local housing supply. It was a goal that, even in progressive Montgomery County, would take six years of constant effort to achieve.

The affordable housing advocates' first strategy focused on designating land as suitable sites for subsidized housing developments. In 1967 they persuaded county council member Ida Mae Garrott, a former League of Women

Voters president, to sponsor an amendment to the county's zoning ordinance. The amendment would require developers of "new towns" or "planned neighborhoods" to set aside land on which the county itself would build subsidized housing for low- and moderate-income families. The county attorney, declaring that such a requirement would be "conditional" zoning, promptly derailed the proposal.

Retreating in confusion, the housing advocates spent two years searching for both a new approach and more planning and legal expertise. "Fair housing" had been a civil rights issue argued largely on moral grounds. "Affordable housing" raised complex economic and technical issues. The Montgomery County groups allied themselves with the Metropolitan Washington Planning and Housing Association for professional assistance. Fortified by a grant from the Taconic Foundation, a key supporter of the national civil rights movement, in January 1970 the coalition established the Montgomery County Project for Low- and Moderate-Income Housing.

Meanwhile, the county's pending updated general plan contained two new proposed policies in the "housing element." First, the plan proposed it would be the county's official policy to seek "to house its total labor force as well as those families of low- or moderate-income that were currently living in the county." Second, the county would ensure "the economic feasibility of providing housing for all income levels" by ensuring "the provision of low- and moderate-income housing as part of all large-scale development, and as an option in smaller-scale development."

By mid-1970 the fair housing groups had succeeded in persuading the county council to adopt the proposed housing policy goals. The target shifted then to amending the county's zoning code to require low- and moderate-income housing in all new subdivision construction in Montgomery County, a path-breaking concept for the United States.

At this crucial juncture a startling political development occurred. Running on a unified platform, including a commitment to meet the housing needs of low- and moderate-income families in Montgomery County, Democratic candidates were elected to all seven county council seats in that November's election. The lone incumbent carryover, council member Garrott, became council chair. She immediately urged the housing advocacy groups to develop and submit a proposed ordinance.

After eight months the citizen work group, fortified by volunteer attorneys from one of Washington's top law firms, submitted their proposal. In all new housing developments of fifty or more units, they proposed, 20 percent must be moderately priced; one-third of the so-called MPDUs would be acquired by the county's Housing Opportunities Commission for low-income tenants. To compensate builders for developing one-fifth of their land at below-market potential, builders could negotiate a "density bonus" to allow them to build 20 percent more units on the site than conventional zoning would permit.

Initially positive about the proposal, several council members became skittish in the face of harsh criticism from the Development Advisory Board, a county-appointed group to represent development interests. Zina Greene, a key staff member for the housing advocate groups, remembers the Development Advisory Board well; "In our first meeting they were rude and outrageously inaccurate. . . . They were sure that they could prove that this was a hare-brained, do-gooder effort that certainly couldn't work. After all, if it were possible to build moderately priced housing, their attitude was that they would already be doing it."[5]

"Anyway," Zina continued, "the Development Advisory Board members argued that people like to live with their own kind and wouldn't buy housing in neighborhoods with economic diversity. . . . They even went so far as to warn the County Council about the 'kind of people' who would come to Montgomery County from the 'city' if such housing were available. Their vehement attack hung heavily over some Council members."

With the council's enthusiasm flagging, weeks dragged into months of delay. Only two council members publicly supported the proposal: Ida Mae Garrott and Norman Christeller. Of the five remaining members, one had never supported it, two were worried about citizen association opposition, and the remaining two had been shaken by the vehement criticism of the Development Advisory Board. The proposal had yet to be even formally introduced. Most critically, Garrott's year as council chair had expired, and a new chairperson might never schedule the proposal for introduction.

To that point the housing coalition had always approached council members in a very collegial manner. Now the housing coalition took a calculated risk. In late February 1971, the coalition prompted local newspaper and television to criticize the council's delay editorially. Council members were enraged at both the editorials and the coalition. How could council members be criticized when they were working so hard and were so committed to good government? But after their pique had passed, the legislation was formally introduced and public hearings were scheduled for early summer.

5. Memorandum, Zina Greene to the Metropolitan Washington Planning and Housing Association, October 4, 1972, pp. 53–54. Much of my early history of the MPDU ordinance is drawn from this document.

Now the coalition's effort shifted to mobilizing broad public support. The League of Women Voters and Suburban Maryland Fair Housing's educational efforts went into high gear. They distributed 30,000 educational flyers and circulated petitions of support. A speaker's bureau made dozens of presentations, using a slide and tape show. In a two-day workshop Congregations United for Shelter organized support from thirty local churches.

The grass-roots campaign came to a head in four public hearings in June and July 1972. More than seventy-five business, civic, religious, and housing groups testified in support. Most critical was the support expressed by three very respected homebuilders in the county. They cited current development procedures and showed how the density bonus could reduce costs sufficiently to allow them to build small housing units within the maximum price ceiling.

Opposition arguments fell into three broad categories. Though agreeing with the need for more affordable housing, the Maryland Suburban Home Builders, the Apartment House Council, and several builders argued for a voluntary rather than mandatory program. Several civic organizations objected to the density bonus provisions, fearing a shift in the single-family home character of their neighborhoods. Several opponents questioned the need for more affordable housing at all.

This final objection was countered effectively by the coalition's release of a new survey of local businesses. The county had embarked on an aggressive economic development program to diversify the local economy. It projected an increase of 90,000 jobs over the next decade. The survey showed that the projected increased employment base would generate a demand for 70,000 new housing units. Of the total, the occupational profile suggested, about one-third would have to be moderately priced, and about 10 percent would require public rent subsidies. Indeed, providing affordable housing to complement the county's economic growth and diversification was the central theme of the coalition's public education campaign.

Through the four hearings, buoyed by so much public support, council members increasingly warmed to the program. Council member Christeller took on passage of the MPDU ordinance as a personal crusade. Many months of careful drafting and compromise, however, still lay ahead. The MPDU percentage, for example, was reduced from 20 percent to 15 percent. Both buyers and renters would be subject to maximum income limits set by the county Department of Housing and Community Development. (Originally 80 percent, the upper ceiling for qualifying is now 65 percent of the county's median household income.) Rent limits would be controlled for twenty years.

Sale and resale prices for MPDUs would be controlled for five years (extended later to ten years). A portion of profits from the first resale after expiration of price controls would be recaptured by the county's revolving Housing Initiative Fund. The county's Housing Opportunities Commission would purchase one-third of the MPDUs for deep-subsidy households.

The county executive opposed the proposed ordinance, threatening a veto. The bill would have to have the support of at least five council members to be veto-proof. The final ordinance also had to be crafted to withstand potential court challenges. Above all, proponents were concerned that the MPDU requirement might be judged an unconstitutional taking of the builder's property; the density bonus would be a key defense against constitutional challenges.

Councilman Christeller pressed down hard. Finally, on October 23, 1973, the county council unanimously enacted the revised bill and overrode the county executive's ensuing veto, and on January 21, 1974, the Moderately Priced Dwelling Unit Ordinance became law. Its champions hailed the new ordinance as "the nation's first 'inclusionary' zoning law."

Because land previously subdivided did not contain density bonuses, all pending subdivisions were exempt from the new MPDU requirement. The first affordable housing built under the program was offered for sale to qualified purchasers and the HOC in 1976.

The MPDU Law's Impact

For two decades the Moderately Priced Dwelling Unit Ordinance has helped define how the housing industry does business in Montgomery County. The MPDU program has long since become part of the normal business climate for private builders in Montgomery County. Over the years county officials and builders have worked closely together to improve the program. One amendment in 1989 allowed builders to increase the allowable sales price by 10 percent to allow for design improvements that would make MPDUs more compatible with surrounding units (such as brick facings). Another change currently under consideration is to apply MPDU requirements in very low-density communities (that is, less than one dwelling unit per acre) whenever the property is served by public water and sewer systems.

"MPDU has been good for the county and good for the builders," Eric Larson, the county's MPDU administrator, observed, "and we have to give a lot of credit to the builders for making the program work."[6] During times of

6. Conversation with the author, June 1994.

soft housing markets, for example, some builders have even constructed MPDU allocations (for which there is always strong demand) in advance of their market-rate housing, bridging the slump in the market.

The policy has had a significant impact on the creation of affordable housing in Montgomery County. Through 1997, private developers had built 10,110 housing units under the MPDU policy; these included 7,305 sale units and 2,805 rental units. In the face of some limitations on funds available for purchase, over the years the HOC purchased more than 1,500 units. (Nonprofit organizations, which can now purchase units as well, own another 38 units.) The MPDU policy has been the HOC's largest source of scattered-site rental units for public housing families.

In a five-year period studied (1992–96), developers working under the MPDU policy built 123 rental units and 1,599 sale units. Of the new homes for sale, 8 percent had one bedroom, 23 percent had two bedrooms, and 69 percent had three or more bedrooms. The average sales price was $83,706 in 1996, which is a bargain in a county where the median housing value was $208,000 in 1990.

Turning to the characteristics of MPDU home purchasers, 41 percent were white, 22 percent black, 28 percent Asian, and 7 percent Hispanic. The average household income of MPDU buyers was $27,754 in 1996; only 6 percent of the purchasers even approached the program's income ceiling of $39,900 for a family of four.

When the MPDU program was being debated, a common anxiety expressed was that mixing low- and moderate-income housing (translation: low- and moderate-income *households*) into higher-income neighborhoods would drive down the price or dampen the appreciation of higher-end housing.

Updating an earlier study, in 1998 the Innovative Housing Institute (begun in 1996 by HOC's retired executive director, Bernard Tetreault) examined trends in resale prices of 1,012 nonsubsidized dwellings sold between 1992 and 1996 either within or next to fourteen subdivisions with subsidized housing. Eight were located in Montgomery County and six in neighboring Fairfax County, Virginia (which had adopted its own affordable dwelling unit policy in 1990). The study found that

> Overall, there was no significant difference in price trends between nonsubsidized homes in the subdivisions with subsidized units and the market as a whole—whether measured at the zip code or county-wide level.
>
> Furthermore, there was no difference in price behavior between nonsubsidized houses located within 500 feet of subsidized housing and those farther away in the same or an adjacent subdivision.

Even the price trends of those non-subsidized homes located immediately adjacent to a subsidized dwelling (either next door, back-to-back, across the street, or within 25 feet) were unaffected by their proximity.

"In sum," the study concluded, "the presence or proximity of subsidized housing made no difference in housing values as measured by relative price behavior in a dynamic market."[7]

The Innovative Housing Institute researchers also conducted structured interviews with fifty-six residents of nonsubsidized homes located close to subsidized units in both counties (plus four MPDU owners).[8] The survey found that twenty-eight households were "very satisfied" with the neighborhood, twenty-five were "satisfied," and only four were "a bit dissatisfied" or "very dissatisfied." When asked what they liked best about their neighborhoods, thirty-eight spoke of good neighbors, safety, peace, and quiet. Location, amenities, and good maintenance were mentioned by twenty-four respondents. Only fourteen of the fifty-six respondents specifically mentioned the subsidized units. Of these, six had negative comments (ranging from traffic congestion and overdevelopment to unsupervised children and teenage behavior).

In assessing the study's findings, it is important to remember the overwhelming middle- to upper-middle-class setting of the subsidized housing. Only 15 percent of the housing units are subsidized in the Montgomery County subdivisions and only 20 percent in the Fairfax County subdivisions. The two counties' housing authorities acquire 5 percent and 7.5 percent, respectively, of the units as rental properties for low-income households. Where middle-class households are so dominant, low- and modest-income households blend right in.

The Full Range of Housing Programs

The MPDU program, administered by the Department of Housing and Community Development, was not the county's first foray into the housing field. In 1966 the county council established the Housing Authority of Montgomery County. Initially, the agency was a typical federally supported pub-

---

7. Innovative Housing Institute (1998), p. 5.
8. The IHI researchers adapted the open-ended-field interview form that I had earlier used for my neighborhood interviews in Fallswick.

lic housing authority. Coming into the field relatively late, however, it was able to avoid the mistakes of earlier public housing programs, particularly building large, higher-density projects. The housing agency's earliest activities were building conventional (but relatively small) projects. The family projects ranged in size from 19 to 76 units. Projects for the elderly were slightly larger (96 to 160 units). Two projects mixed younger families and elderly households.

In 1974, as the MPDU policy was coming on line, the county council reorganized the agency as the Housing Opportunities Commission, with Tetreault as its executive director. The restructured organization took on an additional mission as the county's housing finance agency. It would be responsible for all forms of housing support for both low- and moderate-income households.

By fiscal year 1999 the Housing Opportunities Commission's budget had grown to $118 million. The diversity of its revenue sources reflected the diversity of its programs. Only one-third of its budget was federal grants: $8.7 million for operating subsidies for the 1,579 public housing units HOC owned and operated (the largest number acquired under the MPDU policy) and $30.6 million for section 8 rental assistance certificates and vouchers paid to Montgomery County landlords on behalf of 4,095 low-income tenants. Eleven of the public housing units were in the process of being purchased by their tenants (the latest of scores of instances in which HOC has successfully helped public housing tenants become homeowners.)

Interest on the HOC's mortgage revenue bonds yielded $33.4 million (or 28 percent of the agency's budget). These bonds had been issued to build or purchase another 3,067 nonfederally subsidized units under the HOC's "Opportunity Housing" program. (These included housing units dubbed "McHomes" for households whose incomes were just above the federal eligibility ceiling.) Of these the HOC directly managed 977, and it had placed another 2,090 under private management. Another 1,108 units were not owned by the HOC but fell within the program's guidelines.

The agency received $35.2 million in rental income from its various properties, half of which covered mortgage payments on HOC-owned properties. Finally, $9.9 million came from county government appropriations earmarked for special activities or was generated internally from HOC operations (including almost $1 million in net cash flow from HOC properties).

In all, in fiscal 1999 HOC owned or administered 9,849 houses, townhouses, and apartments for low- and moderate-income households. In addition, the agency monitored 35 privately owned multifamily properties with over 8,300 units that had been financed using the federal low income tax credit. Under the federal guidelines, 20 percent of the units were set aside for low- and moderate-income households.

What is most important about the totality of the HOC's programs is the degree to which low-income housing is spread around the county. The county planning department divides the county into eighteen planning areas. With a countywide poverty rate of 4.2 percent in 1990, HOC-assisted housing accounts for between 1.9 percent and 6.8 percent of all housing units in fifteen of the eighteen planning areas. The exceptions are downtown Silver Spring (where HOC units represent 11.6 percent of all housing units), Bethesda-Chevy Chase (largely built-out before the 1970s), where HOC has only twelve units, and the northern third of the county that is permanently protected as farmland. (Even in the rural areas, HOC has 151 highly scattered housing units, 1.2 percent of the total housing supply.)

Saving Farms by Saving Cities

As much as I have studied Montgomery County, it did not all come together for me until I participated briefly in the Ultimate Farmland Preservation Tour in February 1998. Organized primarily by the Michigan Farm Bureau, the five-day bus tour brought ninety Michigan farmers, public officials, and citizen activists to Maryland and south central Pennsylvania to study those states' farmland preservation programs and, in Montgomery County, its mixed-income housing programs as well.

The group's stamina and motivation were amazing. Arriving after a twelve-hour bus trip from Lansing to Gaithersburg, they still had the energy for a three-hour dinner meeting, peppering county representatives with detailed questions about Montgomery County's transferable development rights and mixed-income housing programs. County officials explained that two decades earlier the county's comprehensive plan had designated the northern third of the county (almost 90,000 acres) as permanent farmland. Initial "agricultural zoning" had required minimum 5-acre lots for each housing unit. Recognizing that such small lot size was promoting rural sprawl rather than farmland protection, in the 1980s the county planning commission raised the minimum requirement to 25 acres—but left the rezoned farmland with residual development rights. In other words, a 100-acre farm would have the right to have four housing units on it but would retain sixteen units of transferable development rights (that is, marketable for off-site construction but not buildable on-site). Some 40,000 acres were now protected by permanent development restrictions as the result of sale of transferable development rights.

Our presentations came to life when the ninety participants climbed onto their buses the next morning to tour Hallowell, one of the earliest communities developed under these policies. Hallowell had been a 400-acre farm but was located within the county's planned urban development zone. As "farmland," it still carried its vestigial zoning of one housing unit for every two acres; in light of topological and drainage restraints and right-of-way requirements, existing zoning would have permitted only about 150 housing units to be built.

Standing on the steps of the bandstand in the middle of Hallowell's neighborhood park on a sunny, crisp February morning, William Hussmann described what had happened. "I am chairman of the Montgomery County Planning Commission now," Hussmann explained, "but back then I was the agent for the Hallowell developer. In this hot housing market, it was much more profitable to develop many more housing units on the land. We asked the county planning commission to upgrade the zoning to three or four units per acre. 'We want more intensive development, too,' the planning commission replied, 'but we are not going to upgrade the zoning. If you want to build more housing units, go buy transferable development rights from farmers in the agricultural protection areas.' "

To the knowing smiles and chuckles of the Michigan farmers, Hussmann described haggling on front porches and at kitchen tables with local farmers over buying their farms' development rights. Ultimately, he purchased 750 development rights from thirty-five different farms at about $3,000–$4,000 per development right. This raised Hallowell's development potential to 900 homes.

Complying with the county's MPDU ordinance, the developer set aside the required allocation of affordable housing units, earning a 22 percent density bonus and raising the land's development capacity to 1,100 units. As an integral part of the new community, the developer built 130 MPDUs and then donated sixty unused development rights to the Housing Opportunities Commission for it to construct additional affordable units. (The then-chairman of the planning commission sponsored downzoning the HOC-built townhouses from sixty to forty units, a move, Hussmann speculated, that was "purely political" in preparation for the former chairman's unsuccessful bid for the elected county executive post.)

The end result was that Hallowell was developed as a community of

1,080 single-family homes and townhouses (including 130 MPDUs) and one forty-unit HOC-owned rental complex. Eighty-seven of the MPDUs were owned by moderate-income households and forty-three by the HOC for low-income households. Thirty of the forty rental units were occupied by moderate-income households as well and only ten by low-income households.

From the social perspective, Hallowell was home to a wide range of residents of different racial and ethnic groups and varying income levels. Fifty-three low-income households had been integrated smoothly into this overwhelmingly middle-class community. They were not otherwise obliged to seek low-rent housing in communities like Silver Spring or Langley Park that were already experiencing substantial pressures from lower-income households moving out of Washington into older housing.

From the environmental perspective, homes for 1,120 new households had been created in an urban environment, easing market pressures on further conversion of farmland. The thirty-five farm families had received about $2.5 million in compensation for their development rights—not tax dollars but private dollars. By controlling zoning densities in both the sending areas (the farms) and the receiving area (Hallowell) within a strong housing market, Montgomery County had successfully privatized the cost of permanent farmland preservation.

Over the next hour, as the Michigan group walked and drove along trimly landscaped streets of single-family homes and townhouse complexes, Hussmann challenged us. Which are the owner-occupied MPDUs? Which are the HOC-owned MPDUs? We could not tell. Often we could not even separate out the MPDUs from the market-rate townhouses. Unlike Fallswick, where the MPDUs were grouped together (though tastefully) in one block, market-rate townhouses, owner-occupied MPDUs, and HOC-owned MPDUs were all mixed together. Even the HOC's forty-unit rental complex was simply an architecturally compatible string of townhouses along a street near Hallowell's elementary school and community playground.

That morning, I believe, most of the Michiganders on the tour truly grasped the connection made by the battle cry of Jack Laurie, president of the Michigan Farm Bureau: "To save our farms, we must save our cities."[9]

In mid-1996 I was chatting with Tetreault, who had resigned after twenty-four years as the HOC's executive director to organize the nonprofit Innovative Housing Institute. The institute's mission is to help local govern-

---

9. In the months after the Ultimate Farmland Preservation Tour, the Farm Bureau's leadership forged a strong political alliance with Detroit mayor Dennis Archer, Grand Rapids mayor John Logie, and the mayors of Michigan's other ten largest cities.

ments and housing authorities understand the value—and, as Bernie said, noting the steady demise of federal housing support—the *financial necessity* of income-integrated housing. Through the institute, Bernie is developing videos, slide shows, model procedures and ordinances, and training materials to spread the Montgomery County success story to other communities.[10]

"You know," Bernie said, "over those years the HOC was transformed from a typical, small public housing agency managing 400 project-based apartments to a multifaceted housing developer, mortgage financier, property manager, social services provider, and rental agent. By the time I left, we were managing more than 4,000 housing units and administering another 4,000 federal rent certificates and vouchers.

"But our greatest achievement," Bernie continued, "was the degree to which we developed mixed-income housing ... low- and moderate-income households living in the same neighborhoods with high-income families."

"Yes, I have driven and walked through some of those neighborhoods, such as Fallswick out in Potomac," I said.

"It's funny," Bernie mused. "A place like Fallswick is the kind of neighborhood where the mixed-income concept works best. The whole idea seems to go down better, the wider the gap between the market rate and MPDU houses. Where there is not much difference in value between market rate and MPDU units, market-rate homeowners sometimes show more animosity toward the MPDU and HOC residents. They feel more often that the subsidized households are getting an unfair break that they had to work for themselves. Maybe among higher-income residents there is more sense of noblesse oblige."

"Higher-income homeowners may also recognize that there is not any danger of the modest proportion of MPDUs 'flipping' the neighborhood," I added. "In a place such as Fallswick, there is no prospect that other low- or moderate-income households will be moving in. The thirteen MPDU properties are all there will ever be."

"You may be correct," Bernie said. He grinned. "Do you know what's the best measure of how scattered our mixed-income housing is? The HOC has a line item in its annual budget, about $350,000, I think. It's used to pay annual membership assessments on behalf of our tenants to over 200 private homeowner associations. Just like every other homeowner, the housing authority pays to have the grass mowed in the street medians and private parks or hire lifeguards for the community swimming pool."

10. In October 1997 I joined the board of directors of the Innovative Housing Institute.

Summing Up

The MPDU policy and the full range of the county's low- and moderate-income housing policies and programs have helped the county accommodate—even encourage—a remarkable social transformation. In 1970 Montgomery County had the look of a classic suburban county: wealthy and white (95 percent). By 1990 it had a "rainbow" look: 12 percent black, 7 percent Hispanic, 8 percent Asian. In 1970 the countywide poverty rate was 3.5 percent; by 1990 the nominal poverty rate had inched up to 4.2 percent (but about 5.8 percent, adjusted for its higher cost of living).

Two close twins of Montgomery County are its Northern Virginia neighbor, Fairfax County, and Oakland County, Michigan, outside Detroit (see table 9-1). They are comparable in geographic areas, population, and, adjusted for metro Washington's higher cost of living, average income level and poverty rate. They were also almost identical in racial composition a generation ago; all three were 95 to 97 percent white.

But there the similarities end. With sixty municipalities and townships and a relatively weak county government, the Detroit suburb is a "little box" area while both the Washington suburbs are "big box" governments. Both of the Washington suburbs had moved far along the road to achieving racially integrated neighborhoods and schools by 1990.[11]

With its aggressive mixed-income housing policies, Montgomery County maintained a low and stable level of economic segregation during the two decades (its dissimilarity index was 27 in 1970 and 28 in 1990). By contrast, Fairfax County (from 22 to 31) and Oakland County (from 27 to 38) experienced steadily rising levels of segregation of poor households.[12]

The Montgomery County Public Schools have worked hard to promote diversity without resorting to widespread busing for racial balance. They have relied on the county's diversified housing policies and periodic adjustments in school attendance zone boundaries. The county school system's

11. Specific data on racial enrollment patterns for the Fairfax County Public Schools for 1989–90 were not supplied by the state of Virginia to the National Center for Education Statistics, the source of my nationwide study. However, high school enrollment patterns would adhere closely to housing patterns countywide.

12. Ironically, the Fairfax County Council had adopted its own affordable dwelling unit (ADU) policy before Montgomery County's MPDU policy in the early 1970s. However, Fairfax County's mixed-income housing ordinance was overturned by the state courts, which ruled that, under the Dillon's Rule doctrine, Fairfax County lacked specific state authorization for the measure. Not until 1990 did the county government, having secured special permissive legislation from the Virginia General Assembly, reenact its ADU ordinance.

Table 9-1. *A Tale of Three Counties*

Demographic data	Montgomery County, Maryland	Fairfax County, Virginia	Oakland County, Michigan
Geographic area (square miles)	494.6	395.6	872.7
Total population, 1970	522,809	454,275	907,871
White (percent)	95	96	97
Black (percent)	4	4	3
Asian and other (percent)	1	0	0
Total population, 1997	826,766	914,259	1,166,512
White, 1990 (percent)	72	77	88
Black, 1990 (percent)	12	8	7
Hispanic, 1990 (percent)	7	6	2
Asian, 1990 (percent)	8	8	2
Other, 1990 (percent)	1	1	1
Cost-of-living index, 1989	137	137	99
COLA-adjusted household income, 1989 (dollars)	49,640	50,334	56,059
COLA-adjusted poverty rate, 1989 (percent)	5.8	4.8	5.9
Municipal governments (with planning and zoning powers)	8	0	60
County planning and zoning powers (as percent of county residents)	88	100	0
School districts	1	1	29
Black housing segregation index, 1970	48	51	91
Black housing segregation index, 1990	39	38	76
Black school segregation index, 1990	34	n.a.	81
Segregation index of the poor, 1970	27	22	27
Segregation index of the poor, 1990	28	31	38

Source: Author's calculations based on census reports.
n.a. Not available.

record and policies are not without their critics. However, balance and diversity within Montgomery County's unified "big box" school system is light-years ahead of the pattern within the multiple "little box" school districts in Oakland County and Westchester County, New York, outside New York City,

Table 9-2. *High School Segregation Indexes in Three Counties, 1989–90*

Racial or ethnic group	Montgomery County, Maryland (20)[a]		Oakland County, Michigan (41)[a]		Westchester County, New York (42)[a]	
	Percent	Index	Percent	Index	Percent	Index
All minorities	37.6	27	15.8	64	33.5	51
Black	15.7	34	11.2	81	18.7	63
Hispanic	8.1	32	1.4	54	9.6	56
Asian	13.7	22	2.5	44	5.2	34
Native American	0.3	23	1.0	65	0.1	79

a. The number of high schools in each county.

as shown in table 9-2. For every racial and ethnic group, Montgomery County's high schools are substantially more integrated than Westchester County's. One cannot even talk about degrees of "integration" in Oakland County; its public high schools are two to three times more segregated than Montgomery County's for every minority group except Oakland County's very small Hispanic student population (who are 67 percent more segregated than Hispanics in Montgomery County schools).

Montgomery County is not exempt from the social trends of contemporary America. County officials and residents alike are conscious of substantial economic differences between the poorer eastern part of the county (for example, Silver Spring, Takoma Park, Aspen Hill) and the wealthier western portion (Bethesda, Chevy Chase, Potomac, Gaithersburg, Germantown). All of the county government's planning and zoning efforts have not prevented the steady filtering of older housing in eastern Montgomery County down the household income scale.

However, Montgomery County has not compounded the damage of such market trends through its own housing policies. More than two-thirds of HOC-assisted housing units have been built or acquired in the wealthier western parts of the county. County policies have prevented a steeper decline in the eastern county while bringing much greater racial and class diversity to the western county than laissez-faire market trends would ever have produced. Montgomery County's more egalitarian social fabric is the direct result of its Moderately Priced Dwelling Unit Ordinance and other mixed-income housing policies and programs.

10

Dayton, Ohio's ED/GE: The Rewards (and Limits) of Voluntary Agreements

THE TOWNSHIP SYSTEM may have been an excellent way to settle the Ohio frontier in the eighteenth century, but having so many small governments certainly made it more difficult to manage a complex urban society 200 years later, Montgomery County (Ohio) administrator Don Vermillion thought as he contemplated the problems faced by the Dayton area in mid-1989. The city of Dayton was slowly dying, and Montgomery County was starting to decline with it. Only fifteen to twenty years earlier, the Dayton area had been one of America's most prosperous manufacturing centers. Since then the area had lost 45,000 high-wage, blue-collar jobs, or more than one-quarter of its industrial employment. Traditional mainstays of the region's economy had cut back or closed down. General Motors had dropped from 40,000 to 20,000 jobs. Dayton Tire and Rubber (2,000 jobs) and Dayton Press (3,000 jobs) had vanished, leaving behind only memories of better days and realities of polluted "brownfields."

National Cash Register (NCR), Dayton's flagship company, had released 20,000 employees. Almost as troubling was the possibility that NCR and Dayton's other four Fortune 500 companies might be swallowed up by outsiders in the wave of corporate mergers sweeping Wall Street. A source of Dayton's civic strength had always been its homegrown corporations. Ab-

sentee owners would never have the same civic and philanthropic commitment to the Dayton area as chief executive officers headquartered just up
the street.[1]

With economic hard times, many younger residents had moved away,
and few new families migrated into the area. Having peaked at about 608,000
residents in 1970, Montgomery County's population had fallen to about
575,000 people two decades later. The city of Dayton had lost a quarter of its
inhabitants; its loss accounted for the entire county's population drop. Most
of Dayton's suburbs had continued to grow in both population and jobs,
sustaining a perception of suburban well-being and further distancing them
psychologically from the city's problems.

Vermillion felt this sense of well-being was an illusion. Wealth had moved
to the fringes of Montgomery County and was leaking into neighboring
counties, especially Greene County, the site of Wright-Patterson Air Force
Base. The base commander had promulgated a new rule requiring defense
contractors to have major offices within a fifty-mile radius of the base; the
"fifty-mile rule" was spurring an office boom along the Interstate 675 corridor rather than in downtown Dayton. The region's most rapidly growing
area was Greene County, where Bellbrook and Beavercreek had become the
newest top-of-the-line communities. The newly opened Fairview Commons
Mall in Beavercreek along I-675 was already drawing shoppers away from
older commercial areas in Montgomery County. Average household incomes
in Beavercreek were one-quarter higher than in suburban Kettering, Montgomery County's second largest city, and more than twice Dayton's average
household income.[2]

Interjurisdictional economic competition had always been fierce among
Ohio's cities, villages, and townships—Ohio was known as "the Home Rule
State"—and there were certainly a lot of local competitors. Within Mont-
gomery County alone there were nineteen municipalities: Dayton, a dozen

1. In 1991 AT&T acquired NCR, converting it into AT&T's "GIS Division." The locus of
decisionmaking for Dayton's largest private employer moved from just two miles away from the
Montgomery County Courthouse to AT&T's headquarters on Manhattan's Avenue of the Ameri-
cas, only 550 air-miles from Dayton but light-years away in terms of local commitment. By 1996,
among Dayton's largest homegrown corporations only Mead Corporation maintained its independence and Fortune 500 ranking (256). However, the pendulum was swinging back. IBM re-
stored the "NCR" name and announced plans to spin NCR off as an independent company.

2. Ironically, Kettering could have been part of Dayton. In 1954 Van Buren Township asked to
be annexed by Dayton. The city refused, and the spurned township incorporated as the new city of
Kettering.

suburban cities, and six suburban villages. Many were former townships that had incorporated to frustrate annexation by the city of Dayton. There were still twelve surviving independent townships, now almost fully empowered municipalities in all but official form. Including county government itself, Montgomery County counted thirty-two separate local governments, roughly one for every 18,000 residents. In addition, the county's 105,000 schoolchildren attended seventeen public school systems plus a plethora of private and parochial schools.

The area's political balkanization had been the focus of much local attention in recent years. In 1986 the Community Factors Evaluation Study, funded by the Dayton Area Progress Council and conducted by Wright State University, found the region's business image was suffering and that efforts to attract new or expanding companies were faltering as a result of duplicate development efforts and political infighting among the region's many local governments. Cleveland State University had prepared a second study for a county-appointed citizens board; this Citizens Financial Task Force Report had projected growing fiscal problems for local governments. Both urged the creation of a new, more cooperative way to pursue economic development. A chamber of commerce committee had recently encouraged the county to investigate tax sharing as a way to promote regional economic development.

Vermillion saw a possible way to make it happen. The Ohio legislature had just authorized Ohio counties to adopt an additional one-half percent sales tax. For Montgomery County, the tax would yield an estimated $210 million in revenues over the ten-year period authorized. The three Montgomery County commissioners had already called for a long-term, cost-cutting fiscal plan. Using the new revenues to retire high-interest bonds, upgrade law enforcement facilities, and rebuild depleted general fund reserves would rank high on the commissioners' list. Perhaps, however, buttressed by these studies, Vermillion could persuade them to set aside some of the money as a cooperative economic development fund. If there were enough money— perhaps $5 million a year—it might be sufficient incentive for most of Montgomery County's local governments to sign on to some tax-sharing arrangement as well. A quid pro quo, Vermillion thought. To qualify for economic development grants, a local government would have to agree to revenue sharing. It might just work.

Could the tough political controversies ahead for such an unusual initiative be overcome? Vermillion wondered. He himself was relatively young (thirty-four years old) with only one year as Montgomery County administrator behind him. He was a professional public manager, however, trained in the University of Kansas's renowned public administration program, and had already served as city manager of suburban Miamisburg. One of the essential tools of a successful city or county manager is skill in providing leadership behind the scenes. Vermillion knew that he had an excellent county commission. Commission president Paula MacIlwaine was a former League of Women Voters president. Commissioner Charles Curran, a former state senator, understood regional issues well. Commissioner Donna Moon, a former Kettering school board member, realized that faster economic growth was needed to sustain good public school systems. The county commission was progressive, open to new ideas, and, Vermillion felt, willing to move in new directions.

Forging Regional Collaboration

And so it was. That summer the county commission enacted the local option sales tax for a ten-year period, effective in October 1989. Of the $210 million in projected revenues, the commissioners earmarked $140 million for debt reduction, general fund reserves, and law enforcement facilities. However, they set aside $5 million a year, or a total of $50 million, for an experimental countywide economic development program. (They also reserved $20 million to be split between an affordable housing fund and an arts and cultural fund, both for the entire county.)

The commissioners recognized that the greatest political hurdle would be to get all the other local governments to participate. Township and municipal officials might reject any program promoted solely as a county government initiative, the commissioners believed. County government would need some other organization to take the lead publicly in shaping the program.

The Community Cooperation Task Force might be just the group, they decided. It was a sort of civic advisory board recently organized by the Dayton Area Chamber of Commerce at the behest of the Montgomery County Township Association. The townships had wanted the new group to help mediate annexation disputes with area municipalities. The Community Cooperation Task Force included the mayor of Dayton, three suburban mayors, the three county commissioners, three township trustees, one township clerk, one village council member, three private sector members (a CEO of a large construction firm, a university president, and a newspaper editor), and five area school board members. If the group's focus could be shifted

from inherently bitter annexation disputes to a more constructive, cooperative agenda, the Community Cooperation Task Force would be the perfect
broadly based team to help forge an agreement among so many diverse local
governments historically jealous of their independence.

In August 1989 the county commission invited the Community Cooperation Task Force to take the lead in developing a joint economic development and tax-sharing program. Tom Heine, the Dayton chamber of
commerce president, would serve as facilitator. After five months of struggling with the technical complexity of the task, the task force volunteers
finally asked county staff to undertake the necessary analysis, develop a tax-
sharing methodology, and report back regularly to the task force. Reluctantly, for it was still wary of adverse reaction to a "county-driven" program,
the county set up a technical advisory group composed of Vermillion, the
county's budget director, and the county's economic development director;
three leading businessmen in the area; William Dodge, an outside strategic
planning consultant; the director of Ohio's State and Local Government
Commission (who had studied other tax-sharing models); and a Wright State
University professor, Jack Dustin, also an expert in tax-sharing programs.

The technical advisory group reached agreement quickly on two major
points. Though some local government officials on the task force had wanted
access to the economic development fund without participating in tax sharing, the two programs were tied together. And though Dayton wanted a tax-
sharing distribution formula based on relative need (using per capita income,
unemployment and poverty rates, and tax effort as measures), the technical
advisory group agreed on using simple population percentage as the distribution formula.

The real struggle revolved around the tax-sharing contribution formula.
First, what revenues would be shared? How much? The members of the
technical advisory group were very familiar with Minnesota's fiscal disparities plan. (Vermillion himself had first studied the program at the University of Kansas.) They decided, however, against the Twin Cities' formula
because it involved sharing growth only in the commercial and industrial
property tax base; the technical group felt that it was equally important to
share growth in the residential property tax base. Moreover, incremental
growth should be based both on new investment and the appreciation of
existing property if the program was to put a dent in fiscal disparities.

When the technical group presented its initial recommendations to the
task force, some of the task force members, particularly township representatives, were troubled by the formula, since it focused on property taxes alone.

They asked that a second advisory group (the technical advisory subcommittee) be organized to broaden the base of local government involvement. The technical advisory subcommittee brought to the table two township administrators and four city managers; all but one had not been involved in the prior discussions. (In all, nine of the county's thirty-one local governments—those with the largest populations and largest shares of commercial and industrial development—were involved directly in one of the two advisory groups.) With Wright State's Dustin assisting in the discussion of various alternatives, the local officials sought to hammer out a revised tax-sharing formula with the three county administrators.

City and township members challenged again the idea of sharing tax revenues at all; "government equity" ought to be abandoned. They argued that nobody (even the wealthiest communities among them) had surplus revenues to share and that revenue sharing would penalize the more "efficient" local governments to reward the "inefficient." Where would the shared revenue really come from? How fast would the commitment build up? Each was fearful of giving up too much. City and township members urged that most of the revenues from the county's half-cent sales tax increase should just flow through to local governments rather than fund the county's regional initiatives. Reluctant to oppose outright the county's effort to foster cooperative economic development efforts, however, the city and township members did not walk out of the talks.

For two months they argued back and forth. City and township administrators constantly sought to limit the amount of tax revenues shared. County administrators wanted a tax-sharing pool large enough to equal the county's $5 million a year economic development fund. The two sides could not compromise. Finally, the county yielded. Residential property included in the contribution formula would be limited to 25 percent of the increase in assessed valuation, and the contribution to the pool would not exceed the previous year's property tax growth. Even with these concessions, the group could not reach unanimity, and the debate moved back to the broader-based task force.

It was now December 1990, and the county's timetable was running out. The county had wanted to implement the economic development and revenue-sharing plan in 1991, after the first year of the new tax collections, but major issues were still unresolved. Township officials were particularly upset. Including only property taxes in the formula, they felt, favored municipalities over townships. In Ohio payroll taxes account for 50 to 85 percent of municipal revenues, but cannot be levied by townships, which are dependent on the property tax for more than 80 percent of township revenues. If cities and villages did not have to share part of their largest revenue source (payroll taxes), why should townships share theirs (property taxes)? Moreover, though property taxes most accurately reflect place-specific new investments, in Ohio property taxes are heavily earmarked for specified purposes, such as police, fire, and road improvements. Property taxes are also subject to sunset provisions; they must be reauthorized periodically by local voters. The amount of property tax that could actually be pooled was questionable.

The Task Force compromised; growth in payroll taxes would be added to the pool as well. The maximum contribution for any jurisdiction would be capped at 13 percent of the growth in payroll and property tax revenues. It was decided that the base year from which incremental growth in taxes would be calculated would always be only three years before the year of distribution. Municipal and township administrators alike were very concerned that a large increase in the tax base early in the program—from a major business expansion, for example—would leave their jurisdiction a net contributor for the remaining life of the program. They demanded that the base year be recalibrated every year. A sliding base year would keep the amount of pooled revenues from ever growing very large. In general, the difference between the contribution and distribution formulas would result in net distributions for declining, stable, or slow-growth jurisdictions and net contributions for fast-growth jurisdictions.

The final plan was dubbed the ED/GE plan (Economic Development/ Government Equity). The Community Cooperation Task Force recommended that the Montgomery County Commission adopt the ED/GE plan. It was publicly launched at a chamber of commerce dinner in January 1991. The county commission then set a deadline of July 1, 1991, for local governments to sign up.

Last-Minute Compromises

Major hurdles still remained. Even after the kick-off dinner several city managers remained concerned that their suburban cities would end up in a precarious position if they were constantly net contributors but received no offsetting economic development funds for projects in their communities. (The precarious position they feared was probably more political than fiscal in nature.) They threatened to reject the program.

The city of Kettering played a key leadership role among the suburban municipalities. Al Jordan, Kettering's assistant city manager, had been an early supporter of the ED/GE negotiations. Now he was balking. Dustin and Jordan met for lunch. "Kettering's an aging suburb now," the Wright State professor argued. "In the next decade you'll begin facing some of Dayton's problems: continuing job losses from GM's DELCO division, retail customers deserting Kettering's stores for new malls and strip centers in Greene County, aging housing stock and infrastructure, more fixed income households. Kettering will need the economic development grants to help attract new jobs to offset the losses. You might even be a net recipient of revenue-sharing funds as the end of the decade approaches."

Jordan was not persuaded. "It's hard to support the program when it's sure to cost us scarce tax dollars right away. What do we say to our citizens? How do we explain what the money was for? What do we do if we come up seriously short in the city budget?"

Dustin returned to his office and returned a phone call from one of the chamber of commerce committee members, who informed Dustin of an emergency meeting with the disaffected municipalities. "Kettering's still balking," Dustin casually mentioned to the chamber leader. "They're afraid of losing revenues."

The next day, when Dustin arrived at the emergency session, Jordan whispered to him, "Whatever you said, it worked." After more than a year of negotiations, Kettering had tried to offer an entirely new program. Chamber of commerce president Tom Heine, the task force's chairman, was not about to see all the effort go down the drain. Were Kettering and others worried about loss of revenues? Heine hammered out a final compromise. Any jurisdiction that had been a net contributor for three straight years was assured of having an economic development grant approved every third year for an equivalent amount of money. This "settle-up" accord would hold net contributors harmless. (Of course, it would also make moot any net effect of revenue sharing.)

Though twenty-seven of the local governments originally executed contracts, four municipalities filed suit, stalling ED/GE's implementation. On June 25, 1992, the Ohio state supreme court let stand lower court rulings rejecting all the municipalities' claims, and the program was officially implemented in the fall of 1992, after communities had been given time to recommit to the program.

As of mid-1996, twenty-eight of Montgomery County's twenty-nine townships and municipalities had voluntarily signed a nine-year contract with the county to participate in the ED/GE program.[3] Vandalia, one of the four jurisdictions that sued unsuccessfully to block the program, remains the sole holdout. Adjacent to the Dayton International Airport and located at the interchange of I-70 and I-75 ("the crossroads of America"), Vandalia is booming economically.[4]

Economic Development Collaboration

After such a long and arduous gestation, how has the ED/GE program actually performed? Its goals are lofty: to create and retain jobs in the county; enhance jurisdictional and county tax bases; compete successfully as a region in national and international markets; and share the benefits of areawide economic prosperity among all jurisdictions in the county.[5]

Each year Montgomery County has allocated $5 million to the economic development fund from the special countywide sales tax. Grants are awarded to (or through) participating governments to establish or expand commercial, industrial, and research facilities and to create and preserve employment opportunities. The fund supports primarily public infrastructure improvements critical to particular economic development projects, but it has also funded other legally allowable activities that foster economic development.

Each year 85 percent of the allocation ($4.25 million) is committed to projects in individual jurisdictions. Another 10 percent ($500,000) is reserved for special projects to take advantage of "newly emerging economic opportunities." A final 5 percent ($250,000) is reserved for "unexpected economic opportunities or threats that occur between funding cycles."

Certain policy guidelines and selection criteria, recommended originally by the Community Cooperation Task Force, are considered in evaluating applications for funding. The grant awards are approved annually by the county commission on the basis of the recommendations of the ED/GE advisory committee. The committee consists of fifteen members (six representing cities and villages; four representing townships; three private sector members; and two county commissioners). Dayton and Kettering have per-

---

3. In the 1990s Mad River and Madison Townships merged with the cities of Riverside and Trotwood, respectively.

4. Vandalia's mayor had led the dissenting municipalities. In the next election, however, a strong supporter of regional cooperation almost upset her.

5. Montgomery County (1991).

manent seats; other membership rotates annually among different participating governments.

The ED/GE advisory committee assesses project proposals on the basis
of their potential to retain or expand local businesses or attract new businesses from outside Montgomery County. The advisory committee gives
priority to proposals that create or help retain jobs, preserve or enhance the
local tax base, and have a private business as a committed end user.

The ED/GE program emphasizes sectors that have high growth potential within the regional economy, such as aerospace and avionics, automo-
tive components, communications, computer information technology, health
care, manufacturing research and development, and transportation-related
activities (for example, warehousing and distribution).

Special consideration is given to collaborative efforts that involve two
or more communities or that encourage growth in areas already served by
basic public infrastructure, such as water and sanitary sewer lines or existing roads. Projects are encouraged to leverage other public and private investment and should not substitute economic development funds for other
funding. They must be ready to begin implementation (typically within six
months of approval, with a completion date within twenty-four months).
Finally, the advisory committee strongly discourages projects that would
simply relocate businesses from one jurisdiction to another within Montgomery County.

New Jobs, Retained Jobs

What has been the economic development fund's impact? After seven funding cycles (1992–98) the results "on the ground" are impressive. Drive past
General Motors' new Clear Coat Paint Line Facility at the GM Truck and
Bus Plant in the city of Moraine. In 1992–93, $1 million in ED/GE funds
helped expand the plant, thereby retaining an estimated 3,500 jobs and creating another 65 new jobs. General Motors had been considering closing the
Moraine facility and moving its operations to Shreveport, Louisiana, or Lin-
den, New Jersey.

Out in the city of Huber Heights, $530,000 in 1992 helped build an
access road connecting a state highway with a new industrial park to accommodate ABF, a trucking firm, and this effort kept 600 jobs and created 400
more. A former department store in Kettering had closed. Some $650,000 in
ED/GE funds for site and leasehold improvements helped convert the aban-

doned store into a new telephone order-taking center for Victoria's Secret, creating 1,000 new jobs.

Other ED/GE investments are not as visible as a GM plant, a trucking company's marshaling yard, or a Victoria's Secret catalog center but have been just as crucial to the region's economy. With 22,000 military and civilian personnel, the Dayton area's primary employer is Wright-Patterson Air Force Base.[6] In 1994 ED/GE provided $135,000 to fund a local task force to defend Wright-Patterson against any cutbacks or even outright closure being considered by the Defense Department's Base Realignment and Closure Commission. "Wright-Pat" suffered no major cutbacks in the 1995 round of defense cuts. As a result, the base was available to serve as the high-security site of the Bosnian peace talks later that year, giving rise to the "Dayton Accords," a more substantive source of worldwide publicity for the Dayton area than hosting a Super Bowl or Miss USA pageant.

By September 1998 the economic development fund had gone through seven project funding cycles and committed over $34 million to 152 projects. ED/GE money had been matched by over $1 billion in other local, state, and federal funds, and private investment. The county's 1997 summary of ED/GE's achievements stated that 26,058 existing jobs will be retained, and 16,009 new jobs are expected to be created through the projects funded thus far. Taken at face value, the ED/GE program had been fabulously successful; the cost in ED/GE grants had been about $2,100 for each new job created. By contrast, in its wildest dreams, Detroit's federally bankrolled Empowerment Community program hopes to create 6,800 new jobs in its target zone at a federal cost of $300 million in grants and tax incentives—which translates to some $44,000 per new job created.

Reviewing the ED/GE program's glowing results, my thoughts wandered back to my years as mayor of Albuquerque (1977–81). I had worked closely with Albuquerque Economic Development, our community's private sector–based organization for promoting business. During those years we had persuaded many national corporations—Intel, Signetics, Honeywell, for example—to set up new manufacturing plants in Albuquerque.

In particular, I remember our negotiations with Ethicon, a subsidiary of Johnson & Johnson, the country's leading medical supply company. Ethicon was interested in building a new plant in Albuquerque to produce ultrasterile surgical sutures. Their proposed site lay south of the city limits

---

6. In 1946 Wright-Patterson's employment had peaked at 49,000 military and civilian personnel.

on a rolling bluff overlooking the University of New Mexico's South Golf Course, a visually spectacular location. The Ethicon Plant would also be the first tenant of the city's proposed South Valley Industrial Park located near the poorest, almost semirural, traditionally Hispanic neighborhoods in the Albuquerque area.

Laying in new city water and sewer lines was essential to opening up the site for industrial development, yet the city's regular policies would have required Ethicon to pay utility extension charges that would have added about $1.2 million to the plant's cost. Ethicon proposed that the cost of utility expansion be covered by a federal urban development action grant (UDAG). Complying with the federal program's conditions, Ethicon was willing to hire 75 percent of its future employees from the South Valley.

The problem was that Albuquerque did not qualify as a UDAG community. Like many cities of the Sun Belt, Albuquerque had rapidly annexed new, middle-class suburban neighborhoods into the city. Even though it had a large number of poorer neighborhoods, Albuquerque's citywide poverty statistics were too low for the city as a whole to qualify for the grant.

At that time the so-called Sun Belt–Rust Belt rivalry was in full swing. Unlike many other Sun Belt mayors, I did not object to seeing the bulk of federal antipoverty funds targeted on cities in the Northeast and Middle West. As a former civil rights and antipoverty staffer with the Washington Urban League, I knew that such cities had far greater social and fiscal problems than Albuquerque. (Moreover, I knew that, with Kirtland Air Force Base and Sandia National Laboratories, Albuquerque actually received defense dollars that far outweighed any shortfall in our "fair share" of federal antipoverty funds.) Rather than support an all-out Sun Belt assault on Frost Belt–favoring distribution formulas, I suggested that a modest slice of UDAG funds be earmarked for "pockets of poverty," a notion that appealed politically to my fellow Sun Belt mayors. We successfully lobbied Congress and the Carter administration to amend UDAG eligibility criteria. And Albuquerque became the first community to receive a "pocket of poverty" UDAG grant: $1.2 million earmarked for utility extension costs into the city's South Valley Industrial Park.

Within several weeks of receiving the UDAG grant, I found myself turning over the ceremonial shovelful of dirt at the groundbreaking of the new plant. Some eighteen months later the plant went into production, ultimately hiring 500 workers. Ethicon met all its local hiring commitments and has been an exemplary employer and civic citizen.

Was the $1.2 million UDAG grant essential to the plant project? At the time Johnson & Johnson executives claimed that it was. Johnson & Johnson's initial $9 million investment, however, dwarfed the UDAG grant's contribution. And Albuquerque's primary attraction was not inexpensive land but a labor pool that was reasonably well educated, highly motivated, and not unionized. (In the late 1980s Ethicon's Albuquerque employees rejected an effort by the Teamsters Union to organize the plant by a more than 2 to 1 margin.)

Did the $1.2 million really "create" 500 new jobs in Albuquerque in 1980? Did $34 million in ED/GE grants really "create" 16,009 new jobs in Dayton–Montgomery County, and "retain" another 26,058 existing jobs in 1992–98? Who knows? Probably a hard-nosed evaluation would downgrade both programs' claims significantly. But by any standard, the economic development fund has been a successful economic tool in Dayton-Montgomery County.

Limited Revenue Sharing

The government equity fund has also been a great success from the perspective of most local finance officers, whose goal is to minimize revenue sharing's impact. Because of the cap on contributions and the sliding base year, the amount of incremental revenues shared through the government equity fund has been modest. By the sixth year, fiscal 1998, the total funds redistributed in any one year had grown to only $712,680, contributed by fourteen of the twenty-eight participating jurisdictions; over the first six years a total of $2,902,262 had been distributed.

The government equity fund has had a modest redistributive effect. Over the first six years, communities with high fiscal capacity were, in fact, net contributors. The city of Oakwood contributed a cumulative total of $148,246; Miami Township, $190,125; Washington Township, $285,208; the city of Miamisburg, $412,161; the city of Centerville, $394,290; and the city of Kettering, $793,681. Communities with low fiscal capacity were, in fact, the largest net recipients, with Jefferson Township receiving $124,427; the city of Huber Heights, $271,371; the newly consolidated city of Riverside, $281,546; the city of Trotwood, $336,731; Harrison Township, $418,138; and the city of Dayton, $1,189,089.

As the above summary demonstrates, however, the actual impact of revenue sharing through the government equity fund is indeed modest. About a half-million dollars a year in shared revenues is a tiny fraction of the total budgets of the twenty-eight participating governments. County administrator Vermillion himself candidly characterized the government equity fund as "symbolic" revenue sharing.

The voluntary, locally negotiated Government Equity program amounts to about $1 a year per resident of Montgomery County in shared revenues. By contrast, the nation's largest, state-mandated, regional revenue-sharing program—the Twin Cities fiscal disparities plan—has grown to over $150 a year per resident of the seven-county, 186-municipality Minneapolis-Saint Paul region.

Moreover, even consistent net contributors to the Dayton area's government equity fund are being made whole over time through the eleventh-hour "settle-up" provision, under which no jurisdiction will contribute more to the government equity fund than it will receive from the economic development fund. The first "settle-up" occurred in 1995, with others to follow in 1998 and 2001 (the ED/GE program's final year). With annual economic development fund allocations being ten times the size of the annual equity fund's pool, "settle-up" will be an easy commitment to fulfill.

Other Regional Collaborations

However, the true value of the ED/GE program is that it has opened the way to an unusual level of intergovernmental cooperation in Montgomery County. Local officials cooperate constantly in the administration of the program, in particular, through service on the ED/GE advisory committee, which evaluates annual project applications.

Concurrent with ED/GE's authorization, in 1989 the county commission established the Dayton/Montgomery County Housing Commission (now the Affordable Housing Fund). Its mission was to develop regionwide approaches to meeting the need for low- and moderate-income housing. With an annual allocation of $1 million in county sales tax funds, by 1998 the Housing Commission had leveraged $7.5 million into $97 million of private mortgage commitments and renovation loans.

In the same year, the county commission also established the Montgomery County Regional Arts and Cultural District (MCRACD) to focus on the public side of arts funding, with an allocation of $1 million per year as incentive funds for the arts. Over the first six years (1990–95) MCRACD provided $3 million in operating support for fourteen arts and cultural organizations, such as Dayton Public TV, the Dayton Philharmonic, and the Museum of Natural History; made over 100 small, one-time grants to art and cultural groups, totaling $877,000 (and generating another $802,000 in matching funds from other sources); contributed $2 million for a new Metropolitan Arts Center in Dayton, which leveraged another $6.5 million in city and state grants; and spent $455,000 to promote a merger of Arts Dayton and the Miami Valley Arts Council into Culture Works, a regionwide United Way for the arts, which will also provide management and technical assistance to local arts organizations. In all, an independent evaluation estimated that from 1990 to 1995 MCRACD's $6.4 million investment had had an aggregate economic impact of $21.3 million on the Miami Valley economy.[7]

In the economic development arena, beyond ED/GE itself, the economic development directors from all thirty jurisdictions have joined forces in the I-70/I-75 Development Association. In 1995 a regional sports council was established to strengthen the area's professional minor league sports.

Even recent head-to-head battles have lost some of their traditional bareknuckles, take-no-prisoners character. In the mid-1990s Kettering and Dayton were locked in fierce competition over the location of Banc One's credit-processing facility. To ensure that Banc One's bank office operation would remain in Montgomery County, ED/GE laid $1 million of incentive funds on the table, available regardless of which local city was chosen by bank officials. However, advisory committee members pressured both cities to work out a supplemental tax-sharing agreement. Kettering won out, but is now sharing a percentage of the payroll taxes collected with Dayton in partial compensation for 600 jobs shifted from the city.

Replicating ED/GE

The ED/GE program is important for the lessons it provides for other communities. The lessons were drawn for me by Jack Dustin, ED/GE's academic godfather and now a member of Wright State University's Department of Urban Affairs:

> Linking economic development funding to tax sharing gives local governments a powerful incentive to discuss tax equity as an objective of cooperative and coordinated economic development. Politics is politics, of course, and there is always some behind-the-scenes political horse-trading on

7. Stock (1996).

project proposals. However, local government sponsors must identify what benefits their proposed projects bring to the county as a whole. The selection process favors projects with broad impact. The application and selection process keeps regional impact at stage center. ED/GE sends a clear message: each local government's fortunes are tied to their neighbors' well-being.

An areawide authority can best provide leadership in getting communities to opt into a tax-sharing plan. County governments represent, for example, a higher level of authority over local governments and have a history of promoting equity and cooperation. But tax sharing needs to be conveyed in a nonthreatening way. Working through other organizations, such as chambers of commerce, universities, or private consulting firms, helps facilitate the decisionmaking process. If the facilitating group is seen as balanced and fair and is well respected, it can inhibit parochial interests and discourage 'get even' inclinations among local governments.

Pondering the strong resistance encountered in ED/GE's negotiations, Jack continued:

Even when coupled with economic development funding, tax sharing is a risky step for local governments. . . . In effect, local governments need to be asked how they think tax sharing can work and then a consensus must be developed.

The technical details of developing tax-sharing formulas are best left to fiscal, tax, and legal professionals. . . . Most business persons and other community leaders have neither the time nor the technical expertise to formulate complex formulas.

Sound methodology will be important in establishing only a baseline of who contributes and who receives. . . . Contributions to a regional tax pool will be based more on negotiation than pure mathematics. . . . Differences in perception of fairness between municipal, suburban, and township representatives may require modifying the "ideal" formula to keep the coalition of communities together.

Despite a powerful economic incentive, local governments will seek to minimize their contribution to a tax-sharing pool. As a result, some provisions to minimize financial burden, regardless of fiscal capacity, will have to be considered. If regional cooperation is a worthwhile goal of local governments, as almost all claim it is, then some cost should be expected and acceptable.

The county administrator, Don Vermillion, highlighted the most crucial lesson for me in a conversation in 1996. "The key is having elected officials with vision and political courage," he observed. "These qualities are
just as important for those who must stay with the program as those who
make the original decision. We've had six different county commissioners
since ED/GE began. Majority control has shifted from Democrats to Republicans. We've had several tough fiscal years when other tax receipts were
falling and there were lots of budget pressures on behalf of more traditional
county programs. But all the commissioners have stuck by ED/GE, the affordable housing fund, the regional arts fund.

"'We've seen our larger community improve as the result of working
together rather than working against each other,' they've said. 'We're going
to keep on with these collective efforts.'"

Lessons of ED/GE

At least two principal lessons can be drawn from this chapter. The first relates to the enormous complications of achieving meaningful collaboration
among multiple units of local government in "little box" regions.

As a speaker and consultant who is often described as a proponent of
"metropolitan government," I have occasionally been admonished by my
hosts to "remember, David, that here in Connecticut [or Ohio . . . or North
Carolina . . . or Texas . . . or whatever state I am visiting] we have a very
strong commitment to home rule." Well, *everybody* in this nation has a strong
commitment to home rule, if that phrase is understood to mean the desire
of citizens to have a say in what happens in their local community. How that
basic democratic need is satisfied simply varies in scale from community to
community and state to state. In Albuquerque, New Mexico (1996 population: 420,000), city council candidates campaign door-to-door in council
districts that average about 45,000 residents; groups of neighbors numbering a few hundred to a few thousand band together in nonprofit neighborhood associations in order to carry out voluntary community projects or
influence their city government. In Kent County, Michigan (1997 population: 539,000), with thirty-four independent municipal and township governments, Grand Rapids mayor John Logie has calculated that there are 637
local elected officials—one for about every 845 residents—and 100 more
than are elected, Mayor Logie notes, to run the U.S. government.

A state's basic system of local government is something that has rarely been determined in living memory. It has simply been inherited from the past, often shaped by historical circumstances that preceded the creation of the very states and localities affected.[8] Ohioans have not only 88 counties and 942 municipal governments but also 1,314 township governments because that is the hand that history dealt them.

No Ohioan of the twentieth century (or even the nineteenth century) decided that townships should be a primary form of local government. The Continental Congress decreed that the Ohio Territory should be divided into townships when it enacted the Land Ordinance of 1785 (under the authority of the Articles of Confederation). The Continental Congress needed to pay off the officers and soldiers of the victorious revolutionary army as expeditiously as possible with the grants of western lands promised. The Congress adopted the scheme offered by Thomas Hutchins. In 1764, as a young captain in the Sixtieth Royal Regiment, Hutchins had made an expedition to the Ohio. He had conceived of a plan of military colonies north of the Ohio as protection against the Indians, based on an almost Roman-like sense of order.

Appointed as first geographer of the United States as reward for his services during the revolution (he sided with the rebels), Hutchins headed a corps of surveyors that divided "the said territory into townships of 6 miles square, by lines running due north and south, and others crossing these at right angles, as near as may be. . . . The plats of the townships respectively shall be marked by subdivisions into lots of one mile square or 640 acres, the same direction as the external lines, and numbered from 1 to 36."

One-seventh of the lots were reserved by the Congress to fulfill its commitments to the officers and soldiers of the Continental Army. Additional lots were allocated by lottery to fulfill the individual states' promised bounties to their revolutionary militias. "Lots Nos. 8, 11, 26, 29, in all townships . . . were reserved to the United States for future sale"—the fiscal salvation of the fledgling central government.

The geographer's whole design was eagerly embraced by the New England delegations, especially Massachusetts and Connecticut, which had long organized their own states into townships. Despite cession of most of their western claims, they saw the Ohio Territories as extensions of themselves. Indeed, they had insisted that the Land Ordinance declare that "there shall

---

8. Slicing the democratic pie into smaller and smaller pieces is no guarantee of greater citizen participation. For the "big box" Albuquerque Public Schools, voter turnout averages 8–10 percent, while voter turnout for the nineteen school districts in "little box" Kent County, Michigan, averages 5–6 percent—neither turnout exactly a shining example of grass-roots democracy.

be reserved the lot No. 16 of every township for the maintenance of public schools." And in light of its proposed Western Reserve, Connecticut had insisted that townships there be laid out Connecticut style—five miles on a side rather than six.[9]

When the Ohio Territory was organized as a state in 1803, the survey townships ordained by the Continental Congress were converted into actual local governments. Township government built and cared for country roads, maintained the peace, and promoted local economic development. Townships gave rural citizens instruments of local government below county governments (though in southern and western states, county governments alone sufficed to meet rural citizens' need for representative democracy; again, county government was a function of *their* historical traditions).

For several generations, more densely settled municipalities viewed surrounding townships largely as land banks. Ohio municipalities annexed township lands when annexation served municipalities' needs. With the advent of rapid suburbanization after World War II, however, many townships were no longer composed of just farms and open lands. Townships themselves had become semi-urbanized communities with sophisticated local governments. Covetous of their positions, township officials increasingly resisted annexation. The Ohio legislature, in turn, strengthened townships' independence, eroding the annexation powers of municipalities and, in 1991, endowing townships with home rule status.

In Ohio the result was not only a highly balkanized political map (to 2,344 local general governments can be added 666 independent school systems) but the emergence of what Jack Dustin terms an ethic of highly competitive "civic individualism." Local communities competed—often bitterly—both to secure the tools that would support economic growth (canals, roads, railroads, tax abatement powers) and to attract and hold on to private businesses. How and when do such local governments reverse course and say they must no longer compete but must learn to work together? How do they come to share rather than lock themselves in fierce interjurisdictional competition and continue to bid away the benefits of regional economic growth?

Vertical intergovernmental revenue sharing is widespread. Throughout the United States the federal and state governments provide more than one-third of all local government revenues. Of $721 billion (fiscal 1994) in local

9. South of the Ohio River, in the lands claimed by Virginia, the Carolinas, and Georgia, those states' system of organizing local government into much larger counties rather than by smaller townships prevailed.

government revenues direct federal grants-in-aid totaled about $30 billion and state aid (including pass-through federal funds) totaled about $212 billion.[10]

Horizontal revenue sharing between local governments is far less prevalent. There are scattered examples of negotiated, bilateral revenue-sharing agreements between two governments. The city of Louisville and Jefferson County, Kentucky, have a multiyear "compact" to split local income tax revenues. The city of Charlottesville and Albemarle County, Virginia, split the growth in property taxes in return for Charlottesville's "no annexation" pledge. And there are numerous situations in which county governments collect local option taxes and redistribute them to municipalities under a negotiated formula; Georgia's "local option sales tax" would be an example. Another would be Monroe County, New York's apportioning sales tax to Rochester and twenty-nine other local governments and eighteen school districts.

By contrast, local *multijurisdictional* revenue sharing is very rare. All cases I know about are based on sharing revenues derived from incremental growth. One prominent example was spurred by construction of a new home stadium for the National Football League's New York Giants. In 1972 fourteen New Jersey townships created the Intermunicipal Tax Sharing Account to share revenue from the development of the Meadowlands sports complex in Hackensack, New Jersey; the program distributes approximately 40 percent of the growth in property tax revenues. Under a recent Ohio state law, Akron and Springfield have established successful joint economic development districts with local townships; in return for extension of municipal utilities to township-based industrial parks, the city collects payroll taxes from new industries while the townships harvest increased property taxes in a win-win arrangement.

Dayton-Montgomery County's ED/GE program is the nation's best example of a voluntary revenue-sharing compact among multiple local governments. Given the region's highly fragmented local governance, the ED/GE program is a significant achievement; the fruits of greater cooperation, rather than competition, on economic development issues have been substantial.

Limitations of Voluntary Compacts

Yet the second lesson of this chapter is that, in spite of herculean efforts, ED/GE's tax-sharing impact is negligible. To achieve significant regional rev-

10. Bureau of the Census (1997, tables 478, 482).

enue sharing (as described in this chapter), regional land use planning (as in chapter 8), and regional mixed-income housing (as in chapter 9) across multiple jurisdictions that jealously guard their local sovereignty, the legal ground rules under which they operate need to change.

The federal government can shape local government responsibilities to a limited degree. Through Congress and the federal courts the federal government can define local governments' responsibilities regarding those rights guaranteed their residents as national citizens; the Civil Rights Act of 1964, the Voting Rights Act of 1965, and the Americans with Disabilities Act of 1990 are excellent examples. Congress, of course, can also attach reasonable strings to its grants-in-aid to local governments. Federal writ follows the federal dollar.

But how local governments are organized and what respective powers they have are the domain of state governments. The U.S. Constitution is silent on the issue of local government; therefore, under the Tenth Amendment, determining the form and duties of local government is a power reserved to the states. The problem is that U.S. legislatures rarely exercise their authority to deal constructively with the growing complexity of governance in metropolitan areas. Typically, legislatures give considerable deference to local governments and local authority, heavily influenced by the American enshrinement of "home rule." (Home rule arguments become paramount, however, only when it suits legislators' political and ideological convenience.)[11]

Chapter 11 presents a case study of the regional reform movement in the Minnesota legislature. The reformers have been addressing all the key issues highlighted in the preceding chapters: urban sprawl, the concentration of poverty, fiscal disparities, fair share affordable housing. But Minnesota reformers have not tried to create broad, authorizing statutes to encourage voluntary cooperation among local governments. They have decided to change the statutory rules of the game. And they have demonstrated that success is based on building political coalitions among central cities, older suburbs, and rural areas appealing to the oldest motivation in the political book: raw, political self-interest.

11. Under the Canadian constitution, provincial governments have full authority over the conduct of local government affairs. In contrast to American state legislatures, Canadian provincial parliaments are much more robust in the exercise of their constitutional responsibilities regarding the form of local governance. Provincial governments not only established Metro Toronto (further combining and reorganizing municipal governments in the process), but also decreed regional arrangements for Montreal, Winnipeg, Edmonton, Vancouver, and several other Canadian urban areas.

11

Minneapolis-Saint Paul, Minnesota: The Winning Coalition

MYRON ORFIELD LOOKS as if he stepped out of a casting call into an updated remake of *Mr. Smith Goes to Washington,* Frank Capra's 1939 classic film of a small-town Everyman confounding the forces of reaction and privilege in the U.S. Congress. Lean, Nordic-handsome, six-foot-two, with a boyish earnestness to match Jimmy Stewart's original screen portrayal, Orfield is a four-term, Democratic Farmer Labor (DFL) party state legislator from Minneapolis. In his thirties, married, and father of a young son, Orfield is a true son of Minnesota. His Minnesota roots reach back three generations to his grandfather, Anders Ortfjeld, who emigrated from Trondheim, Norway, to a farm near Bellevue, Minnesota, in 1880.

The youngest of six children of a Minneapolis insurance agent, Orfield still lives in the Lyndale-Farmstead neighborhood that he grew up in and that he now represents in the Minnesota House of Representatives. After graduating from the University of Minnesota with a degree in history and political science, he studied American history at Princeton, then got his law degree from the University of Chicago in 1987. When not in the Minnesota legislature, he has taught courses on Fourth Amendment issues and legislative process as an adjunct professor at the University of Minnesota and Hamline University law schools.

A local newspaper profile has characterized Orfield as "more bookish than charismatic . . . [with] an academician's reserve. At public meetings, Orfield is more apt to give tutorials than speeches."[1] (And with a rapid-fire delivery, I might add. Orfield's verbal style sharply contrasts with the "Outstate" Minnesota languor so deftly captured in the 1996 film *Fargo*.) Orfield is a polite, but persistent, debater, controlling his emotions under even the harshest public attacks. One is sure that he was raised in the best "Minnesota Nice" tradition.

In short, Myron Orfield does not look or act like what he really is: the most revolutionary politician in urban America.

Orfield has forged the first enduring political alliance between the nation's declining central cities and older, threatened, blue-collar suburbs. A few academicians and journalists may have pointed out that urban poverty is spreading from inner city to inner suburb, but Orfield has developed the most compelling and comprehensive documentation of this trend and translated it into effective political action. The political coalition he has organized between legislators from Minneapolis-Saint Paul, their declining blue-collar suburbs, and what Orfield terms "developing, low-tax-capacity suburbs" has become a dominant force in the Minnesota legislature. Orfield has split the suburbs politically.

"Orfield's political strategy is the first new idea on the urban scene in many years," Tony Downs, the Brookings Institution's renowned urban guru, has noted. "He's making a vital contribution."[2]

Maps as Political Tools

Orfield has also pioneered a new political tool: maps. To be specific, multi-colored maps that, jurisdiction by jurisdiction, trace the decline of central cities and many older, inner-ring suburbs and the rise of affluent outer-ring suburbs. In place of the typical personal attacks on one's opponents that masquerade today as "negative campaigning," Orfield has substituted "fact attacks." With the help of staff from the legislature and state planning agencies, Orfield has produced plenty of maps—300 of the Twin Cities area alone. "No matter how skeptical listeners are," the same newspaper profile commented, "Orfield perseveres with more maps, more data, more explanations.

1. "Urban Visionary or Suburban Villain?" *Saint Paul Pioneer Press*, April 17, 1994, pp. 1b–2b.
2. Conversation with the author, April 22, 1996.

His detractors tire, retreat, and devise new assaults. Orfield, the Energizer Bunny of urban policy, keeps going and going and going."

Orfield is spreading the gospel of alliances between central cities and older suburbs—and his mapping acumen—across the country. Since his political breakthrough in the Minnesota legislature, he has been invited to speak in dozens of metro areas. With local foundation support, the non-profit group Orfield heads has mapped metrowide economic and social trends in Atlanta, Baltimore, Chicago, Cleveland, Detroit, Gary-Hammond, Grand Rapids, Los Angeles, Miami, Milwaukee, Philadelphia, Pittsburgh, Portland, Seattle, San Francisco, and Washington.[3]

The case Orfield's maps make for regional reform is graphic and compelling. Equally important, his credibility as a successful politician who has converted analysis into public policy makes him an even more effective expert witness in presenting his own material. Though focused on the Twin Cities, his first book, *Metropolitics,* lays out a comprehensive case for regional policy reforms.[4] Looking census tract by census tract across the 7 counties and 187 municipalities that form the bulk of the Twin Cities region, Orfield charts the widest array of demographic, educational, economic, and fiscal trends. The list ranges from poverty among children under the age of five to the allocation of state highway funds. It is truly a checklist of critical concerns that would add up to a comprehensive portrait of vast disparities in many metropolitan areas. Public policy activists and concerned citizens anywhere can use *Metropolitics* as an analytical starting point for their own communities. *Metropolitics* serves as a detailed road map for analyzing and understanding most urban regions in America.

Orfield's political odyssey began with his first campaign for the legislature in 1990. He faced heavy political odds. "Though someone on every block knew one of my relatives," he says, he was just twenty-eight, a political unknown, and facing better-known Democratic party insiders. He first won the DFL nomination, then the general election by knocking on every door in his district (some 17,000 doors) three times, asking residents for their vote and listening to their concerns.

"I grew up in Lyndale-Farmstead, but I was really shocked when I started going around the entire legislative district. I found a lot of people who were

---

3. Orfield's mapping operations outside Minnesota were initially carried out through the Metropolitan Area Program, a nonprofit subsidiary of the National Growth Management Leadership Project. In 1998 MAP was established as a separate, nonprofit organization, the Metropolitan Area Research Corporation, on whose board of directors I serve.

4. Orfield (1997).

really hurting, a lot of poverty. And it was getting worse," Orfield told me later. "The neighborhoods were changing fast for some reason, and something had to be done."

A Freshman Legislator's Debut

After his surprise victory, Orfield entered the Minnesota House of Representatives as the most junior of freshman legislators. Both houses were solidly under DFL control in 1991–92, Orfield's first term. Orfield's DFL colleagues held about 60 percent of the seventy-three House seats and thirty-six Senate seats from the Twin Cities area. All of Minneapolis and Saint Paul's seats and almost half the suburban seats were held by DFL members. Slightly more than half of suburban seats were filled by Independent-Republicans (IR).[5]

Like most state legislative bodies, the tradition in the Minnesota legislature is that freshmen should be seen, not heard, and must vote right (that is, with their party's leadership). But the young representative leaped right into the fray in his first session. Concerned about the rising poverty he had seen in his district, Orfield introduced and passed a bill to study the economic health of the Twin Cities and its inner-ring suburbs.

In the 1992 session Orfield's next bite at the apple was a tougher task. A metrowide system for financing sewers and sewage treatment plants had been created years ago. All householders in the Twin Cities region were being assessed a uniform fee for systemwide debt service, varying only by the size of each customer's sewer hook-up. As a result, householders and businesses in established core communities were forced to pay for new sewer extensions and treatment plant expansions on the urban fringe at the same rate as the residents of the new suburbs. In Orfield's eyes, many of the region's poorest households were subsidizing the creation of elite, suburban enclaves for many of the region's wealthiest residents.

In January 1992 Orfield introduced the Metropolitan Infrastructure Stability Act. He urged the legislature to overturn the uniform regional debt service system and require new developments to cover the true costs of their

5. In Minnesota both national political parties have recast their state-level images. The Democratic Farmer Labor party was formed by a coalition of all of Minnesota's rich tradition of left-of-center political parties just after World War II, a merger in which Minneapolis's youthful mayor, Hubert H. Humphrey, played a key role. After a crushing legislative defeat in 1974, the state's Republican party restyled itself the Independent-Republican party, trying to distance itself from Watergate and the disgraced President Richard Nixon.

own sewer expansion. Developers and suburban officials howled and succeeded in rapidly killing the Senate version. With the active support of the Local Government Committee chairman, however, Orfield's bill reached the House floor. In an eleventh-hour compromise, Orfield and his supporters agreed to withdraw the bill in return for a commitment of $400,000 in state funds for the University of Minnesota to make an independent study of freeway and sewer financing.

Having once been a freshman legislator myself in New Mexico, I can attest that passing even study bills is no small achievement. But Orfield, the "Energizer Bunny," was not content to wait for the results of the two studies. He had already embarked on his own exhaustive analysis of Twin Cities regional trends. He had an excellent mentor right at hand. Myron's older brother, Gary Orfield (now a Harvard University professor) had long been the nation's leading academic authority on school desegregation. An advocate of metrowide education strategies, Gary told his younger brother to focus on census tract data, particularly poverty rates among children. What the young legislator found would ultimately stun the Twin Cities area.

Twin Cities' Decline

For decades Minnesotans had prided themselves on the notion that they were exempt from the social problems that afflicted other urban communities. To begin with, the Twin Cities region saw itself as a prosperous and racially homogeneous society. In the 1990 census, the 2.5 million-resident Twin Cities area was 91 percent white. The region's median family income ($43,252, the 1990 census reported) ranked twenty-ninth highest among all 320 metro areas, while the region's 8 percent poverty rate fell far below the nation's 12 percent level.

The Twin Cities area also had a long and proud history of progressive government. Neither Minneapolis nor Saint Paul had ever fallen under the sway of big-city machine politics. The respected Citizens League was just one of many "good government" groups that embodied a high level of civic activism.

For a generation the Twin Cities area had been held forth as one of the nation's models of regional governance. In 1967 the Minnesota legislature had created the Metropolitan Council to bring some coherence to development planning for a region fragmented into 7 counties and 187 municipalities and townships. The "Met Council" was composed of seventeen citizens appointed by the governor, drawn from districts into which the region was divided. Supported by an excellent professional staff, the Met Council had been empowered by the legislature to coordinate regional airport policy, devise a regional sewage collection and treatment system, and develop regional land use policies. In the 1970s the Met Council successfully encouraged suburban communities to accept some subsidized housing. And, though not administered by the Met Council itself, the Twin Cities region benefited from the legislatively established fiscal disparities plan (1971), the nation's most significant regional revenue-sharing program.

In his research, however, Orfield discovered that during the "me decade" of the 1980s the Twin Cities had fallen prey to urban blight. Despite regional prosperity, poverty rates within the central cities were climbing. The 1990 census had reported poverty rates of 16.7 percent for Saint Paul and 18.5 percent for Minneapolis, both more than twice the regional poverty rate. In just a decade, the percentage of children receiving free lunches in the Minneapolis Public Schools increased from 33 percent to 52 percent. Across the Mississippi River (narrow so far north), in the Saint Paul Public Schools, the rate had increased from 28 percent to 55 percent.

But, as Orfield has told many audiences, "when poverty is seen as 'just an inner-city problem,' it has no political legs. It's when poverty becomes a suburban problem that you can do something politically." So Orfield shifted his analytic focus to the Twin Cities suburbs. He found that fortune smiled on only a part of suburbia: a band of suburbs to the south and west, which Orfield dubbed the "Fertile Crescent." Lying along Interstate 494, the Twin Cities' beltway, and stretching from Eagan on its eastern end to Maple Grove on its western terminus, the Fertile Crescent accounted for only 27 percent of the region's population but 61 percent of its job growth. Benefiting from the transfer of 88 percent of state and federal road construction funds during the 1980s, the Fertile Crescent's commercial and industrial tax base had soared 240 percent (compared with a 143 percent increase for the rest of the region). By 1992 the Fertile Crescent's commercial and industrial tax base per household was 62 percent higher than that of the rest of the region. The Fertile Crescent's median household incomes were 45 percent higher than the average of other communities.

Another quarter of the region's population lived in the "inner-ring" suburbs. Built up in the early postwar years, blue-collar suburbs such as Columbia Heights and Brooklyn Park were hurting. They lagged the Fertile Crescent by every indicator: they had captured only 18 percent of the region's new jobs, their household incomes were 30 percent below the Fertile

Crescent's, and they had only two-thirds of the Fertile Crescent's property tax base per household (even after the revenue-shifting impact of the fiscal disparities plan).

Most ominous was the rapid increase in economically stressed households in the inner-ring suburbs. During the 1980s, the number of married couples with children had dropped by one-quarter, while the percentage of single mothers had escalated to almost one-fifth of all families. Eleven percent of all inner-ring children lived in poverty, well below the 32 percent child poverty rate of the central cities but almost three times the percentage of poor children in the Fertile Crescent. Clearly, the sprawl machine in the Twin Cities area was victimizing inner-ring suburbs as well as Minneapolis and Saint Paul.

Building the Metropolitics Coalition

Orfield captured all these trends (and many more) in his maps and set out to recruit allies. It would, he realized, be difficult to persuade many suburbs "even if they were *in extremis*." "Allying politically with the cities," he later told me, "is foreign to their world view . . . a sort of political degradation to them." Throughout 1992, Orfield carried his maps and arguments to more than 100 meetings, first with individuals, then with larger groups. He targeted three key constituencies: community development corporations, church organizations, and inner-ring suburban officials.

During the autumn months, Orfield met regularly with inner-city community development corporations, Legal Aid representatives, and other neighborhood activists. He led them carefully through an understanding of regional development trends and their dire effects on inner-city communities. Orfield's maps graphically confirmed what many inner-city activists had long suspected: huge public expenditures were subsidizing the growth of exclusive communities on the metropolitan fringe to the severe detriment of central-city neighborhoods.

Getting inner-city groups to embrace a suburb-oriented reform agenda was a difficult task, however. Too often around the country the typical response is "Just send *us* more money to rebuild *our* neighborhoods." To many inner-city activists, regional strategies look like another plot to dilute black or Hispanic voting strength and undermine their own influence and position. At last, however, the Twin City groups committed their support for a package of regional reform bills, in particular, the proposed regional fair share housing act.

A second crucial component of the budding coalition was added when the North Metro Mayors Association (NMMA) publicly endorsed Orfield's reform package. The NMMA is an organization of northern suburban communities that banded together in 1982. Its membership includes both inner-ring suburbs and outer-ring communities that are rapidly developing new residential subdivisions. With most business expansion occurring in the Fertile Crescent, however, these modest-income bedroom communities lack adequate commercial and industrial tax bases to deal with the fiscal demands of rapid growth.

Throughout 1992, Orfield courted NMMA members in both individual and group meetings. By January 1993, on the eve of the legislative session, the NMMA was ready to act. At a large public meeting Orfield again displayed his maps and outlined his plans. The NMMA and its seventeen member cities endorsed his program. Their support would be crucial since these suburban cities had twenty-six House members (compared with only eighteen from Minneapolis and Saint Paul).

It was about this time that I first came in contact with Myron. One wintry afternoon just before Christmas 1992 I received a call from a youngish-sounding state legislator from Minnesota. He had heard about a book I was writing, *Cities without Suburbs*, from George Latimer, former mayor of Saint Paul and new chairman of the National Civic League, to whom I had sent a manuscript version. Could I send Myron a manuscript copy as well? I readily did.

I heard nothing further until four or five months later. My telephone rang one late spring morning. "Dave, this is Myron. I just finished reading your book last night. It proves all the things we have been fighting about up here. I sat down on my stairs for a moment to start to read it, and I got so engrossed that I didn't get up until I finished it.[6] Boy, I only wish that I had read it before the legislative session. But we had a lot of excitement here. Let me tell you about it."

The Battle Is Joined

And what a story Myron had to tell! His previous effort to reform the way the regional sewer system was financed had been criticized as too narrow.

6. Myron is not only a speed-talker but probably a speed-reader. However, Delcia did enjoin me that, if I wanted people to actually read *Cities without Suburbs*, it should not be long. At just 130 pages, my first book fit her formula.

For the 1993 session he proposed a broad package of six bills, collectively called the Metropolitan Community Stability Act. The bills were designed to promote fair share housing, reform the Met Council, tighten the regional land use planning system and reform the tax code affecting agricultural lands, strengthen the Met Council's role in transportation planning and transit services, reinvest more funds in inner-city revitalization, and stiffen the work requirements in Minnesota's welfare system. From Myron's retelling (and the evidence of dozens of news articles I subsequently reviewed) it was clear that the Metropolitan Community Stability Act—with its centerpiece, the fair share housing bill—had been a major battleground in the Minnesota legislature's 1993 session.

The Comprehensive Choice Housing Act (CCH) had been carefully devised with the advice of inner-city community groups, housing advocates, and the northern suburban mayors throughout the previous fall. It directed the Met Council to set "fair share" affordable housing goals for each of the area's 187 local communities. Communities would be credited for their existing supply of affordable housing. Minneapolis, Saint Paul, and many older, blue-collar suburbs would already have their "fair share," and the CCH's provisions would have no further effect on them.

For nonconforming communities, however, the CCH imposed three requirements: reduce unreasonable barriers embedded in restrictive zoning codes, development agreements, and practices; support public or private affordable housing providers; and ensure that affordable housing would continue to be affordable to low- and moderate-income renters. Communities that failed to make progress faced stiff penalties—the loss of general state financial aid, a freeze on state-assisted road and sewer construction, and prohibition on access to tax-increment financing.[7] In light of the severity of these penalties, the bill provided that final housing goals would be set by an administrative law judge, assuring local governments of due process (a political condition of the North Metro Mayors Association's support).

Finally, the bill directed that the Met Council focus its compliance activities first on those communities farthest from meeting their fair share goal. This "worst go first" rule assured some wavering blue-collar suburbs

---

7. Tax-increment financing permits a local community to front-end construction costs by bonding against a future revenue stream from properties whose value would be enhanced by the project. Instead of distributing enhanced property tax yields to the local school district or other public agencies, a city government will retain the "incremental" tax collections in a special category ("a tax-increment district") to pay off the bonds. Tax-increment financing had been a popular device of some Fertile Crescent cities to finance their own commerce-creating beltway interchanges.

that the Met Council would not follow a path of least resistance and load up their cities with even more low- and moderate-income housing; the primary targets would be the wealthy communities of the Fertile Crescent.

Throughout the four-month session the legislature battled over the Metropolitan Community Stability Act package. Voting blocs formed according to whether or not legislators thought their districts would benefit. Minneapolis, Saint Paul, the blue-collar suburbs, and rural areas with a poor tax base would clearly benefit. Of the forty-five House members from these regions, all but six were DFL. Orfield and colleagues worked strenuously to secure support from the six IR representatives from these areas; in the end, only one Republican House member (from inner-ring Saint Louis Park) voted for the housing bill. In the face of implacable opposition from Fertile Crescent IR members, Orfield concluded later, "it was simply too difficult for these [inner-ring] Republican members to oppose their normal allies on so controversial an issue."[8]

Most of the controversy surrounded the housing bill. The DFL-controlled legislature potentially had the votes to pass the housing bill and the other measures in Orfield's package. However, one big vote loomed ahead, that of popular IR Governor Arne Carlson. Early in the session Governor Carlson announced that he would be guided by the Met Council's views. Orfield took heart. In drafting the housing bill Orfield had made dozens of changes suggested by the Met Council staff. "By the time the bill was introduced," Orfield would write, "it was as much the council's bill as ours."[9]

But as Fertile Crescent opposition intensified, IR appointees on the Met Council wavered. Having supported the housing bill when first introduced, the Met Council now backtracked. Then, after the *Minneapolis Star Tribune* thundered editorially, "The Met Council Takes a Housing Dive," the council reversed course yet again and testified in support.

A Gubernatorial Veto

Governor Carlson's vote, however, would ultimately be determined not by the Met Council's position but by straightforward partisan politics. In mid-April the IR legislative caucus held a tumultuous closed-door meeting with the governor. Veto the housing bill, they told him, or we will not sustain any

8. Orfield (1997, p. 116).
9. Orfield (1997, p. 117).

of your other vetoes in the DFL-controlled legislature, particularly, the DFL-sponsored campaign finance reform bill that Carlson, a potent fund-raiser facing a reelection campaign, strongly opposed.

After the IR caucus meeting, Governor Carlson's opposition crystallized, and he issued a letter on April 23 outlining his objections to the housing bill and urging its withdrawal. The term "barriers to affordable housing" was not well defined, the governor claimed. The bill failed to deal with "the single most destructive barrier to low-income housing—land cost." It infringed on local governments' home rule prerogatives while overexpanding the Met Council's powers. Finally, the bill relied excessively on penalties rather than on incentives (he ignored the fact that his budget-cutting administration had already rejected any new spending or tax incentives).

Orfield and his colleagues countered the governor's objections and sought any possible compromise. The governor's door had shut. The much-amended Comprehensive Choice Housing Act passed the House 79 to 51, eleven votes short of overriding the promised veto. All but four DFL members voted in favor. (The four DFL dissenters all represented Fertile Crescent constituencies.)

The housing bill's supporters sought to create a veto-proof strategy in the Senate. They would graft the housing provisions into the omnibus state government appropriations bill. The governor would not veto the whole state appropriations bill over the housing provisions, they reasoned.

But they were wrong. After an IR-sponsored motion to delete the housing provisions failed by a single vote, the Senate had passed the appropriations bill. But, during the House-Senate conference committee in the session's waning hours, the governor's chief lobbyist made clear Carlson's unbending opposition. To each offered compromise, the lobbyist intoned, "That is a veto item." Finally, at 2:30 A.M., with all hope of compromise dead, the housing provisions were extracted from the appropriations bill.

Senate supporters made one last effort. The House-passed CCH was brought back to the floor and amended to meet all the governor's earlier objections. The result, Orfield later wrote, was "a toothless housing bill [that was] essentially a 'request' (without penalties) to communities to remove their housing barriers." The modified CCH was passed in the session's final hours, and just as promptly vetoed May 23 by the governor.

A few other parts of the Metropolitan Community Stability Act had fared somewhat better. A provision protecting farmers in urbanizing areas from storm sewer and road assessments became law, the last surviving provision of a more sweeping Metropolitan Land Use Policy Act. The package's welfare reform component passed as well, raising monthly stipends for single, able-bodied adults from $203 to $408 in return for twenty hours a week working at minimum wage in jobs that would rehabilitate depressed neighborhoods.[10]

However, the package's transportation planning bill was also vetoed. It had required the Met Council to assess whether traffic congestion could better be solved by expanding public transit than by building new or wider roads. In addition, each highway expansion would have to be evaluated for its impact on linking core area residents with expanding job opportunities out in the urban fringe. The bill was supported by the Met Council, the Minnesota Department of Transportation, and, in Orfield's phrase, "virtually every imaginable interest group." But it fell victim to the Fertile Crescent's paranoia that the Met Council's expanded powers might lead to some kind of fair share housing regulations or new curbs on development.

Falling short by just one vote—the governor's—obscured what a remarkable maiden session the coalition between the inner city and the inner ring had. A strong fair share housing bill, transportation and transit planning reform, limitations on farm infrastructure assessments and tax-increment financing, and welfare reform had all passed. The coalition had fallen apart on only one issue: the bill to convert Met Council membership from gubernatorial appointment to direct election. Fierce lobbying by the state's association of counties persuaded rural DFLers that an elected Met Council would shift too much power to the Twin Cities area to the detriment of rural interests. With its rural votes fading away, the coalition was unable to get the Met Council reorganization bill to the floors for a vote in either legislative chamber.

After such a bitterly fought legislative session, Governor Carlson was willing to extend one small olive branch. He agreed to appoint a state commission, the Advisory Commission on Metropolitan Governance, to be cochaired by Orfield and state Senator Carol Flynn (DFL-Minneapolis), who had sponsored the advisory commission notion. The seventeen-member commission would meet in the interim, then report its findings and recommendations for action in the 1994 session.

10. Welfare rights and inner-city organizations had strongly protested the measure. However, Orfield noted, the bill was "enormously popular among the middle-class suburban legislators" and passed unanimously as part of the omnibus health and human services act. Costing an estimated $25 million over its first two years, the program was not funded, however.

A Visit to the Twin Cities

The advisory commission's opening session in mid-September was the occasion of my first of four trips to the Twin Cities area. Myron and local supporters put together an extensive schedule for me and Neal Peirce, a veteran nationally syndicated columnist and coauthor of *Citistates,* another strong call for regionalism.[11] The highlight was the public forum Neal and I shared at the Landmark Center, a nineteenth-century Romanesque castle in downtown Saint Paul. It was my first direct exposure to the vibrant climate of civic participation that characterizes the Twin Cities region. The 250-seat auditorium was filled to capacity for a lunch-hour lecture series.

Neal outlined the central thesis of the just-published *Citistates,* namely, that communities must work together as a whole region in order to compete effectively in the emerging global economy. (After hearing Neal's arguments and talking further with him during that trip, I myself began to focus more on the issue of regional economic competitiveness.)

I followed with the themes of *Cities without Suburbs,* illustrated with extensive data about the Twin Cities area itself. Discussing the "Point of No Return" always grabbed an audience's attention. How did the Twin Cities measure up? Major population loss? Minneapolis down 30 percent, Saint Paul down 13 percent. Disproportionate minority population? Minneapolis 23 percent minority, Saint Paul 27 percent. This was not very high by many cities' standards, but within such an overwhelmingly white regional population, the central cities were clearly becoming catch basins for minorities. City-suburb income ratio? Minneapolis 84 percent, Saint Paul 78 percent. Well above the critical 70 percent threshold but both trending steadily downward.

"Unlike a Hartford, Newark, or Detroit, for example, the Twin Cities numbers are not horrifying," I told the Landmark audience, "but they make me just plain mad. I see the patterns I've described above and say 'Darn! These people ought to be doing a better job. They've got so much going for them.'" But I had also learned my new lesson well from Myron. I continued:

> This decline is rooted in the very patterns of ever increasing suburban sprawl that have dominated American lifestyles over the past forty years. And my analysis is too simplistic. It is not just the traditional central cities that are victimized by this steady process of withdrawal and abandonment by the

11. Peirce and Johnson (1993).

middle class. As state Representative Myron Orfield and his legislative allies have shown so convincingly, older, inner-ring suburbs are victimized as well. What we too superficially classify as "inner-city" problems are spreading out into older, blue-collar suburbs.

I reminded them that these older suburbs have fewer assets to call upon to fight growing crime, poverty, and family disintegration. Unlike the great old cities, these suburbs do not have prestigious neighborhoods where wealthy people still choose to live or the endowment of wonderful parks, museums, and other civic facilities that are the legacy of past glory, or downtown areas that are employment centers for the region. Although the Twin Cities area and the state had pioneered some of the most notable initiatives in building a metropolitan *community,* I told them that they had let wise policies slip away. To get back on track, they had to address a key, but simple, question:

> Is the Twin Cities area going to continue to become a society increasingly segregated by income? Are the most advantaged going to keep segregating themselves more and more in enclaves of privilege farther and farther out? Are the most disadvantaged going to be segregated more and more in decaying inner-city neighborhoods and declining inner-ring suburbs?

The choice they faced, I said, was whether to strengthen their sense of community or continue down a path of ever more fragmented governance: "Fragmented governance promotes fragmented citizenship—the withdrawal of the middle class from the practice of civic responsibility and the isolation of the poor from the example of personal responsibility."

Then I drew upon an anecdote that tells of three medieval stonemasons who were once asked what they did. The first said he was paid to cut stone. The second stated that he applied his talent and skill to extract extraordinary shapes from blocks of marble. The third smiled and said simply, "I build cathedrals." The Twin Cities had the conditions and the right tools, I told them. If they had the courage and the vision, they, too, could build a cathedral.

Expanding the Metropolitics Coalition

Myron and his colleagues needed no cathedral-building guidance from me. Between sessions they recruited allies from the Twin Cities religious community. The strongest support came from the Saint Paul Ecumenical Alliance, which sponsored two large public rallies in February 1994 supporting the regional reform movement. Shortly thereafter the Joint Ministries Project in Minneapolis signed on, followed by the Interfaith Action Organization and the Metropolitan Interfaith Coalition for Affordable Housing. Guided by Archbishop John Roach's powerful public statements, the Catholic Office for Social Justice was particularly influential in developing suburban support for fair share housing.

By mid-1994 the coalition building took on new institutional solidity with the formation of the Alliance for Metropolitan Stability. The alliance brought together church groups, environmental organizations concerned about managing growth, inner-city antipoverty groups, and neighborhood associations. Funded by local foundations, the alliance became a focal point for rallying broadly based political support for the regional reform agenda.

The Advisory Commission on Metropolitan Governance, however, had not proved to be the "watershed" I had prophesied. Characterized by the same partisan politics that divided the legislature, the advisory commission was unable to reach agreement on hot issues such as fair share housing or expanding the fiscal disparities plan. After several months of meetings, its only significant recommendation was that the legislature end the semi-independent status of three regional agencies—the Regional Transit Board, the Metropolitan Transit Commission, and the Metropolitan Waste Control Commission—and make them operating divisions of the Met Council. The advisory commission also recommended the direct election of Met Council members, but by so narrow a margin that the recommendation would carry little political weight.

The growing base of public support for the regional reform agenda was softening some of the Fertile Crescent's opposition. In the wake of a bitter public controversy over fair share housing in Maple Grove, one of the fastest-growing Fertile Crescent cities, three IR House members introduced the Metropolitan Poverty Reduction Act of 1994, immediately dubbed "Orfield Lite" by the press.

The suburban IR bill was a pastiche of different provisions. To promote affordable housing, it proposed reducing the building materials tax on low-income housing developments and better coordinating existing affordable housing programs and funding. It recommended support for a pilot project in Eden Prairie, another Fertile Crescent city that was already planning such a local initiative. And "Orfield Lite" would strengthen the region's "reverse commute" programs, under which more than 2,000 central-city workers were

being transported daily to Fertile Crescent job sites. (Reverse commuting programs are often easily embraced by suburban officials. In effect, their message to inner-city residents is "Come work here—just don't try to live here.")

The forces behind fair share housing praised the housing provisions of
the Metropolitan Poverty Reduction Act, despite their modest impact. It
represented a significant change in Fertile Crescent rhetoric, Orfield thought.
Whereas the previous position had been "nothing, no time, never," the conservatives' bill represented "a symbolic acceptance of suburban affordable-
housing policy and regional responsibility for the problems of the city and
older suburbs."[12]

The killer provision of the "Orfield Lite" package, however, was that its
IR sponsors tied the housing provisions to Governor Carlson's sweeping reform of the state's troubled workmen's compensation program. They argued that the state's costly workmen's benefits hurt job creation. Cutting
those costs would greatly help to create more jobs, reduce unemployment,
and revitalize inner-city neighborhoods.

Workmen's compensation had become a litmus test issue in Minnesota
politics. For a generation, a DFL-labor union alliance had squared off against
an IR-business coalition. Both sides were unyielding. When IR sponsors refused to support their own modest housing proposals without full enactment of the governor's workmen's compensation reforms, the Metropolitan
Poverty Reduction Act was pronounced "dead on arrival" in the DFL-controlled 1994 legislative session.

Looking for opportunities for compromise, the pro-housing coalition
reintroduced the previously vetoed Comprehensive Choice Housing Act.
Public support had grown. Beyond the church coalitions, the League of
Women Voters, and other community organizations, the Association of
Metropolitan Municipalities, representing 85 percent of the region's population, endorsed the bill. The *Minneapolis Star Tribune* editorialized eight
times in support, while three times the *Saint Paul Pioneer Press* called editorially for a housing compromise.

The governor's opposition was unyielding. In desperation, the pro-housing forces unilaterally stripped the bill of the penalty provisions and passed
it on straight party-line votes. Governor Carlson just as promptly vetoed it
for the second straight year, despite the fact that the penalties (his principal
objection) had been dropped. Orfield commented that the governor's game
was one that no one could win.

12. Orfield (1997, p. 129).

The regional agenda had moved forward with one modest success. The advisory commission had introduced its bill to elect Met Council members and place the three regional agencies directly under the council. An elected Met Council faced fierce opposition from both the Association of Metropolitan Counties (which feared loss of county government power in Hennepin, Ramsey, and other metro counties) and the statewide county association, which argued again that a more powerful regional government would dry up state aid for outstate Minnesota. The counties' lobbying efforts stripped at least ten DFL votes from Orfield's coalition, and the measure was defeated on the House floor by a 65 to 64 vote.

However, there was bipartisan support for the advisory commission's second recommendation: folding the independent regional agencies into the Met Council structure. The defeated bill was called back to the floor, stripped of the elected council provisions, and passed overwhelmingly.

So ended the second session of "Metropolitics" (as Orfield had begun to call the coalition). Again, in the short 1994 session, the coalition had succeeded in passing a regional fair share housing bill, to be frustrated by the governor's veto. The effort to convert the Met Council from a gubernatorially appointed state agency to a popularly elected regional government had failed by the narrowest of margins. With the addition of the three regional agencies, however, the Met Council would have operating authority over regional road, transit, and sewer agencies with a combined annual budget of over $400 million. Second only in budgetary size to Hennepin County itself, the Met Council had been turned into a more powerful force for regional unity. Most important, for the first time in its history the Met Council combined all major land use planning and transportation responsibilities. With its greatly expanded powers, if the Met Council could be converted into a directly elected body, or the governor's appointees shaken out of their conservatism, the Met Council could exercise tremendous power on behalf of regional reforms, Orfield judged.

Strengthening Regional Tax Base Sharing

The 1994 election brought new challenges to Metropolitics. Faced with a weak DFL candidate, Governor Carlson won a landslide reelection for a second term. Nor was Minnesota otherwise exempt from the Republican tide that swept the nation. Though the state Senate was not up for reelection, IR candidates scored major gains in the House. The DFL lost thirteen seats, bringing the House to sixty-nine DFL members and sixty-five IR members. Six DFL seats were lost in inner-ring and low-tax-capacity outer-ring suburbs, and two DFL incumbents lost their seats in Fertile Crescent districts.

The elections did not seem to have been influenced directly by the legislative battles over the regional reform package. Nevertheless, Orfield and his allies had lost the DFL-based margin needed to pass a housing bill. Any success for the regional agenda would have to be based on issues that could attract some IR votes, especially among newly elected freshman representatives from inner-ring swing districts. Orfield turned his efforts to revising the region's fiscal disparities plan.

The fiscal disparities plan has been the Twin Cities region's greatest claim to fame among progressive "good government" circles for a generation. It is worth examining its history and impact at some length before turning to the reform efforts in the 1995 legislative session.

The fiscal disparities plan was enacted by the Minnesota legislature in 1971 (by a one-vote margin in the House), but court challenges delayed its implementation until 1975. Fertile Crescent legislators have made repeated efforts ever since to repeal the program.

The Met Council has described the plan's rationale succinctly:

> From a regional perspective the Twin Cities is one economy. Large commercial-industrial developments tend to concentrate in a few locations, drawing workers and clients from a market area that is larger than the city it is located in. Access to these concentrations, primarily highways, is a prime determinant of where these developments locate. Cities with such access are the ones most likely to get commercial-industrial development.
>
> Since the property tax is the primary source of local government revenues, certain types of development—office space, headquarters buildings, up-scale housing—are attractive because they typically generate more revenue than it costs to serve them. Not all cities can expect to attract such development, but most participate in financing the regional facilities serving these developments. The ideas underlying tax-base sharing is to allow all cities to share in the commercial-industrial development that is, to a large extent, the result of the regional market and public investments made at the regional and state levels.[13]

13. Metropolitan Council (1995).

The law requires all taxing jurisdictions in a seven-county area, including 186 cities, villages, and townships, 48 school districts, and about 60 other taxing authorities, to contribute 40 percent of the *increase* in the assessed value of commercial-industrial property into a common pool. (A community's pre-1971 assessed valuation is totally exempted.) The pool is taxed at a common millage, and revenues are redistributed among all local governments on the basis of each jurisdiction's population and its "tax capacity" (per capita market value of commercial and industrial property) in relation to the regionwide tax capacity. A jurisdiction with below-average tax capacity receives a relatively larger distribution from the regional pool, and a jurisdiction with above-average tax capacity receives somewhat less.

By 1998 the annual fiscal disparities fund had reached $410 million, almost 30 percent of the region's total commercial-industrial property tax collections.[14] Among cities, villages, and townships, 137 were net recipients, while 49 were net contributors. Over the years the net contributors had consistently been the Twin Cities' wealthiest suburbs, such as Bloomington, Minnetonka, Eden Prairie, Edina, and Plymouth. Giant shopping malls, office towers, garden-like industrial parks had sprouted vigorously along the interstate highways that cut through these Fertile Crescent cities or lay adjacent to the Minneapolis–Saint Paul International Airport.

The major recipients were Saint Paul, many inner-ring suburbs in Hennepin and Ramsey Counties, and virtually all towns and villages lying well beyond the suburban beltways. Fueled by its downtown office boom, Minneapolis moved from largest net recipient in 1980 to second largest net contributor in 1990. (Its $19 million net contribution in 1991 represented 6.5 percent of its total commercial and industrial tax capacity.) With the devaluation of its downtown office buildings during the 1990s bust, however, by 1995 Minneapolis was once again the second largest net recipient.

Orfield and his allies made an abortive attempt to expand the fiscal disparities concept in the 1994 session. Their Metropolitan Reinvestment Act would have included residential property in regional tax base sharing for the first time. The bill specified that all cities would keep the full tax base on

14. The relative value of the shared pool has fallen from a peak 31.8 percent of all commercial and industrial property taxes in 1992. Commercial and industrial assessed valuation and rates fell in some communities, often because of court rulings in contested assessments. In its first year (1975) the shared pool represented 6.7 percent of commercial and industrial valuation. By 1998, the polled revenues distributed reached $410 million (about 28 percent of all commercial and industrial property taxes).

all homes up to $150,000 in value, but any increment above $150,000 would be contributed to a regional pool. Orfield calculated this would have yielded a net $113 million for redistribution in 1994.

The differential impact of residential tax base sharing, if anything, would be greater than the redistribution of the commercial and industrial tax base under the existing fiscal disparities plan. Measured by population, only 24 percent of the region's cities would contribute to the remaining 76 percent. Most net givers would be in the Fertile Crescent; the net recipients would be Minneapolis and Saint Paul, inner-ring cities, and outer-ring suburbs with a low tax capacity. Even after the tax pool, however, the Fertile Crescent would have high tax bases to support local services.

Unlike the existing fiscal disparities plan, however, the pooled funds would not be redistributed for general government services. The funds would be targeted toward housing issues. One-third of the pool would be allocated to suburbs that had not met affordable housing goals; they could either use the funds to provide the housing locally or turn implementation over to the Minnesota Housing Finance Agency. Two-thirds of the pool would flow to cities that had already exceeded their fair share of affordable housing. They could use the funds for reinvestment in and redevelopment of declining neighborhoods.

Introducing the bill late in the short session, Orfield had admittedly not prepared the political ground well. The usual suspects—Fertile Crescent legislators and Governor Carlson—quickly lined up in violent opposition, but some of the presumed beneficiaries were critical as well. Saint Paul and many northern suburbs were convinced they would receive more back than they contributed, but they really preferred to get their money back without housing-related strings attached.

As political support eroded, the sponsors cut the strings loose and placed the housing-based revenues directly into the fiscal disparities plan. This attracted enormous support; the revised bill had, in Orfield's words, "the momentum of a rodeo bull in a steel chute."[15] Faced with certain veto, however, the bill became trade bait. Senate leadership killed it in exchange for votes on a controversial measure for decommissioning a nuclear power plant. They promised to support tax-sharing reform in the 1995 session.

For the 1995 session Orfield upped the ante. The abortive 1994 effort had shown that, with the right formula, regional tax sharing was a political silver bullet. Orfield decided to move for approval of a Metro Fair Tax Base

15. Orfield (1997, p. 139).

Act that would create a unified regional tax base and redistribute almost $1 billion, which was four times the impact of the fiscal disparities plan. The bill would require net recipient cities to use half the tax base received as the basis for a property tax cut. "The Metro Fair Tax Base Act offered recipient cities and their politicians exactly what American politicians always promise," Myron commented to me, "a tax cut and better services."

The North Metro Mayors Association held a summit meeting and quickly declared its support, as did virtually all member groups of the Alliance for Metropolitan Stability. Major efforts were made to wean IR representatives from low-tax-capacity suburbs away from the Fertile Crescent–dominated IR caucus, particularly an IR House member from low-tax-capacity Anoka, whose House predecessor a generation before had been a key sponsor of the original Fiscal Disparities Act. To no avail. Hardball tactics within the IR caucus prevented any early IR support.

Faced with across-the-board rejection by potential IR recruits and widespread controversy fanned by incendiary television news coverage and right-wing talk show hosts, the sponsors scaled the bill back. They decided to leave the existing commercial and industrial-oriented fiscal disparities plan untouched. Then they scaled back residential coverage first to home values over $150,000 (the 1994 bill's level), then to home values over $200,000, finally to just new *growth* of the residential tax base above $200,000. The concessions would shrink the annual pool to just $44 million but shift the ratio between net givers and net recipients from 26–74 to 17–83, which would bring more legislators into the ranks of supporters. These compromises allowed moderate members of both parties to support the bill but by no means reduced the violent opposition from the Fertile Crescent.

"Take no prisoners" was the order of the day in both camps. Opponents vilified Orfield and his allies as "communists" and "Marxists." Noting that the original fiscal disparities plan had been enacted in 1971 with key Republican support, proponents countered that the Metro Fair Tax Base Act, as now amended, was simply "a gentle enhancement of a good Republican idea." Expert studies volleyed back and forth.

After long and acrimonious hearings and floor debate, the scaled-back Metro Fair Tax Base Act passed the House 71 to 63. All DFL members except four from high-tax-capacity districts voted in favor. In a key move three IR representatives from low-tax-capacity districts joined in support. After a procedural misadventure, the bill passed the Senate 36 to 30. The weakened Metro Fair Tax Base Act was, of course, promptly vetoed by Governor Carlson.

A Compromise Housing Bill

After Governor Carlson's reelection and the loss of key DFL seats in the House, Orfield had despaired of getting meaningful fair share housing legislation past the governor's veto pen. State Senator Ted Mondale (DFL-Saint Louis Park), son of former Vice President Walter Mondale, stepped into the breach. In negotiations through the summer and fall of 1994, Mondale and Curt Johnson, Governor Carlson's former chief of staff and newly appointed Met Council chairman, labored to devise a regional affordable housing bill acceptable to the governor.[16]

The result was the Metropolitan Livable Communities Act, which was introduced at the outset of the 1995 session. The initial bill gave the Met Council the power to "negotiate" affordable housing goals with all regional jurisdictions in order to carry out the Met Council's Regional Blueprint. (The twice-vetoed Comprehensive Choice Housing Act would have allowed the Met Council to set such goals through an administrative hearing procedure.) Mondale and Johnson adopted a variation of the failed Metropolitan Reinvestment Act's provisions for pooling the tax base. Rather than pool home values above $150,000, the new bill would require each jurisdiction to pool all home values above an amount equal to twice the value of the jurisdiction's average home. The result would have created a modest pool of funds (about $2.4 million in the initial year) that would have grown slowly but steadily over time. Local jurisdictions could choose either to send their contributions to a regional affordable housing fund or to administer their contributions themselves to meet their own jurisdictions' negotiated targets. If they already met their targets, the funds would be used to upgrade deteriorated housing stock. Two of the bill's other provisions would promote broadly defined environmental cleanup goals and fund a $5 million model low-income housing project.

"The Mondale-Johnson compromise," Orfield would observe, "was just the beginning" of compromise.[17] House IR leaders still thought the bill too strong and demanded further concessions. First, pooling taxes on high-value homes was made voluntary. Mondale and Johnson argued that there would still be incentives for local jurisdictions to contribute, above all, because the

---

16. Johnson is also a regular collaborator in the series of community studies known as Peirce Reports and is a principal of the Citistates Group, with which I am affiliated.

17. Orfield (1997, p. 151).

bill authorized the Met Council to take into consideration local nonparticipation in its allocation of sewer and road funds. Second, power over the proposed housing pool (to the extent that any community voluntarily contributed) was shifted from the Met Council to county governments. With that concession, counties that should have more affordable suburban housing (for example, Hennepin and Carver) probably would not, and counties that would (for example, Ramsey and Anoka) probably should not. The only metro county well positioned to use the fund would be Dakota County (which I believe has one of the most progressive suburban housing authorities in the nation).

As the Metropolitan Livable Communities Act reached the floor, there was little controversy left. Weary of the long battle, the two metropolitan dailies hailed the bill and called for its approval. It would give the Met Council the statutory authority to negotiate goals and the ability to withhold infrastructure grants from cities that did not participate voluntarily in the regional housing program. The bill passed handily, and, at long last, a regional affordable housing bill was signed into law by Governor Carlson at the close of the 1995 session.

"In the end," observed Orfield, who had carried the battle for suburban affordable housing for so long, "the victory was more symbolic than substantive (much like the 1957 Civil Rights Act, the weak precursor of the 1964 act). The [Metropolitan Livable Communities Act] broke the deadlock, and the basic approach of the [Comprehensive Choice Housing Act] was accepted. Like the 1957 Civil Rights Act, the Metropolitan Livable Communities Act was a platform on which a stronger and more enforceable act can be built." Orfield concluded, "It also put the southwestern suburbs on notice: if things do not happen under the voluntary system, fair housing forces will be back."[18]

An Elected Met Council

Both sides, however, rested during the 1996 session, in part out of exhaustion, in part to let implementation of the compromise housing bill get started. In 1997, however, the Metropolitics coalition enacted what Orfield would call "the most important measure yet": popular election of Met Council members. Defeated in the 1994 session, making the Met Council account-

18. Orfield (1997, p. 152).

able not to the governor but to the citizens directly was a cause that had since gained new support. Thanks to the Metropolitics coalition's successful expansion of the Met Council's powers, the Met Council's $418 million budget in fiscal 1997 was second only to that of Hennepin County among Minnesota's local governments. The Met Council's property tax level was $107 million, and it had $687 million in bonded indebtedness. The council designates where all major roads will be built, annually constructs tens of millions of dollars of new sewer projects, runs the transit system, and supervises the airport authority. The cry for ending "taxation without representation" had gained new force among many more conservative legislators.

The elected Met Council bill passed both the House and, surprisingly, the Senate. (State senators traditionally feared that, with much larger constituencies than senate districts, elected Met Council members might become more politically influential than state senators.)

Governor Carlson's press secretary predicted another veto. The governor, he said, objected to adding another layer of "elected bureaucracy." He also objected to public financing of Met Council election campaigns (about 10 cents per voter, the bill's proponents pointed out).[19] Though expressing some support, Curt Johnson, the current Met Council chairman, observed: "I worry that if you start electing people to these positions, it will be difficult and often impossible to get the members to look across the jurisdictional lines and consistently vote for what makes sense for the whole region."[20] "No Met Council could be more 'parochial,'" a *Minneapolis Star Tribune* editorial countered, "than the present body, which consists wholly of gubernatorial appointees who must constantly toe the governor's line on regional issues or risk getting immediately fired."[21]

"Signing the bill would be consistent with his votes in support of an elected Metropolitan Council back in the early 1970s, when Carlson served as a member of the Minnesota House.[22] The ideal of regional government of the people, by the people, and for the people that Rep. Carlson embraced then deserves no less support from Gov. Carlson now."[23]

19. Contributions from land developers, homebuilders, and contractors played major roles in Minnesota politics. Six of the Met Council's seventeen members in 1997 were land developers.

20. "House OKs Bill to Elect Met Council Members," *Minneapolis Star Tribune*, May 7, 1997.

21. "Metro Democracy: Carlson Shouldn't Get in the Way," *Minneapolis Star Tribune*, May 13, 1997.

22. As a state representative, Arne Carlson had sponsored an elected Met Council bill in 1971 and voted for similar bills in 1973 and 1975.

23. "Metro Election: One Step Down, Two to Go," *Minneapolis Star Tribune*, May 9, 1997.

On May 15, 1997, Governor Carlson vetoed the bill despite his earlier support of an elected Met Council when he was a legislator. It was yet another proof of the adage "where you stand depends on where you sit." Responded Representative Orfield: "The bill will be brought forth again."

Lessons of Metropolitics

Metropolitics is a continuing process, of course, a story without a last chapter. But Orfield and his allies have already taught urban America some vital lessons, above all about the real political arena in which regional reform movements must be prepared to do battle: the state legislature. Even though citizens may believe that local home rule is sacrosanct, throughout the nation local government is, in reality, "the child of state government." State legislatures control local governments' scope of powers, particularly in the areas of tax policy and land use planning and development regulation. "Home rule" states (like Ohio) afford local governments broad flexibility. "Dillon's Rule" states (like Virginia) maintain a tight rein over local governments.

In a democratic society all sovereignty ultimately flows from the people. I have heard it argued that the voters in federal elections, state elections, and local elections are all the same people with presumably the same personal values and self-interests. That is true. How can a state legislature be expected to do collectively what local governments would not do individually if both are accountable to the same voters? How can legislators be expected to overcome the intense factionalism of highly fragmented urban areas?

I was led to the best answer by a historical reference made by a forgotten speaker at a conference I attended but can no longer identify. As so often happens, it is one of the Founding Fathers who provided the crucial insight, in this instance, James Madison's Federalist Paper 10, arguing for approval of the newly proposed Constitution of the United States. As Myron's brother, Gary, summarized Madison's argument,

> James Madison wrote that the best way to cure the evil of narrow factions pursuing narrow interests that undermine the interest of the broader community is to expand the scope of the community. By bringing a wider diversity of interests into a larger government, he said, there would be less likelihood of the tyranny of a narrow majority and greater likelihood of a full debate leading to the pursuit of broader community-wide interests. Madison reasoned that "the smaller the society" devising a policy, the more

likely that a local majority, not balanced by other forces and considerations, will "concert and execute their plans of oppression."[24]

In highly fragmented metro areas, without the creation of an elected regional government like Portland Metro, there is no public body to speak to the interests of the entire region. It is only at the state level that local citizens' interests are placed in a framework that addresses their interests as citizens of the entire state or of a substate metropolitan region. State legislatures *must* serve as regional policy bodies because they are the only ones that can. Legislatures must set new ground rules for how the myriad local governments must share common responsibilities for common problems.

The second lesson from Metropolitics is that communities seldom make progress on hard, divisive issues through friendly, consensual agreement. They do so by building political coalitions. And those coalitions are most durable when based on each member's political self-interest—that is, their perception of the interests of the constituencies they represent. The glue that held Metropolitics together was social, economic, and political self-interest.

"The politics of self-interest were particularly apparent in the housing bill," Orfield observed about the legislative battles:

> The decisive suburban political support was largely defensive in character. Civil rights and access to opportunity were an important part of the housing bill's rationale. But most suburban members—and city members, for that matter—supported fair housing, largely to protect their communities from an "unfair" burden of low-income housing and from future neighborhood decline. These members were resigned to the fact that their communities had poor people. They believed that the [Fertile Crescent] must also accept their fair share of poor residents and accompanying social costs.[25]

The third lesson is that the mathematics of local self-interest would by and large provide Metropolitics coalitions with the potential to win. University of Minnesota geographer John Adams has shown that almost every large metro area is characterized by "the Favored Quarter," a slice of the region where most high-end commercial and residential development occurs. In Chicago, the Favored Quarter is the northwestern suburbs around Schaumberg

24. Orfield (1996).
25. Orfield (1997, p. 116).

and Hoffman Estates. In Memphis, the Favored Quarter extends through East Memphis to Germantown and Collierville. In Atlanta, the Favored Quarter grows out through the Buckhead area of North Atlanta into Cobb County. And so on, in almost every metro area that I have visited.

In three short years Minnesota's Metropolitics coalition racked up a remarkable legislative record. It enacted three fair share housing bills, approved a new regional revenue-sharing formula pooling tax revenues from high-end housing, restructured regional sewer and transportation agencies with annual budgets totaling $400 million, changed the tax code, expanded the Met Council's powers, and converted the Met Council from an appointed to an elected body. The coalition most often was stymied by one vote: Governor Carlson's. Only his vetoes prevented more sweeping redefinition of regional benefit sharing and regional burden sharing.

Portland may be the nation's model for regional land use planning and growth management. Maryland's Montgomery County may offer the widest range of exemplary mixed-income housing policies. The Twin Cities fiscal disparities plan may be the nation's most extensive regional revenue-sharing program. But the Minnesota legislature has been engaged in the battle over all the crucial regional issues. And Orfield and his colleagues have shown how to put together the winning coalition. Metropolitics itself is the most important regional reform model in the nation.

PART THREE

Changing the Rules of the Game

PART 2 OUTLINED policies that have proved effective against urban sprawl, concentrated poverty, and fiscal disparities. What Portland, Montgomery County, Maryland, or Minnesota have accomplished is not unique. Other examples could be cited from other communities.

However, these are probably the best, in part because these communities have had almost a quarter of a century's experience with a regional growth boundary, a countywide mandatory mixed-income housing policy, or a regional tax-base sharing program. Their long-term success makes them all the more persuasive and reliable models for other states and communities to adopt and emulate.

What rules need to be changed or what the new rules should be seems clear enough. What is lacking is the political will to act in state legislatures, county courthouses, and township and city halls around the country. Part 3 focuses on the coalitions needed to move the political system to act. Chapter 13 provides case studies of faith-based movements (the Northwest Indiana Federation of Interfaith Organizations), business-driven groups (Virginia's Urban Partnership), the role of activist academics (the Ohio Housing Research Network), and grass-roots citizens' groups (Rochester's Metropolitan Forum). Attention is also given to the vital role (and limitations) of philanthropic foundations in helping finance reform movements, and also to the many city mayors (whose constituents have the most to gain) who, like reluctant warriors, generally stand on the sidelines of regional reform movements.

But first chapter 12 recounts the halting efforts to redirect federal public housing policy, an example of good intentions gone terribly awry. For three crucial decades federal public housing policy has been the greatest promoter of economic and racial segregation in America's urban areas.

12

Changing Federal Public Housing Policies

AT FIRST THE television screen showed puffs of smoke shooting from the base of the giant shape. Then the explosive cloud billowed outward, engulfing the lower half of the multistoried structure, which shuddered and then slowly crumpled downward into a huge pile of dust and rubble.

It was 1972, and the television pictures might have been of the failed launching of a giant Saturn 5 rocket. But all the launches succeeded, carrying U.S. astronauts to their rendezvous with the moon. Each rocket would recede like a flaming meteor in reverse and, shortly thereafter, vanish from earthbound view. Within minutes the space capsule would break free of Earth's grip, carrying the hopes of the human race soaring into the heavens.

No, this was not the launching of a moonshot on the television screen. This was an image of humankind's hopes, gripped by the hard, earthly realities of poverty and discrimination, crumbling into dust. This was the dynamiting of the massive, high-rise, Pruitt-Igoe public housing project in Saint Louis. Headlining network broadcasts across America, the demolition of Pruitt-Igoe was one of the era's unforgettable images.

What stunned many viewers was that Pruitt-Igoe was not some decades-old structure, now technologically obsolescent. The apartment complex had been built only seventeen years before, in 1955, and had been lauded for its state-of-the-art design by federal and local housing officials and community leaders alike. The design won an award from the American Institute of Architects.

Why were these buildings being destroyed so soon? Very simply, Pruitt-Igoe had spawned an untenable social environment. With Saint Louis's poorest families warehoused in its multistory towers, civilized life in Pruitt-Igoe had disintegrated. Fear and violence ruled the dimly lit hallways and stalked dirt expanses littered with broken glass surrounding the buildings.

Pruitt-Igoe was much more than a failure of architecture or property management. It was the failure of a concept: the belief that the most poverty-stressed families could be housed successfully in such high concentration. After experimenting with several management approaches, the Saint Louis Housing Authority and officials from the federal Department of Housing and Urban Development reached a painful conclusion. Pruitt-Igoe could never be made to work. It was better to level it than to continue trying to make it a suitable environment for mothers to raise young children.

Demolishing Big Mistakes

It took HUD twenty-three more years to really learn the lesson of Pruitt-Igoe. Not until 1995 did major demolition of high-density public housing projects begin again. On local television I watched Baltimore's Lafayette Courts and Lexington Terrace implode in seconds. They had become familiar to me during my many visits to Baltimore while I researched and wrote *Baltimore Unbound.*[1]

Closer to home, wrecking balls leveled Ellen Wilson Homes, a bleak complex of thirteen barracks-like apartment buildings in Southeast Washington, on the edges of upscale Capitol Hill. And out of my personal viewing range (demolition of public housing no longer making network news), the Vaughn Apartments in Saint Louis (next to the vacant Pruitt-Igoe site) came tumbling down, joined by Newark's Christopher Columbus Homes, Chicago's notorious Cabrini-Green and Henry Horner Homes, and two-score other projects, including the granddaddy of them all, Atlanta's Techwood, the nation's first public housing project, built in 1936.

By the end of 1996 HUD had approved the demolition of nearly 43,000 units in the nation's worst public housing complexes, "a 4-year pace," proclaimed a HUD booklet issued during President Clinton's reelection campaign, "that dwarfs the 20,000 units demolished in the previous 10 years

1. Rusk (1995).

combined."[2] HUD Secretary Henry Cisneros set a target of 100,000 units to be demolished by the year 2000.

In part, many demolitions were made possible by a technical change in federal law. At the behest of low-income housing advocates, Congress had stipulated that no unit of public housing could be demolished without one-for-one replacement by a new project. Soaring construction costs and intense local controversies over new sites slowed the cycle of demolition and replacement to 1,600 units a year by the early 1990s.

Progress was paralyzed in a gridlock of good intentions. On the one hand, nearly everyone recognized that, in Cisneros's words, "change is needed. Concrete high-rises have become half vacant shells, scarring the urban landscape. Other projects are beset by crime and gang activity. The very names of some places—Cabrini-Green, Robert Taylor Homes, Desire—haunt the American imagination."[3] On the other hand, public housing's most enthusiastic champions could count four other eligible poor persons for every tenant in existing units. They resisted any reduction in the supply of public housing units, however miserable the social and physical living conditions in many projects might be.

While HUD lobbied the Congress for permanent changes in authorizing legislation, Cisneros achieved a temporary breakthrough in the appropriations committees. For fiscal 1996 Congress allowed a suspension of the one-for-one rule (a measure subsequently carried over into fiscal 1997). This action legally freed HUD to act.

Perhaps even more significant was a major shift in HUD's own philosophy toward public housing. While noting that public housing projects provided essential shelter for 1.3 million of America's poorest households, HUD asserted that

> the current public housing system is plagued by deeply rooted, systemic problems.... Perhaps the most destructive of these fundamental problems is that public housing concentrates the very poor. Misguided policies that required housing authorities to restrict assistance to the poorest Americans have robbed public housing communities of the working families whose example is so crucial. The average income of the public housing communities has fallen from 35 percent of area median income in 1990 to less than 17 percent today. This concentration of poverty has left much

2. U.S. Department of Housing and Urban Development (1996, p. 9).
3. HUD (1996, p. 1).

urban public housing prey to an array of economic and social problems that destabilize families and neighborhoods.

In addition, public housing is itself concentrated in high-poverty neighborhoods. The politics of project location have led to the physical, social, and racial isolation of public housing in many cities, cutting off the residents from jobs, basic services, and a wide range of social contacts.[4]

"We've learned our lesson," Secretary Cisneros swore at the demolition of the Vaughn complex in Saint Louis. "We're changing the model."[5] How was the model being changed?

—Designed as bare, utilitarian boxes and constructed on an inhuman scale, many public housing projects stood out from their surroundings and stigmatized the families that lived there. The new model would replace failed high-rises with lower-density townhouses and garden-style apartments more compatible with surrounding neighborhoods.

—In keeping with the "Garden City" ideal of the 1950s and 1960s, many projects were sited in massive "superblocks" that cut off city streets and inhibited normal circulation within the community. Under the new model, urban street grids would be reintroduced, and "defensible space" strategies would be used to enhance community safety.

—Starved for operating funds, many projects had become simply warehouses of poverty, isolating the community's poorest households from educational and training facilities, employment opportunities, and essential services. Under the new model, supportive services designed to foster self-sufficiency would become integral parts of public housing developments.

—And, most important, for two decades federal policy had given preference to the poorest of the poor, excluding from public housing working families "who are the role models and social glue of stable communities." Under the new model, high-density projects would be replaced with more human-scale, mixed-income communities. A proportion of former tenants would be provided rent vouchers to be used throughout the region while many of the new units would be marketed to attract working, middle-income families. "Any effort to reverse the social consequences of concentrated poverty in public housing," HUD stated, "must include a reassertion of the paramount importance of income integration so that the very poor can live next door to working class families."[6]

4. HUD (1996, p. 5).
5. HUD (1996, p. 9).
6. HUD (1996, pp. 11, 27).

If You Build It, Will They Come?

Attracting working-class families to live next door to public housing tenants: that is the crux of the challenge for HUD's new model for public housing communities. If you build it, will they—middle-income households—come?

Putting the "new model" into practice in Baltimore provides an instructive guide to the evolution of the thinking of both local and federal public housing officials—and the useful role played by a class action suit in federal court.[7] In my judgment, Baltimore's Inner Harbor is the most successful downtown redevelopment project in the country. It is a jewel, however, set in a precarious setting, immediately surrounded by some of the highest poverty areas in the city. In the 1950s the Housing Authority of Baltimore City (HABC) built four massive, high-rise, family public housing complexes— Lexington Terrace (677 units), George P. Murphy Homes (758 units), Lafayette Courts (807 units), and Flag House Courts (487 units)—that, west to east, ring downtown and the Inner Harbor. "Our city leaders' worst nightmare," a veteran civic activist once confided to me, "would be two or three high-visibility shootings right down here in the Inner Harbor. All these people," he said, sweeping his hand toward the Inner Harbor, thronged with festive tourists and happy local sports fans, "could disappear overnight."

With $193 million in federal HOPE VI grants from HUD, plus $65 million in state funds and $35 million in city funds, HABC is tearing down and recreating the four public housing developments. "We want to use this largest, one-time chunk of federal cash available in the 1990s to rebuild our city," Van Johnson, HABC's HOPE VI director, told me in October 1998.

Lafayette Courts is the first "new" community completed. Although the architecture is new and attractive, the renamed Pleasant View Gardens is a

---

7. In 1995 the American Civil Liberties Union filed a class action suit, *Thompson* v. *HUD*, charging that HUD, the Housing Authority of Baltimore City, and the city of Baltimore had maintained a racially segregated public housing program for decades. Any litigation can create harsh feelings among the parties, and this suit was vigorously pursued by the ACLU. Nevertheless, the basic facts were uncontested, and all parties shared basic values and similar goals. As remedy, the ACLU sought additional section 8 rent vouchers to substitute for the 16,000 project-based units owned by HABC. The vouchers could be used by low-income city residents for rental housing anywhere in metro Baltimore, achieving complete deconcentration of HABC tenants. The case was settled in early 1996, elaborating on plans HUD and HABC had already initiated to dismantle HABC's four major housing projects under the HOPE VI program. The settlement added 1,342 new HUD-financed rent vouchers, plus additional state and city funds for homeownership opportunities, to be used by HABC tenants to secure rental housing in "non-impacted areas": census tracts with less than a 10 percent poverty rate and less than 25 percent African American residents.

traditional public housing community with some new bells and whistles attached. A central goal of this earliest HOPE VI grant was to reduce project density by 60 percent. That was certainly achieved. The high-rise towers were "imploded" in 1995 and replaced by 228 townhouses and a 110-unit, four-story apartment building for senior citizens by mid-1997.

Over 90 percent of the residents of Pleasant View Gardens are very low-income households. Only 27 of the townhouses (all of which were quickly sold) are owner-occupied. However, HABC and HUD set a low income ceiling for the new homeowners: 60 percent of the city's median family income (which means the owners must fall in the lowest quarter on the region's income scale). Another 103 of the townhouses are legally organized into a condominium arrangement in hopes that the more successful tenants can graduate into owning their own units.

Lexington Terrace's redevelopment represents a more decisive step toward a mixed-income community. The 677 units in five high-rise and twenty-five low-rise properties were leveled in July 1996. By fall 1998 construction had begun on 203 townhouses for public housing tenants and 100 for-sale townhouses to be known as "The Townes at The Terraces." (A prominent sign along Martin Luther King Jr. Boulevard advertises "new homes from the $40s"; about $60,000 is the top sale price, Van Johnson tells me.) With no model townhouse even completed for inspection by potential homebuyers, there are already contracts on 90 percent of the sites. To qualify, buyers cannot exceed 115 percent of the city's median family income (in other words, about twice the maximum income of purchasers at Pleasant View Gardens.) Thus, for the Terraces, the income mix has shifted to 67 percent public housing tenants and 33 percent moderate-income homeowners. The Terraces will be ready for occupancy in 1999.

Flag House Courts will be yet another step forward. Sometime in 2000 all 487 units in three high-rise and fifteen low-rise buildings will be demolished. In accordance with the consent decree in the federal law suit, the redevelopment plan will include a maximum of 125 public housing rental units and a minimum of 125 market-rate units. Purchasers of the market-rate units will not be subject to maximum income ceilings. For the new Flag House Courts the income mix will be at most 50 percent public housing tenants and 50 percent market-rate homeowners.

The redevelopment plan for the George P. Murphy Homes probably goes as far as HUD and Congress will allow in shifting the income mix away from 100 percent public housing tenancy. After the Terraces project is completed and reoccupied, 758 units in four high-rise and twenty low-rise buildings of Murphy Homes and twenty-three two-story buildings of adjacent Emerson Julian Gardens will be demolished. They will be replaced by 210 single-family homes in the form of townhouses and detached two- and three-story buildings. Seventy-five units scattered throughout the new community will be reserved for public housing tenants. The remaining 135 homes will be sold to moderate- and middle-income households. In short, for the last project, the income mix will shift to 35 percent public housing and 65 percent moderate-income (that is, subject to some income ceiling) and market-rate households (subject to no income ceiling).

Architecturally, the new Murphy-Julian homes should have strong market appeal. They are designed by UDA Architects of Pittsburgh, one of the nation's most renowned "new urbanist" firms. Having demonstrated its creative talents in designing many HOPE VI projects for housing authorities around the nation, UDA Architects was selected by the Disney Corporation to design the "pattern book" for Celebration, Disney's 5,000-home "new urbanist" community near Orlando, Florida. (Celebration will be twenty times the size of Seaside, Florida, the real-life set for Jim Carrey's fantasy movie, *The Truman Show*.) "Socially and architecturally, the new Murphy-Julian homes will be a transforming event for Baltimore," Van concluded.

Despite the dramatic reduction in concentration of poor households at specific sites (for example, a hypothetical 90 percent reduction at Murphy-Julian homes), redeveloping public housing projects has not led to casting displaced poor households out onto the streets. First of all, many high-density public housing projects had become so inhospitable that many otherwise desperate households would not live in them. (As of January 1997, for example, at least three years before planned demolition, 40 percent of units at Flag House Courts were vacant.)

For families actually needing temporary or permanent relocation, HABC has filled the gap with rent vouchers or relocation into small, HABC-owned scattered-site units. The shortfall of public housing units at Pleasant View Gardens was filled by 345 rent vouchers and 168 projected ownership opportunities in nonpoverty neighborhoods throughout the region and 50 small, scattered-site HABC-owned units in nonpoverty areas. The reduction of 1,639 public housing units in the remaining three projects would be offset by 1,452 new rent vouchers (used regionwide) plus 188 new units built at several other city locations with state and city funds.

Van Johnson and I toured Pleasant View Gardens on a crisp October 1998 morning. HABC's HOPE VI chief glowed with understandable pride as we drove slowly along streets lined by new, brick-faced, two-story townhouses. Some blocks echoed Baltimore's trademark rows of white stoops leading up to each front door. Other blocks broke up the traditional theme with more varied placement of townhouses. The twenty-seven owner-occupied townhouses, though all grouped along an exterior street, were architecturally indistinguishable from the HABC rental townhouses.

As we drove down streets and around New Hope Circle (the neighborhood's focal point), Van pointed out different community facilities: a large brick and glass community health facility operated by the Greater Baltimore Medical Center; a multipurpose community building housing the management office, a police substation, and community meeting rooms; a large day care center for 120 children, complete with colorful playground; and an even larger youth development center managed by the Boys and Girls Club of Central Maryland, including a computer learning center, multipurpose rooms, and a gymnasium.

"And Pleasant View Gardens is one of HUD's new 'Learning Communities,'" Van added. "Every townhouse is equipped with a computer and Internet hook-up."

"Well, if an almost 100 percent public housing community can create a successful social environment, Pleasant View Gardens certainly ought to be the place," I responded. "Personally, I'll still put my money on Murphy-Julian Homes."

"Yes," Van smiled. "You really have to get the income mix."

The Three *A*s and Three *S*s

The key to success in luring middle-class families back to inner-city neighborhoods, I heard urban consultant Marc Bendick Jr. tell an Allentown, Pennsylvania, audience, is to satisfy the three *A*s and the three *S*s.[8] The three *A*s are ready *access* to high-quality job centers—a condition easily fulfilled by the locations of Lafayette Courts and Lexington Terrace, adjacent to Baltimore's Johns Hopkins Medical Center, Inner Harbor, and revitalized downtown, or the Village at Techwood (in downtown Atlanta), or Cabrini-Green (just north of Chicago's Loop); high-quality *amenities* in the neighborhood, a combination of both quality design features (restoring street grids, attractive landscaping and street furniture) and new facilities (parks, recre-

8. Bendick was project director and author of Committee for Economic Development (1995).

ation centers, new shopping areas); and high *affordability* of the redeveloped housing destined for middle-income buyers and renters, a difficult balance that HUD, local authorities, and private developers must strike between sales prices and rents low enough to attract middle-income clients seeking bargains and prices high enough to meet the public and private cash-flow and profitability requirements.

Harder to satisfy—and much more critical—are, according to Bendick, what middle-class households seek in terms of the three Ss, beginning with adequate internal *space* within the new apartments and townhouses. That issue will be within the private developers' control only if HUD, housing authorities, and private financiers are truly prepared to meet competitive market standards in the new, mixed-income developments.

Next are quality *schools*, the critical decision point for most middle-class families with children. This will prove to be a very difficult hurdle even in developments such as Atlanta's Village at Techwood, where local authorities are committed to creating a new magnet elementary school. Despite enhanced curricula and showcase facilities, the proportion of children from low-income households will probably have to fall below 20 percent to 30 percent before middle-class parents will be convinced that the local school provides a suitable environment for their own children. In light of the typical 60-40 target income ratio in HUD's HOPE VI developments, achieving predominantly middle-class enrollments will be impossible if they are drawn solely from the HUD communities' own populations. The key to success may be enrolling a high proportion of middle-class children of downtown office workers into nearby magnet schools.

Last, and most important, is *safety*. Public housing has created its own variation of Gresham's law: bad neighbors drive out good neighbors. Private housing around major public housing projects often declines because of rising crime, delinquency, and neighborhood vandalism. Unless the new developments create an environment of safety and security, HUD's vision of mixed-income communities will rapidly evaporate.

Perhaps the most dramatic shift in federal policy has occurred in the selection of public housing tenants. As an example of past good intentions terribly misplaced, in 1992 Congress opened up senior citizens' complexes to disabled applicants of any age. Most remarkably, the new federal law defined the disabled as including supposedly recovering alcoholics and drug addicts. The results were predictable. Aggressive young men and women, sometimes still actively engaged in drug trafficking, destroyed the atmosphere of peace and safety in many senior housing projects. Tenant satisfaction plummeted, and elderly tenants began to leave voluntarily, a previously unheard-of phenomenon.

Civilizing the Projects

Today HUD's guiding philosophy is that "public housing is a privilege, and it would be wrong to subordinate the safety of decent, law-abiding public housing residents in favor of the very residents who are terrorizing their neighborhoods." Local housing authorities are urged to screen out potential applicants with recent criminal records and evict tenants engaged in drug and other criminal activity. As President Clinton proclaimed in his 1996 State of the Union address, "From now on, the rule for residents who commit crimes and peddle drugs should be one strike and you're out."

In many housing authorities, significant improvement has occurred. Faced with a sudden severe crack epidemic, Georgia's Macon Housing Authority instituted a tougher crime strategy in 1989 that included one of the country's earlier One Strike policies. People applying for admission to public housing faced strict screening procedures: in 1995 about 280 applicants out of 1,000 were denied admission because of their criminal history. In 1989 the Macon Housing Authority evicted 59 residents for drug-related activities. By 1995, after six years of effective screening and strict lease enforcement, evictions for drug-related offenses had dwindled to only 8 cases. In a 1994 survey of over 100 resident leaders, more than 80 percent reported feeling safe in their community.

Similar trends are reported in Toledo, Ohio, by the Lucas Metropolitan Housing Authority. As a result of tougher tenant screening policy, 330 out of 2,300 applicants were rejected for criminal history in a recent twelve-month period. After a One Strike eviction policy was implemented in 1994, drug-related evictions rose from 0 in 1993 to 41 in 1995. As a result of these and other anticrime activities, incidents of drug-related crime dropped by one-fourth between 1993 and 1995; reports on non-drug-related crime plummeted by two-thirds. By 1995, 76 percent of surveyed residents reported feeling safe, an increase from 46 percent in 1993.

Many public housing projects are located in—and have helped create—America's poorest, most crime-ridden neighborhoods. Not all crimes committed in public housing communities are perpetrated by public housing residents. In New Haven, for example, 85 percent of those arrested on public housing property in the late 1980s did not live there. Likewise, 77 percent of persons arrested on Cincinnati's public housing property were not public housing residents.

HUD has added funds to fight public housing crime at the street level. HUD's public housing drug elimination program has provided grants to more than 500 community-based anticrime initiatives in public housing developments nationwide. The grants put additional police on public housing beats, support resident patrols, give young residents positive alternatives to gangs and drugs through diversion and prevention efforts, and make "defensible space" improvements to public housing facilities.

Operation Safe Haven targets federal, state, and local law enforcement agencies, public housing staff, and residents to stamp out the worst infestation of gangs, drugs, and violent crime in public housing projects and surrounding neighborhoods. In its first two years, Operation Safe Haven resulted in more than 8,000 arrests and the confiscation of $3 million in drugs, almost $2 million in cash, and more than 1,000 weapons.

Dramatically reducing crime in public housing communities has a twofold positive impact. Nobody has a greater stake in reducing the violence and chaos of crime-ridden public housing communities than their current residents. But improving both the image—and reality—of neighborhoods with high percentages of public housing households is the key to attracting middle-class households back to future mixed-income developments.

Cisneros's Legacy

"HUD's Cisneros to Leave a Legacy of Public Housing Reform," headlined the *Washington Post* story. Cisneros had just announced his resignation in late November 1996 after four years as, in my view, the most successful of the ten secretaries of Housing and Urban Development since the cabinet agency was formed in 1965. It is ironic that public housing reform was seen as Cisneros's principal achievement. Through two terms as mayor of San Antonio, Cisneros had paid minimal attention to San Antonio's public housing program. Upon his designation as President-elect Clinton's HUD secretary, he had to seek out several local public housing administrators and tenant activists for a crash course in public housing issues.

I could readily understand Cisneros's inattention to public housing as mayor of San Antonio. I acted the same way as mayor of Albuquerque, and I, unlike Cisneros, was a full-time chief executive. Albuquerque Housing Services was a line agency under the mayor's office. Under San Antonio's council-manager system, Cisneros was a part-time mayor presiding over city council meetings. San Antonio's public housing agency was an independent authority.

But in the eyes of both Cisneros and myself, public housing really functioned as a federally operated program in a local setting (almost like a Veterans Administration hospital). HUD rules and regulations governed almost all decisions. During the 1970s and 1980s there was little room for local flexibility. Mayors allocate time and attention to issues they have to decide. No decisions, no time and attention.

Cisneros and I also shared another common experience. We had both been mayors of Sun Belt cities that aggressively annexed large shares of sprawling regional growth. He had been born in San Antonio at the outset of the postwar suburban era and had witnessed its vast transformation. As Cisneros told me in December 1994, when we were collaborating on an essay on regionalism in which he recalled the small, compact world of San Antonio in the 1950s, with downtown at its center: "At that time only half-a-million people lived in the entire area—80 percent within the city's 70 square miles."[9]

Cisneros explained how San Antonio escaped the fate of many other American cities after the Second World War: the state's liberal annexation laws allowed it to expand and follow its sprawling suburban development. In this way, San Antonio increased its municipal territory nearly fivefold, adding more than 260 square miles and bringing in new middle-class subdivisions, shopping centers, offices, and industrial parks:

> Through expansion the city remains home to over 70 percent of the metropolitan area's population and has maintained a strong middle class, a broad tax base, and a high municipal bond rating. . . .[10]
>
> Through annexation, the city of San Antonio *is* largely its own suburbs. But the Detroits, the Clevelands, the Hartfords—for many inner-city residents of such cities, achieving the American Dream requires opening up to them all the metropolitan area's resources and opportunities.[11]

---

9. HUD published the essay as a series of pamphlets by the secretary. See Cisneros (1995).

10. By 1990 metro San Antonio's three-county area had over 1.3 million residents. The urbanized core covered 438 square miles (75 percent within San Antonio's expanded city limits).

11. Cisneros (1995, pp. 3–4).

Metropolitan solutions, regionalism, linking cities and suburbs, ending the economic and social isolation of inner cities—these were persistent themes sounded by Cisneros throughout his years at HUD, particularly during his first two years, from his confirmation hearing onward. Yet Cisneros's intellectual commitment to metropolitan strategies (the "outside game") was constantly counterbalanced by the greater emotional and political attractiveness of community development strategies (the "inside game"). Part of the inside game's appeal was rooted in Cisneros's own local history. San Antonio's traditional Anglo-dominated politics had been reshaped by the organizing activities of COPS (Communities Organized for Public Service), a local arm of Saul Alinsky's Industrial Areas Foundation. Working through Catholic parishes and largely Hispanic union locals, COPS had helped forge San Antonio's Hispanic residents into an effective political force. COPS had been a key part of the coalition that elected Cisneros as San Antonio's first Hispanic mayor. Cisneros knew firsthand the political muscle of grass-roots movements, but he also knew how rarely poor neighborhoods escape the grip of poverty.

Another part of the inside game's appeal, however, was purely bureaucratic. Since the National Housing and Demonstration Cities Act of 1965, community development was one of HUD's significant bureaucratic missions. The signature institutions of the Great Society's War on Poverty were independent community action agencies that were often at political odds with city hall. The model cities program had been Lyndon Johnson's way of cutting the mayors directly into a piece of the antipoverty action. Spawned by the community action program, neighborhood associations continued to play key planning roles in model cities, but local model cities bureaucracies were direct agencies of city government.

To take the Great Society logo off the program, in 1974 the Nixon administration recast model cities as community development block grants (CDBGs). Postured as more flexible block grants, CDBGs had enough conservative camouflage (plus city hall support) to survive the Reagan years. Though CDBG funding had eroded, by the time of Cisneros's arrival in 1993 the CDBG program still amounted to $2.5 billion. With a young and aggressive Andrew Cuomo as assistant secretary for community development, HUD's own inside game would always demand attention and support.[12]

12. At the outset of the second Clinton administration Cuomo became the eleventh secretary of Housing and Urban Development.

Clinton White House: Playing the Inside Game

Finally, and most important, the White House had chosen to play the inside game. President Clinton's earliest congressional defeat had been the stinging rejection of the new administration's $15 billion "economic stimulus package" in mid-1993. Faced with unanimous Republican opposition, the Democratic-led Congress backed down. The economy was already rebounding from the 1991–92 recession, some argued. More telling was widespread characterization of the package as "just another pork barrel for big city mayors." Critics cited a document compiled by the U.S. Conference of Mayors of ready-to-go projects in different member cities. The Conference of Mayors staff naively believed the document would demonstrate persuasively both the pressing needs of cities and their ability to spend new federal funds quickly. Instead, the mayors' conference inadvertently created Exhibit A for the opposition. Among the hundreds of proposals were an outdoor ice skating rink, a swimming pool, and midnight basketball—all "antirecession" projects widely derided by conservative pundits and congressional opponents.

In the aftermath of that defeat, the White House searched for some strategy to help big cities that could gain a modicum of conservative support. It settled on the idea of federally sponsored "enterprise zones," a largely Republican notion that had been ardently championed by Jack Kemp, the Bush administration's HUD secretary. With a facility that Republicans were to rue by the time of his 1996 reelection campaign, Clinton embraced Republican ideology on enterprise zones, added $1 billion to the previous array of proposed federal tax incentives, and rechristened the package "empowerment communities."

In late 1993 the White House secured congressional approval for the new program, and HUD launched the contest for what was dubbed "the last big federal giveaway." Throughout 1994, hundreds of cities and rural areas packaged their proposals. On December 20, 1994, Cisneros announced the winners: New York, Detroit, Chicago, Atlanta, Baltimore, and Philadelphia-Camden. These were designated "empowerment communities," and each was awarded $100 million cash grants and an estimated $200 million in tax incentives. Smaller cash grants and lesser tax incentives were awarded to Los Angeles and Cleveland as "supplemental empowerment zones" and to Boston, Houston, Kansas City, and Oakland as "enhanced enterprise communities." Almost 100 cities and rural areas were awarded $3 million grants and their target neighborhoods were dubbed "enterprise zones."

As a loyal soldier of the Clinton administration—and with genuine enthusiasm—Cisneros set forth to administer the new empowerment community and enterprise zone program.

Since taking office, however, his main goal had been to gain congressional approval for a major redirection of HUD's programs, particularly, the troubled public housing program. HUD had fallen into political scandal and bureaucratic disarray during the Reagan years. During the Bush years Secretary Jack Kemp had labored mightily to clean out the Augean stables. For the first time in a dozen years the Democrats controlled both the White House and Capitol Hill. The moment was right, Cisneros believed, to push for wide-ranging reform of all HUD's authorizing legislation.

The draft legislation went far beyond seeking reforms solely in public housing policy. HUD sought congressional authorization to raise significantly the eligibility ceiling for the FHA's mortgage insurance program, to secure greater flexibility for community development block grants, to promote greater homeownership, and to expand a host of other HUD programs. HUD organized a coalition of a wide range of interest groups to support the omnibus bill. In early 1994 hearings began before friendly, Democratic-controlled subcommittees in the House and Senate.

The Godfathers Strike

By the late summer of 1994 the legislation was reaching the critical stage. The vote on the omnibus bill would come first in the House. The legislative path was tricky, as HUD was trying to achieve parallel reform language in both authorization and appropriations legislation moving through the House. Particularly sensitive were HUD's proposals to raise the FHA's maximum mortgage insurance limits. This proposal was actively opposed by the Mortgage Insurance Companies of America (MICA), Washington lobbyist for major private mortgage insurers. The private mortgage insurers provided "Cadillac insurance" (mortgage insurance for homes above FHA's limit). The higher FHA's ceiling, the lower their members' profits, as MICA saw it. For all the controversial measures in the omnibus bill, raising FHA's ceiling was the only provision that drew highly organized opposition.

August 20, 1994, was a truly historic day—the founding meeting of the National Partners in Homeownership, another of Cisneros's major initiatives. "Everybody was there—all the top brass from the National Association of Home Builders, Fannie Mae, Freddie Mac, all the leadership of the home building and home financing industry in one room for the first time," one HUD participant remembered. "Except MICA. They were represented by some third-level staffer."

Unbeknownst to HUD, at that very moment, all of MICA's big guns were on Capitol Hill, lobbying members of the House Appropriations Subcommittee on HUD. Midway through the National Partners in Homeownership session, Cisneros was called out of the room to take a call from Representative Louis Stokes, subcommittee chairman. A few minutes later he returned, ashen-faced. "MICA's pressure is too great," Stokes told Cisneros. "The Appropriations Subcommittee's going to have to cave in and not raise FHA's mortgage limits in the money bill."

It was a tableau right out of *The Godfather*. While Al Pacino prays publicly at the baptism of his newborn child, his henchmen are out slaughtering the opposition. In this case, given the realities of legislative warfare, a henchman was dispatched to pray at the baptism while the industry's godfathers were off on their murderous mission.

The omnibus authorization act and the HUD appropriations bill, with conflicting FHA provisions, both passed the House. The Senate speedily agreed to the HUD appropriations. If the omnibus bill were now approved by the Senate, as legislation enacted later, its higher FHA ceiling would prevail. To achieve its ultimate goal, MICA would have to make an all-out effort to defeat the omnibus bill.

"Drop raising the FHA ceiling from the bill," some HUD insiders argued. "The rest of the bill will just sail through. We can fight the FHA battle another day." "We've come this far together," others argued. "We should not break faith with any members of our coalition by dropping any part of the omnibus bill. Besides, Senate leaders assure us that they have enough votes to pass the omnibus bill even over MICA's opposition."

Cisneros decided to press for Senate approval of the House-passed omnibus bill with its higher FHA ceiling. The Senate Democrats were right. They did have the votes, if they could just get the omnibus bill on the floor. But getting a vote scheduled was the problem. The Senate was deadlocked over Clinton's health reform bill. The Republicans were determined to deny the president even a face-saving vote on a greatly scaled-down version of the administration's ambitious health care reform. They filibustered day after day to block a health care vote.

Under the Senate rules, when a filibuster blocks action on the regular agenda, any other Senate business, in order to be considered, must be placed on the consent calendar. That required unanimous consent. MICA lobbied its supporters to block unanimous consent on the omnibus housing bill.

One Republican senator would withhold unanimous consent, citing some minor issue. HUD would negotiate a compromise, then find another Republican senator with yet another minor objection. HUD was dying the death of a thousand cuts. Each time HUD met a critic halfway, it could not get closer to its goal: a floor vote. Finally, Senator Phil Gramm, already positioning for his 1996 presidential run, made it clear that he was unalterably opposed to the omnibus bill and would never assent to its being placed on the consent calendar.

In mid-October Congress adjourned. The omnibus housing bill died on adjournment. It had never reached the Senate floor. Key congressional Democrats, one HUD insider recalled, were "amazingly complacent." "Don't worry," they said. "We've held all the hearings necessary. After the 1994 elections, we'll just reintroduce the omnibus housing bill and run it right through."

Cisneros's Finest Hour

On Election Day the political earthquake struck. From Maine to California the ground beneath congressional Democrats shook and heaved. By midnight a yawning chasm had swallowed the Democratic majorities. The Republicans captured the Senate 53 to 47 for the first time since 1986. By a margin of 230 to 204 the Republicans ended forty years of Democratic control of the House of Representatives.

The headlines highlighted the most visible leadership changes. Bob Dole replaced George Mitchell as Senate Majority Leader. Newt Gingrich was handed the Speaker's gavel, but not by his predecessor, Tom Foley. Foley had not even made it back to the 104th Congress, dumped by his Spokane constituents after twenty-eight years.

From HUD's perspective, the changes were, if anything, more stunning. Gone as chairman of the House Banking, Finance, and Urban Affairs Committee was Representative Henry B. Gonzalez, a long-time member whose first job had been with the San Antonio Housing Authority.

There were, of course, no Republican members who had ever chaired House committees and subcommittees. Moreover, with freshmen and sophomores (first elected in 1992) composing more than half of the Republicans, key leadership roles fell to virtual newcomers. Chairing the housing subcommittee was Representative Rick Lazio from New York, beginning only his second term.

It was not just that the new Republican majority lacked institutional memory. They gloried in that fact. Many had been elected on an explicit anti-Washington platform. Many not only did not know the facts; they did not want to know the facts. They had their agenda. And the central item on that agenda was to cut back the size and scope of the federal government. Within two weeks of the election, the Republican leadership announced their immediate targets: abolish five cabinet departments: Commerce, Labor, Energy, Education, and HUD.

Running scared after the stunning election results, the Clinton White House sharpened its own ax as well. The White House budget cutters, it was reported, had HUD on the administration's kill list. In the 104th Congress HUD would not be fighting for passage of the aborted omnibus housing act after all. HUD would be fighting for its very existence. It would be Henry Cisneros's finest hour.

The shadow of the gallows concentrates the mind marvelously. Drawing together the best ideas of an able cadre of young assistant secretaries, Cisneros launched a preemptive strike. On December 19, 1994, Cisneros announced a sweeping "Reinvention Blueprint" of HUD. (His press conference came the day before the much-anticipated award of empowerment community and enterprise zone grants.)

Believing both in the critical nature of HUD's mission and the need to carry it out more efficiently and effectively, Cisneros proposed three major reforms. First, consolidate more than sixty major HUD grant programs into three "performance funds" decentralized to states and local governments. HUD would "preapprove" local plans to ensure compliance with national goals. Second, convert the Federal Housing Administration into an independent but government-owned Federal Housing Corporation, consolidating its many statutory programs into a few broad, flexible activities directed to three general markets: single-family homeownership, multifamily rental housing, and health care facilities. And third, totally transform the nation's public housing program. Cisneros pulled every page out of the Republican book except that chapter advocating total abolition of the federal government's housing assistance for the poor.

He vowed to create a real launching pad for families trying to raise themselves from squalid conditions and improve their lives. His blueprint for reinventing HUD would create housing certificates to give public housing residents a genuine market choice between public housing and the private rental market; break the monopoly of local housing authorities over federal housing resources by forcing housing authorities to compete in the marketplace with private landlords to attract renters with housing certificates; give preference to families that are moving toward self-sufficiency by already working or participating in "work-ready" and education programs; and end inner-city blight caused by many public housing projects by accelerating the demolition of uninhabitable and nonviable properties. Nor would new developments be targeted exclusively at the very poor.

Over a three-year transition period HUD would get out of the direct funding of public housing by converting project-based public housing subsidies to tenant-based rental assistance. During fiscal 1996 and 1997 HUD would deregulate more than 3,000 well-performing local authorities, work to reform more than 100 severely troubled authorities, and, for 10 to 15 of the most troubled local authorities beyond any reasonable hope of improvement, divest them of their properties and management control. During fiscal 1996 HUD would consolidate all public housing funds into a Capital Fund and Operating Subsidies Fund. States and localities could opt to receive all housing funds as housing certificates. By fiscal 1998 all former project-based public housing subsidies would be completely portable housing certificates awarded to eligible low-income households.

Even by the standards of the Republicans' Contract with America, Cisneros's proposals were a bold stroke. More important, HUD's reinvention blueprint came just six weeks after the Republicans' stunning election victory. Beyond rattling their sabers at HUD, congressional Republicans had not had time to develop their own plans.

Cisneros drew on his close personal ties to President Clinton and Vice President Al Gore to get their imprimatur on HUD's reinvention blueprint. "The reinvention of HUD," Cisneros stated, "flows from the work of the National Performance Review [Vice President Gore's 'reinventing government' initiative], the most sweeping and ambitious effort to revitalize the Federal Government in half a century."

Cisneros had blunted the assaults on HUD. It would be another matter to sell his reinvention plan, which was "viewed with skepticism by many conservatives and near horror by some liberals."[13] The new Republican majority's first budget action was a harbinger of things to come. Congress slashed more than $15 billion from the federal government's fiscal 1995 budget already in effect; $7.2 billion, almost half the cuts, was taken away from HUD alone. Most was in funds for section 8 certificates and vouchers.

13. Guy Gugliotta, "Doubts on Reinvention: GOP Casts Skeptical Eye on Housing Overhaul," *Washington Post*, March 9, 1995, p. A19.

Republican budget cutters argued that not a single poor person would be evicted and put out on the street as a result. Technically, they were correct. The money was as yet "uncommitted." It was still on its way from HUD to 3,400 different local housing authorities. But it was the first time since the inception of the section 8 program that the flow of rent subsidy funds was being reduced. The pipeline of rental assistance was drying up. Cisneros called the rescission "callous and short-sighted."

"We have been waiting for a sound proposal," said Senator Christopher S. Bond (R-Mo.), chairman of the HUD Appropriations Subcommittee. "What is touted as a 'reinvention blueprint' is more press release than working plan." Bond also expressed doubts about HUD's plan to deregulate local housing authorities and voucherize completely all housing assistance. Bond feared that deregulating a "good stock" of public housing could cripple many authorities and also questioned whether vouchers, which "cost twice as much" per family as public housing, could serve as many people as the current system.[14]

Senator Bond's criticisms were echoed by influential groups such as the National Association of Housing and Redevelopment Officials (NAHRO), the Washington-based trade association of the country's 3,400 local housing authorities. While always seeking greater flexibility under federal regulations for local authorities, NAHRO opposed Cisneros's proposal to phase out federal operating subsidies for its members over a three-year period. In response, HUD modified its plan in early 1995. Smaller public housing authorities (PHAs) (less than 100 units) would enter the new world of 100 percent tenant-based subsidies by fiscal 1998; medium-sized PHAs (100–250 units) by fiscal 2000; the larger PHAs (more than 250 units) by fiscal 2002. This would allow larger PHAs to renovate many of their larger projects to compete for voucher-bearing tenants and middle-class households.

Of Cisneros's three original initiatives, two failed to leave the starting gate. Combining all HUD programs into three "performance funds" and converting the FHA into the FHC never even received a hearing in the Republican-controlled Congress. Transforming public housing, however, was another matter.

Transforming Public Housing

Total voucherization of public housing assistance was not seriously considered. As I had written in *Baltimore Unbound*, "the philosophy of Cisneros's

14. Gugliotta, "Doubts on Reinvention."

plan [that is, voucherization] should appeal to the new Republican congressional majority. The politics of Cisneros's plan probably will not."[15] Suburban-based Republican members of Congress were not about to unleash a diaspora of black and Hispanic housing project residents into private rental apartments in their suburban districts.

But much of the rest of HUD's proposals for reforming public housing were attractive. After months of negotiation and debate between HUD and Capitol Hill, Representative Lazio reported out the United States Housing Act of 1996.

—The new bill consolidated dozens of public housing funds into two block grants for PHAs, one for capital investment and the other for operating expenses. This wiped out in one stroke dozens of regulatory bottlenecks that crippled the administration of the federal public housing program for years.

—The new bill provided permanent authority for PHAs to use rehabilitation funds to demolish deteriorated projects rather than rebuild them at immense cost. It also authorized housing authorities to give rent subsidy vouchers to tenants in condemned public housing complexes so they can move to privately owned housing instead of waiting for years for a new public housing complex to be built.

—The bill softened rent preferences for the poorest households, repealed the Brooke amendment setting rents at 30 percent of tenants' incomes, and lowered the marginal tax on tenants' additional earnings—all measures designed to attract working-class families back to public housing.

The United States Housing Act of 1996 passed the House of Representatives by a vote of 315 to 107 on May 9, 1996. The final vote obscured how bitterly House members had fought over key details. A floor effort to reinstate the Brooke amendment failed by a relatively narrow vote of 196 to 222, with some Republicans swayed by Democratic fears that repealing it would enable housing authorities to raise rents well beyond the ability of poor tenants to pay and thereby lead to evictions and homelessness.

Overall, the bill was a triumph for Cisneros. The House bill headed to a House-Senate conference committee for reconciliation with a less sweeping and "softer" Senate-passed bill. Cisneros said he was "looking forward" to working with House and Senate conferees "to create a public housing reform bill that can be signed by the president."[16]

15. Rusk (1995, p. 145).

16. This quotation and the material in the previous paragraphs are drawn from Guy Gugliotta, "House Votes for Overhaul in Housing," *Washington Post*, May 10, 1996, pp. A1, A23.

The bill's substance was more favorable than its timing. In 1992 candidate Clinton had pledged "to end welfare as we know it." The Republican Congress overcame Democratic opposition to send President Clinton the welfare reform bill in early August, just before the Democratic presidential convention. In the face of strong liberal opposition and the resignation of three high-level administrators at the Health and Human Services Department, Clinton signed the welfare reform bill.

Conservative Republicans were also determined "to end public housing as we know it." The wide-ranging reforms just enacted were too complicated for campaign-year sound bites. They needed a simple, easily explained symbol. The House conferees demanded that any compromise House-Senate bill repeal the Wagner-Steagall Act, the New Deal legislation that had launched the federal public housing program.

That was too much for the White House. President Clinton's signature on the welfare reform law wiped out a sixty-year federal commitment to provide the country's poorest families with a basic minimum income. The president was not about to tear down another New Deal monument. Cisneros invoked a sure presidential veto if the final package contained Wagner-Steagall repeal. Influential senators made clear their opposition and ability to block any such action. Once again, when Congress adjourned in mid-October for the final weeks of the 1996 campaign, a comprehensive public housing reform law died.

"Issues of race, class, and poverty remain the unresolved agenda for America," Henry Cisneros wrote me in December 1996, as he was preparing to leave office. With his departure (and that of Labor Secretary Robert Reich), the Clinton administration lost its strongest champions of the poor.

Efforts to transform the federal public housing program moved forward, but on flimsy legal foundations. Suspension of the one-for-one replacement law, greater local flexibility in using federal capital funds, authority to develop public housing as part of private mixed-income developments, greater rent flexibility, repeal of federal admissions priorities to attract more working families—all were legally permissible only because the fiscal 1997 HUD appropriations act had provided one-year authority for these policies. Without a comprehensive housing bill, continuing reforms down this path would be dependent upon language in the annual appropriations acts suspending permanent laws on the books.

For a strategy that would systematically shift poor black families—mostly mothers and children—out of inner-city projects into voucher-subsidized private rental housing located in nonpoor neighborhoods, there was not only no congressional consensus, there was hardly any support at all.

The Death of Moving to Opportunity

That was brutally demonstrated in the sad history of HUD's Moving to Opportunity national demonstration project. With special appropriations from fiscal 1992 and 1993, HUD originally planned to conduct a careful, ten-year study of combining vouchers and intensive counseling to enable a small number of families living in high-poverty areas to find housing in low-poverty areas. In each of five major metropolitan areas—Baltimore, Boston, Chicago, Los Angeles, and New York—130 public housing families would receive vouchers and special intensive counseling, another 130 would receive vouchers and normal counseling support, and a third group would serve as the control group. Test families would have to move from high-poverty neighborhoods (more than 40 percent poverty) to low-poverty neighborhoods (less than 10 percent poverty). In fiscal 1994 HUD hoped to expand the program to additional families in the test communities. The goal was to study definitively the impact that low-poverty communities have on the employment, income, education, and social well-being of poor, inner-city families.

In the five metro areas the small projects quietly got under way. Then all hell broke loose surrounding the Baltimore project. Political campaigns had begun for the Baltimore County commission. Moving to Opportunity was an irresistible target for several conservative candidates. They began beating the tribal drums. They raised the specter of hordes of black public housing residents from Baltimore City invading hard-pressed, largely white, working-class suburbs in eastern Baltimore County. Right-wing talk show hosts jumped aboard. Angry protest meetings were organized in Essex and Dundalk. HUD, city, and county officials (who had quietly agreed to cooperate) came under public siege.

Finally, Maryland's U.S. senators, Barbara Mikulski and Paul Sarbanes, stepped in. Though card-carrying liberal Democrats, they were alarmed during an election year. The fact that Moving to Opportunity's rules would prevent any participants from moving into moderate-poverty communities such as Essex and Dundalk carried no weight with the senators. They were not interested in trying to quell racial fears with facts. They were interested in eliminating the issue. Through Mikulski's membership on the Senate Appropriations Committee, they canceled Moving to Opportunity's $149 million for fiscal 1994, shifting the money to a noncontroversial program. They had heard the voice of the people, they claimed, and had killed Moving to Opportunity (though the five already funded projects continued).

"Boy, it's tough when even your supposed friends won't stand up for what's right," said one HUD insider. "Cosmetics aside, the congressional message was clear: 'We don't want to hear anything more about HUD programs to move poor blacks into white neighborhoods.' Frankly, where HUD has been able to move decisively against segregating poor blacks, it has been in response to federal court orders. Whenever HUD has sought legislative support for fighting racism, the Congress has backed off."

Breaking the Impasse

As I noted in 1995, Cisneros's proposals to convert all public housing assistance to a client-based voucher system might be very attractive ideologically to the new Republican congressional majority, but I doubted that the politics of dispersing poor, often minority, households into suburban areas would appeal to that majority.

In an early draft of this book, in 1996, I projected again that:

> The federal housing dollar is shrinking. Balancing the federal budget by fiscal 2002—while leaving social security and medicare substantially untouched—makes big cuts in HUD's housing assistance programs unavoidable. And they are politically weak. The only major constituency for conventional public housing is NAHRO and its local housing authority membership (although the construction trades are always ready to lobby for construction and major renovation funds). Private owners of project-based section 8 apartments may be a more formidable interest group. They, after all, are private investors and, unlike local housing authorities, make political campaign contributions.
>
> And there is *no* political constituency for the policy that makes the most sense: Cisneros's proposal to completely voucherize whatever federal housing assistance remains. Poor families receiving housing vouchers must be among the most powerless groups in American society, and poor households that do not now but might receive vouchers in the future exist merely as bloodless abstractions in the eyes of many politicians. After all, no family will be put out on the street, the budget cutters assured their congressional colleagues in rescinding $7 billion in HUD's section 8 budget for fiscal 1995.

In October 1998 the Republican Congress and President Clinton agreed on a $500 billion appropriations bill for fiscal year 1999. The bill included

$24.5 billion for HUD without cutting any HUD program. Most significant was an increase of $2.7 billion for section 8 rental assistance, providing an increase of 90,000 rent vouchers over the previous level—the first increase in four years.

In a "Dear Colleague" letter I received, HUD Secretary Andrew Cuomo commented that "in 1996, the *New York Times Magazine* ran a cover story called 'The Year That Housing Died,' describing the consequences of the halt over the previous few years in issuing new rental assistance vouchers. Today I believe that 1998 could well be labeled 'The Year That Housing Was Reborn.'"[17]

In addition to funds for 90,000 additional vouchers in fiscal year 1999, Cuomo noted, Congress authorized another 100,000 vouchers in fiscal year 2000 and an extra 100,000 more in fiscal year 2001.

"Under the deconcentration provisions of the bill," Cuomo continued, "more moderate-income working families will be admitted to public housing in lower-income developments, while at the same time lower-income families will be given the chance to move into higher-income developments [through rent vouchers]. . . . HUD will also be allowed to continue tearing down failed public housing projects and replace them with new townhouse-style developments, through the HOPE VI program [whose annual appropriation was boosted from $550 million to $625 million]. . . . These reforms implement President Clinton's visionary plans to transform public housing from segregated ghettos of poverty and despair into economically integrated communities of opportunity."

So clearly both the *New York Times* and I were overly pessimistic—at least, temporarily. The booming American economy, feeding the tax increases enacted in the 1990 and 1993 budget agreements, ballooned federal revenues so much that "balancing" the budget was achieved not painfully by 2002 but painlessly by 1998.[18] In such flush times the Republican-controlled

17. Letter from Secretary of Housing and Urban Development Andrew Cuomo, October 8, 1998.

18. In an op-ed column in the *Washington Post* William G. Gale, a senior fellow at the Brookings Institution, wrote that "the projected surpluses are substantial, roughly $1.5 trillion over the next decade. But they arise from the peculiarities of government budget accounting, which focuses on annual cash flows, not from underlying economic reality. Over the next several decades, because of the pressure that retiring baby boomers will put on Social Security and Medicare, the government faces large economic deficits, rather than surpluses. Even with no tax cuts [as proposed by Congressional Republicans], the accruing surpluses will not be sufficient to pay for future liabilities. . . . Put differently, if the government kept its books like a business, it would show a shortfall under current circumstances, not a surplus." "A 'Surplus' We Need," *Washington Post*, October 16, 1998, p. A27.

Congress aped the self-styled conservative stereotype of past Democratic-controlled Congresses. The opening of the fiscal floodgates had begun earlier in 1998 with enactment of a $220 billion highway and transit assistance bill, and the fiscal tsunami carried HUD's programs right along with it.

Such largess will likely be seen in a different light when the American economy inevitably cools again, and Congress begins to deal seriously with the consequences of the aging baby boom on social security and medicare. However, the concept of deconcentrating the poor through a combination of vouchers, demolition of massive projects, and modest mixed-income redevelopment appears to be embraced by a significant congressional majority. If HUD meets its target of 100,000 high-density units demolished by 2000, the next census should record a significant reduction in high-poverty neighborhoods.

That will be good news indeed for America's ailing cities—and for many victims of the poverty machine.

13

Building Regional Coalitions

"THIS PLAN ONLY affects the unincorporated areas of Lake County. This matter only concerns 'south county' residents." The chairman of the Lake County (Indiana) Plan Commission was clearly upset. He had expected a routine meeting of the twelve commissioners to approve the proposed Lake County comprehensive plan. There had been no controversy and little public interest in the plan; only a dozen citizens had turned out at the plan commission's previous public hearing in mid-June 1996.

Now, two weeks later, the planning commissioners were confronted by a delegation of about fifty determined citizens. And the group was not just large, it was very different from the smattering of developers, builders, and bureaucrats who were regulars at plan commission meetings. This group was about evenly divided between blacks and whites, a rare enough occurrence in Northwest Indiana (the nation's most racially segregated metro area, according to the Census Bureau). Also, these were mostly Protestant ministers, Catholic priests, rabbis, a Muslim imam—all leaders of the Northwest Indiana Federation of Interfaith Organizations. They had driven down from Gary, Hammond, and East Chicago to the county seat in Crown Point for this meeting.

"We disagree," responded the Reverend Victor Davis, pastor of Gary's Spirit of God Fellowship Church. The former Iowa Hawkeye running back, still trim and athletic, warmed to his argument. "We don't feel this plan addresses urban sprawl. We feel that sprawl needs to be reversed or stopped. Suburban sprawl into rural areas lures residents from Gary, Hammond, and East Chicago, eroding their tax bases, and leading to further deterioration of infrastructure. And older suburban communities often take the greatest hit as development continues in the cornfields. The interfaith federation asks that action on the plan be postponed until another hearing is held in Gary or Hammond so that 'north county' residents can have their say," Reverend Davis concluded.[1]

Though obviously annoyed, plan commission members agreed to post-pone action until their August meeting in order to hold the hearing requested. It was a modest request and only a small concession, hardly on the order of a "shot heard round the world." But out of small events—a weary Rosa Parks refusing to move to the back of that Montgomery, Alabama, bus, for in-stance—mighty movements can grow. The federation's very appearance that night marked an opening shot in a new phenomenon. Urban church activ-ists were beginning to challenge the sprawl machine.

The Churches

The interfaith federation was, itself, a relative newcomer. Its church-based constituent groups had existed in Chicago's Indiana suburbs for some years: the United Citizens Organization of East Chicago, the Interfaith Action Coali-tion of Gary, and the Interfaith Citizens Organization of Hammond. But traditional political rivalries and race had kept apart the movements in East Chicago (48 percent Hispanic), Gary (80 percent black), and Hammond (78 percent white).

Joining together across jurisdictional and racial lines had created a po-tent political force in Lake County. Using civil rights–style political action, the federation blocked relocating the county juvenile courts from Gary to Crown Point. More impressively, they overcame the determination of two federal district judges to move the federal courthouse out of Hammond. Their grass-roots muscle was further highlighted in April 1996 when the federation mobilized more than 1,000 members of their congregations for a public rally at the Hammond Civic Center. The mayors of the three cities were all present as well as most other prominent Lake County politicians.

---

1. "Urban Group Wants Decision on County Plan Delayed," *Hammond Times,* July 2, 1996.

"We must change the way we think about this region," Reverend Davis urged at the rally. "We are a single metropolitan region, with a shared history and a shared economy. We must act as an entire region on critical issues like the need for a regional transportation system and a tax-base sharing system to address growing tax rate disparities."[2]

Higher tax rates in Gary, Hammond, and East Chicago were also critical concerns of Inland Steel, USX's Gary Works, Amoco, and Northwest Indiana Public Service Company, the region's major industries. With giant facilities anchored in the lakeshore communities, they were the deep pockets called upon to bail out the poverty-stricken cities. "We're going to lose one of these industries very soon if we don't address the inequities of the tax system," Tom Reis, another federation member, warned.[3]

The local church coalitions themselves were members of a larger movement, spearheaded by the Chicago-based Gamaliel Foundation. Patterning its organizing approach on the teachings of the late Saul Alinsky (whose Industrial Areas Foundation had been organizing working-class neighborhoods since the 1930s), the Gamaliel Foundation had organizers and affiliates in seventeen communities. Its target communities were Chicago and its depressed southern suburbs, Joliet, Peoria, Iowa's Quad Cities, Detroit, Saginaw, Minnesota's Twin Cities and the Iron Range, Saint Louis and East Saint Louis, Cleveland, Columbus, Cincinnati, Milwaukee, Racine, Buffalo—almost a roll call of the Midwest's hardest-hit industrial areas.[4]

All the local church alliances in Northwest Indiana had had their neighborhood victories. Some had even reshaped major policies and programs of their city governments. But year after year they could see their communities declining in spite of their efforts. Stable middle-class families moved away. Remaining residents were proportionally poorer and poorer. Local stores closed. Salvation Army stores replaced supermarkets and pawnshops replaced pharmacies. Factories large and small would close down overnight. City services declined even as tax rates went up. Crime, drugs, and booze flourished. What was happening? Why could they win battles but never win the war?

Myron Orfield laid out the full picture for a national meeting of Gamaliel's organizers in December 1995. Using Minnesota's Metropolitics to illustrate his points, he showed how sprawling development patterns, increasing segregation by income class, continued racial discrimination, local

---

2. "Leaders Address Region's Ills," *Hammond Times*, May 1, 1996.
3. "Leaders Address Region's Ills."
4. The seventeenth community was Oakland, California.

fiscal disparities, and other factors flowed together to constantly defeat grass-roots efforts to stabilize inner-city neighborhoods. The Gamaliel staffers were very impressed, particularly Paul Scully, assigned to support the Northwest Indiana movement. He invited Myron and me to Gary for a two-day workshop for 150 ministers, lay leaders, and business representatives in early June 1996.

The Metropolitan Summit for Redevelopment was hailed by the local papers. The *Gary Post-Tribune* called the summit "a giant step toward promoting a broader understanding.... The twin centers of dispute these days—landfills and casino money—are just the latest targets in a war that has seen issues come and go. They are no more or less important than other problems that have divided the industrial north from the suburban and rural south. Each side views its needs as being greater than those of the other, but truthfully they are linked to each other. Only the most narrow vision fails to recognize that an apple is only as strong as its core."[5]

The *Hammond Times* sounded a similar theme. "Promoting 'Buffington Harbor' as the site of a spanking new riverboat casino cannot alter the fact, unpalatable as it may be to some, that it really is in Gary, whose hospitality they want to enjoy, whose resources they want to exploit, but whose public mention they want to shut out.... That mentality has to be reversed. It is a mentality of escape; and there is no escape."[6] Local leaders, the *Times* concluded, should focus on the problems of the region as a whole.

Two weeks later the federation won a temporary pause in the Lake County comprehensive plan's apparently well-greased path to approval. But an emotional battle royal was shaping up over the site of a new county landfill. The issue would pit north county against south county again.

Battling the Garbage Dump

Over the previous year the Lake County Solid Waste Management District had evaluated possible sites. By a hotly disputed 12 to 11 vote, the district board had approved a 560-acre site in the midst of farmland in Eagle Creek Township on the county's southern boundary. As an alternative site they rejected the "J-Pit," an abandoned sand quarry on the Gary-Hammond boundary.

5. "North vs. South: Lake County's Regional Feud Must End," *Gary Post-Tribune*, June 21, 1996.
6. "No Town Is an Island," *Hammond Times*, June 25, 1996.

The Eagle Creek site, however, required a county zoning change and was fiercely opposed by South County Residents Opposed to Dumps (SCROD). The group prevailed with the plan commission, which, composed almost entirely of south county commissioners and residents, voted 12 to 0 against the Eagle Creek site at its August meeting. Heavy lobbying by the federation convinced the Lake County Council to reverse the planning group's action by a 4 to 3 vote in late September. The swing vote was cast by the county councilwoman from Hammond. She switched in the last seventy-two hours because she tried, but failed, to get assurances that Gary's J-Pit would not be used if the Eagle Creek location was rejected: "I could not get these assurances. I live near the J-Pit. I need to protect my environment. I have no choice."[7]

SCROD was incensed. It promised further court challenges. A meeting was held to consider having the southern townships secede from Lake County, perhaps joining rural (and white) Newton County. (Secession would require an amendment to the state constitution, experts advised.) Letters to the editor bombarded the papers. Some were sorrowful in tone: "When will the day come when our leaders' foresight is greater than the vision of a garbage mountain stuck in the middle of pristine farmland?"[8]

Others letters were spiteful, even hateful, especially those criticizing the Reverend Rick Orlinsky, the priest of Saint Catherine of Siena in Hammond and a leading federation spokesman. A South County resident wrote: "I, too was at the county council meeting where the Rev. Rick Orlinsky led his three busloads of north Lake County followers to endorse the murder by poison and pollution of south county children and residents. If he is a spokesman for the Catholic Church, then they can no longer preach pro-life because of this crude messiah of the north who has discredited his church. Strip off your cassock, Orlinsky, and put on your grave digging clothes, because once the dump is operational, you'll be able to bury a lot of south county residents who you despise."[9]

7. "Council OKs Landfill Rezoning," *Hammond Times*, September 27, 1996.
8. "A Chance to Show Unity Was Lost," *Hammond Times*, October 14, 1996.
9. "Priest Helped Put South County at Risk," *Gary Post-Tribune*, October 23, 1996. More serious were the efforts to silence Father Orlinsky through political pressure on the Catholic Church. The *Hammond Times* revealed ("Church Asked to Muzzle Priest," December 8, 1996) that, before the landfill vote, a South County councilman had contacted Bishop Dale Melczek, who had refused to intervene. The bishop said that Orlinsky was speaking on behalf of Interfaith, not the Catholic Church. "While Melczek makes a strict distinction between the diocese and Interfaith," the *Times* reported, "he speaks highly of the group, which receives some of its funding from the Campaign for Human Development, an arm of the National Conference of Bishops. 'They fund self-help groups

Responded one grandmother in Gary: "I speak for a group of citizens who never wished a 'dump' on anyone. We have been dumped on by so many different things, we know what it is to be taken advantage of and ignored. The funny thing was, there was no one to care, to offer help, until we had to come to grips with it ourselves. Our cancer rate is very high, so are those of heart problems, breathing problems, etc. For our children and our grandchildren, the future looks rather bleak. We can't survive another dump [in Gary]."[10]

Amending the Land Use Plan

Throughout the months of pitched battle over the landfill, the Lake County comprehensive plan plowed its way inexorably forward. The federation thought it had a commitment for a new hearing to be held in north county; a plan commission staff member rescheduled the hearing for Crown Point again as "the most centrally located point." The federation boycotted the hearing in protest. At the same August meeting, when the plan commission (with its central and south county membership) voted unanimously to oppose the Eagle Creek landfill, its members also recommended unanimously that the county council adopt the comprehensive plan.

The next round, however, belonged to the federation. "Against long odds," the *Hammond Times* reported, "urban activists won a temporary victory over suburban sprawl [September 3] ... when the County Council narrowly voted to defer a vote on the plan until the federation leaders have a chance to voice their concerns and suggest changes."[11]

Aided by a volunteer city planner, the federation weighed in with three pages of proposed amendments by mid-October. The *Hammond Times,* which had praised the federation's metropolitan summit and had endorsed the Eagle Creek landfill site, came unglued. "Wanted: Red Light along I-65," its banner headline screamed. "Economics of Envy," it editorialized. The federation's proposed amendments are "a document dripping with unconcealed hostility toward the south part of the county. . . . It is not so much a

---

that assist the voiceless in expressing themselves on public policies,' Melczek said. 'That is what [Interfaith] is doing.'"

10. "Interfaith Group Acted with Best Interest of People," *Hammond Times,* November 3, 1996. More than 500 families lived within a half-mile of the J-Pit on the Gary-Hammond border; only seventeen families lived that close to the Eagle Creek site in south county. Indeed, tipping fees from the Eagle Creek landfill would provide $4 million to clean up and close Gary's existing municipal dump.

11. "Vote Deferred on Plan for Land," *Hammond Times,* September 4, 1996.

plan for equitable development as a declaration of war. . . . The unabashed aim is to stop the wheels of progress in south county and to force them to come to the north."

The *Times*'s editorial vitriol was easily exceeded by the county council's sole representative on the plan commission: "I think the Interfaith people should mind their own damn business, take care of their churches and their communities, and keep their youth away from crime. We don't stick our nose into Gary or Hammond or East Chicago. Why should they stick their nose into the unincorporated areas?" Commenting on the federation's call for "fair share" affordable housing in new subdivisions, the south county councilman concluded, "Those people can't afford these homes. They can't even afford a gallon of paint."[12]

The federation was stung. Its proposed amendments, in its view, had been modest and moderate; within the group, members who wanted no further development in south county had been argued down. It had recommended that the county wait to approve any new roads until the Northwest Indiana Regional Planning Commission completed the regional 2020 transportation plan. The federation had suggested that the amount of farmland immediately rezoned for residential development around southern Cedar Lake, Lowell, and unincorporated Saint John Township be reasonably limited to that necessary to accommodate the next ten years of projected population growth. It had recommended deleting proposals for new industrial zoning and holding commercial rezoning along Interstate 65 and U.S. 231, in the county's southern section, to a maximum of twenty acres. The federation had opposed a county proposal to have developers of new south county subdivisions contribute to an "off-site" affordable housing fund; instead, it argued for a minimum of 10 percent affordable housing as an integral part of new subdivisions.[13] "There is nothing radical, divisive, vengeful, or extreme about this document," the federation argued in an op-ed response to the *Times*.

> Nowhere does it talk about killing development in south Lake County to force development into Gary, East Chicago, and Hammond. In fact, the

12. "Wanted: Red Light along I-65," *Hammond Times*, October 20, 1996.
13. "Off-site affordable housing will tend to concentrate low-income housing in one particular area and actually increase exclusionary effects," the federation argued in its amendments. "On-site affordable housing will encourage inclusionary developments and reduce the heavy burden on one community." The federation's proposal was drawn from my metropolitan summit presentation on Montgomery County, Maryland's moderately priced dwelling unit policy (see chapter 9).

document talks about preserving and stabilizing the second ring of sub-urbs such as Highland, Griffith, Lake Station, and Merrillville, the com-munities most at risk from the current development trends. These communities are already seeing the same patterns of decline experienced by their northern neighbors in the last two decades. The only difference is that these towns don't have the industrial tax base to fall back on when their residential tax base slowly erodes. . . . If we follow the blueprint pro-duced by the plan commission, what will [the *Times* propose] to protect the property values of its readers in [these suburbs]? What about their prop-erty rights?

The issues we are working on and the solutions we are proposing are in the interest of the entire region. They aim to promote stability in the suburbs, redevelopment in the cities, preservation of agricultural space, economic diversity in our housing, and tax rate equity between munici-palities.[14]

The federation concluded its statement by challenging the *Times* to work with it to convene a conference to discuss its proposals "for the Lake County plan and the future of Lake County" in a gathering of the mayors, town managers, city council members, planners and county officials from the cit-ies and suburbs for "a rational and factual conversation about the danger-ous development trends taking place in our region and the solutions to deal with them."

And that, indeed, was the path taken. Recognizing that there was little public understanding of the consequences of suburban sprawl—and less political support within the county council—the federation opted for longer-term education rather than short-term conflict. When pro-plan supporters geared up for another donnybrook public hearing in mid-December, the federation's president, the Reverend Vincent L. McCutcheon, announced: "We will not participate in an event designed to provoke a north/south con-frontation." Instead, the federation held a countywide prayer breakfast "to promote understanding and fellowship." Successfully persuading the county council to attach an amendment to the comprehensive plan requiring a con-sideration of potential amendments in June 1997, the federation watched quietly as the county council adopted the plan at its December meeting.

---

14. "Officials of Interfaith Federation Criticize *Times* Editorial," *Hammond Times*, November 1996.

A Legislative Victory (Indirectly)

The year's battles had one other immediate result. Success caused the federation to become a principal target in a key Lake County legislative race. Running for a vacant, traditionally Republican House seat in south county, the Republican candidate broadcast a flyer that claimed the federation was "a political action group for North Lake County Democrats. They seek the environmental and economic destruction of South Lake and Porter Counties. Interfaith already controls four of the seven members of the Lake County Council. *They are now supporting a Merrillville Democrat for State Representative.* If they are successful, Democrats will control the Indiana State house. Interfaith's Gary and East Chicago allies will be in charge of important House committees and gain even greater control of South County." For the future of "our families and businesses," the flyer urged, the district's residents should vote Republican.

"It's funny," mused Paul Scully, the federation's senior staffer, in a conversation with me several weeks after the election. "The federation never even talked to the Democratic candidate, much less actively supported him. But he won, and his victory did shift control of the Indiana House. So, I suppose, in a way, we did gain greater influence."

It had been a bruising short course on the politics of regional development. The landfill battle was somewhat familiar ground for federation veterans. But the vehemence of the response to their proposed land use plan amendments startled federation leadership. The message was clear: "Stick to your own sandbox and we'll tolerate you . . . barely. Mess with our turf and we'll cut your heads off."

Breaking into a Closed System

Decisionmaking within the sprawl machine was a closely held process, the federation realized. Legally, the county council's planning and zoning powers apply only to unincorporated territory. Lake County's eighteen incorporated municipalities conduct their own planning and zoning. It was, perhaps, understandable that the plan commission was dominated by residents of south county, where most unincorporated land was found, but that precluded strong voices asserting that south county sprawl had a direct impact on north county stability and vitality.

The system was infused with conflicts of interest. Most striking was the revelation by the *Gary Post-Tribune* that the plan commission's staff director was himself an investor in a proposed subdivision within two miles of the Eagle Creek landfill site.[15] He had been a "ferocious" critic of the landfill, had blasted it as a potential safety hazard, and had voted against the Eagle Creek site as a member of the Lake County Solid Waste Management Board. Now he declared his twenty-four-townhouse Tucson Subdivision to be "a nice little project. We have sewer, well water, sidewalks and full utilities. . . . We are on the opposite side of Interstate 65. The highway's elevated there so you couldn't see the landfill if it was 400 feet high."

Swapping his planning director hat for his developer hat, he remarked: "Do I think I'm exposing them [future homeowners] to anything? I hope not. The water is chlorinated and there are all kinds of safeguards." Referring to the prospect of protracted litigation before the Indiana Department of Environmental Management and in the state courts, the planning director–developer perhaps reflected the typical attitude of area developers: "People are still safe building down there for a little while because you never know. Even if they prove me wrong, they've still got all this litigation to go through so they have another five years."

It was as if the federation's recommendations were written in a foreign language, the federation found. By the standards of communities with active growth management policies in place, the federation's proposals were exceedingly modest. They proposed no urban growth boundaries as in Portland, Seattle, or San Jose; just do not rezone more farmland than you need, they suggested. They were not seeking to ban further freeways or highways, but simply asking local authorities to wait for the transportation planners' study. Their minimum target of 10 percent affordable housing in new subdivisions was well below Montgomery County, Maryland's 15 percent or the 20 percent minimum required in Fairfax County or Loudoun County, Virginia (hardly radical hotbeds).

Most vexing was that the principal beneficiaries of the federation's amendments would probably not be Gary, Hammond, and East Chicago, but the band of older suburban communities south of them, which had traditionally been antagonistic to the three cities. The concern was based, in part, on data I developed for the federation's metropolitan summit in June 1996. It showed that several major suburbs had already joined the downward income trend taking place in the three cities (table 13-1).

15. "Residential Developers Undaunted by Landfill Concerns," *Gary Post-Tribune*, November 10, 1996.

Table 13-1. *Change in Relative Household Income in Lake County, 1970–90*
Percent

Area of county	Household income as percentage of metro mean	
	1970	1990
East Chicago	83	69
Gary	88	69
Hammond	113	82
Griffith	116	108
Highland	128	118
Hobart	113	107
Lake Station	95	81
Merrillville	133	112
Whiting	90	76

Source: Author's calculations based on census reports.

The federation's opposition to new industrial zones along Interstate 65 and U.S. 235 was, indeed, designed to encourage industrial reinvestment in vacant industrial sites in the three cities, which were already served by shipping on Lake Michigan, extensive rail lines, and Interstates 80 and 90. But the federation's desire to restrain new commercial development was designed to "ensure the viability of U.S. 30 as the commercial hub," the corridor five miles south of Gary and Hammond where the shopping centers and regional malls were the core of the tax bases among the first ring of suburbs.

Assessing their six months' effort, the federation realized that it was still too vulnerable politically. Inner-city groups had to do more than just argue for the interests of inner suburbs. They would have to enlist suburban congregations actively in the federation's ranks. In early 1997 they stepped up efforts to reach out to suburban churches. They also moved to repair relationships with the local press, particularly the *Times*.

Recruiting Suburban Support

The 1997 metropolitan summit of Northwest Indiana showed how far the federation had come in spreading the message in just one year. The first metropolitan summit had been held in inner-city Gary. The second metropolitan summit took place in suburban Merrillville in the commercial heart of Lake County. The first summit was sponsored solely by the federation. For the second summit, the federation was joined by the Calumet District of the United Methodist Church, the Roman Catholic Diocese of Gary, the Jewish Federation of Northwest Indiana, and the Merrillville Clergy Association. At the first summit most of the 150 participants were residents of Gary, Hammond, and East Chicago. At least half of the almost 300 participants in the second summit were residents of first-ring—and even second-ring—suburbs.

The program was packed with information and provocative ideas. Indianapolis Mayor Stephen Goldsmith keynoted the conference, emphasizing the necessity for regional collaboration. john powell, director of the University of Minnesota's Institute on Poverty and Race, talked quietly but eloquently about race in America. Memorably, he quoted South Africa's Bishop Desmond Tutu: "It is very difficult to wake up a man who is pretending to be asleep."

The federation had commissioned Myron Orfield's Metropolitan Area Program to map trends in Northwest Indiana. With a dozen multicolored maps based on census data, tax records, and school reports, Orfield hammered away at uneven development patterns, rising child poverty, and growing fiscal disparities affecting both the cities and many first-ring suburbs.

My initial role was to reemphasize Orfield's themes. The Lake County economy has revived modestly, with lower-paying service jobs steadily substituting for higher-paying industrial jobs. Unemployment is lower, but the concentration of poverty grows and spreads outward from central cities to many older suburbs. Though racial barriers are slowly dropping, economic segregation is growing because of prevailing patterns of new development. New investment in new subdivisions and shopping centers is largely offset by disinvestment in older communities. Without strong land use policies, today's winners become tomorrow's losers. Ultimately, all of Lake County loses.

After the box lunch break, it was my task to offer a six-point action plan for "overcoming uncontrolled suburban sprawl in Northwest Indiana." The first recommendation was that the Lake County Council should adopt a strong, sprawl-controlling, comprehensive land use plan that includes urban growth boundaries. Lake County's reform movement should seek a tricounty alliance with concerned groups in neighboring Porter and LaPorte Counties and recruit allies throughout the state (thus the invitation to Indianapolis Mayor Goldsmith). Second in order of priority, reformers should press the Indiana legislature to adopt a strong, Oregon-type land use law.

Third, the new Lake County plan should require a modest amount of low- and moderate-income housing in all new subdivisions in unincorporated areas. Fourth, the land use plan should be buttressed by a special tax-base-sharing district for unincorporated areas. Existing municipalities would only qualify for revenues from the tax base pool by adopting land use, zoning, and mixed-income housing ordinances that were consistent with county policies. Recommendation five was that the Lake County Council develop a transportation policy to support a comprehensive land use plan, including a countywide tax levy to support an expanded, multicommunity bus system. ("Transportation problems do *not* have transportation solutions," I cautioned. "They have land use solutions.")

The last recommendation was that "grass-roots coalitions make land use and transportation planning a more open, democratic process." Membership on the Lake County Plan Commission should be diversified to reflect the stake of older, northern communities in future development patterns. County government should increase the plan commission's budget to allow it to hire disinterested, full-time, professional staff. Membership on the Northwest Indiana Regional Planning Commission should be reformed to reflect one-person, one-vote principles; vital transportation decisions are currently weighted against larger urban population centers. Above all, grass-roots coalitions should make the Lake County comprehensive land use plan *the* key issue in 1998's county council elections.

The conference participants went into breakout sessions to plan the next steps. The Reverend Dan Estes, president of the Merrillville Clergy Association, led the report session. What will the business community do? What will the political leadership do? What will the faith community do? Enthusiastic and committed, Reverend Estes gathered pledges for specific next steps.[16]

A Spanish refrain cautions, "Entre dicho y hecho hay gran trecho" (there is a big gap between what is said and what is done). The Northwest Indiana Federation of Interfaith Organizations has a long, hard path ahead of it. But if new alliances can indeed be forged across racial lines, across class lines, across city and suburb boundaries in metro Gary-Hammond, Indiana, the nation's most racially divided metro area, such alliances can be forged anywhere.

16. The success of their organizational efforts is illustrated by the fact that the third metropolitan summit, held in June 1998 in the largest Lutheran church in suburban Merrillville, attracted 1,500 participants. The newspaper reported that the line of cars waiting to turn into the church parking lot that Saturday afternoon extended a mile and a half down the road.

Over the two-year period, the efforts to curb Father Rick Orlinsky's advocacy through political pressure on the Catholic Church hierarchy had been the ugliest episode of the federation's campaign. Fortunately, the local bishop had stood fast in support of the activist priest. In fact, more vigorous advocacy was developing within the Catholic Church nationally. In early 1996 Anthony M. Pilla, bishop of the Diocese of Cleveland, issued an extraordinary message titled "The Church in the City." After a sophisticated analysis of the impact of suburban sprawl and out-migration from central cities and many inner suburbs, he turned from demographics and economics to theology to show that a common mission links the urban and the suburban church.

It would not be enough to promote mutual philanthropy and interactions between city and suburban parishes. The Catholic Church was targeting issues—sprawl, fiscal disparities, segregated housing—that required political action. Although the church had a role to play, it could not address these issues by itself but would have to join with many others in that undertaking. Bishop Pilla urged his supporters not to be bowed by a sense of hopelessness in the face of a challenge of enormous magnitude, "involving deeply rooted attitudes and beliefs." "If anything," he said, "reason for hope is greatest when we face reality. So let us face it, and let us join with our neighbors, public officials and community leaders in the hopeful undertaking of building a new urban future for Northeast Ohio."[17]

Bishop Pilla's potential influence clearly reaches beyond Northeast Ohio. In 1996 he became president of the National Conference of Catholic Bishops. In fact, at their national leadership meeting in December 1996, the Gamaliel Foundation's Catholic activists voted to encourage Bishop Pilla to push his views more forcefully with his fellow bishops.

The Business Community

"The Regional Competitiveness Act is the first thing I've seen in 30 years that can work to bring municipalities together," said former Virginia Governor Linwood Holton, spokesman for the Urban Partnership.[18] In the 1996 session the Regional Competitiveness Act passed both houses of the Vir-

17. Pilla (1996, p. 5).
18. "Momentum Builds as Regions Form Partnerships," *Urban Impact* (Virginia Center for Urban Development, Fall 1996).

ginia General Assembly by overwhelming majorities. "As a symbol of the General Assembly's willingness to implement the concept," Holton said, "they've already put $3 million into the Regional Incentive Fund despite the fact that they didn't have anything extra to play with."

The Urban Partnership had sought first-year funding of $10 million, rising to $100 million by the third year. Holton expressed his confidence that the General Assembly would fully implement the legislation by allocating, in an always-cautious politician's parlance, "an appropriate amount into the fund."

Other state legislatures have provided incentive funds for intergovernmental cooperation, and the ultimate impact of Virginia's law may well depend on the size of the incentive available.[19] But what is fascinating about Virginia's Regional Competitiveness Act is the way policies and services are ranked for local collaboration. In order to qualify for any incentive funds, a "regional partnership" must collaborate on joint undertakings earning at least twenty points under the new law. The law specified the maximum points the state agency managing the program can assign to different activities: regional revenue sharing, ten; education, ten; human services, eight; local land use, eight; housing, eight; special education, six; transportation, five; law enforcement, five; economic development, four; solid waste, four; water and sewer services, four; corrections, three; fire and emergency medical services, three; libraries, two; and parks and recreation, two.

There would be no "soft path" to regionalism in Virginia. Cities and counties would not be able to qualify with a laundry list of less controversial services and infrastructure compacts. In fact, the top-rated items virtually mirrored the dictum of Don Hutchinson, president of the business-based Greater Baltimore Committee, who has said, "If regionalism isn't dealing with land use, fiscal disparities, housing, and education, regionalism isn't dealing with the issues that really matter."[20]

The Regional Competitiveness Act was not the Urban Partnership's only achievement. Five of seven bills it sponsored were enacted, including broad authorization of revenue and tax base–sharing agreements among local governments, authority for the Virginia Housing Development to finance mixed-income housing throughout the state on an 80-20 formula, and several other housing-related measures. A proposed constitutional amendment to remove

19. By 1998 the General Assembly had raised the appropriation to $10 million.
20. Remarks made at the meeting of the Regionalism Task Force of the Greater Baltimore Committee, September 30, 1996.

the referendum currently required for counties to enter into revenue and tax base–sharing agreements was carried over to the 1997 session.[21]

Forming the Urban Partnership

Remarkable as the Urban Partnership's success was in its initial legislative foray, the group's history and membership were equally noteworthy. The partnership was formally organized in July 1994 after a year of discussions between the political and business leadership of Virginia's major cities. Core members were the mayors, city managers, and chamber of commerce presidents of fifteen major Virginia cities. Lending additional business muscle were top executives from many of the state's major corporations, among them Bell Atlantic, Crestar Financial, First Union Bank, Norfolk Southern, Virginia Power, and American Tobacco Company. Cochairs were Jean Clary, chairman of the statewide Virginia Chamber of Commerce, and Mayor James Eason of Hampton. Staff support was provided by Neal Barber, a veteran Richmond chamber staff member, and Virginia Commonwealth University's Center for Urban Development. With major business support as well as local government contributions, the partnership raised a $375,000 war chest and targeted the 1996 legislative session. "The basic premise of the Urban Partnership is simple," announced Jean Clary. "Virginia needs healthy cities for a healthy economy."

The emergence of the Urban Partnership in Virginia and its philosophy came as no personal surprise. Over the previous two years I had been invited to Richmond, Norfolk, and Roanoke over a dozen times for speeches and workshops by the Richmond Chamber of Commerce, Forward Hampton Roads, and other business and civic groups. I sounded all my themes of city and suburban interdependence, illustrated with census data for each community, themes that were further documented by excellent local scholars such as William Lucy of the University of Virginia and Michael Pratt of Virginia Commonwealth University.

My most useful contribution, however, may have come as lead witness before Governor Douglas Wilder's Advisory Commission on Revitalization of Virginia's Urban Areas in July 1993. In comparison with the highly fragmented northern states, local government in Virginia could be characterized as the "big box" model. With more than 6 million residents, Virginia

---

21. In an antitax climate, the legislature narrowly rejected the proposed amendment in the next session.

has only 95 counties, 41 independent cities, and 189 town governments (which are part of their surrounding counties). Its 136 school districts are coterminous with—and fiscally accountable to—counties or independent cities.[22]

The General Assembly, however, had dealt Virginia's forty-one independent cities a cruel blow when in 1979 it required that any further city annexations had to be approved by the county government affected. "Affected" is, perhaps, too mild a word, for under Virginia's unique system, "independent cities" are not part of the surrounding counties. When an independent city annexes unincorporated territory, it takes everything away from the county. The county loses residents and tax base. Students shift from county schools to city schools. The county assessor, county treasurer, county clerk, the county sheriff—all see their budgets and staffs shrink. It is not surprising that, since 1979 only Danville among Virginia's largest cities has succeeded in getting county approval for proposed annexations.

Losing Out to North Carolina

From 1979 onward (that is, after the General Assembly's freeze on annexations), I told the governor's advisory commission, one can document the steady population, income, and fiscal decline of Virginia's principal cities, especially by comparison with North Carolina's principal cities, which exercise the nation's most liberal annexation powers. During the 1980s average city incomes had slid eight percentage points lower, to an average of only 85 percent of suburban incomes for Virginia's five primary central cities. By contrast, North Carolina's five primary central cities had maintained an average of 107 percent of their suburban incomes. North Carolina's major cities all had AA+ or AAA credit ratings. Wall Street was slowly downgrading Virginia's cities.

Most important, while the real income growth of North Carolina's city residents (22 percent) had clearly swamped Virginia's city residents (9 percent), as entire metropolitan areas the real income growth rate of North Carolina's "elastic" regions (22 percent) had steadily outstripped Virginia's "inelastic" regions (16 percent). Clearly, city and suburbs were economically intertwined.

22. By contrast, with 5 million residents, Wisconsin has 57 counties, 583 municipalities, 1,267 townships, and 430 independent school districts.

I was able to make the lesson more tangible in Norfolk in a talk to Forward Hampton Roads in October 1993. "Several years ago you set a goal of landing a major league sports team for the Hampton Roads area. What progress have you made?" Hampton Roads was not among the final five for two new National Football League franchises, I reminded the audience, confessing that I had just served as a consultant on Charlotte's bid. "As a region, Virginia's Tidewater-Richmond axis has the population and economy to be considered among the finalists. You haven't yet shown that you can pull together the resources of all your communities in order to compete." I predicted that Charlotte would be awarded its NFL franchise and speculated that Jacksonville could well be the other choice. To almost no one's surprise, the next day the NFL announced its choice of the Carolina Panthers. Thirty days later, to almost everyone's surprise, it awarded the second coveted franchise to the Jacksonville Jaguars (ranked second in my study ahead of Baltimore, Saint Louis, and Memphis).[23]

My data had given Virginians hard evidence of what they already felt: Virginia was losing ground to North Carolina. The theme was carried forward in further research commissioned by the partnership. "In three of the six metropolitan regions of Virginia, earnings per private sector job have fallen (Norfolk-Virginia Beach-Newport News, Charlottesville, and Roanoke). North Carolina regions have lost no ground," the partnership reported. "Family poverty rates increased in five out of six central cities in Virginia from 1970 to 1990. In North Carolina family poverty rates declined in central cities in five of its six metropolitan areas."[24] It was all quietly galling to Virginia's pride.[25]

Another research presentation by William Lucy and David Phillips of the University of Virginia also captured the partnership's attention. Many neighborhoods in suburban counties were declining as well. Beyond the evident erosion of the central cities, population and income were declining in many parts of older suburban counties. For example, during the 1980s Henrico and Chesterfield Counties, which abut Richmond, lost population in almost one-half and one-quarter of their census tracts, respectively. Similarly, median family incomes as a percentage of the Richmond regional av-

23. In recounting this history to later audiences, I told them, "You've just heard me pull the old politician's trick: 'Shoot at anything that flies; claim anything that falls.'"

24. Lucy and Phillips (1994, pp. 8, 10).

25. Located between Virginia and South Carolina, North Carolina was once described as "a vale of humility between two mountains of conceit."

erage fell in 71 percent of Henrico's census tracts and 63 percent of Chester-field's.[26] Urban decline was not a phenomenon of only growth-constricted core cities. High-end growth was also moving outward, from inner counties such as Henrico and Chesterfield to outer counties such as Hanover and Goochland.

Hammering Out the Legislative Agenda

In mid-1994 the partnership formed its committees and went to work. The Research and Issues Development Committee commissioned a wide-ranging set of "policy scans" and struggled to thin out long laundry lists of policy proposals into a recommended legislative agenda. The Government Affairs Committee charted a sustained lobbying strategy targeted on the 1996 General Assembly session. The committee called for "bold, significant, and dramatic" recommendations that would be "the top legislative priority of our member localities."

In December 1994 the partnership held an urban summit in Richmond, attended by 400 business and political leaders from across the state.[27] Business leaders emphasized that all parts of a region need to be healthy for the region to be competitive in a global economy. Keynote speaker Anthony Downs of the Brookings Institution emphasized that "it is up to suburban leaders to change attitudes about mutual interdependence and mutual membership in a single metropolitan community." Representative Norman Sisisky observed that "our destinies are linked together whether we like it or not."[28] Cooperation is the key, he emphasized, and the best solutions are ones that are hammered out in meetings rather than mandated.

What was in danger of being hammered out of committee meetings, however, was active business participation. Several chief executives, accustomed to more of a command psychology, were becoming restless with the more leisurely pace set by their public partners, particularly some of the city managers. Particularly vexing was the reluctance of many governmental members to address major reforms on jurisdictional issues. "We've been looking at regional cooperation when a real major barrier to significant progress is the artificial political boundaries that separate city from county or city

26. Lucy and Phillips (1994, pp. 7, 9).

27. "Counties Already Feeling Cities' Ills," *Richmond Times-Dispatch,* December 9, 1994.

28. "Expert: Growth Patterns Lead to Suburban Linkage with Central Cities," and "Common Themes from a Congressman and Business Leaders," *Urban Impact,* February 1995.

from city," one executive stressed.[29] Ultimately, however, the innate caution and stubborn turf protection of mayors and managers prevailed. Aside from suggestions that independent cities could revert to town status—and by becoming part of counties again, regain annexation powers—the partnership members could not agree on basic governance reforms.

After the second urban summit the following June in Norfolk, the Urban Partnership settled on its seven-point agenda for the 1996 legislative session. The initial program, staff director Neal Barber wrote me later, was "modest against your standards."[30] Like all good lobbyists, the partnership realized that the best lobbying is done before the beginning of the session. General information and summaries of its research had been sent to all legislators that spring. Personal visits and phone calls were made to all legislators (often by major business leaders) after the partnership's board approved its legislative program. Throughout the summer and fall, follow-up visits were made with General Assembly members and candidates to reinforce the importance of the proposals. Postelection visits were made to successful candidates between mid-November and mid-December to reinforce the partnership's message.

As noted above, the Urban Partnership's initial legislative proposals met with remarkable success, far more than is typically experienced by the Virginia League of Municipalities or the Virginia Association of Counties. It was business leadership that made the difference.

Building Regional Business Coalitions

Business leaders are practically the only natural constituency for regionalism. Business groups tend to think in terms of economic regions and labor market areas. This is particularly true of local chambers of commerce. Most are regional bodies, though there may be subunits for smaller jurisdictions.

The nature of local business leadership is changing dramatically, however. With its big steel plants and refineries, Gary-Hammond-East Chicago

---

29. "Common Themes from a Congressman and Business Leaders."

30. Letter to the author March 4, 1996. I had made a presentation to the Partnership's Governmental Affairs Committee in February 1995, hoping to help it focus its priorities. I had urged that it focus on the high concentration of poverty in older city and inner-suburb neighborhoods. I urged the partnership to lobby Virginia's congressional delegation to support HUD's proposed transformation of public housing, seek to convert Virginia's "fair share" housing law from permissive authorization to mandatory requirement, and have the General Assembly establish Minnesota-type tax base–sharing programs in all metro areas. Though their final legislative package addressed these priority concerns, the partnership (probably realistically) set more limited goals.

is the exception. In many regions dominant industrialists are gone: moved, merged, or bankrupt.

Akron is a good example. For half a century Akron was the rubber capital of the world, and "Big Rubber"—Firestone, Goodyear, B. F. Goodrich, and General Tire—ran the town. At the end of World War II, the Big Four employed 70,000 workers in the Akron area. In the next four decades the Akron area lost tens of thousands of tire and rubber jobs. By 1995 only Goodyear maintained a major presence (5,000 employees). Bridgestone/Firestone had shrunk to barely 900 employees; B. F. Goodrich to less than 600. Acquired by Michelin, General Tire had closed local operations completely.

In his 1967 film debut, *The Graduate*, young Dustin Hoffman received one word of poolside advice from his father's business partner: "plastics." It was Akron that took the advice to heart. Akron has now successfully converted from the world's rubber capital to the world's polymer capital with more than 400 companies engaged in plastics research, development, and production. But they are all relatively small-scale operations. Not one polymer company ranked among the Akron area's fifty largest employers in 1995. Big Plastic cannot gather in one room and shape the Akron area's future; Big Plastic does not exist.

In Akron and many other communities, the core leadership of the chamber of commerce is no longer a region's major manufacturers. Local business leaders now generally come from businesses more dependent geographically on the local market: the gas, electric, and telephone companies; locally owned banks; local newspapers; even major hospitals (which act like for-profit businesses more and more). Such companies are important, but they do not command the power that major industrialists once had to get things done at city hall or in state capitols. The era has passed when, for example, a single captain of industry, John Patterson, chairman of National Cash Register, could imperiously demand that Dayton throw out its mayor and city council and establish the nation's first commission–city manager form of government in 1914.[31] Acting in coalitions, however, as

31. Those days are not altogether gone, however. Founded in 1906, Kellogg, the country's largest breakfast cereal company, grew up in Battle Creek. The Kellogg Company and the Kellogg Foundation (the United States' second richest) needed new headquarters buildings. "We're not going to invest $70 million in a new building in the midst of a dying, Midwestern industrial city," William LaMothe, Kellogg Company's CEO, in effect, announced in 1982. "We're tired of all the constant, petty bickering between the city and suburban Battle Creek township. Either you two merge or we're out of here and off to the Carolinas." That giant corporate hammer pounded out a new political alignment. City and township merged into one (by a 9 to 1 vote in the city, 3 to 1 in the township). The consolidated government set a uniform tax rate for its new unified tax base: a

Virginia's Urban Partnership shows, business leadership can still wield clout. And harnessing such business groups to regional reform is a key to political success.

Perhaps the next significant, statewide, business-driven regional reform movement is emerging in Pennsylvania, where a statewide Alliance of Midsized Cities began forming in 1996. It may fill a crucial power vacuum, for Pennsylvania politics has traditionally been dominated by "everyone else against Philadelphia and Pittsburgh." In the crunch, the needs of Pennsylvania's "third-class cities" are often ignored.

Now CEO-dominated business groups such as the Lehigh Valley Partnership, the Lancaster Alliance, Scranton Tomorrow, the Erie Conference on Community Development, and the Greater Johnstown Committee are joining together. "Our common bond is that we are all local business leaders deeply concerned about the future of our cities," explains Tom Wolf, president of Better York and a leading voice of the nascent statewide alliance. "However, we've come to realize that what happens *inside* our cities is largely determined by what happens *outside* our cities. While we are right to appreciate the virtues of our system of local government, the future health of our county will be determined in large part by how we address the issue of regional interdependence now."

Speaking of his own York County, Wolf continued: "We will never solve regional problems like traffic congestion by purely local action. We will never develop a rational land use plan for the region if we continue to rely exclusively on local planning efforts. And we will never assure our region of long-term prosperity if we continue to condemn our older communities to make do with declining tax bases, increasing poverty, and long-term economic stagnation."[32]

In the fall of 1996 I was invited to give several speeches in Lancaster, the Lehigh Valley, and York. For Better York I undertook a larger task, writing a "York Report," which was published as a twenty-four-page tabloid by the York *Daily Record*. The report targeted three key problems:

---

30 percent tax increase for former township property owners, a 30 percent tax cut for former city property owners, including Kellogg and other major industries. Rather than just pocketing the tax cut, however, Kellogg contributed an equivalent amount to a new economic development fund. Several dozen other companies followed suit. Matched dollar for dollar by the Kellogg Foundation, their contributions built a $10 million economic development fund over the next five years and helped trigger a major revival of the Battle Creek economy.

32. "For Renewal, County Must Consider Some Regionalizing," *York Daily Record*, November 20, 1996.

—Urban sprawl: in the past thirty years York County had lost 30 percent of its farmland to suburban development.

—Concentrated poverty: though just five miles square, York City housed 91 percent of the county's poor minorities.

—Fiscal disparities: York City had less than half the tax base per capita of suburban Spring Garden township.

With slight shifts in data, the York Report might have described conditions in Lancaster, Reading, Allentown, and all of Pennsylvania's midsized cities as well.

The York Report laid out a program of land use reforms, regional revenue sharing, mixed-income housing, and policies to spur a socially balanced restoration of York City's historic neighborhoods. To Better York's leadership, however, I argued their top priority should be to control sprawl. With many neighborhood homes abandoned, once-strong neighborhood shopping areas closed down, and nearby factories long gone, often to the suburbs, the results of suburban sprawl were painfully apparent to the residents of all of Pennsylvania's central cities and of most boroughs.

Controlling the sprawl, I argued, would help revive central cities, boroughs, and many inner suburban townships by gradually turning development away from greenfields toward established communities. There would be many potential allies, including Pennsylvania's growing environmental movement, in the campaign for a strong statewide land use law. "Regional land use planning tends to be a vehicle for regional fair share affordable housing and regional revenue sharing anyway," I pointed out. "Strong state laws like those of Oregon and Washington set fair share affordable housing as one of the state goals, and revenue sharing can be developed as the 'glue' that helps build support for growth management." In early 1997 the business leaders' Alliance of Midsized Cities made it their top priority to work for a strict, statewide land use law such as Oregon's, and they began the long, arduous task of building legislative support.

Universities

Surrounded by the whirring and clicking of television cameras and press photographers assembled in the Rose Garden in August 1997, the president of the United States beamed. With short strokes from a couple of dozen pens, President Clinton signed the compromise budget and tax bills that would balance the federal budget by the year 2002. The ceremonial pens were handed to congressional leaders and administration stalwarts as mementos of the momentous occasion.

At least one souvenir pen should have been handed out to a small band of academic researchers in Ohio. They were the true authors of one important tax reform in the 1997 budget-balancing law: repeal of virtually all capital gains taxation on sales of private homes. But the academics did not get a pen. Nor were they even invited to the Rose Garden ceremony. Back home in Ohio, they would have to be content with having leveraged a superb piece of policy research into a major change in national policy.

Both President Clinton and the Republican candidate, Senator Bob Dole, had embraced repealing capital gains on home sales during the 1996 campaign. Dole's proposal was part of the Republicans' determination to roll back capital gains taxes across the board. The president's proposal was cast as a broad appeal to the interests of middle-class homeowners, another example of the centrist stance that would carry him to second-term victory. His words, however, cloaked the true origins of the proposal: two words that would be absent from the presidential campaign, "urban policy."

Key Housing Research

The idea of exempting home sales from capital gains taxation had been advanced by its original authors as a tool for slowing suburban sprawl and reinvigorating the demand for older housing in central cities and inner suburbs. The key research had been carried out by the Ohio Housing Research Network, a branch of the Ohio Urban Universities Program. Throughout 1992 researchers from seven state universities, led by Tom Bier of Cleveland State University, had pored through county court house records.[33] They had tracked every sale and purchase of a home in the counties surrounding Ohio's seven largest cities in 1991. Their research yielded important insights into metropolitan housing markets. First, 80.5 percent of all sellers (city and suburban) took advantage of the capital gain provision—that is, they "rolled over" any capital gain by buying a new house equal to or greater in value than the house they had just sold. Second, of the 80.5 percent of homesellers who bought more expensive homes, 84.2 percent moved farther out from

33. The members of the Ohio Housing Research Network are the University of Akron's Center for Urban Studies, the University of Cincinnati's School of Planning, Cleveland State University's Urban Center, Ohio State University's Department of City and Regional Planning, the University of Toledo's Department of Geography and Planning, Wright State University's Center for Urban and Public Affairs, and Youngstown State University's Center for Urban Studies.

the region's urban core; only 15.8 percent moved inward toward the city center to purchase their next home. Third, of the 19.5 percent who bought less expensive homes, 36.1 percent moved inward toward the center. This number was 2.3 times greater than those who met the capital gain rollover requirement.

"By requiring homesellers to purchase a home priced at least equal to the one sold in order to shelter their capital gain," the Ohio researchers wrote, "Section 1034 [of the Internal Revenue Code] obstructs movement to lower-priced homes (and rental units), and it penalizes people who are forced to make such a move. In urban areas where the geographic pattern of home values is one of increasing value with distance from the center, the provision encourages movement out and away from the center, and discourages movement toward it, which exacerbates urban decline." In other words, the provision reduced the options for sellers who move inward by 38 percent, the researchers concluded. Hence, they argued, "Section 1034 should be changed to remove the tax penalty against sellers who move down in price."[34]

Selling Homesellers Tax Reform

The policy recommendations that flowed from this insightful work were simple and straightforward, and I was determined to spread the word around Washington policy circles. An opportunity came in March 1994, when Michael Stegman, HUD's assistant secretary for policy development and research, asked me to organize a round table on regionalism. Attendees would be two dozen members of the Urban Policy Report Working Group: representatives from the White House staff, the Council of Economic Advisers, the Office of Management and Budget, the Treasury, and a half dozen other cabinet departments. (The most important participant, it turned out, was the Health and Human Services Department's David Garrison, who became a real champion of capital gains tax repeal on home sales.) I invited Tom Bier, Myron Orfield, and Jefferson Davis, a Connecticut legislator leading the regionalism effort in his state, to make presentations. With his quiet, factual, clear presentation, Bier, in particular, stirred the audience's interest.

However, there is a season for all things in Washington, and despite my fairly persistent efforts to push the Ohio researchers' home sales capital gains tax exemption forward, it did not catch fire immediately. After the Republican takeover of Congress following the 1994 elections, the Contract with

34. Ohio Housing Research Network (1994, p. iii).

America's pledge to cut capital gains taxes 50 percent across the board dominated the political debate. Democrats were rather solidly opposed, seeing the House Republicans' plan as another giveaway to the wealthiest rather than real help to middle-class families.

"A compromise that would leave the overall capital gains tax unchanged, but eliminate capital gains entirely on sale of homes . . . would be good fiscal policy, good urban policy, good environmental policy, good family policy, and good politics," I told Senator Pete Domenici, influential chairman of the Senate Budget Committee and the most popular figure in New Mexico politics.[35] It would be good fiscal policy because "the federal treasury collects only about $3 billion a year from capital gains tax on home sales because four out of five homesellers reinvest any gain in a new house of equal or greater value. *In short, the tax's impact on homeseller/homebuyer conduct is several times greater than its actual impact on federal revenues.*" It would be good urban policy because "the capital gains tax adds to the abandonment of older city neighborhoods and older inner suburbs. It is possible that repeal might [substantially increase] the demand for central-city/older suburban housing. This could do far more to revitalize older, distressed communities than empowerment and enterprise zones can ever dream of."

Furthermore, it would be good environmental policy because "America is overhoused, and urban sprawl is gobbling up agricultural land voraciously. . . . Removing an obstacle for households to buy down or become renters diminishes the incentive to move out, eases development pressures on the periphery, and strengthens use of existing neighborhoods and infrastructure." It would be good family policy because "their home is typically a family's biggest investment and asset, yet current tax policy locks that value away from a family's use (unless they take out a home equity loan). Not penalizing homesellers for buying a cheaper home or becoming renters allows them interest-free liquidity. Families could invest in starting a new business, pay for further education or training (for parents or children), or otherwise reinvest their funds. It opens up more options for families to manage their own lives better in an ever-changing world." And it would be good politics because a "repeal of the capital gains tax on homesellers primarily targets working-age, middle-class households, whose modest wealth is largely tied

35. This and subsequent quotations are from the author's memorandum to Senator Pete Domenici, January 23, 1995.

up in their home, rather than wealthier households who invest in stocks, bonds, art works, and other such items."

Whatever the strength of other arguments, the good politics of exempting homesellers from capital gains finally took hold in the middle of the presidential campaign. In August 1996 Tom Bier suddenly received a flurry of calls from White House and HUD officials asking for additional copies of his research report. President Clinton publicly launched the proposal en route to accepting the Democratic nomination in Chicago. Debated sporadically, the proposal was the closest thing to "urban policy" discussed in the campaign and was presented to the Congress as part of the administration's fiscal 1998 budget request.

Universities as Regional Reform Organizers

The success of the Ohio Housing Research Network's efforts illustrates just one role that universities play in the regionalism movement: they conduct research of direct concern to public policy issues. Through conferences and workshops, university-based programs also build broad understanding of critical issues among a wide range of participants. Many, such as Michigan State University's Urban Affairs Department or Wayne State University's College of Labor, Urban, and Metropolitan Affairs, conduct regular training programs for business leaders and public officials and administrators. Portland State University's Institute of Portland Metropolitan Studies is engaged in conducting leading-edge analyses of developments in that region. Virginia Commonwealth University's Center for Urban Studies provides key staff support for Virginia's Urban Partnership.

One of the most comprehensive and coordinated university-based projects being conducted on a statewide basis is the Ohio Urban Universities Program. Supported by both the Board of Regents of the statewide system and a line-item appropriation from the state legislature, the program links local research efforts by the major state universities in Cleveland, Columbus, Cincinnati, Akron, Dayton, Toledo, and Youngstown.

I had twice been in the Cleveland area through the sponsorship of Cleveland State University. In mid-1995 Tom Bier secured a grant from the Urban Universities Program to support my visiting and speaking in the other six major metro areas. The goal was to sound some common themes throughout the state: the impact of uncontrolled sprawl, decline of central cities,

growing distress in many inner-ring suburbs, the growth of poverty neighborhoods, the need for regional strategies.

Throughout the fall of 1995 and the spring of 1996 I traveled to the six
other communities. The Housing Research Network members took me under their wing, organizing a wide range of activities. Each visit featured a
major lecture on campus for students, faculty, and citizens alike, but the
professors organized many other events as well: speeches at established civic
forums such as Columbus's Metropolitan Club or the annual luncheon of
Toledo's Corporation for Effective Government, breakfast or luncheon presentations to business leaders or groups of local elected officials, editorial
board briefings, interviews on the local public television or radio station,
and in each community a two- to three-hour windshield tour by car so that
I could put some real-life images behind the data I had amassed or the reports they had sent me.

The themes I sounded and the data I presented were no surprise, certainly not to the professors. Their own studies had often called attention to
the same trends. In many respects, I was simply the "hired gun," the "national expert" brought in to give visibility to community conditions their
own work had previously highlighted. And I certainly learned a great deal
both about and from each community. My Ohio tour was a wonderful postgraduate course in the problems of urban America (at least, Midwest-style).

In May 1996, with all the visits completed, we all took stock at a statewide, one-day conference held in Columbus. It was billed as the Ohio Regional Forum on Land Use and Development Patterns. About 100 persons
attended from the seven metro areas: professors, local officials, key state
agency personnel, a half-dozen state legislators, several journalists. Most had
been involved in the local meetings.

We reviewed common statewide trends, beginning with unchecked urban sprawl. In one generation Ohio had consumed land at almost five times
the rate of population growth, a ratio second only to that of Michigan and
Pennsylvania. The suburban areas around every metropolitan city in Ohio
were more sparsely settled than the national average for suburbs. The next
trend was city decline. All of Ohio's central cities except still-annexing Columbus had lost population and dropped further down the income scale.
Ohio's city-to-suburb income ratio ranked the third worst among all the
states, and its fair share of poverty index was the sixth most burdensome. In
the area of racial segregation, Ohio's metro areas averaged the second worst
in housing markets and the fourth worst in public schools. As for the concentration of poverty, more than 82 percent of the state's poor African Ameri-

cans lived in poverty neighborhoods, compared with 34 percent of poor whites (a comparatively high percentage for poor whites and a reflection of widespread factory layoffs in recent decades). The number of poverty neighborhoods had grown by 50 to 100 percent in every metro area.

Today's Winners Become Tomorrow's Losers

But most important were the data on the decline of older suburbs along with the cities. If "today's winners become tomorrow's losers," "tomorrow" had arrived decades ago in Cleveland and East Cleveland. It was now arriving for many of Cleveland's inner suburbs ringing the high ground around the lakeshore cities: Bedford Heights, Garfield Heights, Maple Heights, Parma Heights, and Warrensville Heights, among two dozen declining suburbs. Suburban Norwood, North College Hill, Reading, and Sharonville, for example, were following Cincinnati's slow downward slide, as were West Carrollton, Shiloh, and Englewood, among others, in the Dayton area.

With its aggressive annexations, Columbus, Ohio's capital and now most populous city, had stabilized its economic position (at about 85 percent of the regional average household income). However, suburban Whitehall's average income had plummeted, while Gahanna, Grove City, Reynoldsburg, and Blacklick Estates were trending downward. Even Upper Arlington, long Columbus's premier suburb, could be destabilized by the emergence of New Albany, now the region's recognized top-of-the-line new town. A similar story was being played out in all of Ohio's metro areas. Somewhere between two-thirds and three-fourths of its atomized suburbs were on a downward demographic and economic path as development patterns spawned Ohio's own "favored quarters."

Our joint yearlong campaign had clearly heightened awareness of regional trends and reform needs, the Housing Research Network members judged. When, just a few weeks later, Governor George Voinevich appointed a new state commission to study ways to preserve Ohio's fast-vanishing farmland, the organizers felt it was a direct reflection of the year's work. The campaign had succeeded in pushing the regional reform agenda forward.

Of course, state-supported universities do not formally lobby causes in state legislatures (except on behalf of their own budgets). But political movements are driven by ideas, as Speaker Newt Gingrich so effectively demonstrated in projecting his controversial college-based television lectures into the Republican takeover of the U.S. House of Representatives. College and university faculties are key groups shaping the ideas driving regional reform movements, and, in their individual capacities as community citizens, academics can be found at the heart of almost all civic reform movements.

Grass-Roots Citizens' Groups

In September 1995, Rochester, New York, hosted golf's Ryder Cup competition. Pitting an all-star team of U.S. professionals against Europe's best golfers, the Ryder Cup was billed as one of the world's premier sporting events, just behind the Olympic Games and international soccer's World Cup. It brought an estimated 30,000 spectators and 1,400 journalists for a week to Rochester, generated an estimated $40 million in revenues, and showcased Rochester's Oak Hills Golf Club to hundreds of millions of television viewers around the world. With the European golfers storming from far back to win seven of eight last-day matches and eke out a half-point victory, longtime fans pronounced this Ryder Cup the most exciting ever.

The Reality Cup

In the weeks leading up to and through Ryder Cup week, the Rochester area was also the venue for the Reality Cup, an event designed to showcase not the face of wealth and prosperity in Rochester, but the city's struggling community, and to bring attention to the poor throughout the county. Among the events staged for the Reality Cup was a challenge to the winning Ryder Cup squad for eighteen holes of miniature golf, with the proceeds to go to charity. The Reality Cup cocaptain was a Catholic nun whose House of Mercy serves 5,000 needy people a year. When asked what she thought was the best part of her game, Sister replied "the windmill." (Having been beaten by the Europeans, a chastened team of American pros packed up quickly and moved on to the next PGA tour stop without taking up Sister's challenge.)

A Corporate Citizenship essay contest was also held for the fifty-two corporations that anted up $12 million in fees for corporate hospitality tents at the Oak Hill Country Club. Essays were to describe the corporation's contributions to the solution of local community problems in 500 words or less, typed double-spaced on plain white paper. The winning CEO would receive a plaque, a cash prize, and an all-expenses paid tour of Rochester neighborhoods, including lunch at the House of Mercy. (Not surprisingly, there were no corporate entrants.) A steady stream of thoughtful and thought-provoking op-ed articles and letters were also sent to the editors of supportive metropolitan dailies and specialized weeklies.

Of all the Reality Cup events, my personal favorite was "Other Half Tours—A Self-Guided Tour of the Greater Rochester Community." The tour pamphlet laid out in gently ironic tones the daily tragedy of many American cities.

Anyone can show you the glitz and the glitter or the quaint country towns of the World's Image Center [Rochester's slogan]. But you are more than a tourist to us. We want you to feel at home like you live here. So here are some local spots that can help you understand our community.

1. The first stop is in the Town of Pittsford, the host of this year's Ryder Cup. At the center of the town find the Phoenix Hotel Building. This former hotel was a well-known stop on the "underground railroad," the network that assisted runaway slaves during the time of slavery in America. It was also the time that Pittsford had its highest concentration of African-American residents. But Pittsford is not alone in maintaining its racial homogeneity. [Pittsford is now 98 percent white.] While the city of Rochester is over 40 percent African-American or Hispanic, only one of the twenty suburban towns has a minority population greater than 4 percent.

2. Next drive out route 31 to Perinton and see the Wegman's Supermarket and the Top's Superstore under construction across the street. Altogether that's nearly 200,000 square feet of groceries! Contrast this with the availability of groceries in the city. Wegman's has just closed two stores and the city has spent nearly 3 million tax dollars supporting efforts to bring food to its residents. All this in the town that is the home of what national business publications describe as the country's best grocery chain!

3. Now take route 590 north to route 104 west and get off at the Seneca exit. Welcome to the town of Irondequoit. Find Rogers Elementary School at 219 Northfield Street. Check out the basketball courts behind the school: the nets and hoops and backboards were taken down because too many kids from the city were coming across the border to play basketball. It's a perfect symbol of problem solving in a county with 1 city, 20 towns, 10 villages, and 19 separate school districts.

4. Now drive south into Northeast Rochester. In this section of the city, young men are 60 times more likely to be murdered than people living elsewhere across the community. If you are at the 500 block of Clinton Avenue you are within a fifteen-minute walk of roughly 70 percent of the murders that occurred across the county in the past three years.

5. Turn east and head for the North Street Recreation Center. It's one of the city's excellent recreation facilities and it's in the heart of this troubled section of the city. Just don't go there in the evenings after eight or on Sun-

days. It won't be open. Despite all the discussion of the importance of recreation and other services, it's mostly a 9 to 5 world. Opening the centers
late at night is a problem that just can't be solved.

6. Now go across the inner loop, that not-so-natural boundary between the business district and the places where most people live. Here's
where you'll find the problems that can be solved. Like at the War Memo-
rial, the home of Rochester's hockey team, the "Americans." The "Amerks"
owners will soon be the beneficiaries of a $500,000 investment by the City.
Or consider the community development money that has gone into the
Hyatt Hotel or the High Falls area. And see the construction site of the new,
publicly funded baseball stadium to replace the one in Northeast Rochester, the home of the Rochester Redwings.

7. Here is an example of economic development that is worth its own
stop. Find the Rochester headquarters of Monro Muffler. The president of
the corporation has been doing "pride in Rochester" public service an-
nouncements. One reason he may be happy is that, in his deal with the City
of Rochester, in exchange for locating his headquarters in the city, the company won't pay any city taxes for ten years and won't pay its full share for
twenty years. The city did, however, get the PSAs.

8. Well, it's time to head back toward the golf course. Head out East
Avenue and see how the community of Susan B. Anthony and Frederick
Douglass grew. Drive out to Oak Hill Country Club, the site of the Ryder
Cup, which is expected to bring 30–50 million dollars to town and from
which, as the head of the Chamber of Commerce said, many poor people
will benefit because the hotels and restaurants where they work will be
filled for the whole week.

The Reality Cup activities drew the ire of the chamber of commerce
and a number of Rochester area citizens. The Reality Cup did seem to stub
its toe when New York City's controversial Reverend Al Sharpton virtually
invited himself to a Rochester rally, drawing a torrent of negative letters to
the editor, and then at the last minute decided not to show up. But an editorial in the *Democrat and Chronicle* probably best summed up the Reality
Cup's message and the reaction of many area residents. Those who had staged
the Reality Cup, it said, were merely reminding everyone of "the reality of
poverty in Rochester," reminding them of all those who "won't be attending
the Ryder Cup. Not with tickets selling for $1,000 and up," who have to work
two jobs to make ends meet, have no health insurance, no paid vacation, no
pension.

And that's all the Reality Cup people are saying. They've gone out of their way to say they don't oppose the Ryder Cup itself. Go ahead and have the party. Have a good time. But after the celebrities have gone home and the corporations have folded up their $200,000 hospitality tents, remember the reality of [those] people. . . .

If Rochester can mobilize for an international golf tournament, it can also mobilize to provide health care for the working poor, get its big businesses more involved in the education of poor children and train people for jobs that pay a living wage.[36]

The Metropolitan Forum

The "party-poopers" who staged the Reality Cup, said the editorial, were actually "the ones most likely to get something done." Indeed, the event was the idea of an energetic and creative group of people calling themselves the Metropolitan Forum. With no budget (aside from small contributions from members) and no staff, but with the power of their ideas and vision, the Metropolitan Forum has been pushing forward the need for regional strategies to deal with sprawl, fiscal disparities, and concentrated poverty.

Key members include Jim Gocker, an attorney; Ralph Sell, deputy director of the Center for Governmental Research; Bob Bonn, former employment and youth services director for the Rochester Urban League and now a health agency executive; John Klofas, a criminology professor at the Rochester Institute of Technology; and Mary Anna Towler, editor and publisher of *City,* Rochester's alternative weekly. The weekly paper, in particular, has kept up a steady stream of stories about the social and economic costs of the region's fragmentation.

Like all of New York State, the Rochester area is an exceptionally difficult institutional and political environment in which to champion regionalism. Since 1963, article 9 of the state constitution has set forth a "Local Government Bill of Rights." As a practical matter, local governments are guaranteed that there will be no change in local government boundaries without a vote of approval by residents of any city, town, or village affected. The geopolitical map of New York State has been frozen for almost half a century. As a consequence, given each region's sprawling development patterns, older communities are doomed to a slow, steady decline. The state has

---

36. "After the Party's Over," *Rochester Democrat and Chronicle,* August 27, 1995.

fifty-seven counties outside of New York City (whose five boroughs are really counties). Of the fifty-seven principal municipalities in each county, some forty-four lost population and fifty-six lost income in relation to their neighboring towns over the period from 1950 to 1990. The only principal municipality in any county in New York that was stronger regionally in 1990 than it was in 1950 was the spa and racetrack community of Saratoga Springs. State law guarantees that at the heart of every urban region will be a city growing weaker and weaker with each decade.

Rochester's institutional rigidity is compounded by partisan political conflict. Rochester Mayor William Johnson, former Urban League chief, is one of the few African American mayors to publicly espouse regional strategies. Johnson, a Democrat, is stymied at every turn by the Monroe County Republican party. Fearing that Johnson, the region's most popular political figure, might challenge the Republican Monroe County executive in a future election, the county Republican party has put out the word to suburban town and village governments: Don't cooperate with the city of Rochester on anything! No joint purchasing agreements, no mutual aid compacts, no regional public works projects—much less any collaboration on the really tough issues dealing with sprawl, fiscal disparities, housing and education.[37] The only headway Mayor Johnson has made is through negotiations with the few suburban jurisdictions headed by Democratic officials.

Nevertheless, the constant, creative agitation of the Metropolitan Forum has moved the public debate over regionalism forward. And its efforts in Rochester have met with a sympathetic response in urban communities in Upstate New York. In 1996 an all-but-bankrupt Utica City agreed to Oneida County's "regionalizing" the city-owned water system and auditorium. The Syracuse mayor and Onondaga County executive have publicly explored various forms of city-county consolidation or joint review. Joel Giambra, Buffalo's elected comptroller, publicly champions that city's merger with Erie County.[38] A "thruway alliance" seems to be developing critical support for major governance reforms in New York State.[39]

37. From an earlier era, the Rochester area does still have the Morin-Ryan Plan, a county–local government tax sharing agreement, in place. A supplemental agreement, distributing additional sales tax revenues, was added for 1995–99.

38. In 1997 Giambra commissioned the Rochester-based Center for Governmental Research to assess merger possibilities. Rejecting outright consolidation as infeasible, the institute recommended that Buffalo contract Erie County to take over delivering about 90 percent of municipal services. Without anticipating any rank-and-file downsizing, the institute estimated that Buffalo could save 9 percent to 15 percent of its budget just by eliminating duplicative administrative layers and cutting down on Buffalo's high costs of city officialdom.

39. The growing interest in regionalism was certified by the success of the Chautauqua Con-

Where such growing ferment over regionalization in New York will ultimately lead is an open question. Years ago a famous *New Yorker* magazine
cover depicted the United States as seen from New York City, with Brooklyn
and Queens lying humbly in the foreground, and Manhattan dominating
the Earth, while just west of the Hudson River the rest of America disappears
as terra incognita. New York's approach to local governance reform mirrors
that *New Yorker* cover. Past state commissions have been composed exclusively of New Yorkers, staffed by New Yorkers, drawing upon New York academics, and examining only New York alternative models. Is New York prepared to learn from other parts of the country? If its political establishment
listens to citizen groups such as Rochester's Metropolitan Forum, it may.

Foundations: Key Regionalism Supporters

One other set of partners in regional coalition building deserves special
mention: local philanthropic foundations. In general, I have been critical of
the focus of most philanthropic giving: helping poor people try to run up
the down escalator (see chapter 3). However, local foundations are becoming more and more supportive of the regional agenda. In my own case, for
example, Baltimore's Abell Foundation commissioned *Baltimore Unbound*.
It provided a follow-up grant to the Citizens Planning and Housing Association for Myron Orfield's mapping studies of the Baltimore region and
helped finance the Greater Baltimore Committee's initiatives for regional
reform. The foundation's president, Robert Embry, is one of the nation's
most knowledgeable experts on housing and metropolitan development. For
many years he was housing chief for Baltimore City and later assistant secretary for community development during the Carter administration.[40]

One could not have a better local sponsor in Baltimore than Bob Embry
and the Abell Foundation. They combine all the desirable qualities of the
perfect sponsor—deep knowledge, deep commitment, deep pockets—with
one crucial exception. As a charitable, tax-exempt organization, the founda-

ference on Regional Governance in June 1997. Organized by Buffalo attorney-activist Kevin Gaughn,
the conference brought more than 200 concerned citizens from western New York, plus a substantial attendance from around the country, for three days of lectures and discussions at the famed
Chautauqua Institution. The faculty was an all-star cast of noted speakers and practitioners of
regionalism, including Neal Peirce and Curt Johnson, Ted Hirshfield of the University of Pennsylvania, Richard Nathan of the Rockefeller Institute, Myron Orfield, and myself.

40. We first met in 1980 when I was mayor of Albuquerque, pursuing a "pocket of poverty"
urban development action grant for a new factory in Albuquerque's South Valley; see chapter 9.

tion cannot lobby actively for legislation. A foundation cannot publicly lead the reform movement. A foundation's activities must be undertaken with a view to providing the public with information about the issues.

The same institutional limitation applies to other foundations that are beginning to support the regional agenda, such as the MacArthur Foundation in Chicago, the Gund Foundation in Cleveland, the Heinz Endowments in Pittsburgh, or the Kellogg Foundation in Battle Creek. They can support, but they cannot lead. Foundations cannot fill the leadership gap.

Mayors: Missing in (In)Action

That leadership gap is not being filled by big city mayors either. There are exceptions, such as Rochester's William Johnson, Grand Rapids's John Logie, or Richmond's Larry Chavis. (The latter two are both part-time mayors who chair their city councils under council-manager governments. For them, being mayor is not a career.)

To my knowledge, only one of the mayors of America's fifty largest central cities has taken a vigorous stand, for example, in favor of formal city-county consolidation. In 1991 W. W. Herenton, former city school superintendent, became the first black mayor of Memphis. Through about 1980 Memphis had always annexed most new development in Shelby County. Then the process stopped abruptly.[41] Despite the creation of prestigious new downtown neighborhoods such as Harbor Town (on Mud Island in the middle of the Mississippi) and the Bluffs, Memphis was unable to capture most new high-end growth without annexations. With the city stagnating and new suburbs such as Germantown and Collierville soaring, Memphis's average income plummeted precipitously, from 97 percent of suburban levels in 1979 to just 76 percent in 1989.[42]

Annexations were always hotly contested (even though Memphis, like Charlotte, has formally defined future "annexation reserves" with five of six

41. By about 1980 a majority-black Memphis City Council may have consciously put the brakes on annexations, which kept adding overwhelmingly white subdivisions to the city electorate. By 1990, 55 percent of Memphis's residents were black. Herenton won the mayor's chair by a bare handful of votes in an election sharply split along racial lines. Very popular throughout his first term, Mayor Herenton won reelection with almost 80 percent of all votes cast in 1995.

42. The twenty-one-point drop was the largest experienced by any central city during the 1980s, a fact I highlighted in comparing Memphis with Baltimore, Saint Louis, Jacksonville, and Charlotte (my client) in a report to the National Football League's Expansion Committee in October 1993.

suburban municipalities). After a year in office, Herenton had a different suggestion: dissolve the city of Memphis—turn in its municipal charter— and make Shelby County the government for the area. Shelby County as a whole—755 square miles, 826,000 residents, and growing—would loom larger on the national scene than the city of Memphis itself. Future politics? "I'll just run for mayor of Shelby County," Herenton suggested.[43]

The new mayor's proposal was assailed from all sides. Many white residents of unincorporated Shelby County, believing they had successfully fled the city's problems, violently rejected possible unification with Memphis. Many black residents were equally critical. "We've just captured control of City Hall," they said. "What are you *doing* suggesting that Memphis be dissolved? Let's enjoy our victory a while!" After a face-saving exploration of whether Memphis could simply "turn in its charter" (a citizens' committee cited many legal complications), Mayor Herenton put his proposal on the back burner.

He continues to see city-county consolidation in Memphis's future, however. "It just makes too much sense. City-county consolidation is inevitable," he told a Leadership Memphis workshop in November 1996. "Besides, within a decade black residents will be in the majority in Shelby County."[44]

And therein lies the issue. Herenton, his city's first black mayor, can embrace city-county consolidation, in part, because he believes African Americans will still be very electable in the consolidated entity. To many black political leaders, regionalism—whether formal (consolidation) or functional (power sharing)—looks like twofold dilution, both of the black community's voting power and of a mayor's political influence.

I know the latter feeling. As mayor of Albuquerque I was a sporadic and generally reluctant participant in the activities of the Middle Rio Grande Council of Governments (COG). Composed of elected officials from a four-county area, COG's principal activity was recommending the annual allocation of federal transportation assistance. In part, my lack of enthusiasm for

43. Shelby County is governed by a thirteen-member county council and an elected county executive, who is formally styled mayor of Shelby County. Thus Memphis advertises itself as "the city with two mayors."

44. A decade may be nine years too late. In July 1997, in an eleventh-hour, almost secret maneuver, the Tennessee legislature suspended the state's ban on new incorporations outside major cities' boundaries for a year. Instantly, local movements sprang up to incorporate seven new, independent municipalities in Shelby County outside Memphis ("toy towns," the newspapers dubbed them). Mayor Herenton and allies fought hard against the separatist movement and managed to get the state Supreme Court to overturn the hastily enacted law.

COG's activities was based on my belief that a strong city of Albuquerque was the best guarantor of a strong Middle Rio Grande region. (That was virtually a truism; Albuquerque accounted for more than two-thirds of the four-county region's population when I was mayor.) In part, also, my discomfort was based on internal city government politics. In Albuquerque's strong mayor-council system, the mayor headed the executive branch, and the city council was the legislative branch. In effect, the mayor had one vote, the council one vote.[45] But within the voluntary council of governments the mayor was just another vote in a five-member Albuquerque delegation. Under the COG structure, a mayor had less leverage on any issue that fell within its purview. It was a scene that I generally avoided.

So it is easy for me to understand why many mayors approach regionalism skeptically and reluctantly. Mayoral resistance is doubly understandable when some "national expert" like myself blows into town, citing census statistics that show, for instance, a dramatic increase in poverty since 1970, despite a city government's best efforts. ("Old data" is the rejoinder. "We've turned things around since then.") Or even worse, that outsider may state that the mayor's city has passed a statistical point of no return. (Such a judgment is often dismissed as "an unproven *theory*," despite the fact that the point of no return is a set of statistical observations whose downward trend is thus far unreversed in at least two dozen instances. "My city will prove that Rusk is wrong," some mayors respond.)

Actually, I would like nothing better than to be proven wrong about the point of no return. Yet I am reminded of an experience in June 1996, when I was conducting a workshop in Gary for the Northwest Indiana Federation of Interfaith Organizations mentioned earlier in the chapter. Toward the end of an invigorating day, a familiar face dropped by. It was Richard Hatcher, former mayor of Gary. Hatcher had been the first African American mayor of a major American city. His long mayoralty (1968–88) and my short one (1977–81) had overlapped, and we had come to know each other in meetings of the U.S. Conference of Mayors.

We reminisced about old times, in particular, the joint appearance we had made on *Meet the Press* (I believe) in 1978 during a mayors' conference

---

45. The Albuquerque City Council could always have the last word whenever it could cast six votes (out of nine) to override the mayor's veto. The veto power was rarely used, however. Under New Mexico law, the city of Albuquerque is a municipal corporation whose governing body is the city council. I constantly deferred publicly to the council's status and independence, while succeeding in gaining its approval for virtually all of my administration's agenda.

in Atlanta. In my mind's eye I recalled the youthful mayor, exuding optimism, energy, and confidence. Now that the black community has gained control of city hall, the mayor had said, we are going to turn Gary around. We are going to make a difference. Twenty years later, neither Mayor Hatcher nor his successors had really made a difference. All their efforts had not turned back the various waves of change eroding Gary: abandoned factories, vacant stores and offices, empty houses, the handiwork of sprawl and race.

Yet how can new mayors anywhere *not* believe that their administrations will make a difference? Optimism and self-confidence are prerequisites for the job. With energy (and some luck) most mayors can point to tangible achievements when they leave office: a new sports stadium, a renovated historic hotel, a new downtown office complex, a riverfront park, a festival marketplace, a tourist-attracting aquarium. It is the Tale of the Tracts that tells the other story, a story of the city's steady strangulation by poverty-stricken neighborhoods.

It is as if a mayor of Gary (or Cleveland or Hartford or Detroit) is invited to play poker, deuces wild. Around the table are his suburban counterparts: township supervisors, county commissioners, village administrators. Every time the cards are dealt, the mayor must fill an inside straight to win. His suburban competitors are always dealt a wild card. Once in a while, the mayor will successfully draw to fill the inside straight (a downtown ballpark, for example) and win a hand. But the odds are overwhelming that the mayor will lose many, many more hands than he wins. He is playing against a stacked deck.

Each new mayor thinks he or she can beat the odds. The record shows that it cannot be done. It is a game that cannot be won. What can be done is to change the rules of the game, to get a chance to play with a fair deck. That is what the regional strategies advanced in this book are all about. The political rules will not change until a few more players at the table—usually inner suburbanites and their state legislators—come to recognize that they are no longer being automatically dealt the wild cards either.

—14—
Changing Attitudes, Changing Laws

I HAVE ARGUED that two major factors have shaped America's urban areas today: sprawl and race. My analysis has revolved around racial poles. In the preceding chapters the terms "race" and "racial" have appeared numerous times. There have been constant references to "colored," "Negro," "black," and "African American" (depending on the era about which I am writing). I have used "Hispanic" as a general term covering "Latino," "Puerto Rican," "Mexican American" and other terms defining Hispanic origin many times. "Whites" and "Anglos" have been mentioned constantly. Of the thirty tables and figures that appear in the previous chapters or the appendix, almost half document racially based social and economic trends.

In all of this book's discussion of racial issues, however, there are two words that I have not used: *racist* and *racism.* Nor, to my recollection, have I ever used these two words in the hundreds of speeches, talks, and workshops that I have given over the past six years.

Some readers—in particular, some African American readers—may dismiss my practice as an example of just another white man who refuses to acknowledge what they see as the fundamental and unchanging reality of American society. Others may discern in my approach the propensity of a politician (even a defrocked one like myself) to avoid alienating potential supporters.

I myself am naturally reluctant to brand the attitudes of persons or audiences that I do not know well, and, for me, the words "racist" and "racism" are terms inextricably linked to personal attitudes, feelings, and values. Yet, the best explanation for my practice is that, as America stands on the threshold of the twenty-first century, I doubt that the precipitous deterioration of urban ghettos and barrios is based primarily on continued racism in American society.

I recall an incident from the mid-1950's when I was a teenager. President Eisenhower had been criticized heavily in liberal circles for his hands-off attitude toward enforcing the Supreme Court's rulings desegregating public schools and for his failure to submit a civil rights bill to the Congress. "You can't legislate morality," Ike proclaimed.

You may not be able to legislate morality, I reflect now, thinking back to that time, but you can legislate conduct, particularly, public conduct. Changing society's formal rules may not eliminate prejudice (what individuals *feel*), but changing the rules can greatly diminish discrimination (what individuals and institutions *do*). In time, new social circumstances—integrated offices, integrated factories, integrated restaurants, integrated theaters, integrated schools, and integrated neighborhoods—change private attitudes. Less discrimination leads to less prejudice. Racism wanes.

That is just what has happened, I believe. Four decades after Ike's dismissive remark, America's most popular public figure (Colin Powell), America's most popular entertainer (Oprah Winfrey, by income, or Bill Cosby, by sentiment), and America's most idolized athlete (Michael Jordan) are all African American.

Is it naïve to attach importance to that simple list of "mosts"? I do not think so. Granted, Colin Powell is a victorious general (albeit on a lesser scale than Ike was) with a Horatio Alger life story, but is it conceivable that any Negro could have become America's most respected public figure thirty or forty years ago? Outside of the readership of *Ebony* and *Jet*, who knew back then of General Benjamin O. Davis Sr.? For that matter, almost thirty years ago, Martin Luther King Jr. was assassinated, probably more reviled than revered at the time by white Americans.

Of course, there were popular colored and Negro entertainers in earlier eras, but they were invariably cast in race roles. Some performers—such as Stepin Fetchit or Butterfly McQueen, who perpetuated minstrel show stereotypes—would make most white moviegoers squirm in embarrassment today (as I suspect they made many in black audiences cringe at the time). Many other entertainers, such as Harry Belafonte and Lena Horne, were popular not just because they were highly talented but because they were,

well, so *white*. What strikes me as remarkable about Bill Cosby or, in particular, about Oprah Winfrey, is that their appeal transcends—no, obliter-
ates—race with most of their vast audiences.

And Michael Jordan? And the stratospheric success of the National Basketball Association (NBA), the world's most popular professional sports
league, with more than 80 percent of its rosters now African American? When
I first began to follow the NBA in 1952–53 as a New York Knicks fan, Nate
"Sweetwater" Clifton was the Knicks' only Negro player (and just the second
in the entire league).

In fact, looking back, the most remarkable sports-linked racial controversy of my youth might have revolved around a college football game. The
University of Pittsburgh was invited to play Georgia Tech in the Sugar Bowl
in New Orleans on New Year's Day, 1956. The Georgia legislature was thrown
into a frenzy when legislators realized that Pitt had a Negro second-string
fullback who was likely to play. Defile the sacred fields of Southern man-
hood by allowing a colored boy to step on the same gridiron with our young
white men? Outrageous! The aroused, all-white legislature almost succeeded
in pulling Georgia Tech out of the Sugar Bowl.

In retrospect, what was so truly remarkable about that episode was not
the race-baiting demagoguery of Dixiecrat politicians or Georgia Tech's lily-
white football team but that as late as 1956 Pitt had only two Negro players
on the roster.[1]

By contrast, for the 1998 season, 43 percent of the Pitt Panthers' football squad was African American, a figure exceeded by Georgia Tech's 49
percent. And the Georgia legislature has thirty-three black state representatives and eleven black senators—about one-fifth of the legislative seats. (As
a reminder of the distance still to be traveled in contemporary America,
however, all but two of the black Georgia legislators represent majority-black
districts.)

Integrating Neighborhoods

Recently, a feature writer in the *Washington Post* dug back through the files
of the long-defunct Roper poll.[2] The writer found a 1939 report on attitudes

---

1. For that matter, as a college freshman, I cheered the Golden Bears of the University of
California at Berkeley on to the 1958–59 NCAA national basketball championship, and Cal did not
have a single Negro player on the team.
2. Richard Morin, "The Ugly Way We Were," *Washington Post*, April 6, 1997, p. C-5.

of 5,146 randomly selected Americans toward racially integrated neighbor-hoods. Some 41 percent believed that "there should be laws compelling Negroes to live in certain districts." While not advocating formal laws, an-other 42 percent polled believed that "there should be no laws, but there should be an unwritten understanding, backed by social pressure, to keep Negroes out of the neighborhoods where white people live." Only 13 per-cent of those polled (including, presumably, most Negroes whose opinions were sampled, if any) held that "Negroes should be allowed to live wherever they want to live."

Almost sixty years later, a 1997 Gallup poll reported that, if a black fam-ily moved in next door, only 1 percent of whites stated that they would move out. Undoubtedly, that 1 percent is an understatement. Probably it is a more accurate measure of how socially unacceptable it is today to utter outright racist sentiments.[3] Despite integration of factories and offices, theaters and restaurants, city halls and county courthouses, for example, many white Americans are still uncomfortable with living in biracial communities.

A compelling reminder was provided by a thoughtful *Dateline* televi-sion special, hosted by NBC's Tom Brokaw, in June 1997. Titled "Why Can't We Live Together?" *Dateline* noted that, despite progress in other fields, hous-ing remains the most racially segregated aspect of American life. The one-hour special report examined Matteson, Illinois, a solidly middle-class suburb of Chicago. A village of 12,000 residents, Matteson has been undergoing steady racial change. Virtually an all-white community in the 1970s, by the mid-1990s Matteson had become about 50 percent African American. The Board of Realtors reported black home seekers outnumbered white home seekers by about 25 to 1. Spurred by that report, the Matteson village coun-cil began advertising actively for white homebuyers to try to stabilize and maintain a racially balanced community. "Yet after more than a year of the village's advertising campaign," Brokaw reported, "only a few whites have moved in, and a few dozen more have left."

Why were whites steadily moving out? NBC reporters asked scores of current and former white residents. Rising crime, declining schools, falling

3. Fifty years ago Jackie Robinson was bombarded with racist abuse from opposing baseball fans and dugouts alike. Compare that with the incident involving golf pro Fuzzy Zoeller at the 1997 Master's Tournament when the forty-something veteran referred to the twenty-one-year-old win-ner, Tiger Woods, as a "little boy" and flippantly cracked that Woods should not select fried chicken as the menu for the champions' banquet on the eve of the next year's tournament. Engulfed by an avalanche of criticism, Zoeller issued an immediate public apology, withdrew voluntarily from fur-ther tournament competition until he could apologize face to face to the young, multiracial phe-nomenon, and, to boot, lost a $2 million endorsement contract from a longtime sponsor.

home values were the most frequent answers. NBC checked the facts behind white perceptions. The village police chief reported that the "crime rate has been pretty stable over the last 22 years."[4] The principal at Rich Central High School (now 80 percent black) reported no actual change in student achievement levels (a statement seconded by NBC). Finally, "there was no evidence," the network's own researchers concluded, "that the price of houses in Matteson had fluctuated any more than in most other Chicago suburbs." NBC cited a 32 percent increase in housing prices in Matteson from 1990 to 1995.

One particular interview, perhaps, reached the heart of the issue. Brokaw was questioning a former white resident, by all appearances a well-educated, upper-middle-class woman named Sallie, about why she had recently moved from Matteson. She conceded that she and her husband had never encountered any problems. She professed not to be surprised by Brokaw's statement that Matteson's crime rate, school performance, and housing values had all been stable. Coming any more to Lincoln Mall, where the majority of shoppers were black, she observed, just made her "uncomfortable."

"How do we get beyond that, Sallie, you know, that you don't feel 'comfortable'?" Brokaw asked.

"I don't know . . . I think . . . I don't know how you do that?" she confessed. "I mean, it's just a fact of life, and unfortunately, I think, a lot of people just move, and they keep moving away from it. They know it's here, and they don't want to live around it. So they move away, move somewhere else where it's not going to happen for a few more years."

Watching the show that evening, I realized that I had probably never heard a more compelling, man-on-the-street connection between the issues of race and sprawl. Quoting an unidentified black resident of Matteson, Brokaw suggested that "whites don't like the idea of becoming a minority in their school, their community, or anywhere else."

Yet what was really the "it" to which Sallie referred? Was "it" just having black neighbors today? That did not quite seem to be the case. Many current and former white residents interviewed, instead, were concerned with what might happen tomorrow. Rising crime, declining schools, falling home values—these might not be happening in Matteson *yet*, many white residents moving out conceded. However, as *Dateline* itself depicted, that was the current reality in many black neighborhoods in Chicago itself or suburbs closer

4. The opening of the Lincoln Mall in 1975 had boosted petty crimes such as shoplifting and bad check writing ever since, the police chief noted.

in. Many were the places—once all-white neighborhoods—where a large number of white Matteson residents or their parents had once lived. In earlier decades, realtors' block-busting tactics, playing on white fears, caused panic selling, tumbling home values and accelerating white flight, first from Chicago, then from many inner suburbs. "Get out of Matteson while the getting's still good" seemed to be the common, if unspoken, motivation of many white movers today.

"Matteson is known as a town that is changing color in a country where color counts," Brokaw noted. Then, introducing a more upbeat note, he concluded that "yet it is important to remember that half of the whites are still here. It's safe to say that a large portion of them are here because they want to be. Other towns are watching to see if these folks can live together—black and white—in the same neighborhoods. There still may be time before the last door closes on the last white to leave Matteson." The Matteson story illustrates how deeply embedded in white consciousness are past racial attitudes and reactions. As William Faulkner wrote, "The past is never dead. It isn't even past."

Racial Segregation, Economic Segregation

I have presented many statistics in this book. The most significant, I believe, appear in appendix table A-5, which reports my calculations of the percentages of poor persons who in 1990 lived in poverty neighborhoods (that is, in census tracts with more than a 20 percent poverty rate). For the fifty-eight metro areas I studied (preparing for local speeches and workshops), one out of four poor whites lived in a poverty neighborhood. By contrast, one-half of poor Hispanics and three-quarters of poor blacks lived in poverty neighborhoods.

The contrast by race was even greater for high-poverty neighborhoods (that is, tracts with more than a 40 percent poverty rate in 1990). Only 5 percent of all poor whites lived in high-poverty neighborhoods compared with 22 percent of poor Hispanics and 33 percent of poor African Americans.

With such a clear racial bias in the geography of poverty, how can I argue that the accelerating collapse of high-poverty ghettos and barrios is not based primarily on continued racism? One reason is aptly summarized by john powell, former national director of the American Civil Liberties Union and currently director of the University of Minnesota's Institute on Race and Poverty: "So many middle-class African Americans have moved out of high-poverty neighborhoods that it's hard to label whites as racists when they do the same."

I would not totally absolve whites from the charge of racism just because black middle-class families are now making the same choices white middle-class families made two or three decades earlier. Because of the civil rights revolution, middle-class blacks now have choices they were denied before. They have every right to seize those opportunities.

A racist act, to me, must be based on more than a racially warped worldview. A racist act must also be an *irrational* act. It might be argued, for instance, that racism is at work in the resegregation of Matteson.[5] Many former white residents of Matteson irrationally rejected all objective evidence that contradicted their fears.

But is it irrational to want to get out of high-poverty neighborhoods? No. It is neither irrational nor racist to want to move out of a high-crime neighborhood. It is neither irrational nor racist to seek a safer, better school environment for your child. It is neither irrational nor racist to want a better house that may well appreciate in value, will have better nearby shopping, and may be closer to your job. In this book I have documented the destructive impact of high-poverty neighborhoods.

All parents—white or black—have the right and responsibility to do what is best for their families. That often compels the decision to leave such literally deadly neighborhoods. The sad irony, of course, is that each such individual decision to move out deprives the remaining residents of the local buying power, the social stability, and often the community leadership that the now-departed family represented. The neighborhood's downward spiral continues. The constant outward flight of people and investment, the abandonment of poverty-stricken neighborhoods, the growing concentration of poverty, and the associated decline of many central cities are, at the level of the *individual*, neither racist nor irrational acts. But from the perspective of *society* as a whole, these trends are immensely wasteful and tragically unnecessary.

Throughout this book I have sought to illustrate how wasteful the conjunction of sprawl and race is. We are wasting our natural heritage of wilderness lands, clear skies, and clean rivers and lakes; productive farm and forestlands; nonrenewable energy resources, in particular through our pro-

---

5. Albeit a very polite form of racism. Commenting on the same *Dateline* show, the *Washington Post*'s William Raspberry, nationally syndicated columnist, wrote that the whites interviewed were so *likable*.

digious consumption of gasoline made necessary by sprawling development patterns; tax dollars through the duplication of costly infrastructure; older housing in older neighborhoods; and tax dollars for greater social welfare programs and the criminal justice systems. Most of all, we are wasting the potential talents and productive capabilities of millions of children trapped in high-poverty ghettos, barrios, and slums.

Some may argue that these are just the necessary costs of the American way. It is not, however, Stuttgart's way, or Lyons's way, or Osaka's way, the way of major international competitors of our own regions. By the mid-1990s, the American economy is once again outpacing those of our international competitors. I would argue, however, that our current achievements are in spite of—not because of—our wasteful systems.

More to the point of this book, the core of our nation's urban problem—the concentration of poor minorities—is just plain unnecessary. America is not a third world county in which the poor are many and the middle classes are few. On the contrary, the middle classes are many and the poor are relatively few. The growing segregation of America's urban areas by income reflects the same convergence of public policy reinforcing private prejudice that was the structure of officially sanctioned racial segregation in an earlier era.

I do not claim, however, that classism has replaced racism in American society either. Race still shapes the concentration of poverty. The overall poverty rate in America's metropolitan areas in 1990 was 12 percent. Out of every hundred residents of the typical metro area only six were poor and white, yet only about one of those six poor whites lived in poverty neighborhoods. Roughly five out of six poor whites lived in nonpoor communities. Most poor whites are "mainstreamed." Few lived in slums, ghettos, and barrios.

By contrast, out of every hundred residents of the typical metro area only six were poor and black or poor and Hispanic. Yet four or five out of those six poor minorities lived in poverty neighborhoods, and two probably lived in high-poverty neighborhoods. Most poor minorities are segregated away from mainstream communities in poverty-stricken ghettos and barrios.

If American society simply functioned for poor minorities the way it functions for poor whites, the opportunities—and odds—for many minorities to escape poverty would be substantially improved. The growing isolation of poor blacks and Hispanics resists civil rights–type legislation. The forces shaping the growth of high-poverty ghettos and barrios are embedded in metropolitan development and housing patterns that promote greater and greater economic segregation even as purely racial isolation slowly recedes.

New housing developments only for above-average-income households, new shopping centers and regional malls, new office and industrial parks—all constantly mushrooming on the urban periphery—have been a part of the metropolitan scene for so long that these development patterns are viewed as if, as Myron Orfield has quipped, "they were ordained by God and Adam Smith."

In fact, as I illustrated in chapter 5 ("The Sprawl Machine"), a complex system of laws was created to shape and foster the suburbanization of America. While America was officially dismantling Jim Crow by race, it was substituting Jim Crow by income. Throughout the nation (North and South), suburban zoning boards, usually filled with earnest, likable citizen volunteers, assumed the functional role of the stereotypical Southern rural sheriff.

Across the country, from the federal government down to the most modest township, transportation, land development, and housing policies are at work that divide our society more and more by income, with tragic consequences for poor black and Hispanic households in a still racialized society.

Changing the Regional Rules

By the mid-1960s the civil rights movement had succeeded in changing the rules in order to advance the cause of racial opportunity. By the mid-1970s the environmental movement had succeeded in changing the rules in order to advance the cause of clean air and water and to protect endangered animals and plant life from extinction.

It is time to change the rules again if our country is to slow the voracious consumption of our countryside, the steady decline of cities and older suburbs, and the rapid growth of "deadly neighborhoods" that destroy good people (mostly blacks and Hispanics).

In part 2 of this book, I offered models of what I consider to be the essential components of changing the rules: regional land use planning and growth management, regional fair-share low- and moderate-income housing requirements for all new construction, and regional tax base or revenue sharing. Other issues could be added to the mix. These three, however, are the key ones.

The federal government certainly has had a major influence in shaping national land use and housing patterns. However, the 1997 agreement to balance the federal budget by the year 2002 cravenly sidestepped once again the long-term crisis in social security and medicare. Without major cutbacks in these almost sacrosanct middle-class entitlements, federal expenditures for all other discretionary domestic programs will shrink year by year.

In *Cities without Suburbs* I proposed a four-part agenda for federal action. It was based on two principles. "First, echoing the old Hippocratic oath, 'do no more harm.' Second, echoing the apparent message of the 1994 congressional elections, 'spend no more money.' " Those recommendations called for incentives for metropolitan reorganization, conditions on federal infrastructure grants in order to slow rather than accelerate urban sprawl, changes in other federal anticity policies (including tax policies), and an end to traditional high-density public housing projects.

Since 1993 there has been modest progress on that agenda. The Intermodal Surface Transportation Efficiency Act (ISTEA) was reauthorized in 1998 despite the campaign of traditional highway lobbies to roll back the regional planning process. Congress and President Clinton embraced the research of the Ohio Housing Research Network (if not its "urban policy" motivation) and repealed capital gains taxation on home sales in 1997 (see chapter 13). The country's worst high-density public housing ghettos are literally being dynamited and replaced by (somewhat) mixed-income, more human-scale townhouse and garden apartment complexes. However, appropriations for HUD's most effective tool for deconcentrating poor households—rent vouchers used regionwide—always face an uncertain future.

In the face of the devastating baby boomer impact on social security and medicare, the federal government's traditional leverage—the strings attached to federal grants to state and local government—will grow weaker and weaker. Unlike activists' principal target during the civil rights movement of the 1960s or the environmental movement of the 1970s, Washington is not "where it's at."

"Where it's at" is state legislatures. State legislatures set the rules for local governments' land use planning power (that is, potential antisprawl controls), zoning powers (potential mixed-income housing mandates), and intergovernmental agreements (potential revenue or tax base–sharing agreements). The next decade's battle must be fought in the statehouses.

Among the three basic policies I have recommended (regional growth management, fair-share affordable housing, and revenue sharing), which should be the priority? If I could wave a magic political wand across this country, I have no doubt which would be the most important policy: a mandatory mixed-income housing policy for all new residential construction.

Back to the Future: FHA's Rules

Albert Einstein conceived his general and special theories of relativity by playing mind games in his imagination. Let us play our own mind game. Imagine that the year is 1934, and the Federal Housing Administration is being established. Franklin Roosevelt and his advisers are considering the basic rules to govern the country's new federal mortgage insurance program. Alternative A bows to contemporary racism. The FHA will insure mortgages only in racially segregated communities and will favor new construction. Alternative B would be a bold departure. The FHA will insure mortgages only in racially *integrated* communities and will treat new construction and older housing equally.

Adopting Alternative B was, of course, politically impossible in the 1930s. A fundamental building block of FDR's New Deal coalition was the white, segregationist Solid South. A decade later, as commander in chief, FDR still fought World War II with a segregated army and navy.

But think what adopting Alternative B—limiting FHA insurance to racially integrated communities—would have meant. It would have shredded the practice of racial covenants in housing deeds that were not declared unconstitutional by the U.S. Supreme Court until 1948. It would have steadily promoted racially integrated neighborhoods in both cities and new suburbs. In fact, racial integration would probably have been the hallmark of postwar America's suburbanization. In turn, local schools would be much more racially integrated as a reflection of integrated housing patterns. Outside the South, still largely segregated neighborhoods are the structural basis for de facto segregation of schools and many local community institutions. Within the South, specifically integrated housing developments would probably have hastened the dismantling of the whole structure of Jim Crow.

Nationwide, a much more racially integrated society would probably be a less economically segregated society as well. We might anticipate that the economic isolation of poor minorities would be no greater than that of poor whites. I would argue that a major reason that overall white poverty rates (less than 8 percent) are so much lower than Hispanic and black poverty rates (24 percent and 28 percent, respectively) is the mainstreaming of most poorer white households in middle-class communities. Mainstreaming more poor minorities would lead to lower poverty rates among blacks and Hispanics overall. High-poverty black ghettos and Hispanic barrios would be as rare as high-poverty white slums. The high crime rates bred by concentrated poverty would be diminished. A vast array of social ills—and the higher taxes to counteract them—would be greatly reduced.

America would have no cities "past the point of no return." In effect, fiscal disparities between all central cities and their suburbs would be no greater than the modest gaps that exist between cities and suburbs in "white America."[6] Without high-poverty concentrations, many more city neighborhoods would have been able to attract and hold middle-class families.

In short, a different set of rules in just this one (though major) federal policy would have transformed social patterns in today's America. Adopting a Montgomery County–type policy even today would transform the social face of America over the first decades of the twenty-first century.

Regional Fair-Share Housing

Of course, a policy favoring racial integration could not politically have been adopted in the mid-1930s, and a housing policy favoring economic integration will not be widely adopted in the late 1990s. I have identified only several dozen communities that require a certain percentage of affordable units in new housing developments. In many of these the goal of integrating lower-income families into middle-income communities is subtly subverted. Faced with statewide requirements, local governments in Massachusetts and New Jersey, for example, meet their targets largely by building senior citizen housing. Other communities, such as Tallahassee, allow developers to make cash payments into an affordable housing fund in lieu of incorporating a percentage of affordable units in new subdivisions. Almost all developers opt to make cash payments. As a result, the city builds more low-income housing in already low-income neighborhoods. Still other communities make clear that "affordable housing" really means housing for modest-income households but not poor households. The Loudoun County, Virginia, program, for example, sets both maximum and *minimum* income eligibility standards.

By contrast, Montgomery County, Maryland, specifically requires that a percentage of all new housing constructed be acquired by its public hous-

6. In fifty-two metro areas that are at least 93 percent "Anglo," incomes of central-city residents equaled suburban residents' incomes in 1990.

ing agency for poor households. That local policy was adopted in 1973. The policy is a time-tested, proven success, yet, as far as I can determine, no state and only one other local community (Fairfax County, Virginia) has adopted a similar policy. Part of the problem is that outside of a small circle of affordable housing advocates, Montgomery County's policy has not been widely known. Over the past six years, however, I personally have probably been its most constant publicist. I have talked about the policy of moderately priced dwelling units to hundreds of audiences, often showing pictures of mixed-income neighborhoods. Persons in many audiences have been intrigued, even excited by the possibilities. I have provided copies of evaluation reports and Montgomery County's ordinances to a dozen communities and legislators in several states.

But no one has acted yet. I am sure that widely held public fears cause good people to shrink from taking decisive action. It is a fear that seems to be justified by local television newscasts every night ("crime, weather, and sports"). Most middle-class white Americans cannot look past the color of the face of crime to see the impact of concentrated poverty.

And, frankly, I have no confidence that facts will dispel fear. All the careful academic studies will not put a dent in the political resistance. Fighting for widespread adoption of genuine mixed-income housing policies is tilting at windmills. What would best solve America's urban problems is also the hardest policy to achieve politically.

Regional Revenue Sharing

As an alternative, Myron Orfield argues that regional revenue sharing ought to be the first item on the regional reform agenda. It is essential to split the suburbs politically, Myron explains, and that can be most easily accomplished through regional revenue sharing. Revenue sharing is the foundation on which Myron and his allies cemented the coalition of the central cities and the inner suburbs in the Minnesota legislature.

Tax systems, of course, vary from state to state, but the politics of regional tax reform are straightforward. Question: What is the best revenue-sharing formula? Answer: Whatever can get a majority of the votes in the legislature. Whatever the formula, the analysis of underlying fiscal disparities is unambiguous and dramatic. A properly crafted bill can provide both a modicum of tax relief and additional money for better services. Regional revenue sharing can arm its proponents with a politically irresistible argument to make to legislators from potential net recipient districts: vote for this bill and your district will get lower taxes and better services. It is an argument that cuts effectively right across ideological, partisan, and, most important, racial lines.

Moreover, pushing for regional revenue sharing ought to work almost everywhere. Most larger metro areas have their "favored quarter," and, by implication, their "unfavored three quarters." Opponents may charge that revenue-sharing advocates are engaging in "Robin Hood politics," robbing the rich to pay the poor. Proponents have a ready rebuttal. The great bulk of tax-supported state and local investments have probably subsidized the favored quarter's growth; in effect, the poor have been taxed to subsidize the growing wealth of the rich. But casting the dispute as rich versus poor obscures the real political power of regional revenue sharing. It is blue-collar and pink-collar communities that will most benefit from revenue sharing. (Protecting the pocketbooks of the rich has rarely been a winning argument in American politics anyway.)

Standing alone, however, regional revenue sharing is merely a palliative. It has negligible impact on slowing suburban sprawl. It has no impact on dispersing the concentration of poverty. Regional revenue sharing merely shores up the fiscal health of communities that are already in social and economic decline.

Helping troubled communities provide a better level of services and perhaps reducing their high tax rates (made necessary by declining tax bases) are undeniably positive outcomes. But, standing alone, making regional revenue sharing the reform priority suggests that the region's problems would be solved by just giving the "inside game" more money. They would not. It is much more important to help the poor move to opportunity than to move more money to the poor.

Myron and I have discussed this many times. Our differences revolve around political strategy. "The key is to split the suburbs," Myron reminds me. "You can do that easiest around revenue sharing. Once you build that coalition, you can get your suburban allies to support anything that is in their self-interest: fair share affordable housing, urban growth boundaries, anything."

I have to respect Myron's experience as a successful politician. After all, he, not I, succeeded in building that coalition in Minnesota. Through his Metropolitan Area Program, he has mapped social, economic, and fiscal trends in almost two dozen major metropolitan areas. We share a common view of the core problems of metropolitan America. Yet I cannot bring myself to advocate regional revenue sharing as the cutting-edge issue. One reason is that I have read many times the dictum of the great turn-of-the-century urban planner Daniel Burnham. "Make no small plans," Burnham preached. "They have no power to move men's souls."

Regional Growth Management

I see fighting urban sprawl through regional growth management laws as the issue that can move men's souls. It is the lesson of my experience in more than sixty local communities in the past six years. You cannot win the inside game without controlling the outside game, and there is potentially a broader coalition of common interests that can be organized around growth management than around the other two strategies.

Regional growth management is the most politically achievable way to rewire that down escalator. How directly and quickly better growth management can be achieved will vary from state to state and region to region. "Big box" regions such as Tallahassee-Leon County (Florida), Charlotte-Mecklenburg County (North Carolina), Memphis-Shelby County (Tennessee), or Albuquerque-Bernalillo County (New Mexico) already have many tools available. Though suburbanization is now accelerating beyond the jurisdictional boundaries of their "big boxes," these core communities can still substantially call the development tune in their regions. The reformers' goal must be to develop greater political will to adopt more rigorous growth management policies within existing local government structures.

In "little box" regions, however, it is virtually impossible to achieve decisive action voluntarily among so many independent local governments. The regional reform priority must be to secure legislative passage of Oregon-type statewide growth management laws.

This is no easy task. After a quarter century of effort, largely by environmental advocates, only twelve states have any form of statewide growth management laws.[7] "My God, getting growth management laws through a legislature is really tough," one veteran state lawmaker once told me. "I put in a little bill last session. The Speaker and the majority leader called me into the Speaker's private office. They'd been supportive of some of my other legislation, but land use controls! They both shouted at me for an hour.

7. By 1998 states with growth management laws were Hawaii, Vermont, Florida, Oregon, Georgia, Washington, Maryland, Maine, Rhode Island, Delaware, New Jersey, and Tennessee.

'What do you think you're *doing*?' they screamed. They pulled out lists and showed me how much money affluent developers had contributed to our campaigns that helped us keep control of the House. You introduce a land use law, it gets really tough. They come after you with chain saws!"

Controlling sprawl is a cause that has the power to move souls in many, many communities. And the potential coalition is becoming much broader by the late 1990s. In earlier decades growth management laws were primarily the cause of the "greens"—the many-faceted environmental movement. Three new waves of recruits have now emerged in the 1990s, however, to lend their weight to the push for strong land use controls.

Declining Suburbs

First, the truth is that, with uncontrolled sprawl, "today's winners become tomorrow's losers." Central-city problems have moved out into the inner suburbs. The social, economic, and fiscal decline of many inner suburbs is becoming more and more evident. In scores of metro areas I have documented the decade-to-decade downward trends of inner suburbs: falling household incomes, rising poverty rates, declining tax bases, flagging home values, escalating percentages of poor children in suburban schools. For some suburban officials accustomed complacently to measuring their communities against their central cities, the statistical evidence comes as a shock. For more astute suburban leaders, the numbers confirm what they already know: their communities are in trouble.

For half a century the "suburbs" have faced off politically with the "cities" in state and national legislatures. I fell into that trap myself. That dual polarity shaped the approach of *Cities without Suburbs*, my first book. As I acknowledged in chapter 10, I myself first learned about "metropolitics" from Myron. Metropolitics can become a dominant political force in many state legislatures. The facts are there on which to build coalitions of common interest. A corps of advocates and publicists is at work. Citizen coalitions are forming. Missing from the action thus far are enough politicians.

Disenchantment in Paradise

The second new development is that more and more suburbanites are becoming disenchanted with the suburban dream. During my travels someone mentioned to me the so-called 20-70 rule. Under the 20-70 rule, when only 20 percent of a new suburban area is developed (let's call it Happy

Acres), it is paradise. Happy Acres' new homeowners look out over their back fences at rolling countryside. The kids can play kids' games in the still-vacant lots. There are not that many nearby stores, but the basics are all there—the supermarket, drugstore, dry cleaners, a few chain restaurants and fast food outlets—and they are easy to reach along uncluttered new roads. Happy Acres Elementary School has just opened and class sizes are small. The morning commute is quick, at least until you drive inside the beltway, where traffic slows down.

But the Good Life seems to melt away by the time 70 percent of Happy Acres has been built. Now that original Happy Acres homeowner looks over his back fence and sees somebody else's house, and then more and more of Happy Acres stretching off toward the horizon. The kids now have to be driven to soccer practice at Happy Acres Municipal Soccer and Tennis Complex several miles away. There are plenty of shopping choices, too many. Despite the best intentions of the planners, strip commercial centers line almost all the major arterial roads. Traffic (particularly, weekend traffic) is a nightmare, swelled by thousands of autos headed for the new Mid-America Mall four miles away. Happy Acres Elementary is overcrowded, and the Board of Education is purchasing temporary classrooms that will further shrink playground space. The morning rush-hour traffic jam begins just three blocks away as cars are lined up to turn into the first collector street (which is still a long way from the interstate). You can smell the smog on hot, muggy, windless summer days.

The Happy Acres Neighborhood Association rises up in arms at the planning commission meeting. Most of Happy Acres has single-family homes on half-acre lots. The original development plan envisioned several blocks of townhouses and an apartment complex, including some senior housing, on the still-vacant land. A thousand times no, screams the neighborhood association leadership. Won't maintain the "character" of the community. Will lower home prices. Too many new children for the already overcrowded school. Too much new traffic.

The planning commission bows. The original development plan is never completed. A few more single-family homes are built on the final lots, or the acreage may even be left vacant. (The neighborhood association will lobby for years to try to get a bond issue approved to build more sports fields.) And Happy Acres, built for a single type of household and age group, moves into a future unprepared for changes in family composition, age, and tastes.

Of course, a lot of the traffic that is jamming the arterial streets is not even coming from a more built-up Happy Acres. It is coming from Elysian

Fields, a thousand-home, even higher-income community three miles to the west whose development began ten years after Happy Acres. (In fact, the advent of Elysian Fields was a principal reason for the construction of the Mid-America Mall, and some higher-income Happy Acres residents have moved up to Elysian Fields.)

Under regional revenue sharing Happy Acres would probably be a net contributor into the regional pool. Elysian Fields would certainly be a net contributor, and the regional mall itself would be a crown jewel. Happy Acres (much less Elysian Fields) will not voluntarily embrace fair-share affordable housing. (Its residents will not even countenance market-rate town homes.)

But a considerable portion of those residents find that the suburban dream has soured on them. Something has gone wrong. *The plan was wrong.* What we need is better planning, not so much for Happy Acres, which is largely finished, but to control better what is happening out at Elysian Fields. In fact, there are likely to be some potential allies among new residents of Elysian Fields. And they will all be opposed to the plans for the 10,000-unit planned community called Paradise Valley (ten miles farther west), which is now being considered by the planning commission of the next county out.

So there are more potential recruits for regional growth management now than was the case in past decades: inner suburbs struggling to survive and some upper-crust new suburbanites worried about the erosion of their quality of life.

Faith Can Move (Political) Mountains

The third wave of new growth management advocates is perhaps the most politically potent of all: coalitions of central-city and suburban churches. In chapter 13, I profiled one such movement, the Northwest Indiana Federation of Interfaith Organizations. But there are many organizing, often under the auspices of the Chicago-based Gamaliel Foundation: Metropolitan Congregations United for Saint Louis, MOSES in Detroit, WECAN in Cleveland, and a dozen more.

Church-based coalitions bring three new strengths to the regional reform movement. First, they bring the potential for mobilizing thousands of parishioners and congregation members for political action. When city council members, county commissioners, and state legislators walk into a meeting with hundreds of aroused constituents, the politicians listen.

Second, the inner-city church activists open a political path to get around the turf protection of central-city politicians. However steep the decline of a

Saint Louis, a Detroit, a Gary may be, there is still power and prestige in being a mayor or city council member. Regional strategies raise the specter of the loss of power—as instinctively resisted by central-city politicians (whose communities would be clear beneficiaries) as by suburban politicians (for whose communities benefits may be less obvious). The people power of organized churches can either get established politicians to move or move them out of the way.

And third, the church coalitions bring an invaluable missing dimension to the debate. Building new roads, water lines, sewers, and schools versus maintaining older infrastructure, trends in real home values, the value of agricultural land versus new subdivisions, the social costs of high-poverty ghettos and barrios—the debates can get mired in dry, technical language. The churches raise the moral argument. Like Cleveland's Bishop Pilla, church leaders can speak to the issues of our moral responsibility, of responsible stewardship of our natural environment, of our stewardship toward our fellow human beings. The moral dimension is necessary to push the calculus of common political self-interest to the point of critical mass.

In *Cities without Suburbs,* I wrote:

> Redeeming inner cities and the urban underclass requires reintegration of city and suburb. . . . Sustained change will require a grass-roots movement like the civil rights movement or the environmental movement. This new movement will be tougher to begin. The civil rights movement in the 1960s mobilized moral outrage against Jim Crow laws. The environmental movement in the 1970s reflected compelling concern with human survival on a despoiled planet.[8]

I was wrong. What I have learned in the scores of communities that I have worked with over the past six years is that the civil rights movement and the environmental movement *can merge to become* the regionalism movement. The issues of social stewardship and environmental stewardship are inextricably interwoven. The connecting link is America's environmentally and socially destructive land development patterns. To win today's civil rights battles as well as today's environmental battles one needs to change the same set of rules.

In December 1996 I was in Milwaukee for a training workshop for field staff and church leaders from seventeen communities organized by the

8. Rusk (1995, pp. 128, 131).

Gamaliel Foundation. At the end of a long but energizing day, one of the participants offered a novel suggestion. "What our movement needs," he said, "are some new songs."

By the Second Metropolitan Summit in Saint Louis in June 1997, the church leaders of Metropolitan Communities United had the first new song. As the composer and lyricist, the Reverend Sylvester Laudermill, jokingly confessed, "You can't really sing 'control urban sprawl.'" Several hundred persons—black and white, Protestant, Catholic, Jewish, Muslim, city and suburb—joined in singing:

> This is God's world.
> We are God's people.
> We've been entrusted.
> This land is in our hands.
> "We must live together,"
> Our children are calling.
> Black, white, rich, or poor,
> For our future let's do more.

A new reform movement is beginning to move across the face of the land. "Our Song" was its first new anthem. It will not be the last. I believe that the chorus of voices will rise, region by region, across the nation until a new set of rules has been created, state by state, for most communities. These rules will emphasize our mutual responsibilities and the reality of our interdependence within America's urban regions. "E Pluribus Unum," "one nation, under God, indivisible, with liberty and justice for all"—these are the true definitions of the American dream. They still have the power to move our souls.

Appendix

Table A-1. *Population and Economic Trends in Communities Served by Twenty-Three Newer CDCs, 1980–90*

Percent unless otherwise noted

Community development corporation and year of incorporation	Poverty rate				Mean household income as percent of metro mean		Total number of households		Racial or ethnic composition						Change in total real income, 1980–90
	Family		Individual						Black		Hispanic		Asian		
	1980	1990	1980	1990	1980	1990	1980	1990	1980	1990	1980	1990	1980	1990	
East Boston Community Development Corporation (Boston, 1971)	15	17	17	20	61	56	11,977	12,432	0	3	3	18	0	4	26
Urban Edge Housing Corporation (Boston, 1974)	27	20	26	22	73	76	11,314	11,747	30	33	24	33	1	2	43
Bethel Housing, Inc. (Chicago, 1978)	35	37	36	40	57	48	16,192	11,852	98	99	1	1	0	0	–34
Greater South West Development Corporation (Chicago, 1974)	12	16	15	20	81	70	54,177	50,195	29	36	10	23	1	1	–12
Hispanic Housing, Inc. (Chicago, 1975)	21	27	24	28	67	59	142,136	126,143	19	26	47	53	1	2	–14
The Neighborhood Institute (Chicago, 1978)	17	21	18	23	75	63	38,748	32,504	86	92	7	6	0	0	–24
Walnut Hills Redevelopment Foundation (Cincinnati, 1977)	35	37	39	41	43	44	4,511	4,229	90	88	1	0	0	0	1

Organization															
Detroit Shoreway Community Development Corporation (Cleveland, 1973)	24	37	26	39	62	46	6,449	6,261	1	8	11	18	2	4	−25
Miles Ahead, Inc. (Cleveland, 1972)	10	11	12	16	89	73	1,740	1,755	98	98	1	1	0	0	−16
Denver Community Development Organization (Denver, 1971)	16	22	19	26	69	64	49,690	47,321	3	4	40	48	2	3	−12
Eastside Community Investments Inc. (Indianapolis, 1976)	19	26	22	28	62	56	14,161	13,051	5	13	3	3	3	3	−11
Blue Hills Home Corporation (Kansas City, 1974)	18	23	21	24	70	69	6,776	5,970	81	86	2	1	1	1	−19
Rehab Project Inc. (Lima, Ohio, 1977)	12	18	15	21	81	74	13,955	12,515	13	17	1	1	0	0	−19
Pacific Asian Community Development Corporation (Los Angeles, 1974)	26	30	28	32	53	47	73,076	65,147	8	6	60	72	14	18	−3
Vermont-Slausson Economic Development Corporation (Los Angeles, 1979)	29	31	31	33	53	50	83,050	81,062	68	45	26	52	2	2	15
Project for Pride in Living (Minneapolis, 1972)	15	25	18	26	63	58	66,037	63,487	14	23	2	3	1	6	−3

(table continues)

Table A-1 (continued)

Community development corporation and year of incorporation	Poverty rate				Mean household income as percent of metro mean		Total number of households		Racial or ethnic composition						Change in total real income, 1980–90
	Family		Individual						Black		Hispanic		Asian		
	1980	1990	1980	1990	1980	1990	1980	1990	1980	1990	1980	1990	1980	1990	
MBD Community Housing Corporation (Bronx, 1975)	45	43	47	45	43	41	5,850	6,279	47	41	51	57	0	0	37
Banana Kelly Community Development Corporation (Bronx, 1977)	49	51	46	53	46	37	9,897	11,698	21	18	76	83	0	0	28
La Casa de Don Pedro (Newark, 1972)	39	29	43	30	47	46	2,734	2,103	14	14	63	81	1	1	–3
Omaha Economic Development Corporation (Omaha, 1978)	21	28	24	31	68	58	18,582	18,394	55	62	2	2	0	0	–13
Mission Housing Development Corporation (San Francisco, 1971)	19	19	22	22	59	60	20,200	19,922	6	5	35	52	13	14	29
Chinese Community Housing Corporation (San Francisco, 1978)	13	15	19	18	88	80	9,671	10,566	2	2	3	3	60	61	28
Marshall Heights Community Development Corporation (Washington, 1979)	19	17	17	20	63	56	30,981	27,976	95	97	1	1	0	0	–4
Unweighted average	23	26	25	29	64	58	30,082	27,943	38	40	20	27	4	5	0

Table A-2. *Population and Economic Trends in Communities Served by Eleven Older CDCs, 1970–90*

Percent unless otherwise noted

Community development corporation and year of incorporation	Poverty rate				Mean household income as percent of metro mean		Total number of households		Racial or ethnic composition						Change in total real income, 1970–90
	Family		Individual						Black		Hispanic		Asian		
	1970	1990	1970	1990	1970	1990	1970	1990	1970	1990	1970[a]	1990	1970	1990	
Bickerdike Redevelopment Corporation (Chicago, 1967)	17	31	21	32	64	55	39,224	28,767	4	11	39	62	n.a.	1	–32
Community Development Corporation of Kansas City (Kansas City, 1970)	17	26	23	30	62	52	42,578	29,214	48	52	2	5	n.a.	1	–37
East Los Angeles Community Union (Los Angeles, 1968)	16	22	17	22	75	62	81,675	73,575	2	1	75	88	n.a.	5	17
New Community Corporation (Newark, 1968)	30	30	33	31	44	40	6,199	3,613	88	87	6	10	n.a.	0	–36
Bedford Stuyvesant Restoration Corporation (Brooklyn, 1967)	24	34	28	34	62	56	114,887	94,879	81	82	15	14	n.a.	1	–12
West Harlem Community Organization (New York, 1965)	25	40	30	42	48	43	14,415	7,891	98	88	2	13	n.a.	1	–42

(table continues)

Table A-2 (continued)

Community development corporation and year of incorporation	Poverty rate				Mean household income as percent of metro mean		Total number of households		Racial or ethnic composition						Change in total real income, 1970–90
	Family		Individual						Black		Hispanic		Asian		
	1970	1990	1970	1990	1970	1990	1970	1990	1970	1990	1970ᵃ	1990	1970	1990	
Harlem Community Council (New York, 1969)	18	29	23	33	59	56	98,531	78,828	75	68	8	25	n.a.	3	–18
Greater Jamaica Development Corporation (Queens, 1967)	9	11	12	14	91	85	30,826	30,345	43	52	10	26	n.a.	10	8
Spanish Speaking Unity Council (Oakland, 1964)	12	19	16	20	72	60	14,509	14,658	20	32	19	34	n.a.	21	11
Chicanos Por La Causa (Phoenix, 1969)	24	41	30	44	43	44	21,620	13,458	15	10	33	65	n.a.	1	–43
Realty House West (San Francisco, 1969)	14	26	22	26	46	31	15,668	13,979	4	11	5	11	n.a.	34	–17
Unweighted average	19	28	23	30	61	53	402,607	389,207	44	45	19	32	n.a.	7	–18

n.a. Not available.
a. Hispanics in 1970 may be double counted under other categories.

Table A-3. *Changes in Poverty Rates and Total Real Household Income in Seventeen Metropolitan Areas Served by Thirty-Four CDCs, 1970–90*

Percent

Metropolitan area	Poverty rate						Change in total real household income	
	Family			Individual				
	1970	1980	1990	1970	1980	1990	1980–90	1970–90
Boston	...	7.3	5.9	...	9.4	8.3	38	...
Chicago	6.8	8.8	9.5	9.3	11.3	12.4	13	26
Cincinnati	...	8.1	8.8	...	10.3	11.3	18	...
Cleveland	...	7.9	9.2	...	9.9	11.8	4	...
Denver	...	5.9	9.2	...	8.4	9.7	19	...
Indianapolis	...	7.1	7.2	...	9.3	9.6	22	...
Kansas City	6.8	6.6	6.7	9.1	9.0	8.9	6	32
Lima	...	6.8	8.8	...	8.6	10.8	2	...
Los Angeles	8.2	10.5	11.6	10.9	13.4	15.1	35	54
Minneapolis-St. Paul	...	4.9	5.7	...	6.8	8.1	33	...
Newark	6.8	8.8	6.7	9.1	10.8	8.9	24	36
New York	11.0	14.1	9.1	14.3	17.0	11.7	36	23
Oakland	7.5	...	6.2	9.9	...	9.0	...	85
Omaha	...	6.8	7.3	...	9.1	9.6	10	...
Phoenix	8.9	...	8.8	11.9	...	12.3	...	199
San Francisco	6.8	6.9	6.2	9.6	9.5	9.0	35	57
Washington	...	6.0	4.3	...	8.2	6.4	47	...
Unweighted average	7.9	7.9	7.7	10.5	10.3	10.2	22	64

Table A-4. *Measures of Urban Sprawl in Fifty-Eight Urbanized Areas, 1950–90*

Urbanized area	Growth in urbanized population (percent)	Growth in urbanized land (percent)	Land-to-population growth ratio	Density of new growth in 1980s (persons per square mile)	Density of central cities in 1950 (persons per square mile)
Akron OH	44	162	4 to 1	747	4,778
Albuquerque NM[a]	106	189	2 to 1	1,440[b]	3,580
Allentown–Bethlehem–Easton PA-NJ	82	188	2 to 1	1,879	5,017
Athens GA	n.a.	n.a.	n.a.	n.a.	n.a.
Atlanta GA	325	977	3 to 1	2,577	7,822
Baltimore MD	63	290	5 to 1	2,695	12,067
Battle Creek MI	n.a.	n.a.	n.a.	n.a.	n.a.
Buffalo NY	7	133	20 to 1	–429	12,879
Charlotte NC	223	601	3 to 1	2,029[b]	4,468
Chattanooga TN	77	410	5 to 1	871	4,680
Chicago IL	38	124	3 to 1	4,328	12,919
Cincinnati OH-KY-IN	49	250	5 to 1	1,198	6,711
Cleveland OH	21	112	5 to 1	–756	12,197
Columbus OH	116	435	4 to 1	2,797[b]	9,541
Dayton OH	77	337	4 to 1	2,160	9,755
Springfield OH[c]	8	170	22 to 1	561	6,488
Detroit MI	34	165	5 to 1	–144	12,066
Erie PA	17	94	6 to 1	1,453	6,958
Fort Wayne IN	77	365	5 to 1	1,496	7,107
Fort Worth TX[d]	274	451	2 to 1	4,587[b]	3,467
Gainesville FL[a]	82	111	1 to 1	2,440[b]	2,472

Gary-Hammond IN[e]	n.a.	n.a.	n.a.	n.a.	n.a.
Grand Rapids MI	92	378	4 to 1	920	7,543
Hartford CT	82	356	4 to 1	784	10,195
Indianapolis IN	82	418	5 to 1	1,823	7,739
Jamestown-Dunkirk NY	n.a.	n.a.	n.a.	n.a.	n.a.
Kalamazoo MI	97	300	3 to 1	1,251	6,557
Kansas City MO-KS	83	411	5 to 1	2,287	5,647
Lancaster PA	154	965	6 to 1	1,769	14,831
Lorain-Elyria OH[a]	50	78	2 to 1	1,488	3,490
Louisville KY-IN	60	324	5 to 1	1,400	9,251
Memphis TN-AR-MS	103	211	2 to 1	2,423	3,676
Minneapolis-St. Paul MN-WI	111	360	3 to 1	3,514	7,859
Mobile AL	64	458	7 to 1	260	5,079
Muskegon MI[a]	11	138	12 to 1	1,516	5,369
Nashville TN	121	800	7 to 1	673	7,923
New Haven-Meriden CT	84	301	4 to 1	2,152	9,187
New Orleans LA	58	148	3 to 1	535	6,633
Niagara Falls NY[f]	n.a.	n.a.	n.a.	n.a.	n.a.
Norfolk-Virginia Beach-Newport News VA[a]	85	162	2 to 1	4,648	3,217
Oklahoma City OK	185	865	5 to 1	557	4,927
Peoria IL	57	289	5 to 1	-1,522	6,857
Pittsburgh PA	10	207	22 to 1	-1,095	12,622
Portland OR-WA	129	242	2 to 1	3,744[b]	5,720
Reading PA	20	127	6 to 1	1,875	12,423
Richmond VA	129	525	4 to 1	2,219	6,208

(table continues)

345

Table A-4 (*continued*)

Urbanized area	Growth in urbanized population (percent)	Growth in urbanized land (percent)	Land-to-population growth ratio	Density of new growth in 1980s (persons per square mile)	Density of central cities in 1950 (persons per square mile)
Rochester NY	51	241	5 to 1	1,369	9,236
Saginaw MI	32	168	5 to 1	100	5,597
San Antonio TX	151	388	3 to 1	2,194[b]	5,877
Springfield MA	49	80	2 to 1	1,165	5,123
St. Louis MO-IL	39	220	6 to 1	1,351	10,968
Tallahassee FL[a]	31	29	1 to 1	1,827	2,755
Toledo OH	34	177	5 to 1	1,221	7,927
Utica-Rome NY	–14	51	–5 to 1	1,050	6,426
Washington DC	161	429	3 to 1	4,465	10,979
Worcester MA	44	218	5 to 1	1,495	5,500
York PA	81	529	7 to 1	1,752	14,275
Youngstown-Warren OH	–6	12	–2 to 1	214	5,132
Unweighted mean	80	305	4 to 1	1,573	7,504

n.a. Not available.

a. Data from 1960 to 1990, except for Gainesville and Tallahassee (1970–90).

b. Both suburban and elastic central-city growth.

c. I have consistently provided separate treatment for Springfield, Ohio (Clark County), which is otherwise a part of the Dayton metropolitan area.

d. Fort Worth and Dallas urbanized areas are combined.

e. Gary-Hammond urbanized area is included in Chicago urbanized area.

f. Niagara Falls urbanized area is included in Buffalo urbanized area.

Table A-5. *Segregation and Concentration of Poverty, by Race, in Poverty Tracts in Fifty-Eight Metropolitan Areas, 1990*
Percent unless otherwise noted

Metropolitan area	Metro poverty level	Black residential segregation index	Poor whites in poverty tracts[a]	Poor blacks in poverty tracts[a]	Poor Hispanics in poverty tracts[a]	Poor whites in high-poverty tracts[b]	Poor blacks in high-poverty tracts[b]	Poor Hispanics in high-poverty tracts[b]
Akron OH	12.1	69	34.1	75.0	61.7	15.9	28.0	27.7
Albuquerque NM	14.1	39	34.9	74.9	59.8	3.7	14.1	6.4
Allentown-Bethlehem-Easton PA-NJ	7.2	49	12.3	50.5	67.6	3.8	10.6	19.1
Athens GA[c]	12.0	45	7.5	50.3	n.a.	5.1	28.6	n.a.
Atlanta GA	10.0	68	10.4	64.9	25.8	2.1	30.3	8.2
Baltimore MD	10.1	71	23.7	72.3	39.6	4.9	33.4	14.0
Battle Creek MI	14.3	63	40.7	81.5	54.6	2.3	22.7	3.4
Buffalo NY	12.2	82	38.0	91.4	84.8	6.4	55.4	42.1
Charlotte NC-SC	9.6	53	9.9	54.1	29.3	0.8	21.3	12.8
Chattanooga TN-GA	13.6	72	37.3	91.0	28.0	9.5	41.9	5.5
Chicago IL	12.4	86	16.3	82.9	62.3	2.4	46.4	12.6
Cincinnati OH-KY-IN	11.4	76	33.7	77.2	43.4	9.7	51.9	21.8
Cleveland OH	11.8	85	37.3	91.0	79.4	9.5	41.9	33.4
Columbus OH	11.8	67	38.2	78.4	68.5	17.6	43.0	27.8
Dayton-Springfield OH	11.9	75	40.8	82.1	44.7	8.5	45.3	18.5
Springfield OH[d]	13.4	67	51.5	71.0	28.8	1.7	2.0	2.0
Detroit MI	12.9	88	30.2	89.8	82.9	12.7	54.2	32.1
Erie PA	12.9	65	40.1	90.1	47.3	9.8	50.7	25.7

(table continues)

Table A-5 (*continued*)

Metropolitan area	Metro poverty level	Black residential segregation index	Poor whites in poverty tracts[a]	Poor blacks in poverty tracts[a]	Poor Hispanics in poverty tracts[a]	Poor whites in high-poverty tracts[b]	Poor blacks in high-poverty tracts[b]	Poor Hispanics in high-poverty tracts[b]
Fort Wayne IN	7.6	73	14.0	60.2	54.4	1.3	24.5	13.6
Fort Worth TX	11.0	62	18.2	66.6	44.2	4.0	26.2	8.8
Gainesville FL[c]	14.2	38	24.6	47.9	n.a.	6.8	20.9	n.a.
Gary-Hammond IN	12.2	90	23.7	87.2	43.1	5.0	25.5	15.6
Grand Rapids MI	8.3	72	26.6	78.9	47.1	1.6	22.2	2.3
Hartford CT	7.1	70	11.8	78.6	87.2	2.9	62.4	47.2
Indianapolis IN	9.6	74	25.5	71.6	41.0	1.3	21.2	6.1
Jamestown-Dunkirk NY	13.8	52	32.8	46.9	59.4	14.1	32.3	8.4
Kalamazoo MI[c]	8.9	53	39.6	85.3	n.a.	7.5	44.5	n.a.
Kansas City MO-KS	9.8	73	17.5	80.1	60.8	3.9	19.7	23.6
Lancaster PA	8.0	64	4.7	76.2	73.0	1.2	31.0	23.6
Lorain-Elyria OH	11.5	56	34.3	73.5	66.2	3.2	2.8	1.7
Louisville KY-IN	12.7	69	31.0	81.0	42.4	6.3	22.5	12.4
Memphis TN-AR-MS	18.3	69	24.3	78.4	45.1	5.0	48.6	21.8
Minneapolis-St. Paul MN-WI	8.1	62	24.1	68.4	54.5	8.1	33.3	25.0
Mobile AL	19.9	66	31.2	83.3	48.6	4.2	54.7	16.0
Muskegon MI	15.3	77	27.4	89.6	52.9	10.1	48.7	17.3
Nashville TN	11.3	61	19.1	75.3	41.6	3.7	34.6	16.7
New Haven-Meriden CT	8.2	68	17.1	74.8	64.2	1.2	8.6	10.6
New Orleans LA	21.2	69	41.7	87.0	59.6	6.4	49.0	16.0

Niagara Falls NY	10.7	66	25.3	76.0	26.5	3.4	43.9	9.3
Norfolk-Virginia Beach-Newport News VA	11.5	50	13.1	59.5	22.5	4.3	29.3	7.9
Oklahoma City OK	13.9	60	34.2	66.1	62.0	7.8	21.6	20.6
Peoria IL	11.8	70	27.2	81.5	56.0	5.5	43.3	24.8
Pittsburgh PA	12.2	71	31.6	79.5	48.9	4.5	45.5	19.6
Portland OR-WA	10.0	66	19.8	56.1	15.4	3.2	25.5	4.0
Reading PA	8.0	63	25.2	82.3	79.8	2.6	21.1	34.1
Richmond VA	9.8	59	26.9	70.7	37.8	7.7	30.8	11.3
Rochester NY	9.8	67	28.1	79.4	69.8	3.0	27.1	31.8
Saginaw-Bay City-Midland MI	14.8	82	30.0	94.1	63.1	4.3	63.6	30.9
San Antonio TX	19.5	54	34.9	62.4	80.1	6.5	27.9	35.8
Springfield-Holyoke MA	12.3	68	20.8	80.2	79.1	9.0	41.4	60.3
St. Louis MO-IL	10.8	77	19.1	81.9	42.5	3.2	39.6	13.1
Tallahassee FL[c]	11.7	52	19.0	61.0	n.a.	3.0	22.0	n.a.
Toledo OH	13.9	74	39.7	84.6	66.5	11.7	36.9	26.9
Utica-Rome NY	12.2	68	31.7	74.5	45.7	2.8	17.4	3.5
Washington DC-MD-VA	6.4	66	7.1	43.5	13.2	0.5	6.6	1.1
Worcester MA	8.7	52	10.0	85.0	79.0	3.0	18.0	31.0
York PA	6.4	71	14.3	69.4	60.5	0.0	0.0	0.0
Youngstown-Warren OH	13.8	76	33.2	93.0	74.1	9.2	52.6	48.9
Unweighted mean	11.7	66	26.2	74.8	54.0	5.5	32.2	18.8

n.a. Not available.
a. More than 20 percent poverty.
b. More than 40 percent poverty.
c. Family poverty data rather than individual.
d. See table A-4.

Table A-6. *Poverty and High-Poverty Census Tracts in Fifty-Eight Metropolitan Areas, 1970–90*

Metropolitan area	Metro poverty level (percent)		Number of poverty tracts		Number of high-poverty tracts[a]	
	1970	1990	1970	1990	1970	1990
Akron OH	8.6	12.1	17	40	3	20
Albuquerque NM	16.3	14.1	25	30	6	5
Allentown-Bethlehem-Easton PA-NJ	7.5	7.2	7	14	0	2
Athens GA[b]	11.8	12.0	6	8	0	4
Atlanta GA	11.7	10.0	56	91	19	36
Baltimore MD	11.3	10.1	73	103	24	38
Battle Creek MI	10.6	14.3	4	11	1	1
Buffalo NY	9.3	12.2	24	60	1	23
Charlotte NC-SC	13.0	9.6	21	24	7	9
Chattanooga TN-GA	16.4	13.6	22	27	7	7
Chicago IL	9.3	12.4	234	440	47	182
Cincinnati OH-KY-IN	10.6	11.4	59	92	16	33
Cleveland OH	9.0	11.8	64	153	17	62
Columbus OH	10.7	11.8	45	88	6	24
Dayton-Springfield OH	8.3	11.9	29	52	4	17
Springfield OH[c]	9.6	13.4	5	13	0	1
Detroit MI	8.5	12.9	164	305	24	151
Erie PA	9.5	12.9	8	16	0	5
Fort Wayne IN	7.5	7.6	7	12	0	2
Fort Worth TX	10.3	11.0	23	65	6	16
Gainesville FL[b]	15.3	14.2	9	7	0	3

City						
Gary-Hammond IN	8.8	12.2	12	44	1	11
Grand Rapids MI	8.2	8.3	12	22	0	4
Hartford CT	6.9	7.1	14	31	4	10
Indianapolis IN	8.8	9.6	38	54	5	10
Jamestown-Dunkirk NY	n.a.	13.8	n.a.	7	n.a.	2
Kalamazoo MI[b]	5.8	8.9	1	8	0	3
Kansas City MO-KS	9.6	9.8	65	98	9	25
Lancaster PA	9.2	8.0	5	7	0	2
Lorain-Elyria OH	7.5	11.5	3	15	1	2
Louisville KY-IN	11.3	12.7	43	57	15	8
Memphis TN-AR-MS	21.9	18.3	58	87	25	46
Minneapolis-St. Paul MN-WI	6.7	8.1	44	90	6	32
Mobile AL	23.3	19.9	64	57	21	26
Muskegon MI	10.0	15.3	5	12	0	5
Nashville TN	14.3	11.3	39	43	5	11
New Haven-Meriden CT	9.8	8.2	13	17	0	3
New Orleans LA	20.2	21.2	109	178	31	67
Niagara Falls NY	8.2	10.7	4	10	0	2
Norfolk-Virginia Beach-Newport News VA	15.6	11.5	71	61	23	23
Oklahoma City OK	12.5	13.9	46	72	10	20
Peoria IL	7.9	11.8	10	21	0	6
Pittsburgh PA	9.5	12.2	82	144	14	38
Portland OR-WA	9.7	10.0	23	35	3	9
Reading PA	7.8	8.0	6	14	0	2
Richmond VA	12.1	9.8	24	35	5	9

(table continues)

Table A-6 (continued)

Metropolitan area	Metro poverty level (percent)		Number of poverty tracts		Number of high-poverty tracts[a]	
	1970	1990	1970	1990	1970	1990
Rochester NY	7.4	9.8	23	54	0	16
Saginaw-Bay City-Midland MI	9.3	14.8	6	29	1	11
San Antonio TX	20.0	19.5	75	104	21	31
Springfield-Holyoke MA	9.0	12.3	17	23	2	11
St. Louis MO-IL	10.9	10.8	75	112	19	40
Tallahassee FL[b]	13.7	11.7	8	9	1	3
Toledo OH	9.2	13.9	18	48	5	16
Utica-Rome NY	9.8	12.2	10	20	1	4
Washington DC-MD-VA	8.3	6.4	60	72	8	10
Worcester MA	7.7	8.7	3	12	0	2
York PA	8.3	6.4	5	9	1	0
Youngstown-Warren OH	8.3	13.8	21	43	2	18
Unweighted mean	10.7	11.7	1,970	3,405	421	1,179

n.a. Not available.
a. More than 40 percent poverty.
b. Family poverty data rather than individual.
c. See table A-4.

352

Table A-7. *Average Home Value per Dollar of Income for Black and White Homeowners in Fifty-Eight Metropolitan Areas, 1990*

Metropolitan area	Residential segregation index	Home value per dollar of income (dollars)		Ratio of black home value per dollar of income to white (percent)	Segregation tax (percent)[a]
		Black	White		
Akron OH	69	1.36	1.79	76	−24
Albuquerque NM	39	2.36	2.25	105	5
Allentown-Bethlehem-Easton PA-NJ	49	2.30	2.62	88	−12
Athens GA	45	1.80	2.01	90	−10
Atlanta GA	68	1.84	2.08	89	−11
Baltimore MD	71	1.68	2.40	70	−30
Battle Creek MI	63	1.07	1.40	76	−24
Buffalo NY	82	1.51	1.99	76	−24
Charlotte NC-SC	53	1.70	2.09	81	−19
Chattanooga TN-GA	72	1.69	1.86	91	−9
Chicago IL	86	1.75	2.46	71	−29
Cincinnati OH-KY-IN	76	1.70	1.86	91	−9
Cleveland OH	85	1.51	1.98	76	−24
Columbus OH	67	1.62	1.90	85	−15
Dayton-Springfield OH	75	1.46	1.79	82	−18
Springfield OH[b]	75	1.28	1.64	78	−22
Detroit MI	88	1.02	1.78	57	−43
Erie PA	65	1.27	1.62	79	−21
Fort Wayne IN	73	1.21	1.59	76	−24
Fort Worth TX	62	1.71	1.82	94	−6

(table continues)

Table A-7 (continued)

Metropolitan area	Residential segregation index	Home value per dollar of income (dollars)		Ratio of black home value per dollar of income to white (percent)	Segregation tax (percent)[a]
		Black	White		
Gainesville FL	38	1.88	1.90	99	−1
Gary-Hammond IN	90	1.18	1.69	70	−30
Grand Rapids MI	72	1.39	1.79	78	−22
Hartford CT	70	3.06	3.11	98	−2
Indianapolis IN	74	1.43	1.72	83	−17
Jamestown-Dunkirk NY	n.a.	1.29	1.63	79	−21
Kalamazoo MI	53	1.24	1.58	79	−21
Kansas City MO-KS	73	1.42	1.73	82	−18
Lancaster PA	64	1.75	2.26	77	−23
Lorain-Elyria OH	56	1.62	1.85	88	−12
Louisville KY-IN	69	1.32	1.70	78	−22
Memphis TN-AR-MS	69	1.73	1.87	92	−8
Minneapolis-St. Paul MN-WI	62	1.92	1.99	96	−4
Mobile AL	66	1.86	1.88	99	−1
Muskegon MI	77	1.29	1.56	83	−17
Nashville TN	61	1.93	2.08	93	−7
New Haven-Meriden CT	68	2.95	3.38	87	−13
New Orleans LA	69	2.17	2.07	105	5
Niagara Falls NY	66	1.21	1.82	66	−34
Norfolk-Virginia Beach-Newport News VA	50	2.03	2.32	87	−13

354

Oklahoma City OK	60	1.62	1.60	101	1
Peoria IL	70	1.17	1.41	83	-17
Pittsburgh PA	71	1.33	1.66	80	-20
Portland OR-WA	66	1.66	1.88	88	-12
Reading PA	63	1.26	2.17	58	-42
Richmond VA	59	1.74	1.99	87	-13
Rochester NY	67	1.64	2.04	80	-20
Saginaw-Bay City-Midland MI	82	1.09	1.46	74	-26
San Antonio TX	54	1.69	1.81	93	-7
Springfield-Holyoke MA	68	2.60	2.98	87	-13
St. Louis MO-IL	77	1.51	1.92	79	-21
Tallahassee FL	52	1.90	1.92	99	-1
Toledo OH	74	1.24	1.71	73	-27
Utica-Rome NY	68	1.50	2.07	72	-28
Washington DC-MD-VA	66	2.46	2.93	84	-16
Worcester MA	52	2.73	3.05	89	-11
York PA	71	1.42	2.12	67	-33
Youngstown-Warren OH	76	1.26	1.60	78	-22
Unweighted mean	66	1.66	1.99	83	-17

n.a. Not available.

a. Inverse of fourth column.

b. See table A-4.

Table A-8. *Nonpoor Married Couples with Children, by Race, in Fifty-Eight Metropolitan Areas, 1990*

Percent unless otherwise noted

Metropolitan area	Racial or ethnic group			Ranking by percentage of black married couples
	White	Black	Hispanic	
Akron OH	96	89	95	26
Albuquerque NM	96	90	84	15
Allentown-Bethlehem-Easton PA-NJ	98	90	78	15
Athens GA	93	89	88	26
Atlanta GA	97	92	88	13
Baltimore MD	98	94	95	5
Battle Creek MI	94	93	87	8
Buffalo NY	97	86	68	43
Charlotte NC-SC	97	93	94	8
Chattanooga TN-GA	93	90	79	15
Chicago IL	98	89	86	26
Cincinnati OH-KY-IN	96	90	94	15
Cleveland OH	96	89	82	26
Columbus OH	96	89	90	26
Dayton-Springfield OH	95	88	92	35
Springfield OH[a]	93	84	90	50
Detroit MI	96	89	90	26
Erie PA	96	83	62	53
Fort Wayne IN	97	93	97	8
Fort Worth TX	96	88	81	35
Gainesville FL	93	85	85	47
Gary-Hammond IN	97	90	92	15
Grand Rapids MI	97	90	87	15
Hartford CT	99	95	89	4
Indianapolis IN	96	90	96	15
Jamestown-Dunkirk NY	93	76	56	58
Kalamazoo MI	96	87	89	41
Kansas City MO-KS	96	90	93	15
Lancaster PA	96	94	87	5
Lorain-Elyria OH	96	84	83	50
Louisville KY-IN	95	89	94	26

Metropolitan area	Racial or ethnic group			Ranking by percentage of black married couples
	White	Black	Hispanic	
Memphis TN-AR-MS	96	85	83	47
Minneapolis-St. Paul MN-WI	98	88	94	35
Mobile AL	93	78	86	57
Muskegon MI	94	86	84	43
Nashville TN	96	93	94	8
New Haven-Meriden CT	99	97	95	1
New Orleans LA	93	82	87	56
Niagara Falls NY	95	87	96	41
Norfolk-Virginia Beach-Newport News VA	97	92	95	13
Oklahoma City OK	93	89	80	26
Peoria IL	95	83	89	53
Pittsburgh PA	94	86	85	43
Portland OR-WA	96	85	85	49
Reading PA	98	88	83	35
Richmond VA	98	94	100	5
Rochester NY	97	89	94	26
Saginaw-Bay City-Midland MI	94	83	85	53
San Antonio TX	95	90	78	15
Springfield-Holyoke MA	97	93	72	8
St. Louis MO-IL	97	88	94	35
Tallahassee FL	97	90	87	15
Toledo OH	95	86	81	43
Utica-Rome NY	94	88	87	35
Washington DC-MD-VA	99	97	93	1
Worcester MA	98	97	84	1
York PA	98	90	78	15
Youngstown-Warren OH	94	84	81	50
Unweighted mean	96	89	87	...

a. See table A-4.

Table A-9. *Poor Single Mothers with Children, by Race, in Fifty-Eight Metropolitan Areas, 1990*

Percent unless otherwise noted

Metropolitan area	Racial or ethnic group			Ranking by percentage of black single mothers
	White	Black	Hispanic	
Akron OH	44	65	54	47
Albuquerque NM	27	51	49	16
Allentown-Bethlehem- Easton PA-NJ	25	51	81	16
Athens GA	35	59	89	38
Atlanta GA	20	43	36	5
Baltimore MD	24	47	30	9
Battle Creek MI	43	57	54	33
Buffalo NY	42	61	72	40
Charlotte NC-SC	24	46	17	6
Chattanooga TN-GA	24	46	17	6
Chicago IL	22	52	52	22
Cincinnati OH-KY-IN	37	61	58	40
Cleveland OH	32	55	70	29
Columbus OH	35	51	35	16
Dayton-Springfield OH	38	58	55	37
Springfield OH[a]	42	54	82	28
Detroit MI	37	57	60	33
Erie PA	48	69	85	53
Fort Wayne IN	25	36	25	2
Fort Worth TX	21	49	43	12
Gainesville FL	40	63	21	44
Gary-Hammond IN	37	62	60	43
Grand Rapids MI	32	52	60	22
Hartford CT	16	39	69	3
Indianapolis IN	28	48	74	11
Jamestown-Dunkirk NY	49	64	82	45
Kalamazoo MI	38	57	53	33
Kansas City MO-KS	27	49	41	12
Lancaster PA	24	49	70	12
Lorain-Elyria OH	41	66	78	48
Louisville KY-IN	35	60	62	39

Metropolitan area	Racial or ethnic group			Ranking by percentage of black single mothers
	White	Black	Hispanic	
Memphis TN-AR-MS	26	57	45	33
Minneapolis-St. Paul MN-WI	32	66	52	48
Mobile AL	41	70	35	55
Muskegon MI	49	67	57	52
Nashville TN	28	52	31	22
New Haven-Meriden CT	22	46	65	6
New Orleans LA	39	66	43	48
Niagara Falls NY	45	61	70	40
Norfolk-Virginia Beach-Newport News VA	29	55	43	29
Oklahoma City OK	36	56	62	32
Peoria IL	44	70	52	55
Pittsburgh PA	43	64	54	45
Portland OR-WA	30	51	42	16
Reading PA	23	40	77	4
Richmond VA	22	47	28	9
Rochester NY	34	55	73	29
Saginaw-Bay City-Midland MI	50	73	65	57
San Antonio TX	28	53	58	25
Springfield-Holyoke MA	35	51	76	16
St. Louis MO-IL	31	53	41	25
Tallahassee FL	28	53	56	25
Toledo OH	37	66	62	48
Utica-Rome NY	42	75	83	58
Washington DC-MD-VA	13	25	24	1
Worcester MA	32	50	70	15
York PA	25	51	81	16
Youngstown-Warren OH	46	69	65	53
Unweighted mean	33	56	56	...

a. See table A-4.

Table A-10. *Ratio of All Married-Couple Families with Children to All Single-Mother Families, by Race, in Fifty-Eight Metropolitan Areas, 1990*
Percent unless otherwise noted

Metropolitan area	Number of married couples per 100 single mothers			Ranking by ratio of black married couples to black single mothers
	White	Black	Hispanic	
Akron OH	449	66	380	40
Albuquerque NM	425	227	275	1
Allentown-Bethlehem-				
Easton PA-NJ	678	100	173	10
Athens GA	517	79	473	22
Atlanta GA	602	103	565	8
Baltimore MD	520	74	411	28
Battle Creek MI	323	56	272	53
Buffalo NY	467	48	103	57
Charlotte NC-SC	564	102	393	9
Chattanooga TN-GA	500	74	424	28
Chicago IL	630	68	379	37
Cincinnati OH-KY-IN	471	62	270	46
Cleveland OH	518	69	190	35
Columbus OH	469	75	333	27
Dayton-Springfield OH	446	74	386	28
Springfield OH[a]	418	85	271	17
Detroit MI	473	60	219	48
Erie PA	413	55	161	54
Fort Wayne IN	565	72	403	32
Fort Worth TX	543	110	578	6
Gainesville FL	377	64	703	44
Gary-Hammond IN	561	77	313	24
Grand Rapids MI	586	64	320	44
Hartford CT	587	71	66	33
Indianapolis IN	477	84	369	18
Jamestown-Dunkirk NY	483	127	97	3
Kalamazoo MI	391	55	624	54
Kansas City MO-KS	475	84	394	18
Lancaster PA	776	88	136	15
Lorain-Elyria OH	492	88	260	15
Louisville KY-IN	419	67	560	38

Metropolitan area	Number of married couples per 100 single mothers			Ranking by ratio of black married couples to black single mothers
	White	Black	Hispanic	
Memphis TN-AR-MS	479	81	364	21
Minneapolis-St. Paul MN-WI	613	65	229	42
Mobile AL	484	79	551	22
Muskegon MI	455	45	172	58
Nashville TN	513	77	269	24
New Haven-Meriden CT	557	69	110	35
New Orleans LA	413	76	342	26
Niagara Falls NY	479	53	278	56
Norfolk-Virginia Beach-Newport News VA	553	122	590	4
Oklahoma City OK	439	100	500	10
Peoria IL	458	59	312	51
Pittsburgh PA	495	60	305	48
Portland OR-WA	456	93	327	13
Reading PA	655	82	81	20
Richmond VA	528	108	268	7
Rochester NY	486	67	204	38
Saginaw-Bay City-Midland MI	439	59	165	51
San Antonio TX	457	131	281	2
Springfield-Holyoke MA	418	65	53	42
St. Louis MO-IL	526	70	417	34
Tallahassee FL	366	89	394	14
Toledo OH	469	66	258	40
Utica-Rome NY	476	61	139	47
Washington DC-MD-VA	638	115	429	5
Worcester MA	475	73	72	31
York PA	678	100	173	10
Youngstown-Warren OH	443	60	196	48
Unweighted mean	501	80	310	...

a. See table A-4.

Table A-11. *Ratio of Married-Couple Families to Single-Mother Families in Poorest Census Tracts in Fifty-Eight Metropolitan Areas, 1990*

Metropolitan area	Married couples with children per 100 single mothers		Ranking by ratio of all married couples to all single mothers in poorest tracts
	Poorest tracts	Rest of metro area	
Akron OH	51	389	19
Albuquerque NM	174	345	3
Allentown-Bethlehem-Easton PA-NJ	62	575	13
Athens GA	49	375	20
Atlanta GA	26	370	49
Baltimore MD	24	322	52
Battle Creek MI	25	282	51
Buffalo NY	26	370	49
Charlotte NC-SC	30	402	43
Chattanooga TN-GA	17	414	56
Chicago IL	35	369	37
Cincinnati OH-KY-IN	31	405	42
Cleveland OH	37	348	35
Columbus OH	37	398	35
Dayton-Springfield OH	16	374	58
Springfield OH[a]	60	356	14
Detroit MI	41	347	27
Erie PA	56	416	16
Fort Wayne IN	47	475	22
Fort Worth TX	75	467	8
Gainesville FL	105	287	5
Gary-Hammond IN	27	424	48
Grand Rapids MI	32	492	41
Hartford CT	19	400	55
Indianapolis IN	46	375	24
Jamestown-Dunkirk NY	91	478	6
Kalamazoo MI	54	377	17
Kansas City MO-KS	48	383	21
Lancaster PA	66	667	11
Lorain-Elyria OH	219	410	2
Louisville KY-IN	33	338	39

Metropolitan area	Married couples with children per 100 single mothers		Ranking by ratio of all married couples to all single mothers in poorest tracts
	Poorest tracts	Rest of metro area	
Memphis TN-AR-MS	38	276	33
Minneapolis-St. Paul MN-WI	67	490	10
Mobile AL	45	383	25
Muskegon MI	42	343	26
Nashville TN	24	408	52
New Haven-Meriden CT	28	342	46
New Orleans LA	39	287	32
Niagara Falls NY	33	438	39
Norfolk-Virginia Beach- Newport News VA	29	386	45
Oklahoma City OK	80	391	7
Peoria IL	30	434	43
Pittsburgh PA	28	442	46
Portland OR-WA	72	427	9
Reading PA	59	543	15
Richmond VA	23	340	54
Rochester NY	41	402	27
Saginaw-Bay City- Midland MI	41	395	27
San Antonio TX	148	368	4
Springfield-Holyoke MA	47	256	22
St. Louis MO-IL	38	390	33
Tallahassee FL	34	260	38
Toledo OH	64	370	12
Utica-Rome NY	40	440	30
Washington DC-MD-VA	17	368	56
Worcester MA	40	416	30
York PA	0	0	1
Youngstown-Warren OH	54	408	17
Total	43	347	...

a. See table A-4.

References

All data presented are author's calculations from decennial reports of the U.S. Bureau of the Census, unless otherwise indicated.

Bureau of the Census. 1970. *Statistical Abstract of the United States, 1970.* Government Printing Office.
———. 1975. *Historical Statistics of the United States: Colonial Times to 1970.* Series Q 148–162.
———. 1994. *Statistical Abstract of the United States, 1994.* Government Printing Office.
———. 1996. *Statistical Abstract of the United States, 1996.* Government Printing Office.
———. 1997. *Statistical Abstract of the United States, 1997.* Government Printing Office.
Byrum, Oliver. 1992. *Old Problems in New Times: Urban Strategies for the 1990s.* Chicago, Ill.: American Planning Association.
Cisneros, Henry G. 1995. *Regionalism: The New Geography of Opportunity.* Department of Housing and Urban Development.
Clinton, Hillary. 1996. *It Takes a Village: And Other Lessons Children Teach Us.* Simon and Schuster.
Coleman, James S., and others. 1966. *Equality of Educational Opportunity.* U.S. Department of Health, Education and Welfare, Office of Education.
Committee for Economic Development. 1995. "Rebuilding Inner City Communities: A New Approach to the Nation's Urban Crisis."
Downs, Anthony. 1994. *New Visions for Metropolitan America.* Brookings.
Garreau, Joel. 1991. *Edge City: Life on the New Frontier.* Doubleday.
Hacker, Andrew. 1992. *Two Nations: Black and White, Separate, Hostile, Unequal.* Charles Scribner's Sons.
Harrington, Michael. 1962. *The Other America: Poverty in the United States.* Macmillan.
Innovative Housing Institute. 1998. "The House Next Door: A Study of the Impact of Subsidized Housing on Property Values of Private Market-Rate Housing in Mixed-Income Environments in Montgomery County, Maryland and Fairfax County, Virginia."

Jargowsky, Paul A. 1994. "Ghetto Poverty among Blacks in the 1980s." *Journal of Policy Analysis and Management* 13: 288–310.

———. 1996. "Take the Money and Run: Economic Segregation in U.S. Metropolitan Areas." *American Sociological Review* 61 (December): 984–98.

———. 1997. *Poverty and Place: Ghettos, Barrios, and the American City.* New York: Russell Sage.

Kasarda, John D., and Kwok-fai Ting. 1996. "Joblessness and Poverty in America's Central Cities: Causes and Policy Prescriptions." *Housing Policy Debate* 7 (2): 387–419.

Ladd, Helen F., and John Yinger. 1991. *America's Ailing Cities: Fiscal Health and the Design of Urban Policy.* Johns Hopkins University Press.

Leinberger, Christopher B. 1996. "Metropolitan Development Trends of the Late 1990s: Social and Environmental Implications." In *Land Use in America: The Report of the Sustainable Use of Land Project,* edited by Henry L. Diamond and Patrick F. Noonan, 203–22. Cambridge, Mass.: Lincoln Institute of Land Policy.

Lucy, William, and David Phillips. 1994. "The Urban Partnership: Energizing Virginia." Richmond: Cullen Management Services.

McDevitt, Suzanne. 1992. "Community Development Corporations: Antecedents, Influences, Results." Ph.D. dissertation, University of Northern Iowa.

Metropolitan Council. 1995. "Tax Base Sharing in the Twin Cities Metropolitan Area: Taxes Payable in 1995." February.

Metroscape. 1996. "The Revenge of the Baristas." Portland State University.

Montgomery County, Ohio. 1991. *The Economic Development and Government Equity Program: The Competitive ED/GE in Montgomery County: Municipal and Township Officials Handbook.* January.

Moore, Stephen, and Dean Stensel. 1993. "The Myth of America's Underfunded Cities." Washington: Cato Institute, February 22.

Moynihan, Daniel Patrick. 1965. "The Negro Family: The Case for National Action." U.S. Department of Labor.

Murray, Charles A. 1984. *Losing Ground. American Social Policy, 1950–80.* Basic Books.

Ohio Housing Research Network. 1994. *The IRS Homeseller Capital Gain Provision: Contributor to Urban Decline.* Ohio University.

Oliver, Melvin L., and Thomas M. Shapiro. 1995. *Black Wealth/White Wealth: A New Perspective on Racial Inequality.* London: Routledge.

1000 Friends of Oregon and HomeBuilders Association of Metropolitan Portland. 1991. "Managing Growth to Promote Affordable Housing: Revisiting Oregon's Goal 10: Executive Summary." September.

Orfield, Gary. 1996. "In Pursuit of a Dream Deferred: Linking Housing and Education; Metropolitan School Desegregation: Impacts on Metropolitan Society." *Minnesota Law Review* 80 (April): 834–85.

Orfield, Myron. 1997. *Metropolitics: A Regional Agenda for Community and Stability.* Brookings and Lincoln Institute of Land Policy.

Orlebeke, Charles J. 1997. *New Life at Ground Zero: New York, Home Ownership, and the Future of American Cities.* Albany, N.Y.: Rockefeller Institute Press.

Peirce, Neal R., and Curt Johnson. 1993. *Citistates: How Urban America Can Prosper in a Competitive World.* Washington: Seven Locks Press.

Pilla, Bishop Anthony M. 1996. "The Church in the City." Archdiocese of Cleveland and Akron.

Rusk, David. 1995. *Cities without Suburbs*. 2d. ed. Johns Hopkins University Press.

———. 1996. *Baltimore Unbound*. Johns Hopkins University Press.

Rusk, David, and Jeff Mosley. 1994. "The Academic Performance of Public Housing Children: Does Living in Middle Class Neighborhoods and Attending Middle Class Neighborhood Schools Make a Difference?" Urban Institute, May.

Stock, Richard D. 1996. "The Economic Impact of the Montgomery County Regional Arts and Cultural District." University of Dayton, School of Business Administration, October.

Thernstrom, Stephen, and Abigail Thernstrom. 1997. *America in Black and White: One Nation, Indivisible: Race in Modern America*. Simon and Schuster.

U.S. Department of Housing and Urban Development. 1996. "Public Housing That Works: The Transformation of America's Public Housing." Government Printing Office, May.

Vitullo-Martin, Julia. 1996. "Housing and Neighborhoods." In *Breaking Away: The Future of Cities: Essays in Memory of Robert F. Wagner, Jr.*, edited by Julia Vitullo-Martin, 105. New York: Twentieth Century Fund Press.

Welfeld, Irving. 1988. *Where We Live: A Social History of American Housing*. Simon and Schuster.

Wilson, William Julius. 1987. *The Truly Disadvantaged: The Inner City, the Underclass, and Public Policy*. University of Chicago Press.

———. 1996. *When Work Disappears: The World of the New Urban Poor*. Knopf.

Index

Objects First with Java™

A Practical Introduction Using BlueJ

Indianapolis   New York   San Francisco   Hoboken

Amsterdam Cape Town Dubai London Madrid Milan Munich Paris Montreal Toronto
Delhi Mexico City Sao Paulo Sydney Hong Kong Seoul Singapore Taipei Tokyo

Vice President, Editorial Director, ECS: *Marcia Horton*
Executive Editor: *Tracy Dunkelberger*
Editorial Assistant: *Kristy Alaura*
Vice President of Marketing: *Christy Lesko*
Director of Field Marketing: *Tim Galligan*
Product Marketing Manager: *Bram Van Kempen*
Field Marketing Manager: *Demetrius Hall*
Marketing Assistant: *Jon Bryant*
Director of Product Management: *Erin Gregg*
Team Lead, Program and Project Management:
   Scott Disanno
Program Manager: *Carole Snyder*
Project Manager: *Camille Trentacoste*

Senior Specialist, Program Planning and Support:
   Maura Zaldivar-Garcia
Acquisitions Editor, Global Edition: *Sourabh Maheshwari*
Project Editor, Global Edition: *Amrita Naskar*
Senior Media Editor, Global Edition: *Gargi Banerjee*
**Senior Manufacturing Controller, Production, Global
Edition:** *Trudy Kimber*
Cover Designer: *Lumina Datamatics Ltd.*
Cover Art: *brm1949/Fotolia*
Inventory Manager: *Ann Lam*
Media Project Manager: *Leslie Sumrall*
Full-Service Project Management, Composition, and Art:
   Chandrasekar Subramanian, SPi Global

Pearson Education Limited
Edinburgh Gate
Harlow
Essex CM20 2JE
England

and Associated Companies throughout the world

Visit us on the World Wide Web at:
www.pearsonglobaleditions.com

© Pearson Education Limited 2017

ISBN 10: 1-292-15904-9

ISBN 13: 978-1-292-15904-1

British Library Cataloguing-in-Publication Data

A catalogue record for this book is available from the British Library

10 9 8 7 6 5 4 3 2 1

Printed in Malaysia (CTP-VVP)

To my wife Helen,

djb

To K.W.

mk

Contents

Foreword

by James Gosling, creator of Java

Watching my daughter Kate and her middle-school classmates struggle through a Java course using a commercial IDE was a painful experience. The sophistication of the tool added significant complexity to the task of learning. I wish that I had understood earlier what was happening. As it was, I wasn't able to talk to the instructor about the problem until it was too late. This is exactly the sort of situation for which BlueJ is a perfect fit.

BlueJ is an interactive development environment with a mission: it is designed to be used by students who are learning how to program. It was designed by instructors who have been in the classroom facing this problem every day. It's been refreshing to talk to the folks who developed BlueJ: they have a very clear idea of what their target is. Discussions tended to focus more on what to leave out, than what to throw in. BlueJ is very clean and very targeting.

Nonetheless, this book isn't about BlueJ. It is about programming.

In Java.

Over the past several years Java has become widely used in the teaching of programming. This is for a number of reasons. One is that Java has many characteristics that make it easy to teach: it has a relatively clean definition; extensive static analysis by the compiler informs students of problems early on; and it has a very robust memory model that eliminates most "mysterious" errors that arise when object boundaries or the type system are compromised. Another is that Java has become commercially very important.

This book confronts head-on the hardest concept to teach: objects. It takes students from their very first steps all the way through to some very sophisticated concepts.

It manages to solve one of the stickiest questions in writing a book about programming: how to deal with the mechanics of actually typing in and running a program. Most books silently skip over the issue, or touch it lightly, leaving the instructor with the burden of figuring out how to relate the book's material to the actual steps that students have to go through to solve the exercises. Instead, this book assumes the use of BlueJ and is able to integrate the tasks of understanding the concepts with the mechanics of how students can explore them.

I wish it had been around for my daughter last year. Maybe next year . . .

New to the sixth edition

This is the sixth edition of this book, and—as always with a new edition—the content has been adapted to the latest developments in object-oriented programs.

Many of the changes this time can, on the surface, be attributed to a new version of Java: Java 8. This version was released in 2014 and is now very widely used in practice. In fact, it is the fastest adoption of any new Java version ever released; so it is time also to change the way we teach novice students.

The changes are, however, more than merely the addition of a few new language constructs. The most significant new aspects in Java 8 center around new constructs to support a (partial) functional programming style. And it is the growing popularity of functional programming that is driving this change. The difference is much deeper, and much more fundamental, than just adding new syntax. And it is the renaissance of the functional ideas in modern programming generally—not only the existence of Java 8—that makes it timely to cover these aspects in a modern edition of a programming textbook.

The ideas and techniques of functional programming, while fairly old and well known in principle, have seen a marked boost of popularity in recent years, with new languages being developed and selected functional techniques being incorporated into existing, traditionally imperative languages. One of the primary reasons for this is the change in computing hardware available, and also the changing nature of problems we wish to tackle.

Almost all programming platforms now are concurrent. Even mid-range laptops and mobile phones now have processors with multiple cores, making parallel processing a real possibility on everyday devices. But, in practice this is not happening on a large scale.

Writing applications that make optimal use of concurrent processing and multiple processors is very, very difficult. Most applications available today do not exploit current hardware to a degree approaching anything that is theoretically possible.

This is not going to change much: the opportunity (and challenge) of parallel hardware will remain, and programming these devices with traditional imperative languages will not get any easier.

This is where functional programming enters the picture.

With functional language constructs, it is possible to automate some concurrency very efficiently. Programs can potentially make use of multiple cores without much effort on the side of the programmer. Functional constructs have other advantages—more elegant expression for certain problems and often clearer readability—but it is the ability to deal with parallelism that will ensure that functional aspects of programming are going to stay with us for a long time to come.

Every teacher who wants to prepare their students for the future should give them some understanding of functional aspects as well. Without it, one will no longer be able to become a master programmer. A novice certainly does not have to master all of functional programming, but a basic understanding of what it is—and what we can achieve with it—is rapidly becoming essential.

Exactly when functional techniques should be introduced is an interesting question. We do not believe that there is a single right answer for this; various sequences are possible. Functional programming could be covered as an advanced topic at the end of the traditional corpus of this book, or it could be addressed when we first encounter the topics where it is applicable, as an alternative to the imperative techniques. It could even be covered first.

An additional question is how to treat the traditional style of programming in those areas where functional constructs are now available: should they be replaced, or do both need to be covered?

For this book, we recognize that different teachers will have different constraints and preferences. Therefore, we have designed a structure that—we hope—allows different approaches, depending on the preference of the learner or teacher.

- We have not replaced the "old-style" techniques. We cover the new, functional approach in addition to the existing material. Functional constructs in Java are most prominent when working with collections of objects, and the mastering traditional approach—using loops and explicit iteration—is still essential for any programmer. Not only are there millions of lines of code out there that are written in this style—and will be continued to be written in this style—but there are also specific cases where it is necessary to use these techniques even if one generally favors the new functional constructs. Mastering both is the goal.

- We present the new functional-construct-oriented material in the book where we discuss the problems that these constructs address. For example, we address functional collection processing as soon as we encounter collections.

- Chapters and sections covering this new material are, however, clearly marked as "advanced," and are structured in a manner that they can safely be skipped on first reading (or left out altogether).

- The previous two points enable different approaches to studying this book: if time permits, it can be read in the sequence it is presented, covering the full scope of material—including functional approaches as alternatives to imperative ones—as the problems are encountered which they address. If time is short, these advanced sections can be skipped, and emphasis can be placed on a thorough grounding in imperative, object-oriented programming. (We should emphasize that *functional* is not a contradiction to *object-oriented*: whether the functional material is included in the study, or the course emphasis is largely on imperative techniques, every reader of this book will emerge with a good understanding of object orientation!) Yet another way to approach the material is to skip the advanced sections initially, and cover them as a separate unit at a later time. They present alternative approaches to other constructs and can be covered independently.

We hope this makes clear that this book provides flexibility where readers want it, but also guidance where a reader has no clear preference: just read it in the sequence it is written.

Apart from the major changes described so far, this edition also presents numerous minor improvements. The overall structure, tone, and approach of the book is unchanged; it has worked very well in the past, and there is no reason to deviate from it. However, we continuously re-evaluate and seek to improve where we see opportunities. We now have almost 15 years of continuous experience teaching with this book, and this is reflected in the many minor improvements throughout.

This book is an introduction to object-oriented programming for beginners. The main focus of the book is general object-oriented and programming concepts from a software engineering perspective.

While the first chapters are written for students with no programming experience, later chapters are suitable for more advanced or professional programmers as well. In particular, programmers with experience in a non-object-oriented language who wish to migrate their skills into object orientation should also be able to benefit from the book.

We use two tools throughout the book to enable the concepts introduced to be put into practice: the Java programming language and the Java development environment BlueJ.

Java

Java was chosen because of both its language design and its popularity. The Java programming language itself provides a clean implementation of most of the important object-oriented concepts, and serves well as an introductory teaching language. Its popularity ensures an immense pool of support resources.

In any subject area, having a variety of sources of information available is very helpful, for teachers and students alike. For Java in particular, countless books, tutorials, exercises, compilers, environments, and quizzes already exist, in many different kinds and styles. Many of them are online and many are available free of charge. The huge amount of high quality support material makes Java an excellent choice as an introduction to object-oriented programming.

With so much Java material already available, is there still room for more to be said about it? We think there is, and the second tool we use is one of the reasons . . .

BlueJ

BlueJ deserves much comment. This book is unique in its completely integrated use of the BlueJ environment.

BlueJ is a Java development environment that is being developed and maintained by the Computing Education Research Group at the University of Kent in Canterbury, UK, explicitly as an environment for teaching introductory object-oriented programming. It is better suited to introductory teaching than other environments for a variety of reasons:

- The user interface is much simpler. Beginning students can typically use the BlueJ environment in a competent manner after 20 minutes of introduction. From then on, instruction can concentrate on the important concepts at hand—object orientation and Java—and no time needs to be wasted talking about environments, file systems, class paths, or DLL conflicts.

- The environment supports important teaching tools not available in other environments. One of them is visualization of class structure. BlueJ automatically displays a UML-like diagram representing the classes and relationships in a project. Visualizing these important concepts is a great help to both teachers and students. It is hard to grasp the concept of an object when all you ever see on the screen is lines of code! The diagram notation is a simple subset of UML, tailored to the needs of beginning students. This makes it easy to understand, but also allows migration to full UML in later courses.

- One of the most important strengths of the BlueJ environment is the user's ability to directly create objects of any class, and then to interact with their methods. This creates the opportunity for direct experimentation with objects, with little overhead in the environment. Students can almost "feel" what it means to create an object, call a method, pass a parameter, or receive a return value. They can try out a method immediately after it has been written, without the need to write test drivers. This facility is an invaluable aid in understanding the underlying concepts and language details.

- BlueJ includes numerous other tools and characteristics that are specifically designed for students of software development. Some are aimed at helping with understanding fundamental concepts (such as the scope highlighting in the editor), some are designed to introduce additional tools and techniques, such as integrated testing using JUnit, or teamwork using a version control system, such as Subversion, once the students are ready. Several of these features are unique to the BlueJ environment.

BlueJ is a full Java environment. It is not a cut-down, simplified version of Java for teaching. It runs on top of Oracle's Java Development Kit, and makes use of the standard compiler and virtual machine. This ensures that it always conforms to the official and most up-to-date Java specification.

The authors of this book have many years of teaching experience with the BlueJ environment (and many more years without it before that). We both have experienced how the use of BlueJ has increased the involvement, understanding, and activity of students in our courses. One of the authors is also the development lead of the BlueJ system.

Real objects first

One of the reasons for choosing BlueJ was that it allows an approach where teachers truly deal with the important concepts first. "Objects first" has been a battle cry for many textbook authors and teachers for some time. Unfortunately, the Java language does not make this noble goal very easy. Numerous hurdles of syntax and detail have to be overcome before the first experience with a living object arises. The minimal Java program to create and call an object typically includes

- writing a class;
- writing a main method, including concepts such as static methods, parameters, and arrays in the signature;
- a statement to create the object ("new");
- an assignment to a variable;
- the variable declaration, including variable type;
- a method call, using dot notation;
- possibly a parameter list.

As a result, most textbooks typically either

- have to work their way through this forbidding list, and only reach objects somewhere around the fourth chapter; or
- use a "Hello, world"-style program with a single static main method as the first example, thus not creating any objects at all.

With BlueJ, this is not a problem. A student can create an object and call its methods as the very first activity! Because users can create and interact with objects directly, concepts such as classes, objects, methods, and parameters can easily be discussed in a concrete manner before looking at the first line of Java syntax. Instead of explaining more about this here, we suggest that the curious reader dip into Chapter 1—things will quickly become clear then.

An iterative approach

Another important aspect of this book is that it follows an iterative style. In the computing education community, a well-known educational design pattern exists that states that important concepts should be taught early and often.[1] It is very tempting for textbook authors to try and say everything about a topic at the point where it is introduced. For example, it is common, when introducing types, to give a full list of built-in data types, or to discuss all available kinds of loop when introducing the concept of a loop.

These two approaches conflict: we cannot concentrate on discussing important concepts first, and at the same time provide complete coverage of all topics encountered. Our experience with textbooks is that much of the detail is initially distracting, and has the effect of drowning the important points, thus making them harder to grasp.

---

[1] The "Early Bird" pattern, in J. Bergin: "Fourteen Pedagogical Patterns for Teaching Computer Science," *Proceedings of the Fifth European Conference on Pattern Languages of Programs* (EuroPLop 2000), Irsee, Germany, July 2000.

In this book we touch on all of the important topics several times, both within the same chapter and across different chapters. Concepts are usually introduced at a level of detail necessary for understanding and applying to the task at hand. They are revisited later in a different context, and understanding deepens as the reader continues through the chapters. This approach also helps to deal with the frequent occurrence of mutual dependencies between concepts.

Some teachers may not be familiar with the iterative approach. Looking at the first few chapters, teachers used to a more sequential introduction will be surprised about the number of concepts touched on this early. It may seem like a steep learning curve.

It is important to understand that this is not the end of the story. Students are not expected to understand everything about these concepts immediately. Instead, these fundamental concepts will be revisited again and again throughout the book, allowing students to get a deeper understanding over time. Since their knowledge level changes as they work their way forward, revisiting important topics later allows them to gain a deeper understanding overall.

We have tried this approach with students many times. Sometimes students have fewer problems dealing with it than some long-time teachers. And remember: a steep learning curve is not a problem as long as you ensure that your students can climb it!

No complete language coverage

Related to our iterative approach is the decision not to try to provide complete coverage of the Java language within the book.

The main focus of this book is to convey object-oriented programming principles in general, not Java language details in particular. Students studying with this book may be working as software professionals for the next 30 or 40 years of their life—it is a fairly safe bet that the majority of their work will not be in Java. Every serious textbook must attempt to prepare them for something more fundamental than the language flavor of the day.

On the other hand, many Java details are essential to actually doing practical programming work. In this book we cover Java constructs in as much detail as is necessary to illustrate the concepts at hand and implement the practical work. Some constructs specific to Java have been deliberately left out of the discussion.

We are aware that some instructors will choose to cover some topics that we do not discuss in detail. However, instead of trying to cover every possible topic ourselves (and thus blowing the size of this book out to 1500 pages), we deal with it using *hooks*. Hooks are pointers, often in the form of questions that raise the topic and give references to an appendix or outside material. These hooks ensure that a relevant topic is brought up at an appropriate time, and leave it up to the reader or the teacher to decide to what level of detail that topic should be covered. Thus, hooks serve as a reminder of the existence of the topic, and as a placeholder indicating a point in the sequence where discussion can be inserted.

Individual teachers can decide to use the book as it is, following our suggested sequence, or to branch out into sidetracks suggested by the hooks in the text.

Chapters also often include several questions suggesting discussion material related to the topic, but not discussed in this book. We fully expect teachers to discuss some of these questions in class, or students to research the answers as homework exercises.

Project-driven approach

The introduction of material in the book is project driven. The book discusses numerous programming projects and provides many exercises. Instead of introducing a new construct and then providing an exercise to apply this construct to solve a task, we first provide a goal and a problem. Analyzing the problem at hand determines what kinds of solutions we need. As a consequence, language constructs are introduced as they are needed to solve the problems before us.

Early chapters provide at least two discussion examples. These are projects that are discussed in detail to illustrate the important concepts of each chapter. Using two very different examples supports the iterative approach: each concept is revisited in a different context after it is introduced.

In designing this book we have tried to use a lot of different example projects. This will hopefully serve to capture the reader's interest, and also illustrate the variety of different contexts in which the concepts can be applied. We hope that our projects serve to give teachers good starting points and many ideas for a wide variety of interesting assignments.

The implementation for all our projects is written very carefully, so that many peripheral issues may be studied by reading the projects' source code. We are strong believers in learning by reading and imitating good examples. For this to work, however, it's important that the examples are well written and worth imitating. We have tried to create great examples.

All projects are designed as open-ended problems. While one or more versions of each problem are discussed in detail in the book, the projects are designed so that further extensions and improvements can be done as student projects. Complete source code for all projects is included. A list of projects discussed in this book is provided on page xxv.

Concept sequence rather than language constructs

One other aspect that distinguishes this book from many others is that it is structured along fundamental software development tasks, not necessarily according to the particular Java language constructs. One indicator of this is the chapter headings. In this book you will not find traditional chapter titles such as "Primitive data types" or "Control structures." Structuring by fundamental development tasks allows us to present a more general introduction that is not driven by intricacies of the particular programming language utilized. We also believe that it is easier for students to follow the motivation of the introduction, and that it makes much more interesting reading.

As a result of this approach, it is less straightforward to use the book as a reference book. Introductory textbooks and reference books have different, partly competing, goals. To a certain extent a book can try to be both, but compromises have to be made at certain points. Our book is clearly designed as a textbook, and wherever a conflict occurred, the textbook style took precedence over its use as a reference book.

We have, however, provided support for use as a reference book by listing the Java constructs introduced in each chapter in the chapter introduction.

Chapter sequence

Chapter 1 deals with the most fundamental concepts of object orientation: objects, classes, and methods. It gives a solid, hands-on introduction to these concepts without going into the details of Java syntax. We briefly introduce the concept of abstraction. This will be a thread that runs through many chapters. Chapter 1 also gives a first look at some source code. We do this by using an example of graphical shapes that can be interactively drawn, and a second example of a simple laboratory class enrollment system.

Chapter 2 opens up class definitions and investigates how Java source code is written to create behavior of objects. We discuss how to define fields and implement methods, and point out the crucial role of the constructor in setting up an object's state as embodied in its fields. Here, we also introduce the first types of statement. The main example is an implementation of a ticket machine. We also investigate the laboratory class example from Chapter 1 a bit further.

Chapter 3 then enlarges the picture to discuss interaction of multiple objects. We see how objects can collaborate by invoking each other's methods to perform a common task. We also discuss how one object can create other objects. A digital alarm clock display is discussed that uses two number display objects to show hours and minutes. A version of the project that includes a GUI picks up on a running theme of the book—that we often provide additional code for the interested and able student to explore, without covering it in detail in the text. As a second major example, we examine a simulation of an email system in which messages can be sent between mail clients.

In Chapter 4 we continue by building more extensive structures of objects and pick up again on the themes of abstraction and object interaction from the preceding chapters. Most importantly, we start using collections of objects. We implement an organizer for music files and an auction system to introduce collections. At the same time, we discuss iteration over collections, and have a first look at the *for-each* and *while* loops. The first collection being used is an `ArrayList`.

Chapter 5 presents the first advanced section (a section that can be skipped if time is short): It is an introduction to functional programming constructs. The functional constructs present an alternative to the imperative collection processing discussed in Chapter 4. The same problems can be solved without these techniques, but functional constructs open some more elegant ways to achieve our goals. This chapter gives an introduction to the functional approach in general, and introduces a few of Java's language constructs.

Chapter 6 deals with libraries and interfaces. We introduce the Java library and discuss some important library classes. More importantly, we explain how to read and understand the library documentation. The importance of writing documentation in software development projects is discussed, and we end by practicing how to write suitable documentation for our own classes. `Random`, `Set`, and `Map` are examples of classes that we encounter in this chapter. We implement an *Eliza*-like dialog system and a graphical simulation of a bouncing ball to apply these classes.

Chapter 7 concentrates on one specific—but very special—type of collection: arrays. Arrays processing and the associated types of loops are discussed in detail.

In Chapter 8 we discuss more formally the issues of dividing a problem domain into classes for implementation. We introduce issues of good class design, including concepts such as responsibility-driven design, coupling, cohesion, and refactoring. An interactive, text-based adventure game (*World of Zuul*) is used for this discussion. We go through several iterations of improving the internal class structure of the game and extending its functionality, and end with a long list of proposals for extensions that may be done as student projects.

Chapter 9 deals with a whole group of issues connected to producing correct, understandable, and maintainable classes. It covers issues ranging from writing clear code (including style and commenting) to testing and debugging. Test strategies are introduced, including formalized regression testing using JUnit, and a number of debugging methods are discussed in detail. We use an example of an online shop and an implementation of an electronic calculator to discuss these topics.

Chapters 10 and 11 introduce inheritance and polymorphism, with many of the related detailed issues. We discuss a part of a social network to illustrate the concepts. Issues of code inheritance, subtyping, polymorphic method calls, and overriding are discussed in detail.

In Chapter 12 we implement a predator/prey simulation. This serves to discuss additional abstraction mechanisms based on inheritance, namely interfaces and abstract classes.

Chapter 13 develops an image viewer and a graphical user interface for the music organizer (first encountered in Chapter 4). Both examples serve to discuss how to build graphical user interfaces (GUIs).

Chapter 14 then picks up the difficult issue of how to deal with errors. Several possible problems and solutions are discussed, and Java's exception-handling mechanism is discussed in detail. We extend and improve an address book application to illustrate the concepts. Input/output is used as a case study where error-handling is an essential requirement.

Chapter 15 discusses in more detail the next level of abstraction: How to structure a vaguely described problem into classes and methods. In previous chapters we have assumed that large parts of the application structure already exist, and we have made improvements. Now it is time to discuss how we can get started from a clean slate. This involves detailed discussion of what the classes should be that implement our application, how they interact, and how responsibilities should be distributed. We use Class/Responsibilities/Collaborators (CRC) cards to approach this problem, while designing a cinema booking system.

In Chapter 16 we to bring everything together and integrate topics from the previous chapters of the book. It is a complete case study, starting with the application design, through design of the class interfaces, down to discussing many important functional and non-functional characteristics and implementation details. Concepts discussed in earlier chapters (such as reliability, data structures, class design, testing, and extendibility) are applied again in a new context.

Supplements

VideoNotes: VideoNotes are Pearson's visual tool designed to teach students key programming concepts and techniques. These short step-by-step videos demonstrate how to solve problems from design through coding. VideoNotes allow for self-paced instruction with easy navigation including the ability to select, play, rewind, fast-forward, and stop within each VideoNote exercise.

VideoNotes are located at `www.pearsonglobaleditions.com/Barnes`. Twelve months of prepaid access are included with the purchase of a new textbook.

Book website: All projects used as discussion examples and exercises in this book are available for download on the book's website, at `http://www.bluej.org/objects-first/`. The website also provides links to download BlueJ, and other resources.

Companion website for students: The following resources are available to all readers of this book at its Companion Website, located at `www.pearsonglobaleditions.com/Barnes`:

- Program style guide for all examples in the book

- Links to further material of interest

- Complete source code for all projects

Instructor resources: The following supplements are available to qualified instructors only:

- Solutions to end-of-chapter exercises

- PowerPoint slides

Visit the Pearson Instructor Resource Center at www.pearsonglobaleditions.com/Barnes to register for access or contact your local Pearson representative.

The Blueroom

Perhaps more important than the static web site resources is a very active community forum that exists for instructors who teach with BlueJ and this book. It is called the *Blueroom* and can be found at

```
http://blueroom.bluej.org
```

The Blueroom contains a resource collection with many teaching resources shared by other teachers, as well as a discussion forum where instructors can ask questions, discuss issues, and stay up-to-date with the latest developments. Many other teachers, as well as developers of BlueJ and the authors of this book, can be contacted in the Blueroom.

List of Projects Discussed in Detail in This Book

Figures (Chapter 1)

Simple drawing with some geometrical shapes; illustrates creation of objects, method calling, and parameters.

House (Chapter 1)

An example using shape objects to draw a picture; introduces source code, Java syntax, and compilation.

Lab-classes (Chapter 1, 2, 10)

A simple example with classes of students; illustrates objects, fields, and methods. Used again in Chapter 10 to add inheritance.

Ticket-machine (Chapter 2)

A simulation of a ticket vending machine for train tickets; introduces more about fields, constructors, accessor and mutator methods, parameters, and some simple statements.

Book-exercise (Chapter 2)

Storing details of a book. Reinforcing the constructs used in the ticket-machine example.

Clock-display (Chapter 3)

An implementation of a display for a digital clock; illustrates the concepts of abstraction, modularization, and object interaction. Includes a version with an animated GUI.

Mail system (Chapter 3)

A simple simulation of an email system. Used to demonstrate object creation and interaction.

Music-organizer (Chapter 4, 11)

An implementation of an organizer for music tracks; used to introduce collections and loops. Includes the ability to play MP3 files. A GUI is added in Chapter 11.

Auction (Chapter 4)

An auction system. More about collections and loops, this time with iterators.

Animal-monitoring (Chapter 5, 6)

A system to monitor animal populations, e.g., in a national park. This is used to introduce functional processing of collections.

Tech-support (Chapter 6, 14)

An implementation of an *Eliza*-like dialog program used to provide "technical support" to customers; introduces use of library classes in general and some specific classes in particular; reading and writing of documentation.

Scribble (Chapter 6)

A shape-drawing program to support learning about classes from their interfaces.

Bouncing-balls (Chapter 6)

A graphical animation of bouncing balls; demonstrates interface/implementation separation and simple graphics.

Weblog-analyzer (Chapter 7, 14)

A program to analyze web access log files; introduces arrays and for loops.

Automaton (Chapter 7)

A series of examples of a cellular automaton. Used to gain practice with array programming.

Brain (Chapter 7)

A version of *Brian's Brain*, which we use to discuss two-dimensional arrays.

World-of-zuul (Chapter 8, 11, 14)

A text-based, interactive adventure game. Highly extendable, makes a great open-ended student project. Used here to discuss good class design, coupling, and cohesion. Used again in Chapter 11 as an example for use of inheritance.

Online-shop (Chapter 9)

The early stages of an implementation of a part of an online shopping website, dealing with user comments; used to discuss testing and debugging strategies.

Calculator (Chapter 9)

An implementation of a desk calculator. This example reinforces concepts introduced earlier, and is used to discuss testing and debugging.

Bricks (Chapter 9)

A simple debugging exercise; models filling pallets with bricks for simple computations.

Network (Chapter 10, 11)

Part of a social network application. This project is discussed and then extended in great detail to introduce the foundations of inheritance and polymorphism.

Foxes-and-rabbits (Chapter 12)

A classic predator–prey simulation; reinforces inheritance concepts and adds abstract classes and interfaces.

Image-viewer (Chapter 13)

A simple image-viewing and -manipulation application. We concentrate mainly on building the GUI.

Music-player (Chapter 13)

A GUI is added to the *music-organizer* project of Chapter 4 as another example of building GUIs.

Address-book (Chapter 14)

An implementation of an address book with an optional GUI interface. Lookup is flexible: entries can be searched by partial definition of name or phone number. This project makes extensive use of exceptions.

Cinema-booking-system (Chapter 15)

A system to manage advance seat bookings in a cinema. This example is used in a discussion of class discovery and application design. No code is provided, as the example represents the development of an application from a blank sheet of paper.

Taxi-company (Chapter 16)

The taxi example is a combination of a booking system, management system, and simulation. It is used as a case study to bring together many of the concepts and techniques discussed throughout the book.

Acknowledgments

Many people have contributed in many different ways to this book and made its creation possible.

First, and most importantly, John Rosenberg must be mentioned. It is only by coincidence of circumstance that John is not one of the authors of this book. He was one of the driving forces in the development of BlueJ and the ideas and pedagogy behind it from the very beginning, and we talked about the writing of this book for several years. Much of the material in this book was developed in discussions with John. Simply the fact that there are only twenty-four hours in a day, too many of which were already taken up with too much other work, prevented him from actually writing this book. John contributed significantly to the original version of this text and helped improve it in many ways. We have appreciated his friendship and collaboration immensely.

Several other people have helped make BlueJ what it is: Bruce Quig, Davin McCall, and Andrew Patterson in Australia, and Ian Utting, Poul Henriksen, and Neil Brown in England. All have worked on BlueJ for many years, improving and extending the design and implementation in addition to their other work commitments. Without their work, BlueJ would never have reached the quality and popularity it has today, and this book might never have been written.

Another important contribution that made the creation of BlueJ and this book possible was very generous support first from Sun Microsystems and now from Oracle. Sun has very generously supported BlueJ for many years, and when Oracle acquired Sun this support has continued. We are very grateful for this crucial contribution.

The Pearson team also has done a terrific job in making this book happen, managing to bring it into the world and avert every author's worst fear—that his book might go unnoticed. Particular thanks are due to our editor, Tracy Johnson, and to Camille Trentacoste and Carole Snyder, who supported us through the writing and production process.

David would like to add his personal thanks to both staff and students of the School of Computing at the University of Kent. The students who have taken his introductory OO course have always been a privilege to teach. They also provide the essential stimulus and motivation that makes teaching so much fun. Without the valuable assistance of knowledgeable and supportive postgraduate supervisors, running classes would be impossible.

Michael would like to thank Davin and Neil who have done such excellent work in building and maintaining BlueJ and our community web sites. Without such a great team none of this could work.

Part 1

Foundations of Object Orientation

Main concepts discussed in this chapter:

- objects
- methods
- classes
- parameters

It's time to jump in and get started with our discussion of object-oriented programming. Learning to program requires a mix of some theory and a lot of practice. In this book, we will present both, so that the two reinforce each other.

At the heart of object orientation are two concepts that we have to understand first: *objects* and *classes*. These concepts form the basis of all programming in object-oriented languages. So let us start with a brief discussion of these two foundations.

1.1   Objects and classes

Concept

Java **objects** model objects from a problem domain.

If you write a computer program in an object-oriented language, you are creating, in your computer, a model of some part of the world. The parts that the model is built up from are the *objects* that appear in the problem domain. These objects must be represented in the computer model being created. The objects from the problem domain vary with the program you are writing. They may be words and paragraphs if you are programming a word processor, users and messages if you are working on a social-network system, or monsters if you are writing a computer game.

Objects may be categorized. A class describes,—in an abstract way,—all objects of a particular kind.

We can make these abstract notions clearer by looking at an example. Assume you want to model a traffic simulation. One kind of entity you then have to deal with is cars. What is a car in our context? Is it a class or an object? A few questions may help us to make a decision.

What color is a car? How fast can it go? Where is it right now?

You will notice that we cannot answer these questions until we talk about one specific car. The reason is that the word "car" in this context refers to the *class* car; we are talking about cars in general, not about one particular car.

If I speak of "my old car that is parked at home in my garage," we can answer the questions above. That car is red, it doesn't go very fast, and it is in my garage. Now I am talking about an object—about one particular example of a car.

We usually refer to a particular object as an *instance*. We shall use the term "instance" quite regularly from now on. "Instance" is roughly synonymous with "object"; we refer to objects as instances when we want to emphasize that they are of a particular class (such as "this object is an instance of the class car").

Before we continue this rather theoretical discussion, let us look at an example.

1.2 Creating objects

Start BlueJ and open the example named *figures*.[1] You should see a window similar to that shown in Figure 1.1.

In this window, a diagram should become visible. Every one of the colored rectangles in the diagram represents a class in our project. In this project, we have classes named **Circle**, **Square**, **Triangle**, **Person**, and **Canvas**.

Right-click on the **Circle** class and choose

    new Circle()

Figure 1.1

The *figures* project in BlueJ

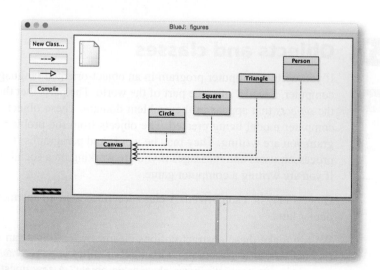

---

[1] We regularly expect you to undertake some activities and exercises while reading this book. At this point, we assume that you already know how to start BlueJ and open the example projects. If not, read Appendix A first.

Figure 1.2
An object on the
object bench

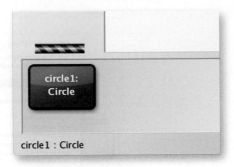

from the pop-up menu. The system asks you for a "name of the instance"; click OK—the default name supplied is good enough for now. You will see a red rectangle toward the bottom of the screen labeled "circle1" (Figure 1.2).

> **Convention** We start names of classes with capital letters (such as `Circle`) and names of objects with lowercase letters (such as `circle1`). This helps to distinguish what we are talking about.

You have just created your first object! "Circle," the rectangular icon in Figure 1.1, represents the class `Circle`; `circle1` is an object created from this class. The area at the bottom of the screen where the object is shown is called the *object bench*.

> **Exercise 1.1** Create another circle. Then create a square.

1.3 Calling methods

Right-click on one of the circle objects (not the class!), and you will see a pop-up menu with several operations (Figure 1.3). Choose `makeVisible` from the menu—this will draw a representation of this circle in a separate window (Figure 1.4).

You will notice several other operations in the circle's menu. Try invoking `moveRight` and `moveDown` a few times to move the circle closer to the corner of the screen. You may also like to try `makeInvisible` and `makeVisible` to hide and show the circle.

> **Concept**
>
> We can communicate with objects by invoking **methods** on them. Objects usually do something if we invoke a method.

> **Exercise 1.2** What happens if you call `moveDown` twice? Or three times? What happens if you call `makeInvisible` twice?

The entries in the circle's menu represent operations that you can use to manipulate the circle. These are called *methods* in Java. Using common terminology, we say that these

Figure 1.3
An object's pop-up
menu, listing its
operations

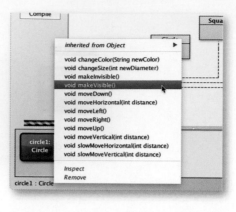

Figure 1.4
A drawing of a circle

methods are *called* or *invoked*. We shall use this proper terminology from now on. We might ask you to "invoke the **moveRight** method of **circle1**."

1.4 Parameters

Now invoke the **moveHorizontal** method. You will see a dialog appear that prompts you for some input (Figure 1.5). Type in 50 and click OK. You will see the circle move 50 pixels to the right.[2]

Concept

Methods can
have **param-
eters** to pro-
vide additional
information for
a task.

The **moveHorizontal** method that was just called is written in such a way that it requires some more information to execute. In this case, the information required is the distance—how far the circle should be moved. Thus, the **moveHorizontal** method is more flexible than the **moveRight** and **moveLeft** methods. The latter always move the circle a fixed distance, whereas **moveHorizontal** lets you specify how far you want to move the circle.

---

[2] A pixel is a single dot on your screen. Your screen is made up of a grid of single pixels.

Figure 1.5
A method-call dialog

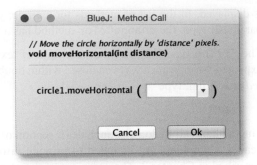

> **Concept**
>
> The method name and the parameter types of a method are called its **signature**. They provide the information needed to invoke that method.

The additional values that some methods require are called *parameters*. A method indicates what kinds of parameters it requires. When calling, for example, the **moveHorizontal** method as shown in Figure 1.5, the dialog displays the line near the top.

```
void moveHorizontal(int distance)
```

This is called the *header* of the method. The header provides some information about the method in question. The part enclosed by parentheses (**int distance**) is the information about the required parameter. For each parameter, it defines a *type* and a *name*. The header above states that the method requires one parameter of type **int** named **distance**. The name gives a hint about the meaning of the data expected. Together, the name of a method and the parameter types found in its header are called the method's *signature*.

1.5 Data types

> **Concept**
>
> Parameters have **types**. The type defines what kinds of values a parameter can take.

A type specifies what kind of data can be passed to a parameter. The type **int** signifies whole numbers (also called "integer" numbers, hence the abbreviation "int").

In the example above, the signature of the **moveHorizontal** method states that, before the method can execute, we need to supply a whole number specifying the distance to move. The data entry field shown in Figure 1.5 then lets you enter that number.

In the examples so far, the only data type we have seen has been **int**. The parameters of the move methods and the **changeSize** method are all of that type.

Closer inspection of the object's pop-up menu shows that the method entries in the menu include the parameter types. If a method has no parameter, the method name is followed by an empty set of parentheses. If it has a parameter, the type and name of that parameter is displayed. In the list of methods for a circle, you will see one method with a different parameter type: the **changeColor** method has a parameter of type **String**.

The **String** type indicates that a section of text (for example, a word or a sentence) is expected. Strings are always enclosed within double quotes. For example, to enter the word *red* as a string, type

```
"red"
```

The method-call dialog also includes a section of text called a *comment* above the method header. Comments are included to provide information to the (human) reader and are described in Chapter 2. The comment of the **changeColor** method describes what color names the system knows about.

Exercise 1.4 Invoke the **changeColor** method on one of your circle objects and enter the string **"red"**. This should change the color of the circle. Try other colors.

Exercise 1.5 This is a very simple example, and not many colors are supported. See what happens when you specify a color that is not known.

Exercise 1.6 Invoke the **changeColor** method, and write the color into the parameter field *without* the quotes. What happens?

Pitfall A common error for beginners is to forget the double quotes when typing in a data value of type **String**. If you type **green** instead of **"green"**, you will get an error message saying something like "Error: cannot find symbol - variable green."

Java supports several other data types, including decimal numbers and characters. We shall not discuss all of them right now, but rather come back to this issue later. If you want to find out about them now, see at Appendix B.

1.6 Multiple instances

Once you have a class, you can create as many objects (or instances) of that class as you like. From the class **Circle**, you can create many circles. From **Square**, you can create many squares.

Exercise 1.7 Create several circle objects on the object bench. You can do so by selecting **new Circle()** from the pop-up menu of the **Circle** class. Make them visible, then move them around on the screen using the "move" methods. Make one big and yellow; make another one small and green. Try the other shapes too: create a few triangles, squares, and persons. Change their positions, sizes, and colors.

Concept

Multiple instances. Many similar objects can be created from a single class.

Every one of those objects has its own position, color, and size. You change an attribute of an object (such as its size) by calling a method on that object. This will affect this particular object, but not others.

You may also notice an additional detail about parameters. Have a look at the **changeSize** method of the triangle. Its header is

```
void changeSize(int newHeight, int newWidth)
```

Here is an example of a method with more than one parameter. This method has two, and a comma separates them in the header. Methods can, in fact, have any number of parameters.

1.7 State

Concept

Objects have state. The **state** is represented by storing values in fields.

The set of values of all attributes defining an object (such as *x*-position, *y*-position, color, diameter, and visibility status for a circle) is also referred to as the object's *state*. This is another example of common terminology that we shall use from now on.

In BlueJ, the state of an object can be inspected by selecting the *Inspect* function from the object's pop-up menu. When an object is inspected, an *object inspector* is displayed. The object inspector is an enlarged view of the object that shows the attributes stored inside it (Figure 1.6).

Exercise 1.8 Make sure you have several objects on the object bench, and then inspect each of them in turn. Try changing the state of an object (for example, by calling the **moveLeft** method) while the object inspector is open. You should see the values in the object inspector change.

Some methods, when called, change the state of an object. For example, **moveLeft** changes the **xPosition** attribute. Java refers to these object attributes as *fields*.

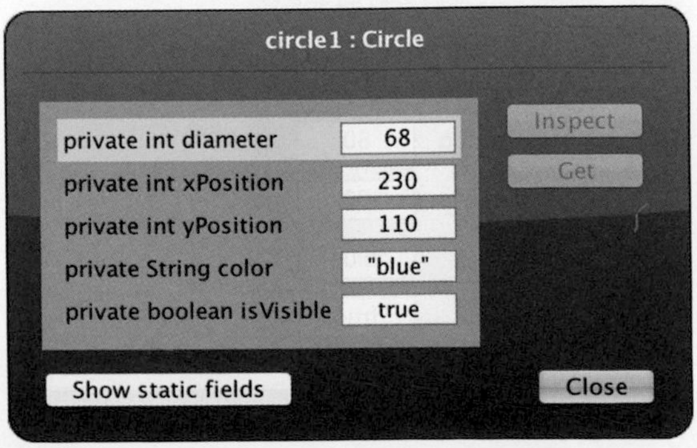

Figure 1.6
An object inspector, showing details of an object

circle1 : Circle	
private int diameter	68
private int xPosition	230
private int yPosition	110
private String color	"blue"
private boolean isVisible	true

Inspect

Get

Show static fields | Close

1.8 ## What is in an object?

On inspecting different objects, you will notice that objects of the *same* class all have the same fields. That is, the number, type, and names of the fields are the same, while the actual value of a particular field in each object may be different. In contrast, objects of a *different* class may have different fields. A circle, for example, has a "diameter" field, while a triangle has fields for "width" and "height."

The reason is that the number, types, and names of fields are defined in a class, not in an object. So the class **Circle** defines that each circle object will have five fields, named **diameter**, **xPosition**, **yPosition**, **color**, and **isVisible**. It also defines the types for these fields. That is, it specifies that the first three are of type **int**, while the color is of type **String** and the **isVisible** flag is of type **boolean**. (**boolean** is a type that can represent two values: **true** and **false**. We shall discuss it in more detail later.)

When an object of class **Circle** is created, the object will automatically have these fields. The values of the fields are stored in the object. That ensures that each circle has a color, for instance, and each can have a different color (Figure 1.7).

Figure 1.7
A class and its objects with fields and values

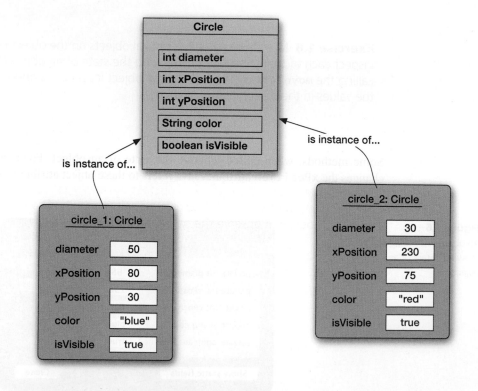

Figure 1.8
Two images created
from a set of shape
objects

 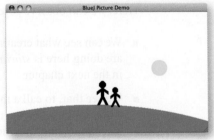

The story is similar for methods. Methods are defined in the class of the object. As a result, all objects of a given class have the same methods. However, the methods are invoked on objects. This makes it clear which object to change when, for example, a `moveRight` method is invoked.

Exercise 1.9 Figure 1.8 shows two different images. Choose one of these images and recreate it using the shapes from the *figures* project. While you are doing this, write down what you have to do to achieve this. Could it be done in different ways?

1.9 Java code

When we program in Java, we essentially write down instructions to invoke methods on objects, just as we have done with our figure objects above. However, we do not do this interactively by choosing methods from a menu with the mouse, but instead we type the commands down in textual form. We can see what those commands look like in text form by using the BlueJ Terminal.

Exercise 1.10 Select *Show Terminal* from the *View* menu. This shows another window that BlueJ uses for text output. Then select *Record method calls* from the terminal's *Options* menu. This function will cause all our method calls (in their textual form) to be written to the terminal. Now create a few objects, call some of their methods, and observe the output in the terminal window.

Using the terminal's *Record method calls* function, we can see that the sequence of creating a person object and calling its `makeVisible` and `moveRight` methods looks like this in Java text form:

```
Person person1 = new Person();
person1.makeVisible();
person1.moveRight();
```

Here, we can observe several things:

- We can see what creating an object and giving it a name looks like. Technically, what we are doing here is *storing the Person object into a variable*; we will discuss this in detail in the next chapter.

- We see that, to call a method on an object, we write the name of the object, followed by a dot, followed by the name of the method. The command ends with a parameter list— an empty pair of parentheses if there are no parameters.

- All Java statements end with a semicolon.

Instead of just looking at Java statements, we can also type them. To do this, we use the *Code Pad*. (You can switch off the *Record method calls* function now and close the terminal.)

> **Exercise 1.11** Select *Show Code Pad* from the *View* menu. This should display a new pane next to the object bench in your main BlueJ window. This pane is the *Code Pad*. You can type Java code here.

In the Code Pad, we can type Java code that does the same things we did interactively before. The Java code we need to write is exactly like that shown above.

> **Exercise 1.12** In the Code Pad, type the code shown above to create a Person object and call its **makeVisible** and **moveRight** methods. Then go on to create some other objects and call their methods.

Tip

You can recall previously used commands in the Code Pad by using the up arrow.

Typing these commands should have the same effect as invoking the same command from the object's menu. If instead you see an error message, then you have mistyped the command. Check your spelling. You will note that getting even a single character wrong will cause the command to fail.

1.10 Object interaction

For the next section, we shall work with a different example project. Close the *figures* project if you still have it open, and open the project called *house*.

> **Exercise 1.13** Open the *house* project. Create an instance of class **Picture** and invoke its **draw** method. Also, try out the **setBlackAndWhite** and **setColor** methods.
>
> **Exercise 1.14** How do you think the **Picture** class draws the picture?

Five of the classes in the *house* project are identical to the classes in the *figures* project. But we now have an additional class: `Picture`. This class is programmed to do exactly what we have done by hand in Exercise 1.9.

In reality, if we want a sequence of tasks done in Java, we would not normally do it by hand. Instead, we would create a class that does it for us. This is the `Picture` class.

The `Picture` class is written so that, when you create an instance, the instance creates two square objects (one for the wall, one for the window), a triangle, and a circle. Then, when you call the `draw` method, it moves them around and changes their color and size, until the canvas looks like the picture we see in Figure 1.8.

> **Concept**
>
> **Method calling.** Objects can communicate by **calling** each other's **methods**.

The important points here are that: objects can create other objects; and they can call each other's methods. In a normal Java program, you may well have hundreds or thousands of objects. The user of a program just starts the program (which typically creates a first object), and all other objects are created—directly or indirectly—by that object.

The big question now is this: How do we write the class for such an object?

1.11 Source code

> **Concept**
>
> The **source code** of a class determines the structure and behavior (the fields and methods) of each of the objects of that class.

Each class has some *source code* associated with it. The source code is text that defines the details of the class. In BlueJ, the source code of a class can be viewed by selecting the *Open Editor* function from the class's pop-up menu, or by double-clicking the class icon.

> **Exercise 1.15** Look at the pop-up menu of class `Picture` again. You will see an option labeled *Open Editor*. Select it. This will open a text editor displaying the source code of the class.

The source code is text written in the Java programming language. It defines what fields and methods a class has, and precisely what happens when a method is invoked. In the next chapter, we shall discuss exactly what the source code of a class contains, and how it is structured.

A large part of learning the art of programming is learning how to write these class definitions. To do this, we shall learn to use the Java language (although there are many other programming languages that could be used to write code).

When you make a change to the source code and close the editor, the icon for that class appears striped in the diagram.[3] The stripes indicate that the source has been changed. The class now needs to be compiled by clicking the *Compile* button. (You may like to read the "About compilation" note for more information on what is happening when you compile a class.) Once a class has been compiled, objects can be created again and you can try out your change.

---

[3] In BlueJ, there is no need to explicitly save the text in the editor before closing. If you close the editor, the source code will automatically be saved.

About compilation When people write computer programs, they typically use a "higher-level" programming language such as Java. A problem with that is that a computer cannot execute Java source code directly. Java was designed to be reasonably easy to read for humans, not for computers. Computers, internally, work with a binary representation of a machine code, which looks quite different from Java. The problem for us is that it looks so complex that we do not want to write it directly. We prefer to write Java. What can we do about this?

The solution is a program called the *compiler*. The compiler translates the Java code into machine code. We can write Java and run the compiler—which generates the machine code—and the computer can then read the machine code. As a result, every time we change the source code, we must first run the compiler before we can use the class again to create an object. Otherwise, the machine code version that the computer needs will not exist.

Exercise 1.16 In the source code of class **Picture**, find the part that actually draws the picture. Change it so that the sun will be blue rather than yellow.

Exercise 1.17 Add a second sun to the picture. To do this, pay attention to the field definitions close to the top of the class. You will find this code:

```
private Square wall;
private Square window;
private Triangle roof;
private Circle sun;
```

You need to add a line here for the second sun. For example:

```
private Circle sun2;
```

Then write the appropriate code in two different places for creating the second sun and making it visible when the picture is drawn.

Exercise 1.18 *Challenge exercise* (This means that this exercise might not be solved quickly. We do not expect everyone to be able to solve this at the moment. If you do, great. If you don't, then don't worry. Things will become clearer as you read on. Come back to this exercise later.) Add a sunset to the single-sun version of **Picture**. That is, make the sun go down slowly. Remember: The circle has a method **slowMoveVertical** that you can use to do this.

Exercise 1.19 *Challenge exercise* If you added your sunset to the end of the **draw** method (so that the sun goes down automatically when the picture is drawn), change this now. We now want the sunset in a separate method, so that we can call **draw** and see the picture with the sun up, and then call **sunset** (a separate method!) to make the sun go down.

Exercise 1.20 *Challenge exercise* Make a person walk up to the house after the sunset.

1.12 Another example

In this chapter, we have already discussed a large number of new concepts. To help in understanding these concepts, we shall now revisit them in a different context. For this, we use another example. Close the *house* project if you still have it open, and open the *lab-classes* project.

This project is a simplified part of a student database designed to keep track of students in laboratory classes, and to print class lists.

Exercise 1.21 Create an object of class **Student**. You will notice that this time you are prompted not only for a name of the instance, but also for some other parameters. Fill them in before clicking OK. (Remember that parameters of type **String** must be written within double quotes.)

1.13 Return values

As before, you can create multiple objects. And again, as before, the objects have methods that you can call from their pop-up menu(s).

Exercise 1.22 Create some **Student** objects. Call the **getName** method on each object. Explain what is happening.

When calling the **getName** method of the **Student** class, we notice something new: methods may return a result value. In fact, the header of each method tells us whether or not it returns a result, and what the type of the result is. The header of **getName** (as shown in the object's pop-up menu) is defined as

```
String getName()
```

The word **String** before the method name specifies the return type. In this case, it states that calling this method will return a result of type **String**. The header of **changeName** states:

```
void changeName(String replacementName)
```

The word **void** indicates that this method does not return any result.

Methods with return values enable us to get information from an object via a method call. This means that we can use methods either to change an object's state, or to find out about its state. The return type of a method is not part of its signature.

> **Concept**
>
> **Result.** Methods may return information about an object via a **return value**.

1.14 Objects as parameters

Exercise 1.23 Create an object of class **LabClass**. As the signature indicates, you need to specify the maximum number of students in that class (an integer).

Exercise 1.24 Call the **numberOfStudents** method of that class. What does it do?

Exercise 1.25 Look at the signature of the **enrollStudent** method. You will notice that the type of the expected parameter is **Student**. Make sure you have two or three students and a **LabClass** object on the object bench, then call the **enrollStudent** method of the **LabClass** object. With the input cursor in the dialog entry field, click on one of the student objects; this enters the name of the student object into the parameter field of the **enrollStudent** method (Figure 1.9). Click OK and you have added the student to the **LabClass**. Add one or more other students as well.

Exercise 1.26 Call the **printList** method of the **LabClass** object. You will see a list of all the students in that class printed to the BlueJ terminal window (Figure 1.10).

Figure 1.9
Adding a student to
a **LabClass**

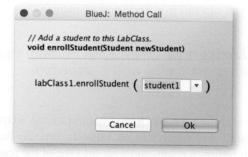

```
● ● ●              BlueJ: Method Call

// Add a student to this LabClass.
void enrollStudent(Student newStudent)


labClass1.enrollStudent ( student1  ▼ )


              Cancel          Ok
```

Figure 1.10
Output of the
LabClass class
listing

```
● ○ ○                BlueJ: Terminal Window – lab-classes
Lab class Fri 10:00
Instructor: M. O. Delmar    Room: 4E
Class list:
Wolfgang Amadeus Mozart, student ID: 547364, credits: 0
Ludwig van Beethoven, student ID: 290034, credits: 0
Johann Sebastian Bach, student ID: 188563, credits: 0
Number of students: 3
```

As the exercises show, objects can be passed as parameters to methods of other objects. In the case where a method expects an object as a parameter, the expected object's class name is specified as the parameter type in the method signature.

Explore this project a bit more. Try to identify the concepts discussed in the *figures* example in this context.

> **Exercise 1.27** Create three students with the following details:
>
> > *Snow White*, student ID: *A00234*, credits: *24*
> >
> > *Lisa Simpson*, student ID: *C22044*, credits: *56*
> >
> > *Charlie Brown*, student ID: *A12003*, credits: *6*
>
> Then enter all three into a lab and print a list to the screen.
>
> **Exercise 1.28** Use the inspector on a `LabClass` object to discover what fields it has.
>
> **Exercise 1.29** Set the instructor, room, and time for a lab, and print the list to the terminal window to check that these new details appear.

1.15 Summary

In this chapter, we have explored the basics of classes and objects. We have discussed the fact that objects are specified by classes. Classes represent the general concept of things, while objects represent concrete instances of a class. We can have many objects of any class.

Objects have methods that we use to communicate with them. We can use a method to make a change to the object or to get information from the object. Methods can have parameters, and parameters have types. Methods have return types, which specify what type of data they return. If the return type is **void**, they do not return anything.

Objects store data in fields (which also have types). All the data values of an object together are referred to as the object's state.

Objects are created from class definitions that have been written in a particular programming language. Much of programming in Java is about learning to write class definitions. A large Java program will have many classes, each with many methods that call each other in many different ways.

To learn to develop Java programs, we need to learn how to write class definitions, including fields and methods, and how to put these classes together well. The rest of this book deals with these issues.

Terms introduced in this chapter:

> **object, class, instance, method, signature, parameter, type, state, source code, return value, compiler**

Concept summary

- **object** Java objects model objects from a problem domain.

- **class** Objects are created from classes. The class describes the kind of object; the objects represent individual instances of the class.

- **method** We can communicate with objects by invoking methods on them. Objects usually do something if we invoke a method.

- **parameter** Methods can have parameters to provide additional information for a task.

- **signature** The method name and the parameter types of a method are called its signature. They provide the information needed to invoke that method.

- **type** Parameters have types. The type defines what kinds of values a parameter can take.

- **multiple instances** Many similar objects can be created from a single class.

- **state** Objects have state. The state is represented by storing values in fields.

- **method calling** Objects can communicate by calling each other's methods.

- **source code** The source code of a class determines the structure and behavior (the fields and methods) of each of the objects of that class.

- **result** Methods may return information about an object via a return value.

Exercise 1.30 In this chapter we have mentioned the data types `int` and `String`. Java has more predefined data types. Find out what they are and what they are used for. To do this, you can check Appendix B, or look it up in another Java book or in an online Java language manual. One such manual is at

```
http://download.oracle.com/javase/tutorial/java/nutsandbolts/
datatypes.html
```

Exercise 1.31 What are the types of the following values?

```
0

"hello"

101

-1

true

"33"

3.1415
```

Exercise 1.32 What would you have to do to add a new field, for example one called `name`, to a circle object?

Exercise 1.33 Write the header for a method named **send** that has one parameter of type `String`, and does not return a value.

Exercise 1.34 Write the header for a method named **average** that has two parameters, both of type `int`, and returns an `int` value.

Exercise 1.35 Look at the book you are reading right now. Is it an object or a class? If it is a class, name some objects. If it is an object, name its class.

Exercise 1.36 Can an object have several different classes? Discuss.

2

Understanding Class Definitions

Main concepts discussed in this chapter:

- fields
- constructors
- parameters
- methods (accessor, mutator)
- assignment and conditional statement

Java constructs discussed in this chapter:

field, constructor, comment, parameter, assignment (=), block, return statement, **void**, compound assignment operators (+=, −=), if-statement

In this chapter, we take our first proper look at the source code of a class. We will discuss the basic elements of class definitions: *fields*, *constructors*, and *methods*. Methods contain statements, and initially we look at methods containing only simple arithmetic and printing statements. Later, we introduce *conditional statements* that allow choices between different actions to be made within methods.

We shall start by examining a new project in a fair amount of detail. This project represents a naíve implementation of an automated ticket machine. As we start by introducing the most basic features of classes, we shall quickly find that this implementation is deficient in a number of ways. So we shall then proceed to describe a more sophisticated version of the ticket machine that represents a significant improvement. Finally, in order to reinforce the concepts introduced in this chapter, we take a look at the internals of the *lab-classes* example encountered in Chapter 1.

2.1 Ticket machines

Train stations often provide ticket machines that print a ticket when a customer inserts the correct money for their fare. In this chapter, we shall define a class that models something like these ticket machines. As we shall be looking inside our first Java example classes, we shall keep our simulation fairly simple to start with. That will give us the opportunity to ask some questions about how these models differ from the real-world versions, and how we might change our classes to make the objects they create more like the real thing.

Our ticket machines work by customers "inserting" money into them and then requesting a ticket to be printed. Each machine keeps a running total of the amount of money it has collected throughout its operation. In real life, it is often the case that a ticket machine offers a selection of different types of ticket, from which customers choose the one they want. Our simplified machines print tickets of only a single price. It turns out to be significantly more complicated to program a class to be able to issue tickets of different values, than it does to offer a single price. On the other hand, with object-oriented programming it is very easy to create multiple instances of the class, each with its own price setting, to fulfill a need for different types of tickets.

2.1.1 Exploring the behavior of a naïve ticket machine

Concept

Object creation: Some objects cannot be constructed unless extra information is provided.

Open the *naíve-ticket-machine* project in BlueJ. This project contains only one class—**TicketMachine**—which you will be able to explore in a similar way to the examples we discussed in Chapter 1. When you create a **TicketMachine** instance, you will be asked to supply a number that corresponds to the price of tickets that will be issued by that particular machine. The price is taken to be a number of cents, so a positive whole number such as 500 would be appropriate as a value to work with.

Exercise 2.1 Create a **TicketMachine** object on the object bench and take a look at its methods. You should see the following: **getBalance**, **getPrice**, **insertMoney**, and **printTicket**. Try out the **getPrice** method. You should see a return value containing the price of the tickets that was set when this object was created. Use the **insertMoney** method to simulate inserting an amount of money into the machine. The machine stores as a balance the amount of money inserted. Use **getBalance** to check that the machine has kept an accurate record of the amount just inserted. You can insert several separate amounts of money into the machine, just like you might insert multiple coins or bills into a real machine. Try inserting the exact amount required for a ticket, and use **getBalance** to ensure that the balance is increased correctly. As this is a simple machine, a ticket will not be issued automatically, so once you have inserted enough money, call the **printTicket** method. A facsimile ticket should be printed in the BlueJ terminal window.

Exercise 2.2 What value is returned if you get the machine's balance after it has printed a ticket?

Exercise 2.3 Experiment with inserting different amounts of money before printing tickets. Do you notice anything strange about the machine's behavior? What happens if you insert too much money into the machine—do you receive any refund? What happens if you do not insert enough and then try to print a ticket?

Exercise 2.4 Try to obtain a good understanding of a ticket machine's behavior by interacting with it on the object bench before we start looking, in the next section, at how the **TicketMachine** class is implemented.

Exercise 2.5 Create another ticket machine for tickets of a different price; remember that you have to supply this value when you create the machine object. Buy a ticket from that machine. Does the printed ticket look any different from those printed by the first machine?

2.2 Examining a class definition

The exercises at the end of the previous section reveal that **TicketMachine** objects only behave in the way we expect them to if we insert the exact amount of money to match the price of a ticket. As we explore the internal details of the class in this section, we shall see why this is so.

Take a look at the source code of the **TicketMachine** class by double-clicking its icon in the class diagram within BlueJ. It should look something like Figure 2.1.

The complete text of the class is shown in Code 2.1. By looking at the text of the class definition piece by piece, we can flesh out some of the object-oriented concepts that discussed in Chapter 1. This class definition contains many of the features of Java that we will see over and over again, so it will pay greatly to study it carefully.

Figure 2.1
The BlueJ editor window

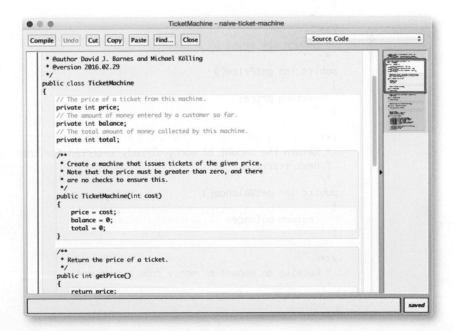

Code 2.1

The **TicketMachine** class

```java
/**
 * TicketMachine models a naive ticket machine that issues
 * flat-fare tickets.
 * The price of a ticket is specified via the constructor.
 * It is a naive machine in the sense that it trusts its users
 * to insert enough money before trying to print a ticket.
 * It also assumes that users enter sensible amounts.
 *
 * @author David J. Barnes and Michael Kölling
 * @version 2016.02.29
 */
public class TicketMachine
{
    // The price of a ticket from this machine.
    private int price;
    // The amount of money entered by a customer so far.
    private int balance;
    // The total amount of money collected by this machine.
    private int total;

    /**
     * Create a machine that issues tickets of the given price.
     * Note that the price must be greater than zero, and there
     * are no checks to ensure this.
     */
    public TicketMachine(int cost)
    {
        price = cost;
        balance = 0;
        total = 0;
    }

    /**
     * Return the price of a ticket.
     */
    public int getPrice()
    {
        return price;
    }

    /**
     * Return the amount of money already inserted for the
     * next ticket.
     */
    public int getBalance()
    {
        return balance;
    }

    /**
     * Receive an amount of money from a customer.
     */
```

**Code 2.1
continued**

The
TicketMachine
class

```
public void insertMoney(int amount)
{
    balance = balance + amount;
}

/**
 * Print a ticket.
 * Update the total collected and
 * reduce the balance to zero.
 */
public void printTicket()
{
    // Simulate the printing of a ticket.
    System.out.println("##################");
    System.out.println("# The BlueJ Line");
    System.out.println("# Ticket");
    System.out.println("# " + price + " cents.");
    System.out.println("##################");
    System.out.println();

    // Update the total collected with the balance.
    total = total + balance;
    // Clear the balance.
    balance = 0;
}
}
```

2.3 The class header

The text of a class can be broken down into two main parts: a small outer wrapping that simply names the class (appearing on a green background), and a much larger inner part that does all the work. In this case, the outer wrapping appears as follows:

```
public class TicketMachine
{
    Inner part of the class omitted.
}
```

The outer wrappings of different classes all look much the same. The outer wrapping contains the class header, whose main purpose is to provide a name for the class. By a widely followed convention, we always start class names with an uppercase letter. As long as it is used consistently, this convention allows class names to be easily distinguished from other sorts of names, such as variable names and method names, which will be described shortly. Above the class header is a comment (shown as blue text) that tells us something about the class.

Exercise 2.6 Write out what you think the outer wrappers of the **Student** and **LabClass** classes might look like; do not worry about the inner part.

Exercise 2.7 Does it matter whether we write

```
public class TicketMachine
```

or

```
class public TicketMachine
```

in the outer wrapper of a class? Edit the source of the **TicketMachine** class to make the change, and then close the editor window. Do you notice a change in the class diagram?

What error message do you get when you now press the *Compile* button? Do you think this message clearly explains what is wrong?

Change the class back to how it was, and make sure that this clears the error when you compile it.

Exercise 2.8 Check whether or not it is possible to leave out the word **public** from the outer wrapper of the **TicketMachine** class.

Exercise 2.9 Put back the word **public**, and then check whether it is possible to leave out the word **class** by trying to compile again. Make sure that both words are put back as they were originally before continuing.

2.3.1 Keywords

The words "public" and "class" are part of the Java language, whereas the word "Ticket-Machine" is not—the person writing the class has chosen that particular name. We call words like "public" and "class" *keywords* or *reserved words* – the terms are used frequently and interchangeably. There are around 50 of these in Java, and you will soon be able to recognize most of them. A point worth remembering is that Java keywords never contain uppercase letters, whereas the words we get to choose (like "TicketMachine") are often a mix of upper- and lowercase letters.

2.4 Fields, constructors, and methods

The inner part of the class is where we define the *fields*, *constructors*, and *methods* that give the objects of that class their own particular characteristics and behavior. We can summarize the essential features of those three components of a class as follows:

- The fields store data persistently within an object.

- The constructors are responsible for ensuring that an object is set up properly when it is first created.

- The methods implement the behavior of an object; they provide its functionality.

In BlueJ, fields are shown as text on a white background, while constructors and methods are displayed as yellow boxes.

In Java, there are very few rules about the order in which you choose to define the fields, constructors, and methods within a class. In the **TicketMachine** class, we have chosen to list the fields first, the constructors second, and finally the methods (Code 2.2). This is the order that we shall follow in all of our examples. Other authors choose to adopt different styles, and this is mostly a question of preference. Our style is not necessarily better than all others. However, it is important to choose one style and then use it consistently, because then your classes will be easier to read and understand.

Code 2.2

Our ordering of fields, constructors, and methods

```
public class ClassName
{
    Fields
    Constructors
    Methods
}
```

Exercise 2.10 From your earlier experimentation with the ticket machine objects within BlueJ, you can probably remember the names of some of the methods—**printTicket**, for instance. Look at the class definition in Code 2.1 and use this knowledge, along with the additional information about ordering we have given you, to make a list of the names of the fields, constructors, and methods in the **TicketMachine** class. *Hint:* There is only one constructor in the class.

Exercise 2.11 What are the two features of the constructor that make it look significantly different from the methods of the class?

2.4.1 Fields

Concept

Fields store data for an object to use. Fields are also known as instance variables.

Fields store data persistently within an object. The **TicketMachine** class has three fields: **price**, **balance**, and **total**. Fields are also known as *instance variables*, because the word *variable* is used as a general term for things that store data in a program. We have defined the fields right at the start of the class definition (Code 2.3). All of these variables are associated with monetary items that a ticket-machine object has to deal with:

- **price** stores the fixed price of a ticket;

- **balance** stores the amount of money inserted into the machine by a user prior to asking for a ticket to be printed;

- **total** stores the total amount of money inserted into the machine by all users since the machine object was constructed (excluding any current balance). The idea is that, when a ticket is printed, any money in the balance is transferred to the total.

Code 2.3

The fields of the **TicketMachine** class

```
public class TicketMachine
{
    private int price;
    private int balance;
    private int total;

    Constructors and methods omitted.

}
```

Fields are small amounts of space inside an object that can be used to store data persistently. Every object will have space for each field declared in its class. Figure 2.2 shows a diagrammatic representation of a ticket-machine object with its three fields. The fields have not yet been assigned any values; once they have, we can write each value into the box representing the field. The notation is similar to that used in BlueJ to show objects on the object bench, except that we show a bit more detail here. In BlueJ, for space reasons, the fields are not displayed on the object icon. We can, however, see them by opening an inspector window (Section 1.7).

Figure 2.2

An object of class **TicketMachine**

Each field has its own declaration in the source code. On the line above each in the full class definition, we have added a single line of text—a *comment*—for the benefit of human readers of the class definition:

```
// The price of a ticket from this machine.
private int price;
```

Concept

Comments are inserted into the source code of a class to provide explanations to human readers. They have no effect on the functionality of the class.

A single-line comment is introduced by the two characters "//", which are written with no spaces between them. More-detailed comments, often spanning several lines, are usually written in the form of multiline comments. These start with the character pair "/*" and end with the pair "*/". There is a good example preceding the header of the class in Code 2.1.

The definitions of the three fields are quite similar:

■ All definitions indicate that they are *private* fields of the object; we shall have more to say about what this means in Chapter 6, but for the time being we will simply say that we always define fields to be private.

- All three fields are of type **int**. **int** is another keyword and represents the data type integer. This indicates that each can store a single whole-number value, which is reasonable given that we wish them to store numbers that represent amounts of money in cents.

Fields can store values that can vary over time, so they are also known as *variables*. The value stored in a field can be changed from its initial value if required. For instance, as more money is inserted into a ticket machine, we shall want to change the value stored in the **balance** field. It is common to have fields whose values change often, such as **balance** and **total**, and others that change rarely or not at all, such as **price**. The fact that the value of **price** doesn't vary once set does not alter the fact that it is still called a variable. In the following sections, we shall also meet other kinds of variables in addition to fields, but they will all share the same fundamental purpose of storing data.

The **price**, **balance**, and **total** fields are all the data items that a ticket-machine object needs to fulfill its role of receiving money from a customer, printing tickets, and keeping a running total of all the money that has been put into it. In the following sections, we shall see how the constructor and methods use those fields to implement the behavior of naïve ticket machines.

Exercise 2.12 What do you think is the *type* of each of the following fields?

```
private int count;

private Student representative;

private Server host;
```

Exercise 2.13 What are the *names* of the following fields?

```
private boolean alive;

private Person tutor;

private Game game;
```

Exercise 2.14 From what you know about the naming conventions for classes, which of the type names in Exercises 2.12 and 2.13 would you say are class names?

Exercise 2.15 In the following field declaration from the **TicketMachine** class

```
private int price;
```

does it matter which order the three words appear in? Edit the **TicketMachine** class to try different orderings. After each change, close the editor. Does the appearance of the class diagram after each change give you a clue as to whether or not other orderings are possible? Check by pressing the *Compile* button to see if there is an error message.

Make sure that you reinstate the original version after your experiments!

Exercise 2.16 Is it always necessary to have a semicolon at the end of a field declaration? Once again, experiment via the editor. The rule you will learn here is an important one, so be sure to remember it.

Exercise 2.17 Write in full the declaration for a field of type **int** whose name is **status**.

From the definitions of fields we have seen so far, we can begin to put a pattern together that will apply whenever we define a field variable in a class:

- They usually start with the reserved word **private**.
- They include a type name (such as **int**, **String**, **Person**, etc.)
- They include a user-chosen name for the field variable.
- They end with a semicolon.

Remembering this pattern will help you when you write your own classes.

Indeed, as we look closely at the source code of different classes, you will see patterns such as this one emerging over and over again. Part of the process of learning to program involves looking out for such patterns and then using them in your own programs. That is one reason why studying source code in detail is so useful at this stage.

2.4.2 Constructors

Concept

Constructors allow each object to be set up properly when it is first created.

Constructors have a special role to fulfill. They are responsible for ensuring that an object is set up properly when it is first created; in other words, for ensuring that an object is ready to be used immediately following its creation. This construction process is also called *initialization*.

In some respects, a constructor can be likened to a midwife: it is responsible for ensuring that the new object comes into existence properly. Once an object has been created, the constructor plays no further role in that object's life and cannot be called again. Code 2.4 shows the constructor of the **TicketMachine** class.

One of the distinguishing features of constructors is that they have the same name as the class in which they are defined—**TicketMachine** in this case. The constructor's name immediately follows the word **public**, with nothing in between.[1]

We should expect a close connection between what happens in the body of a constructor and the fields of the class. This is because one of the main roles of the constructor is to initialize the fields. It will be possible with some fields, such as **balance** and **total**, to set sensible initial values by assigning a constant number—zero in this case. With others, such as the ticket price, it is not that simple, as we do not know the price that tickets from

---

[1] While this description is a slight simplification of the full Java rule, it fits the general rule we will use in the majority of code in this book.

a particular machine will have until that machine is constructed. Recall that we might wish to create multiple machine objects to sell tickets with different prices, so no one initial price will always be right. You will know from experimenting with creating **Ticket-Machine** objects within BlueJ that you had to supply the cost of the tickets whenever you created a new ticket machine. An important point to note here is that the price of a ticket is initially determined *externally* and then has to be *passed into* the constructor. Within BlueJ, you decide the value and enter it into a dialog box. Part of the task of the constructor is to receive that value and store it in the **price** field of the newly created ticket machine, so the machine can remember what that value was without you having to keep reminding it.

Code 2.4

The constructor of the **Ticket Machine** class

```
public class TicketMachine
{

    Fields omitted.

    /**
     * Create a machine that issues tickets of the given price.
     * Note that the price must be greater than zero, and there
     * are no checks to ensure this.
     */
    public TicketMachine(int cost)
    {
        price = cost;
        balance = 0;
        total = 0;
    }

    Methods omitted.

}
```

We can see from this that one of the most important roles of a field is to remember external information passed into the object, so that that information is available to an object throughout its lifetime. Fields, therefore, provide a place to store long-lasting (i.e., persistent) data.

Figure 2.3 shows a ticket-machine object after the constructor has executed. Values have now been assigned to the fields. From this diagram, we can tell that the ticket machine was created by passing in 500 as the value for the ticket price.

In the next section, we discuss how values are received by an object from outside.

Note In Java, all fields are automatically initialized to a default value if they are not explicitly initialized. For integer fields, this default value is zero. So, strictly speaking, we could have done without setting **balance** and **total** to zero, relying on the default value to give us the same result. However, we prefer to write the explicit assignments anyway. There is no disadvantage to it, and it serves well to document what is actually happening. We do not rely on a reader of the class knowing what the default value is, and we document that we really want this value to be zero and have not just forgotten to initialize it.

Figure 2.3
A `TicketMachine` object after initialization (created for 500-cent tickets)

We distinguish between the parameter *names* inside a constructor or method, and the parameter *values* outside, by referring to the names as *formal parameters* and the values as *actual parameters*. So **cost** is a formal parameter, and a user-supplied value such as 500 is an actual parameter.

2.5 Parameters: receiving data

Constructors and methods play quite different roles in the life of an object, but the way in which both receive values from outside is the same: via *parameters*. You may recall that we briefly encountered parameters in Chapter 1 (Section 1.4). Parameters are another sort of variable, just as fields are, so they are also used to hold data. Parameters are variables that are defined in the header of a constructor or method:

```
public TicketMachine(int cost)
```

This constructor has a single parameter, **cost**, which is of type **int**—the same type as the **price** field it will be used to set. A parameter is used as a sort of temporary messenger, carrying data originating from outside the constructor or method, and making it available inside it.

Figure 2.4 illustrates how values are passed via parameters. In this case, a BlueJ user enters the external value into the dialog box when creating a new ticket machine (shown on the left), and that value is then copied into the **cost** parameter of the new machine's constructor. This is illustrated with the arrow labeled (A). The box in the **TicketMachine** object in Figure 2.4, labeled "TicketMachine (constructor)," represents additional space for the object that is created only when the constructor executes. We shall call it the *constructor space* of the object (or *method space* when we talk about methods instead of constructors, as the situation there is the same). The constructor space is used to provide space to store the values for the constructor's parameters. In our diagrams, all variables are represented by white boxes.

We distinguish between the parameter *names* inside a constructor or method, and the parameter *values* outside, by referring to the names as *formal parameters* and the values as *actual parameters*. So **cost** is a formal parameter, and a user-supplied value such as 500 is an actual parameter.

Concept

The **scope** of a variable defines the section of source code from which the variable can be accessed.

A formal parameter is available to an object only within the body of a constructor or method that declares it. We say that the *scope* of a parameter is restricted to the body of the constructor or method in which it is declared. In contrast, the scope of a field is the whole of the class definition–it can be accessed from anywhere in the same class. This is a very important difference between these two sorts of variables.

Concept

The **lifetime** of a variable describes how long the variable continues to exist before it is destroyed.

A concept related to variable scope is variable *lifetime*. The lifetime of a parameter is limited to a single call of a constructor or method. When a constructor or method is called, the extra space for the parameter variables is created, and the external values copied into that space. Once that call has completed its task, the formal parameters disappear and the values they held are lost. In other words, when the constructor has finished executing, the whole constructor space is removed, along with the parameter variables held within it (see Figure 2.4).

In contrast, the lifetime of a field is the same as the lifetime of the object to which it belongs. When an object is created, so are the fields, and they persist for the lifetime of the object. It follows that if we want to remember the cost of tickets held in the **cost** parameter, we must store the value somewhere persistent—that is, in the **price** field.

Just as we expect to see a close link between a constructor and the fields of its class, we expect to see a close link between the constructor's parameters and the fields, because external values will often be needed to set the initial values of one or more of those fields. Where this is the case, the parameter types will closely match the types of the corresponding fields.

Figure 2.4

Parameter passing (A) and assignment (B)

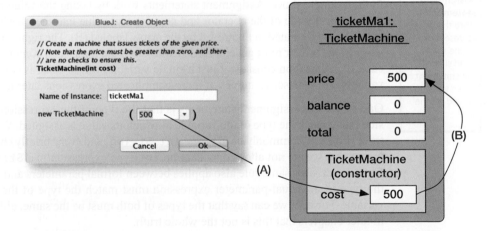

Exercise 2.18 To what class does the following constructor belong?

```
public Student(String name)
```

Exercise 2.19 How many parameters does the following constructor have, and what are their types?

```
public Book(String title, double price)
```

Exercise 2.20 Can you guess what types some of the **Book** class's fields might be, from the parameters in its constructor? Can you assume anything about the names of its fields?

2.5.1 Choosing variable names

One of the things you might have noticed is that the variable names we use for fields and parameters have a close connection with the purpose of the variable. Names such as **price**, **cost**, **title**, and **alive** all tell you something useful about the information being stored in that variable. This, makes it easier to understand what is going on in the program. Given that we have a large degree of freedom in our choice of variable names, it is worth following this principle of choosing names that communicate a sense of purpose rather than arbitrary and meaningless combinations of letters and numbers.

2.6 Assignment

In the previous section, we noted the need to copy the short-lived value stored in a parameter variable into somewhere more permanent—a field variable. In order to do this, the body of the constructor contains the following *assignment statement*:

```
price = cost;
```

> **Concept**
>
> **Assignment statements** store the value represented by the right-hand side of the statement in the variable named on the left.

Assignment statements are used frequently in programming, as a means to store a value into a variable. They can be recognized by the presence of an assignment operator, such as "=" in the example above. Assignment statements work by taking the value of what appears on the right-hand side of the operator and copying that value into the variable on the left-hand side. This is illustrated in Figure 2.4 by the arrow labeled (B). The right-hand side is called an *expression*. In their most general form, expressions are things that compute values, but in this case, the expression consists of just a single variable, whose value is copied into the **price** variable. We shall see examples of more-complicated expressions later in this chapter.

One rule about assignment statements is that the type of the expression on the right-hand side must match the type of the variable to which its value is assigned. We have already met three different, commonly used types: **int**, **String**, and (very briefly) **boolean**. This rule means that we are not allowed to store an **int**-type expression in a **String**-type variable, for instance. This same rule also applies between formal parameters and actual parameters: the type of an actual-parameter expression must match the type of the formal-parameter variable. For now, we can say that the types of both must be the same, although we shall see in later chapters that this is not the whole truth.

> **Exercise 2.21** Suppose that the class **Pet** has a field called **name** that is of the type **String**. Write an assignment statement in the body of the following constructor so that the **name** field will be initialized with the value of the constructor's parameter.
>
> ```
> public Pet(String petsName)
> {
> }
> ```
>
> **Exercise 2.22** *Challenge exercise* The following object creation will result in the constructor of the **Date** class being called. Can you write the constructor's header?
>
> ```
> new Date("March", 23, 1861)
> ```
>
> Try to give meaningful names to the parameters.

2.7 Methods

The **TicketMachine** class has four methods: **getPrice**, **getBalance**, **insertMoney**, and **printTicket**. You can see them in the class's source code (Code 2.1) as yellow boxes. We shall start our look at the source code of methods by considering **getPrice** (Code 2.5).

Code 2.5
The **getPrice**
method

```
public class TicketMachine
{
    Fields omitted.
    Constructor omitted.

    /**
     * Return the price of a ticket.
     */
    public int getPrice()
    {
        return price;
    }

    Remaining methods omitted.
}
```

Concept

Methods consist of two parts: a header and a body.

Methods have two parts: a *header* and a *body*. Here is the method header for **getPrice**, preceded by a descriptive comment:

```
/**
 * Return the price of a ticket.
 */
public int getPrice()
```

It is important to distinguish between method headers and field declarations, because they can look quite similar. We can tell that **getPrice** is a method and not a field because method headers always include a pair of parentheses–"(" and ")"–and no semicolon at the end of the header.

The method body is the remainder of the method after the header. It is always enclosed by a matching pair of curly brackets: "{" and "}". Method bodies contain the *declarations* and *statements* that define what an object does when that method is called. Declarations are used to create additional, temporary variable space, while statements describe the actions of the method. In **getPrice**, the method body contains a single statement, but we shall soon see examples where the method body consists of many lines of both declarations and statements.

Any set of declarations and statements between a pair of matching curly brackets is known as a *block*. So the body of the **TicketMachine** class, the bodies of the constructor, and all of the methods within the class are blocks.

There are at least two significant differences between the headers of the `TicketMachine` constructor and the `getPrice` method:

```
public TicketMachine(int cost)

public int getPrice()
```

- The method has a *return type* of `int`; the constructor has no return type. A return type is written just before the method name. This is a difference that applies in all cases.

- The constructor has a single formal parameter, `cost`, but the method has none—just a pair of empty parentheses. This is a difference that applies in this particular case.

It is an absolute rule in Java that a constructor may not have a return type. On the other hand, both constructors and methods may have any number of formal parameters, including none.

Within the body of `getPrice` there is a single statement:

```
return price;
```

This is called a *return statement*. It is responsible for returning an integer value to match the `int` return type in the method's header. Where a method contains a return statement, it is always the final statement of that method, because no further statements in the method will be executed once the return statement is executed.

Return types and return statements work together. The `int` return type of `getPrice` is a form of promise that the body of the method will do something that ultimately results in an integer value being calculated and returned as the method's result. You might like to think of a method call as being a form of question to an object, and the return value from the method being the object's answer to that question. In this case, when the `getPrice` method is called on a ticket machine, the question is, What do tickets cost? A ticket machine does not need to perform any calculations to be able to answer that, because it keeps the answer in its `price` field. So the method answers by just returning the value of that variable. As we gradually develop more-complex classes, we shall inevitably encounter more-complex questions that require more work to supply their answers.

2.8 Accessor and mutator methods

We often describe methods such as the two "get" methods of `TicketMachine` (`getPrice` and `getBalance`) as *accessor methods* (or just *accessors*). This is because they return information to the caller about the state of an object; they provide access to information about the object's state. An accessor usually contains a return statement in order to pass back that information.

There is often confusion about what "returning a value" actually means in practice. People often think it means that something is printed by the program. This is not the case at all— we shall see how printing is done when we look at the `printTicket` method. Rather, returning a value means that some information is passed internally between two different parts of the program. One part of the program has requested information from an object via a method call, and the return value is the way the object has of passing that information back to the caller.

The `get` methods of a ticket machine perform similar tasks: returning the value of one of their object's fields. The remaining methods—`insertMoney` and `printTicket`—have a

Exercise 2.23 Compare the header and body of the `getBalance` method with the header and body of the `getPrice` method. What are the differences between them?

Exercise 2.24 If a call to `getPrice` can be characterized as "What do tickets cost?" how would you characterize a call to `getBalance`?

Exercise 2.25 If the name of `getBalance` is changed to `getAmount`, does the return statement in the body of the method also need to be changed for the code to compile? Try it out within BlueJ. What does this tell you about the name of an accessor method and the name of the field associated with it?

Exercise 2.26 Write an accessor method `getTotal` in the `TicketMachine` class. The new method should return the value of the `total` field.

Exercise 2.27 Try removing the return statement from the body of `getPrice`. What error message do you see now when you try compiling the class?

Exercise 2.28 Compare the method headers of `getPrice` and `printTicket` in Code 2.1. Apart from their names, what is the main difference between them?

Exercise 2.29 Do the `insertMoney` and `printTicket` methods have return statements? Why do you think this might be? Do you notice anything about their headers that might suggest why they do not require return statements?

Concept

Mutator methods change the state of an object.

much more significant role, primarily because they *change* the value of one or more fields of a ticket-machine object each time they are called. We call methods that change the state of their object *mutator methods* (or just *mutators*).

In the same way as we think of a call to an accessor as a request for information (a question), we can think of a call to a mutator as a request for an object to change its state. The most basic form of mutator is one that takes a single parameter whose value is used to directly overwrite what is stored in one of an object's fields. In a direct complement to "get" methods, these are often called "set" methods, although the `TicketMachine` does not have any of those, at this stage.

One distinguishing effect of a mutator is that an object will often exhibit slightly different behavior before and after it is called. We can illustrate this with the following exercise.

Exercise 2.30 Create a ticket machine with a ticket price of your choosing. Before doing anything else, call the `getBalance` method on it. Now call the `insertMoney` method (Code 2.6) and give a non-zero positive amount of money as the actual parameter. Now call `getBalance` again. The two calls to `getBalance` should show different outputs, because the call to `insertMoney` had the effect of changing the machine's state via its `balance` field.

The header of **insertMoney** has a **void** return type and a single formal parameter, **amount**, of type **int**. A **void** return type means that the method does not return any value to its caller. This is significantly different from all other return types. Within BlueJ, the difference is most noticeable in that no return-value dialog is shown following a call to a **void** method. Within the body of a **void** method, this difference is reflected in the fact that there is no return statement.[2]

Code 2.6

The **insert-Money** method

```
/**
 * Receive an amount of money from a customer.
 */
public void insertMoney(int amount)
{
    balance = balance + amount;
}
```

In the body of **insertMoney**, there is a single statement that is another form of assignment statement. We always consider assignment statements by first examining the calculation on the right-hand side of the assignment symbol. Here, its effect is to calculate a value that is the sum of the number in the **amount** parameter and the number in the **balance** field. This combined value is then assigned to the **balance** field. So the effect is to increase the value in **balance** by the value in **amount**.[3]

> **Exercise 2.31** How can we tell from just its header that **setPrice** is a method and not a constructor?
>
> ```
> public void setPrice(int cost)
> ```
>
> **Exercise 2.32** Complete the body of the **setPrice** method so that it assigns the value of its parameter to the **price** field.
>
> **Exercise 2.33** Complete the body of the following method, whose purpose is to add the value of its parameter to a field named **score**.
>
> ```
> /**
>  * Increase score by the given number of points.
>  */
> public void increase(int points)
> {
>     ...
> }
> ```

---

[2] In fact, Java does allow **void** methods to contain a special form of return statement in which there is no return value. This takes the form

```
return;
```

and simply causes the method to exit without executing any further code.

[3] Adding an amount to the value in a variable is so common that there is a special **compound assignment operator** to do this: +=. For instance:

```
balance += amount;
```

Exercise 2.34 Is the `increase` method a mutator? If so, how could you demonstrate this?

Exercise 2.35 Complete the following method, whose purpose is to subtract the value of its parameter from a field named `price`.

```
/**
 * Reduce price by the given amount.
 */
public void discount(int amount)
{
    ...
}
```

2.9 Printing from methods

Code 2.7 shows the most complex method of the class: `printTicket`. To help your understanding of the following discussion, make sure that you have called this method on a ticket machine. You should have seen something like the following printed in the BlueJ terminal window:

```
##################
# The BlueJ Line
# Ticket
# 500 cents.
##################
```

This is the longest method we have seen so far, so we shall break it down into more manageable pieces:

- The header indicates that the method has a **void** return type, and that it takes no parameters.

- The body comprises eight statements plus associated comments.

- The first six statements are responsible for printing what you see in the BlueJ terminal window: five lines of text and a sixth blank line.

- The seventh statement adds the balance inserted by the customer (through previous calls to `insertMoney`) to the running total of all money collected so far by the machine.

- The eighth statement resets the balance to zero with a basic assignment statement, in preparation for the next customer.

Code 2.7

The **print-**

Ticket method

```java
/**
 * Print a ticket.
 * Update the total collected and reduce the balance to zero.
 */
public void printTicket()
{
    // Simulate the printing of a ticket.
    System.out.println("################");
    System.out.println("# The BlueJ Line");
    System.out.println("# Ticket");
    System.out.println("# " + price + " cents.");
    System.out.println("################");
    System.out.println();

    // Update the total collected with the balance.
    total = total + balance;
    // Clear the balance.
    balance = 0;
}
```

Concept

The method **System.out. println** prints its parameter to the text terminal.

By comparing the output that appears with the statements that produced it, it is easy to see that a statement such as

```java
System.out.println("# The BlueJ Line");
```

literally prints the string that appears between the matching pair of double-quote characters. The basic form of a call to `println` is

```java
System.out.println(something-we-want-to-print);
```

where *something-we-want-to-print* can be replaced by any arbitrary string, enclosed between a pair of double-quote characters. For instance, there is nothing significant in the "#" character that is in the string—it is simply one of the characters we wish to be printed.

All of the printing statements in the **printTicket** method are calls to the **println** method of the **System.out** object that is built into the Java language, and what appears between the round brackets is the parameter to each method call, as you might expect. However, in the fourth statement, the actual parameter to **println** is a little more complicated and requires some more explanation:

```java
System.out.println("# " + price + " cents.");
```

What it does is print out the price of the ticket, with some extra characters on either side of the amount. The two "+" operators are being used to construct a single actual parameter, in the form of a string, from three separate components:

- the string literal: **"# "** (*note the space character after the hash*);
- the value of the **price** field (note that there are no quotes around the field name because we want the field's value, not its name);
- the string literal: **" cents."** (note the space character before the word **"cents"**).

When used between a string and anything else, "+" is a string-concatenation operator (i.e., it concatenates or joins strings together to create a new string) rather than an arithmetic-addition operator. So the numeric value of price is converted into a string and joined to its two surrounding strings.

Note that the final call to **println** contains no string parameter. This is allowed, and the result of calling it will be to leave a blank line between this output and any that follows after. You will easily see the blank line if you print a second ticket.

Exercise 2.36 Write down exactly what will be printed by the following statement:

```
System.out.println("My cat has green eyes.");
```

Exercise 2.37 Add a method called **prompt** to the **TicketMachine** class. This should have a **void** return type and take no parameters. The body of the method should print the following single line of output:

```
Please insert the correct amount of money.
```

Exercise 2.38 What do you think would be printed if you altered the fourth statement of **printTicket** so that **price** also has quotes around it, as follows?

```
System.out.println("# " + "price" + " cents.");
```

Exercise 2.39 What about the following version?

```
System.out.println("# price cents.");
```

Exercise 2.40 Could either of the previous two versions be used to show the price of tickets in different ticket machines? Explain your answer.

Exercise 2.41 Add a **showPrice** method to the **TicketMachine** class. This should have a **void** return type and take no parameters. The body of the method should print:

```
The price of a ticket is xyz cents.
```

where **xyz** should be replaced by the value held in the **price** field when the method is called.

Exercise 2.42 Create two ticket machines with differently priced tickets. Do calls to their **showPrice** methods show the same output, or different? How do you explain this effect?

2.10 Method summary

It is worth summarizing a few features of methods at this point, because methods are fundamental to the programs we will be writing and exploring in this book. They implement the core actions of every object.

A method with parameters will receive data passed to it from the method's caller, and will then use that data to help it perform a particular task. However, not all methods take parameters; many simply use the data stored in the object's fields to carry out their task.

If a method has a non-**void** return type, it will return some data to the place it was called from—and that data will almost certainly be used in the caller for further calculations or program manipulations. Many methods, though, have a **void** return type and return nothing, but they still perform a useful task within the context of their object.

Accessor methods have non-**void** return types and return information about the object's state. Mutator methods modify an object's state. Mutators often take parameters whose values are used in the modification, although it is still possible to write a mutating method that does not take parameters.

2.11 Summary of the naíve ticket machine

We have now examined the internal structure of the naíve **TicketMachine** class in some detail. We have seen that the class has a small outer layer that gives a name to the class, and a more substantial inner body containing fields, a constructor, and several methods. Fields are used to store data that enable objects to maintain a state that persists between method calls. Constructors are used to set up an initial state when an object is created. Having a proper initial state will enable an object to respond appropriately to method calls immediately following its creation. Methods implement the defined behavior of the class's objects. Accessor methods provide information about an object's state, and mutator methods change an object's state.

We have seen that constructors are distinguished from methods by having the same name as the class in which they are defined. Both constructors and methods may take parameters, but only methods may have a return type. Non-**void** return types allow us to pass a value out of a method to the place where the method was called from. A method with a non-**void** return type must have at least one return statement in its body; this will often be the final statement. Constructors never have a return type of any sort—not even **void**.

> Before attempting these exercises, be sure that you have a good understanding of how ticket machines behave and how that behavior is implemented through the fields, constructor, and methods of the class.
>
> **Exercise 2.43** Modify the constructor of **TicketMachine** so that it no longer has a parameter. Instead, the price of tickets should be fixed at 1,000 cents. What effect does this have when you construct ticket-machine objects within BlueJ?

Exercise 2.44 Give the class two constructors. One should take a single parameter that specifies the price, and the other should take no parameter and set the price to be a default value of your choosing. Test your implementation by creating machines via the two different constructors.

Exercise 2.45 Implement a method, `empty`, that simulates the effect of removing all money from the machine. This method should have a **void** return type, and its body should simply set the **total** field to zero. Does this method need to take any parameters? Test your method by creating a machine, inserting some money, printing some tickets, checking the total, and then emptying the machine. Is the `empty` method a mutator or an accessor?

2.12 Reflecting on the design of the ticket machine

From our study of the internals of the **TicketMachine** class, you should have come to appreciate how inadequate it would be in the real world. It is deficient in several ways:

- It contains no check that the customer has entered enough money to pay for a ticket.

- It does not refund any money if the customer pays too much for a ticket.

- It does not check to ensure that the customer inserts sensible amounts of money. Experiment with what happens if a negative amount is entered, for instance.

- It does not check that the ticket price passed to its constructor is sensible.

If we could remedy these problems, then we would have a much more functional piece of software that might serve as the basis for operating a real-world ticket machine.

In the next few sections, we shall examine the implementation of an improved ticket machine class that attempts to deal with some of the inadequacies of the naïve implementation. Open the *better-ticket-machine* project. As before, this project contains a single class: **TicketMachine**. Before looking at the internal details of the class, experiment with it by creating some instances and see whether you notice any differences in behavior between this version and the previous naïve version.

One specific difference is that the new version has an additional method, **refundBalance**. Take a look at what happens when you call it.

Code 2.8
A more
sophisticated
TicketMachine

```
/**
 * TicketMachine models a ticket machine that issues
 * flat-fare tickets.
 * The price of a ticket is specified via the constructor.
 * Instances will check to ensure that a user only enters
 * sensible amounts of money, and will only print a ticket
 * if enough money has been input.
 *
```

Code 2.8 continued

A more sophisticated `TicketMachine`

```java
 * @author David J. Barnes and Michael Kölling
 * @version 2016.02.29
 */
public class TicketMachine
{
    // The price of a ticket from this machine.
    private int price;
    // The amount of money entered by a customer so far.
    private int balance;
    // The total amount of money collected by this machine.
    private int total;

    /**
     * Create a machine that issues tickets of the given price.
     */
    public TicketMachine(int cost)
    {
        price = cost;
        balance = 0;
        total = 0;
    }

    /**
     * @Return The price of a ticket.
     */
    public int getPrice()
    {
        return price;
    }

    /**
     * Return The amount of money already inserted for the
     * next ticket.
     */
    public int getBalance()
    {
        return balance;
    }

    /**
     * Receive an amount of money from a customer.
     * Check that the amount is sensible.
     */
    public void insertMoney(int amount)
    {
        if(amount > 0) {
            balance = balance + amount;
        }
        else {
            System.out.println("Use a positive amount rather than: " +
                                amount);
        }
    }
}
```

Code 2.8
continued

A more
sophisticated
`TicketMachine`

```java
/**
 * Print a ticket if enough money has been inserted, and
 * reduce the current balance by the ticket price. Print
 * an error message if more money is required.
 */
public void printTicket()
{
    if(balance >= price) {
        // Simulate the printing of a ticket.
        System.out.println("##################");
        System.out.println("# The BlueJ Line");
        System.out.println("# Ticket");
        System.out.println("# " + price + " cents.");
        System.out.println("##################");
        System.out.println();

        // Update the total collected with the price.
        total = total + price;
        // Reduce the balance by the price.
        balance = balance - price;
    }
    else {
        System.out.println("You must insert at least: " +
                           (price - balance) + " more cents.");
    }
}

/**
 * Return the money in the balance.
 * The balance is cleared.
 */
public int refundBalance()
{
    int amountToRefund;
    amountToRefund = balance;
    balance = 0;
    return amountToRefund;
}
```

2.13 Making choices: the conditional statement

Code 2.8 shows the internal details of the better ticket machine's class definition. Much of this definition will already be familiar to you from our discussion of the naïve ticket machine. For instance, the outer wrapping that names the class is the same, because we have chosen to give this class the same name. In addition, it contains the same three fields to maintain object state, and these have been declared in the same way. The constructor and the two **get** methods are also the same as before.

The first significant change can be seen in the **insertMoney** method. We recognized that the main problem with the naïve ticket machine was its failure to check certain conditions. One of those missing checks was on the amount of money inserted by a customer, as it was possible for a negative amount of money to be inserted. We have remedied that failing by making use of a *conditional statement* to check that the amount inserted has a value greater than zero:

```
if(amount > 0) {
    balance = balance + amount;
}
else {
    System.out.println("Use a positive amount rather than: " +
                        amount);
}
```

Conditional statements are also known as *if-statements*, from the keyword used in most programming languages to introduce them. A conditional statement allows us to take one of two possible actions based upon the result of a check or test. If the test is true, then we do one thing; otherwise, we do something different. This kind of either/or decision should be familiar from situations in everyday life: for instance, if I have enough money left, then I shall go out for a meal; otherwise, I shall stay home and watch a movie. A conditional statement has the general form described in the following *pseudo-code*:

```
if(perform some test that gives a true or false result) {
    Do the statements here if the test gave a true result
}
else {
    Do the statements here if the test gave a false result
}
```

Certain parts of this pseudo-code are proper bits of Java, and those will appear in almost all conditional statements–the keywords **if** and **else**, the round brackets around the test, and the curly brackets marking the two blocks–while the other three italicized parts will be fleshed out differently for each particular situation being coded.

Only one of the two blocks of statements following the test will ever be performed following the evaluation of the test. So, in the example from the **insertMoney** method, following the test of an inserted amount we shall only either add the amount to the balance or print the error message. The test uses the *greater-than operator*, ">", to compare the value in **amount** against zero. If the value is greater than zero, then it is added to the balance. If it is not greater than zero, then an error message is printed. By using a conditional statement, we have, in effect, protected the change to **balance** in the case where the parameter does not represent a valid amount. Details of other Java operators can be found in Appendix C. The obvious ones to mention at this point are "<" (less-than), "<=" (less-than or equal-to), and ">=" (greater-than or equal-to). All are used to compare two numeric values, as in the **printTicket** method.

The test used in a conditional statement is an example of a *boolean expression*. Earlier in this chapter, we introduced arithmetic expressions that produced numerical results. A boolean expression has only two possible values (**true** or **false**): the value of **amount** is either greater than zero (**true**) or it is not greater (**false**). A conditional statement makes use of those two possible values to choose between two different actions.

Exercise 2.46 Check that the behavior we have discussed here is accurate by creating a `TicketMachine` instance and calling `insertMoney` with various actual parameter values. Check the balance both before and after calling `insertMoney`. Does the balance ever change in the cases when an error message is printed? Try to predict what will happen if you enter the value zero as the parameter, and then see if you are right.

Exercise 2.47 Predict what you think will happen if you change the test in `insertMoney` to use the *greater-than or equal-to operator:*

```
if(amount >= 0)
```

Check your predictions by running some tests. What is the one situation in which it makes a difference to the behavior of the method?

Exercise 2.48 Rewrite the if-else statement so that the method still behaves correctly but the error message is printed if the boolean expression is true but the balance is increased if the expression is false. You will obviously have to rewrite the condition to make things happen this way around.

Exercise 2.49 In the *figures* project we looked at in Chapter 1 we used a `boolean` field to control a feature of the circle objects. What was that feature? Was it well suited to being controlled by a type with only two different values?

2.14 A further conditional-statement example

The `printTicket` method contains a further example of a conditional statement. Here it is in outline:

```
if(balance >= price) {
    Printing details omitted.
    // Update the total collected with the price.
    total = total + price;
    // Reduce the balance by the price.
    balance = balance - price;
}
else {
    System.out.println("You must insert at least: " +
                       (price - balance) + " more cents.");
}
```

With this if-statement, we fix the problem that the naíve version makes no check that a customer has inserted enough money for a ticket before printing. This version checks that the value in the **balance** field is at least as large as the value in the **price** field. If it is, then it is okay to print a ticket. If it is not, then we print an error message instead.

The printing of the error message follows exactly the same pattern as we saw for printing the price of tickets in the `printTicket` method; it is just a little more verbose.

```
System.out.println("You must insert at least: " +
                   (price - balance) + " more cents.");
```

The single actual parameter to the `println` method consists of a concatenation of three elements: two string literals on either side of a numeric value. In this case, the numeric value is a subtraction that has been placed in parentheses to indicate that it is the resulting value we wish to concatenate with the two strings.

Exercise 2.50 In this version of `printTicket`, we also do something slightly different with the **total** and **balance** fields. Compare the implementation of the method in Code 2.1 with that in Code 2.8 to see whether you can tell what those differences are. Then check your understanding by experimenting within BlueJ.

Exercise 2.51 Is it possible to remove the else part of the if-statement in the `printTicket` method (i.e., remove the word **else** and the block attached to it)? Try doing this and seeing if the code still compiles. What happens now if you try to print a ticket without inserting any money?

The `printTicket` method reduces the value of **balance** by the value of **price**. As a consequence, if a customer inserts more money than the price of the ticket, then some money will be left in the balance that could be used toward the price of a second ticket. Alternatively, the customer could ask to be refunded the remaining balance, and that is what the **refundBalance** method does, as we shall see in section 2.16.

2.15 Scope highlighting

You will have noticed by now that the BlueJ editor displays source code with some additional decoration: colored boxes around some elements, such as methods and if-statements (see, for example, Code 2.8).

These colored annotations are known as *scope highlighting*, and they help clarify logical units of your program. A *scope* (also called a *block*) is a unit of code usually indicated by a pair of curly brackets. The whole body of a class is a scope, as is the body of each method and the *if* and *else* parts of an if-statement.

As you can see, scopes are often nested: the if-statement is inside a method, which is inside a class. BlueJ helps by distinguishing different kinds of scopes with different colors.

One of the most common errors in the code of beginning programmers is getting the curly brackets wrong—either by having them in the wrong place, or by having a bracket missing altogether. Two things can greatly help in avoiding this kind of error:

- Pay attention to proper indentation of your code. Every time a new scope starts (after an open curly bracket), indent the following code one level more. Closing the scope brings the indentation back. If your indentation is completely out, use BlueJ's "Auto-layout" function (find it in the editor menu!) to fix it.

■ Pay attention to the scope highlighting. You will quickly get used to the way well-structured code looks. Try removing a curly bracket in the editor or adding one at an arbitrary location, and observe how the coloring changes. Get used to recognizing when scopes look wrong.

Exercise 2.52 After a ticket has been printed, could the value in the **balance** field ever be set to a negative value by subtracting **price** from it? Justify your answer.

Exercise 2.53 So far, we have introduced you to two arithmetic operators, **+** and **−**, that can be used in arithmetic expressions in Java. Take a look at Appendix C to find out what other operators are available.

Exercise 2.54 Write an assignment statement that will store the result of multiplying two variables, **price** and **discount**, into a third variable, **saving**.

Exercise 2.55 Write an assignment statement that will divide the value in **total** by the value in **count** and store the result in **mean**.

Exercise 2.56 Write an if-statement that will compare the value in **price** against the value in **budget**. If **price** is greater than **budget**, then print the message "Too expensive"; otherwise print the message "Just right".

Exercise 2.57 Modify your answer to the previous exercise so that the message includes the value of your budget if the price is too high.

2.16 Local variables

So far, we have encountered two different sorts of variables: fields (instance variables) and parameters. We are now going to introduce a third kind. All have in common that they store data, but each sort of variable has a particular role to play.

Section 2.7 noted that a method body (or, in general, a *block*) can contain both declarations and statements. To this point, none of the methods we have looked at contain any declarations. The **refundBalance** method contains three statements and a single declaration. The declaration introduces a new kind of variable:

```java
public int refundBalance()
{
    int amountToRefund;
    amountToRefund = balance;
    balance = 0;
    return amountToRefund;
}
```

What sort of variable is **amountToRefund**? We know that it is not a field, because fields are defined outside methods. It is also not a parameter, as those are always defined in the method header. The **amountToRefund** variable is what is known as a *local variable*, because it is defined *inside* a method body.

Local variable declarations look similar to field declarations, but they never have **private** or **public** as part of them. Constructors can also have local variables. Like formal parameters, local variables have a scope that is limited to the statements of the method to which they belong. Their lifetime is the time of the method execution: they are created when a method is called and destroyed when a method finishes.

You might wonder why there is a need for local variables if we have fields. Local variables are primarily used as temporary storage, to help a single method complete its task; we think of them as data storage for a single method. In contrast, fields are used to store data that persists through the life of a whole object. The data stored in fields is accessible to all of the object's methods. We try to avoid declaring as fields variables that really only have a local (method-level) usage, whose values don't have to be retained beyond a single method call. So even if two or more methods in the same class use local variables for a similar purpose, it is not appropriate to define them as fields if their values don't need to persist beyond the end of the methods.

In the **refundBalance** method, **amountToRefund** is used briefly to hold the value of the **balance** immediately prior to the latter being set to zero. The method then returns the remembered value of the balance. The following exercises will help to illustrate why a local variable is needed here, as we try to write the **refundBalance** method without one.

It is quite common to initialize local variables within their declaration. So we could abbreviate the first two statements of **refundBalance** as

```
int amountToRefund = balance;
```

but it is still important to keep in mind that there are two steps going on here: declaring the variable **amountToRefund**, and giving it an initial value.

Pitfall A local variable of the same name as a field will prevent the field being accessed from within a constructor or method. See Section 3.13.2 for a way around this when necessary.

Exercise 2.58 Why does the following version of **refundBalance** not give the same results as the original?

```
public int refundBalance()
{
    balance = 0;
    return balance;
}
```

What tests can you run to demonstrate that it does not?

Exercise 2.59 What happens if you try to compile the `TicketMachine` class with the following version of `refundBalance`?

```
public int refundBalance()
{
    return balance;
    balance = 0;
}
```

What do you know about return statements that helps to explain why this version does not compile?

Exercise 2.60 What is wrong with the following version of the constructor of `TicketMachine`?

```
public TicketMachine(int cost)
{
    int price = cost;
    balance = 0;
    total = 0;
}
```

Try out this version in the *better-ticket-machine* project. Does this version compile? Create an object and then inspect its fields. Do you notice something wrong about the value of the `price` field in the inspector with this version? Can you explain why this is?

2.17 Fields, parameters, and local variables

With the introduction of **amountToRefund** in the `refundBalance` method, we have now seen three different kinds of variables: fields, formal parameters, and local variables. It is important to understand the similarities and differences between these three kinds. Here is a summary of their features:

■ All three kinds of variables are able to store a value that is appropriate to their defined types. For instance, a defined type of `int` allows a variable to store an integer value.

■ Fields are defined outside constructors and methods.

■ Fields are used to store data that persist throughout the life of an object. As such, they maintain the current state of an object. They have a lifetime that lasts as long as their object lasts.

■ Fields have class scope: they are accessible throughout the whole class, so they can be used within any of the constructors or methods of the class in which they are defined.

- As long as they are defined as **private**, fields cannot be accessed from anywhere outside their defining class.

- Formal parameters and local variables persist only for the period that a constructor or method executes. Their lifetime is only as long as a single call, so their values are lost between calls. As such, they act as temporary rather than permanent storage locations.

- Formal parameters are defined in the header of a constructor or method. They receive their values from outside, being initialized by the actual parameter values that form part of the constructor or method call.

- Formal parameters have a scope that is limited to their defining constructor or method.

- Local variables are defined inside the body of a constructor or method. They can be initialized and used only within the body of their defining constructor or method. Local variables must be initialized before they are used in an expression—they are not given a default value.

- Local variables have a scope that is limited to the block in which they are defined. They are not accessible from anywhere outside that block.

New programmers often find it difficult to work out whether a variable should be defined as a field or as a local variable. Temptation is to define all variables as fields, because they can be accessed from anywhere in the class. In fact, the opposite approach is a much better rule to adopt: define variables local to a method unless they are clearly a genuine part of an object's persistent state. Even if you anticipate using the same variable in two or more methods, define a separate version locally to each method until you are absolutely sure that persistence between method calls is justified.

Exercise 2.61 Add a new method, **emptyMachine**, that is designed to simulate emptying the machine of money. It should reset **total** to be zero, but also return the value that was stored in **total** before it was reset.

Exercise 2.62 Rewrite the **printTicket** method so that it declares a local variable, **amountLeftToPay**. This should then be initialized to contain the difference between **price** and **balance**. Rewrite the test in the conditional statement to check the value of **amountLeftToPay**. If its value is less than or equal to zero, a ticket should be printed; otherwise, an error message should be printed stating the amount left to pay. Test your version to ensure that it behaves in exactly the same way as the original version. Make sure that you call the method more than once, when the machine is in different states, so that both parts of the conditional statement will be executed on separate occasions.

Exercise 2.63 *Challenge exercise* Suppose we wished a single **TicketMachine** object to be able to issue tickets of different prices. For instance, users might press a button on the physical machine to select a discounted ticket price. What further methods and/or fields would need to be added to **TicketMachine** to allow this kind of functionality? Do you think that many of the existing methods would need to be changed as well?

Save the *better-ticket-machine* project under a new name, and implement your changes in the new project.

2.18 Summary of the better ticket machine

In developing a better version of the **TicketMachine** class, we have been able to address the major inadequacies of the naïve version. In doing so, we have introduced two new language constructs: the conditional statement and local variables.

■ A conditional statement gives us a means to perform a test and then, on the basis of the result of that test, perform one or the other of two distinct actions.

■ Local variables allow us to calculate and store temporary values within a constructor or method. They contribute to the behavior that their defining method implements, but their values are lost once that constructor or method finishes its execution.

You can find more details of conditional statements and the form their tests can take in Appendix D.

2.19 Self-review exercises

This chapter has covered a lot of new ground, and we have introduced a lot of new concepts. We will be building on these in future chapters, so it is important that you are comfortable with them. Try the following pencil-and-paper exercises as a way of checking that you are becoming used to the terminology that we have introduced in this chapter. Don't be put off by the fact that we suggest that you do these on paper rather than within BlueJ. It will be good practice to try things out without a compiler.

Exercise 2.64 List the name and return type of this method:

```
public String getCode()
{
    return code;
}
```

Exercise 2.65 List the name of this method and the name and type of its parameter:

```
public void setCredits(int creditValue)
{
    credits = creditValue;
}
```

Exercise 2.66 Write out the outer wrapping of a class called **Person**. Remember to include the curly brackets that mark the start and end of the class body, but otherwise leave the body empty.

Exercise 2.67 Write out definitions for the following fields:

- a field called **name** of type **String**
- a field of type **int** called **age**
- a field of type **String** called **code**
- a field called **credits** of type **int**

Exercise 2.68 Write out a constructor for a class called **Module**. The constructor should take a single parameter of type **String** called **moduleCode**. The body of the constructor should assign the value of its parameter to a field called **code**. You don't have to include the definition for **code**, just the text of the constructor.

Exercise 2.69 Write out a constructor for a class called **Person**. The constructor should take two parameters. The first is of type **String** and is called **myName**. The second is of type **int** and is called **myAge**. The first parameter should be used to set the value of a field called **name**, and the second should set a field called **age**. You don't have to include the definitions for the fields, just the text of the constructor.

Exercise 2.70 Correct the error in this method:

```
public void getAge()
{
    return age;
}
```

Exercise 2.71 Write an accessor method called **getName** that returns the value of a field called **name**, whose type is **String**.

Exercise 2.72 Write a mutator method called **setAge** that takes a single parameter of type **int** and sets the value of a field called **age**.

Exercise 2.73 Write a method called **printDetails** for a class that has a field of type **String** called **name**. The **printDetails** method should print out a string of the form "The name of this person is", followed by the value of the **name** field. For instance, if the value of the **name** field is "Helen", then **printDetails** would print:

```
The name of this person is Helen
```

If you have managed to complete most or all of these exercises, then you might like to try creating a new project in BlueJ and making up your own class definition for a **Person**. The class could have fields to record the name and age of a person, for instance. If you were unsure how to complete any of the previous exercises, look back over earlier sections in this chapter and the source code of **TicketMachine** to revise what you were unclear about. In the next section, we provide some further review material.

2.20 Reviewing a familiar example

By this point in the chapter, you have met a lot of new concepts. To help reinforce them, we shall now revisit a few in a different but familiar context. Along the way, though, watch out for one or two further new concepts that we will then cover in more detail in later chapters!

Open the *lab-classes* project that we introduced in Chapter 1, and then examine the **Student** class in the editor (Code 2.9).

Code 2.9
The **Student** class

```
/**
 * The Student class represents a student in a student administration system.
 * It holds the student details relevant in our context.
 *
 * @author Michael Kölling and David Barnes
 * @version 2016.02.29
 */
public class Student
{
    // the student's full name
    private String name;
    // the student ID
    private String id;
    // the amount of credits for study taken so far
    private int credits;
```

Code 2.9
continued
The **Student**
class

```
/**
 * Create a new student with a given name and ID number.
 */
public Student(String fullName, String studentID)
{
    name = fullName;
    id = studentID;
    credits = 0;
}

/**
 * Return the full name of this student.
 */
public String getName()
{
    return name;
}

/**
 * Set a new name for this student.
 */
public void changeName(String replacementName)
{
    name = replacementName;
}

/**
 * Return the student ID of this student.
 */
public String getStudentID()
{
    return id;
}

/**
 * Add some credit points to the student's accumulated credits.
 */
public void addCredits(int additionalPoints)
{
    credits += additionalPoints;
}

/**
 * Return the number of credit points this student has accumulated.
 */
public int getCredits()
{
    return credits;
}

/**
 * Return the login name of this student. The login name is a combination
 * of the first four characters of the student's name and the first three
 * characters of the student's ID number.
 */
```

**Code 2.9
continued**

The **Student**
class

```
public String getLoginName()
{
    return name.substring(0,4) + id.substring(0,3);
}

/**
 * Print the student's name and ID number to the output terminal.
 */
public void print()
{
    System.out.println(name + ", student ID: " + id + ", credits: " + credits);
}
}
```

In this small example, the pieces of information we wish to store for a student are their name, their student ID, and the number of course credits they have obtained so far. All of this information is persistent during their time as a student, even if some of it changes during that time (the number of credits). We want to store this information in fields, therefore, to represent each student's state.

The class contains three fields: **name**, **id**, and **credits**. Each of these is initialized in the single constructor. The initial values of the first two are set from parameter values passed into the constructor. Each of the fields has an associated **get** accessor method, but only **name** and **credits** have associated mutator methods. This means that the value of an **id** field remains fixed once the object has been constructed. If a field's value cannot be changed once initialized, we say that it is *immutable*. Sometimes we make the complete state of an object immutable once it has been constructed; the **String** class is an important example of this.

2.21 Calling methods

The **getLoginName** method illustrates a new feature that is worth exploring:

```
public String getLoginName()
{
    return name.substring(0,4) +
           id.substring(0,3);
}
```

We are seeing two things in action here:

- Calling a method on another object, where the method returns a result.

- Using the value returned as a result as part of an expression.

Both **name** and **id** are **String** objects, and the **String** class has a method, **substring**, with the following header:

```
/**
 * Return a new string containing the characters from
 * beginIndex to (endIndex-1) from this string.
 */
public String substring(int beginIndex, int endIndex)
```

An index value of zero represents the first character of a string, so **getLoginName** takes the first four characters of the **name** string and the first three characters of the **id** string, then concatenates them together to form a new string. This new string is returned as the method's result. For instance, if **name** is the string **"Leonardo da Vinci"** and **id** is the string **"468366"**, then the string **"Leon468"** would be returned by this method.

We will learn more about method calling between objects in Chapter 3.

Exercise 2.74 Draw a picture of the form shown in Figure 2.3, representing the initial state of a **Student** object following its construction, with the following actual parameter values:

```
new Student("Benjamin Jonson", "738321")
```

Exercise 2.75 What would be returned by **getLoginName** for a student with name **"Henry Moore"** and id **"557214"**?

Exercise 2.76 Create a **Student** with name **"djb"** and id **"859012"**. What happens when **getLoginName** is called on this student? Why do you think this is?

Exercise 2.77 The **String** class defines a **length** accessor method with the following header:

```
/**
 * Return the number of characters in this string.
 */
public int length()
```

so the following is an example of its use with the **String** variable **fullName**:

```
fullName.length()
```

Add conditional statements to the constructor of **Student** to print an error message if either the length of the **fullName** parameter is less than four characters, or the length of the **studentId** parameter is less than three characters. However, the constructor should still use those parameters to set the **name** and **id** fields, even if the error message is printed. *Hint:* Use if-statements of the following form (that is, having no **else** part) to print the error messages.

```
if(perform a test on one of the parameters) {
    Print an error message if the test gave a true result
}
```

See Appendix D for further details of the different types of if-statements, if necessary.

Exercise 2.78 *Challenge exercise* Modify the **getLoginName** method of **Student** so that it always generates a login name, even if either the **name** or the **id** field is not strictly long enough. For strings shorter than the required length, use the whole string.

2.22 Experimenting with expressions: the Code Pad

In the previous sections, we have seen various expressions to achieve various computations, such as the `total + price` calculation in the ticket machine and the `name.substring(0,4)` expression in the **Student** class.

In the remainder of this book, we shall encounter many more such operations, sometimes written with operator symbols (such as "+") and sometimes written as method calls (such as **substring**). When we encounter new operators and methods, it often helps to try out with different examples what they do.

The Code Pad, which we briefly used in Chapter 1, can help us experiment with Java expressions (Figure 2.5). Here, we can type in expressions, which will then be immediately evaluated and the results displayed. This is very helpful for trying out new operators and methods.

> **Exercise 2.79** Consider the following expressions. Try to predict their results, and then type them in the Code Pad to check your answers.
>
> ```
> 99 + 3
> "cat" + "fish"
> "cat" + 9
> 9 + 3 + "cat"
> "cat" + 3 + 9
> "catfish".substring(3,4)
> "catfish".substring(3,8)
> ```
>
> Did you learn anything you did not expect from the exercise? If so, what was it?

Figure 2.5
The BlueJ Code Pad

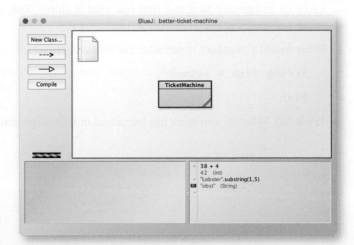

When the result of an expression in the Code Pad is an object (such as a **String**), it will be marked with a small red object symbol next to the line showing the result. You can double-click this symbol to inspect it or drag it onto the object bench for further use. You can also declare variables and write complete statements in the Code Pad.

Whenever you encounter new operators and method calls, it is a good idea to try them out here to get a feel for their behavior.

You can also explore the use of variables in the Code Pad. Try the following:

```
sum = 99 + 3;
```

You will see the following error message:

```
Error: cannot find symbol - variable sum
```

This is because Java requires that every variable (**sum**, in this case) be given a type before it can be used. Recall that every time a field, parameter, or local variable has been introduced for the first time in the source, it has had a type name in front of it, such as **int** or **String**. In light of this, now try the following in the Code Pad:

```
int sum = 0;

sum = 99 + 3;
```

This time there is no complaint, because **sum** has been introduced with a type and can be used without repeating the type thereafter. If you then type

```
sum
```

on a line by itself (with no semicolon), you will see the value it currently stores.

Now try this in the Code Pad:

```
String swimmer = "cat" + "fish";

swimmer
```

One again, we have given an appropriate type to the variable **swimmer**, allowing us to make an assignment to it and find out what it stores. This time we chose to set it to the value we wanted at the same time as declaring it.

What would you expect to see after the following?

```
String fish = swimmer;

fish
```

Try it out. What do you think has happened in the assignment?

Exercise 2.80 Open the Code Pad in the *better-ticket-machine* project. Type the following in the Code Pad:

```
TicketMachine t1 = new TicketMachine(1000);

t1.getBalance()

t1.insertMoney(500);

t1.getBalance()
```

Take care to type these lines exactly as they appear here; pay particular attention to whether or not there is a semicolon at the end of the line. Note what the calls to **getBalance** return in each case.

Exercise 2.81 Now add the following in the Code Pad:

```
TicketMachine t2 = t1;
```

What would you expect a call to **t2.getBalance()** to return? Try it out.

Exercise 2.82 Add the following:

```
t1.insertMoney(500);
```

What would you expect the following to return? Think carefully about this before you try it, and be sure to use the **t2** variable this time.

```
t2.getBalance()
```

Did you get the answer you expected? Can you find a connection between the variables **t1** and **t2** that would explain what is happening?

2.23 Summary

In this chapter, we have covered the basics of how to create a class definition. Classes contain fields, constructors, and methods that define the state and behavior of objects. Within the body of a constructor or method, a sequence of statements implements that part of its behavior. Local variables can be used as temporary data storage to assist with that. We have covered assignment statements and conditional statements, and will be adding further types of statements in later chapters.

Terms introduced in this chapter:

field, instance variable, constructor, method, method header, method body, actual parameter, formal parameter, accessor, mutator, declaration, initialization, block, statement, assignment statement, conditional statement, return statement, return type, comment, expression, operator, variable, local variable, scope, lifetime

Concept summary

- **object creation** Some objects cannot be constructed unless extra information is provided.

- **field** Fields store data for an object to use. Fields are also known as instance variables.

- **comment** Comments are inserted into the source code of a class to provide explanations to human readers. They have no effect on the functionality of the class.

- **constructor** Constructors allow each object to be set up properly when it is first created.

- **scope** The scope of a variable defines the section of source code from which the variable can be accessed.

- **lifetime** The lifetime of a variable describes how long the variable continues to exist before it is destroyed.

- **assignment statement** Assignment statements store the value represented by the right-hand side of the statement in the variable named on the left.

- **accessor method** Accessor methods return information about the state of an object.

- **mutator method** Mutator methods change the state of an object.

- **println** The method **System.out.println** prints its parameter to the text terminal.

- **conditional statement** A conditional statement takes one of two possible actions based upon the result of a test.

- **boolean expression** Boolean expressions have only two possible values: true and false. They are commonly found controlling the choice between the two paths through a conditional statement.

- **local variable** A local variable is a variable declared and used within a single method. Its scope and lifetime are limited to that of the method.

The following exercises are designed to help you experiment with the concepts of Java that we have discussed in this chapter. You will create your own classes that contain elements such as fields, constructors, methods, assignment statements, and conditional statements.

Exercise 2.83

Below is the outline for a **Book** class, which can be found in the *book-exercise* project. The outline already defines two fields and a constructor to initialize the fields. In this and the next few exercises, you will add features to the class outline.

Add two accessor methods to the class—**getAuthor** and **getTitle**—that return the **author** and **title** fields as their respective results. Test your class by creating some instances and calling the methods.

```
/**
 * A class that maintains information on a book.
 * This might form part of a larger application such
 * as a library system, for instance.
 *
 * @author (Insert your name here.)
 * @version (Insert today's date here.)
 */

public class Book

{
    // The fields.
    private String author;
    private String title;

    /**
     * Set the author and title fields when this object
     * is constructed.
     */
    public Book(String bookAuthor, String bookTitle)

    {
        author = bookAuthor;
        title = bookTitle;
    }

    // Add the methods here...

}
```

Exercise 2.84 Add two methods, **printAuthor** and **printTitle**, to the outline **Book** class. These should print the **author** and **title** fields, respectively, to the terminal window.

Exercise 2.85 Add a field, **pages**, to the **Book** class to store the number of pages. This should be of type **int**, and its initial value should be passed to the single constructor, along with the **author** and **title** strings. Include an appropriate **getPages** accessor method for this field.

Exercise 2.86 Are the **Book** objects you have implemented immutable? Justify your answer.

Exercise 2.87 Add a method, `printDetails`, to the **Book** class. This should print details of the author, title, and pages to the terminal window. It is your choice how the details are formatted. For instance, all three items could be printed on a single line, or each could be printed on a separate line. You might also choose to include some explanatory text to help a user work out which is the author and which is the title, for example

```
Title: Robinson Crusoe, Author: Daniel Defoe, Pages: 232
```

Exercise 2.88 Add a further field, `refNumber`, to the **Book** class. This field can store a reference number for a library, for example. It should be of type **String** and initialized to the zero length string (`""`) in the constructor, as its initial value is not passed in a parameter to the constructor. Instead, define a mutator for it with the following header:

```
public void setRefNumber(String ref)
```

The body of this method should assign the value of the parameter to the `refNumber` field. Add a corresponding **getRefNumber** accessor to help you check that the mutator works correctly.

Exercise 2.89 Modify your `printDetails` method to include printing the reference number. However, the method should print the reference number only if it has been set—that is, if the **refNumber** string has a non-zero length. If it has not been set, then print the string **"ZZZ"** instead. *Hint:* Use a conditional statement whose test calls the `length` method on the **refNumber** string.

Exercise 2.90 Modify your `setRefNumber` mutator so that it sets the `refNumber` field only if the parameter is a string of at least three characters. If it is less than three, then print an error message and leave the field unchanged.

Exercise 2.91 Add a further integer field, **borrowed**, to the **Book** class. This keeps a count of the number of times a book has been borrowed. Add a mutator, **borrow**, to the class. This should update the field by 1 each time it is called. Include an accessor, **getBorrowed**, that returns the value of this new field as its result. Modify **printDetails** so that it includes the value of this field with an explanatory piece of text.

Exercise 2.92 Add a further **boolean** field, **courseText**, to the **Book** class. This records whether or not a book is being used as a text book on a course. The field should be set through a parameter to the constructor, and the field is immutable. Provide an accessor method for it called **isCourseText**.

Exercise 2.93 *Challenge exercise* Create a new project, *heater-exercise*, within BlueJ. Edit the details in the project description—the text note you see in the diagram. Create a class, **Heater**, that contains a single field, **temperature** whose type is *double-precision floating point*—see Appendix B, Section B.1, for the Java type name that corresponds to this description. Define a constructor that takes no parameters. The **temperature** field should be set to the value 15.0 in the constructor. Define the mutators **warmer** and **cooler**, whose effect is to increase or decrease the value of temperature by 5.0° respectively. Define an accessor method to return the value of **temperature**.

Exercise 2.94 *Challenge exercise* Modify your **Heater** class to define three new *double-precision floating point* fields: **min**, **max**, and **increment**. The values of **min** and **max** should be set by parameters passed to the constructor. The value of **increment** should be set to 5.0 in the constructor. Modify the definitions of **warmer** and **cooler** so that they use the value of **increment** rather than an explicit value of 5.0. Before proceeding further with this exercise, check that everything works as before.

Now modify the **warmer** method so that it will not allow the temperature to be set to a value greater than **max**. Similarly modify **cooler** so that it will not allow **temperature** to be set to a value less than **min**. Check that the class works properly. Now add a method, **setIncrement**, that takes a single parameter of the appropriate type and uses it to set the value of **increment**. Once again, test that the class works as you would expect it to by creating some **Heater** objects within BlueJ. Do things still work as expected if a negative value is passed to the **setIncrement** method? Add a check to this method to prevent a negative value from being assigned to **increment**.

In the previous chapters, we have examined what objects are and how they are implemented. In particular, we discussed fields, constructors, and methods when we looked at class definitions.

We shall now go one step further. To construct interesting applications, it is not enough to build individual working objects. Instead, objects must be combined so that they cooperate to perform a common task. In this chapter, we shall build a small application from three objects and arrange for methods to call other methods to achieve their goal.

3.1 The clock example

The project we shall use to discuss interaction of objects is a display for a digital clock. The display shows hours and minutes, separated by a colon (Figure 3.1). For this exercise, we shall first build a clock with a European-style 24-hour display. Thus, the display shows the time from 00:00 (midnight) to 23:59 (one minute before midnight). It turns out on closer inspection that building a 12-hour clock is slightly more difficult than a 24-hour clock; we shall leave this until the end of the chapter.

Figure 3.1
A display of a digital clock

11:03

3.2 Abstraction and modularization

A first idea might be to implement the whole clock display in a single class. That is, after all, what we have seen so far: how to build classes to do a job.

However, here we shall approach this problem slightly differently. We will see whether we can identify subcomponents in the problem that we can turn into separate classes. The reason is *complexity*. As we progress in this book, the examples we use and the programs we build will get more and more complex. Trivial tasks such as the ticket machine can be solved as a single problem. You can look at the complete task and devise a solution using a single class. For more complex problems, that, is too simplistic. As a problem grows larger, it becomes increasingly difficult to keep track of all details at the same time.

The solution we use to deal with the complexity problem is *abstraction*. We divide the problem into sub-problems, then again into sub-sub-problems, and so on, until the individual problems are small enough to be easy to deal with. Once we solve one of the sub-problems, we do not think about the details of that part any more, but treat the solution as a single building block for our next problem. This technique is sometimes referred to as *divide and conquer*.

Let us discuss this with an example. Imagine engineers in a car company designing a new car. They may think about the parts of the car, such as the shape of the outer body, the size and location of the engine, the number and size of the seats in the passenger area, the exact spacing of the wheels, and so on. Another engineer, on the other hand, whose job is to design the engine (team of), think of the many parts of an engine: the cylinders, the injection mechanism, the carburetor, the electronics, etc. They will think of the engine not as a single entity, but as a complex work of many parts. One of these parts may be a spark plug.

Then there is an engineer (maybe in a different company) who designs the spark plug. He will think of the spark plug as a complex artifact of many parts. He might have conducted complex studies to determine exactly what kind of metal to use for the contacts, or what kind of material and production process to use for the insulation.

The same is true for many other parts. A designer at the highest level will regard a wheel as a single part. Another engineer much further down the chain may spend her days thinking about the chemical composition necessary to produce the right materials to make the tires. For the tire engineer, the tire is a complex thing. The car company will just buy the tire from the tire company and then view it as a single entity. This is abstraction.

The engineer in the car company *abstracts from* the details of the tire manufacture to be able to concentrate on the details of the construction of, say, the wheel. The designer designing the body shape of the car abstracts from the technical details of the wheels and the engine to concentrate on the design of the body (he will just be interested in the size of the engine and the wheels).

The same is true for every other component. While someone might be concerned with designing the interior passenger space, someone else may work on developing the fabric that will eventually be used to cover the seats.

The point is, if viewed in enough detail, a car consists of so many parts that it is practically impossible for a single person to know every detail about every part at the same time. If that were necessary, no car could ever be built.

The reason why cars are successfully built is that the engineers use *modularization* and abstraction. They divide the car into independent modules (wheel, engine, gear box, seat, steering wheel, etc.) and get separate people to work on separate modules independently. When a module is built, they use abstraction. They view that module as a single component that is used to build more-complex components.

Modularization and abstraction thus complement each other. Modularization is the process of dividing large things (problems) into smaller parts, while abstraction is the process of ignoring details to focus on the bigger picture.

3.3 Abstraction in software

The same principles of modularization and abstraction discussed in the previous section are used in software development. To help us maintain an overview in complex programs, we try to identify subcomponents that we can program as independent entities. Then we try to use those subcomponents as if they were simple parts, without being concerned about their inner complexities.

In object-oriented programming, these components and subcomponents are objects. If we were trying to construct a car in software, using an object-oriented language, we would try to do what the car engineers do. Instead of implementing the car as a single, monolithic object, we would first construct separate objects for an engine, gearbox, wheel, seat, and so on, and then assemble the car object from those smaller objects.

Identifying what kinds of objects (and with these, classes) you should have in a software system for any given problem is not always easy, and we shall have a lot more to say about that later in this book. For now, we shall start with a relatively simple example. Now, back to our digital clock.

3.4 Modularization in the clock example

Let us have a closer look at the clock-display example. Using the abstraction concepts we have just described, we want to try to find the best way to view this example so that we can write some classes to implement it. One way to look at it is to consider it as consisting of a single display with four digits (two digits for the hours, two for the minutes). If we now abstract away from that very low-level view, we can see that it could also be viewed as two separate two-digit displays (one pair for the hours and one pair for the minutes). One pair starts at 0, increases by 1 each hour, and rolls back to 0 after reaching its limit of 23. The other rolls back to 0 after reaching its limit of 59. The similarity in behavior of these two displays might then lead us to abstract away even further from viewing the hours display and minutes display distinctly. Instead, we might think of them as being objects that can display values from zero up to a given limit. The value can be incremented, but, if the value reaches the limit, it rolls over to zero. Now we seem to have reached an appropriate level of abstraction that we can represent as a class: a two-digit display class.

Figure 3.2
A two-digit number display

For our clock display, we shall first program a class for a two-digit number display (Figure 3.2), then give it an accessor method to get its value, and two mutator methods to set the value and to increment it. Once we have defined this class, we can just create two objects of the class with different limits to construct the entire clock display.

3.5 Implementing the clock display

As discussed above, in order to build the clock display, we will first build a two-digit number display. This display needs to store two values. One is the limit to which it can count before rolling over to zero. The other is the current value. We shall represent both of these as integer fields in our class (Code 3.1).

Code 3.1
Class for a two-digit number display

```
public class NumberDisplay
{
    private int limit;
    private int value;

    Constructor and methods omitted.

}
```

> **Concept**
>
> **Classes define types.** A class name can be used as the type for a variable. Variables that have a class as their type can store objects of that class.

We shall look at the remaining details of this class later. First, let us assume that we can build the class **NumberDisplay**, and then let us think a bit more about the complete clock display. We would build a complete clock display by having an object that has, internally, two number displays (one for the hours, and one for the minutes). Each of the number displays would be a field in the clock display (Code 3.2). Here, we make use of a detail that we have not mentioned before: *classes define types*.

Code 3.2
The **Clock-Display** class containing two **NumberDisplay** fields

```
public class ClockDisplay
{
    private NumberDisplay hours;
    private NumberDisplay minutes;

    Constructor and methods omitted.

}
```

When we discussed fields in Chapter 2, we said that the word "private" in the field declaration is followed by a type and a name for the field. Here we use the class **NumberDisplay** as the type for the fields named **hours** and **minutes**. This shows that class names can be used as types.

The type of a field specifies what kind of values can be stored in the field. If the type is a class, the field can hold objects of that class. Declaring a field or other variable of a class type does not automatically create an object of that type; instead, the field is initially empty. We do not yet have a **NumberDisplay** object. The associated object will have to be created explicitly, and we shall see how this is done when we look at the constructor of the **ClockDisplay** class.

3.6 Class diagrams versus object diagrams

The structure described in the previous section (one **ClockDisplay** object holding two **NumberDisplay** objects) can be visualized in an *object diagram* as shown in Figure 3.3a. In this diagram, you see that we are dealing with three objects. Figure 3.3b shows the *class diagram* for the same situation.

Note that the class diagram shows only two classes, whereas the object diagram shows three objects. This has to do with the fact that we can create multiple objects from the same class. Here, we create two **NumberDisplay** objects from the **NumberDisplay** class.

These two diagrams offer different views of the same application. The class diagram shows the *static view*. It depicts what we have at the time of writing the program. We have two classes, and the arrow indicates that the class **ClockDisplay** makes use of the class **NumberDisplay** (**NumberDisplay** is mentioned in the source code of **ClockDisplay**). We also say that **ClockDisplay** *depends on* **NumberDisplay**.

To start the program, we will create an object of class **ClockDisplay**. We will program the clock display so that it automatically creates two **NumberDisplay** objects for itself. Thus, the object diagram shows the situation at *runtime* (when the application is running). This is also called the *dynamic view*.

The object diagram also shows another important detail: when a variable stores an object, the object is not stored in the variable directly, but rather an *object reference* is stored in the variable. In the diagram, the variable is shown as a white box, and the object reference is shown as an arrow. The object referred to is stored outside the referring object, and the object reference links the two.

Figure 3.3
Object diagram and class diagram for the **ClockDisplay**

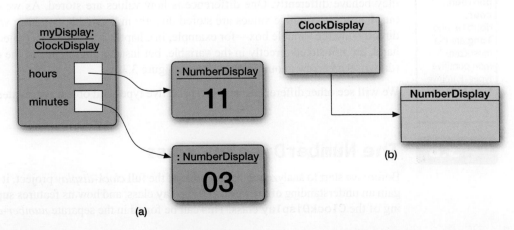

It is very important to understand these two different diagrams and different views. BlueJ displays only the static view. You see the class diagram in its main window. In order to plan and understand Java programs, you need to be able to construct object diagrams on paper or in your head. When we think about what our program will do, we think about the object structures it creates and how these objects interact. Being able to visualize the object structures is essential.

Exercise 3.1 Think again about the *lab-classes* project that we discussed in Chapter 1 and Chapter 2. Imagine that we create a **LabClass** object and three **Student** objects. We then enroll all three students in that lab. Try to draw a class diagram and an object diagram for that situation. Identify and explain the differences between them.

Exercise 3.2 At what time(s) can a class diagram change? How is it changed?

Exercise 3.3 At what time(s) can an object diagram change? How is it changed?

Exercise 3.4 Write a definition of a field named **tutor** that can hold a reference to an object of type **Instructor**.

3.7 Primitive types and object types

Java knows two very different kinds of type: *primitive types* and *object types*. Primitive types are all predefined in the Java language. They include **int** and **boolean**. A complete list of primitive types is given in Appendix B. Object types are those defined by classes. Some classes are defined by the standard Java system (such as **String**); others are those classes we write ourselves.

Both primitive types and object types can be used as types, but there are situations in which they behave differently. One difference is how values are stored. As we could see from our diagrams, primitive values are stored directly in a variable (we have written the value directly into the variable box—for example, in Chapter 2, Figure 2.3). Objects, on the other hand, are not stored directly in the variable, but instead a reference to the object is stored (drawn as an arrow in our diagrams, as in Figure 3.3a).

We will see other differences between primitive types and object types later.

3.8 The NumberDisplay class

Before we start to analyze the source code of the full *clock-display* project, it will help if you gain an understanding of the **NumberDisplay** class, and how its features support the building of the **ClockDisplay** class. This can be found in the separate *number-display* project.

Code 3.3 shows the complete source code of the class **NumberDisplay**. Overall, this class is fairly straightforward, although it does illustrate a few new features of Java. It has the two fields discussed above (Section 3.5), one constructor, and four methods (**getValue**, **setValue**, **getDisplayValue**, and **increment**).

Code 3.3

Implementation of the **Number-Display** class

```
/**
 * The NumberDisplay class represents a digital number display that can hold
 * values from zero to a given limit. The limit can be specified when creating
 * the display. The values range from zero (inclusive) to limit-1. If used,
 * for example, for the seconds on a digital clock, the limit would be 60,
 * resulting in display values from 0 to 59. When incremented, the display
 * automatically rolls over to zero when reaching the limit.
 *
 * @author Michael Kölling and David J. Barnes
 * @version 2016.02.29
 */
public class NumberDisplay
{
    private int limit;
    private int value;

    /**
     * Constructor for objects of class NumberDisplay.
     * Set the limit at which the display rolls over.
     */
    public NumberDisplay(int rollOverLimit)
    {
        limit = rollOverLimit;
        value = 0;
    }

    /**
     * Return the current value.
     */
    public int getValue()
    {
        return value;
    }

    /**
     * Return the display value (that is, the current value as a two-digit
     * String. If the value is less than ten, it will be padded with a leading
     * zero).
     */
    public String getDisplayValue()
    {
        if(value < 10) {
            return "0" + value;
        }
        else {
            return "" + value;
        }
    }
```

Code 3.3

Implementation of the **Number-Display** class

```java
/**
 * Set the value of the display to the new specified value. If the new
 * value is less than zero or over the limit, do nothing.
 */
public void setValue(int replacementValue)
{
    if((replacementValue >= 0) && (replacementValue < limit)) {
        value = replacementValue;
    }
}

/**
 * Increment the display value by one, rolling over to zero if the
 * limit is reached.
 */
public void increment()
{
    value = (value + 1) % limit;
}
}
```

Exercise 3.5 Open the *number-display* project. Select *Show Terminal* from the *View* menu and select *Record method calls*, as you did with the *figures* project in Chapter 1. This will allow you to see the result of your interactions with objects, which will be useful when we look in detail at the full *clock-display* project. Now create a **NumberDisplay** object and give it the name hours, rather than using the default name offered by BlueJ. Use a rollover limit of 24. Open an inspector window for this object. With the inspector open, call the object's **increment** method. Note what is shown in the Terminal window. Repeatedly call the **increment** method until the value in the inspector rolls over to zero. (If you are feeling impatient, you could always create a **Number-Display** object with a lower limit!)

Exercise 3.6 Create a second **NumberDisplay** object with a limit of 60, and give it the name minutes. Call its **increment** method and note how the method calls are represented in the Terminal window. Imagine that the hours and minutes objects on the object bench represent the two **NumberDisplay** objects managed by a **ClockDisplay** object. In effect, you are now performing the role of the **ClockDisplay** object. What should you do each time you call **increment** on minutes to decide whether it has rolled over and whether **increment** should therefore be called on the hours object?

Exercise 3.7 Select *Show Code Pad* from the *View* menu. Create a **Number-Display** object with limit 6 in the Code Pad by typing

```
NumberDisplay nd = new NumberDisplay(6);
```

Then call its **getValue**, **setValue**, and **increment** methods in the Code Pad (e.g., by typing **nd.getValue()**). Note that statements (mutators) need a semi-colon at the end, while expressions (accessors) do not. The call to **setValue** will need to include a numerical parameter value. Use the recorded method calls in the Terminal window to help you with the correct way of writing these method calls.

Exercise 3.8 What error message do you see in the Code Pad if you type the following?

```
NumberDisplay.getValue()
```

Take a careful look at this error message and try to remember it because you will likely encounter something similar on numerous future occasions. Note that the reason for the error is that the class name, **NumberDisplay**, has been used incorrectly to try to call the **getValue** method, rather than the variable name nd.

Exercise 3.9 What error message do you see in the Code Pad if you type the following?

```
nd.setValue(int 5);
```

The error message is not actually very helpful at all. Can you work out what is incorrect about this call to **setValue**, and correct it? It would also be worth remembering this error message because it results from an easy error to make in the early stages of learning.

The constructor receives the roll-over limit as a parameter. If, for example, 24 is passed in as the roll-over limit, the display will roll over to 0 at that value. Thus, the range for the display value would be 0 to 23. This feature allows us to use this class for both hour and minute displays. For the hour display, we will create a **NumberDisplay** with limit 24; for the minute display, we will create one with limit 60. The constructor stores the roll-over limit in a field and sets the current value of the display to 0.

Next follows a simple accessor method for the current display value (**getValue**). This allows other objects to read the current value of the display.

The following sections discuss some new features that have been used in the **setValue**, **getDisplayValue** and **increment** methods.

3.8.1 The logical operators

The following mutator method **setValue** is interesting because it tries to make sure that the starting value of a **NumberDisplay** object is always valid. It reads:

```
public void setValue(int replacementValue)
{
    if((replacementValue >= 0) && (replacementValue < limit)) {
        value = replacementValue;
    }
}
```

Here, we pass the new value for the display as a parameter into the method. However, before we assign the value, we have to check whether the value is legal. The legal range for the value, as discussed above, is zero to one less than the limit. We use an if-statement to check that the value is legal before we assign it. The symbol "**&&**" is a logical "and" operator. It causes the condition in the if-statement to be true if both the conditions on either side of the "**&&**" symbol are true. See the "Logic operators" note that follows for details. Appendix C shows a complete table of logic operators in Java.

Logic operators Logic operators operate on boolean values (true or false) and produce a new boolean value as a result. The three most important logical operators are **and**, **or**, and **not**. They are written in Java as:

&& (and)

|| (or)

! (not)

The expression

a && b

is true if both **a** and **b** are true, and false in all other cases. The expression

a || b

is true if either **a** or **b** or both are true, and false if they are both false. The expression

!a

is true if **a** is false and false if **a** is true.

Exercise 3.10 What happens when the **setValue** method is called with an illegal value? Is this a good solution? Can you think of a better solution?

Exercise 3.11 What would happen if you replaced the "**>=**" operator in the test with "**>**" so that it reads

```
if((replacementValue > 0) && (replacementValue < limit))
```

Exercise 3.12 What would happen if you replaced the **&&** operator in the test with || so that it reads

```
if((replacementValue >= 0) || (replacementValue < limit))
```

Exercise 3.13 Which of the following expressions return *true*?

```
! (4 < 5)
! false
(2 > 2) || ((4 == 4) && (1 < 0))
(2 > 2) || (4 == 4) && (1 < 0)
(34 != 33) && ! false
```

After writing your answers on paper, open the Code Pad in BlueJ and try it out. Check your answers.

Exercise 3.14 Write an expression using boolean variables **a** and **b** that evaluates to *true* when **a** and **b** are either both *true* or both *false*.

Exercise 3.15 Write an expression using boolean variables **a** and **b** that evaluates to *true* when only one of **a** and **b** is *true*, and that is *false* if **a** and **b** are both *false* or both *true*. (This is also called an *exclusive or*.)

Exercise 3.16 Consider the expression (**a && b**). Write an equivalent expression (one that evaluates to *true* at exactly the same values for **a** and **b**) without using the **&&** operator.

3.8.2 String concatenation

The next method, **getDisplayValue**, also returns the display's value, but in a different format. The reason is that we want to display the value as a two-digit string. That is, if the current time is 3:05 a.m., we want the display to read **03:05**, and not **3:5**. To enable us to do this easily, we have implemented the **getDisplayValue** method. This method returns the current value as a string, and it adds a leading 0 if the value is less than 10. Here is the relevant section of the code:

```
if(value < 10) {
    return "0" + value;
}
else {
    return "" + value;
}
```

Note that the zero (**"0"**) is written in double quotes. Thus, we have written the *string* 0, not the *integer number* 0. Then the expression

```
"0" + value
```

"adds" a string and an integer (because the type of **value** is integer). The plus operator, therefore, represents string concatenation again, as seen in Section 2.9. Before continuing, we will now look at string concatenation a little more closely.

The plus operator (**+**) has different meanings, depending on the type of its operands. If both operands are numbers, it represents addition, as we would expect. Thus,

```
42 + 12
```

adds those two numbers, and the result is 54. However, if the operands are strings, then the meaning of the plus sign is string concatenation, and the result is a single string that consists of both operands stuck together. For example, the result of the expression

```
"Java" + "with BlueJ"
```

is the single string

```
"Javawith BlueJ"
```

Note that the system does not automatically add a space between the strings. If you want a space, you have to include it yourself within one of the strings.

If one of the operands of a plus operation is a string and the other is not, then the other operand is automatically converted to a string, and then a string concatenation is performed. Thus,

```
"answer: " + 42
```

results in the string

```
"answer: 42"
```

This works for all types. Whatever type is "added" to a string is automatically converted to a string and then concatenated.

Back to our code in the **getDisplayValue** method. If **value** contains 3, for example, then the statement

```
return "0" + value;
```

will return the string **"03"**. In the case where the value is greater than 9, we have used a little trick:

```
return "" + value;
```

Here, we concatenate **value** with an empty string. The result is that the value will be converted to a string and no other characters will be prefixed to it. We are using the plus operator for the sole purpose of forcing a conversion of the integer value to a value of type **String**.

> **Exercise 3.17** Does the **getDisplayValue** method work correctly in all circumstances? What assumptions are made within it? What happens if you create a number display with limit 800, for instance?

Exercise 3.18 Is there any difference in the result of writing

```
return value + "";
```

rather than

```
return "" + value;
```

in the **getDisplayValue** method?

Exercise 3.19 In Exercise 2.79 you were asked to investigate (among other things) the expressions

```
9 + 3 + "cat"
```

and

```
"cat" + 3 + 9
```

Predict, and then test, the result of these two expressions again. (Did they surprise you?) Explain why the results are what they are.

3.8.3 The modulo operator

The last method in the **NumberDisplay** class increments the display value by 1. It takes care that the value resets to 0 when the limit is reached:

```
public void increment()
{
    value = (value + 1) % limit;
}
```

This method uses the *modulo* operator (%). The modulo operator calculates the remainder of an integer division. For example, the result of the division

```
27 / 4
```

can be expressed in integer numbers as

```
result = 6, remainder = 3
```

The modulo operator returns just the remainder of such a division. Thus, the result of the expression **(27 % 4)** would be **3**.

Exercise 3.20 Explain the modulo operator. You may need to consult more resources (online Java language resources, other Java books, etc.) to find out the details.

Exercise 3.21 What is the result of the expression **(8 % 3)**?

Exercise 3.22 Try out the expression **(8 % 3)** in the Code Pad. Try other numbers. What happens when you use the modulo operator with negative numbers?

Exercise 3.23 What are all possible results of the expression **(n % 5)**, where n is a positive integer variable?

Exercise 3.24 What are all possible results of the expression **(n % m)**, where n and m are positive integer variables?

Exercise 3.25 Explain in detail how the increment method works.

Exercise 3.26 Rewrite the increment method without the modulo operator, using an if-statement. Which solution is better?

3.9 The `ClockDisplay` class

Now that we have seen how we can build a class that defines a two-digit number display, we shall look in more detail at the **ClockDisplay** class—the class that will create two number displays to create a full time display. Code 3.4 shows the complete source code of the **ClockDisplay** class, which can be found in the *clock-display* project.

Code 3.4

Implementation of the **Clock-Display** class

```java
/**
 * The ClockDisplay class implements a digital clock display for a
 * European-style 24 hour clock. The clock shows hours and minutes. The
 * range of the clock is 00:00 (midnight) to 23:59 (one minute before
 * midnight).
 *
 * The clock display receives "ticks" (via the timeTick method) every minute
 * and reacts by incrementing the display. This is done in the usual clock
 * fashion: the hour increments when the minutes roll over to zero.
 *
 * @author Michael Kölling and David J. Barnes
 * @version 2016.02.29
 */
public class ClockDisplay
{
    private NumberDisplay hours;
    private NumberDisplay minutes;
    private String displayString;    // simulates the actual display

    /**
     * Constructor for ClockDisplay objects. This constructor
     * creates a new clock set at 00:00.
     */
    public ClockDisplay()
    {
        hours = new NumberDisplay(24);
        minutes = new NumberDisplay(60);
        updateDisplay();
    }
```

Code 3.4
continued
Implementation
of the **Clock-**
Display class

```java
/**
 * Constructor for ClockDisplay objects. This constructor
 * creates a new clock set at the time specified by the
 * parameters.
 */
public ClockDisplay(int hour, int minute)
{
    hours = new NumberDisplay(24);
    minutes = new NumberDisplay(60);
    setTime(hour, minute);
}

/**
 * This method should get called once every minute - it makes
 * the clock display go one minute forward.
 */
public void timeTick()
{
    minutes.increment();
    if(minutes.getValue() == 0) {  // it just rolled over!
        hours.increment();
    }
    updateDisplay();
}

/**
 * Set the time of the display to the specified hour and
 * minute.
 */
public void setTime(int hour, int minute)
{
    hours.setValue(hour);
    minutes.setValue(minute);
    updateDisplay();
}

/**
 * Return the current time of this display in the format HH:MM.
 */
public String getTime()
{
    return displayString;
}

/**
 * Update the internal string that represents the display.
 */
private void updateDisplay()
{
    displayString = hours.getDisplayValue() + ":" +
                    minutes.getDisplayValue();
}
}
```

Exercise 3.27 Open the *clock-display* project and create a **ClockDisplay** object by selecting the following constructor:

```
new ClockDisplay()
```

Call its **getTime** method to find out the initial time the clock has been set to. Can you work out why it starts at that particular time?

Exercise 3.28 Open an inspector for this object. With the inspector open, call the object's methods. Watch the **displayString** field in the inspector. Read the project comment (by double-clicking the text icon in the class diagram) for more information.

Exercise 3.29 How many times would you need to call the **timeTick** method on a newly created **ClockDisplay** object to make its time reach 01:00? How else could you make it display that time?

In this project, we use the field **displayString** to simulate the actual display device of the clock (as you could see in Exercise 3.28). Were this software to run in a real clock, we would present the output on the real clock display instead. So this string serves as our software simulation for the clock's output device.[1]

In addition to the display string, the **ClockDisplay** class has two more fields: **hours** and **minutes**. Each can hold a reference to an object of type **NumberDisplay**. The logical value of the clock's display (the current time) is stored in these **NumberDisplay** objects. Figure 3.4 shows an object diagram of this application when the current time is 15:23.

Figure 3.4
Object diagram of the clock display

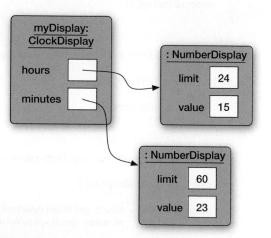

---

[1] The book projects folder also includes a version of this project with a simple graphical user interface (GUI), named *clock-display-with-GUI*. The curious reader may like to experiment with this project; however, it will not be discussed in this book.

3.10	# Objects creating objects

Concept

Object creation. Objects can **create** other **objects**, using the **new** operator.

The first question we have to ask ourselves is: Where do the **NumberDisplay** objects used by the **ClockDisplay** come from? As a *user* of a clock display, when we create a **Clock-Display** object we assume that our clock display has hours and minutes. So by simply creating a clock display, we expect that we have implicitly created two number displays for the hours and minutes.

However, as *writers* of the **ClockDisplay** class, we have to make this happen. To do this, we simply write code in the constructor of the **ClockDisplay** that creates and stores two **NumberDisplay** objects. Because the constructor is automatically executed when a **ClockDisplay** object is created, the **NumberDisplay** objects will automatically be created at the same time. Here is the code of the **ClockDisplay** constructor that makes this work:

```
public class ClockDisplay
{
    private NumberDisplay hours;
    private NumberDisplay minutes;
```

Remaining fields omitted.

```
    public ClockDisplay()
    {
        hours = new NumberDisplay(24);
        minutes = new NumberDisplay(60);
        updateDisplay();
    }
```

Methods omitted.

```
}
```

Each of the first two lines in the constructor creates a new **NumberDisplay** object and assigns it to a variable. The syntax of an operation to create a new object is

```
new ClassName (parameter-list)
```

The **new** operation does two things:

1 It creates a new object of the named class (here, **NumberDisplay**).

2 It executes the constructor of that class.

If the constructor of the class is defined to have parameters, then the actual parameters must be supplied in the new statement. For instance, the constructor of class **NumberDisplay** was defined to expect one integer parameter:

```
public NumberDisplay(int rollOverLimit)
```

Thus, the new operation for the **NumberDisplay** class, which calls this constructor, must provide one actual parameter of type **int** to match the defined constructor header:

```
new NumberDisplay(24);
```

This is the same as for methods discussed in Section 2.5. With this constructor, we have achieved what we wanted: if someone now creates a **ClockDisplay** object, the `ClockDisplay` constructor will automatically execute and create two `NumberDisplay` objects. From the point of view of a user of the `ClockDisplay` class, the creation of the `NumberDisplay` objects is implicit. However, from a writer's point of view, the creation is explicit because they have to write the code to make it happen.

The final statement in the constructor is a call to `updateDisplay` that sets up the `displayString` field. This call is explained in Section 3.12.1. Then the clock display is ready to go.

> **Exercise 3.30** Write Java statements that define a variable named `window` of type `Rectangle`, and then create a `Rectangle` object and assign it to that variable. The `Rectangle` constructor has two `int` parameters.

3.11 Multiple constructors

You might have noticed when you created a `ClockDisplay` object that the pop-up menu offered you two ways to do that:

```
new ClockDisplay()
new ClockDisplay(int hour, int minute)
```

Concept

Overloading. A class may contain more than one constructor, or more than one method of the same name, as long as each has a distinctive set of parameter types.

This is because the `ClockDisplay` class contains two constructors. What they provide are alternative ways of initializing a `ClockDisplay` object. If the constructor with no parameters is used, then the starting time displayed on the clock will be 00:00. If, on the other hand, you want to have a different starting time, you can set that up by using the second constructor. It is common for class definitions to contain alternative versions of constructors or methods that provide various ways of achieving a particular task via their distinctive sets of parameters. This is known as *overloading* a constructor or method.

> **Exercise 3.31** Look at the second constructor in `ClockDisplay`'s source code. Explain what it does and how it does it.
>
> **Exercise 3.32** Identify the similarities and differences between the two constructors. Why is there no call to `updateDisplay` in the second constructor, for instance?

3.12 Method calls

3.12.1 Internal method calls

The last line of the first `ClockDisplay` constructor consists of the statement

```
updateDisplay();
```

Concept

Methods can call other methods of the same class as part of their implementation. This is called an **internal method call**.

This statement is a *method call*. As we have seen above, the **ClockDisplay** class has a method with the following signature:

```
private void updateDisplay()
```

The method call above invokes this method. Because this method is in the same class as the call of the method, we also call it an *internal method call*. Internal method calls have the syntax

```
methodName (parameter-list)
```

An internal method call does not have a variable name and a dot before the method name, which you will have observed in all of the method calls recorded in the Terminal window. A variable is not needed because, with an internal method call, an object calls the method on itself. We contrast internal and external method calls in the next section.

In our example, the method does not have any parameters, so the parameter list is empty. This is signified by the pair of parentheses with nothing between them.

When a method call is encountered, the matching method is executed, and the execution returns to the method call and continues at the next statement after the call. For a method signature to match the method call, both the name and the parameter list of the method must match. Here, both parameter lists are empty, so they match. This need to match against both method name and parameter lists is important, because there may be more than one method of the same name in a class—if that method is overloaded.

In our example, the purpose of this method call is to update the display string. After the two number displays have been created, the display string is set to show the time indicated by the number display objects. The implementation of the **updateDisplay** method will be discussed below.

3.12.2 External method calls

Now let us examine the next method: **timeTick**. The definition is:

```
public void timeTick()
{
    minutes.increment();
    if(minutes.getValue() == 0) { // it just rolled over!
    hours.increment();
    }
    updateDisplay();
}
```

Were this display connected to a real clock, this method would be called once every 60 seconds by the electronic timer of the clock. For now, we just call it ourselves to test the display.

When the **timeTick** method is called, it first executes the statement

```
minutes.increment();
```

This statement calls the **increment** method of the **minutes** object. Thus, when one of the methods of the **ClockDisplay** object is called, it in turn calls a method of another object to do part of the task. A method call to a method of another object is referred to as an *external method call*. The syntax of an external method call is

```
object . methodName ( parameter-list )
```

This syntax is known as *dot notation*. It consists of an object name, a dot, the method name, and parameters for the call. It is particularly important to note that we use the name of an *object* here and not the name of a class. We use the name **minutes** rather than **NumberDisplay**. (This essential principle was illustrated in Exercise 3.8.)

The difference between internal and external method calls is clear—the presence of an object name followed by a dot tells us that the method being called is part of another object. So in the **timeTick** method, the **ClockDisplay** object is asking the **NumberDisplay** objects to carry out part of the overall task. In other words, responsibility for the overall time-keeping task is divided up between the **ClockDisplay** class and the **NumberDisplay** class. This is a practical illustration of the *divide and conquer* principle we referred to earlier in our discussion of abstraction.

> **Concept**
>
> Methods can call methods of other objects using dot notation. This is called an **external method call**.

The **timeTick** method has an if-statement to check whether the hours should also be incremented. As part of the condition in the if-statement, it calls another method of the minutes object: **getValue**. This method returns the current value of the minutes. If that value is zero, then we know that the display just rolled over and we should increment the hours. That is exactly what the code does.

If the value of the minutes is not zero, then we're done. We do not have to change the hours in that case. Thus, the if-statement does not need an *else* part.

We should now also be able to understand the remaining three methods of the **Clock Display** class (see Code 3.4). The method **setTime** takes two parameters—the hour and the minute—and sets the clock to the specified time. Looking at the method body, we can see that it does so by calling the **setValue** methods of both number displays (the one for the hours and the one for the minutes). Then it calls **updateDisplay** to update the display string accordingly, just as the constructor does.

The **getTime** method is trivial—it just returns the current display string. Because we always keep the display string up to date, this is all there is to do.

Finally, the **updateDisplay** method is responsible for updating the display string so that the string correctly reflects the time as represented by the two number display objects. It is called every time the time of the clock changes. Once again, it illustrates external method calls. It works by calling the **getDisplayValue** methods of each of the **NumberDisplay** objects. These methods return the values of each separate number display. The **updateDisplay** method then uses string concatenation to join these two values, separated by a colon, into a single string.

Exercise 3.33 Given a variable

```
Printer p1;
```

which currently holds a reference to a printer object, and two methods inside the **Printer** class with the headers

```
public void print(String filename, boolean doubleSided)
public int getStatus(int delay)
```

write two possible calls to each of these methods.

Exercise 3.34 Open the *house* project from Chapter 1 and review the **Picture** class. What types of object are created by the constructor of **Picture**?

Exercise 3.35 List all of the external method calls that are made in the **draw** method of **Picture** on the **Triangle** object called **roof**.

Exercise 3.36 Does the **Picture** class contain any internal method calls?

Exercise 3.37 Remove the following two statements from the **draw** method of **Picture**:

```
window.changeColor("black");
sun.changeColor("yellow");
```

and make the color setting, instead, via a single call to an internal method called **setColor** (which you need to create).

3.12.3 Summary of the clock display

It is worth looking for a minute at the way this example uses abstraction to divide the problem into smaller parts. Looking at the source code of the class **ClockDisplay**, you will notice that we just create a **NumberDisplay** object without being particularly interested in what that object looks like internally. We can then call methods (**increment**, **getValue**) of that object to make it work for us. At this level, we simply assume that **increment** will correctly increment the display's value, without being concerned with how it does it.

In real-world projects, these different classes are often written by different people. You might already have noticed that all these two people have to agree on is what method signatures the class should have and what they should do. Then one person can concentrate on implementing the methods, while the other person can just use them.

The set of methods an object makes available to other objects is called its *interface*. We shall discuss interfaces in much more detail later in this book.

Exercise 3.38 *Challenge exercise* Change the clock from a 24-hour clock to a 12-hour clock. Be careful: This is not as easy as it might at first seem. In a 12-hour clock, the hours after midnight and after noon are not shown as 00:30, but as 12:30. Thus, the minute display shows values from 0 to 59, while the hour display shows values from 1 to 12!

Exercise 3.39 There are (at least) two ways in which you can make a 12-hour clock. One possibility is to just store hour values from 1 to 12. On the other hand, you can simply leave the clock to work internally as a 24-hour clock but change the display string of the clock display to show **4:23** or **4:23pm** when the internal value is **16:23**. Implement both versions. Which option is easier? Which is better? Why?

Exercise 3.40 Assume a class **Tree** has a field of type **Triangle** called **leaves** and a field of type **Square** called **trunk**. The constructor of **Tree** takes no parameters and its constructor creates the **Triangle** and **Square** objects for its fields. Using the *figures* project from Chapter 1, create a simple **Tree** class to fit this description. You do not need to define any methods in the class and the shapes do not have to be made visible.

Exercise 3.41 *Challenge exercise* Complete the **Tree** class described in the previous exercise, by having the constructor move the trunk square beneath the leaves triangle and then make both shapes visible. Do this by defining a method in the **Tree** class called **setup** and include a call to this method in the constructor of **Tree**. Change the size of the triangle so that it looks more like the leaves of a fir tree growing from the trunk.

3.13   Another example of object interaction

Concept

A **debugger** is a software tool that helps in examining how an application executes. It can be used to find bugs.

We shall now examine the same concepts with a different example, using different tools. We are still concerned with understanding how objects create other objects, and how objects call each other's methods. In the first half of this chapter, we have used the most fundamental technique to analyze a given program: code reading. The ability to read and understand source code is one of the most essential skills for a software developer, and we will need to apply it in every project we work on. However, sometimes it is beneficial to use additional tools in order to help us gain a deeper understanding about how a program executes. One tool we will now look at is a *debugger*.

A debugger is a program that lets programmers execute an application one step at a time. It typically provides functions to stop and start a program at selected points in the source code, and to examine the values of variables.

The name "debugger" Errors in computer programs are commonly known as "bugs." Thus programs that help in the removal of errors are known as "debuggers."

It is not entirely clear where the term "bug" comes from. There is a famous case of what is known as "the first computer bug"—a real bug (a moth, in fact)—which was found inside the Mark II computer by Grace Murray Hopper, an early computing pioneer, in 1945. A logbook still exists in the National Museum of American History of the Smithsonian Institute that shows an entry with this moth taped into the book and the remark "first actual case of bug being found." The wording, however, suggests that the term "bug" had been in use before this real one caused trouble in the Mark II.

To find out more, do a web search for "first computer bug"—you will even find pictures of the moth!

Debuggers vary widely in complexity. Those for professional developers have a large number of functions for sophisticated examination of many facets of an application. BlueJ has a built-in debugger that is much simpler. We can use it to stop our program, step through it one line of code at a time, and examine the values of our variables. Despite the debugger's apparent lack of sophistication, this is enough to give us a great deal of information.

Before we start experimenting with the debugger, we will take a look at the example we will use for debugging: a simulation of an e-mail system.

3.13.1 The mail-system example

We start by investigating the functionality of the *mail-system* project. At this stage, it is not important to read the source, but mainly to execute the existing project to get an understanding of what it does.

Exercise 3.42 Open the *mail-system* project, which you can find in the book's support material. The idea of this project is to simulate the act of users sending mail items to each other. A user uses a mail client to send mail items to a server, for delivery to another user's mail client. First create a **MailServer** object. Now create a **MailClient** object for one of the users. When you create the client, you will need to supply a **MailServer** instance as a parameter. Use the one you just created. You also need to specify a username for the mail client. Now create a second **MailClient** in a similar way, with a different username.

Experiment with the **MailClient** objects. They can be used for sending mail items from one mail client to another (using the **sendMailItem** method) and receiving messages (using the **getNextMailItem** or **printNextMailItem** methods).

Examining the mail system project, we see that:

■ It has three classes: **MailServer**, **MailClient**, and **MailItem**.

- One mail-server object must be created that is used by all mail clients. It handles the exchange of messages.

- Several mail-client objects can be created. Every mail client has an associated user name.

- Mail items can be sent from one mail client to another via a method in the mail-client class.

- Mail items can be received by a mail client from the server one at a time, using a method in the mail client.

- The **MailItem** class is never explicitly instantiated by the user. It is used internally in the mail clients and server to create, store, and exchange messages.

> **Exercise 3.43** Draw an object diagram of the situation you have after creating a mail server and three mail clients. Object diagrams were discussed in Section 3.6.

The three classes have different degrees of complexity. **MailItem** is fairly trivial. We shall discuss only one small detail and leave the rest up to the reader to investigate. **MailServer** is quite complex at this stage; it makes use of concepts discussed only much later in this book. We shall not investigate that class in detail here. Instead, we just trust that it does its job—another example of the way abstraction is used to hide detail that we do not need to be aware of.

The **MailClient** class is the most interesting, and we shall examine it in some detail.

Code 3.5
Fields and constructor of the **MailItem** class

```java
public class MailItem
{
    // The sender of the item.
    private String from;
    // The intended recipient.
    private String to;
    // The text of the message.
    private String message;

    /**
     * Create a mail item from sender to the given recipient,
     * containing the given message.
     * @param from The sender of this item.
     * @param to The intended recipient of this item.
     * @param message The text of the message to be sent.
     */
    public MailItem(String from, String to, String message)
    {
        this.from = from;
        this.to = to;
        this.message = message;
    }

    Methods omitted.

}
```

3.13.2 The this keyword

The only section we will discuss from the **MailItem** class is the constructor. It uses a Java constructor that we have not encountered before. The source code is shown in Code 3.5.

The new Java feature in this code fragment is the use of the **this** keyword:

```
this.from = from;
```

The whole line is an assignment statement. It assigns the value on the right-hand side (**from**) to the variable on the left (**this.from**).

The reason for using this construct is that we have a situation known as *name overloading*—the same name being used for two different entities. The class contains three fields, named **from**, **to**, and **message**. The constructor has three parameters, also named **from**, **to**, and **message**!

So while we are executing the constructor, how many variables exist? The answer is six: three fields and three parameters. It is important to understand that the fields and the parameters are separate variables that exist independently of each other, even though they share similar names. A parameter and a field sharing a name is not really a problem in Java.

The problem we do have, though, is how to reference the six variables so as to be able to distinguish between the two sets. If we simply use the variable name "**from**" in the constructor (for example, in a statement **System.out.println(from)**), which variable will be used—the parameter or the field?

The Java specification answers this question. It specifies that the definition originating in the closest enclosing block will always be used. Because the **from** parameter is defined in the constructor, and the **from** field is defined in the class, the parameter will be used. Its definition is "closer" to the statement that uses it.

Now all we need is a mechanism to access a field when there is a more closely defined variable with the same name. That is what the **this** keyword is used for. The expression **this** refers to the current object. Writing **this.from** refers to the **from** field in the current object. Thus, this construct gives us a means to refer to the field instead of the parameter with the same name. Now we can read the assignment statement again:

```
this.from = from;
```

This statement, as we can see now, has the following effect:

field named **from** = *parameter named* **from**;

In other words, it assigns the value from the parameter to the field with the same name. This is, of course, exactly what we need to do to initialize the object properly.

One last question remains: Why are we doing this at all? The whole problem could easily be avoided just by giving the fields and the parameters different names. The reason is readability of source code.

Sometimes there is one name that perfectly describes the use of a variable—it fits so well that we do not want to invent a different name for it. We want to use it for the parameter, where it serves as a hint to the caller, indicating what needs to be passed. We also want to use it for the field, where it is useful as a reminder for the implementer of the class, indicating what the field is used for. If one name perfectly describes the use, it is reasonable to use it for both and to go through the trouble of using the **this** keyword in the assignment to resolve the name conflict.

3.14 Using a debugger

The most interesting class in the mail-system example is the mail client. We shall now investigate it in more detail by using a debugger. The mail client has three methods: **getNextMailItem**, **printNextMailItem**, and **sendMailItem**. We will first investigate the **printNextMailItem** method.

Before we start with the debugger, set up a scenario we can use to investigate (Exercise 3.44).

> **Exercise 3.44** Set up a scenario for investigation: Create a mail server, then create two mail clients for the users **"Sophie"** and **"Juan"** (you should name the instances **sophie** and **juan** as well so that you can better distinguish them on the object bench). Then use Sophie's **sendMailItem** method to send a message to Juan. Do not read the message yet.

After the setup in Exercise 3.44, we have a situation where one mail item is stored on the server for Juan, waiting to be picked up. We have seen that the **printNextMailItem** method picks up this mail item and prints it to the terminal. Now we want to investigate exactly how this works.

3.14.1 Setting breakpoints

To start our investigation, we set a breakpoint (Exercise 3.45). A breakpoint is a flag attached to a line of source code that will stop the execution of a method at that point when it is reached. It is represented in the BlueJ editor as a small stop sign (Figure 3.5).

You can set a breakpoint by opening the BlueJ editor, selecting the appropriate line (in our case, the first line of the **printNextMailItem** method) and then selecting *Set/Clear Breakpoint* from the *Tools* menu of the editor. Alternatively, you can also simply click into the area next to the line of code where the breakpoint symbol appears, to set or clear breakpoints. Note that the class has to be compiled to do this.

> **Exercise 3.45** Open the editor for the **MailClient** class and set a breakpoint at the first line of the **printNextMailItem** method, as shown in Figure 3.5.

Once you have set the breakpoint, invoke the **printNextMailItem** method on Juan's mail client. The editor window for the **MailClient** class and a debugger window will pop up (Figure 3.6).

Figure 3.5
A breakpoint in the
BlueJ editor

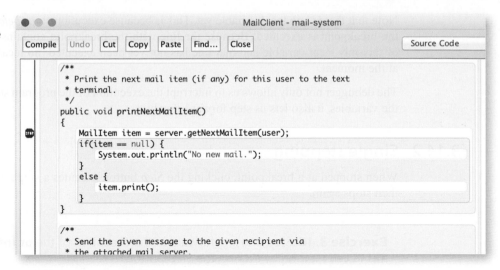

Figure 3.6
The debugger
window, execution
stopped at a
breakpoint

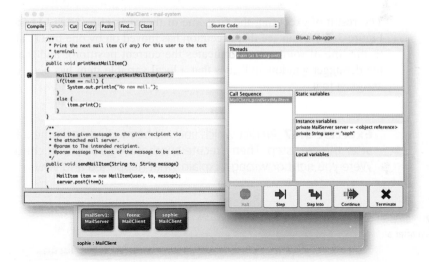

Along the bottom of the debugger window are some control buttons. They can be used to continue or interrupt the execution of the program. (For a more detailed explanation of the debugger controls, see Appendix F.)

On the right-hand side of the debugger window are three areas for variable display, titled *static variables*, *instance variables*, and *local variables*. We will ignore the static-variable area for now. We will discuss static variables later, and this class does not have any.

We see that this object has two instance variables (or fields), **server** and **user**, and we can see the current values. The **user** variable stores the string **"juan"**, and the **server** variable stores a reference to another object. The object reference is what we have drawn as an arrow in the object diagrams.

Note that there is no local variable yet. This is because execution stops *before* the line with the breakpoint is executed. Because the line with the breakpoint contains the declaration of the only local variable and that line has not yet been executed, no local variable exists at the moment.

The debugger not only allows us to interrupt the execution of the program so we can inspect the variables, it also lets us step forward slowly.

3.14.2 Single stepping

When stopped at a breakpoint, clicking the *Step* button executes a single line of code and then stops again.

> **Exercise 3.46** Step one line forward in the execution of the `printNext MailItem` method by clicking the *Step* button.

The result of executing the first line of the `printNextMailItem` method is shown in Figure 3.7. We can see that execution has moved on by one line (a small black arrow next to the line of source code indicates the current position), and the local variable list in the debugger window indicates that a local variable item has been created, and an object assigned to it.

> **Exercise 3.47** Predict which line will be marked as the next line to execute after the next step. Then execute another single step and check your prediction. Were you right or wrong? Explain what happened and why.

Figure 3.7
Stopped again after a single step

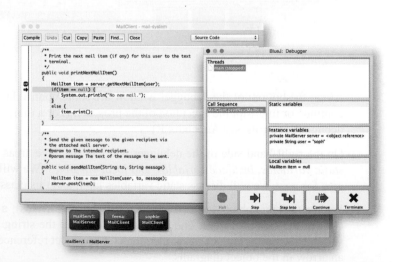

We can now use the *Step* button repeatedly to step to the end of the method. This allows us to see the path the execution takes. This is especially interesting in conditional statements: we can clearly see which branch of an if-statement is executed and use this to see whether it matches our expectations.

> **Exercise 3.48** Call the same method (`printNextMailItem`) again. Step through the method again, as before. What do you observe? Explain why this is.

3.14.3 Stepping into methods

When stepping through the `printNextMailItem` method, we have seen two method calls to objects of our own classes. The line

```
MailItem item = server.getNextMailItem(user);
```

includes a call to the `getNextMailItem` method of the `server` object. Checking the instance variable declarations, we can see that the `server` object is declared of class `MailServer`.

The line

```
item.print();
```

calls the `print` method of the `item` object. We can see in the first line of the `printNext-Mail Item` method that `item` is declared to be of class `MailItem`.

Using the *Step* command in the debugger, we have used abstraction: we have viewed the `print` method of the `item` class as a single instruction, and we could observe that its effect is to print out the details (sender, recipient, and message) of the mail item.

If we are interested in more detail, we can look further into the process and see the print method itself execute step by step. This is done by using the *Step Into* command in the debugger instead of the *Step* command. *Step Into* will step into the method being called and stop at the first line inside that method.

> **Exercise 3.49** Set up the same test situation as we did before. That is, send a message from Sophie to Juan. Then invoke the `printNextMailItem` message of Juan's mail client again. Step forward as before. This time, when you reach the line
>
> ```
> item.print();
> ```
>
> use the *Step Into* command instead of the *Step* command. Make sure you can see the text terminal window as you step forward. What do you observe? Explain what you see.

3.15 Method calling revisited

In the experiments in Section 3.14, we have seen another example of object interaction similar to one we saw before: objects calling methods of other objects. In the **print-NextMailItem** method, the **MailClient** object made a call to a **MailServer** object to retrieve the next mail item. This method (**getNextMailItem**) returned a value—an object of type **MailItem**. Then there was a call to the **print** method of the mail item. Using abstraction, we can view the **print** method as a single command. Or, if we are interested in more detail, we can go to a lower level of abstraction and look inside the **print** method.

In a similar style, we can use the debugger to observe one object creating another. The **sendMessage** method in the **MailClient** class shows a good example. In this method, a **MailItem** object is created in the first line of code:

```
MailItem item = new MailItem(user, to, message);
```

The idea here is that the mail item is used to encapsulate a mail message. The mail item contains information about the sender, the recipient, and the message itself. When sending a message, a mail client creates a mail item with all this information, then stores the mail item on the mail server. There it can later be picked up by the mail client of the recipient.

In the line of code above, we see the **new** keyword being used to create the new object, and we see the parameters being passed to the constructor. (Remember: Constructing an object does two things—the object is being created, and the constructor is executed.) Calling the constructor works in a very similar fashion to calling methods. This can be observed by using the *Step Into* command at the line where the object is being constructed.

Exercise 3.50 Set a breakpoint in the first line of the **sendMailItem** method in the **MailClient** class. Then invoke this method. Use the *Step Into* function to step into the constructor of the mail item. In the debugger display for the **MailItem** object, you can see the instance variables and local variables that have the same names, as discussed in Section 3.13.2. Step further to see the instance variables get initialized.

Exercise 3.51 Use a combination of code reading, execution of methods, breakpoints, and single stepping to familiarize yourself with the **MailItem** and **MailClient** classes. Note that we have not yet discussed enough for you to understand the implementation of the **MailServer** class, so you can ignore this for now. (You can, of course, look at it if you feel adventurous, but don't be surprised if you find it slightly baffling . . .) Explain in writing how the **MailClient** and **MailItem** classes interact. Draw object diagrams as part of your explanations.

3.16   Summary

In this chapter, we have discussed how a problem can be divided into sub-problems. We can try to identify subcomponents in those objects that we want to model, and we can implement subcomponents as independent classes. Doing so helps in reducing the complexity of implementing larger applications, because it enables us to implement, test, and maintain individual classes separately.

We have seen how this approach results in structures of objects working together to solve a common task. Objects can create other objects, and they can invoke each other's methods. Understanding these object interactions is essential in planning, implementing, and debugging applications.

We can use pen-and-paper diagrams, code reading, and debuggers to investigate how an application executes or to track down bugs.

Terms introduced in this chapter

> **abstraction, modularization, divide and conquer, class diagram, object diagram, object reference, overloading, internal method call, external method call, dot notation, debugger, breakpoint**

Concept summary

- **abstraction** Abstraction is the ability to ignore details of parts, to focus attention on a higher level of a problem.

- **modularization** Modularization is the process of dividing a whole into well-defined parts that can be built and examined separately and that interact in well-defined ways.

- **classes define types** A class name can be used as the type for a variable. Variables that have a class as their type can store objects of that class.

- **class diagram** The class diagram shows the classes of an application and the relationships between them. It gives information about the source code and presents the static view of a program.

- **object diagram** The object diagram shows the objects and their relationships at one moment in time during the execution of an application. It gives information about objects at runtime and presents the dynamic view of a program.

- **object references** Variables of object types store references to objects.

- **primitive type** The primitive types in Java are the non-object types. Types such as `int`, `boolean`, `char`, `double`, and `long` are the most common primitive types. Primitive types have no methods.

- **object creation** Objects can create other objects, using the **new** operator.

- **overloading** A class may contain more than one constructor, or more than one method of the same name, as long as each has a distinctive set of parameter types.

- **internal method call** Methods can call other methods of the same class as part of their implementation. This is called an internal method call.

- **external method call** Methods can call methods of other objects using dot notation. This is called an external method call.

- **debugger** A debugger is a software tool that helps in examining how an application executes. It can be used to find bugs.

Exercise 3.52 Use the debugger to investigate the *clock-display* project. Set breakpoints in the **ClockDisplay** constructor and each of the methods, and then single-step through them. Does it behave as you expected? Did this give you new insights? If so, what were they?

Exercise 3.53 Use the debugger to investigate the **insertMoney** method of the *better-ticket-machine* project from Chapter 2. Conduct tests that cause both branches of the if-statement to be executed.

Exercise 3.54 Add a subject line for an e-mail to mail items in the *mail-system* project. Make sure printing messages also prints the subject line. Modify the mail client accordingly.

Exercise 3.55 Given the following class (only shown in fragments here),

```java
public class Screen
{
    public Screen(int xRes, int yRes)
    { ...
    }
    public int numberOfPixels()
    { ...
    }
    public void clear(boolean invert)
    { ...
    }
}
```

write some lines of Java code that create a **Screen** object. Then call its **clear** method if (and only if) its number of pixels is greater than two million. (Don't worry about things being logical here; the goal is only to write something that is syntactically correct—i.e., that would compile if we typed it in.)

Exercise 3.56 Describe the changes that would be required to the **Clock-Display** class in order to be able to display hours, minutes, and seconds. How many **NumberDisplay** objects would a **ClockDisplay** object need to use?

Exercise 3.57 Write the code for the **timeTick** method in **ClockDisplay** that displays hours, minutes, and seconds, or even implement the whole class if you wish.

Exercise 3.58 Discuss whether the current design of the **ClockDisplay** class would support the display of hours, minutes, seconds, tenths of a second, and hundredths of a second. Consider how the **timeTick** method would be coded in this case, for instance.

Exercise 3.59 *Challenge exercise* In the current design of **ClockDisplay**, a **ClockDisplay** object is responsible for detecting when a **NumberDisplay** object has rolled over to zero and then telling another **NumberDisplay** object to increment. In other words, there is no direct link between **NumberDisplay** objects. Would it be possible to have one **NumberDisplay** object tell another that it has rolled over, and that the other **NumberDisplay** object should then increment? For instance, have the minutes object tell the hour object that another hour has passed, or have the seconds object tell the minutes object that another sixty seconds have elapsed. Which of these objects would the **timeTick** method interact with? What fields would a **NumberDisplay** object have? What should the hour object do when a whole day has elapsed? Discuss the issues involved in this alternative design and, if you really feel like a challenge, try implementing it! Note that you might need to find out about the Java **null** keyword, which we don't cover until late in Chapter 4.

The main focus of this chapter is to introduce some of the ways in which objects may be grouped together into collections. In particular, we discuss the **ArrayList** class as an example of flexible-size collections. Closely associated with collections is the need to iterate over the elements they contain. For this purpose, we introduce two new control structures: the for-each loop and the while loop.

This chapter is both long and important. You may not succeed in becoming a good programmer without fully understanding the contents of this chapter. You will likely need longer to study it than was the case for previous chapters. Do not be tempted to rush through it; take your time and study it thoroughly.

4.1 Building on themes from Chapter 3

As well as introducing new material on *collections* and *iteration*, we will also be revisiting two of the key themes that were introduced in Chapter 3: *abstraction* and *object interaction*. There we saw that abstraction allows us to simplify a problem by identifying discrete components that can be viewed as a whole, rather than being concerned with their detail. We will see this principle in action when we start making use of the *library classes* that are available in Java. While these classes are not, strictly speaking, a part of the language, some of them are so closely associated with writing Java programs that they are often thought of in that way. Most people writing Java programs will constantly check the libraries to see if someone has already written a class that they can make use of. That way, they save a huge amount of effort that can be better used in working on other parts of the program. The same principle applies with most other programming languages, which also tend to have libraries of useful classes. So it pays to become familiar with the contents of the library and how to use the most common classes. The power of abstraction is that we don't usually need to know much (if anything, indeed!) about what the class looks like inside to be able to use it effectively.

If we use a library class, it follows that we will be writing code that creates instances of those classes, and then our objects will be interacting with the library objects. Therefore, object interaction will figure highly in this chapter, also.

You will find that the chapters in this book continually revisit and build on themes that have been introduced in previous chapters. We refer to this in the preface as an "iterative approach." One particular advantage of the approach is that it will help you to gradually deepen your understanding of topics as you work your way through the book.

In this chapter, we also extend our understanding of abstraction to see that it does not just mean hiding detail, but also means seeing the common features and patterns that recur again and again in programs. Recognizing these patterns means that we can often reuse part or all of a method or class we have previously written in a new situation. This particularly applies when looking at collections and iteration.

4.2 The collection abstraction

One of the abstractions we will explore in this chapter is the idea of a *collection*—the notion of grouping things so that we can refer to them and manage them all together. A collection might be large (all the students in a university), small (the courses one of the students is taking), or empty even (the paintings by Picasso that I own!).

If we own a collection of stamps, autographs, concert posters, ornaments, music, or whatever, then there are some common actions we will want to perform to the collection from time to time, regardless of what it is we collect. For instance, we will likely want to *add to* the collection, but we also might want to *reduce it*—say if we have duplicates or want to raise money for additional purchases. We also might want to *arrange it* in some way—by date of acquisition or value, perhaps. What we are describing here are typical *operations* on a collection.

> **Concept**
>
> **Collection**
> A collection object can store an arbitrary number of other objects.

In a programming context, the collection abstraction becomes a class of some sort, and the operations would be methods of that class. A particular collection (my music collection) would be an instance of the class. Furthermore, the items stored in a collection instance would, themselves, be objects.

Here are some further collection examples that are more obviously related to a programming context:

- Electronic calendars store event notes about appointments, meetings, birthdays, and so on. New notes are added as future events are arranged, and old notes are deleted as details of past events are no longer needed.

- Libraries record details about the books and journals they own. The catalog changes as new books are bought and old ones are put into storage or discarded.

- Universities maintain records of students. Each academic year adds new records to the collection, while the records of those who have left are moved to an archive collection. Listing subsets of the collection will be common: all the students taking first-year CS, or all the students due to graduate this year, for instance.

The number of items stored in a collection will vary from time to time. So far, we have not met any features of Java that would allow us to group together arbitrary numbers of items. We could, perhaps, define a class with a lot of individual fields to cover a fixed but very large number of items, but programs typically have a need for a more general solution than this provides. A proper solution would not require us either to know in advance how many items we wish to group together, or to fix an upper limit to that number.

So we will start our exploration of the Java library by looking at a class that provides the simplest possible way of grouping objects, an unsorted but ordered flexible-sized list: `ArrayList`. In the next few sections, we shall use the example of keeping track of a personal music collection to illustrate how we can group together an arbitrary number of objects in a single container object.

4.3 An organizer for music files

We are going to write a class that can help us organize our music files stored on a computer. Our class won't actually store the file details; instead, it will delegate that responsibility to the standard `ArrayList` library class, which will save us a lot of work. So, why do we need to write our own class at all? An important point to bear in mind when dealing with library classes is that they have not been written for any particular application scenario—they are general-purpose classes. One `ArrayList` might store student-record objects, while another stores event reminders. This means that it is the classes that we write for using the library classes that provide the scenario-specific operations, such as the fact that we are dealing with music files, or playing a file that is stored in the collection.

For the sake of simplicity, the first version of this project will simply work with the file names of individual music tracks. There will be no separate details of title, artist, playing time, etc. That means we will just be asking the `ArrayList` to store `String` objects representing the file names. Keeping things simple at this stage will help to avoid obscuring the key concepts we are trying to illustrate, which are the creation and usage of a collection object. Later in the chapter, we will add further sophistication to make a more viable music organizer and player.

We will assume that each music file represents a single music track. The example files we have provided with the project have both the artist's name and the track's title embedded in the file name, and we will use this feature later. For the time being, here are the basic operations we will have in the initial version of our organizer:

- It allows tracks to be added to the collection.

- It has no predetermined limit on the number of tracks it can store, aside from the memory limit of the machine on which it is run.

- It will tell us how many tracks are in the collection.

- It will list all the tracks.

We shall find that the `ArrayList` class makes it very easy to provide this functionality from our own class.

Notice that we are not being too ambitious in this first version. These features will be sufficient for illustrating the basics of creating and using the `ArrayList` class, and later versions will then build further features incrementally until we have something more sophisticated. (Most importantly, perhaps, we will later add the possibility of playing the music files. Our first version will not be able to do that.) This modest, incremental approach is much more likely to lead to success than trying to implement everything all at once.

Before we analyze the source code needed to make use of such a class, it is helpful to explore the starting behavior of the music organizer.

Exercise 4.1 Open the *music-organizer-v1* project in BlueJ and create a `MusicOrganizer` object. Store the names of a few audio files into it—they are simply strings. As we are not going to play the files at this stage, any file names will do, although there is a sample of audio files in the *audio* folder of the chapter that you might like to use.

Check that the number of files returned by `numberOfFiles` matches the number you stored. When you use the `listFile` method, you will need to use a parameter value of **0** (zero) to print the first file, **1** (one) to print the second, and so on. We shall explain the reason for this numbering in due course.

Exercise 4.2 What happens if you create a new `MusicOrganizer` object and then call `removeFile(0)` before you have added any files to it? Do you get an error? Would you expect to get an error?

Exercise 4.3 Create a `MusicOrganizer` and add two file names to it. Call `listFile(0)` and `listFile(1)` to show the two files. Now call `removeFile(0)` and then `listFile(0)`. What happened? Is that what you expected? Can you find an explanation of what might have happened when you removed the first file name from the collection?

4.4 Using a library class

Code 4.1 shows the full definition of our `MusicOrganizer` class, which makes use of the library class `ArrayList`. Note that library classes do not appear in the BlueJ class diagram.

Class libraries One of the features of object-oriented languages that makes them powerful is that they are often accompanied by *class libraries*. These libraries typically contain many hundreds or thousands of different classes that have proved useful to developers on a wide range of different projects. Java calls its libraries *packages*. Library classes are used in exactly the same way as we would use our own classes. Instances are constructed using **new**, and the classes have fields, constructors, and methods.

Code 4.1
The **Music-Organizer** class

```java
import java.util.ArrayList;

/**
 * A class to hold details of audio files.
 *
 * @author David J. Barnes and Michael Kölling
 * @version 2016.02.29
 */
public class MusicOrganizer
{
    // An ArrayList for storing the file names of music files.
    private ArrayList<String> files;

    /**
     * Create a MusicOrganizer
     */
    public MusicOrganizer()
    {
        files = new ArrayList<>();
    }

    /**
     * Add a file to the collection.
     * @param filename The file to be added.
     */
    public void addFile(String filename)
    {
        files.add(filename);
    }

    /**
     * Return the number of files in the collection.
     * @return The number of files in the collection.
     */
    public int getNumberOfFiles()
    {
        return files.size();
    }

    /**
     * List a file from the collection.
     * @param index The index of the file to be listed.
     */
    public void listFile(int index)
    {
        if(index >= 0 && index < files.size()) {
            String filename = files.get(index);
            System.out.println(filename);
        }
    }
}
```

```
/**
 * Remove a file from the collection.
 * @param index The index of the file to be removed.
 */
public void removeFile(int index)
{
    if(index >= 0 && index < files.size()) {
        files.remove(index);
    }
}
}
```

4.4.1 Importing a library class

The very first line of the class file illustrates the way in which we gain access to a library class in Java, via an *import statement*:

```
import java.util.ArrayList;
```

This makes the **ArrayList** class from the **java.util** package available to our class definition. Import statements must always be placed before class definitions in a file. Once a class name has been imported from a package in this way, we can use that class just as if it were one of our own classes. So we use **ArrayList** at the head of the **MusicOrganizer** class to define a **files** field:

```
private ArrayList<String> files;
```

Here, we see a new construct: the mention of **String** in angle brackets: **<String>**. The need for this was alluded to in Section 4.3, where we noted that **ArrayList** is a *general-purpose* collection class—i.e., not restricted in what it can store. When we create an **ArrayList** object, however, we have to be specific about the type of objects that will be stored in that particular instance. We can store whatever type we choose, but we have to designate that type when declaring an **ArrayList** variable. Classes such as **ArrayList**, which get parameterized with a second type, are called *generic classes* (we will discuss them in more detail later).

When using collections, therefore, we always have to specify two types: the type of the collection itself (here: **ArrayList**) and the type of the elements that we plan to store in the collection (here: **String**). We can read the complete type definition **ArrayList<String>** as "*ArrayList of String.*" We use this type definition as the type for our **files** variable.

As you should now have come to expect, we see a close connection between the body of the constructor and the fields of the class, because the constructor is responsible for initializing the fields of each instance. So, just as the **ClockDisplay** created **NumberDisplay** objects for its two fields, here we see the constructor of the **MusicOrganizer** creating an object of type **ArrayList** and storing it in the **files** field.

4.4.2 Diamond notation

Note that when creating the **ArrayList** instance, we have written the following statement:

```
files = new ArrayList<>();
```

This is the so-called *diamond notation* (because the two angle brackets create a diamond shape) and it looks unusual. We have seen earlier that the **new** statement has the following form:

```
new type-name(parameters)
```

and we have also seen that the full type name for our collection is

```
ArrayList<String>
```

Therefore, with an empty parameter list, the statement to create the new collection object should look as follows:

```
files = new ArrayList<String>();
```

Indeed, writing this statement would work as well. The first version, using the diamond notation (thus leaving out the mention of the **String** type) is merely a shortcut notation for convenience. If the creation of the collection object is combined with an assignment, then the compiler can work out the type of the collection elements from the type of the variable on the left hand side of the assignment, and Java allows us to skip defining it again. The element type is automatically inferred from the variable type.

Using this form does not change the fact that the object being created will only be able to store **String** objects; it is just a convenience that saves us some typing and makes our code shorter.

4.4.3 Key methods of ArrayList

The **ArrayList** class defines quite a lot of methods, but we shall make use of only four at this stage, to support the functionality we require: **add**, **size**, **get**, and **remove**.

The first two are illustrated in the relatively straightforward **addFile** and **getNumber-OfFiles** methods, respectively. The **add** method of an **ArrayList** stores an object in the list, and the **size** method tells us how many items are currently stored in it. We will look at how the **get** and **remove** methods work in Section 4.7, though you will probably get some idea beforehand simply by reading through the code of the **listFile** and **removeFile** methods.

4.5 Object structures with collections

To understand how a collection object such as an **ArrayList** operates, it is helpful to examine an object diagram. Figure 4.1 illustrates how a **MusicOrganizer** object might appear with two filename strings stored in it. Compare Figure 4.1 with Figure 4.2, where a third file name has been stored.

There are at least three important features of the **ArrayList** class that you should observe:

- It is able to increase its internal capacity as required: as more items are added, it simply makes enough room for them.

- It keeps its own private count of how many items it is currently storing. Its **size** method returns that count.

- It maintains the order of items you insert into it. The **add** method stores each new item at the end of the list. You can later retrieve them in the same order.

Figure 4.1
A **Music-Organizer** containing two file names

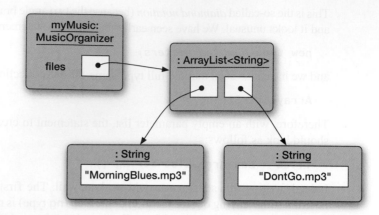

Figure 4.2
A **Music-Organizer** containing three file names

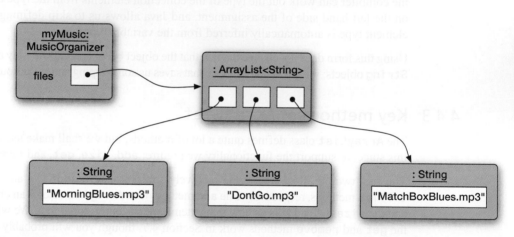

We notice that the **MusicOrganizer** object looks quite simple—it has only a single field that stores an object of type **ArrayList<String>**. All the difficult work is done in the **ArrayList** object. This is one of the great advantages of using library classes: someone has invested time and effort to implement something useful, and we are getting access to this functionality almost for free by using this class.

At this stage, we do not need to worry about *how* an **ArrayList** is able to support these features. It is sufficient to appreciate just how useful this ability is. Remember: This suppression of detail is a benefit that abstraction gives us; it means that we can utilize **ArrayList** to write any number of different classes that require storage of an arbitrary number of objects.

The second feature—the **ArrayList** object keeping its own count of inserted objects—has important consequences for the way in which we implement the **MusicOrganizer** class. Although an organizer has a **getNumberOfFiles** method, we have not actually defined a specific field for recording this information. Instead, an organizer *delegates* the responsibility for keeping track of the number of items to its **ArrayList** object.

This means that an organizer does not duplicate information that is available to it from elsewhere. If a user requests from the organizer information about the number of file names in it, the organizer will pass the question on to the **files** object, and then return whatever answer it gets from there.

Duplication of information or behavior is something we often work hard to avoid. Duplication can represent wasted effort, and can lead to inconsistencies where two things that should be identical turn out not to be, through error. We will have a lot more to say about duplication of functionality in later chapters.

4.6 Generic classes

The new notation using the angle brackets deserves a little more discussion. The type of our **files** field was declared as:

```
ArrayList<String>
```

The class we are using here is simply called **ArrayList**, but it requires a second type to be specified as a parameter when it is used to declare fields or other variables. Classes that require such a type parameter are called *generic classes*. Generic classes, in contrast to other classes we have seen so far, do not define a single type in Java, but potentially many types. The **ArrayList** class, for example, can be used to specify an *ArrayList of String*, an *ArrayList of Person*, an *ArrayList of Rectangle*, or an **ArrayList** of any other class that we have available. Each particular **ArrayList** is a separate type that can be used in declarations of fields, parameters, and return values. We could, for example, define the following two fields:

```
private ArrayList<Person> members;
private ArrayList<TicketMachine> machines;
```

These definitions state that **members** refers to an **ArrayList** that can store **Person** objects, while **machines** can refer to an **ArrayList** to store **TicketMachine** objects. Note that **ArrayList<Person>** and **ArrayList<TicketMachine>** are different types. The fields cannot be assigned to each other, even though their types were derived from the same **ArrayList** class.

Exercise 4.4 Write a declaration of a private field named **library** that can hold an **ArrayList**. The elements of the **ArrayList** are of type **Book**.

Exercise 4.5 Write a declaration of a local variable called **cs101** that can hold an **ArrayList** of **Student**.

Exercise 4.6 Write a declaration of a private field called **tracks** for storing a collection of **MusicTrack** objects.

Exercise 4.7 Write assignments to the **library**, **cs101**, and **track** variables (which you defined in the previous three exercises) to create the appropriate **ArrayList** objects. Write them once using diamond notation and once without diamond notation, specifying the full type.

Generic classes are used for a variety of purposes; we will encounter more of them later in the book. For now, collections such as **ArrayList**, and some other collections that we shall encounter shortly, are the only generic classes we need to deal with.

4.7 Numbering within collections

When exploring the *music-organizer-v1* project in the first few exercises, we noted that it was necessary to use parameter values starting at 0 to list and remove file names in the collection. The reason behind this requirement is that items stored in **ArrayList** collections have an implicit numbering, or positioning, that starts from 0. The position of an object in a collection is more commonly known as its *index*. The first item added to a collection is given index number 0, the second is given index number 1, and so on. Figure 4.3 illustrates the same situation as above, with index numbers shown in the **ArrayList** object.

This means that the last item in a collection has the index *size-1*. For example, in a list of 20 items, the last one will be at index 19.

The **listFile** and **removeFile** methods both illustrate the way in which an index number is used to gain access to an item in an **ArrayList**: one via its **get** method, and the other via its **remove** method. Note that both methods make sure that their parameter value is in the range of valid index values **[0 . . . size()-1]** before passing the index on to the **ArrayList** methods. This is a good stylistic validation habit to adopt, as it prevents failure of a library-class method call when passing on parameter values that could be invalid.

> **Pitfall** If you are not careful, you may try to access a collection element that is outside the valid indices of the **ArrayList**. When you do this, you will get an error message and the program will terminate. Such an error is called an *index-out-of-bounds* error. In Java, you will see a message about an **IndexOutOfBoundsException**.

Figure 4.3
Index numbers of elements in a collection

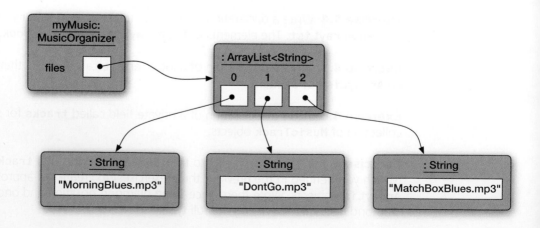

Exercise 4.8 If a collection stores 10 objects, what value would be returned from a call to its **size** method?

Exercise 4.9 Write a method call using **get** to return the fifth object stored in a collection called items.

Exercise 4.10 What is the index of the last item stored in a collection of 15 objects?

Exercise 4.11 Write a method call to add the object held in the variable **favoriteTrack** to a collection called **files**.

4.7.1   The effect of removal on numbering

As well as adding items to a collection, it is common to want to remove items, as we saw with the **removeFile** method in Code 4.1. The **ArrayList** class has a **remove** method that takes the index of the object to be removed. One detail of the removal process to be aware of is that it can change the index values at which other objects in the collection are stored. If an item with a low index number is removed, then the collection moves all subsequent items along by one position to fill in the gap. As a consequence, their index numbers will be decreased by 1.

Figure 4.4 illustrates the way in which some of the index values of items in an **ArrayList** are changed by the removal of an item from the middle of the list. Starting with the situation depicted in Figure 4.3, the object with index 1 has been removed. As a result, the object originally at index number 2 has changed to 1, whereas the object at index number 0 remains unchanged.

Furthermore, we shall see later that it is possible to insert items into an **ArrayList** at a position other than the end of it. This means that items already in the list may have their index numbers increased when a new item is added. Users need to be aware of this possible change of indices when adding or removing items.

Figure 4.4

Index number changes following removal of an item

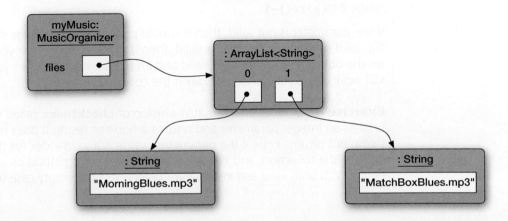

4.7.2 The general utility of numbering with collections

The use of integer index values to access objects in a collection is something that we will see over and over again—not just with **ArrayList**s but also with several different types of collections. So it is important to understand what we have seen of this so far: that the index values start at zero; that the objects are numbered sequentially; and that there are usually no gaps in the index values of consecutive objects in the collection.

Using integer values as indices also makes it easy to express expressions in program code such as "the next item" and "the previous item" with respect to an item in the collection. If an item is at index **p**, then "the next" one will be at index **(p+1)** and "the previous" one is now at index **(p−1)**. We can also map natural-language selections such as "the first three" to program-related terminology. For example, "the items at indices **0**, **1**, and **2**" or "the last four" could be "the items at indices **(list.size()-4)** to **(list.size()-1)**".

We could even imagine working our way through the entire collection by having an integer index variable whose value is initially set to zero and is then successively increased by 1, passing its value to the **get** method to access each item in the list in order (stopping when it goes beyond the final index value of the list).

But we are getting a little ahead of ourselves. Nevertheless, in a little while we will see how all this works out in practice when we look at *loops* and *iteration*.

Exercise 4.12 Write a method call to remove the third object stored in a collection called **dates**.

Exercise 4.13 Suppose that an object is stored at index 6 in a collection. What will be its index after the objects at index 0 and index 9 are removed?

Exercise 4.14 Add a method called **checkIndex** to the **MusicOrganizer** class. It takes a single integer parameter and checks whether it is a valid index for the current state of the collection. To be valid, the parameter must lie in the range **0** to **size()−1**.

If the parameter is not valid, then it should print an error message saying what the valid range is. If the index is valid, then it prints nothing. Test your method on the object bench with both valid and invalid parameters. Does your method still work when you check an index if the collection is empty?

Exercise 4.15 Write an alternative version of **checkIndex** called **validIndex**. It takes an integer parameter and returns a boolean result. It does not print anything, but returns **true** if the parameter's value is a valid index for the current state of the collection, and **false** otherwise. Test your method on the object bench with both valid and invalid parameters. Test the empty case too.

Exercise 4.16 Rewrite both the `listFile` and `removeFile` methods in `MusicOrganizer` so that they use your `validIndex` method to check their parameter, instead of the current boolean expression. They should only call `get` or `remove` on the `ArrayList` if `validIndex` returns true.

<table>
<tr><td>**4.8**</td><td># Playing the music files</td></tr>
</table>

A nice feature of our organizer, beyond keeping a list of music files, would allow us to play them. Once again, we can use abstraction to help us here. If we have a class that has been written specifically to play audio files, then our organizer class would not need to know anything about how to do that; it could simply hand over the name of the file to the player class and leave it to do the rest.

Unfortunately, the standard Java library does not have a class that is suitable for playing mp3 files, which is the audio format we want to work with. However, many individual programmers are constantly writing their own useful classes and making them available for other people to use. These are often called "third-party libraries," and they are imported and used in the same way as are standard Java library classes.

For the next version of our project, we have made use of a set of classes from **javazoom. net** to write our own music-player class. You can find this in the version called *music-organizer-v2*. The three methods of the **MusicPlayer** class we shall be using are **play-Sample**, **startPlaying**, and **stop**. The first two take the name of the audio file to play. The first plays some seconds of the beginning of the file and returns when it has finished playing, while the second starts its playing in the background and then immediately returns control back to the organizer—hence the need for the **stop** method, in case you want to cancel playing. Code 4.2 shows the new elements of the **MusicOrganizer** class that access some of this playing functionality.

Code 4.2

Playing functionality of the **Music-Organizer** class

```
import java.util.ArrayList;

/**
 * A class to hold details of audio files.
 * This version can play the files.
 *
 * @author David J. Barnes and Michael Kölling
 * @version 2016.02.29
 */
public class MusicOrganizer
{
    // An ArrayList for storing the file names of music files.
    private ArrayList<String> files;
    // A player for the music files.
    private MusicPlayer player;
```

Code 4.2 continued

Playing functionality of the **Music-Organizer** class

```
/**
 * Create a MusicOrganizer
 */
public MusicOrganizer()
{
    files = new ArrayList<>();
    player = new MusicPlayer();
}

/**
 * Start playing a file in the collection.
 * Use stopPlaying() to stop it playing.
 * @param index The index of the file to be played.
 */
public void startPlaying(int index)
{
    String filename = files.get(index);
    player.startPlaying(filename);
}

/**
 * Stop the player.
 */
public void stopPlaying()
{
    player.stop();
}

Other details omitted.
}
```

Exercise 4.17 Create a **MusicOrganizer** object in the second version of our project. Experiment with adding some files to it and playing them.

If you want to use the files provided in the *audio* folder within the chapter, you must include the folder name in the filename parameter, as well as the file name and suffix. For example, to use the file *BlindBlake-EarlyMorningBlues.mp3* from the *audio* folder, you must pass the string `"../audio/BlindBlake-EarlyMorningBlues.mp3"` to the **addFile** method.

You can use your own mp3 files by placing them into the *audio* folder. Remember to use the folder name as part of the file name.

Also experiment with file names that do not exist. What happens when you use those?

4.8.1 Summary of the music organizer

We have made good progress with the basics of organizing our music collection. We can store the names of any number of music files and even play them. We have done this with relatively little coding effort, because we have been able to piggyback on the functionality provided by library classes: **ArrayList** from the standard Java library, and a music player that uses a third-party class library. We have also been able to do this with relatively little knowledge of the internal workings of these library classes; it was sufficient to know the names, parameter types, and return types of the key methods.

However, there is still some key functionality missing if we want a genuinely useful program—most obvious is the lack of any way to list the whole collection, for instance. This will be the topic of the next section, as we introduce the first of several Java loop-control structures.

4.9   Processing a whole collection

At the end of the last section, we said that it would be useful to have a method in the music organizer that lists all of the file names stored in the collection. Knowing that each file name in the collection has a unique index number, one way to express what we want would be to say that we wish to display the file name stored at consecutive increasing index numbers starting from zero. Before reading further, try the following exercises to see whether we can easily write such a method with the Java that we already know.

Exercise 4.18 What might the header of a **listAllFiles** method in the **MusicOrganizer** class look like? What sort of return type should it have? Does it need to take any parameters?

Exercise 4.19 We know that the first file name is stored at index zero in the **ArrayList**, and the list stores the file names as strings, so could we write the body of **listAllFiles** along the following lines?

```
System.out.println(files.get(0));
System.out.println(files.get(1));
System.out.println(files.get(2));
etc.
```

How many **println** statements would be required to complete the method?

You have probably noticed that it is not really possible to complete Exercise 4.19, because it depends on how many file names are in the list at the time they are printed. If there are three, then three **println** statements would be required; if there are four, then four statements would be needed; and so on. The **listFile** and **removeFile** methods illustrate that the range of valid index numbers at any one time is **[0 to (size()−1)]**. So a **listAllFiles** method would also have to take that dynamic size into account in order to do its job.

What we have here is the requirement to do something several times, but the number of times depends upon circumstances that may vary—in this case, the size of the collection. We shall meet this sort of requirement in nearly every program we write, and most programming languages have several ways to deal with it through the use of *loop statements*, which are also known as *iterative control structures*.

The first loop we will introduce to list the files is a special one for use with collections, which completely avoids the need to use an index variable at all: this is called a *for-each loop*.

4.9.1 The for-each loop

A *for-each loop* is one way to perform a set of actions repeatedly on the items in a collection, but without having to write out those actions more than once, as we saw was a problem in Exercise 4.19. We can summarize the Java syntax and actions of a for-each loop in the following pseudo-code:

```
for (ElementType element : collection) {
    loop body
}
```

The main new piece of Java is the word **for**. The Java language has two variations of the **for** loop: one is the *for-each loop*, which we are discussing here; the other one is simply called a *for loop* and will be discussed in Chapter 7.

A for-each loop has two parts: a loop header (the first line of the loop statement) and a loop body following the header. The body contains those statements that we wish to perform over and over again.

The for-each loop gets its name from the way we can read this loop: if we read the keyword **for** as "for each" and the colon in the loop header as "in," then the code structure shown above starts to make more sense, as in this pseudo-code:

```
for each element in collection do: {
    loop body
}
```

When you compare this version to the original pseudo-code in the first version, you notice that *element* was written in the form of a variable declaration as **ElementType element**. This section does indeed declare a variable that is then used for each collection element in turn. Before discussing further, let us look at an example of real Java code.

Code 4.3 shows an implementation of a **listAllFiles** method that lists all file names currently in the organizer's **ArrayList** that use such a for-each loop.

Code 4.3

Using a for-each loop to list the file names

```
/**
 * Show a list of all the files in the collection.
 */
public void listAllFiles()
{
    for(String filename : files) {
        System.out.println(filename);
    }
}
```

In this for-each loop, the loop body—consisting of a single **System.out.println** statement —is executed repeatedly, once for each element in the **files ArrayList**. If, for example, there were four strings in the list, the **println** statement would be executed four times.

Each time before the statement is executed, the variable **filename** is set to hold one of the list elements: first the one at index **0**, then the one at index **1**, and so on. Thus, each element in the list gets printed out.

Let us dissect the loop in a little more detail. The keyword **for** introduces the loop. It is followed by a pair of parentheses, within which the loop details are defined. The first of the details is the declaration **String filename**; this declares a new local variable **filename** that will be used to hold the list elements in order. We call this variable the *loop variable*. We can choose the name of this variable just as we can that of any other variable; it does not have to be called "filename." The type of the loop variable must be the same as the declared element type of the collection we are going to use—**String** in our case.

Then follows a colon and the variable holding the collection that we wish to process. From this collection, each element will be assigned to the loop variable in turn; and for each of those assignments, the loop body is executed once. In the loop body, we then use the loop variable to refer to each element.

To test your understanding of how this loop operates, try the following exercises.

Exercise 4.20 Implement the **listAllFiles** method in your version of the music-organizer project. (A solution with this method implemented is provided in the *music-organizer-v3* version of this project, but to improve your understanding of the subject, we recommend that you write this method yourself.)

Exercise 4.21 Create a **MusicOrganizer** and store a few file names in it. Use the **listAllFiles** method to print them out; check that the method works as it should.

Exercise 4.22 Create an **ArrayList<String>** in the Code Pad by typing the following two lines:

```
import java.util.ArrayList;
new ArrayList<String>()
```

If you write the last line without a trailing semicolon, you will see the small red object icon. Drag this icon onto the object bench. Examine its methods and try calling some (such as **add**, **remove**, **size**, **isEmpty**). Also try calling the same methods from the Code Pad. You can access objects on the object bench from the Code Pad by using their names. For example, if you have an **ArrayList** named **al1** on the object bench, in the Code Pad you can type:

```
al1.size()
```

Exercise 4.23 If you wish, you could use the debugger to help you understand how the statements in the body of the loop in **listAllFiles** are repeated. Set a breakpoint just before the loop, and step through the method until the loop has processed all elements and exits.

Exercise 4.24 *Challenge exercise* The for-each loop does not use an explicit integer variable to access successive elements of the list. Thus, if we want to include the index of each file name in the listing, then we would have to declare our own local integer variable (**position**, say) so that we can write in the body of the loop something like:

```
System.out.println(position + ": " + filename);
```

See if you can complete a version of **listAllFiles** to do this. *Hint:* You will need a local variable declaration of **position** in the method, as well as a statement to update its value by one inside the for-each loop.

This exercise illustrates the for-each loop really intended to be used with a separate index variable.

We have now seen how we can use a for-each loop to perform some operation (the loop body) on every element of a collection. This is a big step forward, but it does not solve all our problems. Sometimes we need a little more control, and Java provides a different loop construct to let us do more: the *while loop*.

4.9.2 Selective processing of a collection

The **listAllFiles** method illustrates the fundamental usefulness of a for-each loop: it provides access to every element of a collection, in order, via the variable declared in the loop's header. It does not provide us with the index position of an element, but we don't always need that, so that is not necessarily a problem.

Having access to every item in the collection, however, does not mean we have to do the same thing to every one; we can be more selective than that. For instance, we might want to only list the music by a particular artist, or need to find all the music with a particular phrase in the title. There is nothing to stop us doing this, because the body of a for-each loop is just an ordinary block, and we can use whatever Java statements we wish inside it. So using an if-statement in the body to select the files we want should be easy.

Code 4.4 shows a method to list only those file names in the collection that contain a particular string.

Code 4.4

Printing selected items from the collection

```
/**
 * List the names of files matching the given search string.
 * @param searchString The string to match.
 */
public void listMatching(String searchString)
{
    for(String filename : files) {
        if(filename.contains(searchString)) {
            // A match.
            System.out.println(filename);
        }
    }
}
```

Using an if-statement and the **boolean** result of the **contains** method of the **String** class, we can "filter" which file names are to be printed and which are not. If the file name does not match, then we just ignore it—no **else** part is needed. The filtering criterion (the test in the if-statement) can be whatever we want.

> **Exercise 4.25** Add the **listMatching** method in Code 4.4 to your version of the project. (Use *music-organizer-v3* if you do not already have your own version.) Check that the method only lists matching files. Also try it with a search string that matches none of the file names. Is anything at all printed in this case?
>
> **Exercise 4.26** *Challenge exercise* In **listMatching**, can you find a way to print a message, once the for-each loop has finished, if no file names matched the search string? *Hint:* Use a **boolean** local variable.
>
> **Exercise 4.27** Write a method in your version of the project that plays samples of all the tracks by a particular artist, one after the other. The **listMatching** method illustrates the basic structure you need for this method. Make sure that you choose an artist with more than one file. Use the **playSample** method of the **MusicPlayer** (provided in *music-organizer-v3*). The **playSample** method plays the beginning of a track (about 15 seconds) and then returns.
>
> **Exercise 4.28** Write out the header of a for-each loop to process an **ArrayList<Track>** called **tracks**. Don't worry about the loop's body.

4.9.3 A limitation of using strings

By this point we can see that simply having file name strings containing all the details of the music track is not really satisfactory. For instance, suppose we wanted to find all tracks with the word "love" in the title. Using the unsophisticated matching technique described above, we will also find tracks by artists whose names happen to have that sequence of characters in them (e.g., Glover). While that might not seem like a particularly big problem, it does have a rather "cheap" feel about it, and it should be possible to do better with just a little more effort. What we really need is a separate class, such as **Track**, say—that stores the details of artist and title independently from the file name. Then we could more easily match titles separately from artists. The **ArrayList<String>** in the organizer would then become an **ArrayList<Track>**.

As we develop the music-organizer project in later sections, we will eventually move towards a better structure by introducing a **Track** class.

4.9.4 Summary of the for-each loop

The for-each loop is always used to iterate over a collection. It provides us with a way to access every item in the collection in sequence, one by one, and process those items in whatever way we want. We can choose to do the same thing to each item (as we did when printing the full listing) or we can be selective and filter the list (as we did when we printed only a subset of the collection). The body of the loop can be as complicated as we like.

With its essential simplicity necessarily comes some limitations. For instance, one restriction is that we cannot change what is stored in the collection while iterating over it, either by adding new items to it or removing items from it. That doesn't mean, however, that we cannot change the states of objects already within the collection.

We have also seen that the for-each loop does not provide us with an index value for the items in the collection. If we want one, then we have to declare and maintain our own local variable. The reason for this has to do with abstraction, again. When dealing with collections and iterating over them, it is worth bearing two things in mind:

■ A for-each loop provides a general control structure for iterating over different types of collection.

■ There are some types of collections that do not naturally associate integer indices with the items they store. We will meet some of these in Chapter 6.

So the for-each loop abstracts the task of processing a complete collection, element by element, and is able to handle different types of collection. We do not need to know the details of how it manages that.

One of the questions we have not asked is whether a for-each loop can be used if we want to stop partway through processing the collection. For instance, suppose that instead of playing every track by our chosen artist, we just wanted to find the first one and play it, without going any further. While in principle it *is* possible to do this using a for-each loop, our practice and advice is not to use a for-each loop for tasks that might not need to process the whole collection. In other words, we recommend using a for-each loop only if you *definitely* want to process *the whole collection*. Again, stated in another way, once the loop starts, you know for sure how many times the body will be executed—this will be equal to the size of the collection. This style is often called *definite iteration*. For tasks where you might want to stop partway through, there are more appropriate loops to use—for instance, the *while loop*, which we will introduce next. In these cases, the number of times the loop's body will be executed is less certain; it typically depends on what happens during the iteration. This style is often called *indefinite iteration*, and we explore it next.

4.10 Indefinite iteration

Using a for-each loop has given us our first experience with the principle of carrying out some actions repeatedly. The statements inside the loop body are repeated for each item in the associated collection, and the iteration stops when we reach the end of the collection. A for-each loop provides *definite iteration*; given the state of a particular collection, the loop body will be executed the number of times that exactly matches the size of that collection. But there are many situations where we want to repeat some actions, but we cannot predict in advance exactly how many times that might be. A for-each loop does not help us in those cases.

Imagine, for instance, that you have lost your keys and you need to find them before you can leave the house. Your search will model an indefinite iteration, because there will be many different places to look, and you cannot predict in advance how many places you will have to search before you find the keys; after all, if you could predict that, you would go straight to where they are! So you will do something like mentally composing a list of possible places they could be, and then visit each place in turn until you find them. Once found, you want to stop looking rather than complete the list (which would be pointless).

What we have here is an example of *indefinite iteration*: the (search) action will be repeated an unpredictable number of times, until the task is complete. Scenarios similar to key searching are common in programming situations. While we will not always be searching for something, situations in which we want to keep doing something until the repetition is no longer necessary are frequently encountered. Indeed, they are so common that most programming languages provide at least one—and commonly more than one—loop construct to express them. Because what we are trying to do with these loop constructs is typically more complex than just iterating over a complete collection from beginning to end, they require a little more effort to understand. But this effort will be well rewarded from the greater variety of things we can achieve with them. Our focus here will be on Java's *while loop*, which is similar to loops found in other programming languages.

4.10.1   The while loop

A *while loop* consists of a header and a body; the body is intended to be executed repeatedly. Here is the structure of a while loop where *boolean condition* and *loop body* are pseudo-code, but all the rest is the Java syntax:

```
while(boolean condition) {
    loop body
}
```

The loop is introduced with the keyword `while`, which is followed by a boolean condition. The condition is ultimately what controls how many times a particular loop will iterate. The condition is evaluated when program control first reaches the loop, and it is re-evaluated each time the loop body has been executed. This is what gives a while loop its indefinite character—the re-evaluation process. If the condition evaluates to *true*, then the body is executed; and once it evaluates to *false*, the iteration is finished. The loop's body is then skipped over and execution continues with whatever follows immediately after the loop. Note that the condition could actually evaluate to *false* on the very first time it is tested. If this happens, the body won't be executed at all. This is an important feature of the while loop: the body might be executed zero times, rather than always at least once.

Before we look at a proper Java example, let us look at a pseudo-code version of the key hunt described earlier, to try to develop a feel for how a while loop works. Here is one way to express the search:

```
while(the keys are missing)  {
    look in the next place
}
```

When we arrive at the loop for the first time, the condition is evaluated: the keys are missing. That means we enter the body of the loop and look in the next place on our mental list. Having done that, we return to the condition and re-evaluate it. If we have found the keys, the loop is finished and we can skip over the loop and leave the house. If the keys are still missing, then we go back into the loop body and look in the next place. This repetitive process continues until the keys are no longer missing.[1]

Note that we could equally well express the loop's condition the other way around, as follows:

```
while(not (the keys have been found))  {
    look in the next place
}
```

The distinction is subtle—one expressed as a status to be changed, and the other as a goal that has not yet been achieved. Take some time to read the two versions carefully to be sure you understand how each works. Both are equally valid and reflect choices of expression we will have to make when writing real loops. In both cases, what we write inside the loop when the keys are finally found will mean the loop conditions "flip" from *true* to *false* the next time they are evaluated.

Exercise 4.29 Suppose we express the first version of the key search in pseudo-code as follows:

```
boolean missing = true;
while(missing) {
    if(the keys are in the next place)  {
        missing = false;
    }
}
```

---

[1] At this stage, we will ignore the possibility that the keys are not found, but taking this kind of possibility into account will actually become very important when we look at real Java examples.

Try to express the second version by completing the following outline:

```
boolean found = false;
while(...) {
    if(the keys are in the next place) {
        ...
    }
}
```

4.10.2 Iterating with an index variable

For our first while loop in correct Java code, we shall write a version of the `listAllFiles` method shown in Code 4.3. This does not really illustrate the indefinite character of while loops, but it does provide a useful comparison with the equivalent, familiar for-each example. The while-loop version is shown in Code 4.5. A key feature is the way that an integer variable (`index`) is used both to access the list's elements and to control the length of the iteration.

Code 4.5

Using a while loop to list the tracks

```
/**
 * Show a list of all the files in the collection.
 */
public void listAllFiles()
{
    int index = 0;
    while(index < files.size()) {
        String filename = files.get(index);
        System.out.println(filename);
        index++;
    }
}
```

It is immediately obvious that the while-loop version requires more effort on our part to program it. Consider:

- We have to declare a variable for the list index, and we have to initialize it ourselves to 0 for the first list element. The variable must be declared outside the loop.

- We have to work out how to express the loop's condition in order to ensure that the loop stops at the right time.

- The list elements are not automatically fetched out of the collection and assigned to a variable for us. Instead, we have to do this ourselves, using the `get` method of the `ArrayList`. The variable `filename` will be local to the body of the loop.

- We have to remember to increment the counter variable (`index`) ourselves, in order to ensure that the loop condition will eventually become *false* when we have reached the end of the list.

The final statement in the body of the while loop illustrates a special operator for incrementing a numerical variable by 1:

```
index++;
```

This is equivalent to

```
index = index + 1;
```

So far, the for-each loop is clearly nicer for our purpose. It was less trouble to write, and it is safer. The reason it is safer is that it is always guaranteed to come to an end. In our while-loop version, it is possible to make a mistake that results in an *infinite loop*. If we were to forget to increment the index variable (the last line in the loop body), the loop condition would never become *false*, and the loop would iterate indefinitely. This is a typical programming error that catches even experienced programmers from time to time. The program will then run forever. If the loop in such a situation does not contain an output statement, the program will appear to "hang": it seems to do nothing, and does not respond to any mouse clicks or key presses. In reality, the program does a lot. It executes the loop over and over, but we cannot see any effect of this, and the program seems to have died. In BlueJ, this can often be detected by the fact that the red-and-white-striped "running" indicator remains on while the program appears to be doing nothing.

So what are the benefits of a while loop over a for-each loop? They are twofold: first, the while loop does not need to be related to a collection (we can loop on any condition that we can write as a boolean expression); second, even if we are using the loop to process the collection, we do not need to process every element—instead, we could stop earlier if we wanted to by including another component in the loop's condition that expresses why we would want to stop. Of course, strictly speaking, the loop's condition actually expresses whether we want to continue, and it is the negation of this that causes the loop to stop.

A benefit of having an explicit index variable is that we can use its value both inside and outside the loop, which was not available to us in the for-each examples. So we can include the index in the listing if we wish. That will make it easier to choose a track by its position in the list. For instance:

```
int index = 0;
while(index < files.size()) {
    String filename = files.get(index);
    // Prefix the file name with the track's index.
    System.out.println(index + ": " + filename);
    index++;
}
```

Having a local index variable can be particularly important when searching a list, because it can provide a record of where the item was located, which is still available once the loop has finished. We shall see this in the next section.

4.10.3 Searching a collection

Searching is one of the most important forms of iteration you will encounter. It is vital, therefore, to have a good grasp of its essential elements. The sort of loop structures that result occur again and again in practical programming situations.

The key characteristic of a search is that it involves *indefinite iteration*; this is necessarily so, because if we knew exactly where to look, we would not need a search at all! Instead, we have to initiate a search, and it will take an unknown number of iterations before we succeed. This implies that a for-each loop is inappropriate for use when searching, because it will complete its full set of iterations.[2]

In real search situations, we have to take into account the fact that the search might fail: we might run out of places to look. That means that we typically have two finishing possibilities to consider when writing a searching loop:

- The search succeeds after an indefinite number of iterations.

- The search fails after exhausting all possibilities.

Both of these must be taken into account when writing the loop's condition. As the loop's condition should evaluate to *true* if we want to iterate one more time, each of the finishing criteria should, on their own, make the condition evaluate to *false* to stop the loop.

The fact that we end up searching the whole list when the search fails does not turn a failed search into an example of definite iteration. The key characteristic of definite iteration is that you can determine the number of iterations *when the loop starts*. This will not be the case with a search.

If we are using an index variable to work our way through successive elements of a collection, then a failed search is easy to identify: the index variable will have been incremented beyond the final item in the list. That is exactly the situation that is covered in the `listAll-Files` method in Code 4.5, where the condition is:

```
while(index < files.size())
```

The condition expresses that we want to continue as long as the index is within the valid index range of the collection; as soon as it has been incremented out of range, then we want the loop to stop. This condition works even if the list is completely empty. In this case, `index` will have been initialized to zero, and the call to the `size` method will return zero too. Because zero is not less than zero, the loop's body will not be executed at all, which is what we want.

We also need to add a second part to the condition that indicates whether we have found the search item yet and stops the search when we have. We saw in Section 4.10.1 and Exercise 4.29 that we can often express this positively or negatively, via appropriately set boolean variables:

- A variable called `searching` (or `missing`, say) initially set to *true* could keep the search going until it is set to *false* inside the loop when the item is found.

- A variable called `found`, initially set to *false* and used in the condition as `!found`, could keep the search going until set to *true* when the item is found.

Here are the two corresponding code fragments that express the full condition in both cases:

```
int index = 0;
boolean searching = true;
while(index < files.size() && searching)
```

---

[2] While there are ways to subvert this characteristic of a for-each loop, and they are used quite commonly, we consider them to be bad style and do not use them in our examples.

or

```
int index = 0;
boolean found = false;
while(index < files.size() && !found)
```

Take some time to make sure you understand these two fragments, which accomplish exactly the same loop control, but expressed in slightly different ways. Remember that the condition *as a whole* must evaluate to *true* if we want to continue looking, and *false* if we want to stop looking, for any reason. We discussed the "and" operator **&&** in Chapter 3, which only evaluates to *true* if *both* of its operands are *true*.

The full version of a method to search for the first file name matching a given search string can be seen in Code 4.6 (*music-organizer-v4*). The method returns the index of the item as its result. Note that we need to find a way to indicate to the method's caller if the search has failed. In this case, we choose to return a value that cannot possibly represent a valid location in the collection—a negative value. This is a commonly used technique in search situations: the return of an *out-of-bounds* value to indicate failure.

Code 4.6

Finding the first matching item in a list

```
/**
 * Find the index of the first file matching the given
 * search string.
 * @param searchString The string to match.
 * @return The index of the first occurrence, or -1 if
 *         no match is found.
 */
public int findFirst(String searchString)
{
    int index = 0;
    // Record that we will be searching until a match is found.
    boolean searching = true;

    while(searching && index < files.size()) {
        String filename = files.get(index);
        if(filename.contains(searchString)) {
            // A match. We can stop searching.
            searching = false;
        }
        else {
            // Move on.
            index++;
        }
    }
    if(searching) {
        // We didn't find it.
        return -1;
    }
    else {
        // Return where it was found.
        return index;
    }
}
```

It might be tempting to try to have just one condition in the loop, even though there are two distinct reasons for ending the search. A way to do this would be to artificially arrange for the value of index to be too large if we find what we are looking for. This is a practice we discourage, because it makes the termination criteria of the loop misleading, and clarity is always preferred.

4.10.4 Some non-collection examples

Loops are not only used with collections. There are many situations were we want to repeat a block of statements that does not involve a collection at all. Here is an example that prints out all even numbers from 0 up to 30:

```
int index = 0;
while(index <= 30) {
    System.out.println(index);
    index = index + 2;
}
```

In fact, this is the use of a while loop for definite iteration, because it is clear at the start how many numbers will be printed. However, we cannot use a for-each loop, because they can only be used when iterating over collections. Later we will meet a third, related loop—the *for loop*—that would be more appropriate for this particular example.

To test your own understanding of while loops aside from collections, try the following exercises.

Exercise 4.30 Write a while loop (for example, in a method called `multiplesOfFive`) that prints out all multiples of 5 between 10 and 95.

Exercise 4.31 Write a while loop to add up the values 1 to 10 and print the sum once the loop has finished.

Exercise 4.32 Write a method called **sum** with a while loop that adds up all numbers between two numbers **a** and **b**. The values for **a** and **b** can be passed to the **sum** method as parameters.

Exercise 4.33 *Challenge exercise* Write a method `isPrime(int n)` that returns *true* if the parameter **n** is a prime number, and *false* if it is not. To implement the method, you can write a while loop that divides **n** by all numbers between **2** and **(n–1)** and tests whether the division yields a whole number. You can write this test by using the modulo operator (**%**) to check whether the integer division leaves a remainder of 0 (see the discussion of the modulo operator in Section 3.8.3).

Exercise 4.34 In the `findFirst` method, the loop's condition repeatedly asks the `files` collection how many files it is storing. Does the value returned by `size` vary from one check to the next? If you think the answer is no, then rewrite the method so that the number of files is determined only once and stored in a local variable prior to execution of the loop. Then use the local variable in the loop's condition rather than the call to `size`. Check that this version gives the same results. If you have problems completing this exercise, try using the debugger to see where things are going wrong.

4.11 Improving structure—the Track class

We have seen in a couple of places that using strings to store all of the track details is not entirely satisfactory, and gives our music player a rather cheap feel. Any commercial player would allow us to search for tracks by artist, title, album, genre, etc., and would likely include additional details, such as track playing time and track number. One of the powers of object orientation is that it allows us to design classes that closely model the inherent structure and behaviors of the real-world entities we are often trying to represent. This is achieved through writing classes whose fields and methods match the attributes. We know enough already about how to write basic classes with fields, constructors, and accessor and mutator methods that we can easily design a `Track` class that has fields for storing separate artist and title information, for instance. In this way, we will be able to interact with the objects in the music organizer in a way that feels more natural.

So it is time to move away from storing the track details as strings, because having a separate `Track` class is the most appropriate way to represent the main data items—music tracks—that we are using in the program. However, we will not be too ambitious. One of the obvious hurdles to overcome is how to obtain the separate pieces of information we wish to store in each `Track` object. One way would be to ask the user to input the artist, title, genre, etc., each time they add a music file to the organizer. However, that would be fairly slow and laborious, so for this project, we have chosen a set of music files that have the artist and title as part of the file name. We have written a helper class for our application (called `TrackReader`) that will look for any music files in a particular folder and use their file names to fill in parts of the corresponding `Track` objects. We will not worry about the details of how this is done at this stage. (Later in this book, we will discuss the techniques and library classes used in the `TrackReader` class.) An implementation of this design is in *music-organizer-v5*.

Here are some of the key points to look for in this version:

■ The main thing to review is the changes we have made to the **MusicOrganizer** class, in going from storing **String** objects in the **ArrayList** to storing **Track** objects (Code 4.7). This has affected most of the methods we developed previously.

■ When listing details of the tracks in `listAllTracks`, we request the **Track** object to return a **String** containing its details. This shows that we have designed the **Track** class to be responsible for providing the details to be printed, such as artist and title. This is an example of what is called *responsibility-driven design*, which we cover in more detail in a later chapter.

■ In the `playTrack` method, we now have to retrieve the file name from the selected **Track** object before passing it on to the player.

■ In the music library, we have added code to automatically read from the *audio* folder and some print statements to display some information.

Code 4.7
Using **Track**
in the **Music-
Organizer** class

```java
import java.util.ArrayList;

/**
 * A class to hold details of audio tracks.
 * Individual tracks may be played.
 *
 * @author David J. Barnes and Michael Kölling
 * @version 2016.02.29
 */
public class MusicOrganizer
{
    // An ArrayList for storing music tracks.
    private ArrayList<Track> tracks;
    // A player for the music tracks.
    private MusicPlayer player;
    // A reader that can read music files and load them as tracks.
    private TrackReader reader;

    /**
     * Create a MusicOrganizer
     */
    public MusicOrganizer()
    {
        tracks = new ArrayList<>();
        player = new MusicPlayer();
        reader = new TrackReader();
        readLibrary("../audio");
        System.out.println("Music library loaded. " + getNumberOfTracks() +
                            " tracks.");
        System.out.println();
    }

    /**
     * Add a track to the collection.
     * @param track The track to be added.
     */
    public void addTrack(Track track)
    {
        tracks.add(track);
    }

    /**
     * Play a track in the collection.
     * @param index The index of the track to be played.
     */
    public void playTrack(int index)
    {
        if(indexValid(index)) {
            Track track = tracks.get(index);
            player.startPlaying(track.getFilename());
            System.out.println("Now playing: " + track.getArtist() +
                                " - " + track.getTitle());
        }
    }
}
```

Code 4.7
continued
Using **Track**
in the **Music-**
Organizer class

```java
/**
 * Show a list of all the tracks in the collection.
 */
public void listAllTracks()
{
    System.out.println("Track listing: ");

    for(Track track : tracks) {
        System.out.println(track.getDetails());
    }
    System.out.println();
}
```

Other methods omitted.

}

While we can see that introducing a **Track** class has made some of the old methods slightly more complicated, working with specialized **Track** objects ultimately results in a much better structure for the program as a whole, and allows us to develop the **Track** class to the most appropriate level of detail for representing more than just audio file names. The information is not only better structured; using a **Track** class also allows us to store richer information if we choose to, such as an image of an album cover.

With a better structuring of track information, we can now do a much better job of searching for tracks that meet particular criteria. For instance, if we want to find all tracks that contain the word "love" in their title, we can do so as follows without risking mismatches on artists' names:

```java
/**
 * List all tracks containing the given search string in their title.
 * @param searchString The search string to be found.
 */
public void findInTitle(String searchString)
{
    for(Track track : tracks) {
        String title = track.getTitle();
        if(title.contains(searchString)) {
            System.out.println(track.getDetails());
        }
    }
}
```

Exercise 4.35 Add a `playCount` field to the **Track** class. Provide methods to reset the count to zero and to increment it by one.

Exercise 4.36 Have the **MusicOrganizer** increment the play count of a track whenever it is played.

Exercise 4.37 Add a further field, of your choosing, to the **Track** class, and provide accessor and mutator methods to query and manipulate it. Find a way to use this information in your version of the project; for instance, include it in a track's details string, or allow it to be set via a method in the **Music-Organizer** class.

Exercise 4.38 If you play two tracks without stopping the first one, both will play simultaneously. This is not very useful. Change your program so that a playing track is automatically stopped when another track is started.

4.12 The Iterator type

Iteration is a vital tool in almost every programming project, so it should come as no surprise to discover that programming languages typically provide a wide range of features that support it, each with their own particular characteristics suited for different situations.

> **Concept**
>
> An **iterator** is an object that provides functionality to iterate over all elements of a collection.

We will now discuss a third variation for how to iterate over a collection that is somewhat in the middle between the while loop and the for-each loop. It uses a while loop to perform the iteration, and an *iterator object* instead of an integer index variable to keep track of the position in the list. We have to be very careful with naming at this point, because **Iterator** (note the uppercase *I*) is a Java *class*, but we will also encounter a *method* called **iterator** (lowercase *i*), so be sure to pay close attention to these differences when reading this section and when writing your own code.

Examining every item in a collection is so common that we have already seen a special control structure—the for-each loop—that is custom made for this purpose. In addition, Java's various collection library classes provide a custom-made common type to support iteration, and **ArrayList** is typical in this respect.

The **iterator** method of **ArrayList** returns an **Iterator** object. **Iterator** is also defined in the **java.util** package, so we must add a second import statement to the class file to use it:

```
import java.util.ArrayList;
import java.util.Iterator;
```

An **Iterator** provides just four methods, and two of these are used to iterate over a collection: **hasNext** and **next**. Neither takes a parameter, but both have non-**void** return types, so they are used in expressions. The way we usually use an **Iterator** can be described in pseudo-code as follows:

```
Iterator<ElementType> it = myCollection.iterator();
while(it.hasNext()) {
    call it.next() to get the next element
    do something with that element
}
```

In this code fragment, we first use the **iterator** method of the **ArrayList** class to obtain an **Iterator** object. Note that **Iterator** is also a generic type, so we parameterize it with the type of the elements in the collection we are iterating over. Then we use that **Iterator** to repeatedly check whether there are any more elements, **it.hasNext**(), and to get the next element, **it.next**(). One important point to note is that it is the **Iterator** object that we ask to return the next item, and not the collection object. Indeed, we tend not to refer directly to the collection at all in the body of the loop; all interaction with the collection is done via the **Iterator**.

Using an **Iterator**, we can write a method to list the tracks, as shown in Code 4.8. In effect, the **Iterator** starts at the beginning of the collection and progressively works its way through, one object at a time, each time we call its **next** method.

Code 4.8

Using an **Iterator** to list the tracks

```
/**
 * List all the tracks.
 */
public void listAllTracks()
{
    Iterator<Track> it = tracks.iterator();
    while(it.hasNext()) {
        Track t = it.next();
        System.out.println(t.getDetails());
    }
}
```

Take some time to compare this version to the one using a for-each loop in Code 4.7, and the two versions of **listAllFiles** shown in Code 4.3 and Code 4.5. A particular point to note about the latest version is that we use a while loop, but we do not need to take care of the **index** variable. This is because the **Iterator** keeps track of how far it has progressed through the collection, so that it knows both whether there are any more items left (**hasNext**) and which one to return (**next**) if there is another.

One of the keys to understanding how an **Iterator** works is that the call to **next** causes the **Iterator** to return the next item in the collection *and then move past that item*. Therefore, successive calls to **next** on an **Iterator** will always return distinct items; you cannot go back to the previous item once **next** has been called. Eventually, the **Iterator** reaches the end of the collection and then returns *false* from a call to **hasNext**. Once **hasNext** has returned *false*, it would be an error to try to call **next** on that particular **Iterator** object—in effect, the **Iterator** object has been "used up" and has no further use.

On the face of it, **Iterator** seems to offer no obvious advantages over the previous ways we have seen to iterate over a collection, but the following two sections provide reasons why it is important to know how to use it.

4.12.1 Index access versus iterators

We have seen that we have at least three different ways in which we can iterate over an **ArrayList**. We can use a for-each loop (as seen in Section 4.9.1), the **get** method with an integer index variable (Section 4.10.2), or an **Iterator** object (this section).

Figure 4.5
An iterator, after
one iteration,
pointing to the
next item to be
processed

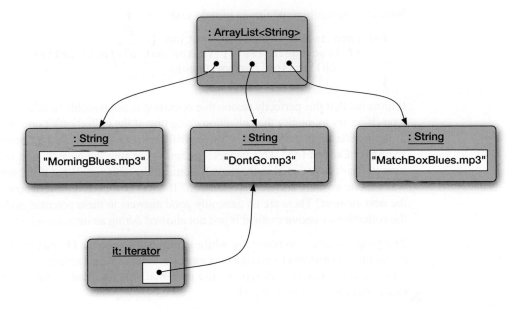

From what we know so far, all approaches seem about equal in quality. The first one was maybe slightly easier to understand, but the least flexible.

The first approach, using the for-each loop, is the standard technique used if all elements of a collection are to be processed (i.e., definite iteration), because it is the most concise for that case. The two latter versions have the benefit that iteration can more easily be stopped in the middle of processing (indefinite iteration), so they are preferable when processing only a part of the collection.

For an **ArrayList**, the two latter methods (using the while loops) are in fact equally good. This is not always the case, though. Java provides many more collection classes besides the **ArrayList**. We shall see several of them in the following chapters. For some collections, it is either impossible or very inefficient to access individual elements by providing an index. Thus, our first while loop version is a solution particular to the **ArrayList** collection and may not work for other types of collections.

The most recent solution, using an **Iterator**, is available for all collections in the Java class library and thus is an important *code pattern* that we shall use again in later projects.

4.12.2 Removing elements

Another important consideration when choosing which looping structure to use comes in when we have to remove elements from the collection while iterating. An example might be that we want to remove all tracks from our collection that are by an artist we are no longer interested in.

We can quite easily write this in pseudo-code:

```
for each track in the collection {
    if track.getArtist() is the out-of-favor artist:
        collection.remove(track)
}
```

It turns out that this perfectly reasonable operation is not possible to achieve with a for-each loop. If we try to modify the collection using one of the collection's **remove** methods while in the middle of an iteration, the system will report an error (called a **ConcurrentModificationException**). This happens because changing the collection in the middle of an iteration has the potential to thoroughly confuse the situation. What if the removed element was the one we were currently working on? If it has now been removed, how should we find the next element? There are no generally good answers to these potential problems, so using the collection's **remove** method is just not allowed during an iteration with the for-each loop.

The proper solution to removing while iterating is to use an **Iterator**. Its third method (in addition to **hasNext** and **next**) is **remove**. It takes no parameter and has a **void** return type. Calling **remove** will remove the item that was returned by the most recent call to **next**. Here is some sample code:

```
Iterator<Track> it = tracks.iterator();
while(it.hasNext()) {
    Track t = it.next();
    String artist = t.getArtist();
    if(artist.equals(artistToRemove)) {
        it.remove();
    }
}
```

Once again, note that we do not use the **tracks** collection variable in the body of the loop. While both **ArrayList** and **Iterator** have **remove** methods, we must use the **Iterator**'s **remove** method, not the **ArrayList**'s.

Using the **Iterator**'s **remove** is less flexible–we cannot remove arbitrary elements. We can remove only the last element we retrieved from the **Iterator**'s **next** method. On the other hand, using the **Iterator**'s **remove** is allowed during an iteration. Because the **Iterator** itself is informed of the removal (and does it for us), it can keep the iteration properly in sync with the collection.

Such removal is not possible with the for-each loop, because we do not have an **Iterator** there to work with. In this case, we need to use the while loop with an **Iterator**.

Technically, we can also remove elements by using the collection's **get** method with an index for the iteration. This is not recommended, however, because the element indices can change when we add or delete elements, and it is quite easy to get the iteration with indices wrong when we modify the collection during iteration. Using an **Iterator** protects us from such errors.

Exercise 4.39 Implement a method in your music organizer that lets you specify a string as a parameter, and then removes all tracks whose titles contain that string.

4.13 Summary of the music-organizer project

In the music organizer we have seen how we can use an **ArrayList** object, created from a class out of the class library, to store an arbitrary number of objects in a collection. We do not have to decide in advance how many objects we want to store, and the **ArrayList** object automatically keeps track of the number of items stored in it.

We have discussed how we can use a loop to iterate over all elements in the collection. Java has several loop constructs—the two we have used here are the *for-each loop* and the *while loop*. We typically use a for-each loop when we want to process the whole collection, and the while loop when we cannot predetermine how many iterations we need or when we need to remove elements during iteration.

With an **ArrayList**, we can access elements either by index, or we can iterate over all elements using an **Iterator** object. It will be worthwhile for you to review the different circumstances under which the different types of loop (for-each and while) are appropriate and why an **Iterator** is to be preferred over an integer index, because these sorts of decisions will have to be made over and over again. Getting them right can make it a lot easier to solve a particular problem.

Exercise 4.40 Use the *club* project to complete this and the following exercises. Your task is to complete the **Club** class, an outline of which has been provided in the project. The **Club** class is intended to store **Membership** objects in a collection.

Within **Club**, define a field for an **ArrayList**. Use an appropriate **import** statement for this field, and think carefully about the element type of the list. In the constructor, create the collection object and assign it to the field. Make sure that all the files in the project compile before moving on to the next exercise.

Exercise 4.41 Complete the **numberOfMembers** method to return the current size of the collection. Until you have a method to add objects to the collection, this will always return zero, of course, but it will be ready for further testing later.

Exercise 4.42 Membership of a club is represented by an instance of the **Membership** class. A complete version of **Membership** is already provided for you in the *club* project, and it should not need any modification. An instance contains details of a person's name and the month and year in which they joined the club. All membership details are filled out when an instance is created. A new **Membership** object is added to a **Club** object's collection via the **Club** object's **join** method, which has the following description:

```
/**
 * Add a new member to the club's collection of members.
 * @param member The member object to be added.
 */
public void join (Membership member)
```

Complete the **join** method.

When you wish to add a new **Membership** object to the **Club** object from the object bench, there are two ways you can do this. Either create a new **Membership** object on the object bench, call the **join** method on the **Club** object, and click on the **Membership** object to supply the parameter or call the **join** method on the **Club** object and type into the method's parameter dialog box:

```
new Membership ("member name ...", month, year)
```

Each time you add one, use the **numberOfMembers** method to check both that the **join** method is adding to the collection and that the **numberOfMembers** method is giving the correct result.

We shall continue to explore this project with some further exercises later in the chapter.

Exercise 4.43 *Challenge exercise* This and the following exercises present a challenge because they involve using some things that we have not covered explicitly. Nevertheless, you should be able to make a reasonable attempt at them if you have a comfortable grasp of the material covered so far. They involve adding something that most music players have: a "shuffle," or "random-play," feature.

The **java.util** package contains the **Random** class whose **nextInt** method will generate a positive random integer within a limited range. Write a method in the **MusicOrganizer** class to select a single random track from its list and play it.

Hint: You will need to import **Random** and create a **Random** object, either directly in the new method, or in the constructor and stored in a field. You will need to find the API documentation for the **Random** class and check its methods to choose the correct version of **nextInt**. Alternatively, we cover the **Random** class in Chapter 6.

Exercise 4.44 *Challenge exercise* Consider how you might play multiple tracks in a random order. Would you want to make sure that all tracks are played equally or prefer favorite tracks? How might a "play count" field in the **Track** class help with this task? Discuss the various options.

Exercise 4.45 *Challenge exercise* Write a method to play every track in the track list exactly once, in random order.

Hint: One way to do this would be to shuffle the order of the tracks in the list—or, perhaps better, a copy of the list—and then play through from start to finish. Another way would be to make a copy of the list and then repeatedly choose a random track from the list, play it, and remove it from the list until the list is empty. Try to implement one of these approaches. If you try the first, how easy is it to shuffle the list so that it is genuinely in a new random order? Are there any library methods that could help with this?

4.14 Another example: an auction system

In this section, we will follow up some of the new ideas we have introduced in this chapter by looking at them again in a different context.

The *auction* project models part of the operation of an online auction system. The idea is that an auction consists of a set of items offered for sale. These items are called "lots," and each is assigned a unique lot number by the program. A person can try to buy a lot by bidding an amount of money for it. Our auctions are slightly different from other auctions because ours offer all lots for a limited period of time.[3] At the end of that period, the auction is closed. At the close of the auction, the person who bid the highest amount for a lot is considered to have bought it. Any lots for which there are no bids remain unsold at the close. Unsold lots might be offered in a later auction, for instance.

The *auction* project contains the following classes: **Auction**, **Bid**, **Lot**, and **Person**. A close look at the class diagram for this project (Figure 4.6) reveals that the relationships between the various classes are a little more complicated than we have seen in previous projects. This will have a bearing on the way in which information is accessed during the

Figure 4.6
The class structure of the *auction* project

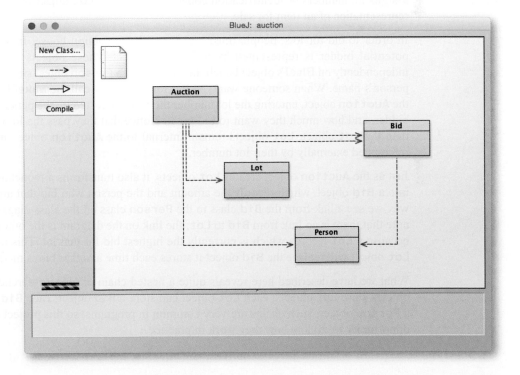

---

[3] For the sake of simplicity, the time-limit aspects of auctions are not implemented within the classes we are considering here.

auction activities. For instance, the diagram shows that **Auction** objects know about all the other types of objects: **Bid**, **Lot**, and **Person**. **Lot** objects know about **Bid** objects, and **Bid** objects know about **Person** objects. What the diagram cannot tell us is exactly how information stored in a **Bid** object, say, is accessed by an **Auction** object. For that, we have to look at the code of the various classes.

4.14.1 Getting started with the project

At this stage, it would be worth opening the *auction* project and exploring the source code before reading further. As well as seeing familiar use of an **ArrayList** and loops, you will likely encounter several things that you do not quite understand at first, but that is to be expected as we move on to new ideas and new ways of doing things.

An **Auction** object is the starting point for the project. People wishing to sell items enter them into the auction via the **enterLot** method, but they only supply a string description. The **Auction** object then creates a **Lot** object for each entered lot. This models the way things work in the real world: it is the auction site, rather than the sellers, for instance, that assigns lot numbers or identification codes to items. So a **Lot** object is the auction site's representation of an item for sale.

In order to bid for lots, people must register with the auction house. In our program, a potential bidder is represented by a **Person** object. These objects must be created independently on BlueJ's object bench. In our project, a **Person** object simply contains the person's name. When someone wants to bid for a lot, they call the **makeABid** method of the **Auction** object, entering the lot number they are interested in, the person object of the bidder, and how much they want to bid for it. Notice that they pass the lot number rather than the **Lot** object; **Lot** objects remain internal to the **Auction** object and are always referenced externally by their lot number.

Just as the **Auction** object creates **Lot** objects, it also transforms a monetary bid amount into a **Bid** object, which records the amount and the person who bid that amount. This is why we see a link from the **Bid** class to the **Person** class on the class diagram. However, note that there is no link from **Bid** to **Lot**; the link on the diagram is the other way around, because a **Lot** records which is currently the highest bid for that lot. This means that the **Lot** object will replace the **Bid** object it stores each time a higher bid is made.

What we have described here reveals quite a nested chain of object references. **Auction** objects store **Lot** objects; each **Lot** object can store a **Bid** object; each **Bid** object stores a **Person** object. Such chains are very common in programs, so this project offers a good opportunity to explore how they work in practice.

Exercise 4.46 Create an auction with a few lots, persons, and bids. Then use the object inspector to investigate the object structure. Start with the auction object, and continue by inspecting any further object references you encounter in the objects' fields.

Because neither the **Person** class nor the **Bid** class initiates any activity within the auction system, we shall not discuss them here in detail. Studying these classes is left as an exercise to the reader. Instead, we shall focus on the source code of the **Lot** and **Auction** classes.

4.14.2 The null keyword

From the discussion above, it should be clear that a **Bid** object is only created when someone actually makes a bid for a **Lot**. The newly created **Bid** object then stores the **Person** making the bid. This means that the **Person** field of every **Bid** object can be initialized in the **Bid** constructor, and the field will always contain a valid **Person** object.

In contrast, when a **Lot** object is created, this simply means it has been entered into the auction and it has no bidders yet. Nevertheless, it still has a **Bid** field, **highestBid**, for recording the highest bid for the lot. What value should be used to initialize this field in the **Lot** constructor?

What we need is a value for the field that makes it clear that there is currently "no object" being referred to by that variable. In some sense, the variable is "empty." To indicate this, Java provides the **null** keyword. Hence, the constructor of **Lot** has the following statement in it:

```
highestBid = null;
```

A very important principle is that, if a variable contains the **null** value, a method call should not be made on it. The reason for this should be clear: as methods belong to objects, we cannot call a method if the variable does not refer to an object. This means that we sometimes have to use an if-statement to test whether a variable contains **null** or not, before calling a method on that variable. Failure to make this test will lead to the very common runtime error called a **NullPointerException**. You will see some examples of this test in both the **Lot** and **Auction** classes.

In fact, if we fail to initialize an object-type field, it will automatically be given the value **null**. In this particular case, however, we prefer to make the assignment explicitly so that there is no doubt in the mind of the reader of the code that we expect **highestBid** to be **null** when a **Lot** object is created.

4.14.3 The Lot class

The **Lot** class stores a description of the lot, a lot number, and details of the highest bid received for it so far. The most complex part of the class is the **bidFor** method (Code 4.9). This deals with what happens when a person makes a bid for the lot. When a bid is made, it is necessary to check that the new bid is higher in value than any existing bid on that lot. If it is higher, then the new bid will be stored as the current highest bid within the lot.

Here, we first check whether this bid is the highest bid. This will be the case if there has been no previous bid, or if the current bid is higher than the best bid so far. The first part of the check involves the following test:

```
highestBid == null
```

Code 4.9

Handle a bid for a lot

```java
public class Lot
{
    // The current highest bid for this lot.
    private Bid highestBid;

    Other fields and constructor omitted.

    /**
     * Attempt to bid for this lot. A successful bid
     * must have a value higher than any existing bid.
     * @param bid A new bid.
     * @return true if successful, false otherwise
     */
    public boolean bidFor(Bid bid)
    {
        if(highestBid == null) {
            // There is no previous bid.
            highestBid = bid;
            return true;
        }
        else if(bid.getValue() > highestBid.getValue()) {
            // The bid is better than the previous one.
            highestBid = bid;
            return true;
        }
        else {
            // The bid is not better.
            return false;
        }
    }

    Other methods omitted.
}
```

This is a test for whether the **highestBid** variable is currently referring to an object or not. As described in the previous section, until a bid is received for this lot, the **highestBid** field will contain the **null** value. If it is still **null**, then this is the first bid for this particular lot and it must clearly be the highest one. If it is not **null**, then we have to compare its value with the new bid. Note that the failure of the first test gives us some very useful information: we now know for sure that **highestBid** is not **null**, so we know that it is safe to call a method on it. We do not need to make a **null** test again in this second condition. Comparing the values of the two bids allows us to choose a higher new bid, or reject the new bid if it is no better.

4.14.4 The Auction class

The **Auction** class (Code 4.10) provides further illustration of the **ArrayList** and for-each loop concepts we discussed earlier in the chapter.

Code 4.10

The **Auction** class

```java
import java.util.ArrayList;

/**
 * A simple model of an auction.
 * The auction maintains a list of lots of arbitrary length.
 *
 * @author David J. Barnes and Michael Kölling.
 * @version 2016.02.29
 */
public class Auction
{
    // The list of Lots in this auction.
    private ArrayList<Lot> lots;
    // The number that will be given to the next lot entered
    // into this auction.
    private int nextLotNumber;

    /**
     * Create a new auction.
     */
    public Auction()
    {
        lots = new ArrayList<>();
        nextLotNumber = 1;
    }

    /**
     * Enter a new lot into the auction.
     * @param description A description of the lot.
     */
    public void enterLot(String description)
    {
        lots.add(new Lot(nextLotNumber, description));
        nextLotNumber++;
    }

    /**
     * Show the full list of lots in this auction.
     */
    public void showLots()
    {
        for(Lot lot : lots) {
            System.out.println(lot.toString());
        }
    }

    /**
     * Make a bid for a lot.
     * A message is printed indicating whether the bid is
     * successful or not.
     *
     * @param lotNumber The lot being bid for.
     * @param bidder The person bidding for the lot.
     * @param value  The value of the bid.
     */
```

**Code 4.10
continued**

The **Auction**
class

```java
public void makeABid(int lotNumber, Person bidder, long value)
{
    Lot selectedLot = getLot(lotNumber);
    if(selectedLot != null) {
        Bid bid = new Bid(bidder, value);
        boolean successful = selectedLot.bidFor(bid);
        if(successful) {
            System.out.println("The bid for lot number " +
                                lotNumber + " was successful.");
        }
        else {
            // Report which bid is higher.
            Bid highestBid = selectedLot.getHighestBid();
            System.out.println("Lot number: " + lotNumber +
                                " already has a bid of: " +
                                highestBid.getValue());
        }
    }
}

/**
 * Return the lot with the given number. Return null
 * if a lot with this number does not exist.
 * @param lotNumber The number of the lot to return.
 */
public Lot getLot(int lotNumber)
{
    if((lotNumber >= 1) && (lotNumber < nextLotNumber)) {
        // The number seems to be reasonable.
        Lot selectedLot = lots.get(lotNumber - 1);
        // Include a confidence check to be sure we have the
        // right lot.
        if(selectedLot.getNumber() != lotNumber) {
            System.out.println("Internal error: Lot number " +
                                selectedLot.getNumber() +
                                " was returned instead of " +
                                lotNumber);
            // Don't return an invalid lot.
            selectedLot = null;
        }
        return selectedLot;
    }
    else {
        System.out.println("Lot number: " + lotNumber +
                            " does not exist.");
        return null;
    }
}
```

The **lots** field is an **ArrayList** used to hold the lots offered in this auction. Lots are entered in the auction by passing a simple description to the **enterLot** method. A new lot is created by passing the description and a unique lot number to the constructor of **Lot**. The new **Lot** object is added to the collection. The following sections discuss some additional, commonly found features illustrated in the **Auction** class.

4.14.5 Anonymous objects

The **enterLot** method in **Auction** illustrates a common idiom—anonymous objects. We see this in the following statement:

```
lots.add(new Lot(nextLotNumber, description));
```

Here, we are doing two things:

- We are creating a new **Lot** object.
- We are also passing this new object to the **ArrayList**'s **add** method.

We could have written the same statement in two lines, to make the separate steps more explicit:

```
Lot newLot = new Lot(nextLotNumber, description);
lots.add(newLot);
```

Both versions are equivalent, but if we have no further use for the **newLot** variable, then the original version avoids defining a variable with such a limited use. In effect, we create an anonymous object—an object without a name—by passing it straight to the method that uses it.

Exercise 4.47 The **makeABid** method includes the following two statements:

```
Bid bid = new Bid(bidder, value);
boolean successful = selectedLot.bidFor(bid);
```

The **bid** variable is only used here as a placeholder for the newly created **Bid** object before it is passed immediately to the lot's **bidFor** method. Rewrite these statements to eliminate the bid variable by using an anonymous object as seen in the **enterLot** method.

4.14.6 Chaining method calls

In our introduction to the *auction* project, we noted a chain of object references: **Auction** objects store **Lot** objects; each **Lot** object can store a **Bid** object; each **Bid** object stores a **Person** object. If the **Auction** object needs to identify who currently has the highest bid on a **Lot**, then it would need to ask the **Lot** to return the **Bid** object for that lot, then ask the **Bid** object for the **Person** who made the bid, and then ask the **Person** object for its name.

Ignoring the possibility of **null** object references, we might see something like the following sequence of statements in order to print the name of a bidder:

```
Bid bid = lot.getHighestBid();
Person bidder = bid.getBidder();
String name = bidder.getName();
System.out.println(name);
```

Because the **bid**, **bidder**, and **name** variables are being used here simply as staging posts to get to the bidder's name, it is common to see sequences like this compressed through the use of anonymous object references. For instance, we can achieve the same effect with the following:

```
System.out.println(lot.getHighestBid().getBidder().getName());
```

This looks as if methods are calling methods, but that is not how this must be read. Bearing in mind that the two sets of statements are equivalent, the chain of method calls must be read strictly from left to right:

```
lot.getHighestBid().getBidder().getName()
```

The call to **getHighestBid** returns an anonymous **Bid** object, and the **getBidder** method is then called on that object. Similarly, **getBidder** returns an anonymous **Person** object, so **getName** is called on that person.

Such chains of method calls can look complicated, but they can be unpicked if you understand the underlying rules. Even if you choose not to write your code in this more concise fashion, you should learn how to read it, because you may come across it in other programmers' code.

Exercise 4.48 Add a **close** method to the **Auction** class. This should iterate over the collection of lots and print out details of all the lots. Use a for-each loop. Any lot that has had at least one bid for it is considered to be sold, so what you are looking for is **Lot** objects whose **highestBid** field is not **null**. Use a local variable inside the loop to store the value returned from calls to the **getHighestBid** method, and then test that variable for the **null** value.

For lots with a bidder, the details should include the name of the successful bidder and the value of the winning bid. For lots with no bidder, print a message that indicates this.

Exercise 4.49 Add a **getUnsold** method to the **Auction** class with the following header:

```
public ArrayList<Lot> getUnsold()
```

This method should iterate over the **lots** field, storing unsold lots in a new **ArrayList** local variable. What you are looking for is **Lot** objects whose **highestBid** field is **null**. At the end of the method, return the list of unsold lots.

Exercise 4.50 Suppose the **Auction** class includes a method that makes it possible to remove a lot from the auction. Assuming the remaining lots do not have their **lotNumber** fields changed when a lot is removed, write down what you think the impact would be on the **getLot** method.

Exercise 4.51 Rewrite `getLot` so that it does not rely on a lot with a particular number being stored at index **(number-1)** in the collection. For instance, if lot number 2 has been removed, then lot number 3 will have been moved from index 2 to index 1, and all higher lot numbers will also have been moved by one index position. You may assume that lots are always stored in increasing order according to their lot numbers.

Exercise 4.52 Add a `removeLot` method to the **Auction** class, having the following header:

```
/**
 * Remove the lot with the given lot number.
 * @param number The number of the lot to be removed.
 * @return The Lot with the given number, or null if
 * there is no such lot.
 */
public Lot removeLot(int number)
```

This method should not assume that a lot with a given number is stored at any particular location within the collection.

Exercise 4.53 The `ArrayList` class is found in the `java.util` package. That package also includes a class called **LinkedList**. Find out what you can about the **LinkedList** class, and compare its methods with those of `ArrayList`. Which methods do they have in common, and which are different?

4.14.7 Using collections

The **ArrayList** collection class (and others like it) is an important programming tools, because many programming problems involve working with variable-sized collections of objects. Before moving on to the next chapters, it is important that you become familiar and comfortable with how to work with them. The following exercises will help you do this.

Exercise 4.54 Continue working with the *club* project from Exercise 4.40. Define a method in the **Club** class with the following description:

```
/**
 * Determine the number of members who joined in the given
 * month.
 * @param month The month we are interested in.
 * @return The number of members who joined in that month.
 */
public int joinedInMonth(int month)
```

If the **month** parameter is outside the valid range of 1 to 12, print an error message and return zero.

Exercise 4.55 Define a method in the **Club** class with the following description:

```
/**
 * Remove from the club's collection all members who
 * joined in the given month,
 * and return them stored in a separate collection object.
 * @param month The month of the membership.
 * @param year The year of the membership.
 * @return The members who joined in the given month and year.
 */
public ArrayList<Membership> purge(int month, int year)
```

If the **month** parameter is outside the valid range of 1 to 12, print an error message and return a collection object with no objects stored in it.

Note: The **purge** method is significantly harder to write than any of the others in this class.

Exercise 4.56 Open the *products* project and complete the **StockManager** class through this and the next few exercises. **StockManager** uses an **Array-List** to store **Product** items. Its **addProduct** method already adds a product to the collection, but the following methods need completing: **delivery**, **find-Product**, **printProductDetails**, and **numberInStock**.

Each product sold by the company is represented by an instance of the **Product** class, which records a product's ID, name, and how many of that product are currently in stock. The **Product** class defines the **increaseQuantity** method to record increases in the stock level of that product. The **sellOne** method records that one item of that product has been sold, by reducing the quantity field level by 1. **Product** has been provided for you, and you should not need to make any alterations to it.

Start by implementing the **printProductDetails** method to ensure that you are able to iterate over the collection of products. Just print out the details of each **Product** returned, by calling its **toString** method.

Exercise 4.57 Implement the **findProduct** method. This should look through the collection for a product whose **id** field matches the ID argument of this method. If a matching product is found, it should be returned as the method's result. If no matching product is found, return **null**.

This differs from the **printProductDetails** method, in that it will not necessarily have to examine every product in the collection before a match is found. For instance, if the first product in the collection matches the product ID, iteration can finish and that first **Product** object can be returned. On the other hand, it is possible that there might be no match in the collection. In that case, the whole collection will be examined without finding a product to return. In this case, the **null** value should be returned.

When looking for a match, you will need to call the **getID** method on a **Product**.

Exercise 4.58 Implement the `numberInStock` method. This should locate a product in the collection with a matching ID and return the current quantity of that product as a method result. If no product with a matching ID is found, return zero. This is relatively simple to implement once the `findProduct` method has been completed. For instance, `numberInStock` can call the `findProduct` method to do the searching and then call the `getQuantity` method on the result. Take care with products that cannot be found, though.

Exercise 4.59 Implement the `delivery` method using a similar approach to that used in `numberInStock`. It should find the product with the given ID in the list of products and then call its `increaseQuantity` method.

Exercise 4.60 *Challenge exercise* Implement a method in **StockManager** to print details of all products with stock levels below a given value (passed as a parameter to the method).

Modify the **addProduct** method so that a new product cannot be added to the product list with the same ID as an existing one.

Add to **StockManager** a method that finds a product from its name rather than its ID:

```
public Product findProduct(String name)
```

In order to do this, you need to know that two **String** objects, **s1** and **s2**, can be tested for equality with the boolean expression

```
s1.equals(s2)
```

More details about comparing `String`s can be found in Chapter 6.

4.15 Summary

We have seen that classes such as `ArrayList` conveniently allow us to create collections containing an arbitrary number of objects. The Java library contains more collections like this, and we shall look at some of the others in Chapter 6. You will find that being able to use collections confidently is an important skill in writing interesting programs. There is hardly an application we shall see from now on that does not use collections of some form.

When using collections, the need arises to iterate over all elements in a collection to make use of the objects stored in them. For this purpose, we have seen the use of loops and iterators.

Loops are also a fundamental concept in computing that you will be using in every project from now on. Make sure you familiarize yourself sufficiently with writing loops—you will not get very far without them. When deciding on the type of loop to use in a particular situation, it is often useful to consider whether the task involves definite iteration, or indefinite iteration. Is there certainty or uncertainty about the number of iterations that will be required?

As an aside, we have mentioned the Java class library, a large collection of useful classes that we can use to make our own classes more powerful. We shall need to study the library in some more detail to see what else is in it that we should know about. This will be the topic of a future chapter.

Terms introduced in this chapter

collection, iterator, for-each loop, while loop, index, import statement, library, package, anonymous object, definite iteration, indefinite iteration

Concept summary

- **collection** A collection object can store an arbitrary number of other objects.

- **loop** A loop can be used to execute a block of statements repeatedly without having to write them multiple times.

- **iterator** An iterator is an object that provides functionality to iterate over all elements of a collection.

- **null** The Java reserved word **null** is used to mean "no object" when an object variable is not currently referring to a particular object. A field that has not explicitly been initialized will contain the value **null** by default.

Exercise 4.84 Java provides another type of loop: the *do-while loop*. Find out how this loop works and describe it. Write an example of a do-while loop that prints out the numbers from 1 to 10. To find out about this loop, find a description of the Java language (for example, at

`http://download.oracle.com/javase/tutorial/java/nutsandbolts/`

in the section "Control Flow Statements").

Exercise 4.85 Rewrite the `listAllFiles` method in the **MusicOrganizer** class from **music-organizer-v3** by using a do-while loop rather than a for-each loop. Test your solution carefully. Does it work correctly if the collection is empty?

Exercise 4.86 *Challenge exercise* Rewrite the `findFirst` method in the **MusicOrganizer** class from *music-organizer-v4* by using a do-while loop rather than a while loop. Test your solution carefully. Try searches that will succeed and others that will fail. Try searches where the file to be found is first in the list, and also where it is last in the list.

Exercise 4.87 Find out about Java's *switch-case statement*. What is its purpose? How is it used? Write an example. (This is also a *control flow statement*, so you will find information in similar locations as for the *do-while loop*.)

CHAPTER

5

Functional Processing of Collections (Advanced)

Main concepts discussed in this chapter:

- functional programming
- lambdas
- streams
- pipelines

Java constructs discussed in this chapter:

`Stream`, `lambda`, `filter`, `map`, `reduce`, `->`

This chapter introduces some advanced concepts. The advanced sections in this book (there will be some others later) can be skipped on first reading if you wish. In this chapter, we will discuss some alternative techniques to achieve the same tasks as discussed in the previous chapters. These techniques were not available in the Java language prior to version 8.

5.1 An alternative look at themes from Chapter 4

In Chapter 4, we started to look at techniques to process collections of objects. Handling collections is one of the fundamental techniques in programming; almost all computer programs process collections of some sort, and we will see much more of this throughout this book. Being able to do this well is essential.

However, learning about collections in programming has become more complicated in recent years through the introduction of new programming techniques into mainstream programming languages. These techniques can make your *program* simpler, but they make *learning* more work—there are simply more different constructs to master.

The "new" techniques are not really new—they are only new in this particular kind of language. There have always been different kinds of languages: Java, for example, is an *imperative object-oriented* language, and the style of collection processing we started to introduce in Chapter 4 is the typical imperative way to do things.

Another class of language is *functional languages*; these have been around for a long time, and they use a different style of programming. It turns out, for reasons we will discuss later, that the functional style of processing collections has advantages in some situations over the imperative style. As a result, the designers of the Java language decided at some point to add some elements of functional programming to the Java language. They did this in version 8 of the language (Java 8, released in 2014). The new techniques that were added are *streams* and *lambdas* (sometimes also called *closures*). This makes Java technically a hybrid language: a mostly imperative language with some functional elements.

For proficient programmers, this is a great thing. The new functional language constructs allow us to write more elegant and expressive programs. For learners, it creates more work: we now have to study two different ways to achieve a similar goal.

The new functional style, which we cover in this chapter, is quickly becoming popular and will likely be the dominant style of writing new code in Java within a short space of time. The imperative style covered in the previous chapter, however, is still the way most code is written today, and is still considered the "standard" Java way to do things. When you work with existing code written by other programmers (as you will most of the time), it is essential that you understand and can work with the imperative style. When you write your own code, you can choose your style: the functional and imperative styles are two different ways to solve the same problem, and one can replace the other. Going forward, we will often prefer the functional style, because it is more concise and more elegant.

In short, for a learner to become a good programmer, it is necessary to become familiar with both styles of processing collections. In this book, we present the imperative style first, and introduce the functional style in 'advanced' sections (such as this chapter).

These advanced sections can be skipped (you can now skip ahead to Chapter 6 if you want), and you will still learn how to program, and will still be able to solve the problems we present. They could also be read out of sequence (skip them now, but come back to them later) if you are short of time and want to make progress with other constructs first. For a full picture, they can be read in sequence, where they are, and you will learn the alternative constructs as you go along.

5.2 Monitoring animal populations

As before, we will use an example program to introduce and discuss the new constructs. Here, we will look at a system to monitor animal populations.

An important element of animal conservation and the protection of endangered species is the ability to monitor population numbers, and to detect when levels are healthy or in decline. Our project processes reports of sightings of different types of animal, sent back by spotters from various different places. Each sighting report consists of the name of the animal that has been seen, how many have been seen, who is sending the report (an integer ID), which area the sighting was made in (an integer), and an indication of when the sighting was made (a simple numerical value which might be the number of days since the experiment started).

The simple data requirements make it easy for spotters in remote locations to send back relatively small amounts of valuable information—perhaps in the form of a text message—to a base that is then able to aggregate the data and create reports or direct the field workers to different areas.

This approach fits well with both highly managed projects—such as might be undertaken by a National Park and involve motion triggered cameras and people evaluating the camera footage—and with loosely organized crowd-sourcing activities—such as national bird-counting days, where a large group of volunteers uses phone apps to send data.

We provide a partial implementation of such a system under the name *animal-monitoring-v1* in the book projects.

Code 5.1 shows the `Sighting` class we will be using to record details of each sighting report, from a single spotter for a particular animal, once the sighting details have been processed. In this chapter, we will not be concerning ourselves directly with format of the data sent in by the spotter. In keeping with the theme that this chapter explores, more advanced Java concepts, you are encouraged to read through the full source code of the project to find things that we have not explored in detail yet, and to use them for your own personal development. The `Sighting` class, however, is very straightforward.

Code 5.1

The **Sighting** class

```java
/**
 * Details of a sighting of a type of animal by an individual spotter.
 *
 * @author David J. Barnes and Michael Kölling
 * @version 2016.02.29
 */
public class Sighting
{
    // The animal spotted.
    private final String animal;
    // The ID of the spotter.
    private final int spotter;
    // How many were seen.
    private final int count;
    // The ID of the area in which they were seen.
    private final int area;
    // The reporting period.
    private final int period;

    /**
     * Create a record of a sighting of a particular type of animal.
     * @param animal The animal spotted.
     * @param spotter The ID of the spotter.
     * @param count How many were seen (>= 0).
     * @param area The ID of the area in which they were seen.
     * @param period The reporting period.
     */
```

Code 5.1 continued
The **Sighting** class

```java
public Sighting(String animal, int spotter, int count,
                int area, int period)
{
    this.animal = animal;
    this.spotter = spotter;
    this.count = count;
    this.area = area;
    this.period = period;
}
```

Some accessors omitted.

```java
/**
 * Return a string containing details of the animal, the number seen,
 * where they were seen, who spotted them and when.
 * @return A string giving details of the sighting.
 */
public String getDetails()
{
    return animal +
        ", count = " + count +
        ", area = " + area +
        ", spotter = " + spotter +
        ", period = " + period;
}
}
```

Code 5.2 shows part of the `AnimalMonitor` class that is used to aggregate the individual sightings into a list. At this point, all of the sightings from all the different spotters and areas are held together in a single collection. Among other things, the class contains methods to print the list, count the total number of sightings of a given animal, list all of the sightings by a particular spotter, remove records containing no sightings, and so on. All of these methods have been implemented using the techniques described in Chapter 4 for basic list manipulation: iteration over the full list; processing selected elements of the list based on some condition (filtering); and removal of elements. The methods implemented here are not complete for an application of this kind, but have been implemented to show examples of these different kinds of list processing.

Code 5.2
The **Animal-Monitor** class

```java
import java.util.ArrayList;
import java.util.Iterator;

/**
 * Monitor counts of different types of animal.
 * Sightings are recorded by spotters.
 *
 * @author David J. Barnes and Michael Kölling
 * @version 2016.02.29 (imperative)
 */
public class AnimalMonitor
{
    // Records of all the sightings of animals.
    private ArrayList<Sighting> sightings;
```

Code 5.2

continued

The **Animal-**
Monitor class

```
/**
 * Create an AnimalMonitor.
 */
public AnimalMonitor()
{
    this.sightings = new ArrayList<>();
}


/**
 * Add the sightings recorded in the given filename to the current list.
 * @param filename A CSV file of Sighting records.
 */
public void addSightings(String filename)
{
    SightingReader reader = new SightingReader();
    sightings.addAll(reader.getSightings(filename));
}


/**
 * Print details of all the sightings.
 */
public void printList()
{
    for(Sighting record : sightings) {
        System.out.println(record.getDetails());
    }
}
```

Other methods omitted.

```
}
```

So far, this code, uses the imperative collection processing techniques introduced in Chapter 4. We will use this as a basis to gradually make changes to replace the list processing code with functional constructs.

Exercise 5.1 Open the *animal-monitoring-v1 project* and create an instance of the AnimalMonitor class. The file sightings.csv in the project directory contains a small sample of sighting records in *comma-separated values* (CSV) format. Pass the name of this file (*"sightings.csv"*) to the addSightings method of the AnimalMonitor object and then call printList to show details of the data that has been read.

Exercise 5.2 Try out the other methods of the AnimalMonitor object, using animal names, spotter and area IDs shown in the output from printList.

Exercise 5.3 Read through the full source code of the AnimalMonitor class to understand how the methods work. The class only uses techniques we have covered in previous chapters, so you should be able to work out the details.

> **Exercise 5.4** Why does the `removeZeroCounts` method use a while loop with an iterator, instead of a for-each loop as used in the other methods? Could it be written with a for-each loop? Could the other methods be written using a while loop?

5.3 A first look at lambdas

Central to the new functional style of processing a collection is the concept of a *lambda*.

The basic new idea is that we can pass *a segment of code* as a parameter to a method, which can then execute this piece of code later when it needs to.

Up to now, we have seen various types of parameters—integers, strings, objects—but all these were pieces of *data*, not pieces of *code*. The ability to pass code as a parameter was new in Java 8, and it allows us to do some very useful things.

5.3.1 Processing a collection with a lambda

When we were processing our collections in Chapter 4, we wrote a loop to retrieve the collection elements one by one, and then we did something to each element. The code structure is always similar to the following pseudo-code:

```
loop (for each element in the collection):
    get one element;
    do something with the element;
end loop
```

It does not matter whether we use a for loop, a for-each loop, or a while loop, or whether we use an iterator or an index to access the elements—the principle is the same.

When using a lambda, we approach the problem differently. We pass a bit of code to the collection and say "Do this to each element in the collection." The code structure looks something like this:

```
collection.doThisForEachElement(some code);
```

We can see that the code looks much simpler. Most importantly: the loop has disappeared completely. In fact, it is not gone—it has just been moved into the *doThisForEachElement* method—but it has disappeared from our own code; we do not need to write it every time anymore.

We have made the collections more powerful: Instead of just being able to hand out their elements to us, so that we can do some work on them, the collection is now able to do work on the elements for us. This makes our life easier.

We can think about it like this: Imagine you need to give every child in a school class a haircut. In the old style, you say to the teacher: *Send me the first child*. Then you give the child a haircut. Then you say: *Send me the next child*. Another hair cutting session. And so it continues, until there are no more children left. This is the old style loop of next item/process.

In the new style, you do the following: You write down instructions for how to give a haircut, and then you give this to the teacher and say: *Do this to every child in your class.* (The teacher, here, represents the collection.) In fact, an interesting side-effect of this approach is that we don't even need to know how the teacher will complete the task. For instance, instead of cutting the hair themselves, they could decide to sub-contract the task to a separate person for each individual child, so that every child's hair is cut at the same time. The teacher would just pass on the instructions you gave them.

Your life is suddenly much easier. The teacher is doing much of the work for you. That is exactly what the new collections in Java 8 can do for you.

5.3.2 Basic syntax of a lambda

A lambda is, in some ways, similar to a method: it is a segment of code that is defined to do something, but not immediately executed. However, unlike a method, it does not belong to a class, and we will not give it a name. It is useful to compare the syntax of a lambda with that of a method performing a similar task.

A method to print out the details of a sighting might look like this:

```
public void printSighting(Sighting record)
{
    System.out.println(record.getDetails());
}
```

The equivalent lambda looks like this:

```
(Sighting record) ->
{
    System.out.println(record.getDetails());
}
```

You can now easily see the differences and the similarities. The differences are:

- There is no `public` or `private` keyword—the visibility is assumed to be `public`.

- There is no return type specified. This is because that can be worked out by the compiler from the final statement in the lambda's body. In this case, the `println` method is `void` so the lambda's return type is `void`.

- There is no name given to the lambda; it starts with the parameter list.

- An arrow (`->`) separates the parameter list from the lambda's body—this is the distinctive notation for a lambda.

You will find that lambdas are often used for relatively simple, one-off tasks that do not require the complexity of a full class. Some of the information about a lambda is provided by default or inferred from the context—its visibility and return type—and we have no choice over this. Furthermore, since a lambda has no associated class, there are also no instance fields and no constructor. That makes for very specialized usage of lambdas. Because of the lack of a name, lambdas are also known as *anonymous functions*.

We will encounter lambdas and function parameters several times later in this book, for example when we introduce *functional interfaces* in Chapter 12 and when we write graphical user interfaces (GUIs) in Chapter 13. For the time being, however, we will explore how to use lambdas with our collections.

5.4   The `forEach` method of collections

When introducing the idea of a lambda above, we mentioned the idea of a `doThisForEach-Element` method in the collection class. This method in Java is actually called `forEach`.

If we have a collection called `myList`, we can write

    `myList.forEach`(... *some code to apply to each element of list* ...)

The parameter to this method will be a lambda—a piece of code—with the syntax as we have seen it above. The `forEach` method will then execute the lambda for each list element, passing each list element as a parameter to the lambda in turn.

Let us look at some concrete code. The `printList` method from our `AnimalMonitor` class looks like this:

```
/**
 * Print details of all the sightings.
 */
public void printList()
{
    for(Sighting record : sightings) {
        System.out.println(record.getDetails());
    }
}
```

We can now write the following lambda-based version of this method:

```
/**
 * Print details of all the sightings.
 */
public void printList()
{
    sightings.forEach(
        (Sighting record) ->
        {
            System.out.println(record.getDetails());
        }
    );
}
```

The body of this new version of `printList` consists of a single statement (even though it spans six lines), which is a call to the `forEach` method of the `sightings` list. Admittedly, this does not yet look simpler than before, but we will get there in a moment. It is important to notice that there is no explicit loop statement in this version, unlike in the previous version—the iteration is handled *implicitly* by the `forEach` method.

The parameter of the `forEach` is a lambda. The lambda itself has a parameter, named `record`. Every element of the `sightings` list will be used as a parameter to this lambda in turn, and the body of the lambda executes. This way, the details of every element will be printed.

This style of syntax is completely unlike any you will have met in previous chapters of this book, so make sure that you take some time to understand this first example of a lambda in action. Although we will shortly show some slight modifications to the syntax used here, it does illustrate a typical use of lambdas, and the fundamental ideas will be repeated in all future examples:

■ A lambda starts with a list of parameters;

■ An arrow symbol follows the parameters;

■ Statements to be executed follow the arrow symbol.

> **Exercise 5.5:** Open the *animal-monitoring-v1* project and rewrite the `printList` method in your version of the **AnimalMonitor** class to use a lambda, as shown above. Test that it still works and performs the same as before.

5.4.1 Variations of lambda syntax

One goal of the lambda syntax in Java is to allow us to write code clearly and concisely. The ability to omit the `public` access modifier, for example, and the return type, are a start of this. The compiler, however, allows us to go further: Several other elements can be omitted where the compiler can work them out by itself.

The first is the type of the parameter to the lambda (`record`, in our case). Since the type of the lambda parameter must always match the type of the collection elements, the compiler can work this out, and we are allowed to omit it. Our code then looks like this:

```
sightings.forEach(
    (record) ->
    {
        System.out.println(record.getDetails());
    }
);
```

The next simplification concerns parentheses and curly brackets:

■ If the parameter list contains only a single parameter, then the parentheses may be omitted.

■ If the body of the lambda contains only a single statement, then the curly brackets may be omitted.

Applying both of these simplifications the code now becomes short enough to fit in a single line, and we can write the `forEach` call as:

```
sightings.forEach(record -> System.out.println(record.getDetails()));
```

This is the version we shall prefer in our own code.

Once again, we encourage you to make sure you understand how this reduced syntax fits the description, as many lambdas are written in this form in practice.

The *animal-monitoring-v2* project is written using the functional style as discussed here and can be used in case you want to check your solutions to some of these exercises. However, do the exercises yourself, and use this project only if you really get stuck.

> **Benefit of lambdas** In practice, when we use lambdas, the lambda code is often short and simple, and the shortcut notation just discussed here can be used. This makes our code short and clear, and easy to write. Also, because we do not write the loop ourselves anymore, we are less likely to make errors—if we don't write the loop, it cannot be wrong.
>
> There are, however, other benefits in addition to this. One is that this allows the use of streams, discussed in the next section. Another benefit is the use of concurrency (also called parallel programming).
>
> Most computers today have multiple cores and are capable of parallel processing. However, writing code that makes good use of these multiple cores is extremely difficult. Most of our programs will just use one core most of the time, and the rest of the available processing power is wasted. Learning to write code to use all cores is a very advanced subject, and many programmers never master it.
>
> By using lambdas and moving the loop into the collection, we can now potentially use collections that handle the parallel processing for us. When we want parallelism, we just use an appropriate collection, and all the hard parallel processing code is hidden inside the collection class, written for us. Our code looks short and simple. Suddenly, using all your cores in your laptop becomes possible, with very little extra effort.
>
> We will not discuss parallel programming much in this book. However, it is interesting to know that mastering lambdas and streams prepares you well to progress to using concurrent collection classes later on.

5.5 Streams

The forEach method of ArrayList (and related collection classes) is just one particular example of a method that makes use of the *streams* feature introduced in Java 8. Streams are a little like collections, but with some important differences:

Concept

Streams unify the processing of elements of a collection and other sets of data. A stream provides useful methods to manipulate these data sets.

- Elements in a stream are not accessed via an index, but usually sequentially.

- The contents and ordering of the stream cannot be changed—changes require the creation of a new stream.

- A stream could potentially be infinite!

The stream concept is used to unify the processing of sets of data, independent of where this data set comes from. It could be the processing of elements from a collection (as we have discussed), processing messages coming in over a network, processing lines of text from a text file, or all characters from a string. It does not matter what the source of the data is—we can view any of these as a stream, then use the same techniques and methods to process the elements.

Streams add one further significant new feature over previous facilities in Java for the processing of collections: the potential for safe parallel processing. There are many situations in which the order elements in a collection are processed does not matter, or when the processing of an element in the collection is largely independent of the other elements. Where these conditions apply, parallelization of collection processing can offer significant acceleration when dealing with large amounts of data. However, we will not discuss this any further here.

An `ArrayList` is not, itself, a stream, but we can ask it to provide the source of a stream by calling its `stream` method. The stream returned will contain all the elements of the `ArrayList` in index order. If we ignore the issue of parallelization, streams do not actually enable us to do anything that we could not already program, using language features we have already met. However, streams neatly capture many of the most commonly-occurring tasks we want to perform on collections, in a form that makes them much simpler to program than we have become used to, as well as being easier to understand. In particular, we will see that operations on streams eliminate the need to write explicit loops when processing a collection—just as we see in the rewrite of the `printList` method in Exercise 5.6.

> **Exercise 5.6** Modify your own `printList` method as discussed here: try out all the syntax variations for lambdas that we have shown. Recompile and test the project with each variation to check that you have the syntax correct.

We have already seen some of that with the `forEach` method; in the remainder of this chapter we will explore the `filter`, `map`, and `reduce` methods defined on streams.

5.5.1 Filters, maps and reductions

We noted above that the contents of a stream cannot be modified, so changes require a new stream to be created. Many varied kinds of processing of streams can be achieved with only three different kinds of functions: *filter*, *map*, and *reduce*. By varying and combining these, we can do most of what we will ever need.

Before looking at the specific Java methods, we will discuss the basic idea of these functions. All of them are applied to a stream to process it in a certain way. All are very common and useful.

The filter function

The *filter* function takes a stream, selects some of it elements, and creates a new stream with only the selected elements (Figure 5.1). Some elements are *filtered out*. The result is a stream with fewer elements (a subset of the original).

An example from our collection of animal sightings could be to select the sightings of elephants out of all sightings recorded. We start with all sightings, apply a filter that only selects elephants, and we are left with a stream of all elephant sightings.

Concept

We can **filter** a stream to select only specific elements.

Figure 5.1
Applying a filter to a stream

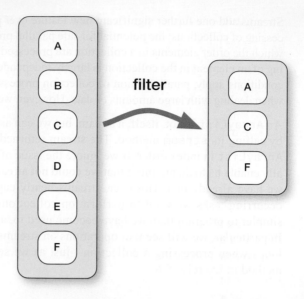

The map function

The *map* function takes a stream and creates a new stream, where each element of the original stream is mapped to a new, different element in the new stream (Figure 5.2). The new stream will have the same number of elements, but the type and content of each element can be different; it is derived in some way from the original element.

In our project, an example is to replace every sighting object in the original stream with the number of animals spotted in this sighting. We start with a stream of sighting objects, and we end with a stream of integers.

Figure 5.2
Applying a map to a stream

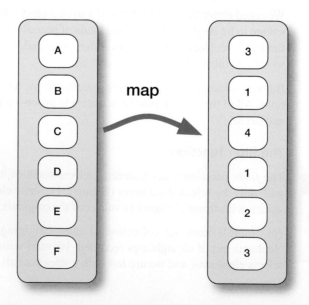

Functional Processing of Collections (advanced)

The reduce function

> **Concept**
>
> We can **reduce** a stream; reducing means to apply a function that takes a whole stream and delivers a single result.

The *reduce* function takes a stream and collapses all elements into a single result (Figure 5.3). This could be done in different ways, for example by adding all elements together, or selecting just the smallest element from the stream. We start with a stream, and we end up with a single result.

In our animal monitoring project, this would be useful for counting how many elephants we have seen: Once we have a stream of all elephant sightings, we can use *reduce* to add them all up. (Remember: each sighting instance can be of multiple animals.)

5.5.2 Pipelines

> **Concept**
>
> A **pipeline** is the combination of two or more stream functions in a chain, where each function is applied in turn.

Streams, and the stream functions, become even more useful when several functions are combined into a *pipeline*. A pipeline is the chaining of two or more of these kinds of function, so that they are applied one after the other.

Let us assume we want to find out how many elephant sightings we have recorded. We can do this by applying a filter, map, and reduce function one after the other (Figure 5.4).

In this example, we first *filter* all sightings to select only elephant sightings, then we *map* each sighting object to the number of elephants spotted in this sighting, and finally we add them all up with a *reduce* function. Notice that after the *map* function has been applied, we are no longer dealing with a stream of `Sighting` objects, but with a stream of integer values. This form of transformation between input stream and output stream is very common with the *map* function.

Figure 5.3
Applying a reduction to a stream

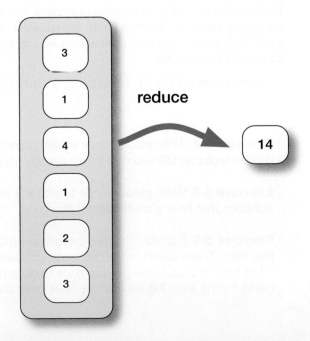

Figure 5.4
A pipeline of stream functions

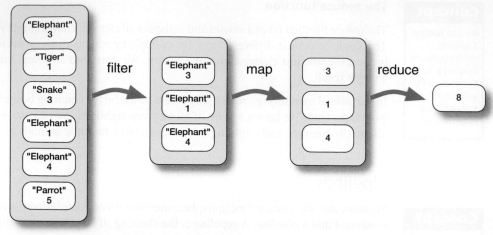

We can write this, using pseudo-code, as follows:

```
sightings.filter(name == elephant).map(count).reduce(add up);
```

This is not correct Java syntax, but you get the idea. We will look at correct Java code below.

By combining these functions in different ways, many different operations can be achieved. If we, for example, wanted to know how many reports a given spotter has made on a given day, we can do the following:

```
sightings.filter(spotter == spotterID)
         .filter(period == dayID)
         .reduce(count elements);
```

Pipelines always start with a *source* (a stream), followed by a sequence of operations. The operations are of two different kinds: *intermediate operations* and *terminal operations*. In a pipeline, the last operation must always be a terminal operation, and all others must be intermediate operations:

```
source.inter1(...).inter2(...).inter3(...).terminal(...);
```

Exercise 5.7 Write pseudo-code to determine how many elephants a particular spotter (`spotterID`) saw on a particular day (`dayID`).

Exercise 5.8 Write pseudo-code to create a stream containing only those sightings that have a count greater than 0.

Exercise 5.9 Consider the *music-organizer* project from Chapter 4 and assume that each `Track` object in the collection contains a count of how many times it has been played. Write pseudo-code to determine the total number of times tracks by the artist Big Bill Broonzy have been played.

Intermediate operations always produce a new stream to which the next operation can be applied, while terminal operations produce a result, or are void (such as `forEach` which is a terminal operation). The documentation for the stream methods always tells you whether an operation is intermediate or terminal.

We will now go on to discuss the Java syntax for the methods that implement these functions. This is where streams and lambdas meet: the parameter to each of the methods is a lambda.

5.5.3 The `filter` method

As discussed, the `filter` method creates a subset of the original stream. Typically that subset will be those elements that fulfill some condition; i.e., there is something about those particular elements that means we want to retain and act on them rather than the others. With the *music-organizer* project we might want to find all the tracks by a particular artist. With the *animal-monitoring* project we might want to find all the sightings of a given animal. Both involve iterating over their respective lists, and making a test of each element to see if it fulfills a particular requirement. If the required condition is met then we will go on to process the element in some way.

The `filter` method of a stream is an intermediate operation that passes on to its output stream only those elements from the input stream that fulfill a given condition. The method takes a lambda that receives an element and returns a `boolean` result. (A lambda that takes an element and returns *true* or *false* is called a *predicate*.) If the result is *true*, the element is included in the output stream, otherwise it is left out. For instance, we might want to select only those `Sighting` objects that relate to elephants. Here is how that might be done:

```
sightings.stream()
        .filter(s -> "Elephant".equals(s.getAnimal()))
        . . . .
```

Notice that we have to first create a stream from the sightings list, in order to be able to apply the filter function. We do not need to specify the type of the lambda's parameter, because the compiler knows that an `ArrayList<Sighting>` will deliver a stream of `Sighting` objects, so the parameter to the predicate will have the type `Sighting`.

More generally, it makes sense to make filtering part of a method that could select different types of animal, so here is how we would rewrite the `printSightingsOf` method of our original project in a stream-based version:

```
/**
 * Print details of all the sightings of the given animal.
 * @param animal The type of animal.
 */
public void printSightingsOf(String animal)
{
    sightings.stream()
            .filter(s -> animal.equals(s.getAnimal()))
            .forEach(s -> System.out.println(s.getDetails()));
}
```

It is important to know that each operation of the stream leaves its input stream unmodified. Each operation creates a fresh stream, based on its input and the operation, to pass on to the next operation in the sequence. Here the terminal operation is a `forEach` that results in the sightings that survived the previous filtering process being printed. The `forEach` method is a terminal operation because it does not return another stream as a result—it is a `void` method.

Exercise 5.10 Rewrite the `printSightingsOf` method in your `Animal-Monitor` class to use streams and lambdas, as shown above. Test to make sure the project still works as before.

Exercise 5.11 Write a method in the `AnimalMonitor` class to print details of all the sightings recorded on a particular `dayID`, which is passed as a parameter to the method.

Exercise 5.12 Write a method that uses two `filter` calls to print details of all the sightings of a particular animal made on a particular day—the method takes the animal name and day ID as parameters.

Exercise 5.13 Does the order of the two `filter` calls matter in your solution to the previous exercise? Justify your answer.

5.5.4 The map method

The `map` method is an intermediate operation that creates a stream with different objects, possibly of a different type, by mapping each of the original elements to a new element in the new stream.

To illustrate this, consider that when we are printing the details of a sighting, we are only actually interested in the string returned from the `getDetails` method, and not the `Sighting` object itself. An alternative to the code above (where we called `getDetails()` within the `System.out.println` call) would be to map the `Sighting` object to the details string first. The terminal operation can then just print those details:

```
/**
 * Print all the sightings by the given spotter.
 * @param spotter The ID of the spotter.
 */
public void printSightingsBy(int spotter)
{
    sightings.stream()
            .filter(sighting -> sighting.getSpotter() == spotter)
            .map(sighting -> sighting.getDetails())
            .forEach(details -> System.out.println(details));
}
```

This example is equivalent to the version we have seen before. The other example we have mentioned above—mapping to the number of animals spotted in each sighting—would look like this:

```
sightings.stream()
        .filter(sighting -> sighting.getSpotter() == spotter)
        .map(sighting -> sighting.getCount())
        . ...
```

This code segment would result in a stream of integers, which we could then process further.

Exercise 5.14 Rewrite the `printSightingsBy` method in your project as discussed above.

Exercise 5.15 Write a method to print the counts of all sightings of a particular animal. Your method should use the `map` operation as part of the pipeline.

Exercise 5.16 If a pipeline contains a `filter` operation and a `map` operation, does the order of the operations matter to the final result? Justify your answer.

Exercise 5.17 Rewrite the `printEndangered` method in your project to use streams. Test. (To test this method, it may be easiest to write a test method that creates an `ArrayList` of animal names and calls the `printEndangered` method with it.)

Exercise 5.18 *Challenge exercise* The `printSightingsBy` method of `AnimalMonitor` contains the following terminal operation:

```
forEach(details -> System.out.println(details));
```

Replace it with the following:

```
forEach(System.out::println);
```

Take care to use the exact syntax. Does this change the operation of the method? What can you deduce from your answer to this? If you are not sure, try to find out what "::" means when using Java lambdas. We will look at this in the advanced sections of Chapter 6.

5.5.5 The reduce method

The intermediate operations we have seen so far take a stream as input and output a stream. Sometimes, however, we need an operation that will "collapse" its input stream to just a single object or value, and this is the function of the `reduce` method, which is a terminal operation.

The complete code for the example given above—selecting all animals of a given type, then mapping to the number of animals in each sighting, and finally adding all numbers—is as follows:

```
public int getCount(String animal)
{
    return sightings.stream()
        .filter(sighting -> animal.equals(sighting.getAnimal()))
        .map(sighting -> sighting.getCount())
        .reduce(0, (total, count) -> return total + count);
}
```

We can see that the parameters to the reduce method look a bit more elaborate than for the filter and map methods. There are two aspects here:

■ The reduce method has two parameters. The first one in our example is 0, and the second is a lambda.

■ The lambda used here itself has two parameters, called total and count.

To understand how this works, it might be useful to look at the code for adding all counts as if we were writing it in the traditional way. We would write a loop that looks like this:

```
public int getCount(String animal)
{
    int total = 0;
    for(Sighting sighting : sightings) {
        if(animal.equals(sighting.getAnimal())) {
            total = total + sighting.getCount();
        }
    }
    return total;
}
```

The process of calculating the sum involves the following steps:

■ Declare a variable to hold the final value and give it an initial value of 0.

■ Iterate over the list and determine which sighting records relate to the particular animal we are interested in (the filtering step).

■ Obtain the count from the identified sighting (the mapping step).

■ Add the count to the variable.

■ Return the sum that has been accumulated in the variable over the course of the iteration.

The key point that is relevant to writing a stream-based version of this process is to recognize that the variable total acts as a form of "accumulator": each time a relevant count is identified, it is added into the value accumulated so far in total to give a new value that will be used the next time around the loop. For the process to work, total obviously has to be given an initial value of 0 for the first count to be added to.

The reduce method takes two parameters: a starting value and a lambda. Formally, the starting value is called an *identity*. It is the value to which our running total is initialized. In our code, we have passed 0 for this parameter.

The second parameter is a lambda with two parameters: one for the running total, and one for the current element of the stream. The lambda we have written in our code is:

```
(total, count) -> return total + count
```

The body of the lambda should return the result of combining the running total and the element. In our example, "combining" means just to add them. The affect of applying this `reduce` method then is to initialize a running total to zero, add each element of the stream to it, and return the total at the end.

Because there is no explicit loop in our code anymore, it might be a little tricky to understand at first, but the overall process contains all of the same elements as the version using the for-each loop.

> **Exercise 5.19** Rewrite your `getCount` method using streams, as shown here.
>
> **Exercise 5.20** Add a method to `AnimalMonitor` that takes three parameters: `animal`, `spotterID`, and `dayID`, and returns a count of how many sightings of the given animal were made by the spotter on a particular day.
>
> **Exercise 5.21** Add a method to `AnimalMonitor` that takes two parameters—`spotterID` and `dayID`—and returns a `String` containing the names of the animals seen by the spotter on a particular day. You should include only animals whose sighting count is greater than zero, but don't worry about excluding duplicate names if multiple non-zero sighting records were made of a particular animal. *Hint*: The principles of using `reduce` with `String` elements and a `String` result are very similar to those when using integers. Decide on the correct *identity* and formulate a two-parameter lambda that combines the running "sum" with the next element of the stream.

5.5.6 Removing from a collection

We have noted that the `filter` method does not actually change the underlying collection from which a stream was obtained. However, predicate lambdas make it relatively easy to remove all the items from a collection that match a particular condition. For instance, suppose we wish to delete from the `sightings` list all of those `Sighting` records where the count is zero. The following code makes use of the `removeIf` method of the collection:

```
/**
 * Remove from the sightings list all of those records with
 * a count of zero.
 */
public void removeZeroCounts()
{
    sightings.removeIf(sighting -> sighting.getCount() == 0);
}
```

Once again, the iteration is implicit. The `removeIf` method passes each element of the list, in turn, to the predicate lambda, then removes all those for which the lambda returns `true`. Note that this is a method of the collection (not of a stream) and it does modify the original collection.

> **Exercise 5.22** Rewrite the `removeZeroCounts` method using the `removeIf` method, as shown above.
>
> **Exercise 5.23** Write a method `removeSpotter` that removes all records reported by a given spotter.

5.5.7 Other stream methods

We have said that many common tasks can be achieved with these three kinds of operations: *filter*, *map*, and *reduce*. In practice, Java offers many more methods on streams, and we will see some of them later in this book. However, most of these are just variations of the three operations introduced here, even though they have different names.

The `Stream` class, for example, has methods called `count`, `findFirst`, and `max`—these are all variants of a reduce operation—and methods called `limit` and `skip`, which are examples of a filter.

> **Exercise 5.24** Find the API documentation for Stream in the `java.util.stream` package and read about the `count`, `findFirst`, and `max` methods. These can be called on any stream.
>
> **Exercise 5.25** Write a method in the `AnimalMonitor` class that takes a single parameter, `spotterID`, and returns a count of how many sighting records have been made by the given spotter. Use the stream's `count` method to do this.
>
> **Exercise 5.26** Write a method that takes an animal name as a parameter and returns the largest count for that animal in a single `Sighting` record.
>
> **Exercise 5.27** Write a method that takes an animal name and spotter ID and returns the first `Sighting` object stored in the `sightings` collection for that combination.
>
> **Exercise 5.28** Read about the `limit` and `skip` methods of streams and devise some methods of your own to make use of them.

5.6 Summary

In this chapter, we have introduced some new concepts that are relatively advanced for this stage of the book, but that are closely associated with the concepts covered in Chapter 4. We have looked at a *functional style* for processing streams of data. In this style, we do not write loops to process the elements in a collection. Instead, we apply a *pipeline* of operations to a stream derived from a collection, in order to transform the sequence into the form we want. Each operation in the pipeline defines what is to be done with a single element of the sequence. The most common sequence transformations are performed via the `filter`, `map`, and `reduce` methods.

Operations in a pipeline often take *lambdas* as parameters in order to specify what is to be done with each element of the sequence. A lambda is an anonymous function that takes zero or more parameters and has a block of code that performs the same role as a method body.

Looking at the *animal-monitoring-v1* project that you have been working on, you may have noticed that there are two methods left using for-each loops that we have not rewritten yet using streams. These are the methods that return new collections as method results; we have not yet discussed how to create a new collection from a stream. We will come back to this in Chapter 6, where we shall see how to create a new collection out of the transformed sequence.

Terms introduced in this chapter:

functional programming, lambda, stream, pipeline, filter, map, reduce

Concept summary

- **lambda** A lambda is a segment of code that can be stored and executed later.

- **functional style** In the functional style of collection processing, We do not retrieve each element to operate on it. Instead, we pass a code segment to the collection to be applied to each element.

- **streams** Streams unify the processing of elements of a collection and other sets of data. A stream provides useful methods to manipulate these data sets.

- **filter** We can filter a stream to select only specific elements.

- **map** We can map a stream to a new stream, where each element of the original stream is replaced with a new element derived from the original.

- **reduce** We can reduce a stream; reducing means to apply a function that takes a whole stream and delivers a single result.

- **pipeline** A pipeline is the combination of two or more stream functions in a chain, where each function is applied in turns.

Exercise 5.29 Take a copy of *music-organizer-v5* from Chapter 4. Rewrite the `listAllTracks` and `listByArtist` methods of the `MusicOrganizer` class to use streams and lambdas.

Main concepts discussed in this chapter:

- using library classes
- writing documentation

- reading documentation

Java constructs discussed in this chapter:

`String`, `Random`, `HashMap`, `HashSet`, `Iterator`, `static`, `final`, autoboxing, wrapper classes

In Chapter 4, we introduced the class `ArrayList` from the Java class library. We discussed how this enabled us to do something that would otherwise be hard to achieve (in this case, storing an arbitrary number of objects).

This was just a single example of a useful class from the Java library. The library consists of thousands of classes, many of which are generally useful for your work, and many of which you may probably never use.

For a good Java programmer, it is essential to be able to work with the Java library and make informed choices about which classes to use. Once you have started work with the library, you will quickly see that it enables you to perform many tasks more easily than you would otherwise have been able to. Learning to work with library classes is the main topic of this chapter.

The items in the library are not just a set of unrelated, arbitrary classes that we all have to learn individually, but are often arranged in relationships, exploiting common characteristics. Here, we again encounter the concept of abstraction to help us deal with a large amount of information. Some of the most important parts of the library are the collections, of which the `ArrayList` class is one. We will discuss other sorts of collections in this chapter and see that they share many attributes among themselves, so that we can often abstract from the individual details of a specific collection and talk about collection classes in general.

New collection classes, as well as some other useful classes, will be introduced and discussed. Throughout this chapter, we will work on the construction of a single application (the *TechSupport* system), which makes use of various different library classes. A complete implementation containing all the ideas and source code discussed here, as well as several intermediate versions, is included in the book projects. While this enables you to study the complete solution, you are encouraged to follow the path through the exercises in this chapter. These will, after a brief look at the complete program, start with a very simple initial version of the project, then gradually develop and implement the complete solution.

The application makes use of several new library classes and techniques—each requiring study individually—such as hash maps, sets, string tokenization, and further use of random numbers. You should be aware that this is not a chapter to be read and understood in a single day, but that it contains several sections that deserve a few days of study each. Overall, when you finally reach the end and have managed to undertake the implementation suggested in the exercises, you will have learned about a good variety of important topics.

6.1 Documentation for library classes

The Java standard class library is extensive. It consists of thousands of classes, each of which has many methods, both with and without parameters, and with and without return types. It is impossible to memorize them all and all of the details that go with them. Instead, a good Java programmer should know:

■ some of the most important classes and their methods from the library by name (**ArrayList** is one of those important ones) and

■ how to find out about other classes and look up the details (such as methods and parameters).

In this chapter, we will introduce some of the important classes from the class library, and further library classes will be introduced throughout the book. More importantly, we will show you how you can explore and understand the library on your own. This will enable you to write much more interesting programs. Fortunately, the Java library is quite well documented. This documentation is available in HTML format (so that it can be read in a web browser). We shall use this to find out about the library classes.

Reading and understanding the documentation is the first part of our introduction to library classes. We will take this approach a step further, and also discuss how to prepare our own classes so that other people can use them in the same way as they would use standard library classes. This is important for real-world software development, where teams have to deal with large projects and maintenance of software over time.

One thing you may have noted about the **ArrayList** class is that we used it without ever looking at the source code. We did not check how it was implemented. That was not necessary for utilizing its functionality. All we needed to know was the name of the class, the names of the methods, the parameters and return types of those methods, and what exactly these methods do. We did not really care how the work was done. This is typical for the use of library classes.

The same is true for other classes in larger software projects. Typically, several people work together on a project by working on different parts. Each programmer should concentrate on her own area and need not understand the details of all the other parts (we discussed this in Section 3.2 where we talked about abstraction and modularization).

In effect, each programmer should be able to use the classes of other team members as if they were library classes, making informed use of them without the need to know how they work internally.

For this to work, each team member must write documentation about his class similar to the documentation for the Java standard library, which enables other people to use the class without the need to read the code. This topic will also be discussed in this chapter.

6.2 The *TechSupport* system

As always, we shall explore these issues with an example. This time, we shall use the *TechSupport* application. You can find it in the book projects under the name *tech-support1*.

TechSupport is a program intended to provide technical support for customers of the fictitious DodgySoft software company. Some time ago, DodgySoft had a technical support department with people sitting at telephones. Customers could call to get advice and help with their technical problems with the DodgySoft software products. Recently, though, business has not been going so well, and DodgySoft decided to get rid of the technical support department to save money. They now want to develop the *TechSupport* system to give the impression that support is still provided. The system is supposed to mimic the responses a technical-support person might give. Customers can communicate with the technical-support system online.

6.2.1 Exploring the *TechSupport* system

Exercise 6.1 Open and run the project *tech-support-complete*. You run it by creating an object of class **SupportSystem** and calling its **start** method. Enter some problems you might be having with your software to try out the system. See how it behaves. Type "bye" when you are done. You do not need to examine the source code at this stage. This project is the complete solution that we will have developed by the end of this chapter. The purpose of this exercise is only to give you an idea of what we plan to achieve.

Eliza The idea of the *TechSupport* project is based on the ground-breaking artificial intelligence program, Eliza, developed by Joseph Weizenbaum at Massachusetts Institute of Technology in the 1960s. You can find out more about the original program by searching the web for "Eliza" and "Weizenbaum."

We will now start our more detailed exploration by using the *tech-support1* project. It is a first, rudimentary implementation of our system. We will improve it throughout the chapter. This way, we should arrive at a better understanding of the whole system than we would by just reading the complete solution.

Figure 6.1
A first *TechSupport* dialog

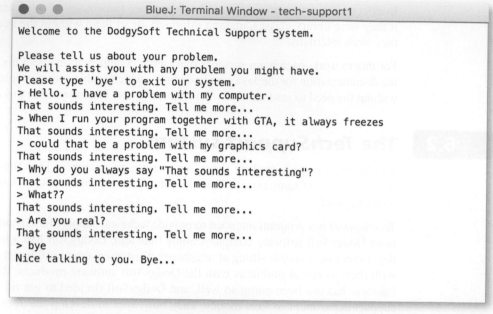

```
● ● ●              BlueJ: Terminal Window - tech-support1

Welcome to the DodgySoft Technical Support System.

Please tell us about your problem.
We will assist you with any problem you might have.
Please type 'bye' to exit our system.
> Hello. I have a problem with my computer.
That sounds interesting. Tell me more...
> When I run your program together with GTA, it always freezes
That sounds interesting. Tell me more...
> could that be a problem with my graphics card?
That sounds interesting. Tell me more...
> Why do you always say "That sounds interesting"?
That sounds interesting. Tell me more...
> What??
That sounds interesting. Tell me more...
> Are you real?
That sounds interesting. Tell me more...
> bye
Nice talking to you. Bye...
```

In Exercise 6.1, you have seen that the program essentially holds a dialog with the user. The user can type in a question, and the system responds. Try the same with our prototype version of the project, *tech-support1*.

In *TechSupport*'s complete version, the system manages to produce reasonably varied responses—sometimes they even seem to make sense! In the prototype version we are using as a starting point, the responses are much more restricted (Figure 6.1). You will notice very quickly that the response is always the same:

"That sounds interesting. Tell me more ..."

This is, in fact, not very interesting at all, and not very convincing when trying to pretend that we have a technical-support person sitting at the other end of the dialog. We will shortly try to improve this. However, before we do this, we shall explore further what we have so far.

The project diagram shows us three classes: **SupportSystem**, **InputReader**, and **Responder** (Figure 6.2). **SupportSystem** is the main class, which uses the **InputReader** to get some input from the terminal and the **Responder** to generate a response.

Examine the **InputReader** further by creating an object of this class and then looking at the object's methods. You will see that it has only a single method available, called **getInput**, which returns a string. Try it out. This method lets you type a line of input in the terminal, then returns whatever you typed as a method result. We will not examine how this works internally at this point, but just note that the **InputReader** has a **getInput** method that returns a string.

Do the same with the **Responder** class. You will find that it has a **generateResponse** method that always returns the string **"That sounds interesting. Tell me more..."**. This explains what we saw in the dialog earlier.

Now let us look at the **SupportSystem** class a bit more closely.

Figure 6.2
TechSupport class
diagram

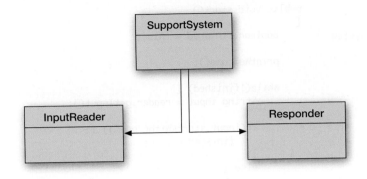

6.2.2 Reading the code

The complete source code of the **SupportSystem** class is shown in Code 6.1. Code 6.2
shows the source code of class **Responder**.

Code 6.1

The
SupportSystem
source code

```
/**
 * This class implements a technical support system. It is the top level class
 * in this project. The support system communicates via text input/output
 * in the text terminal.
 *
 * This class uses an object of class InputReader to read input from the user,
 * and an object of class Responder to generate responses. It contains a loop
 * that repeatedly reads input and generates output until the users wants to
 * leave.
 *
 * @author    Michael Kölling and David J. Barnes
 * @version   0.1 (2016.02.29)
 */
public class SupportSystem
{
    private InputReader reader;
    private Responder responder;

    /**
     * Creates a technical support system.
     */
    public SupportSystem()
    {
        reader = new InputReader();
        responder = new Responder();
    }

    /**
     * Start the technical support system. This will print a welcome
     * message and enter into a dialog with the user, until the user
     * ends the dialog.
     */
```

Code 6.1
continued

The SupportSystem source code

```java
public void start()
{
    boolean finished = false;

    printWelcome();

    while(!finished) {
        String input = reader.getInput();

        if(input.startsWith("bye")) {
            finished = true;
        }
        else {
            String response = responder.generateResponse();
            System.out.println(response);
        }
    }

    printGoodbye();
}

/**
 * Print a welcome message to the screen.
 */
private void printWelcome()
{
    System.out.println("Welcome to the DodgySoft Technical Support System.");
    System.out.println();
    System.out.println("Please tell us about your problem.");
    System.out.println("We will assist you with any problem you might have.");
    System.out.println("Please type 'bye' to exit our system.");
}

/**
 * Print a good-bye message to the screen.
 */
private void printGoodbye()
{
    System.out.println("Nice talking to you. Bye...");
}
}
```

Looking at Code 6.2, we see that the **Responder** class is trivial. It has only one method, and that always returns the same string. This is something we shall improve later. For now, we will concentrate on the **SupportSystem** class.

SupportSystem declares two instance fields to hold an **InputReader** and a **Responder** object, and it assigns those two objects in its constructor.

At the end, it has two methods called **printWelcome** and **printGoodbye**. These simply print out some text—a welcome message and a good-bye message, respectively.

The most interesting piece of code is the method in the middle: **start**. We will discuss this method in some more detail.

```
/**
 * The responder class represents a response generator object.
 * It is used to generate an automatic response to an input string.
 *
 * @author     Michael Kölling and David J. Barnes
 * @version    0.1 (2016.02.29)
 */
public class Responder
{
    /**
     * Construct a Responder - nothing to do
     */
    public Responder()
    {
    }

    /**
     * Generate a response.
     * @return    A string that should be displayed as the response
     */
    public String generateResponse()
    {
        return "That sounds interesting. Tell me more...";
    }
}
```

Toward the top of the method is a call to **printWelcome**, and at the end is a call to **printGoodbye**. These two calls take care of printing these sections of text at the appropriate times. The rest of this method consists of a declaration of a boolean variable and a while loop. The structure is as follows:

```
boolean finished = false;
while(!finished) {
    do something
    if(exit condition) {
        finished = true;
    }
    else {
        do something more
    }
}
```

This code pattern is a variation of the while-loop idiom discussed in Section 4.10. We use **finished** as a flag that becomes **true** when we want to end the loop (and with it, the whole program). We make sure that it is initially **false**. (Remember that the exclamation mark is a *not* operator!)

The main part of the loop—the part that is done repeatedly while we wish to continue—consists of three statements if we strip it of the check for the exit condition:

```
String input = reader.getInput();
...
String response = responder.generateResponse();
System.out.println(response);
```

Thus, the loop repeatedly

- reads some user input,

- asks the responder to generate a response, and

- prints out that response.

(You may have noticed that the response does not depend on the input at all! This is certainly something we shall have to improve later.)

The last part to examine is the check of the exit condition. The intention is that the program should end once a user types the word "bye". The relevant section of source code we find in the class reads

```
String input = reader.getInput();
if(input.startsWith("bye")) {
    finished = true;
}
```

If you understand these pieces in isolation, then it is a good idea to look again at the complete **start** method in Code 6.1 and see whether you can understand everything together.

In the last code fragment examined above, a method called **startsWith** is used. Because that method is called on the **input** variable, which holds a **String** object, it must be a method of the **String** class. But what does this method do? And how do we find out?

We might guess, simply from seeing the name of the method, that it tests whether the input string starts with the word "bye". We can verify this by experiment. Run the *TechSupport* system again and type "bye bye" or "bye everyone". You will notice that both versions cause the system to exit. Note, however, that typing "Bye" or " bye"—starting with a capital letter or with a space in front of the word—is not recognized as starting with "bye". This could be slightly annoying for a user, but it turns out that we can solve these problems if we know a bit more about the **String** class.

How do we find out more information about the **startsWith** method or other methods of the **String** class?

6.3 Reading class documentation

The class **String** is one of the classes of the standard Java class library. We can find out more details about it by reading the library documentation for the **String** class.

To do this, choose the *Java Class Libraries* item from the BlueJ *Help* menu. This will open a web browser displaying the main page of the Java API (Application Programming Interface) documentation.[1]

The web browser will display three frames. In the one at the top left, you see a list of packages. Below that is a list of all classes in the Java library. The large frame on the right is used to display details of a selected package or class.

Concept

The Java **class library documentation** shows details about all classes in the library. Using this documentation is essential in order to make good use of library classes.

---

[1] By default, this function accesses the documentation through the Internet. This will not work if your machine does not have network access. However, BlueJ can be configured to use a local copy of the Java API documentation. This is recommended, because it speeds up access and can work without an Internet connection. For details, see Appendix A.

Figure 6.3
The Java class library
documentation

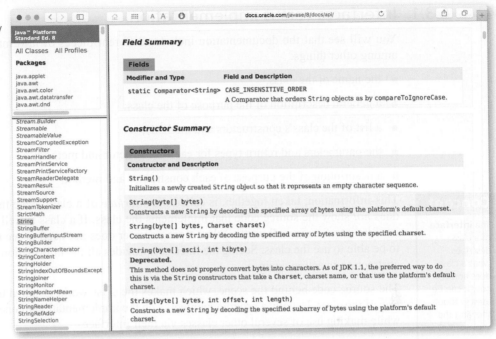

In the list of classes on the left, find and select the class **String**. The frame on the right then displays the documentation of the **String** class (Figure 6.3).

Exercise 6.2 Investigate the **String** documentation. Then look at the documentation for some other classes. What is the structure of class documentation? Which sections are common to all class descriptions? What is their purpose?

Exercise 6.3 Look up the **startsWith** method in the documentation for **String**. There are two versions. Describe in your own words what they do and the differences between them.

Exercise 6.4 Is there a method in the **String** class that tests whether a string ends with a given suffix? If so, what is it called, and what are its parameters and return type?

Exercise 6.5 Is there a method in the **String** class that returns the number of characters in the string? If so, what is it called, and what are its parameters?

Exercise 6.6 If you found methods for the two tasks above, how did you find them? Is it easy or hard to find methods you are looking for? Why?

6.3.1 Interfaces versus implementation

You will see that the documentation includes different pieces of information. They are, among other things:

- the name of the class;

- a general description of the purpose of the class;

- a list of the class's constructors and methods;

- the parameters and return types for each constructor and method;

- a description of the purpose of each constructor and method.

> **Concept**
>
> The **interface** of a class describes what a class does and how it can be used without showing the implementation.

This information, taken together, is called the *interface* of a class. Note that the interface does *not* show the source code that implements the class. If a class is well described (that is, if its interface is well written) then a programmer does not need to see the source code to be able to use the class. Seeing the interface provides all the information needed. This is abstraction in action again.

The source code behind the scene, which makes the class work, is called the *implementation* of the class. Usually a programmer works on the implementation of one class at a time, while making use of several other classes via their interfaces.

> **Concept**
>
> The complete source code that defines a class is called the **implementation** of that class.

This distinction between the interface and the implementation is a very important concept, and it will surface repeatedly in this and later chapters of this book.

> **Note** The word *interface* has several meanings in the context of programming and Java. It is used to describe the publicly visible part of a class (which is how we have just been using it here), but it also has other meanings. The user interface (often a graphical user interface) is sometimes referred to as just *the interface*, but Java also has a language construct called interface (discussed in Chapter 12) that is related but distinct from our meaning here.
>
> It is important to be able to distinguish among the different meanings of the word *interface* in a particular context.

The interface terminology is also used for individual methods. For example, the **String** documentation shows us the interface of the **length** method:

```
public int length()
```

Returns the length of this string. The length is equal to the number of Unicode code units in the string.

Specified by:

length in interface CharSequence

Returns:

the length of the sequence of characters represented by this object.

The interface of a method consists of the *header* of the method and a comment (shown here in italics). The header of a method includes (in this order):

- an access modifier (here **public**), which we shall discuss below;

- the return type of the method (here **int**);

- the method name;

- a list of parameters (which is empty in this example); the name and parameters together are also called the *signature* of the method.

The interface provides everything we need to know to make use of this method.

6.3.2 Using library-class methods

Back to our *TechSupport* system. We now want to improve the processing of input a little. We have seen in the discussion above that our system is not very tolerant: if we type "Bye" or " bye" instead of "bye", for instance, the word is not recognized. We want to change that by adjusting the text read in from a user so that these variations are all recognized as "bye".

The documentation of the **String** class tells us that it has a method called **trim** to remove spaces at the beginning and the end of the string. We can use that method to handle the second problem case.

> **Exercise 6.7** Find the **trim** method in the **String** class's documentation. Write down the header of that method. Write down an example call to that method on a **String** variable called **text**.

Concept

An object is said to be **immutable** if its contents or state cannot be changed once it has been created. Strings are an example of immutable objects.

One important detail about String objects is that they are *immutable*—that is, they cannot be modified once they have been created. Note carefully that the **trim** method, for example, returns a new string; it does not modify the original string. Pay close attention to the following "Pitfall" comment.

> **Pitfall** A common error in Java is to try to modify a string—for example by writing
>
> ```
> input.toUpperCase();
> ```
>
> This is incorrect (strings cannot be modified), but this unfortunately does not produce an error. The statement simply has no effect, and the input string remains unchanged.
>
> The **toUpperCase** method, as well as other string methods, does not modify the original string, but instead returns a *new* string that is similar to the original one, with some changes applied (here, with characters changed to uppercase). If we want our input variable to be changed, then we have to assign this new object back into the variable (discarding the original one), like this:
>
> ```
> input = input.toUpperCase();
> ```
>
> The new object could also be assigned to another variable or processed in other ways.

After studying the interface of the **trim** method, we can see that we can remove the spaces from an input string with the following line of code:

```
input = input.trim();
```

This code will request the **String** object stored in the **input** variable to create a new, similar string with the leading and trailing spaces removed. The new **String** is then stored in the **input** variable because we have no further use for the old one. Thus, after this line of code, **input** refers to a string without spaces at either end.

We can now insert this line into our source code so that it reads

```
String input = reader.getInput();
input = input.trim();
if(input.startsWith("bye")) {
    finished = true;
}
else {
    Code omitted.
}
```

The first two lines can also be merged into a single line:

```
String input = reader.getInput().trim();
```

The effect of this line of code is identical to that of the first two lines above. The right-hand side should be read as if it were parenthesized as follows:

```
(reader.getInput()).trim()
```

Which version you prefer is mainly a matter of taste. The decision should be made mainly on the basis of readability: use the version that you find easier to read and understand. Often, novice programmers will prefer the two-line version, whereas more experienced programmers get used to the one-line style.

Exercise 6.8 Implement this improvement in your version of the *tech-support1* project. Test it to confirm that it is tolerant of extra space around the word "bye".

Now we have solved the problem caused by spaces surrounding the input, but we have not yet solved the problem with capital letters. However, further investigation of the **String** class's documentation suggests a possible solution, because it describes a method named **toLowerCase**.

Exercise 6.9 Improve the code of the **SupportSystem** class in the *tech-support1* project so that case in the input is ignored. Use the **String** class's **toLowerCase** method to do this. Remember that this method will not actually change the **String** it is called on, but result in the creation of a new one being created with slightly different contents.

6.3.3 Checking string equality

An alternative solution would have been to check whether the input string *is* the string "bye" instead of whether it *starts with* the string "bye". An (incorrect!) attempt to write this code could look as follows:

```
if(input == "bye") { // does not always work!
    ...
}
```

The problem here is that it is possible for several independent **String** objects to exist that all represent the same text. Two **String** objects, for example, could both contain the characters "bye". The equality operator (**==**) checks whether each side of the operator refers to *the same object*, not whether they have the same value! That is an important difference.

In our example, we are interested in the question of whether the input variable and the string constant "bye" represent the same value, not whether they refer to the same object. Thus, using the **==** operator is wrong. It could return false, even if the value of the input variable is "bye".[2]

The solution is to use the **equals** method, defined in the **String** class. This method correctly tests whether the contents of two **String** objects are the same. The correct code reads:

```
if(input.equals("bye")) {
    ...
}
```

This can, of course, also be combined with the **trim** and **toLowerCase** methods.

Pitfall Comparing strings with the **==** operator can lead to unintended results. As a general rule, strings should almost always be compared with **equals**, rather than with the **==** operator.

Exercise 6.10 Find the **equals** method in the documentation for class **String**. What is the return type of this method?

Exercise 6.11 Change your implementation to use the **equals** method instead of **startsWith**.

6.4 Adding random behavior

So far, we have made a small improvement to the *TechSupport* project, but overall it remains very basic. One of the main problems is that it always gives the same response, regardless of the user's input. We shall now improve this by defining a set of plausible phrases with which to respond. We will then have the program randomly choose one of

---

[2] Unfortunately, Java's implementation of strings means that using == will often misleadingly give the "right" answer when comparing two different **String** objects with identical contents. However, you should *never* use == between **String** objects when you want to compare their contents.

them each time it is expected to reply. This will be an extension of the **Responder** class in our project.

To do this, we will use an **ArrayList** to store some response strings, generate a random integer number, and use the random number as an index into the response list to pick one of our phrases. In this version, the response will still not depend on the user's input (we'll do that later), but at least it will vary the response and look a lot better.

First, we have to find out how to generate a random integer number.

> **Random and pseudo-random** Generating random numbers on a computer is actually not as easy to do as one might initially think. Because computers operate in a very well-defined, deterministic way that relies on the fact that all computation is predictable and repeatable, they provide little space for real random behavior.
>
> Researchers have, over time, proposed many algorithms to produce seemingly random sequences of numbers. These numbers are typically not really random, but follow complicated rules. They are therefore referred to as *pseudo-random* numbers.
>
> In a language such as Java, the pseudo-random number generation has fortunately been implemented in a library class, so all we have to do to receive a pseudo-random number is to make some calls to the library.
>
> If you want to read more about this, do a web search for "pseudo-random numbers."

6.4.1 The **Random** class

The Java class library contains a class named **Random** that will be helpful for our project.

> **Exercise 6.12** Find the class **Random** in the Java class library documentation. Which package is it in? What does it do? How do you construct an instance? How do you generate a random number? Note that you will probably not understand everything that is stated in the documentation. Just try to find out what you need to know.
>
> **Exercise 6.13** Write a small code fragment (on paper) that generates a random integer number using this class.

To generate a random number, we have to:

- create an instance of class **Random** and
- make a call to a method of that instance to get a number.

Looking at the documentation, we see that there are various methods called **next**_Something_ for generating random values of various types. The one that generates a random integer number is called **nextInt**.

The following illustrates the code needed to generate and print a random integer number:

```
Random randomGenerator;
randomGenerator = new Random();
int index = randomGenerator.nextInt();
System.out.println(index);
```

This code fragment creates a new instance of the **Random** class and stores it in the **randomGenerator** variable. It then calls the **nextInt** method to receive a random number, stores it in the index variable, and eventually prints it out.

Exercise 6.14 Write some code (in BlueJ) to test the generation of random numbers. To do this, create a new class called **RandomTester**. You can create this class in the *tech-support1* project, or you can create a new project for it. In class **RandomTester**, implement two methods: **printOneRandom** (which prints out one random number) and **printMultiRandom(int howMany)** (which has a parameter to specify how many numbers you want, and then prints out the appropriate number of random numbers).

Your class should create only a single instance of class **Random** (in its constructor) and store it in a field. Do not create a new **Random** instance every time you want a new number.

6.4.2 Random numbers with limited range

The random numbers we have seen so far were generated from the whole range of Java integers (−2147483648 to 2147483647). That is okay as an experiment, but seldom useful. More often, we want random numbers within a given limited range.

The **Random** class also offers a method to support this. It is again called **nextInt**, but it has a parameter to specify the range of numbers that we would like to use.

Exercise 6.15 Find the **nextInt** method in class **Random** that allows the target range of random numbers to be specified. What are the possible random numbers that are generated when you call this method with 100 as its parameter?

Exercise 6.16 Write a method in your **RandomTester** class called **throwDie** that returns a random number between 1 and 6 (inclusive).

Exercise 6.17 Write a method called **getResponse** that randomly returns one of the strings **"yes"**, **"no"**, or **"maybe"**.

Exercise 6.18 Extend your **getResponse** method so that it uses an **ArrayList** to store an arbitrary number of responses and randomly returns one of them.

When using a method that generates random numbers from a specified range, care must be taken to check whether the boundaries are *inclusive* or *exclusive*. The **nextInt (int n)** method in the Java library **Random** class, for example, specifies that it generates a number from **0** (inclusive) to **n** (exclusive). That means that the value **0** is included in the possible results, whereas the specified value for **n** is not. The highest number possibly returned by this call is **n–1**.

> **Exercise 6.19** Add a method to your **RandomTester** class that takes a parameter **max** and generates a random number in the range 1 to **max** (inclusive).
>
> **Exercise 6.20** Add a method to your **RandomTester** class that takes two parameters, **min** and **max**, and generates a random number in the range **min** to **max** (inclusive). Rewrite the body of the method you wrote for the previous exercise so that it now calls this new method to generate its result. Note that it should not be necessary to use a loop in this method.
>
> **Exercise 6.21** Look up the details of the **SecureRandom** class that is defined in the **java.security** package. Could this class be used instead of the **Random** class? Why are random numbers important for cryptographic security?

6.4.3 Generating random responses

Now we can look at extending the **Responder** class to select a random response from a list of predefined phrases. Code 6.2 shows the source code of class **Responder** as it is in our first version.

We shall now add code to this first version to:

■ declare a field of type **Random** to hold the random number generator;

■ declare a field of type **ArrayList** to hold our possible responses;

■ create the **Random** and **ArrayList** objects in the **Responder** constructor;

■ fill the responses list with some phrases;

■ select and return a random phrase when **generateResponse** is called.

Code 6.3 shows a version of the **Responder** source code with these additions.

Code 6.3
The **Responder**
source code with
random responses

```
import java.util.ArrayList;
import java.util.Random;

/**
 * The responder class represents a response generator object. It is used
 * to generate an automatic response. This is the second version of this
 * class. This time, we generate some random behavior by randomly selecting
 * a phrase from a predefined list of responses.
 *
 * @author    Michael Kölling and David J. Barnes
 * @version   0.2 (2016.02.29)
 */
```

Code 6.3 continued

The **Responder** source code with random responses

```java
public class Responder
{
    private Random randomGenerator;
    private ArrayList<String> responses;

    /**
     * Construct a Responder
     */
    public Responder()
    {
        randomGenerator = new Random();
        responses = new ArrayList<>();
        fillResponses();
    }

    /**
     * Generate a response.
     *
     * @return  A string that should be displayed as the response
     */
    public String generateResponse()
    {
        // Pick a random number for the index in the default response
        // list. The number will be between 0 (inclusive) and the size
        // of the list (exclusive).
        int index = randomGenerator.nextInt(responses.size());
        return responses.get(index);
    }

    /**
     * Build up a list of default responses from which we can pick one
     * if we don't know what else to say.
     */
    private void fillResponses()
    {
        responses.add("That sounds odd. Could you describe this in more detail?");
        responses.add("No other customer has ever complained about this \n" +
                        "before. What is your system configuration?");
        responses.add("I need a bit more information on that.");
        responses.add("Have you checked that you do not have a dll conflict?");
        responses.add("That is covered in the manual. Have you read the manual?");
        responses.add("Your description is a bit wishy-washy. Have you got \n" +
                        "an expert there with you who could describe this better?");
        responses.add("That's not a bug, it's a feature!");
        responses.add("Could you elaborate on that?");
        responses.add("Have you tried running the app on your phone?");
        responses.add("I just checked StackOverflow - they don't know either.");
    }
}
```

In this version, we have put the code that fills the response list into its own method, named **fillResponses**, which is called from the constructor. This ensures that the responses list will be filled as soon as a **Responder** object is created, but the source code for filling the list is kept separate to make the class easier to read and understand.

The most interesting code segment in this class is in the **generateResponse** method. Leaving out the comments, it reads

```
public String generateResponse()
{
    int index = randomGenerator.nextInt(responses.size());
    return responses.get(index);
}
```

The first line of code in this method does three things:

- It gets the size of the response list by calling its **size** method.

- It generates a random number between 0 (inclusive) and the size (exclusive).

- It stores that random number in the local variable **index**.

If this seems a lot of code for one line, you could also write

```
int listSize = responses.size();
int index = randomGenerator.nextInt(listSize);
```

This code is equivalent to the first line above. Which version you prefer, again, depends on which one you find easier to read.

It is important to note that this code segment will generate a random number in the range **0** to **listSize−1** (inclusive). This fits perfectly with the legal indices for an **ArrayList**. Remember that the range of indices for an **ArrayList** of size **listSize** is **0** to **listSize−1**. Thus, the computed random number gives us a perfect index to randomly access one from the complete set of the list's elements.

The last line in the method reads

```
return responses.get(index);
```

This line does two things:

- It retrieves the response at position **index** using the **get** method.

- It returns the selected string as a method result, using the **return** statement.

If you are not careful, your code may generate a random number that is outside the valid indices of the **ArrayList**. When you then try to use it as an index to access a list element, you will get an **IndexOutOfBoundsException**.

6.4.4 Reading documentation for parameterized classes

So far, we have asked you to look at the documentation for the **String** class from the **java.lang** package, and the **Random** class from the **java.util** package. You might have noticed when doing this that some class names in the documentation list look slightly different, such as **ArrayList<E>** or **HashMap<K, V>**. That is, the class name is followed by some extra information in angle brackets. Classes that look like this are called *parameterized classes* or *generic classes*. The information in the brackets tells us that when we use these classes, we must supply one or more type names in angle brackets to complete the definition. We have already seen this idea in practice in Chapter 4, where we used **ArrayList** by parameterizing it with type names such as **String**. They can also be parameterized with any other type:

```
private ArrayList<String> notes;
private ArrayList<Student> students;
```

Because we can parameterize an **ArrayList** with any other class type that we choose, this is reflected in the API documentation. So if you look at the list of methods for **ArrayList<E>**, you will see methods such as:

```
boolean add(E o)
E get(int index)
```

This tells us that the type of objects we can **add** to an **ArrayList** depends on the type used to parameterize it, and the type of the objects returned from its **get** method depends on this type in the same way. In effect, if we create an **ArrayList<String>** object and then the documentation tells us that the object has the following two methods:

```
boolean add(String o)
String get(int index)
```

whereas if we create an **ArrayList<Student>** object, then it will have these two methods:

```
boolean add(Student o)
Student get(int index)
```

We will ask you to look at the documentation for further parameterized types in later sections in this chapter.

6.5 Packages and import

There are still two lines at the top of the source file that we need to discuss:

```
import java.util.ArrayList;
import java.util.Random;
```

We encountered the import statement for the first time in Chapter 4. Now is the time to look at it a little more closely.

Java classes that are stored in the class library are not automatically available for use, like the other classes in the current project. Rather, we must state in our source code that we would like to use a class from the library. This is called *importing* the class, and is done using the **import** statement. The **import** statement has the form

    import *qualified-class-name*;

Because the Java library contains several thousand classes, some structure is needed in the organization of the library to make it easier to deal with the large number of classes. Java uses *packages* to arrange library classes into groups that belong together. Packages can be nested (that is, packages can contain other packages).

The classes `ArrayList` and `Random` are both in the package `java.util`. This information can be found in the class documentation. The *full name* or *qualified name* of a class is the name of its package, followed by a dot, followed by the class name. Thus, the qualified names of the two classes we used here are `java.util.ArrayList` and `java.util.Random`.

Java also allows us to import complete packages with statements of the form

```
import package-name.*;
```

So the following statement would import all class names from the `java.util` package:

```
import java.util.*;
```

Listing all used classes separately, as in our first version, is a little more work in terms of typing but serves well as a piece of documentation. It clearly indicates which classes are actually used by our class. Therefore, we shall tend to use the style of the first example, listing all imported classes separately.

There is one exception to these rules: some classes are used so frequently that almost every class would import them. These classes have been placed in the package `java.lang`, and this package is automatically imported into every class. So we do not need to write import statements for classes in `java.lang`. The class `String` is an example of such a class.

Exercise 6.22 Implement in your version of the *tech-support* system the random-response solution discussed here.

Exercise 6.23 What happens when you add more (or fewer) possible responses to the responses list? Will the selection of a random-response still work properly? Why or why not?

The solution discussed here is also in the book projects under the name *tech-support2*. We recommend, however, that you implement it yourself as an extension of the base version.

6.6 Using maps for associations

We now have a solution to our technical-support system that generates random responses. This is better than our first version, but is still not very convincing. In particular, the input of the user does not influence the response in any way. It is this area that we now want to improve.

The plan is that we shall have a set of words that are likely to occur in typical questions, and we will associate these words with particular responses. If the input from the user contains one of our known words, we can generate a related response. This is still a very crude method, because it does not pick up any of the meaning of the user's input, nor does it recognize a context. Still, it can be surprisingly effective, and it is a good next step.

To do this, we will use a **HashMap**. You will find the documentation for the class **HashMap** in the Java library documentation. **HashMap** is a specialization of a **Map**, which you will also find documented. You will see that you need to read the documentation of both to understand what a **HashMap** is and how it works.

> **Exercise 6.24** What is a **HashMap**? What is its purpose and how do you use it? Answer these questions in writing, and use the Java library documentation of **Map** and **HashMap** for your responses. Note that you will find it hard to understand everything, as the documentation for these classes is not very good. We will discuss the details later in this chapter, but see what you can find out on your own before reading on.
>
> **Exercise 6.25** **HashMap** is a parameterized class. List those of its methods that depend on the types used to parameterize it. Do you think the same type could be used for both of its parameters?

6.6.1 The concept of a map

Concept

A **map** is a collection that stores key/value pairs as entries. Values can be looked up by providing the key.

A map is a collection of key/value pairs of objects. As with the **ArrayList**, a map can store a flexible number of entries. One difference between the **ArrayList** and a **Map** is that with a **Map** each entry is not an object, but a *pair* of objects. This pair consists of a *key* object and a *value* object.

Instead of looking up entries in this collection using an integer index (as we did with the **ArrayList**), we use the key object to look up the value object.

An everyday example of a map is a contacts list. A contacts list contains entries, and each entry is a pair: a name and a phone number. You use a contacts list by looking up a name and getting a phone number. We do not use an index—the position of the entry in the contacts list—to find it.

A map can be organized in such a way that looking up a value for a key is easy. In the case of a contacts list, this is done using alphabetical sorting. By storing the entries in the alphabetical order of their keys, finding the key and looking up the value is easy. Reverse lookup (finding the key for a value—i.e., finding the name for a given phone number) is not so easy with a map. As with a contacts list, reverse lookup in a map is possible, but it takes a comparatively long time. Thus, maps are ideal for a one-way lookup, where we know the lookup key and need to know a value associated with this key.

6.6.2 Using a **HashMap**

HashMap is a particular implementation of **Map**. The most important methods of the **HashMap** class are **put** and **get**.

The **put** method inserts an entry into the map, and **get** retrieves the value for a given key. The following code fragment creates a **HashMap** and inserts three entries into it. Each entry is a key/value pair consisting of a name and a telephone number.

```
HashMap<String, String> contacts = new HashMap<>();
contacts.put("Charles Nguyen", "(531) 9392 4587");
contacts.put("Lisa Jones", "(402) 4536 4674");
contacts.put("William H. Smith", "(998) 5488 0123");
```

As we saw with **ArrayList**, when declaring a **HashMap** variable and creating a **HashMap** object, we have to say what type of objects will be stored in the map and, additionally, what type of objects will be used for the key. For the contacts list, we will use strings for both the keys and the values, but the two types will sometimes be different.

As we have seen in Section 4.4.2, when creating objects of generic classes and assigning them to a variable, we need to specify the generic types (here **<String, String>**) only once on the left hand side of the assignment, and can use the diamond operator in the object construction on the right; the generic types used for the object construction are then copied from the variable declaration.

The following code will find the phone number for Lisa Jones and print it out.

```
String number = contacts.get("Lisa Jones");
System.out.println(number);
```

Note that you pass the key (the name "Lisa Jones") to the **get** method in order to receive the value (the phone number).

Read the documentation of the **get** and **put** methods of class **HashMap** again and see whether the explanation matches your current understanding.

Exercise 6.26 How do you check how many entries are contained in a map?

Exercise 6.27 Create a class **MapTester** (either in your current project or in a new project). In it, use a **HashMap** to implement a contacts list similar to the one in the example above. (Remember that you must import **java.util.HashMap**.) In this class, implement two methods:

```
public void enterNumber(String name, String number)
```

and

```
public String lookupNumber(String name)
```

The methods should use the **put** and **get** methods of the **HashMap** class to implement their functionality.

Exercise 6.28 What happens when you add an entry to a map with a key that already exists in the map?

Exercise 6.29 What happens when you add two entries to a map with the same value and two different keys?

Exercise 6.30 How do you check whether a given key is contained in a map? (Give a Java code example.)

> **Exercise 6.31** What happens when you try to look up a value and the key does not exist in the map?
>
> **Exercise 6.32** How do you print out all keys currently stored in a map?

6.6.3 Using a map for the *TechSupport* system

In the *TechSupport system*, we can make good use of a map by using known words as keys and associated responses as values. Code 6.4 shows an example in which a **HashMap** named **responseMap** is created and three entries are made. For example, the word "slow" is associated with the text

> *"I think this has to do with your hardware. Upgrading your processor should solve all performance problems. Do you have a problem with our software?"*

Now, whenever somebody enters a question containing the word "slow", we can look up and print out this response. Note that the response string in the source code spans several lines but is concatenated with the **+** operator, so a single string is entered as a value into the **HashMap**.

Code 6.4

Associating selected words with possible responses

```java
private HashMap<String, String> responseMap;

...

public Responder()
{
    responseMap = new HashMap<>();
    fillResponseMap();
}
```

```java
/**
 * Enter all the known keywords and their associated responses
 * into our response map.
 */
private void fillResponseMap()
{
    responseMap.put("slow",
                "I think this has to do with your hardware. Upgrading\n" +
                "your processor should solve all performance problems.\n" +
                "Have you got a problem with our software?");
    responseMap.put("bug",
                "Well, you know, all software has some bugs. But our\n" +
                "software engineers are working very hard to fix them.\n" +
                "Can you describe the problem a bit further?");
    responseMap.put("expensive",
                "The cost of our product is quite competitive. Have you\n" +
                "looked around and really compared our features?");
}
```

A first attempt at writing a method to generate the responses could now look like the **generateResponse** method below. Here, to simplify things for the moment, we assume that only a single word (for example, "slow") is entered by the user.

```java
public String generateResponse(String word)
{
    String response = responseMap.get(word);
    if(response != null) {
        return response;
    }
    else {
        // If we get here, the word was not recognized. In
        // this case, we pick one of our default responses.
        return pickDefaultResponse();
    }
}
```

In this code fragment, we look up the word entered by the user in our response map. If we find an entry, we use this entry as the response. If we don't find an entry for that word, we call a method called **pickDefaultResponse**. This method can now contain the code of our previous version of **generateResponse**, which randomly picks one of the default responses (as shown in Code 6.3). The new logic, then, is that we pick an appropriate response if we recognize a word, or a random response out of our list of default responses if we don't.

> **Exercise 6.33** Implement the changes discussed here in your own version of the *TechSupport* system. Test it to get a feel for how well it works.

This approach of associating keywords with responses works quite well as long as the user does not enter complete questions, but only single words. The final improvement to complete the application is to let the user enter complete questions again, and then pick matching responses if we recognize any of the words in the questions.

This poses the problem of recognizing the keywords in the sentence that was entered by the user. In the current version, the user input is returned by the **InputReader** as a single string. We shall now change this to a new version in which the **InputReader** returns the input as a set of words. Technically, this will be a set of strings, where each string in the set represents a single word that was entered by the user.

If we can do that, then we can pass the whole set to the **Responder**, which can then check every word in the set to see whether it is known and has an associated response.

To achieve this in Java, we need to know about two things: how to cut a single string containing a whole sentence into words, and how to use sets. These issues are discussed in the next two sections.

6.7 Using sets

The Java standard library includes different variations of sets implemented in different classes. The class we shall use is called **HashSet**.

> **Exercise 6.34** What are the similarities and differences between a **HashSet** and an **ArrayList**? Use the descriptions of **Set**, **HashSet**, **List**, and **ArrayList** in the library documentation to find out, because **HashSet** is a special case of a **Set**, and **ArrayList** is a special case of a **List**.

The two types of functionality that we need are the ability to enter elements into the set, and retrieve the elements later. Fortunately, these tasks contain hardly anything new for us. Consider the following code fragment:

```
import java.util.HashSet;
...
HashSet<String> mySet = new HashSet<>();
mySet.add("one");
mySet.add("two");
mySet.add("three");
```

Compare this code with the statements needed to enter elements into an **ArrayList**. There is almost no difference, except that we create a **HashSet** this time instead of an **ArrayList**. Now let us look at iterating over all elements:

```
for(String item : mySet) {
    do something with that item
}
```

Again, these statements are the same as the ones we used to iterate over an **ArrayList** in Chapter 4.

In short, using collections in Java is quite similar for different types of collections. Once you understand how to use one of them, you can use them all. The differences really lie in the behavior of each collection. A list, for example, will keep all elements entered in the desired order, provides access to elements by index, and can contain the same element multiple times. A set, on the other hand, does not maintain any specific order (the elements may be returned in a for-each loop in a different order from that in which they were entered) and ensures that each element is in the set at most once. Entering an element a second time simply has no effect.

6.8 Dividing strings

Now that we have seen how to use a set, we can investigate how we can cut the input string into separate words to be stored in a set of words. The solution is shown in a new version of the **InputReader**'s **getInput** method (Code 6.5).

```
/**
 * Read a line of text from standard input (the text terminal),
 * and return it as a set of words.
 *
 * @return  A set of Strings, where each String is one of the
 *          words typed by the user
 */
public HashSet<String> getInput()
{
    System.out.print("> ");                          // print prompt
    String inputLine = reader.nextLine().trim().toLowerCase();

    String[] wordArray = inputLine.split(" ");  // split at spaces

    // add words from array into hashset
    HashSet<String> words = new HashSet<>();
    for(String word : wordArray) {
        words.add(word);
    }
    return words;
}
```

Here, in addition to using a **HashSet**, we also use the **split** method, which is a standard method of the **String** class.

The **split** method can divide a string into separate substrings and return those in an array of strings. (Arrays will be discussed in more detail in the next chapter.) The parameter to the **split** method defines at what kind of characters the original string should be split. We have defined that we want to cut our string at every space character.

The next few lines of code create a **HashSet** and copy the words from the array into the set before returning the set.[3]

> **Exercise 6.35** The **split** method is more powerful than it first seems from our example. How can you define exactly how a string should be split? Give some examples.
>
> **Exercise 6.36** How would you call the **split** method if you wanted to split a string at either space or tab characters? How might you break up a string in which the words are separated by colon characters (:)?

---

[3] There is a shorter, more elegant way of doing this. One could write
```
HashSet<String> words = new HashSet<>(Arrays.asList(wordArray));
```
to replace all four lines of code. This uses the **Arrays** class from the standard library and a *static method* (also known as *class method*) that we do not really want to discuss just yet. If you are curious, read about *class methods* in Section 6.15, and try to use this version.

Exercise 6.37 What is the difference in the result of returning the words in a **HashSet** compared with returning them in an **ArrayList**?

Exercise 6.38 What happens if there is more than one space between two words (e.g., two or three spaces)? Is there a problem?

Exercise 6.39 *Challenge exercise* Read the footnote about the **Arrays. asList** method. Find and read the sections later in this chapter about class variables and class methods. Explain in your own words how this works.

Exercise 6.40 *Challenge exercise* What are examples of other methods that the **Arrays** class provides?

Exercise 6.41 *Challenge exercise* Create a class called **SortingTest**. In it, create a method that accepts an array of **int** values as a parameter and prints the elements sorted out to the terminal (smallest element first).

6.9 Finishing the *TechSupport* system

To put everything together, we also have to adjust the **SupportSystem** and **Responder** classes to deal correctly with a set of words rather than a single string. Code 6.6 shows the new version of the **start** method from the **SupportSystem** class. It has not changed very much. The changes are:

- The **input** variable receiving the result from **reader.getInput()** is now of type **HashSet**.

- The check for ending the application is done using the **contains** method of the **HashSet** class, rather than a **String** method. (Look this method up in the documentation.)

- The **HashSet** class has to be imported using an **import** statement (not shown here).

Finally, we have to extend the **generateResponse** method in the **Responder** class to accept a set of words as a parameter. It then has to iterate over these words and check each of them with our map of known words. If any of the words is recognized, we immediately return the associated response. If we do not recognize any of the words, as before, we pick one of our default responses. Code 6.7 shows the solution.

This is the last change to the application discussed here in this chapter. The solution in the project *tech-support-complete* contains all these changes. It also contains more associations of words to responses than are shown in this chapter.

Many more improvements to this application are possible. We shall not discuss them here. Instead, we suggest some, in the form of exercises, to the reader. Some of these are quite challenging programming exercises.

Code 6.6
Final version of the
start method

```
public void start()
{
    boolean finished = false;

    printWelcome();

    while(!finished) {
        HashSet<String> input = reader.getInput();

        if(input.contains("bye")) {
            finished = true;
        }
        else {
            String response = responder.generateResponse(input);
            System.out.println(response);
        }
    }
    printGoodbye();
}
```

Code 6.7
Final version of the
generateResponse
method

```
public String generateResponse(HashSet<String> words)
{
    for (String word : words) {
        String response = responseMap.get(word);
        if(response != null) {
            return response;
        }
    }
    // If we get here, none of the words from the input line was recognized.
    // In this case we pick one of our default responses (what we say when
    // we cannot think of anything else to say...)
    return pickDefaultResponse();
}
```

Exercise 6.42 Implement the final changes discussed above in your own version of the program.

Exercise 6.43 Add more word/response mappings into your application. You could copy some out of the solutions provided and add some yourself.

Exercise 6.44 Ensure that the same default response is never repeated twice in a row.

Exercise 6.45 Sometimes two words (or variations of a word) are mapped to the same response. Deal with this by mapping synonyms or related expressions to the same string, so that you do not need multiple entries in the response map for the same response.

Exercise 6.46 Identify multiple matching words in the user's input, and respond with a more appropriate answer in that case.

Exercise 6.47 When no word is recognized, use other words from the user's input to pick a well-fitting default response: for example, words such as "why", "how", and "who".

6.10 Autoboxing and wrapper classes

We have seen that, with suitable parameterization, the collection classes can store objects of any object type. There remains one problem: Java has some types that are not object types.

As we know, the simple types—such as `int`, `boolean`, and `char`—are separate from object types. Their values are not instances of classes, and it would not normally be possible to add them into a collection.

This is unfortunate. There are situations in which we might want to create a list of `int` values or a set of `char` values, for instance. What can we do?

Java's solution to this problem is *wrapper classes*. Every primitive type in Java has a corresponding wrapper class that represents the same type but is a real object type. The wrapper class for `int`, for example, is called `Integer`. A complete list of simple types and their wrapper classes is given in Appendix B.

The following statement explicitly wraps the value of the primitive `int` variable `ix` in an `Integer` object:

```
Integer iwrap = new Integer(ix);
```

And now `iwrap` could obviously easily be stored in an `ArrayList<Integer>` collection, for instance. However, storing of primitive values into an object collection is made even easier through a compiler feature known as *autoboxing*.

> **Concept**
>
> **Autoboxing** is performed automatically when a primitive-type value is used in a context requiring a wrapper type.

Whenever a value of a primitive type is used in a context that requires a wrapper type, the compiler automatically wraps the primitive-type value in an appropriate wrapper object. This means that primitive-type values can be added directly to a collection:

```
private ArrayList<Integer> markList;
...
public void storeMarkInList(int mark)
{
    markList.add(mark);
}
```

The reverse operation—*unboxing*—is also performed automatically, so retrieval from a collection might look like this:

```
int firstMark = markList.remove(0);
```

Autoboxing is also applied whenever a primitive-type value is passed as a parameter to a method that expects a wrapper type, and when a primitive-type value is stored in a wrapper-type variable. Similarly, unboxing is applied when a wrapper-type value is passed as a parameter to a method that expects a primitive-type value, and when stored in a primitive-type variable. It is worth noting that this almost makes it appear as if primitive types can be stored in collections. However, the type of the collection must still be declared using the wrapper type (e.g., **ArrayList<Integer>**, not **ArrayList<int>**).

6.10.1 Maintaining usage counts

Combining a map with autoboxing provides an easy way to maintain usage counts of objects. For instance, suppose that the company running the *TechSupport* system is receiving complaints from its customers that some of its answers bear no relation to the question being asked. The company might decide to analyze the words being used in questions and add further specific responses for those being used most frequently that it does not have ready responses for. Code 6.8 shows part of the **WordCounter** class that can be found in the *tech-support-analysis* project.

Code 6.8

The **WordCounter** class, used to count word frequencies

```java
import java.util.HashMap;
import java.util.HashSet;

/**
 * Keep a record of how many times each word was entered by users.
 *
 * @author      Michael Kölling and David J. Barnes
 * @version     1.0 (2016.02.29)
 */
public class WordCounter
{
    // Associate each word with a count.
    private HashMap<String, Integer> counts;

    /**
     * Create a WordCounter
     */
    public WordCounter()
    {
        counts = new HashMap<>();
    }

    /**
     * Update the usage count of all words in input.
     * @param input A set of words entered by the user.
     */
```

Code 6.8 continued

The **WordCounter** class, used to count word frequencies

```
public void addWords(HashSet<String> input)
{
    for(String word : input) {
        int counter = counts.getOrDefault(word, 0);
        counts.put(word, counter + 1);
    }
}
}
```

The **addWords** method receives the same set of words that are passed to the **Responder**, so that each word can be associated with a count. The counts are stored in a map of **String** to **Integer** objects.

Notice the use of the **getOrDefault** method of the **HashMap**, which takes two parameters: a key and a default value. If the key is already in use in the map then this method returns its associated value, but if the key is not in use then it will return the default value rather than **null**. This avoids having to write two different follow-up actions depending on whether the key was in use or not. Using **get**, instead, we would have had to write something like:

```
Integer counter = counts.get(word);
if(counter == null) {
    counts.put(word, 1);
}
else {
    counts.put(word, counter + 1);
}
```

Notice how autoboxing and unboxing are used multiple times in these examples.

Exercise 6.48 What does the **putIfAbsent** method of **HashMap** do?

Exercise 6.49 Add a method to the **WordCounter** class in *tech-support-analysis* to print the usage count of each word after the "goodbye" message has been printed.

Exercise 6.50 Print counts of only those words that are not already keys in the **responseMap** in the **Responder** class. You will need to provide an accessor method for **responseMap**.

6.11 Writing class documentation

When working on your projects, it is important to write documentation for your classes as you develop the source code. It is common for programmers not to take documentation seriously enough, and this frequently creates serious problems later.

If you do not supply sufficient documentation, it may be very hard for another programmer (or yourself some time later!) to understand your classes. Typically, what you have to do in that case is to read the class's implementation and figure out what it does. This may work with a small student project, but it creates problems in real-world projects.

> **Concept**
>
> The **docu-mentation** of a class should be detailed enough for other program-mers to use the class with-out the need to read the implementation.

It is not uncommon for commercial applications to consist of hundreds of thousands of lines of code in several thousand classes. Imagine that you had to read all that in order to understand how an application works! You would never succeed.

When we used the Java library classes, such as **HashSet** or **Random**, we relied exclusively on the documentation to find out how to use them. We never looked at the implementation of those classes. This worked because these classes were sufficiently well documented (although even this documentation could be improved). Our task would have been much harder had we been required to read the classes' implementation before using them.

In a software development team, the implementation of classes is typically shared between multiple programmers. While you might be responsible for implementing the **SupportSystem** class from our last example, someone else might implement the **InputReader**. Thus, you might write one class while making calls to methods of other classes.

The same argument discussed for library classes holds true for classes that you write: if we can use the classes without having to read and understand the complete implementation, our task becomes easier. As with library classes, we want to see just the public interface of the class, instead of the implementation. It is therefore important to write good class documentation for our own classes as well.

Java systems include a tool called **javadoc** that can be used to generate such an interface description from source files. The standard library documentation that we have used, for example, was created from the classes' source files by **javadoc**.

6.11.1 Using javadoc in BlueJ

The BlueJ environment uses **javadoc** to let you create documentation for your class in two ways:

- You can view the documentation for a single class by switching the pop-up selector at the top right of the editor window from *Source Code* to *Documentation* (or by using *Toggle Documentation View* from the editor's *Tools* menu).

- You can use the *Project Documentation* function from the main window's *Tools* menu to generate documentation for all classes in the project.

The BlueJ tutorial provides more detail if you are interested. You can find the BlueJ tutorial in BlueJ's *Help* menu.

6.11.2 Elements of class documentation

The documentation of a class should include at least:

- the class name
- a comment describing the overall purpose and characteristics of the class
- a version number

- the author's name (or authors' names)
- documentation for each constructor and each method

The documentation for each constructor and method should include:

- the name of the method
- the return type
- the parameter names and types
- a description of the purpose and function of the method
- a description of each parameter
- a description of the value returned

In addition, each complete project should have an overall project comment, often contained in a "ReadMe" file. In BlueJ, this project comment is accessible through the text note displayed in the top left corner of the class diagram.

Exercise 6.51 Use BlueJ's *Project Documentation* function to generate documentation for your *TechSupport* project. Examine it. Is it accurate? Is it complete? Which parts are useful? Which are not? Do you find any errors in the documentation?

Some elements of the documentation, such as names and parameters of methods, can always be extracted from the source code. Other parts, such as comments describing the class, methods, and parameters, need more attention, as they can easily be forgotten, be incomplete, or be incorrect.

In Java, **javadoc** comments are written with a special comment symbol at the beginning:

```
/**
    This is a javadoc comment.
 */
```

The comment start symbol must have two asterisks to be recognized as a **javadoc** comment. Such a comment immediately preceding the class declaration is read as a class comment. If the comment is directly above a method signature, it is considered a method comment.

The exact details of how documentation is produced and formatted are different in different programming languages and environments. The content, however, should be more or less the same.

In Java, using **javadoc**, several special key symbols are available for formatting the documentation. These key symbols start with the @ symbol and include

```
@version
@author
@param
@return
```

Exercise 6.52 Find examples of `javadoc` key symbols in the source code of the *TechSupport* project. How do they influence the formatting of the documentation?

Exercise 6.53 Find out about and describe other `javadoc` key symbols. One place where you can look is the online documentation of Oracle's Java distribution. It contains a document called *javadoc—The Java API Documentation Generator* (for example, at `http://download.oracle.com/javase/8/docs/technotes/tools/windows/javadoc.html`). In this document, the key symbols are called *javadoc tags*.

Exercise 6.54 Properly document all classes in your version of the *TechSupport* project.

6.12 Public versus private

Concept

Access modifiers define the visibility of a field, constructor, or method. Public elements are accessible from inside the same class and from other classes; private elements are accessible only from within the same class.

It is time to discuss in more detail one aspect of classes that we have already encountered several times without saying much about it: *access modifiers*.

Access modifiers are the keywords **public** or **private** at the beginning of field declarations and method signatures. For example:

```
// field declaration
private int numberOfSeats;

// methods
public void setAge(int replacementAge)
{ ...
}

private int computeAverage()
{ ...
}
```

Fields, constructors, and methods can all be either public or private, although so far we have seen mostly private fields and public constructors and methods. We shall come back to this below.

Access modifiers define the visibility of a field, constructor, or method. If a method, for example, is public, it can be invoked from within the same class or from any other class. Private methods, on the other hand, can be invoked only from within the class in which they are declared. They are not visible to other classes.

Now that we have discussed the difference between the interface and the implementation of a class (Section 6.3.1), we can more easily understand the purpose of these keywords.

Remember: The interface of a class is the set of details that another programmer using the class needs to see. It provides information about how to use the class. The interface includes constructor and method signatures and comments. It is also referred to as the *public* part of a class. Its purpose is to define *what* the class does.

The implementation is the section of a class that defines precisely *how* the class works. The method bodies, containing the Java statements, and most fields are part of the implementation. The implementation is also referred to as the *private* part of a class. The user of a class does not need to know about the implementation. In fact, there are good reasons why a user *should be prevented from knowing* about the implementation (or at least from making use of this knowledge). This principle is called *information hiding*.

The `public` keyword declares an element of a class (a field or method) to be part of the interface (i.e., publicly visible); the `private` keyword declares it to be part of the implementation (i.e., hidden from outside access).

6.12.1 Information hiding

> **Concept**
>
> **Information hiding** is a principle that states that internal details of a class's implementation should be hidden from other classes. It ensures better modularization of an application.

In many object-oriented programming languages, the internals of a class—its implementation—are hidden from other classes. There are two aspects to this. First, a programmer making use of a class should *not need to know* the internals; second, a user should *not be allowed to know* the internals.

The first principle—*not need to know*—has to do with abstraction and modularization as discussed in Chapter 3. If it were necessary to know all internals of all classes we need to use, we would never finish implementing large systems.

The second principle—*not being allowed to know*—is different. It also has to do with modularization, but in a different context. The programming language does not allow access to the private section of one class by statements in another class. This ensures that one class does not depend on exactly how another class is implemented.

This is very important for maintenance work. It is a very common task for a maintenance programmer to later change or extend the implementation of a class to make improvements or fix bugs. Ideally, changing the implementation of one class should not make it necessary to change other classes as well. This issue is known as *coupling*. If changes in one part of a program do not make it necessary to also make changes in another part of the program, this is known as weak coupling or loose coupling. Loose coupling is good, because it makes a maintenance programmer's job much easier. Instead of understanding and changing many classes, she may only need to understand and change one class. For example, if a Java systems programmer makes an improvement to the implementation of the **ArrayList** class, you would hope that you would not need to change your code using this class. This will work, because you have not made any references to the implementation of **ArrayList** in your own code.

So, to be more precise, the rule that a user should not be allowed to know the internals of a class does not refer to the programmer of another class, but to the class itself. It is not usually a problem if a programmer knows the implementation details, but a class should not "know" (depend on) the internal details of another class. The programmer of both classes might even be the same person, but the classes should still be loosely coupled.

The issues of coupling and information hiding are very important, and we shall have more to say about them in later chapters.

For now, it is important to understand that the **private** keyword enforces information hiding by not allowing other classes access to this part of the class. This ensures loose coupling, and makes an application more modular and easier to maintain.

6.12.2 Private methods and public fields

Most methods we have seen so far were public. This ensures that other classes can call these methods. Sometimes, though, we have made use of private methods. In the **SupportSystem** class of the *TechSupport* system, for instance, we saw the methods **printWelcome** and **printGoodbye** declared as private methods.

The reason for having both options is that methods are actually used for different purposes. They are used to provide operations to users of a class (public methods), and they are used to break up a larger task into several smaller ones to make the large task easier to handle. In the second case, the subtasks are not intended to be invoked directly from outside the class, but are placed in separate methods purely to make the implementation of a class easier to read. In this case, such methods should be private. The **printWelcome** and **printGoodbye** methods are examples of this.

Another good reason for having a private method is for a task that is needed (as a subtask) in several of a class's methods. Instead of writing the code multiple times, we can write it once in a single private method, and then call this method from several different places. We shall see an example of this later.

In Java, fields can also be declared private or public. So far, we have not seen examples of public fields, and there is a good reason for this. Declaring fields public breaks the information-hiding principle. It makes a class that is dependent upon that information vulnerable to incorrect operation if the implementation changes. Even though the Java language allows us to declare public fields, we consider this bad style and will not make use of this option. Some other object-oriented languages do not allow public fields at all.

A further reason for keeping fields private is that it allows an object to maintain greater control over its state. If access to a private field is channeled through accessor and mutator methods, then an object has the ability to ensure that the field is never set to a value that would be inconsistent with its overall state. This level of integrity is not possible if fields are made public.

In short, fields should always be private.

Java has two more access levels. One is declared by using the **protected** keyword as access modifier; the other one is used if no access modifier at all is declared. We shall discuss these in later chapters.

6.13 Learning about classes from their interfaces

We shall briefly discuss another project to revisit and practice the concepts discussed in this chapter. The project is named *scribble*, and you can find it in the Chapter 6 folder of the book projects. This section does not introduce any new concepts, so it consists in large part of exercises, with some commentary sprinkled in.

Figure 6.4
The *scribble* project

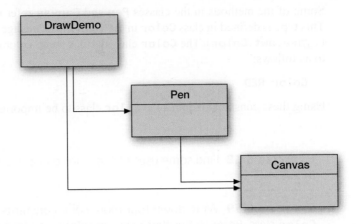

6.13.1 The *scribble* demo

The *scribble* project provides three classes: **DrawDemo**, **Pen**, and **Canvas** (Figure 6.4).

The **Canvas** class provides a window on screen that can be used to draw on. It has operations for drawing lines, shapes, and text. A canvas can be used by creating an instance interactively or from another object. The **Canvas** class should not need any modification. It is probably best to treat it as a library class: open the editor and switch to the documentation view. This displays the class's interface with the **javadoc** documentation.

The **Pen** class provides a pen object that can be used to produce drawings on the canvas by moving the pen across the screen. The pen itself is invisible, but it will draw a line when moved on the canvas.

The **DrawDemo** class provides a few small examples of how to use a pen object to produce a drawing on screen. The best starting point for understanding and experimenting with this project is the **DrawDemo** class.

Exercise 6.55 Create a **DrawDemo** object and experiment with its various methods. Read the **DrawDemo** source code and describe (in writing) how each method works.

Exercise 6.56 Create a **Pen** object interactively using its default constructor (the constructor without parameters). Experiment with its methods. While you do this, make sure to have a window open showing you the documentation of the **Pen** class (either the editor window in *Documentation* view or a web-browser window showing the project documentation). Refer to the documentation to be certain what each method does.

Exercise 6.57 Interactively create an instance of class **Canvas** and try some of its methods. Again, refer to the class's documentation while you do this.

Some of the methods in the classes **Pen** and **Canvas** refer to parameters of type **Color**. This type is defined in class **Color** in the **java.awt** package (thus, its fully qualified name is **java.awt.Color**). The **Color** class defines some color constants, which we can refer to as follows:

```
Color.RED
```

Using these constants requires the **Color** class to be imported in the using class.

> **Exercise 6.58** Find some uses of the color constants in the code of class **DrawDemo**.
>
> **Exercise 6.59** Write down four more color constants that are available in the **Color** class. Refer to the class's documentation to find out what they are.

When calling methods interactively that expect parameters of the **Color** class, we have to refer to the class slightly differently. Because the interactive dialog has no import statement (and thus the **Color** class is not automatically known), we have to write the fully qualified class name to refer to the class (Figure 6.5). This enables the Java system to find the class without using an import statement.

Now that we know how to change the color for pens and canvases, we can do some more exercises.

> **Exercise 6.60** Create a canvas. Using the canvas's methods interactively, draw a red circle near the center of the canvas. Now draw a yellow rectangle.
>
> **Exercise 6.61** How do you clear the whole canvas?

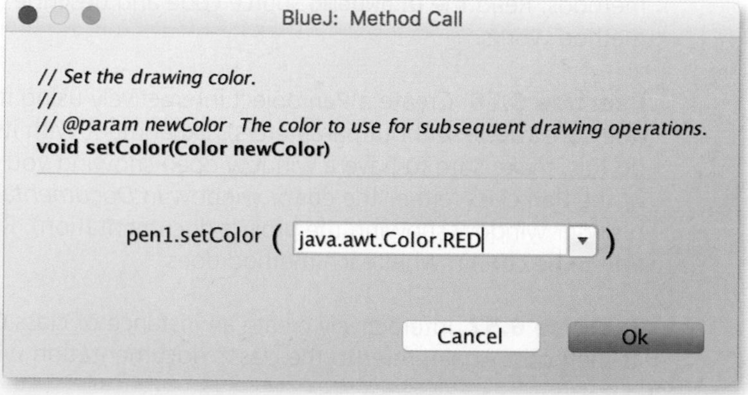

Figure 6.5
A method call with a fully qualified class name

```
BlueJ: Method Call

// Set the drawing color.
//
// @param newColor  The color to use for subsequent drawing operations.
void setColor(Color newColor)


pen1.setColor ( java.awt.Color.RED        ▼ )


                        Cancel        Ok
```

As you have seen, we can either draw directly on to the canvas or we can use a pen object to draw. The pen provides us with an abstraction that holds a current position, rotation, and color, and this makes producing some kinds of drawings easier. Let us experiment with this a bit more, this time by writing code in a class instead of using interactive calls.

> **Exercise 6.62** In class **DrawDemo**, create a new method named **drawTriangle**. This method should create a pen (as in the **drawSquare** method) and then draw a green triangle.
>
> **Exercise 6.63** Write a method **drawPentagon** that draws a pentagon.
>
> **Exercise 6.64** Write a method **drawPolygon(int n)** that draws a regular polygon with **n** sides (thus, n=3 draws a triangle, n=4 draws a square, etc.).
>
> **Exercise 6.65** Write a method called **spiral** that draws a spiral (see Figure 6.6).

6.13.2 Code completion

Often, we are reasonably familiar with a library class that we are using, but we still cannot remember the exact names of all methods or the exact parameters. For this situation, development environments commonly offer some help: code completion.

Code completion is a function that is available in BlueJ's editor when the cursor is behind the dot of a method call. In this situation, typing *CTRL-space* will bring up a pop-up listing all methods in the interface of the object we are using in the call (Figure 6.7).

Figure 6.6
A spiral drawn on the canvas

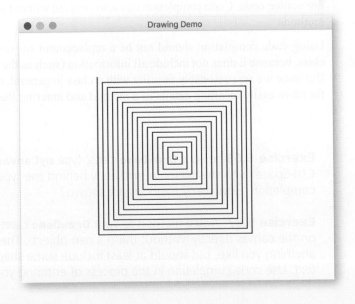

Figure 6.7

Code completion

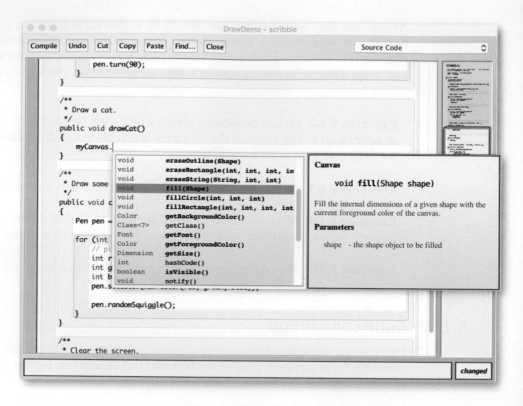

When the code completion pop-up is displayed, we can type the beginning of the method name to narrow down the method list. Hitting *Return* enters the selected method call into our source code. Code completion can also be used without a preceding object to call local methods.

Using code completion should not be a replacement for reading the documentation of a class, because it does not include all information (such as the introductory class comment). But once we are reasonably familiar with a class in general, code completion is a great aid for more easily recalling details of a method and entering the call into our source.

Exercise 6.66 In your **DrawDemo** class, type **myCanvas.er** and then press Ctrl-Space (with the cursor immediately behind the typed text) to activate code completion. How many methods are shown?

Exercise 6.67 Add a method to your **DrawDemo** class that produces a picture on the canvas directly (without using a pen object). The picture can show anything you like, but should at least include some shapes, different colors, and text. Use code completion in the process of entering your code.

6.13.3 The *bouncing-balls* demo

Open the *bouncing-balls* project and find out what it does. Create a **BallDemo** object and execute its **bounce** method.

> **Exercise 6.68** Change the method **bounce** in class **BallDemo** to let the user choose how many balls should be bouncing.

For this exercise, you should use a collection to store the balls. This way, the method can deal with 1, 3, or 75 balls—any number you want. The balls should initially be placed in a row along the top of the canvas.

Which type of collection should you choose? So far, we have seen an **ArrayList**, a **HashMap**, and a **HashSet**. Try the next two exercises first, before you write your implementation.

> **Exercise 6.69** Which type of collection (**ArrayList**, **HashMap**, or **HashSet**) is most suitable for storing the balls for the new **bounce** method? Discuss in writing, and justify your choice.
>
> **Exercise 6.70** Change the **bounce** method to place the balls randomly anywhere in the top half of the screen.
>
> **Exercise 6.71** Write a new method named **boxBounce**. This method draws a rectangle (the "box") on screen and one or more balls inside the box. For the balls, do not use **BouncingBall**, but create a new class **BoxBall** that moves around inside the box, bouncing off the walls of the box so that the ball always stays inside. The initial position and speed of the ball should be random. The **boxBounce** method should have a parameter that specifies how many balls are in the box.
>
> **Exercise 6.72** Give the balls in **boxBounce** random colors.

6.14 Class variables and constants

So far, we have not looked at the **BouncingBall** class. If you are interested in really understanding how this animation works, you may want to study this class as well. It is reasonably simple. The only method that takes some effort to understand is **move**, where the ball changes its position to the next position in its path.

We shall leave it largely to the reader to study this method, except for one detail that we want to discuss here. We start with an exercise.

> **Exercise 6.73** In class **BouncingBall**, you will find a definition of gravity (a simple integer). Increase or decrease the gravity value; compile and run the bouncing ball demo again. Do you observe a change?

The most interesting detail in this class is the line

```
private static final int GRAVITY = 3;
```

This is a construct we have not seen yet. This one line, in fact, introduces two new keywords, which are used together: **static** and **final**.

6.14.1 The **static** keyword

Concept

Classes can have fields. These are known as **class variables** or **static variables**. Exactly one copy exists of a class variable at all times, independent of the number of created instances.

The keyword **static** is Java's syntax to define *class variables*. Class variables are fields that are stored in a class itself, not in an object. This makes them fundamentally different from instance variables (the fields we have dealt with so far). Consider this segment of code (a part of the **BouncingBall** class):

```
public class BouncingBall
{
    // Effect of gravity.
    private static final int GRAVITY = 3;
    private int xPosition;
    private int yPosition;
    Other fields and method omitted.

}
```

Now imagine that we create three **BouncingBall** instances. The resulting situation is shown in Figure 6.8.

As we can see from the diagram, the instance variables (**xPosition** and **yPosition**) are stored in each object. Because we have created three objects, we have three independent copies of these variables.

The class variable **GRAVITY**, on the other hand, is stored in the class itself. As a result, there is always exactly one copy of this variable, independent of the number of created instances.

Source code in the class can access (read and set) this kind of variable, just as it can an instance variable. The class variable can be accessed from any of the class's instances. As a result, the objects share this variable.

Class variables are frequently used if a value should always be the same for all instances of a class. Instead of storing one copy of the same value in each object, which would be a waste of space and might be hard to coordinate, a single value can be shared among all instances.

Java also supports *class methods* (also known as *static methods*), which are methods that belong to a class. We shall discuss those in a separate section later.

Figure 6.8
Instance variables
and a class variable

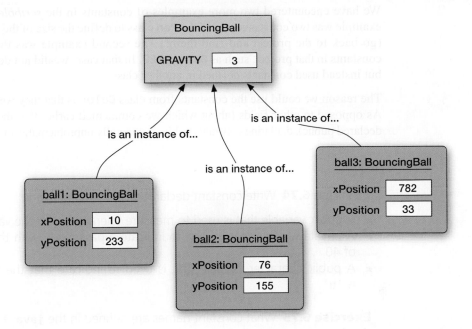

6.14.2 Constants

One frequent use for the **static** keyword is to define *constants*. Constants are similar to variables, but they cannot change their value during the execution of an application. In Java, constants are defined with the keyword **final**. For example:

```
private final int SIZE = 10;
```

Here, we define a constant named **SIZE** with the value 10. We notice that constant declarations look similar to field declarations, with two differences:

- they include the keyword **final** before the type name; and
- they must be initialized with a value at the point of declaration.

If a value is intended not to change, it is a good idea to declare it **final**. This ensures that it cannot accidentally be changed later. Any attempt to change a constant field will result in a compile-time error message. Constants are, by convention, often written in capital letters. We will follow that convention in this book.

In practice, it is frequently the case that constants apply to all instances of a class. In this situation, we declare *class constants*. Class constants are constant class fields. They are declared by using a combination of the **static** and **final** keywords. For example:

```
private static final int SIZE = 10;
```

The definition of **GRAVITY** from our bouncing-ball project is another example of such a constant. This is the style in which constants are defined most of the time. Instance-specific constants are much less frequently used.

We have encountered two more examples of constants in the *scribble* project. The first example was two constants used in the **Pen** class to define the size of the "random squiggle" (go back to the project and find them!) The second example was the use of the color constants in that project, such as `Color.RED`. In that case, we did not define the constants, but instead used constants defined in another class.

The reason we could use the constants from class **Color** is that they were declared public. As opposed to other fields (about which we commented earlier that they should never be declared public), declaring constants public is generally unproblematic and sometimes useful.

> **Exercise 6.74** Write constant declarations for the following:
>
> - A public variable that is used to measure tolerance, with the value 0.001.
> - A private variable that is used to indicate a pass mark, with the integer value of 40.
> - A public character variable that is used to indicate that the help command is `'h'`.
>
> **Exercise 6.75** What constant names are defined in the `java.lang.Math` class?
>
> **Exercise 6.76** In a program that uses the constant value 73.28166 in ten different places, give reasons why it makes sense to associate this value with a variable name.

6.15 Class methods

So far, all methods we have seen have been *instance methods*: they are invoked on an instance of a class. What distinguishes class methods from instance methods is that class methods can be invoked without an instance—having the class is enough.

6.15.1 Static methods

In Section 6.14, we discussed class variables. Class methods are conceptually related and use a related syntax (the keyword **static** in Java). Just as class variables belong to the class rather than to an instance, so do class methods.

A class method is defined by adding the keyword **static** in front of the type name in the method's header:

```java
public static int getNumberOfDaysThisMonth()
{
    . . .
}
```

Such a method can then be called by specifying the name of the class in which it is defined, before the dot in the usual dot notation. If, for instance, the above method is defined in a class called **Calendar**, the following call invokes it:

```
int days = Calendar.getNumberOfDaysThisMonth();
```

Note that the name of the class is used before the dot—no object has been created.

Exercise 6.77 Read the class documentation for class **Math** in the package **java.lang**. It contains many static methods. Find the method that computes the maximum of two integer numbers. What does its header look like?

Exercise 6.78 Why do you think the methods in the **Math** class are static? Could they be written as instance methods?

Exercise 6.79 Write a test class that has a method to test how long it takes to count from 1 to 10000 in a loop. You can use the method **currentTimeMillis** from class **System** to help with the time measurement.

Exercise 6.80 Can a static method be called from an instance method? Can an instance method be called from a static method? Can a static method be called from another static method? Answer these questions on paper, then create a test project to check your answers and try it. Explain in detail your answers and observations.

Exercise 6.81 The **Collections** class in the **java.util** packages contains a large number of static methods that can be used with collections such as **ArrayList**, **LinkedList**, **HashMap** and **HashSet**. Read the class documentation for the **min**, **max**, and **sort** methods, for instance. While you might not fully understand the explanations or the notation used, being aware that these methods exist will be useful to you.

6.15.2 Limitations of class methods

Because class methods are associated with a class rather than an instance, they have two important limitations. The first limitation is that a class method may not access any instance fields defined in the class. This is logical, because instance fields are associated with individual objects. Instead, class methods are restricted to accessing class variables from their class. The second limitation is like the first: a class method may not call an instance method from the class. A class method may only invoke other class methods defined in its class.

You will find that we write very few class methods in the examples in this book.

6.16 Executing without BlueJ

When we finish writing a program, we might want to pass it on to someone else to use. To do this, it would be nice if people could use it without the need to start BlueJ. For this to be the case, we need one more thing: a specific class method known as *the main method*.

6.16.1 The main method

If we want to start a Java application without BlueJ, we need to use a class method. In BlueJ, we typically create an object and invoke one of its methods, but without BlueJ, an application starts without any object in existence. Classes are the only things we have initially, so the first method that can be invoked must be a class method.

The Java definition for starting applications is quite simple: the user specifies the class that should be started, and the Java system will then invoke a method called **main** in that class. This method must have a specific signature:

```
public static void main(String[] args)
```

If such a method does not exist in that class, an error is reported. Appendix E describes the details of this method and the commands needed to start the Java system without BlueJ.

> **Exercise 6.82** Add a **main** method to your **SupportSystem** class in the *tech-support* project. The method should create a **SupportSystem** object and invoke the **start** method on it. Test the **main** method by invoking it from BlueJ. Class methods can be invoked from the class's pop-up menu.
>
> **Exercise 6.83** Execute the program without BlueJ.
>
> **Exercise 6.84** Can a class count how many instances have been created of that class? What is needed to do this? Write some code fragments that illustrate what needs to be done. Assume that you want a static method called **numberOfInstances** that returns the number of instances created.

6.17 Further advanced material

In the previous chapter, we introduced material that we described as "advanced" and suggested that this material could be skipped on first reading, if desired. In this section, we introduce some further advanced material and the same advice applies.

6.17.1 Polymorphic collection types (Advanced)

By now we have introduced several different collection classes from the **java.util** package, such as **ArrayList**, **HashMap** and **HashSet**. Each has a number of distinctive features that make it appropriate for particular situations. However, they also have a considerable number of similarities and methods in common. This suggests that they might be related in some way. In object-oriented programming, relationships between classes are expressed via *inheritance*. We will cover this topic in full in Chapters 10 and 11, but it may be instructive to touch briefly on it here to deepen your understanding of the different types of collection.

When trying to understand how the various collection classes are used, and the relationships between them, it helps to pay close attention to their names. From its name, it is tempting to assume that a **HashSet** must be very similar to a **HashMap**. In fact, as we have illustrated, a **HashSet** is actually much closer in usage to an **ArrayList**. Their names consist of two parts, e.g., "array" and "list." The second half tells us *what kind* of collection we are dealing with (**List**, **Map**, **Set**), and the first tells us *how it is implemented* (for instance, using an array (covered in Chapter 7) or hashing (covered in Chapter 11).

For using collections, the type of the collection (the second part) is the more important. We have discussed before that we can often abstract from the implementation; i.e., we do not need to think about it in much detail. Thus, for our purposes, a **HashSet** and a **TreeSet** are very similar. They are both sets, so they behave in the same way. The main difference is in their implementation, which is important only when we start thinking about efficiency: one implementation will perform some operations much faster than another. However, efficiency concerns come much later, and only when we have either very large collections or applications in which performance is critical.

One consequence of this similarity is that we can often ignore details of the implementation when declaring a variable that will refer to a particular collection object. In other words, we can declare the variable to be of a more abstract type, such as **List**, **Map**, or **Set**, rather than the more concrete type—**ArrayList**, **LinkedList**, **HashMap**, **TreeSet**, etc. For instance,

```
List<Track> tracks = new LinkedList<>();
```

or

```
Map<String, String> responseMap = new HashMap<>();
```

Here, the variable is declared to be of type **List**, even though the object created and stored in it is of type **LinkedList** (and the same for **Map** and **HashMap**).

Variables like **tracks** and **responseMap** in these examples are called *polymorphic variables*, because they are capable of referring to objects of different, but related, types. The variable **tracks** could refer to either an **ArrayList** or a **LinkedList**, while **responseMap** could refer to a **HashMap** or a **TreeMap**. The key point behind declaring them like this is that the way in which the variables are used in the rest of the code is independent of the exact, concrete type of the object to which they refer. A call to **add**, **clear**, **get**, **remove**, or **size** on **tracks** would all have the same syntax, and all have the same effect on the associated collection. The exact type rarely matters in any given situation. One advantage of using polymorphic variables in this way is that if we ever wished to change from one concrete type to another, the only place in the code requiring a change is the place where the object is created. Another advantage is that code that we write does not have to know the concrete type that might have been used in code written by someone else – we only need to know the abstract type: `List`, `Map`, `Set`, etc. Both of these advantages *reduce the coupling* between different parts of a program, which is a good thing and something we explore more deeply in Chapter 8.

We will explore the mechanism behind polymorphic variables in detail in Chapters 10 and 11.

6.17.2 The `collect` method of streams (Advanced)

In this section, we continue the discussion of Java 8 streams and lambdas that we started in the previous (Advanced) chapter. We explained there that it is important to know that each operation of the stream leaves its input stream unmodified. Each operation creates a fresh stream, based on its input and the operation, to pass on the next operation in the sequence. However, we will often want to use stream operations to create a fresh version of an original collection that is a modified copy—typically by filtering the original contents to either select desired objects or reject those that are not required. For this we need to use the `collect` method of a stream. The `collect` method is a *terminal operation* and so it will appear as the final operation in a pipeline of operations. It can be used to insert the elements resulting from a stream operation back into a new collection.

There are actually two versions of the `collect` method, but we will concentrate on just the simplest. Indeed, we will choose to focus on just its role in enabling us to create a new collection object as the final operation of a pipeline, and leave further exploration to the interested reader. Even the most basic usage involves multiple concepts that are already advanced for this relatively early stage of this book: streams, static methods, and polymorphism.

The `collect` method takes a `Collector` as a parameter. Essentially, this has to be something that can progressively *accumulate* the elements of its input stream in some way. There are similarities in this accumulation idea to the stream `reduce` operation we covered in the previous chapter. There we saw that a stream of numbers could be reduced to a single number; here we will reduce a stream of objects to a single object, which is another collection. Since we often won't be particularly concerned about whether the collection is an `ArrayList`, a `LinkedList`, or some other form of list type we have not met before, we can ask the `Collector` to return the collection in the form of the polymorphic type `List`.

The easiest way to obtain a `Collector` is use one of the `static` methods defined in the `Collectors` class of the `java.util.stream` package: `toList`, `toMap`, and `toSet`.

Code 6.9 shows a method from the *national-park* project we looked at in Chapter 5. This method filters the full list of `Sighting` objects to create a new `List` of only those for a specific animal. In our version in the *animal-monitoring-v1* project, this method was written in the iterative style, using a for-each loop. Here, it is rewritten in the functional style, using the `collect` method.

Code 6.9

A functional version of the **getSightingsOf** method

```
/**
 * Return a list of all the sightings of the given animal.
 * @param animal The type of animal.
 * @return A list of all sightings of the given animal.
 */
public List<Sighting> getSightingsOf(String animal)
{
    return sightings.stream()
                    .filter(record -> animal.equals(record.getAnimal()))
                    .collect(Collectors.toList());
}
```

A subtle point to note is that the **toList** method of **Collectors** does not actually return a **List** object to be passed into the **collect** method. Rather, it returns a **Collector** that ultimately leads to the creation of a suitable concrete **List** object.

> **Exercise 6.85** Implement this version of the **getSightingsOf** method in your own *animal-monitoring* project.
>
> **Exercise 6.86** Rewrite the **getSightingsInArea** method from the original *animal-monitoring* project in the functional style.

6.17.3 Method references (Advanced)

Suppose that we wish to collect the objects from a filtered stream into a particular concrete type of collection, such as an **ArrayList**, rather than a polymorphic type. This requires a variation of the approach used in the previous section. We still need to pass a **Collector** to the **collect** operation, but we must obtain it in a different way. Code 6.10 shows how this might be done.

Code 6.10

Another version of the **getSightingsOf** method

```
/**
 * Return a list of all the sightings of the given animal.
 * @param animal The type of animal.
 * @return A list of all sightings of the given animal.
 */
public List<Sighting> getSightingsOf(String animal)
{
    return sightings.stream()
                    .filter(record -> animal.equals(record.getAnimal()))
                    .collect(Collectors.toCollection(ArrayList::new));
}
```

This time we have called the static **toCollection** method of **Collectors**, which requires a single parameter whose type is **Supplier**. The parameter we have used introduces a new notation which is called a *method reference*, whose distinctive syntax is a pair of adjacent colon characters.

Method references are a convenient shorthand for some lambdas. They are often used where the compiler can easily infer the full call of a method without having to specify its details explicitly. There are four cases of method references:

a) A reference to a constructor, as we have used here:

```
ArrayList::new
```

(Note that, strictly speaking, a constructor is not actually a method.) This is a shorthand for the lambda:

```
() -> new ArrayList<>()
```

b) A reference to a method call on a particular object:

```
System.out::println
```

This would be a shorthand for the lambda:

```
str -> System.out.println(str)
```

Note that **System.out** is a **public static** variable of the **System** class and the parameter **str** would be supplied by the context in which the method reference is used, for instance, as the terminal operation of a stream pipeline:

```
forEach(System.out::println)
```

c) A reference to a static method:

```
Math::abs
```

This would be a shorthand for:

```
x -> Math.abs(x)
```

The parameter **x** would be supplied by the context in which the method reference is used, for instance, as part of the mapping of a stream:

```
map(Math::abs)
```

d) A reference to an instance method of a particular type:

```
String::length
```

This would be shorthand for:

```
str -> str.length()
```

Once again, **str** would be supplied by context. Note that it is important to distinguish between this usage, which involves an instance method, and both usage b), which involve a specific instance, and usage c), which involves a static method.

Here we have illustrated only the simplest examples for the use of method references. More complex cases involving multiple parameters will also be encountered in the more general examples.

6.18 Summary

Dealing with class libraries and class interfaces is essential for a competent programmer. There are two aspects to this topic: reading class library descriptions (especially class interfaces) and writing them.

It is important to know about some essential classes from the standard Java class library and to be able to find out more when necessary. In this chapter, we have presented some of the most important classes, and have discussed how to browse the library documentation.

It is also important to be able to document any class that is written, in the same style as the library classes, so that other programmers can easily use the class without the need to understand the implementation. This documentation should include good comments for every project, class, and method. Using **javadoc** with Java programs will help you to do this.

Terms introduced in this chapter:

> **interface, implementation, map, set, autoboxing, wrapper classes, javadoc, access modifier, information hiding, class variable, class method, main method, static, constant, final, polymorphic variable, method reference**

Concept summary

- **Java library** The Java standard class library contains many classes that are very useful. It is important to know how to use the library.

- **library documentation** The Java class library documentation shows details about all classes in the library. Using this documentation is essential in order to make good use of library classes.

- **interface** The interface of a class describes what a class does and how it can be used without showing the implementation.

- **implementation** The complete source code that defines a class is called the implementation of that class.

- **immutable** An object is said to be immutable if its contents or state cannot be changed once it has been created. Strings are an example of immutable objects.

- **map** A map is a collection that stores key/value pairs as entries. Values can be looked up by providing the key.

- **set** A set is a collection that stores each individual element at most once. It does not maintain any specific order.

- **autoboxing** Autoboxing is performed automatically when a primitive-type value is used in a context requiring a wrapper type.

- **documentation** The documentation of a class should be detailed enough for other programmers to use the class without the need to read the implementation.

- **access modifier** Access modifiers define the visibility of a field, constructor, or method. Public elements are accessible from inside the same class and from other classes; private elements are accessible only from within the same class.

- **information hiding** Information hiding is a principle that states that internal details of a class's implementation should be hidden from other classes. It ensures better modularization of an application.

- **class variable, static variable** Classes can have fields. These are known as class variables or static variables. Exactly one copy exists of a class variable at all times, independent of the number of created instances.

Exercise 6.87 There is a rumor circulating on the Internet that George Lucas (the creator of the *Star Wars* movies) uses a formula to create the names for the characters in his stories (Jar Jar Binks, ObiWan Kenobi, etc.). The formula—allegedly—is this:

Your Star Wars *first name:*
1. Take the first three letters of your last name.
2. Add to that the first two letters of your first name.

Your Star Wars *last name:*
1. Take the first two letters of your mother's maiden name.
2. Add to this the first three letters of the name of the town or city where you were born.

And now your task: Create a new BlueJ project named *star-wars*. In it create a class named **NameGenerator**. This class should have a method named **generateStarWarsName** that generates a *Star Wars* name, following the method described above. You will need to find out about a method of the **String** class that generates a substring.

Exercise 6.88 The following code fragment attempts to print out a string in uppercase letters:

```
public void printUpper(String s)
{
    s.toUpperCase();
    System.out.println(s);
}
```

This code, however, does not work. Find out why, and explain. How should it be written properly?

Exercise 6.89 Assume that we want to swap the values of two integer variables, **a** and **b**. To do this, we write a method

```
public void swap(int i1, int i2)
{
    int tmp = i1;
    i1 = i2;
    i2 = tmp;
}
```

Then we call this method with our **a** and **b** variables:
```
swap(a, b);
```

Are **a** and **b** swapped after this call? If you test it, you will notice that they are not! Why does this not work? Explain in detail.

Main concepts discussed in this chapter:

■ arrays   ■ for loop

Java constructs discussed in this chapter:

array, for loop, **++**, conditional operator, **? :**

The main focus of this chapter is the use of array objects for fixed-size collections and the for loop.

7.1   Fixed-size collections

In Chapter 4, we looked at the way in which library classes, such as **ArrayList**, allow us to maintain collections of objects. We also looked at further collection types in Chapter 6, such as **HashSet** and **HashMap**. A significant feature of all of these collection types is that their capacity is flexible—we never have to specify how many items a particular collection will hold, and the number of items stored can be varied arbitrarily throughout the life of the collection.

This chapter is about collections that are not flexible but fixed in their capacity—at the point the collection object is created, we have to specify the maximum number of items it can store, and this cannot be changed. At first, this might seem like an unnecessary restriction, however, in some applications we know in advance exactly how many items we wish to store in a collection, and that number typically remains fixed for the life of the collection. In such circumstances, we have the option of choosing to use a specialized fixed-size collection object to store the items.

7.2 Arrays

Concept

An **array** is a special type of collection that can store a fixed number of items.

A fixed-size collection is called an *array*. Although the fixed-size nature of arrays can be a significant disadvantage in many situations, they do have at least two compensating advantages over the flexible-size collection classes:

■ Access to the items held in an array is often more efficient than access to the items in a comparable flexible-size collection.

■ Arrays are able to store either objects or primitive-type values. Flexible-size collections can store only objects.[1]

Another distinctive feature of arrays is that they have special syntactic support in Java; they can be accessed using a custom syntax different from the usual method calls. The reason for this is mostly historical: arrays are the oldest collection structure in programming languages, and syntax for dealing with arrays has developed over many decades. Java uses the same syntax established in other programming languages to keep things simple for programmers who are used to arrays already, even though it is not consistent with the rest of the language syntax.

In the following sections, we shall show how arrays can be used to maintain collections of fixed size. We shall also introduce a new loop structure that is often closely associated with arrays—the *for loop*. (Note that the *for loop* is different from the *for-each loop*.)

7.3 A log-file analyzer

Web servers typically maintain log files of client accesses to the web pages that they store. Given suitable tools, these logs enable web service managers to extract and analyze useful information such as:

■ which are the most popular pages they provide

■ which sites brought users to this one

■ whether other sites appear to have broken links to this site's pages

■ how much data is being delivered to clients

■ the busiest periods over the course of a day, a week, or a month

Such information might help administrators to determine, for instance, whether they need to upgrade to more-powerful server machines, or when the quietest periods are in order to schedule maintenance activities.

The *weblog-analyzer* project contains an application that performs an analysis of data from such a web server. The server writes a line to a log file each time an access is made. A

---

[1] Although the autoboxing feature described in Chapter 6 provides a mechanism that also lets us store primitive values in flexible-size collections, it is nonetheless true that only arrays can directly store them.

sample log file called *weblog.txt* is provided in the project folder. Each line records the date and time of the access in the following format:

```
year month day hour minute
```

For instance, the line below records an access at 03:45am on 7 June 2015:

```
2015 06 07 03 45
```

The project consists of five classes: **LogAnalyzer**, **LogfileReader**, **LogEntry**, **LoglineTokenizer**, and **LogfileCreator**. We shall spend most of our time looking at the **LogAnalyzer** class, as it contains examples of both creating and using an array (Code 7.1). Later exercises will encourage you to examine and modify **LogEntry**, because it also uses an array. The **LogReader** and **LogLineTokenizer** classes use features of the Java language that we have not yet covered, so we shall not explore those in detail. The **LogfileCreator** class allows you to create your own log files containing random data.

Code 7.1

The log-file analyzer

```java
/**
 * Read web server data and analyse hourly access patterns.
 *
 * @author David J. Barnes and Michael Kölling.
 * @version    2016.02.29
 */
public class LogAnalyzer
{
    // Where to calculate the hourly access counts.
    private int[] hourCounts;
    // Use a LogfileReader to access the data.
    private LogfileReader reader;

    /**
     * Create an object to analyze hourly web accesses.
     */
    public LogAnalyzer()
    {
        // Create the array object to hold the hourly
        // access counts.
        hourCounts = new int[24];
        // Create the reader to obtain the data.
        reader = new LogfileReader();
    }

    /**
     * Analyze the hourly access data from the log file.
     */
    public void analyzeHourlyData()
    {
        while(reader.hasNext()) {
            LogEntry entry = reader.next();
            int hour = entry.getHour();
            hourCounts[hour]++;
        }
    }
}
```

```
/**
 * Print the hourly counts.
 * These should have been set with a prior
 * call to analyzeHourlyData.
 */
public void printHourlyCounts()
{
    System.out.println("Hr: Count");
    for(int hour = 0; hour < hourCounts.length; hour++) {
        System.out.println(hour + ": " + hourCounts[hour]);
    }
}

/**
 * Print the lines of data read by the LogfileReader
 */
public void printData()
{
    reader.printData();
}
}
```

The analyzer currently uses only part of the data stored in a server's log line. It provides information that would allow us to determine which hours of the day, on average, tend to be the busiest or quietest for the server. It does this by counting how many accesses were made in each one-hour period over the duration covered by the log.

Exercise 7.1 Explore the *weblog-analyzer* project by creating a **LogAnalyzer** object and calling its **analyzeHourlyData** method. Follow that with a call to its **printHourlyCounts** method, which will print the results of the analysis. Which are the busiest times of the day?

Over the course of the next few sections, we shall examine how this class uses an array to accomplish this task.

7.3.1 Declaring array variables

The **LogAnalyzer** class contains a field that is of an array type:

```
private int[] hourCounts;
```

The distinctive feature of an array variable's declaration is a pair of square brackets as part of the type name: **int[]**. This indicates that the **hourCounts** variable is of type *integer array*. We say that **int** is the *base type* of this particular array, which means that the array object will store values of type **int**. It is important to distinguish between an array-variable declaration and a similar-looking simple-variable declaration:

```
int hour; // A single int variable.
int[] hourCounts; // An int-array variable.
```

Here, the variable **hour** is able to store a single integer value, whereas **hourCounts** will be used to refer to an array object once that object has been created. An array-variable declaration does not itself create the array object. That takes place in a separate stage using the **new** operator, as with other objects.

It is worth looking at the unusual syntax again for a moment. The declaration **int[]** would in more conventional syntax appear, maybe, as **Array<int>**. That it does not has historical rather than logical reasons. You should still get used to reading it in the same way: as "array of int."

Exercise 7.2 Write a declaration for an array variable **people** that could be used to refer to an array of **Person** objects.

Exercise 7.3 Write a declaration for an array variable **vacant** that could be used to refer to an array of boolean values.

Exercise 7.4 Read through the **LogAnalyzer** class and identify all the places where the **hourCounts** variable is used. At this stage, do not worry about what all the uses mean, as they will be explained in the following sections. Note how often a pair of square brackets is used with the variable.

Exercise 7.5 What is wrong with the following array declarations? Correct them.

```
[]int counts;
boolean[5000] occupied;
```

7.3.2 Creating array objects

The next thing to look at is how an array variable is associated with an array object.

The constructor of the **LogAnalyzer** class includes a statement to create an **int** array object:

```
hourCounts = new int[24];
```

Once again, notice how different the syntax is from that of normal object creation. For instance, there are no round brackets for a constructor's parameters, because an array object does not have a constructor. This statement creates an array object that is able to store 24 separate integer values and makes the **hourCounts** array variable refer to that object. The value of 24 is the size of the array, and not a constructor parameter. Figure 7.1 illustrates the result of this assignment.

Figure 7.1
An array of 24
integers

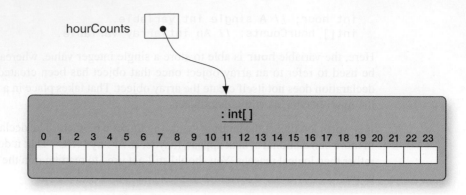

The general form of an array object's construction is

```
new type[integer-expression]
```

The choice of *type* specifies what type of items are to be stored in the array. The *integer expression* specifies the size of the array—that is, the fixed number of items that can be stored in it.

When an array object is assigned to an array variable, the type of the array object must match the declared type of the variable. The assignment to **hourCounts** is allowed because the array object is an integer array, and **hourCounts** is an integer-array variable. The following declares a string-array variable and makes it refer to an array that has a capacity of 10 strings:

```
String[] names = new String[10];
```

It is important to note that the creation of the array assigned to **names** does not actually create 10 strings. Rather, it creates a fixed-size collection that is able to have 10 strings stored within it. Those strings will probably be created in another part of the class to which **names** belongs. Immediately following its creation, an array object can be thought of as empty. If it is an array for objects, then the array will contain **null** values for all elements. If it is an **int** array, then all elements will be set to zero. In the next section, we shall look at the way in which items are stored into (and retrieved from) arrays.

Exercise 7.6 Given the following variable declarations,

```
double[] readings;
String[] urls;
TicketMachine[] machines;
```

write assignments that accomplish the following tasks: (a) Make the **readings** variable refer to an array that is able to hold 60 **double** values; (b) Make the **urls** variable refer to an array that is able to hold 90 **String** objects; (c) Make the **machines** variable refer to an array that is able to hold 5 **TicketMachine** objects.

Exercise 7.7 How many **String** objects are created by the following declaration?

```
String[] labels = new String[20];
```

Exercise 7.8 What is wrong with the following array creation? Correct it.

```
double[] prices = new double(50);
```

7.3.3 Using array objects

The individual elements of an array are accessed by *indexing* the array. An index is an integer expression written between square brackets following the name of an array variable. For instance:

```
labels[6]
machines[0]
people[x + 10 - y]
```

The valid values for an index expression depend upon the length of the array on which they are used. As with other collections, array indices always start at zero and go up to one less than the length of the array. So, the valid indices for the **hourCounts** array are 0 to 23, inclusive.

Pitfall Two very common errors are to think that the valid indices of an array start at 1, and to use the value of the length of the array as an index. Using indices outside the bounds of an array will lead to a runtime error called an **ArrayIndexOutOfBoundsException**.

Expressions that select an element from an array can be used anywhere that a variable of the base type of the array could be used. This means that we can use them on both sides of assignments, for instance. Here are some examples that use array expressions in different places:

```
labels[5] = "Quit";
double half = readings[0] / 2;
System.out.println(people[3].getName());
machines[0] = new TicketMachine(500);
```

Using an array index on the left-hand side of an assignment is the array equivalent of a mutator (or **set** method), because the contents of the array will be changed. Using one anywhere else represents the equivalent of an accessor (or **get** method).

7.3.4 Analyzing the log file

The **hourCounts** array created in the constructor of **LogAnalyzer** is used to store an analysis of the access data. The data is stored into it in the **analyzeHourlyData** method, and displayed from it in the **printHourlyCounts** method. As the task of the **analyze** method is to count how many accesses were made during each hour period, the array needs 24 locations—one for each hour period in a 24-hour day. The analyzer delegates the task of reading its log file to a **LogfileReader**.

The **LogfileReader** class is quite complex, and we suggest that you do not spend too much time investigating its implementation. Its role is to handle the task of breaking up each log line into separate data values, but we can abstract from the implementation details by considering just the headers of two of its methods:

```
public boolean hasNext()
public LogEntry next()
```

These exactly match the methods we have seen with the **Iterator** type, and a **LogfileReader** can be used in exactly the same way, except that we do not permit the **remove** method to be used. The **hasNext** method tells the analyzer whether there is at least one more entry in the log file, and the **next** method then returns a **LogEntry** object containing the values from the next log line.

From each **LogEntry**, the **analyzeHourlyData** method of the analyzer obtains the value of the hour field:

```
int hour = entry.getHour();
```

We know that the value stored in the local variable **hour** will always be in the range 0 to 23, which exactly matches the valid range of indices for the **hourCounts** array. Each location in the array is used to represent an access count for the corresponding hour. So each time an hour value is read, we wish to update the count for that hour by 1. We have written this as

```
hourCounts[hour]++;
```

Note that it is the value stored in the array element that is being incremented and not the **hour** variable. The following alternatives are both equivalent, as we can use an array element in exactly the same way as we would an ordinary variable:

```
hourCounts[hour] = hourCounts[hour] + 1;
hourCounts[hour] += 1;
```

By the end of the **analyzeHourlyData** method, we have a complete set of cumulative counts for each hour of the log period.

In the next section, we look at the **printHourlyCounts** method, as it introduces a new control structure that is well suited to iterating over an array.

7.4 The for loop

Java defines two variations of for loops, both of which are indicated by the keyword *for* in source code. In Section 4.9, we introduced the first variant, the *for-each loop*, as a convenient means to iterate over a flexible-size collection. The second variant, the *for loop*, is an alternative iterative control structure[2] that is particularly appropriate when:

---

[2] Sometimes, if people want to make clearer the distinction between the for loop and the for-each loop, they also talk about the former as the "old-style for loop," because it has been in the Java language longer than the for-each loop. The for-each loop is sometimes referred to as the "enhanced for loop."

- we wish to execute a set of statements a fixed number of times

- we need a variable inside the loop whose value changes by a fixed amount—typically increasing by 1—on each iteration

The for loop is well suited to situations requiring *definite iteration*. For instance, it is common to use a for loop when we wish to do something to every element in an array, such as printing the contents of each element. This fits the criteria, as the fixed number of times corresponds to the length of the array and the variable is needed to provide an incrementing index into the array.

A for loop has the following general form:

```
for (initialization; condition; post-body action) {
    statements to be repeated
}
```

The following concrete example is taken from the **printHourlyCounts** method of the **LogAnalyzer**:

```
for(int hour = 0; hour < hourCounts.length; hour++) {
    System.out.println(hour + ": " + hourCounts[hour]);
}
```

The result of this will be that the value of each element in the array is printed, preceded by its corresponding hour number. For instance:

```
 0: 149
 1: 149
 2: 148
   . . .
23: 166
```

When we compare this for loop to the for-each loop, we notice that the syntactic difference is in the section between the parentheses in the loop header. In this for loop, the parentheses contain three separate sections, separated by semicolons.

From a programming-language design point of view, it would have been nicer to use two different keywords for these two loops, maybe **for** and **foreach**. The reason that **for** is used for both of them is, again, a historical accident. Older versions of the Java language did not contain the for-each loop, and when it was finally introduced, Java designers did not want to introduce a new keyword at this stage, because this could cause problems with existing programs. So they decided to use the same keyword for both loops. This makes it slightly harder for us to distinguish these loops, but we will get used to recognizing the different header structures.

Even though the for loop is often used for definite iteration, the fact that it is controlled by a general boolean expression means that it is actually closer to the while loop than to the for-each loop. We can illustrate the way that a for loop executes by rewriting its general form as an equivalent while loop:

```
    initialization;
    while(condition) {
        statements to be repeated
        post-body action
    }
```

So the alternative form for the body of **printHourlyCounts** would be

```
    int hour = 0;
    while(hour < hourCounts.length) {
        System.out.println(hour + ": " + hourCounts[hour]);
        hour++;
    }
```

From this rewritten version, we can see that the post-body action is not actually executed until after the statements in the loop's body, despite the action's position in the for loop's header. In addition, we can see that the initialization part is executed only once—immediately before the condition is tested for the first time.

In both versions, note in particular the condition

```
    hour < hourCounts.length
```

This illustrates two important points:

- All arrays contain a field **length** that contains the value of the fixed size of that array. The value of this field will always match the value of the integer expression used to create the array object. So the value of **length** here will be 24.

- The condition uses the less-than operator, **<**, to check the value of **hour** against the length of the array. So in this case, the loop will continue as long as **hour** is less than 24. In general, when we wish to access every element in an array, a for-loop header will have the following general form:

```
    for(int index = 0; index < array.length; index++)
```

This is correct, because we do not wish to use an index value that is equal to the array's length; such an element will never exist.

7.4.1 Arrays and the for-each loop

Could we also rewrite the for loop shown above with a for-each loop? The answer is: almost. Here is an attempt:

```
    for(int value : hourCounts) {
        System.out.println(": " + value);
    }
```

This code will compile and execute. (Try it out!) From this fragment, we can see that arrays can, in fact, be used in for-each loops just like other collections. We have, however, one problem: we cannot easily print out the hour in front of the colon. This code fragment simply omits printing the hour, and just prints the colon and the value. This is because the for-each loop does not provide access to a loop-counter variable, which we need in this case to print the hour.

To fix this, we would need to define our own counter variable (similar to what we did in the while loop example). Instead of doing this, we prefer using the old-style for loop because it is more concise.

7.4.2 The for loop and iterators

In Section 4.12.2, we showed the necessity of using an **Iterator** if we wished to remove elements from a collection. There is a special use of the for loop with an **Iterator** when we want to do something like this. Suppose that we wished to remove every music track by a particular artist from our music organizer. The point here is that we need to examine every track in the collection, so a for-each loop would seem appropriate, but we know already that we cannot use it in this particular case. However, we can use a for loop as follows:

```
for(Iterator<Track> it = tracks.iterator(); it.hasNext(); ) {
    Track track = it.next();
    if(track.getArtist().equals(artist)) {
        it.remove();
    }
}
```

The important point here is that there is no post-body action in the loop's header—it is just blank. This is allowed, but we must still include the semicolon after the loop's condition. By using a for loop instead of a while loop, it is a little clearer that we intend to examine every item in the list.

Which loop should I use? We have discussed three different loops: the for-each loop, the while loop, and the for loop. As you have seen, in many situations you have a choice of using any one of these to solve your task. Usually, one loop could be rewritten using another. So how do you decide which one to use at any given point? Here are some guidelines:

- If you need to iterate over all elements in a collection, the for-each loop is almost always the most elegant loop to use. It is clear and concise (but it does not give you a loop counter).
- If you have a loop that is not related to collections (but instead performs some other action repeatedly), the for-each loop is not useful. Your choice will be between the for loop and the while loop. The for-each loop is only for collections.
- The for loop is good if you know how many iterations you need at the start of the loop (that is, how often you need to loop around). This information can be in a variable, but should not change during the loop execution. It is also very good if you need to use the loop counter explicitly.
- The while loop should be preferred if, at the start of the loop, you don't know how often you need to loop. The end of the loop can be determined on the fly by some condition (for example, repeatedly read one line from a file until we reach the end of the file).
- If you need to remove elements from the collection while looping, use a for loop with an **Iterator** if you want to examine the whole collection, or a while loop if you might want to finish before reaching the end of the collection.

Exercise 7.9 Check to see what happens if the for loop's condition is incorrectly written using the **<=** operator in **printHourlyCounts**:

```
for(int hour = 0; hour <= hourCounts.length; hour++)
```

Exercise 7.10 Rewrite the body of **printHourlyCounts** so that the for loop is replaced by an equivalent while loop. Call the rewritten method to check that it prints the same results as before.

Exercise 7.11 Correct all the errors in the following method.

```
/**
 * Print all the values in the marks array that are
 * greater than mean.
 * @param marks An array of mark values.
 * @param mean The mean (average) mark.
 */
public void printGreater(double marks, double mean)
{
    for(index = 0; index <= marks.length; index++) {
        if(marks[index] > mean) {
            System.out.println(marks[index]);
        }
    }
}
```

Exercise 7.12 Modify the **LogAnalyzer** class so that it has a constructor that can take the name of the log file to be analyzed. Have this constructor pass the file name to the constructor of the **LogfileReader** class. Use the **LogfileCreator** class to create your own file of random log entries, and analyze the data.

Exercise 7.13 Complete the **numberOfAccesses** method, below, to count the total number of accesses recorded in the log file. Complete it by using a for loop to iterate over **hourCounts**:

```
/**
 * Return the number of accesses recorded in the log file.
 */
public int numberOfAccesses()
{
    int total = 0;
    // Add the value in each element of hourCounts to
    // total.
    . . .
    return total;
}
```

Exercise 7.14 Add your **numberOfAccesses** method to the **LogAnalyzer** class and check that it gives the correct result. *Hint*: You can simplify your checking by having the analyzer read log files containing just a few lines of data. That way you will find it easier to determine whether or not your method gives the correct answer. The **LogfileReader** class has a constructor with the following header, to read from a particular file:

```
/**
 * Create a LogfileReader that will supply data
 * from a particular log file.
 * @param filename The file of log data.
 */
public LogfileReader(String filename)
```

Exercise 7.15 Add a method **busiestHour** to **LogAnalyzer** that returns the busiest hour. You can do this by looking through the **hourCounts** array to find the element with the biggest count. *Hint:* Do you need to check every element to see if you have found the busiest hour? If so, use a for loop or a for-each loop. Which one is better in this case?

Exercise 7.16 Add a method **quietestHour** to **LogAnalyzer** that returns the number of the least busy hour. *Note:* This sounds almost identical to the previous exercise, but there is a small trap for the unwary. Be sure to check your method with some data in which every hour has a non-zero count.

Exercise 7.17 Which hour is returned by your **busiestHour** method if more than one hour has the biggest count?

Exercise 7.18 Add a method to **LogAnalyzer** that finds which two-hour period is the busiest. Return the value of the first hour of this period.

Exercise 7.19 *Challenge exercise* Save the *weblog-analyzer* project under a different name so that you can develop a new version that performs a more extensive analysis of the available data. For instance, it would be useful to know which days tend to be quieter than others, Are there any seven-day cyclical patterns, for instance? In order to perform analysis of daily, monthly, or yearly data, you will need to make some changes to the **LogEntry** class. This already stores all the values from a single log line, but only the hour and minute values are available via accessors. Add further methods that make the remaining fields available in a similar way. Then add a range of additional analysis methods to the analyzer.

Exercise 7.20 *Challenge exercise* If you have completed the previous exercise, you could extend the log-file format with additional numerical fields. For instance, servers commonly store a numerical code that indicates whether an access was successful or not. The value 200 stands for a successful access, 403 means that access to the document was forbidden, and 404 means that the document could not be found. Have the analyzer provide information on the number of successful and unsuccessful accesses. This exercise is likely to be very challenging, as it will require you to make changes to every class in the project.

Exercise 7.21 In the *lab-classes* project that we have discussed in previous chapters, the **LabClass** class includes a **students** field to maintain a collection of **Student** objects. Read through the **LabClass** class in order to reinforce some of the concepts we have discussed in this chapter.

Exercise 7.22 The **LabClass** class enforces a limit to the number of students who may be enrolled in a particular tutorial group. In view of this, do you think it would be more appropriate to use a fixed-size array rather than a flexible-size collection for the **students** field? Give reasons both for and against the alternatives.

Exercise 7.23 Rewrite the **listAllFiles** method in the **MusicOrganizer** class from *music-organizer-v3* by using a for loop, rather than a for-each loop.

7.5 The *automaton* project

In the following sections, we will extend our coverage of arrays to provide some further typical illustrations of their use. We will use two projects based on *cellular automata*. These are relatively simple computational structures that exhibit both interesting and intriguing patterns of "behavior." We will start with some one-dimensional examples, and then extend to two dimensions in order to explore use of two-dimensional arrays.

A cellular automaton consists of a grid of "cells" Each cell maintains a simple state consisting of a limited range of values—often just the values 0 and 1. These values might be interpreted as meaning "off" and "on," for instance, or "dead" and "alive"—although the meaning is actually arbitrary. While we could implement a cell as a class definition containing a single boolean field plus an accessor and mutator, this would likely be overkill for a basic automaton, and we prefer to represent the automaton as an array of type **int[]**. The choice of **int** over **boolean** will make it simpler to calculate the changes to state values that are required by this particular application.

At each step of the model, a new state is computed for each cell based on its previous state and the states of its neighbors. For a 1D automaton, the neighbors are the two cells to its left and right. In other words, for the cell at index i, the neighbors are at indices $(i - 1)$ and $(i + 1)$. We will refer to the cell at index i as the "center" cell. What makes automata interesting is the widely differing effects that different rules to calculate new state based on those three values have on the overall behavior of the automaton over the course of multiple steps.

Code 7.2 shows a first attempt at implementing an automaton based on these principles, which can be found in the project *automaton-v1*. The rule used to calculate a cell's new state is to add the state values of a cell's two neighbors to the cell's state value and produce a result modulo 2, to force the new value to be either 0 or 1. Figure 7.2 shows the result of repeatedly applying this update rule to every cell, from a starting point at step 0 of a single cell with a value of 1, and all others with a value of 0. After the initial step, the original 1-value cell has remained with a value of 1, but its two 0-value neighbors have both become 1, while all other cells remain at 0. Subsequent steps induce further changes in the form of a symmetrical pattern.

Code 7.2

The Automaton class

```java
import java.util.Arrays;

/**
 * Model a 1D elementary cellular automaton.
 *
 * @author David J. Barnes and Michael Kölling
 * @version  2016.02.29 - version 1
 */
public class Automaton
{
    // The number of cells.
    private final int numberOfCells;
    // The state of the cells.
    private int[] state;

    /**
     * Create a 1D automaton consisting of the given number of cells.
     * @param numberOfCells The number of cells in the automaton.
     */
    public Automaton(int numberOfCells)
    {
        this.numberOfCells = numberOfCells;
        state = new int[numberOfCells];
        // Seed the automaton with a single 'on' cell in the middle.
        state[numberOfCells / 2] = 1;
    }

    /**
     * Print the current state of the automaton.
     */
    public void print()
    {
        for(int cellValue : state) {
            if(cellValue == 1) {
                System.out.print("*");
            }
            else {
                System.out.print(" ");
            }
        }
        System.out.println();
    }
```

**Code 7.2
continued**

The Automaton
class

```java
/**
 * Update the automaton to its next state.
 */
public void update()
{
    // Build the new state in a separate array.
    int[] nextState = new int[state.length];
    // Naively update the state of each cell
    // based on the state of its two neighbors.
    for(int i = 0; i < state.length; i++) {
        int left, center, right;
        if(i == 0) {
            left = 0;
        }
        else {
            left = state[i - 1];
        }
        center = state[i];
        if(i + 1 < state.length) {
            right = state[i + 1];
        }
        else {
            right = 0;
        }
        nextState[i] = (left + center + right) % 2;
    }
    state = nextState;
}

/**
 * Reset the automaton.
 */
public void reset()
{
    Arrays.fill(state, 0);
    // Seed the automaton with a single 'on' cell.
    state[numberOfCells / 2] = 1;

}
}
```

Figure 7.2

The first few steps
of the automaton
implemented in
automaton-v1

Step	Cell states—blank cells are in state 0.														
0								*							
1							*	*	*						
2						*		*		*					
3					*	*		*		*	*				
4				*				*				*			
5			*	*	*		*	*	*		*	*	*		
6		*		*				*				*		*	
7	*	*		*	*		*	*	*		*	*		*	*

Exercise 7.24 Open the *automaton-v1* project and create an `AutomatonController` object. A line containing a single * should be output in the terminal window, representing the initial state of the automaton. Call the `step` method a few times to see how the state progresses. Then try the `run` method.

Exercise 7.25 After running the automaton, call the `reset` method and repeat the process in the previous exercise. Do exactly the same patterns emerge?

Exercise 7.26 How many versions of the `fill` method are there in the `java.util.Arrays` class that take a parameter of type `int[]`? What is the purpose of those methods? How is one of those methods used in the `reset` method of **Automaton**?

Exercise 7.27 Alter the constructor of **Automaton** so that more than one cell is initially in the 1-state. Do different patterns emerge this time? Are those patterns *deterministic*—i.e., does a particular starting state for the automaton always result in the same pattern?

7.5.1 The conditional operator

While the version of the automaton in *automaton-v1* works and produces interesting results, there are some improvements that we can make to its implementation. We will start by introducing a new operator that can often be used to simplify the expression of if-else statements.

You might have noticed that in Code 7.2 there are three if-else statements with a very similar structure of the following form:

```
if(condition) {
    do something;
}
else {
    do something similar;
}
```

For instance, in the `print` method we have:

```
if(cellValue == 1) {
    System.out.print("*");
}
else {
    System.out.print(" ");
}
```

and in the **update** method there is a two if-else statement assigning to the variables **left** and **right**, where the alternative actions differ only in the right-hand side expressions.

In situations such as these, we can often make use of a *conditional operator* which, in Java, consists of the two characters ? and :. This operator is called a *ternary operator* because it actually takes three operands, in contrast to the binary operators we have seen, such as +

and *, which take two. This operator is used to select one of two alternative values, based on the evaluation of a boolean expression and the general form is:

```
condition ? value1 : value2
```

If the condition is **true**, then the value of the whole expression will be *value1*, otherwise it will be *value2*. For instance, we could rewrite the body of the for-loop in the **print** method as follows:

```
String whatToPrint = cellValue == 1 ? "*" : " ";
System.out.print(whatToPrint);
```

or, more concisely:

```
System.out.print(cellValue == 1 ? "*" : " ");
```

Exercise 7.28 Rewrite the two if-else statements in the loop of the **update** method of the **Automaton** class of *automaton-v1* so that the assignments to **left** and **right** use conditional operators.

Exercise 7.29 Why have we created a new array, **nextState**, in the **update** method, rather than using the **state** array directly? Change the assignment to **nextState** to be an assignment to **state** in the loop body, to see if it makes any different to the automaton's behavior. If it does, can you explain why?

Exercise 7.30 Can you find a way to avoid the problems illustrated in the previous exercise without using a new array? *Hint:* how many cells' old values need to be retained on each iteration? In your opinion, which version is better: using a complete array or your solution? Justify your answer.

7.5.2 First and last iterations

The most significant improvement we can make to the Automaton class in Code 7.2 is the structure of the body of the for-loop in the **update** method. At the moment, the code there is very awkward because we have to take special care when dealing with the first cell (**[0]**) and the last cell (**[numberOfCells-1]**) in order to avoid trying to access non-existent elements of the array (**[-1]** to the left of the first cell and **[numberOfCells]** to the right of the last cell). For those non-existent elements, we use a state value of 0 so that we always use three values when calculating the next state of a cell.

Whenever a loop contains code to test for the special case of the first or last iteration, we should review it carefully because, those special cases can be handled differently and the checks avoided. What we really want to see in the body of a loop are statements to be executed on every iteration, and we want to avoid special cases as far as possible. It will not always be possible to eliminate exceptions, but those applying on just the first or the last iterations are those we will most likely be able to avoid.

You might also have observed about this iteration process that the "center" cell will always become the "left" neighbor the next time around; and the "right" neighbor will become the next "center" cell. This opens up the possibility of setting up the next values of **left** and **center** at the end of the loop body ready for the next iteration; i.e.:

```
nextState[i] = (left + center + right) % 2;
left = center;
center = right;
```

That only leaves **right** to be set up explicitly from the **state** array on the next iteration. Interestingly, this modification also provides a route to solving the problem of what to do about assigning to **left** on the first iteration of the loop. This change means that when the loop body is entered on all but the first iteration, **left** and **center** have already been set from the previous iteration to the values they should have for the next-state calculation. So we can simply make sure that **left** has already been set to 0, for the non-existent cell, and **center** has been set to **state[0]** immediately before the loop is entered for the first time:

```
int left = 0;
int center = state[0];
for(int i = 0; i < state.length; i++) {
    int right = i + 1 < state.length ? state[i + 1] : 0;
    nextState[i] = (left + center + right) % 2;
    left = center;
    center = right;
}
```

Notice that the variable declarations for **left** and **center** have had to be moved from inside the loop, so that their values are retained between iterations.

The next exercise asks you to implement these changes in your own version of the project. A version with all of these changes can be found in *automaton-v2* in case you have trouble or want to check your solution; make sure, however, that you make these changes yourself before looking at this.

Exercise 7.31 Rewrite the **update** method as discussed above.

Exercise 7.32 Add a method **calculateNextState** to the **Automaton** class that takes the three values, **left**, **center**, and **right**, and returns the calculation of the value of the next state. The next state of a cell was previously calculated using the following line of code:

```
nextState[i] = (left + center + right) % 2;
```

Change this line to make use of your new method instead.

Exercise 7.33 Experiment with different ways to calculate the next state of a cell through combining the values of **left**, **center**, and **right**, always ensuring that the result is calculated modulo 2. You don't need to include all three values in the calculation. Here are a couple of ways you might like to try:

- **(left + right) % 2**
- **(center + right + center * right + left * center * right) % 2**

How many different sets of unique rules do you think there are to calculate a cell's next 0 or 1 state given the three binary values in **left**, **center**, and **right**? Is there an infinite number of possibilities?

The final improvement we would like to make to the automaton is to avoid having to keep testing for the end of the array when setting **right**. There is a commonly used solution to this—extend the array by one element! At first this sounds like cheating but, used thoughtfully and appropriately, extending an array by a single element can sometimes lead to clearer code. The idea here is that the extra element will contain the value 0 in order to serve as the right-hand neighbor of the last cell. However, that neighbor will not, itself, be included as a cell of the automaton. It will never be changed. The revised version of the body of **update** is:

```
int left = 0;
int center = state[0];
for(int i = 0; i < numberOfCells; i++) {
    int right = state[i + 1];
    nextState[i] = calculateNextState(left, center, right);
    left = center;
    center = right;
}
```

Notice very carefully that the condition of the loop has been changed, because the index variable should no longer be compared against the length of the (extended) array, but the true number of cells of the automaton. This change is essential to ensure that **[i+1]** never exceeds the bounds of the array when setting the value of **right**.

A version of the project including this code can also be found in the project *automaton-v3*.

Exercise 7.34 Make this improvement in your own code.

7.5.3 Lookup tables

In Chapter 6, we discussed the **HashMap** class, which allows associations to be created between objects in the form of a *(key, value) pair*. A map is a general form of a *lookup table*: the key is used to lookup an associated value in the map. Arrays are often a convenient and efficient way to implement specialised lookup tables, in applications where the key is a value from an integer range rather than an object. To fit with the way collections are indexed, the range should have 0 as its smallest value, although a range whose smallest value is non-zero can be easily converted into a 0-based range by the addition of a positive or a negative offset to all values in the range. As long as the size of the range is known, a fixed-size array can be created to hold the values of the (key, value) pair, where the key is a 0-based integer index.

We can illustrate the concept of a lookup table via the cellular automaton. If you have experimented with different formulas for the calculation of a cell's next state, then you might have noticed already that the 1D automaton we have implemented does not actually have an infinite number of ways to decide a cell's next state. The limitation is based on the following two features:

- There are only eight possible different combinations of the left, center and right values of 1 and 0: 000, 001, 010, . . . , 111

- For each of the eight combinations, the outcome can be one of only two possibilities: 0 or 1.

Taken together, these features mean that there are actually only 256 (i.e., 2^8) automata behaviors. In fact, the number of unique behaviors is considerably fewer than this—88 in total.

Wolfram codes In 1983, Stephen Wolfram published a study of all possible 256 elementary cellular automata. He proposed a numerical system for defining the behavior of each type of automaton, and the code assigned to each is known as a *Wolfram code*. Given the numerical code, it is very easy to work out the applicable rule for state changes, given the values of a cell and its two neighbors, because the code itself encodes the rules. See Exercise 7.36, below, for how this works in practice, or do a web search for "elementary cellular automata".

This relatively modest number of possibilities makes it possible to implement determination of a cell's next state, via a lookup table rather than evaluation of a function. Two things are needed:

- A way to turn a (left, center, right) triplet into a number in the range 0–7. These values will be used as the index key of the lookup table.

- An 8-element integer array storing the next-state values for the eight triplet combinations. This will be the table.

The following expression illustrates how we can turn the triplet into an integer index in the range 0–7:

```
left * 4 + center * 2 + right
```

and a state table can be set up as follows:

```
int[] stateTable = new int[] {
    0, 1, 0, 0, 1, 0, 0, 1,
};
```

This illustrates the use of an *array initializer*—a list of the values to be stored in a newly-created array, enclosed in curly brackets. Notice that the size of the array being created does not need to be specified in the square brackets of **new int[]**, because the compiler is able to count how many items there are in the initializer and will make the array object exactly that size. Notice, too, the trailing comma after the final value in the initializer; the trailing comma is optional. An implementation of this version can be found in *automaton-v4*.

> **Exercise 7.35** Experiment with different initialization patterns of the lookup table in *automaton-v4*.
>
> **Exercise 7.36** *Challenge exercise* This exercise involves setting up the state table based on an additional integer parameter passed to the constructor of **Automaton**. The eight 1/0 values in the lookup table could be interpreted as eight binary digits encoding a single numerical value in the range 0–255, in much the same way as we have interpreted the triplet of cell states as representing an integer in the range 0–7. The least-significant bit would be the value in **stateTable[0]** and the most significant bit in **stateTable[7]**. So the pattern used in the initialization of **stateTable**, above, would be an encoding of the value 146 (128 + 16 + 2). In fact, that is exactly how the 256 Wolfram codes are used—a code in the range 0–255 is turned into its 8-bit binary representation and the binary digits are used as the settings of the state table. Add an integer parameter that holds a Wolfram code to the constructor of **Automaton** and use it to initialize **stateTable**. To do this you will need to find out how to extract the individual binary digits from an integer. Use the least-significant bit to set element 0 of the lookup table, the next to set element 1, and so on. *Hint*: You could either do this using integer operations such as **%** and **/**, or bit-manipulation operators such as **>>** and **&**.

7.6 Arrays of more than one dimension (advanced)

This section is an advanced section in this book. You can safely skip it at this point without missing anything you need for later chapters. We will discuss two-dimensional arrays, a specialized but useful data structure. If you were interested in the *automaton* project discussed above, you may enjoy this richer variant.

Arrays of more than one dimension are simply an extension of the one-dimensional concept. For instance, a two-dimensional array is a 1D array of 1D arrays. It is conventional to consider the first dimension of a 2D array as representing the rows of a grid, and the second dimension as representing the columns. Although we won't explore this particular feature any further, the fact that there are arrays of arrays means that two-dimensional arrays do not have to be rectangular: each row may have a different number of elements in it. In this section, we will limit our discussion of multi-dimensional arrays to two dimensions because additional dimensions simply follow the same conventions.

7.6.1 The *brain* project

There are many ways in which we could extend the sort of rules we saw with the 1D automata into two dimensions. Probably the most famous example of a 2D automaton is Conway's *Game of Life*, where the cell states are also binary (i.e., either 1 or 0). However, we will implement a slightly more sophisticated cellular automaton, which is known as *Brian's Brain* because it was devised by Brian Silverman. This time we will use a class to represent the cells because the behaviors and interactions will be significantly more complex than those of the elementary automata we looked at in the previous section.

> **Exercise 7.37** Open the *brain* project, create an **Environment** object and use the GUI controls to create a random initial setup for the automaton. Then either single-step it or run/pause it to obtain a feel for how it behaves (Figure 7.3).

Figure 7.3
A two-dimensional automaton as shown with the *brain* project

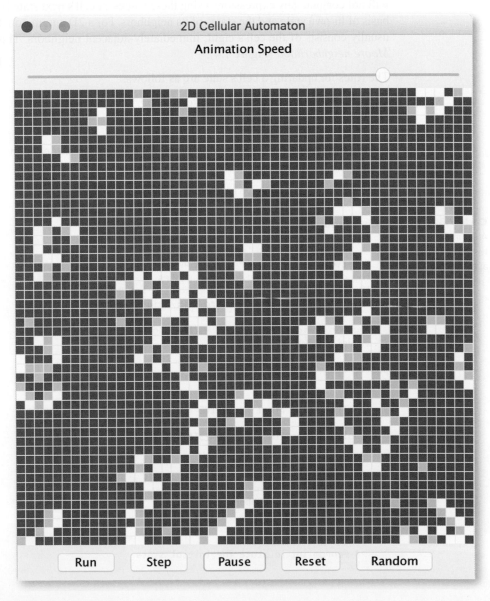

Figure 7.4
The outer grey cells are the Moore neighborhood of the central cell

Cells in *Brian's Brain* are always in one of three possible states, which are described as *alive*, *dying* or *dead*, shown in our project using different colors. However, we should make clear that these are simply convenient labels and have no objective meaning. We will use the arbitrary values 0, 1 and 2 to represent these states although, unlike the 1D automaton, we will not compute any expressions using these values. A cell's next state is calculated on the basis of its own state and the states of its neighbors. For a 2D automaton, the neighborhood usually consists of the cell's eight, immediately-adjacent neighbors. This is known as the *Moore neighborhood* (Figure 7.4).

The rules for updating a cell's state are as follows:

- A cell that is *alive* changes its state to *dying*.

- A cell that is *dying* changes its state to *dead*.

- A cell that is *dead* changes its state to *alive* if exactly two of its neighbors are *alive*, otherwise it remains *dead*.

Code 7.3 shows the class **Cell** class that implements these concepts.

Code 7.3
A cell in a two-dimensional automaton

```java
import java.util.*;

/**
 * A cell in a 2D cellular automaton.
 * The cell has multiple possible states.
 * This is an implementation of the rules for Brian's Brain.
 * @see https://en.wikipedia.org/wiki/Brian%27s_Brain
 *
 * @author David J. Barnes and Michael Kölling
 * @version  2016.02.29
 */
public class Cell
{
    // The possible states.
    public static final int ALIVE = 0, DEAD = 1, DYING = 2;
    // The number of possible states.
    public static final int NUM_STATES = 3;

    // The cell's state.
    private int state;
    // The cell's neighbors.
    private Cell[] neighbors;

    /**
     * Set the initial state.
     * @param initialState The initial state
     */
```

```
public int getNextState()
{
    if(state == DEAD) {
        // Count the number of neighbors that are alive.
        int aliveCount = 0;
        for(Cell n : neighbors) {
            if(n.getState() == ALIVE) {
                aliveCount++;
            }
        }
        return aliveCount == 2 ? ALIVE : DEAD;
    }
    else if(state == DYING) {
        return DEAD;
    }
    else {
        return DYING;
    }
}

/**
 * Receive the list of neighboring cells and take
 * a copy.
 * @param neighborList Neighboring cells.
 */
public void setNeighbors(ArrayList<Cell> neighborList)
{
    neighbors = new Cell[neighborList.size()];
    neighborList.toArray(neighbors);
}
```

Other methods omitted.

```
}
```

Each cell maintains a record of its neighbors in an array. The array is setup following a call to the **setNeighbors** method. The method receives a list of cells and copies the list into an array object via the list's **toArray** method.

7.6.2 Setting up the array

Code 7.4 shows some of those elements of the **Environment** class that set up the 2D array of **Cell** objects to model the automaton.

```
public class Environment
{
    // The grid of cells.
    private Cell[][] cells;
    // Visualization of the environment.
    private final EnvironmentView view;
```

Code 7.4
continued

The Environment
class

```
/**
 * Create an environment with the given size.
 * @param numRows The number of rows.
 * @param numCols The number of cols;
 */
public Environment(int numRows, int numCols)
{
    setup(numRows, numCols);
    randomize();
    view = new EnvironmentView(this, numRows, numCols);
    view.showCells();
}
```

Various other methods omitted.

```
/**
 * Setup a new environment of the given size.
 * @param numRows The number of rows.
 * @param numCols The number of cols;
 */
private void setup(int numRows, int numCols)
{
    cells = new Cell[numRows][numCols];
    for(int row = 0; row < numRows; row++) {
        for (int col = 0; col < numCols; col++) {
            cells[row][col] = new Cell();
        }
    }
    setupNeighbors();
}
```

The syntax for declaring an array variable of more than one dimension is an extension of the single-dimension case—a pair of empty square brackets for each dimension:

```
Cell[][] cells;
```

Similarly, the creation of the array object via **new** specifies the length of each dimension:

```
cells = new Cell[numRows][numCols];
```

Remember that no **Cell** objects are actually created at this point—only the array object that will be able to store the **Cell** objects once they are created.

The **setup** method uses a typical code pattern to iterate through all elements of a two-dimensional array: a nested for loop. The pattern looks like this:

```
for(int row = 0; row < numRows; row++) {
    for (int col = 0; col < numCols; col++) {
        . . . // do something with every element
    }
}
```

In this loop, it then sets up each cell by creating the cell object and assigning it to the current position in the array:

```
cells[row][col] = new Cell();
```

Finally, the **setup** method calls a separate **setupNeighbors** method in order to pass to each **Cell** its Moore neighborhood of adjacent cells.

You will recall from the discussion of the 1D automaton that we needed to be careful at the left- and right-hand ends of the automaton to provide a full set of neighbors for the cells at the edge. We must address the same issue with the 2D automaton. For instance, the **Cell** at location **cells[0][0]** only has three neighbors rather than eight. One approach we could have taken would have been to extend the 2D array with an extra row at the top and bottom and an extra column at the left and right—making it **(numRows+2)** by **(numCols+2)**—with a dummy *dead* cell in each of those locations. Instead, we prefer to use a "wraparound" approach to calculating the neighborhood—in other words, cells in the top row have neighbors in the bottom row and cells in the leftmost column have neighbors in the rightmost column (and vice-versa). This is also known as a *toroidal arrangement*. This way, every cell in the automaton has the full Moore neighborbood of eight cells. All that remains is to find a way to handle the cases around the edge that do not have to resort to special-case code.

If we ignore the edges for the moment, the neighbors of a cell at location **[row][col]** can be found at all the **+1** and **-1** offsets from row and col; e.g. **[row+1][col]**, **[row+1][col+1]**, **[row-1][col]**, etc. So we might write something like the following to build a list of neighbors:

```
Cell cell = cells[row][col];
for(int dr = -1; dr <= 1; dr++) {
  for(int dc = -1; dc <= 1; dc++) {
      add the neighbor at cells[row + dr][col + dc];
  }
}
```

Notice that when both **dr** and **dc** are zero, then the "neighbor" is actually **cell** and this should not be included in the neighbor list, so that is something to be addressed.

What we now need to ensure is that when **row + 1 == numRows** we obtain the value **0**, and when **row + -1 == -1** we obtain **(numRows – 1)** (similarly for **col**). The solution to the first requirement is relatively easy—the modulus operator does exactly that. But this does not cover both requirements because **(-1 % numRows)** gives –1 instead of **(numRows – 1)**. However, we can use a little trick based on the fact that **((x + numRows) % numRows) == (x % numRows)** when **x** is not negative, which means that **((row + 1 + numRows) % numRows)** gives the same result as **((row + 1) % numRows)**. But we do not see the same effect if **x** is negative, and if we add **numRows** before taking the modulus then **((-1 + numRows) % numRows)** gives **(numRows – 1)**, which is what we want. So the expression **((row + dr + numRows) % numRows)** will provide the index we need in both positive and negative cases, in order to determine the neighborhood of a cell in a wraparound grid.

Code 7.5 shows the full version of the **setupNeighbors** method of the Environment class that uses this technique. Notice that a cell is removed from its own neighborhood list before the list is passed to the cell to get around the problem when **dr** and **dc** are both zero.

Code 7.5

Setting up the
neighboring cells

```java
/**
 * Give to a cell a list of its neighbors.
 */
private void setupNeighbors()
{
    int numRows = cells.length;
    int numCols = cells[0].length;
    // Allow for 8 neighbors plus the cell.
    ArrayList<Cell> neighbors = new ArrayList<>(9);
    for(int row = 0; row < numRows; row++) {
        for(int col = 0; col < numCols; col++) {
            Cell cell = cells[row][col];
            // This process will also include the cell.
            for(int dr = -1; dr <= 1; dr++) {
                for(int dc = -1; dc <= 1; dc++) {
                    int nr = (numRows + row + dr) % numRows;
                    int nc = (numCols + col + dc) % numCols;
                    neighbors.add(cells[nr][nc]);
                }
            }
            // The neighbours should not include the cell at
            // (row,col) so remove it.
            neighbors.remove(cell);
            cell.setNeighbors(neighbors);
            neighbors.clear();
        }
    }
}
```

Exercise 7.38 Conway's *Game of Life* is a much simpler automaton than *Brian's Brain*. In the *Game of Life*, a cell has only two states: alive and dead. Its next state is determined as follows:

- A count is taken of the number of its neighbors that are alive.
- If the cell is dead and has exactly three live neighbors then its next state will be alive, otherwise its next state will be dead.
- If the cell is alive then its next state also depends on the number of live neighbors. If there are fewer than two or more than three then the next state will be dead; otherwise it will be alive.

Save a copy of the *brain* project as *game-of-life* and modify the **Cell** class so that it implement's the rules for the *Game of Life*. It should not be necessary to modify any other classes.

Exercise 7.39 Modify the **Environment** class in your version of the Game of Life so that the environment is not toroidal. In other words, the next state of a cell at an outer row or column of the environment is determined by assuming that "neighbors" beyond outside the bounds of the environment are always dead. Do you observe much difference between the behavior of this version and the toroidal one?

Exercise 7.40 Use a copy of either the *brain* project or your *game-of-life* project to implement a new project in which cells can be either alive or dead. Alive cells should appear to "wander" semi-randomly through the 2D environment. Associate a movement direction with a cell. A cell that is alive should "move" in its associated direction at each step—in other words, a cell that is alive should cause one of its neighbors to be alive at the next step, and itself will become dead—this should give the appearance of movement. When an alive cell at the edge of the environment would try to "move" beyond the edge, it should instead sets its direction randomly and remain alive at the next step; i.e., it will not change the state of a neighbor.

Check your implementation of these rules by having just a single live cell in the environment at the start. When you have multiple live cells, you will need to think about what you want to happen if one cell tries to "move" into a location just vacated by another cell, or when two cells try to occupy the same neighboring cell.

7.7 Arrays and streams (advanced)

The principles of stream processing introduced in Chapter 5 apply equally well to arrays as they do to flexible collections. A stream is obtained from the contents of an array by passing the array to the static **stream** method of **java.util.Arrays**. If the array is of type **int[]** then an object of type **java.util.stream.IntStream** is returned:

```
int[] nums = { 1, 2, 3, 4, 5, };
IntStream stream = Arrays.stream(nums);
```

DoubleStream and **LongStream** types exist for equivalent stream versions of **double[]** and **long[]** arrays. Otherwise, the stream version of an array of type **T** will be of type **Stream<T>**.

The standard stream operations, such as **filter**, **limit**, **map**, **reduce**, **skip**, etc. are all available on the resulting stream, of course, so the data in a fixed-size collection can be processed in exactly the same ways as that in a flexible collection, once converted to a stream.

The static **range** method of the **IntStream** class is often used to create a stream of the integer indices of a collection; for instance:

```
IntStream indices = IntStream.range(0, nums.length);
```

The value of **nums.length** will be excluded from the stream. The following example illustrates how we might identify the indices of values in an array that are above a particular threshold. Note that it is the indices we are interested in and not the values, in this particular case:

```
int[] above = IntStream.range(0, hourCounts.length)
                        .filter(i -> hourCounts[i] > threshold)
                        .toArray();
```

The terminal **toArray** method of the stream returns an array containing the index values remaining after filtering.

7.8 Summary

In this chapter, we have discussed arrays as a means to create fixed-size collection objects. Single-dimension arrays are a collection type that is well suited for those situations in which the number of items to be stored is fixed and known in advance. They are also slightly more syntactically lightweight than flexible-sized collections, such as **ArrayList**, particularly when used to store values of the primitive types. However, aside from those specific situations, they do not offer any features that are not also readily available with collections such as lists, maps, and sets.

Terms introduced in this chapter:

array, for loop, conditional operator, lookup table

Concept summary

- **array** An array is a special type of collection that can store a fixed number of elements.
- **for loop** An iterative control structure that is often used when an index variable is required to select consecutive elements from a collection, such as an ArrayList or an array.

Exercise 7.41 Rewrite the following by using the static **arraycopy** method of the **System** class:

```
int[] copy = new int[original.length];
for(int i = 0; i < original.length; i++) {
    copy[i] = original[i];
}
```

Exercise 7.42 Describe what the following static methods of the **java.util. Arrays** class do: **asList**, **binarySearch**, **fill**, and **sort**? Where there are multiple versions of a method, use one that operates on an integer array as the example.

Exercise 7.43 Try to write some example code to use each of the methods mentioned in the previous exercise.

Exercise 7.44 Write statements to copy all of the elements of the 2D integer array, `original`, into a new array called `copy`. You should include the statements to create the `copy` array.

Exercise 7.45 Investigate some other 2D cellular automata and implement their rules in the *brain* project.

Exercise 7.43 Try to write some example code to use each of the methods mentioned in the previous exercise.

Exercise 7.44 Write statements to copy all of the elements of the 2D image array, orig_img, into a new array called copy. You should include the statements to create the copy array.

Exercise 7.45 Investigate some other 2D cellular automata and implement their rules in the barn project.

Main concepts discussed in this chapter:

- ■ responsibility-driven design
- ■ coupling
- ■ cohesion
- ■ refactoring

Java constructs discussed in this chapter:

enumerated types, `switch`

In this chapter, we look at some of the factors that influence the design of a class. What makes a class design either good or bad? Writing good classes can take more effort in the short term than writing bad classes, but in the long term that extra effort will almost always be justified. To help us write good classes, there are some principles that we can follow. In particular, we introduce the view that class design should be responsibility-driven, and that classes should encapsulate their data.

This chapter is, like many of the chapters before, structured around a project. It can be studied by just reading it and following our line of argument, or it can be studied in much more depth by doing the project exercises in parallel while working through the chapter.

The project work is divided into three parts. In the first part, we discuss the necessary changes to the source code and develop and show complete solutions to the exercises. The solution for this part is also available in a project accompanying this book. The second part suggests more changes and extensions, and we discuss possible solutions at a high level (the class-design level), but leave it to readers to do the lower-level work and to complete the implementation. The third part suggests even more improvements in the form of exercises. We do not give solutions—the exercises apply the material discussed throughout the chapter.

Implementing all parts makes a good programming project over several weeks. It can also be used very successfully as a group project.

8.1 Introduction

It is possible to implement an application and get it to perform its task with badly designed classes. Simply executing a finished application does not usually indicate whether it is well structured internally or not.

The problems typically surface when a maintenance programmer wants to make some changes to an existing application. If, for example, a programmer attempts to fix a bug or wants to add new functionality to an existing program, a task that might be easy and obvious with well-designed classes may well be very hard and involve a great deal of work if the classes are badly designed.

In larger applications, this effect occurs earlier on, during the initial implementation. If the implementation starts with a bad structure, then finishing it might later become overly complex, and the complete program may either not be finished contain bugs, or take a lot longer to build. In reality, companies often maintain, extend, and sell an application over many years. It is not uncommon that an implementation for software that we can buy in a software store today was started more than ten years ago. In this situation, a software company cannot afford to have badly structured code.

Because many of the effects of bad class design become most obvious when trying to adapt or extend an application, we shall do exactly that. In this chapter, we will use an example called *world-of-zuul*, which is a rudimentary implementation of a text-based adventure game. In its original state, the game is not actually very ambitious—for one thing, it is incomplete. By the end of this chapter, however, you will be in a position to exercise your imagination and design and implement your own game and make it really fun and interesting.

world-of-zuul Our *world-of-zuul* game is modeled on the original *Adventure* game that was developed in the early 1970s by Will Crowther and expanded by Don Woods. The original game is also sometimes known as the *Colossal Cave Adventure*. This was a wonderfully imaginative and sophisticated game for its time, involving finding your way through a complex cave system, locating hidden treasure, using secret words, and other mysteries, all in an effort to score the maximum number of points. You can read more about it at sites such as http://jerz.setonhill.edu/if/canon/Adventure.htm and http://www.rickadams.org/adventure/, or try doing a web search for "Colossal Cave Adventure."

While we work on extending the original application, we will take the opportunity to discuss aspects of its existing class design. We will see that the implementation we start with contains examples of bad design, and we will be able to see how this impacts on our tasks and how we can fix them.

In the project examples for this book, you will find two versions of the *zuul* project: *zuul-bad* and *zuul-better*. Both implement exactly the same functionality, but some of the class structure is different, representing bad design in one project and better design in the other. The fact that we can implement the same functionality in either a good way or a bad way illustrates the fact that bad design is not usually a consequence of having a difficult problem to solve. Bad design has more to do with the decisions that we make when solving a particular problem. We cannot use the argument that there was no other way to solve the problem as an excuse for bad design.

So, we will use the project with bad design so that we can explore why it is bad, and then improve it. The better version is an implementation of the changes we discuss here.

Exercise 8.1 Open the project *zuul-bad*. (This project is called "bad" because its implementation contains some bad design decisions, and we want to leave no doubt that this should not be used as an example of good programming practice!) Execute and explore the application. The project comment gives you some information about how to run it.

While exploring the application, answer the following questions:

- What does this application do?
- What commands does the game accept?
- What does each command do?
- How many rooms are in the scenario?
- Draw a map of the existing rooms.

Exercise 8.2 After you know what the whole application does, try to find out what each individual class does. Write down for each class its purpose. You need to look at the source code to do this. Note that you might not (and need not) understand all of the source code. Often, reading through comments and looking at method headers is enough.

8.2 The *world-of-zuul* game example

From Exercise 8.1, you have seen that the *zuul* game is not yet very adventurous. It is, in fact, quite boring in its current state. But it provides a good basis for us to design and implement our own game, which will hopefully be more interesting.

We start by analyzing the classes that are already there in our first version and trying to find out what they do. The class diagram is shown in Figure 8.1.

The project shows five classes. They are **Parser**, **CommandWords**, **Command**, **Room**, and **Game**. An investigation of the source code shows, fortunately, that these classes are quite well documented, and we can get an initial overview of what they do by just reading the class comment at the top of each class. (This fact also serves to illustrate that bad design involves something deeper than simply the way a class looks or how good its documentation is.) Our understanding of the game will be assisted by having a look at the source code

Figure 8.1

Zuu1 class diagram

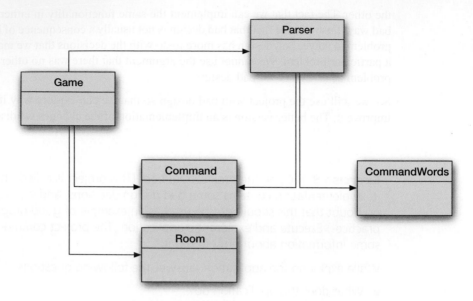

to see what methods each class has and what some of the methods appear to do. Here, we summarize the purpose of each class:

- *CommandWords* The **CommandWords** class defines all valid commands in the game. It does this by holding an array of **String** objects representing the command words.

- *Parser* The parser reads lines of input from the terminal and tries to interpret them as commands. It creates objects of class **Command** that represent the command that was entered.

- *Command* A **Command** object represents a command that was entered by the user. It has methods that make it easy for us to check whether this was a valid command and to get the first and second words of the command as separate strings.

- *Room* A **Room** object represents a location in a game. Rooms can have exits that lead to other rooms.

- *Game* The **Game** class is the main class of the game. It sets up the game and then enters a loop to read and execute commands. It also contains the code that implements each user command.

Exercise 8.3 Design your own game scenario. Do this away from the computer. Do not think about implementation, classes, or even programming in general. Just think about inventing an interesting game. This could be done with a group of people.

The game can be anything that has as its base structure a player moving through different locations. Here are some examples:

- You are a white blood cell traveling through the body in search of viruses to attack ...
- You are lost in a shopping mall and must find the exit ...
- You are a mole in its burrow and you cannot remember where you stored your food reserves before winter ...
- You are an adventurer who searches through a dungeon full of monsters and other characters ...
- You are on the bomb squad and must find and defuse a bomb before it goes off ...

Make sure that your game has a goal (so that it has an end and the player can "win"). Try to think of many things to make the game interesting (trap doors, magic items, characters that help you only if you feed them, time limits... whatever you like). Let your imagination run wild.

At this stage, do not worry about how to implement these things.

8.3 Introduction to coupling and cohesion

If we are to justify our assertion that some designs are better than others, then we need to define some terms that will allow us to discuss the issues that we consider to be important in class design. Two terms are central when talking about the quality of a class design: *coupling* and *cohesion.*

Concept

The term **coupling** describes the interconnectedness of classes. We strive for loose coupling in a system—that is, a system where each class is largely independent and communicates with other classes via a small, well-defined interface.

The term *coupling* refers to the interconnectedness of classes. We have already discussed in earlier chapters that we aim to design our applications as a set of cooperating classes that communicate via well-defined interfaces. The degree of coupling indicates how tightly these classes are connected. We strive for a low degree of coupling, or *loose coupling.*

The degree of coupling determines how hard it is to make changes in an application. In a tightly coupled class structure, a change in one class can make it necessary to change several other classes as well. This is what we try to avoid, because the effect of making one small change can quickly ripple through a complete application. In addition, finding all the places where changes are necessary, and actually making the changes, can be difficult and time consuming.

In a loosely coupled system, on the other hand, we can often change one class without making any changes to other classes, and the application will still work. We shall discuss particular examples of tight and loose coupling in this chapter.

The term *cohesion* relates to the number and diversity of tasks for which a single unit of an application is responsible. Cohesion is relevant for units of a single class and an individual method.[1]

---

[1] We sometimes also use the term *module* (or *package* in Java) to refer to a multi-class unit. *Cohesion* is relevant at this level too.

Concept

The term **cohesion** describes how well a unit of code maps to a logical task or entity. In a highly cohesive system, each unit of code (method, class, or module) is responsible for a well-defined task or entity. Good class design exhibits a high degree of cohesion.

Ideally, one unit of code should be responsible for one cohesive task (that is, one task that can be seen as a logical unit). A method should implement one logical operation, and a class should represent one type of entity. The main reason behind the principle of cohesion is reuse: if a method or a class is responsible for only one well-defined thing, then it is much more likely it can be used again in a different context. A complementary advantage of following this principle is that, when change *is* required to some aspect of an application, we are likely to find all the relevant pieces located in the same unit.

We shall discuss with examples below how cohesion influences the quality of class design.

Exercise 8.4 Draw (on paper) a map for the game you invented in Exercise 8.3. Open the *zuul-bad* project and save it under a different name (e.g., *zuul*). This is the project you will use for making improvements and modifications throughout this chapter. You can leave off the *-bad* suffix, because it will (hopefully) soon not be that bad anymore.

As a first step, change the **createRooms** method in the **Game** class to create the rooms and exits you invented for your game.

8.4 Code duplication

Code duplication is an indicator of bad design. The **Game** class shown in Code 8.1 contains a case of code duplication. The problem with code duplication is that any change to one version must also be made to another if we are to avoid inconsistency. This increases the amount of work a maintenance programmer has to do, and it introduces the danger of bugs. It very easily happens that a maintenance programmer finds one copy of the code and, having changed it, assumes that the job is done. There is nothing indicating that a second copy of the code exists, and it might incorrectly remain unchanged.

Code 8.1

Selected sections of the (badly designed) Game class

```
public class Game
{

    Some code omitted.

    private void createRooms()
    {
        Room outside, theater, pub, lab, office;

        // create the rooms
        outside = new Room("outside the main entrance of the university");
        theater = new Room("in a lecture theater");
        pub = new Room("in the campus pub");
        lab = new Room("in a computing lab");
        office = new Room("in the computing admin office");
```

Code 8.1
continued
Selected sections of
the (badly designed)
Game class

```
                // initialize room exits
                outside.setExits(null, theater, lab, pub);
                theater.setExits(null, null, null, outside);
                pub.setExits(null, outside, null, null);
                lab.setExits(outside, office, null, null);
                office.setExits(null, null, null, lab);

                currentRoom = outside;  // start game outside
        }
```

Some code omitted.

```
        /**
         * Print out the opening message for the player.
         */
        private void printWelcome()
        {
                System.out.println();
                System.out.println("Welcome to the World of Zuul!");
                System.out.println("Zuul is a new incredibly boring adventure game.");
                System.out.println("Type 'help' if you need help.");
                System.out.println();
                System.out.println("You are " + currentRoom.getDescription());
                System.out.print("Exits: ");
                if(currentRoom.northExit != null) {
                    System.out.print("north ");
                }
                if(currentRoom.eastExit != null) {
                    System.out.print("east ");
                }
                if(currentRoom.southExit != null) {
                    System.out.print("south ");
                }
                if(currentRoom.westExit != null) {
                    System.out.print("west ");
                }
                System.out.println();
        }
```

Some code omitted.

```
        /**
         * Try to go in one direction. If there is an exit, enter
         * the new room, otherwise print an error message.
         */
        private void goRoom(Command command)
        {
                if(!command.hasSecondWord()) {
                    // if there is no second word, we don't know where to go...
                    System.out.println("Go where?");
                    return;
                }
```

Concept

**Code
duplication**
(having the
same segment
of code in an
application
more than
once) is a sign
of bad design.
It should be
avoided.

**Code 8.1
continued**

Selected sections of
the (badly designed)
Game class

```
    String direction = command.getSecondWord();

    // Try to leave current room.
    Room nextRoom = null;
    if(direction.equals("north")) {
        nextRoom = currentRoom.northExit;
    }
    if(direction.equals("east")) {
        nextRoom = currentRoom.eastExit;
    }
    if(direction.equals("south")) {
        nextRoom = currentRoom.southExit;
    }
    if(direction.equals("west")) {
        nextRoom = currentRoom.westExit;
    }

    if (nextRoom == null) {
        System.out.println("There is no door!");
    }
    else {
        currentRoom = nextRoom;
        System.out.println("You are " + currentRoom.getDescription());
        System.out.print("Exits: ");
        if(currentRoom.northExit != null) {
            System.out.print("north ");
        }
        if(currentRoom.eastExit != null) {
            System.out.print("east ");
        }
        if(currentRoom.southExit != null) {
            System.out.print("south ");
        }
        if(currentRoom.westExit != null) {
            System.out.print("west ");
        }
        System.out.println();
    }
}
```

Some code omitted.

```
}
```

Both the **printWelcome** and **goRoom** methods contain the following lines of code:

```
System.out.println("You are" + currentRoom.getDescription());
System.out.print("Exits:");
if(currentRoom.northExit != null) {
    System.out.print("north");
}
if(currentRoom.eastExit != null) {
    System.out.print("east");
}
```

```
    if(currentRoom.southExit != null) {
        System.out.print("south");
    }
    if(currentRoom.westExit != null) {
        System.out.print("west");
    }
    System.out.println();
```

Code duplication is usually a symptom of poor cohesion. The problem here has its roots in the fact that both methods in question do two things: **printWelcome** prints the welcome message and prints the information about the current location, while **goRoom** changes the current location then prints information about the (new) current location.

Both methods print information about the current location, but neither can call the other, because they also do other things. This is bad design.

A better design would use a separate, more cohesive method whose sole task is to print the current location information (Code 8.2). Both the **printWelcome** and **goRoom** methods can then make calls to this method when they need to print this information. This way, writing the code twice is avoided, and when we need to change it, we need to change it only once.

Code 8.2
printLocation-
Info as a separate
method

```
private void printLocationInfo()
{
    System.out.println("You are " + currentRoom.getDescription());
    System.out.print("Exits: ");
    if(currentRoom.northExit != null) {
        System.out.print("north ");
    }
    if(currentRoom.eastExit != null) {
        System.out.print("east ");
    }
    if(currentRoom.southExit != null) {
        System.out.print("south ");
    }
    if(currentRoom.westExit != null) {
        System.out.print("west ");
    }
    System.out.println();
}
```

Exercise 8.5 Implement and use a separate **printLocationInfo** method in your project, as discussed in this section. Test your changes.

8.5 Making extensions

The *zuul-bad* project does work. We can execute it, and it correctly does everything that it was intended to do. However, it is in some respects quite badly designed. A well-designed alternative would perform in the same way; we would not notice any difference just by executing the program.

Once we try to make modifications to the project, however, we will notice significant differences in the amount of work involved in changing badly designed code, compared with changes to a well-designed application. We will investigate this by making some changes to the project. While we are doing this, we will discuss examples of bad design when we see them in the existing source, and we will improve the class design before we implement our extensions.

8.5.1 The task

The first task we will attempt is to add a new direction of movement. Currently, a player can move in four directions: *north*, *east*, *south*, and *west*. We want to allow for multilevel buildings (or cellars, or dungeons, or whatever you later want to add to your game) and add *up* and *down* as possible directions. A player can then type **"go down"** to move, say, down into a cellar.

8.5.2 Finding the relevant source code

Inspection of the given classes shows us that at least two classes are involved in this change: **Room** and **Game**.

Room is the class that stores (among other things) the exits of each room. As we saw in Code 8.1, in the **Game** class the exit information from the current room is used to print out information about exits and to move from one room to another.

The **Room** class is fairly short. Its source code is shown in Code 8.3. Reading the source, we can see that the exits are mentioned in two different places: they are listed as fields at the top of the class, and they get assigned in the **setExits** method. To add two new directions, we would need to add two new exits (**upExit** and **downExit**) in these two places.

Code 8.3

Source code of the (badly designed) Room class

```
public class Room
{
    public String description;
    public Room northExit;
    public Room southExit;
    public Room eastExit;
    public Room westExit;

    /**
     * Create a room described "description." Initially, it has
     * no exits. "description" is something like "a kitchen" or
     * "an open court yard."
     * @param description The room's description.
     */
    public Room(String description)
    {
        this.description = description;
    }
```

**Code 8.3
continued**

Source code of the
(badly designed)
Room class

```
/**
 * Define the exits of this room.  Every direction either leads
 * to another room or is null (no exit there).
 * @param north The north exit.
 * @param east The east east.
 * @param south The south exit.
 * @param west The west exit.
 */
public void setExits(Room north, Room east, Room south, Room west)
{
    if(north != null) {
        northExit = north;
    }
    if(east != null) {
        eastExit = east;
    }
    if(south != null) {
        southExit = south;
    }
    if(west != null) {
        westExit = west;
    }
}

/**
 * @return The description of the room.
 */
public String getDescription()
{
    return description;
}
}
```

It is a bit more work to find all relevant places in the **Game** class. The source code is somewhat longer (it is not fully shown here), and finding all the relevant places takes some patience and care.

Reading the code shown in Code 8.1, we can see that the **Game** class makes heavy use of the exit information of a room. The **Game** object holds a reference to one room in the **currentRoom** variable, and frequently accesses this room's exit information.

- In the **createRoom** method, the exits are defined.

- In the **printWelcome** method, the current room's exits are printed out so that the player knows where to go when the game starts.

- In the **goRoom** method, the exits are used to find the next room. They are then used again to print out the exits of the next room we have just entered.

If we now want to add two new exit directions, we will have to add the *up* and *down* options in all these places. However, read the following section before you do this.

8.6 Coupling

The fact that there are so many places where all exits are enumerated is symptomatic of poor class design. When declaring the exit variables in the **Room** class, we need to list one variable per exit; in the **setExits** method, there is one if statement per exit; in the **goRoom** method, there is one if statement per exit; in the **printLocationInfo** method, there is one if statement per exit; and so on. This design decision now creates work for us: when adding new exits, we need to find all these places and add two new cases. Imagine the effect if we decided to use directions such as northwest, southeast, etc.!

To improve the situation, we decide to use a **HashMap** to store the exits, rather than separate variables. Doing this, we should be able to write code that can cope with any number of exits and does not need so many modifications. The **HashMap** will contain a mapping from a named direction (e.g., **"north"**) to the room that lies in that direction (a **Room** object). Thus, each entry has a **String** as the key and a **Room** object as the value.

This is a change in the way a room stores information internally about neighboring rooms. Theoretically, this is a change that should affect only the *implementation* of the **Room** class (*how* the exit information is stored), not the *interface* (*what* the room stores).

Ideally, when only the implementation of a class changes, other classes should not be affected. This would be a case of *loose* coupling.

In our example, this does not work. If we remove the exit variables in the **Room** class and replace them with a **HashMap**, the **Game** class will not compile any more. It makes numerous references to the room's exit variables, which all would cause errors.

We see that we have a case here of *tight* coupling. In order to clean this up, we will decouple these classes before we introduce the **HashMap**.

8.6.1 Using encapsulation to reduce coupling

One of the main problems in this example is the use of public fields. The exit fields in the **Room** class have all been declared **public**. Clearly, the programmer of this class did not follow the guidelines we have set out earlier in this book ("Never make fields public!"). We shall now see the result. The **Game** class in this example can make direct accesses to these fields (and it makes extensive use of this fact). By making the fields public, the **Room** class has exposed in its interface not only the fact that it has exits, but also exactly how the exit information is stored. This breaks one of the fundamental principles of good class design: *encapsulation*.

The encapsulation guideline (hiding implementation information from view) suggests that only information about *what* a class can do should be visible to the outside, not about *how* it does it. This has a great advantage: if no other class knows how our information is stored, then we can easily change how it is stored without breaking other classes.

We can enforce this separation of *what* and *how* by making the fields private, and using an accessor method to access them. The first stage of our modified **Room** class is shown in Code 8.4.

Code 8.4

Using an accessor
method to decrease
coupling

```
public class Room
{
    private String description;
    private Room northExit;
    private Room southExit;
    private Room eastExit;
    private Room westExit;

    Existing methods unchanged.

    public Room getExit(String direction)
    {
        if(direction.equals("north")) {
            return northExit;
        }
        if(direction.equals("east")) {
            return eastExit;
        }
        if(direction.equals("south")) {
            return southExit;
        }
        if(direction.equals("west")) {
            return westExit;
        }
        return null;
    }
}
```

Having made this change to the **Room** class, we need to change the **Game** class as well. Wherever an exit variable was accessed, we now use the accessor method. For example, instead of writing

```
nextRoom = currentRoom.eastExit;
```

we now write

```
nextRoom = currentRoom.getExit("east");
```

This makes coding one section in the **Game** class much easier as well. In the **goRoom** method, the replacement suggested here will result in the following code segment:

```
Room nextRoom = null;
if(direction.equals("north")) {
    nextRoom = currentRoom.getExit("north");
}
if(direction.equals("east")) {
    nextRoom = currentRoom.getExit("east");
}
if(direction.equals("south")) {
    nextRoom = currentRoom.getExit("south");
}
```

```
if(direction.equals("west")) {
    nextRoom = currentRoom.getExit("west");
}
```

Instead, this whole code segment can now be replaced with:

```
Room nextRoom = currentRoom.getExit(direction);
```

> **Exercise 8.6** Make the changes we have described to the **Room** and **Game** classes.
>
> **Exercise 8.7** Make a similar change to the `printLocationInfo` method of **Game** so that details of the exits are now prepared by the **Room** rather than the **Game**. Define a method in **Room** with the following header:
>
> ```
> /**
>  * Return a description of the room's exits,
>  * for example, "Exits: north west".
>  * @return A description of the available exits.
>  */
> public String getExitString()
> ```

So far, we have not changed the representation of the exits in the **Room** class. We have only cleaned up the interface. The *change* in the **Game** class is minimal—instead of an access of a public field, we use a method call—but the *gain* is dramatic. We can now make a change to the way exits are stored in the room, without any need to worry about breaking anything in the **Game** class. The internal representation in **Room** has been completely decoupled from the interface. Now that the design is the way it should have been in the first place, exchanging the separate exit fields for a **HashMap** is easy. The changed code is shown in Code 8.5.

Code 8.5
Source code of the
Room class

```
import java.util.HashMap;
```

Class comment omitted.

```
public class Room
{
    private String description;
    private HashMap<String, Room> exits;        // stores exits of this room.

    /**
     * Create a room described "description."  Initially, it has no exits.
     * "description" is something like "a kitchen" or "an open court yard."
     * @param description The room's description.
     */
    public Room(String description)
    {
        this.description = description;
        exits = new HashMap<>();
    }
```

Code 8.5
continued

Source code of the
Room class

```
/**
 * Define an exit from this room.
 * @param direction The direction of the exit.
 * @param neighbor  The room to which the exit leads.
 */
public void setExit(Room north, Room east, Room south, Room west)
{
    if(north != null) {
        exits.put("north", north);
    }
    if(east != null) {
        exits.put("east", east);
    }
    if(south != null) {
        exits.put("south", south);
    }
    if(west != null) {
        exits.put("west", west);
    }
}

/**
 * Return the room that is reached if we go from this room in direction
 * "direction." If there is no room in that direction, return null.
 * @param direction The exit's direction.
 * @return The room in the given direction.
 */
public Room getExit(String direction)
{
    return exits.get(direction);
}

/**
 * @return The description of the room
 * (the one that was defined in the constructor).
 */
public String getDescription()
{
    return description;
}
}
```

It is worth emphasizing again that we can make this change now without even checking whether anything will break elsewhere. Because we have changed only private aspects of the **Room** class, which, by definition, cannot be used in other classes, this change does not impact on other classes. The interface remains unchanged.

A by-product of this change is that our **Room** class is now even shorter. Instead of listing four separate variables, we have only one. In addition, the **getExit** method is considerably simplified.

Recall that the original aim that set off this series of changes was to make it easier to add the two new possible exits in the *up* and *down* direction. This has already become much easier. Because we now use a **HashMap** to store exits, storing these two additional directions will work without any change. We can also obtain the exit information via the **getExit** method without any problem.

The only place where knowledge about the four existing exits (*north*, *east*, *south*, *west*) is still coded into the source is in the **setExits** method. This is the last part that needs improvement. At the moment, the method's header is

```
public void setExits(Room north, Room east, Room south, Room west)
```

This method is part of the interface of the **Room** class, so any change we make to it will inevitably affect some other classes by virtue of coupling. We can never completely decouple the classes in an application; otherwise objects of different classes would not be able to interact with one another. Rather, we try to keep the degree of coupling as low as possible. If we have to make a change to **setExits** anyway, to accommodate additional directions, then our preferred solution is to replace it entirely with this method:

```
/**
 * Define an exit from this room.
 * @param direction The direction of the exit.
 * @param neighbor The room in the given direction.
 */
public void setExit(String direction, Room neighbor)
{
    exits.put(direction, neighbor);
}
```

Now, the exits of this room can be set one exit at a time, and any direction can be used for an exit. In the **Game** class, the change that results from modifying the interface of **Room** is as follows. Instead of writing

```
lab.setExits(outside, office, null, null);
```

we now write

```
lab.setExit("north", outside);
lab.setExit("east", office);
```

We have now completely removed the restriction from **Room** that it can store only four exits. The **Room** class is now ready to store *up* and *down* exits, as well as any other direction you might think of (northwest, southeast, etc.).

> **Exercise 8.8** Implement the changes described in this section in your own *zuul* project.

8.7 Responsibility-driven design

We have seen in the previous section that making use of proper encapsulation reduces coupling and can significantly reduce the amount of work needed to make changes to an application. Encapsulation, however, is not the only factor that influences the degree of coupling. Another aspect is known by the term *responsibility-driven design*.

Responsibility-driven design expresses the idea that each class should be responsible for handling its own data. Often, when we need to add some new functionality to an application, we need to ask ourselves in which class we should add a method to implement this new function. Which class should be responsible for the task? The answer is that the class that is responsible for storing some data should also be responsible for manipulating it.

How well responsibility-driven design is used influences the degree of coupling and, therefore, again, the ease with which an application can be modified or extended. As usual, we will discuss this in more detail with our example.

8.7.1 Responsibilities and coupling

The changes to the **Room** class that we discussed in Section 8.6.1 make it quite easy now to add the new directions for up and down movement in the **Game** class. We investigate this with an example. Assume that we want to add a new room (the cellar) under the office. All we have to do to achieve this is to make some small changes to **Game**'s **createRooms** method to create the room and to make two calls to set the exits:

> **Concept**
>
> **Responsibility-driven design** is the process of designing classes by assigning well-defined responsibilities to each class. This process can be used to determine which class should implement which part of an application function.

```
private void createRooms()
{
    Room outside, theater, pub, lab, office, cellar;
    . . .
    cellar = new Room("in the cellar");
    . . .
    office.setExit("down", cellar);
    cellar.setExit("up", office);
}
```

Because of the new interface of the **Room** class, this will work without problems. The change is now very easy and confirms that the design is getting better.

Further evidence of this can be seen if we compare the original version of the **printLocationInfo** method shown in Code 8.2 with the **getExitString** method shown in Code 8.6 that represents a solution to Exercise 8.7.

Because information about its exits is now stored only in the room itself, it is the room that is responsible for providing that information. The room can do this much better than any other object, because it has all the knowledge about the internal storage structure of the exit data. Now, inside the **Room** class, we can make use of the knowledge that exits are stored in a **HashMap**, and we can iterate over that map to describe the exits.

Consequently, we replace the version of **getExitString** shown in Code 8.6 with the version shown in Code 8.7. This method finds all the names for exits in the **HashMap** (the keys in the **HashMap** are the names of the exits) and concatenates them to a single **String**, which is then returned. (We need to import **Set** from **java.util** for this to work.)

Exercise 8.9 Look up the **keySet** method in the documentation of **HashMap**. What does it do?

Exercise 8.10 Explain, in detail and in writing, how the **getExitString** method shown in Code 8.7 works.

```java
/**
 * Return a description of the room's exits,
 * for example, "Exits: north west."
 * @return A description of the available exits.
 */
public String getExitString()
{
    String exitString = "Exits: ";
    if(northExit != null) {
        exitString += "north ";
    }
    if(eastExit != null) {
        exitString += "east ";
    }
    if(southExit != null) {
        exitString += "south ";
    }
    if(westExit != null) {
        exitString += "west ";
    }
    return exitString;
}
```

```java
/**
 * Return a description of the room's exits,
 * for example "Exits: north west."
 * @return A description of the available exits.
 */
public String getExitString()
{
    String returnString = "Exits:";
    Set<String> keys = exits.keySet();
    for(String exit : keys) {
        returnString += " " + exit;
    }
    return returnString;
}
```

Our goal to reduce coupling demands that, as far as possible, changes to the **Room** class do not require changes to the **Game** class. We can still improve this.

Currently, we have still encoded in the **Game** class the knowledge that the information we want from a room consists of a description string and the exit string:

```java
System.out.println("You are " + currentRoom.getDescription());
System.out.println(currentRoom.getExitString());
```

What if we add items to rooms in our game? Or monsters? Or other players?

When we describe what we see, the list of items, monsters, and other players should be included in the description of the room. We would need not only to make changes to the **Room** class to add these things, but also to change the code segment above where the description is printed out.

This is again a breach of the responsibility-driven design rule. Because the **Room** class holds information about a room, it should also produce a description for a room. We can improve this by adding to the **Room** class the following method:

```
/**
 * Return a long description of this room, of the form:
 *      You are in the kitchen.
 *      Exits: north west
 * @return A description of the room, including exits.
 */
public String getLongDescription()
{
    return "You are " + description + ".\n" + getExitString();
}
```

In the **Game** class, we then write

```
System.out.println(currentRoom.getLongDescription());
```

The "long description" of a room now includes the description string and information about the exits, and may in the future include anything else there is to say about a room. When we make these future extensions, we will have to make changes to only the **Room** class.

Concept

One of the main goals of a good class design is that of **localizing change**: making changes to one class should have minimal effects on other classes.

Exercise 8.11 Implement the changes described in this section in your own *zuul* project.

Exercise 8.12 Draw an object diagram with all objects in your game, the way they are just after starting the game.

Exercise 8.13 How does the object diagram change when you execute a *go* command?

8.8 Localizing change

Another aspect of the decoupling and responsibility principles is that of *localizing change*. We aim to create a class design that makes later changes easy by localizing the effects of a change.

Ideally, only a single class needs to be changed to make a modification. Sometimes several classes need change, but we then aim at this being as few classes as possible. In addition, the changes needed in other classes should be obvious, easy to detect, and easy to carry out.

To a large extent, we can achieve this by following good design rules such as using responsibility-driven design and aiming for loose coupling and high cohesion. In addition, however, we should have modification and extension in mind when we create our applications. It is important to anticipate that an aspect of our program might change, in order to make any changes easy.

8.9 Implicit coupling

We have seen that the use of public fields is one practice that is likely to create an unnecessarily tight form of coupling between classes. With this tight coupling, it may be necessary to make changes to more than one class for what should have been a simple modification. Therefore, public fields should be avoided. However, there is an even worse form of coupling: *implicit coupling*.

Implicit coupling is a situation where one class depends on the internal information of another, but this dependence is not immediately obvious. The tight coupling in the case of the public fields was not good, but at least it was obvious. If we change the public fields in one class and forget about the other, the application will not compile any longer, and the compiler will point out the problem. In cases of implicit coupling, omitting a necessary change can go undetected.

We can see the problem arising if we try to add further command words to the game.

Suppose that we want to add the command *look* to the set of legal commands. The purpose of *look* is merely to print out the description of the room and the exits again (we "look around the room"). This could be helpful if we have entered a sequence of commands in a room so that the description has scrolled out of view and we cannot remember where the exits of the current room are.

We can introduce a new command word simply by adding it to the array of known words in the **validCommands** array in the **CommandWords** class:

```
// a constant array that holds all valid command words
private static final String validCommands[] = {
    "go", "quit", "help", "look"
};
```

This shows an example of good cohesion: instead of defining the command words in the parser, which would have been one obvious possibility, the author created a separate class just to define the command words. This makes it very easy for us to now find the place where command words are defined, and it is easy to add one. The author was obviously thinking ahead, assuming that more commands might be added later, and created a structure that makes this very easy.

We can test this already. When we make this change and then execute the game and type the command *look*, nothing happens. This contrasts with the behavior of an unknown command word; if we type any unknown word, we see the reply

```
I don't know what you mean...
```

Thus, the fact that we do not see this reply indicates that the word was recognized, but nothing happens because we have not yet implemented an action for this command.

We can fix this by adding a method for the *look* command to the **Game** class:

```java
private void look()
{
    System.out.println(currentRoom.getLongDescription());
}
```

You should, of course, also add a comment for this method. After this, we only need to add a case for the *look* command in the **processCommand** method, which will invoke the **look** method when the *look* command is recognized:

```java
if(commandWord.equals("help")) {
    printHelp();
}
else if(commandWord.equals("go")) {
    goRoom(command);
}
else if(commandWord.equals("look")) {
    look();
}
else if(commandWord.equals("quit")) {
    wantToQuit = quit(command);
}
```

Try this out, and you will see that it works.

Exercise 8.14 Add the *look* command to your version of the zuul game.

Exercise 8.15 Add another command to your game. For a start, you could choose something simple, such as a command *eat* that, when executed, just prints out "You have eaten now and you are not hungry any more." Later, we can improve this so that you really get hungry over time and you need to find food.

Coupling between the **Game**, **Parser**, and **CommandWords** classes so far seems to have been very good—it was easy to make this extension, and we got it to work quickly.

The problem that was mentioned before—implicit coupling—becomes apparent when we now issue a help command. The output is

```
You are lost. You are alone. You wander
around at the university.
Your command words are:
go quit help
```

Now we notice a small problem. The help text is incomplete: the new command, *look*, is not listed.

This seems easy to fix: we can just edit the help text string in the **Game's printHelp** method. This is quickly done and does not seem a great problem. But suppose we had not noticed this error now. Did you think of this problem before you just read about it here?

This is a fundamental problem, because every time a command is added, the help text needs to be changed, and it is very easy to forget to make this change. The program compiles and runs, and everything seems fine. A maintenance programmer may well believe that the job is finished and release a program that now contains a bug.

This is an example of implicit coupling. When commands change, the help text must be modified (coupling), but nothing in the program source clearly points out this dependence (thus implicit).

A well-designed class will avoid this form of coupling by following the rule of responsibility-driven design. Because the **CommandWords** class is responsible for command words, it should also be responsible for printing command words. Thus, we add the following method to the **CommandWords** class:

```
/**
 * Print all valid commands to System.out.
 */
public void showAll()
{
    for(String command : validCommands) {
        System.out.print(command + " ");
    }
    System.out.println();
}
```

The idea here is that the **printHelp** method in **Game**, instead of printing a fixed text with the command words, invokes a method that asks the **CommandWords** class to print all its command words. Doing this ensures that the correct command words will always be printed, and adding a new command will also add it to the help text without further change.

The only remaining problem is that the **Game** object does not have a reference to the **CommandWords** object. You can see in the class diagram (Figure 8.1) that there is no arrow from **Game** to **CommandWords**. This indicates that the **Game** class does not even know of the existence of the **CommandWords** class. Instead, the game just has a parser, and the parser has command words.

We could now add a method to the parser that hands the **CommandWords** object to the **Game** object so that they could communicate. This would, however, increase the degree of coupling in our application. **Game** would then depend on **CommandWords**, which it currently does not. Also, we would see this effect in the class diagram: **Game** would then have an arrow to **CommandWords**.

The arrows in the diagram are, in fact, a good first indication of how tightly coupled a program is—the more arrows, the more coupling. As an approximation of good class design, we can aim at creating diagrams with few arrows.

Thus, the fact that **Game** did not have a reference to **CommandWords** is a good thing! We should not change this. From **Game's** viewpoint, the fact that the **CommandWords** class exists is an implementation detail of the parser. The parser returns commands, and whether it uses a **CommandWords** object to achieve this or something else is entirely up to the parser's implementation.

A better design just lets the **Game** talk to the **Parser**, which in turn may talk to **Command-Words**. We can implement this by adding the following code to the **printHelp** method in **Game**:

```
System.out.println("Your command words are:");
parser.showCommands();
```

All that is missing, then, is the **showCommands** method in the **Parser**, which delegates this task to the **CommandWords** class. Here is the complete method (in class **Parser**):

```
/**
 * Print out a list of valid command words.
 */
public void showCommands()
{
    commands.showAll();
}
```

Exercise 8.16 Implement the improved version of printing out the command words, as described in this section.

Exercise 8.17 If you now add another new command, do you still need to change the **Game** class? Why?

The full implementation of all changes discussed in this chapter so far is available in your code examples in a project named *zuul-better*. If you have done the exercises so far, you can ignore this project and continue to use your own. If you have not done the exercises but want to do the following exercises in this chapter as a programming project, you can use the *zuul-better* project as your starting point.

8.10 Thinking ahead

The design we have now is an important improvement to the original version. It is, however, possible to improve it even more.

One characteristic of a good software designer is the ability to think ahead. What might change? What can we safely assume will stay unchanged for the life of the program?

One assumption that we have hard-coded into most of our classes is that this game will run as a text-based game with terminal input and output. But will it always be like this?

It might be an interesting extension later to add a graphical user interface with menus, buttons, and images. In that case, we would not want to print the information to the text terminal anymore. We might still have command words, and we might still want to show them when a player enters a help command. But we might then show them in a text field in a window, rather than using `System.out.println`.

It is good design to try to encapsulate all information about the user interface in a single class or a clearly defined set of classes. Our solution from Section 8.9, for example—the `showAll` method in the `CommandWords` class—does not follow this design rule. It would be nice to define that `CommandWords` is responsible for *producing* (but not *printing*!) the list of command words, but that the `Game` class should decide how it is presented to the user.

We can easily achieve this by changing the `showAll` method so that it returns a string containing all command words instead of printing them out directly. (We should probably rename it `getCommandList` when we make this change.) This string can then be printed in the `printHelp` method in `Game`.

Note that this does not gain us anything right now, but we might profit from the improved design in the future.

> **Exercise 8.18** Implement the suggested change. Make sure that your program still works as before.
>
> **Exercise 8.19** Find out what the *model-view-controller* pattern is. You can do a web search to get information, or you can use any other sources you find. How is it related to the topic discussed here? What does it suggest? How could it be applied to this project? (Only *discuss* its application to this project, as an actual implementation would be an advanced challenge exercise.)

8.11 Cohesion

We introduced the idea of cohesion in Section 8.3: a unit of code should always be responsible for one, and only one, task. We shall now investigate the cohesion principle in more depth and analyze some examples.

The principle of cohesion can be applied to classes and methods: classes should display a high degree of cohesion, and so should methods.

8.11.1 Cohesion of methods

When we talk about cohesion of methods, we seek to express the ideal that any one method should be responsible for one, and only one, well-defined task.

We can see an example of a cohesive method in the `Game` class. This class has a private method named `printWelcome` to show the opening text, and this method is called when the game starts in the `play` method (Code 8.8).

Code 8.8

Two methods with a good degree of cohesion

```java
/**
 * Main play routine. Loops until end of play.
 */
public void play()
{
    printWelcome();

    // Enter the main command loop. Here we repeatedly read commands and
    // execute them until the game is over.

    boolean finished = false;
    while (! finished) {
        Command command = parser.getCommand();
        finished = processCommand(command);
    }
    System.out.println("Thank you for playing.  Good bye.");
}
```

```java
/**
 * Print out the opening message for the player.
 */
private void printWelcome()
{
    System.out.println();
    System.out.println("Welcome to the World of Zuul!");
    System.out.println("Zuul is a new, boring adventure game.");
    System.out.println("Type 'help' if you need help.");
    System.out.println();
    System.out.println(currentRoom.getLongDescription());
}
```

Concept

Method cohesion
A cohesive method is responsible for one, and only one, well-defined task.

From a functional point of view, we could have just entered the statements from the **printWelcome** method directly into the **play** method and achieved the same result without defining an extra method and making a method call. The same can, by the way, be said for the **processCommand** method that is also invoked in the **play** method: this code, too, could have been written directly into the **play** method.

It is, however, much easier to understand what a segment of code does and to make modifications if short, cohesive methods are used. In the chosen method structure, all methods are reasonably short and easy to understand, and their names indicate their purposes quite clearly. These characteristics represent valuable help for a maintenance programmer.

8.11.2 Cohesion of classes

The rule of cohesion of classes states that each class should represent one single, well-defined entity in the problem domain.

Concept

Class cohesion
A cohesive class represents one well-defined entity.

As an example of class cohesion, we now discuss another extension to the *zuul* project. We now want to add *items* to the game. Each room may hold an item, and each item has a description and a weight. An item's weight can be used later to determine whether it can be picked up or not.

A naïve approach would be to add two fields to the **Room** class: **itemDescription** and **itemWeight**. We could now specify the item details for each room, and we could print out the details whenever we enter a room.

This approach, however, does not display a good degree of cohesion: the **Room** class now describes both a room and an item. It also suggests that an item is bound to a particular room, which we might not wish to be the case.

A better design would create a separate class for items, probably called **Item**. This class would have fields for a description and weight, and a room would simply hold a reference to an item object.

Exercise 8.20 Extend either your adventure project or the *zuul-better* project so that a room can contain a single item. Items have a description and a weight. When creating rooms and setting their exits, items for this game should also be created. When a player enters a room, information about an item in this room should be displayed.

Exercise 8.21 How should the information be produced about an item present in a room? Which class should produce the string describing the item? Which class should print it? Why? Explain in writing. If answering this exercise makes you feel you should change your implementation, go ahead and make the changes.

The real benefits of separating rooms and items in the design can be seen if we change the specification a little. In a further variation of our game, we want to allow not only a single item in each room, but an unlimited number of items. In the design using a separate **Item** class, this is easy. We can create multiple **Item** objects and store them in a collection of items in the room.

With the first, naïve approach, this change would be almost impossible to implement.

Exercise 8.22 Modify the project so that a room can hold any number of items. Use a collection to do this. Make sure the room has an **addItem** method that places an item into the room. Make sure all items get shown when a player enters a room.

8.11.3 Cohesion for readability

There are several ways in which high cohesion benefits a design. The two most important ones are *readability* and *reuse*.

The example discussed in Section 8.11.1, cohesion of the `printWelcome` method, is clearly an example in which increasing cohesion makes a class more readable and thus easier to understand and maintain.

The class-cohesion example in Section 8.11.2 also has an element of readability. If a separate `Item` class exists, a maintenance programmer will easily recognize where to start reading code if a change to the characteristics of an item is needed. Cohesion of classes also increases readability of a program.

8.11.4 Cohesion for reuse

The second great advantage of cohesion is a higher potential for reuse.

The class-cohesion example in Section 8.11.2 shows an example of this: by creating a separate `Item` class, we can create multiple items and thus use the same code for more than a single item.

Reuse is also an important aspect of method cohesion. Consider a method in the **Room** class with the following header:

```
public Room leaveRoom(String direction)
```

This method could return the room in the given direction (so that it can be used as the new **currentRoom**) and also print out the description of the new room that we just entered.

This seems like a possible design, and it can indeed be made to work. In our version, however, we have separated this task into two methods:

```
public Room getExit(String direction)
public String getLongDescription()
```

The first is responsible for returning the next room, whereas the second produces the room's description.

The advantage of this design is that the separate tasks can be reused more easily. The **getLongDescription** method, for example, is now used not only in the **goRoom** method, but also in **printWelcome** and the implementation of the *look* command. This is only possible because it displays a high degree of cohesion. Reusing it would not be possible in the version with the **leaveRoom** method.

Exercise 8.23 Implement a *back* command. This command does not have a second word. Entering the *back* command takes the player into the previous room he/she was in.

Exercise 8.24 Test your new command. Does it work as expected? Also, test cases where the command is used incorrectly. For example, what does your program do if a player types a second word after the *back* command? Does it behave sensibly?

Exercise 8.25 What does your program do if you type "back" twice? Is this behavior sensible?

Exercise 8.26 *Challenge exercise* Implement the *back* command so that using it repeatedly takes you back several rooms, all the way to the beginning of the game if used often enough. Use a **Stack** to do this. (You may need to find out about stacks. Look at the Java library documentation.)

8.12 Refactoring

Concept

Refactoring is the activity of restructuring an existing design to maintain a good class design when the application is modified or extended.

When designing applications, we should attempt to think ahead, anticipate possible changes in the future, and create highly cohesive, loosely coupled classes and methods that make modifications easy. This is a noble goal, but we cannot always anticipate all future adaptations, and it is not feasible to prepare for all possible extensions we can think of.

This is why *refactoring* is important.

Refactoring is the activity of restructuring existing classes and methods to adapt them to changed functionality and requirements. Often in the lifetime of an application, functionality is gradually added. One common consequence is that, as a side-effect of this, methods and classes slowly grow in length.

It is tempting for a maintenance programmer to add some extra code to existing classes or methods. Doing this for some time, however, decreases the degree of cohesion. When more and more code is added to a method or a class, it is likely that at some stage it will represent more than one clearly defined task or entity.

Refactoring is the rethinking and redesigning of class and method structures. Most commonly, the effect is that classes are split in two or that methods are divided into two or more methods. Refactoring can also include the joining of multiple classes or methods into one, but that is less common than splitting.

8.12.1 Refactoring and testing

Before we provide an example of refactoring, we need to reflect on the fact that, when we refactor a program, we are usually proposing to make some potentially large changes to something that already works. When something is changed, there is a likelihood that errors will be introduced. Therefore, it is important to proceed cautiously; and, prior to refactoring, we should establish that a set of tests exists for the current version of the program. If tests do not exist, then we should first decide how we can reasonably test the functionality of the program and record those tests (for instance, by writing them down) so that we can repeat the same tests later. We will discuss testing more formally in the next chapter. If you are already familiar with automated testing, use automated tests. Otherwise, manual (but systematic) testing is sufficient for now.

Once a set of tests has been decided, the refactoring can start. Ideally, the refactoring should then follow in two steps:

- The first step is to refactor in order to improve the internal structure of the code, but without making any changes to the functionality of the application. In other words, the program should, when executed, behave exactly as it did before. Once this stage is completed, the previously established tests should be repeated to ensure that we have not introduced unintended errors.

- The second step is taken only once we have reestablished the baseline functionality in the refactored version. Then we are in a safe position to enhance the program. Once that has been done, of course, testing will need to be conducted on the new version.

Making several changes at the same time (refactoring and adding new features) makes it harder to locate the source of problems when they occur.

> **Exercise 8.27** What sort of baseline functionality tests might we wish to establish in the current version of the game?

8.12.2 An example of refactoring

As an example, we shall continue with the extension of adding items to the game. In Section 8.11.2, we started adding items, suggesting a structure in which rooms can contain any number of items. A logical extension to this arrangement is that a player should be able to pick up items and carry them around. Here is an informal specification of our next goal:

- The player can pick up items from the current room.

- The player can carry any number of items, but only up to a maximum weight.

- Some items cannot be picked up.

- The player can drop items in the current room.

To achieve these goals, we can do the following:

- If not already done, we add a class **Item** to the project. An item has, as discussed above, a description (a string) and a weight (an integer).

- We should also add a field **name** to the **Item** class. This will allow us to refer to the item with a name shorter than that of the description. If, for instance, there is a book in the current room, the field values of this item might be:

  name: **book**
  description: **an old, dusty book bound in gray leather**
  weight: **1200**

If we enter a room, we can print out the item's description to tell the player what is there. But for commands, the name will be easier to use. For instance, the player might then type *take book* to pick up the book.

■ We can ensure that some items cannot be picked up, by just making them very heavy (more than a player can carry). Or should we have another **boolean** field **canBePickedUp**? Which do you think is the better design? Does it matter? Try answering this by thinking about what future changes might be made to the game.

■ We add commands *take* and *drop* to pick up and drop items. Both commands have an item name as a second word.

■ Somewhere we have to add a field (holding some form of collection) to store the items currently carried by the player. We also have to add a field with the maximum weight the player can carry, so that we can check it each time we try to pick up something. Where should these go? Once again, think about future extensions to help you make the decision.

This last task is what we will discuss in more detail now, in order to illustrate the process of refactoring.

The first question to ask ourselves when thinking about how to enable players to carry items is: Where should we add the fields for the currently carried items and the maximum weight? A quick look over the existing classes shows that the **Game** class is really the only place where it can be fit in. It cannot be stored in **Room**, **Item**, or **Command**, because there are many different instances of these classes over time, which are not all always accessible. It does not make sense in **Parser** or **CommandWords** either.

Reinforcing the decision to place these changes in the **Game** class is the fact that it already stores the current room (information about where the player is right now), so adding the current items (information about what the player has) seems to fit with this quite well.

This approach could be made to work. It is, however, not a solution that is well designed. The **Game** class is fairly big already, and there is a good argument that it contains too much as it is. Adding even more does not make this better.

We should ask ourselves again which class or object this information should belong to. Thinking carefully about the type of information we are adding here (carried items, maximum weight), we realize that this is information about a *player*! The logical thing to do (following responsibility-driven design guidelines) is to create a **Player** class. We can then add these fields to the **Player** class, and create a **Player** object at the start of the game, to store the data.

The existing field **currentRoom** also stores information about the player: the player's current location. Consequently, we should now also move this field into the **Player** class.

Analyzing it now, it is obvious that this design better fits the principle of responsibility-driven design. Who should be responsible for storing information about the player? The **Player** class, of course.

In the original version, we had only a single piece of information for the player: the current room. Whether we should have had a **Player** class even back then is up for discussion.

There are arguments both ways. It would have been nice design, so, yes, maybe we should. But having a class with only a single field and no methods that do anything of significance might have been regarded as overkill.

Sometimes there are gray areas such as this one, where either decision is defensible. But after adding our new fields, the situation is quite clear. There is now a strong argument for a **Player** class. It would store the fields and have methods such as **dropItem** and **pickUpItem** (which can include the weight check and might return false if we cannot carry it).

What we did when we introduced the **Player** class and moved the **currentRoom** field from **Game** into **Player** was refactoring. We have restructured the way we represent our data, to achieve a better design under changed requirements.

Programmers not as well trained as us (or just being lazy) might have left the **currentRoom** field where it was, seeing that the program worked as it was and there did not seem to be a great need to make this change. They would end up with a messy class design.

The effect of making the change can be seen if we think one step further ahead. Assume that we now want to extend the game to allow for multiple players. With our nice new design, this is suddenly very easy. We already have a **Player** class (the **Game** holds a **Player** object), and it is easy to create several **Player** objects and store in **Game** a collection of players instead of a single player. Each player object would hold its own current room, items, and maximum weight. Different players could even have different maximum weights, opening up the even wider concept of having players with quite different capabilities—their carrying capability being just one of many.

The lazy programmer who left **currentRoom** in the **Game** class, however, has a serious problem now. Because the entire game has only a single current room, current locations of multiple players cannot easily be stored. Bad design usually bites back to create more work for us in the end.

Doing good refactoring is as much about thinking in a certain mindset as it is about technical skills. While we make changes and extensions to applications, we should regularly question whether an original class design still represents the best solution. As the functionality changes, arguments for or against certain designs change. What was a good design for a simple application might not be good any more when some extensions are added.

Recognizing these changes and actually making the refactoring modifications to the source code usually saves a lot of time and effort in the end. The earlier we clean up our design, the more work we usually save.

We should be prepared to *factor out* methods (turn a sequence of statements from the body of an existing method into a new, independent method) and classes (take parts of a class and create a new class from it). Considering refactoring regularly keeps our class design clean and saves work in the end. Of course, one of the things that will actually mean that refactoring makes life harder in the long run is if we fail to adequately test the refactored version against the original. Whenever we embark on a major refactoring task, it is essential to ensure that we test well, before and after the change. Doing these tests manually (by creating and testing objects interactively) will get tedious very quickly. We shall investigate how we can improve our testing—by automating it—in the next chapter.

Exercise 8.28 Refactor your project to introduce a separate **Player** class. A **Player** object should store at least the current room of the player, but you may also like to store the player's name or other information.

Exercise 8.29 Implement an extension that allows a player to pick up one single item. This includes implementing two new commands: *take* and *drop*.

Exercise 8.30 Extend your implementation to allow the player to carry any number of items.

Exercise 8.31 Add a restriction that allows the player to carry items only up to a specified maximum weight. The maximum weight a player can carry is an attribute of the player.

Exercise 8.32 Implement an *items* command that prints out all items currently carried and their total weight.

Exercise 8.33 Add a *magic cookie* item to a room. Add an *eat cookie* command. If a player finds and eats the magic cookie, it increases the weight that the player can carry. (You might like to modify this slightly to better fit into your own game scenario.)

8.13 Refactoring for language independence

One feature of the *zuul* game that we have not commented on yet is that the user interface is closely tied to commands written in English. This assumption is embedded in both the **CommandWords** class, where the list of valid commands is stored, and the **Game** class, where the **processCommand** method explicitly compares each command word against a set of English words. If we wish to change the interface to allow users to use a different language, then we would have to find all the places in the source code where command words are used and change them. This is a further example of a form of implicit coupling, which we discussed in Section 8.9.

If we want to have language independence in the program, then ideally we should have just one place in the source code where the actual text of command words is stored and have everywhere else refer to commands in a language-independent way. A programming language feature that makes this possible is *enumerated types*, or *enums*. We will explore this feature of Java via the *zuul-with-enums* projects.

8.13.1 Enumerated types

Code 8.9 shows a Java enumerated type definition called **CommandWord**.

Code 8.9

An enumerated type
for command words

```
/**
 * Representations for all the valid command words for the game.
 *
 * @author  Michael Kölling and David J. Barnes
 * @version 2016.02.29
 */
public enum CommandWord
{
    // A value for each command word, plus one for unrecognized commands.
    GO, QUIT, HELP, UNKNOWN
}
```

In its simplest form, an enumerated type definition consists of an outer wrapper that uses the word **enum** rather than **class**, and a body that is simply a list of variable names denoting the set of values that belong to this type. By convention, these variable names are fully capitalized. We never create objects of an enumerated type. In effect, each name within the type definition represents a unique instance of the type that has already been created for us to use. We refer to these instances as **CommandWord.GO**, **CommandWord.QUIT**, etc. Although the syntax for using them is similar, it is important to avoid thinking of these values as being like the numeric class constants we discussed in Section 6.14. Despite the simplicity of their definition, enumerated type values are proper objects, and are not the same as integers.

How can we use the **CommandWord** type to make a step toward decoupling the game logic of *zuul* from a particular natural language? One of the first improvements we can make is to the following series of tests in the **processCommand** method of **Game**:

```
if(command.isUnknown()) {
    System.out.println("I don't know what you mean...");
    return false;
}
String commandWord = command.getCommandWord();
if(commandWord.equals("help")) {
    printHelp();
}
else if(commandWord.equals("go")) {
    goRoom(command);
}
else if(commandWord.equals("quit")) {
    wantToQuit = quit(command);
}
```

If **commandWord** is made to be of type **CommandWord** rather than **String**, then this can be rewritten as:

```
if(commandWord == CommandWord.UNKNOWN) {
    System.out.println("I don't know what you mean...");
}
else if(commandWord == CommandWord.HELP) {
    printHelp();
}
```

```
    else if(commandWord == CommandWord.GO) {
        goRoom(command);
    }
    else if(commandWord == CommandWord.QUIT) {
        wantToQuit = quit(command);
    }
```

In fact, now that we changed the type to **CommandWord**, we could also use a *switch statement* instead of the series of if statements. This expresses the intent of this code segment a little more clearly.[2]

```
switch (commandWord) {
    case UNKNOWN:
        System.out.println("I don't know what you mean...");
        break;
    case HELP:
        printHelp();
        break;
    case GO:
        goRoom(command);
        break;
    case QUIT:
        wantToQuit = quit(command);
        break;
}
```

The switch statement takes the variable in the parentheses following the **switch** keyword (**commandWord** in our case) and compares it to each of the values listed after the **case** keywords. When a case matches, the code following it is executed. The **break** statement causes the switch statement to abort at that point, and execution continues after the switch statement. For a fuller description of the switch statement, see Appendix D.

Now we just have to arrange for the user's typed commands to be mapped to the corresponding **CommandWord** values. Open the *zuul-with-enums-v1* project to see how we have done this. The most significant change can be found in the **CommandWords** class. Instead of using an array of strings to define the valid commands, we now use a map between strings and **CommandWord** objects:

```
public CommandWords()
{
    validCommands = new HashMap<>();
    validCommands.put("go", CommandWord.GO);
    validCommands.put("help", CommandWord.HELP);
    validCommands.put("quit", CommandWord.QUIT);
}
```

---

[2] In fact, string literals can also be used as case values in switch statements, in order to avoid a long sequence of if-else-if comparisons.

The command typed by a user can now easily be converted to its corresponding enumerated type value.

Exercise 8.34 Review the source code of the *zuul-with-enums-v1* project to see how it uses the **CommandWord** type. The classes **Command**, **CommandWords**, **Game**, and **Parser** have all been adapted from the *zuul-better* version to accommodate this change. Check that the program still works as you would expect.

Exercise 8.35 Add a *look* command to the game, along the lines described in Section 8.9.

Exercise 8.36 "Translate" the game to use different command words for the **GO** and **QUIT** commands. These could be from a real language or just made-up words. Do you only have to edit the **CommandWords** class to make this change work? What is the significance of this?

Exercise 8.37 Change the word associated with the HELP command and check that it works correctly. After you have made your changes, what do you notice about the welcome message that is printed when the game starts?

Exercise 8.38 In a new project, define your own enumerated type called **Direction** with values NORTH, SOUTH, EAST, and WEST.

8.13.2 Further decoupling of the command interface

The enumerated **CommandWord** type has allowed us to make a significant decoupling of the user interface language from the game logic, and it is almost completely possible to translate the commands into another language just by editing the **CommandWords** class. (At some stage, we should also translate the room descriptions and other output strings, probably by reading them from a file, but we shall leave this until later.) There is one further piece of decoupling of the command words that we would like to perform. Currently, whenever a new command is introduced into the game, we must add a new value to the **CommandWord**, and an association between that value and the user's text in the **CommandWords** classes. It would be helpful if we could make the **CommandWord** type self-contained—in effect, move the text–value association from **CommandWords** to **CommandWord**.

Java allows enumerated type definitions to contain much more than a list of the type's values. We will not explore this feature in much detail, but just give you a flavor of what is possible. Code 8.10 shows an enhanced **CommandWord** type that looks quite similar to an ordinary class definition. This can be found in the *zuul-with-enums-v2* project.

Code 8.10

Associating command strings with enumerated type values

```java
/**
 * Representations for all the valid command words for the game
 * along with a string in a particular language.
 *
 * @author  Michael Kölling and David J. Barnes
 * @version 2016.02.29
 */
public enum CommandWord
{
    // A value for each command word along with its
    // corresponding user interface string.
    GO("go"), QUIT("quit"), HELP("help"), UNKNOWN("?");

    // The command string.
    private String commandString;

    /**
     * Initialize with the corresponding command string.
     * @param commandString The command string.
     */
    CommandWord(String commandString)
    {
        this.commandString = commandString;
    }

    /**
     * @return The command word as a string.
     */
    public String toString()
    {
        return commandString;
    }
}
```

The main points to note about this new version of **CommandWord** are that:

- Each type value is followed by a parameter value—in this case, the text of the command associated with that value.

- Unlike the version in Code 8.9, a semicolon is required at the end of the list of type values.

- The type definition includes a constructor. This does not have the word **public** in its header. Enumerated type constructors are never public, because we do not create the instances. The parameter associated with each type value is passed to this constructor.

- The type definition includes a field, **commandString**. The constructor stores the command string in this field.

- A **toString** method has been used to return the text associated with a particular type value.

With the text of the commands stored in the **CommandWord** type, the **CommandWords** class in *zuul-with-enums-v2* uses a different way to create its map between text and enumerated values:

```
validCommands = new HashMap<String, CommandWord>();
for(CommandWord command : CommandWord.values()) {
    if(command != CommandWord.UNKNOWN) {
        validCommands.put(command.toString(), command);
    }
}
```

Every enumerated type defines a **values** method that returns an array filled with the value objects from the type. The code above iterates over the array and calls the **toString** method to obtain the command **String** associated with each value.

> **Exercise 8.39** Add your own *look* command to *zuul-with-enums-v2*. Do you only need to change the **CommandWord** type?

> **Exercise 8.40** Change the word associated with the *help* command in **CommandWord**. Is this change automatically reflected in the welcome text when you start the game? Take a look at the **printWelcome** method in the **Game** class to see how this has been achieved.

8.14 Design guidelines

An often-heard piece of advice to beginners about writing good object-oriented programs is, "Don't put too much into a single method" or "Don't put everything into one class." Both suggestions have merit, but frequently lead to the counter-questions, "How long should a method be?" or "How long should a class be?"

After the discussion in this chapter, these questions can now be answered in terms of cohesion and coupling. A method is too long if it does more than one logical task. A class is too complex if it represents more than one logical entity.

You will notice that these answers do not give clear-cut rules that specify exactly what to do. Terms such as *one logical task* are still open to interpretation, and different programmers will decide differently in many situations.

These are *guidelines*—not cast-in-stone rules. Keeping these in mind, though, will significantly improve your class design and enable you to master more complex problems and write better and more interesting programs.

> *It is important to understand the following exercises as suggestions, not as fixed specifications. This game has many possible ways in which it can be extended, and you are encouraged to invent your own extensions. You do not need to do all the exercises here to create an interesting game; you may want to do more,*

or you may want to do different ones. Here are some suggestions to get you started.

Exercise 8.41 Add some form of time limit to your game. If a certain task is not completed in a specified time, the player loses. A time limit can easily be implemented by counting the number of moves or the number of entered commands. You do not need to use real time.

Exercise 8.42 Implement a trapdoor somewhere (or some other form of door that you can only cross one way).

Exercise 8.43 Add a *beamer* to the game. A beamer is a device that can be *charged* and *fired*. When you charge the beamer, it memorizes the current room. When you fire the beamer, it transports you immediately back to the room it was charged in. The beamer could either be standard equipment or an item that the player can find. Of course, you need commands to charge and fire the beamer.

Exercise 8.44 Add locked doors to your game. The player needs to find (or otherwise obtain) a key to open a door.

Exercise 8.45 Add a transporter room. Whenever the player enters this room, he/she is randomly transported into one of the other rooms. Note: Coming up with a good design for this task is not trivial. It might be interesting to discuss design alternatives for this with other students. (We discuss design alternatives for this task at the end of Chapter 11. The adventurous or advanced reader may want to skip ahead and have a look.)

8.15 Summary

In this chapter, we have discussed what are often called the *nonfunctional aspects* of an application. Here, the issue is not so much to get a program to perform a certain task, but to do this with well-designed classes.

Good class design can make a huge difference when an application needs to be corrected, modified, or extended. It also allows us to reuse parts of the application in other contexts (for example, for other projects) and thus creates benefits later.

There are two key concepts under which class design can be evaluated: coupling and cohesion. Coupling refers to the interconnectedness of classes, cohesion to modularization into appropriate units. Good design exhibits loose coupling and high cohesion.

One way to achieve a good structure is to follow a process of responsibility-driven design. Whenever we add a function to the application, we try to identify which class should be responsible for which part of the task.

When extending a program, we use regular refactoring to adapt the design to changing requirements and to ensure that classes and methods remain cohesive and loosely coupled.

Terms introduced in this chapter:

code duplication, coupling, cohesion, encapsulation, responsibility-driven design, implicit coupling, refactoring

Concept summary

- **coupling** The term *coupling* describes the interconnectedness of classes. We strive for *loose coupling* in a system—that is, a system where each class is largely independent and communicates with other classes via a small, well-defined interface.

- **cohesion** The term *cohesion* describes how well a unit of code maps to a logical task or entity. In a *highly cohesive* system, each unit of code (method, class, or module) is responsible for a well-defined task or entity. Good class design exhibits a high degree of cohesion.

- **code duplication** Code duplication (having the same segment of code in an application more than once) is a sign of bad design. It should be avoided.

- **encapsulation** Proper encapsulation in classes reduces coupling and thus leads to a better design.

- **responsibility-driven design** Responsibility-driven design is the process of designing classes by assigning well-defined responsibilities to each class. This process can be used to determine which class should implement which part of an application function.

- **localizing change** One of the main goals of a good class design is that of localizing change: making changes to one class should have minimal effects on other classes.

- **method cohesion** A cohesive method is responsible for one, and only one, well-defined task.

- **class cohesion** A cohesive class represents one well-defined entity.

- **refactoring** Refactoring is the activity of restructuring an existing design to maintain a good class design when the application is modified or extended.

- **switch statement** A switch statement selects a sequence of statements for execution from multiple different options.

Exercise 8.46 *Challenge exercise* In the **processCommand** method in **Game**, there is a switch statement (or a sequence of if statements) to dispatch commands when a command word is recognized. This is not a very good design, because every time we add a command, we have to add a case here. Can you improve this design? Design the classes so that handling of commands is more modular and new commands can be added more easily. Implement it. Test it.

Exercise 8.47 Add characters to the game. Characters are similar to items, but they can talk. They speak some text when you first meet them, and they may give you some help if you give them the right item.

Exercise 8.48 Add moving characters. These are like other characters, but every time the player types a command, these characters can move into an adjoining room.

Exercise 8.49 Add a class called **GameMain** to your project. Define just a **main** method within it and have them method create a **Game** object and call its **play** method.

9

Well-Behaved Objects

Main concepts discussed in this chapter:

- testing
- debugging
- unit testing
- test automation

Java constructs introduced in this chapter:

(No new Java constructs are introduced in this chapter.)

9.1 Introduction

If you have followed the previous chapters in this book, and if you have implemented the exercises we have suggested, then you have written a good number of classes by now. One observation that you will likely have made is that a class you write is rarely perfect after the first attempt to write its source code. Usually, it does not work correctly at first, and more work is needed to complete it.

The problems you are dealing with will shift over time. Beginners typically struggle with Java *syntax errors*. Syntax errors are errors in the structure of the source code itself. They are easy to spot, because the compiler will highlight them and display some sort of error message.

More experienced programmers who tackle more complicated problems usually have less difficulty with the language syntax. They are more concerned with *logical errors* instead.

A logical error is a problem where the program compiles and executes without an obvious error, but delivers the wrong result. Logical problems are much more severe and harder to find than syntax errors. In fact, it is sometimes not easy to detect that there is an error in the first place.

Writing syntactically correct programs is relatively easy to learn, and good tools (such as compilers) exist to detect syntax errors and point them out. Writing logically correct programs, on the other hand, is very difficult for any nontrivial problem, and proof that a

Concept

Testing is the activity of finding out whether a piece of code (a method, class, or program) produces the intended behavior.

program is correct cannot, in general, be automated. It is so hard, in fact, that most software that is commercially sold is known to contain a significant number of bugs.

Thus, it is essential for a competent software engineer to learn how to deal with correctness, and how to reduce the number of errors in a class.

In this chapter, we shall discuss a variety of activities that are related to improving the correctness of a program. These include testing, debugging, and writing for maintainability.

Testing is an activity that is concerned with finding out whether a segment of code contains any errors. Testing well is not easy, and there is much to think about when testing a program.

Debugging comes after testing. If tests have shown that an error is present, we use debugging techniques to find out exactly where the error is and how to fix it. There can be a significant amount of work between knowing that an error exists, finding the cause, and fixing it.

Concept

Debugging is the attempt to pinpoint and fix the source of an error.

Writing for maintainability is maybe the most fundamental topic. It is about trying to write code in such a way that errors are avoided in the first place and, if they still slip in, that they can be found as easily as possible. Code style and commenting are part of it, as are the code quality principles that we have discussed in the previous chapter. Ideally, code should be easy to understand so that the original programmer avoids introducing errors and a maintenance programmer can easily find possible errors.

In practice, this is not always simple. But there are big differences between few and many errors, and also between the effort it takes to debug well-written code and not-so-well-written code.

9.2 Testing and debugging

Testing and debugging are crucial skills in software development. You will often need to check your programs for errors, then locate the source of those errors when they occur. In addition, you might also be responsible for testing other people's programs or modifying them. In the latter case, the debugging task is closely related to the process of understanding someone else's code, and there is a lot of overlap in the techniques you might use to do both. In the sections that follow, we shall investigate the following testing and debugging techniques:

- manual unit testing within BlueJ
- test automation
- manual walkthroughs
- print statements
- debuggers

We shall look at the first two testing techniques in the context of some classes that you might have written for yourself, and the remaining debugging techniques in the context of understanding someone else's source code.

Unit testing within BlueJ

Concept

unit testing refers to tests of the individual parts of an application, such as methods and classes.

The term *unit testing* refers to a test of the individual parts of an application, as opposed to *application testing*, which is testing of the complete application. The units being tested can be of various sizes. They may be a group of classes, a single class, or even a single method. It is worth observing that unit testing can be done long before an application is complete. Any single method, once written and compiled, can (and should) be tested.

Because BlueJ allows us to interact directly with individual objects, it offers unique ways to conduct testing on classes and methods. One of the points we want to stress in this section is that it is never too early to start testing. There are several benefits in early experimentation and testing. First, they give us valuable experience with a system; this can make it possible to spot problems early enough to fix them at a much lower cost than if they had not been uncovered until much later in the development. Second, we can start building up a series of test cases and results that can be used over and over again as the system grows. Each time we make a change to the system, these test cases allow us to check that we have not inadvertently introduced errors into the rest of the system as a result of the changes.

In order to illustrate this form of testing within BlueJ, we shall use the *online-shop* project, which represents an early stage in the development of software for an online sales shop (such as Amazon.com). Our project contains only a very small part of this application, namely the part that deals with customer comments for sales items.

Open the *online-shop* project. Currently, it contains only two classes: **SalesItem** and **Comment**. The intended functionality of this part of the application—concentrating solely on handling customer comments—is as follows:

- Sales items can be created with a description and price.

- Customer comments can be added to and removed from sales items.

- Comments include a comment text, an author's name, and a rating. The rating is in the range of 1 to 5 (inclusive).

- Each person may leave only one comment. Subsequent attempts to leave a comment by the same author are rejected.

- The user interface (not implemented in this project yet) will include a question asking, "Was this comment helpful to you?" with Yes and No buttons. A user clicking Yes or No is known as *upvoting* or *downvoting* the comment. The balance of up and down votes is kept for comments, so that the most useful comments (the ones with the highest vote balance) can be displayed at the top.

The **Comment** class in our project stores information about a single comment. For our testing, we shall concentrate on the **SalesItem** class, shown in Code 9.1. Objects of this class represent a single sales item, including all comments left for this item.

As part of our testing, we should check several parts of the intended functionality, including:

- Can comments be added and removed from a sales item?

- Does the **showInfo** method correctly show all the information stored about a sales item?

- Are the constraints (ratings must be 1 to 5, only one comment per person) enforced correctly?

- Can we correctly find the most helpful comment (the one with the most votes)?

We shall find that all of these can be tested conveniently using the object bench within BlueJ. In addition, we shall see that the interactive nature of BlueJ makes it possible to simplify some of the testing by making controlled alterations to a class under test.

Code 9.1
The `SalesItem` class

```java
import java.util.ArrayList;
import java.util.Iterator;

/**
 * The class represents sales items on an online e-commerce site (such as
 * Amazon.com). SalesItem objects store all information relevant to this item,
 * including description, price, customer comments, etc.
 *
 * NOTE: The current version is incomplete! Currently, only code dealing with
 * customer comments is here.
 *
 * @author Michael Kölling and David J. Barnes
 * @version 0.1 (2016.02.29)
 */
public class SalesItem
{
    private String name;
    private int price;  // in cents
    private ArrayList<Comment> comments;

    /**
     * Create a new sales item.
     */
    public SalesItem(String name, int price)
    {
        this.name = name;
        this.price = price;
        comments = new ArrayList<>();
    }

    /**
     * Return the name of this item.
     */
    public String getName()
    {
        return name;
    }

    /**
     * Return the price of this item.
     */
    public int getPrice()
    {
        return price;
    }
```

Code 9.1
continued

The SalesItem class

```java
/**
 * Return the number of customer comments for this item.
 */
public int getNumberOfComments()
{
    return comments.size();
}

/**
 * Add a comment to the comment list of this sales item. Return true if
 * successful; false if the comment was rejected.
 *
 * The comment will be rejected if the same author has already left a
 * comment, or if the rating is invalid. Valid ratings are numbers between
 * 1 and 5 (inclusive).
 */
public boolean addComment(String author, String text, int rating)
{
    if(ratingInvalid(rating)) {   // reject invalid ratings
        return false;
    }

    if(findCommentByAuthor(author) != null) {
        // reject mutiple comments by same author
        return false;
    }

    comments.add(new Comment(author, text, rating));
    return true;
}

/**
 * Remove the comment stored at the index given. If the index is invalid,
 * do nothing.
 */
public void removeComment(int index)
{
    if(index >=0 && index < comments.size()) { // if index is valid
        comments.remove(index);
    }
}

/**
 * Upvote the comment at "index." That is: count this comment as more
 * helpful. If the index is invalid, do nothing.
 */
public void upvoteComment(int index)
{
    if(index >=0 && index < comments.size()) { // if index is valid
        comments.get(index).upvote();
    }
}
```

Code 9.1 continued

The `SalesItem` class

```java
/**
 * Downvote the comment at "index." That is: count this comment as less
 * helpful. If the index is invalid, do nothing.
 */
public void downvoteComment(int index)
{
    if(index >=0 && index < comments.size()) { // if index is valid
        comments.get(index).downvote();
    }
}

/**
 * Show all comments on screen. (Currently, for testing purposes: print
 * to the terminal. Modify later for web display.)
 */
public void showInfo()
{
    System.out.println("*** " + name + " ***");
    System.out.println("Price: " + priceString(price));
    System.out.println();
    System.out.println("Customer comments:");
    for(Comment comment : comments) {
        System.out.println("-------------------------------------------");
        System.out.println(comment.getFullDetails());
    }
    System.out.println();
    System.out.println("=========================================");
}

/**
 * Return the most helpful comment. The most useful comment is the one
 * with the highest vote balance. If there are multiple comments with
 * equal highest balance, return any one of them.
 */
public Comment findMostHelpfulComment()
{
    Iterator<Comment> it = comments.iterator();
    Comment best = it.next();
    while(it.hasNext()) {
        Comment current = it.next();
        if(current.getVoteCount() > best.getVoteCount()) {
            best = current;
        }
    }
    return best;
}

/**
 * Check whether the given rating is invalid. Return true if it is
 * invalid. Valid ratings are in the range [1..5].
 */
private boolean ratingInvalid(int rating)
{
    return rating < 0 || rating > 5;
}
```

```
/**
 * Find the comment by the author with the given name.
 *
 * @return The comment if it exists; null if it doesn't.
 */
private Comment findCommentByAuthor(String author)
{
    for(Comment comment : comments) {
        if(comment.getAuthor().equals(author)) {
            return comment;
        }
    }
    return null;
}

/**
 * For a price given as an int, return a readable String representing the
 * same price. The price is given in whole cents. For example for
 * price==12345, the following String is returned: $123.45
 */
private String priceString(int price)
{
    int dollars = price / 100;
    int cents = price - (dollars*100);
    if(cents <= 9) {
        return "$" + dollars + ".0" + cents;   // zero padding
    }
    else {
        return "$" + dollars + "." + cents;
    }
}
}
```

9.3.1 Using inspectors

When testing interactively, using object inspectors is often very helpful. In preparation for our testing, create a **SalesItem** object on the object bench and open its inspector by selecting the *Inspect* function from the object's menu. Select the **comments** field and open its inspector as well (Figure 9.1). Check that the list has been created (is not null) and is initially of size 0. Check also that the size grows as you add comments. Leave the comment-list inspector open to assist with subsequent tests.

An essential component of testing classes that use data structures is checking that they behave properly both when the data structures are empty and—if appropriate—when they are full. Testing for full data structures only applies to those that have a fixed limit, such as arrays. In our case, where we use an **ArrayList**, testing for the list being full does not apply, because the list expands as needed. However, making tests with an empty list is important, as this is a special case that needs special treatment.

A first test that can be performed on **SalesItem** is to call its **showInfo** method before any comments have been added. This should correctly show the item's description and price, and no comments.

Figure 9.1
Inspector for the
comments list

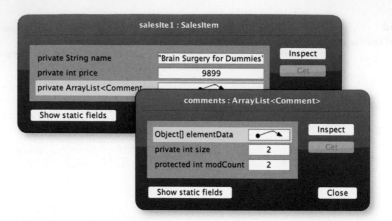

A key feature of good testing is to ensure that *boundaries* are checked, because these are often the points at which things go wrong. The boundaries associated with the **SalesItem** class are, for example, the empty comment list. Boundaries set for the **Comment** class include the restriction of the rating to the range 1 to 5. Ratings at the top and bottom of this range are boundary cases. It will be important to check not only ratings in the middle of this range, but also the maximum and minimum possible rating.

In order to conduct tests along these lines, create a **SalesItem** object on the object bench and try the following as initial tests of the comment functionality. If you perform these tests carefully, they should uncover two errors in our code.

Exercise 9.1 Add several comments to the sales item while keeping an eye on the inspector for the comments list. Make sure the list behaves as expected (that is, its size should increase). You may also like to inspect the *elementData* field of the ArrayList object.

Exercise 9.2 Check that the **showInfo** method correctly prints the item information, including the comments. Try this both for items with and without comments.

Exercise 9.3 Check that the **getNumberOfComments** method works as expected.

Exercise 9.4 Now check that duplicate authors are correctly handled—i.e., that further comments by the same author are rejected. When trying to add a comment with an author name for whom a comment already exists, the **addComment** method should return **false**. Check also that the comment was not added to the list.

Exercise 9.5 Perform boundary checking on the rating value. That is, create comments not only with medium ratings, but also with top and bottom ratings. Does this work correctly?

Exercise 9.6 Good boundary testing also involves testing values that lie just beyond the valid range of data. Test 0 and 6 as rating values. In both cases, the comment should be rejected (**addComment** should return **false**, and the comment should not be added to the comment list).

Exercise 9.7 Test the **upvoteComment** and **downvoteComment** methods. Make sure that the vote balance is correctly counted.

Exercise 9.8 Use the **upvoteComment** and **downvoteComment** methods to mark some comments as more or less helpful. Then test the **findMostHelpfulComment** method. This method should return the comment that was voted most helpful. You will notice that the method returns an object reference. You can use the *Inspect* function in the method result dialog to check whether the correct comment was returned. Of course, you will need to know which is the correct comment in order to check whether you get the right result.

Exercise 9.9 Do boundary testing of the **findMostHelpfulComment** method. That is, call this method when the comments list is empty (no comments have been added). Does this work as expected?

Exercise 9.10 The tests in the exercises above should have uncovered two bugs in our code. Fix them. After fixing these errors, is it safe to assume that all previous tests will still work as before? Section 9.4 will discuss some of the testing issues that arise when software is corrected or enhanced.

From these exercises, it is easy to see how valuable interactive method invocations and inspectors are in giving immediate feedback on the state of an object, often avoiding the need to add print statements to a class when testing or debugging it.

9.3.2 Positive versus negative testing

> **Concept**
>
> **Positive testing** is the testing of cases that are expected to succeed.

When deciding about what to test, we generally distinguish *positive* and *negative* test cases. Positive testing is the testing of functionality that we expect to work. For example, adding a comment by a new author with a valid rating is a positive test. When testing positive test cases, we have to convince ourselves that the code did indeed work as expected.

Negative testing is the test of cases that we expect to fail. Using an invalid rating, or attempting to store a second comment from the same author, are both negative tests. When testing negative cases, we expect the program to handle this error in some specified, controlled way.

> **Pitfall** It is a very common error for inexperienced testers to conduct only positive tests. Negative tests—testing that what should go wrong indeed does go wrong, and does so in a well-defined manner—are crucial for a good test procedure.

Concept

Negative testing is the testing of cases that are expected to fail.

> **Exercise 9.11** Which of the test cases mentioned in the previous exercises are positive tests and which are negative? Make a table of each category. Can you think of further positive tests? Can you think of further negative ones?

9.4 Test automation

Concept

test automation simplifies the process of regression testing.

One reason why thorough testing is often neglected is that it is both a time-consuming and a relatively boring activity, if done manually. You will have noticed, if you did all exercises in the previous section, that testing thoroughly can become tedious very quickly. This particularly becomes an issue when tests have to be run not just once but possibly hundreds or thousands of times. Fortunately, there are techniques available that allow us to automate repetitive testing, and so remove much of the drudgery associated with it. The next section looks at test automation in the context of *regression testing*.

9.4.1 Regression testing

It would be nice if we could assume that correcting errors only ever improves the quality of a program. Sadly, experience shows that it is all too easy to introduce further errors when modifying software. Thus, fixing an error at one spot may introduce another error at the same time.

As a consequence, it is desirable to run *regression tests* whenever a change is made to software. Regression testing involves rerunning tests that have previously passed, to ensure that the new version still passes them. It is much more likely to be performed if it can be automated. One of the easiest ways to automate regression tests is to write a program that acts as a *test rig*, or *test harness*.

9.4.2 Automated testing using JUnit

Support for regression testing is integrated in BlueJ (and many other development environments) using a testing system called JUnit. JUnit is a testing framework devised by Erich Gamma and Kent Beck for the Java language, and similar systems are now available for many other programming languages.

> **JUnit** JUnit is a popular testing framework to support organized unit testing and regression testing in Java. It is available independent of specific development environments, as well as integrated in many environments. JUnit was developed by Erich Gamma and Kent Beck. You can find the software and a lot of information about it at `http://www.junit.org`.

Figure 9.2

A project with a test class

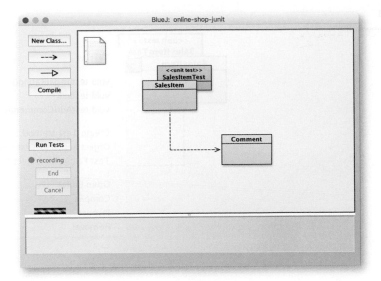

To start investigating regression testing with our example, open the *online-shop-junit* project. This project contains the same classes as the previous one, plus an additional class, **SalesItemTest**.

SalesItemTest is a test class. The first thing to note is that its appearance is different from what we have seen previously (Figure 9.2). It is annotated as a **<<unit test>>**, its color is different from that of the ordinary classes in the diagram, and it is attached to the **SalesItem** class (it will be moved with this class if **SalesItem** is moved in the diagram).

You will note that Figure 9.2 also shows some additional controls in the main window, below the *Compile* button. These allow you to use the built-in regression testing tools. If you have not used JUnit in BlueJ before, the testing tools are switched off, and the buttons will not yet be visible on your system. You should switch on these testing tools now. To do this, open the *Interface* tab in your *Preferences* dialog, and ensure that the *Show unit testing tools* option is selected.

A further difference is apparent in the menu that appears when we right-click the test class (Figure 9.3). There are three new sections in the menu instead of a list of constructors.

Using test classes, we can automate regression testing. The test class contains code to perform a number of prepared tests and check their results. This makes repeating the same tests much easier.

A test class is usually associated with an ordinary project class. In this case, **SalesItemTest** is associated with the **SalesItem** class, and we say that **SalesItem** is the *reference class* for **SalesItemTest**.

In our project, the test class has already been created, and it already contains some tests. We can now execute these tests by clicking the *Run Tests* button.

Figure 9.3

The pop-up menu for a test class

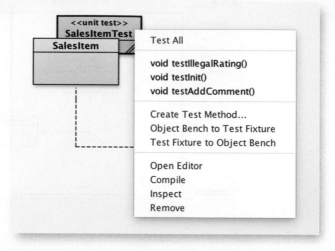

Exercise 9.12 Run the tests in your project, using the *Run Tests* button. You should see a window similar to Figure 9.4, summarizing the results of the tests.

Figure 9.4 shows the result of running three tests named **testAddComment**, **testInit**, and **testIllegalRating**, which are defined in the test class. The ticks immediately to the left of the test names indicate that the tests succeeded. You can achieve the same result by selecting the *Test All* option from the pop-up menu associated with the test class, or running the tests individually by selecting them from the same menu.

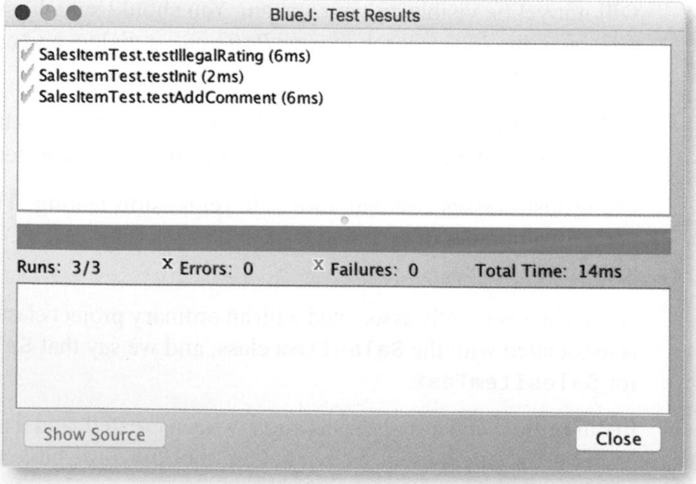

Figure 9.4

The Test Results window

Test classes are clearly different in some way from ordinary classes, and if you open the source code of **SalesItemTest**, you will notice that it has some new features. At this stage of the book, we are not going to discuss in detail how test classes work internally, but it is worth noting that although the source code of **SalesItemTest** could have been written by a person, it was, in fact, *automatically generated* by BlueJ. Some of the comments were then added afterwards to document the purpose of the tests.

Each test class typically contains tests for the functionality of its reference class. It is created by using the right mouse button over a potential reference class and selecting *Create Test Class* from the pop-up menu. Note that **SalesItem** already has a test class, so this additional menu item does not appear in its class menu, but the one for **Comment** does have this option, as it currently has no associated test class.

The test class contains source code both to run tests on a reference class and to check whether the tests were successful or not. For instance, here is one of the statements from **testInit** that checks that the price of the item is 1000 at that point:

```
assertEquals(1000, salesIte1.getPrice());
```

When such tests are run, BlueJ is able to display the results in the window shown in Figure 9.4.

In the next section, we shall discuss how BlueJ supports creation of tests so that you can create your own automated tests.

> **Exercise 9.13** Create a test class for the **Comment** class in the *online-shop-junit* project.
>
> **Exercise 9.14** What methods are created automatically when a new test class is created?

9.4.3 Recording a test

As we discussed at the beginning of Section 9.4, test automation is desirable because manually running and re-running tests is a time-consuming process. BlueJ makes it possible to combine the effectiveness of manual unit testing with the power of test automation, by enabling us to record manual tests, then replay them later for the purposes of regression testing. The **SalesItemTest** class was created via this process.

Suppose that we wanted to thoroughly test the **addComment** method of the **SalesItem** class. This method, as we have seen, adds customer comments if they are valid. There are several tests we would like to make, such as:

- adding a first comment to an empty comment list (positive)

- adding further comments when other comments already exist (positive)

- attempting to add a comment with an author who has already submitted a comment (negative)

- attempting to add a comment with an invalid rating (negative)

The first of these already exists in the **SalesItemTest** class. We will now describe how to create the next one using the *online-shop-junit* project.

A test is recorded by telling BlueJ to start recording, performing the test manually, and then signaling the end of the test. The first step is done via the menu attached to a test class. This tells BlueJ which class you wish the new test to be stored in. Select *Create Test Method . . .* from the **SalesItemTest** class's pop-up menu. You will be prompted for a name for the test method. By convention, we start the name with the prefix "test." For example, to create a method that tests adding two comments, we might call that method **testTwoComments**.[1]

Once you have entered a name and clicked *OK,* a red recording indicator appears to the left of the class diagram, and the *End* and *Cancel* buttons become available. *End* is used to indicate the end of the test-creation process and *Cancel* to abandon it.

Once recording is started, we just carry out the actions that we would with a normal manual test:

- Create a **SalesItem** object.

- Add a comment to the sales item.

Once **addComment** has been called, a new dialog window will appear (Figure 9.5). This is an extended version of the normal method result window, and it is a crucial part of the automated testing process. Its purpose is to allow you to specify what the result of the method call *should be.* This is called an *assertion.*

Figure 9.5
The Method Result dialog with assertion facility

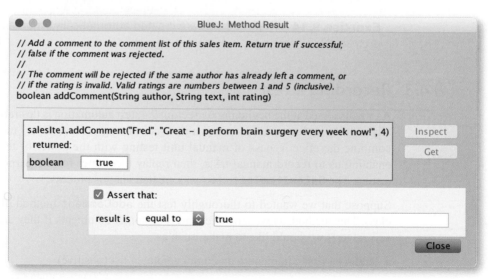

In this case, we expect the method return value to be *true*, and we want to include a check in our test to make sure that this is really the case. We can now make sure that the *Assert that* checkbox is checked, enter *true* in the dialog, and select the *Close* button.

- Add a second comment to your sales item. Make sure the comments are valid (they have unique authors and the rating is valid). Assert that the result is true for the second comment addition as well.

- We now expect two comments to exist. To test that this is indeed the case, call the **getNumberOfComments** method and assert that the result is 2.

This is the final stage of the test. We then press the *End* button to stop the recording. At that point, BlueJ adds source code to the **SalesItemTest** class for our new method, **testTwoComments**, then compiles the class and clears the object bench. The resulting generated method is shown in Code 9.2.

Code 9.2

An automatically generated test method

```
@Test
public void testTwoComments()
{
    SalesItem salesIte1 = new SalesItem("Java book", 12345);
    assertEquals(true, salesIte1.addComment("James Duckling",
                                            "Great book!", 4));
    assertEquals(true, salesIte1.addComment("Fred", "Like it", 3));
    assertEquals(2, salesIte1.getNumberOfComments());
}
```

As can be seen, the method contains statements that reproduce the actions made when recording it: a **SalesItem** object is created, and the **addComment** and **getNumberOf-Comments** methods are called. The call to **assertEquals** checks that the result returned by these methods matches the expected value. You can also see a new construct, **@Test**, before the method. This is an *annotation* that identifies this method as a test method.

The exercises below are provided so that you can try this process for yourself. They include an example to show what happens if the actual value does not match the expected value.

Exercise 9.15 Create a test to check that **addComment** returns **false** when a comment from the same author already exists.

Exercise 9.16 Create a test that performs negative testing on the boundaries of the rating range. That is, test the values 0 and 6 as a rating (the values just outside the legal range). We expect these to return **false**, so assert **false** in the result dialog. You will notice that one of these actually (incorrectly) returns **true**. This is the bug we uncovered earlier in manual testing. Make sure that you assert **false** anyway. The assertion states the *expected* result, not the *actual* result.

Exercise 9.17 Run all tests again. Explore how the *Test Result* dialog displays the failed test. Select the failed test in the list. What options do you have available to explore the details of the failed test?

Exercise 9.18 Create a test class that has **Comment** as its reference class. Create a test that checks whether the author and rating details are stored correctly after creation. Record separate tests that check whether the **upvote** and **downvote** methods work as expected.

Exercise 9.19 Create tests for **SalesItem** that test whether the **find-MostHelpfulComment** method works as expected. Note that this method returns a **Comment** object. During your testing, you can use the *Get* button in the method result dialog to get the result object onto the object bench, which then allows you to make further method calls and add assertions for this object. This allows you to identify the comment object returned (e.g., by checking its author). You can also assert that the result is *null* or *not null*, depending on what you expect.

9.4.4 Fixtures

Concept

A **fixture** is a set of objects in a defined state that serves as a basis for unit tests.

As a set of test methods is built up, it is common to find yourself creating similar objects for each one. For instance, every test of the **SalesItem** class will involve creating at least one **SalesItem** and initializing it, often by adding one or more comments. An object or a group of objects that is used in more than one test is known as a *fixture*. Two menu items associated with a test class enable us to work with fixtures in BlueJ: *Object Bench to Test Fixture* and *Test Fixture to Object Bench*. In your project, create two **SalesItem** objects on the object bench. Leave one without any comments, and add two comments to the other. Now select *Object Bench to Test Fixture* from **SalesItemTest**. The objects will disappear from the object bench, and if you examine the source code of **SalesItemTest**, you will see that its **setUp** method looks something like Code 9.3, where **salesItem1** and **salesItem2** have been defined as fields.

Code 9.3

Creating a fixture

```
/**
 * Sets up the test fixture.
 *
 * Called before every test case method.
 */
@Before
public void setUp()
{
    salesItem1 = new SalesItem("Java book", 12345);
    salesItem2 = new SalesItem("Harry Potter", 1250);
    salesItem2.addComment("Fred", "Best book ever", 5);
}
```

The significance of the `setUp` method is that it is automatically called immediately before every test method is called. (The `@Before` annotation above the method header ensures this.) This means that the individual test methods no longer need to create their own versions of the fixture objects.

Once we have a fixture associated with a test class, recording tests becomes significantly simpler. Whenever we create a new test method, the objects from the fixture will automatically appear on the object bench—there is no longer a need to create new test objects manually each time.

Should we wish to add further objects to the fixture at any time, one of the easiest ways is to select *Test Fixture to Object Bench*, add further objects to the object bench in the usual way, then select *Object Bench to Test Fixture*. We could also edit the `setUp` method in the editor and add further fields directly to the test class.

Test automation is a powerful concept because it makes it more likely that tests will be written in the first place, and more likely that they will be run and rerun as a program develops. You should try to get into the habit of starting to write unit tests early in the development of a project, and of keeping them up to date as the project progresses. In Chapter 14, we shall return to the subject of assertions in the context of error handling.

Exercise 9.20 Add further automated tests to your project until you reach a point where you are reasonably confident of the correct operation of the classes. Use both positive and negative tests. If you discover any errors, be sure to record tests that guard against recurrence of these errors in later versions.

In Section 9.6, we look at debugging—the activity that starts when we have noticed the existence of an error and we need to find and fix it.

9.5 Refactoring to use streams (advanced)

In previous advanced sections of this book, we have introduced streams as an alternative to loops when processing collections. The *online-shop* project provides an opportunity for another exercise in rewriting traditional loops using streams. If you have worked through the previous advanced exercises, you may also like to do this one.

Exercise 9.21 Rewrite all loops in the `SalesItem` class using streams. When you are finished, this class should not contain any explicit loop anymore. Once you are finished, rerun your tests to convince yourself that your rewriting of the code has not broken any of the intended functionality.

9.6 Debugging

Testing is important, and testing well helps uncover the existence of errors. However, testing alone is not enough. After detecting the existence of an error, we also have to find its cause and fix it. That's where debugging comes in.

To discuss various approaches to debugging, we use a hypothetical scenario. Imagine that you have been asked to join an existing project team that is working on an implementation of a software calculator (Figure 9.6). You have been drafted in because a key member of the programming team, Hacker T. Largebrain, has just been promoted to a management position on another project. Before leaving, Hacker assured the team you are joining that his implementation of the part of the calculator he was responsible for was finished and fully tested. He had even written some test software to verify that this was the case. You have been asked to take over the class and ensure that it is properly commented prior to integration with the classes being written by other members of the team.

The software for the calculator has been carefully designed to separate the user interface from the calculator logic, so that the calculator might be used in different contexts later on. The first version, which we are looking at here, will run with a graphical user interface, as shown in Figure 9.6. However, in later extensions to the project, it is intended that the same calculator implementation should be able to run in a web browser or on a mobile device. In preparation for this, the application has been split into separate classes, most importantly **UserInterface**, to implement the graphical user interface, and **CalcEngine**, to implement the calculation logic. It is the latter class for which Hacker was responsible. This class should remain unchanged when the calculator runs with a different user interface.

To investigate how the **CalcEngine** class is used by other classes, it is useful to look at its *interface*. Confusingly, we are now not talking about the *user interface*, but about the *class interface*. This double meaning of the term *interface* is unfortunate, but it is important to understand both meanings.

Figure 9.6

The user interface of a software calculator

The class interface is the summary of the public-method headers that other classes can use. It is what other classes can see and how they can interact with our class. The interface is shown in the **javadoc** documentation of a class and in the *Documentation* view in the editor. Code 9.4 shows the interface of the **CalcEngine** class.

Code 9.4

The interface of
the arithmetic
logic unit

```
/**
 * @return The value currently displayed on the calculator.
 */
public int getDisplayValue();
```

```
/**
 * A number button was pressed.
 * @param number The single digit.
 */
public void numberPressed(int number);
```

```
/**
 * The '+' button was pressed.
 */
public void plus();
```

```
/**
 * The '-' button was pressed.
 */
public void minus();
```

```
/**
 * The '=' button was pressed.
 */
public void equals();
```

```
/**
 * The 'C' (clear) button was pressed.
 */
public void clear();
```

Such an interface can be written before the full classes are implemented. It represents a simple form of contract between the **CalcEngine** class and other parts of the program that wish to use it. The **CalcEngine** class provides the implementation of this interface. The interface describes a minimum set of methods that will be implemented in the logic component, and for each method the return type and parameters are fully defined. Note that the interface gives no details of exactly what its implementing class will do internally when notified that a plus operator has been pressed; that is left to its implementers. In addition, the implementing class might well have additional methods not listed here.

In the sections that follow, we shall look at Hacker's attempt to implement this interface. In this case, we decide that the best way to understand Hacker's software prior to documenting it is to explore its source and the behavior of its objects.

Commenting and style

Open the *calculator-engine* project to view the classes. This is Hacker's own version of the project, containing only the calculator engine and a test class, but not the user interface class. The **CalcEngineTester** class takes the place of the user interface at this stage of development. This illustrates another positive feature of defining interfaces between classes: it becomes easier to develop mock-ups of the other classes for the purpose of testing.

If you take a look at the **CalcEngine** class, you will find that its author has paid attention to some important areas of good style:

■ The class has been given a multiline comment at the top, indicating the purpose of the class. Also included are annotations indicating author and version number.

■ Each method of the interface has a comment indicating its purpose, parameters, and return type. This will certainly make it easier to generate project documentation for the interface, as discussed in Chapter 6.

■ The layout of the class is consistent, with appropriate amounts of white-space indentation used to indicate the distinct levels of nested blocks and control structures.

■ Expressive variable names and method names have been chosen.

Although these conventions may seem time-consuming during implementation, they can be of enormous benefit in helping someone else to understand your code (as we have to in this scenario), or in helping you to remember what a class does if you have taken a break from working on it.

We also note another detail that looks less promising: Hacker has not used a specialized unit test class to capture his tests, but has written his own test class. As we know about unit test support in BlueJ, we wonder why.

This does not necessarily have to be bad. Handwritten test classes may be just as good, but it makes us a little suspicious. Did Hacker really know what he was doing? We shall come back to this point a bit later.

So, maybe Hacker's abilities are as great as he thinks they are, and in that case you will not have much to do to make the class ready for integration with the others! Try the following exercises to see if this is the case.

Exercise 9.22 Make sure the classes in the project are compiled, and then create a **CalcEngineTester** object within BlueJ. Call the **testAll** method. What is printed in the terminal window? Do you believe the final line of what it says?

Exercise 9.23 Using the object you created in the previous exercise, call the **testPlus** method. What result does it give? Is that the same result as was printed by the call to **testAll**? Call **testPlus** one more time. What result does it give now? Should it always give the same answer? If so, what should that answer be? Take a look at the source of the **testPlus** method to check.

Exercise 9.24 Repeat the previous exercise with the `testMinus` method. Does it always give the same result?

The experiments above should have alerted you to the fact that not all seems to be right with the `CalcEngine` class. It looks like it contains some errors. But what are they, and how can we find them? In the sections that follow, we shall consider a number of different ways in which we can try to locate where errors are occurring in a class.

9.8 Manual walkthroughs

Manual walkthroughs are a relatively underused technique, perhaps because they are a particularly "low-tech" debugging and testing technique. However, do not let this fool you into thinking that they are not useful. A manual walkthrough involves printing copies of the classes you are trying to understand or debug, then getting away from your computer! It is all too easy to spend a lot of time sitting in front of a computer screen not making much progress in trying to deal with a programming problem. Relocating and refocusing your efforts can often free your mind to attack a problem from a completely different direction. We have often found that going off to lunch or cycling home from the office brings enlightenment that has otherwise eluded us through hours of slogging away at the keyboard.

> **Concept**
>
> A **walk-through** is an activity of working through a segment of code line by line while observing changes of state and other behavior of the application.

A walkthrough involves both reading classes and tracing the flow of control between classes and objects. This helps us understand both how objects interact with one another and how they behave internally. In effect, a walkthrough is a pencil-and-paper simulation of what happens inside the computer when you run a program. In practice, it is best to focus on a narrow portion of an application, such as a single logical grouping of actions or even a single method call.

9.8.1 A high-level walkthrough

We shall illustrate the walkthrough technique with the *calculator-engine* project. You might find it useful to print out copies of the `CalcEngine` and `CalcEngineTester` classes in order to follow through the steps of this technique.

We shall start by examining the `testPlus` method of the `CalcEngineTester` class, as it contains a single logical grouping of actions that should help us gain an understanding of how several methods of the `CalcEngine` class work together to fulfill the computation role of a calculator. As we work our way through it, we shall often make penciled notes of questions that arise in our minds.

1. For this first stage, we do not want to delve into too much detail. We simply want to look at how the `testPlus` method uses an engine object, without exploring the internal details of the engine. From earlier experimentation, it would appear that there are some errors to be found, but we do not know whether the errors are in the tester or the engine. So the first step is to check that the tester appears to be using the engine appropriately.

2. We note that the first statement of **testPlus** assumes that the **engine** field already refers to a valid object:

   ```
   engine.clear();
   ```

   We can verify that this is the case by checking the tester's constructor. It is a common error for an object's fields not to have been initialized properly, either in their declarations or in a constructor. If we attempt to use a field with no associated object, then a **NullPointerException** is a likely runtime error.

3. The first statement's call to **clear** appears to be an attempt to put the calculator engine into a valid starting state, ready to receive instructions to perform a calculation. This looks like a reasonable thing to do, equivalent to pressing a "reset" or "clear" key on a real calculator. At this stage, we do not look at the engine class to check exactly what the **clear** method does. That can wait until we have achieved a level of confidence that the tester's actions are reasonable. Instead, we simply make a penciled note to check that **clear** puts the engine into a valid starting state as expected.

4. The next statement in **testPlus** is the entry of a digit via the **numberPressed** method:

   ```
   engine.numberPressed(3);
   ```

   This is reasonable, as the first step in making a calculation is to enter the first operand. Once again, we do not look to see what the engine does with the number. We simply assume that it stores it somewhere for later use in the calculation.

5. The next statement calls **plus**, so we now know that the full value of the left operand is 3. We make a penciled note of this fact on the printout, or make a tick against this assertion in one of the comments of **testPlus**. Similarly, we should note or confirm that the operation being executed is addition. This seems like a trivial thing to do, but it is very easy for a class's comments to get out of step with the code they are supposed to document. So checking the comments at the same time as we read the code can help us avoid being misled by them later.

6. Next, another single digit is entered as the right operand by a further call to **numberPressed**.

7. Completion of the addition is requested by a call to the **equals** method. We make a penciled note that, from the way it has been used in **testPlus**, the **equals** method appears not to return the expected result of the calculation. This is something else that we can check when we look at **CalcEngine**.

8. The final statement of **testPlus** obtains the value that should appear in the calculator's display:

   ```
   return engine.getDisplayValue();
   ```

   Presumably, this is the result of the addition, but we cannot know that for sure without looking in detail at **CalcEngine**. Once again, we make a note to check that this is indeed the case.

With our examination of **testPlus** completed, we have gained a reasonable degree of confidence that it uses the engine appropriately: that is, simulating a recognizable sequence of key presses to complete a simple calculation. We might remark that the method is not particularly ambitious—both operands are single-digit numbers, and only a single operator is used. However, that is not unusual in test methods, because it is important to test for the most basic functionality before testing more complex combinations. Nevertheless, some more complex tests should be added to the tester at some stage.

> **Exercise 9.25** Perform a similar walkthrough of your own with the **test-Minus** method. Does that raise any further questions in your mind about things you might like to check when looking at **CalcEngine** in detail?

Before looking at the **CalcEngine** class, it is worth walking through the **testAll** method to see how it uses the **testPlus** and **testMinus** methods we have been looking at. From this, we observe the following:

1 The **testAll** method is a straight-line sequence of print statements.

2 It contains one call to each of **testPlus** and **testMinus**, and the values they return are printed out for the user to see. We might note that there is nothing to tell the user what the results should be. This makes it hard for the user to confirm that the results are correct.

3 The final statement boldly states:

    `All tests passed.`

but the method contains no tests to establish the truth of this assertion! There should be a proper means of establishing both what the result values should be, and whether they have been calculated correctly or not. This is something we should remedy as soon as we have the chance to get back to the source of this class.

At this stage, we should not be distracted by the final point into making changes that do not directly address the errors we are looking for. If we make those sorts of changes, we could easily end up masking the errors. One of the crucial requirements for successful debugging is to be able to trigger the error you are looking for easily and reproducibly. When that is the case, it is much easier to assess the effect of an attempted correction.

Having checked over the test class, we are in a position to examine the source of the **CalcEngine** class. We can do so armed with a reasonable sequence of method calls to explore from the walkthrough of the **testPlus** method, as well as with a set of questions thrown up by it.

9.8.2 Checking state with a walkthrough

A `CalcEngine` object is quite different in style from its tester. This is because the engine is a completely passive object. It initiates no activity of its own, but simply responds to external method calls. This is typical of the server style of behavior. Server objects often rely heavily on their state to determine how they should respond to method calls. This is particularly true of the calculator engine. So an important part of conducting the walkthrough is to be sure that we always have an accurate representation of its state. One way to do this on paper is by making up a table of an object's fields and their values (Figure 9.7). A new line can be entered to keep a running log of the values following each method call.

This technique makes it quite easy to check back if something appears to go wrong. It is also possible to compare the states after two calls to the same method.

1   As we start the walkthrough of `CalcEngine`, we document the initial state of the engine, as in the first row of values in Figure 9.7. All of its fields are initialized in the constructor. As we observed when walking through the tester, object initialization is important, and we make a note here to check that the default initialization is sufficient—particularly as the default value of `previousOperator` would appear not to represent a meaningful operator. Furthermore, this makes us think about whether it really is meaningful to have a *previous* operator before the first real operator in a calculation. In noting these questions, we do not necessarily have to try to discover the answers right away, but they provide prompts as we discover more about the class.

2   The next step is to see how a call to `clear` changes the engine's state. As shown in the second data row of Figure 9.7, the state remains unchanged at this point because `displayValue` is already set to 0. But we note another question here: Why is the value of only one of the fields set by this method? If this method is supposed to implement a form of reset, why not clear all of the fields?

3   Next, a call to **numberPressed** with an actual parameter of 3 is investigated. The method multiplies an existing value of `displayValue` by 10 and then adds in the new digit. This correctly models the effect of appending a new digit onto the right-hand end of an existing number. It relies on `displayValue` having a sensible initial value of 0 when the first digit of a new number is entered, and our investigation of the `clear` method gives us confidence that this will be the case. So this method looks all right.

4   Continuing to follow the order of calls in the **testPlus** method, we next look at **plus**. Its first statement calls the **applyPreviousOperator** method. Here we have to decide whether to continue ignoring nested method calls or whether to break off and see what it does. Taking a quick look at the **applyPreviousOperator** method, we can see that

Figure 9.7

Informal tabulation of an object's state

Method called	displayValue	leftOperand	previousOperator
initial state	0	0	' '
clear	0	0	' '
numberPressed(3)	3	0	' '

it is fairly short. Furthermore, it is clearly going to alter the state of the engine, and we shall not be able to continue documenting the state changes unless we follow it up. So we would certainly decide to follow the nested call. It is important to remember where we came from, so we mark the listing just inside the `plus` method before following through the `applyPreviousOperator` method. If following a nested method call is likely to lead to further nested calls, we need to use something more than a simple mark to help us find our way back to the caller. In that case, it is better to mark the call points with ascending numerical values, reusing previous values as calls return.

5 The `applyPreviousOperator` method gives us some insights into how the `previousOperator` field is used. It also appears to answer one of our earlier questions: whether having a space as the initial value for the previous operator was satisfactory. The method explicitly checks to see whether `previousOperator` contains either a + or a − before applying it. So another value will not result in an incorrect operation being applied. By the end of this method, the value of `leftOperand` will have been changed, so we note its new value in the state table.

6 Returning to the `plus` method, the remaining two fields have their values set, so the next row of the state table contains the following values:

> plus   0   3   '+'

The walkthrough of the engine can be continued in a similar fashion, by documenting the state changes, gaining insights into its behavior, and raising questions along the way. The following exercises should help you complete the walkthrough.

Exercise 9.26 Complete the state table based on the following subsequent calls found in the `testPlus` method:

```
numberPressed(4);
equals();
getDisplayValue();
```

Exercise 9.27 When walking through the `equals` method, did you feel the same reassurances that we felt in `applyPreviousOperator` about the default value of `previousOperator`?

Exercise 9.28 Walkthrough a call to `clear` immediately following the call to `getDisplayValue` at the end of your state table, and record the new state. Is the engine in the same state as it was at the previous call to `clear`? If not, what impact do you think this could have on any subsequent calculations?

Exercise 9.29 In the light of your walkthrough, what changes do you think should be made to the `CalcEngine` class? Make those changes to a paper version of the class, and then try the walkthrough all over again. You should not need to walk through the `CalcEngineTester` class, just repeat the actions of its `testAll` method.

Exercise 9.30 Try a walkthrough of the following sequence of calls on your corrected version of the engine:

```
clear();
numberPressed(9);
plus();
numberPressed(1);
minus();
numberPressed(4);
equals();
```

What should the result be? Does the engine appear to behave correctly and leave the correct answer in **displayValue**?

9.8.3 Verbal walkthroughs

Another way in which the walkthrough technique can be used to find errors in a program is to try explaining to another person what a class or method does. This works in two completely different ways:

■ The person you explain the code to might spot the error for you.

■ You will often find that the simple act of trying to put into words what a piece of code should do is enough to trigger in your own mind an understanding of why it does not.

This latter effect is so common that it can often be worth explaining a piece of code to someone who is completely unfamiliar with it—not in anticipation that *they* will find the error, but that *you* will!

9.9 Print statements

Probably the most common technique used to understand and debug programs—even amongst experienced programmers—is to annotate methods temporarily with print statements. Print statements are popular because they exist in most languages, they are available to everyone, and they are very easy to add with any editor. No additional software or language features are required to make use of them. As a program runs, these additional print statements will typically provide a user with information such as:

■ which methods have been called

■ the values of parameters

■ the order in which methods have been called

■ the values of local variables and fields at strategic points

Code 9.5 shows an example of how the **numberPressed** method might look with print statements added. Such information is particularly helpful in providing a picture of the way in which the state of an object changes as mutators are called. To help support this, it is often worth including a debugging method that prints out the current values of all the fields of an object. Code 9.6 shows such a **reportState** method for the **CalcEngine** class.

Code 9.5

A method with debugging print statements added

```
/**
 * A number button was pressed.
 * @param number The single digit.
 */
public void numberPressed(int number)
{
    System.out.println("numberPressed called with: " + number);

    displayValue = displayValue * 10 + number;

    System.out.println("displayValue is: " + displayValue +
                        "at end of numberPressed");
}
```

Code 9.6

A state-reporting method

```
/**
 * Print the values of this object's fields.
 * @param where Where this state occurs.
 */
public void reportState(String where)
{
    System.out.println("displayValue: " + displayValue +
                        " leftOperand: " + leftOperand +
                        " previousOperator: " + previousOperator +
                        " at " + where);
}
```

If each method of **CalcEngine** contained a print statement at its entry point and a call to **reportState** at its end, Figure 9.8 shows the output that might result from a call to the tester's **testPlus** method. (This was generated from a version of the calculator engine that can be found in the *calculator-engine-print* project.) Such output allows us to build up a picture of how control flows between different methods. For instance, we can see from the order in which the state values are reported that a call to **plus** contains a nested call to **applyPreviousOperator**.

Print statements can be very effective in helping us understand programs or locate errors, but there are a number of disadvantages:

- It is not usually practical to add print statements to every method in a class. So they are only fully effective if the right methods have been annotated.

- Adding too many print statements can lead to information overload. A large amount of output can make it difficult to identify what you need to see. Print statements inside loops are a particular source of this problem.

- Once their purpose has been served, it can be tedious to remove them.

- There is also the chance that, having removed them, they will be needed again later. It can be very frustrating to have to put them back in again!

Figure 9.8
Debugging output from a call to **testPlus**

```
clear called
displayValue: 0 leftOperand: 0 previousOperator: at end of clear
numberPressed called with: 3
displayValue: 3 leftOperand: 0 previousOperator: at end of number...
plus called
applyPreviousOperator called
displayValue: 3 leftOperand: 3 previousOperator: at end of apply...
displayValue: 0 leftOperand: 3 previousOperator: + at end of plus
numberPressed called with: 4
displayValue: 4 leftOperand: 3 previousOperator: + at end of number...
equals called
displayValue: 7 leftOperand: 0 previousOperator: + at end of equals
```

Exercise 9.31 Open the *calculator-engine-print* project and complete the addition of print statements to each method and the constructor.

Exercise 9.32 Create a **CalcEngineTester** in the project and run the **testAll** method. Does the output that results help you identify where the problem lies?

Exercise 9.33 Do you feel that the amount of output produced by the fully annotated **CalcEngine** class is too little, too much, or about right? If you feel that it is too little or too much, either add further print statements or remove some until you feel that you have the right level of detail.

Exercise 9.34 What are the respective advantages and disadvantages of using manual walkthroughs or print statements for debugging? Discuss.

9.9.1 Turning debugging information on or off

If a class is still under development when print statements are added, we often do not want to see the output every time the class is used. It is best if we can find a way to turn the printing on or off as required. The most common way to achieve this is to add an extra **boolean** debugging field to the class, then make printing dependent upon the value of the field. Code 9.7 illustrates this idea.

Code 9.7
Controlling whether debugging information is printed or not

```
/**
 * A number button was pressed.
 * @param number The single digit.
 */
public void numberPressed(int number)
{
    if(debugging) {
        System.out.println("numberPressed called with: " + number);
    }
```

**Code 9.7
continued**
Controlling
whether debug-
ging information is
printed or not

```
        displayValue = displayValue * 10 + number;

        if(debugging) {
            reportState();
        }
    }
}
```

A more economical variation on this theme is to replace the direct calls to print statements with calls to a specialized printing method added to the class.[2] The printing method would print only if the **debugging** field is **true**. Therefore, calls to the printing method would not need to be guarded by an if statement. Code 9.8 illustrates this approach. Note that this version assumes that **reportState** either tests the **debugging** field itself or calls the new **printDebugging** method.

Code 9.8
A method for
selectively print-
ing debugging
information

```
/**
 * A number button was pressed.
 * @param number The single digit.
 */
public void numberPressed(int number)
{
    printDebugging("numberPressed called with: " + number);

    displayValue = displayValue * 10 + number;
    reportState();
}
```

```
/**
 * Only print the debugging information if debugging is true.
 * @param info The debugging information.
 */
public void printDebugging(String info)
{
    if(debugging) {
        System.out.println(info);
    }
}
```

As you can see from these experiments, it takes some practice to find the best level of detail to print out to be useful. In practice, print statements are often added to one or a small number of methods at a time, when we have a rough idea in what area of our program an error might be hiding.

---

[2] In fact, we could move this method to a specialized debugging class, but we shall keep things simple in this discussion.

9.10 Debuggers

In Chapter 3, we introduced the use of a debugger to understand how an existing application operates and how its objects interact. In a very similar manner, we can use the debugger to track down errors.

The debugger is essentially a software tool that provides support for performing a walk-through on a segment of code. We typically set a breakpoint at the statement where we want to start our walkthrough and then use the *Step* or *Step Into* functions to do the actual walking.

One advantage is that the debugger automatically takes care of keeping track of every object's state, and, thus, doing this is quicker and less error prone than doing the same manually. A disadvantage is that debuggers typically do not keep a permanent record of state changes, so it is harder to go back and check the state as it was a few statements earlier.

A debugger typically also gives you information about the *call sequence* (or *stack*) at each point in time. The call sequence shows the name of the method containing the current state-ment, the name of the method that the current method was called from, and the name of the method that *that* method was called from, and so on. Thus, the call sequence contains a record of all currently active, unfinished methods—similar to what we have done manually during our walkthrough by writing marks next to method-call statements.

In BlueJ, the call sequence is displayed on the left-hand side of the debugger window (Figure 9.9). Every method name in that sequence can be selected to inspect the current values of that method's local variables.

Figure 9.9

The BlueJ debugger window, with execu-tion stopped at a breakpoint

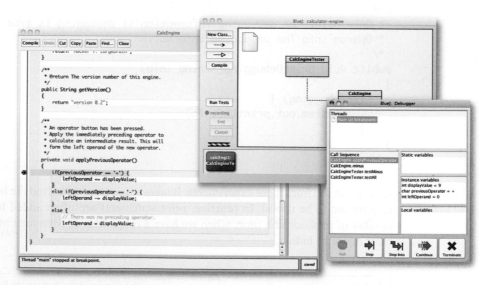

Exercise 9.35 Using the *calculator-engine* project, set a breakpoint in the first line of the **testPlus** method in the **CalcEngineTester** class. Execute this method. When the debugger appears, walk through the code step by step. Experiment with both the *Step* and *Step Into* buttons.

Exercise 9.36 *Challenge exercise* In practice, you will probably find that Hacker T. Largebrain's attempt to program the **CalcEngine** class is too full of errors to be worth trying to fix. Instead, write your own version of the class from scratch. The *calculator-gui* project contains classes that provide the GUI shown in Figure 9.6. You can use this project as the basis for your own implementation of the **CalcEngine** class. Be sure to document your class thoroughly and to create a thorough set of tests for your implementation so that your experience with Hacker's code will not have to be repeated by your successor! Make sure to use a dedicated unit test class for your testing, instead of writing tests into a standard class; as you have seen, this makes asserting the correct results much easier.

9.11 Debugging streams (advanced)

All of the debugging techniques we have described in this chapter apply equally well when writing code that uses streams. The only nuance is the complexity of a typical statement that involves the use of streams. It would not be uncommon for a single statement to contain three or more operations as part of a pipeline, and the ordering and logical flow between those operations will be critical to the correct outcome of the statement. So, it will often be useful to inspect the state of the stream at intermediate points of the pipeline.

The **peek** method is a stream operation that provides the equivalent of using print statements, as a way to examine the state of a pipeline at various points. It is an intermediate operation that can be inserted at any point within a pipeline. It takes a consumer lambda expression as a parameter, but also passes the elements of its input stream unmodified through to its output stream.

For instance, suppose that you are reviewing some reasonably complex code—written by somebody else—in the *animal-monitoring* project. The code is meant to create a list of sightings specific to a particular animal, area, and spotter. They might have written this in a single statement as follows:

```
List<Sighting> result =
    sightings.stream()
            .filter(record -> animal == record.getAnimal() &&
                              area == record.getArea() &&
                              spotter == record.getSpotter())
            .collect(Collectors.toList());
```

Imagine that the list produced by this code is always empty, even though you are using test data with sighting records that should definitely match. Clearly there must be something wrong with the **filter** operation, but you cannot immediately spot the problem. One of the easiest ways to get to the bottom of this would be to split the single filter operation into three separate filters, and to print out fields of the remaining elements after each filtration step. The following version does this:

```
List<Sighting> result =
    sightings.stream()
            .filter(record -> animal == record.getAnimal())
            .peek(r -> System.out.println(r.getAnimal())
            .filter(record -> area == record.getArea()
            .peek(r -> System.out.println(r.getArea())
            .filter(record -> spotter == record.getSpotter())
            .peek(r -> System.out.println(r.getDetails())
            .collect(Collectors.toList());
```

From this version you would be quite likely to find that the first filter operation is not passing on any records to the next, because the test for string equality has not been made using the **equals** method. Once that has been corrected, the tests could be rerun and eventually the **peek** operations removed.

A **peek** operation can also be a convenient way to create a position in the middle of a pipeline sequence for setting a breakpoint for a debugger. In this case, you would be more likely to be interested in the states of the objects rather than having something printed, so a consumer lambda that does nothing would be used as the parameter to **peek**, for instance:

```
peek(r -> { })
```

9.12 Choosing a debugging strategy

We have seen that several different debugging and testing strategies exist: written and verbal walkthroughs, use of print statements (either temporary or permanent, with enabling switches), interactive testing using the object bench, writing your own test class, and using a dedicated unit test class.

In practice, we would use different strategies at different times. Walkthroughs, print statements, and interactive testing are useful techniques for initial testing of newly written code, to investigate how a program segment works, or for debugging. Their advantage is that they are quick and easy to use, they work in any programming language, and they are (except for the interactive testing) independent of the environment. Their main disadvantage is that the activities are not easily repeatable. This is okay for debugging, but for testing we need something better: we need a mechanism that allows easy repetition for regression testing. Using unit test classes has the advantage that—once they have been set up—tests can be replayed any number of times.

So Hacker's way of testing—writing his own test class—was one step in the right direction, but was, flawed. We know now that his problem was that although his class contained reasonable method calls for testing, it did not include any assertions on the method results, and thus did not detect test failure. Using a dedicated unit test class can solve these problems.

Exercise 9.37 Open your project again and add better testing by replacing Hacker's test class with a unit test class attached to the **CalcEngine**. Add similar tests to those Hacker used (and any others you find useful), and include correct assertions.

9.13 Putting the techniques into practice

This chapter has described several techniques that can be used either to understand a new program or to test for errors in a program. The *bricks* project provides a chance for you to try out those techniques with a new scenario. The project contains part of an application for a company producing bricks. Bricks are delivered to customers on pallets (stacks of bricks). The **Pallet** class provides methods telling the height and weight of an individual pallet, according to the number of bricks on it.

Exercise 9.38 Open the *bricks* project. Test it. There are at least four errors in this project. See if you can find them and fix them. What techniques did you use to find the errors? Which technique was most useful?

9.14 Summary

When writing software, we should anticipate that it will contain logical errors. Therefore, it is essential to consider both testing and debugging to be normal activities within the overall development process. BlueJ is particularly good at supporting interactive unit testing of both methods and classes. We have also looked at some basic techniques for automating the testing process and performing simple debugging.

Writing good JUnit tests for our classes ensures that errors are detected early, and they give a good indication which part of the system an error originates in, making the resulting debugging task much easier.

Terms introduced in this chapter:

syntax error, logical error, testing, debugging, unit testing, JUnit, positive testing, negative testing, regression testing, manual walkthrough, call sequence

Concept summary

- **testing** Testing is the activity of finding out whether a piece of code (a method, class, or program) produces the intended behavior.

- **debugging** Debugging is the attempt to pinpoint and fix the source of an error.

- **unit testing** refers to tests of the individual parts of an application, such as methods and classes.

- **positive testing** Positive testing is the testing of cases that are expected to succeed.

- **negative testing** Negative testing is the testing of cases that are expected to fail.

- **test automation** simplifies the process of regression testing.

- **assertion** An assertion is an expression that states a condition that we expect to be true. If the condition is false, we say that the assertion fails. This indicates an error in our program.

- **fixture** A fixture is a set of objects in a defined state that serves as a basis for unit tests.

- **walkthrough** A walkthrough is an activity of working through a segment of code line by line while observing changes of state and other behavior of the application.

Part 2   Application Structures

Part 2

10

Improving Structure with Inheritance

Main concepts discussed in this chapter:

- inheritance
- subtyping

- substitution
- polymorphic variables

Java constructs discussed in this chapter:

extends, super (in constructor), cast, Object

In this chapter, we introduce some additional object-oriented constructs to improve the general structure of our applications. The main concepts we shall use to design better program structures are *inheritance* and *polymorphism*.

Both of these concepts are central to the idea of object orientation, and you will discover later how they appear in various forms in everything we discuss from now on. However, it is not only the following chapters that rely heavily on these concepts. Many of the constructs and techniques discussed in earlier chapters are influenced by aspects of inheritance and polymorphism, and we shall revisit some issues introduced earlier and gain a fuller understanding of the interconnections between different parts of the Java language.

Inheritance is a powerful construct that can be used to create solutions to a variety of different problems. As always, we will discuss the important aspects using an example. In this example, we will first introduce only some of the problems that are addressed by using inheritance structures, and discuss further uses and advantages of inheritance and polymorphism as we progress through this chapter.

The example we discuss to introduce these new structures is called *network*.

10.1   The *network* example

The *network* project implements a prototype of a small part of a social-network application. The part we are concentrating on is the *news feed*—the list of messages that should appear on screen when a user opens the network's main page.

Here, we will start small and simple, with a view to extending and growing the application later. Initially, we have only two types of posts appearing in our news feed: text posts (which we call *messages*), and photo posts consisting of a photo and a caption.

The part of the application that we are prototyping here is the engine that stores and displays these posts. The functionality that we want to provide with this prototype should include at least the following:

■ It should allow us to create text and photo posts.

■ Text posts consist of a message of arbitrary length, possibly spanning multiple lines. Photo posts consist of an image and a caption. Some additional details are stored with each post.

■ It should store this information permanently so that it can be used later.

■ It should provide a search function that allows us to find, for example, all posts by a certain user, or all photos within a given date range.

■ It should allow us to display lists of posts, such as a list of the most recent posts, or a list of all posts by a given user.

■ It should allow us to remove information.

The details we want to store for each message post are:

■ the username of the author

■ the text of the message

■ a time stamp (time of posting)

■ how many people like this post

■ a list of comments on this post by other users

The details we want to store for each photo post are:

■ the username of the author

■ the filename of the image to display

■ the caption for the photo (one line of text)

■ a time stamp (time of posting)

■ how many people like this post

■ a list of comments on this post by other users

10.1.1 The *network* project: classes and objects

To implement the application, we first have to decide what classes to use to model this problem. In this case, some of the classes are easy to identify. It is quite straightforward to decide that we should have a class **MessagePost** to represent message posts, and a class **PhotoPost** to represent photo posts.

Figure 10.1
Fields in **Message-Post** and **Photo-Post** objects

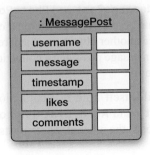
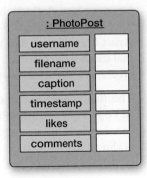

Figure 10.2
Details of the **MessagePost** and **PhotoPost** classes

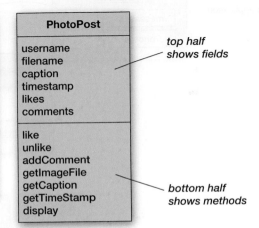

Objects of these classes should then encapsulate all the data we want to store about these objects (Figure 10.1).

Some of these data items should probably also have accessor and mutator methods (Figure 10.2).[1] For our purpose, it is not important to decide on the exact details of all the methods right now, but just to get a first impression of the design of this application. In this figure, we have defined accessor and mutator methods for those fields that may change over time ("liking" or "unliking" a post and adding a comment) and assume for now that the other fields are set in the constructor. We have also added a method called **display** that will show details of a **MessagePost** or **PhotoPost** object.

---

[1] The notation style for class diagrams that is used in this book and in BlueJ is a subset of a widely used notation called UML. Although we do not use everything from UML (by far), we attempt to use UML notation for those things that we show. The UML style defines how fields and methods are shown in a class diagram. The class is divided into three parts that show (in this order from the top) the class name, the fields, and the methods.

Once we have defined the **MessagePost** and **PhotoPost** classes, we can create as many post objects as we need—one object per message post or photo post that we want to store. Apart from this, we then need another object: an object representing the complete news feed that can hold a collection of message posts and a collection of photo posts. For this, we shall create a class called **NewsFeed**.

The **NewsFeed** object could itself hold two collection objects (for example, of types **ArrayList<MessagePost>** and **ArrayList<PhotoPost>**). One of these collections can then hold all message posts, the other all photo posts. An object diagram for this model is shown in Figure 10.3.

Figure 10.3

Objects in the *network* application

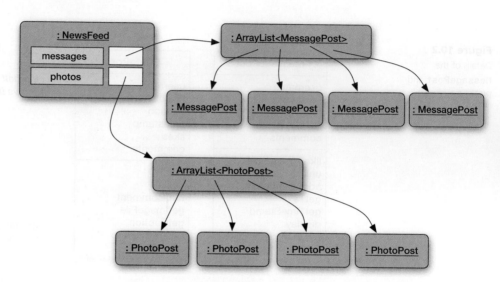

The corresponding class diagram, as BlueJ displays it, is shown in Figure 10.4. Note that BlueJ shows a slightly simplified diagram: classes from the standard Java library (**ArrayList** in this case) are not shown. Instead, the diagram focuses on user-defined classes. Also, BlueJ does not show field and method names in the diagram.

Figure 10.4

BlueJ class diagram of *network*

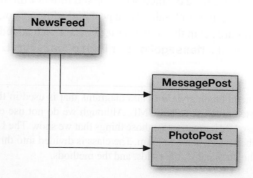

In practice, to implement the full *network* application, we would have more classes to handle things such as saving the data to a database and providing a user interface, most likely through a web browser. These are not very relevant to the present discussion, so we shall skip describing those for now, and concentrate on a more detailed discussion of the core classes mentioned here.

10.1.2 *Network* source code

So far, the design of the three current classes (**MessagePost**, **PhotoPost**, and **News-Feed**) has been very straightforward. Translating these ideas into Java code is equally easy. Code 10.1 shows the source code of the **MessagePost** class. It defines the appropriate fields, sets in its constructor all the data items that are not expected to change over time, and provides accessor and mutator methods where appropriate. It also implements a first, simple version of the **display** method to show the post in the text terminal.

Code 10.1

Source code of the **MessagePost** class

```java
import java.util.ArrayList;

/**
 * This class stores information about a post in a social network.
 * The main part of the post consists of a (possibly multi-line)
 * text message. Other data, such as author and time, are also stored.
 *
 * @author Michael Kölling and David J. Barnes
 * @version 0.1
 */
public class MessagePost
{
    private String username;   // username of the post's author
    private String message;    // an arbitrarily long, multi-line message
    private long timestamp;
    private int likes;
    private ArrayList<String> comments;

    /**
     * Constructor for objects of class MessagePost.
     *
     * @param author    The username of the author of this post.
     * @param text      The text of this post.
     */
    public MessagePost(String author, String text)
    {
        username = author;
        message = text;
        timestamp = System.currentTimeMillis();
        likes = 0;
        comments = new ArrayList<>();
    }

    /**
     * Record one more "Like" indication from a user.
     */
    public void like()
    {
        likes++;
    }
```

Code 10.1 continued

Source code of the **MessagePost** class

```java
/**
 * Record that a user has withdrawn his/her "Like" vote.
 */
public void unlike()
{
    if (likes > 0) {
        likes--;
    }
}

/**
 * Add a comment to this post.
 *
 * @param text   The new comment to add.
 */
public void addComment(String text)
{
    comments.add(text);
}

/**
 * Return the text of this post.
 *
 * @return The post's text.
 */
public String getText()
{
    return message;
}

/**
 * Return the time of creation of this post.
 *
 * @return The post's creation time, as a system time value.
 */
public long getTimeStamp()
{
    return timestamp;
}

/**
 * Display the details of this post.
 *
 * (Currently: Print to the text terminal. This is simulating display
 * in a web browser for now.)
 */
public void display()
{
    System.out.println(username);
    System.out.println(message);
    System.out.print(timeString(timestamp));

    if(likes > 0) {
        System.out.println("  -  " + likes + " people like this.");
    }
    else {
        System.out.println();
    }
```

**Code 10.1
continued**

Source code of the
MessagePost class

```java
        if(comments.isEmpty()) {
            System.out.println("   No comments.");
        }
        else {
            System.out.println("   " + comments.size() +
                            " comment(s). Click here to view.");
        }
    }

    /**
     * Create a string describing a time point in the past in terms
     * relative to current time, such as "30 seconds ago" or "7 minutes ago".
     * Currently, only seconds and minutes are used for the string.
     *
     * @param time  The time value to convert (in system milliseconds)
     * @return      A relative time string for the given time
     */
    private String timeString(long time)
    {
        long current = System.currentTimeMillis();
        long pastMillis = current - time;        // time passed in milliseconds
        long seconds = pastMillis/1000;
        long minutes = seconds/60;
        if(minutes > 0) {
            return minutes + " minutes ago";
        }
        else {
            return seconds + " seconds ago";
        }
    }
}
```

Some details are worth mentioning:

■ Some simplifications have been made. For example, comments for a post are stored as strings. In a more complete version, we would probably use a custom class for comments, as comments also have additional detail such as an author and a time. The "like" count is stored as a simple integer. We are currently not recording which user liked a post. While these simplifications make our prototype incomplete, they are not relevant for our main discussion here, and we shall leave them as they are for now.

■ The time stamp is stored as a single number, of type **long**. This reflects common practice. We can easily get the system time from the Java system, as a **long** value in milliseconds. We have also written a short method, called **timeString**, to convert this number into a relative time string, such as "5 minutes ago." In our final application, the system would have to use real time rather than system time, but again, system time is good enough for our prototype for now.

Note that we do not intend right now to make the implementation complete in any sense. It serves to provide a feel for what a class such as this might look like. We will use this as the basis for our following discussion of inheritance.

Now let us compare the **MessagePost** source code with the source code of class **PhotoPost**, shown in Code 10.2. Looking at both classes, we quickly notice that they are very similar. This is not surprising, because their purpose is similar: both are used to store information about news-feed posts, and the different types of post have a lot in common. They differ only in their details, such as some of their fields and corresponding accessors and the bodies of the **display** method.

Code 10.2

Source code of the **PhotoPost** class

```java
import java.util.ArrayList;

/**
 * This class stores information about a post in a social network.
 * The main part of the post consists of a photo and a caption.
 * Other data, such as author and time, are also stored.
 *
 * @author Michael Kölling and David J. Barnes
 * @version 0.1
 */
public class PhotoPost
{
    private String username;   // username of the post's author
    private String filename;   // the name of the image file
    private String caption;    // a one line image caption
    private long timestamp;
    private int likes;
    private ArrayList<String> comments;

    /**
     * Constructor for objects of class PhotoPost.
     *
     * @param author     The username of the author of this post.
     * @param filename   The filename of the image in this post.
     * @param caption    A caption for the image.
     */
    public PhotoPost(String author, String filename, String caption)
    {
        username = author;
        this.filename = filename;
        this.caption = caption;
        timestamp = System.currentTimeMillis();
        likes = 0;
        comments = new ArrayList<>();
    }

    /**
     * Record one more "Like" indication from a user.
     */
    public void like()
    {
        likes++;
    }

    /**
     * Record that a user has withdrawn his/her "Like" vote.
     */
```

Code 10.2 continued

Source code of the **PhotoPost** class

```java
public void unlike()
{
    if (likes > 0) {
        likes--;
    }
}

/**
 * Add a comment to this post.
 *
 * @param text  The new comment to add.
 */
public void addComment(String text)
{
    comments.add(text);
}

/**
 * Return the file name of the image in this post.
 *
 * @return The post's image file name.
 */
public String getImageFile()
{
    return filename;
}

/**
 * Return the caption of the image of this post.
 *
 * @return The image's caption.
 */
public String getCaption()
{
    return caption;
}

/**
 * Return the time of creation of this post.
 *
 * @return The post's creation time, as a system time value.
 */
public long getTimeStamp()
{
    return timestamp;
}

/**
 * Display the details of this post.
 *
 * (Currently: Print to the text terminal. This is simulating display
 * in a web browser for now.)
 */
```

```
public void display()
{
    System.out.println(username);
    System.out.println("   [" + filename + "]");
    System.out.println("   " + caption);
    System.out.print(timeString(timestamp));

    if(likes > 0) {
        System.out.println("    -  " + likes + " people like this.");
    }
    else {
        System.out.println();
    }

    if(comments.isEmpty()) {
        System.out.println("    No comments.");
    }
    else {
        System.out.println("    " + comments.size() +
                        " comment(s). Click here to view.");
    }
}

/**
 * Create a string describing a time point in the past in terms
 * relative to current time, such as "30 seconds ago" or "7 minutes ago".
 * Currently, only seconds and minutes are used for the string.
 *
 * @param time   The time value to convert (in system milliseconds)
 * @return       A relative time string for the given time
 */
private String timeString(long time)
{
    long current = System.currentTimeMillis();
    long pastMillis = current - time;       // time passed in milliseconds
    long seconds = pastMillis/1000;
    long minutes = seconds/60;
    if(minutes > 0) {
        return minutes + " minutes ago";
    }
    else {
        return seconds + " seconds ago";
    }
}
}
```

Next, let us examine the source code of the **NewsFeed** class (Code 10.3). It, too, is quite simple. It defines two lists (each based on class **ArrayList**) to hold the collection of message posts and the collection of photo posts. The empty lists are created in the constructor. It then provides two methods for adding items: one for adding message posts, one for adding photo posts. The last method, named **show**, prints a list of all message and photo posts to the text terminal.

Code 10.3

Source code of the

NewsFeed class

```java
import java.util.ArrayList;

/**
 * The NewsFeed class stores news posts for the news feed in a social network
 * application.
 *
 * Display of the posts is currently simulated by printing the details to the
 * terminal. (Later, this should display in a browser.)
 *
 * This version does not save the data to disk, and it does not provide any
 * search or ordering functions.
 *
 * @author Michael Kölling and David J. Barnes
 * @version 0.1
 */
public class NewsFeed
{
    private ArrayList<MessagePost> messages;
    private ArrayList<PhotoPost> photos;

    /**
     * Construct an empty news feed.
     */
    public NewsFeed()
    {
        messages = new ArrayList<>();
        photos = new ArrayList<>();
    }

    /**
     * Add a text post to the news feed.
     *
     * @param text  The text post to be added.
     */
    public void addMessagePost(MessagePost message)
    {
        messages.add(message);
    }

    /**
     * Add a photo post to the news feed.
     *
     * @param photo  The photo post to be added.
     */
    public void addPhotoPost(PhotoPost photo)
    {
        photos.add(photo);
    }

    /**
     * Show the news feed. Currently: print the news feed details to the
     * terminal. (To do: replace this later with display in web browser.)
     */
```

**Code 10.3
continued**

Source code of the
NewsFeed class

```java
public void show()
{
    // display all text posts
    for(MessagePost message : messages) {
        message.display();
        System.out.println();    // empty line between posts
    }

    // display all photos
    for(PhotoPost photo : photos) {
        photo.display();
        System.out.println();    // empty line between posts
    }
}
}
```

This is by no means a complete application. It has no user interface yet (so it will not be usable outside BlueJ), and the data entered is not stored to the file system or in a database. This means that all data entered will be lost each time the application ends. There are no functions to sort the displayed list of posts—for example, by date and time or by relevance. Currently, we will always get messages first, in the order in which they were entered, followed by the photos. Also, the functions for entering and editing data, as well as searching for data and displaying it, are not flexible enough for what we would want from a real program.

However, this does not matter in our context. We can work on improving the application later. The basic structure is there, and it works. This is enough for us to discuss design problems and possible improvements.

Exercise 10.1 Open the project *network-v1*. It contains the classes exactly as we have discussed them here. Create some **MessagePost** objects and some **PhotoPost** objects. Create a **NewsFeed** object. Enter the posts into the news feed, and then display the feed's contents.

Exercise 10.2 Try the following. Create a **MessagePost** object. Enter it into the news feed. Display the news feed. You will see that the post has no associated comments. Add a comment to the **MessagePost** object on the object bench (the one you entered into the news feed). When you now list the news feed again, will the post listed there have a comment attached? Try it. Explain the behavior you observe.

10.1.3 Discussion of the *network* application

Even though our application is not yet complete, we have done the most important part. We have defined the core of the application—the data structure that stores the essential information.

This was fairly straightforward so far, and we could now go ahead and design the rest that is still missing. Before doing that, though, we will discuss the quality of the solution so far.

There are several fundamental problems with our current solution. The most obvious one is *code duplication*.

We have noticed above that the **MessagePost** and **PhotoPost** classes are very similar. In fact, the majority of the classes' source code is identical, with only a few differences. We have already discussed the problems associated with code duplication in Chapter 8. Apart from the annoying fact that we have to write everything twice (or copy and paste, then go through and fix all the differences), there are often problems associated with maintaining duplicated code. Many possible changes would have to be done twice. If, for example, the type of the comment list is changed from **ArrayList<String>** to **ArrayList<Comment>** (so that more details can be stored), this change has to be made once in the **MessagePost** class and again in the **PhotoPost** class. In addition, associated with maintenance of code duplication is always the danger of introducing errors, because the maintenance programmer might not realize that an identical change is needed at a second (or third) location.

There is another spot where we have code duplication: in the **NewsFeed** class. We can see that everything in that class is done twice—once for message posts, and once for photo posts. The class defines two list variables, then creates two list objects, defines two **add** methods, and has two almost-identical blocks of code in the **show** method to print out the lists.

The problems with this duplication become clear when we analyze what we would have to do to add another type of post to this program. Imagine that we want to store not only text messages and photo posts, but also activity posts. Activity posts can be automatically generated and inform us about an activity of one of our contacts, such as "Fred has changed his profile picture" or "Jacob is now friends with Feena." Activity posts seem similar enough that it should be easy to modify our application to do this. We would introduce another class, **ActivityPost**, and essentially write a third version of the source code that we already have in the **MessagePost** and **PhotoPost** classes. Then we have to work through the **NewsFeed** class and add another list variable, another list object, another **add** method, and another loop in the **show** method.

We would have to do the same for a fourth type of post. The more we do this, the more the code-duplication problem increases, and the harder it becomes to make changes later. When we feel uncomfortable about a situation such as this one, it is often a good indicator that there may be a better alternative approach. For this particular case, the solution is found in object-oriented languages. They provide a distinctive feature that has a big impact on programs involving sets of similar classes. In the following sections, we will introduce this feature, which is called *inheritance*.

10.2 Using inheritance

Concept

Inheritance allows us to define one class as an extension of another.

Inheritance is a mechanism that provides us with a solution to our problem of duplication. The idea is simple: instead of defining the **MessagePost** and **PhotoPost** classes completely independently, we first define a class that contains everything these two have in common. We shall call this class **Post**. Then we can declare that a **MessagePost** is a **Post** and a **PhotoPost** is a **Post**. Finally, we add those extra details needed for a message post to the **MessagePost** class, and those for a photo post to the **PhotoPost** class. The essential feature of this technique is that we need to describe the common features only once.

Figure 10.5 shows a class diagram for this new structure. At the top, it shows the class **Post**, which defines all fields and methods that are common to all posts (messages and photos). Below the **Post** class, it shows the **MessagePost** and **PhotoPost** classes, which hold only those fields and methods that are unique to each particular class.

This new feature of object-oriented programming requires some new terminology. In a situation such as this one, we say that the class **MessagePost** *inherits from* class **Post**. Class **PhotoPost** also inherits from **Post**. In the vernacular of Java programs, the expression "class **MessagePost** *extends* class **Post**" could be used, because Java uses an **extends** keyword to define the inheritance relationship (as we shall see shortly). The arrows in the class diagram (usually drawn with hollow arrow heads) represent the inheritance relationship.

Concept

A **superclass** is a class that is extended by another class.

Class **Post** (the class that the others inherit from) is called the *parent class* or *superclass*. The inheriting classes (**MessagePost** and **PhotoPost** in this example) are referred to as *child classes* or *subclasses*. In this book, we will use the terms "superclass" and "subclass" to refer to the classes in an inheritance relationship.

Concept

A **subclass** is a class that extends (inherits from) another class. It inherits all fields and methods from its superclass.

Inheritance is sometimes also called an *is-a* relationship. The reason is that a subclass is a specialization of a superclass. We can say that "a message post *is a* post" and "a photo post *is a* post."

The purpose of using inheritance is now fairly obvious. Instances of class **MessagePost** will have all fields defined in class **MessagePost** *and* in class **Post**. (**MessagePost** inherits the fields from **Post**.) Instances of **PhotoPost** will have all fields defined in **PhotoPost** and in **Post**. Thus, we achieve the same as before, but we need to define the fields **username**, **timestamp**, **likes**, and **comments** only once, while being able to use them in two different places.

Figure 10.5
MessagePost and
PhotoPost inherit-
ing from **Post**

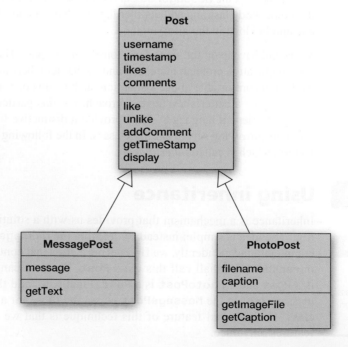

The same holds true for methods: instances of subclasses have all methods defined in both the superclass and the subclass. In general, we can say: because a message post is a post, a message-post object has everything that a post has, and more. And because a photo post is also a post, it has everything that a post has, and more.

Thus, inheritance allows us to create two classes that are quite similar, while avoiding the need to write the identical part twice. Inheritance has a number of other advantages, which we discuss below. First, however, we will take another, more general look at inheritance hierarchies.

10.3 Inheritance hierarchies

Inheritance can be used much more generally than shown in the example above. More than two subclasses can inherit from the same superclass, and a subclass can, in turn, be a superclass to other subclasses. The classes then form an *inheritance hierarchy*.

Concept

Classes that are linked through inheritance relationships form an **inheritance hierarchy**.

The best-known example of an inheritance hierarchy is probably the classification of species used by biologists. A small part is shown in Figure 10.6. We can see that a poodle is a dog, which is a mammal, which is an animal.

We know some things about poodles—for example, that they are alive, they can bark, they eat meat, and they give birth to live young. On closer inspection, we see that we know some of these things not because they are poodles, but because they are dogs, mammals, or animals. An instance of class **Poodle** (an actual poodle) has all the characteristics of a poodle, a dog, a mammal, and an animal, because a poodle is a dog, which is a mammal, and so on.

The principle is simple: inheritance is an abstraction technique that lets us categorize classes of objects under certain criteria and helps us specify the characteristics of these classes.

Exercise 10.3 Draw an inheritance hierarchy for the people in your place of study or work. For example, if you are a university student, then your university probably has students (first-year students, second-year students, . . .), professors, tutors, office personnel, etc.

Figure 10.6
An example of an
inheritance hierarchy

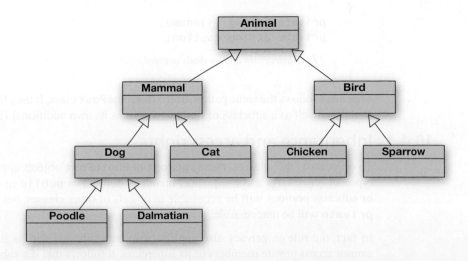

10.4 Inheritance in Java

Before discussing more details of inheritance, we will have a look at how inheritance is expressed in the Java language. Here is a segment of the source code of the **Post** class:

```
public class Post
{
    private String username; // username of the post's author
    private long timestamp;
    private int likes;
    private ArrayList<String> comments;

    // Constructors and methods omitted.

}
```

There is nothing special about this class so far. It starts with a normal class definition and defines **Post**'s fields in the usual way. Next, we examine the source code of the **Message-Post** class:

```
public class MessagePost extends Post
{
    private String message;

    // Constructors and methods omitted.

}
```

There are two things worth noting here. First, the keyword **extends** defines the inheritance relationship. The phrase "**extends Post**" specifies that this class is a subclass of the **Post** class. Second, the **MessagePost** class defines only those fields that are unique to **MessagePost** objects (only **message** in this case). The fields from **Post** are inherited and do not need to be listed here. Objects of class **MessagePost** will nonetheless have fields for **username**, **timestamp**, and so on.

Next, let us have a look at the source code of class **PhotoPost**:

```
public class PhotoPost extends Post
{
    private String filename;
    private String caption;

    // Constructors and methods omitted.

}
```

This class follows the same pattern as the **MessagePost** class. It uses the **extends** keyword to define itself as a subclass of **Post** and defines its own additional fields.

10.4.1 Inheritance and access rights

To objects of other classes, **MessagePost** or **PhotoPost** objects appear just like all other types of objects. As a consequence, members defined as **public** in either the superclass or subclass portions will be accessible to objects of other classes, but members defined as **private** will be inaccessible.

In fact, the rule on privacy also applies between a subclass and its superclass: a subclass cannot access private members of its superclass. It follows that if a subclass method needed to access or change private fields in its superclass, then the superclass would need to provide appropriate accessor and/or mutator methods. However, an object of a subclass may call any public methods defined in its superclass as if they were defined locally in the subclass—no variable is needed, because the methods are all part of the same object.

This issue of access rights between super- and subclasses is one we will discuss further in Chapter 11, when we introduce the **protected** modifier.

Exercise 10.4 Open the project *network-v2*. This project contains a version of the *network* application, rewritten to use inheritance, as described above. Note that the class diagram displays the inheritance relationship. Open the source code of the **MessagePost** class and remove the "**extends Post**" phrase. Close the editor. What changes do you observe in the class diagram? Add the "**extends Post**" phrase again.

Exercise 10.5 Create a **MessagePost** object. Call some of its methods. Can you call the inherited methods (for example, **addComment**)? What do you observe about the inherited methods?

Exercise 10.6 In order to illustrate that a subclass can access non-private elements of its superclass without any special syntax, try the following slightly artificial modification to the **MessagePost** and **Post** classes. Create a method called **printShort-Summary** in the **MessagePost** class. Its task is to print just the phrase "Message post from *NAME*", where *NAME* should show the name of the author. However, because the **username** field is private in the **Post** class, it will be necessary to add a public **getUserName** method to **Post**. Call this method from **printShortSummary** to access the name for printing. Remember that no special syntax is required when a subclass calls a superclass method. Try out your solution by creating a **MessagePost** object. Implement a similar method in the **PhotoPost** class.

10.4.2 Inheritance and initialization

When we create an object, the constructor of that object takes care of initializing all object fields to some reasonable state. We have to look more closely at how this is done in classes that inherit from other classes.

When we create a **MessagePost** object, we pass two parameters to the message post's constructor: the name of the author and the message text. One of these contains a value for a field defined in class **Post**, and the other a value for a field defined in class **MessagePost**. All of these fields must be correctly initialized, and Code 10.4 shows the code segments that are used to achieve this in Java.

Several observations can be made here. First, the class **Post** has a constructor, even though we do not intend to create an instance of class **Post** directly.[2] This constructor receives the

---

[2] Currently, there is nothing actually preventing us from creating a **Post** object, although that was not our intention when we designed these classes. In Chapter 12, we shall see some techniques that allow us to make sure that **Post** objects cannot be created directly, but only **MessagePost** or **PhotoPost** objects.

Code 10.4
Initialization of
subclass and
superclass fields

```java
public class Post
{
    private String username;  // username of the post's author
    private long timestamp;
    private int likes;
    private ArrayList<String> comments;

    /**
     * Constructor for objects of class Post.
     *
     * @param author    The username of the author of this post.
     */
    public Post(String author)
    {
        username = author;
        timestamp = System.currentTimeMillis();
        likes = 0;
        comments = new ArrayList<>();
    }

    Methods omitted.

}
```

```java
public class MessagePost extends Post
{
    private String message;  // an arbitrarily long, multi-line message

    /**
     * Constructor for objects of class MessagePost.
     *
     * @param author    The username of the author of this post.
     * @param text      The text of this post.
     */
    public MessagePost(String author, String text)
    {
        super(author);
        message = text;
    }

    Methods omitted.

}
```

parameters needed to initialize the **Post** fields, and it contains the code to do this initialization. Second, the **MessagePost** constructor receives parameters needed to initialize both **Post** and **MessagePost** fields. It then contains the following line of code:

```java
super(author);
```

The keyword **super** is a call from the subclass constructor to the constructor of the superclass. Its effect is that the **Post** constructor is executed as part of the **MessagePost** constructor's execution. When we create a message post, the **MessagePost** constructor is called, which, in turn, as its first statement, calls the **Post** constructor. The **Post** constructor initializes the post's fields, and then returns to the **MessagePost** constructor, which initializes the remaining field defined in the **MessagePost** class. For this to work, those parameters needed for the initialization of the post fields are passed on to the superclass constructor as parameters to the **super** call.

In Java, a subclass constructor must always call the *superclass constructor* as its first statement. If you do not write a call to a superclass constructor, the Java compiler will insert a superclass call automatically, to ensure that the superclass fields are properly initialized. The inserted call is equivalent to writing

```
super();
```

Inserting this call automatically works only if the superclass has a constructor without parameters (because the compiler cannot guess what parameter values should be passed). Otherwise, an error will be reported.

In general, it is a good idea to always include explicit superclass calls in your constructors, even if it is one that the compiler could generate automatically. We consider this good style, because it avoids the possibility of misinterpretation and confusion in case a reader is not aware of the automatic code generation.

> **Concept**
>
> **Superclass constructor**
> The constructor of a subclass must always invoke the constructor of its superclass as its first statement. If the source code does not include such a call, Java will attempt to insert a call automatically.

> **Exercise 10.7** Set a breakpoint in the first line of the **MessagePost** class's constructor. Then create a **MessagePost** object. When the debugger window pops up, use *Step Into* to step through the code. Observe the instance fields and their initialization. Describe your observations.

10.5   *Network*: adding other post types

Now that we have our inheritance hierarchy set up for the *network* project so that the common elements of the items are in the **Post** class, it becomes a lot easier to add other types of posts. For instance, we might want to add event posts, which consist of a description of a standard event (e.g., "Fred has joined the 'Neal Stephenson fans' group."). Standard events might be a user joining a group, a user becoming friends with another, or a user changing their profile picture. To achieve this, we can now define a new subclass of **Post** named **EventPost** (Figure 10.7). Because **EventPost** is a subclass of **Post**, it automatically inherits all fields and methods that we have already defined in **Post**. Thus, **EventPost** objects already have a username, a time stamp, a likes counter, and comments. We can then concentrate on adding attributes that are specific to event posts, such as the event type. The event type might be stored as an enumeration constant (see Chapter 8) or as a string describing the event.

This is an example of how inheritance enables us to *reuse* existing work. We can reuse the code that we have written for photo posts and message posts (in the **Post** class) so that it

Figure 10.7
Network items with
an **EventPost** class

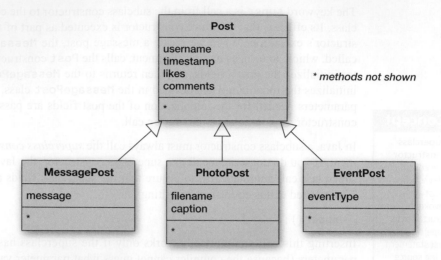

also works for the **EventPost** class. The ability to reuse existing software components is one of the great benefits that we get from the inheritance facility. We will discuss this in more detail later.

This reuse has the effect that a lot less new code is needed when we now introduce additional post types. Because new post types can be defined as subclasses of **Post**, only the code that is actually different from **Post** has to be added.

Now imagine that we change the requirements a bit: event posts in our *network* application will not have a "Like" button or comments attached. They are for information only. How do we achieve this? Currently, because **EventPost** is a subclass of **Post**, it automatically inherits the **likes** and **comments** fields. Is this a problem?

We could leave everything as it is and decide to never display the likes count or comments for event posts—just ignore the fields. This does not feel right. Having the fields present but unused invites problems. Someday, a maintenance programmer will come along who does not realize that these fields should not be used and try to process them.

Or we could write **EventPost** without inheriting from **Post**. But then we are back to code duplication for the **username** and **timestamp** fields and their methods.

The solution is to refactor the class hierarchy. We can introduce a new superclass for all posts that have comments attached (named **CommentedPost**), which is a subclass of **Post** (Figure 10.8). We then shift the **likes** and **comments** fields from the **Post** class to this new class. **MessagePost** and **PhotoPost** are now subclasses of our new **CommentedPost** class, while **EventPost** inherits from **Posts** directly. **MessagePost** objects inherit everything from both superclasses and have the same fields and methods as before. Objects of class **EventPost** will inherit the **username** and **timestamp**, but not the comments.

This is a very common situation in designing class hierarchies. When the hierarchy does not seem to fit properly, we have to refactor the hierarchy.

Figure 10.8
Adding more post
types to *network*

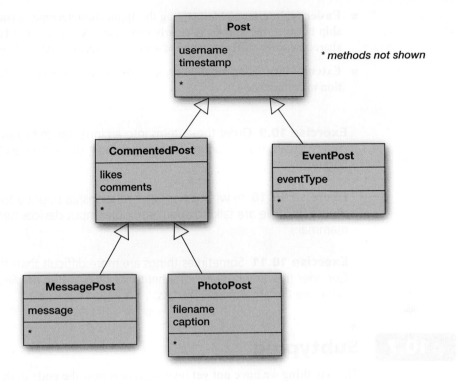

Classes that are not intended to be used to create instances, but whose purpose is exclusively to serve as superclasses for other classes (such as **Post** and **CommentedPost**), are called *abstract classes*. We shall investigate this in more detail in Chapter 12.

Exercise 10.8 Open the *network-v2* project. Add a class for event posts to the project. Create some event-post objects and test that all methods work as expected.

10.6 Advantages of inheritance (so far)

We have seen several advantages of using inheritance for the *network* application. Before we explore other aspects of inheritance, we shall summarize the general advantages we have encountered so far:

- **Avoiding code duplication** The use of inheritance avoids the need to write identical or very similar copies of code twice (or even more often).

- **Code reuse** Existing code can be reused. If a class similar to the one we need already exists, we can sometimes subclass the existing class and reuse some of the existing code, rather than having to implement everything again.

- **Easier maintenance** Maintaining the application becomes easier, because the relationship between the classes is clearly expressed. A change to a field or a method that is shared between different types of subclasses needs to be made only once.

- **Extendibility** Using inheritance, it becomes much easier to extend an existing application in certain ways.

Exercise 10.9 Order these items into an inheritance hierarchy: apple, ice cream, bread, fruit, food item, cereal, orange, dessert, chocolate mousse, baguette.

Exercise 10.10 In what inheritance relationship might a *touch pad* and a *mouse* be? (We are talking about computer input devices here, not a small furry mammal.)

Exercise 10.11 Sometimes things are more difficult than they first seem. Consider this: In what kind of inheritance relationship are *Rectangle* and *Square*? What are the arguments? Discuss.

10.7 Subtyping

The one thing we have not yet investigated is how the code in the **NewsFeed** class was changed when we modified our project to use inheritance. Code 10.5 shows the full source code of class **NewsFeed**. We can compare this with the original source shown in Code 10.3.

Code 10.5
Source code of the
NewsFeed class
(second version)

```java
import java.util.ArrayList;

/**
 * The NewsFeed class stores news posts for the news feed in a
 * social network application.
 *
 * Display of the posts is currently simulated by printing the
 * details to the terminal. (Later, this should display in a browser.)
 *
 * This version does not save the data to disk, and it does not
 * provide any search or ordering functions.
 *
 * @author Michael Kölling and David J. Barnes
 * @version 0.2
 */
public class NewsFeed
{
    private ArrayList<Post> posts;

    /**
     * Construct an empty news feed.
     */
```

Code 10.5

Source code of the **NewsFeed** class (second version)

```java
public NewsFeed()
{
    posts = new ArrayList<>();
}

/**
 * Add a post to the news feed.
 *
 * @param post  The post to be added.
 */
public void addPost(Post post)
{
    posts.add(post);
}

/**
 * Show the news feed. Currently: print the news feed details
 * to the terminal. (To do: replace this later with display
 * in web browser.)
 */
public void show()
{
    // display all posts
    for(Post post : posts) {
        post.display();
        System.out.println();   // empty line between posts
    }
}
}
```

Concept

Subtype As an analog to the class hierarchy, types form a type hierarchy. The type defined by a subclass definition is a subtype of the type of its superclass.

As we can see, the code has become significantly shorter and simpler since our change to use inheritance. Where in the first version (Code 10.3) everything had to be done twice, it now exists only once. We have only one collection, only one method to add posts, and one loop in the **show** method.

The reason why we could shorten the source code is that, in the new version, we can use the type **Post** where we previously used **MessagePost** and **PhotoPost**. We investigate this first by examining the **addPost** method.

In our first version, we had two methods to add posts to the news feed. They had the following headers:

```java
public void addMessagePost(MessagePost message)
public void addPhotoPost(PhotoPost photo)
```

In our new version, we have a single method to serve the same purpose:

```java
public void addPost(Post post)
```

The parameters in the original version are defined with the types **MessagePost** and **PhotoPost**, ensuring that we pass **MessagePost** and **PhotoPost** objects to these methods, because actual parameter types must match the formal parameter types. So far, we have interpreted the requirement that parameter types must match as meaning "must be of the same type"—for instance, that the type name of an actual parameter must be the same as the type name of the corresponding formal parameter. This is only part of the truth, in fact, because an object of a subclass can be used wherever its superclass type is required.

10.7.1 Subclasses and subtypes

We have discussed earlier that classes define types. The type of an object that was created from class **MessagePost** is **MessagePost**. We also just discussed that classes may have subclasses. Thus, the types defined by the classes can have subtypes. In our example, the type **MessagePost** is a subtype of type **Post**.

10.7.2 Subtyping and assignment

When we want to assign an object to a variable, the type of the object must match the type of the variable. For example,

```
Car myCar = new Car();
```

is a valid assignment, because an object of type **Car** is assigned to a variable declared to hold objects of type **Car**. Now that we know about inheritance, we must state the typing rule more completely: a variable can hold objects of its declared type, or of any subtype of its declared type.

> **Concept**
>
> **Variables and subtypes** Variables may hold objects of their declared type or of any subtype of their declared type.

Imagine that we have a class **Vehicle** with two subclasses, **Car** and **Bicycle** (Figure 10.9). In this case, the typing rule allows all the following assignments:

```
Vehicle v1 = new Vehicle();
Vehicle v2 = new Car();
Vehicle v3 = new Bicycle();
```

The type of a variable declares what it can store. Declaring a variable of type **Vehicle** states that this variable can hold vehicles. But because a car is a vehicle, it is perfectly legal to store a car in a variable that is intended for vehicles. (Think of the variable as a garage: if someone tells you that you may park a vehicle in a garage, you would think that parking either a car or a bicycle in the garage would be okay.)

This principle is known as *substitution*. In object-oriented languages, we can substitute a subclass object where a superclass object is expected, because the subclass object is a special case of the superclass. If, for example, someone asks us to give them a pen, we can

Figure 10.9
An inheritance hierarchy

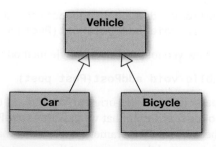

Concept

Substitution Subtype objects may be used wherever objects of a supertype are expected. This is known as substitution.

fulfill the request perfectly well by giving them a fountain pen or a ballpoint pen. Both fountain pen and ballpoint pen are subclasses of pen, so supplying either where an object of class **Pen** was expected is fine.

However, doing it the other way is not allowed:

```
Car c1 = new Vehicle(); // this is an error!
```

This statement attempts to store a **Vehicle** object in a **Car** variable. Java will not allow this, and an error will be reported if you try to compile this statement. The variable is declared to be able to store cars. A vehicle, on the other hand, may or may not be a car—we do not know. Thus, the statement may be wrong, and therefore not allowed.

Similarly:

```
Car c2 = new Bicycle(); // this is an error!
```

This is also an illegal statement. A bicycle is not a car (or, more formally, the type **Bicycle** is not a subtype of **Car**), and thus the assignment is not allowed.

> **Exercise 10.12** Assume that we have four classes: **Person**, **Teacher**, **Student**, and **PhDStudent**. **Teacher** and **Student** are both subclasses of **Person**. **PhDStudent** is a subclass of **Student**.
>
> a. Which of the following assignments are legal, and why or why not?
>
> ```
> Person p1 = new Student();
> Person p2 = new PhDStudent();
> PhDStudent phd1 = new Student();
> Teacher t1 = new Person();
> Student s1 = new PhDStudent();
> ```
>
> b. Suppose that we have the following legal declarations and assignments:
>
> ```
> Person p1 = new Person();
> Person p2 = new Person();
> PhDStudent phd1 = new PhDStudent();
> Teacher t1 = new Teacher();
> Student s1 = new Student();
> ```
>
> Based on those just mentioned, which of the following assignments are legal, and why or why not?
>
> ```
> s1 = p1
> s1 = p2
> p1 = s1;
> t1 = s1;
> s1 = phd1;
> phd1 = s1;
> ```

> **Exercise 10.13** Test your answers to the previous question by creating bare-bones versions of the classes mentioned in that exercise and trying it out in BlueJ.

10.7.3 Subtyping and parameter passing

Passing a parameter (that is, assigning an actual parameter to a formal parameter variable) behaves in exactly the same way as an assignment to a variable. This is why we can pass an object of type **MessagePost** to a method that has a parameter of type **Post**. We have the following definition of the **addPost** method in class **NewsFeed**:

```
public void addPost(Post post)
{
    . . .
}
```

We can now use this method to add message posts and photo posts to the feed:

```
NewsFeed feed = new NewsFeed();
MessagePost message = new MessagePost(. . .);
PhotoPost photo = new PhotoPost(. . .);
feed.addPost(message);
feed.addPost(photo);
```

Because of subtyping rules, we need only one method (with a parameter of type **Post**) to add both **MessagePost** and **PhotoPost** objects.

We will discuss subtyping in more detail in the next chapter.

10.7.4 Polymorphic variables

Variables holding object types in Java are *polymorphic* variables. The term "polymorphic" (literally, *many shapes*) refers to the fact that a variable can hold objects of different types (namely, the declared type or any subtype of the declared type). Polymorphism appears in object-oriented languages in several contexts—polymorphic variables are just the first example. We will discuss other incarnations of polymorphism in more detail in the next chapter.

For now, we just observe how the use of a polymorphic variable helps us simplify our **show** method. The body of this method is

```
for(Post post : posts) {
    post.display();
    System.out.println(); // empty line between posts
}
```

Here, we iterate through the list of posts (held in an **ArrayList** in the **posts** variable). We get out each post and then invoke its **display** method. Note that the actual posts that we get out of the list are of type **MessagePost** or **PhotoPost**, not of type **Post**. We can, however, use a loop variable of type **Post**, because variables are polymorphic.

The **post** variable is able to hold **MessagePost** and **PhotoPost** objects, because these are subtypes of **Post**.

Thus, the use of inheritance in this example has removed the need for two separate loops in the **show** method. Inheritance avoids code duplication not only in the server classes, but also in clients of those classes.

> **Note** When doing the exercises, you may have noticed that the **show** method has a problem: not all details are printed out. Solving this problem requires some more explanation. We will provide this in the next chapter.

> **Exercise 10.14** What has to change in the **NewsFeed** class when another **Post** subclass (for example, a class **EventPost**) is added? Why?

10.7.5 Casting

Sometimes the rule that we cannot assign from a supertype to a subtype is more restrictive than necessary. If we know that the supertype variable holds a subtype object, the assignment could actually be allowed. For example:

```
Vehicle v;
Car c = new Car();
v = c; // correct
c = v; // error
```

The above statements would not compile: we get a compiler error in the last line, because assigning a **Vehicle** variable to a **Car** variable (supertype to subtype) is not allowed. However, if we execute these statements in sequence, we know that we could actually allow this assignment. We can see that the variable **v** actually contains an object of type **Car**, so the assignment to **c** would be okay. The compiler is not that smart. It translates the code line by line, so it looks at the last line in isolation without knowing what is currently stored in variable **v**. This is called *type loss*. The type of the object in **v** is actually **Car**, but the compiler does not know this.

We can get around this problem by explicitly telling the type system that the variable **v** holds a **Car** object. We do this using a *cast operator*:

```
c = (Car) v; // okay
```

The cast operator consists of the name of a type (here, **Car**) written in parentheses in front of a variable or an expression. Doing this will cause the compiler to believe that the object is a **Car**, and it will not report an error. At runtime, however, the Java system will check that it really is a **Car**. If we were careful, and it is truly is a **Car**, everything is fine. If the object in **v** is of another type, the runtime system will indicate an error (called a **ClassCast-Exception**), and the program will stop.[3]

---

[3] Exceptions are discussed in detail in Chapter 14.

Now consider this code fragment, in which `Bicycle` is also a subclass of `Vehicle`:

```
Vehicle v;
Car c;
Bicycle b;
c = new Car();
v = c; // okay
b = (Bicycle) c; // compile time error!
b = (Bicycle) v; // runtime error!
```

The last two assignments will both fail. The attempt to assign **c** to **b** (even with the cast) will be a compile-time error. The compiler notices that `Car` and `Bicycle` do not form a subtype/supertype relationship, so **c** can never hold a `Bicycle` object—the assignment could never work.

The attempt to assign **v** to **b** (with the cast) will be accepted at compile time, but will fail at runtime. `Vehicle` is a superclass of `Bicycle`, and thus **v** can potentially hold a `Bicycle` object. At runtime, however, it turns out that the object in **v** is not a `Bicycle` but a `Car`, and the program will terminate prematurely.

Casting should be avoided wherever possible, because it can lead to runtime errors, and that is clearly something we do not want. The compiler cannot help us to ensure correctness in this case.

In practice, casting is very rarely needed in a well-structured, object-oriented program. In almost all cases, when you use a cast in your code, you could restructure your code to avoid this cast and end up with a better-designed program. This usually involves replacing the cast with a polymorphic method call (more about this will be covered in the next chapter).

10.8 The `Object` class

Concept

All classes with no explicit superclass have **Object** as their superclass.

All classes have a superclass. So far, it has appeared as if most classes we have seen do not have a superclass. In fact, while we can declare an explicit superclass for a class, all classes that have no superclass declaration implicitly inherit from a class called **Object**.

`Object` is a class from the Java standard library that serves as a superclass for all objects. Writing a class declaration such as

```
public class Person
{
    . . .
}
```

is equivalent to writing

```
public class Person extends Object
{
    . . .
}
```

Figure 10.10
All classes inherit
from **Object**

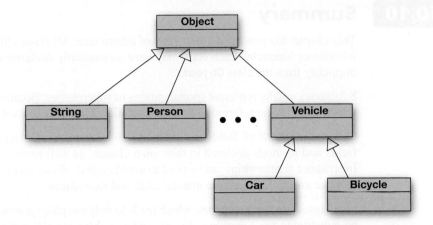

The Java compiler automatically inserts the **Object** superclass for all classes without an explicit **extends** declaration, so it is never necessary to do this for yourself. Every single class (with the sole exception of the **Object** class itself) inherits from **Object**, either directly or indirectly. Figure 10.10 shows some randomly chosen classes to illustrate this.

Having a common superclass for all objects serves two purposes: First, we can declare polymorphic variables of type **Object** to hold any object. Having variables that can hold any object type is not often useful, but there are some situations where this can help. Second, the **Object** class can define some methods that are then automatically available for every existing object. Of particular importance are the methods **toString**, **equals**, and **hashCode** which **Object** defines. This second point becomes interesting a bit later, and we shall discuss this in more detail in the next chapter.

10.9 The collection hierarchy

The Java library uses inheritance extensively in the definition of the collections classes. Class **ArrayList**, for example, inherits from a class called **AbstractList**, which, in turn, inherits from **AbstractCollection**. We shall not discuss this hierarchy here, because it is described in detail at various easily accessible places. One good description is at Oracle's web site at **http://download.oracle.com/javase/tutorial/collections/index.html**.

Note that some details of this hierarchy require an understanding of Java *interfaces*. We discuss those in Chapter 12.

> **Exercise 10.15** Use the documentation of the Java standard class libraries to find out about the inheritance hierarchy of the collection classes. Draw a diagram showing the hierarchy.

10.10 Summary

This chapter has presented a first view of inheritance. All classes in Java are arranged in an inheritance hierarchy. Each class may have an explicitly declared superclass, or it inherits implicitly from the class **Object**.

Subclasses usually represent specializations of superclasses. Because of this, the inheritance relationship is also referred to as an is-a relationship (a car *is-a* vehicle).

Subclasses inherit all fields and methods of a superclass. Objects of subclasses have all fields and methods declared in their own classes, as well as those from all superclasses. Inheritance relationships can be used to avoid code duplication, to reuse existing code, and to make an application more maintainable and extendable.

Subclasses also form subtypes, which leads to polymorphic variables. Subtype objects may be substituted for supertype objects, and variables are allowed to hold objects that are instances of subtypes of their declared type.

Inheritance allows the design of class structures that are easier to maintain and more flexible. This chapter contains only an introduction to the use of inheritance for the purpose of improving program structures. More uses of inheritance and their benefits will be discussed in the following chapters.

Terms introduced in this chapter:

inheritance, superclass (parent), subclass (child), *is-a,* **inheritance hierarchy, abstract class, subtype substitution, polymorphic variable, type loss, cast**

Concept summary

- **inheritance** Inheritance allows us to define one class as an extension of another.

- **superclass** A superclass is a class that is extended by another class.

- **subclass** A subclass is a class that extends (inherits from) another class. It inherits all fields and methods from its superclass.

- **inheritance hierarchy** Classes that are linked through inheritance relationships form an inheritance hierarchy.

- **superclass constructor** The constructor of a subclass must always invoke the constructor of its superclass as its first statement. If the source code does not include such a call, Java will attempt to insert a call automatically.

- **reuse** Inheritance allows us to reuse previously written classes in a new context.

- **subtype** As an analog to the class hierarchy, types form a type hierarchy. The type defined by a subclass definition is a subtype of the type of its superclass.

- **variables and subtypes** Variables may hold objects of their declared type or of any subtype of their declared type.

- **substitution** Subtype objects may be used wherever objects of a supertype are expected. This is known as substitution.

- **object** All classes with no explicit superclass have **Object** as their superclass.

Exercise 10.16 Go back to the *lab-classes* project from Chapter 1. Add instructors to the project (every lab class can have many students and a single instructor). Use inheritance to avoid code duplication between students and instructors (both have a name, contact details, etc.).

Exercise 10.17 Draw an inheritance hierarchy representing parts of a computer system (processor, memory, disk drive, DVD drive, printer, scanner, keyboard, mouse, etc.).

Exercise 10.18 Look at the code below. You have four classes (**O**, **X**, **T**, and **M**) and a variable of each of these.

```
O o;
X x;
T t;
M m;
```

The following assignments are all legal (assume that they all compile):

```
m = t;
m = x;
o = t;
```

The following assignments are all illegal (they cause compiler errors):

```
o = m;
o = x;
x = o;
```

What can you say about the relationships of these classes? Draw a class diagram.

Exercise 10.19 Draw an inheritance hierarchy of **AbstractList** and all its (direct and indirect) subclasses as they are defined in the Java standard library.

The last chapter introduced the main concepts of inheritance by discussing the *network* example. While we have seen the foundations of inheritance, there are still numerous important details that we have not yet investigated. Inheritance is central to understanding and using object-oriented languages, and understanding it in detail is necessary to progress from here.

In this chapter, we shall continue to use the *network* example to explore the most important of the remaining issues surrounding inheritance and polymorphism.

11.1 The problem: *network's* display method

When you experimented with the *network* examples in Chapter 10, you probably noticed that the second version—the one using inheritance—has a problem: the **display** method does not show all of a post's data.

Let us look at an example. Assume that we create a **MessagePost** and a **PhotoPost** object with the following data:

The message post:

Leonardo da Vinci

Had a great idea this morning.
But now I forgot what it was. Something to do with flying . . .

40 seconds ago. 2 people like this.

No comments.

The photo post:

```
Alexander Graham Bell
```

[experiment.jpg]   I think I might call this thing 'telephone'.

```
12 minutes ago. 4 people like this.

No comments.
```

If we enter these objects into the news feed[1] and then invoke the first version of the news feed's **show** method (the one without inheritance), it prints

```
Leonardo da Vinci
Had a great idea this morning.
But now I forgot what it was. Something to do with flying . . .
40 seconds ago - 2 people like this.
    No comments.

Alexander Graham Bell
[experiment.jpg]
I think I might call this thing 'telephone'.
12 minutes ago - 4 people like this.
    No comments.
```

While the formatting isn't pretty (because, in the text terminal, we don't have format-ting options available), all the information is there, and we can imagine how the **show** method might be adapted later to show the data in a nicer formatting in a different user interface.

Compare this with the second *network* version (with inheritance), which prints only

```
Leonardo da Vinci
40 seconds ago - 2 people like this.
    No comments.

Alexander Graham Bell
12 minutes ago - 4 people like this.
    No comments.
```

We note that the message post's text, as well as the photo post's image filename and cap-tion, are missing. The reason for this is simple. The **display** method in this version is implemented in the **Post** class, not in **MessagePost** and **PhotoPost** (Figure 11.1). In the methods of **Post**, only the fields declared in **Post** are available. If we tried to access the **MessagePost**'s **message** field from **Post**'s **display** method, an error would be reported. This illustrates the important principle that inheritance is a one-way street: **MessagePost** inherits the fields of **Post**, but **Post** still does not know anything about fields in its subclasses.

---

[1] The text for the message post is a two-line string. You can enter a multiline text into a string by using "\n" in the string for the line break.

Figure 11.1
Display, version 1:
display method in
superclass

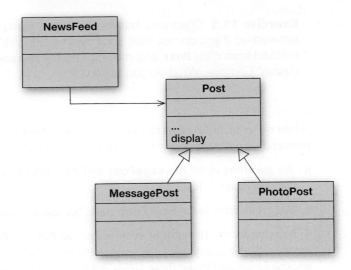

11.2 Static type and dynamic type

Trying to solve the problem of developing a complete polymorphic **display** method leads us into a discussion of *static* and *dynamic types* and *method lookup*. But let us start at the beginning.

A first attempt to solve the display problem might be to move the **display** method to the subclasses (Figure 11.2). That way, because the method would now belong to the **MessagePost** and **PhotoPost** classes, it could access the specific fields of **MessagePost** and **PhotoPost**. It could also access the inherited fields by calling accessor methods defined in the **Post** class. That should enable it to display a complete set of information again. Try out this approach by completing Exercise 11.1.

Figure 11.2
Display, version 2:
display method in
subclasses

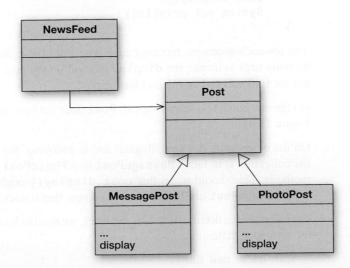

> **Exercise 11.1** Open your last version of the *network* project. (You can use *network-v2* if you do not have your own version yet.) Remove the `display` method from class **Post** and move it into the **MessagePost** and **PhotoPost** classes. Compile. What do you observe?

When we try to move the `display` method from **Post** to the subclasses, we notice that the project does not compile any more. There are two fundamental issues:

■ We get errors in the **MessagePost** and **PhotoPost** classes, because we cannot access the superclass fields.

■ We get an error in the **NewsFeed** class, because it cannot find the `display` method.

The reason for the first sort of error is that the fields in **Post** have private access, and so are inaccessible to any other class—including subclasses. Because we do not wish to break encapsulation and make these fields public, as was suggested above, the easiest way to solve this is to define public accessor methods for them. However, in Section 11.9, we shall introduce a further type of access designed specifically to support the superclass–subclass relationship.

The reason for the second sort of error requires a more detailed explanation, and this is explored in the next section.

11.2.1 Calling `display` from **NewsFeed**

First, we investigate the problem of calling the `display` method from **NewsFeed**. The relevant lines of code in the **NewsFeed** class are:

```
for(Post post : posts) {
    post.display();
    System.out.println();
}
```

The for-each statement retrieves each post from the collection; the first statement inside its body tries to invoke the `display` method on the post. The compiler informs us that it cannot find a `display` method for the post.

On the one hand, this seems logical; **Post** does not have a `display` method any more (see Figure 11.2).

On the other hand, it seems illogical and is annoying. We know that every **Post** object in the collection is in fact a **MessagePost** or a **PhotoPost** object, and both have `display` methods. This should mean that `post.display()` ought to work, because, whatever it is—**MessagePost** or **PhotoPost**—we know that it does have a `display` method.

To understand in detail why it does not work, we need to look more closely at types. Consider the following statement:

```
Car c1 = new Car();
```

We say that the type of **c1** is **Car**. Before we encountered inheritance, there was no need to distinguish whether by "type of **c1**" we meant "the type of the variable **c1**" or "the type of the object stored in **c1**." It did not matter, because the type of the variable and the type of the object were always the same.

Now that we know about subtyping, we need to be more precise. Consider the following statement:

```
Vehicle v1 = new Car();
```

What is the type of **v1**? That depends on what precisely we mean by "type of **v1**." The type of the variable **v1** is **Vehicle**; the type of the object stored in **v1** is **Car**. Through subtyping and substitution rules, we now have situations where the type of the variable and the type of the object stored in it are not exactly the same.

Let us introduce some terminology to make it easier to talk about this issue:

- We call the declared type of the variable the *static type,* because it is declared in the source code—the static representation of the program.

- We call the type of the object stored in a variable the *dynamic type,* because it depends on assignments at runtime—the dynamic behavior of the program.

Thus, looking at the explanations above, we can be more precise: the static type of **v1** is **Vehicle**, the dynamic type of **v1** is **Car**. We can now also rephrase our discussion about the call to the post's **display** method in the **NewsFeed** class. At the time of the call

```
post.display();
```

the static type of **post** is **Post**, while the dynamic type is either **MessagePost** or **PhotoPost** (Figure 11.3). We do not know which one of these it is, assuming that we have entered both **MessagePost** and **PhotoPost** objects into the feed.

Figure 11.3
Variable of type
Post containing
an object of type
PhotoPost

The compiler reports an error because, for type checking, the static type is used. The dynamic type is often only known at runtime, so the compiler has no other choice but to use the static type if it wants to do any checks at compile time. The static type of **post** is **Post**, and **Post** does not have a **display** method. It makes no difference that all known subtypes of **Post** do have a **display** method. The behavior of the compiler is reasonable in this respect, because it has no guarantee that *all* subclasses of **Post** will, indeed, define a **display** method, and this is impossible to check in practice.

In other words, to make this call work, class **Post** must have a **display** method, so we appear to be back to our original problem without having made any progress.

Exercise 11.2 In your *network* project, add a `display` method in class **Post** again. For now, write the method body with a single statement that prints out only the username. Then modify the `display` methods in **MessagePost** and **PhotoPost** so that the **MessagePost** version prints out only the message and the **PhotoPost** version prints only the caption. This removes the other errors encountered above (we shall come back to those below).

You should now have a situation corresponding to Figure 11.4, with `display` methods in three classes. Compile your project. (If there are errors, remove them. This design should work.)

Before executing, predict which of the `display` methods will get called if you execute the news feed's **show** method.

Try it out. Enter a message post and a photo post into the news feed and call the news feed's **show** method. Which `display` methods were executed? Was your prediction correct? Try to explain your observations.

Figure 11.4
Display, version 3:
`display` method
in subclasses and
superclass

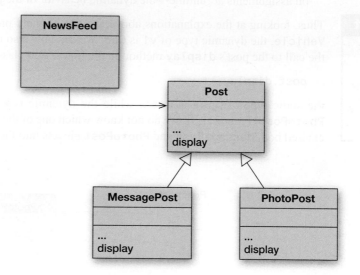

11.3   Overriding

The next design we shall discuss is one where both the superclass and the subclasses have a `display` method (Figure 11.4). The header of all the `display` methods is exactly the same.

Code 11.1 shows the relevant details of the source code of all three classes. Class **Post** has a `display` method that prints out all the fields that are declared in **Post** (those common to message posts and photo posts), and the subclasses **MessagePost** and **PhotoPost** print out the fields specific to **MessagePost** and **PhotoPost** objects, respectively.

Code 11.1
Source code of
the **display**
methods in all
three classes

```java
public class Post
{
    ...
    public void display()
    {
        System.out.println(username);
        System.out.print(timeString(timestamp));

        if(likes > 0) {
            System.out.println("  -  " + likes + " people like this.");
        }
        else {
            System.out.println();
        }

        if(comments.isEmpty()) {
            System.out.println("   No comments.");
        }
        else {
            System.out.println("   " + comments.size() +
                               " comment(s). Click here to view.");
        }
    }
}
```

```java
public class MessagePost extends Post
{
    ...
    public void display()
    {
        System.out.println(message);
    }
}
```

```java
public class PhotoPost extends Post
{
    ...
    public void display()
    {
        System.out.println("  [" + filename + "]");
        System.out.println("   " + caption);
    }
}
```

Concept

Overriding
A subclass
can override
a method
implementa-
tion. To do this,
the subclass
declares a
method with
the same sig-
nature as the
superclass, but
with a different
method body.
The overriding
method takes
precedence for
method calls
on subclass
objects.

This design works a bit better. It compiles, and it can be executed, even though it is not perfect yet. An implementation of this design is provided in the project *network-v3*. (If you have done Exercise 11.2, you already have a similar implementation of this design in your own version.)

The technique we are using here is called *overriding* (sometimes it is also referred to as *redefinition*). Overriding is a situation where a method is defined in a superclass (method `display` in class `Post` in this example), and a method with exactly the same signature is defined in the subclass. The annotation `@Override` may be added before the version in the subclass to make it clear that a new version of an inherited method is being defined.

In this situation, objects of the subclass have two methods with the same name and header: one inherited from the superclass and one from the subclass. Which one will be executed when we call this method?

11.4 Dynamic method lookup

One surprising detail is what exactly is printed once we execute the news feed's `show` method. If we again create and enter the objects described in Section 11.1, the output of the `show` method in our new version of the program is

```
Had a great idea this morning.
But now I forgot what it was. Something to do with flying . . .

[experiment.jpg]
I think I might call this thing 'telephone'.
```

We can see from this output that the `display` methods in `MessagePost` and in `PhotoPost` were executed, but not the one in `Post`.

This may seem strange at first. Our investigation in Section 11.2 has shown that the compiler insisted on a `display` method in class `Post`—methods in the subclasses were not enough. This experiment now shows that the method in class `Post` is then not executed at all, but the subclass methods are. In short:

- Type checking uses the static type, but at runtime, the methods from the dynamic type are executed.

This is a fairly important statement. To understand it better, we look in more detail at how methods are invoked. This procedure is known as *method lookup*, *method binding*, or *method dispatch*. We will use the term "*method lookup*" in this book.

We start with a simple method-lookup scenario. Assume that we have an object of a class `PhotoPost` stored in a variable `v1` declared of type `PhotoPost` (Figure 11.5).

Figure 11.5

Method lookup with a simple object

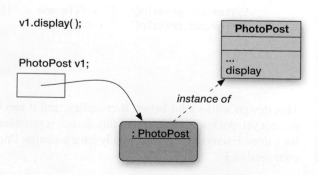

The **PhotoPost** class has a **display** method and no declared superclass. This is a very simple situation—there is no inheritance or polymorphism involved here. We then execute the statement

```
v1.display();
```

When this statement executes, the **display** method is invoked in the following steps:

1. The variable **v1** is accessed.

2. The object stored in that variable is found (following the reference).

3. The class of the object is found (following the "instance of" reference).

4. The implementation of the **display** method is found in the class and executed.

This is all very straightforward and not surprising.

Next, we look at method lookup with inheritance. This scenario is similar, but this time the **PhotoPost** class has a superclass **Post**, and the **display** method is defined only in the superclass (Figure 11.6).

We execute the same statement. The method invocation then starts in a similar way: steps 1 through 3 from the previous scenario are executed again, but then it continues differently:

4. No **display** method is found in class **PhotoPost**.

5. Because no matching method was found, the superclass is searched for a matching method. If no method is found in the superclass, the next superclass (if it exists) is searched. This continues all the way up the inheritance hierarchy to the **Object** class, until a method is found. Note that at runtime, a matching method should definitely be found, or else the class would not have compiled.

6. In our example, the **display** method is found in class **Post**, and will be executed.

Figure 11.6
Method lookup with inheritance

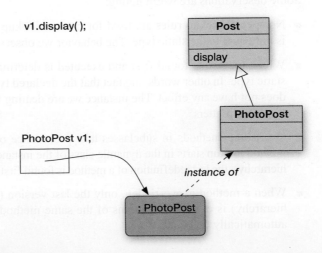

Figure 11.7
Method lookup with
polymorphism and
overriding

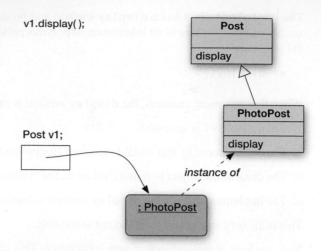

This scenario illustrates how objects inherit methods. Any method found in a superclass can be invoked on a subclass object and will correctly be found and executed.

Next, we come to the most interesting scenario: method lookup with a polymorphic variable and method overriding (Figure 11.7). The scenario is again similar to the one before, but there are two changes:

- The declared type of the variable **v1** is now **Post**, not **PhotoPost**.

- The **display** method is defined in class **Post** and then redefined (overridden) in class **PhotoPost**.

This scenario is the most important one for understanding the behavior of our *network* application, and in finding a solution to our **display** method problem.

The steps in which method execution takes place are exactly the same as steps 1 through 4 from scenario 1. Read them again.

Some observations are worth noting:

- No special lookup rules are used for method lookup in cases where the dynamic type is not equal to the static type. The behavior we observe is a result of the general rules.

- Which method is found first and executed is determined by the dynamic type, not the static type. In other words, the fact that the declared type of the variable **v1** is now **Post** does not have any effect. The instance we are dealing with is of class **PhotoPost**—that is all that matters.

- Overriding methods in subclasses take precedence over superclass methods. Because method lookup starts in the dynamic class of the instance (at the bottom of the inheritance hierarchy), the last redefinition of a method is found first, and this is the one that is executed.

- When a method is overridden, only the last version (the one lowest in the inheritance hierarchy) is executed. Versions of the same method in any superclasses are also not automatically executed.

This explains the behavior that we observe in our *network* project. Only the `display` methods in the subclasses (`MessagePost` and `PhotoPost`) are executed when posts are printed out, leading to incomplete listings. In the next section, we discuss how to fix this.

11.5 super **call in methods**

Now that we know in detail how overridden methods are executed, we can understand the solution to the problem. It is easy to see that what we would want to achieve is for every call to a `display` method of, say, a `PhotoPost` object, to result in both the `display` method of the `Post` class and that of the `PhotoPost` class being executed for the same object. Then all the details would be printed out. (A different solution will be discussed later in this chapter.)

This is, in fact, quite easy to achieve. We can simply use the **super** construct, which we have already encountered in the context of constructors in Chapter 10. Code 11.2 illustrates this idea with the `display` method of the `PhotoPost` class.

Code 11.2
Redefining method
with a **super** call

```
public void display()
{
    super.display();
    System.out.println("   [" + filename + "]");
    System.out.println("   " + caption);
}
```

When `display` is now called on a `PhotoPost` object, initially the `display` method in the `PhotoPost` class will be invoked. As its first statement, this method will in turn invoke the `display` method of the superclass, which prints out the general post information. When control returns from the superclass method, the remaining statements of the subclass method print the distinctive fields of the `PhotoPost` class.

There are three details worth noting:

- Contrary to the case of **super** calls in constructors, the method name of the superclass method is explicitly stated. A **super** call in a method always has the form

    super.*method-name*(*parameters*)

- The parameter list can, of course, be empty.

- Again, contrary to the rule for **super** calls in constructors, the **super** call in methods may occur anywhere within that method. It does not have to be the first statement.

- And contrary to the case of **super** calls in constructors, no automatic **super** call is generated and no **super** call is required; it is entirely optional. So the default behavior gives the effect of a subclass method completely hiding (i.e., overriding) the superclass version of the same method.

Exercise 11.3 Modify your latest version of the *network* project to include the super call in the `display` method. Test it. Does it behave as expected? Do you see any problems with this solution?

It is worth reiterating what was illustrated in Exercise 10.6: that in the absence of method overriding, the non-private methods of a superclass are directly accessible from its subclasses without any special syntax. A **super** call only has to be made when it is necessary to access the superclass version of an *overridden* method.

If you completed Exercise 11.3, you will have noticed that this solution works, but is not perfect yet. It prints out all details, but in a different order from what we wanted. We will fix this last problem later in the chapter.

1.6 Method polymorphism

Concept

Method polymorphism.
Method calls in Java are polymorphic. The same method call may at different times invoke different methods, depending on the dynamic type of the variable used to make that call.

What we have just discussed in the previous sections (Sections 11.2–11.5) is yet another form of polymorphism. It is what is known as *polymorphic method dispatch* (or *method polymorphism* for short).

Remember that a polymorphic variable is one that can store objects of varying types (every object variable in Java is potentially polymorphic). In a similar manner, Java method calls are polymorphic, because they may invoke different methods at different times. For instance, the statement

```
post.display();
```

could invoke the **MessagePost**'s **display** method at one time and the **PhotoPost**'s **display** method at another, depending on the dynamic type of the **post** variable.

1.7 Object methods: toString

Concept

Every object in Java has a **toString** method that can be used to return a string representation of itself. Typically, to make it useful, an object should override this method.

In Chapter 10, we mentioned that the universal superclass, **Object**, implements some methods that are then part of all objects. The most interesting of these methods is **toString**, which we introduce here (if you are interested in more detail, you can look up the interface for **Object** in the standard library documentation).

Exercise 11.4 Look up **toString** in the library documentation. What are its parameters? What is its return type?

The purpose of the **toString** method is to create a string representation of an object. This is useful for any objects that are ever to be textually represented in the user interface, but also helps for all other objects; they can then easily be printed out for debugging purposes, for instance.

The default implementation of **toString** in class **Object** cannot supply a great amount of detail. If, for example, we call **toString** on a **PhotoPost** object, we receive a string similar to this:

```
PhotoPost@65c221c0
```

The return value simply shows the object's class name and a magic number.[2]

To make this method more useful, we would typically override it in our own classes. We can, for example, define the **Post**'s **display** method in terms of a call to its **toString** method. In this case, the **toString** method would not print out the details, but just create a string with the text. Code 11.3 shows the changed source code.

Code 11.3
toString
method for
Post and
MessagePost

```java
public class Post
{
    ...
    public String toString()
    {
        String text = username + "\n" + timeString(timestamp);
        if(likes > 0) {
            text += "  -  " + likes + " people like this.\n";
        }
        else {
            text += "\n";
        }

        if(comments.isEmpty()) {
            return text + "   No comments.\n";
        }
        else {
            return text + "    " + comments.size() +
                    " comment(s). Click here to view.\n";
        }
    }

    public void display()
    {
        System.out.println(toString());
    }
}
```

---

[2] The magic number is in fact the memory address where the object is stored. It is not very useful except to establish identity. If this number is the same in two calls, we are looking at the same object. If it is different, we have two distinct objects.

**Code 11.3
continued**

toString
method for
Post and
MessagePost

```
public class MessagePost extends Post
{
    ...

    public String toString()
    {
        return super.toString() + message + "\n";
    }

    public void display()
    {
        System.out.println(toString());
    }
}
```

Ultimately, we would plan on removing the **display** methods completely from these classes. A great benefit of defining just a **toString** method is that we do not mandate in the **Post** classes what exactly is done with the description text. The original version always printed the text to the output terminal. Now, any client (e.g., the **NewsFeed** class) is free to do whatever it chooses with this text. It might show the text in a text area in a graphical user interface; save it to a file; send it over a network; show it in a web browser; or, as before, print it to the terminal.

The statement used in the client to print the post could now look as follows:

```
System.out.println(post.toString());
```

In fact, the **System.out.print** and **System.out.println** methods are special in this respect: if the parameter to one of the methods is not a **String** object, then the method automatically invokes the object's **toString** method. Thus we do not need to write the call explicitly and could instead write

```
System.out.println(post);
```

Now consider the modified version of the **show** method of class **NewsFeed** shown in Code 11.4. In this version, we have removed the **toString** call. Would it compile and run correctly?

Code 11.4

New version of
NewsFeed show
method

```
public class NewsFeed
{
    Fields, constructors, and other methods omitted.

    /**
     * Show the news feed. Currently: print the news feed details to the
     * terminal. (To do: replace this later with display in web browser.)
     */
    public void show()
    {
        for(Post post : posts) {
            System.out.println(post);
        }
    }
}
```

In fact, the method *does* work as expected. If you can explain this example in detail, then you probably already have a good understanding of most of the concepts that we have introduced in this and the previous chapter! Here is a detailed explanation of the single `println` statement inside the loop.

- The for-each loop iterates through all posts and places them in a variable with the static type **Post**. The dynamic type is either **MessagePost** or **PhotoPost**.

- Because this object is being printed to **System.out** and it is not a **String**, its **toString** method is automatically invoked.

- Invoking this method is valid only because the class **Post** (the static type!) has a **toString** method. (Remember: Type checking is done with the static type. This call would not be allowed if class **Post** had no **toString** method. However, the **toString** method in class **Object** guarantees that this method is always available for any class.)

- The output appears properly with all details, because each possible dynamic type (**MessagePost** and **PhotoPost**) overrides the **toString** method and the dynamic method lookup ensures that the redefined method is executed.

The **toString** method is generally useful for debugging purposes. Often, it is very convenient if objects can easily be printed out in a sensible format. Most of the Java library classes override **toString** (all collections, for instance, can be printed out like this), and often it is a good idea to override this method for our classes as well.

11.8 Object equality: `equals` and `hashCode`

It is often necessary to determine whether two objects are "the same." The **Object** class defines two methods, **equals** and **hashCode**, that have a close link with determining similarity. We actually have to be careful when using phrases such as "the same"; this is because it can mean two quite different things when talking about objects. Sometimes we wish to know whether two different variables are referring to the same object. This is exactly what happens when an object variable is passed as a parameter to a method: there is only one object, but both the original variable and the parameter variable refer to it. The same thing happens when any object variable is assigned to another. These situations produce what is called *reference equality*. Reference equality is tested for using the **==** operator. So the following test will return **true** if both **var1** and **var2** are referring to the same object (or are both **null**), and **false** if they are referring to anything else:

```
var1 == var2
```

Reference equality takes no account at all of the *contents* of the objects referred to, just whether there is one object referred to by two different variables or two distinct objects. That is why we also define *content equality*, as distinct from reference equality. A test for content equality asks whether two objects are the same internally—that is, whether the internal states of two objects are the same. This is why we rejected using reference equality for making string comparisons in Chapter 6.

What content equality between two particular objects means is something that is defined by the objects' class. This is where we make use of the **equals** method that every class inherits from the **Object** superclass. If we need to define what it means for two objects to be equal according to their internal states, then we must override the **equals** method, which then allows us to write tests such as

```
var1.equals(var2)
```

This is because the **equals** method inherited from the **Object** class actually makes a test for reference equality. It looks something like this:

```
public boolean equals(Object obj)
{
    return this == obj;
}
```

Because the **Object** class has no fields, there is no state to compare, and this method obviously cannot anticipate fields that might be present in subclasses.

The way to test for content equality between two objects is to test whether the values of their two sets of fields are equal. Notice, however, that the parameter of the **equals** method is of type **Object**, so a test of the fields will make sense only if we are comparing fields of the same type. This means that we first have to establish that the type of the object passed as a parameter is the same as that of the object it is being compared with. Here is how we might think of writing the method in the **Student** class of the *lab-classes* project from Chapter 1:

```
public boolean equals(Object obj)
{
    if(this == obj) {
        return true; // Reference equality.
    }
    if(!(obj instanceof Student)) {
        return false; // Not the same type.
    }
    // Gain access to the other student's fields.
    Student other = (Student) obj;
    return name.equals(other.name) &&
           id.equals(other.id) &&
           credits == other.credits;
}
```

The first test is just an efficiency improvement; if the object has been passed a reference to itself to compare against, then we know that content equality must be true. The second test makes sure that we are comparing two students. If not, then we decide that the two objects cannot be equal. Having established that we have another student, we use a cast and another variable of the right type so that we can access its details properly. Finally, we make use of the fact that the private elements of an object are directly accessible to an instance of the same class; this is essential in situations such as this one, because there will not necessarily be accessor methods defined for every private field in a class. Notice that we have consistently used content-equality tests rather than reference-equality tests on the object fields **name** and **id**.

It will not always be necessary to compare every field in two objects in order to establish that they are equal. For instance, if we know for certain that every **Student** is assigned a unique **id**, then we need not test the **name** and **credits** fields as well. It would then be possible to reduce the final statement above to

```
return id.equals(other.id);
```

Whenever the **equals** method is overridden, the **hashCode** method should also be overridden. The **hashCode** method is used by data structures such as **HashMap** and **HashSet** to provide efficient placement and lookup of objects in these collections. Essentially, the **hashCode** method returns an integer value that represents an object. From the default implementation in **Object**, distinct objects have distinct **hashCode** values.

There is an important link between the **equals** and **hashCode** methods in that two objects that are the same as determined by a call to **equals** must return identical values from **hashCode**. This stipulation, or contract, can be found in the description of **hashCode** in the API documentation of the **Object** class.[3] It is beyond the scope of this book to describe in detail a suitable technique for calculating hash codes, but we recommend that the interested reader see Joshua Bloch's *Effective Java*, whose technique we use here.[4] Essentially, an integer value should be computed making use of the values of the fields that are compared by the overridden **equals** method. Here is a hypothetical **hashCode** method that uses the values of an integer field called **count** and a **String** field called **name** to calculate the code:

```
public int hashCode()
{
    int result = 17; // An arbitrary starting value.
    // Make the computed value depend on the order in which
    // the fields are processed.
    result = 37 * result + count;
    result = 37 * result + name.hashCode();
    return result;
}
```

11.9   Protected access

In Chapter 10, we noted that the rules on public and private visibility of class members apply between a subclass and its superclass, as well as between classes in different inheritance hierarchies. This can be somewhat restrictive, because the relationship between a superclass and its subclasses is clearly closer than it is with other classes. For this reason, object-oriented languages often define a level of access that lies between the complete restriction of private access and the full availability of public access. In Java, this is called *protected access* and is provided by the **protected** keyword as an alternative to **public** and **private**. Code 11.5 shows an example of a protected accessor method, which we could add to class **Post**.

---

[3] Note that it is not essential that unequal objects always return distinct hash codes.

[4] Joshua Bloch: *Effective Java*, 2nd edition. Addison-Wesley. ISBN: 0-321-35668-3.

Code 11.5
An example of a `protected` method

```
protected long getTimeStamp()
{
    return timestamp;
}
```

Concepts

Declaring a field or a method **protected** allows direct access to it from (direct or indirect) subclasses.

Protected access allows access to the fields or methods within a class itself and from all its subclasses, but not from other classes.[5] The **getTimeStamp** method shown in Code 11.5 can be called from class **Post** or any subclasses, but not from other classes. Figure 11.8 illustrates this. The oval areas in the diagram show the group of classes that are able to access members in class **SomeClass**.

While protected access can be applied to any member of a class, it is usually reserved for methods and constructors. It is not usually applied to fields, because that would be a weakening of encapsulation. Wherever possible, mutable fields in superclasses should remain private. There are, however, occasional valid cases where direct access by subclasses is desirable. Inheritance represents a much closer form of coupling than does a normal client relationship.

Inheritance binds the classes closer together, and changing the superclass can more easily break the subclass. This should be taken into consideration when designing classes and their relationships.

Figure 11.8
Access levels: private, protected, and public

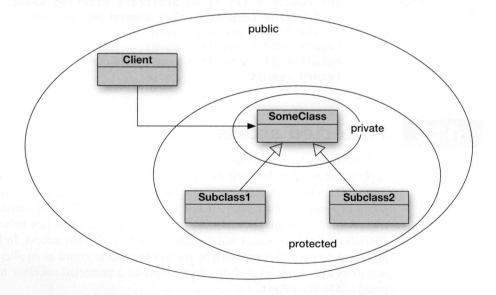

---

[5] In Java, this rule is not as clear-cut as described here, because Java includes an additional level of visibility, called *package level*, but with no associated keyword. We will not discuss this further, and it is more general to consider protected access as intended for the special relationship between superclass and subclass.

Exercise 11.6 The version of `display` shown in Code 11.2 produces the output shown in Figure 11.9. Reorder the statements in the method in your version of the *network* project so that it prints the details as shown in Figure 11.10.

Figure 11.9
Possible output
from `display`:
superclass call at
the beginning of
`display` (shaded
areas printed
by superclass
method).

```
Leonardo da Vinci
40 seconds ago - 2 people like this.
   No comments.
Had a great idea this morning.
But now I forgot what it was. Something to do with flying...
```

Figure 11.10
Alternative output
from `display`
(shaded areas
printed by super-
class method)

```
Had a great idea this morning.
But now I forgot what it was. Something to do with flying...
Leonardo da Vinci
40 seconds ago - 2 people like this.
   No comments.
```

Exercise 11.7 Having to use a superclass call in `display` is somewhat restrictive in the ways in which we can format the output, because it is dependent on the way the superclass formats its fields. Make any necessary changes to the **Post** class and to the `display` method of **MessagePost** so that it produces the output shown in Figure 11.11. Any changes you make to the **Post** class should be visible only to its subclasses. *Hint:* You could add protected accessors to do this.

Figure 11.11
Output from
`display` mix-
ing subclass and
superclass details
(shaded areas rep-
resent superclass
details)

```
Leonardo da Vinci
Had a great idea this morning.
But now I forgot what it was. Something to do with flying...
40 seconds ago - 2 people like this.
   No comments.
```

11.10 The `instanceof` operator

One of the consequences of the introduction of inheritance into the *network* project has been that the **NewsFeed** class knows only about **Post** objects and cannot distinguish between message posts and photo posts. This has allowed all types of posts to be stored in a single list.

However, suppose that we wish to retrieve just the message posts or just the photo posts from the list; how would we do that? Or perhaps we wish to look for a message by a particular author? That is not a problem if the **Post** class defines a **getAuthor** method, but this will find both message and photo posts. Will it matter which type is returned?

There are occasions when we need to rediscover the distinctive dynamic type of an object rather than dealing with a shared supertype. For this, Java provides the **instanceof** operator. The **instanceof** operator tests whether a given object is, directly or indirectly, an instance of a given class. The test

```
obj instanceof MyClass
```

returns **true** if the dynamic type of **obj** is **MyClass** or any subclass of **MyClass**. The left operand is always an object reference, and the right operand is always the name of a class. So

```
post instanceof MessagePost
```

returns **true** only if **post** is a **MessagePost**, as opposed to a **PhotoPost**, for instance.

Use of the **instanceof** operator is often followed immediately by a cast of the object reference to the identified type. For instance, here is some code to identify all of the message posts in a list of posts and to store them in a separate list.

```
ArrayList<MessagePost> messages = new ArrayList<>();
for(Post post : posts) {
    if(post instanceof MessagePost) {
        messages.add((MessagePost) post);
    }
}
```

It should be clear that the cast here does not alter the post object in any way, because we have just established that it already is a **MessagePost** object.

11.11 Another example of inheritance with overriding

To discuss another example of a similar use of inheritance, we go back to a project from Chapter 8: the *zuul* project. In the *world-of-zuul* game, we used a set of **Room** objects to create a scene for a simple game. Exercise 8.45 suggested that you implement a transporter room (a room that beams you to a random location in the game if you try to enter or leave it). We revisit this exercise here, because its solution can greatly benefit from inheritance. If you don't remember this project well, have a quick read through Chapter 8 again, or look at your own *zuul* project.

There is no single solution to this task. Many different solutions are possible and can be made to work. Some are better than others—more elegant, easier to read, and easier to maintain and to extend.

Assume that we want to implement this task so that the player is automatically transported to a random room when she tries to leave the magic transporter room. The most straightforward solution that comes to mind first for many people is to deal with this in the **Game** class, which implements the player's commands. One of the commands is *go*, which is implemented in the **goRoom** method. In this method, we used the following statement as the central section of code:

```
nextRoom = currentRoom.getExit(direction);
```

This statement retrieves from the current room the neighboring room in the direction we want to go. To add our magic transportation, we could modify this in a form similar to the following:

```
if(currentRoom.getName().equals("Transporter room")) {
    nextRoom = getRandomRoom();
}
else {
    nextRoom = currentRoom.getExit(direction);
}
```

The idea here is simple: we just check whether we are in the transporter room. If we are, then we find the next room by getting a random room (of course, we have to implement the **getRandomRoom** method somehow); otherwise, we just do the same as before.

While this solution works, it has several drawbacks. The first is that it is a bad idea to use text strings, such as the room's name, to identify the room. Imagine that someone wanted to translate your game into another language—say, to German. They might change the names of the rooms—"Transporter room" becomes "Transporterraum"—and suddenly the game does not work any more! This is a clear case of a maintainability problem.

The second solution, which is slightly better, would be to use an instance variable instead of the room's name to identify the transporter room. Similar to this:

```
if(currentRoom == transporterRoom) {
    nextRoom = getRandomRoom();
}
else {
    nextRoom = currentRoom.getExit(direction);
}
```

This time, we assume that we have an instance variable **transporterRoom** of class **Room**, where we store the reference to our transporter room.[6] Now the check is independent of the room's name. That is a bit better.

There is still a case for further improvement, though. We can understand the shortcomings of this solution when we think about another maintenance change. Imagine that we want to add two more transporter rooms, so that our game has three different transporter locations.

A very nice aspect of our existing design was that we could set up the floor plan in a single spot, and the rest of the game was completely independent of it. We could easily change the layout of the rooms, and everything would still work—high score for maintainability! With our current solution, though, this is broken. If we add two new transporter rooms, we have to add two more instance variables or an array (to store references to those rooms), and we have to modify our **goRoom** method to add a check for those rooms. In terms of easy changeability, we have gone backwards.

---

[6] Make sure that you understand why a test for reference equality is the most appropriate here.

The question, therefore, is: Can we find a solution that does not require a change to the command implementation each time we add a new transporter room? Following is our next idea.

We can add a method **isTransporterRoom** in the **Room** class. This way, the **Game** object does not need to remember all the transporter rooms—the rooms themselves do. When rooms are created, they could receive a boolean flag indicating whether a given room is a transporter room. The **goRoom** method could then use the following code segment:

```
if(currentRoom.isTransporterRoom()) {
    nextRoom = getRandomRoom();
}
else {
    nextRoom = currentRoom.getExit(direction);
}
```

Now we can add as many transporter rooms as we like; there is no need for any more changes to the **Game** class. However, the **Room** class has an extra field whose value is really needed only because of the nature of one or two of the instances. Special-case code such as this is a typical indicator of a weakness in class design. This approach also does not scale well should we decide to introduce further sorts of special rooms, each requiring its own flag field and accessor method.[7]

With inheritance, we can do better and implement a solution that is even more flexible than this one. We can implement a class **TransporterRoom** as a subclass of class **Room**. In this new class, we override the **getExit** method and change its implementation so that it returns a random room:

```
public class TransporterRoom extends Room
{
    /**
     * Return a random room, independent of the direction
     * parameter.
     * @param direction Ignored.
     * @return A random room.
     */
    public Room getExit(String direction)
    {
        return findRandomRoom();
    }

    /*
     * Choose a random room.
     * @return A random room.
     */
    private Room findRandomRoom()
    {
        ... // implementation omitted
    }
}
```

---

[7] We might also think of using **instanceof**, but the point here is that none of these ideas is the best.

The elegance of this solution lies in the fact that no change at all is needed in either the original **Game** or **Room** classes! We can simply add this class to the existing game, and the **goRoom** method will continue to work as it is. Adding the creation of a **TransporterRoom** to the setup of the floor plan is (almost) enough to make it work. Note, too, that the new class does not need a flag to indicate its special nature—its very type and distinctive behavior supply that information.

Because **TransporterRoom** is a subclass of **Room**, it can be used everywhere a **Room** object is expected. Thus, it can be used as a neighboring room for another room or be held in the **Game** object as the current room.

What we have left out, of course, is the implementation of the **findRandomRoom** method. In reality, this is probably better done in a separate class (say **RoomRandomizer**) than in the **TransporterRoom** class itself. We leave this as an exercise for the reader.

> **Exercise 11.8** Implement a transporter room with inheritance in your version of the *zuul* project.
>
> **Exercise 11.9** Discuss how inheritance could be used in the *zuul* project to implement a player and a monster class.
>
> **Exercise 11.10** Could (or should) inheritance be used to create an inheritance relationship (super-, sub-, or sibling class) between a character in the game and an item?

11.12 Summary

When we deal with classes with subclasses and polymorphic variables, we have to distinguish between the static and dynamic type of a variable. The static type is the declared type, while the dynamic type is the type of the object currently stored in the variable.

Type checking is done by the compiler using the static type, whereas at runtime method lookup uses the dynamic type. This enables us to create very flexible structures by overriding methods. Even when using a supertype variable to make a method call, overriding enables us to ensure that specialized methods are invoked for every particular subtype. This ensures that objects of different classes can react distinctly to the same method call.

When implementing overriding methods, the **super** keyword can be used to invoke the superclass version of the method. If fields or methods are declared with the **protected** access modifier, subclasses are allowed to access them, but other classes are not.

Terms introduced in this chapter:

> **static type, dynamic type, overriding, redefinition, method lookup, method dispatch, method polymorphism, protected**

Concept summary

- **static type** The static type of a variable **v** is the type as declared in the source code in the variable declaration statement.

- **dynamic type** The dynamic type of a variable **v** is the type of the object that is currently stored in **v**.

- **overriding** A subclass can override a method implementation. To do this, the subclass declares a method with the same signature as the superclass, but with a different method body. The overriding method takes precedence for method calls on subclass objects.

- **method polymorphism** Method calls in Java are polymorphic. The same method call may at different times invoke different methods, depending on the dynamic type of the variable used to make that call.

- **toString** Every object in Java has a **toString** method that can be used to return a string representation of itself. Typically, to make it useful, a class should override this method.

- **protected** Declaring a field or a method **protected** allows direct access to it from (direct or indirect) subclasses.

Exercise 11.11 Assume that you see the following lines of code:

```
Device dev = new Printer();
dev.getName();
```

Printer is a subclass of **Device**. Which of these classes must have a definition of method **getName** for this code to compile?

Exercise 11.12 In the same situation as in the previous exercise, if both classes have an implementation of **getName**, which one will be executed?

Exercise 11.13 Assume that you write a class **Student** that does not have a declared superclass. You do not write a **toString** method. Consider the following lines of code:

```
Student st = new Student();
String s = st.toString();
```

Will these lines compile? If so, what exactly will happen when you try to execute?

Exercise 11.14 In the same situation as before (class **Student**, no **toString** method), will the following lines compile? Why?

```
Student st = new Student();
System.out.println(st);
```

Exercise 11.15 Assume that your class **Student** overrides **toString** so that it returns the student's name. You now have a list of students. Will the following code compile? If not, why not? If yes, what will it print? Explain in detail what happens.

```
for(Object st : myList) {
    System.out.println(st);
}
```

Exercise 11.16 Write a few lines of code that result in a situation where a variable **x** has the static type **T** and the dynamic type **D**.

Main concepts discussed in this chapter:

- abstract classes
- multiple inheritance
- interfaces

Java constructs discussed in this chapter:

`abstract`, `implements`, `interface`

In this chapter, we examine further inheritance-related techniques that can be used to enhance class structures and improve maintainability and extensibility. These techniques introduce an improved method of representation of abstractions in object-oriented programs.

The previous two chapters have discussed the most important aspects of inheritance in application design, but several more advanced uses and problems have been ignored so far. We will now complete the picture with a more advanced example.

The project we use for this chapter is a simulation. We use it to discuss inheritance again and see that we run into some new problems. Abstract classes and interfaces are then introduced to deal with these problems.

12.1 Simulations

Computers are frequently used to simulate real systems. These include systems that model traffic flows in a city, forecast weather, simulate the spread of infection, analyze the stock market, do environmental simulations, and much more. In fact, many of the most powerful computers in the world are used for running some sort of simulation.

When creating a computer simulation, we try to model the behavior of a subset of the real world in a software model. Every simulation is necessarily a simplification of the real thing. Deciding which details to leave out and which to include is often a challenging task. The more detailed a simulation is, the more accurate it may be in forecasting the behavior of the real system. But more detail increases the complexity of the model and the requirements for both more computing power and more programmer time. A well-known example is weather forecasting: climate models in weather simulations have been improved by adding more and more detail over the last few decades. As a result, weather forecasts have improved significantly in accuracy (but are far from perfect, as we all have experienced at some time). Much of this improvement has been made possible through advances in computer technology.

The benefit of simulations is that we can undertake experiments that we could not do with the real system, either because we have no control over the real thing (for instance, the weather) or because it is too costly, too dangerous, or irreversible in case of disaster. We can use the simulation to investigate the behavior of the system under certain circumstances or to investigate "what if" questions.

An example of the use of environmental simulations is to try to predict the effects of human activity on natural habitats. Consider the case of a national park containing endangered species and a proposal to build a freeway through the middle of it, completely separating the two halves. The supporters of the freeway proposal claim that splitting the park in half will lead to little actual land loss and make no difference to the animals in it, but environmentalists claim otherwise. How can we tell what the effect is likely to be without building the freeway? Simulation is one option. An essential question in all cases of this kind will be, of course, "How good is the simulation?" One can "prove" just about anything with an ill-designed simulation. Gaining trust in it through controlled experiments will be essential.

The issue in this particular case boils down to whether it is significant for the survival of a species to have a single, connected habitat area, or whether two disjoint areas (with the same total size as the other) are just as good. Rather than building the freeway first and then observing what happens, we will try to simulate the effect in order to make a well-informed decision.[1]

Our simulation will necessarily be simpler than the scenario we have described, because we are using it mainly to illustrate new features of object-oriented design and implementation. Therefore, it will not have the potential to simulate accurately many aspects of nature, but some of the simulation's characteristics are nonetheless interesting. In particular, it will demonstrate the structure of typical simulations. In addition, its accuracy may surprise you; it would be a mistake to equate greater complexity with greater accuracy. It is often the case that a simplified model of something can provide greater insight and understanding than a more complex one, from which it is often difficult to isolate the underlying mechanisms—or even be sure that the model is valid.

12.2 The foxes-and-rabbits simulation

The simulation scenario we have chosen to work with in this chapter uses the freeway example from above as its basis. It involves tracking populations of foxes and rabbits within an enclosed area. This is just one particular example of what are known as *predator–prey*

---

[1] In this particular case, by the way, size does matter: the size of a natural park has a significant impact on its usefulness as a habitat for animals.

simulations. Such simulations are often used to model the variation in population sizes that result from a predator species feeding on a prey species. A delicate balance exists between such species. A large population of prey will potentially provide plenty of food for a small population of predators. However, too many predators could kill off all the prey and leave the hunters with nothing to eat. Population sizes could also be affected by the size and nature of the environment. For instance, a small, enclosed environment could lead to overcrowding and make it easy for the predators to locate their prey, or a polluted environment could reduce the stock of prey and prevent even a modest population of predators from surviving. Because predators in one context are often prey for other species (think of cats, birds, and worms, for instance), loss of one part of the food chain can have dramatic effects on the survival of other parts.

As we have done in previous chapters, we will start with a version of an application that works perfectly well from a user's point of view, but whose internal view is not so good when judged by the principles of good object-oriented design and implementation. We will use this base version to develop several improved versions that progressively introduce new abstraction techniques.

One particular problem that we wish to address in the base version is that it does not make good use of the inheritance techniques that were introduced in Chapter 10. However, we will start by examining the mechanism of the simulation, without being too critical of its implementation. Once we understand how it works, we shall be in a good position to make some improvements.

> **Predator–prey modeling** There is a long history of trying to model predator–prey relationships mathematically before the invention of the computer, because they have economic, as well as environmental, importance. For instance, mathematical models were used in the early twentieth century to explain variations in the level of fish stocks in the Adriatic Sea as a side effect of World War I. To find out more about the background of this topic, and perhaps gain an understanding of population dynamics, do a web search for the Lotka-Volterra model.

12.2.1 The *foxes-and-rabbits* project

Open the *foxes-and-rabbits-v1* project. The class diagram is shown in Figure 12.1.

The main classes we will focus on in our discussion are **Simulator**, **Fox**, and **Rabbit**. The **Fox** and **Rabbit** classes provide simple models of the behavior of a predator and prey, respectively. In this particular implementation, we have not tried to provide an accurate biological model of real foxes and rabbits; rather, we are simply trying to illustrate the principles of typical predator–prey simulations. Our main concerns will be on the aspects that most affect population size: birth, death, and food supply.

The **Simulator** class is responsible for creating the initial state of the simulation, then controlling and executing it. The basic idea is simple: the simulator holds collections of foxes and rabbits, and it repeatedly gives those animals an opportunity to live through one

Figure 12.1

Class diagram of the
foxes-and-rabbits
project

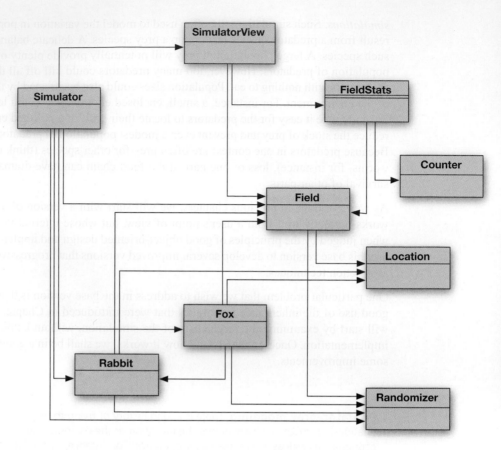

step[2] of their life cycle. At each step, each fox and each rabbit is allowed to carry out the actions that characterize their behaviors. After each step (when all the animals have had the chance to act), the new current state of the field is displayed on screen.

We can summarize the purpose of the remaining classes as follows:

■ **Field** represents a two-dimensional enclosed field. The field is composed of a fixed number of locations, which are arranged in rows and columns. At most, one animal may occupy a single location within the field. Each field location can hold an animal, or it can be empty.

■ **Location** represents a two-dimensional position within the field, specified by a row and a column value.

■ These five classes together (**Simulator**, **Fox**, **Rabbit**, **Field**, and **Location**) provide the model for the simulation. They completely determine the simulation behavior.

---

[2] We won't define how much time a "step" actually represents. In practice, this has to be decided by a combination of such things as what we are trying to discover, what events we are simulating, and how much real time is available to run the simulation.

- The **Randomizer** class provides us with a degree of control over random aspects of the simulation, such as when new animals are born.

- The classes **SimulatorView**, **FieldStats**, and **Counter** provide a graphical display of the simulation. The display shows an image of the field and counters for each species (the current number of rabbits and foxes).

- **SimulatorView** provides a visualization of the state of the field. An example can be seen in Figure 12.2.

- **FieldStats** provides to the visualization counts of the numbers of foxes and rabbits in the field.

- A **Counter** stores a current count for one type of animal to assist with the counting.

Try the following exercises to gain an understanding of how the simulation operates before reading about its implementation.

> **Exercise 12.1** Create a **Simulator** object, using the constructor without parameters, and you should see an initial state of the simulation similar to that in Figure 12.2. The more numerous rectangles represent the rabbits. Does the number of foxes change if you call the **simulateOneStep** method just once?

Figure 12.2
The graphical display of the *foxes-and-rabbits* simulation

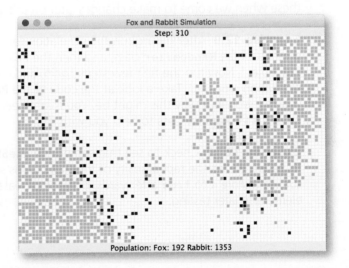

> **Exercise 12.2** Does the number of foxes change on every step? What natural processes do you think we are modeling that cause the number of foxes to increase or decrease?
>
> **Exercise 12.3** Call the **simulate** method with a parameter to run the simulation continuously for a significant number of steps, such as 50 or 100. Do the numbers of foxes and rabbits increase or decrease at similar rates?

Exercise 12.4 What changes do you notice if you run the simulation for a much longer time, say for 4,000 steps? You can use the `runLongSimulation` method to do this.

Exercise 12.5 Use the `reset` method to create a new starting state for the simulation, and then run it again. Is an identical simulation run this time? If not, do you see broadly similar patterns emerging anyway?

Exercise 12.6 If you run a simulation for long enough, do all of the foxes or all of the rabbits ever die off completely? If so, can you pinpoint any reasons why that might be occurring?

Exercise 12.7 In the source code of the `Simulator` class, find the `simulate` method. In its body, you will see a call to a `delay` method that is commented out. Uncomment this call and run the simulation. Experiment with different delays so you can observe the simulation behavior more clearly. At the end, leave it in a state that makes the simulation look useful on your computer.

Exercise 12.8 Make a note of the numbers of foxes and rabbits at each of the first few steps, and at the end of a long run. It will be useful to have a record of these when we come to make changes later on and perform regression testing.

Exercise 12.9 After having run the simulation for a while, call the static `reset` method of the `Randomizer` class, and then the `reset` method of the `Simulator` object. Now run the first few steps again, and you should see the original simulation repeated. Take a look at the code of the `Randomizer` class to see if you can work out why this might be. You might need to look at the API for the `java.util.Random` class to help you with this.

Exercise 12.10 Check to see that setting the `useShared` field in `Randomizer` to `false` breaks the repeatability of the simulations seen in Exercise 12.9. Be sure to restore it to `true` afterwards, because repeatability will be an important element in later testing.

Now that we have a broad, external understanding of what this project does, we will look in detail at the implementation of the **Rabbit**, **Fox**, and `Simulator` classes.

12.2.2 The `Rabbit` class

The source code of the **Rabbit** class is shown in Code 12.1.

The **Rabbit** class contains a number of class variables that define configuration settings that are common to all rabbits. These include values for the maximum age to which a rabbit can live (defined as a number of simulation steps) and the maximum number of offspring

Code 12.1

The **Rabbit** class

Import statement and class comment omitted.

```java
public class Rabbit
{
    // Characteristics shared by all rabbits (class variables).

    // The age at which a rabbit can start to breed.
    private static final int BREEDING_AGE = 5;
    // The age to which a rabbit can live.
    private static final int MAX_AGE = 40;
    // The likelihood of a rabbit breeding.
    private static final double BREEDING_PROBABILITY = 0.12;
    // The maximum number of births.
    private static final int MAX_LITTER_SIZE = 4;
    // A shared random number generator to control breeding.
    private static final Random rand = Randomizer.getRandom();

    // Individual characteristics (instance fields).

    // The rabbit's age.
    private int age;
    // Whether the rabbit is alive or not.
    private boolean alive;
    // The rabbit's position.
    private Location location;
    // The field occupied.
    private Field field;

    /**
     * Create a new rabbit. A rabbit may be created with age
     * zero (a new born) or with a random age.
     *
     * @param randomAge If true, the rabbit will have a random age.
     * @param field The field currently occupied.
     * @param location The location within the field.
     */
    public Rabbit(boolean randomAge, Field field, Location location)
    {
        Body of constructor omitted.
    }

    /**
     * This is what the rabbit does most of the time - it runs
     * around. Sometimes it will breed or die of old age.
     * @param newRabbits A list to return newly born rabbits.
     */
    public void run(List<Rabbit> newRabbits)
    {
        incrementAge();
        if(alive) {
            giveBirth(newRabbits);
            // Try to move into a free location.
            Location newLocation = field.freeAdjacentLocation(location);
            if(newLocation != null) {
                setLocation(newLocation);
            }
    }
```

Code 12.1
continued
The **Rabbit** class

```
            else {
                // Overcrowding.
                setDead();
            }
        }
    }

    /**
     * Indicate that the rabbit is no longer alive.
     * It is removed from the field.
     */
    public void setDead()
    {
        alive = false;
        if(location != null) {
            field.clear(location);
            location = null;
            field = null;
        }
    }

    /**
     * Increase the age.
     * This could result in the rabbit's death.
     */
    private void incrementAge()
    {
        age++;
        if(age > MAX_AGE) {
            setDead();
        }
    }

    /**
     * Check whether or not this rabbit is to give birth at this step.
     * New births will be made into free adjacent locations.
     * @param newRabbits A list to return newly born rabbits.
     */
    private void giveBirth(List<Rabbit> newRabbits)
    {
        // New rabbits are born into adjacent locations.
        // Get a list of adjacent free locations.
        List<Location> free = field.getFreeAdjacentLocations(location);
        int births = breed();
        for(int b = 0; b < births && free.size() > 0; b++) {
            Location loc = free.remove(0);
            Rabbit young = new Rabbit(false, field, loc);
            newRabbits.add(young);
        }
    }

    /**
     * Generate a number representing the number of births,
     * if it can breed.
     * @return The number of births (may be zero).
     */
```

Code 12.1
continued
The **Rabbit** class

```
private int breed()
{
    int births = 0;
    if(canBreed() && rand.nextDouble() <= BREEDING_PROBABILITY) {
        births = rand.nextInt(MAX_LITTER_SIZE) + 1;
    }
    return births;
}
```

Other methods omitted.

```
}
```

it can produce at any one step. Centralized control of random aspects of the simulation is provided through a single, shared **Random** object supplied by the **Randomizer** class. This is what makes possible the repeatability seen in Exercise 12.9. In addition, each individual rabbit has four instance variables that describe its state: its age as a number of steps, whether it is still alive, and its location in a particular field.

Exercise 12.11 Do you feel that omitting gender as an attribute in the **Rabbit** class is likely to lead to an inaccurate simulation? Write down the arguments for and against including it.

Exercise 12.12 Are there other simplifications that you feel are present in our implementation of the **Rabbit** class, compared with real life? Discuss whether these could have a significant impact on the accuracy of the simulation.

Exercise 12.13 Experiment with the effects of altering some or all of the values of the class variables in the **Rabbit** class. For instance, what effect does it have on the populations if the breeding probability of rabbits is much higher or much lower than it currently is?

A rabbit's behavior is defined in its **run** method, which in turn uses the **giveBirth** and **incrementAge** methods and implements the rabbit's movement. At each simulation step, the **run** method will be called and a rabbit will increase its age; if old enough, it might also breed, and it will then try to move. Both the movement and the breeding behaviors have random components. The direction in which the rabbit moves is randomly chosen, and breeding occurs randomly, controlled by the class variable **BREEDING_PROBABILITY**.

You can already see some of the simplifications that we have made in our model of rabbits: there is no attempt to distinguish males from females, for instance, and a rabbit could potentially give birth to a new litter at every simulation step once it is old enough.

12.2.3 The **Fox** class

There is a lot of similarity between the **Fox** and the **Rabbit** classes, so only the distinctive elements of **Fox** are shown in Code 12.2.

Code 12.2

The **Fox** class

Import statements and class comment omitted.

```java
public class Fox
{
    // Characteristics shared by all foxes (class variables).

    // The food value of a single rabbit. In effect, this is the
    // number of steps a fox can go before it has to eat again.
    private static final int RABBIT_FOOD_VALUE = 9;

    Other static fields omitted.

    // Individual characteristics (instance fields).

    // The fox's age.
    private int age;
    // Whether the fox is alive or not.
    private boolean alive;
    // The fox's position.
    private Location location;
    // The field occupied.
    private Field field;
    // The fox's food level, which is increased by eating rabbits.
    private int foodLevel;

    /**
     * Create a fox. A fox can be created as a new born (age zero
     * and not hungry) or with a random age and food level.
     *
     * @param randomAge If true the fox will have random age and hunger level.
     * @param field The field currently occupied.
     * @param location The location within the field.
     */
    public Fox(boolean randomAge, Field field, Location location)
    {
        Body of constructor omitted.

    }

    /**
     * This is what the fox does most of the time: it hunts for
     * rabbits. In the process, it might breed, die of hunger,
     * or die of old age.
     * @param field The field currently occupied.
     * @param newFoxes A list to return newly born foxes.
     */
    public void hunt(List<Fox> newFoxes)
    {
        incrementAge();
        incrementHunger();
```

**Code 12.2
continued**

The **Fox** class

```
        if(alive) {
            giveBirth(newFoxes);
            // Move towards a source of food if found.
            Location newLocation = findFood();
            if(newLocation == null) {
                // No food found - try to move to a free location.
                newLocation = field.freeAdjacentLocation(location);
            }
            // See if it was possible to move.
            if(newLocation != null) {
                setLocation(newLocation);
            }
            else {
                // Overcrowding.
                setDead();
            }
        }
    }

    /**
     * Look for rabbits adjacent to the current location.
     * Only the first live rabbit is eaten.
     * @return Where food was found, or null if it wasn't.
     */
    private Location findFood()
    {
        List<Location> adjacent = field.adjacentLocations(location);
        Iterator<Location> it = adjacent.iterator();
        while(it.hasNext()) {
            Location where = it.next();
            Object animal = field.getObjectAt(where);
            if(animal instanceof Rabbit) {
                Rabbit rabbit = (Rabbit) animal;
                if(rabbit.isAlive()) {
                    rabbit.setDead();
                    foodLevel = RABBIT_FOOD_VALUE;
                    return where;
                }
            }
        }
        return null;
    }
```

Other methods omitted.

```
}
```

For foxes, the **hunt** method is invoked at each step and defines their behavior. In addition to aging and possibly breeding at each step, a fox searches for food (using **findFood**). If it is able to find a rabbit in an adjacent location, then the rabbit is killed and the fox's food level is increased. As with rabbits, a fox that is unable to move is considered dead through overcrowding.

Exercise 12.14 As you did for rabbits, assess the degree to which we have simplified the model of foxes and evaluate whether you feel the simplifications are likely to lead to an inaccurate simulation.

Exercise 12.15 Does increasing the maximum age for foxes lead to a significantly higher numbers of foxes throughout a simulation, or is the rabbit population more likely to be reduced to zero as a result?

Exercise 12.16 Experiment with different combinations of settings (breeding age, maximum age, breeding probability, litter size, etc.) for foxes and rabbits. Do species always disappear completely in some configurations? Are there configurations that are stable—i.e., that produce a balance of numbers for a significant length of time?

Exercise 12.17 Experiment with different sizes of fields. (You can do this by using the second constructor of **Simulator**.) Does the size of the field affect the likelihood of species surviving?

Exercise 12.18 Compare the results of running a simulation with a single large field, and two simulations with fields that each have half the area of the single field. This models something close to splitting an area in half with a freeway. Do you notice any significant differences in the population dynamics between the two scenarios?

Exercise 12.19 Repeat the investigations of the previous exercise, but vary the proportions of the two smaller fields. For instance, try three-quarters and one quarter, or two-thirds and one-third. Does it matter at all how the single field is split?

Exercise 12.20 Currently, a fox will eat at most one rabbit at each step. Modify the **findFood** method so that rabbits in all adjacent locations are eaten at a single step. Assess the impact of this change on the results of the simulation. Note that the **findFood** method currently returns the location of the single rabbit that is eaten, so you will need to return the location of one of the eaten rabbits in your version. However, don't forget to return **null** if there are no rabbits to eat.

Exercise 12.21 Following from the previous exercise, if a fox eats multiple rabbits at a single step, there are several different possibilities as to how we can model its food level. If we add all the rabbit's food values, the fox will have a very high food level, making it unlikely to die of hunger for a very long time. Alternatively, we could impose a ceiling on the fox's food level. This models the effect of a predator that kills prey regardless of whether it is hungry or not. Assess the impacts on the resulting simulation of implementing this choice.

> **Exercise 12.22** *Challenge exercise* Given the random elements in the simulation, argue why the population numbers in an apparently stable simulation could ultimately collapse.

12.2.4 The `Simulator` class: setup

The `Simulator` class is the central part of the application that coordinates all the other pieces. Code 12.3 illustrates some of its main features.

Code 12.3
Part of the
Simulator class

Import statements and class comment omitted.

```
public class Simulator
{
    Static variables omitted.

    // Lists of animals in the field.
    private List<Rabbit> rabbits;
    private List<Fox> foxes;
    // The current state of the field.
    private Field field;
    // The current step of the simulation.
    private int step;
    // A graphical view of the simulation.
    private SimulatorView view;

    /**
     * Create a simulation field with the given size.
     * @param depth Depth of the field. Must be greater than zero.
     * @param width Width of the field. Must be greater than zero.
     */
    public Simulator(int depth, int width)
    {
        if(width <= 0 || depth <= 0) {
            System.out.println("The dimensions must be >= zero.");
            System.out.println("Using default values.");
            depth = DEFAULT_DEPTH;
            width = DEFAULT_WIDTH;
        }

        rabbits = new ArrayList<>();
        foxes = new ArrayList<>();
        field = new Field(depth, width);

        // Create a view of the state of each location in the field.
        view = new SimulatorView(depth, width);
        view.setColor(Rabbit.class, Color.ORANGE);
        view.setColor(Fox.class, Color.BLUE);

        // Setup a valid starting point.
        reset();
    }
```

```java
/**
 * Run the simulation for the given number of steps.
 * Stop before the given number of steps if it ceases to be viable.
 * @param numSteps The number of steps to run for.
 */
public void simulate(int numSteps)
{
    for(int step=1; step <= numSteps && view.isViable(field); step++) {
        simulateOneStep();
        // delay(60);   // uncomment this to run more slowly
    }
}

/**
 * Run the simulation from its current state for a single step. Iterate
 * over the whole field updating the state of each fox and rabbit.
 */
public void simulateOneStep()
{

    Method body omitted.

}

/**
 * Reset the simulation to a starting position.
 */
public void reset()
{
    step = 0;
    rabbits.clear();
    foxes.clear();
    populate();

    // Show the starting state in the view.
    view.showStatus(step, field);
}

/**
 * Randomly populate the field with foxes and rabbits.
 */
private void populate()
{
    Random rand = Randomizer.getRandom();
    field.clear();
    for(int row = 0; row < field.getDepth(); row++) {
        for(int col = 0; col < field.getWidth(); col++) {
            if(rand.nextDouble() <= FOX_CREATION_PROBABILITY) {
                Location location = new Location(row, col);
                Fox fox = new Fox(true, field, location);
                foxes.add(fox);
            }
            else if(rand.nextDouble() <= RABBIT_CREATION_PROBABILITY) {
                Location location = new Location(row, col);
                Rabbit rabbit = new Rabbit(true, field, location);
                rabbits.add(rabbit);
            }
```

**Code 12.3
continued**

Part of the
Simulator class

```
                      // else leave the location empty.
            }
        }
    }

    Other methods omitted.
}
```

The **Simulator** has three important parts: its constructor, the **populate** method, and the **simulateOneStep** method. (The body of **simulateOneStep** is shown in Code 12.4.)

When a **Simulator** object is created, all other parts of the simulation are constructed by it (the field, the lists to hold the different types of animals, and the graphical interface). Once all these have been set up, the simulator's **populate** method is called (indirectly, via the **reset** method) to create the initial populations. Different probabilities are used to decide whether a particular location will contain one of these animals. Note that animals created at the start of the simulation are given a random initial age. This serves two purposes:

1. It represents more accurately a mixed-age population that should be the normal state of the simulation.

2. If all animals were to start with an age of zero, no new animals would be created until the initial population had reached their respective breeding ages. With foxes eating rabbits regardless of the fox's age, there is a risk that either the rabbit population will be killed off before it has a chance to reproduce, or that the fox population will die of hunger.

Exercise 12.23 Modify the **populate** method of **Simulator** to determine whether setting an initial age of zero for foxes and rabbits is always catastrophic. Make sure that you run it a sufficient number of times—with different initial states, of course!

Exercise 12.24 If an initial random age is set for rabbits but not foxes, the rabbit population will tend to grow large while the fox population remains very small. Once the foxes do become old enough to breed, does the simulation tend to behave again like the original version? What does this suggest about the relative sizes of the initial populations and their impact on the outcome of the simulation?

12.2.5 The **Simulator** class: a simulation step

The central part of the **Simulator** class is the **simulateOneStep** method shown in Code 12.4. It uses separate loops to let each type of animal move (and possibly breed or do whatever it is programmed to do). Because each animal can give birth to new animals, lists for these to be stored in are passed as parameters to the **hunt** and **run** methods of **Fox** and **Rabbit**. The newly born animals are then added to the master lists at the end of the step. Running longer simulations is trivial. To do this, the **simulateOneStep** method is called repeatedly in a simple loop.

Code 12.4

Inside the `Simu-lator` class: simulating one step

```java
public void simulateOneStep()
{
    step++;

    // Provide space for newborn rabbits.
    List<Rabbit> newRabbits = new ArrayList<>();
    // Let all rabbits act.
    for(Iterator<Rabbit> it = rabbits.iterator(); it.hasNext(); ) {
        Rabbit rabbit = it.next();
        rabbit.run(newRabbits);
        if(! rabbit.isAlive()) {
            it.remove();
        }
    }

    // Provide space for newborn foxes.
    List<Fox> newFoxes = new ArrayList<>();
    // Let all foxes act.
    for(Iterator<Fox> it = foxes.iterator(); it.hasNext(); ) {
        Fox fox = it.next();
        fox.hunt(newFoxes);
        if(! fox.isAlive()) {
            it.remove();
        }
    }

    // Add the newly born foxes and rabbits to the main lists.
    rabbits.addAll(newRabbits);
    foxes.addAll(newFoxes);

    view.showStatus(step, field);
}
```

In order to let each animal act, the simulator holds separate lists of the different types of animals. Here, we make no use of inheritance, and the situation is reminiscent of the first version of the *network* project introduced in Chapter 10.

Exercise 12.25 Each animal is always held in two different data structures: the **Field** and the **Simulator**'s **rabbits** and **foxes** lists. There is a risk that they could be inconsistent with each other. Check that you thoroughly understand how the **Field** and the animal lists are kept consistent between the **simulateOneStep** method in **Simulator**, **hunt** in **Fox**, and **run** in **Rabbit**.

Exercise 12.26 Do you think it would be better for **Simulator** not to keep separate lists of foxes and rabbits, but to generate these lists again from the contents of the field at the beginning of each simulation step? Discuss this.

Exercise 12.27 Write a test to ensure that, at the end of a simulation step, there is no animal (dead or alive) in the field that is not in one of the lists and vice versa. Should there be any dead animals in any of those places at that stage?

12.2.6 Taking steps to improve the simulation

Now that we have examined how the simulation operates, we are in a position to make improvements to its internal design and implementation. Making progressive improvements through the introduction of new programming features will be the focus of subsequent sections. There are several points at which we could start, but one of the most obvious weaknesses is that no attempt has been made to exploit the advantages of inheritance in the implementation of the **Fox** and **Rabbit** classes, which share a lot of common elements. In order to do this, we shall introduce the concept of an *abstract class*.

Exercise 12.28 Identify the similarities and differences between the **Fox** and **Rabbit** classes. Make separate lists of the fields, methods, and constructors, and distinguish between the class variables (static fields) and instance variables.

Exercise 12.29 Candidate methods for placement in a superclass are those that are identical in all subclasses. Which methods are truly identical in the **Fox** and **Rabbit** classes? In reaching a conclusion, you might like to consider the effect of substituting the values of class variables into the bodies of the methods that use them.

Exercise 12.30 In the current version of the simulation, the values of all similarly named class variables are different. If the two values of a particular class variable (**BREEDING_AGE**, say) were identical, would it make any difference to your assessment of which methods are truly identical?

12.3   Abstract classes

Chapter 10 introduced concepts such as inheritance and polymorphism that we ought to be able to exploit in the simulation application. For instance, the **Fox** and **Rabbit** classes share many similar characteristics that suggest they should be subclasses of a common superclass, such as **Animal**. In this section, we will start to make such changes in order to improve the design and implementation of the simulation as a whole. As with the project in Chapter 10, using a common superclass should avoid code duplication in the subclasses and simplify the code in the client class (here, **Simulator**). It is important to note that we are undertaking a process of refactoring and that these changes should not change the essential characteristics of the simulation as seen from a user's viewpoint.

12.3.1 The `Animal` superclass

For the first set of changes, we will move the identical elements of **Fox** and **Rabbit** to an **Animal** superclass. The project *foxes-and-rabbits-v1* provides a copy of the base version of the simulation for you to follow through the changes we make.

■ Both **Fox** and **Rabbit** define **age**, **alive**, **field**, and **location** attributes. However, at this point we will only move **alive**, **location**, and **field** to the **Animal** superclass, and come back to discuss the **age** field later. As is our normal practice with instance fields, we will keep all of these private in the superclass. The initial values are set in the constructor of **Animal**, with **alive** set to **true**, and **field** and **location** passed via **super** calls from the constructors of **Fox** and **Rabbit**.

■ These fields will need accessors and mutators, so we can move the existing **getLocation**, **setLocation**, **isAlive**, and **setDead** from **Fox** and **Rabbit**. We will also need to add a **getField** method in **Animal** so that direct access to **field** from the subclass methods **run**, **hunt**, **giveBirth**, and **findFood** can be replaced.

■ In moving these methods, we have to think about the most appropriate visibility for them. For instance, **setLocation** is private in both **Fox** and **Rabbit**, but cannot be kept private in **Animal** because **Fox** and **Rabbit** would not be able to call it. So we should raise it to **protected** visibility, to indicate that it is for subclasses to call.

■ In a similar vein, notice that **setDead** was public in **Rabbit**, but private in **Fox**. Should it therefore be public in **Animal**? It was public in **Rabbit** because a fox needs to be able to call a rabbit's **setDead** method when it eats its prey. Now that they are sibling classes of a shared superclass, a more appropriate visibility is **protected**, again indicating that this is a method that is not a part of an animal's general interface—at least at this stage of the project's development.

Making these changes is a first step toward eliminating code duplication through the use of inheritance, in much the same way as we did in Chapter 10.

Exercise 12.31 What sort of regression-testing strategy could you establish before undertaking the process of refactoring on the simulation? Is this something you could conveniently automate?

Exercise 12.32 The **Randomizer** class provides us with a way to control whether the "random" elements of the simulation are repeatable or not. If its **useShared** field is set to **true**, then a single **Random** object is shared between all of the simulation objects. In addition, its **reset** method resets the starting point for the shared **Random** object. Use these features as you work on the following exercise, to check that you do not change anything fundamental about the overall simulation as you introduce an **Animal** class.

Create the **Animal** superclass in your version of the project. Make the changes discussed above. Ensure that the simulation works in a similar manner as before. You should be able to check this by having the old and new versions of the project open side by side, for instance, and making identical calls on **Simulator** objects in both, expecting identical outcomes.

Exercise 12.33 How has using inheritance improved the project so far? Discuss this.

12.3.2 Abstract methods

So far, use of the **Animal** superclass has helped to avoid a lot of the code duplication in the **Rabbit** and **Fox** classes, and has potentially made it easier to add new animal types in the future. However, as we saw in Chapter 10, intelligent use of inheritance should also simplify the client class—in this case, **Simulator**. We shall investigate this now.

In the **Simulator** class, we have used separate typed lists of foxes and rabbits and per-list iteration code to implement each simulation step. The relevant code is shown in Code 12.4. Now that we have the **Animal** class, we can improve this. Because all objects in our animal collections are a subtype of **Animal**, we can merge them into a single collection and hence iterate just once using the **Animal** type. However, one problem with this is evident from the single-list solution in Code 12.5. Although we know that each item in the list is an **Animal**, we still have to work out which type of animal it is in order to call the correct action method for its type—**run** or **hunt**. We determine the type using the **instanceof** operator.

Code 12.5

An unsatisfactory single-list solution to making animals act

```
for(Iterator<Animal> it = animals.iterator(); it.hasNext(); ) {
    Animal animal = it.next();
    if(animal instanceof Rabbit) {
        Rabbit rabbit = (Rabbit) animal;
        rabbit.run(newAnimals);
    }
    else if(animal instanceof Fox) {
        Fox fox = (Fox) animal;
        fox.hunt(newAnimals);
    }
    else {
        System.out.println("found unknown animal");
    }
    // Remove dead animals from the simulation.
    if(! animal.isAlive()) {
        it.remove();
    }
}
```

The fact that in Code 12.5 each type of animal must be tested for and cast separately, and that special code exists for each animal class, is a good sign that we have not taken full advantage of what inheritance has to offer. A better solution is placing a method in the superclass (**Animal**), letting an animal act, and then overriding it in each subclass so that we have a polymorphic method call to let each animal act appropriately, without the need to test for the specific animal types. This is a standard refactoring technique in situations like this, where we have subtype-specific behavior invoked from a context that only deals with the supertype.

Let us assume that we create such a method, called **act**, and investigate the resulting source code. Code 12.6 shows the code implementing this solution.

Code 12.6

The fully improved solution to animal action

```
// Let all animals act.
for(Iterator<Animal> it = animals.iterator(); it.hasNext(); ) {
    Animal animal = it.next();
    animal.act(newAnimals);
    // Remove dead animals from the simulation.
    if(! animal.isAlive()) {
        it.remove();
    }
}
```

Several observations are important at this point:

■ The variable we are using for each collection element (**animal**) is of type **Animal**. This is legal, because all objects in the collection are foxes or rabbits and are all subtypes of **Animal**.

■ We assume that the specific action methods (**run** for **Rabbit**, **hunt** for **Fox**) have been renamed **act**. Instead of telling each animal exactly what to do, we are just telling it to "act," and we leave it up to the animal itself to decide what exactly it wants to do. This reduces coupling between **Simulator** and the individual animal subclasses.

■ Because the dynamic type of the variable determines which method is actually executed (as discussed in Chapter 11), the fox's action method will be executed for foxes, and the rabbit's method for rabbits.

■ Because type checking is done using the static type, this code will compile only if class **Animal** has an **act** method with the right header.

The last of these points is the only remaining problem. Because we are using the statement

animal.act(newAnimals);

and the variable **animal** is of type **Animal**, this will compile only if **Animal** defines an **act** method—as we saw in Chapter 11. However, the situation here is rather different from the situation we encountered with the **display** method in Chapter 11. There, the super-class version of **display** had a useful job to do: print the fields defined in the superclass. Here, although each particular animal has a specific set of actions to perform, we cannot describe in any detail the actions for animals in general. The particular actions depend on the specific subtype.

Our problem is to decide how we should define **Animal**'s **act** method.

The problem is a reflection of the fact that no instance of class **Animal** will ever exist. There is no object in our simulation (or in nature) that is just an animal and not also an instance of a more specific subclass. These kinds of classes, which are not intended for creating objects but serve only as superclasses, are known as *abstract classes*. For animals, for example, we can

Concept

An **abstract method** definition consists of a method header without a method body. It is marked with the keyword **abstract**.

say that each animal can act, but we cannot describe exactly how it acts without referring to a more specific subclass. This is typical for abstract classes, and it is reflected in Java constructs.

For the **Animal** class, we wish to state that each animal has an **act** method, but we cannot give a reasonable implementation in class **Animal**. The solution in Java is to declare the method *abstract*. Here is an example of an abstract **act** method:

```
abstract public void act(List<Animal> newAnimals);
```

An abstract method is characterized by two details:

1. It is prefixed with the keyword **abstract**.

2. It does not have a method body. Instead, its header is terminated with a semicolon.

Because the method has no body, it can never be executed. But we have already established that we do not want to execute an **Animal**'s **act** method, so that is not a problem.

Before we investigate in detail the effects of using an abstract method, we shall introduce more formally the concept of an abstract class.

12.3.3 Abstract classes

It is not only methods that can be declared abstract; classes can be declared abstract as well. Code 12.7 shows an example of class **Animal** as an abstract class. Classes are declared abstract by inserting the keyword **abstract** into the class header.

Code 12.7
Animal as an abstract class

```
public abstract class Animal
{

    Fields omitted.

    /**
     * Make this animal act - that is: make it do whatever it wants/needs
     * to do.
     *
     * @param newAnimals A list to receive newly born animals.
     */
    abstract public void act(List<Animal> newAnimals);

    Other methods omitted.

}
```

Concept

An **abstract class** is a class that is not intended for creating instances. Its purpose is to serve as a superclass for other classes. Abstract classes may contain abstract methods.

Classes that are not abstract (all classes we have seen previously) are called *concrete classes*.

Declaring a class abstract serves several purposes:

- No instances can be created of abstract classes. Trying to use the **new** keyword with an abstract class is an error and will not be permitted by the compiler. This is mirrored in BlueJ: right-clicking on an abstract class in the class diagram will not list any constructors in the pop-up menu. This serves our intention discussed above: we stated that we did not want instances of class **Animal** created directly—this class serves only as a superclass. Declaring the class abstract enforces this restriction.

- Only abstract classes can have abstract methods. This ensures that all methods in concrete classes can always be executed. If we allowed an abstract method in a concrete class, we would be able to create an instance of a class that lacked an implementation for a method.

- Abstract classes with abstract methods force subclasses to override and implement those methods declared abstract. If a subclass does not provide an implementation for an inherited abstract method, it is itself abstract, and no instances may be created. For a subclass to be concrete, it must provide implementations for *all* inherited abstract methods.

Concept

Abstract subclass. For a subclass of an abstract class to become concrete, it must provide implementations for all inherited abstract methods. Otherwise, the subclass will itself be abstract.

Now we can start to see the purpose of abstract methods. Although they do not provide an implementation, they nonetheless ensure that all concrete subclasses have an implementation of this method. In other words, even though class **Animal** does not implement the **act** method, it ensures that all existing animals have an implemented **act** method. This is done by ensuring that

- no instance of class **Animal** can be created directly, and

- all concrete subclasses must implement the **act** method.

Although we cannot create an instance of an abstract class directly, we can otherwise use an abstract class as a type in the usual ways. For instance, the normal rules of polymorphism allow us to handle foxes and rabbits as instances of the **Animal** type. So those parts of the simulation that do not need to know whether they are dealing with a specific subclass can use the superclass type instead.

Exercise 12.34 Although the body of the loop in Code 12.6 no longer deals with the **Fox** and **Rabbit** types, it still deals with the **Animal** type. Why is it not possible for it to treat each object in the collection simply using the **Object** type?

Exercise 12.35 Is it necessary for a class with one or more abstract methods to be defined as abstract? If you are not sure, experiment with the source of the **Animal** class in the *foxes-and-rabbits-v2* project.

Exercise 12.36 Is it possible for a class that has no abstract methods to be defined as abstract? If you are not sure, change **act** to be a concrete method in the **Animal** class by giving it a method body with no statements.

Exercise 12.37 Could it ever make sense to define a class as abstract if it has no abstract methods? Discuss this.

Exercise 12.38 Which classes in the **java.util** package are abstract? Some of them have **Abstract** in the class name, but is there any other way to tell from the documentation? Which concrete classes extend them?

Exercise 12.39 Can you tell from the API documentation for an abstract class which (if any) of its methods are abstract? Do you *need* to know which methods are abstract?

Exercise 12.40 Review the overriding rules for methods and fields discussed in Chapter 11. Why are they particularly significant in our attempts to introduce inheritance into this application?

Exercise 12.41 The changes made in this section have removed the dependencies (couplings) of the **simulateOneStep** method on the **Fox** and **Rabbit** classes. The **Simulator** class, however, is still coupled to **Fox** and **Rabbit**, because these classes are referenced in the **populate** method. There is no way to avoid this; when we create animal instances, we have to specify exactly what kind of animal to create.

This could be improved by splitting the **Simulator** into two classes: one class, **Simulator**, that runs the simulation and is completely decoupled from the concrete animal classes, and another class, **PopulationGenerator** (created and called by the simulator), that creates the population. Only this class is coupled to the concrete animal classes, making it easier for a maintenance programmer to find places where change is necessary when the application is extended. Try implementing this refactoring step. The **PopulationGenerator** class should also define the colors for each type of animal.

The project *foxes-and-rabbits-v2* provides an implementation of our simulation with the improvements discussed here. It is important to note that the change in **Simulator** to processing all the animals in a single list, rather than in separate lists, means that the simulation results in version 2 will not be identical to those in version 1.

In the book projects, you will find a third version of this project: *foxes-and-rabbits-graph*. This project is identical to *foxes-and-rabbits-v2* in its model (i.e., the animal/fox/rabbit/ simulator implementations), but it adds a second view to the project: a graph showing population numbers over time. We will discuss some aspects of its implementation a little later in this chapter; for now, just experiment with this project.

Exercise 12.42 Open and run the *foxes-and-rabbits-graph* project. Pay attention to the *Graph View* output. Explain, in writing, the meaning of the graph you see, and try to explain why it looks the way it looks. Is there a relationship between the two curves?

Exercise 12.43 Repeat some of your experiments with different sizes of fields (especially smaller fields). Does the *Graph View* give you any new insights or help you understand or explain what you see?

If you have done all the exercises in this chapter so far, then your version of the project will be the same as *foxes-and-rabbits-v2* and similar to *foxes-and-rabbits-graph*, except for the graph display. You can continue the exercises from here on with either version of these projects.

12.4 More abstract methods

When we created the **Animal** superclass in Section 12.3.1, we did this by identifying common elements of the subclasses, but we chose not to move the **age** field and the methods associated with it. This might be overly conservative. We could have easily moved the **age** field to **Animal** and provided for it there an accessor and a mutator that were called by subclass methods, such as **incrementAge**. Why didn't we move **incrementAge** and **canBreed** into **Animal**, then? The reason for not moving these is that, although several of the remaining method bodies in **Fox** and **Rabbit** contain textually identical statements, their use of class variables with different values means that they cannot be moved directly to the superclass. In the case of **canBreed**, the problem is the **BREEDING_AGE** variable, while **breed** depends on **BREEDING_PROBABILITY** and **MAX_LITTER_SIZE**. If **canBreed** is moved to **Animal**, for instance, then the compiler will need to have access to a value for the subtype-specific breeding age in class **Animal**. It is tempting to define a **BREEDING_AGE** field in the **Animal** class and assume that its value will be overridden by similarly named fields in the subclasses. However, fields are handled differently from methods in Java: they cannot be overridden by subclass versions.[3] This means that a **canBreed** method in **Animal** would use a meaningless value defined in that class, rather than one that is specific to a particular subclass.

The fact that the field's value would be meaningless gives us a clue as to how we can get around this problem and, as a result, move more of the similar methods from the subclasses to the superclass.

Remember that we defined **act** as abstract in **Animal** because having a body for the method would be meaningless. If we access the breeding age with a method rather than a field, we can get around the problems associated with the age-dependent properties. This approach is shown in Code 12.8.

Code 12.8
The canBreed
method of
Animal

```
/**
 * An animal can breed if it has reached the breeding age.
 * @return true if the animal can breed
 */
public boolean canBreed()
{
    return age >= getBreedingAge();
}
```

```
/**
 * Return the breeding age of this animal.
 * @return The breeding age of this animal.
 */
abstract protected int getBreedingAge();
```

---

[3] This rule applies regardless of whether a field is static or not.

The **canBreed** method has been moved to **Animal** and rewritten to use the value returned from a method call rather than the value of a class variable. For this to work, a method **getBreedingAge** must be defined in class **Animal**. Because we cannot specify a breeding age for animals in general, we can again use an **abstract** method in the **Animal** class and concrete redefinitions in the subclasses. Both **Fox** and **Rabbit** will define their own versions of **getBreedingAge** to return their particular values of **BREEDING_AGE**:

> **Concept**
>
> **Superclass method calls.** Calls to non-private instance methods from within a superclass are always evaluated in the wider context of the object's dynamic type.

```
/**
 * @return The age at which a rabbit starts to breed.
 */
public int getBreedingAge()
{
    return BREEDING_AGE;
}
```

So even though the call to **getBreedingAge** originates in the code of the superclass, the method called is defined in the subclass. This may seem mysterious at first but it is based on the same principles we described in Chapter 11 in using the dynamic type of an object to determine which version of a method is called at runtime. The technique illustrated here makes it possible for each instance to use the value appropriate to its subclass type. Using the same approach, we can move the remaining methods, **incrementAge** and **breed**, to the superclass.

Exercise 12.44 Using your latest version of the project (or the *foxes-and-rabbits-v2* project in case you have not done all the exercises), record the number of foxes and rabbits over a small number of steps, to prepare for regression testing of the changes to follow.

Exercise 12.45 Move the **age** field from **Fox** and **Rabbit** to **Animal**. Initialize it to zero in the constructor. Provide accessor and mutator methods for it and use these in **Fox** and **Rabbit** rather than in direct accesses to the field. Make sure the program compiles and runs as before.

Exercise 12.46 Move the **canBreed** method from **Fox** and **Rabbit** to **Animal**, and rewrite it as shown in Code 12.8. Provide appropriate versions of **getBreedingAge** in **Fox** and **Rabbit** that return the distinctive breeding age values.

Exercise 12.47 Move the **incrementAge** method from **Fox** and **Rabbit** to **Animal** by providing an abstract **getMaxAge** method in **Animal** and concrete versions in **Fox** and **Rabbit**.

Exercise 12.48 Can the **breed** method be moved to **Animal**? If so, make this change.

Exercise 12.49 In light of all the changes you have made to these three classes, reconsider the visibility of each method and make any changes you feel are appropriate.

Exercise 12.50 Was it possible to make these changes without having any impact on any other classes in the project? If so, what does this suggest about the degrees of encapsulation and coupling that were present in the original version?

Exercise 12.51 *Challenge exercise* Define a completely new type of animal for the simulation, as a subclass of **Animal**. You will need to decide what sort of impact its existence will have on the existing animal types. For instance, your animal might compete with foxes as a predator on the rabbit population, or your animal might prey on foxes but not on rabbits. You will probably find that you need to experiment quite a lot with the configuration settings you use for it. You will need to modify the **populate** method to have some of your animals created at the start of a simulation.

You should also define a new color for your new animal class. You can find a list of predefined color names on the API page documenting the **Color** class in the **java.awt** package.

Exercise 12.52 *Challenge exercise* The text of the **giveBirth** methods in **Fox** and **Rabbit** is very similar. The only difference is that one creates new **Fox** objects and the other creates new **Rabbit** objects. Is it possible to use the technique illustrated with **canBreed** to move the common code into a shared **giveBirth** method in **Animal**? If you think it is, try it out. *Hint*: The rules on polymorphic substitution apply to values returned from methods as well as in assignment and parameter passing.

12.5 Multiple inheritance

12.5.1 An **Actor** class

In this section, we discuss some possible future extensions and some programming constructs to support these.

The first obvious extension for our simulation is the addition of new animals. If you have attempted Exercise 12.51 then you will have touched on this already. We should, however, generalize this a bit: maybe not all participants in the simulation will be animals. Our current structure assumes that all acting participants in the simulation are animals and that they inherit from the **Animal** superclass. One enhancement that we might like to make is the introduction of human predators to the simulation, as either hunters or trappers. They do not neatly fit the existing assumption of purely animal-based actors. We might also extend the simulation to include plants eaten by the rabbits, or even some aspects of the weather. The plants as food would influence the population of rabbits (in effect, rabbits become predators of the plants), and the growth of the plants might be influenced by the weather. All these new components would act in the simulation, but they are clearly not animals, so it would be inappropriate to have them as subclasses of **Animal**.

As we consider the potential for introducing further actors into the simulation, it is worth revealing why we chose to store details of the animals in both a **Field** object and an **Animal** list. Visiting each animal in the list is what constitutes a single simulation step. Placing all participants in a single list keeps the basic simulation step simple. However, this clearly duplicates information, which risks creating inconsistency. One reason for this design decision is that it allows us to consider participants in the simulation that are not actually within the field—a representation for the weather might be one example of this.

To deal with more general actors, it seems like a good idea to introduce an **Actor** superclass. The **Actor** class would serve as a superclass to all kinds of simulation participants, independent of what they are. Figure 12.3 shows a class diagram for this part of the simulation. The **Actor** and **Animal** classes are abstract, while **Rabbit**, **Fox**, and **Hunter** are concrete classes.

The **Actor** class would include the common part of all actors. One thing all possible actors have in common is that they perform some kind of action. We will also need to know whether an actor is still active or not. So the only definitions in class **Actor** are those of abstract **act** and **isActive** methods:

```
// all comments omitted
public abstract class Actor
{
    abstract public void act(List<Actor> newActors);
    abstract public boolean isActive();
}
```

This should be enough to rewrite the actor loop in the **Simulator** (Code 12.6), using class **Actor** instead of class **Animal**. (Either the **isAlive** method could be renamed to **isActive**, or a separate **isActive** method in **Animal** could simply call the existing **isAlive** method.)

Figure 12.3
Simulation structure
with **Actor**

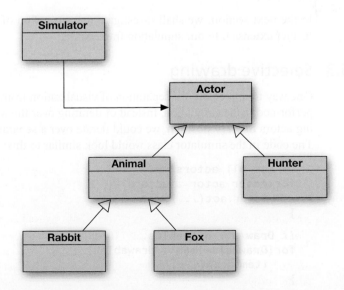

> **Exercise 12.53** Introduce the **Actor** class into your simulation. Rewrite the **simulateOneStep** method in **Simulator** to use **Actor** instead of **Animal**. You can do this even if you have not introduced any new participant types. Does the **Simulator** class compile? Or is there something else that is needed in the **Actor** class?

This new structure is more flexible because it allows easier addition of non-animal actors. In fact, we could even rewrite the statistics-gathering class, **FieldStats**, as an **Actor**—it too acts once every step. Its action would be to update its current count of animals.

12.5.2 Flexibility through abstraction

By moving towards the notion of the simulation being responsible for managing actor objects, we have succeeded in abstracting quite a long way away from our original very specific scenario of foxes and rabbits in a rectangular field. This process of abstraction has brought with it an increased flexibility that may allow us to widen even further the scope of what we might do with a general simulation framework. If we think through the requirements of other similar simulation scenarios, then we might come up with ideas for additional features that we could introduce.

For instance, it might be useful to simulate other predator–prey scenarios such as a marine simulation involving fish and sharks, or fish and fishing fleets. If the marine simulation were to involve modeling food supplies for the fish, then we would probably not want to visualize plankton populations—either because the numbers are too vast, or because their size is too small. Environmental simulations might involve modeling the weather, which, while it is clearly an actor, also might not require visualization in the field cells.

In the next section, we shall investigate the separation of visualization from acting, as a further extension to our simulation framework.

12.5.3 Selective drawing

One way to implement the separation of visualization from acting is to change the way it is performed in the simulation. Instead of iterating over the whole field every time and drawing actors in every position, we could iterate over a separate collection of drawable actors. The code in the simulator class would look similar to this:

```
// Let all actors act.
for(Actor actor : actors) {
    actor.act(...);
}

// Draw all drawables.
for(Drawable item : drawables) {
    item.draw(...);
}
```

Figure 12.4
Actor hierarchy with
Drawable class

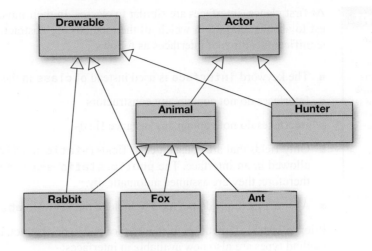

All of the actors would be in the **actors** collection, and those actors we want to show on screen would also be in the **drawables** collection. For this to work, we need another super-class called **Drawable**, which declares an abstract **draw** method. Drawable actors must then inherit from both **Actor** and **Drawable**. (Figure 12.4 shows an example where we assume that we have ants, which act but are too numerous to visualize.)

12.5.4 Drawable actors: multiple inheritance

> **Concept**
>
> **Multiple inheritance.** A situation in which a class inherits from more than one superclass is called multiple inheritance

The scenario presented here uses a structure known as *multiple inheritance*. Multiple inheritance exists in cases where one class has more than one immediate superclass.[4] The subclass then has all the features of both superclasses and those defined in the subclass itself.

Multiple inheritance is quite easy to understand in principle but can lead to significant complications in the implementation of a programming language. Different object-oriented languages vary in their treatment of multiple inheritance: some languages allow the inheritance of multiple superclasses; others do not. Java lies somewhere in the middle. It does not allow multiple inheritance of classes, but provides another construct, called an "interface," that allows a limited form of multiple inheritance. Interfaces are discussed in the next section.

12.6 Interfaces

Up to this point in the book, we have used the term "interface" in an informal sense, to represent that part of a class that couples it to other classes. Java captures this concept more formally by allowing *interface types* to be defined.

---

[4] Don't confuse this case with the regular situation where a single class might have several superclasses in its inheritance hierarchy, such as **Fox**, **Animal**, **Actor**, and **Object**. This is not what is meant by multiple inheritance.

Concept

A Java **interface** is a specification of a type (in the form of a type name and a set of methods). It often does not provide an implementation for most of its methods.

At first glance, interfaces are similar to classes. In their most common form they are closest to abstract classes in which all the methods are abstract. We can summarize the most significant features of interfaces as follows:

- The keyword **interface** is used instead of **class** in the header of the declaration.
- Interfaces do not contain any constructors.
- Interfaces do not contain any instance fields.
- Only fields that are constant class fields (**static** and **final**) with public visibility are allowed in an interface. The **public**, **static**, and **final** keywords may be omitted, therefore; they are assumed automatically.
- Abstract methods do not have to include the keyword **abstract** in their header.

Prior to Java 8, all methods in an interface had to be abstract, but the following non-abstract method types are also now available in interfaces:

- Methods marked with the **default** keyword have a method body.
- Methods marked with the **static** keyword have a method body.

All methods in an interface—whether abstract, concrete or static—have public visibility, so the **public** keyword may be omitted in their definition.

12.6.1 An **Actor** interface

Code 12.9 shows **Actor** defined as an interface type.

Code 12.9

The **Actor** interface

```
/**
 * The interface to be extended by any class wishing
 * to participate in the simulation.
 */
public interface Actor
{
    /**
     * Perform the actor's regular behavior.
     * @param newActors A list for receiving newly created actors.
     */
    void act(List<Actor> newActors);

    /**
     * Is the actor still active?
     * @return true if still active, false if not.
     */
    boolean isActive();
}
```

A class can inherit from an interface in a similar way to that for inheriting from a class. However, Java uses a different keyword—**implements**—for inheriting interfaces.

A class is said to *implement* an interface if it includes an *implements clause* in its class header. For instance:

```
public class Fox extends Animal implements Drawable
{
    Body of class omitted.
}
```

As in this case, if a class both extends a class and implements an interface, then the extends clause must be written first in the class header.

Two of our abstract classes in the example above, **Actor** and **Drawable**, are good candidates for being written as interfaces. Both of them contain only the definition of methods, without method implementations. Thus, they already fit the most abstract definition of an interface perfectly: they contain no instance fields, no constructors, and no method bodies.

The class **Animal** is a different case. It is a real abstract class that provides a partial implementation with instance fields, a constructor and many methods with bodies. It has only a single abstract method in its original version. Given all of these characteristics, it must remain as a class rather than becoming an interface.

Exercise 12.54 Redefine as an interface the abstract class **Actor** in your project. Does the simulation still compile? Does it run? Make any changes necessary to make it runnable again.

Exercise 12.55 Are the fields in the following interface class fields or instance fields?

```
public interface Quiz
{
    int CORRECT = 1;
    int INCORRECT = 0;
    ...
}
```

What visibility do they have?

Exercise 12.56 What are the errors in the following interface?

```
public interface Monitor
{
    private static final int THRESHOLD = 50;
    private int value;
    public Monitor (int initial);
    void update(int reading);
    int getThreshold()
    {
        return THRESHOLD;
    }
    ...
}
```

12.6.2 Default methods in interfaces

A method marked as **default** in an interface will have a method body, which is inherited by all implementing classes. The addition of default methods to interfaces in Java 8 muddied the waters in the distinction between abstract classes and interfaces, since it is no longer true that interfaces never contain method bodies. However, it is important to exercise caution when considering defining a default method in an interface. It should be borne in mind that default methods were added to the language primarily to support the addition of new methods to interfaces in the API that existed before Java 8. Default methods made it possible to change existing interfaces without breaking the many classes that already implemented the older versions of those interfaces.

From the other limitations of interfaces—no constructors and no instance fields—it should be clear that the functionality possible in a default method is strictly limited, since there is no state that can be examined or manipulated directly by them. In general, therefore, when writing our own interfaces we will tend to limit ourselves to purely abstract methods. Furthermore, when discussing features of interfaces in this chapter we will often ignore the case of non-abstract methods for the sake of simplicity.

12.6.3 Multiple inheritance of interfaces

As mentioned above, Java allows any class to extend at most one other class. However, it allows a class to implement any number of interfaces (in addition to possibly extending one class). Thus, if we define both **Actor** and **Drawable** as interfaces instead of abstract classes, we can define class **Hunter** (Figure 12.4) to implement both of them:

```
public class Hunter implements Actor, Drawable
{
    // Body of class omitted.
}
```

The class **Hunter** inherits the methods of all interfaces (**act** and **draw**, in this case) as abstract methods. It must, then, provide method definitions for both of them by overriding the methods, or the class itself must be declared abstract.

The **Animal** class shows an example where a class does not implement an inherited interface method. **Animal**, in our new structure in Figure 12.4, inherits the abstract method **act** from **Actor**. It does not provide a method body for this method, which makes **Animal** itself abstract (it must include the **abstract** keyword in the class header). The **Animal** subclasses then implement the **act** method and become concrete classes.

The presence of default methods in interfaces can lead to complications in the implementation of multiple interfaces by a class. Where a class implements multiple interfaces and two or more of the interfaces have a default method with the same signature then the implementing class *must* override that method—even if the alternative versions of the method are identical. The reason for this is that, in the general case, it needs to be clear exactly which of the alternative implementations should be inherited by the class. The class may override either by calling the preferred version in the overriding method, or by defining a completely different implementation. The header of the overriding method will not contain the **default** keyword, since that is only used in interfaces.

There is a new syntax involving the keyword **super** for calling a default method from one of the interfaces in an overriding method. For instance, suppose the **Actor** and **Drawable** interfaces both define a default method called, **reset**, that has a **void** return type and takes no parameters. If a class implementing both interfaces overrides this method by calling both default versions then the overriding method might be defined as follows:

```
public void reset()
{
    Actor.super.reset();
    Drawable.super.reset();
}
```

In other words, an implementing class that overrides an inherited default method can call that default method using the syntax:

```
InterFaceName.super.methodName( . . . )
```

> **Exercise 12.57** *Challenge exercise* Add a non-animal actor to the simulation. For instance, you could introduce a **Hunter** class with the following properties. Hunters have no maximum age and neither feed nor breed. At each step of the simulation, a hunter moves to a random location anywhere in the field and fires a fixed number of shots into random target locations around the field. Any animal in one of the target locations is killed.
>
> Place just a small number of hunters in the field at the start of the simulation. Do the hunters remain in the simulation throughout, or do they ever disappear? If they do disappear, why might that be, and does that represent realistic behavior?
>
> What other classes required changing as a result of introducing hunters? Is there a need to introduce further decoupling to the classes?

12.6.4 Interfaces as types

When a class implements an interface, it often does not inherit any implementation from it. The question, then, is: What do we actually gain by implementing interfaces?

When we introduced inheritance in Chapter 10, we emphasized two great benefits of inheritance:

1. The subclass inherits the code (method implementations and fields) from the superclass. This allows reuse of existing code and avoids code duplication.

2. The subclass becomes a subtype of the superclass. This allows polymorphic variables and method calls. In other words, it allows different special cases of objects (instances of subclasses) to be treated uniformly (as instances of the supertype).

Interfaces are not primarily used for the first benefit but for the second. An interface defines a type just as a class does. This means that variables can be declared to be of interface types, even though no objects of that type can exist (only subtypes).

In our example, even though **Actor** is now an interface, we can still declare an **Actor** variable in the **Simulator** class. The simulation loop still works unchanged.

Interfaces can have no direct instances, but they serve as supertypes for instances of other classes.

12.6.5 Interfaces as specifications

In this chapter, we have introduced interfaces as a means to implement multiple inheritance in Java. This is one important use of interfaces, but there are others.

The most important characteristic of interfaces is that they almost completely separate the definition of the functionality (the class's "interface" in the wider sense of the word) from its implementation. A good example of how this can be used in practice can be found in the Java collection hierarchy.

The collection hierarchy defines (among other types) the interface **List** and the classes **ArrayList** and **LinkedList** (Figure 12.5). The **List** interface specifies the full functionality of a list, without constraining its underlying structural implementation. The subclasses (**LinkedList** and **ArrayList**) provide two completely different structural implementations of the same interface. This is interesting, because the two implementations differ greatly in the efficiency of some of their functions. Random access to elements in the middle of the list, for example, is much faster with the **ArrayList**. Inserting or deleting elements, however, can be much faster in the **LinkedList**.

Which implementation is better in any given application can be hard to judge in advance. It depends a lot on the relative frequency with which certain operations are performed and on some other factors. In practice, the best way to find out is often to try it out: implement the application with both alternatives and measure the performance.

The existence of the **List** interface makes it very easy to do this. If, instead of using **ArrayList** or **LinkedList** as variable and parameter types, we always use **List**, our application will work independently of the specific type of list we are currently using. Only when we create a new list do we really have to use the name of the specific implementation. We would, for instance, write

```
List<Type> myList = new ArrayList<>();
```

Figure 12.5
The **List** interface and its subclasses

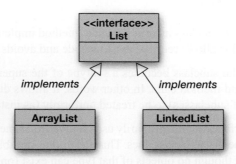

Note that the polymorphic variable's type is just **List** of **Type**. This way, we can change the whole application to use a linked list by just changing **ArrayList** to **LinkedList** in a single location when the list is being created.

12.6.6 Library support through abstract classes and interfaces

In Chapter 6, we pointed out the importance of paying attention to the names of the collection classes: **ArrayList**, **LinkedList**, **HashSet**, **TreeSet**, etc. Now that we have been introduced to abstract classes and interfaces, we can see why these particular names have been chosen. The **java.util** package defines several important collection abstractions in the form of interfaces, such as **List**, **Map**, and **Set**. The concrete class names have been chosen to communicate information about both what kind of interface they conform to and some of the underlying implementation detail. This information is very useful when it comes to making informed decisions about the right concrete class to use in a particular setting. However, by using the highest-level abstract type (be it abstract class or interface) for our variables, wherever possible, our code will remain flexible in light of future library changes—such as the addition of a new **Map** or **Set** implementation, for instance.

In Chapter 13, where we introduce the Java GUI libraries, we will be making enormous use of abstract classes and interfaces as we see how to create quite sophisticated functionality with very little additional code.

Exercise 12.58 Which methods do **ArrayList** and **LinkedList** have that are not defined in the **List** interface? Why do you think that these methods are not included in **List**?

Exercise 12.59 Write a class that can make comparisons between the efficiency of the common methods from the **List** interface in the **ArrayList** and **LinkedList** classes such as **add**, **get**, and **remove**. Use the polymorphic-variable technique described above to write the class so that it only knows it is performing its tests on objects of the interface type **List** rather than on the concrete types **ArrayList** and **LinkedList**. Use large lists of objects for the tests, to make the results significant. You can use the **currentTimeMillis** method of the **System** class for getting hold of the start and finish time of your test methods.

Exercise 12.60 Read the API description for the **sort** methods of the **Collections** class in the **java.util** package. Which interfaces are mentioned in the descriptions? Which methods in the **java.util.List** interface have **default** implementations?

Exercise 12.61 *Challenge exercise* Investigate the **Comparable** interface. This is a *parameterized* interface. Define a simple class that implements **Comparable**. Create a collection containing objects of this class and sort the collection. *Hint*: The **LogEntry** class of the *weblog-analyzer* project in Chapter 7 implements this interface.

12.6.7 Functional interfaces and lambdas (advanced)

Java 8 introduced a special classification for interfaces that contain just a single abstract method (regardless of the number of default and/or static methods they contain). Such an interface is called a *functional interface*. The annotation **@FunctionalInterface** may be included with the declaration to allow the compiler to check that the interface conforms to the rules for functional interfaces.

There is a special relationship between functional interfaces and lambda expressions. Anywhere that an object of a functional interface type is required, a lambda expression may be used instead. In the following chapter, we shall see extensive use of this feature when implementing graphical user interfaces.

This link between lambdas and functional interfaces is important. In particular, it gives us a convenient means to associate a lambda expression with a type, for example to declare a variable that can hold a lambda. The **java.util.function** package defines a large number of interfaces that provide convenience names for the most commonly occurring types of lambda expression. In general, the interface names indicate the return type and the parameter types of their single method, and hence a lambda of that type. For example:

- **Consumer** interfaces relate to lambdas with a **void** return type. For instance, **DoubleConsumer** takes a single **double** parameter and returns no result.

- **BinaryOperator** interfaces take two parameters and return a result of the same type. For instance, **IntBinaryOperator** takes two **int** parameters and returns an **int** result.

- **Supplier** interfaces return a result of the indicated type. For instance, **LongSupplier**.

- **Predicate** interfaces return a **boolean** result. For instance, **IntPredicate**.

All of these interfaces extend the **Function** interface, whose single abstract method is called **apply**. One potentially useful functional interface type, defined in the **java.lang** package, is **Runnable**. This fills a gap in the list of **Consumer** interfaces in that it takes no parameters and has a **void** return type. However, its single abstract method is called **run**.

Functional interface types allow lambdas to be assigned to variables or passed as actual parameters. For example, suppose we have pairs of *name* and *alias* strings that we wish to format in a particular way, such as **"Michelangelo Merisi (AKA Caravaggio)"**. A lambda taking two **String** parameters and returning a **String** result is compatible with the **BinaryOperator** interface, and we might give a type and name to a lambda as follows:

```
BinaryOperator<String> aka =
    (name, alias) -> return name + " (AKA " + alias + ")";
```

This lambda would be used by calling its **apply** method with appropriate parameters, for instance:

```
System.out.println(aka.apply("Michelangelo Merisi",
                             "Caravaggio"));
```

A further example of interfaces

In the previous section, we have discussed how interfaces can be used to separate the specification of a component from its implementation so that different implementations can be "plugged in," thus making it easy to replace components of a system. This is often done to separate parts of a system that are logically only loosely coupled.

We have seen an example of this (without discussing it explicitly) at the end of Section 12.3. There, we investigated the *foxes-and-rabbits-graph* project, which added another view of the populations in the form of a line graph. Looking at the class diagram for this project, we can see that the addition also makes use of a Java interface (Fig 12.6).

The previous versions of the *foxes-and-rabbits* project contained only one **SimulatorView** class. This was a concrete class, and it provided the implementation of a grid-based view of the field. As we have seen, the visualization is quite separate from the simulation logic (the field and the actors), and different visualization views are possible.

For this project, **SimulatorView** was changed from a class to an interface, and the implementation of this view was moved into a class named **GridView**.

GridView is identical to the previous SimulatorView class. The new SimulatorView interface was constructed by searching through the Simulator class to find all methods that are actually called from outside, then defining an interface that specifies exactly those methods. They are:

```
view.setColor(classObject, color);
view.isViable(field);
view.showStatus(step, field);
view.reset();
```

We can now easily define the complete **SimulatorView** interface:

```
import java.awt.Color;
public interface SimulatorView
{
    void setColor(Class<?> animalClass, Color color);
    boolean isViable(Field field);
    void showStatus(int step, Field field);
    void reset();
}
```

Figure 12.6
The **Simulator-
View** interface and
implementing classes

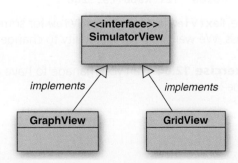

The one slightly tricky detail in the definition above is the use of the type **Class<?>** as the first parameter of the **setColor** method. We will explain that in the next section.

The previous **SimulatorView** class, now called **GridView**, is specified to implement the new **SimulatorView** interface:

```
public class GridView extends JFrame implements SimulatorView
{
    ...
}
```

It does not require any additional code, because it already implements the interface's methods. However, after making these changes, it becomes fairly easy to "plug in" other views for the simulation by providing further implementations of the **SimulatorView** interface. The new class **GraphView**, which produces the line graph, is an example of this.

Once we have more than one view implementation, we can easily replace the current view with another or, as we have in our example, even display two views at the same time. In the **Simulator** class, the concrete subclasses **GridView** and **GraphView** are only mentioned once when each view was constructed. Thereafter, they are stored in a collection holding elements of the **SimulatorView** supertype, and only the interface type is used to communicate with them.

The implementations of the **GridView** and **GraphView** classes are fairly complex, and we do not expect you to fully understand them at this stage. The pattern of providing two implementations for a single interface, however, is important here, and you should make sure that you understand this aspect.

Exercise 12.62 Review the source code of the **Simulator** class. Find all occurrences of the view classes and interfaces, and trace all variables declared using any of these types. Explain exactly how the views are used in the **Simulator** class.

Exercise 12.63 Implement a new class **TextView** that implements **SimulatorView**. **TextView** provides a textual view of the simulation. After every simulation step, it prints out one line in the form

```
Foxes: 121 Rabbits: 266
```

Use **TextView** instead of **GridView** for some tests. (Do not delete the **GridView** class. We want to have the ability to change between different views!)

Exercise 12.64 Can you manage to have all three views active at the same time?

12.8 The Class class

In Chapter 10, we described the paradoxically named **Object** class. It shouldn't surprise you, therefore, that there is also a **Class** class! This is where talking about classes and objects can become very confusing.

We used the **Class** type in defining the **SimulatorView** interface in the previous section. The **Class** class has nothing specifically to do with interfaces; it is a general feature of Java, but we just happen to be meeting it for the first time here. The idea is that each type has a **Class** object associated with it.

The **Object** class defines the method **getClass** to return the **Class** associated with an object. Another way to get the **Class** object for a type is to write ".**class**" after the type name: for instance, **Fox.class** or **int.class**—notice that even the primitive types have **Class** objects associated with them.

The **Class** class is a generic class—it has a type parameter specifying the specific class subtype we are referencing. For example, the type of **String.class** is **Class<String>**. We can use a question mark in place of the type parameter—**Class<?>**—if we want to declare a variable that can hold all class objects of all types.

Class objects are particularly useful if we want to know whether the type of two objects is the same. We use this feature in the original **SimulatorView** class to associate each animal type with a color in the field. **SimulatorView** has the following field to map one to the other:

```
private Map<Class<?>, Color> colors;
```

When the view is set up, the constructor of **Simulator** has the following calls to its **setColor** method:

```
view.setColor(Rabbit.class, Color.ORANGE);
view.setColor(Fox.class, Color.BLUE);
```

We won't go into any further detail about **Class<?>**, but this description should be sufficient to enable you to understand the code shown in the previous section.

12.9 Abstract class or interface?

In some situations, a choice has to be made between whether to use an abstract class or an interface, while in other cases, either abstract classes or interfaces can do the job. Prior to the introduction of default methods in Java 8, the issue appeared to be clearer: if a type needed elements of concrete implementation—such as instance fields, constructors, or method bodies—then an abstract class would have to be used. However, the present availability of default methods in interfaces should not really change the answer to this question in most cases. In general, it is preferable to avoid defining default methods in interfaces except for the purpose of adapting legacy code.

If we have a choice, interfaces are usually preferable. Interfaces are relatively lightweight types that minimize constraints on implementing classes. Furthermore, if we provide a type as an abstract class, then subclasses cannot extend any other classes. Because interfaces allow multiple inheritance, the use of an interface does not create such a restriction. Interfaces cleanly separate the type specification from the implementation, and this creates less coupling. Therefore, using interfaces leads to a more flexible and more extensible structure.

12.10 Event-driven simulations

The style of simulation we have used in this chapter has the characteristic of time passing in discrete, equal-length steps. At each time step, each actor in the simulation was asked to act—i.e., take the actions appropriate to its current state. This style of simulation is sometimes called *time-based*, or *synchronous*, simulation. In this particular simulation, most of the actors will have had something to do at each time step: move, breed, and eat. In many simulation scenarios, however, actors spend large numbers of time steps doing nothing—typically, waiting for something to happen that requires some action on their part. Consider the case of a newly born rabbit in our simulation, for instance. It is repeatedly asked whether it is going to breed, even though it takes several time steps before this is possible. Isn't there a way to avoid asking this unnecessary question until the rabbit is actually ready?

There is also the question of the most appropriate size of the time step. We deliberately left vague the issue of how much real time a time step represents, and the various actions actually require significantly different amounts of time (eating and movement should occur much more frequently than giving birth, for instance). Is there a way to decide on a time-step size that is not so small that most of the time nothing will be happening, or too long that different types of actions are not distinguished clearly enough between time steps?

An alternative approach is to use an *event-based*, or *asynchronous*, simulation style. In this style, the simulation is driven by maintaining a schedule of future events. The most obvious difference between the two styles is that, in an event-based simulation, time passes in uneven amounts. For instance, one event might occur at time t and the next two events occur at times $t + 2$ and time $t + 8$, while the following three events might all occur at time $t + 9$.

For a fox-and-rabbits simulation, the sort of events we are talking about would be birth, movement, hunting, and death from natural causes. What typically happens is that, as each event occurs, a fresh event is scheduled for some point in the future. For instance, when a birth event occurs, the event marking that animal's death from old age will be scheduled. All future events are stored in an ordered queue, where the next event to take place is held at the head of the queue. It is important to appreciate that newly scheduled events will not always be placed at the end of the current queue; they will often have to be inserted somewhere before the end, in order to keep the queue in time order. In addition, some future events will be rendered obsolete by events that occur before them—an obvious example is that the natural-death event for a rabbit will not take place if the rabbit is eaten beforehand!

Event-driven simulations lend themselves particularly well to the techniques we have described in this chapter. For instance, the concept of an event is likely to be implemented as an **Event** abstract class containing concrete details of when the event will occur, but only abstract details of what the event involves. Concrete subclasses of **Event** will then supply the specific details for the different event types. Typically, the main simulation loop will not need to be concerned with the concrete event types, but will be able to use polymorphic method calls when an event occurs.

Event-based simulations are often more efficient and are preferable where large systems and large amounts of data are involved, while synchronous simulations are better for producing time-based visualizations (such as animations of the actors) because time flows more evenly.

> **Exercise 12.65** Find out some more about how event-driven simulations differ from time-based simulations.
>
> **Exercise 12.66** Look at the `java.util` package to see if there are any classes that might be well suited to storing an event queue in an event-based simulation.
>
> **Exercise 12.67** *Challenge exercise* Rewrite the foxes-and-rabbits simulation in the event-based style.

12.11 Summary of inheritance

In Chapters 10 through 12, we have discussed many different aspects of inheritance techniques. These include code inheritance and subtyping as well as inheriting from interfaces, abstract classes, and concrete classes.

In general, we can distinguish two main purposes of using inheritance: we can use it to inherit code (code inheritance), and we can use it to inherit the type (subtyping). The first is useful for code reuse, the second for polymorphism and specialization.

When we inherit from ("extend") concrete classes, we do both: we inherit the implementation and the type. When we inherit from ("implement") interfaces, we separate the two: we inherit a type but (usually) no implementation. For cases where parts of both are useful, we can inherit from abstract classes; here, we inherit the type and a partial implementation.

When inheriting a complete implementation, we can choose to add or override methods. When no or only partial implementation of a type is inherited, the subclass must provide the implementation before it can be instantiated.

Some other object-oriented languages also provide mechanisms to inherit code without inheriting the type. Java does not provide such a construct.

12.12 Summary

In this chapter, we have discussed the fundamental structure of computer simulations. We have then used this example to introduce abstract classes and interfaces as constructs that allow us to create further abstractions and develop more-flexible applications.

Abstract classes are classes that are not intended to have any instances. Their purpose is to serve as superclasses to other classes. Abstract classes may have both abstract methods—methods that have a header but no body—and full method implementations. Concrete subclasses of abstract classes must override abstract methods to provide the missing method implementations.

Another construct for defining types in Java is the interface. Java interfaces are similar to completely abstract classes: they define method headers, but generally provide no implementation. Interfaces define types that can be used for variables.

Interfaces can be used to provide a specification for a class (or part of an application) without stating anything about the concrete implementation.

Java allows multiple inheritance of interfaces (which it calls "implements" relationships) but only single inheritance for classes ("extends" relationships). Multiple inheritance is made more complicated by the presence of conflicting default methods.

Terms introduced in this chapter:

abstract method, abstract class, concrete class, abstract subclass, multiple inheritance, interface (Java construct), implements

Concept summary

- **abstract method** An abstract method definition consists of a method header without a method body. It is marked with the keyword `abstract`.

- **abstract class** An abstract class is a class that is not intended for creating instances. Its purpose is to serve as a superclass for other classes. Abstract classes may contain abstract methods.

- **abstract subclass** For a subclass of an abstract class to become concrete, it must provide implementations for all inherited abstract methods. Otherwise, it will itself be abstract.

- **superclass method calls** Calls to non-private instance methods from within a superclass are always evaluated in the wider context of the object's dynamic type.

- **multiple inheritance** A situation in which a class inherits from more than one superclass is called multiple inheritance.

- **interface** A Java **interface** is a specification of a type (in the form of a type name and a set of methods). It often does not provide an implementation for most of its methods.

Exercise 12.68 Can an abstract class have concrete (non-abstract) methods? Can a concrete class have abstract methods? Can you have an abstract class without abstract methods? Justify your answers.

Exercise 12.69 Look at the code below. You have five types—classes or interfaces—(U, G, B, Z, and X) and a variable of each of these types.

```
U u;
G g;
B b;
Z z;
X x;
```

The following assignments are all legal (assume that they all compile).

```
u = z;
x = b;
g = u;
x = u;
```

The following assignments are all illegal (they cause compiler errors).

```
u = b;
x = g;
b = u;
z = u;
g = x;
```

What can you say about the types and their relationships? (What relationship are they to each other?)

Exercise 12.70 Assume that you want to model people in a university to implement a course management system. There are different people involved: staff members, students, teaching staff, support staff, tutors, technical-support staff, and student technicians. Tutors and student technicians are interesting: tutors are students who have been hired to do some teaching, and student technicians are students who have been hired to help with the technical support.

Draw a type hierarchy (classes and interfaces) to represent this situation. Indicate which types are concrete classes, abstract classes, and interfaces.

Exercise 12.71 *Challenge exercise* Sometimes class/interface pairs exist in the *Java standard library* that define exactly the same methods. Often, the interface name ends with *Listener* and the class name with *Adapter*. An example is **PrintJobListener** and **PrintJobAdapter**. The interface defines some method headers, and the adapter class defines the same methods, each with an empty method body. What might the reason be for having them both?

Exercise 12.72 The collection library has a class named **TreeSet**, which is an example of a sorted set. Elements in this set are kept in order. Carefully read the description of this class, and then write a class **Person** that can be inserted into a **TreeSet**, which will then sort the **Person** objects by age.

Exercise 12.73 Use the API documentation for the **AbstractList** class to write a concrete class that maintains an unmodifiable list.

13 Building Graphical User Interfaces

Main concepts discussed in this chapter:

- constructing GUIs
- interface components
- GUI layout
- event handling

Java constructs discussed in this chapter:

JFrame, JLabel, JButton, JMenuBar, JMenu, JMenuItem, ActionEvent, Color, FlowLayout, BorderLayout, GridLayout, BoxLayout, Box, JOptionPane, EtchedBorder, EmptyBorder, anonymous inner classes

13.1 Introduction

So far in this book, we have concentrated on writing applications with text-based interfaces. The reason is not that text-based interfaces have any great advantage in principle; they just have the one advantage that they are easier to create.

We did not want to distract too much attention from the important software-development issues in the early stages of learning about object-oriented programming. These were issues such as object structure and interaction, class design, and code quality.

Graphical user interfaces (GUIs) are also constructed from interacting objects, but they have a very specialized structure, and we avoided introducing them before discussing object structures in more general terms. Now, however, we are ready to have a look at the construction of GUIs.

Some of the material in this chapter makes extensive use of the *lambda expression* feature that was introduced in Java 8. That feature was covered in detail in Chapter 5 of this book—a chapter that we designated as "Advanced" for that particular point in the book. If you have not yet read that chapter, we recommend that you now do so in order to familiarise yourself with the syntax and usage of lambda expressions. In addition, it would be worth reviewing the advanced material in Chapter 12, as significant use is made of abstract classes and interface types in the Java GUI libraries.

GUIs give our applications an interface consisting of windows, menus, buttons, and other graphical components. They make applications look much more like the "typical" applications people are used to.

Note that we are stumbling about the double meaning of the word *interface* again here. The interfaces we are talking about now are neither interfaces of classes nor the Java interface construct. We are now talking about *user interfaces*—the part of an application that is visible on screen for the user to interact with.

Once we know how to create GUIs with Java, we can develop much-better-looking programs.

13.2 Components, layout, and event handling

The details involved in creating GUIs are extensive. In this book, we will not be able to cover all details of all of the possible things you can do with them, but we shall discuss the general principles and a good number of examples.

All GUI programming in Java is done through the use of dedicated standard class libraries. Once we understand the principles, we can find out all the necessary details by working with the standard library documentation.

The principles we need to understand can be divided into three topic areas:

■ What kinds of elements can we show on screen?

■ How do we arrange those elements?

■ How do we react to user input?

We shall discuss these questions under the keywords *components*, *layout*, and *event handling*.

Components are the individual parts that a GUI is built from. They are things such as buttons, menus, menu items, checkboxes, sliders, text fields, and so on. The Java library contains a good number of ready-made components, and we can also write our own. We shall have to learn what the important components are, how to create them, and how to make them look the way we want them to look.

> **Concept**
>
> A GUI is built by arranging **components** on screen. Components are represented by objects.

Layout deals with the issue of how to arrange the components on screen. Older, more primitive GUI systems handled this with two-dimensional coordinates: the programmer specified *x*- and *y*-coordinates (in pixels) for the position and the size of each component. In more modern GUI systems, this is too simplistic. We have to take into account different screen resolutions, different fonts, users resizing windows, and many other aspects that make layout more difficult. The solution will be a scheme where we can specify the layout in more general terms. We can, for example, specify that a particular component should be below this other one, or that this component should be stretched if the window gets resized but this other should always have a constant size. We shall see that this is done using *layout managers*.

> **Concept**
>
> Arranging the **layout** of components is achieved by using layout managers.

Event handling refers to the technique we shall use to deal with user input. Once we have created our components and positioned them on screen, we also have to make sure that

Concept

The term **event handling** refers to the task of reacting to user events, such as mouse-button clicks or keyboard input.

something happens when a user clicks a button. The model used by the Java library for this is event-based: if a user activates a component (e.g., clicks a button or selects a menu item) the system will generate an event. Our application can then receive a notification of the event (by having one of its methods invoked), and we can take appropriate action.

We shall discuss each of these areas in much more detail later in this chapter. First, however, we shall briefly introduce a bit more background and terminology.

13.3 AWT and Swing

Java has three GUI libraries. The oldest is called *AWT* (Abstract Window Toolkit) and was introduced as part of the original Java API. Later, a much-improved GUI library, called *Swing,* was added to Java. More recently, the *JavaFX* library has been added. In this chapter we shall concentrate on using Swing, but many of the principles we cover will apply equally well to GUI libraries in general.

Swing makes use of some of the AWT classes, replaces some AWT classes with its own versions, and adds many new classes (Figure 13.1). This means that we shall use some AWT classes that are still used with Swing programs, but use the Swing versions of all classes that exist in both libraries.

Wherever there are equivalent classes in AWT and Swing, the Swing versions have been identified by adding the letter *J* to the start of the class name. You will, for example, see classes named **Button** and **JButton**, **Frame** and **JFrame**, **Menu** and **JMenu**, and so on. The classes starting with a *J* are the Swing versions; these are the ones we shall use, and the two should not be mixed in an application.

That is enough background for a start. Let us look at some code.

13.4 The ImageViewer example

As always, we shall discuss the new concepts by using an example. The application we shall build in this chapter is an image viewer (Figure 13.2). This is a program that can open and display image files in JPEG and PNG formats, perform some image transformations, and save the images back to disk.

Figure 13.1
AWT and Swing

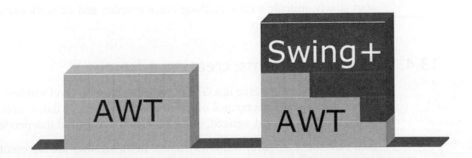

Figure 13.2

A simple image-viewer application

Concept

Image format
Images can be stored in different formats. The differences primarily affect file size and the quality of the image.

As part of this, we shall use our own image class to represent an image while it is in memory, implement various filters to change the image's appearance, and use Swing components to build a user interface. While doing this, we shall concentrate our discussion on the GUI aspects of the program.

If you are curious to see what we will build, you can open and try out the *imageviewer1-0* project—that is the version displayed in Figure 13.2; just create an **ImageViewer** object. There are some sample images in the *images* folder inside the *chapter13* folder (one level up from the project folder). You can, of course, also open your own images. Here, we start slowly, initially with something much simpler, and we work our way to the complete application step by step.

13.4.1 First experiments: creating a frame

Almost everything you see in a GUI is contained in a top-level window. A top-level window is one that is under the control of the operating system's window management and which typically can be moved, resized, minimized, and maximized independently.

Java calls these top-level windows *frames*. In Swing, they are represented by a class called **JFrame**.

Code 13.1

A first version of
an **ImageViewer**
class

```java
import java.awt.*;
import java.awt.event.*;
import javax.swing.*;

/**
 * ImageViewer is the main class of the image viewer application. It builds
 * and displays the application GUI and initialises all other components.
 *
 * To start the application, create an object of this class.
 *
 * @author Michael Kölling and David J. Barnes.
 * @version 0.1
 */
public class ImageViewer
{
    private JFrame frame;

    /**
     * Create an ImageViewer show it on screen.
     */
    public ImageViewer()
    {
        makeFrame();
    }

    // ---- swing stuff to build the frame and all its components ----

    /**
     * Create the Swing frame and its content.
     */
    private void makeFrame()
    {
        frame = new JFrame("ImageViewer");
        Container contentPane = frame.getContentPane();

        JLabel label = new JLabel("I am a label. I can display some text.");
        contentPane.add(label);

        frame.pack();
        frame.setVisible(true);
    }
}
```

To get a GUI on screen, the first thing we have to do is create and display a frame. Code 13.1 shows a complete class (already named **ImageViewer** in preparation for things to come) that shows a frame on screen. This class is available in the book projects as *imageviewer0-1* (the number stands for version 0.1).

> **Exercise 13.1** Open the *imageviewer0-1* project. (This will become the basis of your own image viewer.) Create an instance of class **ImageViewer**. Resize the resulting frame (make it larger). What do you observe about the placement of the text in the frame?

We shall now discuss the **ImageViewer** class shown in Code 13.1 in some detail.

The first three lines in that class are import statements of all classes in the packages **java.awt**, **java.awt.event**, and **javax.swing**.[1] We need many of the classes in these packages for all Swing applications we create, so we shall always import the three packages completely in our GUI programs.

Looking at the rest of the class shows very quickly that all the interesting stuff is in the **make-Frame** method. This method takes care of constructing the GUI. The class's constructor contains only a call to this method. We have done this so that all the GUI construction code is at a well-defined place and is easy to find later (cohesion!). We shall do this in all our GUI examples.

The class has one instance variable of type **JFrame**. This is used to hold the frame that the image viewer wants to show on screen. Let us now take a closer look at the **makeFrame** method.

The first line in this method is

```
frame = new JFrame("ImageViewer");
```

This statement creates a new frame and stores it in our instance variable for later use.

As a general principle, you should, in parallel with studying the examples in this book, look at the class documentation for all classes we encounter. This applies to all the classes we use; we shall not point this out every time from now on, but just expect you to do it.

> **Exercise 13.2** Find the documentation for class **JFrame**. What is the purpose of the **ImageViewer** parameter that we used in the constructor call above?

> **Concept**
>
> Components are placed in a frame by adding them to the frame's **menu bar** or **content pane**.

A frame consists of three parts: the *title bar*, an optional *menu bar,* and the *content pane* (Figure 13.3). The exact appearance of the title bar depends on the underlying operating system. It usually contains the window title and a few window controls.

The menu bar and the content pane are under the control of the application. To both, we can add some components to create a GUI. We shall concentrate on the content pane first.

13.4.2 Adding simple components

Immediately following creation of the **JFrame**, the frame will be invisible and its content pane will be empty. We continue by adding a label to the content pane:

```
Container contentPane = frame.getContentPane();
JLabel label = new JLabel("I am a label.");
contentPane.add(label);
```

The first line gets the content pane from the frame. We always have to do this; GUI components are added to a frame by adding them to the frame's content pane.[2]

---

[1] The **swing** package is really in a package called **javax** (ending with an *x*), not **java**. The reason for this is largely historic—there does not seem to be a logical explanation for it.

[2] Java also has an **add** method for adding components directly in the **JFrame** class, which will also add the component to the content pane. However, we need access to the content pane for other reasons later anyway, so we do the adding of components to the content pane at this point as well.

Figure 13.3
Different parts of a
frame

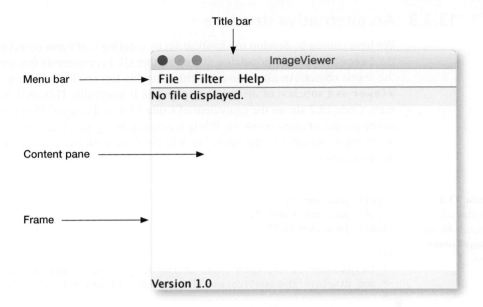

Title bar

Menu bar

Content pane

Frame

ImageViewer

File   Filter   Help

No file displayed.

Version 1.0

The content pane itself is of type **Container**. A container is a Swing component that can hold arbitrary groups of other components—rather like an **ArrayList** can hold an arbitrary collection of objects. We shall discuss containers in more detail later.

We then create a label component (type **JLabel**) and add it to the content pane. A label is a component that can display text and/or an image.

Finally, we have the two lines

```
frame.pack();
frame.setVisible(true);
```

The first line causes the frame to arrange the components inside it properly, and to size itself appropriately. We always have to call the **pack** method on the frame after we have added or resized components.

The last line finally makes the frame visible on screen. We always start out with the frame being invisible so that we can arrange all the components inside the frame without the construction process being visible on screen. Then, when the frame is built, we can show it in a completed state.

Exercise 13.3 Another often-used Swing component is a button (type **JButton**). Replace the label in the example above with a button.

Exercise 13.4 What happens when you add two labels (or two buttons) to the content pane? Can you explain what you observe? Experiment with resizing the frame.

13.4.3 An alternative structure

We have chosen to develop our application by creating a **JFrame** object as an attribute of the **ImageViewer** and populating it with further GUI components that are created outside the frame object. An alternative structure for this top level would be to define **Image-Viewer** as a subclass of **JFrame** and populate it internally. This style is also commonly seen. Code 13.2 shows the equivalent of Code 13.1 in this style. This version is available as the project *imageviewer0-1a*. While it is worth being familiar with both styles, neither is obviously superior to the other. We will continue with our original version in the rest of this chapter.

Code 13.2

An alternative structure for the **ImageViewer** class

```java
import java.awt.*;
import java.awt.event.*;
import javax.swing.*;

/**
 * ImageViewer is the main class of the image viewer application. It builds
 * and displays the application GUI and initialises all other components.
 *
 * To start the application, create an object of this class.
 *
 * @author Michael Kölling and David J. Barnes.
 * @version 0.1a
 */
public class ImageViewer extends JFrame
{
    /**
     * Create an ImageViewer and show it on screen.
     */
    public ImageViewer()
    {
        super("ImageViewer");
        makeFrame();
    }

    // ---- swing stuff to build the frame and all its components ----

    /**
     * Create the Swing frame and its content.
     */
    private void makeFrame()
    {
        Container contentPane = getContentPane();

        JLabel label = new JLabel("I am a label. I can display some text.");
        contentPane.add(label);

        pack();
        setVisible(true);
    }
}
```

13.4.4 Adding menus

Our next step toward building a GUI is to add menus and menu items. This is conceptually easy but contains one tricky detail: How do we arrange to react to user actions, such as the selection of a menu item? We discuss this below.

First, we create the menus. Three classes are involved:

- **JMenuBar**—An object of this class represents a menu bar that can be displayed below the title bar at the top of a window (see Figure 13.3). Every window has at most one **JMenuBar**.[3]

- **JMenu**—Objects of this class represent a single menu (such as the common *File, Edit, or Help* menus). Menus are often held in a menu bar. They could also appear as pop-up menus, but we shall not do that now.

- **JMenuItem**—Objects of this class represent a single menu item inside a menu (such as *Open* or *Save*).

For our image viewer, we shall create one menu bar, and several menus and menu items.

The class **JFrame** has a method called **setJMenuBar**. We can create a menu bar and use this method to attach our menu bar to the frame:

```
JMenuBar menubar = new JMenuBar();
frame.setJMenuBar(menubar);
```

Now we are ready to create a menu and add it to the menu bar:

```
JMenu fileMenu = new JMenu("File");
menubar.add(fileMenu);
```

These two lines create a menu labeled *File* and insert it into our menu bar. Finally, we can add menu items to the menu. The following lines add two items, labeled *Open* and *Quit*, to the *File* menu:

```
JMenuItem openItem = new JMenuItem("Open");
fileMenu.add(openItem);
JMenuItem quitItem = new JMenuItem("Quit");
fileMenu.add(quitItem);
```

Exercise 13.5 Add the menu and menu items discussed here to your image-viewer project. What happens when you select a menu item?

Exercise 13.6 Add another menu called *Help* that contains a menu item named *About ImageViewer*. (Note: To increase readability and cohesion, it may be a good idea to move the creation of the menus into a separate method, perhaps named **makeMenuBar**, which is called from our **makeFrame** method.)

---

[3] In Mac OS, the native display is different: the menu bar is at the top of the screen, not the top of each window. In Java applications, the default behavior is to attach the menu bar to the window. It can be placed at the top of the screen with Java applications by using a Mac OS–specific property.

So far, we have achieved half of our task; we can create and display menus. But the second half is missing—nothing happens yet when a user selects a menu. We now have to add code to react to menu selections. This is discussed in the next section.

13.4.5 Event handling

Swing uses a very flexible model to deal with GUI input: an *event-handling* model with *event listeners*.

The Swing framework itself and some of its components raise events when something happens that other objects may be interested in. There are different types of events caused by different types of actions. When a button is clicked or a menu item is selected, the component raises an **ActionEvent**. When a mouse is clicked or moved, a **MouseEvent** is raised. When a frame is closed or iconified, a **WindowEvent** is generated. There are many other types of events.

Any of our objects can become an event listener for any of these events. When it is a listener, it will get notified about any of the events it listens to. An object becomes an event listener by implementing one of several existing listener interfaces. If it implements the right interface, it can register itself with a component it wants to listen to.

Let us look at an example. A menu item (class **JMenuItem**) raises an **ActionEvent** when it is activated by a user. Objects that want to listen to these events must implement the **ActionListener** interface from the **java.awt.event** package.

There are two alternative styles for implementing event listeners: either a single object listens for events from many different event sources, or each distinct event source is assigned its own unique listener. We shall discuss both styles in the next two sections.

13.4.6 Centralized receipt of events

In order to make our **ImageViewer** object the single listener to all events from the menu, we have to do three things:

1. We must declare in the class header that it implements the **ActionListener** interface.

2. We have to implement a method with the signature

```
public void actionPerformed(ActionEvent e)
```

   This is the only method declared in the **ActionListener** interface.

3. We must call the **addActionListener** method of the menu item to register the **ImageViewer** object as a listener.

Numbers 1 and 2—implementing the interface and defining its method—ensure that our object is a subtype of **ActionListener**. Number 3 then registers our own object as a listener for the menu items. Code 13.3 shows the source code for this in context.

Note especially the lines

```
JMenuItem openItem = new JMenuItem("Open");
openItem.addActionListener(this);
```

Code 13.3

Adding an action
listener to a menu
item

```java
public class ImageViewer
    implements ActionListener
{
```

Fields and constructor omitted.

```java
    /**
     * Receive notification of an action.
     * @param event Details of the action.
     */
    public void actionPerformed(ActionEvent event)
    {
        System.out.println("Menu item: " + event.getActionCommand());
    }
```

```java
    /**
     * Create the Swing frame and its content.
     */
    private void makeFrame()
    {
        frame = new JFrame("ImageViewer");
        makeMenuBar(frame);
```

Other GUI building code omitted.

```java
    }
```

```java
    /**
     * Create the main frame's menu bar.
     * @param frame    The frame that the menu bar should be added to.
     */
    private void makeMenuBar(JFrame frame)
    {
        JMenuBar menubar = new JMenuBar();
        frame.setJMenuBar(menubar);

        // create the File menu
        JMenu fileMenu = new JMenu("File");
        menubar.add(fileMenu);

        JMenuItem openItem = new JMenuItem("Open");
        openItem.addActionListener(this);
        fileMenu.add(openItem);

        JMenuItem quitItem = new JMenuItem("Quit");
        quitItem.addActionListener(this);
        fileMenu.add(quitItem);
    }
}
```

in the code example. Here, a menu item is created, and the current object (the **ImageViewer** object itself) is registered as an action listener by passing **this** as a parameter to the **addActionListener** method.

The effect of registering our object as a listener with the menu item is that our own **action-Performed** method will be called by the menu item each time the item is activated. When our method is called, the menu item will pass along a parameter of type **ActionEvent** that provides some details about the event that has occurred. These details include the exact time of the event, the state of the modifier keys (the shift, control, and meta keys), a "command string," and more.

The command string is a string that somehow identifies the component that caused the event. For menu items, this is by default the label text of the item.

In our example in Code 13.3, we register the same listener object for both menu items. This means that both menu items will invoke the same **actionPerformed** method when they are activated.

In the **actionPerformed** method, we simply print out the command string of the item to demonstrate that this scheme works. Here, we could now add code to properly handle the menu invocation.

This code example, as discussed this far, is available in the book projects as project *imageviewer0-2*.

> **Exercise 13.7** Implement the menu-handling code, discussed above, in your own imageviewer project. Alternatively, open the *imageviewer0-2* project and carefully examine the source code. Describe in writing and in detail the sequence of events that results from activating the *Quit* menu item.
>
> **Exercise 13.8** Add another menu item called *Save*.
>
> **Exercise 13.9** Add three private methods to your class, named **openFile**, **saveFile**, and **quit**. Change the **actionPerformed** method so that it calls the corresponding method when a menu item is activated.
>
> **Exercise 13.10** If you have done Exercise 13.6 (adding a *Help* menu), make sure that its menu item also gets handled appropriately.

We note that this approach works. We can now implement methods to handle menu items to do our various program tasks. There is, however, one other aspect we should investigate: the current solution is not very nice in terms of maintainability and extendibility.

Examine the code that you had to write in the **actionPerformed** method for Exercise 13.9. There are several problems. They are:

■ You probably used an if-statement and the **getActionCommand** method to find out which item was activated. For example, you could write:

```
if(event.getActionCommand().equals("Open")) ...
```

Depending on the item label string for performing the function is not a good idea. What if you now translated the interface into another language? Just changing the text on the menu item would have the effect that the program does not work anymore. (Or you would have to find all places in the code where this string was used and change them all—a tedious and error-prone procedure.)

- Having a central dispatch method (such as our **actionPerformed**) is not a nice structure at all. We essentially make every separate item call a single method, only to write tedious code in that method to call separate methods for every item from there. This is annoying in maintenance terms (for every additional menu item we have to add a new if-statement in **actionPerformed**); it also seems a waste of effort. It would be much nicer if we could make every menu item call a separate method directly.

In the next section, we show how Java 8's lambda expressions can significantly simplify the code for event handling.

13.4.7 Lambda expressions as event handlers

The material in this section makes extensive use of the *lambda expression* feature that was introduced in Java 8, and which was covered in detail in Chapter 5 of this book.

The **ActionListener** interface contains a single abstract method, which means that it fits the definition of a *functional interface*, as discussed in Chapter 12. There we noted that a lambda expression may be used wherever an object of a functional interface type is required. So when calling the **addActionListener** method of a **JMenuItem**, we can use a lambda expression to specify the actions to be taken when the associated **ActionEvent** occurs. The following code shows the full syntax for a lambda expression used as the event handler for the *Open* menu item:

```
openItem.addActionListener(
    (ActionEvent e) -> { openFile(); }
);
```

When a menu item is selected, the associated listener lambda expression will receive an **ActionEvent** object—with which it does nothing—and the body of the listener calls the **openFile** method defined in the enclosing **ImageViewer** class. The body of a lambda expression is able to access any of the members of the enclosing class, including those that are private.

> **Exercise 13.11** Implement menu-item handling with lambda expressions, as discussed here, in your own version of the image viewer.

We can use the simplified syntax for lambda expressions that allows us to leave out the parameter type for lambdas with a single parameter and the curly brackets for a single statement body. The code to add the listener then looks as follows:

```
openItem.addActionListener(e -> openFile());
```

Version 0-3 of the *imageviewer* project implements its listeners in this way.

> **Exercise 13.12** Open the *imageviewer0-3* project and examine it; that is, test it and read its source code. Don't worry about understanding everything, because some new features are the subject of this section.
>
> **Exercise 13.13** You will notice that activating the *Quit* menu item now quits the program. Examine how this is done. Look up the library documentation for any classes and methods involved.

Many of the listener interfaces associated with GUIs are functional interfaces and it will be appropriate to implement listeners using the lambda syntax. We will follow this convention in future versions of the *imageviewer* project. For non-functional interfaces—i.e., those containing more than one abstract method—a different syntax is required, and we cover this in Section 13.8, Inner classes.

Note also that **ImageViewer** does not implement **ActionListener** anymore (we removed its **actionPerformed** method), but the lambda expressions do. (Lambda expressions implement interfaces just by virtue of providing an implementation that matches the signature of the method in the functional interface.) This now allows us to use lambda expressions as action listeners for the menu items.

In summary, instead of having the image-viewer object listen to all action events, we create separate listeners for each possible event—defined by a lambda—where each listener listens to one single event type. As every listener has its own implementation of the **actionPerformed** method, we can now write specific handling code in these methods. Also, because the lambdas are in the scope of the enclosing class, they can make full use of the enclosing class in the implementation of their body, because they can access the enclosing class's private fields and methods.

This structure is cohesive and extendable. If we need an additional menu item, we just add code to create the item and the lambda that handles its function. No listing in a central method is required.

However, using lambdas can make code quite hard to read if the lambda expression is long. It is strongly recommended to use them only for very short handler functionality and for well-established code idioms. For more complex code, it may be best for the lambda to call a separate method defined in the enclosing class—as we have done here—or to consider the use of an *inner class*. Inner classes are discussed in Section 13.8.

13.4.8 Summary of key GUI elements

At the beginning of this chapter, we listed the three areas of GUI construction: components, layout, and event handling. So far, we have concentrated on two of these areas. We have encountered a small number of components (labels, buttons, menus, menu items), and we have discussed the handling of action events in quite some detail.

Getting to the current state (showing a frame with a label and a few menus) was hard work, and had to discuss a lot of background concepts. It gets easier from now on—really! Understanding the event handling for menu items was probably the most difficult detail we had to master for our example.

Adding more menus and other components to the frame will now be quite easy—just more of the same. The one entirely new area we shall have to look at is *layout*: how to arrange the components in the frame.

13.5   ImageViewer 1.0: the first complete version

We shall now work on creating the first complete version—one that can really accomplish the main task: display some images.

13.5.1   Image-processing classes

On the way to the solution, we shall investigate one more interim version: *imageviewer0-4*. Its class structure is shown in Figure 13.4.

As you can see, we have added three new classes: **OFImage**, **ImagePanel**, and **Image-FileManager**. **OFImage** is a class to represent an image that we want to display and manipulate. **ImageFileManager** is a helper class that provides static methods to read an image file (in JPEG or PNG format) from disk and return it in **OFImage** format, then save the **OFImage** back to disk. **ImagePanel** is a custom Swing component to show the image in our GUI.

We shall briefly discuss the most important aspects of each of these classes in some more detail. We shall not, however, explain them completely—that is left as an investigation for the curious reader.

The **OFImage** class is our own custom format for representing an image in memory. You can think of an **OFImage** as a two-dimensional array of pixels. Each of the pixels can

Figure 13.4

The class structure of the image viewer application

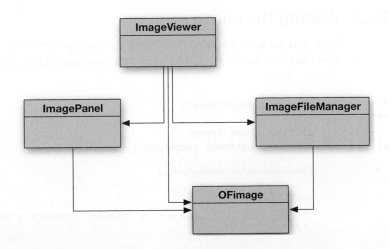

have a color. We use the standard class **Color** (from package **java.awt**) to represent each pixel's color. (Have a look at the documentation of class **Color** as well; we shall need it later.)

OFImage is implemented as a subclass of the Java standard class **BufferedImage** (from package **java.awt.image**). **BufferedImage** gives us most of the functionality we want (it also represents an image as a two-dimensional array), but it does not have methods to set or get a pixel using a **Color** object (it uses different formats for this, which we do not want to use). So we made our own subclass that adds these two methods.

For this project, we can treat **OFImage** like a library class; you will not need to modify this class.

The most important methods from **OFImage** for us are:

- **getPixel** and **setPixel** to read and modify single pixels
- **getHeight** and **getWidth** to find out about the image's size.

The **ImageFileManager** class offers three methods: one to read a named image file from disk and return it as an **OFImage**, one to write an **OFImage** file to disk, and one to open a file-chooser dialog to let a user select an image to open. The methods can read files in the standard JPEG and PNG formats, and the **save** method will write files in JPEG format. This is done using the standard Java image I/O methods from the **ImageIO** class (package **javax.imageio**).

The **ImagePanel** class implements a custom-made Swing component to display our image. Custom-made Swing components can easily be created by writing a subclass of an existing component. As such, they can be inserted into a Swing container and displayed in our GUI like any other Swing component. **ImagePanel** is a subclass of **JComponent**. The other important point to note here is that **ImagePanel** has a **setImage** method that takes an **OFImage** as a parameter to display any given **OFImage**.

13.5.2 Adding the image

Now that we have prepared the classes for dealing with images, adding the image to the user interface is easy. Code 13.4 shows the important differences from previous versions.

Code 13.4
ImageViewer
class with
ImagePanel

```
public class ImageViewer
{
    private JFrame frame;
    private ImagePanel imagePanel;

    Constructor and quit method omitted.

    /**
     * Open function: open a file chooser to select a new image file.
     */
```

**Code 13.4
continued**

ImageViewer
class with
ImagePanel

```
private void openFile()
{
    OFImage image = ImageFileManager.getImage();
    imagePanel.setImage(image);
    frame.pack();
}

/**
 * Create the Swing frame and its content.
 */
private void makeFrame()
{
    frame = new JFrame("ImageViewer");
    makeMenuBar(frame);

    Container contentPane = frame.getContentPane();

    imagePanel = new ImagePanel();
    contentPane.add(imagePanel);

    // building is done - arrange the components and show
    frame.pack();
    frame.setVisible(true);
}
```

makeMenuBar method omitted.

```
}
```

When comparing this code with the previous version, we note that there are only two small changes:

■ In method **makeFrame**, we now create and add an **ImagePanel** component instead of a **JLabel**. Doing this is no more complicated than adding the label. The **ImagePanel** object is stored in an instance field so that we can access it again later.

■ Our **openFile** method has now been changed to actually open and display an image file. Using our image-processing classes, this also is easy now. The **ImageFileManager** class has a method to select and open an image, and the **ImagePanel** object has a method to display that image. One thing to note is that we need to call **frame.pack()** at the end of the **openFile** method, as the size of our image component has changed. The **pack** method will recalculate the frame layout and redraw the frame so that the size change is properly handled.

Exercise 13.14 Open and test the *imageviewer0-4* project. The folder for this chapter's projects also includes a folder called *images*. Here, you can find some test images you can use. Of course, you can also use your own images.

> **Exercise 13.15** What happens when you open an image and then resize the frame? What if you first resize the frame and then open an image?

With this version, we have solved the central task; we can now open an image file from disk and display it on screen. Before we call our project "version 1.0," however, and thus declare it finished for the first time, we want to add a few more improvements (see Figure 13.2).

■ We want to add two labels: one to display the image filename at the top and a status text at the bottom.

■ We want to add a *Filter* menu that contains some filters that change the image's appearance.

■ We want to add a *Help* menu that contains an *About ImageViewer* item. Selecting this menu item should display a dialog with the application's name, version number, and author information.

13.5.3 Layout

First, we shall work on the task of adding two text labels to our interface: one at the top that is used to display the filename of the image currently displayed, and one at the bottom that is used for various status messages.

Creating these labels is easy—they are both simple **JLabel** instances. We store them in instance fields so that we can access them later to change their displayed text. The only question is how to arrange them on screen.

A first (naïve and incorrect) attempt could look like this:

```
Container contentPane = frame.getContentPane();
filenameLabel = new JLabel();
contentPane.add(filenameLabel);
imagePanel = new ImagePanel();
contentPane.add(imagePanel);
statusLabel = new JLabel("Version 1.0");
contentPane.add(statusLabel);
```

The idea here is simple: we get the frame's content pane and add, one after the other, all three components that we wish to display. The only problem is that we did not specify exactly how these three components should be arranged. We might want them to appear next to each other, or one below the other, or in any other possible arrangement. As we did not specify any layout, the container (the content pane) uses a default behavior. And this, it turns out, is not what we want.

Swing uses *layout managers* to arrange the layout of components in a GUI. Each container that holds components, such as the content pane, has an associated layout manager that takes care of arranging the components within that container.

Exercise 13.16 Continuing from your last version of the project, use the code fragment shown above to add the two labels. Test it. What do you observe?

Swing provides several different layout managers to support different layout preferences. The most important are: **FlowLayout**, **BorderLayout**, **GridLayout**, and **BoxLayout**. Each of those is represented by a Java class in the Swing library, and each lays out in different ways the components under its control.

Here follows a short description of each layout. The key differences between them are the ways in which they position components, and how the available space is distributed between the components. You can find the examples illustrated here in the *layouts* project.

A **FlowLayout** (Figure 13.5) arranges all components sequentially from left to right. It will leave each component at its preferred size and center them horizontally. If the horizontal space is not enough to fit all components, they wrap around to a second line. The **FlowLayout** can also be set to align components left or right. Because the components are not resized to fill the available space, there will be spare space around them if the window is resized.

A **BorderLayout** (Figure 13.6) places up to five components in an arranged pattern: one in the center and one each at the top, bottom, right, and left. Each of these positions may be empty, so it may hold fewer than five components. The five positions are named CENTER, NORTH, SOUTH, EAST, and WEST. There is no leftover space with a **BorderLayout** when the window is resized; it is all distributed (unevenly) between the components.

This layout may seem very specialized at first—one wonders how often this is needed. But in practice, this is a surprisingly useful layout that is used in many applications. In BlueJ,

Figure 13.5
FlowLayout

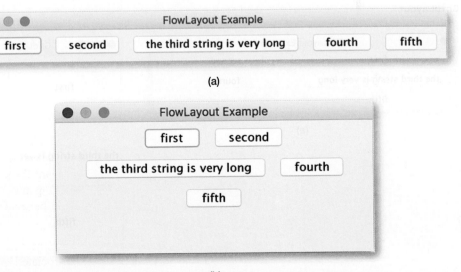

(a)

(b)

Figure 13.6
BorderLayout

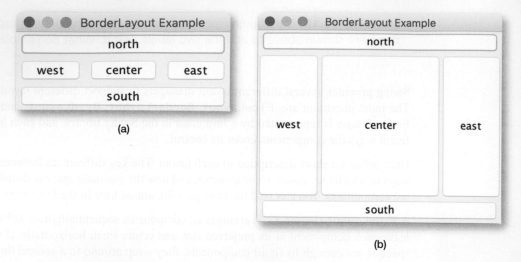

(a)

(b)

for example, both the main window and the editor use a **BorderLayout** as the main layout manager.

When a **BorderLayout** is resized, the middle component is the one that gets stretched in both dimensions. The east and west components change in height but keep their width. The north and south components keep their height, and only the width changes.

As the name suggests, a **GridLayout** (Figure 13.7) is useful for laying out components in an evenly spaced grid. The numbers of rows and columns can be specified, and the **Grid-Layout** manager will always keep all components at the same size. This can be useful to force buttons, for example, to have the same width. The width of **JButton** instances is initially determined by the text on the button—each button is made just wide enough to

Figure 13.7
GridLayout

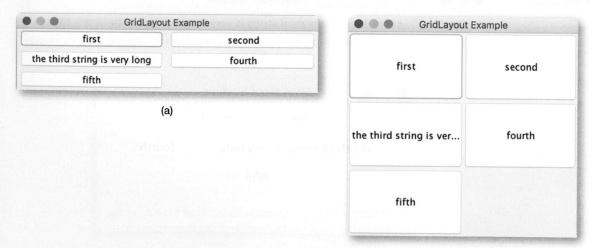

(a)

(b)

Figure 13.8
BoxLayout

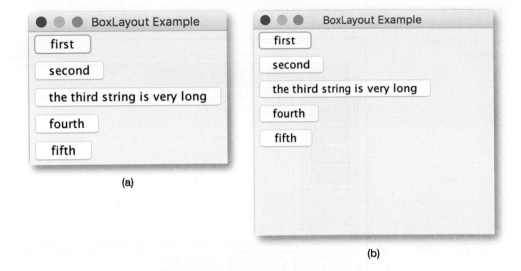

(a)

(b)

display its text. Inserting buttons into a **GridLayout** will result in all buttons being resized to the width of the widest button. If an odd number of equal-size components cannot fill a 2D grid, there may be spare space in some configurations.

A **BoxLayout** lays out multiple components either vertically or horizontally. The components are not resized, and the layout will not wrap components when resized (Figure 13.8). By nesting multiple **BoxLayouts** inside each other, sophisticated two-dimensionally aligned layouts may be built.

> **Exercise 13.17** Using the *layouts* project from this chapter, experiment with the examples illustrated in this section. Add and remove components from the existing classes to get a proper feel for the key characteristics of the different layout styles. What happens if there is no CENTER component with **Border-Layout**, for instance?

13.5.4 Nested containers

All the layout strategies discussed above are fairly simple. The key to building good-looking and well-behaved interfaces lies in one last detail: layouts can be nested. Many of the Swing components are *containers*. Containers appear to the outside as a single component, but they can contain multiple other components. Each container has its own layout manager attached.

The most-used container is the class **JPanel**. A **JPanel** can be inserted as a component into the frame's content pane, and then more components can be laid out inside the **JPanel**. Figure 13.9, for example, shows an interface arrangement similar to that of the BlueJ main window. The content pane of this frame uses a **BorderLayout**, where the EAST position

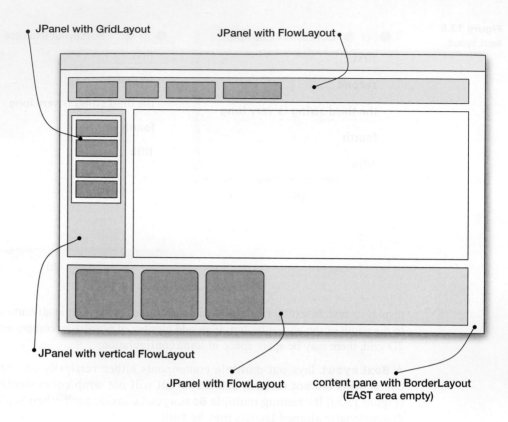

JPanel with GridLayout

JPanel with FlowLayout

JPanel with vertical FlowLayout

JPanel with FlowLayout

content pane with BorderLayout
(EAST area empty)

is unused. The NORTH area of this **BorderLayout** contains a **JPanel** with a horizontal **FlowLayout** that arranges its components (say toolbar buttons) in a row. The SOUTH area is similar: another **JPanel** with a **FlowLayout**.

The button group in the WEST area was first placed into a **JPanel** with a one-column **GridLayout** to give all buttons the same width. This **JPanel** was then placed into another **JPanel** with a **FlowLayout** so that the grid did not extend over the full height of the WEST area. The outer **JPanel** is then inserted into the WEST area of the frame.

Note how the container and the layout manager cooperate in the layout of the components. The container holds the components, but the layout manager decides their exact arrangement on screen. Every container has a layout manager. It will use a default layout manager if we do not explicitly set one. The default is different for different containers: the content pane of a **JFrame**, for example, has by default a **BorderLayout**, whereas **JPanels** use a **FlowLayout** by default.

Exercise 13.18 Look at the GUI of the calculator project used in Chapter 9 (Figure 9.6). What kind of containers/layout managers do you think were used to create it? After answering in writing, open the *calculator-gui* project and check your answer by reading the code.

Exercise 13.19 What kind of layout managers might have been used to create the layout of BlueJ's editor window?

Exercise 13.20 In BlueJ, invoke the *Use Library Class* function from the *Tools* menu. Look at the dialog you see on screen. Which containers/layout managers might have been used to create it? Resize the dialog and observe the resize behavior to get additional information.

It is time to look again at some code for our **ImageViewer** application. Our goal is quite simple. We want to see three components above each other: a label at the top, the image in the middle, and another label at the bottom. Several layout managers can do this. Which one to choose becomes clearer when we think about resizing behavior. When we enlarge the window, we would like the labels to maintain their height and the image to receive all the extra space. This suggests a **BorderLayout**: the labels can be in the NORTH and SOUTH areas, and the image in the CENTER. Code 13.5 shows the source code to implement this.

Two details are worth noting. First, the **setLayout** method is used on the content pane to set the intended layout manager.[4] The layout manager itself is an object, so we create an instance of **BorderLayout** and pass it to the **setLayout** method.

Second, when we add a component to a container with a **BorderLayout**, we use a different **add** method that has a second parameter. The value for the second parameter is one of the public constants **NORTH**, **SOUTH**, **EAST**, **WEST**, and **CENTER**, which are defined in class **BorderLayout**.

Code 13.5
Using a **Border Layout** to arrange components

```
private void makeFrame()
{
    frame = new JFrame("ImageViewer");
    makeMenuBar(frame);

    ...

    Container contentPane = frame.getContentPane();

    contentPane.setLayout(new BorderLayout(6, 6));

    filenameLabel = new JLabel();
    contentPane.add(filenameLabel, BorderLayout.NORTH);

    imagePanel = new ImagePanel();
    contentPane.add(imagePanel, BorderLayout.CENTER);

    statusLabel = new JLabel("Version 1.0");
    contentPane.add(statusLabel, BorderLayout.SOUTH);

    ...
}
```

---

[4] Strictly speaking, the **setLayout** call is not needed here, as the default layout manager of the content pane is already a **BorderLayout**. We have included the call here for clarity and readability.

Exercise 13.21 Implement and test the code shown above in your version of the project.

Exercise 13.22 Experiment with other layout managers. Try in your project all of the layout managers mentioned above, and test whether they behave as expected.

13.5.5 Image filters

Two things remain to be done before our first image-viewer version is finished: adding some image filters, and adding a *Help* menu. Next, we shall do the filters.

The image filters are the first step toward image manipulation. Eventually, we want not only to be able to open and display images, but also to be able to manipulate them and save them back to disk.

Here, we start by adding three simple filters. A filter is a function that is applied to the whole image. (It could, of course, be modified to be applied to a part of an image, but we are not doing that just yet.)

The three filters are named *darker*, *lighter*, and *threshold*. *Darker* makes the whole image darker, and *lighter* makes it lighter. The threshold filter turns the image into a grayscale picture with only a few preset shades of gray. We have chosen a three-level threshold. This means we shall use three colors: black, white, and medium-gray. All pixels that are in the upper-third value range for brightness will be turned white, all that are in the lower third will be turned black, and the middle third will be gray.

To achieve this, we have to do two things:

■ create menu items for each filter with an associated menu listener

■ implement the actual filter operation

First the menus. There is nothing really new in this. It is just more of the same menu-creation code that we already wrote for our existing menu. We need to add the following parts:

■ We create a new menu (class **JMenu**) named *Filter* and add it to the menu bar.

■ We create three menu items (class **JMenuItem**) named *Darker*, *Lighter*, and *Threshold*, and add them to our filter menu.

■ To each menu item, we add an action listener, using lambda expressions as we discussed for the other menu items. The action listeners should call the methods **makeDarker**, **makeLighter**, and **threshold**, respectively.

After we have added the menus and created the (initially empty) methods to handle the filter functions, we need to implement each filter.

The simplest kinds of filters involve iterating over the image and making a change of some sort to the color of each pixel. A pattern for this process is shown in Code 13.6. More-complicated filters might use the values of neighboring pixels to adjust a pixel's value.

> **Exercise 13.23** Add the new menu and the menu items to your version of the *image-viewer0-4* project, as described here. In order to add the action listeners, you need to create the three methods **makeDarker**, **makeLighter**, and **threshold** as private methods in your **ImageViewer** class. They all have a **void** return type and take no parameters. These methods can initially have empty bodies, or they could simply print out that they have been called.

Code 13.6

Pattern for a simple filtering process

```
for(int y = 0; y < height; y++) {
    for(int x = 0; x < width; x++) {
        Color pixel = getPixel(x, y);

        Alter the pixel's color value.

        setPixel(x, y, pixel);
    }
}
```

The filter function itself operates on the image, so following responsibility-driven design guidelines, it should be implemented in the **OFImage** class. On the other hand, handling the menu invocation also includes some GUI-related code (for instance, we have to check whether an image is open at all when we invoke the filter), and this belongs in the **ImageViewer** class.

As a result of this reasoning, we create two methods, one in **ImageViewer** and one in **OFImage**, to share the work (Code 13.7 and Code 13.8). We can see that the **makeDarker** method in **ImageViewer** contains the part of the task that is related to the GUI (checking that we have an image loaded, displaying a status message, repainting the frame), whereas the **darker** method in **OFImage** includes the actual work of making each pixel in the image a bit darker.

Code 13.7

The filter method in the **ImageViewer** class

```
public class ImageViewer
{

    Fields, constructor, and all other methods omitted.

    /**
     * 'Darker' function: make the picture darker.
     */
```

Code 13.7 continued

The filter method in the `ImageViewer` class

```
    private void makeDarker()
    {
        if(currentImage != null) {
            currentImage.darker();
            frame.repaint();
            showStatus("Applied: darker");
        }
        else {
            showStatus("No image loaded.");
        }
    }
}
```

Code 13.8

Implementation of a filter in the `OFImage` class

```
public class OFImage extends BufferedImage
{

    Fields, constructor, and all other methods omitted.

    /**
     * Make this image a bit darker.
     */
    public void darker()
    {
        int height = getHeight();
        int width = getWidth();
        for(int y = 0; y < height; y++) {
            for(int x = 0; x < width; x++) {
                setPixel(x, y, getPixel(x, y).darker());
            }
        }
    }
}
```

Exercise 13.24 What does the method call `frame.repaint()` do, which you can see in the `makeDarker` method?

Exercise 13.25 We can see a call to a method `showStatus`, which is clearly an internal method call. From the name, we can guess that this method should display a status message using the status label we created earlier. Implement this method in your version of the *imageviewer0-4* project. (*Hint*: Look at the `setText` method in the `JLabel` class.)

Exercise 13.26 What happens if the *Darker* menu item is selected when no image has been opened?

Exercise 13.27 Explain in detail how the `darker` method in `OFImage` works. (*Hint*: It contains another method call to a method also called `darker`. Which class does this second method belong to? Look it up.)

Exercise 13.28 Implement the *lighter* filter in **OFImage**.

Exercise 13.29 Implement the *threshold* filter. To get the brightness of a pixel, you can get its red, green, and blue values and add them up. The **Color** class defines static references to suitable black, white, and gray objects.

You can find a working implementation of everything described so far in the *imageviewer1-0* project. You should, however, attempt to do the exercises yourself first, before you look at the solution.

13.5.6 Dialogs

Our last task for this version is to add a *Help* menu that holds a menu item labeled *About ImageViewer* . . . When this item is selected, a dialog should pop up that displays some short information.

Now we have to implement the **showAbout** method so that it displays an "About" dialog.

Exercise 13.30 Again add a menu named *Help*. In it, add a menu item labeled *About ImageViewer* . . .

Exercise 13.31 Add a method stub (a method with an empty body) named **showAbout**, and add an event handler that calls **showAbout** to the *About ImageViewer* . . . menu item.

One of the main characteristics of a dialog is whether or not it is *modal*. A modal dialog blocks all interaction with other parts of the application until the dialog has been closed. It forces the user to deal with the dialog first. Non-modal dialogs allow interaction in other frames while the dialogs are visible.

Dialogs can be implemented in a similar way to our main **JFrame**. They often use the class **JDialog** to display the frame.

For modal dialogs with a standard structure, however, there are some convenience methods in class **JOptionPane** that make it very easy to show such dialogs. **JOptionPane** has, among other things, static methods to show three types of standard dialog. They are:

- *Message dialog:* This is a dialog that displays a message and has an *OK* button to close the dialog.

- *Confirm dialog:* This dialog usually asks a question and has buttons for the user to make a selection—for example, *Yes*, *No*, and *Cancel*.

- *Input dialog:* This dialog includes a prompt and a text field for the user to enter some text.

Our "About" box is a simple message dialog. Looking through the **JOptionPane** documentation, we find that there are static methods named **showMessageDialog** to do this.

Exercise 13.32 Find the documentation for **showMessageDialog**. How many methods with this name are there? What are the differences between them? Which one should we use for the "About" box? Why?

Exercise 13.33 Implement the **showAbout** method in your **ImageViewer** class, using a call to a **showMessageDialog** method.

Exercise 13.34 The **showInputDialog** methods of **JOptionPane** allow a user to be prompted for input via a dialog when required. On the other hand, the **JTextField** component allows a permanent text input area to be displayed within a GUI. Find the documentation for this class. What input causes an **ActionListener** associated with a **JTextField** to be notified? Can a user be prevented from editing the text in the field? Is it possible for a listener to be notified of arbitrary changes to the text in the field? (*Hint*: What use does a **JTextField** make of a **Document** object?)

You can find an example of a **JTextField** in the *calculator* project in Chapter 9.

After studying the documentation, we can now implement our "About" box by making a call to the **showMessageDialog** method. The code is shown in Code 13.9. Note that we have introduced a string constant named **VERSION** to hold the current version number.

Code 13.9

Displaying a modal dialog

```
/**
 * Show the 'About...' dialog.
 */
private void showAbout()
{
    JOptionPane.showMessageDialog(frame,
            "ImageViewer\n" + VERSION,
            "About ImageViewer",
            JOptionPane.INFORMATION_MESSAGE);
}
```

This was the last task to be done to complete "version 1.0" of our image-viewer application. If you have done all the exercises, you should now have a version of the project that can open images, apply filters, display status messages, and display a dialog.

The *imageviewer1-0* project, included in the book projects, contains an implementation of all the functionality discussed thus far. You should carefully study this project and compare it with your own solutions.

In this project, we have also improved the **openFile** method to include better notification of errors. If the user chooses a file that is not a valid image file, we now show a proper error message. Now that we know about message dialogs, this is easy to do.

13.5.7 Summary of layout management

In this section, we have added some custom classes to deal with images, but more importantly for our GUI, we have looked at the layout of components. We have seen how containers and layout managers work together to achieve the exact arrangement we need on screen.

Learning to work with layout managers takes some experience and often some trial-and-error experimentation. Over time, however, you will get to know the layout managers well.

We have now covered the basics of all important areas of GUI programming. For the rest of the chapter, we can concentrate on fine-tuning and improving what we've got.

13.6 ImageViewer 2.0: improving program structure

Version 1.0 of our application has a useable GUI and can display images. It can also apply three basic filters.

The next obvious idea for an improvement of our application is to add some more interesting filters. Before we rush in and do it, however, let us think about what this involves.

With the current structure of filters, we have to do three things for each filter:

1. add a menu item

2. add a method to handle the menu activation in **ImageViewer**

3. add an implementation of the filter in **OFImage**

Numbers 1 and 3 are unavoidable—we need a menu item and a filter implementation. But number 2 looks suspicious. If we look at these methods in the **ImageViewer** class (Code 13.10 shows two of them as an example), this looks a lot like code duplication. These methods are essentially the same (except for some small details), and for each new filter we have to add another one of these methods.

As we know, code duplication is a sign of bad design and should be avoided. We deal with it by refactoring our code. We want to find a design that lets us add new filters without having to add a new dispatch method for the filter every time.

To achieve what we want, we need to avoid hard-coding every filter-method name (**lighter**, **threshold**, etc.) into our **ImageViewer** class. Instead, we shall use a collection of filters and then write a single filter-invocation method that finds and invokes the right filter. This will be similar in style to the introduction of an **act** method when decoupling the simulator from individual actor types in the *foxes-and-rabbits* project in Chapter 12.

In order to do this, filters must themselves become objects, rather than just method names. If we want to store them in a common collection, then all filters will need a common superclass, which we name **Filter** and give an **apply** method (Figure 13.10 shows the structure, Code 13.11 shows the source code).

Code 13.10
Two of the
filter-handling
methods from
`ImageViewer`

```
private void makeLighter()
{
    if(currentImage != null) {
        currentImage.lighter();
        frame.repaint();
        showStatus("Applied: lighter");
    }
    else {
        showStatus("No image loaded.");
    }
}
```

```
private void threshold()
{
    if(currentImage != null) {
        currentImage.threshold();
        frame.repaint();
        showStatus("Applied: threshold");
    }
    else {
        showStatus("No image loaded.");
    }
}
```

Figure 13.10
Class structure for
filters as objects

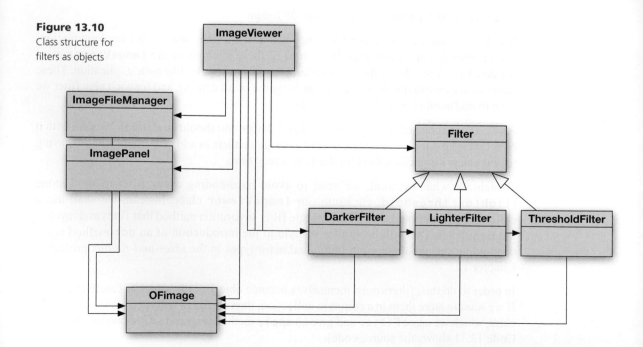

Every filter will have an individual name, and its **apply** method will apply that particular sort of filter to an image. Note that this is an abstract class, as the **apply** method has to be abstract at this level, but the **getName** method can be fully implemented so it is not an interface.

Code 13.11

Abstract class
Filter: Super-
class for all filters

```java
public abstract class Filter
{
    private String name;

    /**
     * Create a new filter with a given name.
     * @param name The name of the filter.
     */
    public Filter(String name)
    {
        this.name = name;
    }

    /**
     * Return the name of this filter.
     * @return   The name of this filter.
     */
    public String getName()
    {
        return name;
    }

    /**
     * Apply this filter to an image.
     * @param  image  The image to be changed by this filter.
     */
    public abstract void apply(OFImage image);
}
```

Once we have written the superclass, it is not hard to implement specific filters as subclasses. All we need to do is provide an implementation for the **apply** method that manipulates an image (passed in as a parameter) using its **getPixel** and **setPixel** methods. Code 13.12 shows an example.

Code 13.12

Implementation
of a specific filter
class

```java
/**
 * An image filter to make the image a bit darker.
 *
 * @author Michael Kölling and David J. Barnes.
 * @version 1.0
 */
public class DarkerFilter extends Filter
{
    /**
     * Constructor for objects of class DarkerFilter.
     * @param name The name of the filter.
     */
```

```
public DarkerFilter(String name)
{
    super(name);
}

/**
 * Apply this filter to an image.
 * @param  image  The image to be changed by this filter.
 */
public void apply(OFImage image)
{
    int height = image.getHeight();
    int width = image.getWidth();
    for(int y = 0; y < height; y++) {
        for(int x = 0; x < width; x++) {
            image.setPixel(x, y, image.getPixel(x, y).darker());
        }
    }
}
}
```

As a side effect of this, the **OFImage** class becomes much simpler, as all of the filter methods can be removed from it. It now only defines the **setPixel** and **getPixel** methods.

Once we have defined our filters like this, we can create filter objects and store them in a collection (Code 13.13).

Code 13.13

Adding a collection of filters

```
public class ImageViewer
{
    Other fields and comments omitted.
    private List<Filter> filters;

    /**
     * Create an ImageViewer show it on screen.
     */
    public ImageViewer()
    {
        filters = createFilters();
        ...
    }
}

/**
 * Create and return a list with all the known filters.
 * @return The list of filters.
 */
```

Code 13.13 continued

Adding a collection of filters

```
private List<Filter> createFilters()
{
    List<Filter> filterList = new ArrayList<>();
    filterList.add(new DarkerFilter("Darker"));
    filterList.add(new LighterFilter("Lighter"));
    filterList.add(new ThresholdFilter("Threshold"));

    return filterList;
}
```

Other methods omitted.

```
}
```

Once we have this structure in place, we can make the last two necessary changes:

- We change the code that creates the filter menu items so that it iterates over the filter collection. For every filter, it creates a menu item and uses the filter's **getName** method to determine the item's label.

- Having done this, we can write a generic **applyFilter** method that receives a filter as a parameter and applies this filter to the current image.

The *imageviewer2-0* project includes a complete implementation of these changes.

> **Exercise 13.35** Open the *imageviewer2-0* project. Study the code for the new method to create and apply filters in class **ImageViewer**. Pay special attention to the **makeMenuBar** and **applyFilter** methods. Explain in detail how the creation of the filter menu items and their activation works. Draw an object diagram.
>
> **Exercise 13.36** What needs to be changed to add a new filter to your image viewer?
>
> **Exercise 13.37** *Challenge exercise* You might have observed that the **apply** methods of all of the **Filter** subclasses have a very similar structure: iterate over the whole image and change the value of each pixel independently of surrounding pixels. It should be possible to isolate this duplication in much the same way as we did in creating the **Filter** class.
>
> Create a method in the **Filter** class that iterates over the image and applies a filter-specific transformation to each individual pixel. Replace the bodies of the **apply** methods in the three **Filter** subclasses with a call to this method, passing the image and something that can apply the appropriate transformation.

In this section, we have done pure refactoring. We have not changed the functionality of the application at all, but have worked exclusively at improving the implementation structure so that future changes become easier.

Now, after finishing the refactoring, we should test that all existing functionality still works as expected. In all development projects, we need phases like this. We do not always make perfect design decisions at the start, and applications grow and requirements change. Even though our main task in this chapter is to work with GUIs, we needed to step back and refactor our code before proceeding. This work will pay off in the long run by making all further changes easier.

Sometimes it is tempting to leave structures as they are, even though we recognize that they are not good. Putting up with a bit of code duplication may be easier in the short term than doing careful refactoring. One can get away with that for a short while, but for projects that are intended to survive for a longer time, this is bound to create problems. As a general rule: Take the time; keep your code clean!

Now that we have done this, we are ready to add some more filters.

Exercise 13.38 Add a *grayscale* filter to your project. The filter turns the image into a black-and-white image in shades of gray. You can make a pixel any shade of gray by giving all three color components (red, green, blue) the same value. The brightness of each pixel should remain unchanged.

Exercise 13.39 Add a *mirror* filter that flips the image horizontally. The pixel at the top left corner will move to the top right, and vice versa, producing the effect of viewing the image in a mirror.

Exercise 13.40 Add an *invert* filter that inverts each color. "Inverting" a color means replacing each color value x with $255 - x$.

Exercise 13.41 Add a *smooth* filter that "smoothes" the image. A smooth filter replaces every pixel value with the average of its neighboring pixels and itself (nine pixels in total). You have to be careful at the image's edges, where some neighbors do not exist. You also have to make sure to work with a temporary copy of the image while you process it, because the result is not correct if you work on a single image. (Why is this?) You can easily obtain a copy of the image by creating a new **OFImage** with the original as the parameter to its constructor.

Exercise 13.42 Add a *solarize* filter. Solarization is an effect one can create manually on photo negatives by re-exposing a developed negative. We can simulate this by replacing each color component of each pixel that has a value v of less than 128 with $255 - v$. The brighter components (value of 128 or more) we leave unchanged. (This is a very simple solarization algorithm—you can find more-sophisticated ones described in the literature.)

Exercise 13.43 Implement an *edge detection* filter. Do this by analyzing the nine pixels in a three-by-three square around each pixel (similar to the smooth filter), and then set the value of the middle pixel to the difference between the highest and the lowest value found. Do this for each color component (red, green, blue). This also looks good if you invert the image at the same time.

Exercise 13.44 Experiment with your filters on different pictures. Try applying multiple filters, one after another.

Once you have implemented some more filters of your own, you should change the version number of your project to "version 2.1."

13.7   ImageViewer 3.0: more interface components

Before we leave the image-viewer project behind us, we want to add a few last improvements, and in the process look at two more GUI components: buttons and borders.

13.7.1   Buttons

We now want to add functionality to the image viewer to change the size of the image. We do this by providing two functions: *larger*, which doubles the image size, and *smaller*, which halves the size. (To be exact, we double or halve both the width and the height, not the area.)

One way to do this is to implement filters for these tasks. But we decide against it. So far, filters never change the image size, and we want to leave it like that. Instead, we introduce a toolbar on the left side of our frame with two buttons in it labeled *Larger* and *Smaller* (Figure 13.11). This also gives us a chance to experiment a bit with buttons, containers, and layout managers.

So far, our frame uses a **BorderLayout**, where the **WEST** area is empty. We can use this area to add our toolbar buttons. There is one small problem, though. The **WEST** area of a **BorderLayout** can hold only one component, but we have two buttons.

The solution is simple. We add a **JPanel** to the frame's **WEST** area (as we know, a **JPanel** is a container), and then place the two buttons in the **JPanel**. Code 13.14 shows the code to do this.

Code 13.14

Adding a toolbar panel with two buttons

```
// Create the toolbar with the buttons
JPanel toolbar = new JPanel();

smallerButton = new JButton("Smaller");
toolbar.add(smallerButton);

largerButton = new JButton("Larger");
toolbar.add(largerButton);

contentPane.add(toolbar, BorderLayout.WEST);
```

Exercise 13.45 Add two buttons labeled *Larger* and *Smaller* to your latest version of the project, using code similar to Code 13.14. Test it. What do you observe?

Figure 13.11

Image viewer with
toolbar buttons

When we try this out, we see that it works partially but does not look as expected. The reason is that a **JPanel** uses, by default, a **FlowLayout**, and a **FlowLayout** arranges its components horizontally. We would like them arranged vertically.

We can achieve this by using another layout manager. A **GridLayout** does what we want. When creating a **GridLayout**, constructor parameters determine how many rows and columns we wish to have. A value of zero has a special meaning here, standing for "as many as necessary."

Thus, we can create a single column **GridLayout** by using 0 as the number of rows and 1 as the number of columns. We can then use this **GridLayout** for our **JPanel** by using the panel's **setLayout** method immediately after creating it:

```
JPanel toolbar = new JPanel();
toolbar.setLayout(new GridLayout(0, 1));
```

Alternatively, the layout manager can also be specified as a constructor parameter of the container:

```
JPanel toolbar = new JPanel(new GridLayout(0, 1));
```

Exercise 13.46 Change your code so that your toolbar panel uses a **GridLayout**, as discussed above. Test. What do you observe?

If we try this out, we can see that we are getting closer, but we still do not have what we want. Our buttons now are much larger than we intended. The reason is that a container in a **BorderLayout** (our toolbar **JPanel** in this case) always covers its whole area (the **WEST** area in our frame). And a **GridLayout** always resizes its components to fill the whole container.

A **FlowLayout** does not do this; it is quite happy to leave some empty space around the components. Our solution is therefore to use both: the **GridLayout** to arrange the buttons in a column, and a **FlowLayout** around it to allow some space. We end up with a **GridLayout** panel inside a **FlowLayout** panel inside a **BorderLayout**. Code 13.15 shows this solution. Constructions like this are very common. You will often nest various containers inside other containers to create exactly the look you want.

Code 13.15

Using a nested **GridLayout** container inside a **FlowLayout** container

```
// Create the toolbar with the buttons
JPanel toolbar = new JPanel();
toolbar.setLayout(new GridLayout(0, 1));

smallerButton = new JButton("Smaller");
toolbar.add(smallerButton);

largerButton = new JButton("Larger");
toolbar.add(largerButton);

// Add toolbar into panel with flow layout for spacing
JPanel flow = new JPanel();
flow.add(toolbar);

contentPane.add(flow, BorderLayout.WEST);
```

Our buttons now look quite close to what we were aiming for. Before adding the finishing polish, we can first focus on making the buttons work.

We need to add two methods for instance, **makeLarger** and **makeSmaller**, to do the actual work, and we need to add action listeners to the buttons that invoke these methods.

Exercise 13.47 In your project, add two method stubs named **makeLarger** and **makeSmaller**. Initially, put just a single **println** statement into these method bodies to see when they have been called. The methods can be private.

Exercise 13.48 Add lambda event handlers to the two buttons that invoke the two new methods. Adding event handlers to buttons is identical to adding them to menu items. You can essentially copy the code pattern from there. Test it. Make sure your **makeSmaller** and **makeLarger** methods get called by activating the buttons.

Exercise 13.49 Properly implement the **makeSmaller** and **makeLarger** methods. To do this, you have to create a new **OFImage** with a different size, copy the pixels from the current image across (while scaling it up or down), and then set the new image as the current image. At the end of your method, you should call the frame's **pack** method to rearrange the components with the changed size.

Exercise 13.50 All Swing components have a **setEnabled(boolean)** method that can enable and disable the component. Disabled components are usually displayed in light gray and do not react to input. Change your image viewer so that the two toolbar buttons are initially disabled. When an image is opened, they should be enabled, and when it is closed, they should be disabled again.

13.7.2 Borders

The last polish we want to add to our interface is some internal borders. Borders can be used to group components, or just to add some space between them. Every Swing component can have a border.

Some layout managers also accept constructor parameters that define their spacing, and the layout manager will then create the requested space between components.

The most used borders are **BevelBorder**, **CompoundBorder**, **EmptyBorder**, **EtchedBorder**, and **TitledBorder**. You should familiarize yourself with these.

We shall do three things to improve the look of our GUI:

- add some empty space around the outside of the frame
- add spacing between the components of the frame
- add a line around the image

The code to do this is shown in Code 13.16. The **setBorder** call on the content pane, with an **EmptyBorder** as a parameter, adds empty space around the outside of the frame. Note

Code 13.16

Adding spacing with gaps and borders

```
JPanel contentPane = (JPanel)frame.getContentPane();
contentPane.setBorder(new EmptyBorder(12, 12, 12, 12));

// Specify the layout manager with nice spacing
contentPane.setLayout(new BorderLayout(6, 6));

// Create the image pane in the center
imagePanel = new ImagePanel();
imagePanel.setBorder(new EtchedBorder());
contentPane.add(imagePanel, BorderLayout.CENTER);
```

that we now cast the **contentPane** to a **JPanel**, as the supertype **Container** does not have the **setBorder** method.[5]

Creating the **BorderLayout** with two **int** parameters adds spacing between the components that it lays out. And finally, setting an **EtchedBorder** for the **imagePanel** adds a line with an "etched" look around the image. (Borders are defined in the package **javax. swing.border**—we have to add an import statement for this package.)

All the improvements discussed in the section have been implemented in the next version of this application in the book projects: *imageviewer3-0*. In that version, we have also added a *Save As* function to the file menu so that images can be saved back to disk.

And we have added one more filter, called *Fish Eye*, to give you some more ideas about what you can do. Try it out. It works especially well on portraits.

13.8 Inner classes

Up to this point, we have implemented event-handling listeners using lambda notation. This has been possible because the listener interfaces have been functional interfaces—i.e., they have consisted of a single abstract method. However, this will not be the case with all listener interfaces. For instance, the **KeyListener**, **MouseListener** and **MouseMotionListener** interfaces in the **java.awt.event** package all consist of more than one abstract method, and so we cannot use lambda expressions to supply their implementations.

13.8.1 Named inner classes

The obvious approach, in such cases, is to define a separate class to implement the required interface, and then create an instance to act as the listening object. However, there are several drawbacks to this approach if we simply implement the interface as a normal class within a project, at the same level as all the other classes:

- There is usually a very tight *coupling* between a listener and the object managing the multiple components of the full GUI. The listener will often need to access and modify private elements of the GUI object's state. This degree of coupling cannot be avoided, but it would be more palatable if we could find a way to identify its existence more clearly among the multiple classes of a project.

- We have seen that a lambda expression has full access to even the private elements of the enclosing GUI class—this is how the very tight coupling arises. This would not be possible for an external class without the addition of accessor and mutator methods in the GUI class, likely provided solely for the listener's benefit. Furthermore, the methods' existence could invite unintended coupling to other classes.

- We often create just a single instance of a listener class, and a full-blown external class will often look like overkill for this sort of usage pattern.

---

[5] Using a cast in this way only works because the dynamic type of the content pane is already **JPanel**. The cast does not transform the content-pane object into a **JPanel**.

Fortunately, Java provides a construct that mitigates all of these problems. It is a construct that we have not discussed before: *inner classes*. Inner classes are classes that are declared textually inside another class:

```
class EnclosingClass
{
    . . .
    class InnerClass
    {
        . . .
    }
}
```

Instances of the inner class are attached to instances of the enclosing class; they can only exist together with an enclosing instance, and they exist conceptually *inside* the enclosing instance. It is immediately clear from this construct that the tight coupling between inner listener class and the enclosing GUI class is explicit. A further feature is that statements in methods of the inner class can see and access private fields and methods of the enclosing class—just as a lambda expression is able to do. The inner class is considered to be a part of the enclosing class just as are any of the enclosing class's methods. This deals effectively with the second problem we described above.

We can now use this construct to implement a **MouseListener**, say, within the **ImageViewer** class. The structure looks like this:

```
public class ImageViewer
{
    . . .

    private class MouseHandler implements MouseListener
    {
        public void mouseClicked(MouseEvent event)
        {
            // perform click action
        }

        public void mouseEntered(MouseEvent event)
        {
            // perform entered action
        }

        ... remaining MouseListener methods omitted ...
    }
}
```

(As a style guide, we usually write inner classes at the end of the enclosing class—after the methods.) Note that we have given the inner class private visibility to reinforce the sense that it is performing a task that is highly specific to the **ImageViewer** class and should not be considered independent of it.

Once we have defined an inner class we can create instances of it in exactly the same way as for those of any other class:

```
// Detect mouse clicks on the image when the user
// wishes to edit it.
imagePanel.addMouseListener(new MouseHandler());
```

Notice a couple of typical usage characteristics of these listener inner classes:

■ We do not bother storing the instances in variables—so, in effect, they are anonymous objects. Only the component to which they are attached has a reference to their specific listener object, so that they can call the listener's event-handling methods.

■ We often only create just a single object from each of the inner classes, because each is highly specialized for a particular component within a specific GUI.

These characteristics will lead us to explore a further feature of Java in the next section.

Inner classes can generally be used in some cases to improve cohesion in larger projects. The *foxes-and-rabbits* project from Chapter 12, for example, has a class **SimulatorView** that includes an inner class **FieldView**. You might want to study this example to deepen your understanding.

13.8.2 Anonymous inner classes

The solution to implementing multi-method interfaces using inner classes is fairly good, but we want to take it one step further: we can use *anonymous inner classes*. To illustrate this feature we will develop another version of the image viewer project; one that allows simple editing of individual pixels. The idea is that the user can click anywhere on the image to change a pixel to a specific color. There are two aspects to this:

■ Choosing the color to place on the image.

■ Choosing which pixel to replace.

The color will be chosen via a **JColorChooser** dialog, which will appear when the user presses a mouse button with the *Shift* key held down, and the pixel to be replaced is chosen by pressing the mouse without the *Shift* key. Once a color has been chosen, pixels are replaced with that color until a new color is chosen. This is implemented as *imageviewer4-0*.

Clearly, the only mouse event we are interested in is a mouse click, but implementing the **MouseListener** requires that we implement five separate methods. This is a nuisance since four of the five method bodies will be empty, and we will often face similar issues when implementing other multi-method listener interfaces. Fortunately, the implementors of the Java API have recognized this problem and provided no-op implementations of these interfaces in the form of abstract **Adapter** classes; for instance, **MouseAdapter** and **MouseMotionAdapter**. What this means is that we can often create a subclass of an **Adapter** class, rather than implementing the full interface, and just override the one or two methods that we need for a particular task. So, for our example, we will create an inner class that is a subclass of **MouseAdapter**, and just override the **mousePressed** method.

We are now in a position to illustrate anonymous inner classes. The relevant code looks like this:

```
imagePanel = new ImagePanel();
imagePanel.addMouseListener(new MouseAdapter() {
    public void mousePressed(MouseEvent e)
    {
        ... take action on a mouse pressed event ...
    }
});
```

This code fragment looks quite mysterious when you encounter it for the first time, and you will probably have trouble interpreting it, even if you have understood everything we have discussed in this book so far. But don't worry—we shall investigate this slowly.

The idea for this construct is based on the observation that we only use each inner class exactly once to create a single, unnamed instance. For this situation, anonymous inner classes provide a syntactical shortcut: they let us define a class and create a single instance of this class, all in one step. The effect is identical to the inner-class version with the difference that we do not need to define separate named classes for the listeners and that the definition of the listener's methods is closer to the registration of the listener with the GUI component.

The scope coloring in BlueJ's editor gives us some hints that may help in understanding this structure (Figure 13.12). The green shading indicates a class, the yellowish color shows a method definition, and the white background identifies a method body. We can see that the body of the **makeFrame** method contains, very tightly packed, a (strange-looking) class definition, which has a single method definition with a short body.

When using an anonymous inner class, we create an inner class *without naming it* and immediately create a single instance of the class. In the mouse-listener code above, this is done with the code fragment

```
new MouseAdapter() {
    public void mousePressed(MouseEvent e) { ... }
}
```

An anonymous inner class is created by naming a supertype (often an abstract class or an interface—here **MouseAdapter**), followed by a block that contains an implementation for its abstract methods, or any methods we wish to override. This looks unusual, although there are some similarities to the syntax for lambda expressions.

In this example, we create a new subtype of **MouseAdapter** that overrides the **mousePressed** method. This new class does not receive a name. Instead, we precede it with the **new** keyword to create a single instance of this class. This single instance is a mouse-listener object (it is indirectly a subtype of **MouseListener**) and so it can be passed to a GUI component's **addMouseListener** method. Each subtype of **MouseListener** or **MouseAdapter** created in this way represents a unique anonymous class.

Just like lambdas and named inner classes, anonymous inner classes are able to access the fields and methods of their enclosing classes. In addition, because they are defined inside a method, they are able to access the local variables and parameters of that method.

Figure 13.12
Scope coloring with an anonymous inner class

```
/**
 * Create the Swing frame and its content.
 */
private void makeFrame()
{
    frame = new JFrame("ImageViewer");
    JPanel contentPane = (JPanel)frame.getContentPane();
    contentPane.setBorder(new EmptyBorder(12, 12, 12, 12));

    makeMenuBar(frame);

    // Specify the layout manager with nice spacing
    contentPane.setLayout(new BorderLayout(6, 6));

    // Create the image pane in the center
    imagePanel = new ImagePanel();
    imagePanel.setBorder(new EtchedBorder());
    imagePanel.addMouseListener(new MouseAdapter() {
                public void mousePressed(MouseEvent e) { handleMousePressed(e); }
            });
    contentPane.add(imagePanel, BorderLayout.CENTER);

    // Create two labels at top and bottom for the file name and status message
```

It is worth emphasizing some observations about anonymous inner classes that are also shared with lambdas. This structure is nicely cohesive and extendable. If we need an additional menu item, we just add code to create the item and its listener, as well as the method that handles its function.

However, using anonymous inner classes can make code quite hard to read. It is strongly recommended to use them only for very short classes and for well-established code idioms. For instance, it is questionable whether a full implementation of the **MouseListener** interface would be appropriate as an anonymous inner class, in view of the amount of code required; a named inner class would probably be preferable in terms of cohesion. For us, implementing event listeners is the only example in this book where we use this construct.[6]

Exercise 13.51 Review the implementation of the pixel editor in *imageviewer4-0*. Consider whether the current mouse operations used to chose a color or choose a pixel are the most appropriate for a user. Change them if you feel that they are not.

Exercise 13.52 Add a menu to the project that allows a 'brush size' to be specified for the pixel editor. Use the brush size to edit multiple adjacent pixels on each mouse press.

Exercise 13.53 Override further methods of the **MouseAdapter** class to permit free-hand drawing on the image panel. Consider carefully whether to continue with the listener as an anonymous inner class, or whether to make it a named inner class.

---

[6] If you'd like to find out more about inner classes, have a look at these two sections of the online Java tutorial: `http://download.oracle.com/javase/tutorial/java/java0O/nested.html` and `http://download.oracle.com/javase/tutorial/java/java0O/innerclasses.html`.

13.9 Further extensions

Programming GUIs with Swing is a big subject area. Swing has many different types of components and many different containers and layout managers. And each of these has many attributes and methods.

Becoming familiar with the whole Swing library takes time, and is not something done in a few weeks. Usually, as we work on GUIs, we continue to read about details that we did not know before and become experts over time.

The example discussed in this chapter, even though it contains a lot of detail, is only a brief introduction to GUI programming. We have discussed most of the important concepts, but there is still a large amount of functionality to be discovered, most of which is beyond the scope of this book. There are various sources of information available to help you continue. You frequently have to look up the API documentation for the Swing classes; it is not possible to work without it. There are also many GUI/Swing tutorials available, both in print and on the web.

A very good starting point for this, as so often is the case, is the Java Tutorial, available publicly on Oracle's web site. It contains a section titled *Creating a GUI with JFC/Swing* (`http://download.oracle.com/javase/tutorial/uiswing/index.html`).

In this section, there are many interesting subsections. One of the most useful may be the section entitled *Using Swing Components* and in it the subsection *How To . . .* It contains these entries: *How to Use Buttons, Check Boxes, and Radio Buttons*; *How to Use Labels*; *How to Make Dialogs*; *How to Use Panels*; and so on.

Similarly, the top-level section *Laying Out Components within a Container* also has a *How To . . .* section that tells you about all available layout managers.

Exercise 13.54 Find the online Java Tutorial section *Creating a GUI with JFC/ Swing* (the sections are called *trails* on the web site). Bookmark it.

Exercise 13.55 What do **CardLayout** and **GroupLayout** have to offer that is different from the layout managers we have discussed in this chapter?

Exercise 13.56 What is a *slider*? Find a description and summarize. Give a short example in Java code about creating and using a slider.

Exercise 13.57 What is a *tabbed pane*? Find a description and summarize. Give examples of what a tabbed pane might be used for.

Exercise 13.58 What is a *spinner*? Find a description and summarize.

Exercise 13.59 Find the demo application *ProgressBarDemo*. Run it on your computer. Describe what it does.

This is where we shall leave the discussion of the image-viewer example. It can, however, be extended in many directions by interested readers. Using the information from the online tutorial, you can add numerous interface components.

The following exercises give you some ideas, and obviously there are many more possibilities.

Exercise 13.60 Implement an *undo* function in your image viewer. This function reverses the last operation.

Exercise 13.61 Disable all menu items that cannot be used when no image is being displayed.

Exercise 13.62 Implement a *reload* function that discards all changes to the current image and reloads it from disk.

Exercise 13.63 The **JMenu** class is actually a subclass of **JMenuItem**. This means that nested menus can be created by placing one **JMenu** inside another. Add an *Adjust* menu to the menu bar. Nest within it a *Rotate* menu that allows the image to be rotated either 90 or 180 degrees, clockwise or counterclockwise. Implement this functionality. The *Adjust* menu could also contain menu items that invoke the existing *Larger* and *Smaller* functionality, for instance.

Exercise 13.64 The application always resizes its frame in order to ensure that the full image is always visible. Having a large frame is not always desirable. Read the documentation on the **JScrollPane** class. Instead of adding the **ImagePanel** directly to the content pane, place the panel in a **JScrollPane** and add the scroll pane to the content pane. Display a large image and experiment with resizing the window. What difference does having a scroll pane make? Does this allow you to display images that would otherwise be too large for the screen?

Exercise 13.65 Change your application so that it can open multiple images at the same time (but only one image is displayed at any time). Then add a pop-up menu (using class **JComboBox**) to select the image to display.

Exercise 13.66 As an alternative to using a **JComboBox** as in Exercise 13.65, use a tabbed pane (class **JTabbedPane**) to hold multiple open images.

Exercise 13.67 Implement a slide show function that lets you choose a directory and then displays each image in that directory for a specified length of time (say, 5 seconds).

Exercise 13.68 Once you have the slide show, add a slider (class **JSlider**) that lets you select an image in the slide show by moving the slider. While the slide show runs, the slider should move to indicate progress.

13.10 Another example: MusicPlayer

So far in this chapter, we have discussed one example of a GUI application in detail. We now want to introduce a second application to provide another example to learn from. This program introduces a few additional GUI components.

This second example is a music-player application. We shall not discuss it in any great amount of detail. It is intended as a basis for studying the source code largely on your own and as a source of code fragments for you to copy and modify. Here, in this chapter, we shall only point out a few selected aspects of the application that are worth focusing on.

> **Exercise 13.69** Open the *musicplayer* project. Create an instance of **MusicPlayerGUI**, and experiment with the application.

The *musicplayer* project provides a GUI interface to classes based on the *music-organizer* projects from Chapter 4. As there, the program finds and plays MP3 files stored in the *audio* folder inside the chapter folder (one level up from the project folder). If you have sound files of the right format of your own, you should be able to play them by dropping them into the *audio* folder.

The music player is implemented across three classes: **MusicPlayerGUI**, **MusicPlayer**, and **MusicFilePlayer**. Only the first is intended to be studied here. **MusicFilePlayer** can be used essentially as a library class; instances are created along with the name of the MP3 file to be played. Familiarize yourself with its interface, but you do not need to understand or modify its implementation. (You are welcome, of course, to study this class as well if you like, but it uses some concepts that we shall not discuss in this book.)

Following are some noteworthy observations about the *musicplayer* project.

Model/view separation

This application uses a better model/view separation than the previous example. This means that the application functionality (the model) is separated cleanly from the application's user interface (the GUI). Each of those two, the model and the view, may consist of multiple classes, but every class should be clearly in one or the other group to achieve a clear separation. In our example, the view consists of a single GUI class.

Separating the application's functionality from the interface is an example of good cohesion; it makes the program easier to understand, easier to maintain, and easier to adapt to different requirements (especially different user interfaces). It would, for example, be fairly easy to write a text-based interface for the music player, effectively replacing the **MusicPlayerGUI** class and leaving the **MusicPlayer** class unchanged.

Inheriting from JFrame

In this example, we are demonstrating the alternative popular version of creating frames that we mentioned at the start of the chapter. Our GUI class does not instantiate a **JFrame** object; instead, it extends the **JFrame** class. As a result, all the **JFrame** methods we need to call (such as **getContentPane**, **setJMenuBar**, **pack**, **setVisible**, and so on) can now be called as internal (inherited) methods.

There is no strong reason for preferring one style (using a **JFrame** instance) over the other (inheriting from **JFrame**). It is largely a matter of personal preference, but you should be aware that both styles are widely used.

Displaying static images

We often want want to display an image in a GUI. The easiest way to do this is to include in the interface a **JLabel** that has a graphic as its label (a **JLabel** can display either text or a graphic or both). The sound player includes an example of doing this. The relevant source code is

```
JLabel image = new JLabel(new ImageIcon("title.jpg"));
```

This statement will load an image file named "title.jpg" from the project directory, create an icon with that image, and then create a **JLabel** that displays the icon. (The term "icon" seems to suggest that we are dealing only with small images here, but the image can in fact be of any size.) This method works for JPEG, GIF, and PNG images.

Combo boxes

The sound player presents an example of using a **JComboBox**. A combo box is a set of values, one of which is selected at any time. The selected value is displayed, and the selection can be accessed through a pop-up menu. In the sound player, the combo box is used to select a particular ordering for the tracks—by artist, title, etc.

A **JComboBox** may also be editable, in which case the values are not all predefined but can be typed by a user. Ours is not.

Lists

The program also includes an example of a list (class **JList**) for the list of tracks. A list can hold an arbitrary number of values, and one or more can be selected. The list values in this example are strings, but other types are possible. A list does not automatically have a scrollbar.

Scrollbars

Another component demonstrated in this example is the use of scrollbars.

Scrollbars can be created by using a special container, an instance of class **JScrollPane**. GUI objects of any type can be placed into a scroll pane, and the scroll pane will, provide the necessary scrollbars if the held object is too big to be displayed in the available space.

In our example, we have placed our track list into a scroll pane. The scroll pane itself is then placed into its parent container. The scrollbars only become visible when necessary. You can try this by either adding more tracks until they do not fit into the available space, or by resizing the window to make it too small to display the current list.

Other elements demonstrated in this example are the use of a slider (which does not do much), and the use of color (in the list) for changing the look of an application. Each of the GUI's elements has many methods for modifying the component's look or behavior—you should look through the documentation for any component that interests you and experiment with modifying some properties of that component.

Exercise 13.70 Change the music player so that it displays a different image in its center. Find an image on the web to use, or make your own.

Exercise 13.71 Change the colors of the other components (foreground and background colors) to suit the new main image.

Exercise 13.72 Add a new component to display details of the current track when one is playing.

Exercise 13.73 Add a *reload* capability to the music player that rereads the files from the *audio* folder. Then you can drop a new file into the folder and load it without having to quit the player.

Exercise 13.74 Add an *Open* item to the file menu. When activated, it presents a file-selection dialog that lets the user choose a sound file to open. If the user chooses a directory, the player should open all sound files in that directory (as it does now with the *audio* directory).

Exercise 13.75 Modify the slider so that the start and end (and possibly other tick marks) are labeled with numbers. The start should be zero, and the end should be the length of the music file. The `MusicPlayer` class has a `getLength` method. Note that the slider is not currently functional.

Exercise 13.76 Modify the music player so that a double click on a list element in the track list starts playing that track.

Exercise 13.77 Improve the button look. All buttons that have no function at any point in time should be grayed out at that time, and should be enabled only when they can reasonably be used.

Exercise 13.78 The display of tracks is currently simply a `JList` of `String` objects. Investigate whether there are any Swing components available that would provide greater sophistication than this. For instance, can you find a way to provide a header line and align the artist, title, and other parts of the track information? Implement this in your version.

Exercise 13.79 *Challenge exercise* Have the position slider move as a track is being played.

13.11 Summary

In this chapter, we have supplied an introduction to GUI programming using the Swing and AWT libraries. We have discussed the three main conceptual areas: creating GUI components, layout, and event handling.

We have seen that building a GUI usually starts with creating a top-level frame, such as a **JFrame**. The frame is then filled with various components that provide information and functionality to the user. Among the components we have encountered are menus, menu items, buttons, labels, borders, and others.

Components are arranged on screen with the help of containers and layout managers. Containers hold collections of components, and each container has a layout manager that takes care of arranging the components within the container's screen area. Nesting containers, using combinations of different layout managers, is a common way to achieve the desired combination of component size and juxtaposition.

Interactive components (those that can react to user input) generate events when they are activated by a user. Other objects can become event listeners and be notified of such events by implementing standard interfaces. When the listener object is notified, it can take appropriate action to deal with the user event. Event listeners are often implemented using lambda notation.

We have introduced the concept of anonymous inner classes as an alternative modular, extendable technique for writing event listeners. These are particularly useful when a listener interface is not a functional interface (it has more than one abstract method) and cannot be implemented via a lambda expression.

And finally, we have given a pointer to an online reference and tutorial site that may be used to learn about details not covered in the chapter.

Terms introduced in this chapter:

> **GUI, AWT, Swing, component, layout, event, event handling, event listener, frame, menu bar, menu, menu item, content pane, modal dialog, anonymous inner class**

Concept summary

- **components** A GUI is built by arranging components on screen. Components are represented by objects.

- **layout** Arranging the layout of components is achieved by using layout managers.

- **event handling** The term *event handling* refers to the task of reacting to user events, such as mouse-button clicks or keyboard input.

- **image format** Images can be stored in different formats. The differences primarily affect file size and the quality of the image.

- ■ **menu bar, content pane** Components are placed in a frame by adding them to the frame's menu bar, or content pane.

- ■ **event listener** An object can listen to component events by implementing an event-listener interface.

- ■ **anonymous inner classes** Anonymous inner classes are a useful construct for implementing event listeners that are not functional interfaces.

Exercise 13.80 Add a GUI to the *world-of-zuul* project from Chapter 8. Every room should have an associated image that is displayed when the player enters the room. There should be a non-editable text area to display text output. To enter commands, you can choose between different possibilities: you can leave the input text-based and use a text field (class **JTextField**) to type commands, or you can use buttons for command entry.

Exercise 13.81 Add sounds to the *word-of-zuul* game. You can associate individual sounds with rooms, items, or characters.

Exercise 13.82 Design and build a GUI for a text editor. Users should be able to enter text, edit, scroll, etc. Consider functions for formatting (font faces, style, and size) and a character/word-count function. You do not need to implement the *load* and *save* functions just yet—you might want to wait with that until you have read the next chapter.

Main concepts discussed in this chapter:

- defensive programming
- exception throwing and handling
- error reporting
- basic file processing

Java constructs discussed in this chapter:

TreeMap, TreeSet, SortedMap, assert, exception, throw, throws, try, catch, File, FileReader, FileWriter, Path, Scanner, Stream

In Chapter 9, we saw that logical errors in programs are harder to spot than syntactical errors, because a compiler cannot give any help with logical errors. Logical errors arise for several reasons, which may overlap in some situations:

- The solution to a problem has been implemented incorrectly. For instance, a problem involving generating some statistics on data values might have been programmed to find the mean value rather than the median value (the "middle" value).

- An object might be asked to do something it is unable to. For instance, a collection object's **get** method might be called with an index value outside the valid range.

- An object might be used in ways that have not been anticipated by the class designer, leading to the object being left in an inconsistent or inappropriate state. This often happens when a class is reused in a setting that is different from its original one, perhaps through inheritance.

Although the sort of testing strategies discussed in Chapter 9 can help us identify and eliminate many logical errors before our programs are put to use, experience suggests that program failures will continue to occur. Furthermore, even the most thoroughly tested program may fail as a result of circumstances beyond the programmer's control. Consider the case of a web-browser asked to display a web page that does not exist, or a program that tries to write data to a disk that has no more space left. These problems are not the result of logical programming errors, but they could easily cause a program to fail if the possibility of their arising has not been taken into account.

In this chapter, we look at how to anticipate potential errors and how to respond to error situations as they arise during the execution of a program. In addition, we provide some suggestions on how to report errors when they occur. We also provide a brief introduction to how to perform textual input/output, as file processing is one of the situations where errors can easily arise.

14.1 The *address-book* project

We shall use the *address-book* family of projects to illustrate some of the principles of error reporting and error handling that arise in many applications. The projects represent an application that stores personal-contact details—name, address, and phone number— for an arbitrary number of people. Such a contacts list might be used on a mobile phone or in an e-mail program, for instance. The contact details are indexed in the address book by both name and phone number. The main classes we shall be discussing are **AddressBook** (Code 14.1) and **ContactDetails**. In addition, the **AddressBookDemo** class is provided as a convenient means of setting up an initial address book with some sample data.

Code 14.1

The **Address-Book** class

```java
import java.util.Iterator;
import java.util.LinkedList;
import java.util.List;
import java.util.Set;
import java.util.SortedMap;
import java.util.TreeMap;
import java.util.TreeSet;

/**
 * A class to maintain an arbitrary number of contact details.
 * Details are indexed by both name and phone number.
 *
 * @author David J. Barnes and Michael Kölling.
 * @version 2016.02.29
 */
public class AddressBook
{
    // Storage for an arbitrary number of details.
    private TreeMap<String, ContactDetails> book;
    private int numberOfEntries;

    /**
     * Perform any initialization for the address book.
     */
    public AddressBook()
    {
        book = new TreeMap<>();
        numberOfEntries = 0;
    }

    /**
     * Look up a name or phone number and return the
     * corresponding contact details.
     * @param key The name or number to be looked up.
     * @return The details corresponding to the key.
     */
    public ContactDetails getDetails(String key)
    {
        return book.get(key);
    }
```

**Code 14.1
continued**

The Address-
Book class

```java
/**
 * Return whether or not the current key is in use.
 * @param key The name or number to be looked up.
 * @return true if the key is in use, false otherwise.
 */
public boolean keyInUse(String key)
{
    return book.containsKey(key);
}

/**
 * Add a new set of details to the address book.
 * @param details The details to associate with the person.
 */
public void addDetails(ContactDetails details)
{
    book.put(details.getName(), details);
    book.put(details.getPhone(), details);
    numberOfEntries++;
}

/**
 * Change the details previously stored under the given key.
 * @param oldKey One of the keys used to store the details.
 * @param details The replacement details.
 */
public void changeDetails(String oldKey, ContactDetails details)
{
    removeDetails(oldKey);
    addDetails(details);
}

/**
 * Search for all details stored under a key that starts with
 * the given prefix.
 * @param keyPrefix The key prefix to search on.
 * @return An array of those details that have been found.
 */
public ContactDetails[] search(String keyPrefix)
{
    // Build a list of the matches.
    List<ContactDetails> matches = new LinkedList<>();
    // Find keys that are equal-to or greater-than the prefix.
    SortedMap<String, ContactDetails> tail = book.tailMap(keyPrefix);
    Iterator<String> it = tail.keySet().iterator();
    // Stop when we find a mismatch.
    boolean endOfSearch = false;
    while(!endOfSearch && it.hasNext()) {
        String key = it.next();
        if(key.startsWith(keyPrefix)) {
            matches.add(book.get(key));
        }
        else {
            // As the list is sorted, there won't be any more.
            endOfSearch = true;
        }
    }
    ContactDetails[] results = new ContactDetails[matches.size()];
    matches.toArray(results);
    return results;
}
```

Code 14.1 continued

The Address-Book class

```java
    /**
     * Return the number of entries currently in the
     * address book.
     * @return The number of entries.
     */
    public int getNumberOfEntries()
    {
        return numberOfEntries;
    }

    /**
     * Remove an entry with the given key from the address book.
     * @param key One of the keys of the entry to be removed.
     */
    public void removeDetails(String key)
    {
        ContactDetails details = book.get(key);
        book.remove(details.getName());
        book.remove(details.getPhone());
        numberOfEntries--;
    }

    /**
     * Return all the contact details, sorted according
     * to the sort order of the ContactDetails class.
     * @return A sorted list of the details.
     */
    public String listDetails()
    {
        // Because each entry is stored under two keys, it is
        // necessary to build a set of the ContactDetails. This
        // eliminates duplicates.
        StringBuilder allEntries = new StringBuilder();
        Set<ContactDetails> sortedDetails = new TreeSet<>(book.values());
        for(ContactDetails details : sortedDetails) {
            allEntries.append(details).append("\n\n");
        }
        return allEntries.toString();
    }
}
```

New details can be stored in the address book via its **addDetails** method. This assumes that the details represent a new contact, and not a change of details for an existing one. To cover the latter case, the **changeDetails** method removes an old entry and replaces it with the revised details. The address book provides two ways to retrieve entries: the **getDetails** method takes a name or phone number as the key and returns the matching details; the **search** method returns an array of all those details that start with a given search string (for instance, the search string **"084"** would return all entries with phone numbers having that prefix).

There are two introductory versions of the *address-book* project for you to explore. Both provide access to the same version of **AddressBook**, as shown in Code 14.1. The *address-book-v1t* project provides a text-based user interface, similar in style to the interface of the *zuul* game discussed in Chapter 8. Commands are currently available to list the address book's contents, search it, and add a new entry. Probably more interesting as an interface, however, is the *address-book-v1g* version, which incorporates a simple GUI. Experiment with both versions to gain some experience with what the application can do.

Exercise 14.1 Open the *address-book-v1g* project and create an **Address-BookDemo** object. Call its **showInterface** method to display the GUI and interact with the sample address book.

Exercise 14.2 Repeat your experimentation with the text interface of the *address-book-v1t* project.

Exercise 14.3 Examine the implementation of the **AddressBook** class and assess whether you think it has been well-written or not. Do you have any specific criticisms of it?

Exercise 14.4 The **AddressBook** class uses quite a lot of classes from the **java.util** package; if you are not familiar with any of these, check the API documentation to fill in the gaps. Do you think the use of so many different utility classes is justified? Could a **HashMap** have been used in place of the **TreeMap**?

If you are not sure, try changing **TreeMap** to **HashMap** and see if **HashMap** offers all of the required functionality.

Exercise 14.5 Modify the **CommandWords** and **AddressBookTextInterface** classes of the *address-book-v1t* project to provide interactive access to the **getDetails** and **removeDetails** methods of **AddressBook**.

Exercise 14.6 The **AddressBook** class defines a field to record the number of entries. Do you think it would be more appropriate to calculate this value directly, from the number of unique entries in the **TreeMap**? For instance, can you think of any circumstances in which the following calculation would not produce the same value?

```
return book.size() / 2;
```

Exercise 14.7 How easy do you think it would be to add a **String** field for an email address to the **ContactDetails** class, and then to use this as a third key in the **AddressBook**? Don't actually try it, at this stage.

Defensive programming

14.2.1 Client–server interaction

An **AddressBook** is a typical server object, initiating no actions on its own behalf; all of its activities are driven by client requests. Programmers can adopt at least two possible views when designing and implementing a server class:

■ They can assume that client objects will know what they are doing and will request services only in a sensible and well-defined way.

■ They can assume that server objects will operate in an essentially problematic environment in which all possible steps must be taken to prevent client objects from using them incorrectly.

These views clearly represent opposite extremes. In practice, the most likely scenario usually lies somewhere in between. Most client interactions will be reasonable, with the occasional attempt to use the server incorrectly—either as the result of a logical programming error or of misconception on the part of the client programmer. A third possibility, of course, is an intentionally hostile client who is trying to break or find a weakness in the server.

These different views provide a useful base from which to discuss questions such as:

■ How much checking should a server's methods perform on client requests?

■ How should a server report errors to its clients?

■ How can a client anticipate failure of a request to a server?

■ How should a client deal with failure of a request?

If we examine the **AddressBook** class with these issues in mind, we shall see that the class has been written to trust completely that its clients will use it appropriately. Exercise 14.8 illustrates one of the ways in which this is the case, and how things can go wrong.

Exercise 14.8 Using the *address-book-v1g* project, create a new **Address-Book** object on the object bench. This will be completely empty of contact details. Now make a call to its **removeDetails** method with any string value for the key. What happens? Can you understand why this happens?

Exercise 14.9 For a programmer, the easiest response to an error situation arising is to allow the program to terminate (i.e., to "crash"). Can you think of any situations in which simply allowing a program to terminate could be very dangerous?

Exercise 14.10 Many commercially sold programs contain errors that are not handled properly in the software and cause them to crash. Is that unavoidable? Is it acceptable? Discuss this issue.

The problem with the `removeDetails` method is that it assumes that the key passed to it is a valid key for the address book. It uses the supposed key to retrieve the associated contact details:

```
ContactDetails details = book.get(key);
```

However, if the map does not have that particular key, then the `details` variable ends up containing `null`. That, of itself, is not an error; but the error arises from the following statement, where we assume that `details` refers to a valid object:

```
book.remove(details.getName());
```

It is an error to call a method on a variable containing `null`, and the result will be a run-time error. BlueJ reports this as a `NullPointerException` and highlights the statement from which it resulted. Later in this chapter, we shall be discussing exceptions in detail. For now, we can simply say that, if an error such as this were to occur in a running application, then the application would crash—i.e., terminate in an uncontrolled way—before it had completed its task.

There is clearly a problem here, but whose fault is it? Is it the fault of the client object for calling the method with a bad parameter value, or is it the fault of the server object for failing to handle this situation properly? The writer of the client class might argue that there is nothing in the method's documentation to say that the key must be valid. Conversely, the writer of the server class might argue that it is obviously wrong to try to remove details with an invalid key. Our concern in this chapter is not to resolve such disputes, but to try to prevent them from arising in the first place. We shall start by looking at error handling from the point of view of the server class.

Exercise 14.11 Save a copy, to work on, of one of the *address-book-v1* projects under another name. Make changes to the `removeDetails` method to avoid a `NullPointerException` arising if the key value does not have a corresponding entry in the address book. Use an if-statement. If the key is not valid, then the method should do nothing.

Exercise 14.12 Is it necessary to report the detection of an invalid key in a call to `removeDetails`? If so, how would you report it?

Exercise 14.13 Are there any other methods in the **AddressBook** class that are vulnerable to similar errors? If so, try to correct them in your copy of the project. Is it acceptable in all cases for the method simply to do nothing if its parameter values are inappropriate? Do the errors need reporting in some way? If so, how would you do it, and would it be the same way for each error?

14.2.2 Parameter checking

A server object is most vulnerable when its constructor and methods receive external values through their parameters. The values passed to a constructor are used to set up an object's initial state, while the values passed to a method will be used to influence the overall effect of the method call and may change the state of the object and a result the method returns. Therefore, it is vital that a server object knows whether it can trust parameter values to be valid, or whether it needs to check their validity for itself. The current situation in both the **ContactDetails** and **AddressBook** classes is that there is no checking at all on parameter values. As we have seen with the **removeDetails** method, this can lead to a fatal runtime error.

Preventing a **NullPointerException** in **removeDetails** is relatively easy, and Code 14.2 illustrates how this can be done. Note that, as well as improving the source code in the method, we have updated the method's comment, to document the fact that unknown keys are ignored.

Code 14.2

Guarding against an invalid key in **removeDetails**

```
/**
 * Remove the entry with the given key from the address book.
 * The key should be one that is currently in use.
 * @param key One of the keys of the entry to be removed.
 */
public void removeDetails(String key)
{
    if(keyInUse(key)) {
        ContactDetails details = book.get(key);
        book.remove(details.getName());
        book.remove(details.getPhone());
        numberOfEntries--;
    }
}
```

If we examine all the methods of **AddressBook**, we find that there are other places where we could make similar improvements:

■ The **addDetails** method should check that its actual parameter is not **null**.

■ The **changeDetails** method should check both that the old key is one that is in use and that the new details are not **null**.

■ The **search** method should check that the key is not **null**.

These changes have all been implemented in the version of the application to be found in the *address-book-v2g* and *address-book-v2t* projects.

> **Exercise 14.14** Why do you think we have felt it unnecessary to make similar changes to the **getDetails** and **keyInUse** methods?
>
> **Exercise 14.15** In dealing with parameter errors, we have not printed any error messages. Do you think an **AddressBook** *should* print an error message whenever it receives a bad parameter value to one of its methods? Are there any situations where a printed error message would be inappropriate? For instance, do error messages printed to the terminal seem appropriate with the GUI version of the project?

Exercise 14.16 Are there any further checks you feel we should make on the parameters of other methods, to prevent an **AddressBook** object from functioning incorrectly?

14.3 Server error reporting

Having protected a server object from performing an illegal operation through bad parameter values, we could take the view that this is all that the server writer needs to do. However, ideally we should like to avoid such error situations from arising in the first place. Furthermore, it is often the case that incorrect parameter values are the result of some form of programming error in the client that supplied them. Therefore, rather than simply programming around the problem in the server and leaving it at that, it is good practice for the server to make some effort to indicate that a problem has arisen, either to the client itself or to a human user or programmer. In that way, there is a chance that an incorrectly written client will be fixed. But notice that those three "audiences" for the notification will often be completely different.

What is the best way for a server to report problems when they occur? There is no single answer to this question, and the most appropriate answer will often depend upon the context in which a particular server object is being used. In the following sections, we shall explore a range of options for error reporting by a server.

Exercise 14.17 How many different ways can you think of to indicate that a method has received incorrect parameter values or is otherwise unable to complete its task? Consider as many different sorts of applications as you can—for instance: those with a GUI; those with a textual interface and a human user; those with no sort of interactive user, such as software in a vehicle's engine-management system; or software in embedded systems such as a cash machine.

14.3.1 Notifying the user

The most obvious way in which an object might respond when it detects something wrong is to try to notify the application's user in some way. The main options are either to print an error message using **System.out** or **System.err** or to display an error message alert window.

The two main problems with both approaches are:

- They assume that the application is being used by a human user who will see the error message. There are many applications that run completely independently of a human user. An error message, or an error window, will go completely unnoticed. Indeed, the computer running the application might not have any visual-display device connected to it at all.

- Even where there is a human user to see the error message, it will be rare for that user to be in a position to do something about the problem. Imagine a user at an automatic teller machine being confronted with a **NullPointerException**! Only in those cases where the user's direct action has led to the problem—such as supplying invalid input to the application—is the user likely to be able take some appropriate corrective or avoiding action the next time.

Programs that print inappropriate error messages are more likely to annoy their users rather than achieve a useful outcome. Therefore, except in a very limited set of circumstances, notifying the user is not a general solution to the problem of error reporting.

> **Exercise 14.18** The Java API includes a sophisticated collection of error-logging classes in the **java.util.logging** package. The static **getLogger** method of the **Logger** class returns a **Logger** object. Investigate the features of the class for text-based diagnostic error logging. What is the significance of having different logging levels? How does the **info** method differ from the **warning** method? Can logging be turned off and then on again?

14.3.2 Notifying the client object

A radically different approach from those we have discussed so far is for the server object to feedback an indication to the client object when something has gone wrong. There are two main ways to do this:

- A server can use a non-**void** return type of a method to return a value that indicates either success or failure of the method call.

- A server can *throw an exception* if something goes wrong. This introduces a new feature of Java that is also found in some other programming languages. We shall describe this feature in detail in Section 14.4.

Both techniques have the benefit of encouraging the programmer of the *client* to take into account that a method call could fail. However, only the decision to throw an exception will actively prevent the client's programmer from ignoring the consequences of method failure.

The first approach is easy to introduce to a method that would otherwise have a **void** return type, such as **removeDetails**. If the **void** type is replaced by a **boolean** type, then the method can return **true** to indicate that the removal was successful, and **false** to indicate that it failed for some reason (Code 14.3).

Code 14.3

A **boolean** return type to indicate success or failure

```
/**
 * Remove the entry with the given key from the address book.
 * The key should be one that is currently in use.
 * @param key One of the keys of the entry to be removed.
 * @return true if the entry was successfully removed,
 *         false otherwise.
 */
```

Code 14.3 continued

A **boolean** return type to indicate success or failure

```
public boolean removeDetails(String key)
{
    if(keyInUse(key)) {
        ContactDetails details = book.get(key);
        book.remove(details.getName());
        book.remove(details.getPhone());
        numberOfEntries--;
        return true;
    }
    else {
        return false;
    }
}
```

This allows a client to use an if-statement to guard statements that depend on the successful removal of an entry:

```
if(contacts.removeDetails(". . .")) {
    // Entry successfully removed. Continue as normal.
    . . .
}
else {
    // The removal failed. Attempt a recovery, if possible.
    . . .
}
```

Where a server method already has a non-**void** return type—effectively preventing a **boolean** diagnostic value from being returned—there may still be a way to indicate that an error has occurred through the return type. This will be the case if a value from the return type's range is available to act as an error diagnostic value. For instance, the **getDetails** method returns a **ContactDetails** object corresponding to a given key, and the example below assumes that a particular key will locate a valid set of contact details:

```
// Send David a text message.
ContactDetails details = contacts.getDetails("David");
String phone = details.getPhone();
. . .
```

One way for the **getDetails** method to indicate that the key is invalid or not in use is to have it return a **null** value instead of a **ContactDetails** object (Code 14.4).

Code 14.4

Returning an out-of-bounds error diagnostic value

```
/**
 * Look up a name or phone number and return the
 * corresponding contact details.
 * @param key The name or number to be looked up.
 * @return The details corresponding to the key, or
 *         null if the key is not in use.
 *
 */
```

**Code 14.4
continued**

Returning an
out-of-bounds
error diagnostic
value

```
public ContactDetails getDetails(String key)
{
    if(keyInUse(key)) {
        return book.get(key);
    }
    else {
        return null;
    }
}
```

This would allow a client to examine the result of the call, then either continue with the normal flow of control or attempt to recover from the error:

```
ContactDetails details = contacts.getDetails("David");
if(details != null) {
    // Send a text message to David.
    String phone = details.getPhone();
    . . .
}
else {
    // Failed to find the entry. Attempt a recovery, if possible.
    . . .
}
```

It is common for methods that return object references to use the **null** value as an indication of failure or error. With methods that return primitive-type values, there will sometimes be an *out-of-bounds value* that can fulfill a similar role: for instance, the **indexOf** method of the **String** class returns a negative value to indicate that it has failed to find the character sought.

Exercise 14.19 Do you think the different interface styles of the *v2t* and *v2g* *address-book* projects mean that there should be a difference in the way errors are reported to users?

Exercise 14.20 Using a copy of the *address-book-v2t* project, make changes to the **AddressBook** class to provide failure information to a client when a method has received incorrect parameter values, or is otherwise unable to complete its task.

Exercise 14.21 Do you think that a call to the **search** method that finds no matches requires an error notification? Justify your answer.

Exercise 14.22 What combinations of parameter values would it be inappropriate to pass to the constructor of the **ContactDetails** class?

Exercise 14.23 Does a constructor have any means of indicating to a client that it cannot correctly set up the new object's state? What should a constructor do if it receives inappropriate parameter values?

Clearly, an out-of-bounds value cannot be used where all values from the return type already have valid meanings to the client. In such cases, it will usually be necessary to resort to the alternative technique of *throwing an exception* (see Section 14.4), which does, in fact, offer some significant advantages. To help you appreciate why this might be, it is worth considering two issues associated with the use of return values as failure or error indicators:

- Unfortunately, there is no way to require the client to check the return value for its diagnostic properties. As a consequence, a client could easily carry on as if nothing has happened, and could then end up terminating with a `NullPointerException`. Worse than that, it could even use the diagnostic return value as if it were a normal return value, creating a difficult-to-diagnose logical error!

- In some cases, we may be using the diagnostic value for two quite different purposes. This is the case in the revised `removeDetails` (Code 14.3) and `getDetails` (Code 14.4). One purpose is to tell the client whether its request was successful or not. The other is to indicate that there was something wrong with its request, such as passing bad parameter values.

In many cases, an *unsuccessful* request will not represent a logical programming error, whereas an *incorrect* request almost certainly does. We should expect quite different follow-up actions from a client in these different situations. Unfortunately, there is no general satisfactory way to resolve the conflict simply by using return values.

14.4   Exception-throwing principles

Throwing an exception is the most effective way a server object has of indicating that it is unable to fulfill a call on one of its methods. One of the major advantages this has over using a special return value is that it is (almost) impossible for a client to ignore the fact that an exception has been thrown and carry on regardless. Failure by the client to handle an exception will result in the application terminating immediately.[1] In addition, the exception mechanism is independent of the return value of a method, so it can be used for all methods, irrespective of the return type.

An important point to bear in mind throughout the following discussion is that, where exceptions are involved, the place where an error is discovered will be distinct from where recovery (if any) is attempted. Discovery will be in the server's method, and recovery will be in the client. If recovery were possible at the point of discovery, then there would be no point in throwing an exception.

14.4.1 Throwing an exception

Code 14.5 shows how an exception is thrown using a *throw statement*. Here, the `getDetails` method is throwing an exception to indicate that passing a `null` value for the key does not make sense because it is not a valid key.

---

[1] This is exactly what you will have experienced whenever your programs inadvertently died because of a `NullPointerException` or `IndexOutOfBoundsException`.

```
/**
 * Look up a name or phone number and return the corresponding
 * contact details.
 * @param key The name or number to be looked up.
 * @return The details corresponding to the key,
 *          or null if there are none matching.
 * @throws IllegalArgumentException if the key is invalid.
 */
public ContactDetails getDetails(String key)
{
    if(key == null){
        throw new IllegalArgumentException("null key in getDetails");
    }
    return book.get(key);
}
```

There are two stages to throwing an exception. First, an exception object is created using the **new** keyword (in this case, an **IllegalArgumentException** object); then the exception object is thrown using the **throw** keyword. These two stages are almost invariably combined in a single statement:

```
throw new ExceptionType("optional-diagnostic-string");
```

When an exception object is created, a diagnostic string may be passed to its constructor. This string is later available to the receiver of the exception via the exception object's **getMessage** and **toString** methods. The string is also shown to the user if the exception is not handled and leads to the termination of the program. The exception type we have used here, **Illegal-ArgumentException**, is defined in the **java.lang** package and is regularly used to indicate that an inappropriate actual parameter value has been passed to a method or constructor.

Code 14.5 also illustrates that the **javadoc** documentation for a method can be expanded to include details of any exceptions it throws, using the **@throws** tag.

14.4.2 Checked and unchecked exceptions

An exception object is always an instance of a class from a special inheritance hierarchy. We can create new exception types by creating subclasses in this hierarchy (Figure 14.1). Strictly speaking, exception classes are always subclasses of the **Throwable** class that is defined in the **java.lang** package. We shall follow the convention of defining and using exception classes that are subclasses of the **Exception** class, also defined in **java.lang**.[2] The **java.lang** package defines a number of commonly seen exception classes that you might already have run across inadvertently in developing programs, such as **Null-PointerException**, **IndexOutOfBoundsException**, and **ClassCastException**.

Java divides exception classes into two categories: *checked exceptions* and *unchecked exceptions*. All subclasses of the Java standard class **RuntimeException** are unchecked exceptions; all other subclasses of **Exception** are checked exceptions.

---

[2] **Exception** is one of two direct subclasses of **Throwable**; the other is **Error**. Subclasses of **Error** are usually reserved for runtime-system errors rather than errors over which the programmer has control.

Figure 14.1
The exception class
hierarchy

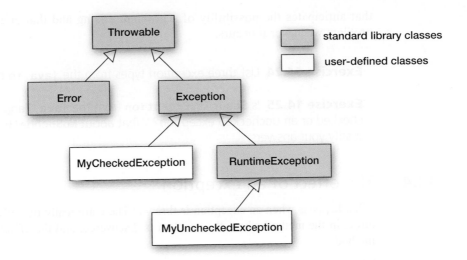

Slightly simplified, the difference is this: checked exceptions are intended for cases where the client should expect that an operation could fail (for example, if it tries to write to a disk, it should anticipate that the disk could be full). In such cases, the client will be forced to check whether the operation was successful. Unchecked exceptions are intended for cases that should never fail in normal operation—they usually indicate a program error. For instance, a programmer would never knowingly try to get an item from a position in a list that does not exist, so when they do, it elicits an unchecked exception.

Unfortunately, knowing which category of exception to throw in any particular circumstance is not an exact science, but we can offer the following general advice:

- One rule of thumb is to use unchecked exceptions for situations that should lead to program failure—typically because it is suspected that there is a logical error in the program that will prevent it from continuing any further. It follows that checked exceptions should be used where there may be a possibility of the client effecting a recovery. One problem with this policy is that it assumes that the server is aware enough of the context in which it is being used to be able to determine whether client recovery is likely or unlikely to be possible.

- Another rule of thumb is to use unchecked exceptions for situations that could reasonably be avoided. For instance, calling a method on a variable containing **null** is the result of a logical programming error that is completely avoidable, and the fact that **NullPointerException** is unchecked fits this model. It follows that checked exceptions should be used for failure situations that are beyond the control of the programmer, such as a disk becoming full when trying to write to a file or a network operation failing because a wireless network connection has dropped out.

The formal Java rules governing the use of exceptions are significantly different for unchecked and checked exceptions, and we shall outline the differences in detail in Sections 14.4.4 and 14.5.1, respectively. In simplified terms, the rules ensure that a client object calling a method that could throw a checked exception will contain code that anticipates the possibility of a problem arising and that attempts to handle the problem whenever it occurs.[3]

Exercise 14.24 List three exception types from the **java.io** package.

Exercise 14.25 Is **SecurityException** from the **java.lang** package a checked or an unchecked exception? What about **NoSuchMethodException**? Justify your answers.

14.4.3 The effect of an exception

What happens when an exception is thrown? There are really two effects to consider: the effect in the method where the problem is discovered, and the effect in the caller of the method.

When an exception is thrown, the execution of the throwing method finishes immediately; it does not continue to the end of the method body. A consequence of this is that a method with a non-**void** return type is not required to execute a return statement on a route that throws an exception. This is reasonable, because throwing an exception is an indication of the throwing method's inability to continue normal execution, which includes not being able to return a valid result. We can illustrate this principle with the following alternative version of the method body shown in Code 14.5:

```
if(key == null) {
    throw new IllegalArgumentException("null key in getDetails");
}
else {
    return book.get(key);
}
```

The absence of a return statement in the route that throws an exception is acceptable. Indeed, the compiler will indicate an error if any statements are written following a throw statement, because they could never be executed.

The effect of an exception on the point in the program that called the problem method is a little more complex. In particular, the full effect depends upon whether or not any code has been written to *catch* the exception. Consider the following contrived call to **getDetails**:

```
AddressDetails details = contacts.getDetails(null);
// The following statement will not be reached.
String phone = details.getPhone();
```

We *can* say that, in all cases, the execution of these statements will be left incomplete; the exception thrown by **getDetails** will interrupt the execution of the first statement, and no assignment will be made to the **details** variable. As a result, the second statement will not be executed either.

---

[3] In fact, it is still all too easy for the writer of the client to adhere to the rules in principle, but to fail to attempt a proper recovery from the problem, which rather subverts their purpose!

This neatly illustrates the power of exceptions to prevent a client from carrying on, regardless of the fact that a problem has arisen. What actually happens next depends upon whether or not the exception is caught. If it isn't caught, then the program will simply terminate with an indication that an uncaught `IllegalArgumentException` has been thrown. We shall discuss how to catch an exception in Section 14.5.2.

14.4.4 Using unchecked exceptions

Concept

An **unchecked exception** is a type of exception whose use will not require checks from the compiler.

Unchecked exceptions are the easiest to use from a programmer's point of view, because the compiler enforces few rules on their use. This is the meaning of *unchecked*: the compiler does not apply special checks, either on the method in which an unchecked exception is thrown or on the place from which the method is called. An exception class is unchecked if it is a subclass of the `RuntimeException` class, defined in the `java.lang` package. All of the examples we have used so far to illustrate exception throwing have involved unchecked exceptions. So there is little further to add here about how to throw an unchecked exception—simply use a throw statement.

If we also follow the convention that unchecked exceptions should be used in those situations where we expect the result to be program termination—i.e., the exception is not going to be caught—then there is also nothing further to be discussed about what the method's caller should do, because it will do nothing and let the program fail. However, if there is a need to catch an unchecked exception, then an exception handler *can* be written for it, exactly as for a checked exception. How to do this is described in Section 14.5.2.

We have already seen use of the unchecked `IllegalArgumentException`; this is thrown by a constructor or method to indicate that its parameter values are inappropriate. For instance, the `getDetails` method might also choose to throw this if the key string passed to it is a blank string (Code 14.6).

Code 14.6

Checking for an illegal parameter value

```java
/**
 * Look up a name or phone number and return the corresponding
 * contact details.
 * @param key The name or number to be looked up.
 * @throws IllegalArgumentException if the key is invalid.
 * @return The details corresponding to the key,
 *         or null if there are none matching.
 */
public ContactDetails getDetails(String key)
{
    if(key == null) {
        throw new IllegalArgumentException("null key in getDetails");
    }
    if(key.trim().length() == 0) {
        throw new IllegalArgumentException(
                        "Empty key passed to getDetails");
    }
    return book.get(key);
}
```

It is well worth having a method conduct a series of validity checks on its parameters before proceeding with the main purpose of the method. This makes it less likely that a method will get partway through its actions before having to throw an exception because of bad parameter values. A particular reason for avoiding this situation is that partial mutation of an object is likely to leave it in an inconsistent state for future use. If a method fails for any reason, the object on which it was called should ideally be left in the state it was before the operation was attempted.

The static `requireNonNull` method of the `java.util.Objects` class provides a convenient shorthand for testing an expression and throwing an exception if the expression is `null`. The following will throw a `NullPointerException`, with the associated string, if the value of **key** is `null`; otherwise it will do nothing:

```
Objects.requireNonNull(key, "null key passed to getDetails");
```

Exercise 14.26 Review all of the methods of the **AddressBook** class and decide whether there are any additional situations in which they should throw an `IllegalArgumentException`. Add the necessary checks and throw statements.

Exercise 14.27 If you have not already done so, add javadoc documentation to describe any exceptions thrown by methods in the **AddressBook** class.

Exercise 14.28 `UnsupportedOperationException` is an unchecked exception defined in the `java.lang` package. How might this be used in an implementation of the `java.util.Iterator` interface to prevent removal of items from a collection that is being iterated over? Try this out in the **LogfileReader** class of the *weblog-analyzer* project from Chapter 7.

14.4.5 Preventing object creation

An important use for exceptions is to prevent objects from being created if they cannot be placed in a valid initial state. This will usually be the result of inappropriate parameter values being passed to a constructor. We can illustrate this with the **ContactDetails** class. The constructor is currently fairly forgiving of the parameter values it receives: it does not reject **null** values but replaces them with empty strings. However, the address book needs at least a name or phone number from each entry to use as a unique index value, so an entry with both **name** and **phone** fields blank would be impossible to index. We can reflect this requirement by preventing construction of a **ContactDetails** object with no valid key details. The process of throwing an exception from a constructor is exactly the same as throwing one from a method. Code 14.7 shows the revised constructor that will prevent an entry from ever having both **name** and **phone** fields blank.

An exception thrown from a constructor has the same effect on the client as an exception thrown from a method. So the following attempt to create an invalid **ContactDetails** object will completely fail; it will *not* result in a **null** value being stored in the variable:

```
ContactDetails badDetails = new ContactDetails("", "", "");
```

Code 14.7

The constructor of the **Contact-Details** class

```
/**
 * Set up the contact details. All details are trimmed to remove
 * trailing white space.
 * @param name The name.
 * @param phone The phone number.
 * @param address The address.
 * @throws IllegalStateException If both name and phone are blank.
 */
public ContactDetails(String name, String phone, String address)
{
    // Use blank strings if any of the arguments is null.
    if(name == null) {
        name = "";
    }
    if(phone == null) {
        phone = "";
    }
    if(address == null) {
        address = "";
    }

    this.name = name.trim();
    this.phone = phone.trim();
    this.address = address.trim();

    if(this.name.isEmpty() && this.phone.isEmpty()) {
        throw new IllegalStateException(
                "Either the name or phone must not be blank.");
    }
}
```

14.5 Exception handling

The principles of exception throwing apply equally to unchecked and checked exceptions, but the rules of Java mean that exception handling is a requirement only with checked exceptions. A checked exception class is one that is a subclass of **Exception**, but not of **RuntimeException**. There are several more rules to follow when using checked exceptions, because the compiler enforces checks both in a method that throws a checked exception and in any caller of that method.

14.5.1 Checked exceptions: the throws clause

The first requirement of the compiler is that a method throwing a checked exception must declare that it does so in a *throws clause* added to the method's header. For instance, a method throwing a checked **IOException** from the **java.io** package might have the following header:[4]

```
public void saveToFile(String destinationFile)
    throws IOException
```

It is permitted to use a throws clause for unchecked exceptions, but the compiler does not require one. We recommend that a throws clause be used only to list the checked exceptions thrown by a method.

It is important to distinguish between a throws clause in the header of a method, and the **@throws** javadoc comment that precedes the method; the latter is completely optional for both types of exception. Nevertheless, we recommend that javadoc documentation be included for both checked and unchecked exceptions. In that way, as much information as possible will be available to someone wishing to use a method that throws an exception.

14.5.2 Anticipating exceptions: the try statement

The second requirement, when using checked exceptions, is that a caller of a method, that throws a checked exception must make provision for dealing with the exception. This usually means writing an *exception handler* in the form of a *try statement*. Most practical try statements have the general form shown in Code 14.8. This introduces two new Java keywords—**try** and **catch**—which mark a *try block* and a *catch block*, respectively.

Code 14.8

The try and catch blocks of an exception handler

```
try {

    Protect one or more statements here.

}
catch(Exception e) {

    Report and recover from the exception here.

}
```

Suppose we have a method that saves the contents of an address book to a file. The user is requested in some way for the name of a file (perhaps via a GUI dialog window), and the address book's **saveToFile** method is then called to write out the list to the file. If we did not have to take exceptions into account, then this would be written as follows:

```
String filename = request-a-file-from-the-user;
addressbook.saveToFile(filename);
```

However, because the writing process could fail with an exception, the call to **saveToFile** must be placed within a try block to show that this has been taken into account. Code 14.9 illustrates how we would tend to write this, anticipating possible failure.

---

[4] Note that the keyword here is **throws** and not **throw**.

Code 14.9

An exception
handler

```
String filename = null;
boolean successful;
try {
    filename = request-a-file-from-the-user;
    addressbook.saveToFile(filename);
    successful = true;
}
catch(IOException e) {
    System.out.println("Unable to save to " + filename);
    successful = false;
}
```

Any number of statements can be included in a try block, so we tend to place there not just the single statement that could fail, but all of the statements that are related to it in some way. The idea is that a try block represents a sequence of actions we wish to treat as a logical whole but recognize that they might fail at some point.[5] The catch block will then attempt to deal with the situation or report the problem if an exception arises from any statement within the associated try block. Note that, because both the try and catch blocks make use of the **filename** and **successful** variables, they have to be declared outside the try statement in this example, for reasons of scope.

In order to understand how an exception handler works, it is essential to appreciate that *an exception prevents the normal flow of control from being continued in the caller*. An exception interrupts the execution of the caller's statements, and hence any statements immediately following the problem statement will not be executed. The question then arises, "Where is execution resumed in the caller?" A try statement provides the answer: if an exception arises from a statement called in the try block, then execution is resumed in the corresponding catch block. So, if we consider the example in Code 14.9, the effect of an **IOException** being thrown from the call to **saveToFile** will be that control will transfer from the try block to the catch block, as shown in Code 14.10.

Code 14.10

Transfer of control
in a try statement

1. Exception thrown from here   2. Control transfers to here

```
try {
    filename = request-a-file-from-the-user;
    addressbook.saveToFile(filename);
    successful = true;
}
catch(IOException e) {
    System.out.println("Unable to save to " + filename);
    successful = false;
}
```

---

[5] See Exercise 14.31 for an example of what can happen if a statement that might result in an exception is treated in isolation from the statements around it.

Statements in a try block are known as *protected statements*. If no exception arises during execution of protected statements, then the catch block will be skipped over when the end of the try block is reached. Execution will continue with whatever follows the complete try/catch statement.

A catch block names the type of exception it is designed to deal with in a pair of parentheses immediately following the **catch** word. As well as the exception type name, this also includes a variable name (traditionally, simply **e** or **ex**) that can be used to refer to the exception object that was thrown. Having a reference to this object can be useful in providing information that will support recovery from, or reporting of, the problem—e.g., accessing any diagnostic message placed in it by the throwing method. Once the catch block has been completed, control does *not* return to the statement that caused the exception.

Exercise 14.29 The *address-book-v3t* project includes some throwing of unchecked exceptions if parameter values are **null**. The project source code also includes the checked exception class **NoMatchingDetailsException**, which is currently unused. Modify the **removeDetails** method of **AddressBook** so that it throws this exception if its key parameter is not a key that is in use. Add an exception handler to the **remove** method of **AddressBookTextInterface** to catch and report occurrences of this exception.

Exercise 14.30 Make use of **NoMatchingDetailsException** in the **changeDetails** method of **AddressBook**. Enhance the user interface so that the details of an existing entry may be changed. Catch and report exceptions in **AddressBookTextInterface** that arise from use of a key that does not match any existing entry.

Exercise 14.31 Why is the following not a sensible way to use an exception handler? Will this code compile and run?

```
Person p = null;
try {
    // The lookup could fail.
    p = database.lookup(details);
}
catch(Exception e) {
}
System.out.println("The details belong to: " + p);
```

Note that in all the examples of try statements you have seen, the exception is not thrown *directly* by the statements in the try block, which is in the client object. Rather, the exception arises *indirectly*, passed back from a method in the server object, which is called from the statements within the try block. This is the usual pattern, and it would almost certainly be a programming error to enclose a throw statement directly within a try statement.

14.5.3 Throwing and catching multiple exceptions

Sometimes a method throws more than one type of exception in order to indicate different sorts of problems. Where these are checked exceptions, they must all be listed in the throws clause of the method, separated by commas. For instance:

```
public void process()
        throws EOFException, FileNotFoundException
```

An exception handler must cater for all checked exceptions thrown from its protected statements, so a try statement may contain multiple catch blocks, as shown in Code 14.11. Note that the same variable name can be used for the exception object in each case.

Code 14.11
Multiple catch blocks in a try statement

```
try {
    ...
    ref.process();
    ...
}
catch(EOFException e) {
    // Take action appropriate to an end-of-file exception.
    ...
}
catch(FileNotFoundException e) {
    // Take action appropriate to a file-not-found exception.
    ...
}
```

When an exception is thrown by a method call in a try block, the catch blocks are checked in the order in which they are written until a match is found for the exception type. So, if an **EOFException** is thrown, then control will transfer to the first catch block, and if a **FileNotFoundException** is thrown, then control will transfer to the second. Once the end of a single catch block is reached, execution continues following the last catch block.

Polymorphism can be used to avoid writing multiple catch blocks, if desired. However, this could be at the expense of being able to take type-specific recovery actions. In Code 14.12, the single catch block will handle *every* exception thrown by the protected statements. This is because the exception-matching process that looks for an appropriate catch block simply checks that the exception object is an instance of the type named in the block. As all exceptions are subtypes of the **Exception** class, the single block will catch everything, whether checked or unchecked. From the nature of the matching process, it follows that the order of catch blocks in a single try statement matters, and that a catch block for one exception type cannot follow a block for one of its supertypes (because the earlier supertype block will always match before the subtype block is checked). The compiler will report this as an error.

Code 14.12

Catching all exceptions in a single catch block

```
try {
    ...
    ref.process();
    ...
}
catch(Exception e) {
    // Take action appropriate to all exceptions.
    ...
}
```

A better way to handle multiple exceptions with the same recovery or reporting action is to list the exception types together, separated by the "|" symbol, in front of the exception variable name. See Code 14.13.

Code 14.13

Catching multiple exceptions

```
try {
    ...
    ref.process();
    ...
}
catch(EOFException | FileNotFoundException e) {
    // Take action appropriate to both exceptions.
    ...
}
```

Exercise 14.32 Enhance the try statements you wrote as solutions to Exercises 14.29 and 14.30 so that they handle checked and unchecked exceptions in different catch blocks.

Exercise 14.33 What is wrong with the following try statement?

```
Person p = null;
try {
    p = database.lookup(details);
    System.out.println("The details belong to: " + p);
}
catch(Exception e) {
    // Handle any checked exceptions . . .
    . . .
}
catch(RuntimeException e) {
    // Handle any unchecked exceptions . . .
    . . .
}
```

14.5.4 Propagating an exception

So far, we have suggested that an exception must be caught and handled at the earliest possible opportunity. That is, an exception thrown in a method **process** would have to be caught and handled in the method that called **process**. In fact, this is not strictly the case, as Java allows an exception to be *propagated* from the client method to the caller of the client method, and possibly beyond. A method propagates an exception simply by not including an exception handler to protect the statement that might throw it. However, for a checked exception, the compiler requires that the propagating method include a throws clause, even though it does not itself create and throw the exception. This means that you will sometimes see a method that has a throws clause, but with no throw statement in the method body. Propagation is common where the calling method is either unable to, or does not need to, undertake any recovery action itself, but this might be possible or necessary from within higher-level calls. It is also common in constructors, where a constructor's actions in setting up a new object fail and the constructor cannot recover from this.

If the exception being propagated is unchecked, then the throws clause is optional, and we prefer to omit it.

14.5.5 The finally clause

A try statement can include a third component that is optional. This is the *finally clause* (Code 14.14), and it is often omitted. The finally clause provides for statements that should be executed whether an exception arises in the protected statements or not. If control reaches the end of the try block, then the catch blocks are skipped and the finally clause is executed. Conversely, if an exception is thrown from the try block, the appropriate catch block is executed, and this is then followed by execution of the finally clause.

Code 14.14

A try statement with a finally clause

```
try {
        Protect one or more statements here.
}
catch(Exception e) {
        Report and recover from the exception here.
}
finally {
        Perform any actions here common to whether or not
        an exception is thrown.
}
```

At first sight, a finally clause would appear to be redundant. Doesn't the following example illustrate the same flow of control as Code 14.14?

```
try {
        Protect one or more statements here.
}
```

```
catch(Exception e) {
    Report and recover from the exception here.
}

Perform any actions here common to whether or not an exception is
thrown.
```

In fact, there are at least two cases where these two examples would have different effects:

■ A finally clause is executed even if a return statement is executed in the try or catch blocks.

■ If an exception is thrown in the try block but not caught, then the finally clause is still executed.

In the latter case, the uncaught exception could be an unchecked exception that does not require a catch block, for instance. However, it could also be a checked exception that is not handled by a catch block but propagated from the method, to be handled at a higher level in the call sequence. In such a case, the finally clause would still be executed.

It is also possible to omit the catch blocks in a try statement that has both a try block and a finally clause if the method is propagating all exceptions:

```
try {
    Protect one or more statements here.
}
finally {
    Perform any actions here common to whether or not
    an exception is thrown.
}
```

14.6   Defining new exception classes

Where the standard exception classes do not satisfactorily describe the nature of an error condition, new, more-descriptive exception classes can be defined using inheritance. New checked exception classes can be defined as subclasses of any existing checked exception class (such as **Exception**), and new unchecked exceptions would be subclasses of the **RuntimeException** hierarchy.

All existing exception classes support the inclusion of a diagnostic string passed to a constructor. However, one of the main reasons for defining new exception classes is to include further information within the exception object to support error diagnosis and recovery. For instance, some methods in the *address-book* application, such as **changeDetails**, take a **key** parameter that should match an existing entry. If no matching entry can be found, then this represents a programming error, as the methods cannot complete their task. In reporting the exception, it is helpful to include details of the key that caused the error. Code 14.15 shows a new checked exception class that is defined in the *address-book-v3t* project. It receives the key in its constructor and then makes it available through both the diagnostic string and a dedicated accessor method. If this exception were to be caught by an exception handler in the caller, the key would be available to the statements that attempt to recover from the error.

Code 14.15

An exception class
with extra diag-
nostic information

```java
/**
 * Capture a key that failed to match an entry in the address book.
 *
 * @author David J. Barnes and Michael Kölling.
 * @version 2016.02.29
 */
public class NoMatchingDetailsException extends Exception
{
    // The key with no match.
    private String key;

    /**
     * Store the details in error.
     * @param key The key with no match.
     */
    public NoMatchingDetailsException(String key)
    {
        this.key = key;
    }

    /**
     * @return The key in error.
     */
    public String getKey()
    {
        return key;
    }

    /**
     * @return A diagnostic string containing the key in error.
     */
    public String toString()
    {
        return "No details matching: " + key + " were found.";
    }
}
```

The principle of including information that could support error recovery should be kept
in mind particularly when defining new checked exception classes. Defining formal
parameters in an exception's constructor will help to ensure that diagnostic information is
available. In addition, where recovery is either not possible or not attempted, ensuring that
the exception's **toString** method is overridden to include appropriate information will
help in diagnosing the reason for the error.

Exercise 14.34 In the *address-book-v3t* project, define a new checked exception class: **DuplicateKeyException**. This should be thrown by the **addDetails**
method if either of the non-blank key fields of its actual parameter is already
currently in use. The exception class should store details of the offending key(s).
Make any further changes to the user interface class that are necessary to catch
and report the exception.

> **Exercise 14.35** Do you feel that `DuplicateKeyException` should be a checked or unchecked exception? Give reasons for your answer.

14.7 Using assertions

14.7.1 Internal consistency checks

When we design or implement a class, we often have an intuitive sense of things that should be true at a given point in the execution, but rarely state them formally. For instance, we would expect a `ContactDetails` object to always contain at least one non-blank field, or, when the `removeDetails` method is called with a particular key, we would expect that key to no longer be in use at the end of the method. Typically, these are conditions we wish to establish while developing a class, before it is released. In one sense, the sort of testing we discussed in Chapter 9 is an attempt to establish whether we have implemented an accurate representation of what a class or method should do. Characteristic of that style of testing is that the tests are *external* to the class being tested. If a class is changed, then we should take the time to run regression tests in order to establish that it still works as it should; it is easy to forget to do that. The practice of checking parameters, which we have introduced in this chapter, slightly shifts the emphasis from wholly external checking to a combination of external and internal checking. However, parameter checking is primarily intended to protect a server object from incorrect usage by a client. That still leaves the question of whether we can include some internal checks to ensure that the server object behaves as it should.

One way we could implement internal checking during development would be through the normal exception-throwing mechanism. In practice, we would have to use unchecked exceptions, because we could not expect regular client classes to include exception handlers for what are essentially internal server errors. We would then be faced with the issue of whether to remove these internal checks once the development process has been completed, in order to avoid the potentially high cost of runtime checks that are almost certainly bound to pass.

14.7.2 The assert statement

In order to deal with the need to perform efficient internal consistency checks, which can be turned on in development code but off in released code, an *assertion facility* is available in Java. The idea is similar to what we saw in Chapter 9 with JUnit testing, where we asserted the results we expected from method calls, and the JUnit framework tested whether or not those assertions were confirmed.

The *address-book-assert* project is a development version of the *address-book* projects that illustrates how assertions are used. Code 14.16 shows the `removeDetails` method, which now contains two forms of the *assert statement*.

Code 14.16

Using assertions
for internal
consistency checks

```java
/**
 * Remove the entry with the given key from the address book.
 * The key should be one that is currently in use.
 * @param key One of the keys of the entry to be removed.
 * @throws IllegalArgumentException If the key is null.
 */
public void removeDetails(String key)
{
    if(key == null) {
        throw new IllegalArgumentException(
                            "Null key passed to removeDetails.");
    }
    if(keyInUse(key)) {
        ContactDetails details = book.get(key);
        book.remove(details.getName());
        book.remove(details.getPhone());
        numberOfEntries--;
    }
    assert !keyInUse(key);
    assert consistentSize() : "Inconsistent book size in removeDetails";
}
```

Concept

An **assertion**
is a statement
of a fact that
should be
true in normal
program execu-
tion. We can
use assertions
to state our
assumptions
explicitly and
to detect
programming
errors more
easily.

The **assert** keyword is followed by a boolean expression. The purpose of the statement is to assert something that should be true at this point in the method. For instance, the first assert statement in Code 14.16 asserts that **keyInUse** should return **false** at that point, either because the key wasn't in use in the first place or because it is no longer in use as the associated details have now been removed from the address book. This seemingly obvious assertion is more important than might at first appear; notice that the removal process does not actually involve use of the key with the address book.

Thus, an assert statement serves two purposes. It expresses explicitly what we assume to be true at a given point in the execution, and therefore increases readability both for the current developer and for a future maintenance programmer. Also, it actually performs the check at runtime so that we get notified if our assumption turns out to be incorrect. This can greatly help in finding errors early and easily.

If the boolean expression in an assert statement evaluates to **true**, then the assert statement has no further effect. If the statement evaluates to **false**, then an **Assertion-Error** will be thrown. This is a subclass of **Error** (see Figure 14.1) and is part of the hierarchy regarded as representing unrecoverable errors—hence, no handler should be provided in clients.

The second assert statement in Code 14.16 illustrates the alternative form of assert statement. The string following the colon symbol will be passed to the constructor of **AssertionError** to provide a diagnostic string. The second expression does not have to be an explicit string; any value-giving expression is acceptable, and will be turned into a **String** before being passed to the constructor.

The first assert statement shows that an assertion will often make use of an existing method within the class (e.g., **keyInUse**). The second example illustrates that it might be useful to provide a method specifically for the purpose of performing an assertion test (**consistentSize** in this example). This might be used if the check involves significant computation. Code 14.17 shows the **consistentSize** method, whose purpose is to ensure that the **numberOfEntries** field accurately represents the number of unique details in the address book.

Code 14.17

Checking for internal consistency in the address book

```
/**
 * Check that the numberOfEntries field is consistent with
 * the number of entries actually stored in the address book.
 * @return true if the field is consistent, false otherwise.
 */
private boolean consistentSize()
{
    Collection<ContactDetails> allEntries = book.values();
    // Eliminate duplicates as we are using multiple keys.
    Set<ContactDetails> uniqueEntries = new HashSet<>(allEntries);
    int actualCount = uniqueEntries.size();
    return numberOfEntries == actualCount;
}
```

14.7.3 Guidelines for using assertions

Assertions are primarily intended to provide a way to perform consistency checks during the development and testing phases of a project. They are not intended to be used in released code. It is for this reason that a Java compiler will include assert statements in the compiled code only if requested to do so. It follows that assert statements should never be used to provide normal functionality. For instance, it would be wrong to combine assertions with removal of details, as follows, in the address book:

```
// Error: don't use assert with normal processing!
assert book.remove(details.getName()) != null;
assert book.remove(details.getPhone()) != null;
```

Exercise 14.36 Open the *address-book-assert* project. Look through the **AddressBook** class and identify all of the assert statements to be sure that you understand what is being checked and why.

Exercise 14.37 The **AddressBookDemo** class contains several test methods that call methods of **AddressBook** that contain assert statements. Look through the source of **AddressBookDemo** to check that you understand the tests, and then try out each of the test methods. Are any assertion errors generated? If so, do you understand why?

Exercise 14.38 The `changeDetails` method of **AddressBook** currently has no assert statements. One assertion we could make about it is that the address book should contain the same number of entries at the end of the method as it did at the start. Add an assert statement (and any other statements you might need) to check this. Run the **testChange** method of **AddressBookDemo** after doing so. Do you think this method should also include the check for a consistent size?

Exercise 14.39 Suppose that we decide to allow the address book to be indexed by address as well as name and phone number. If we simply add the following statement to the **addDetails** method

```
book.put(details.getAddress(), details);
```

do you anticipate that any assertions will now fail? Try it. Make any further necessary changes to **AddressBook** to ensure that all of the assertions are now successful.

Exercise 14.40 **ContactDetails** are immutable objects—that is, they have no mutator methods. How important is this fact to the internal consistency of an **AddressBook**? Suppose the **ContactDetails** class had a **setPhone** method, for instance? Can you devise some tests to illustrate the problems this could cause?

14.7.4 Assertions and the BlueJ unit-testing framework

In Chapter 9, we introduced the support that BlueJ provides for the JUnit unit-testing framework. That support is based on the assertion facility we have been discussing in this section. Methods from the framework, such as **assertEquals**, are built around an assertion statement that contains a boolean expression made up from their parameters. If JUnit test classes are used to test classes containing their own assertion statements, then assertion errors from these statements will be reported in the test-results window along with test-class assertion failures. The *address-book-junit* project contains a test class to illustrate this combination. The **testAddDetailsError** method of **AddressBookTest** will trigger an assertion error, because **addDetails** should not be used to change existing details (see Exercise 14.34).

14.8 Error recovery and avoidance

So far, the main focus of this chapter has been on the problem of identifying errors in a server object and ensuring that any problem is reported back to the client if appropriate. There are two complementary issues that go with error reporting: error recovery and error avoidance.

14.8.1 Error recovery

The first requirement of successful error recovery is that clients take note of any error notifications that they receive. This may sound obvious, but it is not uncommon for a programmer to assume that a method call will not fail, and so not bother to check the return value. While ignoring errors is harder to do when exceptions are used, we have often seen the equivalent of the following approach to exception handling:

```
AddressDetails details = null;
try {
    details = contacts.getDetails(. . .);
}
catch(Exception e) {
    System.out.println("Error: " + e);
}
String phone = details.getPhone();
```

The exception has been caught and reported, but no account has been taken of the fact that it is probably incorrect, just to carry on regardless.

Java's try statement is the key to supplying an error-recovery mechanism when an exception is thrown. Recovery from an error will usually involve taking some form of corrective action within the catch block, and then trying again. Repeated attempts can be made by placing the try statement in a loop. An example of this approach is shown in Code 14.18, which is an expanded version of Code 14.9. The efforts to compose an alternative filename could involve trying a list of possible folders, for instance, or prompting an interactive user for different names.

Code 14.18

An attempt at error recovery

```
// Try to save the address book.
boolean successful = false;
int attempts = 0;
do {
    try {
        addressbook.saveToFile(filename);
        successful = true;
    }
    catch(IOException e) {
        System.out.println("Unable to save to " + filename);
        attempts++;
        if(attempts < MAX_ATTEMPTS) {
            filename = an alternative file name;
        }
    }
} while(!successful && attempts < MAX_ATTEMPTS);
if(!successful) {
    Report the problem and give up;
}
```

Although this example illustrates recovery for a specific situation, the principles it illustrates are more general:

- Anticipating an error, and recovering from it, will usually require a more complex flow of control than if an error cannot occur.
- The statements in the catch block are key to setting up the recovery attempt.
- Recovery will often involve having to try again.
- Successful recovery cannot be guaranteed.
- There should be some escape route from endlessly attempting hopeless recovery.

There won't always be a human user around to prompt for alternative input, so it might be the client object's responsibility to log the error, via something like a logging API, so that it will be noticed and can be investigated later.

14.8.2 Error avoidance

It should be clear that arriving at a situation where an exception is thrown will be, at worst, fatal to the execution of a program and, at best, messy to recover from in the client. It can be simpler to try to avoid the error in the first place, but this often requires collaboration between server and client.

Many of the cases where an **AddressBook** object is forced to throw an exception involve **null** parameter values passed to its methods. These represent logical programming errors in the client that could clearly be avoided by simple prior tests in the client. Null parameter values are usually the result of making invalid assumptions in the client. For instance, consider the following example:

```
String key = database.search(zipCode);
ContactDetails university = contacts.getDetails(key);
```

If the database search fails, then the key it returns may well be either blank or **null**. Passing that result directly to the **getDetails** method will produce a runtime exception. However, using a simple test of the search result, the exception can be avoided, and the real problem of a failed zip code search can be addressed instead:

```
String key = database.search(zipCode);
if(key != null && !key.isEmpty()) {
    ContactDetails university = contacts.getDetails(key);
    . . .
}
else {
    Deal with the zipcode error . . .
}
```

In this case, the client could establish for itself that it would be inappropriate to call the server's method. This is not always possible, and sometimes the client must enlist the help of the server.

Exercise 14.34 established the principle that the **addDetails** method should not accept a new set of details if one of the key values is already in use for another set. In order to avoid an inappropriate call, the client could make use of the address book's **keyInUse** method, as follows:

```
// Add what should be a new set of details to the address book.
if(contacts.keyInUse(details.getName()) {
    contacts.changeDetails(details.getName(), details);
}
else if(contacts.keyInUse(details.getPhone()) {
    contacts.changeDetails(details.getPhone(), details);
}
else {
    Add the details . . .
}
```

Using this approach, it is clearly possible to completely avoid a **DuplicateKeyException** being thrown from **addDetails**, which suggests that it could be downgraded from a checked to an unchecked exception.

This particular example illustrates some important general principles:

- If a server's validity-check and state-test methods are visible to a client, the client will often be able to avoid causing the server to throw an exception.

- If an exception can be avoided in this way, then the exception being thrown really represents a logical programming error in the client. This suggests use of an unchecked exception for such situations.

- Using unchecked exceptions means that the client does not have to use a try statement when it has already established that the exception will not be thrown. This is a significant gain, because having to write try statements for "cannot happen" situations is annoying for a programmer and makes it less likely that providing proper recovery for genuine error situations will be taken seriously.

The effects are not all positive, however. Here are some reasons why this approach is not always practical:

- Making a server class's validity-check and state-test methods publicly visible to its clients might represent a significant loss of encapsulation, and result in a higher degree of coupling between server and client than is desirable.

- It will probably not be safe for a server class to assume that its clients *will* make the necessary checks that avoid an exception. As a result, those checks will often be duplicated in both client and server. If the checks are computationally "expensive" to make, then duplication may be undesirable or prohibitive. However, our view would be that it is better to sacrifice efficiency for the sake of safer programming, where the choice is available.

14.9 File-based input/output

An important programming area in which error recovery cannot be ignored is input/output. This is because a programmer may have little direct control over the external environment in which their code is executed. For instance, a required data file may have been accidentally deleted or have become corrupted in some way, before the application is run; or an attempt to store results to the file system may be thwarted by lack of appropriate permissions or exceeding a file-system quota. There are many ways in which an input or output operation could fail at any stage. Furthermore, modern input/output has moved beyond a program simply accessing its local file store to a networked environment in which connectivity to the resources being accessed may be fragile and inconsistent—for example, when in a mobile environment.

The Java API has undergone a number of evolutions over the years, reflecting the increasing diversity of environments in which Java programs have come to be used. The core package for input/output-related classes has always been **java.io**. This package contains numerous classes to support input/output operations in a platform-independent manner. In particular, it defines the checked exception class **IOException** as a general indicator that something has gone wrong with an input/output operation, and almost any input/output operation must anticipate that one of these might be thrown. Instances of checked subclasses of **IOException** may be thrown at times to provide more detailed diagnostic information, such as **FileNotFoundException** and **EOFException**. In more recent versions of Java, a shift has taken place from a number of classes in the **java.io** package to those in the **java.nio** hierarchy, although without completely superseding everything in **java.io**.

A full description of the many different classes in the **java.io** and **java.nio** packages is beyond the scope of this book, but we shall provide some fundamental examples within the context of several of the projects we have already seen. This should give you enough background to experiment with input/output in your own projects. In particular, we shall illustrate the following common tasks:

- obtaining information about a file from the file system

- writing textual output to a file with the **FileWriter** class

- reading textual input from a file with the **FileReader** and **BufferedReader** classes

- anticipating **IOException** exceptions

- parsing input with the **Scanner** class

In addition, we look at reading and writing binary versions of objects as a brief introduction to Java's *serialization* feature.

For further reading on input/output in Java, we recommend Oracle's tutorial, which can be found online at:

`http://download.oracle.com/javase/tutorial/essential/io/index.html`

14.9.1 Readers, writers, and streams

Several of the classes of the **java.io** package fall into one of two main categories: those dealing with text files, and those dealing with binary files. We can think of text files as containing data in a form similar to Java's **char** type—typically simple, line-based, human-readable alphanumeric information. Web pages, written in HTML, are a particular example. Binary files are more varied: image files are one common example, as are executable programs such as word processors and media players. Java classes concerned with processing text files are known as *readers* and *writers*, whereas those concerned with binary files are known as *stream* handlers.[6] In the main, we shall focus on readers and writers.

14.9.2 The `File` class and `Path` interface

A file is much more than just a name and some contents. A file will be located in a particular *folder* or *directory* on a particular disk drive, for instance, and different operating systems have different conventions for which characters are used in file pathnames. The `File` class from `java.io` allows a program to enquire about details of an external file in a way that is independent of the particular file system on which the program is running. The name of the file is passed to the constructor of `File`. Creating a `File` object within a program does not create a file in the file system. Rather, it results in details about a file being stored in the `File` object if the external file exists.

The more modern `Path` interface and `Files` class (note the plural name) in `java.nio.file` fulfill a similar role to the legacy `File` class. Because `Path` is an interface rather than a class, a concrete instance of an implementing class is created via a static `get` method of the `Paths` class (plural again), which is also in the `java.nio.file` package. When working with legacy code, an equivalent `Path` object may be created from a `File` object via the `toPath` method of `File`.

We can sometimes avoid getting into situations that require an exception to be handled, by using the `Files` class and a `Path` object to check whether or not a file exists. The `Files` class has `exists` and `isReadable` methods, which make attempting to open a file less likely to fail if we use them first. However, because opening a file that we know exists *still* requires a potential exception to be handled, many programmers do not bother with checking first.

The `Files` class provides a large number of static methods for querying the attributes of a `Path` object.

Exercise 14.41 Read the API documentation for the `Files` class from the `java.nio.file` package. What sort of information is available on files/paths?

Exercise 14.42 What methods of the `Files` class tell you whether a `Path` represents an ordinary file or a directory (folder)?

Exercise 14.43 Is it possible to determine anything about *the contents* of a particular file using the `Files` class?

---

[6] It is important to note that the input-output `Stream` classes in the `java.io` package are different from the `Stream` classes in the `java.util.stream` package.

14.9.3 File output

There are three steps involved in storing data in a file:

1. The file is opened.

2. The data is written.

3. The file is closed.

The nature of file output means that any of these steps could fail, for a range of reasons, many completely beyond the application programmer's control. As a consequence, it will be necessary to anticipate exceptions being thrown at every stage.

In order to write a text file, it is usual to create a **FileWriter** object, whose constructor takes the name of the file to be written. The file name can be either in the form of a **String** or a **File** object. Creating a **FileWriter** has the effect of opening the external file and preparing it to receive some output. If the attempt to open the file fails for any reason, then the constructor will throw an **IOException**. Reasons for failure might be that file system permissions prevent a user from writing to certain files, or that the given file name does not match a valid location in the file system.

When a file has been opened successfully, then the writer's **write** methods can be used to store characters—often in the form of strings—into the file. Any attempt to write could fail, even if the file has been opened successfully. Such failures are rare, but still possible.

Once all output has been written, it is important for the file to be closed. This ensures that all the data really has been written to the external file system, and it often has the effect of freeing some internal or external resources. Once again, on rare occasions, the attempt to close the file could fail.

The basic pattern that emerges from the above discussion looks like this:

```
FileWriter writer = new FileWriter(" ... name of file ... ");
while(there is more text to write) {
    . . .
    writer.write(next piece of text);
    . . .
}
writer.close();
```

The main issue that arises is how to deal with any exceptions that are thrown during the three stages. An exception thrown when attempting to open a file is really the only one it is likely to be possible to do anything about, and only then if there is some way to generate an alternative name to try instead. As this will usually require the intervention of a human user of the application, the chances of dealing with it successfully are obviously application- and context-specific. If an attempt to write to the file fails, then it is unlikely that repeating the attempt will succeed. Similarly, failure to close a file is not usually worth a further attempt. The consequence is likely to be an incomplete file.

An example of this pattern can be seen in Code 14.19. The **LogfileCreator** class in the *weblog-analyzer* project includes a method to write a number of random log entries to a file whose name is passed as a parameter to the **createFile** method. This uses two different **write** methods: one to write a string, and one to write a character. After writing out the text of the entry as a string, we write a newline character so that each entry appears on a separate line.

Code 14.19

Writing to a text file

```
/**
 * Create a file of random log entries.
 * @param filename The file to write.
 * @param numEntries How many entries.
 * @return true if successful, false otherwise.
 */
public boolean createFile(String filename, int numEntries)
{
    boolean success = false;
    try {
        FileWriter writer = new FileWriter(filename);
        LogEntry[] entries = new LogEntry[numEntries];
        for(int i = 0; i < numEntries; i++) {
            writer.write(entries[i].toString());
            writer.write('\n');
        }

        writer.close();
        success = true;
    }
    catch(IOException e) {
        System.err.println("There was a problem writing to " + filename);
    }
    return success;
}
```

14.9.4 The try-with-resource statement

It is important to close a file once it is finished, and there is a version of the try statement that simplifies the task of ensuring this happens. This form is called *try with resource* or *automatic resource management* (ARM). Code 14.20 shows its use with in the **Logfile-Creator** class in the *weblog-analyzer* project.

The resource object is created in a new parenthesized section immediately after the **try** word. In this case, the resource is associated with a file. Once the try statement is completed, the **close** method will be called automatically on the resource. This version of the try statement is only appropriate for objects of classes that implement the **AutoCloseable** interface, defined in the **java.lang** package. These will predominantly be classes associated with input/output.

Code 14.20

Writing to a text
file using a try-
with-resource
statement

```java
/**
 * Create a file of random log entries.
 * @param filename The file to write.
 * @param numEntries How many entries.
 * @return true if successful, false otherwise.
 */
public boolean createFile(String filename, int numEntries)
{
    boolean success = false;
    try(FileWriter writer = new FileWriter(filename)) {

        Entry creation omitted.

        for(int i = 0; i < numEntries; i++) {
            writer.write(entries[i].toString());
            writer.write('\n');
        }
        success = true;
    }
    catch(IOException e) {
        System.err.println("There was a problem writing to " + filename);
    }
    return success;
}
```

Exercise 14.44 Modify the *world-of-zuul* project so that it writes a script of user input to a text file as a record of the game. There are several different ways that you might think of tackling this:

- You could modify the **Parser** class to store each line of input in a list and then write out the list at the end of the game. This will produce a solution that is closest to the basic pattern we have outlined in the discussion above.
- You could place all of the file handling in the **Parser** class so that, as each line is read, it is written out immediately in exactly the same form as it was read. File opening, writing, and closing will all be separated in time from one another (or would it make sense to open, write, and then close the file for every line that is written?).
- You could place the file handling in the **Game** class and implement a **toString** method in the **Command** class to return the **String** to be written for each command.

Consider each of these possible solutions in terms of responsibility-driven design and the handling of exceptions, along with the likely implications for playing the game if it proves impossible to write the script. How can you ensure that the script file is always closed when the end of the game is reached? This is important to ensure that all of the output is actually written to the external file system.

14.9.5 Text input

The complement to the output of text with a **FileWriter** is the input with a **FileReader**. As you might expect, a complementary set of three input steps is required: opening the file, reading from it, and closing it. Just as the natural units for writing text are characters and strings, the obvious units for reading text are characters and lines. However, although the **FileReader** class contains a method to read a single character,[7] it does not contain a method to read a line. The problem with reading lines from a file is that there is no predefined limit to the length of a line. This means that any method to return the next complete line from a file must be able to read an arbitrary number of characters. For this reason, we usually want to be working with the **BufferedReader** class, which does define a **readLine** method.

A **BufferedReader** is created via the static **newBufferedReader** method of the **Files** class. In addition to a **Path** parameter corresponding to the file to be opened, one complication is that a **Charset** parameter is also required. This is used to describe the character set to which the characters in the file belong. **Charset** can be found in the **java.nio. charset** package. There are a number of standard character sets, such as **US-ASCII** and **ISO-8859-1**, and more details can be found in the API documentation for **Charset**. The line-termination character is always removed from the **String** that **readLine** returns, and a **null** value is used to indicate the end of file.

This suggests the following basic pattern for reading the contents of a text file:

```
Charset charset = Charset.forName("US-ASCII");
Path path = Paths.get(filename);
BufferedReader reader =
    Files.newBufferedReader(path, charset);
String line = reader.readLine();
while(line != null) {
    do something with line
    line = reader.readLine();
}
reader.close();
```

Code 14.21 illustrates the practical use of a **BufferedReader** in the *tech-support* project from Chapter 6. This has been done so that we can read the system's default responses from a file, rather than hardwiring them into the code of the **Responder** class (project: *tech-support-io* in this chapter's folder).

As with output, the question arises as to what to do about any exceptions thrown during the whole process. In this example, we have printed an error message, then provided at least one response in case of a complete failure to read anything.

---

[7] In fact, its **read** method returns each character as an **int** value rather than as a **char**, because it uses an out-of-bounds value, -1, to indicate the end of the file. This is exactly the sort of technique we described in Section 14.3.2.

Code 14.21

Reading from a
text file with a
`BufferedReader`

```java
import java.io.*;
import java.nio.charset.Charset;
import java.nio.file.*;
import java.util.*;

public class Responder
{
    // Default responses to use if we don't recognize a word.
    private List<String> defaultResponses;
    // The name of the file containing the default responses.
    private static final String FILE_OF_DEFAULT_RESPONSES = "default.txt";

    Other fields and methods omitted.

    /**
     * Build up a list of default responses from which we can pick
     * if we don't know what else to say.
     */
    private void fillDefaultResponses()
    {
        Charset charset = Charset.forName("US-ASCII");
        Path path = Paths.get(FILE_OF_DEFAULT_RESPONSES);
        try (BufferedReader reader = Files.newBufferedReader(path, charset)) {
            String response = reader.readLine();
            while(response != null) {
                defaultResponses.add(response);
                response = reader.readLine();
            }
        }
        catch(FileNotFoundException e) {
            System.err.println("Unable to open " + FILE_OF_DEFAULT_RESPONSES);
        }
        catch(IOException e) {
            System.err.println("A problem was encountered reading " +
                            FILE_OF_DEFAULT_RESPONSES);
        }
        // Make sure we have at least one response.
        if(defaultResponses.size() == 0) {
            defaultResponses.add("Could you elaborate on that?");
        }
    }
}
```

There is an even simpler way of reading a complete file of text without having to use
a **BufferedReader**. The **lines** method of the **Files** class takes a **Path** parameter
and returns the contents of the file in the form of a **Stream<String>**. This can be
processed as a stream, converted to a **String** array, or collected in an **ArrayList**,
say, as required.

Exercise 14.45 The file **default.txt** in the project folder of the *tech-support-io* project contains the default responses read in by the **fillDefault-Responses** method. Using any text editor, change the content of this file so that it contains an empty line between any two responses. Then change your code to work correctly again in reading in the responses from this file.

Exercise 14.46 Change your code so that several lines of text found in the file not separated by an empty line are read as one single response. Change the **default.txt** file so that it contains some responses spanning multiple lines. Test.

Exercise 14.47 Modify the **Responder** class of the *tech-support-io* project so that it reads the associations between keywords and responses from a text file, rather than initializing **responseMap** with strings written into the source code in the **fillResponseMap** method. You can use the **fillDefaultResponses** method as a pattern, but you will need to make some changes to its logic, because there are two strings to be read for each entry rather than one—the keyword and the response. Try storing keywords and responses on alternating lines; keep the text of each response on a single line. You may assume that there will always be an even number of lines (i.e., no missing responses).

14.9.5 Scanner: parsing input

So far, we have treated input largely as unstructured lines of text, for which **Buffered-Reader** is the ideal class. However, many applications will then go on to decompose the individual lines into component pieces representing multi-typed data values. For instance, the comma-separated values (CSV) format is a commonly used way to store text files whose lines consist of multiple values, each of which is separated from its neighbors by a comma character.[8] In effect, such lines of text have an implicit structure. Identifying the underlying structure is known as *parsing*, while piecing the individual characters into separate data values is known as *scanning*.

The **Scanner** class, in the **java.util** package, is specifically designed to scan text and convert composite sequences of characters to typed values, such as integers (**nextInt**) and floating-point numbers (**nextDouble**). While a **Scanner** can be used to break up **String** objects, it is also often used to read and convert the contents of files directly instead of using **BufferedReader**. It has constructors that can take **String**, **File**, or **Path** arguments. Code 14.22 illustrates how a text file that is to be interpreted as containing integer data might be read in this way.

---

[8] In practice, any character can be used in place of a comma; for instance, a tab character is frequently used.

Code 14.22

Reading integer data with **Scanner**

```java
/**
 * Read integers from a file and return them as an array.
 * @param filename The file to be read.
 * @return The integers read.
 */
public int[] readInts(String filename)
{
    int[] data;
    try {
        List<Integer> values = new ArrayList<>();
        Scanner scanner = new Scanner(Paths.get(filename));
        while(scanner.hasNextInt()) {
            values.add(scanner.nextInt());
        }
        // Copy them to an array of the exact size.
        data = new int[values.size()];
        Iterator<Integer> it = values.iterator();
        int i = 0;
        while(it.hasNext()) {
            data[i] = it.next();
            i++;
        }
    }
    catch(IOException e) {
        System.out.println("Cannot find file: " + filename);
        data = new int[0];
    }
    return data;
}
```

Note that this method does not guarantee to read the whole file. The **Scanner**'s **hasNextInt** method that controls the loop will return **false** if it encounters text in the file that does not appear to be part of an integer. At that point, the data gathering will be terminated. In fact, it is perfectly possible to mix calls to the different **next** methods when parsing a complete file, where the data it contains is to be interpreted as consisting of mixed types.

Another common use of **Scanner** is to read input from the "terminal" connected to a program. We have regularly used calls to the **print** and **println** methods of **System.out** to write text to the BlueJ terminal window. **System.out** is of type **java.io.PrintStream** and maps to what is often called the *standard output* destination. Similarly, there is a corresponding *standard input* source available as **System.in**, which is of type **java.io.InputStream**. An **InputStream** is not normally used directly when it is necessary to read user input from the terminal, because it delivers input one character at a time. Instead, **System.in** is usually passed to the constructor of a **Scanner**. The **InputReader** class in the *tech-support-complete* project of Chapter 6 uses this approach to read questions from the user:

```java
Scanner reader = new Scanner(System.in);
. . . intervening code omitted . . .
String inputLine = reader.nextLine();
```

The **nextLine** method of **Scanner** returns the next complete line of input from standard input (without including the final newline character).

> **Exercise 14.48** Review the **InputReader** class of *tech-support-complete* to check that you understand how it uses the **Scanner** class.
>
> **Exercise 14.49** Read the API documentation for the **Scanner** class in the **java.util** package. What **next** methods does it have in addition to those we have discussed in this section?
>
> **Exercise 14.50** Review the **Parser** class of *zuul-better* to also see how it uses the **Scanner** class. It does so in two slightly different ways.
>
> **Exercise 14.51** Review the **LoglineTokenizer** class of *weblog-analyzer* to see how it uses a **Scanner** to extract the integer values from log lines.

14.9.7 Object serialization

Concept

Serialization allows whole objects, and object hierarchies, to be read and written in a single operation. Every object involved must be from a class that implements the **Serializable** interface.

In simple terms, serialization allows a whole object to be written to an external file in a single write operation and read back in at a later stage using a single read operation.[9] This works with both simple objects and multi-component objects such as collections. This is a significant feature that avoids having to read and write objects field by field. It is particularly useful in applications with persistent data, such as address books or media databases, because it allows all entries created in one session to be saved and then read back in at a later session. Of course, we have the choice to write out the contents of objects as text strings, but the process of reading the text back in again, converting the data to the correct types, and restoring *the exact state* of a complex set of objects is often difficult, if not impossible. Object serialization is a much more reliable process.

In order to be eligible to participate in serialization, a class must implement the **Serializable** interface that is defined in the **java.io** package. However, it is worth noting that this interface defines no methods. This means that the serialization process is managed automatically by the runtime system and requires little user-defined code to be written. In the *address-book-io* project, both **AddressBook** and **ContactDetails** implement this interface so that they can be saved to a file. The **AddressBookFileHandler** class defines the methods **saveToFile** and **readFromFile** to illustrate the serialization process. Code 14.23 contains the source of **saveToFile** to illustrate how little code is actually required to save the whole address book, in a single write statement. Note too that, because we are writing objects in binary form, a **Stream** object has been used rather than a **Writer**. The **AddressBookFileHandler** class also includes further examples of the basic reading and writing techniques used with text files. See, for instance, its **saveSearchResults** and **showSearchResults** methods.

---

[9] This is a simplification, because objects can also be written and read across a network, for instance, and not just within a file system.

Code 14.23

Serialization
of a complete
Address Book
with all **Contact**
Details

```
public class AddressBookFileHandler
{

    Fields and methods omitted.

    /**
     * Save a binary version of the address book to the given file.
     * If the file name is not an absolute path, then it is assumed
     * to be relative to the current project folder.
     * @param destinationFile The file where the details are to be saved.
     * @throws IOException If the saving process fails for any reason.
     */
    public void saveToFile(String destinationFile)
            throws IOException
    {
        Path destination = Paths.get(destinationFile).toAbsolutePath();
        ObjectOutputStream os = new ObjectOutputStream(
                                    new FileOutputStream(
                                            destination.toString()));
        os.writeObject(book);
        os.close();
    }
}
```

Exercise 14.52 Modify the *network* project from Chapter 11 so that the data
can be stored to a file. Use object serialization for this. Which classes do you
have to declare to be serializable?

Exercise 14.53 What happens if you change the definition of a class by, say,
adding an extra field, and then try to read back serialized objects created from
the previous version of the class?

14.10 Summary

When two objects interact, there is always the chance that something could go wrong, for
a variety of reasons. For instance:

- The programmer of a client might have misunderstood the state or the capabilities of a
  particular server object.

- A server object may be unable to fulfill a client's request because of a particular set of
  external circumstances.

- A client might have been programmed incorrectly, causing it to pass inappropriate parameter values to a server method.

If something does go wrong, a program is likely either to terminate prematurely (i.e., crash!)
or to produce incorrect and undesirable effects. We can go a long way toward avoiding many
of these problems by using exception throwing. This provides a clearly defined way for an

object to report to a client that something has gone wrong. Exceptions prevent a client from simply ignoring the problem, and encourage programmers to try to find an alternative course of action as a workaround if something does go wrong.

When developing a class, assert statements can be used to provide internal consistency checking. These are typically omitted from production code.

Input/output is an area where exceptions are likely to occur. This is primarily because a programmer has little, if any, control over the environments in which their programs are run, but it also reflects the complexity and diversity of the environments in which programs are run.

The Java API supports input/output of both textual and binary data via readers, writers, and streams. More recent versions of Java introduced the **java.nio** packages, which supersede some of the older **java.io** classes.

Terms introduced in this chapter:

> **exception, unchecked exception, checked exception, exception handler, assertion, serialization**

Concept summary

- **exception** An *exception* is an object representing details of a program failure. An exception is thrown to indicate that a failure has occurred.

- **unchecked exception** An *unchecked exception* is a type of exception whose use will not require checks from the compiler.

- **checked exception** A *checked exception* is a type of exception whose use will require extra checks from the compiler. In particular, checked exceptions in Java require the use of throws clauses and try statements.

- **exception handler** Program code that protects statements in which an exception might be thrown is called an *exception handler*. It provides reporting and/or recovery code should one arise.

- **assertion** An *assertion* is a statement of a fact that should be true in normal program execution. We can use assertions to state our assumptions explicitly and to detect programming errors more easily.

- **serialization** Serialization allows whole objects, and object hierarchies, to be read and written in a single operation. Every object involved must be from a class that implements the **Serializable** interface.

Exercise 14.54 Add to the *address-book* project the ability to store multiple e-mail addresses in a **ContactDetails** object. All of these e-mail addresses should be valid keys. Use assertions and JUnit testing through all stages of this process to provide maximum confidence in the final version.

> ## Main concepts discussed in this chapter:
>
> - discovering classes
> - CRC cards
> - designing interfaces
> - patterns
>
> ## Java constructs discussed in this chapter:
>
> (No new Java constructs are introduced in this chapter.)

In previous chapters of this book, we have described how to write good classes. We have discussed how to design them, how to make them maintainable and robust, and how to make them interact. All of this is important, but we have omitted one aspect of the task: finding the classes.

In all our previous examples, we assumed that we more or less know what the classes are that we should use to solve our problems. In a real software project, deciding what classes to use to implement a solution to a problem can be one of the most difficult tasks. In this chapter, we discuss this aspect of the development process.

These initial steps of developing a software system are generally referred to as *analysis and design*. We analyze the problem, and then we design a solution. The first step of design will be at a higher level than the class design discussed in Chapter 8. We will think about what classes we should create to solve our problem, and how exactly they should interact. Once we have a solution to this problem, then we can continue with the design of individual classes and start thinking about their implementation.

15.1 Analysis and design

Analysis and design of software systems is a large and complex problem area. Discussing it in detail is far outside the scope of this book. Many different methodologies have been described in the literature and are used in practice for this task. In this chapter, we aim only to give an introduction to the problems encountered in the process.

We will use a fairly simple method to address these tasks, which serves well for relatively small problems. To discover initial classes, we use the *verb/noun method*. Then we will use *CRC cards* to perform the initial application design.

15.1.1 The verb/noun method

This method is all about identifying classes and objects, and the associations and interactions between them. The nouns in a human language describe "things," such as people, buildings, and so on. The verbs describe "actions," such as writing, eating, etc. From these natural-language concepts, we can see that, in a description of a programming problem, the nouns will often correspond to classes and objects, whereas the verbs will correspond to the things those objects do—that is, to methods. We do not need a very long description to be able to illustrate this technique. The description typically needs to be only a few paragraphs in length.

The example we will use to discuss this process is the design of a cinema booking system.

15.1.2 The cinema booking example

This time, we will not start by extending an existing project. We now assume that we are in a situation where it is our task to create a new application from scratch. The task is to create a system that can be used by a company operating cinemas to handle bookings of seats for movie screenings. People often call in advance to reserve seats. The application should, then, be able to find empty seats for a requested screening and reserve them for the customer.

We will assume that we have had several meetings with the cinema operators, during which they have described to us the functionality they expect from the system. (Understanding what the expected functionality is, describing it, and agreeing about it with a client is a significant problem in itself. This, however, is outside the scope of this book and can be studied in other courses and other books.)

Here is the description we wrote for our cinema booking system:

> *The cinema booking system should store seat bookings for multiple theaters. Each theater has seats arranged in rows. Customers can reserve seats and are given a row number and a seat number. They may request bookings of several adjoining seats.*

> *Each booking is for a particular show (that is, the screening of a given movie at a certain time). Shows are at an assigned date and time and are scheduled for a theater where they are screened. The system stores the customer's telephone number.*

Given a reasonably clear description such as this, we can make a first attempt at discovering classes and methods by identifying the nouns and verbs in the text.

15.1.3 Discovering classes

The first step in identifying the classes is to go through the description and mark all the nouns and verbs in the text. Doing this, we find the following nouns and verbs. (The nouns are shown in the order in which they appear in the text; verbs are shown attached to the nouns they refer to.)

Nouns	Verbs
cinema booking system	*stores* (seat bookings)
	stores (telephone number)
seat booking	
theater	*has* (seats)
seat	
row	
customer	*reserves* (seats)
	is given (row number, seat number)
	requests (seat booking)
row number	
seat number	
show	*is scheduled* (in theater)
movie	
date	
time	
telephone number	

The nouns we identified here give us a first approximation for classes in our system. As a first cut, we can use one class for each noun. This is not an exact method; we might find later that we need a few additional classes or that some of our nouns are not needed. This, however, we will test a bit later. It is important not to exclude any nouns straight away; we do not yet have enough information to make an informed decision.

When we do this exercise with students, some students immediately leave out some nouns. For example, a student leaves out the noun *row* from the previous description. When questioned about this, students often say: "Well, that's just a number, so I just use an **int**. That doesn't need a class." It is really important at this stage not to do this. We really do not have enough information at this point to decide whether *row* should be an **int** or a class. We can make this decision only much later. For now, we just go through the paragraph mechanically, picking out *all* nouns. We make no judgments yet about which are "good ones" and which are not.

You might note that all of the nouns have been written in their singular form. It is typical that the names of classes are singular rather than plural. For instance, we would always choose to define a class as **Cinema** rather than **Cinemas**. This is because the multiplicity is achieved by creating multiple instances of a class.

> **Exercise 15.1** Review projects from earlier chapters in this book. Are there any cases of a class name being a plural name? If so, are those situations justified for a particular reason?

15.1.4 Using CRC cards

The next step in our design process is to work out interactions between our classes. In order to do this, we shall use a method called *CRC cards*.[1]

CRC stands for Class/Responsibilities/Collaborators. The idea is to take cardboard cards (normal index cards do a good job) and use one card for each class. It is important for this activity to do this using real, physical cards, not just a computer or a single sheet of paper. Each card is divided into three areas: one area at the top left, where the name of the class is written; one area below this, to note responsibilities of the class; and one area to the right for writing collaborators of this class (classes that this one uses). Figure 15.1 illustrates the layout of a CRC card.

Figure 15.1

A CRC card

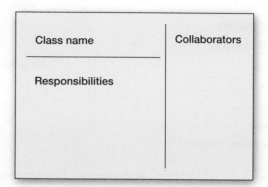

Exercise 15.2 Make CRC cards for the classes in the cinema booking system. At this stage, you need only fill in the class names.

15.1.5 Scenarios

Concept

Scenarios (also known as "use cases") can be used to get an understanding of the inter-actions in a system.

Now we have a first approximation of the classes needed in our system, and a physical representation of them on CRC cards. In order to figure out necessary interactions between the classes in our system, we play through *scenarios*. A scenario is an example of an activity that the system has to carry out or support. Scenarios are also referred to as *use cases*. We do not use that term here because it is often used to denote a more formal way of describing scenarios.

Playing through scenarios is best done in a group. Each group member is assigned one class (or a small number of classes), and that person plays their role by saying out loud what the class is currently doing. While the scenario is played through, the person records on the CRC card everything that is found out about the class in action: what its responsibilities should be and which other classes it collaborates with.

---

[1] CRC cards were first described in a paper by Kent Beck and Ward Cunningham, titled *A Laboratory For Teaching Object-Oriented Thinking*. This paper is worth reading as information supplemental to this chapter. You can find it online at **http://c2.com/doc/oopsla89/paper.html** or by doing a web search for its title.

We start with a simple example scenario:

> A customer calls the cinema and wants to make a reservation for a seats tonight to watch the classic movie *The Shawshank Redemption*. The cinema employee starts using the booking system to find and reserve two seats.

Because the human user interacts with the booking system (represented by the **Cinema BookingSystem** class), this is where the scenario starts. Here is what might happen next:

- The user (the cinema employee) wants to find all showings of *The Shawshank Redemption* that are on tonight. So we can note on the **CinemaBookingSystem** CRC card, as a responsibility: *Can find shows by title and day*. We can also record class **Show** as a collaborator.

- We have to ask ourselves: How does the system find the show? Who does it ask? One solution might be that the **CinemaBookingSystem** stores a collection of shows. This gives us an additional class: the collection. (This might be implemented later by using an **ArrayList**, a **LinkedList**, a **HashSet**, or some other form of collection with additional methods appropriate to showings. We can make that decision later; for now, we just note this as a **ShowCollection**.) This is an example of how we might introduce additional classes during the playing of scenarios. It might happen every now and then that we have to add classes for implementation reasons that we initially overlooked. We add to the responsibilities of the **CinemaBookingSystem** card: *Stores collection of shows*. And we add **ShowCollection** to the collaborators.

> **Exercise 15.3** Make a CRC card for the newly identified **ShowCollection** class, and add it to your system.

- We assume that three shows come up: one at 5:30 p.m., one at 9:00 p.m., and one at 11:30 p.m. The employee informs the customer of the times, and the customer chooses the one at 9:00 p.m. So the employee wants to check the details of that show (whether it is sold out, which theater it runs at, etc.). Thus, in our system, the **CinemaBooking-System** must be able to retrieve and display the show's details. Play this through. The person playing the booking system should ask the person playing the show to tell them the required details. Then we note on the card for **CinemaBookingSystem**: *Retrieves and displays show details*, and on the **Show** card you write: *Provides details about theater and number of free seats*.

- Assume that there are plenty of free seats. The customer chooses seats 13 and 14 in row 12. The employee makes that reservation. We note on the **CinemaBookingSystem** card: *Accepts seat reservations from user*.

- We now have to play through exactly how the seat reservation works. A seat reservation is clearly attached to a particular show, so the **CinemaBookingSystem** should probably tell the show about the reservation; it delegates the actual task of making the reservation to the **Show** object. We can note for the **Show** class: *Can reserve seats*. (You may have noticed that the notion of objects and classes is blurred when playing through CRC scenarios. In effect, the person representing a class is representing its instances too. This is intentional and not usually a problem.)

- Now it is the **Show** class's turn. It has received a request to reserve a seat. What exactly does it do? To be able to store seat reservations, it must have a representation of the seats in the theater. So we assume that each show has a link to a **Theater** object. (Note this on the card: *Stores theater*. This is also a collaborator.) The theater should probably know about the exact number and arrangement of seats it has. (We can also note in the back of our heads, or on a separate piece of paper, that each show must have its own instance of the **Theater** object, because several shows can be scheduled for the same **Theater** and reserving a seat in one does not reserve the same seat for another show. This is something to look out for when **Show** objects are created. We have to keep this in mind so that later, when we play through the scenario of *Scheduling a new show*, we remember to create a theater instance for each show.) The way a show deals with reserving a seat is probably by passing this reservation request on to the theater.

- Now the theater has accepted a request to make a reservation. (Note this on the card: *Accepts reservation request*.) How does it deal with it? The theater could have a collection of seats in it. Or it could have a collection of rows (each row being a separate object), and rows, in turn, hold seats. Which of these alternatives is better? Thinking ahead about other possible scenarios, we might decide to go with the idea of storing rows. If, for example, a customer requests four seats together in the same row, it might be easier to find four adjacent seats if we have them all arranged by rows. We note on the **Theater** card: *Stores rows*. **Row** is now a collaborator.

- We note on the **Row** class: *Stores collection of seats*. And then we note a new collaborator: **Seat**.

- Getting back to the **Theater** class, we have not yet worked out exactly how it should react to the seat reservation request. Let us assume it does two things: find the requested row and then make a reservation request with the seat number to the **Row** object.

- Next, we note on the **Row** card: *Accepts reservation request for seat*. It must then find the right **Seat** object (we can note that as a responsibility: *Can find seats by number*) and can make a reservation for that seat. It would do so by telling the **Seat** object that it is now reserved.

- We can now add to the **Seat** card: *Accepts reservations*. The seat itself can remember whether it has been reserved. We note on the **Seat** card: *Stores reservation status (free/ reserved)*.

> **Exercise 15.4** Play this scenario through on your cards (with a group of people, if possible). Add any other information you feel was left out in this description.

Should the seat also store information about who has reserved it? It could store the name of the customer or the telephone number. Or maybe we should create a **Customer** object as soon as someone makes a reservation, and store the **Customer** object with the seat once the seat has been reserved? These are interesting questions, and we will try to work out the best solution by playing through more scenarios.

This was just the first, simple scenario. We need to play through many more scenarios to get a better understanding of how the system should work.

Playing through scenarios works best when a group of people sit around a table and move the cards around on it. Cards that cooperate closely can be placed close together to give an impression of the degree of coupling in the system.

Other scenarios to play through next would include the following:

- A customer requests five seats together. Work out exactly how five adjoining seats are found.

- A customer calls and says he forgot the seat numbers he was given for the reservation he made yesterday. Could you please look up the seat numbers again?

- A customer calls to cancel a reservation. He can give his name and the show, but has forgotten the seat numbers.

- A customer calls who already has a reservation. She wants to know whether she can reserve another seat next to the ones she already has.

- A show is canceled. The cinema wants to call all customers that have reserved a seat for that show.

These scenarios should give you a good understanding of the seat lookup and reservation part of the system. Then we need another group of scenarios: those dealing with setting up the theater, and scheduling shows. Here are some possible scenarios:

- The system has to be set up for a new cinema. The cinema has two theaters, each of a different size. Theater A has 26 rows with 18 seats each. Theater B has 32 rows. In this theater, the first six rows have 20 seats, the next 10 rows have 22 seats, and the other rows have 26 seats.

- A new movie is scheduled for screening. It will be screened for the next two weeks, three times each day (4:40 p.m., 6:30 p.m., and 8:30 p.m.). The shows have to be added to the system. All shows run in theater A.

> **Exercise 15.5** Play through these scenarios. Note on a separate piece of paper all the questions you have left unanswered. Make a record of all scenarios you have played through.

> **Exercise 15.6** What other scenarios can you think of? Write them down, and then play them out.

Playing through scenarios takes some patience and some practice. It is important to spend enough time doing this. Playing through the scenarios mentioned here could take several hours.

It is very common for beginners to take shortcuts and not question and record every detail about the execution of a scenario. This is dangerous! We will soon move on to developing this system in Java, and if details are left unanswered, it is very likely that *ad hoc* decisions will be made at implementation time that could later turn out to be poor choices.

It is also common for beginners to forget some scenarios. Forgetting to think through a part of the system before starting the class design and implementation can cause a large amount of work later, when an already partially implemented system would have to be changed.

Doing this activity well, carefully stepping through all necessary steps, and recording steps in sufficient detail takes some practice and a lot of discipline. This exercise is harder than it looks and more important than you realize.

> **Exercise 15.7** Make a class design for an airport-control-system simulation. Use CRC cards and scenarios. Here is a description of the system:
>
> *The program is an airport simulation system. For our new airport, we need to know whether we can operate with two runways or whether we need three. The airport works as follows:*
>
> *There are multiple runways. Planes take off and land on runways. Air traffic controllers coordinate the traffic and give planes permission to take off or land. The controllers sometimes give permission right away, but sometimes they tell planes to wait. Planes must keep a certain distance from one another. The purpose of the program is to simulate the airport in operation.*

15.2 Class design

Now it is time for the next big step: moving from CRC cards to Java classes. During the CRC card exercise, you should have gained a good understanding of how your application is structured and how your classes cooperate to solve the program's tasks. You may have come across cases where you had to introduce additional classes (this is often the case with classes that represent internal data structures), and you may have noticed that you have a card for a class that was never used. If the latter is the case, this card can now be removed.

Recognizing the classes for the implementation is now trivial. The cards show us the complete set of classes we need. Deciding on the interface of each class (that is, the set of public methods that a class should have) is a bit harder, but we have made an important step toward that as well. If the playing of the scenarios was done well, then the responsibilities noted for each class describe the class's public methods (and maybe some of the instance fields). The responsibilities of each class should be evaluated according to the class design principles discussed in Chapter 8: Responsibility-Driven Design, Coupling, and Cohesion.

15.2.1 Designing class interfaces

Before starting to code our application in Java, we can once more use the cards to make another step toward the final design by translating the informal descriptions into method calls and adding parameters.

To arrive at more formal descriptions, we can now play through the scenarios again, this time talking in terms of method calls, parameters, and return values. The logic and the structure of the application should not change any more, but we try to note complete information about method signatures and instance fields. We do this on a new set of cards.

> **Exercise 15.8** Make a new set of CRC cards for the classes you have identified. Play through the scenarios again. This time, note exact method names for each method you call from another class, and specify in detail (with type and name) all parameters that are passed and the methods' return values. The method signatures are written on the CRC card instead of the responsibilities. On the back of the card, note the instance fields that each class holds.

Once we have done the exercise described above, writing each class's interface is easy. We can translate directly from the cards into Java. Typically, all classes should be created and *method stubs* for all public methods should be written. A method stub is a placeholder for the method that has the correct signature and an empty method body.[2]

Many students find doing this in detail tedious. At the end of the project, however, you will hopefully come to appreciate the value of these activities. Many software development teams have realized after the fact that time saved at the design stage had to be spent many times over to fix mistakes or omissions that were not discovered early enough.

Inexperienced programmers often view the writing of the code as the "real programming." Doing the initial design is seen as, if not superfluous, at least annoying, and people cannot wait to get it over with so that the "real work" can start. This is a very misguided picture.

The initial design is one of the most important parts of the project. You should plan to spend at least as much time working on the design as on the implementation. Application design is not something that comes before the programming—it *is* (the most important part of) programming!

Mistakes in the code itself can later be fixed fairly easily. Mistakes in the overall design can, at best, be expensive to put right and, at worst, be fatal to the whole application. In unlucky cases, they can be almost unfixable (short of starting all over again).

---

[2] If you wish, you can include trivial return statements in the bodies of methods with non-**void** return types. Just return a **null** value for object-returning methods and a zero, or **false**, value for primitive types.

15.2.2 User interface design

One part that we have left out of the discussion so far is the design of the user interface.[3] At some stage, we have to decide in detail what users see on the screen and how they interact with our system.

In a well-designed application, this is quite independent of the underlying logic of the application, so it can be done independently of designing the class structure for the rest of the project. As we saw in the previous chapters, BlueJ gives us the means of interacting with our application before a final user interface is available, so we can choose to work on the internal structure first.

The user interface may be a GUI (graphical user interface) with menus and buttons, it can be text based, or we can decide to run the application using the BlueJ method-call mechanism. Maybe the system runs over a network, and the user interface is presented in a web browser on a different machine.

For now, we shall ignore the user-interface design and use BlueJ method invocation to work with our program.

15.3 Documentation

After identifying the classes and their interfaces, and before starting to implement the methods of a class, the interface should be documented. This involves writing a class comment and method comments for each class in the project. These should be described in sufficient detail to identify the overall purpose of each class and method.

Along with analysis and design, documentation is a further area that is often neglected by beginners. It is not easy for inexperienced programmers to see why documentation is so important. The reason is that inexperienced programmers usually work on projects that only have a handful of classes and are written in the span of a few weeks or months. A programmer can get away with bad documentation when working on these mini-projects.

However, even experienced programmers often wonder how it is possible to write the documentation before the implementation. This is because they fail to appreciate that good documentation focuses on high-level issues such as what a class or method does rather than on low-level issues such as exactly how it is done. This is usually symptomatic of viewing the implementation as being more important than the design.

If a software developer wants to progress to more interesting problems and starts to work professionally on real-life applications, it is not unusual to work with dozens of other people on an application over several years. The *ad hoc* solution of just "having the documentation in your head" does not work anymore.

---

[3] Note carefully the double meaning of the term *designing interfaces* here! Above, we were talking about the interfaces of single classes (a set of public methods); now, we talk about the *user interface*—what the user sees on screen to interact with the application. Both are very important issues, and unfortunately the term *interface* is used for both.

> **Exercise 15.9** Create a BlueJ project for the cinema booking system. Create the necessary classes. Create method stubs for all methods.
>
> **Exercise 15.10** Document all classes and methods. If you have worked in a group, assign responsibilities for classes to different group members. Use the `javadoc` format for comments, with appropriate `javadoc` tags to document the details.

15.4 Cooperation

> **Pair programming** Implementation of classes is traditionally done alone. Most programmers work on their own when writing the code, and other people are brought in only after the implementation is finished, to test or review the code.
>
> More recently, pair programming has been suggested as an alternative that is intended to produce better-quality code (code with better structure and fewer bugs). Pair programming is also one of the elements of a technique known as *Extreme Programming*. Do a web search for "pair programming" or "extreme programming" to find out more.

Software development is usually done in teams. A clean object-oriented approach provides strong support for teamwork, because it allows for the separation of the problem into loosely coupled components (classes) that can be implemented independently.

Although the initial design work was best done in a group, it is now time to split it up. If the definition of the class interfaces and the documentation was done well, it should be possible to implement the classes independently. Classes can now be assigned to programmers, who can work on them alone or in pairs.

In the remainder of this chapter, we shall not discuss the implementation phase of the cinema booking system in detail. That phase largely involves the sorts of task we have been doing throughout this book in previous chapters, and we hope that by now readers can determine for themselves how to continue from here.

15.5 Prototyping

Instead of designing and then building the complete application in one giant leap, *prototyping* can be used to investigate parts of a system.

A prototype is a version of the application where one part is simulated in order to experiment with other parts. You may, for example, implement a prototype to test a graphical user interface. In that case, the logic of the application may not be properly implemented. Instead, we would write simple implementations for those methods that simulate the task. For example, when calling a method to find a free seat in the cinema system, a method could always return *seat 3, row 15* instead of actually implementing the search. Prototyping allows us to

Concept

Prototyping is the construction of a partially working system in which some functions of the application are simulated. It serves to provide an understanding early in the development process of how the system will work.

quickly develop an executable (but not fully functional) system so that we can investigate parts of the application in practice.

Prototypes are also useful for single classes to aid a team development process. Often when different team members work on different classes, not all classes take the same amount of time to be completed. In some cases, a missing class can hold up continuation of development and testing of other classes. In those cases, it can be beneficial to write a class prototype. The prototype has implementations of all method stubs, but instead of containing full, final implementations, the prototype only simulates the functionality. Writing a prototype should be possible quickly, and development of client classes can then continue using the prototype until the class is implemented.

As we discuss in Section 15.6, one additional benefit of prototyping is that it can give the developers insights into issues and problems that were not considered at an earlier stage.

Exercise 15.11 Outline a prototype for your cinema-system example. Which of the classes should be implemented first, and which should remain in prototype stage?

Exercise 15.12 Implement your cinema-system prototype.

15.6 Software growth

Several models exist for how software should be built. One of the most commonly known is often referred to as the *waterfall model* (because activity progresses from one level to the next, like water in a cascading waterfall—there is no going back).

15.6.1 Waterfall model

In the waterfall model, several phases of software development are done in a fixed sequence:

■ analysis of the problem

■ design of the software

■ implementation of the software components

■ unit testing

■ integration testing

■ delivery of the system to the client

If any phase fails, we might have to step back to the previous phase to fix it (for example, if testing shows failure, we go back to implementation), but there is never a plan to revisit earlier phases.

This is probably the most traditional, conservative model of software development, and it has been in widespread use for a long time. However, numerous problems have been discovered with this model over the years. Two of the main flaws are that it assumes that developers understand the full extent of the system's functionality in detail from the start, and that the system does not change after delivery.

In practice, both assumptions are typically not true. It is quite common that the design of a system's functionality is not perfect at the start. This is often because the client, who knows the problem domain, does not know much about computing, and because the software engineers, who know how to program, have only limited knowledge of the problem domain.

15.6.2 Iterative development

One possibility to address the problems of the waterfall model is to use early prototyping and frequent client interaction in the development process. Prototypes of the systems are built that do not do much, but give an impression of what the system would look like and what it would do, and clients comment regularly on the design and functionality. This leads to a more circular process than the waterfall model. Here, the software development iterates several times through an *analysis/design/prototype -implementation–client-feedback* cycle.

Another approach is captured in the notion that good software is not designed, it is *grown*. The idea behind this is to design a small and clean system initially and get it into a working state in which it can be used by end users. Then additional features are gradually added (the software grows) in a controlled manner, and "finished" states (meaning states in which the software is completely usable and can be delivered to clients) are reached repeatedly and fairly frequently.

In reality, growing software is, of course, not a contradiction to designing software. Every growth step is carefully designed. What the software growth model does not try to do is design the complete software system right from the start. Even more, the notion of a complete software system does not exist at all!

The traditional waterfall model has as its goal the delivery of a complete system. The software growth model assumes that complete systems that are used indefinitely in an unchanged state do not exist. There are only two things that can happen to a software system: either it is continuously improved and adapted, or it will disappear.

This discussion is central to this book, because it strongly influences how we view the tasks and skills required of a programmer or software engineer. You might be able to tell that the authors of this book strongly favor the iterative development model over the waterfall model.[4]

As a consequence, certain tasks and skills become much more important than they would be in the waterfall model. Software maintenance, code reading (rather than just writing),

---

[4] An excellent book describing the problems of software development and some possible approaches to solutions is *The Mythical Man-Month* by Frederick P. Brooks Jr., Addison-Wesley. Even though the original edition is 40 years old, it makes for entertaining and very enlightening reading.

designing for extensibility, documentation, coding for understandability, and many other issues we have mentioned in this book take their importance from the fact that we know there will be others coming after us who have to adapt and extend our code.

Viewing a piece of software as a continuously growing, changing, adapting entity, rather than a static piece of text that is written and preserved like a novel, determines our views about how good code should be written. All the techniques we have discussed throughout this book work toward this.

Exercise 15.13 In which ways might the cinema booking system be adapted or extended in the future? Which changes are more likely than others? Write down a list of possible future changes.

Exercise 15.14 Are there any other organizations that might use booking systems similar to the one we have discussed? What significant differences exist between the systems?

Exercise 15.15 Do you think it would be possible to design a "generic" booking system that could be adapted or customized for use in a wide range of different organizations with booking needs? If you were to create such a system, at what point in the development process of the cinema system would you introduce changes? Or would you throw that one away and start again from scratch?

15.7 Using design patterns

In earlier chapters, we have discussed in detail some techniques for reusing some of our work and making our code more understandable to others. So far, a large part of these discussions has remained at the level of source code in single classes.

> **Concept**
>
> A **design pattern** is a description of a common computing problem and a description of a small set of classes and their interaction structure that help to solve that problem.

As we become more experienced and move on to design larger software systems, the implementation of single classes is not the most difficult problem any more. The structure of the overall system—the complex relationships between classes—becomes harder to design and to understand than the code of individual classes.

It is a logical step that we should try to achieve the same goals for class structures that we attempted for source code. We want to reuse good bits of work, and we want to enable others to understand what we have done.

At the level of class structures, both these goals can be served by using *design patterns*. A design pattern describes a common problem that occurs regularly in software development and then describes a general solution to that problem that can be used in many different contexts. For software design patterns, the solution is typically a description of a small set of classes and their interactions.

Design patterns help in our task in two ways. First, they document good solutions to problems so that these solutions can be reused later for similar problems. The reuse in this case is not at the level of source code, but at the level of class structures.

Second, design patterns have names and thus establish a vocabulary that helps software designers talk about their designs. When experienced designers discuss the structure of an application, one might say, "I think we should use a Singleton here." *Singleton* is the name of a widely known design pattern, so if both designers are familiar with the pattern, being able to talk about it at this level saves explanation of a lot of detail. Thus, the pattern language introduced by commonly known design patterns introduces another level of abstraction, one that allows us to cope with complexity in ever-more-complex systems.

Software design patterns were made popular by a book published in 1995 that describes a set of patterns, their applications, and benefits.[5] This book is still today one of the most important works about design patterns. Here, we do not attempt to give a complete overview of design patterns. Rather, we discuss a small number of patterns to give readers an impression of the benefits of using design patterns, and then we leave it up to the reader to continue the study of patterns in other literature.

15.7.1 Structure of a pattern

Descriptions of patterns are usually recorded using a template that contains some minimum information. A pattern description is not only information about a structure of some classes, but also includes a description of the problem(s) this pattern addresses and competing forces for or against use of the pattern.

A description of a pattern includes at least:

- a **name** that can be used to conveniently talk about the pattern

- a description of the **problem** that the pattern addresses (often split into sections such as *intent*, *motivation*, and *applicability*)

- a description of the **solution** (often listing *structure*, *participants*, and *collaborations*)

- the **consequences** of using the pattern, including results and trade-offs

In the following section, we shall briefly discuss some commonly used patterns.

15.7.2 Decorator

The *Decorator* pattern deals with the problem of adding functionality to an existing object. We assume that we want an object that responds to the same method calls (has the same interface) as the existing object, but has added or altered behavior. We may also want to add to the existing interface.

One way this could be done is by using inheritance. A subclass may override the implementation of methods and add additional methods. But using inheritance is a static solution: once created, objects cannot change their behavior.

A more dynamic solution is the use of a Decorator object. The Decorator is an object that encloses an existing object and can be used instead of the original (it usually implements

---

[5] *Design Patterns: Elements of Reusable Object-Oriented Software* by Erich Gamma, Richard Helm, Ralph Johnson, and John Vlissides, Addison-Wesley, 1995.

Figure 15.2
Structure of the
decorator pattern

the same interface). Clients then communicate with the Decorator instead of with the original object directly (without a need to know about this substitution). The Decorator passes the method calls on to the enclosed object, but it may perform additional actions. We can find an example in the Java input/output library. There, a **BufferedReader** is used as a Decorator for a **Reader** (Figure 15.2). The **BufferedReader** implements the same interface and can be used instead of an unbuffered **Reader**, but it adds to the basic behavior of a **Reader**. In contrast to using inheritance, decorators can be added to existing objects.

15.7.3 Singleton

A common situation in many programs is to have an object of which there should be only a single instance. In our *world-of-zuul* game, for instance, we want only a single parser. If we write a software development environment, we might want only a single compiler or a single debugger.

The *Singleton* pattern ensures that only one instance will be created from a class, and it provides unified access to it. In Java, a Singleton can be defined by making the constructor private. This ensures that it cannot be called from outside the class, and thus client classes cannot create new instances. We can then write code in the Singleton class itself to create a single instance and provide access to it (Code 15.1 illustrates this for a **Parser** class).

Code 15.1
The Singleton
pattern

```java
public class Parser
{
    private static Parser instance = new Parser();

    public static Parser getInstance()
    {
        return instance;
    }

    private Parser()
    {
        ...
    }
}
```

In this pattern:

- The constructor is private so that instances can be created only by the class itself. This has to be in a static part of the class (initializations of static fields or static methods), because no instance will otherwise exist.

- A private static field is defined and initialized with the (sole) instance of the parser.

- A static **getInstance** method is defined, which provides access to the single instance.

Clients of the Singleton can now use that static method to gain access to the parser object:

```
Parser parser = Parser.getInstance();
```

In fact, Java offers an even easier way to obtain the fundamental features of a singleton —an enum with a single value (Code 15.2).

Code 15.2

A Singleton definition using a Java enum

```
public enum Parser
{
    INSTANCE;

    Parser-specific methods added here.

}
```

The singleton instance would then be accessed as **Parser.INSTANCE**. Since arbitrary additional functionality can be included in an enum definition in the same way as in a class, this approach, rather than a hand-crafted approach, is well worth considering in Java.

15.7.4 Factory method

The *Factory method* pattern provides an interface for creating objects, but lets subclasses decide which specific class of object is created. Typically, the client expects a superclass or an interface of the actual object's dynamic type, and the factory method provides specializations.

Iterators of collections are an example of this technique. If we have a variable of type **Collection**, we can ask it for an **Iterator** object (using the **iterator** method) and then work with that iterator (Code 15.3). The **iterator** method in this example is the Factory method.

Code 15.3

A use of the Factory method

```
public void process(Collection<Type> coll)
{
    Iterator<Type> it = coll.iterator();
    ...
}
```

From the client's point of view (in the code shown in Code 15.3), we are dealing with objects of type **Collection** and **Iterator**. In reality, the (dynamic) type of the collection may be **ArrayList**, in which case the **iterator** method returns an object of type **ArrayList-Iterator**. Or it may be a **HashSet**, and **iterator** returns a **HashSetIterator**. The Factory method is specialized in subclasses to return specialized instances to the "official" return type.

We can make good use of this pattern in our *foxes-and-rabbits* simulation from Chapter 12, to decouple the **Simulator** class from the specific animal classes. (Remember: In our version, **Simulator** was coupled to classes **Fox** and **Rabbit**, because it creates the initial instances.) Instead, we can introduce an interface **ActorFactory** and classes implementing this interface for each actor (for example, **FoxFactory** and **RabbitFactory**). The **Simulator** would simply store a collection of **ActorFactory** objects, and it would ask each of them to produce a number of actors. Each factory would, of course, produce a different kind of actor, but the **Simulator** talks to them via the **ActorFactory** interface.

15.7.5 Observer

In the discussions of several of the projects in this book, we have tried to separate the internal model of the application from the way it is presented on screen (the view). The *Observer* pattern provides one way of achieving this model/view separation.

More generally, the Observer pattern defines a one-to-many relationship so that when one object changes its state, many others can be notified. It achieves this with a very low degree of coupling between the observers and the observed object.

The Observer pattern not only supports a decoupled view on the model, but it also allows for multiple different views (either as alternatives or simultaneously). As an example, we can again use our *foxes-and-rabbits* simulation.

In the simulation, we presented the animal populations on screen in a two-dimensional animated grid. There are other possibilities. We might have preferred to show the population as a graph of population numbers along a timeline, or as an animated bar chart (Figure 15.3). We might even like to see all representations at the same time.

Figure 15.3

Multiple views of one subject

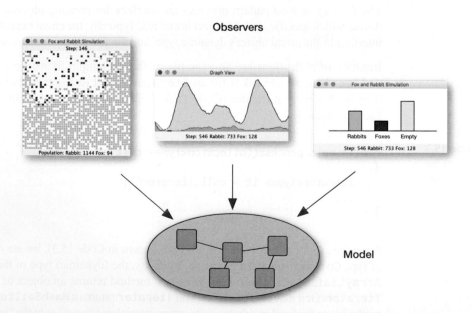

Figure 15.4
Structure of the
Observer pattern

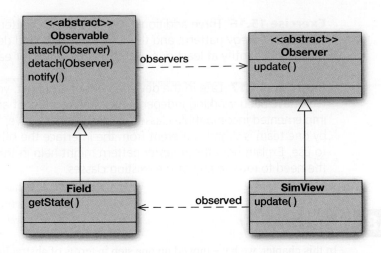

For the Observer pattern, we use two types: **Observable** and **Observer**.[6] The observable entity (the **Field** in our simulation) extends the **Observable** class, and the observer (**SimulatorView**) implements the **Observer** interface (Figure 15.4).

The **Observable** class provides methods for observers to attach themselves to the observed entity. It ensures that the observers' **update** method is called whenever the observed entity (the field) invokes its inherited **notify** method. The actual observers (the viewers) can then get a new, updated state from the field and redisplay.

The Observer pattern can also be used for problems other than a model/view separation. It can always be applied when the state of one or more objects depends on the state of another object.

15.7.6 Pattern summary

Discussing design patterns and their applications in detail is beyond the scope of this book. Here, we have presented only a brief idea of what design patterns are, and we have given an informal description of some of the more common patterns.

We hope, however, that this discussion serves to show where to go from here. Once we understand how to create good implementations of single classes with well-defined functionality, we can concentrate on deciding what kinds of classes we should have in our application and how they should cooperate. Good solutions are not always obvious, so design patterns describe structures that have proven useful over and over again for solving recurring classes of problems. They help us in creating good class structures.

The more experienced you get as a software developer, the more time you will spend thinking about higher-level structure rather than about implementation of single methods.

---

[6] In the Java **java.util** package, **Observer** is actually an interface with a single method, **update**.

Exercise 15.16 Three additional commonly used patterns are the *State* pattern, the *Strategy* pattern, and the *Visitor* pattern. Find descriptions of each of these, and identify at least one example application for each.

Exercise 15.17 Late in the development of a project, you find that two teams who have been working independently on two parts of an application have implemented incompatible classes. The interface of several classes implemented by one team is slightly different from the interface the other team is expecting to use. Explain how the *Adapter* pattern might help in this situation by avoiding the need to rewrite any of the existing classes.

15.8 Summary

In this chapter, we have moved up one step in terms of abstraction levels, away from thinking about the design of single classes (or cooperation between two classes) and toward the design of an application as a whole. Central to the design of an object-oriented software system is the decision about the classes to use for its implementation and the communication structures between these classes.

Some classes are fairly obvious and easy to discover. We have used as a starting point a method of identifying nouns and verbs in a textual description of the problem. After discovering the classes, we can use CRC cards and played-out scenarios to design the dependences and communication details between classes, and to flesh out details about each class's responsibilities. For less-experienced designers, it helps to play through scenarios in a group.

CRC cards can be used to refine the design down to the definition of method names and their parameters. Once this has been achieved, classes with method stubs can be coded in Java and the classes' interfaces can be documented.

Following an organized process such as this one serves several purposes. It ensures that potential problems with early design ideas are discovered before much time is invested in implementation. It also enables programmers to work on the implementation of several classes independently, without having to wait for the implementation of one class to be finished before implementation of another can begin.

Flexible, extensible class structures are not always easy to design. Design patterns are used to document generally good structures that have proven useful in the implementation of different classes of problems. Through the study of design patterns, a software engineer can learn a lot about good application structures and improve application design skills.

The larger a problem, the more important is a good application structure. The more experienced a software engineer becomes, the more time he or she will spend designing application structures rather than just writing code.

Terms introduced in this chapter:

> **analysis and design, verb/noun method, CRC card, scenario, use case, method stub, design pattern**

Concept summary

- **verb/noun** Classes in a system roughly correspond to nouns in the system's description. Methods correspond to verbs.

- **scenarios** Scenarios (also known as "use cases") can be used to get an understanding of the interactions in a system.

- **prototyping** Prototyping is the construction of a partially working system in which some functions of the application are simulated. It serves to provide an understanding early in the development process of how the system will work.

- **design pattern** A design pattern is a description of a common computing problem, and a description of a small set of classes and their interaction structure that help to solve that problem.

Exercise 15.18 Assume that you have a school management system for your school. In it, there is a class called **Database** (a fairly central class) that holds objects of type **Student**. Each student has an address that is held in an **Address** object (i.e., each **Student** object holds a reference to an **Address** object).

Now, from the **Database** class, you need to get access to a student's street, city, and zip code. The **Address** class has accessor methods for these. For the design of the **Student** class, you now have two choices:

Either you implement **getStreet**, **getCity**, and **getZipCode** methods in the **Student** class—which just pass the method call on to the **Address** object and hand the result back—or you implement a **getAddress** method in **Student** that returns the complete **Address** object to the **Database** and lets the **Database** object call the **Address** object's methods directly.

Which of these alternatives is better? Why? Make a class diagram for each situation and list arguments either way.

CHAPTER

16

A Case Study

> **Main concepts discussed in this chapter:**
>
> ■ whole-application development
>
> **Java constructs discussed in this chapter:**
>
> (No new Java constructs are introduced in this chapter.)

In this chapter, we draw together many of the object-oriented principles that we have introduced in this book by presenting an extended case study. We shall take the study from the initial discussion of a problem, through class discovery, design, and an iterative process of implementation and testing. Unlike previous chapters, it is not our intention here to introduce any major new topics. Rather, we are seeking to reinforce those topics that have been covered in the second half of the book, such as inheritance, abstraction techniques, error handling, and application design.

16.1 The case study

The case study we will be using is the development of a model for a taxi company. The company is considering whether to expand its operations into a new part of a city. It operates taxis and shuttles. Taxis drop their passengers at their target locations before taking on new passengers. Shuttles may collect several passengers from different locations on the same trip, taking them to similar locations (such as collecting several guests from different hotels and taking them to different terminals at the airport). Based on estimates of the number of potential customers in the new area, the company wishes to know whether an expansion would be profitable, and how many cabs it would need in the new location in order to operate effectively.

16.1.1 The problem description

The following paragraph presents an informal description of the taxi company's operating procedures, arrived at following several meetings with them.

The company operates both individual taxis and shuttles. The taxis are used to transport an individual (or small group) from one location to another. The shuttles are used to pick up individuals from different locations and transport them to their several destinations. When the company receives a call from an individual, hotel, entertainment venue, or tourist organization, it tries to schedule a vehicle to pick up the fare. If it has no free vehicles, it does not operate any form of queuing system. When a vehicle arrives at a pickup location, the driver notifies the company. Similarly, when a passenger is dropped off at their destination, the driver notifies the company.

As we suggested in Chapter 12, one of the common purposes of modeling is to help us learn something about the situation being modeled. It is useful to identify at an early stage what we wish to learn, because the resulting goals may well have an influence on the design we produce. For instance, if we are seeking to answer questions about the profitability of running taxis in this area, then we must ensure that we can obtain information from the model that will help us assess profitability. Two issues we ought to consider, therefore, are: how often potential customers are lost because no vehicle is available to collect them, and, at the opposite extreme, how much time taxis remain idle for lack of passengers. These influences are not found in the basic description of how the taxi company normally operates, but they do represent scenarios that will have to be played through when we draw up the design.

So we might add the following paragraph to the description:

The system stores details about passenger requests that cannot be satisfied. It also provides details of how much time vehicles spend in each of the following activities: carrying passengers, going to pickup locations, and being idle.

However, as we develop our model, we shall focus on just the original description of the company's operating procedures, and leave the additional features as exercises.

Exercise 16.1 Is there any additional data that you feel it would be useful to gather from the model? If so, add these requirements to the descriptions given above and use them in your own extensions to the project.

16.2   Analysis and design

As suggested in Chapter 15, we will start by seeking to identify the classes and interactions in the system's description, using the verb/noun method.

16.2.1 Discovering classes

The following (singular versions of) nouns are present in the description: company, taxi, shuttle, individual, location, destination, hotel, entertainment venue, tourist organization, vehicle, fare, pickup location, driver, and passenger.

The first point to note is that it would be a mistake to move straight from this list of nouns to a set of classes. Informal descriptions are rarely written in a way that suits that sort of direct mapping.

One refinement that is commonly needed in the list of nouns is to identify any *synonyms*: different words used for the same entity. For instance, "individual" and "fare" are both synonyms for "passenger."

A further refinement is to eliminate those entities that do not really need to be modeled in the system. For instance, the description identified various ways in which the taxi company might be contacted: by individuals, hotels, entertainment venues, and tourist organizations. Will it really be necessary to maintain these distinctions? The answer will depend upon the information we want from the model. We might wish to arrange discounts for hotels that provide large numbers of customers or send publicity material to entertainment venues that do not. If this level of detail is not required, then we can simplify the model by just "injecting" passengers into it according to some statistically reasonable pattern.

> **Exercise 16.2** Consider simplifying the number of nouns associated with the vehicles. Are "vehicle" and "taxi" synonyms in this context? Do we need to distinguish between "shuttle" and "taxi"? What about between the type of vehicle and "driver"? Justify your answers.
>
> **Exercise 16.3** Is it possible to eliminate any of the following as synonyms in this context: "location," "destination," and "pickup location"?
>
> **Exercise 16.4** Identify the nouns from any extensions you have added to the system, and make any necessary simplifications.

16.2.2 Using CRC cards

Figure 16.1 contains a summary of the noun and verb associations we are left with once some simplification has been performed on the original description. Each of the nouns should now be assigned to a CRC card, ready to have its responsibilities and collaborators identified.

Figure 16.1
Noun and verb associations in the taxi company

Nouns	Verbs
company	*operates taxis and shuttles*
	receives a call
	schedules a vehicle
taxi	*transports a passenger*
shuttle	*transports one or more passengers*
passenger	
location	
passenger-source	*calls the company*
vehicle	*picks up passenger*
	arrives at pickup location
	notifies company of arrival
	notifies company of drop-off

From that summary, it is clear that "taxi" and "shuttle" are distinct specializations of a more general vehicle class. The main distinction between a taxi and a shuttle is that a taxi is only ever concerned with picking up and transporting a single passenger or coherent group, but a shuttle deals with multiple *independent* passengers concurrently. The relationship between these two vehicles is suggestive of an inheritance hierarchy, where "taxi" and "shuttle" represent subtypes of vehicle.

Exercise 16.5 Create physical CRC cards for the nouns/classes identified in this section, in order to be able to work through the scenarios suggested by the project description.

Exercise 16.6 Do the same for any of your own extensions you wish to follow through in the next stage.

16.2.3 Scenarios

The taxi company does not actually represent a very complex application. We shall find that much of the total interaction in the system is explored by taking the fundamental scenario of trying to satisfy a passenger request to go from one location to another. In practice, this single scenario will be broken down into a number of steps that are followed in sequence, from the initial call to the final drop-off.

■ We have decided that a passenger source creates all new passenger objects for the system. So a responsibility of **PassengerSource** is *Create a passenger*, and a collaborator is **Passenger**.

■ The passenger source calls the taxi company to request a pickup for a passenger. We note **TaxiCompany** as a collaborator of **PassengerSource** and add *Request a pickup* as a responsibility. Correspondingly, we add to **TaxiCompany** a responsibility to *Receive a pickup request*. Associated with the request will be a passenger and a pickup location. So **TaxiCompany** has **Passenger** and **Location** as collaborators. When it calls the company with the request, the passenger source could pass the passenger and pickup location as separate objects. However, it is preferable to associate closely the pickup location with the passenger. So a collaborator of **Passenger** is **Location**, and a responsibility will be *Provide pickup location*.

■ From where does the passenger's pickup location originate? The pickup location and destination could be decided when the **Passenger** is created. So add to **Passenger-Source** the responsibility *Generate pickup and destination locations for a passenger*, with **Location** as a collaborator; and add to **Passenger** the responsibilities *Receive pickup and destination locations* and *Provide destination location*.

■ On receipt of a request, the **TaxiCompany** has a responsibility to *Schedule a vehicle*. This suggests that a further responsibility is *Store a collection of vehicles*, with **Collection** and **Vehicle** as collaborators. Because the request might fail—there may be no vehicles free—a success or failure indication should be returned to the passenger source.

■ There is no indication whether the company seeks to distinguish between taxis and shuttles when scheduling, so we do not need to take that aspect into account here.

However, a vehicle can be scheduled only if it is free. This means that a responsibility of **Vehicle** will be *Indicate whether free*.

- When a free vehicle has been identified, it must be directed to the pickup location. **TaxiCompany** has the responsibility *Direct vehicle to pickup*, with the corresponding responsibility in **Vehicle** being *Receive pickup location*. **Location** is added as a collaborator of **Vehicle**.

- On receipt of a pickup location, the behavior of taxis and shuttles may well differ. A taxi will have been free only if it was not already on its way to either a pickup or a destination location. So the responsibility of **Taxi** is *Go to pickup location*. In contrast, a shuttle has to deal with multiple passengers. When it receives a pickup location, it may have to choose between several possible alternative locations to head to next. So we add the responsibility to **Shuttle** to *Choose next target location*, with a **Collection** collaborator to maintain the set of possible target locations to choose from. The fact that a Vehicle moves between locations suggests that it has a responsibility to *Maintain a current location*.

- On arrival at a pickup location, a **Vehicle** must *Notify the company of pickup arrival*, with **TaxiCompany** as a collaborator; **TaxiCompany** must *Receive notification of pickup arrival*. In real life, a taxi meets its passenger for the first time when it arrives at the pickup location, so this is the natural point for the vehicle to receive its next passenger. In the model, it does so from the company, which received it originally from the passenger source. **TaxiCompany** responsibility: *Pass passenger to vehicle*; **Vehicle** responsibility: *Receive passenger*, with **Passenger** added as a collaborator to **Vehicle**.

- The vehicle now requests the passenger's intended destination. **Vehicle** responsibility: *Request destination location*; **Passenger** responsibility: *Provide destination location*. Once again, at this point the behavior of taxis and shuttles will differ. A **Taxi** will simply *Go to passenger destination*. A shuttle will *Add location to collection of target locations* and choose the next one.

- On arrival at a passenger's destination, a **Vehicle** has responsibilities to *Offload passenger* and *Notify the company of passenger arrival*. The **TaxiCompany** must *Receive notification of passenger arrival*.

The steps we have outlined represent the fundamental activity of the taxi company, repeated over and over as each new passenger requests the service. An important point to note, however, is that our computer model needs to be able to restart the sequence for each new passenger as soon as each fresh request is received, even if a previous request has not yet run to completion. In other words, within a single step of the program, one vehicle could still be heading to a pickup location while another could be arriving at a passenger's destination, and a new passenger might be requesting a pickup.

> **Exercise 16.7** Review the problem description and the scenario we have worked through. Are there any further scenarios that need to be addressed before we move on to class design? Have we adequately covered what happens, for instance, if there is no vehicle available when a request is received? Complete the scenario analysis if you feel there is more to be done.

Exercise 16.8 Do you feel that we have described the scenario at the correct level of detail? For instance, have we included too little or too much detail in the discussion of the differences between taxis and shuttles?

Exercise 16.9 Do you feel it is necessary to address *how* vehicles move between locations at this stage?

Exercise 16.10 Do you think that a need for further classes will emerge as the application is developed—classes that have no immediate reference in the problem description? If so, why is this the case?

16.3 Class design

In this section, we shall start to make the move from a high-level abstract design on paper to a concrete outline design within a BlueJ project.

16.3.1 Designing class interfaces

In Chapter 15, we suggested that the next step was to create a fresh set of CRC cards from the first, turning the responsibilities of each class into a set of method signatures. Without wishing to de-emphasize the importance of that step, we shall leave it for you to do and move directly to a BlueJ project outline containing stub classes and methods. This should provide a good feel for the complexity of the project and whether we have missed anything crucial in the steps taken so far.

It is worth pointing out that, at every stage of the project life cycle, we should expect to find errors or loose ends in what we have done in earlier stages. This does not necessarily imply that there are weaknesses in our techniques or abilities. It is more a reflection of the fact that project development is often a discovery process. It is only by exploring and trying things out that we gain a full understanding of what it is we are trying to achieve. So discovering omissions actually says something positive about the process we are using!

16.3.2 Collaborators

Having identified collaborations between classes, one issue that will often need to be addressed is how a particular object obtains references to its collaborators. There are usually three distinct ways in which this happens, and these often represent three different patterns of object interaction:

■ A collaborator is received as an argument to a constructor. Such a collaborator will usually be stored in one of the new object's fields so that it is available through the new object's life. The collaborator may be shared in this way with several different objects. Example: A **PassengerSource** object receives the **TaxiCompany** object through its constructor.

- A collaborator is received as an argument to a method. Interaction with such a collaborator is usually transitory—just for the period of execution of the method—although the receiving object may choose to store the reference in one of its fields, for longer-term interaction. Example: **TaxiCompany** receives a **Passenger** collaborator through its method to handle a pickup request.

- The object constructs the collaborator for itself. The collaborator will be for the exclusive use of the constructing object, unless it is passed to another object in one of the previous two ways. If constructed in a method, the collaboration will usually be short term, for the duration of the block in which it is constructed. However, if the collaborator is stored in a field, then the collaboration is likely to last the full lifetime of the creating object. Example: **TaxiCompany** creates a collection to store its vehicles.

> **Exercise 16.11** As the next section discusses the *taxi-company-outline* project, pay particular attention to where objects are created and how collaborating objects get to know about each other. Try to identify at least one further example of each of the patterns we have described.

16.3.3 The outline implementation

The project *taxi-company-outline* contains an outline implementation of the classes, responsibilities, and collaborations that we have described as part of the design process. You are encouraged to browse through the source code and associate the concrete classes with the corresponding descriptions of Section 16.2.3. Code 16.1 shows an outline of the Vehicle class from the project.

Code 16.1

An outline of the **Vehicle** class

```
/**
 * Capture outline details of a vehicle.
 *
 * @author David J. Barnes and Michael Kölling
 * @version 2016.02.29
 */

public abstract class Vehicle
{
    private TaxiCompany company;
    // Where the vehicle is.
    private Location location;
    // Where the vehicle is headed.
    private Location targetLocation;

    /**
     * Constructor of class Vehicle
     * @param company The taxi company. Must not be null.
     * @param location The vehicle's starting point. Must not be null.
     * @throws NullPointerException If company or location is null.
     */
```

Code 16.1
continued

An outline of the
Vehicle class

```java
public Vehicle(TaxiCompany company, Location location)
{
    if(company == null) {
        throw new NullPointerException("company");
    }
    if(location == null) {
        throw new NullPointerException("location");
    }
    this.company = company;
    this.location = location;
    targetLocation = null;
}

/**
 * Notify the company of our arrival at a pickup location.
 */
public void notifyPickupArrival()
{
    company.arrivedAtPickup(this);
}

/**
 * Notify the company of our arrival at a
 * passenger's destination.
 * @param passenger The passenger who has arrived.
 */
public void notifyPassengerArrival(Passenger passenger)
{
    company.arrivedAtDestination(this, passenger);
}

/**
 * Receive a pickup location.
 * How this is handled depends on the type of vehicle.
 * @param location The pickup location.
 */
public abstract void setPickupLocation(Location location);

/**
 * Receive a passenger.
 * How this is handled depends on the type of vehicle.
 * @param passenger The passenger being picked up.
 */
public abstract void pickup(Passenger passenger);

/**
 * Is the vehicle free?
 * @return Whether or not this vehicle is free.
 */
public abstract boolean isFree();

/**
 * Offload any passengers whose destination is the
 * current location.
 */
public abstract void offloadPassenger();

/**
 * Get the location.
 * @return Where this vehicle is currently located.
 */
```

**Code 16.1
continued**

An outline of the
Vehicle class

```
public Location getLocation()
{
    return location;
}

/**
 * Set the current location.
 * @param location Where it is. Must not be null.
 * @throws NullPointerException If location is null.
 */
public void setLocation(Location location)
{
    if(location != null) {
        this.location = location;
    }
    else {
        throw new NullPointerException();
    }
}

/**
 * Get the target location.
 * @return Where this vehicle is currently headed, or null
 *          if it is idle.
 */
public Location getTargetLocation()
{
    return targetLocation;
}

/**
 * Set the required target location.
 * @param location Where to go. Must not be null.
 * @throws NullPointerException If location is null.
 */
public void setTargetLocation(Location location)
{
    if(location != null) {
        targetLocation = location;
    }
    else {
        throw new NullPointerException();
    }
}

/**
 * Clear the target location.
 */
public void clearTargetLocation()
{
    targetLocation = null;
}
```

The process of creating the outline project raised a number of issues. Here are some of them:

- You should expect to find some differences between the design and the implementation, owing to the different natures of design and implementation languages. For instance, discussion of the scenarios suggested that **PassengerSource** should have the responsibility

Generate pickup and destination locations for a passenger, and **Passenger** should have the responsibility *Receive pickup and destination locations*. Rather than mapping these responsibilities to individual method calls, the more natural implementation in Java is to write something like

```
new Passenger(new Location( . . . ), new Location( . . . ))
```

■ We have ensured that our outline project is complete enough to compile successfully. That is not always necessary at this stage, but it does mean that undertaking incremental development at the next stage will be a little easier. However, it does have the corresponding disadvantage of making missing pieces of code potentially harder to spot, because the compiler will not point out the loose ends.

■ The shared and distinct elements of the **Vehicle**, **Taxi**, and **Shuttle** classes only really begin to take shape as we move towards their implementation. For instance, the different ways in which taxis and shuttles respond to a pickup request is reflected in the fact that **Vehicle** defines **setPickupLocation** as an abstract method, which will have separate concrete implementations in the subclasses. On the other hand, even though taxis and shuttles have different ways of deciding where they are heading, they can share the concept of having a single target location. This has been implemented as a **targetLocation** field in the superclass.

■ At two points in the scenario, a vehicle is expected to notify the company of its arrival at either a pickup point or a destination. There are at least two possible ways to organize this in the implementation. The direct way is for a vehicle to store a reference to its company. This would mean that there would be an explicit association between the two classes on the class diagram.

■ An alternative is to use the *Observer* pattern introduced in Chapter 15, with **Vehicle** extending the **Observable** class and **TaxiCompany** implementing the **Observer** interface. Direct coupling between **Vehicle** and **TaxiCompany** is reduced, but implicit coupling is still involved, and the notification process is a little more complex to program.

■ Up to this point, there has been no discussion about how many passengers a shuttle can carry. Presumably there could be different-sized shuttles. This aspect of the application has been deferred until a later resolution.

There is no absolute rule about exactly how far to go with the outline implementation in any particular application. The purpose of the outline implementation is not to create a fully working project, but to record the design of the outline structure of the application (which has been developed through the CRC card activities earlier). As you review the classes in the *taxi-company-outline* project, you may feel that we have gone too far in this case, or maybe even not far enough. On the positive side, by attempting to create a version that at least compiles, we certainly found that we were forced to think about the **Vehicle** inheritance hierarchy in some detail: in particular, which methods could be implemented in full in the superclass, and which were best left as abstract. On the negative side, there is always the risk of making implementation decisions too early: for instance, committing to particular sorts of data structures that might be better left until later or, as we did here, choosing to reject the *Observer* pattern in favor of the more direct approach.

Exercise 16.12 For each of the classes in the project, look at the class interface and write a list of JUnit tests that should be used to test the functionality of the class.

Exercise 16.13 The *taxi-company-outline* project defines a **Demo** class to create a pair of **PassengerSource** and **TaxiCompany** objects. Create a **Demo** object and try its `pickupTest` method. Why is the **TaxiCompany** object unable to grant a pickup request at this stage?

Exercise 16.14 Do you feel that we should have developed the source code further at this stage, to enable at least one pickup request to succeed? If so, how much further would you have taken the development?

16.3.4 Testing

Having made a start on implementation, we should not go too much further before we start to consider how we shall test the application. We do not want to make the mistake of devising tests only when the full implementation is complete. We can already put some tests in place that will gradually evolve as the implementation is evolved. Try the following exercises to get a feel for what is possible at this early stage.

Exercise 16.15 The *taxi-company-outline-testing* project includes some simple initial JUnit tests. Try them out. Add any further tests you feel are appropriate at this stage of the development, to form the basis of a set of tests to be used during future development. Does it matter if the tests we create fail at this stage?

Exercise 16.16 The **Location** class currently contains no fields or methods. How is further development of this class likely to affect existing test classes?

16.3.5 Some remaining issues

One of the major issues that we have not attempted to tackle yet is how to organize the sequencing of the various activities: passenger requests, vehicle movements, and so on. Another is that locations have not been given a detailed concrete form, so movement has no effect. As we further develop the application, resolutions of these issues and others will emerge.

16.4 Iterative development

We obviously still have quite a long way to go from the outline implementation developed in *taxi-company-outline* to the final version. However, rather than being overwhelmed by the magnitude of the overall task, we can make things more manageable by identifying some discrete steps to take toward the ultimate goal and undertaking a process of iterative development.

16.4.1 Development steps

Planning some development steps helps us to consider how we might break up a single large problem into several smaller problems. Individually, these smaller problems are likely to be both less complex and more manageable than the one big problem, but together they should combine to form the whole. As we seek to solve the smaller problems, we might find that we need to also break up some of them. In addition, we might find that some of our original assumptions were wrong or that our design is inadequate in some way. This process of discovery, when combined with an iterative development approach, means that we obtain valuable feedback on our design and on the decisions we make, at an early enough stage for us to be able to incorporate it back into a flexible and evolving process.

Considering what steps to break the overall problem into has the added advantage of helping to identify some of the ways in which the various parts of the application are interconnected. In a large project, this process helps us to identify the interfaces between components. Identifying steps also helps in planning the timing of the development process.

It is important that each step in an iterative development represent a clearly identifiable point in the evolution of the application toward the overall requirements. In particular, we need to be able to determine when each step has been completed. Completion should be marked by the passing of a set of tests and a review of the step's achievements, so as to be able to incorporate any lessons learned into the steps that follow.

Here is a possible series of development steps for the taxi company application:

- Enable a single passenger to be picked up and taken to her destination by a single taxi.

- Provide sufficient taxis to enable multiple independent passengers to be picked up and taken to their destinations concurrently.

- Enable a single passenger to be picked up and taken to his destination by a single shuttle.

- Ensure that details are recorded of passengers for whom there is no free vehicle.

- Enable a single shuttle to pick up multiple passengers and carry them concurrently to their destinations.

- Provide a GUI to display the activities of all active vehicles and passengers within the simulation.

- Ensure that taxis and shuttles are able to operate concurrently.

- Provide all remaining functionality, including full statistical data.

We will not discuss the implementation of all of these steps in detail, but we will complete the application to a point where you should be able to add the remaining functionality yourself.

Exercise 16.17 Critically assess the list of steps we have outlined, with the following questions in mind. Do you feel the order is appropriate? Is the level of complexity of each too high, too low, or just right? Are there any steps missing? Revise the list as you see fit, to suit your own view of the project.

Exercise 16.18 Are the completion criteria (tests on completion) for each stage sufficiently obvious? If so, document some tests for each.

16.4.2 A first stage

For the first stage, we want to be able to create a single passenger, have them picked up by a single taxi, and have them delivered to their destination. This means that we shall have to work on a number of different classes: **Location**, **Taxi**, and **TaxiCompany**, for certain, and possibly others. In addition, we shall have to arrange for simulated time to pass as the taxi moves within the city. This suggests that we might be able to reuse some of the ideas involving actors that we saw in Chapter 12.

The *taxi-company-stage-one* project contains an implementation of the requirements of this first stage. The classes have been developed to the point where a taxi picks up and delivers a passenger to their destination. The **run** method of the **Demo** class plays out this scenario. However, more important at this stage are really the test classes—**LocationTest**, **PassengerTest**, **PassengerSourceTest**, and **TaxiTest**—which we discuss in Section 16.4.3.

Rather than discuss this project in detail, we shall simply describe here some of the issues that arose from its development out of the previous outline version. You should supplement this discussion with a thorough reading of the source code.

The goals of the first stage were deliberately set to be quite modest, yet still relevant to the fundamental activity of the application—collecting and delivering passengers. There were good reasons for this. By setting a modest goal, the task seemed achievable within a reasonably short time. By setting a relevant goal, the task was clearly taking us closer toward completing the overall project. Such factors help to keep our motivation high.

We have borrowed the concept of actors from the *foxes-and-rabbits* project of Chapter 12. For this stage, only taxis needed to be actors, through their **Vehicle** superclass. At each step a taxi either moves toward a target location or remains idle (Code 16.2). Although we did not have to record any statistics at this stage, it was simple and convenient to have vehicles record a count of the number of steps for which they are idle. This anticipated part of the work of one of the later stages.

The need to model movement required the **Location** class to be implemented more fully than in the outline. On the face of it, this should be a relatively simple container for a two-dimensional position within a rectangular grid. However, in practice, it also needs to provide both a test for coincidence of two locations (**equals**), and a way for a vehicle to find out where to move to next, based on its current location and its destination (**nextLocation**). At this stage, no limits were put on the grid area (other than that coordinate values should be positive), but this raises the need in a later stage for something to record the boundaries of the area in which the company operates.

Code 16.2

The **Taxi** class as an actor

```java
/**
 * A taxi is able to carry a single passenger.
 *
 * @author David J. Barnes and Michael Kölling
 * @version 2016.02.29
 */

public class Taxi extends Vehicle
{
    private Passenger passenger;

    /**
     * Constructor for objects of class Taxi
     * @param company The taxi company. Must not be null.
     * @param location The vehicle's starting point. Must not be null.
     * @throws NullPointerException If company or location is null.
     */
    public Taxi(TaxiCompany company, Location location)
    {
        super(company, location);
    }

    /**
     * Carry out a taxi's actions.
     */
    public void act()
    {
        Location target = getTargetLocation();
        if(target != null) {
            // Find where to move to next.
            Location next = getLocation().nextLocation(target);
            setLocation(next);
            if(next.equals(target)) {
                if(passenger != null) {
                    notifyPassengerArrival(passenger);
                    offloadPassenger();
                }
                else {
                    notifyPickupArrival();
                }
            }
        }
        else {
            incrementIdleCount();
        }
    }

    /**
     * Is the taxi free?
     * @return Whether or not this taxi is free.
     */
    public boolean isFree()
    {
        return getTargetLocation() == null && passenger == null;
    }
```

Code 16.2
continued
The **Taxi** class as
an actor

```java
/**
 * Is the taxi free?
 * @return Whether or not this taxi is free.
 */
public boolean isFree()
{
    return getTargetLocation() == null && passenger == null;
}

/**
 * Receive a pickup location. This becomes the
 * target location.
 * @param location The pickup location.
 */
public void setPickupLocation(Location location)
{
    setTargetLocation(location);
}

/**
 * Receive a passenger.
 * Set their destination as the target location.
 * @param passenger The passenger.
 */
public void pickup(Passenger passenger)
{
    this.passenger = passenger;
    setTargetLocation(passenger.getDestination());
}

/**
 * Offload the passenger.
 */
public void offloadPassenger()
{
    passenger = null;
    clearTargetLocation();
}

/**
 * Return details of the taxi, such as where it is.
 * @return A string representation of the taxi.
 */
public String toString()
{
    return "Taxi at " + getLocation();
}
}
```

One of the major issues that had to be addressed was how to manage the association between a passenger and a vehicle, between the request for a pickup and the point of the vehicle's arrival. Although we were required only to handle a single taxi and a single passenger, we tried to bear in mind that ultimately there could be multiple pickup requests outstanding at any one time. In Section 16.2.3, we decided that a vehicle should receive its passenger when it notifies the company that it has arrived at the pickup point. So, when a notification is received, the company needs to be able to work out which passenger has been assigned to that vehicle. The solution we chose was to have the company store a *vehicle:passenger* pairing in a map. When the vehicle notifies the company that it has arrived, the company passes the corresponding passenger to it. However, there are various reasons why this solution is not perfect, and we shall explore this issue further in the exercises below.

One error situation we addressed was that there might be no passenger found when a vehicle arrives at a pickup point. This would be the result of a programming error, so we defined the unchecked **MissingPassengerException** class.

As only a single passenger was required for this stage, development of the **Passenger-Source** class was deferred to a later stage. Instead, passengers were created directly in the **Demo** and **Test** classes.

Exercise 16.19 If you have not already done so, take a thorough look through the implementation in the *taxi-company-stage-one* project. Ensure that you understand how movement of the taxi is effected through its **act** method.

Exercise 16.20 Do you feel that the **TaxiCompany** object should keep separate lists of those vehicles that are free and those that are not, to improve the efficiency of its scheduling? At what points would a vehicle move between the lists?

Exercise 16.21 The next planned stage of the implementation is to provide multiple taxis to carry multiple passengers concurrently. Review the **Taxi-Company** class with this goal in mind. Do you feel that it already supports this functionality? If not, what changes are required?

Exercise 16.22 Review the way in which *vehicle:passenger* associations are stored in the assignments' map in **TaxiCompany**. Can you see any weaknesses in this approach? Does it support more than one passenger being picked up from the same location? Could a vehicle ever need to have multiple associations recorded for it?

Exercise 16.23 If you see any problems with the current way in which *vehicle:passenger* associations are stored, would creating a unique identification for each association help—say a "booking number"? If so, would any of the existing method signatures in the **Vehicle** hierarchy need to be changed? Implement an improved version that supports the requirements of all existing scenarios.

16.4.3 Testing the first stage

As part of the implementation of the first stage, we have developed two test classes: **Loca-tionTest** and **TaxiTest**. The first checks basic functionality of the **Location** class that is crucial to correct movement of vehicles. The second is designed to test that a passenger is picked up and delivered to her destination in the correct number of steps, and that the taxi becomes free again immediately afterwards. In order to develop the second set of tests, the **Location** class was enhanced with the **distance** method, to provide the number of steps required to move between two locations.[1]

In normal operation, the application runs silently, and without a GUI there is no visual way to monitor the progress of a taxi. One approach would be to add print statements to the core methods of classes such as **Taxi** and **TaxiCompany**. However, BlueJ does offer the alternative of setting a breakpoint within the **act** method of, say, the **Taxi** class. This would make it possible to "observe" the movement of a taxi by inspection.

Having reached a reasonable level of confidence in the current state of the implementation, we have simply left print statements in the notification methods of **TaxiCompany** to provide a minimum of user feedback.

As testimony to the value of developing tests alongside implementation, it is worth recording that the existing test classes enabled us to identify and correct two serious errors in our code.

> **Exercise 16.24** Review the tests implemented in the test classes of *taxi-company-stage-one*. Should it be possible to use these as regression tests during the next stages, or would they require substantial changes?
>
> **Exercise 16.25** Implement additional tests and further test classes that you feel are necessary to increase your level of confidence in the current implementation. Fix any errors you discover in the process of doing this.

16.4.4 A later stage of development

It is not our intention to discuss in full the completion of the development of the taxi company application, as there would be little for you to gain from that. Instead, we shall briefly present the application at a later stage, and we encourage you to complete the rest from there.

This more advanced stage can be found in the *taxi-company-later-stage* project. It handles multiple taxis and passengers, and a GUI provides a progressive view of the movements of both (Figure 16.2). Here is an outline of some of the major developments in this version from the previous one.

- A **Simulation** class now manages the actors, much as it did in the *foxes-and-rabbits project*. The actors are the vehicles, the passenger source, and a GUI provided by the **CityGUI** class. After each step, the simulation pauses for a brief period so that the GUI does not change too quickly.

- The need for something like the **City** class was identified during development of stage one. The **City** object defines the dimensions of the city's grid and holds a collection of all the items of interest that are in the city—the vehicles and the passengers.

---

[1] We anticipate that this will have an extended use later in the development of the application as it should enable the company to schedule vehicles on the basis of which is closest to the pickup point.

Figure 16.2
A visualization of
the city

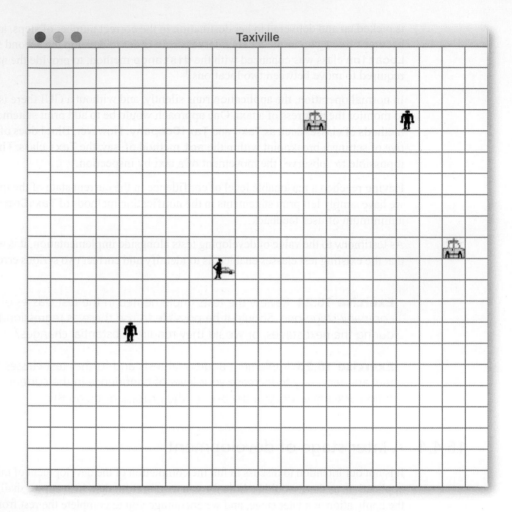

- Items in the city may optionally implement the **DrawableItem** interface, which allows the GUI to display them. Images of vehicles and people are provided in the **images** folder within the project folder for this purpose.

- The Taxi class implements the **DrawableItem** interface. It returns alternative images to the GUI, depending on whether it is occupied or empty. Image files exist in the **images** folder for a shuttle to do the same.

- The **PassengerSource** class has been refactored significantly from the previous version, to better fit its role as an actor. In addition, it maintains a count of missed pickups for statistical analysis.

- The **TaxiCompany** class is responsible for creating the taxis to be used in the simulation.

As you explore the source code of the *taxi-company-later-stage* project, you will find illustrations of many of the topics we have covered in the second half of this book: inheritance, polymorphism, abstract classes, interfaces, and error handling.

Exercise 16.26 Add assertion and exception-throwing consistency checks within each class, to guard against inappropriate use. For instance, ensure that a **Passenger** is never created with pickup and destination locations that are the same; ensure that a taxi is never requested to go to a pickup when it already has a target location; etc.

Exercise 16.27 Report on the statistical information that is being gathered by taxis and the passenger source; also on taxi idle time and missed pickups. Experiment with different numbers of taxis to see how the balance between these two sets of data varies.

Exercise 16.28 Adapt the vehicle classes so that records are kept of the amount of time spent traveling to pickup locations and passenger destinations. Can you see a possible conflict here for shuttles?

16.4.5 Further ideas for development

The version of the application provided in the *taxi-company-later-stage* project represents a significant point in the development toward full implementation. However, there is still a lot that can be added. For instance, we have hardly developed the **Shuttle** class at all, so there are plenty of challenges to be found in completing its implementation. The major difference between shuttles and taxis is that a shuttle has to be concerned with multiple passengers, whereas a taxi has to be concerned with only one. The fact that a shuttle is already carrying a passenger should not prevent it from being sent to pick up another. Similarly, if it is already on its way to a pickup, it could still accept a further pickup request. These issues raise questions about how a shuttle organizes its priorities. Could a passenger end up being driven back and forth while the shuttle responds to competing requests, the passenger never getting delivered? What does it mean for a shuttle not to be free? Does it mean that it is full of passengers, or that it has enough pickup requests to fill it? Suppose at least one of those pickups will reach their destination before the final pickup is reached: Does that mean it could accept more pickup requests than its capacity?!

Another area for further development is vehicle scheduling. The taxi company does not operate particularly intelligently at present. How should it decide which vehicle to send when there may be more than one available? No attempt is made to assign vehicles on the basis of their distance from a pickup location. The company could use the **distance** method of the **Location** class to work out which is the nearest free vehicle to a pickup. Would this make a significant difference to the average waiting time of passengers? How might data be gathered on how long passengers wait to be picked up? What about having idle taxis move to a central location, ready for their next pickup, in order to reduce potential waiting times? Does the size of the city have an impact on the effectiveness of this approach? For instance, in a large city, is it better to have idle taxis space themselves out from one another, rather than have all gather at the center?

Could the simulation be used to model competing taxi companies operating in the same area of the city? Multiple **TaxiCompany** objects could be created and the passenger source allocate passengers to them competitively on the basis of how quickly they could be picked up. Is this too fundamental a change to graft onto the existing application?

16.4.6 Reuse

Currently, our goal has been to simulate the operation of vehicles in order to assess the commercial viability of expanding a business into a new area of the city. You may have noticed that substantial parts of the application may actually be useful once the expansion is in operation.

Assuming that we develop a clever scheduling algorithm for our simulation to decide which vehicle should take which call, or that we have worked out a good scheme for deciding where to send the vehicles to wait while they are idle, we might decide to use the same algorithms when the company actually operates in the new area. The visual representation of each vehicle's location could also help.

In other words, there is potential to turn the simulation of the taxi company into a taxi management system used to help the real company in its operations. The structure of the application would change, of course: the program would not control and move the taxis, but rather record their positions, which it might receive from GPS (global positioning system) receivers in each vehicle. However, many of the classes developed for the simulation could be reused with little or no change. This illustrates the power of reuse that we gain from good class structure and class design.

16.5 Another example

There are many other projects that you could undertake along similar lines to the taxi company application. A popular alternative is the issue of how to schedule elevators in a large building. Coordination between elevators becomes particularly significant here. In addition, within an enclosed building, it may be possible to estimate numbers of people on each floor and hence to anticipate demand. There are also time-related behaviors to take account of: morning arrivals, evening departures, and local peaks of activity around lunchtimes.

Use the approach we have outlined in this chapter to implement a simulation of a building with one or more elevators.

16.6 Taking things further

We can only take you so far by presenting our own project ideas and showing you how we would develop them. You will find that you can go much further if you develop your own ideas for projects and implement them in your own way. Pick a topic that interests you, and work through the stages we have outlined: analyze the problem, work out some scenarios, sketch out a design, plan some implementation stages, and then make a start.

Designing and implementing programs is an exciting and creative activity. Like any worthwhile activity, it takes time and practice to become proficient at it. So do not become discouraged if your early efforts seem to take forever or are full of errors. That is normal, and you will gradually improve with experience. Do not be too ambitious to start with, and expect to have to rework your ideas as you go; that is all part of the natural learning process.

Most of all: Have fun!

APPENDIX

A

Working with a BlueJ Project

A.1 Installing BlueJ

To work with BlueJ, you must download and install the BlueJ system. It is available for free download from `http://www.bluej.org/`. The download for Windows and Mac OS includes a copy of the JDK (the Java system)—this does not need to be installed separately. On Linux, the package dependencies will automatically install the right JDK version when you install BlueJ, if necessary.

A.2 Opening a project

You can download all of the example projects from the companion website for this book at `http://www.bluej.org/objects-first/`

Download the zip file and uncompress it to give you a folder called *projects*. After installing and starting BlueJ by double-clicking its icon, select *Open . . .* from the *Project* menu. Navigate to the projects folder and select a project. (You can have multiple projects open at the same time.) Each project folder contains a `bluej.project` file that, when associated with BlueJ, can be double-clicked to open a project directly.

More information about the use of BlueJ is included in the BlueJ Tutorial. The tutorial is accessible via the *BlueJ Tutorial* item in BlueJ's *Help* menu.

A.3 The BlueJ debugger

Information on using the BlueJ debugger may be found in Appendix F and in the BlueJ Tutorial. The tutorial is accessible via the *BlueJ Tutorial* item in BlueJ's *Help* menu.

A.4 Configuring BlueJ

Many of the settings of BlueJ can be configured to better suit your personal situation. Some configuration options are available through the *Preferences* dialog in the BlueJ system, but many more configuration options are accessible by editing the "BlueJ definitions file." The location of that file is *<bluej_home>/lib/bluej.defs*, where *<bluej_home>* is the folder where the BlueJ system is installed.[1]

---

[1] On Mac OS, the *bluej.defs* file is inside the application bundle. See the "Tips archive" for instructions how to find it.

Configuration details are explained in the "Tips archive" on the BlueJ web site. You can access it at

`http://www.bluej.org/help/archive.html`

Following are some of the most common things people like to configure. Many more configuration options can be found by reading the `bluej.defs` file.

A.5 Changing the interface language

You can change the interface language to one of several available languages. To do this, open the `bluej.defs` file and find the line that reads

`bluej.language=english`

Change it to one of the other available languages. For example:

`bluej.language=spanish`

Comments in the file list all available languages. They include at least Afrikaans, Catalan, Chinese, Czech, Danish, Dutch, English, French, German, Greek, Italian, Japanese, Korean, Portuguese, Russian, Slovak, Spanish, and Swedish.

A.6 Using local API documentation

You can use a local copy of the Java class library (API) documentation. That way, access to the documentation is faster and you can use the documentation without being online. To do this, download the Java documentation file from `http://www.oracle.com/technetwork/java/javase/downloads/` (a zip file) and unzip it at a location where you want to store the Java documentation. This will create a folder named *docs*.

Then open a web browser, and, using the *Open File . . . .* (or equivalent) function, open the file *docs/api/index.html*. Once the API view is correctly displayed in the browser, copy the URL (web address) from your browser's address field, open BlueJ, open the *Preferences* dialog, go to the *Miscellaneous* tab, and paste the copied URL into the field labeled *JDK documentation URL*. Using the *Java Class Libraries* item from the *Help* menu should now open your local copy.

A.7 Changing the new class templates

When you create a new class, the class's source is set to a default source text. This text is taken from a template and can be changed to suit your preferences. Templates are stored in the folders

`<bluej_home>/lib/<language>/templates/ and`
`<bluej_home>/lib/<language>/templates/newclass/`

where *<bluej_home>* is the BlueJ installation folder and *<language>* is your currently used language setting (for example, *english*).

Template files are pure text files and can be edited in any standard text editor.

B

Java Data Types

Java's type system is based on two distinct kinds of types: primitive types, and object types.

Primitive types are stored in variables directly, and they have value semantics (values are copied when assigned to another variable). Primitive types are not associated with classes and do not have methods.

In contrast, an object type is manipulated by storing a reference to the object (not the object itself). When assigned to a variable, only the reference is copied, not the object.

B.1   Primitive types

The following table lists all the primitive types of the Java language:

Type name	Description	Example literals		
Integer numbers				
byte	byte-sized integer (8 bit)	24	-2	
short	short integer (16 bit)	137	-119	
int	integer (32 bit)	5409	-2003	
long	long integer (64 bit)	423266353L	55L	
Real numbers				
float	single-precision floating point	43.889F		
double	double-precision floating point	45.63	2.4e5	
Other types				
char	a single character (16 bit)	'm'	'?'	'\u00F6'
boolean	a boolean value (true or false)	true	false	

Notes:

- A number without a decimal point is generally interpreted as an int but automatically converted to byte, short, or long types when assigned (if the value fits). You can declare a literal as long by putting an L after the number. (l, lowercase L, works as well but should be avoided because it can easily be mistaken for a one (1).)
- A number with a decimal point is of type double. You can specify a float literal by putting an F or f after the number.
- A character can be written as a single Unicode character in single quotes or as a four-digit Unicode value, preceded by "\u".
- The two boolean literals are true and false.

Because variables of the primitive types do not refer to objects, there are no methods associated with the primitive types. However, when used in a context requiring an object type, autoboxing might be used to convert a primitive value to a corresponding object. See Section B.4 for more details.

The following table details minimum and maximum values available in the numerical types.

Type name	Minimum	Maximum
byte	−128	127
short	−32768	32767
int	−2147483648	2147483647
long	−9223372036854775808	9223372036854775807
	Positive minimum	**Positive maximum**
float	1.4e−45	3.4028235e38
double	4.9e−324	1.7976931348623157e308

B.2 Casting of primitive types

Sometimes it is necessary to convert a value of one primitive type to a value of another primitive type—typically, a value from a type with a particular range of values to one with a smaller range. This is called *casting*. Casting almost always involves loss of information—for example, when converting from a floating-point type to an integer type. Casting is permitted in Java between the numeric types, but it is not possible to convert a boolean value to any other type with a cast, or vice versa.

The cast operator consists of the name of a primitive type written in parentheses in front of a variable or an expression. For instance,

```
int val = (int) mean;
```

If mean is a variable of type double containing the value 3.9, then the statement above would store the integer value 3 (conversion by truncation) in the variable val.

B.3 Object types

All types not listed in Section B.1, Primitive types, are object types. These include class and interface types from the Java library (such as String) and user-defined types.

A variable of an object type holds a reference (or "pointer") to an object. Assignments and parameter passing have reference semantics (i.e., the reference is copied, not the object). After assigning a variable to another one, both variables refer to the same object. The two variables are said to be aliases for the same object. This rule applies in simple assignment between variables, but also when passing an object as an actual parameter to a method. As a consequence, state changes to an object via a formal parameter will persist, after the method has completed, in the actual parameter.

Classes are the templates for objects, defining the fields and methods that each instance possesses.

Arrays behave like object types; they also have reference semantics. There is no class definition for arrays.

B.4 Wrapper classes

Every primitive type in Java has a corresponding wrapper class that represents the same type but is a real-object type. This makes it possible to use values from the primitive types where object types are required, through a process known as *autoboxing*. The following table lists the primitive types and their corresponding wrapper type from the `java.lang` package. Apart from `Integer` and `Character`, the wrapper class names are the same as the primitive-type names, but with an uppercase first letter.

Whenever a value of a primitive type is used in a context that requires an object type, the compiler uses autoboxing to automatically wrap the primitive-type value in an appropriate wrapper object. This means that primitive-type values can be added directly to a collection, for instance. The reverse operation—*unboxing*—is also performed automatically when a wrapper-type object is used in a context that requires a value of the corresponding primitive type.

Primitive type	Wrapper type
byte	Byte
short	Short
int	Integer
long	Long
float	Float
double	Double
char	Character
boolean	Boolean

B.5 Casting of object types

Because an object may belong to an inheritance hierarchy of types, it is sometimes necessary to convert an object reference of one type to a reference of a subtype lower down the inheritance hierarchy. This process is called *casting* (or *downcasting*). The cast operator consists of the name of a class or interface type written in parentheses in front of a variable or an expression. For instance,

```
Car c = (Car) veh;
```

If the declared (i.e., static) type of variable `veh` is `Vehicle` and `Car` is a subclass of `Vehicle`, then this statement will compile. A separate check is made at runtime to ensure that the object referred to by `veh` really is a `Car` and not an instance of a different subtype.

It is important to appreciate that casting between object types is completely different from casting between primitive types (Section B.2, above). In particular, casting between object types involves *no change* of the object involved. It is purely a way of gaining access to type information that is already true of the object—that is, part of its full dynamic type.

C

Operators

C.1 Arithmetic expressions

Java has a considerable number of operators available for both arithmetic and logical expressions. Table C.1 shows everything that is classified as an operator, including things such as type casting and parameter passing. Most of the operators are either binary operators (taking a left and a right operand) or unary operators (taking a single operand). The main binary arithmetic operations are:

+ *addition*
− *subtraction*
* *multiplication*
/ *division*
% *modulus*, or *remainder after division*

The results of both division and modulus operations depend on whether their operands are integers or floating-point values. Between two integer values, division yields an integer result and discards any remainder, but between floating-point values, a floating-point value is the result:

```
5 / 3 gives a result of 1
5.0 / 3 gives a result of 1.6666666666666667
```

(Note that only one of the operands needs to be of a floating-point type to produce a floating-point result.)

When more than one operator appears in an expression, then *rules of precedence* have to be used to work out the order of application. In Table C.1, those operators having the highest precedence appear at the top, so we can see that multiplication, division, and modulus all take precedence over addition and subtraction, for instance. This means that both of the following examples give the result 100:

```
51 * 3 − 53
154 − 2 * 27
```

Binary operators with the same precedence level are evaluated from left to right, and unary operators with the same precedence level are evaluated right to left.

When it is necessary to alter the normal order of evaluation, parentheses can be used. So both of the following examples give the result 100:

```
(205 − 5) / 2
2 * (47 + 3)
```

The main unary operators are -, !, ++, --, [ ], and new. You will notice that ++ and -- appear in each of the top two rows in Table C.1. Those in the top row take a single operand on their left, while those in the second row take a single operand on their right.

Table C.1
Java operators, highest precedence at the top

[ ]	.		++	--	(*parameters*)						
++	--		+	-	!	~					
new	(*cast*)										
*	/		%								
+	-										
<<	>>		>>>								
<	>		>=	<=	instanceof						
==	!=										
&											
^											
&&											
||											
?:											
=	+=	-=	*=	/=	%=	>>=	<<=	>>>=	&=	|=	^=

C.2 Boolean expressions

In boolean expressions, operators are used to combine operands to produce a value of either true or false. Such expressions are usually found in the test expressions of if-else statements and loops.

The relational operators usually combine a pair of arithmetic operands, although the tests for equality and inequality are also used with object references. Java's relational operators are:

== equal to   != not equal to
< less than   <= less than or equal to
> greater than   >= greater than or equal to

The binary logical operators combine two boolean expressions to produce another boolean value. The operators are:

&& and
|| or
^ exclusive or

In addition,
! not

takes a single boolean expression and changes it from true to false and vice versa.

C.3 Short-circuit operators

Both && and || are slightly unusual in the way they are applied. If the left operand of && is false, then the value of the right operand is irrelevant and will not be evaluated. Similarly, if the left operand of || is true, then the right operand is not evaluated. Thus, they are known as short-circuit operators.

D.1 Control structures

Control structures affect the order in which statements are executed. There are two main categories: *selection statements* and *loops*.

A selection statement provides a decision point at which a choice is made to follow one route through the body of a method or constructor rather than another route. An *if-else statement* involves a decision between two different sets of statements, whereas a *switch statement* allows the selection of a single option from among several.

Loops offer the option to repeat statements, either a definite or an indefinite number of times. The former is typified by the *for-each loop* and *for loop*, while the latter is typified by the *while loop* and *do loop*.

In practice, exceptions to the above characterizations are quite common. For instance, an *if-else statement* can be used to select from among several alternative sets of statements if the *else* part contains a nested if-else statement, and a *for loop* can be used to loop an indefinite number of times.

D.2 Selection statements

D.2.1 if-else

The *if-else statement* has two main forms, both of which are controlled by the evaluation of a boolean expression:

```
if(expression) {
    statements
}
```

```
if(expression) {
    statements
}
else {
    statements
}
```

In the first form, the value of the boolean expression is used to decide whether or not to execute the statements. In the second form, the expression is used to choose between two alternative sets of statements, only one of which will be executed.

Examples:

```
if(field.size() == 0) {
    System.out.println("The field is empty.");
}

if(number < 0) {
    reportError();
}
else {
    processNumber(number);
}
```

It is very common to link if-else statements together by placing a second if-else in the else part of the first. This can be continued any number of times. It is a good idea to always include a final else part.

```
if(n < 0) {
    handleNegative();
}
else if(n == 0) {
    handleZero();
}
else {
    handlePositive();
}
```

D.2.2 switch

The *switch statement* switches on a single value to one of an arbitrary number of cases. Two possible patterns of use are:

```
switch(expression) {                      switch(expression) {
    case value: statements;                   case value1:
                break;                        case value2:
    case value: statements;                   case value3:
                break;                            statements;
    further cases possible                        break;
    default: statements;                      case value4:
             break;                           case value5:
}                                                 statements;
                                                  break;
                                              further cases possible
                                              default:
                                                  statements;
                                                  break;
                                          }
```

Notes:

- A *switch statement* can have any number of case labels.
- The break instruction after every case is needed, otherwise the execution "falls through" into the next label's statements. The second form above makes use of this. In this case,

all three of the first values will execute the first *statements* section, whereas values four and five will execute the second *statements* section.

- The `default` case is optional. If no default is given, it may happen that no case is executed.
- The `break` instruction after the default (or the last case, if there is no default) is not needed but is considered good style.
- The expression used to switch on and the case labels may be strings.
- The expression and case labels may be of an enumerated type. The type name is omitted from the labels.

Examples:

```java
switch(day) {
    case 1: dayString = "Monday";
            break;
    case 2: dayString = "Tuesday";
            break;
    case 3: dayString = "Wednesday";
            break;
    case 4: dayString = "Thursday";
            break;
    case 5: dayString = "Friday";
            break;
    case 6: dayString = "Saturday";
            break;
    case 7: dayString = "Sunday";
            break;
    default: dayString = "invalid day";
            break;
}
```

```java
switch(dow.toLowerCase()) {
    case "mon":
    case "tue":
    case "wed":
    case "thu":
    case "fri":
        goToWork();
        break;
    case "sat":
    case "sun":
        stayInBed();
        break;
}
```

D.3 Loops

Java has three loops: *while, do-while,* and *for.* The for loop has two forms. Both while and do-while are well suited for indefinite iteration. The *for-each loop* is intended for definite iteration over a collection, and the *for loop* falls somewhere between the two. Except for the *for-each* loop, repetition is controlled in each with a boolean expression.

D.3.1 While

The *while loop* executes a block of statements as long as a given expression evaluates to *true*. The expression is tested *before* execution of the loop body, so the body may be executed zero times (i.e., not at all). This capability is an important feature of the while loop.

```
while(expression) {
    statements
}
```

Examples:

```
System.out.print("Please enter a filename: ");
input = readInput();
while(input == null) {
    System.out.print("Please try again: ");
    input = readInput();
}


int index = 0;
boolean found = false;
while(!found && index < list.size()) {
    if(list.get(index).equals(item)) {
        found = true;
    }
    else {
        index++;
    }
}
```

D.3.2 do-while

The *do-while loop* executes a block of statements as long as a given expression evaluates to *true*. The expression is tested *after* execution of the loop body, so the body always executes at least once. This is an important difference from the *while loop*.

```
do {
    statements
} while(expression);
```

Example:

```
do {
    System.out.print("Please enter a filename: ");
    input = readInput();
} while(input == null);
```

D.3.3 for

The *for loop* has two different forms. The first form is also known as a *for-each loop* and is used exclusively to iterate over elements of a collection. The loop variable is assigned the value of successive elements of the collection on each iteration of the loop.

```
for(variable-declaration : collection) {
    statements
}
```

Example:

```
for(String note : list) {
    System.out.println(note);
}
```

No associated index value is made available for the elements of the collection. A *for-each loop* cannot be used if the collection is to be modified while it is being iterated over.

The second form of for loop executes as long as a *condition* evaluates to *true*. Before the loop starts, an *initialization statement* is executed exactly once. The *condition* is evaluated before every execution of the loop body (so the statements in the loop's body may execute zero times). An *increment statement* is executed after each execution of the loop body.

```
for(initialization; condition; increment) {
    statements
}
```

Example:

```
for(int i = 0; i < text.size(); i++) {
    System.out.println(text.get(i));
}
```

Both types of for loop are commonly used to execute the body of the loop a definite number of times—for instance, once for each element in a collection—although a *for loop* is actually closer in effect to a *while loop* than to a *for-each loop*.

D.4 Exceptions

Throwing and catching exceptions provides another pair of constructs to alter control flow. However, exceptions are primarily used to anticipate and handle error situations, rather than the normal flow of control.

```
try {
    statements
}
catch(exception-type name) {
    statements
}
finally {
    statements
}
```

Example:

```
try {
    FileWriter writer = new FileWriter("foo.txt");
    writer.write(text);
    writer.close();
}
catch(IOException e) {
    Debug.reportError("Writing text to file failed.");
    Debug.reportError("The exception is: " + e);
}
```

An exception statement may have any number of *catch clauses*. They are evaluated in order of appearance, and only the first matching clause is executed. (A clause matches if the dynamic type of the exception object being thrown is assignment-compatible with the declared exception type in the catch clause.) The *finally clause* is optional.

Java 7 introduced two mainstream additions to the try statement: multi-catch and try-with-resources, or automatic resource management (ARM).

Multiple exceptions may be handled in the same catch clause by writing the list of exception types separated by the "|" symbol.

Example:

```
try {
    ...
    var.doSomething();
    ...
}
catch(EOFException | FileNotFoundException e) {
    ...
}
```

Automatic resource management—also known as "try-with-resource"—recognizes that try statements are often used to protect statements that use resources that should be closed when their use is complete, both upon success and failure. The header of the try statement is amended to include the opening of the resource—often a file—and the resource will be closed automatically at the end of the try statement.

Example:

```
try (FileWriter writer = new FileWriter(filename)){
    ...
    Use the writer . . .
    ...
}
catch(IOException e) {
    ...
}
```

D.5 Assertions

Assertion statements are primarily used as a testing tool during program development rather than in production code. There are two forms of assert statement:

```
assert boolean-expression ;
assert boolean-expression : expression;
```

Examples:

```
assert getDetails(key) != null;
assert expected == actual:
       "Actual value: " + actual +
       "does not match expected value: " + expected;
```

If the assertion expression evaluates to *false*, then an `AssertionError` will be thrown.

A compiler option allows assertion statements to be rendered inactive in production code without having to remove them from the program source.

APPENDIX

E

Throughout this book, we have used BlueJ to develop and execute our Java applications. There is a good reason for this: BlueJ gives us tools to make some development tasks very easy. In particular, it lets us execute individual methods of classes and objects easily; this is very useful if we want to quickly test a segment of new code.

We separate the discussion of working without BlueJ into two categories: executing an application without BlueJ, and developing without BlueJ.

E.1 Executing without BlueJ

Usually, when applications are delivered to end users, they are executed differently than from within BlueJ. They then have one single starting point, which defines where execution begins when a user starts an application.

The exact mechanism used to start an application depends on the operating system. Usually, this is done by double-clicking an application icon, or by entering the name of the application on a command line. The operating system then needs to know which method of which class to invoke to execute the complete program.

In Java, this problem is solved using a convention. When a Java program is started, the name of the class is specified as a parameter of the start command, and the name of the method is main. The name "main" is arbitrarily chosen by the Java developers, but it is fixed—the method must have this name. (The choice of "main" for the name of the initial method actually goes back to the C language, from which Java inherits much of its syntax.)

Let us consider, for example, the following command, entered at a command line such as the Windows command prompt or a Unix terminal:

```
java Game
```

The java command starts the Java virtual machine. It is part of the Java Development Kit (JDK), which must be installed on your system. Game is the name of the class that we want to start.

The Java system will then look for a method in class Game with exactly the following signature:

```
public static void main(String[] args)
```

The method has to be `public` so that it can be invoked from the outside. It also has to be `static`, because no objects exist when we start off. Initially, we have only classes, so static methods are all we can call. This static method then typically creates the first object. The return type is `void`, as this method does not return a value.

The parameter is a `String` array. This allows users to pass in additional arguments. In our example, the value of the `args` parameter will be an array of length zero. The command line starting the program can, however, define arguments:

```
java Game 2 Fred
```

Every word after the class name in this command line will be read as a separate `String` and be passed into the main method as an element in the string array. In this case, the `args` array would contain two elements, which are the strings `"2"` and `"Fred"`. Command-line parameters are not very often used with Java.

The body of the main method can theoretically contain any statements you like. Good style, however, dictates that the length of the main method should be kept to a minimum. Specifically, it should not contain anything that is part of the application logic.

Typically, the main method should do exactly what you did interactively to start the same application in BlueJ. If, for instance, you created an object of class `Game` and invoked a method named `start` to start an application, you should add the following main method to the `Game` class:

```
public static void main(String[] args)
{
    Game game = new Game();
    game.start();
}
```

Now, executing the main method will mimic your interactive invocation of the game.

Java projects are usually stored each in a separate directory. All classes for a project are placed inside this directory. When you execute the command to start Java and execute your application, make sure that the project directory is the active directory in your command terminal. This ensures that the classes will be found.

If the specified class cannot be found, the Java virtual machine will generate an error message similar to this one:

```
Could not find or load main class game
```

If you see a message like this, make sure that you have typed the class name correctly, and that the current directory actually contains this class. The class is stored in a file with the suffix `.class`. The code for class `Game`, for example, is stored in a file named `Game.class`.

If the class is found but does not contain a main method (or the main method does not have the right signature), you will see a message similar to this one:

```
Main method not found in class Game, please define the main method
as:
public static void main(String[] args)
```

In that case, make sure that the class you want to execute has a correct main method.

E.2　Creating executable `.jar` files

Java projects are typically stored as a collection of files in a directory (or "folder"). We shall briefly discuss the different files below.

To distribute applications to others, it is often easier if the whole application is stored in a single file. Java's mechanism for doing this is the Java Archive (`.jar`) format. All of the files of an application can be bundled into a single file, and they can still be executed. (If you are familiar with the "zip" compression format, it might be interesting to know that the format is, in fact, the same. "Jar" files can be opened with zip programs and vice versa.)

To make a `.jar` file executable, it is necessary to specify the `main` class somewhere. (Remember: The executed method is always `main`, but we need to specify the class this method is in.) This is done by including a text file in the `.jar` file (the *manifest file*) with this information. Luckily, BlueJ takes care of this for you.

To create an executable `.jar` file in BlueJ, use the *Project—Create Jar File* function, and specify in the resulting dialog the class that contains the main method. (You must still write a main method exactly as discussed above.)

For details with this function, read the BlueJ tutorial, which you can get through the BlueJ menu *Help—Tutorial* or from the BlueJ web site.

Once the executable `.jar` file has been created, it can be executed by double-clicking it. The computer that executes this `.jar` file must have the JDK or JRE (Java Runtime Environment) installed and associated with `.jar` files.

E.3　Developing without BlueJ

If you want not only to execute but also develop your programs without BlueJ, you will need to edit and compile the classes. The source code of a class is stored in a file ending in `.java`. For example, class `Game` is stored in a file called `Game.java`. Source files can be edited with any text editor. There are many free or inexpensive text editors around. Some, such as *Notepad* or *WordPad*, are distributed with Windows, but if you really want to use the editor for more than a quick test, you will soon want to get a better one. Be careful with word processors, though. Word processors typically do not save text in plain text format, and the Java system will not be able to read it.

The source files can then be compiled from a command line with the Java compiler that is included with the JDK. It is called `javac`. To compile a source file named `Game.java`, use the command

```
javac Game.java
```

This command will compile the `Game` class and any other classes it depends on. It will create a file called `Game.class`. This file contains the code that can be executed by the Java virtual machine. To execute it, use the command

```
java Game
```

Note that this command does not include the `.class` suffix.

The BlueJ debugger provides a set of basic debugging features that are intentionally simplified yet genuinely useful, both for debugging programs and for gaining an understanding
of the runtime behavior of programs.

The debugger window can be accessed by selecting the *Show Debugger* item from the *View*
menu or by pressing the right mouse button over the work indicator and selecting *Show
Debugger* from the pop-up menu. Figure F.1 shows the debugger window.

Figure F.1
The BlueJ debug-
ger window

The debugger window contains five display areas and five control buttons. The areas and buttons become active only when a program reaches a breakpoint or halts for some other reason. The following sections describe how to set breakpoints, how to control program execution, and the purpose of each of the display areas.

F.1 Breakpoints

A breakpoint is a flag attached to a line of code (Figure F.2). When a breakpoint is reached during program execution, the debugger's displays and controls become active, allowing you to inspect the state of the program and control further execution.

Breakpoints are set via the editor window. Either press the left mouse button in the breakpoint area to the left of the source text, or place the cursor on the line of code where the breakpoint should be and select *Set/Clear Breakpoint* from the editor's *Tools* menu. Breakpoints can be removed by the reverse process. Breakpoints can be set only within classes that have been compiled.

Figure F.2
A breakpoint attached to a line of code

```
 * The '=' button was pressed.
 */
public void equals()
{
    // This should completes the building of a second operand,
    // so ensure that we really have a left operand, an operator
    // and a right operand.
    if(haveLeftOperand &&
            lastOperator != '?' &&
            buildingDisplayValue) {
        calculateResult();
        lastOperator = '?';
        buildingDisplayValue = false;
    }
    else {
        keySequenceError();
    }
```

F.2 The control buttons

Figure F.3 shows the control buttons that are active at a breakpoint.

Figure F.3
Active control buttons at a breakpoint

F.2.1 Halt

The *Halt* button is active when the program is running, thus allowing execution to be interrupted should that be necessary. If execution is halted, the debugger will show the state of the program as if a breakpoint had been reached.

F.2.2 Step

The *Step* button resumes execution at the current statement. Execution will pause again when the statement is completed. If the statement involves a method call, the complete method call is completed before the execution pauses again (unless the call leads to another explicit breakpoint).

F.2.3 Step Into

The *Step Into* button resumes execution at the current statement. If this statement is a method call, then execution will "step into" that method and be paused at the first statement inside it.

F.2.4 Continue

The *Continue* button resumes execution until the next breakpoint is reached, execution is interrupted via the *Halt* button, or the execution completes normally.

F.2.5 Terminate

The *Terminate* button aggressively finishes execution of the current program such that it cannot be resumed again. If it is simply desired to interrupt the execution in order to examine the current program state, then the *Halt* operation is preferred.

F.3 The variable displays

Figure F.4 shows all three variable display areas active at a breakpoint, in an example taken from the predator–prey simulation discussed in Chapter 12. Static variables are displayed in the upper area, instance variables in the middle area, and local variables in the lower area.

Figure F.4
Active-variable
displays

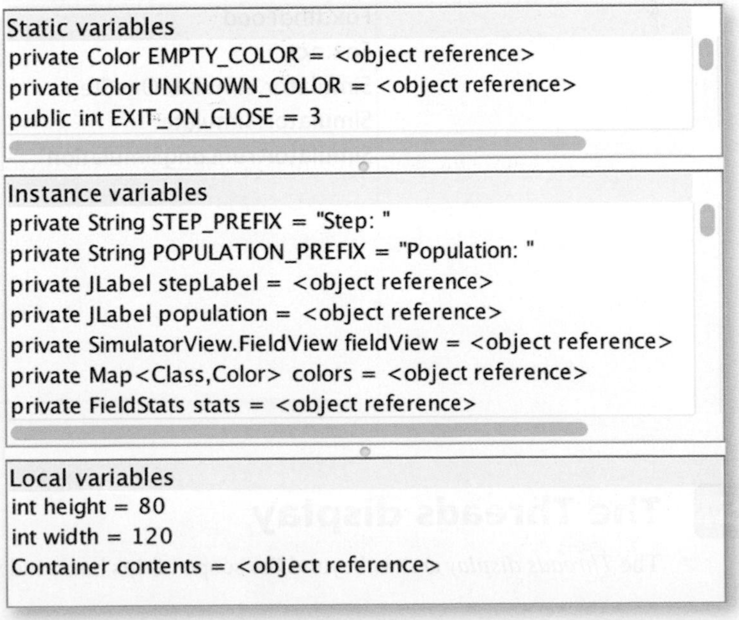

```
Static variables
private Color EMPTY_COLOR = <object reference>
private Color UNKNOWN_COLOR = <object reference>
public int EXIT_ON_CLOSE = 3
```

```
Instance variables
private String STEP_PREFIX = "Step: "
private String POPULATION_PREFIX = "Population: "
private JLabel stepLabel = <object reference>
private JLabel population = <object reference>
private SimulatorView.FieldView fieldView = <object reference>
private Map<Class,Color> colors = <object reference>
private FieldStats stats = <object reference>
```

```
Local variables
int height = 80
int width = 120
Container contents = <object reference>
```

When a breakpoint is reached, execution will be halted at a statement of an arbitrary object within the current program. The *Static variables* area displays the values of the static variables defined in the class of that object. The *Instance variables* area displays the values of that particular object's instance variables. Both areas also include any variables inherited from superclasses.

The *Local variables* area displays the values of local variables and parameters of the currently executing method or constructor. Local variables will appear in this area only once they have been initialized, as it is only at that point that they come into existence within the virtual machine.

A variable in any of these areas that is an object reference may be inspected by double-clicking on it.

F.4 The Call Sequence display

Figure F.5 shows the *Call Sequence* display, containing a sequence six methods deep. Methods appear in the format `Class.method` in the sequence, irrespective of whether they are static methods or instance methods. Constructors appear as `Class.<init>` in the sequence.

The call sequence operates as a *stack*, with the method at the top of the sequence being the one where the flow of execution currently lies. The variable display areas reflect the details of the method or constructor currently highlighted in the call sequence. Selecting a different line of the sequence will update the contents of the other display areas.

Figure F.5

A call sequence

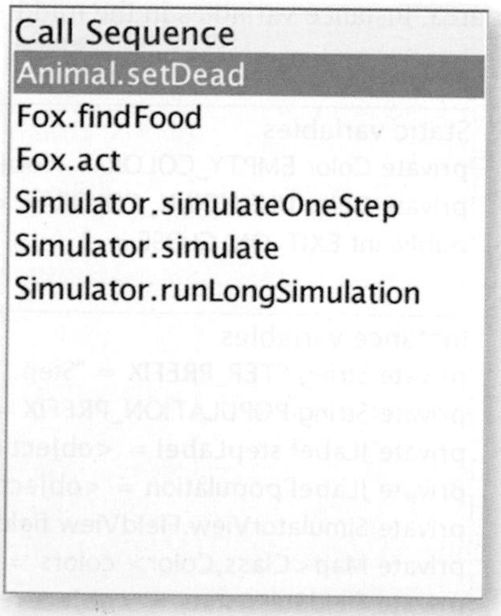

```
Call Sequence
Animal.setDead
Fox.findFood
Fox.act
Simulator.simulateOneStep
Simulator.simulate
Simulator.runLongSimulation
```

F.5 The Threads display

The *Threads display* area is beyond the scope of this book and will not be discussed further.

In this appendix, we give a brief outline of the main features of BlueJ's support for JUnit-style unit testing. More details can be found in the testing tutorial that is available from the BlueJ web site.

G.1 Enabling unit-testing functionality

In order to enable the unit-testing functionality of BlueJ, it is necessary to ensure that the *Show unit testing tools* box is ticked under the *Tools–Preferences–Miscellaneous* menu. The main BlueJ window will then contain a number of extra buttons that are active when a project is open.

G.2 Creating a test class

A test class is created by right-clicking a class in the class diagram and choosing *Create Test Class*. The name of the test class is determined automatically by adding Test as a suffix to the name of the associated class. Alternatively, a test class may be created by selecting the *New Class . . .* button and choosing *Unit Test* for the class type. In this case, you have a free choice over its name.

Test classes are annotated with <<unit test>> in the class diagram, and they have a color distinct from ordinary classes.

G.3 Creating a test method

Test methods can be created interactively. A sequence of user interactions with the class diagram and object bench are recorded, then captured as a sequence of Java statements and declarations in a method of the test class. Start recording by selecting *Create Test Method* from the pop-up menu associated with a test class. You will be prompted for the name of the new method. Earlier versions of JUnit, up to version 3, required the method names to start with the prefix "test". This is not a requirement in current versions. The *recording* symbol to the left of the class diagram will then be colored red, and the *End* and *Cancel* buttons become available.

Once recording has started, any object creations or method calls will form part of the code of the method being created. Select *End* to complete the recording and capture the test, or select *Cancel* to discard the recording, leaving the test class unchanged.

Test methods have the annotation `@Test` in the source of the test class.

G.4 Test assertions

While recording a test method, any method calls that return a result will bring up a *Method Result* window. This offers the opportunity to make an assertion about the result value by ticking the *Assert that* box. A drop-down menu contains a set of possible assertions for the result value. If an assertion is made, this will be encoded as a method call in the test method which is intended to lead to an `AssertionError` if the test fails.

G.5 Running tests

Individual test methods can be run by selecting them from the pop-up menu associated with the test class. A successful test will be indicated by a message in the main window's status line. An unsuccessful test will cause the *Test Results* window to appear. Selecting *Test All* from the test class's pop-up menu runs all tests from a single test class. The *Test Results* window will detail the success or failure of each method.

G.6 Fixtures

The contents of the object bench may be captured as a *fixture* by selecting *Object Bench to Test Fixture* from the pop-up menu associated with the test class. The effect of creating a fixture is that a field definition for each object is added to the test class, and statements are added to its `setUp` method that re-create the exact state of the objects as they were on the bench. The objects are then removed from the bench.

The `setUp` method has the annotation `@Before` in the test class and the method is automatically executed before the run of any test method, so all objects in a fixture are available for all tests.

The objects of a fixture may be re-created on the object bench by selecting *Test Fixture to Object Bench* from the test class's menu.

A `tearDown` method, with the annotation `@After`, is called following each test method. This can be used to conduct any post-test housekeeping or clean-up operations, should they be needed.

In this appendix, we briefly describe the tools available to support teamwork.

BlueJ includes teamwork support tools based on a source-code-repository model. In this model, a repository server is set up that is accessible over the Internet from the machines the users work on.

The server needs to be set up by an administrator. BlueJ supports both Subversion and CVS repositories.

H.1 Server setup

The setup of the repository server should normally be done by an experienced administrator. Detailed instructions can be found in the document, BlueJ Teamwork Repository Configuration, which is accessible via the *BlueJ Tutorial* item in BlueJ's *Help* menu.

H.2 Enabling teamwork functionality

The teamwork tools are initially hidden in BlueJ. To show the tools, open the *Preferences* dialog and, in the *Miscellaneous* tab, tick the *Show teamwork controls* box. The BlueJ interface then contains three extra buttons (*Update*, *Commit*, *Status*) and an additional submenu titled *Team* in the *Tools* menu.

H.3 Sharing a project

To create a shared project, one team member creates the project as a standard BlueJ project. The project can then be shared by using the *Share this Project* function from the *Team* menu. When this function is used, a copy of the project is placed into the central repository. The server name and access details need to be specified in a dialog; ask your administrator (the one who set up the repository) for the details to fill in here.

H.4 Using a shared project

Once a user has created a shared project in the repository, other team members can use this project. To do this, select *Checkout Project* from the *Team* menu. This will place a copy of the shared project from the central server into your local file system. You can then work on the local copy.

H.5   Update and commit

Every now and then, the various copies of the project that team members have on their local disks need to be synchronized. This is done via the central repository. Use the *Commit* function to copy your changes into the repository, and use the *Update* function to copy changes from the repository (which other team members have committed) into your own local copy. It is good practice to commit and update frequently so that the changes at any step do not become too substantial.

H.6   More information

More detailed information is available in the Team Work Tutorial, which is accessible via the *BlueJ Tutorial* item in BlueJ's *Help* menu.

Writing good documentation for class and interface definitions is an important complement to writing good-quality source code. Documentation allows you to communicate your intentions to human readers in the form of a natural-language, high-level overview, rather than forcing them to read relatively low-level source code. Of particular value is documentation for the `public` elements of a class or interface, so that programmers can make use of it without having to know the details of its implementation.

In all of the project examples in this book, we have used a particular commenting style that is recognized by the `javadoc` documentation tool, which is distributed as part of the JDK. This tool automates the generation of class documentation in the form of HTML pages in a consistent style. The Java API has been documented using this same tool, and its value is appreciated when using library classes.

In this appendix, we give a brief summary of the main elements of the documentation comments that you should get into the habit of using in your own source code.

I.1 Documentation comments

The elements of a class to be documented are the class definition as a whole, its fields, constructors, and methods. Most important from the viewpoint of a user of your class is to have documentation for the class and its public constructors and methods. We have tended not to provide javadoc-style commenting for fields, because we regard these as private implementation-level details, and not something to be relied upon by users.

Documentation comments are always opened with the character triplet "/**" and closed by the character pair "*/". Between these symbols, a comment can have a *main description* followed by a *tag section*, although both are optional.

I.1.1 The main description

The main description for a class should be a general description of the purpose of the class. Code I.1 shows part of a typical main description, taken from the `Game` class of the *world-of-zuul* project. Note how the description includes details of how to use this class to start the game.

Code I.1

The main
description of a
class comment

```
/**
 * This class is the main class of the "World of Zuul".
 * application.
 *
 * "World of Zuul" is a very simple, text-based adventure game.
 * Users can walk around some scenery. That's all. It should
 * really be extended to make it more interesting!
 * To play this game, create an instance of this class and call
 * the "play" method.
 */
```

The main description for a method should be kept fairly general, without going into a lot of detail about how the method is implemented. Indeed, the main description for a method will often only need to be a single sentence, such as

```
/**
 * Create a new passenger with distinct pickup and
 * destination locations.
 */
```

Particular thought should be given to the first sentence of the main description for a class, interface, or method, as it is used in a separate summary at the top of the generated documentation.

Javadoc also supports the use of HTML markup within these comments.

I.1.2 The tag section

Following the main description comes the *tag section*. Javadoc recognizes around 20 tags, of which we discuss only the most important here (Table I.1). Tags can be used in two forms: *block tags* and *in-line tags*. We shall only discuss block tags, as these are the most commonly used. Further details about in-line tags and the remaining available tags can be found in the *javadoc* section of the *Tools and Utilities* documentation that is part of the JDK.

Table .1

Common
javadoc tags

Tag	Associated text
@author	author name(s)
@param	parameter name and description
@return	description of the return value
@see	cross-reference
@throws	exception type thrown and the circumstances
@version	version description

The @author and @version tags are regularly found in class and interface comments and cannot be used in constructor, method, or field comments. Both are followed by freetext, and there is no required format for either. Examples are

```
@author Hacker T. Largebrain
@version 2012.12.03
```

The @param and @throws tags are used with methods and constructors, whereas @return is just used with methods. Examples are

```
@param limit The maximum value allowed.
@return A random number in the range 1 to limit (inclusive).
@throws IllegalLimitException If limit is less than 1.
```

The @see tag has several different forms and may be used in any documentation comment. It provides a way to cross-reference a comment to another class, method, or other form of documentation. A *See Also* section is added to the item being commented. Here are some typical examples:

```
@see "The Java Language Specification, by Joy et al"
@see <a href="http://www.bluej.org/">The BlueJ web site</a>
@see #isAlive
@see java.util.ArrayList#add
```

The first simply embeds a text string with no hyperlink; the second embeds a hyperlink to the specified document; the third links to the documentation for the isAlive method in the same class; the fourth links to the documentation for the add method in the ArrayList class of the java.util package.

I.2   BlueJ support for javadoc

If a project has been commented using the javadoc style, then BlueJ provides support for generating the complete HTML documentation. In the main window, select the *Tools/ Project Documentation* menu item, and the documentation will be generated (if necessary) and displayed within a browser window.

Within the BlueJ editor, the source-code view of a class can be switched to the documentation view by changing the *Source Code* option to *Documentation* at the right of the window (Figure I.1), or by using *Toggle Documentation View* from the editor's *Tools* menu. This provides a quick preview of the documentation, but will not contain references to documentation of superclasses or used classes.

Figure I.1

The *Source Code* and *Documentation* view option

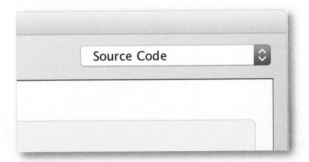

More details are available at:

```
http://www.oracle.com/technetwork/java/javase/documentation/
index-137868.html
```

J.1 Naming

J.1.1 Use meaningful names

Use descriptive names for all identifiers (names of classes, variables, and methods). Avoid ambiguity. Avoid abbreviations. Simple mutator methods should be named *setSomething*(. . .). Simple accessor methods should be named *getSomething*(. . .). Accessor methods with `boolean` return values are often called *isSomething*(. . .)—for example, `isEmpty()`.

J.1.2 Class names start with a capital letter

J.1.3 Class names are singular nouns

J.1.4 Method and variable names start with lowercase letters

All three—class, method, and variable names—use capital letters to begin each word after the first in order to increase readability of compound identifiers, e.g. `numberOfItems`.

J.1.5 Constants are written in UPPERCASE

Constants occasionally use underscores to indicate compound identifiers:

`MAXIMUM_SIZE`.

J.2 Layout

J.2.1 One level of indentation is four spaces

J.2.2 All statements within a block are indented one level

J.2.3 Braces for classes and methods are alone on one line

The braces for class and method blocks are on separate lines and are at the same indentation level. For example:

```
public int getAge()
{
    statements
}
```

J.2.4 For all other blocks, braces open at the end of a line

All other blocks open with braces at the end of the line that contains the keyword defining the block. The closing brace is on a separate line, aligned under the keyword that defines the block. For example:

```
while(condition) {
    statements
}

if(condition) {
    statements
}
else {
    statements
}
```

J.2.5 Always use braces in control structures

Braces are used in if statements and loops even if the body is only a single statement.

J.2.6 Use a space before the opening brace of a control structure's block

J.2.7 Use a space around operators

J.2.8 Use a blank line between methods (and constructors)

Use blank lines to separate logical blocks of code; this means at least between methods, but also between logical parts within a method.

J.3 Documentation

J.3.1 Every class has a class comment at the top

The class comment contains at least:

- a general description of the class

- the author's name(s)

- a version number

Every person who has contributed to the class has to be named as an author or has to be otherwise appropriately credited.

A version number can be a simple number, a date, or other format. The important thing is that a reader must be able to recognize whether two versions are different, and to determine which one is newer.

J.3.2   Every method has a method comment

J.3.3   Comments are Javadoc-readable

Class and method comments must be recognized by Javadoc. In other words, they should start with the comment symbol "/**".

J.3.4   Code comments (only) where necessary

Comments in the code should be included where the code is not obvious or is difficult to understand (and preference should be given to make the code obvious or easy to understand where possible) and where comments facilitate understanding of a method. Do not comment obvious statements—assume that your reader understands Java!

J.4   Language-use restrictions

J.4.1   Order of declarations: fields, constructors, methods

The elements of a class definition appear (if present) in the following order: package statement; import statements; class comment; class header; field definitions; constructors; methods; inner classes.

J.4.2   Fields may not be public (except for final fields)

J.4.3   Always use an access modifier

Specify all fields and methods as either `private`, `public`, or `protected`. Never use default (package private) access.

J.4.4   Import classes separately

Importing statements explicitly naming every class are preferred over importing whole packages. For example:

```
import java.util.ArrayList;
import java.util.HashSet;
```

is better than

```
import java.util.*;
```

J.4.5   Always include a constructor (even if the body is empty)

J.4.6   Always include a superclass constructor call

In constructors of subclasses, do not rely on automatic insertion of a superclass call. Include the `super()` call explicitly, even if it would work without it.

J.4.7   Initialize all fields in the constructor

Include assignments of default values. This makes it clear to a reader that the correct initialization of all fields has been considered.

J.5 Code idioms

J.5.1 Use iterators with collections

To iterate over a complete collection, use a for-each loop. When the collection must be changed during iteration, use an `Iterator` with a while loop or a for loop, not an integer index.

APPENDIX

K

Important Library Classes

The Java platform includes a rich set of libraries that support a wide variety of programming tasks.

In this appendix, we briefly summarize details of some classes and interfaces from the most important packages of the Java API. A competent Java programmer should be familiar with most of these. This appendix is only a summary, and it should be read in conjunction with the full API documentation.

K.1 The `java.lang` package

Classes and interfaces in the `java.lang` package are fundamental to the Java language, as this package is automatically imported implicitly into any class definition.

Package `java.lang` —Summary of the most important classes

interface `Comparable`	Implementation of this interface allows comparison and ordering of objects from the implementing class. Static utility methods such as `Arrays.sort` and `Collections.sort` can then provide efficient sorting in such cases, for instance.
interface `Runnable`	An interface that takes no parameters and returns no result and used as the type for lambdas with those characteristics.
class `Math`	`Math` is a class containing only static fields and methods. Values for the mathematical constants e and π are defined here, along with trigonometric functions and others such as `abs`, `min`, `max`, and `sqrt`.
class `Object`	All classes have `Object` as a superclass at the root of their class hierarchy. From it, all objects inherit default implementations for important methods such as `equals` and `toString`. Other significant methods defined by this class are `clone` and `hashCode`.
class `String`	Strings are an important feature of many applications, and they receive special treatment in Java. Key methods of the `String` class are `charAt`, `equals`, `indexOf`, `length`, `split`, and `substring`. Strings are immutable objects, so methods such as `trim` that appear to be mutators actually return a new `String` object representing the result of the operation.
class `StringBuilder`	The `StringBuilder` class offers an efficient alternative to `String` when it is required to build up a string from a number of components: e.g., via concatenation. Its key methods are `append`, `insert`, and `toString`.

K.2 The `java.util` package

The `java.util` package is a relatively incoherent collection of useful classes and interfaces.

Package `java.util` —Summary of the most important classes and interfaces

interface `Collection`	This interface provides the core set of methods for most of the collection-based classes defined in the `java.util` package, such as `ArrayList`, `HashSet`, and `LinkedList`. It defines signatures for the `add`, `clear`, `iterator`, `remove`, and `size` methods.
interface `Iterator`	`Iterator` defines a simple and consistent interface for iterating over the contents of a collection. Its three core methods are `hasNext`, `next`, and `remove`.
interface `List`	`List` is an extension of the `Collection` interface and provides a means to impose a sequence on the selection. As such, many of its methods take an index parameter: for instance, `add`, `get`, `remove`, and `set`. Classes such as `ArrayList` and `LinkedList` implement `List`.
interface `Map`	The `Map` interface offers an alternative to list-based collections by supporting the idea of associating each object in a collection with a *key* value. Objects are added and retrieved via its `put` and `get` methods. Note that a `Map` does not return an `Iterator`, but its `keySet` method returns a `Set` of the keys, and its `values` method returns a `Collection` of the objects in the map.
interface `Set`	`Set` extends the `Collection` interface with the intention of mandating that a collection contain no duplicate elements. It is worth pointing out that `Set` has no implication to enforce this restriction. This means that `Set` is actually provided as a marker interface to enable collection implementers to indicate that their classes fulfill this particular restriction.
class `ArrayList`	`ArrayList` is an implementation of the `List` interface that uses an array to provide efficient direct access via integer indices to the objects it stores. If objects are added or removed from anywhere other than the last position in the list, then following items have to be moved to make space or close the gap. Key methods are `add`, `get`, `iterator`, `remove`, `removeIf`, `size`, and `stream`.
class `Collections`	`Collections` contains many useful static methods for manipulating collections. Key methods are `binarySearch`, `fill`, and `sort`.
class `HashMap`	`HashMap` is an implementation of the `Map` interface. Key methods are `get`, `put`, `remove`, and `size`. Iteration over a `HashMap` is usually a two-stage process: obtain the set of keys via its `keySet` method, and then iterate over the keys.
class `HashSet`	`HashSet` is a hash-based implementation of the `Set` interface. Key methods are `add`, `remove`, and `size`.
class `LinkedList`	`LinkedList` is an implementation of the `List` interface that uses an internal linked structure to store objects. Direct access to the ends of the list is efficient, but access to individual objects via an index is less efficient than with an `ArrayList`. On the other hand, adding objects or removing them from within the list requires no shifting of existing objects. Key methods are `add`, `getFirst`, `getLast`, `iterator`, `removeFirst`, `removeIf`, `removeLast`, `size`, and `stream`.
class `Random`	The `Random` class supports generation of pseudo-random values—typically, random numbers. The sequence of numbers generated is determined by a *seed value*, which may be passed to a constructor or set via a call to `setSeed`. Two Random objects starting from the same seed will return the same sequence of values to identical calls. Key methods are `nextBoolean`, `nextDouble`, `nextInt`, and `setSeed`.
class `Scanner`	The `Scanner` class provides a way to read and parse input. It is often used to read input from the keyboard. Key methods are `next` and `hasNext`.

K.3   The `java.io` **and** `java.nio.file` **packages**

The `java.io` and `java.nio.file` packages contain classes that support input and output and access to the file system. Many of the input/output classes in `java.io` are distinguished by whether they are *stream-based* (operating on binary data) or *readers* and *writers* (operating on characters). The `java.nio` package supplies several classes that support convenient access to the file system.

Package `java.io` —Summary of the most important classes and interfaces

interface `Serializable`	The `Serializable` interface is an empty interface requiring no code to be written in an implementing class. Classes implement this interface in order to be able to participate in the serialization process. `Serializable` objects may be written and read as a whole to and from sources of output and input. This makes storage and retrieval of persistent data a relatively simple process in Java. See the `ObjectInputStream` and `ObjectOutputStream` classes for further information.
class `BufferedReader`	`BufferedReader` is a class that provides buffered character-based access to a source of input. Buffered input is often more efficient than unbuffered, particularly if the source of input is in the external file system. Because it buffers input, it is able to offer a `readLine` method that is not available in most other input classes. Key methods are `close`, `read`, and `readLine`.
class `BufferedWriter`	`BufferedWriter` is a class that provides buffered character-based output. Buffered output is often more efficient than unbuffered, particularly if the destination of the output is in the external file system. Key methods are `close`, `flush`, and `write`.
class `File`	The `File` class provides an object representation for files and folders (directories) in an external file system. Methods exist to indicate whether a file is readable and/or writeable, and whether it is a file or a folder. A `File` object can be created for a nonexistent file, which may be a first step in creating a physical file on the file system. Key methods are `canRead`, `canWrite`, `createNewFile`, `createTempFile`, `getName`, `getParent`, `getPath`, `isDirectory`, `isFile`, and `listFiles`.
class `FileReader`	The `FileReader` class is used to open an external file ready for reading its contents as characters. A `FileReader` object is often passed to the constructor of another reader class (such as a `BufferedReader`) rather than being used directly. Key methods are `close` and `read`.
class `FileWriter`	The `FileWriter` class is used to open an external file ready for writing character-based data. Pairs of constructors determine whether an existing file will be appended to, or its existing contents discarded. A `FileWriter` object is often passed to the constructor of another Writer class (such as a `BufferedWriter`) rather than being used directly. Key methods are `close`, `flush`, and `write`.
class `IOException`	`IOException` is a checked exception class that is at the root of the exception hierarchy of most input/output exceptions.

Package `java.nio.file` —Summary of the most important classes and interfaces	
interface Path	The Path interface provides the key methods for accessing information about a file in the file system. Path is, in effect, a replacement for the older File class of the java.io package.
class Paths	The Paths class provides get methods to return concrete instances of the Path interface.
class Files	Files is a class that provides static methods to query attributes of files and directories (folders), as well as to manipulate the file system—e.g., creating directories and changing file permissions. It also includes methods for opening files, such as newBufferedReader.

K.4 The `java.util.function` package

The java.util.function package contains only interfaces. It supplies the commonly recurring types that are associated with lambdas and method references. Among these are consumer, supplier and predicate interfaces, as well as those for binary operators, for instance. All of the interfaces are important and we describe only a small selection here.

Package java.util.function —Summary of some of the typical interfaces	
interface BiFunction	The BiFunction interface takes two parameters and returns a result. The types of the parameters and result may be all different, so this is a generalization of the BinaryOperator interface.
interface BinaryOperator	The BinaryOperator interface takes two parameters of its parameterized type and returns a result of the same type. This is commonly used in *reduce* operations.
interface Consumer	The Consumer interface takes a single parameter of its parameterized type and has a void result.
interface Predicate	The Predicate interface takes a single parameter of its parameterized type and returns a boolean result. This is commonly used in *filter* operations.
interface Supplier	The Supplier interface takes no parameter and returns a result of its parameterized type.

K.5 The `java.net` package

The java.net package contains classes and interfaces supporting networked applications. Most of these are outside the scope of this book.

Package java.net —Summary of the most important classes	
class URL	The URL class represents a Uniform Resource Locator. In other words, it provides a way to describe the location of something on the Internet. In fact, it can also be used to describe the location of something on a local file system. We have included it here because classes from the java.io and javax.swing packages often use URL objects. Key methods are getContent, getFile, getHost, getPath, and openStream.

K.6 Other important packages

Other important packages are:

```
java.awt
java.awt.event
javax.swing
javax.swing.event
```

These are used extensively when writing graphical user interfaces (GUIs), and they contain many useful classes that a GUI programmer should become familiar with.

Index